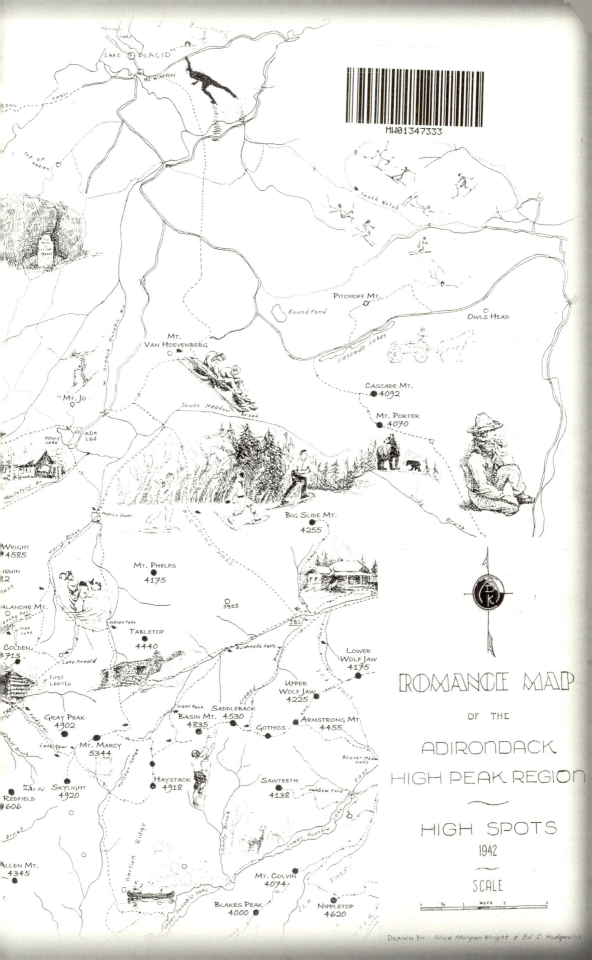

Heaven Up-h'isted-ness!

The History of the Adirondack Forty-Sixers

and the

High Peaks of the Adirondacks

Copyright © 2011 Adirondack Forty-Sixers, Inc.

All rights reserved. No part of this publication may be used, reproduced, or transmitted in any form whatsoever without the written approval of the Adirondack Forty-Sixers, Inc.

Photo Credits:

The color photographs which appear on pages 209 to 224 are copyrighted and remain the property of their creators. All black and white photos in this volume which are not already in the public domain are copyrighted by the Adirondack Forty-Sixers with the exception of the following, which have been printed with permission:

Pages 14, 19, 28, 31–36, 38, 39, 44–51, 55, 57, 59, 61, 63, 66, 137, 243, 244, 247, 248, 259, 278, 280, 321, 345, 349, 350, 359, 375, 396, 421, 430, 452, 458, 482, 487, 504, 505 – from the photo collection of Grace Hudowalski;

Pages 21, 22, and 25 – courtesy of Nancy Montville;

Pages 26 and 551 – courtesy of the Saranac Lake Public Library Adirondack Collection;

Pages 68, 117, 292, 293, 294, 481, and 536 – courtesy of Brooke Dittmar;

Pages 70, 92, and 93 – courtesy of James A. Goodwin, Jr.;

Page 193 – courtesy of Adirondack Research Center Library, Schenectady, New York;

Pages 227, 346, 409, and 559 – courtesy of Britt Moss;

Page 310 – courtesy of Williams College, Williamstown, Massachusetts;

Page 331 – courtesy of Barbara Harris;

Page 408 – courtesy of Gretel H. Schueller;

Page 434 (top) – courtesy of Ken Marcinowski;

Page 489 – courtesy of Douglas Arnold; and

Page 557 – courtesy of George Sloan.

Endpapers: A portion of the "Romance Map of the Adirondack High Peak Region," designed and drawn by Alice Morgan Wright and Edward C. Hudowalski. The full map first appeared in the Adirondack Mountain Club's publication, *High Spots*, 1942.

Adirondack Forty-Sixers, Inc.
P.O. Box 180
Cadyville, NY 12918-0180
www.adk46r.org

First Edition
2011

Library of Congress Control Number: 2010917212

ISBN: 978-0-615-34489-8

We have made a commitment to being environmentally and socially responsible: This publication was manufactured by Villanti & Sons, Printers, Inc. using Green-e® Certified renewable energy and is printed on paper that is certified to the FSC® standard. Inks used in manufacturing were high solid, soy based, and low VOC (containing less than 1% VOC).

Heaven Up-h'isted-ness!

Charles Dudley Warner wrote an essay about Old Mountain Phelps, "The Primitive Man," for the May 1878 edition of the *Atlantic Monthly*. In it, Warner wrote that "Phelps loved his mountains. He was the discoverer of Marcy, and caused the first trail to be cut to its summit, so that others could enjoy the noble views from its round and rocky top. To him it was, in noble symmetry and beauty, the chief mountain of the globe. To stand on it gave him, as he said, 'a feeling of heaven up-h'isted-ness.'"

Forty-sixers know that Phelps was not the "discoverer" of Mount Marcy, but they share with Phelps a love for "their" mountains and understand the "feeling of heaven up-h'isted-ness" – the feeling of having been hoisted up to heaven – when they stand upon Marcy and the other high peaks of the Adirondacks. Hence, this volume of Forty-Sixer history and the stories of the forty-six peaks has as its principal title, *Heaven Up-h'isted-ness!*

Dedication

We dedicate this book to three individuals in appreciation of the contributions they have made both to our organization and to the Adirondack High Peaks. They truly exemplify the stewardship spirit of the Adirondack Forty-Sixers:

James A. Goodwin – 46er #24
Guide, Trailmaster, Director
ATIS Leader

Dr. Edwin H. "Ketch" Ketchledge – 46er #507
Past President, Summit Seeding Program Initiative
Summit Steward Program Creator

Glenn W. Fish – 46er #536
Past President, 46ers and ADK
Mountain Clean-up Project
Search & Rescue Program

Forty-Sixers Song

Where Tahawus' lofty summit
        reaches for the sky
With old Gray Peak on his shoulder,
        Skylight following nigh.
There will we gaze with joy and rev'rence,
        from every hill and vale
That surrounds the grand old monarch,
        as we tramp the trail.

Where the Opalescent plunges
        down its rough-hewn course,
Fed by Uphill Brook and Feldspar,
        Hudson's highest source;
There let me look on old Algonquin,
        kissed by setting sun,
There I'll light my evening campfire,
        when the day is done.

Where old Seward spreads his shadow
        o'er Ouluska's den,
With its dark and hidden caverns,
        far from haunts of men,
There let me tramp 'til early nightfall
        bids me stop and rest,
There with pals and God and Nature,
        will my soul be blest.

        – The Rev. E. R. Ryder (#7)

Table of Contents

Introduction
    by James A. (Tony) Goodwin, Jr. (#211) .... Page 7

The History of the Adirondack Forty-Sixers
    by Suzanne Lance (#1802W) 13
    Part I: The First Forty-Sixers 15
    Part II: The Forty-Sixers of Troy and the Adirondack Forty-Sixers 30
    Part III: The 1970s – Giving Something Back to the Mountains 76
    Part IV: The 1980s – Decade of Growth 98
    Part V: The 1990s – End of an Era 108
    Part VI: The 2000s – Looking Toward the Future 124
    Conclusion 135
    Adirondack Peeks 148

The History of the High Peaks of the Adirondacks 153

Mount Marcy
    by Tim Tefft (#616) 155

Notes About Summit Elevation Figures 208

Mountain Images
    Color photographs by various artists 209

Skylight and Gray Peak
    by John Konowitz, Jr. 225

Mount Colden
    by Tim Singer (#1038) 231

Cliff, Redfield, and Allen
    by Tom Wheeler (#3356W) 244

Santanoni, Panther, and Couchsachraga
    by Phil Corell (#224W) 269

The Seward Range
    by John Sharp Swan, Jr. (#566W) 287

Street and Nye
    by Barbara Harris (#2824W) 327

The MacIntyre Range
    by Sean O'Donnell (#5120W) 345

Mount Phelps, Tabletop, and Big Slide
    by Ron Konowitz (#487) 392

Cascade and Porter
    by Gretel H. Schueller 408

Giant and Rocky Peak Ridge
    by Chuck Gibson (#251) 419

The Dix Range
    by Daniel Eagan (#4666) 433

Nippletop and Dial
    by Sally Hoy (#2924W) 465

Sawteeth, Mount Colvin, and Blake's Peak
    by Douglas Arnold (#4693W) 478

The Upper Range
    by Christine Bourjade (#4967W) 500

The Lower Range
    by Mary Lou Recor (#2214W) 530

Whiteface and Esther
    by Tim Tefft (#616) 539

The Membership Roster of the Adirondack Forty-Sixers
    Prepared by Mike Becker (#1889W) 565

Index 681

INTRODUCTION

What other mountainous area has spawned a club that has created not one but now four volumes dedicated to the experience of climbing those forty-six peaks? What other "peak-bagging" organization demands so much (aside from the physical effort) of those who want to join and then gets so much back in return from those same members? Finally, how is it that places such as a thickly wooded bump with nothing but a small marker reading "Nye Mt." can become sacred ground to be visited time and again? There probably are no good answers to the above questions; but given the unique geologic and social history of the Adirondacks, it shouldn't be all that surprising that the Adirondacks has given rise to an organization as unique as the Adirondack 46ers.

To start at the very beginning, the geologic history of the Adirondacks is totally different from the surrounding Green, White, and Catskill mountains. As an extension of the Canadian Shield, the exposed Adirondack bedrock is some of the oldest rock in the world. Formed deep underground and allowed to cool slowly before rising to and above the surface, Adirondack anorthosite granite is less brittle than other granites. It therefore is less likely to crack and create opportunities for vegetation to firmly affix to the mountainside. As a result, the bare summits exhibit mostly nothing but smooth rock. There are also frequent slides when the accumulated growth can no longer stick on the smooth rock. Outside of the High Peaks, the Canadian Shield is characterized by vast areas of relatively flat, poorly-drained soils. Referred to as "drowned lands" by the early explorers, these areas supported much wildlife including beavers, but were mostly unsuited for agriculture. Except for the major river corridors, travel across this country was difficult and resulted in much of the Adirondacks being unknown long after surrounding areas had been fully explored and populated.

In 1609, eleven years before the Pilgrims landed on Plymouth Rock, Samuel de Champlain came down the lake that now bears his name. Champlain's journals note the presence of high mountains on both sides of the lake, but neither he nor any of the other French explorers and missionaries that followed him made any forays into what was then a thickly-wooded wilderness. By contrast, it was only 22 years after Plymouth Rock that Darby Field reached the summit of Mt. Washington, 195 years before the first ascent of Mt. Marcy.

Part of the reason for this great disparity would be that the mountains of New England could easily be seen from the ocean. Furthermore, during the colder climate of the sixteenth and seventeenth centuries, the White Mountains probably "advertised" their height with glistening snowfields that stood out prominently for much of each year. Additionally, as early as 1623 there were settlements at both today's Portsmouth, New Hampshire, and, more importantly, at the mouth of the Saco River – the river that Darby Field followed to get to the base of Mt. Washington. Still, there had to be something else about the Adirondacks that kept even the explorers away for so long.

Although the Adirondacks could certainly be seen from Lake Champlain, and Giant and Rocky Peak were clearly quite high, surely another factor was the lack of any settlement along the shore of Lake Champlain until the latter part of the eighteenth century. Competing claims by the Algonquin and the Iroquois tribes (and by extension between France and England) made it difficult to actually claim land for a settlement. Additionally, even after settlements were established along Lake Champlain, the monolithic Canadian Shield rock that underlies much of the Adirondacks meant anyone venturing much beyond the Champlain Valley found mostly unfertile and poorly-drained soils not conducive to agriculture. Most early farmers thus stuck to the periphery of the Adirondacks. Those few that did venture further inland were probably locked in a life and death battle for survival and had no time or interest in exploring the adjacent mountains.

There has always been speculation about whether Native Americans ever penetrated the interior of the High Peaks, but according to Stephen Sulavik's careful research *[Adirondack: Of Indians and Mountains, 1535-1838]* so far there is no evidence that there were any permanent settlements in any part of the Adirondacks. Before the arrival of Europeans, Native Americans did travel through areas west of the High Peaks, following the Raquette, Saranac, and Oswegatchie rivers. Thus the name "Indian Carry" for the portage between the Raquette River and Upper Saranac Lake is apparently appropriate, but "Indian Pass" was not likely ever used by Native Americans until long after the arrival of Europeans.

In writing of his explorations in 1838, William Redfield does say,

> Traces have been discovered near McIntyre [iron works] of a rout, which the natives sometimes pursued through this mountain region, by way of Lakes Sanford and Henderson, and thence to the Preston Ponds and the headwaters of the Racket*[sic]*. But these savages had no inducement to make the laborious ascent of sterile mountain peaks, which they held in superstitious dread, or to explore the hidden sources of the rivers they send forth. Even the more hardy huntsman of later times, who, when trapping for northern furs, has marked his path into the recesses of these elevated forests, has left no traces of his axe higher than the borders of Lake Colden, where some few marks of this description may be perceived.

Of the "northern furs" mentioned by Redfield, the most significant one was beaver, but his reference to "later times" indicates that only the tremendous European demand for this fur caused Native Americans to push far into the Adirondack wilderness. The generally accepted meaning of "Couchsachraga" is "dismal wilderness," but Sulavik's research indicates the meaning may actually be "at the place of beaver dams." Sulavik does concede, however, that anyone having to travel through the "drowned lands" where beavers are most numerous would surely consider their surroundings to be truly a "dismal wilderness." Indeed, the infamous swamp between Panther and Couchsachraga, while not actually beaver-caused, gives one a sense of how areas of beaver activity would be perceived by those required to travel through them.

As for actually climbing the mountains above these areas of dismal wilderness, at first it was only the land surveyors (whose work required them to go over whatever mountain lay in their path) who climbed the peaks. The most notable of these surveyors was Charles Broadhead who in 1797 bagged several first ascents, climbing Giant, Tabletop, and Boundary as he ran the north boundary of the Totten and Crossfield Purchase from east to west. Broadhead was working for Alexander McComb who needed to determine the boundaries of his 1792 "Great Purchase." Broadhead started near New Russia and headed west on a line that was the south bounds of the Old Military Tract and the north bounds of the Totten and Crossfield Purchase. He attempted to find the east end of the line that was started, but never finished, by Archibald Campbell in 1772 when he surveyed the Totten and Crossfield Purchase. Once past Wallface Mt., that line became the south boundary of Macomb's Purchase.

While Broadhead never did find Campbell's line, his field notes offer terse but telling details about what the land was like. He frequently refers to long stretches of "coal land," which is the piney duff that covers so many of the higher slopes. "Coal land" also indicated land not suited to agriculture. He found two feet of snow on Giant's summit on June 2. On Tabletop, he noted, "Top the mountain – very rough chief of the timber fallen down by the wind." We therefore know that, aside from a herdpath, some things in the High Peaks haven't changed in more than 200 years. Given that he described only the poor land and difficulty of travel – making no mention of the views from Giant or Boundary, or of the great cliff on Wallface – it is little wonder that few, if any, were encouraged to go into the mountains.

Thus it was finally the scientific curiosity of Ebenezer Emmons and William Redfield that led to the determination that Mount Marcy, and not Slide Mt. in the Catskills, was the highest point in New York State. His report on his climb did spark at least some momentary interest in climbing the higher peaks. Most notably, the author Charles Fenno Hoffman tried to ascend Marcy a mere month after Redfield and company's ascent. Even though he failed, he gave us "Opalescent," "Hanging Spear" and, of course, "Tahawus" as poetic additions to Adirondack lore. So even though the Adirondacks were now "known" as high mountains with sublime scenery, there was no immediate rush since the place was still pretty inaccessible.

By 1837 when Mt. Marcy was first climbed, Mt. Washington had had a trail to its summit for nearly 20 years along with a few stone shelters on the summit. Within three years there was a bridle trail to summit. By 1861, when Orson "Old Mountain" Phelps cut the first primitive trail up Marcy, Mt. Washington already had a carriage road and two summit hotels. The cog railway was under construction and not far behind in reaching the summit as well. South of the Adirondacks, the Catskills had the Catskill Mountain House as early as 1823 with good trails soon built for the benefit of its guests. With easy access via Hudson River steamboats, there was little incentive for anyone to travel beyond to the trailless, "hotelless," and nearly road-less Adirondacks.

Nature, as they say, "abhors a vacuum" and it was only a matter of time before someone would "discover" the Adirondacks as a place where it was still possible to escape from the increasingly industrialized civilization of the post Civil War era. That "someone" was William H. H. Murray (a.k.a. "Adirondack" Murray) whose *Adventures in the Wilderness,* published in 1869, started the great rush of "Murray's fools." While Keene Valley and Lake Placid had been quietly attracting summer visitors for some years before, it wasn't until the 1870s that the boom in hotel construction began. Hotels outside of the High Peaks tended to be situated on an attractive lake with fishing and boating the primary pursuits of the guests. In the mountains, however, it was hiking and camping that drew the guests. To better accommodate their guests, the hoteliers thus became trail builders who additionally cultivated locals to become guides.

Suddenly, there were trails to the summits of peaks like Giant, Noonmark, Gothics, Cascade, Whiteface, Algonquin and, of course, Marcy. Most of those trails, however, were crudely constructed; and maintenance was up to the whim of the hotelier or guide who originally constructed them. By contrast, the formation of the Appalachian Mountain Club in 1876 and later the formation of the Randolph Mountain Club meant the White Mountains would have good trails and even huts for hikers before the Adirondacks had much more than a few crude trails. One could go on detailing the summit hotels, bridle trails and carriage roads constructed in other mountain ranges during the nineteenth century; but the main point is that as late as the 1920s the Marshalls could still be true explorers as they set out to climb all the 4,000 foot peaks in the Adirondacks. In the process, the Marshalls and their guide Herbert Clark were the first to climb six of those peaks.

The Marshalls' accounts of their explorations in 1922, even before they finished all of the peaks, inspired Russell M. L. Carson to begin writing about the history and naming of the peaks. Carson's initial goal was to create a contest that would stimulate better attendance at the weekly meetings of the Glens Falls Rotary Club. Soon, however, he became a partner of the Marshalls as he worked to publish his weekly sketches of the "peak of the week." And it was Carson who suggested peaks that should be added to the original list of 42. These were Gray Peak, because it had been named by Colvin after a famous nineteenth century botanist (famous enough that he occasionally still shows up in crossword puzzles) and the peaks that had just a 4,000 foot contour line.

What apparently intrigued the Glens Falls Rotary Club, and later those who bought *Peaks and People of the Adirondacks,* was that there were so many high mountains so close by that had never been climbed or even named. How could it be that even in the age of automobiles and after railroads had reached seemingly every corner of the country, there was unexplored terrain right here in what was then the nation's most populous state?

Those inspired to follow the Marshalls found that, despite the information gained and shared by the Marshalls, there was still a sense of true exploration in attempting to reach those summits. It is probably not too much of a stretch to say that when the next ten Forty-Sixers climbed those six peaks first ascended by the Marshalls, they were recording the next ten ascents. And from the early accounts, it appears the constantly changing mazes of lumber roads made any route description quickly obsolete and every ascent a unique exercise in route finding. Even as the number of Forty-Sixers climbed into the hundreds, the routes to half the peaks remained obscure enough that each ascent was still a bit of personal exploration.

This shared sense of true adventure and exploration created a core group of founders whose intensely shared experiences forged a bond so strong that the traditions they established have extended through the membership to the present day. Needless to say, the effort required to finish one's ascents of the forty-six has become somewhat less over the years, but the traditions established many years ago help to keep up the excitement as the newest aspirants close in on their goal.

I can well remember the final two weeks of the summer of 1961 as I hiked nearly every day to achieve my goal of finishing before having to return to Hartford, Connecticut, and school. I have therefore often smiled, forty or more years later, as an aspirant breathlessly explains what they have just hiked and what they will soon be hiking to finish. Tradition established; excitement undiminished.

So now the question may be, "Why do we need yet another book to help continue that excitement?" The answer obviously is ultimately in the pages themselves, but this volume goes beyond the previous three in many ways. If Dr. Suess could write *On Beyond Zebra,* then this book could be subtitled "On Beyond Carson." This is in no sense said to belittle Carson whose research gave life to the peaks that we all climb; but modern research (and a rich history of climbing since Carson) has allowed authors to provide the reader with the most comprehensive histories of these peaks ever written. The club's history even reveals that George Marshall spent three months in a federal prison in 1950.

Taken together, the biographies of those twenty individuals whose names adorn our peaks provide a wonderful slice of nineteenth century life and politics – a perspective that many would miss if it didn't relate to the naming of a summit they had struggled to attain. And with only six of those twenty named for politicians, I think we can say that the Adirondacks are less "political" than the White Mountains with their Presidential Range and a total of eleven of their forty-eight 4,000 footers named for political figures. Suffice it to say that the research in this volume on the naming, first ascents, and subsequent lore adds a depth to each of these peaks that helps to make each subsequent ascent special.

The second major element in this book is Suzanne Lance's club history. Lance's contribution describes a truly dynamic organization that has often debated its purpose, subsequently altering its mission to remain relevant to changed conditions. Indeed, about the only aspect of the 46ers left unchanged is the peaks to be climbed.

As is noted elsewhere, the original list compiled by the Marshalls became "obsolete" when the 1953 series of topographic maps lowered four peaks of the original 46 and raised one previously shown as less than 4,000 feet high. This created somewhat of a dilemma for the organization. Writing long afterwards, Laura and Guy Waterman mischievously imagined Adirondack peak baggers assembled in the parking lot at Adirondak Loj as the Executive Committee of the 46ers met inside in secret conclave to decide how to deal with the revised elevations. All eyes were focused on the smoke coming from the Loj's chimney as a change in the color would indicate that a decision had been reached. Finally, the color changed and a representative emerged onto the balcony to solemnly announce, "We will continue to climb the same peaks we have always climbed."

Of course over time (relatively short by geological standards) there have been significant and noticeable changes. The "Big Blow" of 1950 totally altered the routes to be followed, and made some peaks practically inaccessible for many years afterwards. Additionally, violent rain storms have brought down many slides. Adirondack geology has favored smooth slabs of bedrock with very few cracks so that trees cannot take root in anything but the thin, organic topsoil. When enough rain falls, the soil becomes heavy and rain runs under the topsoil to act as a lubricant. With no tree firmly anchored to any bedrock, the only logical result is a major slide. The most notable slides have been on Macomb in 1946; Giant in 1963; Colden east side and Gothics "True North" in 1991; Bennies Brook and Kilburn in 1995; and Avalanche Pass, Angel, and numerous other smaller slides in 1999.

Given the changes in the Adirondacks in general and Adirondack hiking in particular since the founding of the original "46-Rs of Troy," it is to this organization's credit that change has occurred – even if the list of peaks never changed. Who would have thought that a small group, formed essentially for the purpose of congratulating themselves for their accomplishment of climbing 46 peaks, could become a significant force for preserving the environment traversed by those same climbers? The answer probably lies in the debates, often intense, that have continued through the years and which are well documented by Suzanne's history.

We learn, for instance, that early on George Marshall opposed the placement of canisters on the summits. Placed they were, however, and for many years those registers fulfilled a useful purpose. Then, after much debate, the organization decided to remove them – ultimately for many of the reasons Marshall originally opposed them. When herdpaths were "discovered" in the early 1960s, a debate raged about whether the organization should even continue to exist. The main argument was that the damage caused by the creation of herdpaths occurred only because hikers wanted to join the organization and receive a patch. A secondary argument was that the challenge was now much less and therefore not as deserving of recognition.

Many were persuaded by these arguments, and there was even serious talk of disbanding at the round number of 1,000 members. Countering them were those who believed another organization would soon spring up to replace a disbanded 46ers. Others said that an organization of dedicated, experienced hikers could make a big difference in a landscape that was rapidly changing. We thus ended up with Wilderness Leadership Workshops to train neophyte leaders, trail maintainers to help reverse the deterioration of the trails we hiked, and legions of seed/lime/fertilizer carriers that have helped to restore denuded areas of our alpine summits. Suzanne's history offers many more interesting details on how we have come to have the organization we have today and to be around still to produce the book you hold in your hands.

Through all of these changes was the often unseen, but still evident guiding hand of Grace Hudowalski. Her mantra "It's not whether you make the summit, it's how you do the climb" made sure that those who corresponded with her knew that climbing was more than just about reaching the summit. This saying seemed to translate easily to an ethic that could be paraphrased "It's not that you've climbed all 46, it's what you do afterwards that's important." With her constant letter writing and special attention to the youngest climbers, Grace was our link to the early spirit of adventure, and sometimes hardship, that has defined this organization. I remain honored that my oldest child finished in time to receive a personal letter from Grace when he applied for membership.

So, will this fourth book be the last? My answer is that, if the organization declined to disband at 1,000 members, then why should this book, even though it is the most comprehensive, be the end? There will always be new adventures to chronicle. Additionally, the mountains themselves will continue to change. Sometimes it will be the sudden, cataclysmic change that we saw on Giant in 1963. A less sudden, but still rapid change can be the appearance of thick undergrowth after an event such as the ice storm of 1998 or Hurricane Floyd in 1999. Other times it will be the slow change of natural tree growth that finally obscures a remembered view, or a restored canopy that reduces undergrowth and again makes traveling easier.

As a group, 46ers have seen it all. The cycle between second, third, and now fourth books has been about 20 years. Who knows what the discussions will be like in 2030? While we probably can't imagine the details, we can be sure that the discussions will be about the mountains, why we climb them, what the currently perceived problems are, and how can this organization help to mitigate any problems so that we can continue to enjoy these mountains as we always have.

James A. (Tony) Goodwin, Jr.
Forty-Sixer #211
Keene Valley, New York

The History of the Adirondack Forty-Sixers

By Suzanne Lance
Forty-Sixer #1802W

The Adirondack 46ers at Adirondak Loj - May 28, 1949

The Forty-Sixers gathered together on May 28, 1949, at Adirondak Loj for their second annual spring meeting. Among those in attendance were the 46ers above. In front: Roy Snyder, George Trapp, Chrissie Wendell (canine), and Dick Wendell. Seated: Charles Trapp, Jr., Mary Dittmar, Dot Haeusser, Kay Flickinger, Werner Bachli, Jack McKenzie, Lil McKenzie, Bob Denniston, and Nell Plum. Standing: Charles Trapp, Sr., Roland Wendell, Herbert Malcomb, Orra Phelps, A. G. Dittmar, P. F. Loope, Ed Harmes, Rudy Clements, Helen Menz, Ed Hudowalski, Ray Hall, and Grace Hudowalski.

Part I: The First Forty-Sixers

When Herbert Clark and Robert and George Marshall reached the summit of Mt. Emmons on June 10, 1925, they became the first people to have climbed the 46 peaks over 4,000 feet in northern New York's Adirondack Mountains. Although the trio could not have anticipated the effects their hiking feat would have, their personal journey has in many ways played a part in shaping the history of the Adirondacks. As of the beginning of 2010, as many as 6,677 people have duplicated their accomplishment of climbing the 46 High Peaks for the distinction of being able to call themselves Forty-Sixers.

Throughout the past few decades, issues relating to over-usage similar to those that confront many of our nation's National Parks have plagued the Adirondack High Peaks region. The popularity of the area and the problems associated with the increasing volume of visitors are sometimes said to be a case of the Adirondacks being "loved to death." While the nature of the Adirondack Park, with its 20 developed trailheads and numerous undeveloped access points, makes it difficult to pinpoint accurate usage estimates, the New York State Department of Environmental Conservation (DEC) has documented a clear trend of increased use, particularly in the High Peaks area. The data show usage tripling within that area from some 57,000 visitors a year in the early 1980s to as many as 170,000 visitors each year in the early 2000s. While those aspiring to become Forty-Sixers are by no means the only people enjoying the Adirondack High Peaks Region, the effects of "forty-sixing" have been part of the discourse on wilderness preservation, land management, and conservation within the area.

The growth of the Forty-Sixer organization in many ways parallels the state's response to the increased usage of the High Peaks area itself. Both the Forty-Sixers and the DEC have sought solutions to problems relating to trail litter, the impact of camping, the proliferation of herdpaths on the twenty untrailed peaks, trail erosion, and maintaining the wilderness experience in an area which continues to grow in popularity. How the Forty-Sixer club has recognized and responded to these challenges is a major part of its history. "Forty-sixing" has evolved from three friends who hiked the High Peaks for fun and adventure to an enterprise that is integral to the care and preservation of the region. As the theme of the club's 46th anniversary celebration expressed, today's Forty-Sixers play the dual role of "hiking partners, mountain stewards."

> They are set on fire with the idea that they have found something very precious in life, which a lot of folks don't even know exists. Thrills. Adventure. Health. Beauty. Fellowship. Courage. God. Not any one of these things alone but a blend – a blend that is as individual as each snowflake yet as kindred as snow.
>
> — David H. Beetle, Editor,
> *The Knickerbocker News*, Albany, New York, December 1, 1957[1]

Hiking Partners: Herbert Clark and Robert and George Marshall

Two young brothers, Robert and George Marshall, and their friend and guide, Herbert Clark, 30 years their senior, started their quest to climb the 46 Adirondack High Peaks with a trip up Whiteface Mountain on August 1, 1918. Growing up and living at opposite ends of the state – the Marshalls from New York City, and Herb Clark from Saranac Lake – their backgrounds were as different as the landscape in which they hiked, but what they shared was a sense of adventure and a deep love of the wilderness. The trio hiked at a time when only twelve of the 46 peaks had trails (but no trail markers and few signboards to guide their way), when large expanses of forest had been denuded by the timber industry and scarred by logging slash and the ravages of fires, and when one could spend all day hiking and not see another person. They hiked not for recognition or to gain membership to an elite club, but for the sense of adventure and the pure joy derived from exploring the wilderness around them. Their seemingly insignificant personal accomplishment caught the attention of like-minded adventurers who also were captivated by the wilds of the Adirondacks, and it eventually spurred the establishment of the Adirondack Forty-Sixers, a club whose members have literally followed in their footsteps to climb the Adirondack 46 High Peaks.

Robert and George Marshall were the sons of Louis Marshall, a German immigrant, and Florence Lowenstein Marshall. The couple married on May 6, 1895, and had four children: James, the eldest; Ruth, known as "Pootie"[2]; Robert, who was almost always called Bob, born January 2, 1901; and George, born February 11, 1904. A family of wealth and prominence, they lived in a brownstone on East 72nd Street in New York City. Louis Marshall was well known as a brilliant constitutional lawyer who argued numerous cases before the U. S. Supreme Court. He was a champion of minority causes, often providing free legal counsel, a respected Jewish leader, an amateur naturalist, and a staunch defender of wilderness. As a delegate to the New York State Constitutional Convention in 1894, he played a leading role in the passage of Article VII, the "Forever Wild" amendment to the state's constitution. Article VII provided protection for the Adirondack and Catskill Forest Preserves, which had been established in 1885, stating, "The lands of the state, now owned or hereafter acquired, constituting the Forest Preserve as now fixed by law, shall be forever kept as wild forest lands. They shall not be leased, sold or exchanged, or be taken by any corporation, public or private, nor shall the timber thereon be sold, removed or destroyed."[3]

Bob Marshall

For Bob and George, their father's love of the outdoors and respect for protecting wilderness, along with their early experiences climbing in the Adirondacks, led to lifetimes of advocacy on behalf of wilderness preservation and conservation. Bob, in particular, developed a passionate, almost obsessive, love for the outdoors and a keen understanding of the need to minimize human impact on the environment and set aside and protect wild areas from human intervention. In his book *A Wilderness Original: The Life of Bob Marshall*, James Glover speculates that this attitude was reinforced not only by Louis Marshall's efforts on behalf of wilderness preservation but also by the nineteenth century doctrine of romanticism, which Bob studied in school. Romanticism was a philosophy that valued the spirituality of nature and the need for the human spirit to use the outdoors as a tonic for mental and physical rejuvenation. Bob was also influenced by the book *Pioneer Boys of the Great Northwest*, which he read while recovering from a bout of pneumonia at the age of eleven.[4] The book, which he reread several times, was an adventure story based on the Lewis and Clark expedition. Bob also discovered a copy of Adirondack surveyor Verplanck Colvin's multi-volume *Report of the Topographical Survey of the Adirondack Wilderness* on a bookshelf at Knollwood, his family's summer retreat on Lower Saranac Lake. The accounts of wilderness exploration captivated him, and he spent the rest of his life trying to match firsthand the exhilaration he felt when reading about uncharted wilderness.[5]

Bob Marshall

Glover provides an excellent examination of Bob Marshall and the significant role he played not only in encouraging hiking in the Adirondack High Peaks but also in guiding the course for wilderness preservation in the United States. Glover described Bob as having a "sturdy but slightly pear-shaped frame, square shoulders, wavy brown hair" and a distinctive "rapid gait." His customary hiking attire consisted of "loose-fitting blue-denim jeans, high-topped sneakers, and faded cotton shirt."[6]

With an obsessive and hyperactive personality, Bob put his whole being into everything he did. He had a passion for keeping detailed records on everything – from baseball statistics to descriptions of the flora and fauna he saw while hiking, to lists of his most enjoyable hikes, the prettiest Adirondack ponds, and the most impressive mountain views. Bob recorded it all. He also had a passion for long hikes. Bob was famous for taking 30 to 40-mile, sometimes upwards of 60-mile day hikes. Many of those expeditions were off-trail in uncharted wilderness.[7] Although he did engage in "peak-bagging" expeditions to see how many mountains he could climb in a given amount of time, his motivation, he claimed, was for the pure fun of being active and to experience as much of what nature had to offer as possible. Those long trips also seemed to have been a way to satisfy his need to expend an enormous amount of energy. If after one of those long hikes he felt he hadn't traveled enough miles, he would walk up and down the road by his residence to add on more miles. In 1928 he sent a formal announcement to his friends of his accomplishment: "Mr. Robert Marshall takes pleasure in announcing that he walked 30 or more miles in one day for the 100th time on Sunday, January 1, 1928, in Yellowstone National Park."[8]

In 1932 Bob set out to see how many peaks he could climb in one day in the Adirondacks. Beginning his hike at 3:30 a.m. and finishing at 10:30 p.m., he climbed 14 peaks and ascended a total of 13,600 feet. In writing about his 19-hour hike he said, "Yesterday I ascended fourteen Adirondack peaks… [This] would fit perfectly in a class with flagpole sitting and marathon dancing as an entirely useless type of record, made only to be broken, were it not that I had such a thoroughly glorious time out of the entire day…"[9]

In July 1932 Bob was asked to attend a conference to establish rules for the "sport" of breaking records while climbing in the Adirondacks. He was unable to attend but did offer his views on the subject: "As for making standards for record climbing, I'm afraid that that is a rather futile pastime, because record climbing loses its significance as soon as it ceases to be merely an exhilaration thoroughly paying for itself, regardless of records established, and becomes just an effort for records."[10]

Bob decided at an early age to extend his passion for exploring wilderness to a career as a forester. In 1920 he enrolled in the New York State College of Forestry at Syracuse University. His father had been instrumental in establishing the College of Forestry and served as its first president. Bob's time at the school helped him formulate his philosophy on wilderness preservation and the benefits to human health of untouched wild places to relieve the stresses of urban living. He graduated in 1924 and went on to study for a Masters of

Forestry degree at Harvard Forest (part of Harvard University) in Petersham, Massachusetts. He completed the masters program in 1925. From 1925 to 1928 he worked at the Northern Rocky Mountain Forest Experiment Station along the Montana-Idaho border. It was there that he earned his reputation for taking long walks. Thirty-mile day-hikes were routine and forty-milers were nothing unusual.[11] In 1940, to honor him and his work, a 950,000-acre roadless area in the Flathead and Lewis and Clark National Forest in Montana, an area which Bob had extensively explored, was designated as the Bob Marshall Wilderness Area.

Bob returned to the East Coast in 1928 to attend Johns Hopkins University to work on a doctorate degree in plant physiology. At the end of his first year he traveled to Alaska, where he explored a 15,000-acre section of the Brooks Range and subsequently published a book describing the trip, *Alaska Wilderness*. This was just one of many books and journal articles he published throughout his life recounting his explorations and expounding about issues of wilderness preservation. He finished his Ph.D. in 1930 and returned to Alaska for over a year to live among the Eskimos and continue his exploration of the Brooks Range. The result of that stay was the book *Arctic Village*, his most popular and well-known publication. Altogether, Bob spent more than 200 days exploring the Brooks Range, climbing peaks previously unclimbed, and mapping and assigning names to important physical formations in over 12,000 square miles of uncharted wilderness. The heart of the area was subsequently set aside as the Gates of the Arctic National Park.

Bob Marshall was appointed Director of the Indian Forest Service in 1933. In that position he visited reservations from Minnesota to Arizona and advised on problems of land and wildlife management and grazing practices. Despite the fact that he worked for the federal government, he often found his personal convictions at odds with official policy. He was opposed to the building of Skyline Drive in the Shenendoah National Park in 1934 and advised against it. The Park Service's decision to go ahead with the road was one of the major factors in Marshall's efforts to create a national wilderness group to fight for wilderness preservation throughout the United States. In January 1935, he, along with seven friends and preservationists who shared his concern, created the Wilderness Society, for which Marshall provided the majority of the early funding. Today, with more than 250,000 members, the Wilderness Society has become a leading advocate for preserving wild lands in the United States, and it continues to carry out Marshall's visions.

In 1937 Marshall became Director of Recreation and Lands for the Forest Service. In that position he was able to make significant contributions to changing the philosophies and policies of the Forest Service to promote responsible stewardship of wild lands and to make national parks and public lands open to all people. During the 1930s some resorts on National Park land openly discriminated against African Americans and Jews. Bob protested the inequity, claiming that the national parks and the wilderness belonged to all Americans and should be accessible to all, regardless of race, color, or religious affiliation.

Bob Marshall died unexpectedly on November 10, 1939. He was traveling by train from Washington, D.C., to New York City to visit his brothers, George and Jim, and was found dead in his berth when the train arrived at Penn Station.[12] He was not quite 39 years old. Bob had lived his passion and he had made no compromise in his quest for wilderness preservation. He articulated a sentiment and a philosophy that all who seek inspiration from the wilds can appreciate: "...the enjoyment of solitude, complete independence, and the beauty of undefiled panoramas is absolutely essential to happiness."[13]

Although he had hiked all over the country, he once wrote to a friend, "in spite of the more rugged mountains in a few parts of the west, the Adirondacks are still my favorites."[14]

George Marshall

While he did not follow his older brother into a vocation involving wilderness preservation, George Marshall demonstrated a strong advocacy for preserving wild places through his volunteer activities. He also embraced his father's passion for advancing minority causes and had a long, and, in part, painful history of social activism.

Along with Bob, George attended the Ethical Culture School in New York City, a walk across Central Park from their East Side brownstone. Florence Marshall died of cancer when George was 12 years old and his sister Ruth filled the role of a surrogate mother for the family.

George attended Columbia College, where he received his B.A. (Phi Beta Kappa) in 1926 and M.A. in 1927. He then went on to the Brookings Institution in Washington, D.C., where he received his Ph.D. in economics in 1930, a year after his father's death. He worked as assistant editor of the *Encyclopedia of Social Sciences* from 1929 to 1931; as an economist for the Consumer Division of the Bureau of Labor Statistics from 1934 to 1937; and as a consultant to the Natural Resources Council from 1937 to 1938.

In 1930 George married Elisabeth (Betty) Dublin, a Phi Beta Kappa Barnard graduate whose father would become a vice president of the Metropolitan Life Insurance Company. The marriage was put to the test in 1931 when George contracted tuberculosis. The couple moved to South Carolina in an effort to facilitate his recuperation from the disease. To continue his recovery, they moved to Garmisch Partenkirken in Germany, where they witnessed the rise of Hitler and the Nazi party. Recognizing the dangers of remaining in Germany at that time, they returned to New York, where George shifted his focus from academics to political engagement. Following his father's advocacy for minority causes, George became involved in the defense of civil liberties and civil rights, fighting for the elimination of such practices as the lynching of blacks in the South and the poll tax.[15] He served as chairman of the National Federation for Constitutional Liberties and its successor organization, the Civil Rights Congress, which between 1946 and 1956 was the leading organization in the emerging Civil Rights Movement. George gave the keynote address at the founding meeting of the Civil Rights Congress in Detroit in 1946. He worked closely with Paul Robeson, Dashiel Hammett, and William L. Patterson defending black civil rights and the civil liberties of American Communists following World War II.[16]

George Marshall

In April 1946, George was called before the House Un-American Activities Committee, a committee (1938–1975) of the U.S. House of Representatives created to investigate disloyalty and subversive organizations. Refusing to cooperate with the committee's investigation by turning over organizational records of the National Federation for Constitutional Liberties, he was cited for contempt of Congress. He was convicted and his case went to the Supreme Court, which refused to hear his appeal. He served three months in federal prison in Ashland, Kentucky, in 1950.

In the years following his incarceration, George turned his attention to his other passion, environmental conservation. He had an active interest in wilderness preservation and conservation issues and wrote numerous articles on the subject. In 1937 he joined his brother, Bob, on the board of directors of the Wilderness Society. He was a member of the national council of the Wilderness Society for more than 50 years and served at various times on its executive committee. He served as the managing editor of the society's publication *The Living Wilderness* between 1957 and 1961 and also served as president of the society, 1971-72. George was a charter member of the Adirondack Mountain Club (ADK) and an active member of its conservation committee and board of directors for many years. He was assistant editor of the ADK publication *Ad-i-ron-dac* from 1955 to 1959.

After moving to California in 1959, George became active with the Sierra Club, serving on its board of directors, 1959-68, as secretary, 1965-66, and again, 1967-68, and as the club's president, 1966-67.

In 1978 George and Betty moved to London, England, where they resided until Betty's death in 1993, at which time George moved back to New York. He died on May 21, 2000, at the age of 96, after a long battle with Parkinson's Disease.

The Knollwood Club, Saranac Lake

In 1899 Louis Marshall and five friends bought a tract of 500 acres along the northeast shore of Lower Saranac Lake. The camp complex that they built on a forested hillside overlooking the lake was known as the Knollwood Club. The six families hired a local Saranac Lake architect, William Coulter, to design individual camps and several community buildings. Coulter was well known in the area for designing rustic structures in what is now known as the Adirondack "Great Camp" style. When construction was completed in 1900, the Knollwood Club consisted of six two-and-a-half story cottages, one for each family; a central building that served as a communal dining and recreation facility, known as the Casino; a two-story boat house; and a baseball field. Each cottage had two levels of log porches that wrapped around three sides. The gables above each upper porch were decorated with a unique geometric pattern of native timber. Wooden boardwalks through the woods connected the buildings. Knollwood was considered "one of the most carefully planned and executed of the Great Camps."[17]

The Marshall family spent their summers at Knollwood, with Louis commuting from New York City by train on Fridays and returning on Sunday evenings. Knollwood was an active community that offered Bob and George a variety of educational and recreational opportunities including reading, Bible study, basketball, baseball, tennis, swimming, and boating. The boys often accompanied their father on long walks in the woods that surrounded the compound. George and Bob also tramped all over the area by themselves. When George was 14 and Bob 17, they circumnavigated Upper, Middle, and Lower Saranac lakes, a trip of 40 miles, in 11 hours, 38 minutes. They even ran the final three-quarters-of-a-mile from the Knollwood gate to the compound so they would be back in time for dinner. Bob's and George's early boyhood adventures in the Adirondack Mountains served as the perfect landscape for developing their philosophy of environmental protection and conservation as they experienced firsthand the pleasures derived from spending time in the wilderness.

An amateur botanist, Louis taught his children how to identify the native plants and trees and had them inventory the flora around Knollwood each year.[18] Bob in particular displayed a penchant for recording what he observed and kept detailed records. Not only did he keep journals on the plants around Knollwood and what he saw on his walks with his father, but he also kept detailed accounts of the Knollwood Baseball League, writing summaries of each game played and game statistics, which he collected in small handmade booklets. This attention to detail was a skill that served him well in his career as a forester and explorer.

With all the activities available on the grounds of Knollwood, Bob and George could have been entertained without ever leaving the grounds, but what enthralled them most was the vast wilderness that surrounded them and the anticipation of the adventures that were waiting for them if they ventured out to explore it.

Herbert Clark, Friend and Guide

In 1906, the Marshall family hired Herbert Clark, a veteran Adirondack guide, to be their guide at Knollwood during the summer months – to take family members on hiking, hunting, and fishing trips, to teach the children outdoor skills, and to do odd jobs around the property.

Herb Clark was born in Keeseville on July 10, 1870, the ninth of 11 children born to Elizabeth Marion Spence and John Clark. His grandparents had emigrated to Quebec from Scotland and Northern Ireland. According to family history, his Scottish grandmother had been a lady-in-waiting to the Queen. After marrying, his parents lived in Canada before buying a farm outside of Keeseville, which they paid for in gold. The couple prospered until the Civil War. John served in the Army of the Potomac and returned to northern New York with crippling rheumatism, a condition thought to have been brought on by sleeping on the ground throughout his three years of Army service. Elizabeth suffered from tuberculosis. Because of their physical maladies, farm work for them became difficult, and the family fell on hard times. The Clarks sold the farm and bought another piece of land near Augur Pond in the town of Chesterfield during the depression of 1873. The children helped with chores on the farm before going to school and worked outside the farm during the summer to earn extra money for the family. Herb worked odd jobs wherever he could find them to help support the family.

George Marshall and Herb Clark on top of Basin

Bob Marshall provided the most complete picture of Herb Clark's background and his own relationship with him in an article he wrote for the October 1933 edition of the Adirondack Mountain Club's *High Spots*. Of Herb's childhood he wrote:

> In spite of the austerity which this background may suggest, Herb from his childhood was a jocular and dashing young blade. His fondness for poking the keenest sort of satire at hypocrisy and sham, for twisting up blusterers in their own boastful stories, was something which friends who knew Herb in his youth tell me he possessed while he was in the early teens. He apparently was a very handsome young man in those days and a great favorite with the girls whom he rushed by the wholesale.
>
> Herb was also a terribly hard worker, and he had a tremendous sense of loyalty to his family. He contributed materially to its income from the time he was twelve. For about five years he worked on the farm and in such odd jobs as he could pick up around Clintonville. In those days they paid 50 cents for a 12-hour day at loading pulp wood.[19]

Herb Clark on Ampersand Mountain

Marshall went on to list the various jobs that Herb held: haying at Hank Allen's farm in North Elba, working at Miller's old hotel on Lower Saranac Lake and at the old Club House at Bartlett's Carry between Upper Saranac and Round Lake.

> He acted as a night watchman at Bartlett's for two years, then for five summers rowed the freight boat 24 miles between Bartlett's and the Ampersand in the morning and guided in the afternoon, and finally for three years devoted himself exclusively to guiding. The freight boat was a huge Adirondack guide boat, nearly twice the length of the normal crafts of that design, and Herb sometimes rowed as much as 2200 pounds in one load. While at Bartlett's he made the record of having rowed about 65 miles in one day, 24 of them with this freight boat.[20]

Herb was well-known in the area as a champion oarsman, among the top finishers in All-Adirondack rowing competitions on Lower Saranac Lake throughout the early 1900s.

In 1903 Herb married Mary Jane Dowdle from Madrid, New York. They met at the Wawbeek Hotel, one of the finest hotels in its day on Upper Saranac Lake. Mary worked there as a waitress. The couple settled in Saranac Lake and had six children: Gertrude Marion (b. April 13, 1904); George Thomas (b. September 4, 1905); Herbert John (b. May 8, 1908); Irene Elizabeth (b. November 24, 1909); James Robert (b. June 12, 1911); and Francis Vincent (b. January 23, 1919). James, George, and Gertrude Clark also worked at Knollwood during the summer when they were teenagers. James and George were porters and bus boys and Gertrude worked in the dining room and did housekeeping. They also participated in annual staff athletic meets at Knollwood, as did Herb, competing in activities such as rowing, sack, three-legged, potato, and tub races, and pillow fights.

When Clark went to work for the Marshalls at Knollwood, all of the Marshall children were under ten years of age. For the children, particularly Bob and George, Clark became a cherished companion, teacher, and friend. Bob described their relationship:

> ...to me Herb has been not only the greatest teacher that I have ever had, but also the most kindly and considerate friend a person could ever dream about, a constantly refreshing and stimulating

companion with whom to discuss both passing events and the more permanent philosophical relationships, and to top it all, the happy possessor of the keenest of humor I have known...

For my brothers and myself Herb would make up the most amazing fables. A rock on Lower Saranac with a peculiar dent was where Captain Kidd had bumped his head. The Ausable River below the present Olympic ski jump was where the Monitor and Merrimac had fought their famous battle... There were those great heroes of our youth: Sliny Stott, a sort of reverse Paul Bunyan, who did everything inconceivably poorer than you would imagine it could be done; Jacob Whistletricker, a man with many marvelous drugs; Joe McGinnis, who got the fantod, a disease in which one shrinks to the size of a baseball ... Herb is full of songs. Almost every year he adds to his repertoire, which consists either of garbled versions of ancient popular ditties, fitted to suit his needs, or of jingles which he made up expressly for the occasion.[21]

On August 13, 1916, Herb took Bob and George on their first mountain climb: Mt. Ampersand. Bob was 15, George 12, and Herb 46. Years later in an article which appeared in *High Spots,* "Some Reflections on Ampersand Mountain," George Marshall described part of that climb:

Bob and I were frequently looking around as we climbed to try to get a glimpse of Round Lake [Middle Saranac] through the trees. When we came to the ladders, Herb Clark was afraid that if we craned our necks too hard in our effort to see everything, we might fall. So with ever ready wit he told us that it was on these very ladders that Lot's wife was turned into a pillar of salt for disobeying the admonition never to look back, and that if we looked back for a view while on the ladders we might suffer the same sad fate. We were sufficiently impressed to wait for our view until we reached the summit.[22]

That first hike of Ampersand piqued their curiosity about the mountains around them. George later wrote, "We decided to penetrate those mountains, which previously had been accepted as a scenic backdrop along the skyline across the lake, and see what lay beyond."[23] Years later, when completing a questionnaire for the 46ers, he described how he became interested in mountain climbing: "Probably climbing the hemlock hill from Lower Saranac Lake to our cottage to eat lunch the first year I could walk, and then, in the natural course of events, climbing higher and higher hills over the years until one hill was finally tall enough to be called a mountain."

In 1917 the trio started going on overnight camping trips and climbed Baker, Stoney Creek, and Bootbay mountains in the Saranac area. Bob wrote detailed reports on each hike and rated the mountains for views and overall enjoyment of their climbs, a tradition he continued throughout his life.

According to one of Herb's granddaughter's, Herb's wife Mary Jane was very supportive of his work as a guide and his hiking trips with the Marshall boys. Whenever he went on his hikes, Mary Jane would cook him a steak and homefries breakfast at 4 a.m. and send him on his way. Most times he would leave before sun up and return home after dark. Only Herb's son Herbert John followed in his father's footsteps, working as a hunting, fishing, and trapping guide for a period of time.

When he wasn't hiking or working at Knollwood in the summer, Herb maintained a large vegetable garden and was known throughout the Saranac Lake area for having impressive flower beds filled with dahlias, hollyhocks, and phlox. Clark passed away on March 2, 1945, at the age of 74.

The 46 Climbing Challenge Begins

During the summer of 1918, Bob, George, and Herb, and a friend, Carl Poser, climbed Whiteface, the first 4,000-foot peak for all of them. Bob Marshall noted later the irony that although Herb Clark was perhaps best known for his hiking accomplishments in the High Peaks, he had never climbed a 4,000-footer until that climb of Whiteface. Later that summer the trio climbed Marcy, Algonquin (which they knew as MacIntyre), and Iroquois (which they called Herbert).

It wasn't until 1920, when Bob was a freshman at the College of Forestry at Syracuse University that he and George decided that they should climb all the 4,000-foot peaks in the Adirondacks, which at that time was thought to number 42. "For the next six years," Bob said, "Herb, George, and I found Adirondack mountain climbing our greatest joy in life." In the summer of 1921 the three climbed 23 peaks in three major excursions. Eighteen of them were trailless, and eight – Marshall (then known as Iroquois), Allen, Street, Nye, Hough (then known as Middle Dix), East Dix, South Dix, and Couchsachraga – had no records of previous ascents. By the end of the following summer, they had completed all 42 peaks.

George Marshall's records indicate that the three men did not climb every peak together. On a few occasions Herb hiked with just Bob or just George and, a few times, the two brothers hiked together without Herb. However, throughout their five years of climbing the 46, they each climbed them all and completed their final climb together.

Since the Marshall family did not own a car, just getting to the High Peaks was an adventure for the threesome. First, Herb Clark would make use of his expert oarsmanship to row from his house about a mile-and-a-half across Lower Saranac Lake to pick up the boys at Knollwood. Then he would row back across the lake. The trio, on a typical trip, then walked another mile-and-a-half to the Saranac Lake Depot, where they boarded the train to Lake Placid. They then walked down the dirt road to South Meadow, a distance of about eight miles. In later years George Marshall wrote an essay about walking the road to South Meadow, "Approach to the Mountains," which originally appeared in the March-April 1955 edition of *Ad-i-ron-dac*. He considered it "fortunate" that his family did not have an automobile as the threesome enjoyed their time walking the road and considered it preparation, both physically and mentally, for the climbs that lay ahead.

> The joys of road walking in those days before pavements and heavy traffic were to us only second to those of tramping and climbing in the back woods... As we swung along, the dirt rising from our feet, our energy seemed to be kinetic – the more we walked, the easier it seemed to be to walk... On the first trip on which we carried packbaskets, the straps began to pull a bit as the road mounted. Suddenly Herb burst into song:
>
> > I saw three wayworn travelers,
> > In tattered garments clad.
> > They were struggling up the mountain
> > And it seemed that they were sad.
> > Their backs were heavy laden,
> > Their strength was almost gone,
> > And they shouted as they journeyed,
> > "Deliverance will come.
> > Then crowns of victory, palms of glory,
> > Crowns of victory they will wear."

George Marshall and Herb Clark on snowshoes, ready to ascend Algonquin

When we entered these wilder regions, our eight-mile hike to the last frontier at the road's end had prepared us in ways that cannot be equaled today by driving an auto to the beginning of a trail. The road walk was a gradual transition, physically and psychologically, between the twentieth-century world and the primeval...[24]

South Meadow was the jumping-off site for several of their major trips, including their first climb of Marcy, a circling of the MacIntyres, an exploration of Wallface-Scott Pond-Lost Pond plateau, a pack into Panther Gorge to the Upper Range, and a walk to the Saranacs via Indian Pass, Preston Ponds, Big Ampersand, and Kettle Mountain Pass.

One of the trio's most memorable trips was a four-day hike of the Upper Range in 1920, when Bob was 19, George 16, and Herb 50. On the first day the group packed in from Lake Placid and camped at Lake Colden. The second day they climbed Skylight and then dropped down to Panther Gorge to camp. On the third day they climbed Haystack, Basin, Saddleback and Gothics and then retraced their steps to return to their camp in Panther Gorge. That day they walked about 20 miles with a vertical elevation gain and loss of 18,400 feet in nine hours and forty minutes. Bob Marshall described the day as "the hardest, the wildest, and one of the very most enjoyable days of our lives."

> It was 8:23 when we started on what we hoped would be the big day of our trip – the traverse of the range. The ascent to the forks of the trail in the flats between Haystack and Bartlett was a glorious climb through a magnificent coniferous forest... Then we went to the summit [Haystack] and looked over on the heavily wooded valley and mountains on the other side. Our eyes rested on the range we were to traverse, and we realized far better than the map could indicate what a hard day lay before us. As we looked around us we realized that this was one of the few places east of the Rockies where a person could look over miles of territory without seeing civilization... It was just eleven o'clock when, after emerging from the woods and traversing the

George Marshall and Herb Clark

rocky stretch near the top we reached the summit [Basin]. We had descended and then ascended 2000 feet in an hour and three minutes... An easy drop of about three hundred feet and another rise of a couple of hundred, and we were ready for perhaps the steepest part of the whole trip. We could not go very fast, and even Herb continually cautioned us to go carefully... Suddenly I heard George ahead exclaim, 'Well, I've seen pretty many ways of traveling in the mountains but never this before.' Looking over his shoulder I perceived a long rope stretched the length of a 35 or 40-foot slide having a grade of at least 130 percent. Herb was just starting to let himself down. His feet acted slightly as brakes, but he depended mostly upon the rope for support... The climb up Saddleback was about 450 feet, but not hard... Through the trees we could see the bold, sharp aspect of the Gothics, with their awful precipices... The ascent was the rockiest we had ever encountered. It led along a steep slide... Finally we reached the first peak of the Gothics... We soon continued to the main peak, for we were anxious to reach our destination, and in a short time stood on the highest point, ten miles, and 9200 feet by up and down climbing, from Panther Gorge. It was now 1:02. The journey had taken about 4½ hours... we started on the return at 1:42... Despite the fact that there was no hurry, Herb proceeded to set a terrific pace down the very steep, rocky face of the Gothics, all the time admonishing George and myself to go slowly and carefully. We were not a bit bothered by his speed, but decided to take our time, go as he would... We noticed and admired his method. He never stopped or hesitated at the steepest place. It was steadiness that made his speed. George and I would stop every now and then at a bad place, or sit down and gently slide, but never Herb. This sliding, incidentally, put two great holes in my trousers... It was 6:04 when we returned from the hardest day of our lives. We had been gone nine hours and forty minutes... Thus in one day we had climbed a fifth again as high as the climb up Pikes Peak from its base. Counting ascent and descent together, we had done 18,400 feet, or more than 3½ miles just up and down. Our total mileage for the day was about 20 miles. We had seen no one outside our own party in over 24 hours.[25]

As if that wasn't enough, Bob and George reclimbed Haystack the following day, and the trio packed out over Mt. Marcy and out to Woods' farm near North Elba.

Bob Marshall made several other references to Herb Clark's speed and skill as a route-finder in various articles that he wrote about their climbing adventures.

> In our later adventures on trailless peaks.... Herb was really a marvel. At the age of 51 he was the fastest man I have ever known in the pathless woods. Furthermore, he could take one glance at a mountain from some distant point then not be able to see anything 200 feet from where he was walking for several hours, and emerge on the summit by what would almost always be the fastest and easiest route.[26]

Bob also credited Herb with coining the term cripplebrush. He wrote, "I recall once while we were battling our way through the clumps of mountain balsam on Colden, hearing Herb's cheerful voice from far above us booming out:

> 'Don't let the golden moments go,
> Like the sunbeams passing by,
> You'll never miss the cripplebrush
> 'Til ten years after you die.'"[27]

In a letter to Grace Hudowalski, long-time historian of the Adirondack Forty-Sixers, and the club's first president, dated January 12, 1939, in which he approved of Grace's idea of assembling a list of all the people who had climbed the 46 High Peaks, Bob wanted to make sure that Grace understood the special relationship he and George shared with Herb Clark. He wrote that Clark "was more than just a nameless guide. He is just about the most distinctive and individual person I have ever known and also just about the grandest human being I have ever met. As a matter of fact, our relationship on these trips was not that of guide and guided, although Herb was much the most competent of the three of us. However, we would all hold conferences when different problems of route came up... and then decide on which route we would take."

Then in a hand-written P.S. he wrote, "Incidentally I just spent a weekend at Saranac Lake and Herb Clark, who is now 69, accompanied me on 21 miles of a 32-mile walk."

In 1922 Bob and George became charter members of the Adirondack Mountain Club, which was organized that year. To help the club get started, Bob gave them a manuscript he had written, "The High Peaks of the Adirondacks," which the club published. It was the first climbing guide for the High Peaks. In writing the booklet, Bob noted that he wrote only as the scribe and was speaking as much for Herb and George as for himself.

The booklet contained brief trail descriptions and a view rating of each summit. The ratings were compiled through a "secret ballot," taken in writing from George, Herb and Bob himself. Using the wilderness characteristics of a summit as the main criteria for the beauty of the view, the trio considered the views from the summits of Haystack, Santanoni, and Nippletop as the top three mountain vistas, and the views from Phelps, Street, and Nye as the least attractive. While a totally subjective list, which the trio readily acknowledged, the Marshall/Clark view rating has resulted in some good-natured debate and more than a little head-scratching by today's hikers. However, in analyzing the list it must be remembered that much of the Adirondack landscape in the 1920s was scarred by forest fires and lumbering activities. Those blemishes led the Marshalls and Herb Clark to rate some views as much less "beautiful" than they appear today. The one ranking that most hikers still agree with is that of Haystack as having the most impressive view. In a letter to Grace Hudowalski dated September 18, 1968, George Marshall reaffirmed his number one view rating for Haystack after reclimbing the mountain for the first time in 30 years. He said: "The first view of the cone of Tahawus from the ledges on the way to Haystack was very beautiful and unlike anything I have seen in any other part of the world. The view from the top of Haystack itself was magnificent and moving... On the basis of this recent climb, I see no reason to revise our former rating of the views from Haystack as being the finest of any in the Adirondacks – which also means from any peak I have ever been on. There are still almost no signs of civilization from the top..."

A survey of 46ers conducted in 1988 to update the Marshall/Clark view ratings based on the current landscape concurred. More than 60 years after the initial view ratings were published, hikers again bestowed upon Haystack the number one ranking for best view in the High Peaks.[28]

"The High Peaks of the Adirondacks" stimulated interest in hiking the Adirondack 4,000-footers. The pocket-sized booklet also caught the eye of Russell M. L. "Little Mac" Carson, an Adirondack historian and climber. In a letter to Bob Marshall dated November

Bob Marshall

29, 1923, Carson wrote "...no book, large or small, ever quite thrilled me as did yours. It... obsessed me with the Adirondacks." Carson used Marshall's book as an incentive to build membership and attendance at Glens Falls Rotary Club meetings. Carson was the club's first secretary. Each time a member attended one of the club's weekly luncheons, he would be credited with the height of one of the 42 High Peaks. Whoever "climbed" the greatest number of feet won the competition. Carson sparked additional interest by writing a historical sketch of one of the peaks each week. That was the start of Carson's five-year research and study of the High Peaks, which culminated in the publication of *Peaks and People of the Adirondacks* in 1927. In a letter to Bob Marshall dated May 4, 1923, Carson described the evolution of his book from Rotary Club contest to what to this day many consider to be the definitive work on the history of the Adirondack High Peaks.

> Last fall I originated a Mountain Climbing Contest for the Glens Falls Rotary Club for an attendance competition which would extend over the same number of weeks as there were mountains described in "The High Peaks." Although Glens Falls is in the foot hills of the Adirondacks, most of us here are a good deal like the New Yorkers that have not seen the Statue of Liberty, so the club director's asked me to write a short story of the mountain climbed each week for the club letter as part of the stunt. When I started it, I had no idea of anything more than a story about the scenery based on your booklet, Donaldson, Longstreth and my own, still limited experience. But as I got into it, I began, almost without realizing it, searching for the origins of the mountain names, many of which I had wondered about for years. From that first idea, the writing of a set of little historical sketches concerning name sources, first climbs and the cutting of the first trails has evolved.

In the course of his research, Carson "discovered" four peaks which the Marshalls and Clark had overlooked in their climbs. On October 14, 1923, he wrote to Bob urging the threesome to climb Gray Peak, which they no doubt had assumed was just a shoulder of Marcy, as well as Cliff, Blake, and Couchsachraga, all of which at the time were thought to be just 4,000 feet. So the three climbed the remaining four peaks in 1924.

However, in a later climb of Seward and Donaldson, Herb and George discovered that the trio really had not climbed Emmons, so they returned in 1925 to climb that peak on June 10, to officially become the first to climb all 46 of the Adirondack High Peaks. George explained this in his letter to Grace Hudowalski dated March 1, 1951 when he submitted the trio's climbing roster for the newly organized Adirondack Forty-Sixers. He said, "We thought we had climbed Emmons when we climbed Seward and Donaldson on August 23, 1921. Herb and I discovered our mistake when we climbed Seward and Donaldson on August 11, 1924, with Russ Carson and Charlie West. We discovered that in 1921 we thought that what is now Donaldson was South Seward and that North Seward was an intervening peak between it and Seward itself. When we discovered our mistake, we informed Bob and discussed it with him and arranged to climb the real South Seward, now called Emmons, the following summer."

Russell Carson

Carson continued to research the High Peaks through the years uncovering additional information on the history of the area. Philip G. Terrie edited a revised edition of *Peaks and People* that was published in 1986 by the Adirondack Mountain Club. Many of the revisions he included in the new edition were based on Carson's continuing research following the book's original publication in 1927.

A charter member and a president of the Adirondack Mountain Club, Carson helped establish the club's *High Spots* magazine, serving as editor of that publication for a number of years. He wrote numerous articles for *High Spots* and for *The Cloud Splitter*, the ADK Albany Chapter's newsletter. He penned an outdoor recreation column (1928-29), "The Footpath," which was published in the Glens Falls *Post-Star* and five other papers. It is interesting to note that while Carson continued to write extensively on the Adirondacks, for ADK publications and several newspapers, he never became a 46er, climbing only 21 of the High Peaks.

Carson was president and director of his own insurance company in Glens Falls. A civic leader, he was a member of the local Rotary Club and also served on the Glens Falls Union Free School Board for more than 35 years. He served as president of the New York State School Board Association, president of the New York State Association of Local Insurance Agents, chairman of the finance committee of the National Association of Insurance Agents, and for 20 years as a trustee for the Association for the Protection of the Adirondacks. He died in 1961.

Part II: The Forty-Sixers of Troy and the Adirondack Forty-Sixers

During the early 1930s Bob Marshall's booklet, "The High Peaks of the Adirondacks," and Russell Carson's *Peaks and People of the Adirondacks* captured the attention of a small group of outdoor enthusiasts from Grace Methodist Church in Troy, in particular the church's pastor, the Rev. Ernest Ryder (#7), and two parishioners, Grace Hudowalski (#9) and Edward Hudowalski (#6).

Ryder was born in Rensselaer in 1887. His family moved to Vermont in 1894, and there his father entered the ministry. "Love of mountains and lakes was soon awakened in me," Ernest later said. He attended Troy Conference Academy in 1907 and followed his father into the Methodist ministry. He became pastor of Grace Methodist Church in 1930.

Ernest Ryder, with cap and white tie, atop Whiteface with friends, including his fiancée, Letha Matteson (in white sweater), in August 1911

Ryder's first High Peak ascent was of Whiteface, which he climbed dressed in a suitcoat and white tie in August of 1911, seven years before the Marshalls and Herb Clark climbed it, but, as he later wrote, he "didn't enthuse until the early 1930s... *Peaks and People* was the needed tonic." He also wrote, "after climbing a few trailless peaks and reading of the Marshall boys and Herb Clark, I knew it was only a question of time to finish the 46 peaks." His usual hiking partner in his quest was Edward Hudowalski.

Ed was born in 1904 and grew up in Paterson, New Jersey. He became interested in hiking and camping during his Boy Scout days, but he credited his wife Grace's (Grace Leach Hudowalski) "love of the woods" for kindling his interest in mountain climbing. In recounting what spurred his interest in the Adirondack High Peaks, Ed wrote, "Heard a great deal about Marcy from Gracie, who climbed the mountain when she was 15. Became interested. Decided to climb Marcy and the Range with five others because Conservation Department 'Trails to Marcy' said that was the sportiest trip in the Adirondacks. Made trip, liked it and kept coming back for more." Grace, who grew up in the foothills of the Adirondacks recalled, "I'd talked so much about those mountains that finally Ed decided he'd take his Sunday School class to climb Mount Marcy in 1932. That really started the whole thing."

William Lance, one of the members of Ed's Sunday School class, recalled that first trip in July 1932:

> There were six members of this adventurous group – Ed Hudowalski, Charlie Horn, Orville Gowie, Jack Colby, Harry May, and myself. We were all members of Ed's Sunday School class.
>
> Our transportation consisted of two Ford Model A coupes complete with rumble seats. We stored our equipment in luggage racks on the running boards and stashed the pack basket, which contained most of our food, in the rumble seat of Charlie's car. That left room for two in the front seat and two in the rumble seat of Ed's car and two in Charlie's car... Traveling at that time was quite different than it is today. First we had to cross the river to get on Route 9 and then we headed north on a two-lane highway... We proceeded on our way going through Warrensburg, Chestertown, North Hudson and finally reached the turn off to Route 73 over Chapel Pond Road. This section of the trip was over a narrow dirt road...
>
> Catalogs, equipment houses and specialty stores were nonexistent in those days. So we outfitted ourselves through the Boy Scout section of our local department stores and the Army & Navy surplus stores... Most of us preferred a high top shoe (mine were Endicott-Johnson work shoes at $2.95 a pair)... Packs were more or less self-designed. Most consisted of our bedroll (one wool blanket), in which we wrapped an extra shirt, underwear and socks, a wool sweater or jacket, and our cooking and eating utensils. Around all of this we wrapped some support straps so that the whole bundle could be worn over our shoulders.
>
> Ed outlined our climbing procedure: fifty minutes of hiking with a ten-minute rest.[29]

First Forty-Sixers of Troy group at Plateau Lean-to below Marcy's summit

The group packed into Plateau Lean-to (on the VanHoevenberg Trail to Marcy .3 miles before the junction with the Phelps Trail, with the summit dome of Marcy in view), taking turns carrying the pack basket that was filled with canned and fresh food. The neophytes encountered their share of the ubiquitous Adirondack mud.

"We had to traverse a flat stretch of trail that looked innocent enough, but at the first step we were in mud over our shoe tops. Due to the nature of the terrain, we could not go around it but had to slog through. Needless to say, we were muddy halfway to our knees."[30]

Bill Lance, Orville Gowie, Harry May, Jack Colby, Charlie Horn atop Marcy

After a chicken dinner the group bedded down for the night on a deep cushion of balsam boughs placed on the lean-to floorboards by the ranger who patrolled the area. The following morning the group climbed Mt. Marcy and had their first taste of all that the Adirondack wilderness had to offer.

"I was overwhelmed by the expansive vista so magnificently stretched out before me no matter which way I turned. By this time, the mists had lifted, the sun was coming out, and it seemed there was unlimited vision in every compass direction. I was elated and impressed..."[31]

After spending considerable time on the summit consulting their Conservation Department trail map and identifying the surrounding peaks, the group continued to Sno Bird Lean-to (on the Range Trail between Basin and Little Haystack, now a designated campsite) for their second night. The following day they climbed Basin and Saddleback and then descended via the Orebed Brook trail to their cars parked at the Garden. The trip was deemed an unqualified success. Throughout the 1930s Ed and the Reverend Mr. Ryder led numerous trips to climb the High Peaks. Ed's wife, Grace, joined them, finally returning to the area which had captured her attention when she climbed Marcy as a young lady.

Ed and the Rev. Ryder had not, originally, intended to climb all 46. According to Ed, their goal was 25 peaks, but when they hit 27 "by accident," they decided to climb 30. After reaching 30 they decided to climb all of them. The two finished arm-in-arm on Dix in the pouring rain on September 13, 1936. They shared a prayer of praise and thanks for their accomplishment.

Less than six months after the Rev. Ryder and Ed finished their 46, the duo organized a club, comprised mainly of Ed Hudowalski's Sunday School class, known as the Forty-Sixers of Troy. It was Ryder who coined the name "Forty-Sixer." The term first appeared in print in an article in the *Troy Record* newspaper in 1937 announcing the formation of the hiking club: "Troy has its first mountain climbing club, all officers of which have climbed more than thirty of the major peaks in the Adirondacks. The club recently organized will be known as the Forty-sixers..."[32]

Grace Methodist Church

Ryder was elected club president; Ed Hudowalski, vice president; Charles Horn (#11), secretary-treasurer; and Orville Gowie (#8), historian. At that time only Ed and Ryder had climbed all of the 46 High Peaks. Horn had climbed 39 and Gowie 36. Other charter members of the club and the number of peaks climbed at the time were as follows: Clarence Craver, 38; Grace Hudowalski, 32; Louise Goark, 21; William Lance, 7; Janet Ryder, 5; Dorothy Ryder, 5; Mary Davis, 4; and Lethe Ryder, 1. The hope of club members was that the new organization would eventually become a chapter of the Adirondack Mountain Club.

Many of the stories and traditions that are important parts of the Adirondack Forty-Sixers today had their genesis with the Troy club. It was the Rev. Ryder who invented the Skylight legend that placing a rock on the mountain's summit cairn will guarantee good weather. Today the enormous cairn on Skylight's summit attests to the fact that hikers have continued to place their rock offerings on Skylight's top in the hope that the legend is true. Ryder also came up with a little verse to help people remember the order of height of the first ten peaks: "*M*ac *a*nd *S*am *h*ave *g*one *w*here *I d*on't *b*e *g*oing." The first letter in each word matched the first letter of the mountain names – Marcy, Algonquin, Skylight, Haystack, Gray, Whiteface, Iroquois, Dix, Basin, and Gothics. More accurate elevation measurements have made that little ditty obsolete, but it was considered correct at the time.

Ed Hudowalski designed the Forty-Sixers of Troy emblem. He wrote,

Ed Hudowalski

Ed and Grace Hudowalski pause beside a brook.

"The insignia of the club shall be the numerals 4 and 6 with the letter R. These shall be of green upon a circular field of yellow bordered with red." He also designed the current version of the patch (adding the letters "ADK" above the 46-R, which were superimposed over a green mountain) when the Adirondack Forty-Sixers club was formed in 1948. Prior to World War II, Ed led numerous trips to the seldom-climbed trailless peaks, and he was given the affectionate title "Uncle Ed" by fellow climbers.

In much the same spirit and with the same enthusiasm that Bob Marshall had demonstrated for recording details, Grace Hudowalski started keeping track of the climbs of each member of the Forty-Sixers of Troy, noting the dates of each climb and who was on each trip. When C. Howard Nash (#10), a member of the Taconic Hiking Club of Troy, prepared a written summary with pictures to document his feat of climbing the 46 within a six-month period in 1937, the Forty-Sixer tradition of climbers writing to the club to record their climbs began. So, too, began Grace's lifelong commitment to maintaining individual climbing folders for each hiker who was working toward the goal of climbing all of the 46 peaks.

The original 46R patch can be seen above on the pack of its designer: Ed Hudowalski.

Grace Leach Hudowalski

Grace Leach Hudowalski

Grace Dolbeck Leach Hudowalski was born in Ticonderoga on February 25, 1906, and grew up in the surrounding foothills of the Adirondack Mountains. She was the youngest of six children born to James Casper Leach and Alice Luella Dolbeck Leach, who died when Grace was eleven. Her father operated a boat delivery and tourist service on Lake George. In the early 1920s, he bought a hotel/tavern in Minerva and moved the family there. Starting in 1921 Grace lived with her sister, Nora Leach Sproule (#22), ten years her senior, in Troy during the school year so she could attend Troy High School, and while living in Troy, she met her eventual husband, Ed Hudowalski, who was attending Rensselaer Polytechnic Institute. They married on September 5, 1926, after an eleven-month courtship, and settled in Lansingburgh (North Troy). They moved to Albany in the 1940s.

After graduating from RPI in 1927 with a degree in electrical engineering, Ed joined the state Department of Architecture as an electrical draftsman (1928). His state service was interrupted in 1942 when he joined the Army Signal Corps and performed special assignments in Europe, Asia, and the Pacific Theater. He rose to the rank of major and was honorably discharged in 1947. Following the war he returned to state employment in the Department of Public Works as an electrical engineer for the canal system. For 13 years he was Assistant Superintendent of Operations and Maintenance of Canals and Waterways.

Ed and Grace bought a summer home on the eastern side of Schroon Lake in 1954. One of the oldest camps on the lake, it was built in 1910. Although Ed doubted the structural integrity of the camp, the sturdy cedar log building has withstood a century of harsh Adirondack winters. The couple called their rustic camp Boulders, in recognition of the large glacial erratics that dot the property. The camp brought Ed and Grace closer to the area to which they had such strong personal connections. They worked together to promote the Adirondacks and were active in public policy issues that affected the region. Ed, in particular, was very vocal in the debate during the late 1950s over the placement of the Northway (I-87) through the Adirondack Park. The couple also sponsored an annual folklore writing contest for eleventh grade students in the Schroon Lake Central School from 1957 through the mid-1980s. The purpose of the contest was "to uncover early history and folktales of the Town of Schroon and adjacent townships (North Hudson, Minerva, Chester, Ticonderoga, Crown Point)." The essay winners were awarded $50 U.S. Savings Bonds that Grace and Ed donated, and their essays were considered for publication in *New York State Folklore* and *North Country Life* magazines. In 2007 the tradition of the competition was resumed under the leadership of Forty-Sixer Douglas Arnold (#4693W).

Ed passed away at the couple's home in Albany on September 30, 1966, three days before his official retirement from state service, at the age of 62. Grace was at Boulders at the time. Following Ed's death, Boulders became Grace's haven in the mountains. With a view across Schroon Lake of the long ridge of Hoffman Mountain and, in the distance to the north, the Dix Range of the High Peaks, she was in constant visual contact with the mountains she loved. Boulders also became a natural destination for hikers on their way to and from the Adirondacks. During the summer, climbers would often stop by Boulders to share their hiking tales with Grace or to include her in their celebration after finishing the 46.

Grace at work, promoting New York State tourism

Much like Bob Marshall, whose love of the wilderness was his all-consuming passion, Grace devoted her talents and energy, in both her professional and personal life, to promoting the exploration of New York State and in particular the Adirondack Mountains. While in school, Grace developed an interest in storytelling. Following high school she enrolled in evening classes in creative writing and public speaking. Those interests led her to her first job with the New York State Commerce Department in 1945 as a publicity writer. She wrote travel releases highlighting the folklore and history of the state. "[If] I was to sell travel, the easiest way was to sell it by telling about the people who lived and loved and worked here," she explained.[33] She was promoted to Travel Promotion Supervisor for the department in 1948 and served in that position until her retirement in 1961. Representing the state at travel shows throughout the United States and Canada, Grace spoke regularly on radio and television programs across the country. Her boss, Joseph R. Horan, director of the Travel Bureau, referred to her as "a super-saleswoman for New York State."

Many of the human-interest news releases that Grace wrote about tourist destinations across the state as part of her job focused on some aspect of the Adirondack region. Several even highlighted the activities of the Forty-Sixers. For example, she promoted the story of Chrissie Wendell (#60), a black-and-white spaniel-terrier-spitz mix, that was the first canine to be officially recorded as a Forty-Sixer. Chrissie finished on Sawteeth on September 3, 1948, with her family: the Rev. (#63) and Mrs. Roland Wendell and their sons Richard (#62) and David (#61). Grace also used her expertise in public relations and her contacts around the state to invite hiking clubs and government officials to participate in the centennial climb to the summit of Mt. Haystack on August 20, 1949, to commemorate the first known ascent of that mountain. "My job is even more enjoyable since it is the outgrowth of my hobby," she once said.[34]

In her local area, Grace was featured on a weekly broadcast heard on radio station WGY in Schenectady. An expert on folklore, she also presented a regional history program on public television station WMHT in Schenectady and was a much acclaimed and sought after public speaker during the 1950s and 1960s.

Grace's hiking accomplishments and lifelong love of the Adirondack Mountains are legendary. She was the first woman to climb the 46 Adirondack High Peaks and the ninth person to achieve the feat. She made her first ascent of Mt. Marcy, the state's highest peak, on August 2, 1922, and completed her climbs of the 46 high peaks on Mt. Esther on August 26, 1937.[35] Although she loved the outdoors, Grace initially had no intention of climbing the 46. She explained, "When Ed was chalking up the 46 back in the 30's I only went along for the climb, not the score. As a matter of fact, I was happy being in the woods until eventually I got bitten by the 46er bug and had to finish them all."[36]

Grace hiked in men's composition-sole work boots from Montgomery Ward and blue checkered cotton shorts with pearl buttons. The shorts, which she wore on all of her climbs of the 46 high peaks, are part of the collection of the Adirondack Museum in Blue Mountain Lake. She carried a small musette bag, which contained only a few items: lunch, a thermos of tea, a map, a sweater, and long culottes, which she wore when hiking the trailless peaks, and, at the request of her husband, when visiting Adirondack hermit Noah John Rondeau. Grace noted that the availability of hiking equipment when she was climbing was as limited as were her funds to purchase them.

For a woman growing up in the first half of the twentieth century, Grace was clearly a pioneer. Not only did she hold a high-ranking position in state service but she also engaged in a hobby in which relatively few women participated at the time. In an interview that appeared in the *Buffalo Courier Express* in 1955, she encouraged other women to experience the great outdoors.

> Too many women stay indoors. It is good to get out of doors, to get lots of fresh air to bring color to your cheeks and zest to your step. It's more outdoor exercise we women need.
>
> I've never even twisted an ankle climbing the mountains, but last year I smashed my toe in my own home.
>
> How did I get interested in mountain climbing? Well, the mountains just happened to be all around me, so I climbed them.[37]

Grace described her first climb of Mt. Marcy, which quite literally changed her life:

> It was to be three days. Marcy was not considered a one-day climb – not in 1922. We went in through the old Iron Works, which I knew about but I'd never been there... and hiked into the ranger's place where we spent the night. The next day we started for Marcy... It was raining. There were black flies. And every step you'd take and try to get your breath you'd get a mouth full of black flies... Finally we got up to Four Corners lean-to and the boys tried to build a fire... It was still raining. You couldn't see a thing... Finally some of them decided they were going back.

Grace, Mary Davis, Herb Lance, and A. T. Shorey on the trail to Marcy

They didn't want to climb in the rain... But some of them decided they would go on and I decided to go with them because my father had told me originally when I was going – the only advice he gave me – was that it didn't make any difference whether I reached the top or not. The important thing was *how* I made the climb. You know, that sort of inspired me all my life.

It was tough. I was on all fours sometimes. I didn't think I was going to get there. But I had to get to the top – there was some reason. God knows what it was but I had to go on. And on the top just for a fraction of a moment, the clouds lifted while I was there and I looked down and there a mile below me was Lake Tear of the Clouds, the Hudson's highest source. And you know, that did something to me. I had seen something – I felt it. I never forgot the mountain and I never forgot that trip.

From that point on she said, "I never talked about anything but mountains. I talked about them, I wrote about them. I gave speeches about them."

As interest in climbing the Adirondack High Peaks grew, Grace was instrumental in expanding the scope of "46ing" beyond the Forty-Sixers of Troy. She was a founding member of the Adirondack Forty-Sixers, Inc. and helped to organize its first meeting on May 30, 1948. She served as the new club's first president (1948-1951). From the early days of the Forty-Sixers of Troy, Grace also kept detailed records of the ascents of those working on climbing the High Peaks, a task which she continued until she was well into her 90s. She died on March 13, 2004, at the age of 98.

For over 60 years Grace was the guiding spirit and the very embodiment of the Forty-Sixer experience. She encouraged letter-writing and maintained personal correspondence with each climber, a feature unique to the 46ers among hiking clubs. She wrote thousands of letters – as many as 2,000 several years – to those hikers who were reporting their climbs of the 46 Adirondack High Peaks.

Grace's emphasis on personal correspondence is a tradition that the club maintains today to monitor the progress of hikers seeking membership in the club. She considered the climbing of the 46 to be a life-affirming and often life-altering accomplishment that deserved reflection and contemplation. "It's important," she often said, "for hikers to write about what they saw and felt as they climbed and to share that experience with others." "Any mountain worth climbing is worth talking about" was one of her favorite sayings.

In a letter to Noah John Rondeau, the hermit of Cold River, Grace revealed the reverence she held for the mountains and for her hiking companions: "I do love the woods! But can't say that I would want to spend time in them with just any one. The mountains are sacred to me and to enjoy them one needs the right kind of companionship. We don't stand on the brink of heaven so often that when we do it means something special to have a real soul along to hold onto."

She described her views on the quest to become a 46er in a profile that appeared in the Albany *Times Union*: "There is something spiritual in it. The mountains mean something different and special to each person. They are what connect us as a group. But the journey is an inward one, learning about yourself."[38]

Grace was interested in hearing people's stories: what happened and why it happened. She said that she "sold New York State with its stories" in her job with the Commerce Department, and she extended that passion for history and for the tales behind events, places, and people to her work with the Forty-Sixers. Her goal and her reward was to instill in hikers the notion that every mountain, just like every person, is different. "They are individual peaks and they all mean something different," she once said. For Grace it was through the telling of stories from each hiking experience that the differences were revealed.

In her letters she took on the roles of compassionate mother (although she and Ed never had any children), stern teacher, loyal companion, spirited cheerleader, and sage philosopher. In recounting their climbs, hikers shared with her not only the stories of their adventures but also the highlights of their lives. News of marriages, divorces, births, deaths, illnesses, and job changes were related with frequency and with the familiarity and comfort of old friends. Grace in turn shared her sympathetic ear, her encyclopedic knowledge of Adirondack history, accounts of her personal hiking experiences, and her life wisdom. George Sloan (#2651W), president of the Forty-Sixers from 1997 to 2000, described the special relationship Grace had with climbers: "She's so warm and welcoming that people just want to spill their guts to Grace. We are her children and the mountains are her family, her true love."[39]

Receiving a reply from Grace was a highly anticipated event to be savored and enjoyed. She had a special place in her heart for young climbers and always answered their letters first. She made a point of requiring children, no matter how young, to write their own reports about their climbs – even if those "notes" took the form of crayon drawings – and she made sure to address her return letter to each child instead of their parents. While providing encouragement and support, valuable tips on routes up trailless peaks, and reminiscences, her letters could also include gentle but pointed cautions and even scoldings when necessary. Grace's correspondence provides the clearest picture of her devotion to mountain climbing and the natural environment and her esteem for those who were attempting to become Forty-Sixers. The excerpts below provide a sampling of her style and tone:

Grace writing a letter

Just remember that following herd paths, especially on Allen, can be disastrous. Depend on your compass![40]

* * * * * * * * * * * * *

Welcome to Aspiring Forty-Sixer status! I especially appreciate your sharing the Duck Hole trek with me. I know well that one isn't always "in tune" for certain hikes. It is then we call upon every reserve we have to get there. My resource was a hymn we used to sing in Sunday School at Grace Methodist... It was titled "It is better farther on"... I still sing the words of that hymn when I'm in trouble and that does the trick every time – it gets me through.[41]

* * * * * * * * * * * * *

Esther will always remain special for me as it was my 46th and it was a miserable day until I arrived on its summit. Then the sun came out and a spectacular rainbow wound itself around Whiteface.[42]

* * * * * * * * * * * * *

It is a breathtaking morning to sit reading your letter of your three-day trek to become a Forty-Sixer! Boulder Hill is still shaded with trees but softly shining with lovely carpets of fallen leaves. Schroon Lake is deep blue and sun is glowing on the hills above it, calling attention to their Autumn shades. A wonderful background for your becoming-a-46er letter. Thanks for sharing it with me. It has a lot of special meaning for me.[43]

* * * * * * * * * * * * *

Grace, in her 80s, on Cascade

And as for Marshall, the best way to climb it without grief is via Herbert Brook – my favorite way![44]

* * * * * * * * * * * * *

What's the matter with that brother of yours, no reports in ages![45] (Grace insisted that climbers file their own reports as each person experiences the mountains differently.)

* * * * * * * * * * * * *

Your girls are doing fine and you and John should be very proud of them. And how could one find a better way to teach children about life than to share the adventures of climbing the 46 with them. There are so many lessons learned in the mountains all very important to help one in everyday life. I think it's great that you both are spending this time with them in the mountains. Of course, you are enjoying yourselves too, but these treks are planned with them in mind and that's a bonus for parents.[46]

* * * * * * * * * * * * *

But I take exception with your statement now you have finished there is 'nothing left to climb in those areas.' To me, the reclimbs were always the more interesting. I didn't have to get there, and if I did there were certain things I wanted to look for, or views to search out along the way. Every mountain is different every time you climb it and most of the joy comes when you share the thrill of the climb with someone who has never been up the peak before.[47]

* * * * * * * * * * * * *

It might be a good idea to get a notebook to keep your own records in there. If you date the climbs and jot down how you felt about the mountain, you'll be glad you did when you grow older. Our memory can retain only so much and I think you'll find it very special to remember those early days in the mountains. I know how I love to look back to find old references of mine – but in those days one seldom made a record like climbers do today.[48]

* * * * * * * * * * * *

You'll have a great time hiking in to Cold River where the Hermit used to live. Not much is left today of this Hermitage but a few tumble down boards and possibly a flower that reseeds itself as a reminder where he kept a lovely flower garden. Perhaps your father will take you across the dam there. If you get over it you can walk in to the swamp where the Hermit used to show us how to get across when we climbed Couchsachraga. Very few walk there these years.[49]

* * * * * * * * * * * *

There's a good lesson learned on every mountain that one climbs and I guess the best one is, as an old hiking friend said many years ago, "If you bite off more than you can chew, just think carefully, now I've got to chew it."[50]

* * * * * * * * * * * *

I have always been partial to Couchee. It's a very special peak to me as I associate it with Noah John Rondeau, the Hermit, whose Hermitage site you visited last year. We usually climbed it from there. But once I climbed it from Panther as you did, but I dropped down to the Hermit's afterwards and then had to hike out fourteen miles to get to the car that was picking me up there. A long walk at the end of the day!![51]

* * * * * * * * * * * *

I suspect you'll reclimb Street and if the day is a good one you will get that great view again. It's not far from the canister – just look for it. I get very annoyed at climbers who say 'no view' – they don't take the trouble to look.[52]

* * * * * * * * * * * *

This is just the beginning of a life-long friendship with the mountains you have just climbed and the persons whose lives have touched yours in the climbing! You, too, have made a difference to them and thereby hangs a tale! It's not just memories, it's something more like a special warmth of feeling, the sense of belonging to, and being a part of this beautiful country which is ours. No sense trying to put it into words, for there just aren't any! ... We've enjoyed your letters and hope you will continue to let us know what you're doing in the mountains – certainly helping others reach their goal, for one thing and 'giving something back' to the mountains for another.[53]

* * * * * * * * * * * *

Winter, as you know, is not an easy time, nor is it expected to be. One has to gear one's mind to Winter and accept that she'll have to try harder to think she can, then *go for it!*[54]

In her own way Grace passed along what she understood to be the meaning of her father's counsel when he told her before her first climb of Marcy, "It doesn't matter whether you make it to the top. What matters is how you make the climb." His words became her motto for mountain climbing and for life. The correspondence between Grace and those climbing the 46 is housed permanently in the New York State Library Manuscripts and Special Collections to preserve a unique and significant historical record of the High Peaks region.

Grace was also active in other Adirondack region organizations. She served as executive secretary for the Adirondack North Country Association (now the Adirondack Park Association) for 21 years, writing brochures, press releases, and other informational pieces. An active member of the Adirondack Mountain Club, Inc., she was contributing editor of its publications, *High Spots* and *Adirondac*,[55] and editor of the Albany Chapter's newsletter *The Cloud Splitter*. She was also a member of the Outdoor Writers Association of America and a president of the New York Folklore Society.

Grace was very active in Grace Methodist Church, teaching Sunday School classes, playing roles in church-sponsored plays and pageants, singing in the choir, and writing the Sunday

Grace, in her 90s, on Whiteface

bulletin. She had a strong faith in God, which was firmly rooted in her relationship with the mountains and the belief she placed in nature as a guiding and sustaining force. She would be the first to credit "the healing woods" with giving her the strength to deal with a number of adversities in her life, including the loss of Ed at an early age, and her own health issues – an ectopic pregnancy, breast cancer, which resulted in two radical mastectomies, and heart and circulatory problems in her later years.

Strong-willed, stubborn, and self-sufficient, Grace also had her quirks in both her hiking preferences and her personal life, which were a source of constant kidding and amusement among her friends. When hiking she didn't like the sound of water sloshing in a water bottle attached to her belt and she swore that if she drank plain water on the trail it made that same sloshing sound in her stomach. She preferred to drink tea when hiking, which she kept in a Thermos in her pack. While she exhorted aspiring 46ers to use a compass when climbing the trailless peaks, she rarely used one herself. "I did not care for compasses and cared less for maps," she once said. The only map she used was the 1932 "Trails to Mount Marcy" map published by the Conservation Department. "I figured if I just headed in the right direction, I'd get there, and if you weren't sure you were on the top, you'd climb a tree," she explained.

In her daily life she preferred her tossed salad ingredients to be diced instead of sliced. When she made her legendary grilled cheese sandwiches, the bread had to be buttered on both sides. When clearing the table after a meal, plates could never be stacked one on top of the other but had to be individually placed on the counter. Grace also had a few practical guidelines, chief among them this: "Never argue with people. What good does it do?" Her reasoning was that arguments seldom change anyone's opinion and only lead to animosity. However, her opinions were highly valued and respected, and she rarely found herself in the position of having to engage in an argument to get her point across. There was a maxim by which she ordered her life: "*Can't* never accomplished anything."

In 1995 Grace established the Adirondack 46R Conservation Trust, a private charitable endowment with a mission to provide financial support for conservation and educational projects which advance, promote, and encourage the responsible recreational use of the Adirondack High Peaks. In addition to supporting the work of the Forty-Sixers' Office of the Historian and trail maintenance program, the trust is a major source of funding for the Summit Steward program, which places trained educators on the busiest summits – Marcy, Algonquin, Colden, Haystack, and Wright – during the summer months to inform the hiking public about the fragile alpine environment, conduct plant inventories, and assist in restoration projects.

Grace's contributions to the Adirondacks have been repeatedly recognized. The Adirondack Mountain Club, at its annual banquet on March 13, 2004, conferred on Grace its highest honor, the Trail Blazer Award. It was the evening of Grace's passing. In recognition of her lifelong service to the state and the Adirondack region, the Adirondack 46ers have spearheaded an effort to rename East Dix, "Grace Peak," in her honor.

Grace penned a poem that described her personal relationship to the mountains, which was first published in *The Cloud Splitter* in April 1939:

My Mountains!

Soft scented trees sway to and fro
Where laughing brooklets gaily flow.
Majestic, wooded mountains rise
To meet the softly tinted skies,
                            The Adirondacks!

Deep rocky chasms oft extend
And with the hills abruptly blend;
While o'er the hillsides' dotted green
Alluring trails are dimly seen.
                            The Adirondacks!

Transparent, shining lakes repose
Embraced by every breeze that blows.
A silvery moon sends rays that gleam
Where peace and beauty reign supreme–
                            The Adirondacks!

I claim these mountains for my own.
I'm happy here—I am at home!

Activities of the Forty-Sixers of Troy

The first order of business for the newly formed Forty-Sixers of Troy was to create bylaws of organization. Those bylaws stated that the club's purpose was "to bring together Grace Church mountain enthusiasts and their friends who have climbed in the Adirondacks so they may share experiences and cooperate with the spirit of Article VII, Section 7 of the New York State Conservation Law."[56] The aim of club members was "to climb the forty-six major peaks of the Adirondack Mountains," and the club's official name was "The Forty-Sixers." The bylaws outlined club officers: "President – must have climbed the 46 major peaks; Vice President – responsible for the social program at the regular meetings; Secretary – shall keep a complete record of the membership, of all meetings, and handle all correspondence; Treasurer – shall collect all dues and handle all monies; Historian – shall keep records of all club activities and shall write a yearly history to be given at the December meeting; Publicity Chairman – shall care for all publicity."

The group identified four levels of membership. Active Members – those who had climbed at least one high peak during the calendar year – were required to give the Historian a yearly report of their climbs. Those reports were saved as part of each hiker's official climbing folder and the information was used to verify climbs and to assign climbing numbers

Heaven Up-h'isted-ness!

At the trail head… ready to walk to Noah John Rondeau's hermitage

based on the date and time of each hiker's final ascent. Associate Members – those who did not climb a peak during a calendar year – were required to present a paper or talk on some aspect of outdoor life in order to maintain membership in the club. The club recognized Sustaining Members as those who had climbed many of the High Peaks but were unable to continue mountain climbing for some reason, and it also granted Honorary Member status to persons who had performed an outstanding accomplishment pertaining to the Adirondacks. Upon completion of the 46, members were entitled to active membership for life.

Meetings, hosted by a different club member each time, were scheduled for the first Wednesday of the months of February, April, June, October, and December. Dues were set at seventy-five cents a year for active and associate members and $1.25 for sustaining members.

The Rev. Ryder wrote the words to the "Forty-Sixer Song" (1937) which the Troy climbers sang to the tune of Cornell's alma mater at their meetings:

> Where Tahawus' lofty summit
>   Reaches for the sky,
> With old Gray Peak on his shoulder,
>   Skylight following nigh.
> There will we gaze with joy and rev'rence
>   From every hill and vale,
> That surrounds the grand old monarch,
>   As we tramp the trail.
>
> Where the Opalescent plunges
>   Down its rough-hewn course,
> Fed by Uphill Brook and Feldspar,
>   Hudson's highest source.

> There let me look on old Algonquin
>   Kissed by setting sun,
> There I'll light my evening campfire,
>   When the day is done.
>
> Where old Seward spreads his shadow
>   O'er Ouluska's den,
> With its dark and hidden caverns
>   Far from haunts of men.
> There let me tramp 'til early nightfall
>   Bids me stop and rest;
> There with pals and God and Nature
>   Will my soul be blest.

Members of the Troy Forty-Sixers approached their mountains like kids would a candy store. With unbridled enthusiasm they were eager to sample all that the mountains had to offer, and they were equally eager to share their playland with others. While engaged primarily in social activities, club members were also interested in the history and folklore of the Adirondack region and in disseminating that information to the general public. Orville Gowie, the local advertising manager of Troy's *The Record* newspaper, was the club's first historian. He wrote numerous articles about the High Peaks and club activities that appeared regularly in the *Knickerbocker News* and *The Record* throughout the late 1930s. Articles with headlines such as "Trojans on Hike in Upstate Mountains," "46'ers Suffer From Cold in Climb to Adirondack Peaks," "Two Major Peaks Climbed by Trojans," and "Three Trojans Plan to Climb Mt. Allen After 22-Mile Hike," spread the word about the adventures awaiting those who ventured into the region. An article that appeared in the *Troy Record* on September 12, 1936, described the finishing trip of Ed Hudowalski and the Reverend Ryder in detail: "Friday they climbed McComb *[sic, a former spelling]*, South Dix, Marshall, (now known as Hough) and East Dix, all trailless peaks, saving Dix for Saturday. The entire day was consumed in this climb in a pouring rain, the climbers wading through water up to their knees on some portions of the trail."

Display in Chamber of Commerce window

To present mountain climbing as a hobby and give city-bound folks a visual sense of the mountains, club members created a miniature exhibit, which was displayed in the Chamber of Commerce window on Fourth Street in Troy, December 1-10, 1938. It depicted a mountain camp, complete with a forest of trees, a brook, a lean-to, and a campfire with cooking utensils. It also included winter camping equipment and photos of the Great Range. Margery N. Ludlow (#27) was chairperson for the project.

The Troy hikers developed a special relationship with Noah John Rondeau, one of the best-known Adirondack hermits. Born in 1883 and raised near Au Sable Forks, Rondeau began visiting the Cold River area of the western High Peaks in the early 1900s, spending more and more time in the wilderness each year. He eventually built a number of crude structures including two small cabins – "Town Hall" and the "Hall of Records," both measuring approximately eight by ten feet – and a series of wigwams. Town Hall served as Rondeau's

Noah John Rondeau

Louise Goark
on Colden

sleeping quarters during the cold weather. He also stored his personal items, food staples, and a collection of more than 60 books in it. The Hall of Records was his tool and storage shed and doubled as sleeping quarters for visitors. The wigwams provided additional storage, a cooler bedroom during the summer months, and a convenient manner by which to store and dry his wood supply.[57] Rondeau became known as the "Mayor of Cold River." He lived off the land, leaving his hermitage only to replenish basic supplies – staples such as coffee, sugar, flour – and to escape the harshest winter months. His longest continuous stay at Cold River was 381 days, from May 1, 1943, to May 16, 1944.[58]

Ernest Ryder, his brother Harold T. Ryder, and father Willis Ryder, and Charlie Horn were the first of the Troy hiking group to meet Rondeau.[59] On a hike in the Cold River area in the summer of 1934 the men heard someone cutting wood. As they investigated the source of the sound, they came upon Rondeau and his hermitage. In talking with him they discovered that 30 years earlier he had attended the church in Bloomingdale (in northern Essex County near Saranac Lake), at which the Rev. Ryder's father had been pastor, and, in fact, sat in a pew with the Ryder family.

While he was not on any regular postal route, Rondeau did have a post office box in Coreys, which he checked whenever he was in the area to replenish his supplies. Despite the sometimes nine months that would pass between trips to the post office, he managed to stay in touch with a number of people, including Grace Hudowalski, with whom he maintained a seven-year correspondence between 1939 and 1945.

Grace and Louise Goark (#14), were among the first women to visit the hermit. Although he preferred his solitary life and non-traditional life-style, he was not antisocial and did not fit the stereotype of a hermit. He welcomed visitors and shared with them his coffee, fish that he had caught, vegetables from his small garden, and his stories. Once a year in the summer, whenever a trip was planned, the group carried a birthday cake to Rondeau. It was baked by Orville Gowie's mother, Catherine. Usually it was Grace who carried the cake in her hands the 14 miles to the hermitage for one of the celebrations. One of those birthday cakes factored into Rondeau's climb of Seymour on his 55th birthday. In a letter to Grace, whom he addressed as "The Old Lady of the Wigwam," he explained:

Grace Hudowalski looking out from behind Noah John's "Welcome" signs

> July 6th was the anniversary of my age. (55) I resolved that I was a Big Boy now… I had planned for some time, to start on this day, to climb and write up the Major Peaks. So I took eats, blanket, water-can, writing material, my new pipe and new shirt. I started for the Peak of Mount Seymour… Two Hours before sun down I was on the Peak and I stayed 19 hours. The weather was good. After sun down, the Moon was high in the south sky and Venus stood Big and High right over Mount Donaldson. I made my Balsam Bed on the very Peak of Seymour and had the last of my Birthday Cake there.

Club members also carried in supplies for Rondeau on their trips into the area and sent him presents at Christmas time. One year they gave him an oil painting kit and canvases as he had expressed a desire to paint the mountains. Other gifts included a flannel shirt, a tin of tobacco, a dictionary, and money so he could purchase additional supplies. Individual club members also sent him gifts for the holidays. At their October 6, 1937, meeting the club voted to make Rondeau their first honorary member.[60]

Carried in 14 miles by hand

The small club organized an annual banquet at Grace Methodist Church in Troy. It was open to anyone interested in the mountains. The programs at the yearly affairs always related to the Adirondacks and featured such notable speakers as Russell Carson, author of the Forty-Sixer "bible," *Peaks and People of the Adirondacks*, and Lithgow Osborne, commissioner of New York state's Conservation Department. The first banquet was held on Friday, May 13, 1938, with the theme, "Spring Camp Fire." Members of the Taconic Hiking Club and the ADK were invited to the program. The evening's entertainment included talks about climbing Allen and the history of the club and

Cover of Forty-Sixers of Troy May 1939 annual banquet program

a group sing-along. In addition O. Kenneth Parks screened a movie he had made on the trails of Marcy and of the Marcy centennial observance of August 1937, an event in which members of the Troy club had participated. Club members decorated the church hall with 46er emblems, evergreens, and a replica of an Adirondack lean-to.

The theme of the second banquet was "Rig-a-marole of a Random Scoot," a reference to the term coined by noted Adirondack guide Old Mountain Phelps to describe a particularly challenging off-trail bushwhack. Conservation Department Commissioner Osborne was the speaker. The evening's entertainment also included a performance of an original skit written by Orville Gowie. Bark and fir boughs covered the pillars of the hall, and a lean-to and campfire added to the ambience. Russell Carson was the guest speaker at the third banquet on May 10, 1940, with the theme of "Mountains," and each person in attendance received a small first aid kit as a favor. John T. Carr Lowe, a New York attorney and president of the ADK, spoke at the May 9, 1941, banquet, at which the decorations included a built-to-scale replica of Noah John Rondeau's hermitage.

In 1938 several members of the Forty-Sixers of Troy joined the Albany Chapter of the Adirondack Mountain Club. The Albany Chapter's publication, *The Cloud Splitter*, which

The Marcy Centennial celebration was filmed and broadcast over the radio.

Grace Hudowalski edited for a number of years, often carried news of the Forty-Sixers' hiking exploits. Those articles were instrumental in spreading the challenge of 46ing among the members of the ADK. Interest in climbing the 46 high peaks became so strong that the ADK asked C. Howard Nash and Grace to write an article on the best approaches to the 21 trailless summits. Their article appeared in the January 1939 issue of ADK's *High Spots*. In modified form the account was included in the 1941 edition of the ADK's *Guide to Adirondack Trails*.

Though small in number, the Forty-Sixers of Troy had abundant energy and members were not afraid to speak out on issues that concerned the Adirondack wilderness. In 1938 they rallied against a proposed amendment to Article VII Section 7 of the State Constitution that would have permitted the sale of timber on state land. In the fall of 1941 the Trojan hikers staged a strenuous campaign against the construction of a ski center on Whiteface Mountain. They argued that such development represented an exploitation of the forest preserve. They also went on record as supporting the easement which permitted the construction of the railroad from North Creek to the National Lead Company's mines at Lake Sanford, only for the duration of World War II. They felt that the land should revert to wild forest once the war was over and the titanium oxide, extracted from the mine's ore, was no longer crucial to the war effort. They sent a resolution outlining their position to President Franklin D. Roosevelt and other federal authorities.

In addition to their political advocacy to maintain the wilderness character of the Adirondacks and their efforts to popularize the sport of hiking, the Forty-Sixers of Troy were responsible for a number of noteworthy accomplishments. The first was the organization of the Esther Centennial to commemorate the first recorded ascent of Mount Esther. Fifteen-year-old Esther McComb was credited with making the first ascent of the mountain in 1839 while attempting to climb Whiteface, which towered over her family's home. (For additional information, see the chapter in this book about Mount Esther.) While she failed to accomplish her goal, by climbing to the top of Esther, "for the sheer joy of climbing," she became the first woman to reach the summit of a four thousand-foot peak.

It was Bob Marshall who mentioned the anniversary of Esther's climb in a letter to Grace Hudowalski in March 1939 and suggested that a celebration of some sort might be in order. In her May 20, 1939, reply Grace said, "Of course I never would have thought – or for that matter, known – about Esther's anniversary if you hadn't written me. So, thanks to you!"

The Forty-Sixers of Troy sent notices to hiking clubs throughout the region as well as to state dignitaries inviting them to participate in a two-day celebration, July 29 and 30, 1939. Thirty-one people participated. The schedule of activities called for them to climb Whiteface on July 29 and camp out at the lean-to near the summit. To make it easier for hikers, the club made arrangements to have bed rolls and other camping equipment driven to the summit for pick-up by the climbers at the Whiteface Castle. Some hikers camped at the lean-to, others in the observer's cabin which was located nearby, and a hearty few spent the night on the summit.

At 7 a.m. the following morning, Clarence Craver (#15) led the group in a dawn service on Whiteface's summit. Orville Gowie presented a short meditation

Clarence Craver

entitled "I'm Sitting on Top of the World." Setting the tone for the rest of the day's events, he expressed the familiar theme that climbing mountains wasn't just about getting to the top: "Just to get to the top of a mountain and back down again isn't an unusual feat. To have gained knowledge, satisfaction, and inspiration from the trip is far more worthwhile."

Following the service, participants were treated to a breakfast of flapjacks and maple syrup served at the Castle. Those who did not wish to camp out overnight drove to the summit to meet the group. They broke up into small groups to make the trek from Whiteface and came together again on Esther's trailless summit for the centennial ceremony at 1 p.m. In the mist and clouds upon the peak, Arthur S. Hopkins, assistant director of Lands and Forests for the New York State Conservation Department, spoke about the significance of mountain tops and the feelings of humility when experiencing the greatness of nature. Hopkins sported a

Margery Ludlow

five-inch tear on the leg of his white pants, a consequence of Esther's spruce branches. Ed Hudowalski read greetings from Russell Carson and Bob Marshall, who were unable to attend the celebration. George Marshall sent a telegram to Grace to be read at the ceremony:

> Greatly regret unable participate in unveiling of Esther. Not having climbed in past few years think it unwise to climb Whiteface without practice. Pride prevents my driving to top on this occasion. Incidentally doubt Esther was kind of gal who used veils. Breaking bottle elderberry wine over her probably more appropriate. Regards to all centennial climbers. Have grand time.[61]

The highlight of the celebration was the unveiling of a bronze plaque that Ed Hudowalski had affixed to Esther's summit rock. The plaque was made by Margery Ludlow:

1839　Mt. Esther　1939
— 4,270 feet —
to commemorate
the indomitable spirit of
Esther McComb
Age 15
Who made the first recorded
Ascent of this peak
For the
"Sheer joy of climbing."
46-ers, Troy, N.Y.

Together the group joined in singing a song written in honor of Esther McComb for the occasion by Clarence Craver and Grace Hudowalski:

The 1939 Esther group. Grace Hudowalski, wearing a plaid, wool shirt, is sitting at center.

To Esther McComb
Tune: St. Thomas

O Esther, Spirit-brave!
O, Maid, Undaunted, true!
We pay our homage and respect
Upon this mount to you!

Not for renown or fame
You climbed this rugged peak;
But for the joy of drinking in
The virgin beauty deep.

Long may thy spirit flame
In hearts of everyone!
Long may thy deed inspire O Maid,
Who climbed here just for fun!

In 1940 the Forty-Sixers of Troy embarked on what would turn out to be a four-decade mission to formally name a number of the High Peaks that were not registered with the New York State or United States Boards of Geographic Names. The state's 1932 "Map of the Mt. Marcy Region" – the map used most frequently by those climbing in the High Peaks at the time – did not list names for four of the High Peaks as identified by Russell Carson in his book *Peaks and People*. The omitted names included the 4,404-foot peak in the Dix Range, which Carson referred to as Marshall, Blake's Peak, Couchsachraga, and Emmons. In addition, the 1932 map listed the 4,411-foot westernmost peak of the MacIntyre Range as MacIntyre instead of Herbert, the name Carson gave to the peak.

The untimely death of Bob Marshall in 1939 spurred the club to action to secure a peak named for Bob, while at the same time correcting the other omissions of the 1932 map. In a letter dated October 15, 1940, the Forty-Sixers petitioned the state Board of Geographic Names for the official and permanent naming of Blake's Peak, Couchsachraga, and Mount Marshall (in the Dix Range) as designated in Carson's *Peaks and People*. At the time of the 46ers' naming request, there was a state law that prohibited the naming of any mountain, river or other natural formation for a living person. Since Herbert Peak had been named after Herb Clark and since in 1940 Clark was very much alive, the 46ers could not include Herbert Peak in their official request for a permanent name for that mountain. The letter, which was signed by Orville Gowie, C. Howard Nash, and Grace Hudowalski, included detailed descriptions of each peak, their histories, and justifications for each name.

In responding to the request, Supervisor of Public Records and a member of the Secretary of the State's Committee on Geographic Names Hugh M. Flick informed the Forty-Sixers that the mountain in the Dix Range that they referred to as Marshall had already been officially designated as Hough Peak by both the state and federal boards in June 1937. The petition to name the peak Hough (after Dr. Franklin B. Hough, a member of the first New York State Park Commission appointed in 1872 and the first chief of the Division of Forestry of the U.S. Department of Agriculture) came from state Conservation Department Commissioner Lithgow Osborne. He had petitioned the state board at the time of the Fifty Years of Conservation Celebration to honor Dr. Hough. In a letter to Grace explaining the history of the naming of Hough Peak, Director of the Division of Lands and Forests William G. Howard reported that the commissioner's recommendation had been supported by resolutions from several organizations, including the Adirondack Mountain Club. However, there was no record of the official designation in the Conservation Department files and the change had not been widely publicized. Grace asked the ADK for a copy of their resolution. The reply she received from Executive Secretary Paul Doherty revealed that while the ADK board of directors had passed a resolution approving the name of Hough for a peak on April 25, 1936, the peak they were referring to was actually "one of the main mountain peaks near Mt. Evans in Colorado... as shown on the U.S.G.S. Topographical Map of Georgetown, Colorado Quadrangle.[62]

Disappointed by the finding that the mountain they knew as "Marshall" had been officially designated as Hough Peak, the Forty-Sixers of Troy were nonetheless determined to have a High Peak named after Bob Marshall. The question became which peak? After much discussion, the Forty-Sixers were unanimous in their choice to petition that the 4,411-foot mountain in the MacIntyre Range that Russ Carson called Herbert be renamed Mt. Marshall. Though unanimous, a good deal of ambivalence surrounded the decision as Grace Hudowalski explained in a letter to George Marshall outlining the reasoning behind the club's decision:

> There is not one of us who would take Herb Clark's name from a peak. We have a high regard for him and his accomplishments, nevertheless these facts remain – there is the big matter of the not-naming-a-mountain-after-a-living person. Therefore the 46-ers cannot petition for the official naming of this mountain for Herbert Clark. It also is very evident, especially in lieu of how the Dix 4,404 was named, that someone may wish to memorialize a person or event in the near future and they would not have the slightest compunctions about suggesting the peak we now call Herbert. If this was done the mountain would be lost to Herb and Bob alike.
>
> It is not an easy thing to take one name from a mountain and place another. (We are already running into difficulties here with Hough, having never called it anything but Marshall!) We love the Adirondacks, the traditions, and the people who have made them. I believe you know what I am trying to say. One doesn't take naming a mountain lightly. It is a tremendous task. We like

the name of Herbert but there isn't a thing we can do under the present conditions to make sure that this name will be kept for that peak.

Aside from the regulation that prevented the official naming of Herbert since its namesake was still alive, the Forty-Sixers felt it was appropriate to name the mountain *Marshall* since Bob himself had expressed such a strong affection for the peak. In 1938 Grace Hudowalski wrote an article about "random scooting" up Mount Herbert which appeared in the August/September *Bulletin* of the ADK. Bob Marshall read the article and wrote to Grace on December 10, 1938 – the start of their brief collegial correspondence – and commented on his memories of climbing Herbert.

> I have just read with great interest your little article on "random scooting" up Mount Herbert... It brought back most pleasant memories of a "random scoot" which my brother George, Herb Clark and I took up this mountain in June, 1921. We went a different way than you, going from Iroquois straight across to Herbert and then dropping down toward Indian Pass. After seventeen years, what I remember especially about that trip was the freshness of Mount Herbert's summit without a single trace of man, and the marvelous ground cover, especially sphagnum, moss, wood sorrel and dwarf dogwood, which we walked over and sank into as we dropped down the mountain. But your description of freshness and virgin vegetation, while it was mostly of other land, nevertheless brought back splendidly that feeling of a wilderness which one gets so grandly on Herbert.
>
> Incidentally, I might add this and Allan [sic], as I look back upon Adirondack mountain climbing, stand out as my two favorite peaks just because they are so perfect for real wilderness travel.

Based on Bob Marshall's words, the Forty-Sixers of Troy felt justified in petitioning for the name designation.[63] As a token of respect for Herb Clark and in recognition of Clark's role as expert guide, the club's members took to calling the brook on the side of Mt. Marshall that most hikers followed to get to the mountain's summit, Herbert Brook. Just as he had led the Marshalls up the mountain that would eventually bear their name, so would Herbert Brook lead thousands of hikers to the summit for years to come.

Both state Conservation Department Commissioner Lithgow W. Osborne and Division of Lands and Forests Director William G. Howard wrote letters to Hugh M. Flick in support of the Marshall name designation petition. Robert Sterling Yard, president of the Wilderness Society, which Bob Marshall was instrumental in founding, also expressed support for the peak naming. Before continuing with their petition, the Forty-Sixers consulted with both Russell Carson and George Marshall. Both men, believing that Bob himself would have been opposed to it, expressed reservations about the name change. However, neither offered strong opposition or mounted any formal protest to the petition.[64]

In a letter to the state Board of Geographic Names, dated January 6, 1941, the Forty-Sixers of Troy renewed their request for the permanent naming of Blake's Peak and Couchsachraga Mountain and repetitioned that the name "Mt. Marshall" be applied to the "4,411-foot mountain located at the southwestern end of the MacIntyre Mountain Range."

At the same time additional discrepancies were discovered between the names of peaks that appeared on the state Conservation Department maps of the High Peaks and the information from the U.S. Board of Geographic Names. In an attempt to preserve the familiar usage of the names designated in Carson's book, the Forty-Sixers of Troy submitted an additional petition to the state on May 21, 1941. That petition – requesting official designation for peaks "already known to authors and historians of Adirondack literature, natives, mountaineers and lovers of these mountains through common usage" – included Mount Phelps, Mount Emmons, Gray Peak, Mount Wright, Mount Algonquin, and Mount Boundary. Those peaks, along with Blake, Couchsachraga, and Mt. Marshall, were officially named by the state Board of Geographic Names on June 26, 1942, with notification of the decision forwarded to the United States Board of Geographic Names.

The first map that listed all 46 names of the Adirondack High Peaks was the 1942 "Romance Map" printed in ADK's publication *High Spots*. However, when the official U.S. maps were published in 1957, all of the correct mountain names appeared except that of Mt. Marshall, which was replaced with the name Mt. Clinton. Correspondence with the U.S. board at that time revealed that the original notification of the name change had been misplaced. Neither the U.S. board nor the state board had any record of the original petitions. Therefore, a whole new round of petitions and letters of support from the groups and individuals who had submitted the original documentation seventeen years earlier was required to secure the name change.

Efforts to redo the petitions stagnated until 1972 when Philip Terrie took on the task of updating Russell Carson's *Peaks and People* for reprinting. Terrie was instrumental in reviving the cause and documenting the timeline of original correspondence. Grace Hudowalski once again solicited letters of support and provided all the historical background for the formal repetitioning.

Finally, 32 years after the initial request, approval for the name of Mt. Marshall was granted by the U.S. Board on Geographic Names at its December 1972 meeting. The official entry read: "Marshall, Mount: mountain, elevation, 4,360 ft., in the MacIntyre Mountains 3 mi. NE of Henderson Lake; named for Robert Marshall, conservationist who made the first recorded ascent of this mountain; Essex Co., N.Y.: 44°07'40" N, 74°00'50"W. Variant: Mount Clinton."

Two references shed light on how the name Clinton became attached to Mt. Marshall. A letter from Lester F. Dingman, executive secretary, Domestic Geographic Names, U.S. Board on Geographic Names, to Philip Terrie stated, "The Board of Geographic Names records reveal that a U.S. Geological Survey field party in 1953 reported that the name Mount Clinton was used locally for this feature, and we have no record that the New York Board on Geographic Names officially changed the name in 1942 to Mount Marshall." A letter to Dr. John G. Broughton, assistant commissioner, New York State Museum and Sciences Services, from Grace Hudowalski speculated, "This mountain was never known by the name of Clinton although at one time Colvin [surveyor Verplanck Colvin] called the peak in the same range now known as Iroquois that."

The 1950 edition of the Adirondack Mountain Club's *Guide to Adirondack Trails, Northeastern Section* referred to the mountain by three names in describing the MacIntyre Range: "Still further to the S. is another peak that rises 4411 ft. with no official name, Oct. 1949. There is no trail on this. Colvin on one map called it Clinton. ADK'ers call it Herbert for Herb Clark, the guide, who went with Bob and George Marshall when they climbed the 46 peaks over 4000 ft. It may be Marshall officially some day."[65] To further complicate the matter, a small map in the ADK trail guide of the Sanford Lake Region listed the name of the peak as MacIntyre.

James M. Glover, in his book *A Wilderness Original: The Life of Bob Marshall*, recounts a controversy that emerged over the original naming of the 4,404-foot peak in the Dix Range as Mt. Marshall by Russell Carson in honor of both Bob and George. At that time an attorney and ADK member, Theodore Van Wyck Anthony, objected to the name of Mt.

The History of the Adirondack Forty-Sixers

Marshall along with five other peak names proposed by Carson. In fact, according to Glover, Anthony lobbied strongly for the regulation that prevented any natural formation, *i.e.,* mountain or a river, from being named after a living person. Glover also raises the possibility that Anthony's objection to the Marshall name carried an anti-Semitic sentiment. Regardless of Anthony's actual motivation for his objection, it is curious that of the mountain names included in the club's original petition, Mt. Marshall was both the only one absent from the 1957 U.S. Board records and the only one replaced by another name.

While their activities were centered in the Troy area, the Forty-Sixers of Troy were aware that other people from throughout New York state and surrounding states were also attempting to climb the 46 High Peaks. Grace Hudowalski played a major role in contacting hikers who lived beyond the confines of the Troy area and in encouraging all known 46ers to get together beyond the Troy club. Two of the individuals outside of the Troy club who were also drawn to the mountains were P. F. "Fay" Loope (#4) and Herbert L. Malcolm (#5). Fay Loope, a future president of the ADK, lived in Schenectady while he was climbing. He noted in his 46er questionnaire that he became interested in climbing with "the first mountain I saw" and decided to climb the 46 after reading Carson's book *Peaks and People.* The first of the 46 peaks he climbed was Mt. Marcy in May 1927, and he finished on Rocky Peak Ridge in September 1933. Loope's nickname was "Easy Going" for his habit of encouraging hikers by saying, "It's easier going from here on," whether it really was or not.[66]

Herbert Malcolm was from Pompano, Florida. A teacher and school headmaster, he summered for several years in Lake Placid before moving to the White Mountains in New Hampshire and entering the hotel business. His first ascent of a high peak was Whiteface in the fall of 1907, and he finished on Couchsachraga on June 8, 1935. He credited the exploits of the Marshall brothers for piquing his interest in climbing the 46. Malcolm usually hiked alone and became well-known for tackling marathon hikes. An article in the ADK publication *High Spots* concerned an October 7, 1933, hike during which he climbed 18 peaks in just under 24 hours. Starting at the Ausable Club at 12:01 a.m. on October 7, he climbed Giant, Noonmark, Little, Lower and Upper Wolf Jaws, Armstrong, Gothics, Saddleback, Basin, Little Haystack, Haystack, Little Haystack

Herbert Malcolm on Marcy the day of the 1937 centennial celebration

again, Marcy, Skylight, Colden, Algonquin, and, finally, Mt. Jo – twice – for a total of $40^1/_8$ miles and 20,067 feet in ascents. (He climbed Mt. Jo the second time in order to surpass 20,000 feet in vertical elevation gained during his mountain marathon.) At the time, Malcolm was joined in a friendly rivalry of marathon hiking by Bob and George Marshall, James E. Foote, and Ernest S. Griffith.[67]

In the fall of 1940 the Forty-Sixers of Troy made an initial attempt to bring all those interested in climbing the 46 together for an informal meeting: to get acquainted, swap stories, and climb together. A small group met at Adirondak Loj on October 13, 1940, and discussed the possibility of meeting twice a year, keeping records of the 46 ascents, and doing all in their power to keep the trailless peaks without trails.[68]

Activities of the Troy club slowed during the period of World War II, as did the number of hikers finishing their 46. Only three people finished in 1941, two in 1942, none in 1943 and 1944, and one in 1945. After the war ended and as life slowly returned to normal, outdoor recreation picked up with fifteen climbers finishing their 46 in 1946. As 1948 ended, 68 hikers were recorded as having climbed the 46.

The Adirondack Forty-Sixers

Hikers' desires to become Forty-Sixers began to spread. From throughout New York state and the Northeast people took up the challenge. Since a number of those climbing the forty-six were members of the Adirondack Mountain Club, ADK's newsletters and bulletins printed the names of those finishing the 46 and often contained stories of their adventures as well as information about trail conditions and other items of interest.

In October 1947, the ADK Bouquet River Lodge Chapter sent a letter to all known 46ers inviting them to the ADK's 25th anniversary dinner celebration at the Nelson House in Poughkeepsie on the 15th of that month. The letter, signed by Kay [Katherine] Flickinger (#41), encouraged 46ers who were not members of the ADK to get together to "swap tales, compare notes," and discuss "new ideas for trips of exploration."

The 46ers who attended the celebration decided that it would be a good idea to meet "in the woods" and discuss some simple form of organization. Following that get-together, Kay Flickinger and Edward Harmes (#18) sent another letter to all known 46ers informing them that a meeting had been set for the May 29-31, 1948, Memorial Day weekend. Recognizing the existence of the Forty-Sixers of Troy, the letter suggested the possibility of an expansion and consolidation:

> The records we have indicate that the number included in the group has grown to fifty-three, and it is felt that now some simple form of organization should be effected. Important to us all is to decide upon a name. The designation, "46er," was originated, and belongs to a group that includes some, but not all, to whom this letter is addressed. Without their permission, we should not adopt this name, so come with, or send your suggestions... Come with a story about some of your climbs, and help make successful, what we hope will be the charter meeting of a new and growing organization of mountain enthusiasts.

The inaugural meeting of the Adirondack 46ers was held on May 30, 1948, at Adirondak Loj. Twenty people joined together to discuss some simple form of organization. Those present at the meeting were Werner Bachli (#33), Roy Buchanan (#49), Mary Dittmar, (#29), Adolph "Ditt" Dittmar (#31), Katherine "Kay" Flickinger (#41), Orville Gowie (#8),

Edward Harmes (#18), John "Jack" Harmes (#19), Charles Horn (#11), Grace Hudowalski (#9), Bess Little (#30), P. F. Loope (#4), Helen Menz (#42), Orra Phelps (#47), Eleanor "Nell" Plum (#26), Louis Puffer (#50), Nora Sproule (#22), Charles Trapp (#44), Charles Trapp, Jr. (#45), and George Trapp (#46).

With the blessing of those members of the Forty-Sixers of Troy who were in attendance, the name "Adirondack 46ers" was adopted as the official name of the new group, which also adopted the list of 46 peaks as printed in Russell Carson's *Peaks and People of the Adirondacks* as the official list of mountains to be climbed for membership. It was decided that semi-annual meetings would be held on the weekend nearest Decoration Day (Memorial Day) and Columbus Day. The group also decided to prepare a questionnaire to be filled out by all 46ers upon the completion of their hikes in order to record various "data on the climbing of the peaks and the sort of people who do it."

The group selected an executive committee composed of six directors: Ed Harmes, Kay Flickinger, Orra Phelps, Grace Hudowalski, Adolph Dittmar, and Fay Loope. The executive committee then elected the first officers for the club: President, Grace Hudowalski; Secretary, Kay Flickinger; Treasurer, Adolph Dittmar.

Shortly after the inaugural meeting, Ed Hudowalski redesigned the Forty-Sixers of Troy patch and developed a new logo reflecting the new name of the group. The design, which is still used today to identify Forty-Sixers, featured the letters ADK in green on a yellow background, with *46R* in yellow on a green mountain, and the entire design bounded by a red circle. The executive committee recommended that the emblem be worn "as a left shoulder patch, over the left shirt pocket... and/or on one's pack, as desired. It would also be proper to fasten one with cellophane tape to the rear window on one's car."

Orville Gowie

Nora Sproule

Haystack Centennial

The new Adirondack Forty-Sixers club took on the major task of organizing a centennial hike up Mt. Haystack on Saturday, August 20, 1949, to commemorate the one hundredth anniversary of the first documented ascent of that peak. Adirondack guide Orson S. "Old Mountain" Phelps, along with two companions, Almeron Oliver and George Estey, made the first known climb in August 1849. Grace Hudowalski and Orra Phelps planned the celebration and sent invitations to area outing and hiking clubs, all the ADK chapters, hotels and lodges in the High Peaks region, and to 25 special guests. The state Department of Commerce (at which Grace worked at the time) sent out a press release, which was printed in the *New York Times,* announcing the celebration.

Eighty-two people climbed to the summit, a hike of ten miles one way, for a 1 p.m. ceremony. As president of the 46ers, Grace welcomed the hearty crowd who braved 40-degree temperatures and high winds to join the celebration. The Rev. Peter A. Ward (#72), pastor of St. Bernard's Roman Catholic Church, Lyon Mountain, and the Rev. Roland Wendell (#63), pastor of the First Congregational Church, Ogdensburg, both 46ers, presented tributes to Orson Phelps. J. Victor Skiff, deputy commissioner of the Conservation Department, spoke on "The Adirondack Park – A Unique Forest Playground."

At 5 p.m. on Sunday, August 21, one hundred people gathered at Phelps's gravesite at the Estes Family Burial Ground, Keene Valley, for a separate ceremony. Frederica Mitchell, Congregational Minister at Keene Valley, and W. J. Braman of Au Sable Forks, who had known Old Mountain Phelps, spoke. William A. Andrews placed a wreath on his grave.

Discussions at early Forty-Sixer meetings, which were attended by ten to twenty people, often dealt with such routine issues as whether or not to order lapel pins with the 46er insignia, when to hold the semi-annual meetings, and how to encourage younger hikers to become involved in club activities; but there were also heated discussions over more philosophical issues regarding the overall purpose of the club and the impact of hiking on the High Peaks. The first point of discussion focused on the official function of the Adirondack Forty-Sixers. Some felt the group should take on a formal structure with a definite constitution and purpose beyond that of simply meeting twice a year to hike together and swap climbing stories. Others supported a loose organizational format with a strictly social agenda.

Ed Hudowalski supported a formal organization with a definite purpose, and at the May 28, 1949, meeting the club decided to compose a document to define aims and goals for the group. At the October 8-9, 1949, meeting the Forty-Sixers adopted articles of organization and by-laws that defined the purpose of the club:

> To aid the preservation of the wilderness character of the Adirondack Forest preserve; to further interest in mountain climbing and exploration through encouragement, information and example; to explore the mountains within the Adirondack Park; to provide an opportunity for those with similar interests to get together regularly and share past experiences and propose trips; to develop constructive programs of mutual acceptability in these connections.

The by-laws also outlined the dates for the semi-annual meetings; the make-up of the executive committee and term limits; the amount of dues (originally set at one dollar); and designated the "official" list of the 46 High Peaks as those discussed in Carson's *Peaks and People.*

The Canisters: Blight or Blessing

Trail signs at Johns Brook Lodge, 1945

One issue that generated a good deal of discussion and disagreement throughout the early 1950s was the practice by some hikers of leaving personal markers – disks, cans, jars, and scraps of paper which contained their names and addresses – on what they considered to be the highest point of each peak, particularly the trailless ones, to prove they had climbed them. The practice began in 1937 with one of the early 46ers of Troy, C. Howard Nash. Franklin H. Wilson, a Taconic Hiking Club member, bet Nash a pound of his favorite tobacco that he could not climb all of the forty-six peaks in six months. At the age of 57, Nash took up the challenge. To document his ascents, he fastened a special bronze marker, designed by his sister, Margery Ludlow, to a tree at the highest elevation of each summit. Ditt Dittmar from Au Sable Forks also placed three-inch aluminum disks on which he punched the name of each peak, its elevation, and the date he placed it on the summit to attest to his climbs between 1939 and 1945. It became a tradition for those who followed to look for the "white discs" to reassure themselves that they had reached the actual summits.

C. Howard Nash
with his marker on Donaldson

A quartet of women, Agnes Benedix (#34) and Jessie Benedix (#35) from Tuckahoe, Priscilla Chipman (#36), from Weymouth, MA, and Margaret Keating (#37), from Garden City, climbed the 46 together in the mid-1940s and placed ointment cans (similar to today's metal Band Aid boxes) on the summits of the trailless peaks so that people could leave their names in them. (In addition to the ointment cans, the quartet also decorated each summit with a small American flag affixed to a staff, which they stuck into the ground.) Others left peanut tins, milk bottles, and jelly jars with their names inside. Since not everyone agreed on the high points of the trailless peaks, there were often multiple cans and bottles at various locations on the summits. Those who didn't find one of the containers would often leave scraps of paper with their names on them at a spot that they considered to be a true summit. As many as four separate containers were found on Couchsachraga in 1957. In a letter to Grace dated July 2, 1957, Arthur K. Davis (#134) reported finding three containers on the mountain. He wrote, "I brought down the big one and junked it after sending you the contents. The other two are still there... One is a two-ounce instant coffee glass jar... The other is a green tin box, such as might have held an army dressing, the size of a tobacco tin... The two containers are located together, on the ground, under a standing tree trunk..."

While those makeshift registers were not environmentally sound practice, they did serve as an important source of information to identify those who were climbing the 46 peaks in those early days.

Concerned about the proliferation of personal markers on the trailless peaks, the 46ers appointed a committee consisting of Ed Hudowalski, Werner Bachli (#33), Roy Snyder (#48), and Ditt Dittmar to discuss the topic and propose solutions to the problem. The committee suggested the placing of a canister containing a register book on each of the trailless summits. That, they believed, would resolve a number of issues. First, it would mark the true summit of each peak. Hikers who found the canister would know that they had reached the top and would not be tempted to tramp across the summit area searching for a higher spot. The registers would allow hikers to record their names, thus eliminating the practice of leaving individual markers. The overriding view was that the canisters were a practical compromise.[69] The minutes from the June 2, 1951, meeting summarized the prevailing opinion:

> ...it seemed to be the consensus of the meeting, that although it would be nice to stand on a remote summit with a feeling of being one of a very few who had been there without being reminded by a register that many had been there earlier... it would be far better to have an official register rather than a myriad collection of tin cans, milk bottles and other makeshift registers with the ever present possibility of over enthusiastic climbers leaving their own form of marking.

L. Morgan Porter (#69)[70], 46er president at the time, campaigned for the removal of all personal markers from the trailless peaks and even removed several of Ditt Dittmar's and Howard Nash's original markers himself. Convinced of the insensitivity of their previous actions, both Dittmar and Nash climbed the mountains again to remove the rest of their markers — those that hadn't already been claimed as souvenirs. Dittmar had to make repeated climbs of several mountains in order to retrieve all of his markers. His son, Jim, finally located the last of Ditt's High Peaks markers on the summit of Dial in 1963, twenty-two years after he had originally placed it there.

The Forty-Sixers brought their idea of placing canisters on the summits of the trailless peaks to the Conservation Department, which soon thereafter approved a marker register that was unobtrusive and small, in keeping with the wilderness character of the mountains. In 1950 the club voted to place canisters on only the remotest of the trailless peaks, with their main purpose being to mark the true summits.

The first three canisters were made by the state Barge Canal Terminal Shop and were ready for placement during the summer of 1950. The first was placed on Emmons on September 3, 1950; the second, which had to be mounted to one of the summit boulders, on East Dix on October 14, 1950. Tabletop received its first canister on May 30, 1952; Redfield during the Columbus Day weekend 1952; Nye on May 30, 1953; and Allen on September 19, 1953. Made of a four inch steel pipe with a cap on the bottom and a snap-on cover, the canisters were painted yellow with the mountain name in green. Additional canisters were added to the trailless peak summits throughout the 1950s and early 1960s.

The History of the Adirondack Forty-Sixers

The first official 46er register was placed on the summit of Emmons on September 3, 1950. Left to right, Fred Hein, Eleanor Plum, Bill Endicott, and Ditt Dittmar, presenting a Forty-Sixer patch to Endicott. Both Hein and Endicott became 46ers atop Emmons that day.

Because the initial canisters were deemed too heavy, Roy Snyder manufactured a new version made with welded sheet metal. A register book was placed in each canister so climbers could write down their names and the dates they reached the summit. The back cover of the register book contained a brief description of the mountain, how it was named, and a note encouraging climbers to report the names of previous climbers to the Forty-Sixers:

Hi Hiker!

You're on Mount Emmons, 4,216 feet in elevation. This mountain was named for Ebenezer Emmons who made the first recorded ascent of Marcy in 1837 and named these mountains "the Adirondacks."

This register has been placed here by the Adirondack 46ers with the approval of the New York State Conservation Department. This is the first peak to be so marked.

Sign your name and address and secure the register cover.

Ed Hudowalski: "Hi, Hiker!"

You can help us keep an accurate record of ascents by sending a postcard to the Adirondack 46ers, 129 Cardinal Avenue, Albany, NY, with the date, name and address of the last three persons on this register before your party. Be sure to add your own names.

We hope to meet you soon on the trail or at some 46er gathering wearing the above emblem which signifies you've climbed the 46.

                    Good climbing!
                    The Adirondack 46ers.[71]

The pros and cons of the canister/registers became a frequent topic of debate at club meetings throughout the 1950s. George Marshall was the most vocal opponent of the canisters, and he communicated his opposition to the club in a number of letters that were read and discussed. Believing that it was not necessary to leave one's name on a summit, he felt, instead, that a summit free from any traces of man was much more valuable. His article "Trailless Peaks," which appeared in *Ad-i-ron-dac* in the mid 1950s, reiterated his philosophy on trailless peak climbing and summarized his views on the canisters.

Marshall considered the trailless peaks "the most precious features of our wild forest lands" and cautioned against jeopardizing their "rare primeval character" by "careless, thoughtless or egotistical acts." While agreeing that the canisters were preferable to the proliferation of individual markers, still he considered them to be "unnatural elements." In a passionate plea to place a moratorium on the installation of additional canisters on the trailless peaks he wrote, "Do they not interfere with the sense of eternal wilderness which most people seek when they climb trailless peaks? Shall we leave no mountain tops of any great height where we may find no sign of man and his ambitions?"

Recognizing that people who were climbing the 46 high peaks were "record keepers... a reasonable and worthwhile pleasure," he saw no reason why those records should be kept on the mountains. "They are after all, recorded with great care by the Forty-Sixers... and each climber is free to keep a log or journal of his own ascents." Marshall's recommendation was that instead of placing registers on the summits of the trailless peaks, "the Adirondack Forty-Sixers spend the same effort and funds in launching an educational campaign, for climbers of trailless peaks in particular, to leave the summits just as they found them so that the next climbers will see no sign of anyone having been there before... Would it not be well to give such a program a chance before participating further in lessening the sense of wildness on our trailless peaks by leaving our mark upon them?"

In the same article Marshall touched on another issue that Forty-Sixers would debate over the course of the club's history: the proliferation of herdpaths on the trailless peaks. He noted that the herdpaths were "caused by parties of too many people in relation to what the ground cover will stand... a large party going single file over terrain may inadvertently make a trail and thus destroy the trailless quality of the peak it is climbing." Even with the relatively few people, by today's standards, who were hiking the trailless peaks at that time, it is interesting to note that the debate and the desire to maintain the wild character of the trailless peaks began so early.

George Marshall repeated his concern about the herdpaths and canisters in 1958, when he wrote to then 46er president Richard Babcock (#115), "I do feel that there is a special obligation on the part of the 46ers, who have done such splendid work in popularizing an interest in mountain climbing, especially among the trailless peaks, to take leadership in seeing that the good features of this activity do not destroy the possibility of it continuing for all time."

Babcock's October 30, 1958, letter in response to Marshall expressed the 46ers' prevailing view on the canister issue:

> Experience has shown us that people will leave their marks in some form or another on these peaks (I wish you could have seen the top of Couchsachraga in 1956, as I did, before the register was placed there). This being so, it is much better to have one neat inconspicuous register "spoiling" one small spot than to have records of marks in the form of cans, glasses and papers strewn all over the mountain top. Those peaks I have visited since the placing of registers have been notably improved in this respect.

THE HISTORY OF THE ADIRONDACK FORTY-SIXERS

While George Marshall could not convince the 46ers to remove the canisters and leave the trailless peaks free from any sign of human presence, he did succeed in convincing club members to rethink their hobby and the impact it was having on the mountains. As Babcock indicated in the latter part of his response, Marshall had brought an environmental consciousness to the 46ers that the club would build on throughout its organizational growth:

> Up to now the 46ers collectively and individually have emphasized exclusively "climbing" the 46 peaks with little thought being given to the desirability of climbing the trailless peaks in large parties or small, of being guided by someone familiar with a certain route as opposed to finding your own way, or of leaving the woodlands and ridges unmarked by blazes or cairns. Neglect of these considerations is natural in an organization so young and with so few members. But we are maturing and our membership fast increasing so that it behooves us to give more attention to the "how" of climbing, as you have long advocated.

Kay Flickinger, Phyllis Anderson, and Ed Foley on Colden, January 1954

The Fifties

On November 25, 1950, a major storm swept through the Adirondacks.[72] Heavy rains and winds in excess of 100 miles per hour did extensive damage to large sections of the High Peaks. In June of 1951 the Conservation Department closed a significant number of trails in the Cold River area as well as the Lake Colden, Marcy, and MacIntyre area due to safety concerns for hikers and the fire hazard caused by the tangled masses of downed trees. That action effectively closed the summits of more than a dozen High Peaks. The 46er executive committee informed club members that it had decided not to recognize any climbs to summits that were made on restricted trails, thus working in concert with the regulations of the Conservation Department. As a result, information in the canister registers proved useful. The club sent a letter to all hikers who had left their names and addresses in the registers, informing them of the closed trails and the club's efforts to keep hikers out of restricted areas. Trails gradually reopened throughout 1952 and 1953. The club conferred on a regular basis with the Conservation Department to find out which trails had been reopened and which remained restricted and reported that information to members. At the end of December 1954 the Conservation Department announced that all trails in the High Peaks wilderness were again open.

The club held two weekend meetings a year, one in the spring and one in the fall. The spring meeting was always held at Adirondak Loj. Fall meetings, which were less well attended than the spring meetings, were held at various lodges throughout the North Country: Northbrook Lodge on Osgood Lake in Paul Smiths, Elk Lake Lodge, Cedar River House, Indian Lake, Stockton College, Severance on Paradox Lake, Irondequoit Club on Piseco Lake, and even at Boulders, Grace and Ed Hudowalski's camp on Schroon Lake. Saturday daytime activities included planned hikes, canoe trips, boat rides, or visits to a nearby museum or historic site. Spring meeting participants usually spent some time working on maintenance around Adirondak Loj – clearing trails, cutting trees. At the end of the day participants gathered for a meal followed by a business meeting and some entertainment or program: a slide presentation, a talk on some aspect of hiking, or a group sing-along. A traditional vesper service, a holdover from the Forty-Sixers of Troy days and the club's roots in Grace Methodist Church, was held on Sunday morning. Those services included the reading of some inspirational poetry, prose, and Psalms, the singing of songs and hymns, and a brief meditation. Nonsectarian and catholic in nature, the brief services provided an opportunity for members to "join hearts and hands and voices" in praise of mountains and nature. One song frequently sung was Orra Phelps's *Tahawus*, which she wrote to the tune of *Austria*:

> Great Tahawus, we salute Thee,
> Mighty cleaver of the sky.
> Of the summits of the forests
> Thine the crown that towers most high.
> Suns of summer, snows of winter
> Make thy grandeur more sublime.
> We come humbly seeking blessings
> That thou givest all who climb.
>
> On Tahawus' slope we tarry
> Build our evening campfires bright.
> Comrades of the trail together
> Here find shelter for the night.
> Wind for music, stars for wonder,
> Mystic dawn, then glorious day.
> Great Tahawus, strength Thou givest,
> For life's ever upward way.

Club memorabilia – items that displayed the 46er logo – were offered for sale to club members for the first time in 1951. Lapel pins were $2.50, tie clips and tie bars $4.20, and cuff links $5. Only those individuals who had completed the 46 were allowed to purchase those items and wear the insignia.

New U.S. Geological Survey maps released in the mid-1950s indicated that four of the peaks originally measured to be over 4,000 feet in elevation were, in fact, less than 4,000 feet. They were Blake's Peak, Cliff, Nye, and Couchsachraga. In addition, the height of

MacNaughton, originally thought to be 3,976 feet, was adjusted to exactly 4,000 feet. At the September 24-26, 1954, meeting the club passed a resolution stating that it would continue to use Carson's original measurements as the basis for the official climbing list for membership regardless of the corrected elevations.

The club had an unwritten dictum that when the number of recorded 46ers reached 100 it would print an official roster of members. Discussions on what form the printed list would take led to the printing of the first 46er book, *The Adirondack Forty-Sixers,* in 1958. Instead of a modest mimeographed roster of climbers, the club published a 147-page book, printed by the Peters Print of Albany. Four hundred copies were printed with 200 individually numbered so that the first 200 Forty-Sixers could reserve the book number that corresponded with their climbing number.

The book publication committee consisted of Dorothy O. Haeusser (#52), Orra Phelps, Eleanor M. Plum and Grace Hudowalski, chair. Dr. Edgar B. Nixon, a past president of the ADK and the author of the column "Armchair Mountaineer" which appeared in *Ad-i-ron-dac,* edited the material.[73] Pen and ink sketches by Alice Morgan, whose work had enlivened the covers of *The Cloud Splitter*, were used with the permission of the ADK's Albany Chapter. David H. Beetle, editor of *The Knickerbocker News* in Albany (and a 21er at the time), wrote the book's introduction.

The book's dedication read: "To the First Adirondack Forty-Sixers Herbert Clark, Robert and George Marshall and to all Others who wish to attain 'Heaven Up-H'istedness.'"

The term "heaven up-h'isted" was coined by early Adirondack guide Orson "Old Mountain" Phelps to describe his feelings when standing on one of the summits of the High Peaks, or "mountings" as he called them. It is interesting to note that the book jacket flaps contained a brief history of the Adirondack Mountain Club, demonstrating the close relationship between the two clubs at the time.

While intended as a vehicle to publish the roster of 46er finishers – 136 at the time – the book also contained a wealth of information on the High Peaks and the sport of 46ing. Grace Hudowalski wrote a chapter on the history of the 46ers. Edward Harmes contributed brief sketches of each of the 46 high peaks. Katherine Flickinger's chapter, "Climbing the Forty-Six on Snow and Ice," presented a summary of the winter climbing exploits of a small but growing contingent of hearty souls. At the end of her chapter Flickinger noted, "Already there are several people who have well over twenty such trips to remember, and it is entirely feasible that in time there may be an occasional winter Forty-Sixer on the roster." (As of 2010 the number of individuals who have climbed the 46 in winter stood at 471 and counting.) The Rev. Peter Ward wrote an essay entitled "Why We Climb," in which he attempted to put into

Kay Flickinger took this picture of Bob Wiley on his way up Colden, January 2, 1954. Bob's first climb was of Marcy in 1934. He finished the 46 on Whiteface in 1973.

John Siau and Bob Wiley at Bradley Pond Lean-to, April 1955

words the feeling of Old Mountain Phelps's "heaven up-h'isted-ness." Orville C. Gowie penned a short chapter, "Forty-Sixer Footsteps," which was a compilation of interesting statistics on 46er firsts: first father-daughter combination, oldest and youngest persons to finish the 46, first and last mountains climbed by the most number of people, etc.[74] *The Adirondack Forty-Sixers* also included a sample of the traditional vesper service, a copy of the 46er questionnaire, which each hiker had to submit as a prerequisite for membership, the club's Articles of Organization and Bylaws, a list of officers since the club's inception, and the roster of membership. The roster consisted of individual listings of each climber, climbing numbers, and the dates and mountain names of first and finishing ascents.

Those 46ers who purchased copies of the 1958 book were sent supplemental rosters with the names of the new 46ers each year until 1966.

The main topic of discussion at the May 30, 1959, meeting at Adirondak Loj was the need for a "climber's code." President Richard Babcock said that the development of such a code occurred to him as a result of a letter he had received from George Marshall, who had expressed his concern that one of the primary objectives of the club, that of protecting the wilderness characteristics of the trailless peaks, was being neglected. He felt that activities such as sponsoring hikes by large parties to climb the trailless peaks were contrary to the goal of preservation. Marshall, who was living in Los Angeles at the time, wrote, "I have seen some very wonderful country in the West, but none of it, in my opinion, surpasses the Adirondacks. It is because of its unique qualities that I feel the Forest Preserve must be enlarged before it is too late... and that there must be constant vigilance and education to preserve the natural quality of what remains of our Adirondack Wilderness."[75]

Marshall had sounded the alarm years earlier in a letter to ADK president L. Morgan Porter dated November 8, 1952. In that letter he described what he had found on the top of Mt. Marcy, graphically pointing out the little regard for environmental issues that was part of the general climbing culture at that time:

> I climbed Mt. Marcy last August on a misty day, when I knew the chances were that there would be no view from the summit... We did not look forward to a view, but we did look forward to that fresh, stimulating experience and that sense of wilderness which one experiences on an above-timberline peak covered with fog on a windy day. However, when we got to the summit, we found it covered with orange peels and the old shelter[76] literally turned into a garbage dump. This is mighty discouraging and, together with seeing initials carved and painted on top of Ampersand and a moderate amount of litter along the trails, makes me feel that both the Adirondack Mountain Club and the Forty-Sixers in cooperation with the Conservation Department might well consider what program of education would be most effective to stop most of the desecration of beautiful places.[77]

In response to Marshall's concerns, Babcock envisioned a "climber's code" that would outline some basic principles to define the "right way" to climb the 46 peaks. In developing such a code the discussion centered on the seeming mutually exclusive goals of fostering the use of the Forest Preserve while at the same time attempting to maintain its wilderness characteristics. As more and more people took up the challenge of climbing the 46 high peaks, it seemed unquestionable that the increase in usage would have an impact on the natural landscape. The executive committee appointed a special committee consisting of George Marshall, Fay Loope, Ed Hudowalski, and Herbert Allen (#96), with Babcock serving as chair, to grapple with this issue. The committee struggled with the content and tone of the code. They penned a draft document, but the ultimate goal and purpose of the code was never defined and the club never acted on the committee's proposal.

An additional topic of discussion at the spring 1959 meeting was the future growth of the club. A committee consisting of Rudolph Strobel (#98), Grace Hudowalski, and Ditt Dittmar was assigned the task of long-range planning: to discuss issues such as additional venues for meetings, activities to further the aims of the club, and ways to involve more of the membership in club activities.

The Sixties

During 1961 the club explored the feasibility of applying for tax-exempt status as a not-for-profit organization. To do so the club was required to amend its bylaws to reflect educational and service goals. The plan to apply for the status met with some minor opposition. In a letter to club secretary Trudy Healy (#148) dated May 14, 1962, Don Dickinson (#155) expressed his reservations: "Since the tax deduction for the dues is inconsequential... there must be some other schemes afoot... Too bad, it has been refreshing to be a member of an organization, small and informal (and elite!), that was not continually pressing some Grand Strategy in this or that direction."

While Dickinson's opposition was not widely shared by club members, it was indicative of the club's growing pains and conflicting goals. Would the Forty-Sixers be primarily a social club of members with like interests or a service-oriented organization that would play a role in resolving issues concerning the High Peaks region? After much discussion, the aims and objectives of the organization were revised in order to meet requirements for tax-exempt status, and the new bylaws were passed at the May 1962 meeting. Those bylaws stated the objectives of the organization to be "the fostering and protection of the natural resources within the Adirondack Forest Preserve of the State of New York and the preservation of the wilderness character of the region. These objects shall be promoted by... educating the public to the availability and benefits of outdoor activity and the increased use of the Forest Preserve by encouragement, information, and example, and assuring that those who do engage in wilderness endeavors under the aegis of this organization do so well informed and prepared, carrying on their activities in a manner adapted to secure fullest enjoyment, safety, and preservation of the wilderness."

The club received tax-exempt approval from the U.S. Treasury Department, Internal Revenue Service on June 5, 1964.

At the same time, the club made several other changes to the bylaws. In a move to provide continuity in the club positions of secretary and treasurer, the bylaws were amended to allow the individuals serving in those two positions to succeed themselves. The club also formally defined in the by-laws the appointive position of Historian, "whose duties shall consist of tracing and recording the history of the organization and the growth of its membership." Thus Grace Hudowalski was given an official title for the work she had been doing since the inception of the Forty-Sixers of Troy and Ditt Dittmar was allowed to continue as club treasurer, a position he would hold for 53 years, until his retirement in 2001.

Adolph "Ditt" Dittmar

Adolph "Ditt" Dittmar was born in Richmond Hill, New York, on February 5, 1915. He graduated from Hobart College in Geneva and Columbia University School of Dental and Oral Surgery, after which he pursued an internship in dentistry at Albany Medical Center. That move placed him closer to the mountains and to Grace, with whom he had been corresponding. She invited him to an Albany ADK Chapter meeting, and it was at that meeting that he met his future wife Mary Colyer (#29). In late 1941, the day after Pearl Harbor, Ditt enlisted in the Navy, joining the Hospital Corps. He and Mary were married in September 1943 and spent two days of their hiking/camping honeymoon at Noah John Rondeau's hermitage. Ditt was posted to Pensicola, Florida, and later was stationed in Galveston, Texas, and Newport, Rhode Island, before shipping out to serve on a support vessel in the Pacific Theatre as a dental officer. He achieved the rank of lieutenant.

Ditt's first ascent of a High Peak was Mt. Marcy on August 13, 1938. He later described that climb: "My introduction to the Adirondacks came way back in 1938 when, as a counselor at a boy's summer camp, we canoed in the Fulton Chain and then climbed Mt. Marcy. The trail was ankle deep in mud and a thunderstorm was brewing as we hit the lean-to at Four-Corners. I vowed then and there that I would never climb another Adirondack Mountain."[78]

He utterly failed to keep that vow. On a camping trip in the Lake Colden area with the Intercollegiate Outing Club Association, Ditt and his brother Charlie decided to hike

Ditt and Mary Dittmar with son David in pack basket in late 1940s

into the Cold River region in search of the hermit Noah John Rondeau. They found him and Rondeau told Ditt about "46ering" and of a group called the Forty-Sixers of Troy.[79] At Rondeau's suggestion Ditt wrote to Grace Hudowalski and asked her for a list of the 46 high peaks. On July 11, 1945, while on leave from the Navy, he finished the 46 on Seymour... the muddy trail he had encountered on his first hike up Marcy was by then a distant memory. He was the only one to finish the forty-six that year and the first since 1942, when Mary and her friend Elizabeth Little (#30) had completed their forty-sixth peak. Few people were climbing the 46 at that time as evidenced by Ditt's recalling that he "found [his] hat on Allen on my second visit there, which I had left by accident four years before."

In the summer of 1946, after he was discharged from the Navy, Ditt and Mary served as the caretakers at ADK's Johns Brook Lodge. After deciding they wanted to live in the North Country, Ditt looked for a place where he could set up his dental practice. The couple moved to Au Sable Forks in 1947, and Ditt maintained two offices, one in Plattsburgh and one in Au Sable Forks for several years, before moving to Plattsburgh in 1953, when he closed his Au Sable Forks office. He retired in 1988.

Ditt attended the charter meeting of the Adirondack Forty-Sixers and was appointed treasurer. If Grace was the heart and soul of the Adirondack Forty-Sixers, then Ditt was its backbone, providing organizational structure and administrative support for the club. The growth of the 46er club can be traced by the increased workload of the treasurer over the years. "My responsibilities were few in those days," Ditt recalled. There were only sixty-eight members by the end of 1948, seventy-eight by 1949, and eighty-seven by 1950. As the numbers steadily increased, however, in the 1960s and 1970s, so did Ditt's workload. He was responsible for all club mailings; keeping the list of active 46ers; producing the spring and fall meeting notices, special bulletins, and agendas; and maintaining the supply of 46er patches, pins, buttons, note paper, T-shirts, etc., and filling the orders for them. He hand-addressed all correspondence for the mailings for the first 19 years. Then, in 1967, the club purchased a hand-operated Elliot Addressing Machine, which required Ditt to type individual stencils for each member, ink and print them, and then store them for the next mailing. With the help of a computer expert, he moved to punch card data processing around 1969 to produce computer-generated labels. Finally, at the age of 76, he took on the task of learning to use a home computer to manage the club's membership and mailing lists.

Ditt initiated a humorous dues notice, which greatly increased the contributions to the club. His annual reminder to renew membership always included some joke, amusing poem, or lighthearted look at life along with a not-so-subtle request for dues payment. One such notice was "A Treasurer's Dream":

> I fell asleep the other night,
> And while I had a snooze,
> I dreamed each member stepped right up,
> And promptly paid his dues.
> But when I found 'twas but a dream,
> I nearly threw a fit.
> It's up to you to make it true,
> Suggestion: Please remit.[80]

In 1973 Ditt considered retiring from his position as treasurer after 25 years because of the increased amount of time the job required. However, no one came forward to replace him. So the club voted to change his title from Treasurer to Executive Secretary/Treasurer and provide him with a small stipend for his labors. The position eventually involved so much detail that Ditt developed a loose-leaf volume, "Duties of the Executive Secretary/Treasurer" to turn over to an eventual successor. The volume, close to 50 pages, listed 37 separate duties (one of which had eight parts). Despite the increasing time commitment, which even required him to plan family vacations around his workload, Ditt never considered the position a burden. At the age of 80 he said, "If I quit I wouldn't know what to do with my time."

Ditt repeated his climbs of the 46 with each of his five children, David (#201), Katharyn (#564), Brooke (#561), James (#465), and Elizabeth (#563). Ditt was also a violinist and member of the Plattsburgh Community Orchestra, chairman of the Adirondack Boy Scout Council Camping Committee, and a member of the Plattsburgh Rotary and the Adirondack Dental Society.

Internal and External Communication

In 1963 Grace designed a brochure, "Climbing the Adirondack 46," which explained the club's purpose and provided instructions for hikers on how to register their climbs with the club to become 46ers. Illustrated with sketches made by Trudy Healy, it included a list of the mountains and space to record the date of each climb, companions on the hike, and brief comments. Grace consulted with and had the brochure copy approved by the Conservation Department before it was printed and distributed at Adirondak Loj and various tourist attractions throughout the North County. The brochure helped to promote the club and the sport of 46ing. The sketches employed in the climbing folder were also used to create note cards that were made available for members to purchase. They sold for $1 in packets of 12 cards and envelopes and the proceeds from their sale were used to help defray the cost of printing the brochure.[81]

In order to improve communication with its growing membership the Forty-Sixers decided to publish a newsletter: *Adirondack Peeks*. The first issue was distributed in the fall/winter of 1963-64. The editors – Richard Babcock, James Goodwin (#24), and Trudy Healy – described the purpose of the publication in their first issue: "to further the fellowship of the 46ers, promote the conservation of the Adirondack Peaks in their present state, encourage the right kind of climbing... inform 46ers and Aspiring 46ers about each other and their doings... supply current hiking information... serve as a means of communication."

Jim Goodwin, left, guided "Pop" Anderson and the Rev. Will Lewis to the top of Haystack from Panther Gorge in 1926.

The editors encouraged readers to send in articles about their climbs, poems, notices of birth, marriage... and death... "anything as long as it has even a smidgen of relationship to Adirondack 46er peaks or people." Their plan was to publish the newsletter twice a year. The first 16-page mimeographed edition contained an editorial about Conservation Department policies on building new trails in the High Peaks; the Treasurer's Report on club finances; an article by Goodwin on the fresh landslides on Giant that were set off by a major rainstorm on June 29, 1963; minutes from the fall 1963 meeting; a notice about the first winter 46ers, Edgar Bean (#92W), who finished on Blake's Peak on March 10, 1962, and James W. F. Collins (#183W), who finished on Panther on March 16, 1963; brief articles on the climbing exploits of Aspiring 46ers and those who had already finished; a crossword puzzle; and humorous cartoons and mountain sketches drawn by Trudy Healy.

Healy was an avid mountaineer, hiker, skier, photographer, and spelunker. Originally from the Black Forest of Germany, she met her future husband, George Healy, when he was studying at the University of Munich. She came to the United States in 1941. Her first High Peak climb was of Gothics on July 17, 1952, and she became a 46er on Redfield, August 26, 1958. From that point on she was one of the stalwarts of the club, taking on various leadership roles throughout the 1960s and 1970s. In addition to being editor of *Peeks* from 1963 until she moved to Utah in 1974, Trudy was secretary of the club (1959-62 and 1966-67). Her pen and ink drawings often appeared on the cover of *Peeks* as well as other club publications. She was editor and illustrator of *Rock Climber's Guide to the Adirondacks* (1967, 1971) and author of *From the Black Forest to Tibet: One Woman's Mountains* (1993). Trudy organized the first Adirondack Mountain Club rock climbing school in 1965. Having hiked in the White Mountains of New Hampshire, the Rockies, the Alps, and the Andes, she was elected to membership in the American Alpine Club. She completed seven rounds of the Adirondack 46 – her first round and six subsequent rounds with each of her six children.

Peeks became the club's main source of communication with its members, providing a mechanism to disseminate information on club activities, personal hiking achievements, and trail conditions. It also served as the vehicle through which club issues were presented and debated in editorials, letters, and articles.

Herdpaths on the Trailless Peaks

The issue that dominated discussions at Forty-Sixer meetings throughout the mid to late-1960s was the appearance and proliferation of "herd tracks" on many of the trailless peaks and what to do about them. Club members still regarded navigating one's way to the summits of the trailless peaks as an important part of the Forty-Sixer experience, and they were determined to maintain those peaks as pristine wilderness for as long as possible. It became clear to some that the club's efforts to promote the use of the High Peaks was in direct conflict with its desire to protect the wilderness character of the area. Richard Babcock discussed the conundrum in an editorial that appeared in the Fall 1964 (Vol. 1 No. 2) issue of *Peeks*:

> Each year the evidence of man's passage accumulates on the trailless peaks, as each climber or party of climbers, in following the path of least resistance, is channeled along a common way. This has happened over a span of 15 to 20 years during which a typical trailless peak was climbed by (at a rough estimate) anywhere from 10 to 50 people in a year's time. What will happen as time passes, the number of Aspiring 46ers increases, and 100 to 200 people climb a trailless peak in one year?... Aren't the 46ers to a large degree responsible for the climbing that is done on the trailless peaks?... isn't there a fundamental unresolved conflict in the purposes of the 46ers as stated in the Articles of Organization? On the one hand we propose "educating the public to the availability... of outdoor activity in this region" and at the same time we aim at "preservation of the wilderness character of this region."[82]

Babcock went on to suggest that "our promotional activities are getting way ahead of our 'conservation' objective so that we should consider soft-peddling the promotion and work much harder on the preservation of wilderness character." To accomplish that Babcock suggested removing the Forty-Sixer's pamphlet "Climbing the Adirondack 46" from tourist promotion displays. He also proposed that the club sponsor an annual Adirondack hikers' conference aimed at summer camp counselors, Aspiring 46ers, and other groups interested in climbing in the High Peaks to educate them about conservation and wilderness preservation issues.

Also appearing in the Fall 1964 issue of *Peeks* was an article, "Paths on the Trailless Peaks," by Jim Goodwin. In it he wrote, "I am sure that I speak for the majority of 46ers in saying that we want to put off the day as long as possible when all trailless peaks ascents are like climbing Phelps. Half the fun in climbing these mountains is the chance to be one's own 'navigator'..."[83] Phelps was a well-traveled trailless peak, with a herdpath so well-defined that it was as easy to follow as any marked trail. Goodwin bemoaned the then new trend of some hikers and groups of marking the untrailed peaks with illegal blazes, cairns, and string to guide their way. He suggested that people refrain from marking the trailless peaks in any way, which he reasoned could help slow the formation of herdpaths and maintain the fun and challenge of navigating to the summits by oneself.

Paul W. Weld, an Aspiring 46er, continued the discussion on the trailless peaks in the Spring 1965 (Vol. II, No. 1) issue of *Peeks* with an editorial that encouraged people to climb one mountain at a time in order to avoid contributing to the herdpaths that were developing on the ridges between mountains. He also suggested broadening the requirements for membership in the Forty-Sixers to allow some choice of climbs from a greater number of peaks. In addition he suggested the club consider a "herdpath obliteration campaign" to remove the cairns and other markers that denoted the herdpaths.

Jim Goodwin expressed the opinion that while the herdpaths were inevitable, there was still much that the 46ers could do to maintain the character of the trailless peaks. In an editorial that appeared in the Spring 1966 issue of *Peeks* he wrote, "We can't turn history back forty-five years. There are many more people in the world and the trodden paths are here to stay. What we can do however, is to convince the public and the authorities that what is left of the wilderness is precious, and that formal trails should not be constructed up the trailless peaks. We must puncture the myth that the Forty-Sixers are selfish extremists who don't want anyone else to enjoy the wilderness. What we want is to preserve the wilderness for as many people to enjoy as wish to."[84]

Goodwin encouraged 46ers to educate others to leave the peaks as they "are"; refrain from leaving garbage on the summits and from marking the climbing routes; and to discourage the notion of formally marking trails on the trailless peaks.

Discussions concerning the fate of the trailless peaks continued at the Forty-Sixer spring meeting in 1966. On Sunday May 29, a group of concerned 46ers met with some camp counselors from Camp Lincoln and Pok-O-Moonshine to address the issue. Since camp-sponsored hikes tended to involve a counselor leading a large group single file up a trailless peak, they were considered to be major contributors to the creation of herdpaths. Those in attendance at the meeting generally agreed that any markers which encouraged hikers to follow the same route led to the formation of herdpaths as did the sheer number of people following one after the other. Suggested solutions to the problem ranged from eliminating the trailless peaks section from the ADK trail guides, to educating people on map and compass reading so they would be comfortable finding their own route to the summit, to groups walking spaced out three or four abreast instead of in single file.

Focusing on education as the most productive way to inform people about the problems of herdpath proliferation and other conservation issues, the 46ers held a summer camporee for campers and counselors from area boys' and girls' camps July 28 – 29, 1966 at South Meadow. Fifty-nine registrants from five different camps participated in presentations on the history of the Forty-Sixer club, the problem of litter on the trails, ways to avoid adding to the proliferation of herdpaths, alternate peaks to climb outside of the High Peaks, and tips on low impact camping techniques. Forty-Sixer President James "Beetle" Bailey (#233), who had been instrumental in organizing the camporee, noted the interest and enthusiasm that were displayed at the event and recommended that it be conducted annually.

The information imparted at the camporee had a positive impact on reducing the amount of litter found on the trailless summits as well as on the marked trails. However, it also had an unexpected impact on the herdpath issue. The Forty-Sixers' message to refrain from marking herdpaths resulted in some vigilante behavior. Several camp groups, as well as individuals, took it upon themselves to dismantle cairns that marked the start of an approach to a trailless peak. In the case of the well-defined herdpath up Phelps, a group not only went so far as to cover the beginning of the herdpath with logs and brush but also, purposely to mislead hikers, to cut a false herdpath that came to an abrupt end. In a letter on "The Wrecking of Herd Paths" that appeared in the Fall 1966 issue of *Peeks*, Jim Goodwin described a similar trail war that went on at the start of the approach to Rocky Peak Ridge near the summit of Giant Mountain:

> On one day, the cairn would be gone and the path blocked with brush. On the next day, an 'Anti-Forty-Sixer' group would build a bigger cairn and remove the brush. On still another day, the 'Forty-Sixers' would attack again – with resulting counterattack by the 'Antis.' This continued most of the summer. Lots of fun for those involved, but an annoyance for everyone else.[85]

The unfortunate practice brought the 46er organization a good deal of criticism from those who relied on the information in the ADK trail guides to find their way. It also prompted many to pose the question, as Goodwin noted in his letter, "Who gave the Forty-Sixers or any other minority group the right to destroy such a route?"[86]

While the club's desire to preserve the true wilderness character of the trailless peaks was well-intentioned – although in retrospect perhaps a bit unrealistic and idealized with the number of 46ers growing exponentially each year – the resulting overzealous response on the part of some who were eager to solve the problem was a detriment to the cause and image of the organization. As Peggy O'Brien wrote in a letter to the editor that appeared in the Fall 1966 issue of *Peeks*, "It is difficult for me to understand the presumptuous actions of members of the 46er organization in removing well-known signs, cairns, etc. to eliminate herd trails... The trailless peaks of the Adirondacks do not belong to the 46ers alone nor do they have the right to dictate what should be done or not done with them. Their opinion should be regarded equally with others but their ascent of the 46 peaks gives them no dictorial (*sic*) powers."[87]

In many cases, 46ers had originally placed the cairns at the beginning of the access routes to trailless peaks in order to make it easier for those attempting to climb them. Some members felt a degree of justification in removing the markers as a way to slow the establishment of herdpaths. However, a number of the access points had been described in the ADK guidebooks for years and were well known points of reference throughout the hiking community. Alice Waterhouse (#16) provided a more philosophical explanation for the 46ers' attitudes. In an article in *The Knickerbocker News* announcing her completion of the 46 in 1939 she said: "When you reach the top of a difficult peak, you may feel a sense of ownership of all that surrounds you. Sometimes I do."[88]

At the Forty-Sixer fall 1966 meeting, in what again in retrospect appears to have been a public relations folly, club members voted to ask the ADK to remove detailed descriptions of the trailless peak routes from future editions of their trail guide publications and suggest the use of topographical maps to lay out routes instead. In fact, the ADK's Conservation Committee had also recommended the removal of instructions for accessing the trailless peaks. Although the ADK ultimately rejected the idea, they added, as a compromise, an explanation about how to minimize hiker impact.[89]

In 1967 the Forty-Sixers absorbed a blow to their efforts to keep the trailless peaks as trailless and unmarked as possible with the state's designation of Phelps as an official Conservation Department marked and maintained trail. The herdpath debate continued but with a feeling of resignation that well-defined routes were inevitable as more and more people — those attempting to climb the 46 and those just out for an adventure — were climbing in the High Peaks. In a letter that appeared in the Fall 1967 issue of *Peeks*, Mason T. Ingram of East Longmeadow, MA, took a slightly different approach to the problem. Ingram, who had climbed 14 high peaks at the time, felt the real problem with the herdpaths was the proliferation of false ones — well worn pathways, which arrived, eventually at dead ends — that developed when the "correct" herdpaths were not distinct. That, he argued, resulted in a maze of paths in some areas that led nowhere. He suggested the establishment of "wilderness paths," informal trails sparingly marked and marginally maintained that would follow the most ecologically sensible and direct routes to the summits.[90] Ingram also suggested the notion of a point system whereby those seeking to become 46ers could climb an alternate peak outside the High Peak region (such as Jay or Sentinel) of the same relative difficulty as one of the 46 as a substitute for climbing certain high peaks. That, he reasoned, would reduce the foot traffic in the High Peaks and slow the development of the herdpaths.

Ingram's idea was discussed but ultimately dismissed as contrary to the Forty-Sixer ideal of maintaining the special qualities of the trailless peaks. Ironically, as history has shown, Ingram's idea was sound but slightly ahead of its time. Establishing "wilderness paths" on the trailless peaks became a major focus of the 46er trail maintenance efforts in the 2000s.

On Sunday, June 2, 1968, during their spring meeting weekend, Forty-Sixers gathered at the south shore of Marcy Dam to dedicate the Ed Hudowalski Memorial Lean-to. The club had donated the materials to build the lean-to to honor Ed for his years of service to the club. He had passed away a week after the fall meeting in 1966. About forty people attended the brief ceremony of song and remembrances which culminated with his widow, Grace, lighting a fire in the lean-to's fireplace. A plaque affixed to the lean-to wall read:

Memorial Lean-to
"Uncle Ed" Hudowalski
1904 – 1966
Co-Organizer of Adirondack 46ers
and
Designer of 46er Emblem

George Marshall attended the fall 1968 club meeting at Johns Brook Lodge on September 7. While he kept informed about club issues and often expressed his views through his correspondence with members of the club's executive committee, he had rarely been able to attend meetings after moving to California in 1959. He supported a resolution passed by the club at the fall 1968 meeting in opposition to "all current proposals for dams on the Upper Hudson River." Of particular concern was the proposal for the Gooley Dam, which would have flooded most of the village of Newcomb and Hudson River valley in the central Adirondacks to supply water to New York City. The Forty-Sixers joined a number of other conservation groups in expressing opposition to the project. The dam was never built.

In addition to contributing a strong voice of conservation and preservation to the Gooley Dam discussion, Marshall's presence at the fall gathering was a real treat for club members. Those in attendance questioned him about his climbing experiences and some asked for his autograph. If Forty-Sixers were impressed with him, he likewise was impressed by them and the spirit of forty-sixing. In a letter to Grace Hudowalski he expressed his sentiments:

> The group not only has a fine love of mountains and a competence in them, but also seems to have fine conservation attitudes. However, my feeling after all these years are somewhat mixed. On the one hand I was disturbed to hear a term new to me, 'herd ways,' and realized vividly what has happened to our previously trailless peaks as a result of Forty-Sixer enthusiasm, and I am also somewhat disturbed at those who regard Forty-Sixing in a similar way to those who like to check off their visits to all the national parks. On the other hand, I realize that for most of those who have climbed the Forty-Six peaks this has been a fine mountain, and to a degree wilderness experience, which means a great deal to them, and this makes me very happy. When one of the Forty-Sixers present asked me, of all things, to autograph her Mt. Marcy Quadrangle and said that Forty-Sixing had changed her whole life, I was impressed anew by what mountain experience may mean to one's entire outlook.

View from the "Uncle Ed" Hudowalski Lean-to – photo by Joanna R. Donk

Part III: The 1970s – Giving Something Back to the Mountains

The 1970s proved to be a pivotal decade for the 46ers as the club's focus slowly evolved from serving primarily as a social outlet for hiking enthusiasts to improving the environmental health of the Adirondack mountain region. Throughout the 1970s as the numbers of visitors to the High Peaks steadily increased, club members began to witness first hand the deterioration of trails and camping areas. Herdpaths on the trailless peaks and trash on the trails and at campsites vividly documented the environmental strain that was diminishing the wilderness experience. It was becoming readily apparent that remedial intervention would be necessary in order to save and maintain the area's prized wilderness character.

The club grappled with its seeming conflicting values of promoting use of the High Peaks while decrying the loss of true wilderness untouched by the influences of man. While some members suggested removing the summit registers or disbanding the club as the response to those problems, others recognized an opportunity to engage the club in conservation and education programs for the benefit of the High Peaks region. In particular, two 46ers, Glenn Fish (#536) and Dr. Edwin Ketchledge (#507), who both were passionate about decreasing the human impact on the area, steered the club toward its new direction. Just as the club was slowly recognizing the need for action, so, too, was state government. After years of promoting recreational development in the Adirondack Park, state officials began to understand the need to engage in ecological management in order to protect and maintain state lands in their natural condition. Stewardship of the region became a priority.

The club's epiphany combined with the changing role of state government provided the impetus for conservation and education programs which have become the core of the club's stewardship efforts today. The phrase "giving something back to the mountains" began to direct programming priorities.

Mountain Stewards: The New Wilderness Ethic Emerges

By the beginning of the 1970s club members began to accept the inevitability of clearly defined herdpaths on the trailless peaks along with the reality that the pristine wilderness so prized and eloquently described by the Marshalls and other early 46ers was a thing of the past. Discussions began to center on changing the focus of club activities: from simply hiking in the High Peaks to developing programs aimed at conservation and education.

A solution to the herdpath problem continued to vex members and Mason Ingram's idea of the "wilderness paths" on the trailless peaks received additional attention. To gauge attitudes and collect opinions, the club asked members to respond to a questionnaire regarding Ingram's suggestion to mark informally one approach to the summit of each trailless peak. From an active membership of 525, seventy-seven members voiced support for Ingram's solution, 101 were opposed, and 11 were undecided. John Siau (#94) summed up the opinions of those in favor of Ingram's wilderness paths: "An excellent suggestion to reduce destruction and erosion of the whole mountain side. It channels the hikers through a relatively small area."[91] Others in favor of one route noted that a distinct path would be safer and allow more people to enjoy the High Peaks.

Those opposed to Ingram's solution agreed with James Goodwin (#24) who said, "The Wilderness Path Plan would destroy what is unique in the Adirondacks."[92] Other comments in opposition added that semi-marked trails would take the fun and challenge out of hiking the trailless peaks. As Clyde Babb (#448) quipped, "If I wanted trailed mountains, I would go to the White Mountains."[93] Forty-Sixer President William C. Frenette (#216) discussed the proposal with a representative from the state Conservation Department, but since the majority of 46ers who responded to the questionnaire were opposed to the plan, the executive committee voted to take no further action.

On the remaining question of what to do about the proliferation of the herdpaths on the trailless peaks, eighteen people suggested the drastic measures of either removing the summit registers, disbanding the 46er club altogether, or both. Their reasoning was that without the goal of becoming a 46er and the incentive provided by the registers on the trailless peaks, the number of people venturing onto those peaks would decrease. With fewer climbers, the woods could heal, and the herdpaths disappear. Others preferred a less draconian solution and supported an increase in conservation education efforts as the most constructive step the club could take to preserve the wilderness experience for future generations.

Forty-Sixers Publish a Second Book

Forty-Sixer activity during the late 1960s was not limited to discussions about the herdpaths. Members were also hard at work preparing a second book, *The Adirondack High Peaks and the Forty-Sixers*, published in 1970. The book, edited by Grace Hudowalski with drawings by Trudy Healy, was a limited edition volume of 1,200 copies sold mainly to club members. Like the 1958 book, the 1970 version included a history of the club, the roster of climbers,[94] descriptions of the 46 peaks, and chapters on "The Forty-Six in Winter" by David A. Vermilyea (#342W) and "Why We Climb" by Peter A Ward (#72), reprinted from the 1958 volume. The 1970 book also contained scientific material for the layperson on Adirondack alpine flora, birds, geology, mammals and trees, and folklore. Additional chapters included "Adirondack Guides of the High Peak Area" written by George Marshall; "Rock Climbing in the Adirondacks" by James A. Goodwin; "Noah John Rondeau, Hermit of Cold River" by Adolph G. Dittmar; "Legends of the Couchsachrage" by Grace Hudowalski; and "The Adirondack Lean-to" by Maitland C. DeSormo (#339). More than 50 black-and-white photos appeared throughout the book along with a full-page color photo of the summit of Mt. Marcy from Lake Tear-of-the-Clouds.

After the book was published, Paul Jamieson (#146), noted outdoorsman and conservationist, who also had authored a chapter for the new book ("The Class of '58"), expressed the sentiment that perhaps the 46ers should dissolve. In a letter to Grace Hudowalski dated June 5, 1970, Jamieson first praised the new book saying, "Every chapter was a pleasure to read... This is an important book for New York Staters and for everyone interested in the Adirondacks." He then went on to note:

> If it were not for one thing, I'd say let's stop right here, with this fine climax. Let's dissolve the club, remove the canisters, and let the woods quietly heal over the herdways. A few people would continue to climb the trailless peaks for love of it, but with no urgent incentive to finish with the first 600 or 700. The Forty-Sixers have been too successful. It would be nice to retire, bloated with success. But for one thing. Another group would be sure to found Forty-Sixer II.

Jamieson understood, as did other members of the club, that the challenge of climbing the 46 was here to stay regardless of the existence of any club or formal or informal recognition. The book was revised in 1971 with 3,000 copies printed. Those were sold to bookstores, libraries, and the general public.

State Government Enters the Discussion on Overuse in the High Peaks

A major shift in how state government viewed the Adirondack wilderness began to emerge in the late 1960s and early 1970s. Since 1919, when the New York state legislature adopted a formal Forest Preserve recreation plan, the state's emphasis had been on recreational development and ways to promote visitor use of state land.[95] For 50 years, Forest Preserve managers sought to make the High Peaks region more accessible and more convenient for users. The state cut 100 additional miles of trails, erected 90 lean-tos, and built dams and bridges, as well as roads to provide access to the backcountry in the event of forest fires. A cross-country ski trail was cut across Nye Mountain for use during the 1932 Olympics held in Lake Placid. Other ski trails were cut over Whale's Tail near Wright Peak and on the north slope of Mt. Marcy. A horse trail system was constructed with barns, bridges, and corrals in the Cold River area, and motorized equipment was used to conduct trail maintenance. Management programs emphasized visitor numbers, convenience, and enhancement of scenic vistas rather than the wilderness experience.

With the construction of the Adirondack Northway, Interstate 87, which began in the mid-1950s with sections opening throughout the 1960s, seekers of wilderness solitude from large population centers such as New York City and Boston had easy access to the High Peaks region. That convenience, along with increased leisure time, rising incomes, and greater publicity about the area led to a major influx of recreational users of the High Peaks during the 1950s and 1960s. As a result, regular visitors to the area began to see a degradation of the wilderness itself. Litter often lined the trails, garbage pits at lean-to sites – then the accepted places for campers to dispose of their trash – overflowed with refuse, and trail erosion became more and more evident as did deterioration of the alpine vegetation on the mountains with open summits. Those concerns were addressed at public hearings in 1960 held by the Joint Legislative Committee on Natural Resources. Reports generated by the committee recognized the growing problem of overuse of the High Peaks but recommended limited remedial action.

In 1967, following a proposal to create an Adirondack National Park from the state and private lands of the Forest Preserve, Governor Nelson A. Rockefeller appointed a Temporary Study Commission on the Future of the Adirondacks. The commission, chaired by Harold Hochschild, founder of the Adirondack Museum, was charged with exploring both state and private land issues within the Adirondack Park. Its 1970 report contained a number of recommendations, including a call for the creation of an independent bipartisan Adirondack Park Agency (APA) which would be granted general oversight and regulatory powers over the use of both the private and public lands that made up the park. With that recommendation in mind, the state legislature created the Adirondack Park Agency in 1971. One of the APA's first acts (1972) was to create the Adirondack Park State Land Master Plan (APSLMP) for the preservation, management, and use of all state lands within the park. The principle objective was the protection and preservation of the natural resources on those lands. The APSLMP classified the public lands within the park in seven categories according to each area's "characteristics and capacity to withstand use." They were Wilderness; Primitive; Canoe; Wild Forest; Intensive Use; Wild, Scenic, and Recreational Rivers; and Travel Corridors. The High Peaks region was designated as Wilderness, defined as lands that demonstrated "a primeval character without significant improvements or permanent human habitation... where man himself is a visitor who does not remain." The APA established guidelines to manage Wilderness areas in order to protect and maintain those natural conditions.[96]

The creation of the APA and the APSLMP represented a significant change in the state's approach to managing the natural resources of the High Peaks. The emphasis had shifted from providing more facilities to accommodate the increased numbers of users, to reducing facilities and exercising greater controls over user activities in order to preserve wilderness and the wilderness experience.[97] Under the APSLMP, non-conforming structures – firetowers, ranger cabins, telephone lines, and certain lean-tos and roads – in the High Peaks region were scheduled for removal or closure.

Recognizing the need to consolidate all of the agencies that dealt with environmental issues in order to more effectively carry out policy, the state created the Department of Environmental Conservation (DEC) on July 1, 1970. That agency combined the Conservation Department, Water Resources Commission, and Air Pollution Control Board, thereby facilitating a more unified coordination of the state's environmental protection programs.

The APA directed the newly-formed DEC to develop individual unit management plans (UMPs) for each unit of land under its jurisdiction as classified in the APSLMP. Those plans were developed and made available for public comment throughout the 1970s and 1980s. (As of 2008, a number of plans were still in the public comment phase.) The goal of each plan was to assess the natural resources of an area, identify opportunities for recreational use, and make recommendations for maintaining the wilderness integrity of each unit. The DEC was responsible for implementing the policies outlined for each UMP.

With their own discussions about the canisters, the proliferation of herdpaths, and the quandary posed by the club's seeming mutually exclusive purposes, the 46ers' internal debates had presaged the state's changing attitudes regarding the management of its wilderness resources. Discussions at the 46er spring 1970 executive committee meeting centered on the club's response to the state's new approach. The members of the committee discussed the notion of disbanding as well as the possibility of becoming a standing committee or "chapter" of the ADK. There was a concern that the bulk of the club's work was being done by only a few members and that if the club initiated any new programs no one would volunteer to work on them. Some members felt that any conservation projects that the club could initiate would stand a better chance of success if they were coordinated through the more organized, and better-financed and staffed committees of the ADK. However two men, Glenn Fish and Edwin Ketchledge, both of whom would serve as 46er presidents, saw an opportunity for the 46er club to establish itself as a service organization. They believed that club members would volunteer their time and energies to assist with conservation projects on behalf of the High Peaks. Fish and Ketchledge led the discussion and, with patient but pointed determination, redirected the focus of club activities into the areas of conservation, education, and environmental protection.

In 1928, when Glenn Fish was a college freshman, he had already made the decision that he would retire at the age of 55. Having decided when to retire, his next decision was where. That choice became clear a few years later, after he and his new bride Dorothy had honeymooned in the Adirondacks. The couple decided then that upstate New York would become home during their retirement years. So in 1966, Glenn and Dorothy had a retirement home built on the banks of the Hudson River between Warrensburg and North Creek. Two of the contractors working on the house invited Glenn to spend a weekend with them during hunting season at the East River Rod and Gun Club on the Opalescent River. Glenn was an avid fisherman but not a hunter. Nevertheless, he joined the group on November 25, 1966, for a hunting weekend. Foul weather thwarted the group's hunting plans, but Fish wandered out of camp to explore the area on his own. He hiked toward Uphill Brook Lean-to and was intrigued by a "game trail" and decided to follow it. That trail took him to the summit of Mt.

Glenn W. Fish

Redfield, where he found the 46er canister and signed his name in the logbook. Two days later, instead of going hunting with his hosts, he chose to explore again. That time he made his way to the summit of Allen, again finding the 46er canister. He recounted later, "Stimulated by the pleasure of climbing Redfield and Allen over the weekend, it was only natural to write to Grace Hudowalski promptly and indicate my interest in climbing the remainder of the 46 peaks."[98] He completed the 46 on Cliff on July 23, 1969.

Fish was elected president of the 46ers in 1970 and served until 1973. After his term as president ended he became very involved with the ADK, serving as first vice president (1973-74) and then president (1975-76). He also served on ADK's Loj Operating and Finance Committees. His involvement in leadership positions with both the 46ers and the ADK was motivated by his determination to do something about the deterioration of the trails and the proliferation of litter that he witnessed while hiking the 46. In an article in the Fall/Winter 1988-89 issue of *Peeks,* he described the conditions of trails in the late 1960s and early 1970s:

> Trails were sloughs of mud, and litter of every type – paper, glass, metal, plastic – caught the eye at every turn. Even the two-room stone hut on the summit of Marcy had its floor paved with eggshells, orange and banana peels, paper, and worse... You could always tell when you were approaching a lean-to by the abundance of litter scattered about from the garbage pits by animals, the wind, and hikers with poor aims... I felt a growing revulsion for the litter I saw on each trip and absolute disgust for those contributing to it. Not content with just complaining, I began to search for answers.[99]

Fish's search led him to suggest ways to improve the condition of the trails that so disturbed him and to realign the thinking of the hiking public through his work with the 46ers and ADK.

Similarly, it was the deterioration of the fragile vegetation on the alpine summits of the High Peaks which Dr. Edwin Ketchledge found distressing and led him to devote much of his professional career and personal energy to rectifying. Ketchledge's unquenchable interest in the outdoors and the Adirondacks began in his youth, when his family summered at their camp at Canada Lake. It was there that his boyhood interests in fishing, exploring, swimming, and hiking steered him towards a professional career in the scientific study of the natural history and resources of the Adirondack region.

With a masters degree in forest botany from the State University of New York College of Environmental Science and Forestry in Syracuse and a doctorate in biology from Stanford University, Ketchledge joined the faculty of his Syracuse alma mater in 1955. There he taught and conducted research on the ecology of the High Peaks for thirty years. From

1969 through 1979 he served as director of the college's Cranberry Lake Biological Station. He eventually achieved the rank of Distinguished Teaching Professor at the College of Forestry.

Ketchledge's research delineated trail erosion and summit deterioration of the natural environment due to the upsurge in recreational use. In 1964, with support from the United States Forest Service, Ed inventoried the status of trails throughout the High Peaks and outlined steps to correct ecological damage. During the course of his research, Ed found himself on the summits of most of the High Peaks. While he had no intention at that time of becoming a 46er, he finished on Couchsachraga on August 30, 1968, and submitted his documentation at the persistent urging of Trudy Healy.[100] Having climbed to its summit more than 160 times over the course of his research, Ed identified Algonquin as his favorite Adirondack peak.

Ed published more than one hundred forty popular print and technical articles describing his research. His publications include the booklets *Trees of the Adirondack High Peaks Region*, and a companion volume on shrubs of the region, a *Guide to the Natural History of Mt. Jo*, and the *Lost Pond Nature Trail* at Cranberry Lake. He served as president of the 46ers from 1975 to 1978. Ketchledge died on June 30, 2010, at the age of 85.

Like Glenn Fish, Ketchledge was involved in a leadership capacity with the ADK. He served three terms on ADK's board of governors, one term as a vice president, and several years as chairman of the Natural History Committee. Ed also served in various capacities with the Adirondack Nature Conservancy, the Association for the Protection of the Adirondacks, the Lake Placid Olympic Organizing Committee, DEC's High Peaks Advisory Committee, and the Adirondack Park Agency.

Ketchledge wrote a letter to then 46er president Glenn Fish to invite discussion about the future of the 46er organization. While focusing on the damage to the alpine summits, his letter echoed many of Fish's concerns about the ecological damage being done throughout the High Peaks. Fish read Ketchledge's letter to members at the September 19, 1970, club meeting at Adirondak Loj, and it became the main topic of discussion. The letter was subsequently printed in the Fall 1970 (Vol. VII, No. 2) issue of *Peeks*. In it Ketchledge asked the club to become stewards of the High Peaks, to focus their efforts on minimizing the damage done to the area by hikers, and to encourage some sort of ecological management.

While Ketchledge was interested in "finding out ways the ecologists can control environmental degradation caused by overuse" throughout the region in general, his research primarily focused on the damage

Dr. Edwin H. Ketchledge

being done to the fragile summits. He summarized the problem: "There is not a summit that doesn't show damage from man. Some are worse than others. Dix is simply awful; Colden is gullying out badly; and so on down the list."

As he explained, conservationists and ecologists had the technical know-how to repair and control trail erosion on the lower mountain slopes: water bars to channel water off of trails and routing trails on gentle angles upslope. However, the summits, he maintained, presented a "completely different problem, a different ecosystem. Their trespass-capacity is much lower than even the trails on the high slopes."

Ketchledge made the simple but pointed observation, "...if we climb, we kill." He recommended "ecological management... a higher level of trail maintenance than that currently existing in the Adirondack High Peaks region." He continued:

> Everyone of us would prefer to have the woods in a natural, undisturbed condition, without trails and other signs of people, conditions like they were when the 46ers were first started. But for every wilderness traveler in 1930, there are now probably twenty, if not more. And with that number, we as a society have an obligation to the natural world we are enjoying, that we counter and correct the damage we cause so that future generations of people will have the same out-of-door opportunities in the high peaks that we enjoy in 1970... We owe it to the woods; we owe it to tomorrow's generations.

Ketchledge agreed with Mason Ingram's notion of "wilderness paths" – single, well-designed routes to the summits of the trailless peaks – as being ecologically preferable to "five herd paths wandering around a summit. The 'hang-up' some of us have on not seeing a sign of man on the summit we climb is a hollow image from the long-gone past. This is 1970 we live in, a day when hundreds of people share our love of climbing the high peaks. Let's accept the march of time and learn to live with the conditions we now cause, we all who climb the 46."

He suggested that an even greater challenge than climbing the 46 was "to become the one organization in the region that champions the art of trailsmanship. I propose that the 46ers concern themselves with the matter of stewardship for the high peaks, that they set the standards for proper trail maintenance, that they fight for the ecological integrity of Adirondack summits and the trails that lead to them. Wouldn't this be proper re-payment for the joys and happiness experienced over the years in originally climbing the 46?" To start the process, he volunteered to conduct a workshop for interested 46ers to instruct them on issues of trail building and damage control.

Ketchledge's call to action was received with enthusiasm. President Fish shared his views on changing the club's priorities to conservation efforts within the High Peaks region. Three days after the 1970 fall meeting Fish sent a letter to DEC Commissioner Henry L. Diamond to suggest "an effort to secure a liaison with the Department of Environmental Conservation in order that the 46ers might secure guidance, suggestions, possible supervision, or approval for some of the projects being considered to date."[101] He outlined several possible projects including reaching out to summer camps and camp counselors; the distribution at trailheads of "Mountain Manners,"[102] a pamphlet prepared by the club that would list the "dos and don'ts" of responsible wilderness usage; the placement of signs at lean-tos outlining good woods etiquette; and trail maintenance projects, particularly on the trailless peaks.

On May 19, 1971, following an exchange of correspondence with Commissioner Diamond, Fish and Grace Hudowalski met with Victor Glider, director of the Division of Lands and Forests, and two of his aides, Robert Norton and Randy Kerr, to seek department approval for a number of specific projects proposed by the club. That was the first of six trips to the

DEC offices in Albany that Fish spearheaded during 1971 and 1972 to secure state acceptance of 46er conservation project proposals. The projects he presented on behalf of the club included the purchase and distribution of plastic litter bags for hikers to use to pack out their trash; the purchase, construction, and placement of picnic tables at lean-to sites below 3,500 feet; the participation of club members in assisting Dr. Ketchledge with his experimental planting of grasses on certain summits to help curb soil erosion and reestablish the growth of native plants; the establishment of a trail maintenance program with 46er volunteers conducting routine trail work on state trails under the leadership of DEC personnel; and the collection and removal of litter on trails and at lean-to sites with the DEC providing trucks at the trailheads to haul away the refuse.

Fish and Hudowalski received a "thoughtful and considerate reception" from the DEC representatives who expressed an appreciation for the 46ers' interest as well as a willingness to enter into a working relationship to benefit High Peaks ecology. Additional meetings with William Petty, regional director of Ray Brook, were held to work out the details. Plans progressed slowly, hampered by the state bureaucracy or as Fish described it, "...the objections, the foot-dragging, the mumble-jumble of officialese, the simple inertia soon piled higher than the rubble from Wallface in Indian Pass."

The May 29-30, 1971, spring meeting included enthusiastic discussions of the conservation projects that Fish had proposed to the DEC along with the realization that the club might have to consider increasing dues from $1 to $2 to provide financial support for the programs.

As he had offered, Ed Ketchledge held a "Trail Workshop" on Saturday, May 29, 1971, as one of the 46er spring meeting activities. With the assistance of Dr. Ray Leonard of the U.S. Forest Service, Ketchledge described to the 30 participants the work he had been doing to slow the rapid progress of erosion above treeline. Over the previous four years, Ketchledge, along with colleagues and students from the Syracuse College of Forestry, had conducted research and experiments on the summit of Dix that had focused on methods to replace vegetation that had been trampled by hikers criss-crossing the summit. Their research found that some lawn grasses – blue grass and red fescue in particular – when treated with a commercial fertilizer, would grow in the meager soils, protecting the remaining soil from further erosion and providing a platform for native plants to take root. Ketchledge instructed volunteers on sowing techniques and provided each with one pound of grass seed and five pounds of fertilizer for the treatment of 200 square feet of an eroded summit area. Workshop activities continued on Sunday, May 30. DEC Ranger Gary Hodgson demonstrated the proper function of water bars and how to keep them clean and working properly.

Projects Get Underway
Summit Seeding

Ed Ketchledge's summit seeding trial efforts had been successful and, in 1972, he planned to launch an active phase, concentrating on restoration work on four summits: Dix, Colden, Wright, and Algonquin. Based on his research, Ketchledge had refined his seeding procedure to include treating the targeted areas with lime, before spreading the seed and fertilizer, to counteract the acidity of the mountain soils. His goal was to enlist 46er volunteers to help carry the seeding supplies to the mountain summits and spread the material. Students from Paul Smiths and the Ranger School at Wanakena along with a few 46er volunteers participated in the seeding efforts on the summits of Algonquin, Wright, and Colden on May 20 and 21, 1972. They carried 880 pounds of materials up the mountains.

Ketchledge was initially disappointed with the 46ers' response, both in terms of logistical support for the project and in re-directing the club's activities toward a new environmental mission; but he continued to keep the 46ers informed about his summit erosion studies and to solicit volunteers. A wet summer of 1972 reversed some of the progress Ketchledge had made and he had to renew efforts to seed the summits. Fifty volunteers, among them a number of 46ers, packed 935 pounds of seed, fertilizer, and lime to the summits of Algonquin and Wright on May 19, 1973. An early spring snowstorm forced the group to cache much of the material at tree line for use on a more hospitable day. During that summer, Ketchledge saw some success from previous seeding and concluded that his method to restore the ecological damage done by hikers was working. As 46ers began to see the dramatic effect of Ketchledge's summit seeding efforts, they embraced the project and contributed funds to purchase the raw materials. Additionally, volunteers were eager to carry the five-pound packets of seeding materials to the alpine summits. Forty-Sixers became the main source of volunteer labor for the summit seeding program throughout the 1970s and 1980s.

Wilderness Workshop

Information collected in the 46er logbooks on the trailless peaks identified summer camps as sending out some of the largest and most frequent hiking groups to the summits. Consequently, in the fall of 1971 the club reached out once again to camp leaders with a letter and questionnaire concerning the environmental degradation of the trails in the High Peaks and ways to preserve the landscape.

In response to the information gathered from the questionnaire, Marion Fresn (#273), chair of the club's newly formed Education Committee, suggested a weekend program to provide leaders of youth groups, parents, and teachers with the knowledge and skills necessary to be comfortable in the natural environment. She envisioned a series of information sessions at which Forty-Sixer volunteers would offer instruction in map and compass orientation, geology, birds, signs of animal life, and proper sanitation techniques in the wilderness. The executive committee decided to hold a pilot workshop in spring 1972, similar to the 1966 Camporee.

The first 46er Wilderness Leadership Workshop, which was held at Marcy Dam on the weekend of May 14, 1972, provided leaders of youth groups with the information they needed to plan successful hiking and camping trips and gain maximum benefit from their wilderness experience. Topics covered included bird watching, photography, plant life, map and compass, area geology, camp cooking, and camping and hiking equipment. Approximately twenty people attended the inaugural workshop.

The second annual workshop, coordinated again by Marion Fresn, was held May 11-13, 1973. Seventeen participants camped at Heart Lake the first night and at Marcy Dam the second night. Workshop staff and presentation topics included Father Cotter (#229) - "Introduction and Geology"; Ditt Dittmar - "Food Planning, Packaging, and Preparation"; Judy Cameron (#605) - "Nature Observation"; Fred Hunt (#593W) - "Map & Compass"; Phil Corell (#224W) - "Campsites and Backpacking Equipment"; and Dr. Orra Phelps - "Plant Life Around You."

Fresn served as the workshop coordinator for four years. Winifred Lamb (#367) and Judy Cameron took over as co-coordinators in 1976. During its first several years of operation, the workshop was expanded to accommodate growing interest, and the programming was adjusted to meet the needs of the participants.

By the seventh annual Wilderness Leadership Workshop, which was held on May 19-21, 1978, with a full capacity of 47 participants, the workshop had settled into a format that attracted a defined audience. It was advertised as a program "to provide educational and practical experience for persons who are planning to serve as group leaders for wilderness hiking and camping trips in the Adirondacks or other wilderness areas." Participants assembled on Friday evening and attended a talk by DEC Interior Forest Ranger C. Peter "Pete" Fish (#1396) on the use and care of the Adirondack Wilderness. He also treated participants to a peek at what he carried in his pack to ensure a safe trip in the woods. Filled with dark humor and a wealth of practical tips, Pete Fish's lecture became one of the highlights of the weekend workshop.

Following the introductory session, participants then broke into cook groups. On Saturday and Sunday they took part in a series of workshops on topics including use of guidebooks, maps and compass; advanced route finding; trip planning and packing; and campsite cooking. Weekend activities also included a hike up Mt. Jo for talks on Adirondack geology and first aid, and a slide presentation on various aspects of Adirondack history, flora and fauna.

Longtime Outdoor Leadership Workshop Director Phil Corell samples a foil baked supper during his famous cooking and baking demonstration.

Philip Corell and Jules Comeau (#646) took over leadership of the Wilderness Leadership Workshop in 1979. Corell and John Sharpe Swan (#566W) developed a slide presentation for the workshop that introduced participants to the history and beauty of the High Peaks as well as aspects of conserving the area's natural resources and wilderness properties. In 1984 the workshop staff changed the name of the weekend gathering to the "Outdoor Leadership Workshop." Corell provided the impetus for the change. He thought that the term "wilderness" implied a much more advanced course – one that would be more appropriate to the true large wilderness expanses of Alaska or parts of the western U.S. Using the term "outdoor" better reflected the content of the weekend workshop, which offered group leaders the information they needed to organize and conduct a successful trip in the outdoors, whether a backpacking trip in the Adirondacks or a weekend at a campground.

The Outdoor Leadership Workshop (OLW) continues to be the major educational program of the 46ers. While the staff has changed and the specific workshops have been modified over the years, the basic format for the weekend session has remained the same. The program attracts a mix of camp counselors and youth group leaders as well as outdoor enthusiasts interested in honing their skills to make their camping experiences safer and more enjoyable. The workshop is filled to capacity each year and often has a waiting list.

Picnic Table Distribution and Lean-to Cleanup

In 1970 club members placed picnic tables at the Hudowalski Lean-to at Marcy Dam and at the Myers Memorial Lean-to at Johns Brook, as well as at lean-to sites at Bear Brook, Indian Falls, Plateau, and Lake Arnold. The club purchased the materials to build the picnic tables for $15 per table, and the DEC assisted in transporting some of the materials to the sites for assembly. Distribution efforts continued the following summer with the placement of 12 picnic tables at Marcy Dam and five in the Sewards. The placement of additional tables was put on hold after 1971, pending final decisions by the DEC on a proposal to remove a number of lean-tos in the High Peaks for environmental reasons.

As part of the spring meeting on May 25, 1974, the 46ers participated in a major "Clean-up Day" in the High Peaks coordinated by the DEC. Volunteers from several hiking clubs and youth groups gathered to pack out litter found on the trails and at lean-to sites in an effort to stem the assault on the wilderness experience that Glenn Fish had found so objectionable. For years the approved method of disposing of garbage when camping at a lean-to was to burn everything that could be burned and dump the remaining items, such as tin cans, foil, and bottles, in garbage pits that were located at each lean-to site. As the garbage pits filled to capacity and as the amount of litter soiling the trails increased, the DEC adopted the new wilderness ethic of "If you carry it in, carry it out" and mounted a campaign to clean out and fill in the garbage pits. Two hundred and eighty people, including fifty-three 46ers, participated in "Clean-Up Day." They carried out 141 bags of litter from Indian Falls, 21 bags from the Phelps Lean-to, 17 bags from Plateau Lean-to, and 75 bags from Avalanche Lean-tos on the first day. The following day an additional 20 bags were packed out from Lake Arnold and 60 more from Plateau. A total of 303 bags of litter averaging 20-30 pounds each were removed and the garbage cribs at lean-tos were dismantled and filled in. In addition to "Clean-Up Day," Glenn Fish led 46er volunteers on a number of trail improvement outings – nine in the Northville area and 17 in the Warrensburg area – and additional litter pick-up projects under the guidance of the DEC, contributing a total of 535 man days to work projects during 1973.

Search and Rescue Unit

In 1971 Glenn Fish introduced the idea of forming a Search and Rescue Unit comprised of 46er volunteers who would work in cooperation with the State Police and the DEC. He envisioned that such a unit would consist of interested 46ers who had received training in search and rescue techniques and who would be available as called upon by the state to assist in rescue missions.

The first training session for the 46er Search and Rescue Unit was held at the spring 1972 meeting. Representatives from the State Police and the DEC conducted a field exercise to find a "lost" hiker. Additional training, along with a first aid course, was held in the fall of 1972, including an overnight backpacking weekend exercise with other units across the state.

The Search and Rescue Unit was involved with three calls: a lost hunter at Morehouseville on October 30, 1972, that turned out to be a false alarm; two hikers lost on Algonquin on March 12, 1973, who were found at Scott's Clearing; and the search for George Atkinson, 20, of Chicopee, MA, who was lost on Marcy on March 23, 1973, and never located.[103]

By 1973 the 46er Search and Rescue Unit had 42 trained members, and in 1974 the unit was registered with both the State Police and the DEC. In March 1974 members were called to search for a pilot whose plane had gone down in the Tupper Lake area.

After making those initial calls for assistance, the DEC made no additional requests for the services of the 46er Search and Rescue Unit for the next several years. Therefore the unit was discontinued and those interested in continued involvement were encouraged to contact the DEC at Ray Brook.

Litter Bags and "Mountain Manners" Pamphlets

Glenn Fish's idea to distribute litter bags in the High Peaks was modeled after similar programs in Maine's Baxter State Park and in various National Forests in the West, where park rangers distributed heavy drawstring litter bags to campers. The plastic bag that the 46ers suggested to the DEC measured 13" x 24" and had a drawstring at the top. William Petty, district director of Lands and Forests for the High Peaks area was interested in any program that would help reduce the litter problem. However, others within the DEC had a number of concerns about the proposal. One fear was that the bags themselves would become litter. In an effort to prevent that and provide some means of control, the DEC considered applying the hiker's name to the bag with a marker when they received one at distribution points. A second strong objection concerned the non-biodegradable plastic material itself, which could compound the litter problem for years if the bags were discarded in the woods. The DEC advocated a more eco-friendly material.

After discussing possible alternatives, Glenn Fish forwarded another proposal to the DEC for approval: a disposable biodegradable, coated paper bag for one-time use that could be placed inside a reusable plastic drawstring bag. The paper bag would satisfy the DEC's desire for an environmentally friendly material and the plastic outer bag would satisfy the hiker's need for a waterproof container in which to carry refuse in his or her pack. Fish also suggested that the bags be distributed in a distinct area as a pilot project in order to study their effectiveness. The pilot program was approved for the 1973 hiking season by the DEC's Robert Norton, general manager of Forest and Parks, and Randy Kerr, assistant general manager.

With the institution of the litter bag project, Forty-Sixers were encouraged to note how the bags were being used and to report any misuse. Three thousand litter bags were distributed from four locations in 1973, and reports indicated that no bags were refused or misused. The DEC was impressed with the success of the project and allowed distribution at an additional six locations in 1974. The club distributed 6,500 plastic litter bags in 1974 and an even greater number of the inner biodegradable bag liners.

A letter from James O. Preston, director, Division of Lands and Forests, dated April 14, 1975, praised the litter bag initiative: "The Department would like to take this opportunity to congratulate your previous efforts in litter reduction and endorse the continued distribution of Adirondack Forty-Sixer litter bags at two or more distribution points during the 1975 and 1976 seasons." He noted that the litter bag project had been successful in raising awareness of the litter problems in the High Peaks.

Because the DEC's fear that the litter bags themselves would become trash did not materialize, the department rescinded the requirement for the paper inner bag. By the fall of 1979 fifteen thousand plastic litter bags had been distributed to hikers and the club had to order a new supply. Ranger Peter Fish had objected to the graphic on the original plastic bag. It depicted a campfire ring with a stack of firewood next to it. He thought that the picture might encourage hikers to cut down trees to make their own campfires. In response to Ranger Fish's concern, the club redesigned the bags when reordering, replacing the campfire image with a generic mountain scene. Printed in 46er colors – red, yellow, and green – the new bags also included this message:

"Mountain Manners" sketch by Trudy Healy

MOUNTAIN MANNERS
Help keep the Wilderness as you would like to find it... Clean. If you carry it in, carry it out.
Pack out cans, bottles, foil and other refuse. Obey rules and regulations.
Leave a clean camp and a dead fire. Have a safe and good outing.
Provided by the Adirondack Forty-Sixers in the interest of the hiker, camper & the environment.
The Adirondack Forty-Sixers
Adirondack, N.Y. 12808

    The message on the bag was as much an educational tool as the bag itself, and many hikers soon understood their responsibility to the environment and began to practice the accepted backcountry wilderness ethic, "If you carry it in, carry it out."

    As an additional tool to help educate hikers and campers about the new "take only pictures, leave only footsteps" wilderness ethic, the club worked with the DEC on developing a small informational brochure entitled "Mountain Manners: Don'ts, Why Nots, and Dos." Trudy Healy designed the brochure which contained explanations of such "leave no trace" principles as the proper disposal of refuse, safe campfire practices, and camp cleanliness, along with reminders to respect the quiet of the wilderness, to refrain from disturbing any of the flora or fauna, and to sign the DEC registers at trailheads. The brochure was approved by the

DEC's Robert Norton and Randy Kerr in a letter dated December 22, 1970. The club printed 10,000 copies. The modest brochure turned out to be a very effective and popular educational tool. The club issued a press release announcing the availability of "Mountain Manners" and encouraged the public to request copies. A number of individuals and groups took advantage of the offer including the Saranac Village tent campsite and the Rideau Trail Association in Ottawa, Canada. It was also distributed in the Catskills, in particular in the Bear Mountain/Harriman sections of the park. The club has updated and reprinted "Mountain Manners" periodically to reflect changes in DEC hiking and camping regulations.

Trail Maintenance

During the 1972 fall meeting, which was held September 8–10 at Johns Brook Lodge, discussions on the future direction of the club continued. The main concern again centered on the question: Was the club's very existence doing more harm than good? With membership at 866 and swelling, Vern Lamb (#364) suggested that the summit registers were an unnecessary incentive for climbing and should be removed after the membership reached 1,000. Others suggested that the club add a service requirement to cut down on the numbers of climbers who would qualify for membership, and some renewed the call to disband. As he had in previous meetings, Ed Ketchledge spoke on the subject of damage control of the trails and summits. He suggested that the problem wasn't the number of people climbing but the inadequate resources put forth by the state for trail maintenance and improvement. He stressed that the 46ers shouldn't disband but should take on the mission of trailsmanship as their main purpose. Climbing the 46 should be just the first step in becoming a 46er, Ketchledge stressed. The second step should be to become protectors of the Adirondack ecosystem. Ketchledge specifically recommended that the 46ers meet with DEC staff in early summer 1973 to identify a section of trail that the 46ers could adopt and maintain on a regular basis.

Response to Ketchledge's recommendations was favorable and the executive committee voted to present all of the issues mentioned to the general membership in the form of a questionnaire to solicit opinions. A total of 117 members responded to the questionnaire. An overwhelming majority of them rejected the notion of closing membership at 1,000 – eighty-nine were opposed, only 17 in favor – or disbanding when membership reached 1,000 – one hundred three opposed, five in favor. By a vote of 101 to 1, members supported the idea of pursuing service programs and projects.

James "Tony" Goodwin, Jr. (#211) countered the sentiment that the 46ers should disband after the number of registered 46ers had reached 1,000 in an article that appeared in the Spring 1973 issue of *Peeks*, "The Future of the Adirondack Forty-Sixers." He wrote, "The emphasis recently seems to have been on expressing guilt feelings over unleashing a monster (peak bagging) that now cannot be controlled and somehow thinking that all can be made right again if we simply cut our activities off at the conveniently round number of 1,000. The issue of wilderness use, as all issues unfortunately are, is much too complex to yield to simple solutions."[104]

Goodwin noted, as Paul Jamieson had previously, that if the 46ers disbanded, another group would surely pick up the challenge: "… the convenient numbers of '46' and '4000 feet' would doubtless attract climbers anyway (as the Marshalls were once attracted) and now that these peaks have been described and popularized, it is a game that will be hard to stop."[105] Instead of criticizing the sport of 46ing, he pointed to the significant contribution the 46ers could make toward preserving the wilderness by saying, "… groups like the 46ers have a real responsibility to make sure that wise decisions are made regarding our precious open land."[106]

In an effort to put those sentiments into action and build on the successful initiatives the club had already undertaken, Glenn Fish sent correspondence to William Petty, the DEC's Region 5 director, renewing his proposal to have the 46ers work with the DEC on trail maintenance and general protection of the area. In his letter dated January 9, 1973, Fish wrote, "The past several years have exhibited a growing restlessness amongst the members of the Adirondack Forty-Sixers. This unrest is attributable to a growing concern that we, as hikers, have been taking much more from the woods and mountains in our enjoyment of them, and in growing numbers of hikers, and yet have been putting back very little in the way of lessening our impact upon the environment."

As a remedy for that imbalance, Fish again offered to, "produce and sustain, on a continuous basis, a workforce, which, working under proper and authoritative supervision, could do much to counter the adverse effects of our presence in the forests and on the summits." He proposed general trail maintenance such as drainage of low spots, cleaning water bars, rerouting some trails, litter pickup, and maintenance in lean-to areas, all under the supervision of DEC personnel.

The response Fish received from Petty, dated January 11, 1973, was cautiously optimistic. Petty replied, "I think it would be a fine idea, for every little bit helps providing it is properly supervised and the volunteers organized and can be depended upon." He suggested a meeting to discuss the proposal in further detail.

As an incentive to join trail work outings, Fish suggested a "Conservation Patch" that members and nonmembers could earn upon completing 46 hours of work on trail projects. In proposing the award, he noted that the patches would be a visual symbol of the club's commitment to promoting the environmental integrity of the High Peaks and of its active participation in projects to reduce the impact of hikers on the trails. He reasoned that the patch could help counter some of the negative images that some people had of the 46ers as "taking" more out of the mountains than they were "putting back." His hope was that participation in trail work would "become as much pleasure as climbing."

Although his term as 46er president was coming to an end, Fish was eager to continue to reshape the club into a conservation-minded, service-oriented organization. In his message to club members as outgoing president he wrote, "Our environment, and our enjoyment of it as hikers/climbers will certainly be challenged in many ways in the near future, changes will become necessary, concessions required in our approach to our woods use, and 'new ways' must replace 'old ways.' Let each one of us commit ourselves to true concern as to how 46er membership can best serve the common welfare in the most constructive fashion."[107]

Winifred Lamb (#367), who took over as club president in spring 1973, embraced the call for change championed by Fish and Ketchledge. In the Spring 1973 issue of *Peeks* she wrote:

> We are a growing organization and emphasis on environmental education is becoming more important. Many projects in this field have been initiated by the past president Glenn Fish, and I hope that every member will support at least one with enthusiasm and energy...
>
> Hikers who earn the 46er badge need to realize that responsibility goes with this distinction. They need to be willing to accept an obligation to the hiking public and its environment and help support our programs to preserve the beauty and wilderness of the mountains.[108]

By the mid-1970s, the problems associated with the High Peaks area were beginning to receive a good deal of attention from sources outside of the 46ers. In 1974 the DEC created the High Peaks Advisory Committee – an independent, 15-member group that was charged with examining the effects of recreational overuse in the High Peaks. The committee sought solutions to the problems of trail erosion, increased usage, damage to the alpine vegetation, degradation of campsites – all issues that the 46ers were also debating. Members of the High Peaks Advisory Committee (HPAC), which met over the three-year period of 1974-1977, included J. William Adriance; Almy D. Coggeshall, secretary; Harry Eldridge, Jr. (#90W); Glenn Fish, vice chairman; Jerome W. Jensen, chairman and assistant to the director of DEC's Division of Lands and Forests; Ed Ketchledge; Ervin H. Markert; Barbara McMartin; David L. Newhouse (#317); Arthur E. Newkirk; Margaret "Peggy" G. O'Brien (#560); Alfred Obrist (#509); Robert Ringlee; John F. Siau (#94); and Sidney P. Tuthill Jr.

With seven 46ers serving on the committee, including Glenn Fish and Ed Ketchledge, the views of the club were well represented, and in turn the club was well informed about concerns expressed by others with varying interests in the High Peaks.

At their December 14, 1974, meeting in Albany, the High Peaks Advisory Committee adopted a resolution urging the 46ers to consider working with the DEC on repairing the critical damage to the herdpaths on Allen, Donaldson, Hough, Iroquois, and Seymour, as well as other trailless peaks.

The HPAC's resolution coincided with the trail maintenance program proposal that Glenn Fish had already presented to the DEC. In the Summer 1975 issue of *Peeks*, Ketchledge penned a "Call for 46er High Peak Task Force," in which he outlined a plan for the start of an ongoing 46er trail maintenance program. He wrote, "I am... persuaded that those of us who comprise the Adirondack 46ers are a massive, latent force capable of molding and directing the flow of forces influencing our beloved high peak region, capable of becoming a significant, constructive force ourselves in preserving the ecological integrity of our shared wilderness heritage, the Adirondack high country."[109]

Ketchledge proposed a High Peak Task Force, which he volunteered to head. He solicited volunteers who would be willing to work once or twice a year on selected projects approved by the DEC to protect the ecological well-being of the High Peaks. He suggested scheduling projects during the spring and fall meeting weekends when a number of members would already be in the High Peaks area. Additional projects could be scheduled as necessary. As an example of the type of work that the task force would do, he pointed to the HPAC's resolution urging the 46ers to repair the damage to the herdpaths.

While the notion of "managing" the herdpaths on the trailless peaks was something that the 46ers had resisted up to that point, Ketchledge argued that the trailless peaks were joining the trailed peaks in a crisis of deterioration. He argued that there were two ways to approach the problem: either close the trailless peaks to foot traffic to keep them trailless or minimize and correct damage to facilitate the natural recovery process.

Ketchledge and Glenn Fish met with Ranger Gary Hodgson and Interior Ranger Pete Fish to discuss several possible courses of action. Their recommendations included selecting the most ecologically sound herdpaths as the recommended routes, blocking off with brush any undesirable paths, and minimally marking the preferred paths with cairns or special trail markers.

The first project for the High Peak Task Force was to apply those recommendations on the Iroquois herdpath during the spring 1976 meeting weekend. The second was to place DEC-approved and prepared signs at tree line on a number of marked trails. Those signs informed climbers that they should stay on the trails and avoid trampling the fragile vegetation on the high alpine meadows.

During the spring of 1977 task force volunteers participated in several projects, including the removal of the tent platform on Cascade; removal of the Lake Arnold Lean-to; carrying planks three-quarters of the way to Marcy Dam for a future project; and repairing bridges and rotting corduroy[110] sections of the Indian Pass Trail.

In the summer of 1977 the first all-46er volunteer trail crew spent four days working on a swampy one-half mile section of the Lake Arnold Crossover trail near Feldspar Lean-to. They rerouted the trail and built new bridges and a new section of corduroy. The crew consisted of leader Walter "Wally" Herrod (#750), Jules Comeau (#646), Richard Mallinson (#782W) and his wife Chai-Kyou (#1171W), Tom Stanwood (#1405), Donald Hoffman (#1148), Glenn Fish, and Gordon "Big Axe" Shaw (#1108).

At the spring 1978 executive committee meeting, Jim Goodwin made a motion for a "Trail Master Amendment" to formalize the High Peak Task Force work parties that Ed Ketchledge had organized. The motion passed, a new position was created – Trailmaster – and Goodwin was named to the post.

Jim Goodwin, age 9, atop his first peak, Hopkins

In appointing Jim Goodwin to coordinate its fledgling trail maintenance program, the club made a wise choice. Jim Goodwin was born in Hartford, Connecticut, in 1910. His family spent summers in the Adirondacks, first in Lake Placid and then in Keene Valley. Jim's early exposure to the Adirondack region led to a lifetime of mountain adventures and a commitment to work on behalf of the peaks. In 1921, at the age of 11, Goodwin offered his services as a guide, posting his fees on the bulletin board at Interbrook Lodge in the Johns Brook Valley. He charged "fifty cents a half day" for trips to the Porter Ledges or Washbond's Flume; "a dollar a day" for trips up Hopkins, Hurricane or Giant.[111] From the start, his services were in demand. At the age of 12 he led his first hike up Mt. Marcy and earned $2 for doing so, thus establishing himself as a professional guide.[112]

In addition to providing guiding services, Goodwin was also involved in trail building and cutting new routes to summits. He established the Porter Ledges Trail that leads up Porter from the Johns Brook Valley. While the route has changed through the years, it was Goodwin who cut the original route above the main Porter cliffs and along the ridge to the summit. In the late 1930s he worked in the Ausable Valley to connect the W. A. White Trail with Wolf Jaws Notch, and in the 1950s he connected Rooster Comb and the W. A. White Trail with a route over Hedgehog, thus completing the Range Trail. He also worked with the Keene Valley Chapter of the ADK in 1951 to complete the trail over the Brothers to the summit of Big Slide. In 1955 he assisted with the construction of the Giant Ridge Trail.[113] Goodwin served as trail crew foreman for the Adirondack Trail Improvement Society (ATIS), which maintains trails in the Adirondack Mountain Reserve in the Ausable Lakes area, for several years and as chairman of the trails committee for the Keene Valley Chapter of ADK. In 1966 he worked with ATIS on the construction of the Alfred Weld Trail to Gothics over Pyramid Peak from the Lower Ausable Lake.[114]

Jim Goodwin on the Porter Mountain trail he first cut in 1924

Goodwin became a 46er on September 7, 1940, on Street after also climbing Nye. Coincidentally he met Grace and Ed Hudowalski on Street's summit as they were leading Franklin Wilson (#25) on a hike of the two peaks, and the trio joined Goodwin in celebrating the completion of his 46.

Starting in 1957 Goodwin wrote the notes on climbing the trailless peaks for the Adirondack Mountain Club's *Guide to Adirondack Trails High Peak Region*.[115] He provided revisions for subsequent volumes until 1985, when his son, Tony, took over the guidebook editorship.

Goodwin retired in 1975 at the age of 65, after 41 years of teaching at Kingswood School in West Hartford, Connecticut. Retirement allowed him to spend more time in the Adirondacks, particularly in the Keene Valley area. He took on two major projects in retirement: He assumed the presidency of ATIS and he became the 46ers' Trailmaster. He commented about his early involvement as 46er Trailmaster:

> In 1978 Dr. Edwin Ketchledge, who was then president of the 46ers, asked me to organize and lead an ongoing trail maintenance group composed of members of the 46er organization. I agreed to give the project a try, but having seen enthusiasm from similar projects wane after a year or so, expected that the effectiveness of this plan would soon wither as I had seen happen in the past. With the Forty-Sixers, however, it was another story... twenty-five volunteers turned out on Memorial Day weekend to work on our first project, removing down timber from the Indian Pass and Wallface Ponds trails. Many of these people appeared again to work on later weekends throughout the summer. They were enthusiastic and competent and every year more

volunteers turned up, with most of the original workers continuing to work as well... I think that the main strength of the operation lay in the teamwork and camaraderie that developed among the unusually fine people who offered their services.[116]

With his years of experience working on the trails of the High Peaks, Jim Goodwin wasted no time in organizing the 46ers' trail maintenance efforts. In need of assistance to cover all of the state's trails in the Adirondack Park, the DEC asked the 46ers to assume responsibility for regular maintenance of the Dix/Round Pond Trail. In 1978 forty workers assembled and cleared the entire trail of blowdown and side cut portions of overgrown areas. Work continued on a second weekend to build cairns above treeline to mark the route in inclement weather and to keep people on the trail and off the fragile landscape. Not all hikers appreciated the 46ers' efforts, especially the marking of routes above treeline. The cairns were completely destroyed before the group returned to treeline two weeks later.

In the fall of 1978 the club announced the establishment of the Conservation Service Award (CSA). The award, designed by Tom Stanwood, was a rectangular patch of the same colors as the 46er patch bearing the words "ADK 46-R Conservation Service Award." Just as the 46er patch has to be earned by climbing the 46 High Peaks, so, too, the CSA patch has to be earned by accumulating 46 hours of trail maintenance or related service. The award was established to promote volunteerism and to recognize those who commit their time and energy to club projects on behalf of the Adirondack wilderness.

During the summer of 1979 fifty-two volunteers worked with Goodwin on a number of projects, including corduroy construction and drainage work on the Indian Pass Trail, marker replacement and additional side cutting on the Dix/Round Pond Trail, summit seeding on Marcy and Algonquin, and clearing blowdown on the Mr. Van Trail. The DEC noted the significant contribution of the 46er volunteers as the club's efforts came at an opportune time for the department. In the late 1970s the state had drastically reduced its financial support for direct trail maintenance by the DEC trail crews. The DEC was forced to rely on the trail work programs of the 46ers, ADK, and ATIS to provide the necessary trail maintenance.[117]

In addition to its own trail work projects, the club also joined the DEC and International Paper Company in contributing funds to support the ADK paid trail crew led by Jim's son, Tony. That crew worked on the Van Hoevenberg Trail and the Elk Lake-Marcy and Colden trails.

At the end of the 1979 trail work season, six 46ers had accumulated enough hours to earn the Conservation Service Awards. The first recipients were Christian G. Behr (#1453), June Behr (#1455), and Christian M. Behr (#1454), Jim Goodwin (who accepted the award reluctantly), President Wally Herrod, and Bill Myers (#1218).

Jim's initial fear that the trail maintenance program would peter out after a few years due to lack of interest had proved unfounded. In fact, the 46er trail work program has grown in the number of outings, the variety and complexity of tasks, and in participation. Starting with two or three projects a season, the program has expanded to as many as 12 weekend projects scheduled from May through October. Today the 46ers conduct regular maintenance on the entire Dix trail system – the Dix/Round Pond Trail and the Dix/Elk Lake/Hunters Pass Trails – the North Trail to Giant, yearly sweeps of the Indian Pass Trail to Scott's Clearing, and work on the Putnam Pond trail system, an area outside of the High Peaks. Over the years trail crews have installed and relocated privies, constructed and rehabilitated lean-tos, built bridges over streams and stringers over wet, muddy areas, created rock steps on badly eroded sections of trail, and engaged in a battle of wills with beavers who insisted on building their dams in locations that flooded trails. All of the work has been done in the spirit of "giving something back" to the mountains. As of 2008 Forty-Sixer volunteers had contributed more than 52,000 man and woman hours to trail and educational projects that benefit the Adirondack Park.

The success of the program is due in large part to Jim Goodwin, who served as Trailmaster for five seasons. His experience, enthusiasm, and collegial spirit set the tone for the program, making it fun as well as rewarding for the volunteers who joined him on the trails. Why would anyone want to spend a day or a weekend in the woods doing oftentimes strenuous work and give up the opportunity to climb to a nearby summit? Ray Held (#2007W), who contributed over 146 hours working with the 46er trail crews, summed up the attitude of many of the volunteers:

> Why, indeed. Where else can a grown man wallow in mud, play in stream beds, throw rocks all day and receive recognition for having all that fun?... On a more serious side are such reasons as giving something back to the wilderness, helping preserve our trails for future generations to enjoy, and finally, experiencing the camaraderie from sharing hard work for a worthwhile cause with your fellow 46ers.[118]

Issues of the Late 1970s

Despite the early successes of the 46ers' litter bag initiative, Wilderness Workshop, and trail maintenance program, President Ketchledge was concerned about maintaining and building on the momentum of those conservation/education programs. His President's Report in the Summer 1976 issue of *Peeks* again noted that regional recreational growth seriously threatened preservation of the wilderness character and quality of the high peaks environment. In a bold and controversial move, he called for the removal of the 46er canisters on the trailless peaks, calling them a "now-outdated program." He felt it was time the 46ers stopped perpetuating the "former 'peak-bagging' aura that once, in another time, was our *raison d'etre*... We have been over-successful, it turns out, in dramatizing the joys of mountain climbing in the Adirondacks. Our purpose was good, was proper, was commendable, for *those* times. But who would dream '46ing' would eventually become a cancer on the landscape of our prized summits?"[119]

Ketchledge pointed to the growth in membership, the number of 46ers having doubled in each of the last two five-year periods. It took 40 years, from 1925-1965, to grow to approximately 340 members, but only five years, 1966-70 to nearly double that to 615, and five more years, from 1971-75, to double that to almost 1,300 members.

Ketchledge saw the canisters as a visible sign of the old peak-grabbing fad and as a psychological goal for some people, making them rush from one peak to the next. Times had changed, he felt, and "the trailless peaks are no longer the wild, unvisited, unspoiled refuge they once were." Given the growth of membership, he recommended that the club abandon the registers as a symbol of the past and accept a more modern day approach of "personal restraint as essential to the preservation of that which we hold dear."[120]

He received limited feedback concerning his proposal to remove the canisters. Of the 60 people who responded, 38 or 60 percent agreed that the canisters should be removed, 11 or 17 percent disagreed, and an additional 11 were undecided.

The canister issue was discussed at length at the October 2, 1976, meeting, and those in attendance were in favor of keeping the canisters by a margin of 39 to 18. A motion to hold a referendum to poll the entire membership was defeated. All, however, supported the club's commitment to stewardship of the High Peaks. As proof of that commitment President Ketchledge announced a schedule of six summer work parties to tackle the herdpath problems on the trailless peaks.

While club members were not yet ready to remove the canisters from the trailless peaks, they were prepared to eliminate a long tradition of allowing dogs to become 46ers. Six dogs had been officially registered as Forty-Sixers. However, during the mid-1970s the club realized that it was not strictly adhering to an Adirondack Mountain Reserve (AMR) restriction which prohibited dogs on its trails in the St. Huberts valley. While dog owners hiking in that area could bushwhack to the summits from other approaches to avoid using the AMR trail system, several of the mountaintops were also owned by the reserve. To correct the situation, club members voted unanimously at the May 24, 1975, spring meeting to exclude dogs from membership in the Adirondack 46ers. The 1976 Summer issue of *Peeks* included a notice advising members that in order to adhere to and respect the no-dog policy of the AMR, whose private land included all or a portion of the summits of Sawteeth, Haystack, Basin, Saddleback, Gothics, Armstrong, Upper and Lower Wolf Jaws, Dial, Nippletop, Colvin and Blake, dogs would no longer be eligible for membership.

During late 1977 and early 1978 the 46ers found themselves embroiled in several controversial issues that resulted in the club taking public stances concerning the High Peaks and defending its existence and activities.

In the mid-1970s the APA ruled that seven lean-tos on state land over 3,500 feet in elevation were considered "non-conforming structures" and therefore had to be removed. The designated lean-tos were located at some of the most popular camping sites in the High Peaks: Indian Falls, Plateau, Four Corners, Lake Tear, Lake Arnold, and between Basin and Haystack (Sno-Bird). While for many 46ers the decision was unpopular, the club was more concerned with a similar announcement that the interior ranger stations, which were located in high traffic camping areas, were also considered "non conforming structures" in the state's land use master plan and were therefore also targeted for removal. The 46ers were adamantly opposed to the removal of the ranger stations for reasons of hiker safety and crowd control. President Ketchledge sent a letter on behalf of the club to DEC Commissioner Peter A. A. Berle opposing the decision. Joining other recreational and environmental groups in choosing to make their views public, Ketchledge noted that "for the first time in our history" the club was in "*unanimous* disagreement" with the department's plan to remove the cabins. Based on the objections of the 46ers and other groups, the DEC agreed to delay removal of ranger stations pending the actual adoption of the area's Unit Management Plan.

The second issue, which had a more direct impact on the club, concerned the 46ers' trailless summit canisters. The canisters, which were held in high esteem by a majority of club members, were determined to be "illegal under DEC Rules and Regulations, Part 190.8(i), and non-conforming to the APSLMP."[121] While the master plan did not specifically call for the removal of the canisters, it was clear that their continued presence on the summits of the trailless peaks would remain an issue.

The Adirondack Council passed a resolution dated December 21, 1977, requesting that the 46ers "remove the tin cans on summits of trailless peaks... because it is speculated that some hikers climb only to check off one more mountain and to have the opportunity to sign the register..." and "that tin cans on mountain summits in wilderness areas do not contribute to a wilderness experience because they are an unnecessary imprint of man and civilization." The council sent copies of its resolution to 46er President Ketchledge, and DEC Commissioner Berle, as well as to the news media in the Adirondack region.

In response to the request, Ed Ketchledge sent Harold Jerry, chairman of the council, a passionate four-page letter defending the club and the canisters. In the letter Ketchledge outlined the internal debate in which the club had recently engaged concerning the canisters, and he summarized some of the conclusions:

> In brief, the club discovered the canisters were an incidental issue and to focus on them was to miss the critical point: the *real* issue was, instead, protecting the ecological integrity of the former-trailless peaks by eliminating the superfluous herd paths and by making evident the one route determined to be the most environmentally sound. This we have done by sending out work parties that have brushed shut unnecessary, secondary routes and by making somewhat more obvious at questionable turns the one route that does the least damage.[122]

Ketchledge also stated that the Adirondack Forty-Sixers "are *the* most conscientious and active group of recreationists protecting the wilderness character of the Adirondack high peaks," and he outlined the recent service projects instituted by the club in cooperation with the DEC. He offered to take Jerry on a hike up any one of the trailless peaks so he could point out the work that the 46ers had done. He further chastised Jerry for airing issues in public first "rather than resolving them on their relative merits in private dialogue where constructive understandings may be generated without damage to our various programs of public service."

The debate continued with several other letters passing between Ketchledge and Jerry in very spirited and pointed tones. It is interesting to note that while Ketchledge personally favored the removal of the canisters, he passionately defended the majority position of club members to keep them. While the public nature of the controversy resulted in some unwarranted negative publicity for the 46ers, the canister issue eventually died down.

In 1979 the HPAC released the results of its investigation along with its recommendations to DEC Commissioner Berle. The citizen's committee made 47 recommendations for management of the High Peaks, including systematic trail rehabilitation; investigation of user fees and a permit system; and restrictions on camping, group size, and wood fires.

In response to the HPAC's report, the DEC instituted a number of new regulations that affected users of the High Peaks area. Open fires were prohibited above 4,000 feet and camping above 4,000 feet was prohibited except in winter. Camping was also prohibited within 150 feet of trails, streams, ponds or other bodies of water. Camping permits were required if a location was to be used four or more nights in a row or for a group of more than ten members. Visitors were required to carry out all garbage. All users of the High Peaks wilderness area were required to register at a trailhead before entering the forest. The new regulations were considered the "minimal tool" necessary to help preserve wilderness values.

By the end of the 1970s, with its trail maintenance efforts, Wilderness Workshop, and litter bag distribution project, the Forty-Sixers had established several significant service programs, all staffed and operated by volunteers. In recognition of the club's philosophical and organizational shift from a self-congratulatory, social group, to one with a productive purpose, a new item was added to the 46er questionnaire: "Indicate what type of conservation-related activity you would be willing to assist with." The current questionnaire reads: "There are many ways you can assist the Forty-Sixer organization. Please check if you are interested in participating in: Trail work, Clerical work at the Office of the Historian in Schenectady, NY, Other. Perhaps you have a valuable skill you are willing to share with us."

Part IV: The 1980s – Decade of Growth

The 1980s was a decade of growth for the 46ers – both in terms of membership and programs. As the decade began, 1,662 people had registered their climbs of the 46 High Peaks, and by the end of it, membership had risen to 2,712. The surge in numbers proved to be both a benefit and a burden to the club. The burgeoning membership provided the club with a pool of volunteers to staff its various service projects, but the popularity of 46ing presented organizational challenges and increased workloads for the club's officers and staff.

The trail maintenance program continued to expand and made substantive contributions to the state's trail management and conservation efforts. On behalf of the entire hiking community the club also took the lead in negotiating a resolution to a property boundary dispute that threatened to block access to several of the High Peaks.

During the 1980s the state began the process of developing a Unit Management Plan for the High Peaks. That put in motion a series of debates on issues of import not only to the club but also to the well being of the High Peaks that culminated in decisions that would impact the hiking public and the 46ers for years to come.

Managing the Numbers

The ADK Camper/Hiker Building at Adirondak Loj, which had served as the location for the club's annual spring and, sometimes, fall meetings was too small to accommodate the swelling ranks. At the fall 1983 meeting, more than 145 members squeezed into that building set up to seat 79. It was clear that the club had outgrown the space. The executive committee began searching for alternative meeting locations. The 1984 spring meeting was held at the North Country School, south of Lake Placid village, marking the first time that the spring meeting had been held at a location other than the Loj property since the club's organizational meeting in 1948. One hundred sixty-two attendees more than filled the meeting space at the North Country School to hear guest speaker DEC Commissioner Henry G. Williams. Requiring a still larger venue, the club held its fall 1984 meeting at Keene Central School in Keene Valley. The school became the club's annual meeting location for both spring and fall gatherings for the remainder of the 1980s.

Members began to express interest in having items sporting the 46er logo available for purchase to identify them as 46ers. After much discussion on design, colors, order filling, shipping, and inventory storage, the club offered a 46er T-shirt for sale to members for the first time in the fall of 1982. As was the case with the 46er patches and decals, only registered 46ers were allowed to purchase the shirts. The first were Kelly green with a large 46er logo silk-screened on the front in red and yellow. The shirts quickly sold out. During the fall of 1984, Fred Johnson (#1788), designed a new shirt, again Kelly green, which featured an expanded design that displayed a small logo on the right breast complemented by an expanse of white clouds and mountain silhouettes stretching across the remainder of the shirt front. Fred, along with William Kozel (#1529W), Donald Hoffman, and Grace, designed a three-by-two-inch cast brass belt buckle with a raised relief color 46er logo in the center, which was offered to members in 1986. For his conceptualization of those and other memorabilia items that were offered for sale to members throughout the 1980s, Fred earned the title of the 46er "ideas man."

Johnson also played a major role in the printing and distribution of a 46er "Certificate of Accomplishment." At the fall 1985 meeting the executive committee approved the concept, design, and printing of a three-color certificate to present to members upon completing their 46 peaks. The challenge was how to individualize the certificates to include each hiker's name and climbing number. Fred took on the herculean task of hand-lettering the initial certificates using a special transfer process that took him about five minutes per certificate. At the spring 1986 meeting 274 members – an all-time attendance record to date for an annual meeting – saw club historian Grace Hudowalski present the certificates for the first time to approximately 50 new 46ers. The presentations became an annual spring meeting feature during which Grace provided personal tidbits about each hiker as she read off their names. Certificates for the rest of the membership were mailed out at a later date, once Fred had completed the tedious task of lettering all 1,700 of them. For the next several years he used an Apple computer to individualize the certificates for the new 46ers, thus replacing the painstaking hand stenciling process with a less arduous one.

Devon Taylor (#2752) and Nancy Taylor (#2753) created a unique memorabilia item for members: a board game based on climbing the 46 peaks. They presented a sample of the game to the executive committee during the spring 1987 meeting along with the suggestion to mass produce it and offer it for sale to members. The Adirondack High Peaks Adventure Game board included a map of the High Peaks with "trails" to all of the summits. With rolls of dice, players would "climb" the peaks. The object of the Forty-Sixer game was to climb all 46 peaks, of course, visit Adirondak Loj and Johns Brook Lodge, stay two nights in a lean-to and return to the finish square. The game, which was manufactured at a reasonable cost and offered for purchase in 1988, proved immensely popular. Registered 46ers found that it made the perfect gift for aspiring hikers, some of whom used the game board as a "map" to help them chart their progress.

With a growing membership came increased workloads for the club's various appointed positions, especially for Executive Secretary/Treasurer Ditt Dittmar and club Historian Grace Hudowalski. In recognition of their extraordinary dedication and years of service, the club presented both Grace and Ditt with plaques at the fall 1984 meeting. The plaques read, "In recognition and appreciation for your many years of unselfish and dedicated service to the members of the Adirondack Forty-Sixers. Your guidance, inspiration and friendship will always be remembered by each of us." More important than the public recognition for their efforts was the club's attempts to find ways to make their jobs easier.

Grace answered 1,245 letters in 1988, all of her responses composed on a portable electric typewriter. During the fall of 1988 she acknowledged for the first time that the mail from hikers reporting their climbs was piling up and that she could use some assistance in answering the letters. Suzanne Lance (#1802W) and L. John Van Norden (#2110W) volunteered to help her through the busy hiking season, and for the first time in 46er history, a few aspiring 46ers received letters from someone other than Grace. It was apparent that the volume of correspondence would continue to increase during the peak hiking months and that Grace would continue to need assistance at those times.

Two additional items were indicative of the club's growth. In 1987 the club officially incorporated, and dues, which had held steady at $2 per year, were increased to $4 for new members for their initial year of membership only, in order to offset the cost of the certificates.

Trail Maintenance

In the early 1980s the 46ers faced a situation that threatened the very core of the sport of 46ing. Finch Pruyn and Company, Inc. owned timber land bordering the High Peaks Wilderness, including a large tract west of Tahawus, a tract bordering the Opalescent River, and a tract containing the Boreas River watershed in the western High Peaks. In late 1980 the company informed hiking groups and the general public of its intention to close its lands to the public, except for along established and marked state trails. For those attempting to climb the 46, that meant that the usual approaches to the Santanonis (Santanoni, Panther, and Couchsachraga) and Allen, which began on state trails and then veered off onto herdpaths through Finch Pruyn property, would no longer be accessible legally. The reasoning behind Finch Pruyn's decision revolved around the company's practice of leasing some of its lands to private fee-based hunting and fishing clubs. Members of those clubs reportedly objected to the hiking public having free recreational access to Finch Pruyn's land while they were paying rent for the same privilege.

Finch Pruyn urged hikers to respect the rights of the private landowners and refrain from climbing Allen and the Santanonis from the traditional routes. The company threatened not only to pursue legal action against trespassers but also to close the entire Duck Hole/Bradley Pond Trail, a move which would effectively have cut off all access to the Santanonis from the eastern side, if hikers continued to use the old route. For those attempting to climb the 46 High Peaks that would have necessitated much longer trips through areas of thick blowdown and difficult terrain in order to avoid Finch Pruyn property.

Intent on retaining the traditional routes to the Santanonis and Allen, Jim Goodwin, on behalf of the 46ers, approached Finch Pruyn with the idea of flagging new herdpaths along the state/Finch Pruyn land boundaries to establish "legal" routes to those summits. His initial attempts to persuade the company to allow public access to the traditional routes up Allen and the Santanonis were unsuccessful. However, Richard Nason, the company's chief woodlands manager, was sympathetic to the hikers' dilemma and worked with the 46ers and ADK to find a solution to the problem. He sent a lumber crew to cut out a survey line near Bradley Pond to state land on the slopes of Panther Mountain to provide access to the Santanonis. The crew used chain saws to clear severe blowdown from the Big Blow of 1950 and painted blazes to mark the property boundaries. In the summer of 1981 a 46er trail crew followed the route and marked a practical path, diverting from the property line only where necessary to avoid some dangerous cliffs and pinnacles. From the end of Finch Pruyn property, Jim Goodwin led a crew that continued to flag a route to Panther Brook and then up the brook to the Santanoni/Panther ridge. With bright paint blazes, surveyor's tape, and the scars of chain-sawed trees and logs from Finch Pruyn's work, the new path was an assault on both the senses and the wilderness, but it satisfied the landowner and provided a new legal access route to the peaks of the area.

Finch Pruyn also was willing to adopt a similar procedure to create a new route up Allen if the DEC would approve the location of the path where it would intersect with state land. However, at that time the High Peaks Unit Management Plan (HPUMP) had not been approved and until a plan was in place the DEC district director at Ray Brook was reluctant to take any action. The HPUMP was tenth on the state's established priority list, and the state had only finished four of the UMPs in the previous ten years. Consequently, officially, a reroute of the Allen trail was on hold and no resolution was anticipated in the foreseeable future.

Through notices in *Peeks* the club alerted members about the Allen herdpath approach problem. Grace supplied hikers who inquired about a "legal" route up the mountain with a map of a new approach that used the abandoned yellow trail that ran from Twin Brook Lean-to to Uphill Brook Lean-to to bring hikers to the Finch Pruyn/state property line. Once past the Finch Pruyn boundary line the legal route turned right and followed an unnamed brook along the property line. That route gradually veered left to Skylight Brook and then up the brook to an intersection with the old herdpath on the side of Allen Brook.

David Lance helps position a trail "stringer". Behind him on the left are Trailmaster Chris M. Behr and David's sister and then co-editor of *Peeks,* Suzanne Lance.

Jim Goodwin, along with other club members, continued to discuss a trail reroute with Finch Pruyn, and, finally, Richard Nason gave the 46ers permission to flag a route to Allen from Twin Brook Lean-to that reached state land without passing near any of the hunting camps on the company's leased property. With cooperation from Finch Pruyn in hand the club approached the DEC for permission to continue flagging a route on state land that would connect with the old herdpath to Allen. Goodwin sent a letter to the DEC outlining the plan and received a perfunctory response. He persisted and the DEC finally relented, granting the club permission to flag the connector route. Goodwin, along with the husband and wife team of Chris G. and June Behr, who had been regular volunteers on the 46ers' trail maintenance outings, marked the new path in 1983.

While certainly motivated by club goals, the 46ers' persistence with the DEC and Finch Pruyn in negotiating routes to the Santanonis and Allen that satisfied all parties represented a major service to the entire hiking community. Without the club's persistence, in particular the indefatigable efforts of Jim Goodwin, the Santanonis and Allen could have become peaks accessible only by the hardiest hikers.

With the 46er trail maintenance program in full swing, Jim Goodwin decided to step down as Trailmaster in the spring of 1982 so he could spend more time maintaining the 90 miles of ATIS trails in the Ausable Valley. In the fall of that year, Chris G. Behr was appointed to fill the position. He had participated in almost every trail outing since the inception of the program and was a natural choice to succeed Goodwin. Chris's wife June and their son Chris M. joined the Trailmaster team. Jim Goodwin later reflected on the Behr's collective contribution to the trail program saying, "This couple, with their son Chris M. Behr had been the most able and devoted members of the trail crew during my tenure as Trailmaster. They were excellent engineers in devising trail drainage, bridge building and solving other problems. Furthermore, they were outstanding morale builders and leaders. I was especially fortunate that the Behrs agreed to take over Forty-Sixer trail maintenance operations, when after five years, I wanted to give more time to my ATIS obligations."[123]

The first problem that the Behrs faced upon assuming the Trailmaster duties was the lack of tools. Goodwin had always provided equipment that either belonged to him personally or to ATIS for the 46er trail crew volunteers. Through the generosity of 46er members, many of whom contributed a few extra dollars when paying their annual dues, the club was able to purchase tools – axes, bow saws, cross-cut saws, picks and mattocks, shovels, and loppers – that would allow volunteers to tackle a variety of projects.

The leadership of the 46er trail maintenance program became a true family affair for the Behrs with June and Chris M. accompanying Chris G. on almost every outing. In 1985 Chris M. was officially appointed co-Trailmaster. Chris G. explained their approach to leading the 46er trail crews: "Most of all, we tried to keep in mind all we had learned from Jim about how to lead a group of volunteers – make everyone welcome, help everyone learn, let everyone work at their own pace, and make the outing fun."[124] That people-friendly philosophy contributed to an increase in the number of volunteers who participated in trail work outings. It also encouraged an atmosphere of camaraderie and a collegial spirit among the trail workers, many of whom developed close bonds and lasting friendships.

Trail workers coined some new terms to describe aspects of their work. For example, "monolithomania" described the obsession to move a large rock from one location to another, usually uphill. A "wibble-wobble" described an erratic bow saw cut. The notion that it was possible to have fun while "giving something back" to the mountains became the motto of the trail crews.

Donald Hoffman, who was Forty-Sixer president from 1984 to 1987, summed up the club's enthusiasm for the trail work program and the philosophy of "giving something back" in his President's Report in the Spring/Summer 1985 issue of *Peeks*:

> I do not believe that one can come to the High Peaks, climb the 46, and then just completely walk away from them. You just cannot spend the amount of time in the wilderness that is needed to become a 46er without it causing you to develop a deep and everlasting appreciation for these mountains. You also cannot climb these mountains and not realize that your very own presence has, in some very small way, made an impact on the mountain environment. Thus we all have this great love and appreciation for the High Peaks, and coupled with our sincere concern for the future well-being of our mountains will not allow most of us to just turn our back and rest on our laurels. Instead we want to do something constructive for these mountains – to give of ourselves.[125]

The number of volunteers and the number of trail work projects steadily increased throughout the 1980s. Fifty-four people participated in the 1982 trail work season which included the clearing of blowdown on the Elk Lake/Marcy trail, building bridges on Upper Ausable Lake and at Slide Brook, and side-cutting the Dix trails, the Mr. Van Trail, and the Wallface Pond Trail. The 46ers' commitment to trailwork came at an opportune time. DEC personnel cutbacks in the early 1980s reduced the number of Wilderness Rangers in the High Peaks, limiting the state's impact in the regulation and upkeep of the area. As a result the DEC increasingly relied on volunteer trail crews to carry out the routine trail maintenance of state trails.

Ed Ketchledge's summit seeding efforts continued with 46er volunteers spreading 200 pounds of seed and fertilizer on the summit of Algonquin during the 1983 spring meeting weekend.[126] Thirty-two seeding volunteers worked with Ketchledge during the spring of 1984 to distribute an additional 400 pounds of material. In June of 1987 Ketchledge's project received a boost. He wanted to start remedial efforts on the summit of Marcy, the state's highest peak, but to ask volunteers to carry an extra five to ten pounds in their packs

Members of the "46er First Airborne Division" – John Siau , Dr. Edwin Ketchledge, and Joe Urbanczyk atop Marcy. David Lance (#1801) took the photograph.

over the almost eight miles to Marcy's summit seemed extreme. With assistance from the DEC, Ketchledge was able to secure a state helicopter to transport more than 250 pounds of seeding materials along with four volunteers to carry out the work on Marcy's summit. On June 11, a state helicopter picked up four boxes of seed, lime, and fertilizer at Mt. Van Hoevenberg and the "46er First Airborne Division" – Joe Urbanczyk (#2151), David Lance (#1801), John Siau, and Ketchledge. After a stop at the Colden Interior Ranger Station to drop off supplies, the helicopter deposited the seeding materials and the volunteers on the summit ridge of Marcy. The crew spread the materials and then hiked back to Adirondak Loj.

In the spring of 1983 Chris G. Behr formed an emergency trail maintenance team. Dubbed the SWAT team (Special Willingness and Temperament), the group consisted of volunteers who could be available on short notice to take on trail projects that required immediate attention. One SWAT team project in the summer of 1984 involved the installation of a privy at Lake Arnold. The volunteers had to carry the prefabricated privy components, including the side walls and fully-shingled roof, from Marcy Dam to its intended location at Lake Arnold, a distance of 2.6 miles. The extraordinary effort required to accomplish that task prompted SWAT team members to change the nomenclature of SWAT to "Struggles With A Toilet."[127]

Giardiasis Solutions

Prior to the 1980s hikers could feel confident in drinking any moving water encountered along the trails in the High Peaks without filtration or chemical treatment. One of the simple joys of hiking was to dip a cup into a stream and drink the cool, pure Adirondack waters. However, in the early 1980s cases of *Giardiasis*, an intestinal disease carried by the parasite *Giardia lamblia,* were reported from hikers who drank water in some of the heavily traveled areas of the High Peaks. A major factor in the contamination of the water was the improper or inadequate disposal of human waste. High Peaks Forest Ranger Peter Fish first reported the problem of *Giardiasis* to the 46ers at the fall 1982 meeting.

Trowel Project: Novel Approach, Unexpected Results

At the fall 1983 meeting Ranger John Wood also commented on the increasing number of *Giardiasis* cases and suggested that the club consider distributing plastic trowels for hikers to use to bury their waste when a privy was not available. The executive committee discussed the suggestion and voted to pursue the project. With approval from the DEC, the club purchased 10,000 trowels and began distributing them at Adirondak Loj and Johns Brook Lodge. An attached message defined the problem and explained how to use the tool. Between 3,000 and 5,000 trowels and accompanying information sheets were distributed during the summer of 1984. Ranger Fish termed the trowel project a good "gimmick" which had helped disseminate information about water contamination in the High Peaks. The DEC approved a second season of distribution. Unfortunately, the trowels and information sheets, abandoned by hikers after use, began to appear at lean-to sites and along trails, littering the landscape. Created to solve one problem but inadvertently contributing to another, the trowel project was abandoned in the fall of 1985.

Privy Installation

Despite the mixed results of the trowel project, the 46ers stood ready to assist the DEC with another program to help mitigate problems associated with the improper disposal of human waste. The DEC theorized that increasing the number of privies, particularly at lean-to and other camping areas, would help control the contamination of water sources. So the 46er trail maintenance program entered into the privy installation and relocation business. Throughout the 1980s trail crews installed or moved privies at the Lillian Brook, Slide Brook, Boquet River, Twin Brook, and Ouluska Pass lean-to sites, among others.

Trail work volunteers continued their regular maintenance of the Dix trail system from both the Elk Lake and Round Pond access points. In the summer of 1986 the club added the North Trail to Giant to its regular maintenance responsibilities. Trail work skills and ingenuity were put to the test in the summer of 1985 when the crew took on its first lean-to rehabilitation: the Boquet River Lean-to on the Round Pond-Dix trail. The work included the replacement of the lean-to's base logs, the installation of new floor joists, hangers, a solid plank floor, and tar and shingles roof repairs. The DEC had airlifted materials to the site to complete that project. Forty-Sixer engineering and carpentry skills were up to the task and "lean-to rehab" became a specialty of 46er trail crews.

In the summer of 1986 trail volunteers ventured into the Pharaoh Lake area to assist the DEC with projects in that highly used hiking and camping region outside of the High Peaks. It became a popular annual trail work outing as participants had the opportunity to "car camp" at the Putnam Pond state campground. Without having to backpack into a worksite, volunteers were able to take along such luxury items as air mattresses, pillows, lawn chairs, and barbecue grills. No freeze-dried backpacking meals were allowed. The trail crew had the added benefit of being able to partake of hot showers, swimming, games of horseshoes and Frisbee, and any number of libations following a hard day's work.

As cuts in state funding continued to reduce the amount of direct DEC staff-conducted trail work, the 46er trail maintenance program became a major contributor to the work

THE HISTORY OF THE ADIRONDACK FORTY-SIXERS

Sometimes the volunteer trail crews simply moved privies to new locations.

conducted in the High Peaks. The 46ers proved to be enthusiastic, reliable, and skilled workers. From 1979, when record-keeping began on 46er trail work, to the end of 1988 more than three hundred 46ers and friends contributed more than 14,000 hours of volunteer time working on projects that improved the trails and camping areas in the Adirondack Park. The 46er program was so successful that club President Don Hoffman appointed a special committee (Jules Comeau, Joe Urbanczyk, and Glenn Fish) to consider instituting higher recognition levels for the Conservation Service Award beyond the initial 46 hours. At the spring 1987 annual meeting the executive committee approved 146 and 346 hours as additional CSA levels of achievement.

Forest Preserve Centennial Celebration

In 1985 the state celebrated the 100th anniversary of the creation of the Forest Preserve by sponsoring a series of events throughout the year. Groups were encouraged to offer their own programming to highlight the history of the preserve. For its part the Forty-Sixers led 13 day hikes to introduce people to the High Peaks. Coordinated by Ed Ketchledge, the guided hikes were very popular. Trip leaders included Bob Helenek (#1483), Sharp Swan, Ellen Somers (#1751), Ferdinand Ulrich (#1819), Anthony Ulrich (#1818), Ernest Freidow (#1564), Sally Sturner (#1997), Phil Corell, William Kozel, Jules Comeau, Tom Lee (#1452), Fred Johnson, Joseph Carman (#1930) and Carol Carman (#1929).

The club also participated in a three-day festival at Lake Placid, September 13-15, 1985. Twenty 46ers represented the club by marching in the centennial parade. Proudly carrying the 46er banner in front of a float that depicted a wilderness tenting/camping scene, Ditt Dittmar and Don Hoffman led the procession. Glenn Fish coordinated an information booth from which 46er volunteers passed out literature about the 46ers, climbing the High Peaks, litter control, *Giardiasis*, and other environmental concerns.

Left: Trailmaster Chris G. Behr. Above: Trailmaster Chris M. Behr. Below: Crew building new Bushnell Falls Lean-to.

High Peaks Unit Management Plan Moves Forward

As of the spring of 1983 there had been no substantial progress on the HPUMP. However, new DEC Commissioner Henry G. Williams was intent on moving the project forward. Finally, in 1984, the DEC conducted an inventory of the region to identify and assess lean-to sites, camping areas, access points, signs, and trail conditions. The DEC also sought input from the 46ers regarding the management of the region. Recognizing that the HPUMP would eventually contain recommendations that would directly impact hiking and recreational use of the region, the club created a new appointed position – 46er Information Officer. The purpose of the position was to provide a liaison between the DEC and other clubs and organizations throughout the process of formulating the HPUMP. Ed Ketchledge agreed to serve as the club's eyes and ears during that important time.

By the fall of 1987 the DEC had completed the inventory phase of the HPUMP and announced the establishment of a Citizen's Advisory Committee to review and collect input on the findings and recommendations in the draft document. In attempting to respond to the HPUMP draft the club faced a dilemma. With a diverse and growing membership the executive committee became increasingly reluctant to dictate official club policy or offer opinions on issues affecting the Forest Preserve and the High Peaks. Unlike the early days when club leaders publicly expressed their positions on issues concerning the Adirondack Park, during the 1980s the executive committee took a different approach. The committee members saw the club as a social entity with a conservation and educational service component and not as a political action club with a desire to influence public policy. With only two annual meetings the club leadership felt it was too difficult to engage the membership in any meaningful dialogue on issues. While the mountains brought members together for a common purpose, each hiker's background, attitudes, personal agendas, and even reasons for climbing the 46 were widely dissimilar. Reluctant to speak for or to formulate a consensus for a group with such diversity, the executive committee felt that the best approach was to keep the membership informed about the issues and let each member enter the public debate if he or she desired to do so. Some members felt the philosophy represented a head-in-the-sands approach, depriving the DEC of the valuable experiences of the collective club membership. No other group of individuals spent more time in the High Peaks and had more knowledge of trail conditions and hiker behavior. The executive committee's decision to refrain from contributing as a club to the debate on policy issues reduced the 46ers' first hand experience to a minor role in the process.

In the spring of 1988 members of the executive committee did meet with representatives from the DEC to engage in a dialogue on the HPUMP. As a result of that meeting the committee decided to survey the membership. The survey included 31 questions, all relating to specific recommendations or topics under discussion in the HPUMP. It asked for responses to questions concerning such issues as the institution of a user permit and fee system for those hiking and camping in the High Peaks; the closing of the Marcy Dam Ranger Station; group size restrictions; the expansion of the current trail system; restrictions on camping and campfires; placement of lean-tos; and, of course, the future of the trailless peaks and the canisters. A total of 802 members – more than 50 percent of the active membership – responded to the survey. Tabulation of the responses regarding the canisters and the trailless peaks – the two issues of greatest concern to the 46ers – showed overwhelming support for retaining the canisters (701 in support; 49 for removal; 44 undecided) and against maintaining trails on the trailless peaks (581 against; 120 for basic maintenance; 99 undecided). The club shared the results of the entire survey with the APA and DEC but did not issue any official positions on the HPUMP recommendations. Public hearings on the HPUMP began in October 1989. Reports and recommendations were due to be released in April 1990.

Part V: The 1990s – End of an Era

The 1990s represented a particularly tumultuous decade for the Forty-Sixers as the club faced upheavals that threatened to weaken the core of its foundation.

Aspects of the state's High Peaks Unit Management Plan, namely recommendations regarding the status of the herdpaths on the trailless peaks and the fate of the canisters directly affected the club's programs and focus throughout the decade. The 46ers were forced to engage in serious discussions, which at times turned into heated and painful debates, on what actions the club should take in response to the HPUMP.

Not only did the club struggle with the issues brought to the forefront by external influences but it also struggled to address problems involving its organizational structure and growth. As it had throughout the 1980s, the club's membership continued to increase and the resulting workload was becoming unmanageable for Executive Secretary/Treasurer Ditt Dittmar and Historian Grace Hudowalski. Both Ditt and Grace were the only individuals throughout the club's history to ever hold their respective positions and both were octogenarians. Through some magic bestowed upon those stalwarts by the mountains the club had been able to dodge the unthinkable task of finding replacements for those two pivotal officers for many years. However, with the 1990s came the unavoidable realization that change was inevitable. Members of the executive committee held their collective breaths when the subject of how best to accomplish the transitions arose.

Despite the challenges, the decade also heralded a number of celebratory milestones which demonstrated the club's ability to make positive advances in its mission and program priorities.

Club Responds to HPUMP
Trailless Peaks

Throughout the 1990s the club's commitment to trail maintenance continued to expand. Under the direction of the Behr family, each successive year set new records for participation in trail outings and in man/woman-hours contributed. New and more technically sophisticated trail projects were added to the season's schedules, presenting additional opportunities and challenges for volunteers.

In support of the 1992 Adirondack Park Centennial[128] celebration, the 46ers took on the challenge of funding and building a replacement lean-to in the High Peaks area in cooperation with the DEC. With generous support from club members, a grant from the Hudson River Improvement Fund, and a special contribution from the International Paper Company Foundation, the club raised enough funds to purchase three lean-to kits. Up to that time, 46er trail crews had refurbished lean-tos, successfully accomplishing such tasks as installing a new roof, replacing the front base log or "deacon seat," and adding plank flooring; but the crews had not yet built an entire lean-to from scratch. The trail crew regulars eagerly anticipated the new challenge. Thirty-nine volunteers turned out to help build a new lean-to at the Bushnell Falls # 1 site in the summer of 1991. The project involved completely dismantling and burning the old lean-to, relocating the privy, and general cleanup and reclamation of trampled areas at the site in addition to the construction of the lean-to.

A second Centennial lean-to was erected at Feldspar Brook in July 1992. After delays in having the raw material airlifted to the site, the trail crew completed the third Centennial lean-to at Uphill Brook over the course of two weekends during the summer of 1994.

The 1992 trail work season set a number of records: the largest number of scheduled outings, at ten; the largest number of volunteers, at 158; the largest number of first-time participants, at 41; and at 3,504, the most service hours contributed in a trail work season. In 1993, in addition to its own regular trail work outings, the club also contributed $1,600 to support the Summit Stewardship Program (SSP). Initiated by Ed Ketchledge in 1989, the SSP placed trained educators on the summits of Marcy and Algonquin during the high traffic summer months. The Summit Stewards conducted plant inventories of the unique wilderness environment of those high summits, assisted in restoration projects, and informed the public about how they could protect the rare and fragile alpine meadows. The SSP was sponsored by the Adirondack Nature Conservancy, which trained the stewards; the Adirondack Mountain Club, which provided administrative support, equipment, and facilities for the program; and the New York State Department of Environmental Conservation. The 46ers' contribution helped to purchase equipment to outfit the stewards and pay their salaries. The club's support for the important and innovative program was a natural extension of its involvement with Ketchledge's summit seeding/stabilization projects conducted throughout the 1980s.[129]

In the spring of 1995 Chris G. and Chris M. Behr retired as Trailmasters after serving in that position for 12 years. The Behr family had been the architects and catalysts for the significant growth in the frequency and sophistication of projects undertaken by the 46ers' all-volunteer crews. Planners, administrators, and encouragers, they made new participants as well as the seasoned trail work veterans feel welcome and important members of the team. They shared their considerable knowledge with anyone wanting to learn and they were always eager to pick up a new trick or a simpler method from other crew members. They grew in the job, adapted, and expanded the mission and horizon of Forty-Sixer trail crews. Trail stewardship has become one of the defining initiatives of the club in large part due to the examples set by Chris G., Chris M., and June Behr.

Len Grubbs (#2541W), Joe Urbanczyk, and David Hudda (#3018), all of whom had been regular trail work participants, assumed the duties of Trailmaster.

In the fall of 1995 the three Behrs received official recognition for their significant contribution to trail maintenance in the Adirondack Forest Preserve. The DEC presented the 46er Trailmaster family with the Adirondack Stewardship Award. Their work as leaders of the 46ers' trailwork program included participation in outings every other summer weekend for 12 years. Their individual volunteer contribution amounted to more than 2,000 hours of trail work *each*. The DEC also presented the Adirondack Stewardship Award to Ed Ketchledge for his more than 45 years of research concerning the ecology of the open alpine summits in the High Peaks and his remedial work to restore damage done to those areas by hikers. The awards were presented at the fall conference of the Association for the Protection of the Adirondacks held at Silver Bay Conference Center on Lake George.

Of primary concern for the new Trailmasters was the information contained in the HPUMP draft regarding the herdpaths on the trailless peaks. Formal public participation in the development of the HPUMP began in June of 1990 with the appointment of a 26-member citizens' advisory group. The High Peaks Citizens' Advisory Committee (CAC), much like its predecessor, the High Peaks Advisory Committee that had met during the 1970s, was made up of scientists, recreationists, and representatives from environmental groups and local governments. The committee was organized into ten subcommittees to develop and analyze the issues outlined in the HPUMP and to make recommendations to the DEC on how best to manage and maintain the High Peaks Wilderness as an enduring resource. The CAC held

15 group and numerous subcommittee meetings over a two-year period and issued a detailed report to the DEC in July of 1992. That report contained 186 recommendations concerning the management of visitor use while protecting the natural resources of the region. Jules Comeau, who had served as 46er president from 1987 to 1989, represented the 46ers on the CAC.

One issue that the CAC discussed at length was the fate of the herdpaths on the trailless peaks. The main concern was severe erosion that was evident on some of the paths. Herdpaths tended to take the shortest and most direct routes to summits. Those routes were usually the steepest courses and, therefore, most susceptible to erosion. The proliferation of multiple herdpaths as hikers either lost the main tracks, skirted blowdown, or attempted to find easier routes in some spots was also cited as a problem.

The solution proposed by the CAC to address those concerns was to direct herdpaths over the most environmentally sound routes, placing branches or fallen logs across undesirable paths. To keep hikers on the desired path, the committee also suggested minimal trail clearing when necessary and the placement of simple markers at the beginning of a herdpath and at strategic spots along the way. That recommendation was very similar to that of the wilderness paths suggested by Mason Ingram in 1967. The proposal also formalized the work that Ed Ketchledge had initiated in response to a directive by the High Peaks Advisory Committee in the mid 1970s.

The recommendations of the CAC regarding the trailless peaks were particularly troublesome for the club since the recent member survey indicated that a majority continued to disapprove of marking routes up trailless peaks. Tony Goodwin, who served on the CAC Facilities Subcommittee, which focused on such issues as shelters, bridges, campsites, and trails, recognized that the recommendations concerning the trailless peak herdpaths would be unpopular with many 46ers. To alert members to the sensitive issue and to describe the rationale for the CAC's recommendations, he wrote an article that appeared in the Fall/Winter 1991-92 issue of *Peeks*. In "Herdpaths and the High Peaks Management Plan," he expressed the committee's hope that "carefully routed and subtly marked trails will keep the majority of trailless climbers on a route where they will do minimal damage."[130] He noted that change was inevitable given the conditions of the herdpaths, but that the change was for the benefit of the wilderness itself – to preserve it and maintain it for future generations.

In the fall of 1995, the DEC released a draft of the HPUMP which incorporated the recommendations of the CAC. The plan's stated goals were "to preserve, enhance, and restore wilderness conditions in the High Peaks Wilderness Complex. With regard to human use and enjoyment, these activities will be permitted and encouraged, so long as the wilderness resources in their ecological or sociological context are not degraded."

The Fall/Winter 1995-1996 issue of *Peeks* included a summary of the specific items that would have the most impact on the 46ers and on hiking in general in the High Peaks. As expected the HPUMP called for the DEC to work cooperatively with the 46ers to designate the most environmentally suitable paths up the trailless peaks. Less desirable routes would be closed and rehabilitated. It also recommended the removal of the canisters from the trailless peaks, once work to establish sound herdpaths to the summits was completed.

The HPUMP also established general usage restrictions in the eastern and western High Peaks zones, including a maximum camping and day use group size of 10 persons, limiting camping to designated areas only, and prohibiting all open campfires in the Marcy Dam-Lake Colden corridor. It also called for the removal of two lean-tos at Marcy Dam, one of which was the Hudowalski Memorial Lean-to. The lean-tos were dismantled in July 1996. Using the best parts of both structures, DEC personnel built a single lean-to on the bluff northwest of Marcy Brook. They placed the original Hudowalski plaque in it, thus preserving, to an extent, the original memorial to Ed Hudowalski.

In December 1995 Len Grubbs, Joe Urbanczyk, and 46er President Nancy Allen (#2355) met with DEC Supervisor of Natural Resources Dale Huyck and DEC Region 5 Director Stuart Buchanan to seek clarification of the department's plans for the trailless peaks and to outline a course of action. While the final version of the HPUMP would not be released for another four years, it was expected that the plan would be approved with minimal revisions. Therefore it seemed appropriate to begin the discussions. The DEC's plan was to classify the herdpaths on the trailless peaks as Class II trails.[131] As such they would be unmarked or minimally marked and subject only to basic maintenance such as clearing blowdown or rerouting water drainage in order to keep hikers on the desired paths. The DEC expected the rehabilitation efforts to be a long-term endeavor, with work being completed on one trailless peak a year. With 20 trailless peaks, the project would continue over the course of two decades.

The Trailmasters recognized that the trailless peak rehabilitation project would be a major undertaking and that the club would need to broaden support for the initiative and solicit additional manpower and expertise in trail design. In March 1996, in anticipation of the final approval of the HPUMP, Len Grubbs approached the ADK Trails Committee to discuss the possibility of a cooperative effort. As a result the two clubs formed the Trailless Peaks Committee, which included the 46er Trailmasters as well as Phil Corell, ADK Trails Director E. William Brosseau (#2136), and Nathaniel "Nat" Wells (#2685), chairman of the ADK Trails Committee.

During June 1996 the Trailless Peaks Committee met with DEC liaison Phil Johnstone to establish goals and set protocols for a pilot project. The group decided on a general procedure for the rehabilitation projects. Each of the trailless peaks would be surveyed to identify the one route to the summit that would have the least environmental impact. Following the recommendation set forth in the HPUMP, alternate paths would be closed off with brush and downed logs. Remedial work would be undertaken only to mitigate environmental damage, not to make the route easier in an attempt to retain some of the challenge of climbing a "trailless" peak. Small markers would be used only to keep hikers on the desired path in areas where there could be some confusion.

After initially inspecting several peaks known to have severely eroded herdpaths, the committee selected Tabletop as a pilot project. Committee members climbed Tabletop on July 22, 1996, to formally survey the existing path and make recommendations for remedial action. In August the group submitted its recommendations to the DEC for review. The committee returned with Phil Johnstone in September to review the site and receive feedback. On March 22, 1997, based on Johnstone's assessment, the committee submitted a detailed three-phase proposal for Tabletop. The plan called for the following remedial action: clear blowdown that was causing hikers to deviate from the main path and block any secondary paths; re-route approximately 250 feet of the trail on the summit ridge to avoid a wet depression that was subject to erosion; and mark and re-route the beginning of the trail to avoid another wet area.

The DEC formally approved the first two phases of the plan in August and on September 5, 1997, a crew began preliminary work: flagging the blowdown to be removed, paths to be closed, and the re-route section on the summit ridge. The crew returned the following day to complete the work. The re-route of the beginning of the path was approved several weeks later, and the actual work to complete that portion was undertaken during the 1998 trail work season.

Street and Nye, which had vexed hikers for years with their maze of herdpaths in the col between the two summits, were tapped as the next candidates for rehabilitation work. A similar process to that used for the Tabletop project was begun in September 1998. By early May 1999 a crew had completed the work on Street and Nye, which included a 1,013-foot re-route of a lower section of the herdpath. In July members of the Trailless Peaks Committee hiked to Marshall, Redfield, and Cliff to gather data and develop plans for remedial work on those trailless peaks.

In the late summer of 1999 a natural disaster dictated trailwork priorities for the 46ers. Hurricane Floyd swept through the High Peaks on September 16th of that year. Due to an extraordinary amount of rain that drenched the area in a short period of time, a 2,500-foot swath of dirt and trees slid to the base of Mt. Colden in Avalanche Pass – the pass living up to its name – burying the Marcy Dam to Lake Colden trail under 30 feet of muddy debris. Winds from Floyd, which snapped trees apart and uprooted them, also did extensive damage to more than 400 miles of trails in the High Peaks. Despite the devastation to many areas, by a quirk of nature, Floyd turned out to be a blessing for one section. On the shoulder of Noonmark a forest fire that had started on September 2 and had destroyed over 90 acres of forest,[132] had continued to smolder. Floyd's rains fully extinguished the pesky blaze.

After Hurricane Floyd, the 46er Trailmasters surveyed the trails for which the club provided regular maintenance. What they found was staggering. The Round Pond/Dix trail was passable although difficult to navigate due to extensive blowdown. Forty to fifty trees of various sizes blocked sections of the North Trail to Giant, and the Elk Lake/Dix trail was devastated. A half-mile up the Elk Lake/Dix trail, still on Elk Lake Lodge property, Lawrence "Larry" Hokirk (#3332), who had assumed the position of Trailmaster when Dave Hudda stepped down in 1997, was stopped by a massive blowdown. He climbed ten feet to the top of a pile of downed trees and observed more twisted, tangled masses for as far as he could see. The Elk Lake/Dix trail had sustained so much damage that the DEC was forced to close it. One hiker who ventured into the area counted more than 200 downed trees from the trailhead to Slide Brook, a distance of 2.3 miles.

Because the devastation was so extensive, the blowdown had to be removed in a methodical, ordered fashion to prevent injuries from sections collapsing like a pile of pick-up sticks. It was therefore impossible to bring in a large crew to work on the trails despite the enormous amount of work that needed to be done. The Trailmasters, along with a few experienced volunteers, completed most of the clearing. On September 25, 1999, tackling the Round Pond trail, the Trailmasters removed 34 trees between Route 73 and the Boquet River Lean-to. Twenty-two of those trees had been uprooted. At the end of October the Trailmasters and a small crew began the arduous task of clearing the mangled mess of the Elk Lake/Dix trail, and that work extended into the following year.

Despite the challenges of the 1990s, the Trailmasters were able to maintain the regular trail work schedule and even initiate a new program. While part of the crew was involved with the Tabletop rehabilitation on the weekend of July 22, 1996, the remaining Trailmaster led the first all-women trailwork weekend. Fourteen women strapped loppers and saws to their packs to side cut the Hunters Pass trail on Dix. The all-women trail crew weekend was a tremendous success and has become a regular part of the trail maintenance schedule.

The HPUMP and the Canisters

As difficult as it was for many 46ers to accept the HPUMP's proposal regarding the herdpaths on the trailless peaks, the plan's call for the removal of the canisters caused even more feverish debate and a fractional divide among club members.

As indicated by the response to the survey the club conducted in 1988, a majority of 46ers opposed the removal of the canisters. Many considered the tradition of locating the canisters and signing the log books to be the quintessential 46er experience. The canisters represented success, a goal achieved, a job well done. Being able to record one's presence at a location visited by relatively few people seemed to satisfy some deep-seated need of the modern-day adventurer. While reaching the top of any of the trailed 46 provided a sense of accomplishment, somehow finding the canisters on the summits of the trailless peaks made those climbs even more rewarding. While the club had discussed the fate of the canisters on several occasions throughout its history, having the state's plan call for their removal made the prospects of actually losing them a distressing reality.

Tim Tefft (#616), who assumed the presidency of the 46ers in 1992 when Joe Urbanczyk stepped down for health reasons, brought the canister debate to the forefront. He also renewed the discussion concerning the club's overall purpose. Tim had a long history of volunteer work on behalf of the 46ers. For 15 years he had been an Outdoor Leadership Workshop staff member, but his vision for the club's future was very different from that of past presidents and indeed most of the membership.

Tim suggested that the club reexamine its goals within the context of the changing face of the Adirondack wilderness. He was opposed to the summit canisters remaining on the trailless peaks. He thought it was time for the club to abandon its role of serving as the clearinghouse for those who were climbing the 46 peaks. In his President's Report in the Fall/Winter 1992-93 issue of *Peeks* he offered a thought-provoking explanation for his controversial opinions concerning the club's priorities. He said, "We have long since served our purpose in registering climbers who aspire to and eventually complete their jaunts over the Forty-six." Instead of focusing on the accomplishments of individual climbers, he felt that the club should continue to build on its existing trail work and educational efforts and develop other conservation projects. He pointed to the destruction of the once pristine route along the sides of the old slide on Seymour, "the labyrinth of herdpaths between Nye and Street" and "the development of 'Times Square' on the Santanoni/Panther Ridge" as evidence of "what, in large measure, the focus of Forty-sixing has done."[133]

Tim suggested that the 46ers again "redefine" its mission – as the club had done in the early 1970s – away from "an organization which, directly or indirectly, promotes the climbing of a rather limited number of fragile peaks on a small number of ridges just so individuals can call themselves Forty-Sixers and don emblems which declare that accomplishment."[134] While he didn't actually call for the club to disband as had been proposed in previous years, his recommendations did suggest that the club abandon its original purpose – the climbing of the Adirondack 46.

Tefft's message in *Peeks* elicited a wide range of responses. There seemed to be universal concern over the environmental impact of climbing the 46 but disagreement as to what could be done to mitigate the damage. Some members adamantly opposed the notion of disbanding the club and were equally against removing the canisters. Others thought the club's educational and conservation programs had become such major contributors to the ultimate health of the region that ceasing to register climbers would put those programs in jeopardy. Trailmaster Len Grubbs, responded, "Our challenge is not to disband but to continue to grow while encouraging more member participation. We need greater member involvement in our activities so we can harness their ideas, their muscle, their organizational and leadership skills for the preservation of the Adirondacks... A decade hence, I certainly hope a strong, active, committed Forty-Sixer organization exists to welcome my granddaughter and celebrate her membership, if she is so inclined."[135]

Michael Becker (#1889W) also objected to the notion of disbanding and questioned whether "the 46er volunteer base would remain strong for very long with no new members being recognized ..."[136]

On the issue of the canisters, some agreed with Tefft and thought that the club should remove them as a symbol of its dedication to maintaining the wilderness. Jim Poulette (#2729) said, "As a statement of their concern for the protection, future, and wild character of the Adirondacks, the 46ers, in a highly visible and organized manner, should simultaneously dismantle and remove the 20 canisters which they placed on the untrailed summits some years ago. It would represent one of the most significant conservation projects that the 46ers have ever undertaken and would be consistent with the club's objectives of environmental protection and education."[137]

However, a majority of members thought the canisters should stay. Most of the comments in support of the summit registers centered on tradition – the sense of community that the canisters fostered, the anticipation followed by the feeling of accomplishment when finally locating the canister after a long, difficult hike. Others noted that it was simply enjoyable to read the comments left by previous hikers in the logbooks and to add their own thoughts and feelings about their climbs. Greg Davis (#3671) praised the canisters for both their communal and practical purpose. He said, "The canisters provide camaraderie for hikers even if they are alone and are a good marker that you are actually on the peak. This is a good safety feature for a mountain such as Nye with no distinct top."[138] Stephen F. Pecsek (#3517) argued that blaming the canisters for multiple herdpaths was like throwing the baby out with the bathwater. If the main concern was trail erosion on the trailless peaks, then he posed, "what we should perhaps be considering instead of eliminating canisters is replacing the erosion creating herdpaths with well designed trails." He added, "I think dismantling the canisters could lead to a dismantling of the 46er organization which would be much more destructive than herdpath erosion."[139]

Recognizing that he was out of sync with the opinions of the majority, Tim Tefft stepped down as president after serving only one year. Phil Corell, who had previously served as president, from 1981 to 1984, assumed the leadership position.

The merits of Tim's call for discontinuing the registration of 46ers was given a brief, cursory review by the executive committee and quickly rejected. However, the future of the canisters remained a topic of major concern. The "Boulder Report" in the Spring/Summer 1998 issue of *Peeks* mentioned that someone had stolen the canisters on the Dixes, leaving mangled metal brackets and broken treetops. That news prompted another round of discussions on the disposition of the canisters and the goals of the club in general. It wasn't clear whether the vandalism was an act of rebellion against the canisters being on the trailless peaks or an attempt to secure them as souvenirs. Since the club had not changed its position on the canisters, the missing ones were replaced.

Regardless of the strong support for the canisters, there was no denying that the HPUMP called for their removal. With the final approval of the plan expected soon, the issue was not going to fade away. Anticipating the inevitable, the club shifted its discussions to the ramifications of the canisters' eventual removal. For the most part there was little concern that hikers would revert to the undesirable practice of placing their own individual markers on the trailless summits – one of the main reasons the canisters were originally placed on the peaks – if the canisters were removed. Efforts to educate hikers on the "leave no trace" wilderness ethic had been successful. Most hikers followed the maxim "Take only pictures; leave only footprints." However, on several of the trailless peaks with wooded summits, the canisters served the additional purpose of marking the true summit. Club members were concerned that removing the canisters would result in damage to summit areas as hikers criss-crossed the top to make sure they had reached the highpoint. There was a general feeling that if the canisters had to go, they should be replaced with some kind of small marker to designate the true summit. The Trailmasters discussed that concern with the DEC and attempted to negotiate a suitable replacement for the canisters. Until that issue was resolved, the 46ers were reluctant to consider removing them.

With the HPUMP poised for imminent approval, the club renewed its message of conservation in a continuing effort to become part of the solution to the overuse issues of the High Peaks instead of part of the problem. As they had back in the early 1970s and most recently with Tim Tefft's message, the club wrestled with the question of whether the quest for a 46er patch was swelling the hiking ranks to numbers that were detrimental to the region. *Peeks* included several reminders to all climbers that the real work of mountain stewardship was the responsibility of everyone who hiked in the High Peaks. The club urged climbers to be vigilant in their practice of low impact camping and hiking and to educate and encourage others to follow those principles. Climbers were reminded to refrain from placing anything on the summits in the High Peaks or elsewhere and to resist the temptation to mark herdpaths or bushwhack routes. The club also encouraged those who had completed the 46 to expand their personal hiking adventures beyond the high traffic areas. As frequent users of the High Peaks wilderness, all 46ers and those who aspired to membership were challenged to take the lead in mountain stewardship to ensure that the pleasures experienced in the mountains would be available to hikers for generations to come.

On June 18, 1999, the inevitable occurred. The state released the final version of the HPUMP. It included the recommendations for the rehabilitation of the herdpaths on the trailless peaks – work that was already underway – and the removal of the canisters from the summits. Despite its final adoption, the DEC did not press the 46ers for the immediate removal of the canisters as they had not yet made a decision on the club's request for replacement markers. The department's position was that the canisters could be removed as each trailless peak herdpath was rehabilitated. However, a growing number of 46ers felt that the club should take a proactive approach by immediately and voluntarily removing the canisters to demonstrate a true commitment to stewardship of the High Peaks. Additional vandalism of the canisters added to the club's quandary over their future.

Internal Organizational Change

By the end of 1990 there were 2,859 registered 46ers, an increase of more than 1,200 over the previous decade. The historian's correspondence files were bursting at the seams as hikers continued writing in to register their climbs.

During the fall 1990 meeting, the executive committee decided that it was time for the club to enter the computer age and purchase a computer for Executive Secretary/Treasurer Ditt Dittmar. A computer would facilitate Ditt's work with such tasks as maintaining the roster of hikers and climbing numbers, organizing the club's mailing list, generating mailing labels, and recording dues payments. While Ditt was not wildly enthusiastic about computerizing his records, he was excited about the possibility of streamlining a number of his responsibilities.

In the spring of 1991 the club received an IBM PC and printer donated from IBM's Fund for Community Service with the help of recording secretary Mark Turner (#2024), an IBM employee. So, at the age of 76, Ditt embraced the world of computers with the same vigor as he had hiking. With an introductory computer course and some additional assistance to set up a menu-driven system, he quickly made good use of his new electronic assistant.

Providing appropriate assistance for Club Historian Grace Hudowalski presented a different set of challenges. She was not interested in entering the computer age. In 1991, Grace wrote 1,600 individual letters to climbers on her portable electric typewriter. Despite the volume, she did not want to learn how to use a computer, nor did she want to upgrade her typewriter. She also rejected the notion of using form letters to reduce the strain, preferring instead to maintain her personal touch. Her single-minded dedication to her responsibilities did not alter the fact that the workload for the position of club historian had reached a level beyond the capability of one person. In addition to recognizing the work overload, several members of the executive committee began to realize that no one had enough knowledge of what Grace actually did and how she did it to assume the role if she were suddenly unable to carry out her work. Ditt had prepared his own manual that outlined 37 separate duties and the procedures to accomplish them. That document provided the bulk of the information necessary for someone to take over his responsibilities, but Grace's organizational structure was known only to her.

With a sense of deep reluctance and anxiety, members of the executive committee slowly began to discuss not only ways to ease Grace's workload but also the need to document the duties of her position. Out of respect for all that she had done for the club, members of the executive committee were hesitant to suggest the notion of "retirement" to Grace or the need to plan for an eventual transition. Maintaining the records of those climbing the Forty-six had been as vital to her life as eating and breathing. Many felt that it was, in fact, her focus on the mountains that was responsible for her longevity and mental acuity.

Grace approached the inevitability of change with quiet ambivalence. On the one hand, she was loath to admit that quite apart from her advancing years, she was no longer able to handle the workload by herself. On the other hand, she recognized that she would not be the club historian forever. To ensure that the long tradition of registering those who had climbed the 46 continued, she knew that it was in the best interest of the club for her to document her duties to provide a compass for her eventual successors.

In his President's Message in the Fall/Winter 1992-93 issue of *Peeks*, Tim Tefft solicited help for Grace. He first asked for volunteers who would be willing to meet with her "to see and experience first hand what it is she does and then to recommend to the officers and directors what can be done to relieve or assuage her burdens... without the disrupting or upsetting of her routines."[140] In response to that request, five volunteers – Mike Becker, Suzanne Lance, Tom Lee, George Sloan, and Devon Taylor – came forward to form the "Grace Committee." Committee members met with Grace on several occasions to document her responsiblities and assess her need.

The Grace Committee's report came as no surprise when the group presented its findings and recommendations at the 1993 spring executive committee meeting. The committee concluded that because of the growth of the club over the years and the increase in the numbers of people climbing the 46, the duties of the Historian could no longer be managed by one person – regardless of age. The committee suggested that the club adopt a team approach to the Office of the Historian, regarding it as a department with the position of Historian at its head and a staff of volunteers, each of whom would take over a small portion of the job. Several 46ers were already assisting Grace with various tasks. Edward Bunk (#3052W) maintained and replaced the summit canisters and Marilyn Corson (#2686) coordinated the replacement of the log books. For years Helen Menz (#42) had helped Grace assign climbing numbers for those who had finished the 46 each year. Michael Becker prepared the "Peeks Sketches" report for *Peeks,* which provided a statistical summary along with some interesting tidbits from each year's finishers. Grace often called upon Fred

Helen Colyer Menz, left, and Mary Colyer Dittmar on Cascade in 1934

Johnson, Edythe Robbins (#2197) and Charles "Chuck" Bennett (#1934) for help on individual projects such as researching answers to hikers' questions and compiling trailless peak usage numbers. Beyond those jobs, the Grace Committee identified several additional tasks that could be managed by one or more volunteers. Those included preparing the agendas and vesper services for the annual meetings, printing the Certificates of Accomplishment, providing general office assistance, and answering correspondence during the peak hiking/reporting seasons. They also recommended that the executive committee appoint an Assistant Historian to work closely with Grace to learn the duties and procedures of the office.

With specific tasks identified, the club solicited volunteers to assist with the duties. As volunteers came forward to fill the "staff" positions for the Office of the Historian, George Sloan coordinated their work schedules and matched skills and time commitments with various tasks so Grace wouldn't be bogged down with yet another responsibility. As part of their work the Grace Committee had created an 11-page office procedure reference manual which proved to be a very valuable resource for the volunteers.

A number of 46ers answered the call to ease Grace's workload. Marilee Urbanczyk (#3530) and George Sloan prepared the Certificates of Accomplishment for new 46ers. Marilee, along with her husband Joe Urbanczyk, also prepared the vesper services for the annual meetings. Mindaugus "Mindy" Jatulis (#2383) and his wife Linnea, N. Clark (#103W) and Mildred "Millie" Gittinger (#3331), Anton "Tony" Solomon (#3626W), and Jane Nye (#4142) provided general office assistance. Joseph Busch (#3814) prepared a database to manage the assigning of climbing numbers, and Michael Gebhard (#3633) and Mindy Jatulis began answering the bulk of hiker correspondence. Mindy also accepted the responsibility of heading the Office of the Historian. Grace continued to write to young climbers and to send the congratulatory letters to hikers when they reported finishing the 46.

The most time consuming and labor intensive aspect of the job of historian was answering climber correspondence. It was also universally recognized by the Grace Committee and the executive committee to be the most important. When looking for ways to reduce Grace's workload, the club discussed minimizing the personal contact with those climbing the 46 by de-emphasizing letter writing. However, the executive committee, like Grace, believed that it was the correspondence that made the 46ers unique among hiking clubs. The personal contact added to the sense of community among 46ers and offered opportunities to educate hikers and share club news. It also provided a mechanism to monitor hiker activity and trail conditions. Everyone was committed to continuing the tradition of personal correspondence with hikers.

As George Sloan, vice president of the club at the time, said regarding the overwhelming number of letters sent in by aspiring hikers: "We could do what other clubs do – create form letters, or maybe just write back to the climber when he or she is finished… What makes this club different and better is the personal correspondence. The aspiring climber connects with someone who wants to listen and who is willing to give advice and encouragement for the achievement of the 46 peaks."[141]

Many hikers expressed the same sentiment. Alan Robert Kapitzke (#4197) of Higganum, CT, noted in one of his letters: "Writing is something I do not do often but I'm glad the club asks this of people. Many memories fade but now I have (my own and your) letters to reflect on."

It turned out that the 46ers were not the only ones interested in the tradition of hiker correspondence. The sheer volume of climbers' folders was becoming a storage dilemma for Grace, who had maintained and safeguarded the 46er records in her home for more than 60 years. She contacted James Corsaro, the associate librarian at the New York State Library in Albany, to ask if the library would be interested in being a repository for the 46ers' files. Corsaro was eager to add all of the hiker files and climbing folders to the archives. The library viewed the collection as offering unique historical and personal perspectives on the Adirondack High Peaks. The files, which were transferred to the New York State Library Manuscripts and Special Collection in the spring of 1997, filled 65 boxes, or 30 cubic feet, and the individual questionnaires filled an additional 17 boxes. The climber folders of new Forty-Sixers are now transferred to the State Library annually and are available for researchers and the general public to view.

With arrangements made for the disposition of the 46er files and an initial group of volunteers assuming many of her responsibilities, Grace announced her plan to give herself a 90th birthday present by officially retiring as club Historian in 1996. Her announcement had the unforeseen effect of actually increasing her workload. Hikers working on the 46 accelerated their climbing in order to finish while Grace was still Historian. Additional volunteers were sought to assist with the correspondence to aspiring hikers.

As of spring 1997 the mailing address for the 46ers changed from Grace's personal residences to P. O. Box 9046 in Schenectady, NY, symbolizing the operational transition in the Office of the Historian. When Grace's declining health forced her to move into an assisted living residence, the club lost its unofficial "office." L. John Van Norden offered the club space in his law office in Schenectady. All of the current files and equipment were moved there, and volunteers established the space as the 46ers' official headquarters. For the first time since it appeared in the Fall/Winter 1981-82 issue of *Peeks*, the "Boulder Report" in the Spring/Summer 1997 issue was not penned by Grace, as her retirement was all but complete. L. John Van Norden composed the report for several issues before Mindy Jatulis took on the task of compiling the popular summary of hikers' adventures. In the summer of 1998 Mindy turned over the administrative duties of the Office of the Historian to Tony Solomon and Jane Nye, but he remained as one of the main correspondents.

In addition to the personnel and organizational changes within the Office of the Historian, the club also initiated an effort in the fall of 1995 to computerize all 46er records so they could be shared with various club officials. Jan Coffin (#4383), Adella Lamb (#4384), and Barbara Relles (#3745) formulated a database for club records. Jan tackled the enormous task of inputting all of the data from the climbing folders of the more than 3,800 recorded 46ers.

Technological initiatives continued with the development of a website – http://www.adk46r.org – which went online in the spring of 1997. Originally designed and maintained by Alan Ratcliff (#1129) the website contains information on club history, photos of the High Peaks, notices of club events, and links to other hiking-related sites.

Winter Recognition

The 46ers of the 1940s and 1950s speculated that someday an ambitious hiker would earn 46er status by climbing all the peaks in winter. Kay Flickinger, an avid winter mountaineer, concluded her chapter in the first 46er book by saying, " ...it is entirely feasible that in time there may be an occasional winter Forty-Sixer on the roster."[142]

Grace on the porch at Boulders

Climbers had been venturing into the High Peaks during the winter months dating back to the 1890s. In March of 1893 Benjamin Pond and John Otis made a successful ascent of Mt. Marcy after they had been snowshoeing in the Upper Ausable Lake area.[143] During the 1920s and 1930s climbers made it to the summits of Haystack, Giant, Algonquin, Gothics, Whiteface, the Great Range, Nye, Colden, Big Slide, Iroquois, Porter, and Cascade in the winter months. Several college outing clubs participated in winter climbing competitions, venturing to the summits of many of the less accessible trailless peaks in the late 1940s and 1950s. In the 1950s the ADK Winter Activities Committee established the "V-Badge," which was earned by climbing five High Peaks in the winter. By the late 1950s several people had recorded climbing more than 20 High Peaks during the winter season.[144]

The first person to record a complete round of the 46 in winter was Edgar B. Bean, who finished on Blake on March 10, 1962. His first winter climb was Cascade and Porter on February 27, 1954. James W. F. Collins, who climbed many peaks with Bean, was the second to complete the 46 in winter, finishing on March 16, 1963, on Panther. The first woman to climb a winter round was Elsie Chrenko (#766W), who finished on Seymour on March 10, 1973. She and her husband Richard (#118W), who had finished on March 18, 1971, were the first husband and wife couple to climb all 46 in winter.

Many hikers who were already 46ers looked to continue their 46er experience by taking on the challenge of hiking to all of the summits again in winter. By the 1980s the availability of specialized equipment and clothing made the goal a bit more comfortable, if not any easier, for those winter season aspirants, and more and more hikers began to witness first hand the demands and rewards of winter hiking. Compared to the numbers of people who complete the 46 during the spring, summer, and fall months, it is still a relatively rare feat for someone to climb them all in the winter, but the number of winter enthusiasts is growing. In 1969 only five people had completed a winter round. By 1991 ninety-five persons were registered Winter 46ers, and by 1995, one hundred thirty-five. As of the winter of 2009-2010, four hundred seventy-one climbers claim Winter 46 status.

Hikers testing their resolve in the extreme conditions of mountain winters to climb the 46 thought that their efforts deserved special recognition. The executive committee appointed a committee made up of William Embler (#2308) chairman, Robert Helenek (#1483), and John Wiley (#1756W) to study winter recognition. The committee presented the pros and cons of offering special recognition to winter climbers to the executive committee at the fall 1989 meeting. They also suggested several possibilities for appropriate recognition of those who achieved status as Winter Forty-Sixers.

Chief among the executive committee's concerns in rewarding winter climbers was the higher level of risk inherent in winter mountaineering. The club did not want to promote or encourage an activity that involved life-threatening hazards by rewarding those who chose to hike in winter. Of additional concern to the executive committee, as well as other hikers, were several questionable practices that some winter hikers resorted to on their quest to achieve their goal. One of the problems that winter hikers faced was locating the canisters on the summits of the trailless peaks. They were often buried under several feet of snow. Trying to find a summit marker in order to make sure they had actually reached the high point and to record their ascent was often an arduous and time-consuming task. Some winter climbers reverted to the old unacceptable practice of leaving notes in plastic bags tied to a tree on what they thought was the summit, to verify their climb when they failed to locate the canister. Other winter hikers would climb a peak in the late fall before the heavy snows to tie a ribbon or piece of surveyor's tape to the top of the tree to which the canister was attached so they could more easily find it upon their return later in the winter season. Some took to marking routes on the trailless peak herdpaths to facilitate their winter navigation. Those practices were an affront to the wilderness ethic that the club purported to embrace and helped to perpetuate the image of 46ers as self-absorbed "peak-baggers." Concerned with issues of hiker safety and the questionable practices of some winter hikers, the executive committee voted against providing any form of special recognition for winter 46ers.

As would be expected, persistence is a quality necessary for anyone aspiring to climb the 46 in winter. A number of the winter climbers, unhappy with the executive committee's decision, used that never-say-die attitude to continue their lobbying efforts for winter recognition. In 1990 a group of winter 46ers who instituted a letter-writing campaign to then 46er President June Behr encouraged the executive committee to reconsider its decision regarding winter recognition. In an effort to poll the general membership about the issue, the executive committee asked the Trailmasters to prepare a special questionnaire outlining the arguments for and against winter recognition in order to solicit feedback on the subject. The survey included several brief statements outlining the opposing viewpoints along with a series of suggestions for appropriate acknowledgment.

The arguments for recognition pointed to the fact that other hiking clubs such as the Catskill 3500 Club and the Northeast 111 offered special awards for those hiking in winter. It was also noted that winter climbing required specialized equipment and a greater level of preparation, planning, and effort. Proponents of winter recognition argued, "Recognizing winter 46ers would allow the club to take the lead in promoting safe winter hiking practices."

The arguments against formal recognition reasoned that climbing the 46 in any season was an accomplishment and that each season had its own unique set of equipment needs and challenges to overcome. In an attempt to add some levity to the debate, one club member suggested that the infamous Adirondack black fly season was infinitely more challenging than the most severe winter conditions. "Equality of recognition" was also highlighted as one of the unique and special attributes of 46ing. It was feared that offering unique recognition for hiking in winter would set "those 46ers apart from the others, implying that climbing the

46 in winter is somehow, better, more worthy, more of an accomplishment." Opponents to winter recognition also argued that winter climbing is inherently more dangerous than climbing in the other three seasons and that the club should not put itself in the position of sanctioning winter hiking to satisfy patch collectors.

The survey results from 603 responses showed that 64 percent supported some minimal recognition for those completing the 46 in winter; 27 percent believed that special recognition was not necessary. Responding to the wishes of the majority of club members who had expressed an opinion, the executive committee reversed its original decision and voted to recognize those who had climbed all of the 46 in winter with a "W" after their numbers in future rosters and listings. The committee further authorized the creation of a special patch that would be made available to those who had completed a winter round. However, no separate series of numbers indicating the order of finish for the winter 46 would be maintained. Bill Embler and John Wiley designed a simple white and ice blue – colors appropriate to the season – rocker patch with the words "Winter 46er" that could be placed under the regular round 46er patch.

In the late 1990s, in an attempt to eliminate some of the questionable practices of the winter climbers, the Office of the Historian issued a ruling that it was not necessary to sign the canister on the trailless peaks in order to receive credit for a climb. Just as reporting climbs on trailed peaks was done on the honor system, so, too, would climbs of the trailless peaks be accepted by one's word. If in all good faith a climber thought he or she had been on a summit, then that was all that was necessary to record a winter ascent.

Through the years, Winter 46ers and aspiring winter climbers have developed their own fraternity. An informal communications network kicks into high gear during the winter months to keep winter hiking enthusiasts informed about trail conditions and upcoming trips. Winter hikers also organized a gathering at the close of the 1998 winter season to swap stories and make plans for the next winter season. This has become an annual event usually scheduled for the first weekend after the official end of winter.

Celebrations

The 46ers celebrated a number of significant milestones and accomplishments throughout the 1990s, the first of which was the publication of its third book, *Of the Summits, of the Forests,* in June 1991. Six years previously John Nicoll (#1506), Phil Corell, Sharp Swan, and William Kozel hatched the notion of creating a new 46er book. Kozel, a photographer and frequent contributor of articles to *Peeks,* took on the general responsibilities of editor, organizing and conceptualizing the book, finding contributors, editing copy, soliciting artwork, and gathering and selecting photographs. Kozel had completed work on about two-thirds of the new book when he suffered significant injuries in a serious accident, which halted his progress with the book. Tim Tefft took over as editor to complete the project.

The new book was printed and available for sale to members in the fall of 1991. *Of the Summits, of the Forests* took its name from the lyrics of the song *Tahawus,* which was written by Orra Phelps and sung at each vesper service. The book contained information on a wide range of Adirondack topics within its 352 pages. Chapters included profiles of the 46 High Peaks, a history of the club, essays on hiking and the special lure of the region, legends of the Adirondacks, winter mountaineering, and regional geology, zoology, botany, and meteorology. It also contained a complete roster of the 2,859 club members at the time, a section of historic black-and-white photos, a number of stunning recent color photos, pen and ink artwork by Jeaneen Dumers (#2649) and Ann Palen (#2802), and endsheets of a watercolor reproduction, *On Mount Jo,* by John L. Turner (#2102). In a letter to Ditt Dittmar,

George Marshall, who was writing from London, England, where he was residing at the time, called *Of the Summits, of the Forests* "one of the best 46er publications and a splendid addition to Adirondack Literature."[145]

As a tribute to its name and the 46 mountains, the club's executive committee decided to deviate from the traditional 50th year anniversary celebration and instead recognize 46 years of club history. On Sunday September 4, 1994, at the Holiday Inn SunSpree Resort in Lake Placid the club celebrated its 46th anniversary. The theme of the event, "Adirondack 46ers: Hiking Partners, Mountain Stewards" was chosen to highlight hiking as the common bond among members as well as the club's service emphasis on conservation education and environmental protection. The anniversary celebration included a dinner and a program that focused on the club's climbing history and its dedication to "giving something back to the mountains." Special presentations were made to honor several members who had played major roles in the club's founding and development. Phil Corell presented a memorial to Glenn Fish, under whose leadership the club shifted its focus to education and conservation. Ditt Dittmar made a presentation to honor George Marshall (in absentia). Tim Tefft honored Ed Ketchledge for his years of research and remedial action to protect the alpine environment of the High Peaks. Bill Kozel offered a tribute to Executive Secretary/Treasurer Ditt Dittmar, and Ed Bunk (#3052W) presented a testimonial to club Historian Grace Hudowalski. Chris G. Behr honored Jim Goodwin with a special award in appreciation for his years of service as the club's first Trailmaster. Tim Tefft also read a note congratulating the 46ers on the occasion of their 46th anniversary. It came from the White House and was signed by President Bill Clinton.

Dr. Ed Ketchledge greeting summit reseeding volunteers

Adirondack musicians and songwriters Dan Berggren and Peggy Eyres provided entertainment. A video produced by Tim Tefft, *The Adirondack 46: People and Places,* which featured footage of all 46 peaks and many of the service activities of the club, was screened, and a commemorative envelope with a specially designed stamp cancellation was given to the 550 people who attended the event.

The May 25, 1996, spring meeting was again held at the Holiday Inn in Lake Placid as the club hosted a surprise birthday party for Grace, who had turned 90 in February. To keep the celebration a surprise, members went to the extreme of preparing a special spring meeting notice to mail to Grace that eliminated any mention of the event. The rest of the membership received an invitation to the celebration. Members submitted hand-made birthday cards, photos, poems, and thank you notes for all her efforts on behalf of the club, as well as acknowledgments in appreciation of her personal support and friendship. Those were compiled into a commemorative album. More than 500 people attended the birthday party.

As a result of the success of the 46th anniversary and Grace's birthday celebration, the executive committee considered holding the spring meetings at a large hotel in Lake Placid on a regular basis. The spring meeting, which was generally more widely attended than the fall meeting, had outgrown the Keene Central School. With 300 dinner reservations for the

May 23, 1992, spring meeting, the club had reached the capacity of the Keene Central School's facility and was forced to turn away 36 people. Some executive committee members were concerned that the increased cost involved with holding the meetings at a hotel might discourage some members from attending, but others felt that the extra cost was not extravagant and that the change was necessary in order to accommodate the growth in membership.

In the summer of 1997 a group of 46ers organized a special celebration to commemorate the 60th anniversary of Grace's completion of the 46 on Esther on August 26, 1937. More than 80 participants attempted to summit all 46 peaks simultaneously between noon and 1 p.m. on August 26, 1997. The celebrants reached the peaks of 44 of the 46, with Emmons and Donaldson the only ones that weren't climbed. Joyous shouts, bells, and whistles echoed throughout the High Peaks as those who participated conducted celebrations on their respective summits in homage to Grace. John Lange (#3883W), who climbed East Dix, draped red, green, and yellow – 46er colors – streamers all over the summit and secured a pole on the highest point that sported the same color balloons. (He cleared all the decorations from the summit when he left, of course.) Grace herself participated in the celebration. Tony Solomon and Jane Nye drove her to the summit parking area on Whiteface, and she proceeded to climb the last quarter-mile to the summit instead of taking the elevator. A television crew from Plattsburgh met Grace at the peak and interviewed her. All climbers met back at Boulders to share the stories of their hikes and celebrate with their mentor.

Other notable milestones during the 1990s included the 25th anniversary of the Outdoor Leadership Workshop in the spring of 1996, and the 20th year of the club's trail maintenance program. Both represented the 46ers' continuing commitment to education and protecting the magnificent natural resources within the High Peaks region. The milestones were also a tribute to the club's dedicated volunteers who provided the leadership, inspiration, and perspiration to implement those important and worthwhile programs. At the fall meeting on October 10, 1998, the club acknowledged its 50th anniversary with a cake made especially for the occasion.

Adirondack 46R Conservation Trust

With a desire to leave a lasting legacy to the High Peaks and with some concern that the club might seriously consider Tim Tefft's suggestion to stop registering climbers, Grace Hudowalski established the Adirondack 46R Conservation Trust in 1995. Created for charitable and educational purposes, the trust's primary focus is "to provide financial assistance necessary to continue the activities, duties and responsibilities" of the 46ers' Office of the Historian, including "maintaining of files for aspiring Forty-Sixers, correspondence to aspiring Forty-Sixers, and/or maintenance of membership records and other materials, documents, and property of historical significance..."[146]

Beyond the specific mandate to support the continuation of Grace's work as club historian to which she had devoted a significant portion of her life, the trust was also charged with preserving the "forever wild" character of the Adirondack High Peaks through education and conservation. The trust became a public expression of Grace's passionate love for the region, with the "express purpose and intent... to encourage, advance and promote the responsible use, development and management of those lands commonly known and designated as the 'Adirondack Park' ...and to aid, advance and promote the conservation and preservation of that portion of the New York State Forest Preserve situate within the said 'Adirondack Park' as wild forest lands consistent with the spirit and intent of Article XIV of the New York State Constitution."[147]

Managed by Grace's long-time friend and personal advisor Trustee L. John Van Norden and an advisory board of 46ers, the trust is authorized to grant financial support to activities that advance its stated goals.

Since its inception, the trust has provided funding for the operation of the 46ers' Office of the Historian and trail maintenance program. The trust has also supported requests for funding from ATIS to assist with their trail clearing efforts following Hurricane Floyd, and YMCA Camp Chingachgook to support the building of a Hike and Trip Center to serve as a year-round classroom to teach young people skills in leadership, trip planning, environmental conservation, map and compass, and low impact camping. The trust also helped to fund a study by the Residents' Committee to Protect the Adirondacks on illegal ATV usage within the Forest Preserve and a black bear education awareness research program sponsored by the Wildlife Conservation Society aimed at minimizing encounters between humans and black bears in the Adirondack backcountry.

The trust's priority has been to provide a significant portion of the funding for the Summit Steward Program, which was initiated by Dr. Edwin Ketchledge in 1989 as an outgrowth of his efforts to restore alpine habitats. The program places trained educators on the busiest summits – Marcy, Algonquin, Colden, Haystack, and Wright – during the summer months to inform the hiking public on ways to protect the fragile alpine habitats on the high summits. The Summit Steward Program has been successful in educating tens of thousands of hikers about the unique alpine environment and simple things they can do while hiking to protect the fragile plants. To ensure the continuation of the program the trust spearheaded an effort to create a permanent endowment to fund it. Named the "Edwin Ketchledge Summit Steward Endowment," it is both a tribute to Ketchledge's tireless work on behalf of the high summits and an investment in preserving a precious part of the state's natural history.

The Adirondack 46R Conservation Trust held a major fund-raiser in conjunction with the spring 2000 meeting on Sunday May 28, 2000, auctioning vintage and historic Adirondack books and memorabilia from the collection of Grace Hudowalski.

Part VI: The 2000s – Looking Toward the Future

Continued membership growth, leadership transitions, and the HPUMP's new regulations created major challenges for the club as it entered the twenty-first century. In response to the challenges, the Forty-Sixers approached the new millennium with a commitment to maintain its organizational priorities while strengthening its stewardship and educational programs. In concert with the state the club was intent on continuing to offer support and solutions toward minimizing wilderness degradation within the High Peaks. The first years of the decade also saw a final resolution of the canister debate, an issue which had been the topic of more discussions, letters, and opinion surveys, and had stimulated more passion, frustration, criticism, negative publicity, bad feelings, and downright hostility than any other issue throughout the club's history.

Long Range Planning

To help set club policy and respond to the changing environment, the executive committee appointed a Long Range Planning Committee (LRPC). Members included Jan Coffin, Phil

Corell, Adella Lamb, Jane Nye, Martha Precheur (#3316), Mary Lou Recor (#2214W), Patti Schwankert (#4445W), George Sloan, Tony Solomon, Joe Urbanczyk, and L. John Van Norden. The committee's mission was to review the club's existing programs and assess what impact the HPUMP would have – not only on the club but also on recreational activities in the High Peaks in general – and make recommendations for appropriate action. The goal was to position the club as a partner with the DEC and other groups with similar interests to benefit the High Peaks region. To assist with its mission the LRPC developed a survey to solicit membership opinions on a number of important issues including the canisters, the location of meetings, membership requirements, ways to increase member participation, and suggestions for additional conservation and education projects.

Membership participation in the survey was overwhelming. The questionnaire was sent to the club's 3,300 active members and 1,226 of them responded. The LRPC presented a summary of the survey results along with its recommendations to the executive committee and general membership at the fall 2000 meeting.

The survey results pointed to some clear opinions held by a majority of members: 66% opposed the removal of the canisters; 55% supported a DEC recommendation to construct large cairns to mark the summits of the trailless peaks if the canisters were removed. An additional 18% presented a persuasive argument in favor of a small sign bearing the name of the peak as a more appropriate marker; 44% agreed that the club should change the location for the spring meeting to a large hotel in Lake Placid; 62% agreed that the fall meeting should remain at the Keene Central School; 48% opposed the addition of a service requirement for membership, with 35% supporting the notion.

Based on the results of the survey, the LRPC made the following recommendations to the executive committee:

• The club should request a variance from the HPUMP to retain and maintain the canisters on the trailless peaks. Should that request be rejected the club should recommend that the trailless summits be marked by a small sign instead of a cairn;

• The annual spring meeting should be held at a hotel in Lake Placid in order to accommodate the larger attendance at the spring gathering, and the fall meeting should continue to be held at Keene Central School;

• Service to the club should be encouraged but not required for membership; and

• The club should use the *Leave No Trace* brochure to educate hikers on principles of safe and responsible use of the wilderness, and initiate a "Trail Ambassador" program to train volunteers to interact with the public at trailheads and along the trails to reinforce the "leave no trace" philosophy.

In addition, the LRPC supported the continuation of the trail maintenance program, re-institution of the litter bag distribution project, expansion of the Outdoor Leadership Workshop, and improving the number and appeal of outhouses along the trail and at lean-to sites.

Canister Resolution

The survey results and the recommendations of the LRPC presented the executive committee with plenty of agenda items for discussion. The main topic at the fall 2000 meeting – as it had been at so many meetings – was the disposition of the canisters. Despite the overwhelming member support for the canisters' continued presence on the trailless peaks, several members of the executive committee expressed compelling reasons for their removal. Even though the DEC was not pressing the club to remove them, the canisters were in violation of state regulations. The club was in effect perpetuating its negative "peak bagger" image by failing to comply with the directive in the HPUMP for their removal.

While once a useful tool to mark the trailless peaks' true summits, verify climbs, and stop the proliferation of personal markers, the canisters and their log books had outlived their usefulness. The Office of the Historian no longer referred to them to verify climbs. With the dramatic increase in hiker traffic on the trailless peaks, the logbooks needed to be replaced two or three times a year, which presented an increasing logistical challenge for the club; and since paths on most of the trailless peaks were nearly as clear and easy to follow as the regular marked trails, the canisters were no longer an important safety factor. Voluntarily removing the canisters would represent a public demonstration of the club's stewardship commitment to the region.

The executive committee debate centered on whether the club should request a waiver from the DEC to exempt the canisters from non-conforming status or simply remove them. The Trailmasters had engaged the DEC in discussions since the original HPUMP called for the canisters' removal about how best to protect the summits of the trailless peaks once the canisters no longer marked the tops. Both the DEC and the 46ers were concerned that without markers of some sort hikers would destroy much of the fragile vegetation on the summits while looking for the highest point. That would run counter to the state's efforts to reduce the environmental impact on the trails in the High Peaks. The DEC had suggested that a large cairn be built on each summit to mark the high point. The 46ers objected to that proposal since significant damage to the environment would be necessary to "mine" rocks for the raw material to make the cairns. A cairn also would be of little help to winter hikers in locating the high points. Instead, the Trailmasters suggested a small sign as a more appropriate and useful summit marker.

The club was reluctant to remove the canisters until the issue of a replacement marker was resolved, and the DEC seemed in no hurry to make that decision. With no clear timetable for the removal of the canisters or plan from the DEC for a suitable replacement summit marker, the executive committee felt compelled to force the issue by recommending its own solution. After considerable discussion, the committee voted seven to two to support the removal of the canisters, replacing them with signs to mark the summits. It was not a vote to remove the canisters immediately. Instead it was a vote to enable the club to present its position to the DEC and negotiate a settlement. The executive committee also felt that by taking a proactive approach the club would maintain some control over the final disposition of the canisters. In 2000, in an attempt to clarify the state's position, the Trailmasters asked DEC liaison Supervising Forester Kristofer Alberga of the DEC's Division of Lands and Forests, Region 5, for a ruling.

Over the winter of 2000-2001 the DEC approved the club's proposal to replace the canisters with wooden signs which were painted brown with the mountain names in yellow letters. The DEC determined that no signs were necessary for the summits of Esther, South Dix, East Dix, and Hough since those peaks all had clearly discernible high points. With the DEC's approval of acceptable summit markers, the club's main objection to the canisters' removal was resolved. So, after emotional debates and much deliberation, the executive committee finally voted to remove the canisters from the summits of the trailless peaks and replace them with the signs provided by the DEC.

Even more controversial than the vote to remove the canisters was the executive committee's decision to withhold information of the decision from the general membership until after the replacements had been completed. There was a concern that souvenir hunters would help themselves to the canisters if the plan for their removal was announced in advance. Members of the executive committee completed the replacement on most of the summits during the June 23-24, 2001, weekend, and they replaced the others on the few remaining summits over the next two weeks.

As word of the canisters' removal became public, member reaction to the executive committee's decision was mixed. Those who wanted the canisters to remain on the summits felt that the club should have argued more passionately for their existence. Some felt betrayed by the decision and thought that the executive committee had ignored the opinions of a majority of the membership. Others were upset with the secrecy surrounding the decision. However, some members applauded the decision as being in the best interests of the mountains as well as the responsible response to the HPUMP mandate. Most quietly accepted the loss of the canisters with sad resignation and viewed their removal as a sign of the changing times. Regardless of member reaction, an issue that had vexed the club and had consumed countless hours of debate for 50 years – since the first canister was placed on Emmons on September 3, 1950 – had finally been put to rest.

An article in the Spring/Summer 2001 issue of *Peeks*[148] from President Barbara Harris (#2824W) on behalf of the executive committee, informed the membership of the decision and explained the rationale for it. Simply stated, it was made "in the best interest of the 46ers and, more importantly, of the High Peaks... As a club, the 46ers have embarked on a major effort to be responsible stewards of the lands in which our members spend so much time and to educate the public in 'leave no trace' principles. What better example can we give than this action, which expands our commitment to the High Peaks Wilderness?"

The notice explained the history of the canisters, their original purpose, the controversies that for years had surrounded their presence on the trailless peaks, and the state's call for their removal:

> From the beginning, the existence of the canisters has been a controversial issue with a long history of heated exchanges both from within the 46er organization and from outside sources. Opponents of the canisters voiced concern over their "magnetic attraction" to hikers who climbed the trailless peaks to write their name in the log books. Proponents pointed to a safety aspect of the canisters and that their existence has eliminated a litter problem which had previously existed.
>
> The state's call for removing the canisters began in 1972 with the first draft of the Adirondack Park State Land Master Plan and according to the plan the canisters along with other designated non-conforming structures in Wilderness Areas were to be removed by December 31, 1975. With the bureaucracy of the state the canisters got a 30 year reprieve... [The HPUMP, approved in June 1999], reiterated that the canisters be removed as non-conforming structures. While we may question this designation, we believe the 46ers have a responsibility to finally respond to the HPUMP. More importantly, we think we have a duty to set a positive example for stewardship of the High Peaks.[149]

The announcement in *Peeks* also pointed out the club's leadership role in successfully arguing for a small sign as a more appropriate and environmentally sound marker than a cairn as originally proposed by the state. The executive committee also responded to the criticism of the air of secrecy that surrounded their decision:

> The intent of the Executive Committee was to make the announcement of the canister removal and do the actual removal simultaneously. There was a concern that the canisters would become prizes for trophy hunters if the decision to remove them was announced too far in advance of the actual removal. The canisters are the property of the 46er club and the club deserved the right to decide their fate. As it turned out, the Executive Committee's concern was legitimate. Six canisters – those on Allen, Hough, MacNaughton, Macomb, Marshall, and South Dix – disappeared prior to their official removal.[150]

Harris concluded her article by soliciting hikers' cooperation in refraining from leaving bits of paper with their names on them to document their climbs of the trailless peaks as the early climbers had done. "Treat the untrailed summits as you do the trailed peaks. Continue to climb and enjoy these wonderful and special mountains, but 'leave no trace.'"[151]

In an effort to ease the disappointment over the loss of the canisters, the executive committee decided to offer for sale replicas of the white canisters fashioned from PVC pipe. Each would include the 46er emblem along with a bracket and nails for mounting on a wall or tree. Ed Bunk, who had fabricated the PVC versions that had replaced the original metal canisters, volunteered to make the replicas.[152] Edmund Scott (#627), Jeffrey Scott (#490), and James Pugh (#320) also offered to collect photos of each canister on their respective summits and design a poster that could be sold to members as a way to retain a part of 46er history.

Hiker Education

With the DEC's new emphasis on reducing the impact of hikers and campers in the High Peaks, the 46ers looked for ways to assist in educational efforts. In response to the LRPC's recommendation, the Office of the Historian decided to distribute the National Outdoor Leadership School's (NOLS) pamphlet, *Leave No Trace,* to hikers writing into the club for the first time. The pamphlet informed wildland users about the principles of minimum impact camping and hiking. It included useful tips and techniques on the basic principles of the "leave no trace" philosophy including trip planning and preparation, choosing a camping site, packing out garbage, proper disposal of human waste, and minimizing the use and impact of campfires. The Adirondack 46R Conservation Trust paid for a supply of the pamphlets.

While exploring additional avenues for educating trail users, the club realized that most, if not all, of the informational materials distributed by the DEC and other groups were in English. None of the material was in French to service the large numbers of French Canadians who frequented the High Peaks. Thus, the club decided to produce a new brochure in English and French similar to the *Leave No Trace* pamphlet, which would also include information on the new regulations on group size and camping restrictions specific to the High Peaks region. During the fall of 2001 Tim Tefft designed a new brochure entitled *Walk Softly* to replace both the *Leave No Trace* booklet and the club's old *Mountain Manners* pamphlet. The final English language version was ready for distribution in spring 2004. In addition, the club revised its climbing folder, which the correspondents send to all hikers to record their climbs, to reflect the new DEC day hiking and camping rules as well as the removal of the canisters.

To help promote safety and preparedness in the backwoods and increase the number of people who would be qualified to help in case of a medical emergency, the club offered a partial reimbursement of tuition costs for any member who completed an approved Wilderness First Aid course.

Celebrating its 30th year in the spring of 2001, the OLW continued to be the club's core education program. To acknowledge the milestone, President Barbara Harris presented the staff and participants with a commemorative anniversary cake as that year's workshop came to a close.

In the summer of 2000 the club was confronted with a different sort of challenge: that of publicly justifying its existence. The June issue of the *Adirondack Explorer* contained an article by Thomas R. Welch, M.D. criticizing the 46ers. He called for the club to close the books on further membership and disband. Dr. Welch reasoned that the club, by continuing to register hikers who had climbed the 46 High Peaks, was "…implicitly encouraging a 'do it-check it off' mentality more suited for Junior League initiation than for teaching appreciation of the wilderness. We are encouraging people to push into fragile environments for no real reason other than to say that they were there."

Believing that the time for such uninformed criticism of the 46ers was long past, the club went on the offensive to defend its record. President Barbara Harris, responded in a "Letter to the Editor" to the *Adirondack Explorer,* stressing the club's education and conservation programming record as well as the legacies left by the club's earliest members. She wrote, "Does anyone believe the Marshalls, Hudowalskis, and Dittmars are so well regarded just because they made it to the summits of the 46 highest mountains? Of course not. It's how they made their climbs, and what they did during and afterwards to protect and preserve our mountains. That is the legacy the 46ers celebrate and shall continue."[153]

Ed Ketchledge also submitted a rebuttal that the *Explorer* highlighted. Ketchledge felt that it was a perversion of logic to criticize the club when it displayed such a strong volunteer commitment to assisting the DEC with its preservation and educational programs within the High Peaks. He described his work to preserve the alpine summits and praised the 46ers as being his "…greatest allies, every summer sending their field parties out to designated locations, to alpine summits and to spruce/fir forest trails, to help repair and preserve the high country… We try to educate the climbing public after they have individually decided on their own to explore the high Adirondack wilderness. We believe it is more responsible to address a problem than to walk away from it."[154]

While defending itself against outside criticism, the club also engaged in some internal examination and reflection during the early 2000s. Members started to question two hiking trends that were receiving greater and greater attention. The club had a long history of paying homage to personal climbing achievements. The annual "Peeks Sketches" column in *Peeks* noted such categories as the youngest and oldest climber, who took the longest and shortest time to finish, husband/wife, father/son, mother/daughter duos, largest family, etc. In her "Boulder Report" Grace frequently highlighted climbing records, marathon-like hikes, and the accomplishment of personal hiking goals. However, for some time, an unofficial game of one-upmanship had been taking place in the High Peaks. A few hikers were engaged in setting personal records for such feats as climbing the 46 the fastest, being the youngest to finish, completing multiple rounds in all seasons and all months. Others found unique ways of approaching the 46, such as climbing them barefoot, and on nights with a full moon. Stories with a can-you-top-this mentality were creeping into *Peeks* as well as the local media, providing public recognition for those feats. Whatever the motivation for the displays of machismo hiking, the executive committee was concerned that the behaviors, especially when they attracted public attention, would impact negatively on the 46ers.

In the summer of 2002, a record-setting stunt reached epic proportion when self-proclaimed speed hiker and wandering adventurer Ted E. "Cave Dog" Keizer arrived in the Adirondacks. In September 2000 Keizer had smashed the speed record for climbing Colorado's 14,000-foot peaks by topping all 55 summits in ten days, 20 hours, and 26 minutes. In June of 2002 he turned his attention to the Northeast, summitting the 46 Adirondack 4,000-footers in three days, 18 hours, and 14 minutes between 4:15 a.m. on June 24 and 10:29 p.m. on June 27. While not in a position to stop the personal exhibitions and the publicity they garnered, the club wanted to make a statement that climbing for the express purpose of setting records did not represent the true spirit of the 46ers and that club policy was not to promote or reward the climbing-to-set-records mentality. In the fall of 2004 the executive committee voted to revise the club's mission statement to reflect that position by adding: "While the club records climbing accomplishments, it does not advocate, collect, or publicize records involving time, number of rounds climbed, ages, or other arbitrary goals. The club encourages all to climb for personal satisfaction."[155]

The concern over record-setting also extended to one very specific area: that of young children climbing in winter with their sights – or their parents' sights – on achieving the distinction of becoming the youngest Winter 46ers. Considering the dangers inherent in winter climbing, the executive committee was concerned about children hiking in winter in general and certainly did not support children climbing in the winter months for the purpose of setting records. The executive committee felt is was necessary to share their concerns with parents. The following statement appeared in the Fall/Winter 2001-2002 issue of *Peeks* and on the website:

> The Forty-Sixers in no way supports nor promotes extreme winter climbing by children. The severe conditions and added challenges of winter travel can be dangerous and require thoughtful preparation and wise decision-making. We caution all parents to become knowledgeable and experienced winter climbers themselves before exposing their children to snow, ice and sub-freezing conditions. We urge those who do climb with their children in winter to plan trips conservatively and with the utmost care and caution.[156]

Contribution to Trailwork Expands

In the spring and summer of 2000 Forty-Sixer trail crews were back in the woods continuing to clear the Hurricane Floyd damage from their adopted trails in the Dix Range, particularly the Elk Lake trails that had been closed by the DEC. For the first time in many years, the number of hikers finishing the 46 decreased in 2000 due to the closure of several trails and summits that were rendered impassable by Floyd's fury. The trails reopened in 2001.

Work also continued on the rehabilitation of herdpaths on the trailless peaks with crews stabilizing the Marshall path on August 11, 2000. In 2002 trail crews rerouted a section of the Redfield herdpath, moving the route's first half mile away from Uphill Brook. The path's starting point was marked with a large cairn.

Recognizing that hikers would eventually recreate a maze of alternate routes without some minimal maintenance to keep the rehabilitated paths free of blowdown and wet areas, the Trailmasters proposed a Path Adopter Program to the DEC. The program would assign volunteers to perform minimal maintenance on the paths to keep them open and accessible. The program mirrored the ADK's lean-to adoption program through which volunteers conduct annual inspections and cleanup of lean-to sites throughout the Forest Preserve. The Trailmasters recommended that path adopters inspect the newly rehabilitated trailless peak paths twice a year, perform basic trail clearing and drainage, and report more serious problems to the Trailmasters.

In 2003 the DEC approved the Path Adopter Program for the wilderness paths and volunteers were assigned to inspect and provide routine maintenance for the paths on Tabletop, Marshall, Redfield, Street and Nye. Under the DEC's trail classification system, the rehabilitated trails on the trailless peaks were designated Class II trails, or "wilderness paths" to more adequately describe their status. Since the herdpaths to the trailless peaks in most cases had been well established for years, continuing to use the term "trailless" had long since become a misnomer.

Throughout the 2000s the 46ers continued their work on the trailless peaks. To eliminate a maze of paths around a wet, marshy section on the path to Esther, the club paid for and installed a 60-foot-long boardwalk that kept hikers' boots out of the quagmire between

Lookout Mountain and the ridge leading to Esther. The herdpath ascending Gray from Lake Tear-of-the-Clouds was sound and required only minor attention. Traces of a route leading from Gray's summit to Marcy were closed off and the cairns marking the route above treeline were removed to discourage hiker traffic over that environmentally sensitive area. Macomb, which needed extensive blowdown clearing and a reroute to move the trail away from a streambed, was completed in 2005.

In 2007 the beginning of Cliff's path was relocated a few hundred yards up the Redfield route. Temporary flagging was added to lead hikers above an extremely wet, muddy section to rejoin Cliff's established herdpath.

Volunteer trail adopters worked on the various herdpaths in the Slide Brook/Lillian Brook area that offered access to the trailless Dixes. By the end of 2007 all of the herdpaths in that area had been cleared of major blowdown and false paths had been closed off.

With the trails in the Santanonis needing very little rehabilitation, the remaining challenge will be relocating the paths on the upper slopes of Seward and Seymour. Those areas will require DEC approval for major path rerouting.

In the fall of 2002 the DEC formalized the trailwork arrangement it had had with the 46ers for more than 20 years with a contractual agreement, Adopt a Natural Resource. The contract officially assigned stewardship duties for a five-year period to the 46ers for regular maintenance of the trails in the Dix Mountain, Giant Mountain, and High Peaks Wilderness areas and the Wilmington Wild Forest.

In the spring of 2003 the DEC gave public recognition to the 46ers as well as to other participants in the Adopt a Natural Resource Program. The DEC placed signs at the Round Pond and Elk Lake trails to the Dixes and on the North Trail to Giant recognizing the 46ers' long-standing cooperative relationship with the DEC to provide maintenance on those trails.

With its own trail work program continuing its productive efforts, the trailless peak rehabilitation project proceeding successfully, and a healthy balance in the club's treasury, the executive committee sought other opportunities to assist with stewardship projects in the High Peaks. At the direction of the committee, Trailmaster Len Grubbs contacted Wes Lampman, the ADK's director of field programs, to explore possible joint trail work projects. As a result of those discussions the executive committee voted to contribute $3,000 to support the ADK's 2004 spring trail clearing program: a sweep of state trails in the Adirondak Loj area by the ADK's paid trail crew to clear the trails of any winter blowdown or water runoff damage.

In the fall of 2004 the executive committee voted to increase funding support for the ADK's spring 2005 trail sweep to $6,000, fully funding the cost of that work crew. An additional $8,000 was approved for major trail improvements on the Algonquin trail between Whale's Tail Notch and MacIntyre Falls. The work, accomplished by the ADK's professional work crew, included 49 new rock steps, seven rock bars, and 125 feet of drainage ditching.

In the spring of 2005 the club provided funding support of $8,843 toward the building of a bridge at Slide Brook in the Johns Brook Valley, a special Boy Scouts of America Eagle Project organized by Ian McMullen (#5115) in coordination with the DEC.

Just as the hiking community has had to adjust to the newly instituted DEC trails usage regulations, so, too, have the 46er Trailmasters had to adapt to the changing times. The bulk of the 46er trail maintenance efforts take place on the club's adopted trails in the Dix Mountain Wilderness and the Giant Mountain Wilderness Areas. With the final approvals of the Unit Management Plans for both those areas in January 2004, the Trailmasters have to be mindful of the new group size limits established in those areas: fifteen for day use and eight for overnight camping.

A Changing of the Guard

The retirement of Grace Hudowalski and the reorganization of the Office of the Historian were the first of several administrative challenges for the club at the beginning of the 2000s. A number of longtime 46ers chose the start of the new millennium to retire from their staff positions. The first to step down was the only Secretary/Treasurer the club had ever had, Ditt Dittmar. After 53 years of faithful service to the 46ers, following the spring 2001 annual meeting, Ditt retired from the post of Executive Secretary/Treasurer at the age of 86. With the ceremonial passing of the checkbook to Phil Corell, who had already assumed some of the duties of the position at the end of 2000, Ditt officially retired. The club held a surprise celebration to honor Ditt and his wife, Mary, for their over half-century of service. In a letter to the 46er community that appeared in the Spring/Summer 2001 issue of *Peeks,* Ditt listed health concerns as the main reason for his retirement and added, "This has been my life for 53 years."

In a strange twist that symbolically foreshadowed Ditt's retirement, Tony Goodwin made a special presentation to Ditt at the spring 2000 meeting. While surveying fire damage on Noonmark, Goodwin found one of Ditt's original aluminum markers that he had placed on the summits of the peaks as he climbed them. It was dated June 7, 1941. Ditt said that the Noonmark disk was the only marker that he had never been able to find when he reclimbed all of the peaks to remove them. Ditt passed away at the age of 91 on May 22, 2006.

As with Grace's role as club Historian, Ditt's duties as Executive Secretary/Treasurer were so overwhelming that no one person was willing to assume all of the responsibilities. Consequently the position was split into two. Phil Corell took over the treasurer's duties and the tasks of maintaining the 46er mailing list and preparing the meeting notices. Club mailings, which up to that point had been labeled and stuffed by hand by Ditt and Mary and other volunteers, were turned over to a mailing house. A new position, Merchandising Clerk, was created to fill orders for 46er emblem items and maintain an inventory of merchandise. Jean Burks (#4712) volunteered to fill the new position.

Some of those in 46er leadership positions had feared that the retirement of Grace and Ditt, the cornerstones of the organization for so many years, would dramatically alter the character of the club. However, the dreaded transitions had been accomplished with relative ease and the club's traditions and core values remained intact. This seemed to give others who had devoted many years of service to the club an impetus to follow Grace's and Ditt's lead. The club was rocked once again with a series of retirements at the beginning of the decade. In the spring of 2001 Trailmaster Joe Urbanczyk announced his retirement after 19 years of dedicated service helping to coordinate the 46er trail maintenance program. Joe always reminded members to "give something back to the mountains" for all the many hours of joy that they had given each hiker. Peter Hickey (#3202W), who was one of the "regulars" on trailwork crews, took over the position. Tim Tefft resigned as co-chair of the OLW after serving for almost 20 years. He remained as an instructor at the workshop. Donald McMullen stepped into the vacated position.

In the Fall/Winter 2001-2002 issue of *Peeks,* the magazine's editors Suzanne and David Lance announced their retirement after 17 years. The brother and sister duo had started their terms with the Fall/Winter 1985 issue. They agreed to stay on until new editors could be found and assist in the transition. Daniel Eagan (#4666) and Melissa Eagan (#4667) volunteered to take on the task starting with the Spring/Summer 2002 issue.

Dues Increase, But Still a Bargain

Although club dues were set at the bargain price of $5, many members contributed well beyond that small sum to support the club's programs. Traditionally dues had covered the costs for the biannual printing and mailing of *Peeks* as well as the two annual meeting notice mailings. However, by the beginning of 2000, with the rise in printing and mailing costs, the $5 amount was no longer sufficient to cover those basic club expenses. In the fall of 2001 the executive committee voted to increase member dues to $8 per year. Given the extent of the 46ers' programs, the fact that the organization has been able to maintain such a low membership fee is a tribute to the club's all volunteer workforce. A Family Membership at $25 was also established for those with four or more 46ers in the same household as was a Life Membership category at $546.

The executive committee briefly discussed the possibility of trademarking the name of the organization – 46-R, 46er, Forty-Sixer – as the designation started to pop up on everything from a locally-brewed beer to a reading contest.

In response to the tragedy of September 11, 2001, the 46ers donated $2,000 to the Clinton/Franklin County Red Cross Chapter for their Disaster Fund to help families who lost loved ones.

Grace CD

For years Grace Hudowalski had delighted climbers with her hiking stories. Her vivid tales of trail conditions, her crude equipment (by today's standards), and her hiking companions mesmerized listeners and represented a treasure trove of knowledge about Adirondack history and folklore. She also held the institutional memory, particularly of the 46ers of Troy and the formation of the current club. In an effort to preserve the club's history and some of Grace's accounts of what it was like to hike in the Adirondacks over half a century ago, 46er President Barbara Harris initiated a project to produce a CD of Grace talking about her mountain experiences. The idea received enthusiastic support from the executive committee.

During 2001 Harris, along with Kathleen Gill (#1179W) and Robert Zabinski of Arcane Music Studio in Malta, visited Grace, who then resided in a nursing home, and recorded her stories. Her experiences were produced as a CD entitled *Mountain Tales by Grace*. The 80-minute recording, which was offered for sale to members, included descriptions of her first climb up Mt. Marcy, her friendship with Adirondack Hermit Noah John Rondeau, and her hike down Colden's Trap Dike, among others. Grace's remembrances provided a fascinating look at the early days of hiking in the High Peaks as well as insights into the woman herself.

Peak Renaming Effort

L. John Van Norden spearheaded a proposal to rename two of the High Peaks, one in honor of Russell Carson, whose book *Peaks and People of the Adirondacks* was the definitive history of the mountains that had served as an inspiration to the early climbers, and one to recognize Grace Hudowalski for her life-long dedication to promoting the Adirondack Park in both her professional and personal life. The mountains Van Norden had in mind were East Dix, to be renamed Grace Peak, and South Dix, to be renamed Carson Peak. Those peaks were chosen specifically because they did not have their own unique designations. Their names simply reflected their proximity to Dix, the most prominent mountain in the range. Carson himself in *Peaks and People* explained the original naming of those two peaks. In a statement that could prove to be a prophetic irony, he mused over the possibility of a renaming opportunity in the future:

> If Marshall [Bob] had not called them South Dix and East Dix in his booklet ["The High Peaks of the Adirondacks"], in order to identify them, they would still be nameless mountains. The most interesting fact about these two mountains is that their names are not important enough to be retained and that they can be given distinctive titles, when the right occasion comes, without violation of old-established names.[157]

In making that statement it is doubtful that Carson ever considered his own name as an appropriate replacement.

At the fall 2001 meeting, the executive committee voted to form a committee to investigate the feasibility of renaming South and East Dix. A group of 46ers interested in the project joined the "Grace Peak Committee": L. John Van Norden, Barbara Harris, Sue Franklin (#3791), Inge Aiken (#4688W), John Bradley (#4693), John Case (#4499), Ron Konowitz (#487), Alan Via (#1426W), and Douglas Arnold (#4693W), chairman.

Russell Carson on Skylight

The Grace Peak Committee began to research the process of renaming natural landmarks, much as Grace herself had back in the 1940s when the 46ers began their campaign to formally name a number of the mountains in the High Peaks. As was the case 50 years before, the committee determined that the U.S. Board on Geographic Names has the ultimate authority to designate place names. The board requires a five-year waiting period after a person's death before his or her name can be applied to a geographic place. Under that requirement, Carson was already eligible, having died in 1961, but since Grace had passed away in March 2004, the club had to wait until the spring of 2009 to officially submit the request. In the meantime the committee discussed strategies to educate people about the proposed name changes and the reasoning behind them and to seek local support, a major aspect of the process.

Doug Arnold began the education campaign by developing a PowerPoint presentation to inform the public and seek feedback on the idea. In the spring of 2005 the committee also designed and produced two embroidered patches – one for each peak – to increase awareness of the renaming effort. The patches made use of artwork by Trudy Healy. The committee also created a brochure containing information about Grace and Russ Carson and their impact on the Adirondacks and the hiking community.

In addition, the committee worked with Loris Clark, president of the Schroon-North Hudson Historical Society, to reinstate the Hudowalski Essay Contest that Grace and Ed sponsored from 1957 to 1984. In the spring of 2007 thirty-seven students from within the towns of Schroon and North Hudson submitted essays on Adirondack history or environmental issues affecting the region for the renewed contest. Members of the Adirondack 46R Conservation Trust and the Schroon-North Hudson Historical Society judged the essays ranking each submission in the categories of content and organization, proper grammar, application to the Adirondack area, readability and appeal, and overall creativity.

To announce the winners of the new "Grace Hudowalski Essay Contest," the historical society held a Grace Hudowalski Appreciation Day on June 24, 2007 – the 50th anniversary of the original contest – at the Boathouse Theatre in Schroon Lake. The winner in the 10 to 14-year-old category for her essay on the Leland House, the leading hotel on Schroon Lake during the early 1900s, was Amelia Botterbusch. She received a three-week summer campership at the Pok-O-MacCready Camps. In the 15 to 18-year-old age group, Will Thompson received a $1,500 scholarship for his winning essay on acid rain and Andrew Filler received $500 for his second place summary of the history of Schroon. All participants received a commemorative certificate for their efforts.

46ers Publish a Fourth Book

In the fall of 2003 the executive committee decided to pursue publishing a new book. It had been twelve years since the publication of the club's *Of the Summits, of the Forests* (1991). The committee felt that the club had gone through significant changes since the early 1990s that should be documented and that it was also time to update the roster of club members. A book committee was formed consisting of James Barnshaw (#4156W), Phil Corell, Barbara Harris, Suzanne Lance, George Sloan, Sharp Swan, and Tim Tefft, who was appointed editor of the book. Instead of merely updating *Of the Summits, of the Forests,* the book committee envisioned an expanded publication with a different format that would include an extended section on the history of the club. In addition, detailed mountain profiles would be grouped by ranges or proximity and would incorporate information on naming, geology, flora and fauna, first ascents, and local history, information that had been covered in separate chapters in the club's previous books. You now hold in your hands *Heaven Up-h'isted-ness! The History of the Adirondack Forty-Sixers and the High Peaks of the Adirondacks*. It represents unique perspectives on the High Peaks written by individuals who have years of firsthand experience exploring the wonders of the area. All add their own viewpoints on the mountains and what it means to be a 46er.

Conclusion

The history of the Adirondack Forty-Sixers and the sport of 46ing is a story of change: change in the number of people attracted to northern New York's High Peaks; change in the mountain environment itself as increased usage degraded the wilderness; change in state management policy from facilitating access to restricting usage; and change in the club's core philosophy from a recreational/social emphasis to stewardship.

Herb Clark and Bob and George Marshall never envisioned that their pleasant summers exploring the Adirondack High Peaks would capture the spirits of other like-minded adventurers and spawn the sport of 46ing. Since those early days, 6,677 hikers (as of the end of 2009) have literally followed in their footsteps. Currently approximately 215 Forty-Sixers are added to the ranks annually.

The first 46ers encountered a pristine wilderness environment with only 14 marked summit trails and no discernible herdpaths on the other 32 peaks. Hiking all day without meeting another soul was the norm. Today's hikers experience 26 trailed peaks, some with routes to them that are gullied and badly eroded, and 20 untrailed peaks – now more accurately termed Wilderness Paths – accessible along easily discernible routes, and some of those are similarly eroded and worn. At any given time on a summer day well over 100 people can be counted on the summit of Marcy. No summit is free from the influence of human presence. In fact, there is barely a ridge, rock outcropping, slide, stream, or pass that hasn't been explored by someone seeking adventure off the beaten path.

Critics of the sport of 46ing have indicted the club, attributing the deterioration of the High Peaks Wilderness to the influence of 46ing, but blaming the 46ers exclusively for the damage is more than overly simplistic. Those seeking 46er status account for only a fraction of the more than 100,000 yearly visitors to the High Peaks over the past four decades. The beauty of the area is a strong lure for the casual tourist seeking an occasional walk in the woods, the weekend camper seeking an escape, boys' and girls' clubs, summer camp groups, commercial tour groups, and other outdoor recreation clubs, as well as the devotee returning to favorite spots over and over again.

In 1928, twenty years before the formation of the Adirondack Forty-Sixers, Russ Carson struggled with the conundrum of making state land accessible and attractive for recreational use while maintaining its wilderness character. In a speech to the Albany Chapter of the ADK on December 8, 1928, he said, "In all of our thinking about recreational development, we ought constantly to remember that wilderness and natural beauty are the real charm of the Adirondacks, and that preservation is as much our objective as helping more people to share our joy in them." Carson understood the delicate balance between promoting the recreational use of the Forest Preserve for pleasure and advocating for the area's conservation and protection. He understood that these two goals are not mutually exclusive, nor should they be. Finding the balance between use and protection guarantees the wisest use of the land for the optimum benefit of visitors.

By adding volunteer service to its hiking traditions, the Adirondack Forty-Sixers organization has effectively embraced the dual roles of "hiking partners and mountains stewards" – encouraging those who aspire to climb the 46 and engaging in activities to preserve the wilderness character of the Adirondack High Peaks. Through insightful leadership, the organization has evolved from a close-knit group whose members gathered socially to share hiking experiences into an organization committed to conserving and preserving the High Peaks environment. The club's educational programs (Outdoor Leadership Workshop, informational brochures, litterbag distribution, and regular correspondence with hikers) and conservation projects (regular trail maintenance, lean-to rehabilitations, and summit seeding) are now integral to the mission of the 46ers. The vital role that the club plays in the state's overall management of the High Peaks Region is a living tribute to the vision of 46er leadership and the commitment of its members.

Like the 46ers, state government also has revised its role as manager of the High Peaks to achieve a balance between use and preservation. After promoting recreational development of the Adirondack Forest Preserve for over 50 years, the state changed its emphasis in the 1970s toward protecting and preserving the wilderness character of the region. The APSLMP and the regional Unit Management Plans placed limits on user activity in an effort to mitigate environmental damage from overuse and preserve the wilderness experience. Trailhead registration numbers from the DEC indicate that the UMP's restrictions on camping and group size did reduce the numbers of visitors to the High Peaks. In 1998 about 125,000 hikers signed trail registers in the Eastern Region. That number decreased to about 90,000

On the way to Cliff... crossing the Opalescent in 1937

during 2004. Whether the reduction was the result of the new regulations or a natural cyclical occurrence only time will tell.

The connection between recognizing those who climb the 46 peaks and the deterioration of the wilderness will continue to be argued. Perhaps in some idyllic future, humankind will be content to experience the mountains from a distance, satisfied with faraway views or photos from past adventurers. Without the constant footfalls of visitors the wilderness would be allowed to heal itself, but that time is not now. With or without the lure of the 46er patch, the mountain wilderness will continue to attract adventurous hikers and casual tourists who are drawn to the area's natural beauty for the same reasons that originally attracted the early hikers – curiosity, adventure, challenge, peace: all elements intrinsically bound to the human spirit. People will continue to climb the Adirondack 46 High Peaks for physical and spiritual renewal, for the sense of accomplishment and pride, for the sheer fun of it, and, yes, for the privilege of donning the 46er patch.

Despite all the changes to the High Peaks' environment and to the 46er club itself, one feature of 46ing persists: the stories recounting the joys and trials of climbing. Reaching 46er status continues to be a life-changing event for many. In their correspondence, hikers reflect on their experiences with a sense of excitement, wonder, pride, humility, achievement, camaraderie, and respect. As Grace, in her quiet wisdom, understood, it is the stories from hikers reflecting on the meaning of their experience that inspire and compel. For her it was the journey, or as her father told her before her first hike, "how you make the climb" that was and continues to be just as important as summiting a peak or becoming a 46er. The importance of the journey continues today. The sharing of the stories, over and over again, along with the images and emotions that remain in the mind and the heart after the goal has been achieved is the measure of a true 46er. These tales define the essence of 46ing.

Forty-Sixers experience the wilderness on its terms. It's Paul Brach (#2430) witnessing "near treeline, a lynx and a snowshoe hare play*[ing]* out a darting, swift drama... a rare and beautiful event." It's Johanne Hagar (#3037) and Barb Harris (#2824W) on Skylight picking blueberries that they added to their pancake mix the following morning. It's Bill (#2308) and Chris (#2309) Embler who heard the call and sighted a red-throated loon on Preston Pond. It's scores of campers who encountered "Marty" the pine martin, a regular visitor at Uphill Brook Lean-to. It's countless stories of bears visiting campers in the Marcy/Lake Colden corridor. It's Bob Werner (#2207) and John Kennedy (#1571) witnessing the break-up of an ice jam on Twin Brook. It's John Winkler (#1279) and Ray Held (#2207W) abandoning a winter ascent of Tabletop after falling into spruce traps over their heads.

Being a 46er means the hardships willingly endured to meet a personal goal... like Bill Peck (#2677) of Minnesota, who flew some 42,000 miles during the years as he climbed the 46... or Elliott Adams (#4776), who climbed the 46 in bare feet... or Ron Konowitz (#487), who skied to the summits of all 46... or Sam James (#3940), who finished the 46 on Haystack on August 15, 1996, at the age of 81, sixty years after he had climbed his first 46 peak, Mt. Marcy in December 1936... or Wayne Ratowski (#3036W), who climbed the 46 under the glow of full moons. It's Anne E. Dennis (#2529), who made her first climb in 1926 and finished in 1988 at the age of 72. It's Peter Hogan (#4111), who climbed 40 mountains after having a heart attack.

The measure of a true 46er is recognizing that 46ing is not about checking off mountains on a list but about sharing the joy and satisfaction of the adventure with others. As one 46er put it, "My best friends are those I've met by climbing the 46"... or Martha Honeywell (#4389), who celebrated completing the 46 on the summit of Wright by playing "Ode to Joy" on her trumpet accompanied by Vikki Finnin on her clarinet... or Zack Grossman, who carried a 20-pound watermelon to the summit of Dix to celebrate the finishing climb of his parents, Bernard and Christine. It's a group of ten people who all finished various rounds of the 46 together on Allen... or as Scott Reitz recalled "the look of excitement on my mother's face as she got her first peak... and the wonderful lunch that can only be made by a mother"... or Boy Scout Troop #709 from Caughdenoy, celebrating their 200th consecutive monthly camping weekend on March 19, 1988... or, as Grace recalled, her husband, Ed, carrying individual servings of ice cream packed in dry ice up Allen for some 15 or more climbers to enjoy when Eleanor Plum became an Adirondack Forty-Sixer. It's Rick Church (#1778) who wrote his proposal to his wife-to-be in Tabletop's summit register for her to read when she signed her name.

Being a 46er is recognizing all that the mountains have to offer. John Wuillermin (#4452) summed up the varying lures of the mountains when he said, "The Adirondack Park is my gym, my pressure valve, my getaway, my battery charger, my peace, my think-tank, my museum, and my church."

A. Edward Blackmar (#126) described the mixed emotions that greet many hikers on their final climb when he wrote in his questionnaire, "When I reached the summit of Allen, the last of my 46, it was with a sense of disappointment that I could no longer look forward to the prospect of climbing a 46er for the first time."

In the late 1950s the club discussed the idea of developing a climbers' code to remind hikers of their responsibility to protect both the wilderness and their fellow hikers while on the trail. Although never officially endorsed, Dick Babcock did prepare a draft that embodies the dual role of the club today:

> Climb joyfully, filled with the beauty and wonder of the mountains. Climb prepared. Climb with conservation, preserving the wilderness unmarred for those who come after you. Climb generously, sharing with others your strength and your joy as well as your possessions. Climb

thoughtfully, with understanding and humility, grateful that to you a great gift has been given – the opportunity to walk the mountains.

Grace put it more succinctly as she ended one of her "Boulder Reports" with these words that, in effect, reveal the essence of 46ing:

Climb well, with a discerning eye and a soft step in the mountain fastness.
And report your climbs to the Adirondack Forty-Sixers.

Endnotes

Part I: The First Forty-Sixers

1. David H. Beetle, "Introduction" in *The Adirondack Forty-Sixers*, Grace Hudowalski, editor, (Albany, NY: The Peters Print, 1958), pg. 10.
2. Robert Marshall spelled his sister's nickname "Putey."
3. New York State's 1938 Constitutional Convention recodified Article VII to Article XIV and made slight changes in wording without modifying the "forever wild" language.
4. James M. Glover, *A Wilderness Original: The Life of Bob Marshall*, (Seattle: The Mountaineers, 1986), pg. 19.
5. *Ibid*, pgs. 29-30.
6. *Ibid.*, pg. 2.
7. After George and Bob Marshall had completed the Adirondack 46 and lived apart, they wrote long letters to each other describing their latest wilderness treks. In one of George's letters to Bob dated September 30, 1925, he recounted a bushwhack he and Herb Clark took in the Boreas Ponds area, over North River Mountain, eventually to the South Branch of the Opalescent, onto the East River Trail to Hanging Spear Falls, and out to Adirondak Loj. In attempting to figure the mileage of that trip, a good portion of which was not on any marked trail, George queried Bob on his method. "I enjoyed your last letter telling about your dandy forty mile walk. That reminds me; on what do you base mileage in a country in which there are no good maps and in which there is much rough and irregular country? I have tried to calculate our mileage for the North River Mt. Day and I have been unable to settle yet." George Marshall raises a legitimate question concerning the accuracy of Bob's estimates of his long day trips. *(George Marshall Adirondack Collection*, The William Chapman White Memorial Room, Adirondack Research Center, Saranac Lake Free Library, Saranac Lake, New York.)
8. *Ibid.*, pg. 88.
9. Bob Marshall, "Fourteen in One," *High Spots*, Adirondack Mountain Club, October 1932.
10. Glover, pg. 143.
11. Glover, pg. 79.
12. Glover, pg. 267.
13. Glover, pg. 96.
14. Glover, pg. 188.
15. A poll, or "head" tax, is a tax levied equally on every adult in a community. Poll taxes were enacted in Southern states during the late nineteenth and early twentieth centuries as a prerequisite for voting. The tax was adopted to circumvent the Fourteenth and Fifteenth Amendments and deny many African Americans and poor whites the right to vote.
16. In 1951, the Civil Rights Congress presented a denunciation of lynching in the United States, *We Charge Genocide*, to the United Nations. William L. Patterson and Paul Robeson were prominent members of the organization. Robeson was an internationally renowned black singer – one of the most popular singers of his time – actor, orator, and political activist, who experienced the devastating

effects of discrimination first hand. Although trained as a lawyer – a profession he was forced to abandon because of racial tension – he found his notoriety as a cultural leader more useful in his fight for social justice and in defense of civil liberties. His social activism brought him to the attention of the House Un-American Activities Committee. Attempts to silence and discredit him culminated in 1950 when his passport was revoked. Being branded "un-American" and without the freedom to travel abroad, his career as a performer suffered. Patterson was a leader in the Communist Party USA and head of the International Labor Defense. As a lawyer, he offered legal representation to communists, trade unionists, and African Americans in cases involving racial and political discrimination. He was tried twice for contempt of Congress for his condemnation of United States government policies that supported racism and for failing to release information to the House Un-American Activities Committee. Dashiel Hammett, best known as author of the novels *The Maltese Falcon* (1930) and *The Thin Man* (1932), often has been referred to as the father of the modern American detective story. Hammett became involved in left-wing activism in the 1930s, joining the American Communist Party. During the 1950s he was investigated by the House Un-American Activities Committee, which labeled him as an active communist. He was imprisoned for six months for refusing to divulge the names of other American communist activists. He was blacklisted and his career was virtually destroyed.

17. Harvey H. Kaiser, editor, *Great Camps of the Adirondacks,* (Jaffrey, NH: David R. Godine, 1982), pg. 140.

18. Glover, pg. 24.

19. Bob Marshall, "Great Adirondack Guides No. 4 Herbert Clark," *High Spots*, Adirondack Mountain Club, October 1933, pg. 8.

20. *Ibid*, pg. 9.

21. *Ibid*, pg. 9.

22. George Marshall, "Some Reflections on Ampersand Mountain," *High Spots*, Adirondack Mountain Club, July 1934, pg. 4.

23. George Marshall, "Adirondacks to Alaska: A Biographical Sketch of Robert Marshall," *Ad-i-rondac*, Adirondack Mountain Club, May-June 1951, pg. 44.

24. George Marshall, "Approach to the Mountains," *The Adirondack Reader*, editor Paul Jamieson, The Adirondack Mountain Club, Glens Falls, NY, 1982, second edition, pgs. 111-113.

25. Robert Marshall, "A Day on the Gothics: August 11, 1920," *High Spots*, Adirondack Mountain Club Year Book, 1942, pgs. 10-12.

26. "Great Adirondack Guides No. 4 Herbert Clark." pg. 10.

27. *Ibid*, pg. 10.

28. See *Adirondack Peeks* Vol. XXV No. 1, Spring/Summer 1988, pg. 2 for a complete comparison of the Marshall/Clark 1926 view rating and the 1988 modern ranking.

Part II: The Forty-Sixers of Troy and the Adirondack Forty-Sixers

29. William Lance, "First Trip," *Adirondack Peeks*, Vol. XXXI, No. 1 (Spring/Summer 1994), pgs. 31-34.

30. *Ibid*.

31. *Ibid*.

32. *Troy Times Record*, February 15, 1937.

33. Grace Hudowalski speech to New York Folklore Society, Munson-Williams-Proctor Institute, Utica, NY, 9/22/61.

34. Hugh Tuohey, "Mole Hills from Mountains Easy for Albany Woman," *Times Union*, April 17, 1953.

35. In reporting her own climbs of the 46 High Peaks, Grace listed June 1921 as the date of her first climb of Marcy. That date was repeated in the climbing rosters printed in the first two books

published by the Adirondack Forty-Sixers, *The Adirondack Forty-Sixers,* 1958, and *The Adirondack High Peaks and the Forty-Sixers*, 1970. However, a detailed description of the climb of Marcy, prepared by Gertrude H. Carragan, secretary of the Chepontuc Trail Club, dated April 25, 1923, listed the date of the hike as August 1-5, 1922, with the actual summitting of Marcy on August 2nd. The August 2, 1922, date is listed in the climbing roster of the Forty-Sixer book *Of the Summits, of the Forests*, published in 1991.

36. Grace Hudowalski in letter to Mrs. Nelson Dunn, August 6, 1967.

37. Rita I. Smith, "Mountain Climbing Keeps Figure Slim," *Buffalo Courier Express*, March 27, 1955.

38. Paul Grondahl, "Amazing Grace," *Times Union*, October 12, 1997, pg. G1.

39. Grondahl, *Times Union*.

40. Letter from Grace Hudowalski to Suzanne Lance, August 24, 1982.

41. Letter from Grace Hudowalski to George Sloan, May 24, 1988. The hymn Grace was referring to was written by an anonymous author. One of the verses reads:

> Oh, my brother, are you weary
> Of the roughness of the way?
> Does your strength begin to fail you,
> And your vigor to decay?
> Farther on, still go farther,
> Count the milestones one by one,
> Jesus will forsake you never.
> It is better farther on.

42. Letter from Grace Hudowalski to George Sloan, January 28, 1989.

43. Letter from Grace Hudowalski to George Sloan, October 13, 1989.

44. Letter from Grace Hudowalski to Suzanne Lance, August 5, 1982.

45. *Ibid.*

46. Letter from Grace Hudowalski to Marta Bolton, September 11, 1992.

47. Letter from Grace Hudowalski to Kirk Burness, November 18, 1966.

48. Letter from Grace Hudowalski to Jenn Bolton, July 11, 1991.

49. Letter from Grace Hudowalski to Jenn Bolton, April 24, 1992.

50. Letter from Grace Hudowalski to Jenn Bolton, July 21, 1991.

51. Letter from Grace Hudowalski to Renee Bolton, July 20, 1993. The hike that Grace was referring to was a trip she took with Margery Ludlow, C. Howard Nash, Margery's brother, and Franklin Wilson on September 23, 1940. The group climbed Couchsachraga from Tahawus, the typical route for hikers today. At the top of Couchie, which Margery needed to finish the 46, Margery announced that she didn't think she could make it back out to Tahawus. The group decided that Grace and Margery would climb down the northwestern flank of Couchie into the Cold River Valley and go to Rondeau's hermitage where Margery could spend the night and recoup her strength before hiking out the following day. Grace, who was scheduled to be the guest speaker at an event the following evening and therefore could not spend the extra day in the woods, would then hike the 14 miles out to Coreys. The men hiked back to the car at Tahawus and drove to Coreys to pick her up. This resulted in a total day trip mileage of about 25 miles for Grace. In a subsequent letter to Rondeau, she recounted her trip and complained that her legs "wobbled and throbbed" for a week afterward and she couldn't understand why. Rondeau's response to her in a letter dated January 14, 1941, offered the obvious explanation along with his sound advice: "It was too long a day; Under a load; through jungles not fit for a rabbit. (too many miles!) Think of the leverage your poor walking sticks done that day, no wonder they cried out. And you should heed their cries. Every time you over do, you never completely get over it. And the oftener you over do, the more your pains and the slower your speed in 25 years from now. Please conserve that noble strength of yours; not to brake (sic) records in a day, but to enjoy the mountains as long as possible in years."

52. Letter from Grace Hudowalski to Barbara Harris, March 8, 1990.

53. Letter from Grace Hudowalski to Barbara Harris, September 26, 1990.

54. Letter from Grace Hudowalski to Barbara Harris, February 16, 1996.

55. *High Spots* was the ADK's first newsletter, which was published periodically beginning in November 1922. After 1937 *High Spots* became an annual yearbook before being phased out after the 1944 issue. A new bimonthly periodical, ADK *Bulletin,* started in 1937. It was renamed *Ad-i-ron-dac* in 1945, with the hyphens removed in 1962.

56. Article VII, Section 7, now Article XIV, Sections 1 and 2, the "forever wild" clause in the state's constitution, originally created the forest preserve and protected all state land, now owned or subsequently acquired.

57. Maitland C. DeSormo, *Noah John Rondeau: Adirondack Hermit,* (North Country Books, 1969), pgs. 58-59.

58. DeSormo, pg. 60.

59. From Charlie Horn's questionnaire.

60. In October 1940 the club also extended honorary membership to Herb Clark and Bob and George Marshall.

61. Telegram from George Marshall to Grace Hudowalski, July 28, 1939.

62. Letter to Grace Hudowalski from Paul Doherty dated November 6, 1940.

63. In a letter to Mr. Robert Sterling Yard, President and Permanent Secretary of the Wilderness Society, dated February 9, 1941, in which Grace was updating him on the petition to name an Adirondack mountain after Bob Marshall, she described her feelings about Bob. "I wish I could put into words what Bob Marshall means to me. There are times it seems very strange that I never knew him at all for I don't know of any other person who made such an impression on me as he did. When I stop to think about him and read about him or better yet, read something he wrote, I have a difficult time convincing myself that I didn't know him. He seems just as alive to me today as he did when he wrote occasionally. I have an idea that he is one of those immortal persons. My feelings for him went – and goes – deeper than words."

64. Upon notification that the name Marshall had been officially approved by the state and federal Boards of Geographic Names, George Marshall wrote in a letter to Grace Hudowalski dated February 5, 1957: "Naturally I am pleased that there is a mountain in the Adirondacks named for Bob; but I am distressed that Herbert Peak seems to have been lost in the process. I wish something could be done to preserve his name on an Adirondack peak. I do not believe that Bob would have approved this kind of name change." It is interesting to note that the remaining and by far more substantial part of this letter concerned the state's plan to build the Northway through the Adirondacks and the pros and cons of the various routes proposed for the project. George Marshall either chose not to express any further opinion on an issue, which he felt had already been decided, or was more concerned with immediate environmental issues facing the Adirondacks at the time.

65. *Guide to Adirondack Trails: Northeastern Section and Northville-Placid Trail,* 1950 edition, Adirondack Mountain Club, pg. 63.

66. Riford, Ruth Tallmadge, "Faye Loope 46er #4," *Adirondack Peeks*, Summer 1976. Vol. XIII, No. 1, pgs. 9-10.

67. In a letter to Francis P. Farquhar of Berkeley, CA, dated July 1, 1953, George Marshall described the marathon hiking rivalry: "For a few years during the 1930s there were a series of so called mountain marathons – to see how many peaks and feet one could climb in a day... I am afraid Bob and I started it on a nine peak climb for the fun of it, and then others got serious about it. I dropped out (I was not in the class of these other climbers), but Bob, Jim Foote (later with the National Parks Assoc.), Ernest Griffith (on Wilderness Society Council and Chief of Legislative Reference Service of Library of Congress), and Professor Herbert L. Malcolm of Syracuse improved on each other's records several times..."

68. Letter from Grace Hudowalski to Mr. Dellman dated October 23, 1940, describing the meeting.

69. Philip Alan Macklin (#38) had proposed the idea of registers on the trailless peaks when he submitted his questionnaire on September 5, 1946. He said, "Please enter my violent opposition to

any personal markers on peaks – such as the aluminum Dittmar tags. They seem to me completely out of the spirit of things. A permanent register, which in itself could indicate the top, would be a fine idea. Perhaps the maintenance of these registers could be a function of the 46ers."

70. L. Morgan Porter was also chairman of the ADK's Committee on Maps and Guidebooks. He was responsible for the publication of ADK's High Peaks trail guides for 15 years. He traveled more than 1,000 miles on Adirondack trails with a measuring wheel to gather the data on distances for the guidebooks.

71. With the placement of the canisters also came the responsibility of maintaining them. Sometimes a tree on which a canister was attached would blow over, or the canister would be too low on a tree and thereby covered by the winter snow. The registers would be filled with names of climbers with no pages left to record additional names. News of the condition of the canisters and the registers would go to Grace Hudowalski as climbers wrote to her to report their climbs. She would then pass the information along to volunteers who would make the necessary upgrades.

72. The storm was often called "The Big Blow" and "The Blowdown of 1950." It is often referred to as a hurricane; however, most weather experts agree that it was not a true hurricane. Rather, it was, according to Jane Eblen Keller in *Adirondack Wilderness - A Story of Man and Nature* (Syracuse University Press, 1980, pg. 225-226), an "extremely low pressure system." She explained that on "November 25, 1950, the pressures between two air masses dropped so quickly and to such a low point that it caused the most damaging storm in recorded New York history."

73. Dr. Nixon was the archivist-editor at the Franklin D. Roosevelt Library in Hyde Park. He was editor of *Franklin D. Roosevelt and Conservation, 1911-1945*, published by the Franklin D. Roosevelt Library in 1957, and *Franklin D. Roosevelt and Foreign Affairs, 1933-1937*, published by the Harvard University Press in 1969.

74. This statistical analysis grew into a regular column in *Adirondack Peeks*, the newsletter/magazine of the Forty-Sixers called "Peeks Sketches," which lists notable categories for each yearly class of 46er finishers.

75. Letter from George Marshall to Richard Babcock dated November 17, 1958.

76. The shelter on Marcy that George Marshall refers to was the MacDonald Hospice, a stone storm shelter on the leeward side of Marcy's summit. Pirie MacDonald, a famous New York photographer and past president of the ADK, paid for its construction in 1928. He conceived the idea of a shelter on Mt. Marcy "one chilly October day after watching two girl climbers shiver in thin dresses at the summit." The structure, which was approved by the state Conservation Department, was partitioned into two rooms, one for men and one for women. Tip Roseberry, "The Roving Reporter: A New Pirie MacDonald Climbs Famed Mt. Marcy," *Times Union*, July 10, 1953.

77. Porter passed Marshall's comments along to the Conservation Department and suggested fining people for littering and initial carving but noted that catching people in the act and prosecuting them would be difficult.

78. Suzanne Lance, "A 'Treasured' Treasurer," *Adirondack Peaks*, Vol. XXIII, No. 1, Spring/Summer 1986, pg. 9.

79. Ditt visited Rondeau on numerous occasions, once spending a week with him during which time the two made a pack basket from scratch. Ditt also maintained regular correspondence with the hermit.

80. Dues notice December 8, 1962.

81. Members can still purchase "Note Cards by Trudy" at the minimally increased price of $5.50 for three packets of 12 cards and envelopes.

82. Richard Babcock, "Editorial," *Adirondack Peeks*, Vol. I, No. 2, Fall 1964, pg. 2.

83. Jim Goodwin, "Paths on the Trailless Peaks," *Adirondack Peeks*, Vol. I, No. 2, Fall 1964, pg. 6.

84. Jim Goodwin, "Editorial," *Adirondack Peeks*, Vol. III, No. 1, Spring 1966, pg. 5.

85. Jim Goodwin, "The Wrecking of Herd Paths," *Adirondack Peeks*, Vol. III, No. 2, Fall 1966, pg. 6.

86. *Ibid.*

87. *Ibid.*, pg. 7.

88. *The Knickerbocker News*, November 18, 1939, Second Section.

89. Bruce Wadsworth, "ADK Conservation Policy," *Adirondac*, Vol XLVI, No. 9, November 1982, pg. 20.

90. Mason Ingram, "Letters," *Adirondack Peeks,* Vol. IV, No 2, Fall 1967, pg. 9-10.

Part III: The 1970s – Giving Something Back to the Mountains

91. T. H. [Trudy Healy] for William Weissinger, "Report of the Wilderness Path Committee," *Adirondack Peeks* Spring 1970, Vol. VII, No. 1, pg. 8.

92. *Ibid.*

93. *Ibid.*

94. It is interesting to note that for this book George Marshall struggled with the assignment of climbing numbers for his brother Bob, Herb Clark, and himself. In a letter to Grace dated December 31, 1969, regarding the printing of the book he wrote: "For book distribution purposes, I realize that you have to give separate numbers; but actually since we climbed these peaks together and finished climbing the 46th together at the same time, I should think your records should show: 'Herbert Clark, 46er No, 1-3, George Marshall, 46er No. 1-3; and Robert Marshall, 46er No. 1-3.'"

95. *High Peaks Unit Management Plan,* New York State Department of Environmental Conservation, March 1999, pg. 86.

96. The guidelines closely mirrored those of the National Wilderness Preservation System that was established in 1964, for which the Wilderness Society and Bob Marshall had long advocated.

97. *High Peaks Wilderness Complex Unit Management Plan,* pg. 88.

98. Glenn Fish, "Mountain Madness: Or How I Became Hooked on Becoming a 46er," *Adirondack Peeks*, Vol. XVIII, No. 1, Spring/Summer 1981, pg. 10.

99. "46er Trail Work: A Rich History of Stewardship," *Adirondack Peeks*, Vol. XXV, No. 2, Fall/Winter 1988-89, pg. 12. Prior to the "If you carry it in, carry it out" regulation instituted in the 1970s, the DEC sanctioned the use of garbage pits at lean-to sites as a way to consolidate and control the disposal of refuse.

100. Grace Hudowalski also encouraged Ed to finish the 46. He confided to her in a letter that he wasn't sure he wanted to finish the 46 given the nature of his research and the abuses caused to the environment from hiker overuse. Grace attended an ADK Chapter meeting where he made a presentation on his research in the High Peaks. Afterward, she chided him good-naturedly, saying that if he was going to give presentations about the High Peaks, he had better climb them all so he knew what he was talking about.

101. Glenn Fish letter to Henry L. Diamond dated September 22, 1970.

102. The pamphlet "Mountain Manners: Don'ts, Why Nots and Dos" was based on a brochure prepared by James "Beetle" Bailey, then 46er president, for the 1966 Camporee. Trudy Healy updated and redesigned the publication in 1970.

103. On April 12, 1976, Steven Thomas disappeared while climbing Marcy. In July of 1976, Bob and Marilyn Thomas, while searching for their brother, found a sleeping bag, boots, shotgun, and a moss-encrusted skeleton in Panther Gorge. Dental records revealed the remains to be those of George Atkinson. From "Lost on Marcy" by Kate Gurnett, Albany *Times Union*, April 22, 2001, pg. C4.

104. Tony Goodwin, "The Future of the Adirondack Forty-Sixers," *Adirondack Peeks*, Vol. X, No. 1, Spring 1973, pg. 12.

105. *Ibid.*

106. *Ibid.*

107. *Adirondack Peeks*, Spring 1973, Vol. X, No. 1, pg. 3.

108. *Ibid,* pg. 3.

109. E. H. Ketchledge, "Call for a 46er High Peak Task Force," *Adirondack Peeks*, Summer 1975, Vol. XII, No. 1, pg. 3.

110. *Corduroy* – curiously, *Merriam Webster's Collegiate Dictionary* states that the origin of the term *corduroy* is unknown. Its earliest use was to describe a road (or trail) upon which logs were laid, transversely, often over rough or muddy stretches. Legend maintains that the first such applications were on roads in France upon which the King's carriage traveled. Although such roads were less treacherous for vehicles to navigate, they were infamous for being unpleasant – very bumpy – for passengers of vehicles passing over the logs. Later, in this country, for a time, corduroy was refined. Instead of logs being placed over rough sections, milled boards were attached to runners, sometimes along long stretches of roadway. Several such "plank roads" were constructed in the Adirondacks. Corduroy fabric is named for its ribs (wales) which resemble, to a degree, the surface of a corduroy road. Folk etymology suggests that *corduroy* is derived from French: *Cours de Roi*, the *Way of the King*.

111. James A. Goodwin, *And Gladly Guide: Reflections of a Life in the Mountains*, pg. 31. Goodwin's book provides a fascinating look at Keene Valley in the 1920s, a heyday of activity for vacationers. It also reveals the social and political climate of the area at the time.

112. *Ibid.*, pg. 3.

113. *Ibid.*, pgs. 38-39.

114. *Ibid.*, pg. 39.

115. *Ibid.*, pg. 112.

116. *Ibid.*, pgs. 119, 120.

117. At the time the ADK was also actively involved in increasing its trail maintenance activities. ADK's trail program dated back to the summer of 1922 when the club cleared and marked a large portion of he Northville-Lake Placid Trail. When ADK opened Johns Brook Lodge in 1925, its trail building and maintenance efforts shifted to the area surrounding the lodge. Trails were built up Big Slide, Upper Wolf Jaw, and to Klondike Notch. Throughout the 1930s and during World War II volunteer assistance waned and work on the trails diminished. During the 1950s and 1960s as trail deterioration became evident, the ADK began to focus on environmentally sound trail building and maintenance and it prepared a new Trails Maintenance Manual. Rudolph W. Strobel is credited with installing the first water bars on trails near JBL in 1967. Their effectiveness in controlling erosion was immediately apparent and the technique was used throughout the trails in the High Peaks. In 1979 the ADK hired its first paid trail crew to conduct more technically specialized work such as installing rock steps and engineering drainage ditches. Robert D. Hofer, Chairman Trails Committee, "Sixty Years of Trails Activity," *Adirondac*, November 1982, pgs. 24, 25.

118. "Celebrating 10 Years of 46er Trail Maintenance," *Adirondack Peeks*, Vol. XXV, No. 2, Fall/Winter 1988-89, pg. 14.

119. Edwin Ketchledge, "From the President," *Adirondack Peeks*, Vol. XIII, No. 1, Summer 1976, pg. 5

120. *Ibid*, pg. 6.

121. *High Peaks Unit Management Plan Final Draft*, New York State Department of Environmental Conservation, July 1996, pg. 148. DEC Rules and Regulations Part 190.8(i) states, "No person shall erect or post any notice or sign upon State land at any time."

122. Letter from Edwin Ketchledge to Harold Jerry dated January 9, 1978.

Part IV: The 1980s – Decade of Growth

123. James Goodwin, *And Gladly Guide: Reflections of a Life in the Mountains*, pgs. 120-121.

124. "Celebrating 10 Years of 46er Trail Maintenance," *Adirondack Peeks*, Vol. XXV, No. 2, Fall/Winter 1988-89, pg. 18

125. Donald Hoffman, "President's Page," *Adirondack Peeks*, Vol. XXII, No. 1, Spring/Summer 1985, pg. 24.

126. Summit seeding was scheduled during the early spring to take advantage of a small window of optimum weather conditions for the grass seed to germinate and establish roots before the peak summer hiking season.

127. Chris Behr, "46ers Take to the Trails," *Adirondack Peeks*, Vol. XXI, No. 2, Fall/Winter 1984-85, pg. 17.

Part V: The 1990s – End of an Era

128. Chapter 707 of the New York State Laws of 1892 established the 2,800,000-acre Adirondack Park, delineated on a map by a blue line, which has been used ever since on official state maps to outline the boundaries of the park.

129. The Adirondack 46R Conservation Trust, established by Grace Hudowalski, now provides the bulk of the financial support for this successful program.

130. "Herdpaths and the High Peaks Management Plan," Tony Goodwin, *Adirondack Peeks*, Vol. XXVIII, No. 2, Fall/Winter 1991-92, pg. 25.

131. The DEC established a trail classification system to reflect different types of trails and levels of use and to define maintenance standards. The classification system ranges from Class I, unmarked footpaths, to Class V, heavily used and maintained primary trails. Under the DEC trail classification system, the paths on the trailless peaks are officially designated as Class II paths. The acceptable maintenance for these paths is defined as: "Intermittent marking with consideration given to appropriate layout based on drainage, occasional barrier removal only to define appropriate route."

132. "New York: Fire Grows Despite Rain Near Adirondack Resort," *New York Times*, Metro News Briefs, September 7, 1999.

133. "President's Page," *Adirondack Peeks*, Vol. XXIX, No. 2, Fall/Winter 1992-93, pg. 21.

134. *Ibid.*, pg. 21.

135. "Letters," *Adirondack Peeks*, Vol. XXX. No. 1, Spring/Summer 1993, pg. 28.

136. *Ibid.*, pg. 32.

137. *Ibid.*

138. "Letters," *Adirondack Peeks*, Vol. XXX, No. 2, Fall/Winter 1993-94, pg. 27.

139. *Ibid.*, pgs. 27-28.

140. "President's Page," *Adirondack Peeks*, Vol. XXIX, No. 2, Fall/Winter 1992-93, pg. 21.

141. "The Vice Box," *Adirondack Peeks*, Vol. XXXI, No. 2, Fall/Winter 1994-95, pg. 18.

142. Kay Flickinger, "Climbing the Forty-Six on Snow and Ice," *The Adirondack Forty-Sixers*, (The Peters Print, Albany, NY, 1958), pg. 97.

143. *Ibid.*, pg. 89.

144. *Ibid.*, pg. 97.

145. "Letters," *Adirondack Peeks*, Vol. XXIX, No. 2, Fall/Winter 1992-93, pg. 28.

146. Declaration of Trust, Adirondack 46R Conservation Trust, pgs. 3-4

147. *Ibid.*

Part VI: The 2000s – Looking Toward the Future

148. Barbara Harris, "Canister Removal from Un-trailed Peaks," *Adirondack Peeks*, Vol. XXXVIII, No.1, Spring/Summer 2001, pgs. 17-18.

149. *Ibid.*, pg. 17.

150. *Ibid.*, pg. 18.

151. *Ibid.*

152. Fearing that fortune hunters would help themselves to the canisters when the HPUMP, which called for their removal, was finalized, the club had replaced the original metal canisters in the mid-1990s with a new version fabricated from PVC pipe.

153. *Adirondack Explorer*, September 2000. The *Explorer* only printed a very small portion of Barbara Harris's letter. Her original letter outlined the club's service projects saying, "...Many [hikers] check that last mountain off their lists, get their patches and then go home never to be seen again. That is their right. But many 46ers want something more than that, want to be something more than that. These are 46ers who every year spend thousands of man and woman hours toiling, sweating

oceans, wallowing in mud up to their knees to maintain and repair our worn and damaged trails. These are the 46ers who participate in the Outdoor Leadership Workshop where our vast stores of knowledge are shared with camp counselors, scoutmasters, and others who will be leaders in the out of doors. These are the 46ers who advocate and practice "Leave No Trace" principles while enjoying the Adirondacks. "Leave No Trace" principles are now a central part of being a 46er and LNT information is provided to all members and aspiring members. These are the 46ers who spend countless hours in front of their keyboards corresponding with aspiring members, sharing their knowledge and insight into the mountains and our organization... yes, there are challenges but the 46ers have too much to offer the Adirondacks now and for years to come to disband..."

154. *Adirondack Explorer,* September 2000.

155. The club's entire Mission Statement is: "The Adirondack Forty-Sixers consists of hikers who have climbed to the summits of the forty-six major peaks of the Adirondacks. The club is dedicated to protection of the Adirondack environment, to education in the proper usage of the Adirondack wilderness, and to participation in work projects in cooperation with the NYS Department of Environmental Conservation to meet those objectives. While the club records climbing accomplishments, it does not advocate, collect, or publicize records involving time, number of rounds climbed, ages, or other arbitrary goals. The club encourages all to climb for personal satisfaction."

156. "A Shared Concern," *Adirondack Peeks*, Vol. XXXVIII, No. 2, Fall/Winter 2001-2002, pg. 4.

157. Russell M. L. Carson, *Peaks and People of the Adirondacks*, edited by Philip Terrie, 1986, Adirondack Mountain Club, Glens Falls, NY, pg. 223.

About the Author

Suzanne Lance, 46er #1802W, climbed Cascade, her first high peak, in 1962 and finished the 46 twenty years later in gale force winds on Haystack. She reclimbed the 46 with her husband, George Sloan (#2651W), during his quest to become a 46er, and added a winter round with George, finishing on Macomb in March 2007. Suzanne is also a Northeast 111er, having climbed all the peaks in New York and New England above 4,000 feet, as well as a member of the Catskill 3500 Club, having climbed all the peaks in the Catskills above 3,500 feet. With her brother David Lance (#1801), Suzanne served as editor for 17 years, from 1985 to 2002, of *Adirondack Peeks*, the 46ers' biannual magazine. She has participated in numerous 46er trail maintenance projects, earning the club's Conservation Service Award for accumulating over 546 hours of volunteer service. She is Assistant Director of the New York State Writers Institute at the University at Albany.

Adirondack Peeks

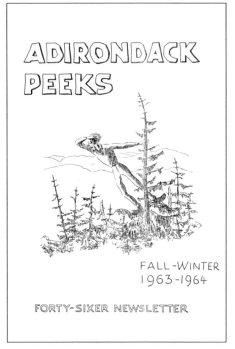

Cover of first issue of *Adirondack Peeks*

In the early 1960s Grace Hudowalski and Trudy Healy discussed how to communicate with a small but growing club membership. Grace suggested a "newsletter" as a way to inform members of club business and to encourage them to report their climbs in between meetings. She envisioned a simple, two-page notice that could be produced inexpensively as a way to share club news. With enthusiastic support from the club's executive committee, Richard Babcock, Trudy Healy, and James Goodwin accepted the challenge of editing the fledgling publication, producing their first issue – a 16-page mimeographed booklet – during the winter of 1963-64. They called the publication *Adirondack Peeks,* a clever homophonic play on words. Early issues of *Peeks* were filled with humorous cartoons, which often commented on controversial issues; members' personal milestones, such as births and marriages; editorials; brief trip reports, creative poems, and silly songs. What the original issues lacked in production and printing sophistication, they more than made up for in content creativity.

Trudy's pen-and-ink drawings of mountain scenes graced the cover of each issue and her small sketches provided the bulk of the graphic content. Trudy retired as editor in fall 1974, but her artwork has provided a visual continuity for the publication as every editor since has used it to highlight stories.

Editors throughout the 1970s – Elly King Strode (#623), and Jeanne and George Amedore (#1354) – continued to produce the mimeographed newsletter with a mix of club news, members' personal tidbits, and short summaries of hiking trips. Improvements in type, format, printing, and binding were made during that period. Content enhancements included the introduction of photographs, a report from the Trailmaster on club trail improvement outings, a summary of the Outdoor Leadership Workshop, and a book review column. A photo appeared for the first time on the cover of the Fall 1974 issue, and, for the same issue, Jeffery Paul Brown contributed artwork, giving Trudy a well-deserved rest. The Spring 1976 issue sported a special color photo on the cover as well as the first commercial advertisement in an effort to defray some of the costs of *Peeks'* production. A small number of ads continued to appear in several subsequent issues in the 1970s. However, ads were dropped after a few issues and since then the publication of *Peeks* has been supported completely by member dues. Photos started to appear inside *Peeks* on a regular basis in the late 1970s when Joseph Turon (#1016), a professional photographer, joined the production team as an assistant editor. For the Summer 1980 issue, *Peeks* was professionally typeset for the first time.

When Joe Turon took over as editor with the Spring/Summer 1981 issue, he incorporated graphic design into the production of the publication and increased the use of photos. Maxine Fabian provided illustrations. Content turned more to feature-length climbing stories from members as opposed to club news or editorials. Joe also introduced the "Boulder Report." Anticipating that readers would be interested in reading about other climbers' adventures, he asked club historian Grace Hudowalski if she would write a summary of highlights from hiker correspondence. That popular column, which has become the heart and soul of *Peeks*, first appeared in the Fall 1981-82 issue and has been a regular feature ever since.

Brother and sister David (#1801) and Suzanne (#1802W) Lance took over the reins of the publication starting with the Fall/Winter 1985-86 issue and continued as editors over the course of 18 years and 33 issues. Under their direction *Peeks* witnessed several enhancements: a redesigned two-color masthead, which first appeared in the Spring/Summer 1987 issue; use of desktop publishing software and computer graphics to aid in design and print production; full color photos on the front and back covers starting with the Spring/Summer 1994 issue; and designating the publication as a magazine instead of a newsletter to more accurately reflect its content. The Lances also designed two special commemorative issues: the Fall 1988-89 volume, that highlighted the 10th anniversary of the 46ers' trail maintenance program, and the Spring/Summer 1994 issue to celebrate the club's 46th anniversary, which included a special pull-out section on club history.

When the Lances retired after the Fall/Winter 2001-2002 issue, husband and wife Daniel (#4666) and Melissa (#4667) Eagan assumed the editors' duties with the Spring/Summer 2002 issue, accomplishing a seamless transition. The Eagans added their own touches to improve the publication including the use of color photography throughout each issue; a striking new cover design with the Spring 2006 issue; contests to engage members; a series of articles profiling current and past 46er leadership; and a question-and-answer column.

Throughout the evolution of *Peeks*, each editorial team has instituted advancements to make it the unique publication that it is today, but one element has remained a constant: the source of the material. *Peeks* has always depended solely on membership participation and submissions for its content. Whether the stories are about climbing one of the 46 or about 46ers' adventures in high spots throughout the world, the articles celebrate the joys, trials, beauty, and satisfaction of mountain climbing.

Peeks, Spring 1967

Heaven Up-h'isted-ness!

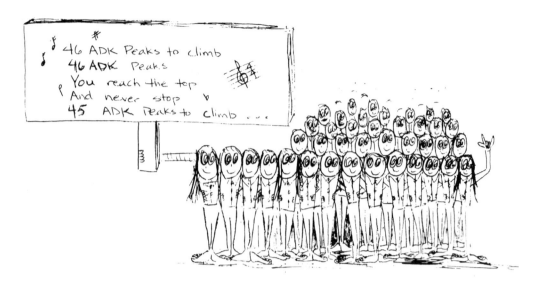

Peeks, Spring/Summer 1981

You've Become a 46er

So you've become a 46er, and you've climbed up all the trails,
And you bumped your head upon the clouds, and slept in lots of dales.
You've listened to the birds that sing, and watched the bears go prowl around.
While you were doing woodside things, did you look upon the ground?
Did you pick up any litter in the miles that you walked?
Or did you do as others do, and talk, and talk and talk,
About our trashy trails, and how something should be done,
As from your fingers fluttered the wrapper from your gum?
Did you go out on a weekend, where the 46ers gather,
And help to fix up some old bridge and work up quite a lather?
Or help to fix a better trail so as you hiked along
Instead of tripping over things, you could hum a little song?
Did you rub some moss against your cheek as on a log it grew,
Or gaze upon a spider web caressed by morning dew?
Or did you walk right through the web, instead of going 'round,
And knock the moss right off the log to grind it in the ground?
Did you from these lovely peaks gaze with wondrous eyes
Upon our Forty-six reaching grandly for the skies
And know, deep down, without your help their trails would fast decay,
With fragile alpine soon destroyed, rain washing all away?
There'd be no place to hike nor sleep, no place for creatures to stay,
Because the people did not keep the land the proper way.
So be kind; do all you can so when you're laid to rest,
"Here lies a 46er," they'll say, "who did his very best."

– Penny Wiktorek (#1584)
Peeks, Summer 1980

Peeks, Fall 1967

The Mountains

They stay the same and never change,
    that row on row of mountain range.
Their beauty is but a brutal thing,
    where trees and moss for life do cling.
So dark and gray as these peaks may seem,
    in the valleys lies a heart of green.
Their face may change by days and weeks
    with rain and snow upon these peaks;
But men are born and empires fall,
    before this place will change at all.
For mountains are a timeless breed,
    and their jagged spires doth time impede.

I come to this place with shoulders bent,
    renewing mind and body spent;
Yet every time that I return
    I see I've changed from things I've learned.
A certain sense of stability
    is what the mountains give to me;
My gain is not an earthly thing,
    instead a song for soul to sing.
Its echoing strength is such to see,
    the mountains are the place for me.

– **Bruce Bandorick (#988)**
Peeks, Summer 1978

Lament of the Lost 46er

(Tune: "My Bonnie Lies Over the Ocean")

The cripple-brush oozes with water,
The clouds are so thick I can't see;
The logs of the blowdown are criss-crossed –
Oh where can that good herdpath be!

Chorus: Bring back, bring back, bring back that herdpath to me, to me,
Bring back, bring back, bring back that herdpath to me.

Last night as I lay in the lean-to
Last night as I lay in my sack
I prayed the Good Lord that tomorrow
I'd stay on that blessed herdpath.
(Chorus)

I know that all herdpaths are objects
Which good Forty-Sixers decry
Yet if I could find one to follow
I sure would stay on it for aye.
(Chorus)

– Jim Goodwin
Peeks, Fall 1967

Peeks, Spring/Summer 1969

The History of the High Peaks of the Adirondacks

View of Mount Marcy from inside the former Lake Tear Lean-to.
The photograph was taken by Ed Hudowalski in the late 1930s.

MOUNT MARCY
Height: 1st — 1,629 meters (5,344 feet)*
By Tim Tefft (#616)

On Friday, August 19, 1836, William C. Redfield "mounted a hill about 150 feet on the south bank" of the Opalescent River about two miles "southeasterly" upstream from the Opalescent's junction with Lake Colden's outlet brook. From the "hill," probably near the Uphill Brook, Redfield saw a "high peak... surmounted by a beautiful dome of rock the whole apparently a difficult ascent." He gave a name, "The High Peak of Essex," to the previously unnamed mountain which many other people had seen before him from various locations – from Lake Sanford at the McIntrye Iron Works; from North Elba; from Burlington, Vermont; from Whiteface Mountain.

On August 22, 1836, Redfield reported, Archibald McIntyre and James Hall "with two men set out on an expedition through the notch *[Indian Pass]* to the northward to visit the slide on Whiteface Mountain." From that vantage point, they would have been able to look to see the mountain summits south of North Elba. Among them, of course, was "The High Peak of Essex."

Professor Ebenezer Emmons and Hall, his assistant, in September climbed to the summit of Whiteface and, gazing south, determined that Redfield's "high peak" was probably in excess of 5,000 feet in elevation and possibly the loftiest mountain in the state of New York. The two were dissuaded from attempting a climb of the high peak to the south because, on September 26, snow had already blanketed the mountains. Emmons felt that they would probably remain snow covered until the following June. However, he was confident that the peak that he and Hall had viewed from Whiteface was the region's highest. In his report to the state legislature for the year 1836 he wrote as follows:

> The highest peak amongst these mountains is about sixteen miles south from Whiteface, and so far as we know, has neither been ascended or measured. Whiteface is generally supposed to be the highest, but erroneously, as is proved by leveling from its summit in range with those southern elevations.

The United States was 60 years old in 1836, Andrew Jackson was its President, and Arkansas had just become its twenty-fifth state. The defenders of the Alamo had died that year, and Texas had won its independence from Mexico after Sam Houston and his army had defeated and captured General Santa Anna at the Battle of San Jacinto. New Hampshire's "White Hills" had been first explored two hundred years earlier, and that state's highest peak, Mount Washington, had first been climbed 194 years before Redfield, Emmons, and Hall first took note of the highest mountain in the state of New York. In fact, three parties of men climbed Mount Washington in 1642. The third group of record to achieve the summit of Mount Marcy did so in 1848.

---

* Turn to Page 208 for a brief explanation of the summit elevation figures used in this book.

Heaven Up-h'isted-ness!

In Albany in 1836 New York Secretary of State John Adams Dix had called for a "natural history" survey of the state, and the idea had been endorsed by Governor William Learned Marcy. He chose Professor Emmons to head the survey party for the second of four survey districts, the one which would cover the northern portion of New York, including the vast wilderness of the Adirondacks, much of which had not previously been explored by anyone other than local hunters.

Until 1836, the "High Peak of Essex" had been but another prominence in a landscape which featured numerous ridges and peaks. Following the 1813 publication of *A Gazetteer of the State of New York* by Horatio Gates Spafford, the peaks and ridges of the Adirondacks were considered less lofty than those of the Catskill Mountains. Spafford relied on various correspondents around the state for the information he compiled in his gazetteer. One such correspondent supplied the information about the Essex County towns of Jay and Elizabethtown, but the accounts included descriptions of only two of the region's highest peaks: Whiteface and Giant of the Valley. Whiteface was considered the highest of the Peruvian Mountains, and both, according to the gazetteer were about 2,500 feet in elevation.[1]

Two years previous to the publication of Spafford's gazetteer, work began on the building of the Elba Iron and Steel Manufacturing Company facility on the Chubb River in the area in present North Elba then known as "The Plains of Abraham." The company was run by Archibald McIntyre and some associates, but it fell on hard times after the "Year Without a Summer" (1816), and it closed in 1817. Nine years later McIntyre's son, John; brothers Malcolm and Duncan McMartin; the McIntyres' African-American servant, Enoch; Archibald's nephew, Dyer Thompson; and his future son-in-law David Henderson were at the abandoned iron works at North Elba, apparently preparing to search for a greater source of wealth than iron: silver.[2] Henderson later wrote to Archibald McIntyre, telling him about a "strapping young Indian," Elijah Lewis, who came to the party at their old works, showed them a large chunk of iron ore, and tempted them thusly: "You want see 'em ore – me know 'em bed, all same." For a plug of tobacco and a dollar and a half, the son of Mitchell Sabattis led the silver-seeking party south, through Indian Pass, and on to what would later be known as the Upper Works. There a vein of iron ore formed a "natural dam" fifty feet in width across a stream descending from the mountains to the northeast. A quick reconnaissance of the ore bed, which rose above the surface of the surrounding ground, convinced Henderson that Elijah had shown them something potentially far more valuable than the rumored vein of silver. Henderson, calling it the "great mother load of iron" of the region, was determined to procure the purchase of the property as quickly as possible.

The land for the Adirondack Iron Works was purchased at Albany by Archibald McIntyre and his associates, and work began on developing the site in 1827. At the Upper Works – first called McIntyre and later Adirondac – the new iron mining concern established a forge, a sawmill, and a boarding house for employees. Prospects looked good for the enterprise, but progress was slow. In 1833 McIntyre lamented, "The ore has not yet been tested, the roads are abominable, and coal wood in the vicinity is very scarce." Soon thereafter, David Henderson traveled from his home at Jersey City, New Jersey, to the works to inspect its operations. While there he embarked on an exploration of the "East River" (the Opalescent) and traveled along its course, past a "splendid perpendicular fall of about sixty feet, the whole river pouring over" it: Hanging Spear Falls. Continuing, he made his way to Lake Colden and contemplated going on to Avalanche Lake but decided, because the weather was wet and miserable, to return to the works via the "ore bed stream," which later became known as Calamity Brook.

Mining operations ceased at the works in 1834, due principally to the expense of transportation of the iron to Lake Champlain and on from there to Jersey City, where it was processed. A caretaker was left in charge of Adirondac while McIntyre and McMartin worked to find investors who might infuse new money into the enterprise. Their salesmanship brought businessman David Colden of Jersey City and successful businessman and scientist William C. Redfield of New York, among others, to the works and, thus, because they were there in August 1836, they were involved in the reconnaissance of Lake Colden, Avalanche Lake, and the upper Opalescent when the "discovery" of the "High Peak of Essex" was made.

The following summer, Emmons set out for the Essex County mountains with the intent of exploring the sources of the Hudson River and the high peaks which he, Hall, and Redfield had reconnoitered the previous summer. His party, including Redfield, left the works on August 3, 1837. They camped at "Cheney's Camp" at Lake Colden that night and began the ascent of the "High Peak of Essex" at 7:45 the next morning, August 4. Following the Opalescent upstream, as Redfield had done the year before, they stayed with the main branch of the stream, or along its forested sides as it cascaded through flumes and rocky chasms. At the "South Elbow," where the Uphill Brook joins the Opalescent, they began their walk through the "High Valley," the relatively level area, upstream. They continued, passing the Feldspar Brook, and tramped along the swampy ground that today's trail from Feldspar Camp to Lake Arnold follows along the narrow river. From the high valley, they went up through a "gorge" through which the Opalescent descends from the east, and at 4:30 in the afternoon stopped for the day at a site which Redfield called "Holt's Camp," after guide Harvey Holt.[3]

The climb resumed at 7:30 the next morning, August 5, 1837. At 8:40 they arrived at a "meadow from which tiny streams flowed in opposite directions, one to the Hudson and the other to the Ausable."[4] This was, undoubtedly, the high meadow later known as Plateau. At noon, according to Redfield's field notes, the party reached the peak of the state's highest mountain; however, other accounts indicate that the summit was achieved earlier, at 10 o'clock. Those attaining the summit were Professor Emmons, Redfield, James Hall,[5] artist Charles Cromwell Ingham,[6] state botanist John Torrey,[7] David Henderson of the iron works, Ebenezer Emmons, Jr., and five guides, most likely including John Cheney and Harvey Holt. Shortly after their arrival on top, the "High Peak of Essex" was formally named, apparently with the approval of all who were there.

Ebenezer Emmons wrote later about the naming:

> The region in which the east branch of the river rises, it seems, had never been explored previous to our visit; and it is not unreasonable to suppose this, for all our writers on geography have uniformly underrated its height, have made incorrect statements in relation to the origin and course of the principal branches of the Hudson, and also in relation to the character of the whole mountain group in which they rise.
>
> This being the case, it is not surprising that names have not been given to the highest points of land in the state. This privilege belongs by common consent to the first explorers. This, to be sure, is but of little consequence; still, as things must have a name, the party saw fit to confer upon a few of the highest summits designations by which they may in future be known. As this tour of exploration was made by gentlemen who were in the discharge of their duties to the state, and under the direction of the present executive, whose interest in the survey has been expressed both by public recommendations and private counsel and advice, it was thought that

The first published view of Mount Marcy – 1841
"The Adirondack Group, as seen from Newcomb" (From Ebenezer Emmon's report, *Geology of New York, Part II, Comprising the Survey of the Second Geological District*.)

a more appropriate name could not be conferred on the highest summit of this group than Mount Marcy.

The name *Marcy* was bestowed upon the mountain to honor William Learned Marcy, who was born December 12, 1786, in Massachusetts and was schooled there and at Brown University in Rhode Island. After teaching school in Newport, Rhode Island, he moved to Troy, New York, where he studied law and, after being admitted to the bar, practiced his profession. As a lieutenant in a company of light infantry during the War of 1812, he was sent to French Mills (now Fort Covington) on the St. Lawrence River and on October 23, 1812, became, at St. Regis, the first American officer to capture enemy forces (and their flag) on land during the war. Marcy, without a doubt, traveled through at least some portion of the Adirondacks during his period of service during the war and may well have seen some of the high peaks while on his way to French Mills and during his return, after completing his service.[8]

During the years which followed, Marcy began his political career. He served two terms as Troy's recorder (1816-1818 and 1821-1823), was the state comptroller (1823-1829), an associate justice of the New York State Supreme Court (1829-1831), and a United States Senator (beginning in 1831) before becoming New York's Governor in 1833. He served in that office for three consecutive terms and was defeated for a fourth by Auburn lawyer William H. Seward.

At the time of the naming of the mountain, Marcy was the state's chief executive, one of its best known politicians, and already known beyond the state for having served as judge during the sensational trial of the alleged murderers of William Morgan (a case which spurred the anti-Masonic movement in the United States) and for having spoken these words regarding the "spoils system" on the floor of the United States Senate in January

1832: "They seeing nothing wrong in the rule, that to the victors belong the spoils of the enemy." Marcy's words, often reduced to "To the victor belongs the spoils," are still cited in *Bartlett's Familiar Quotations*.

William Learned Marcy
when he was Secretary of State
(Photo attributed to Matthew Brady)

Marcy would go on to greater achievements, after the peak was named for him and after he left the office of governor. He served from 1839 to 1842 as a commissioner appointed to settle claims against Mexico, and he was Secretary of War under President James Knox Polk (1845-1849). While in that office he managed the affairs of the Mexican War and helped to settle the dispute ("54°40' or Fight") over the Oregon Territory border. He retired from public service in 1849 but was called back to it by President Franklin Pierce, for whom he served (1853-1857) as Secretary of State. During his tenure in that office (which extended briefly into the Buchanan administration), Marcy may best be remembered for his diplomacy in securing the Gadsden Purchase for the United States. He retired again, in March 1857, to his home in Ballston Spa and died there shortly thereafter – July 4, 1857. An early 1900s edition of *Appleton's Encyclopedia* concluded that "He was regarded among his countrymen of all parties as a statesman of the highest order of administrative and diplomatic ability." Today, however, his life and legacy are rarely considered, but his name is recalled upon the state's highest peak.

The choice of the name, Marcy, drew some criticism, particularly from people who felt that naming any mountain after a politician was inappropriate and from some who earnestly believed that the mountain already had a name, Tahawus, bestowed upon it by "native" people. Those who believed that – and some still do – were – and are – wrong.

Emmons made some observations and took barometric readings while atop Marcy on August 5, 1837. Later he published a calculation of the mountain's height as being 5,467 feet above sea level. The figure was a preliminary one, revised with Emmons' blessing by Farrand Benedict, a University of Vermont professor. Benedict, with botanist George McRae, and John Cheney as their guide, made the second recorded ascent of Marcy on August 14, 1839. Benedict, who was regarded as one of the foremost mathematicians in the United States at the time, took a series of barometric readings from the summit that morning, and later, based upon synchronous readings that had been taken at Burlington, calculated the height of the mountain to be 5,344.69 feet in elevation. His complete report concerning his calculations was published by Professor Emmons in his *Geology of New York, Part II, Comprising the Survey of the Second Geological District* (1841).

Benedict's party was the second to reach the summit of the mountain, but earlier, soon after news of the mountain's first ascent had been printed in New York City newspapers in late August 1837, lawyer, journalist, novelist and poet Charles Fenno Hoffman departed from the city for the McIntyre Iron Works so that he could attempt a climb of the high peak. Hoffman, a literary celebrity and friend of Edgar Allen Poe, proceeded along the trail to Marcy in September in the company of Cheney, but he was unable to go far beyond Lake Colden before he was forced to turn back, disappointed. In 1817, at age eleven, in a boating accident, he had lost a leg. The fact that he made it as far as Lake Colden on a wooden leg demonstrated the degree of his determination, but Charles Fenno Hoffman's association with the Adirondacks might not be remembered today at all had he not penned the following words which appeared first in the *New York Mirror* and later in his book, *Wild Scenes in the Forest and Prairie*, first published in England in 1839. Note that he regarded the name *Mount Marcy* a proper one. Also note his pronunciation of *Tahawus:*

> The highest peak... was measured during the last summer, and found to be nearly six thousand feet in height. Mount Marcy, as it has been christened, not improperly, after the publick *(sic)* functionary who first suggested the survey of this interesting region, presents a perfect pyramidal top, when viewed from Lake Sanford. The sharp cone was sheathed in snow on the day I took a swim in the lake; the woods around displayed as yet but few autumnal tints, and the deep verdure of the adjacent mountains set off the snowy peak in such high contrast, that soaring as it did far above them, and seeming to pierce, as it were, the blue sky which curtained them, the poetick *(sic)* Indian epithet of TAH-A-Wus, *He splits the sky,* was hardly extravagant to characterize its particular grandeur.

Charles Fenno Hoffman, the man who "named" Tahawus

Hoffman never wrote that the mountain had been called Tahawus by natives of the area – Mohawks or Abenakis – but some who read his account decided that Tahawus was the name of the mountain before it was designated Marcy. In 1847, Charles Lanman was dismayed that "the beautiful name of Tahawus," if Emmons was "to have his way," would be "superseded by that of Marcy." Also in the 1840s novelist Richard Henry Dana and author Joel Headley favored the name Tahawus, and Headley used it instead of Marcy in his 1849 volume *The Adirondack; or Life in the Woods,* which contains a description of his ascent of the peak in 1846. In 1847, the "Lower Works" of the McIntyre mining operation became known as "Tahawus" as well.

Unfortunately, once something is written in a publication which attains some degree of popularity, it tends to take on a life of its own. Other authors read the misinformation and repeat it in their works, and, eventually, a fallacy becomes an accepted "fact." Thus, even though respected historians and Adirondack experts, including Alfred B. Street and Verplanck Colvin, understood that the high peak had never been called Tahawus by Native Americans, false interpretation of Hoffman's description of the mountain as he had seen it from Lake Sanford made it so. The bronze plaque on the summit rock of Mount Marcy, commemorating the first ascent by the Emmons party, tells those who reach that summit that Marcy is "Also Known by the Indian Name TAHAWUS meaning CLOUD-SPLITTER." Even the Forty-Sixers are not exempt from preserving the error. Orra A. Phelps (#47) wrote the words for "Tahawus," a hymn still sung at club vespers services. Tahawus, by the way, is most likely derived from the language of the Seneca, who occupied a large portion of western-most New York state. It, apparently, was never applied by members of that tribe to a place; rather, according to a former state archaeologist, Dr. Arthur C. Parker, it was an "abstract word of religion."[9]

Charles Fenno Hoffman also contributed to the literature of the Adirondacks and the lore of Mount Marcy when he quoted "a hunter," presumably his guide, John Cheney, concerning the view from Marcy's summit:

It makes a man feel what it is to have all creation under his feet. There are woods there which it would take a lifetime to hunt over, mountains that seem shouldering each other to boost the one whereon you stand, up and away Heaven knows where. Thousands of little lakes are let in among them so light and clean. Old Champlain, though fifty miles away, glistens below you like a strip of white birch when slicked up by the moon on a frosty night, and the Green Mountains of Vermont beyond it fade and fade away until they disappear as gradually as a cold scent when the dew rises.

Joel Tyler Headley

So far as is known, the third successful ascent of Marcy was made by a party which included Farrand Benedict's cousin, Joel Tyler Headley, on July 12, 1846. Cheney was the principal guide for the party. After floundering through fir trees which "grew thicker and more dwarfish" as they "ascended, til they became mere shrubs, and literally matted together, so that you could not see two feet in advance of you," Headley and the others "passed over the bed of a moose, which (they) doubtless roused from his repose, for the rank grass was still matted where he had lain."

Headley continued his description in his volume *The Adirondack; or Life in the Woods* (1849):

> At length, we emerged upon the brow of a cliff, across a gulf at the base of which arose a bare, naked pyramid, that pushed its rocky forehead high into the heavens. This was the summit of Tahawus. A smooth grey rock, shaped like an inverted bowl, stood before us, as if on purpose to mock all our efforts. Halfway up this was S—th, looking no larger than a dog, as with his pack on his back he crawled on all fours over the rocks. Hitherto nothing could knock the fun out of him; and as he from time to time stumbled on a log, or heard the complaint of some one behind, he would sing in a comical sort of a chorus, *"go-in-up,"* followed by his hearty ha-ha-ha, as if he were impervious to fatigue. To every halloo we sent after him, he would return that everlasting *"go-in-up,"* sung out so funnily that we invariably echoed back his laugh, till the mountains rang again. But now he was silent – the *"go-in-up"* had become a serious matter, and it required all his breath to enable him to "go up."

Headley wrote that a "chill wind swept by like a December blast" as they ascended the "bald cone." He noted that the trees "gradually dwindled away, till they were not taller than your finger, and *[then]* disappeared altogether; for nothing but naked rock could resist the climate of this high region." He continued,

> At length we reached the top; and oh, what a view spread out before, or rather below us. Here we were more than a mile up in the heavens on the highest point of land in the Empire State; and with one exception the highest in the Union;[10] and in the centre of a chaos of mountains, the like of which I never saw before. It was wholly different from the Alps.[11] There were no snow peaks and shining glaciers; but all was grey, or green, or black, as far as the vision could extend. It looked as if the Almighty had once set this vast earth rolling like the sea; and then, in the midst of its maddest flow, bid all the gigantic billows stop and congeal in their places. And there they stood, just as He froze them – grand and gloomy. There was the long swell – and there the cresting, bursting billow – and there, too, the deep, black cavernous gulf.

According to his account, Headley and his party climbed to the peak in a single day. They began their trek from the iron works at 7 a.m. and reached the summit at 4 p.m.

In *The Adirondack,* Headley provided an account of the death of David Henderson when, in describing the route to Mount Marcy, he wrote, "The first few miles there is a rough path, which was cut last summer, in order to bring out the body of Mr. Henderson. It is a great help, but filled with sad associations."

He continued,

> At length we came to the spot where twenty-five workmen watched with the body in the forest all night. It was too late to get through, and here they kindled their camp-fire, and stayed. The rough poles are still there, on which the corpse rested. "Here," says Cheney, "on this log I sat all night, and held Mr. Henderson's little son, eleven years of age, in my arms. Oh, how he cried to be taken in to his mother; but it was impossible to find our way through the woods; and he, at length, cried himself to sleep in my arms. Oh, it was a dreadful night." A mile further on, and we came to the rock where he was shot. It stands by a little pond, and was selected by them to dine upon. Cheney was standing on the other side of the pond, with the little boy, whither they had gone to make a raft, on which to take some trout, when he heard the report of a gun, and then a scream; and looking across, saw Mr. Henderson clasp his arms twice over his breast, exclaiming, "I am shot!" The son fainted by Cheney's side; but in a few moments all stood round the dying man, who murmured, "What an accident, and in such a place!" In laying down his pistol, with the muzzle unfortunately towards him, the hammer struck the rock, and the cap exploding, the entire contents were lodged in his body. After commending his soul to his Maker, and telling his son to be a good boy, and give his love to his mother, he leaned back and died. It made us sad to gaze on the spot; and poor Cheney, as he drew a long sigh, looked the picture of sorrow...

Henderson had died while engaged in an exploration, attempting to find a water source which could be diverted for use by the iron works for the motive power to drive the bellows that supplied the blast furnaces and the waterwheels of the forge. Plans were being made to dig a half-mile-long canal to join the upper Opalescent River to what later became known as the Calamity Brook. On September 3, 1845, the company's engineer, Daniel Taylor went with Henderson, Henderson's son Archie, Cheney, and another guide, Tone Snyder, up the Calamity Brook to the pond where Henderson lost his life, now Calamity Pond. Snyder quickly returned to the village at the Upper Works to gather a rescue party - the "workmen" that Headley wrote about. They cut the path that Headley's party followed the next year. The stone memorial which was erected along the trail to Lake Colden within a few years of Henderson's death, reads as follows: "This monument erected in filial affection To the memory of our dear father David Henderson who accidentally lost his life on this spot 3rd September 1845."

Artist and writer Charles Lanman[12] ventured into the "Adirondac Mountains" in 1847. He traveled from Lyndsey's Tavern at "Scaroon" (Schroon Lake) by way of the "mettle of his legs... about fifteen miles, through a hilly, thickly wooded, and houseless wilderness," to the Boreas River with "a pair of temporary companions, who were going into the interior to see their friends, and have a few days' sport in the way of fishing and hunting." They stopped to camp together along the river in "a ruined shantee" in "a lonely spot at about three o'clock in the afternoon," and Lanman and one of his companions proceeded to go fishing. In his account of the trip in *Adventures in the Wilds of the United States and British American Provinces* (1856), Lanman reported that he "threw a red hackle for upwards of three hours" and had the "rare luck" of catching 34 trout, "twenty-one of which averaged three-quarters of a pound, and the remaining thirteen were regular two-pounders." He returned to the shanty with his catch and found his companions there, "one of them sitting before a blazing fire and fiddling, and the other busily employed in cleaning the trout he had taken." Following their sumptuous dinner, the three "spent the following hours in smoking and telling stories, and having made a bed of spruce boughs... retired to repose!"[13] The next morning, they "shouldered" their "knapsacks, and started for the Hudson." They reached the "noble river at the embryo city of Tahawus," where they found "a log house and an unfinished saw-mill" and a canoe which they used to travel upstream to Lake Sanford. From the end of the lake they followed a "mountain road... about four miles" to "the famous Newcomb Farm," occupied by Steuben Hewitt and his family. Lanman wrote that...

>Newcomb Farm is well worth visiting, if for no other purpose than to witness the panorama of mountains which it commands. On every side but one may they be seen, fading away to mingle their deep blue with the lighter hue of the sky, but the chief among them is old Tahawus, King of the Adirondacs. The country out of which this mountain rises, is an imposing Alpine wilderness, and as it has long since been abandoned by the red man, the solitude of its deep valleys and lonely lakes for the most part, is now more impressive than that of the far off Rocky Mountains... Though Tahawus is not quite so lofty as its New England brother *(Mount Washington)*, yet its form is by far the more picturesque and imposing...
>
>For nine months of the year old Tahawus is covered with a crown of snow, but there are spots among its fastnesses where you may gather ice and snow even in the dog days. The base of this mountain is covered with a luxuriant forest of pine, spruce and hemlock, while the summit is clothed in a net-work of creeping trees, and almost destitute of the green which should characterize them. In ascending its sides when near the summit, you are impressed with the idea that your pathway may be smooth; but as you proceed, you are constantly annoyed by pit-falls, into which your legs are foolishly poking themselves, to the great annoyance of your back bone and other portions of your body which are naturally straight.

Lanman "ascended Tahawus, as a matter of course, and in making the trip... travelled some twenty miles on foot and through the pathless woods, employing for the same the better part of two days." His only companion, apparently, on the "expedition was John Cheney," who so impressed him that he devoted an entire chapter of his book to the "Nimrod" and his stories about his dogs and his hunts, including his having shot two moose on the side of Mount Marcy with a single ball.

"The view from Tahawus," Lanman described in a single sentence, mentioning that "it looks down upon what appears to be an uninhabited wilderness." He and Cheney spent only "one hour gazing upon the panorama from the top, and then descended about half way down the mountain where" they "built their watch fire" and settled down for the night. There, Cheney – "a remarkably amiable and intelligent man... small in stature, bearing more the appearance of a modest and thoughtful student, gentle in his manners, and as devoted a lover of nature and solitude as ever lived" – told Lanman "the manner in which certain distinguished gentlemen have ascended Mount Tahawus, for it must be known that he officiates as the guide of all travellers in this wild region."

>Among those to whom he alluded were Ingham and Cole,[14] the artists, and Hoffman and Headley, the travellers. He told me that Mr. Ingham fainted a number of times in making the ascent, but became so excited with all he saw, he determined to persevere, and finally succeeded in accomplishing the difficult task. Mr. Hoffman, he said, in spite of his lameness, would not be

persuaded by words that he could not reach the summit; and when he finally discovered that this task was utterly beyond his accomplishment, his disappointment seemed to have no bounds."

A "regular built rain-storm" disturbed the rest of the two hikers that night, but they were awakened the next morning "from a short but refreshing sleep, by the singing of birds, and when the cheerful sunlight had reached the bottom of the ravines, *[they]* were enjoying a comfortable breakfast" back at the village of McIntyre, where "the prominent individual, and only remarkable man" who lived there was "the mighty hunter of the Adirondacs," Lanman's guide, John Cheney.

On October 19, 1847, the Tahawian Association was established at Elizabethtown, apparently at the urging of Dr. David P. Holton[15] of New York City. Those present at the meeting – including Orlando Kellogg,[16] A. C. Hand,[17] and Byron Pond[18] of Elizabethtown, Wendell Lansing[19]; Archibald McIntyre[20] of Albany – considered "the propriety of cutting a pedestrian road through the wilderness in the western section of Essex County to the tops of Tahawus and Whiteface by way of the Adirondac Pass *(Indian Pass).*"

> After a free interchange of sentiments, regarding the geological and geographical relations of these regions, and the topographical bearings of the proposed road, and the advantages, which would accrue to the health seeking pedestrians," the members of the association resolved to "prepare a pedestrian road from Keene Flats, westward to the summit of Tahawus, estimated distance ten miles; thence down to the Adirondac and Tahawus Iron Works, fifteen miles; thence northward through the Adirondac Pass to Lake Placid, seventeen miles; thence eastward to the top of Whiteface and down to Wilmington eight miles – the whole distance estimated fifty miles.

The group also resolved to make "efforts" to fund an "educational convention on Tahawus, the second week of August 1848, or such other time as the Executive Committee" might designate. A "suitable sum" was to be appropriated "to pay for engraving on Tahawus the names of all who give not less than one dollar in money or two days' work upon the road." Fifty "Testaments, in Phonotypes of Dr. Comstock"[21] were to be purchased and a copy, each, presented to "any gentleman or lady" who would present an "Address, Essay, or Poem upon any department of the moral, intellectual, or physical condition and progress of man" approved by the association. Left over money was to go to the construction of the "road" and to the "erecting" of shanties "at suitable stages." If any other money remained, it was to go to the purchase of "Testaments in phonotypes" for clergymen "within a circuit, Tahawus being the centre..."

Although the "pedestrian road" proposed by the Tahawian Association was not built, the "educational convention on Tahawus" actually took place. In his "Reminiscences," Dr. Holton reported as follows:

> In celebrating the seventy-first anniversary of American Independence, Saturday, 3d of July, 1847, it was my privilege to accompany several school-teachers to the top of Whiteface mountain in the western section of Essex Co. N.Y., and there to engrave the symbols of these elementary sounds, giving on that occasion an address upon the "Aid which Phonotypes will be in translating the Bible into the languages of the heathen..."
>
> One month later, August 3d, similar exercises were had at the school district of the *Adirondack Iron Works,* and on Tahawus (Mount Marcy), August 4th and 5th...

If phonetic symbols were actually "engraved" on the summit of Mount Marcy in August 1847, they apparently did not last long. Old Mountain Phelps told Verplanck Colvin that he had seen them in 1849, but no other mention of them has ever been recorded. However, the word *Tahawus* was chiseled into the summit's anorthosite at about the time Holton and his party of phonotypists visited the mountain.

Richard Henry Dana,[22] author of *Two Years Before the Mast,* made an expedition to New York's highest peak by way of Westport, Elizabethtown, Keene, North Elba, Indian Pass, and the iron works at Adirondac in 1849. For Dana, before he "had seen the Yosemite Valley," Wallface Mountain's "cliffs satisfied" his "ideal of steep mountain walls." He remarked about "a wintry chill" that pervaded the air in Indian Pass and wrote about refreshing himself "with water dripping from out of ice-caverns" and walking "over banks of snow which lie here through the year, preserved by the exclusion of the sun."

Dana and his companions on his trek spent several days in the vicinity of Adirondac in the company of Dan Gates, Tone Snyder, Jack Wright, and John Cheney – "names redolent in memory of rifles and sable-traps, and hemlock camps and deer, and trout and hard walks and good talks."

He wrote,

> The scenery here is as different from that of the White Mountains as if these were in a different hemisphere. Here the mountains wave with woods, and are green with bushes to their summits; torrents break down into the valleys on all sides; lakes of various sizes and shapes glitter in the landscape, bordered by bending woods whose roots strike through the waters. There is none of that dreary, barren grandeur that marks the White Mountains, although Tahawus, the highest, is about forty-four hundred feet high...
>
> We spent two days and nights in the ascent of Tahâwus and the return, camping out under hemlock boughs, cooking our trout and venison in the open air, and enjoying it all as I verily believe none can so thoroughly as they who escape from city life.

In the midst of lamenting about the naming of the mountain for Governor Marcy, Dana mentioned that "a company of travellers have chiselled the old Indian name into rocks at its summit." Perhaps the letters of the name *Tahawus* were what Orson Phelps saw that same year, 1849.

In the years that followed, Marcy – still called Tahawus, according to Dana, by the "woodsmen" – was climbed frequently from the iron works. Among those who made the climb were artists Jervis McEntee and Joseph Tubby in 1851,[23] and T. Addison Richards[24] about 1859. Richards wrote and illustrated an account of a climb for *Harper's Monthly*. His party reportedly included four women, but, if they did complete the climb to the summit, as Richards said they did, they were not the first females to do so.[25] Mary Cook and Fannie Newton were credited with that honor when in 1858 they climbed to the summit, along the Panther Gorge route from the Upper Ausable Lake, with Harvey Holt, Orson S. Phelps, William and Riley Peacock, William and Marvin Washbund, and Theodore White, all of Keene Flats (now Keene Valley). Russell Carson later wrote in *Peaks and People,* "It was a difficult climb, especially for Miss Cook, who was of generous proportions, but she is said to have refused the aid of a rope around her waist to help her up the slides."[26] Several years later, again in the company of Phelps, Miss Cook climbed the mountain again.

Following the death of David Henderson at Calamity Pond in 1845, the Adirondack Iron and Steel Company[27] experienced a period of boom (1848 to 1853) and one of bust (1854 to 1858). The property, which then included a cupola furnace, an "old" blast furnace, and a puddling furnace,[28] was purchased in 1853 by a syndicate of businessmen represented by Benjamin C. Butler of Luzerne for a princely sum, more than half a million dollars. The following year the mine added its latest improvement, the "new" blast furnace which is extant, a preserved ruin, along the road to the Upper Works. It was first "fired" on August 20, 1854. Its capacity was "14 tons of iron per day." Iron from the mine was shipped, with great difficulty to Jersey City; there much of it was worked to become table flatware at the Adirondac Steel Manufacturing Company owned by Archibald McIntyre, Archibald Robertson, Dudley S. Gregory, and the estate of David Henderson. The company's product, the first steel manufactured in this country, won a gold medal at the 1850 Exposition at the Crystal

The Henderson Monument by Lossing

Palace in London. The man who managed to make steel of McIntyre iron was Joseph Dixon (1799-1869), who later perfected the manufacture of lead (graphite) pencils and the plumbago crucibles which assured the century-long success of the American steel industry. Dixon left the company in 1852.[29]

One of the principal problems the mining operation had faced, that of the difficulty of transportation to and from its markets, had seemed on the verge of solution when, in 1848, the Sackett's Harbor and Saratoga Railroad was chartered. The line, between the two locations, would have passed within a reasonable distance of the iron works, and if it had been built, a branch line would have been run to the Upper Works; however, by the mid 1850s, hope that the railroad would be built began to fade. Without it, Harold Hochschild wrote in his *The MacIntyre Mine - From Failure to Fortune,* "the mine could not make a profit. It was compelled to cart its ore to Lake Champlain for barge transportation to Jersey City... The excessive cost of this long haul by horse and wagon made it impossible to compete with imported Scotch pig iron."

The syndicate which had purchased the McIntyre property made only the first of ten annual payments and, Hochschild continued, "The railroad did not come, and without it the McIntyre enterprise lost its attraction to the syndicate members. The purchase contract lapsed and the title remained with the Adirondack Iron and Steel Company."

Disaster struck in August 1856, when heavy rains created a flood on the Opalescent. It destroyed the dam at Adirondac and both the dam and a sawmill at the Lower Works. The following year was marked by a nationwide financial crisis. Archibald McIntyre died in May 1858. Archibald Robertson died in September 1858. In *The Story of Adirondac* (1923), Arthur H. Masten wrote, "The cessation of operations, whenever they occurred, was a sudden step. Work was dropped just as it was... The last cast from the furnace was still in the sand and the tools were left leaning against the wall of the cast house."

By 1859, the Adirondack Iron and Steel Company was out of business. Adirondac had been deserted, the company's former workers had scattered. Only Robert Hunter, a former bricklayer for the company, and his family remained at the old village. He was retained as the property's caretaker, according to John Burroughs in *Wake Robin,* "at a dollar a day..." to live there "and see that things were not wantonly destroyed, but allowed to decay properly and decently."

In *The Hudson from the Wilderness to the Sea,* Benson Lossing described his 1859 excursion to the top of Mount Marcy in the company of his wife, a Mr. Buckingham, and their two guides, Mitchell Sabattis and William Preston. They...

set out from Adirondack on the afternoon of the 30th of August, our guides with their packs leading the way... We crossed the Hudson three-fourths of a mile below Henderson Lake, upon a rude bridge, made our way through a clearing tangled with tall raspberry shrubs full of fruit, for nearly half a mile, and then entered the deep and solemn forest... Our way was over a level for three-fourths of a mile, to the outlet of Calamity Pond. We crossed it at a beautiful cascade, and then commenced ascending by a sinuous mountain path, across which many a huge tree had been cast by the wind. It was a weary journey of almost four miles... for in many places the soil was hidden by boulders covered with thick moss, over which we were compelled to climb. Towards sunset we reached a pleasant little lake, embosomed in the dense forest, its low wet margin fringed with brilliant yellow flowers, beautiful in form but without perfume. At the head of that little lake, where the inlet comes flowing sluggishly from a dark ravine scooped from the mountain slope, we built a bark cabin, and encamped the night.

Lossing and company had made it, their first day on the trail, as far as Calamity Pond. They feasted that evening and at breakfast the next morning on "over two dozen trout" which Sabattis and Buckingham had caught in the pond from a "rough raft."

Resuming their trek on August 31, the party had to proceed "a much rougher" way, "for there was nothing but a dim and obstructed hunter's trail to follow." They "pursued" it to the outlet of Lake Colden and "walked more than four miles in the bed" of the drought-reduced Opalescent "upon boulders."

"Departure for Tahawus" by Lossing

We crossed it *(the Opalescent)* a hundred times or more, picking our way, and sometimes compelled to go into the woods in passing a cascade. The stream is broken into falls and swift rapids the whole distance that we followed it, and, when full, it must present a grand spectacle. At one place the river had assumed the bed of a displaced trap dyke, by which the rock has been intersected. The walls are perpendicular, and only a few feet apart – so near that the branches of the trees on the summits interlace. Through this the water rushes for several rods, and then leaps into a dark chasm, full fifty feet perpendicular, and emerges among a mass of immense boulders.

The falls Lossing described: Hanging Spear. He included a sketch of it, "Fall in the Opalescent River," in his book.

The party followed the Opalescent, Lossing wrote, "to the foot of the Peak of Tahawus, on the borders of the high valley which separates that mountain from Mount Colden, at an elevation nine hundred feet above the highest peaks of the Cattskill range on the Lower Hudson":

"Fall in the Opalescent River"

> There the water is very cold, the forest trees are somewhat stunted and thickly planted, and the solitude complete. The silence was almost oppressive. Game-birds and beasts of the chase are there almost unknown. The wildcat and wolverine alone prowl over that lofty valley, where rises one of the chief fountains of the Hudson, and we heard the voice of no living creature excepting the hoarse croak of the raven.
>
> It was noon when we reached this point of departure for the summit of Tahawus. We had been four hours travelling six miles, and yet in that pure mountain air we felt very little fatigue. There we found an excellent bark "camp," and traces of recent occupation. Among them was part of a metropolitan newspaper, and light ashes. We dined upon bread and butter and maple sugar, in a sunny spot in front of the cabin, and then commenced the ascent, leaving our provisions and other things at the camp, where we intended to repose for the night. The journey upward was two miles, at an angle of forty-five degrees to the base of the rocky pinnacle. We had no path to follow. The guides "blazed" the larger trees (striking off chips with their axes), that they might with more ease find their way back to the camp. Almost the entire surface was covered with boulders, shrouded in the most beautiful alpine mosses. From among these shot up dwarfing pines and spruces, which diminished in height at every step. Through their thick horizontal branches it was difficult to pass. Here and there among the rocks was a free spot, where the bright trifoliolate oxalis, or wood-sorel, flourished, and the shrub of the wild currant, and gooseberry, and the tree-cranberry appeared. At length we reached the foot of the open rocky pinnacle, where only thick mosses, lichens, a few alpine plants, and little groves of dwarfed balsam, are seen. The latter trees, not more than five feet in height, are, most of them, centenarians. Their stems, not larger than a strong man's wrist, exhibited, when cut, over one hundred concentric rings, each of which indicates the growth of a year. Our journey now became still more difficult, at the same time more interesting, for, as we emerged from the forest, the magnificent panorama of mountains that lay around us burst upon the vision. Around steep rocky slopes and ledges, and around and beneath huge stones a thousand tons in weight, some of them apparently poised, as if ready for a sweep down the mountain, we made our way cautiously, having at times no other support than the strong moss, and occasionally a gnarled shrub that sprung from the infrequent fissures. We rested upon small terraces, where the dwarf balsams grew. Upon one of those, within a hundred feet of the summit, we found a spring of very cold water, and near it quite thick ice. This spring is one of the remote sources of the

Lossing's "Climbing Tahawus" – First published view of the climb

Hudson. It bubbles from the base of a huge mass of loose rocks (which, like all the other portions of the peak, are composed of beautiful labradorite), and sends down a little stream into the Opalescent River, from whose bed we had just ascended.

A few minutes later, behind Mr. Buckingham, Lossing and his wife achieved the summit, "forgetful, in the exhilaration of the moment, of every fatigue and danger" they "had encountered." Lossing wrote, "Indeed it was a triumph for us all, for few persons have ever attempted the ascent of that mountain, lying in a deep wilderness, hard to penetrate, the nearest point of even a bridle path, on the side of our approach, being ten miles from the base of its peak."

Lossing described the summit spur whose face today holds the Marcy plaque and compared it to "the heel of an upturned boot." He wrote, "In a nook on the southern side of this heel, was a small hut, made of loose stones gathered from the summit, and covered with moss. It was erected the previous year by persons from New York, and had been occupied by others a fort-night before our visit. Within the hut we found a piece of paper, on which was written: – 'This hospice, erected by a party from New York, August 19, 1858, is intended for the use and comfort of visitors to Tahawus. – F.S.P. – M.C. – F.M.N.' Under this was written: – 'This hospice was occupied over night of August 14, 1859, by A.G.C. and T.R.D. Sun rose fourteen minutes to five.' Under this: – 'Tahawus House Register, August 14, 1859, Alfred G. Compton, and Theodore R. Davis,[30] New York. August 16, Charles Newman, Stamford, Connecticut; Charles Bedfield, Elizabeth Town, New York.' To these we added our own names, and those of the guides."

Sketch of "Hospice on the Peak of Tahawus" by Lossing

Sandra Weber (#5227) in *Mount Marcy, The High Peak of New York,* identifies the builders of the "hospice," mentioning that the initials recorded by Lossing correspond to the names of "artist Frederick S. Perkins,[31] Mary Cook, and Fannie Newton, who climbed from Keene Valley." The shelter did not last many years.

Lossing devoted several pages of his book to a description of the view from the summit, both topographic and historic. He wrote, "It required little exercise of the imagination to behold the stately procession of historic men and events, passing through" the Champlain Valley "to the east."

Because the "cold increased every moment as the sun declined," the party remained atop Marcy only an hour before descending to the camp where they had left their packs earlier, and there they spent the night. They reached Lake Colden and "dined" there the next day. They were back at Calamity Pond by three o'clock in the afternoon, and "just before sunset emerged from the forest into the open fields near Adirondack village." The following day, they visited Indian Pass and returned to "Mr. Hunter's" that evening. In four days' time, Lossing reported, "we had travelled thirty miles on foot in the tangled forest, camped out two nights, and seen some of nature's wildest and grandest lineaments." He went on to tell his readers that the wilderness gave "the tourist most exquisite sensations, and the physical system appears to take in health at every pore. Invalids go in with hardly strength enough to reach some quiet log-house in a clearing, and come out with strong quick pulse and elastic muscles... It has been called by the uninformed the 'Siberia of New York;' it may more properly be called the 'Switzerland of the United States.'"

The approach to Mount Marcy along the Calamity Brook and Opalescent River was fully established by the time of the Civil War, and the route would remain a standard one until Verplanck Colvin pioneered the short approach by way of the Feldspar Brook to Lake Tear-of-the-Clouds and Four Corners in the 1870s.

Starting from "Scott's" at North Elba with guides Loyal A. Merrill and Robert Scott Blinn, Alfred B. Street ascended Marcy via Indian Pass and the "abandoned village of the Upper Works" along the "original" route in 1865. Carson wrote that Street and his two guides followed "the second Marcy trail... cut between 1859 and 1865, following the Opalescent River farther north than the present trail does and going on to the summit from the northwest," not by way of the Feldspar Brook, which Redfield had observed in 1837 and had thought might "afford the shortest route to Marcy."

Street stopped at Hunter's home "for a few days" to make himself "comfortable" after having developed an "incipient limp" along the way from North Elba. With his "foot being healed, thanks to the magic ointment of kind Mrs. Hunter and the yellow plasters of a very nice, friendly young Philadelphian who, with his bright-eyed brothers, was passing the summer at the village," he decided "to start for Tahawus, fifteen miles distant." He "donned" a "copper shoe" he had had made for his hiking and began the trek with his guides and Hunter, who went along as far as the "splendid Iron Dam."

The trio passed by the Henderson Monument at Calamity Pond and, as sunset "smiled" upon them, reached "a little hunter's shanty near Lake Colden." The following day "was devoted to Lake Avalanche," the "savage lake." They attempted to navigate Lake Colden upon a cedar raft Merrill and Blinn had constructed the night before, but it became stuck in a "shallow" and they were obliged to wade ashore. They took to the Colden side of the lake and began what Street described as a "frightful journey across the flank of the almost precipitous summit," to Avalanche Lake, eventually coming across and following "a line of fresh panther-tracks (deep, huge, showing the enormous size of the creature)." Street, thrilled by the sublime nature of the wilderness, as he constantly was throughout his accounts in *The Indian Pass* (1869), wrote about "the almost absolute certainty of *[their]* being the first for many years, to attempt the visit of this most recluse, untamed, and almost unknown lake."[32]

As "everything comes to an end at last," so did their trek to the lake that had, Street surmised, been last visited by Professor Emmons in 1837: "Our level path leading through tall herbage, was soon trod, and wading through a few bushes, we ascended a small acclivity, and the deep, black waters of Avalanche were before us."

> I made my way to a tall rock, emerald with moss and gray with lichen, on the immediate shore of the pure, transparent lake, and sat down to stamp the scene upon my heart. The ragged fracture of the great Trap Dyke, so famous among geologists, calling forth their warmest enthusiasm, and cut so deeply (one hundred feet) into the flinty ashy gray hypersthene of Mount Colden, frowned directly opposite.

Rain soon descended. The party returned to their camp at Lake Colden and took up the ascent of Mount Marcy the next day, crossing on a "fallen tree, bridging a foaming watercourse" from the lake "which dashed into the Opalescent directly from the roots of old Tahawus... Then up, up, the fierce river brawling in its wide, glary, rocky channel..." They climbed for "a mile" along "the famous 'Flume' of the Opalescent," and "at length came to a little green dell, bare of trees... Then the trail suddenly turned, leaving the river..." Street thought they "were probably a mile from its source, which lies... in a small meadow on the lofty flank of Tahawus." The trail "became immediately steep," and the three men stopped for a "cordial tea" before starting up again: "Up, up, up, without intermission!"

Drawing ourselves by pendent boughs, inserting our feet into fissures of the rocks, clutching wood-sprouts and knotted roots, and dangling by little saplings, up, up, up, with not a solitary level spot, we went, climbing thus our mountain-ladder. Loftier, as we went, rose the grand breast of an opposite mountain that we set down as Mount Colden. Up, up, up! the magnificent flank of Colden now heaving on high like an enormous ocean billow piled from hundreds of its fellows. It was awful, the sight of that mountain! its frown fairly chilled my blood. But up, up, still up. The trees that had hitherto towered into the sky, dwindled perceptibly, warning us that something was to happen. Up, up, still up. Lower and lower the trees. Barer and barer the rocks… Owing to the difficulties of the route, clinging to every object that presents, I cannot look upward! Steeper, if possible, the trail! See! the shrub I clutch, to drag myself ponderously upward…

Up, up, still up! The shrub lies flat, a stiff verdant wreath, a mere crawling vine, a thing of wire, with scarce life sufficient to keep life!

After a while, Street saw "Bob Blin!" above and "Merrill following. And so I followed too."

Showers of stones, loosened by my guides, rattled past. Still up I went. Over the precipitous rock by clambering its cracks and crannies, through its tortuous galleries, along the dizzy edges of the chasms. A score of times I thought the summit was just in front, but no; on still went my guides, and on still I followed. I began to think the nearer I approached the farther I was off. But at last Merrill and Blin both became stationary, in fact seated themselves, – their figures sharply relieved against the sky. Surmounting a steep acclivity, then turning into a sort of winding gallery, and passing a large mass of rock, I placed myself at their side, and lo, the summit!

Merrill and Blinn fired their rifles from the summit "for the echo. The sounds were like two short taps, or rather asthmatic coughs. A minute followed of blank silence – then a faint tone struggled from a distant gorge." Street observed, "And such is fame. We shout our names aloud to arrest the attention of the world, and lo, but stifled tones are heard, succeeded by feeble reverberation, and all is still and soon forgotten."

The three men stayed upon the summit until after sunset and Street, making no mention of the shelter Lossing had observed, considered, "How romantic would prove the night, to lie here on the brow of the stately Titan, listening to the long, deep breathings of its slumber, as the breeze heaved the forest, and waiting for the coming of the dawn!" But, concluding that it would be "awfully cold!" they descended to "encamp not far from the summit" so that they might return to it the next morning to view the sunrise.

He, Merrill, and Blinn did so and took in the view replete with "gauzes of mist" that "glimmered between the peaks." Merrill, with a hammer, carved their names "on the peak," and Street, seeing "a point or headland jutting out below from where he stood, "resolved to reach it" to see what its prospect might reveal.

Merrill attempted to dissuade him, saying "Don't go there, I entreat! It is dangerous." Nonetheless, Street "persevered" through "the most terrible twine of bayonet-pointed chevaux de frise" but could not penetrate it to reach the headland. He turned and struggled back to reach his companions. Had he reached the "point," he might have been inspired to write a dozen or more pages about what he would have seen: the side of Haystack as it plunges into Panther Gorge.

The article concluded, "Forcing our way through the thicket... out from every leafy barrier we pass, and stand in the midst of barrenness and desolation. Awhile we throw ourselves down on a bed of lichens, panting almost breathless from fatigue... The summit is in sight and surely near. To our utter incredulity we are told that it is yet two hundred feet above us... But excitement could carry us on now, and before noon we stand on the topmost stone of Marcy... A countryman on first reaching this point exclaimed, 'By golly, there's nothing but mountains, and where they couldn't get in a big one they sharpened up a little one and stuck it in.' No language can describe the glory and the magnificence of the view."

In his 1874 edition of *The Adirondacks Illustrated,* Seneca Ray Stoddard wrote about climbing Marcy with Old Mountain Phelps from Keene Valley by way of the Upper Ausable Lake and his trail over Bartlett Mountain to Marcy Brook... "then up toward the west or through Panther Gorge." Giving Phelps "the floor," he quoted the guide as follows:

  Well, I guess I kin show you the way, fur I've been up there near a hundred times, I 'spose. Let's see, we're in Panther Gorge now, I believe, and before we go up Marcy, I want to show you a sight up here from the side of Haystack that is worth seeing, where we can look right down into the gulf below. See that precipice on the Marcy side? It is one continuous wall of rock a mile in length, circling around to the head of the gorge with Castle Column at its head; that is one of the wildest places in the Adirondacks, where, after a heavy rain or in the spring, streams pour down it from all sides. You see that water-course over there in the centre? I have seen an almost unbroken sheet of water, six feet wide, pouring over that to the bottom of the gorge, almost a thousand feet below. Now we will pass on up the trail once more, just stopping to notice those shafts of rock across on the Haystack side. There are three of them, entirely detached from the wall near by, about ten feet square, and one of them near fifty feet high, with a loose cap-stone on top of it. The soft rock must have crumbled away between them and the main ledge while they were left standing. Now, out at the upper end and we begin to climb Marcy, striking the John's Brook trail that goes down to Keene Flats near its centre. Up here, on the side of the mountain, we find a little marsh, which is the head of the longest branch of the Ausable; but our trees are getting stunted and we will soon be able to see over the tops of them; it's about like going through a thrashing machine trying to get along before they are chopped out; but here we are at last at the top, and you will see the place to see things; down there at Marcy Brook, where we turned to go through Panther Gorge, comes the other trail up this way, running spirally up the south side from east to west until it strikes the smooth rock that has been swept clean by the avalanche; then up that, across back and forth to its head. It is about as steep as the roof of a house, and when it is wet and slippery it's bad getting along, but when it's dry it sticks to your boots like sand paper.

Much of what follows, though abbreviated by Stoddard, is very similar to the description of the view from Marcy that Phelps wrote in the manuscript, "The High Peaks of Essex." In his transcription of a portion of the manuscript's text, Bill Healy found Phelps to have written, "As I have had more opportunity than any other one to obsurve different views from the summit of Tahawus some of them may be of interest. A view of a clear atmosphere is the view most sought but seldom obtained in the many times and days I have been on its summit which is nearly a hundred in all I never have but three times could see the outlines of two of the summits of the White Mts in New Hampshire which must be at least 150 miles distant."

In Stoddard's version, that text became "In the many times and days I have been on its summit, I have but three times had what I call a first-class clear view, then I could see the outlines of two of the summits of the White Mountains in New Hampshire, which must be at least 150 miles distant."

Another quote from the manuscript as transposed by Healy: "I once saw the clearing up of a thunder shower at sunset there was a tornado of a wind sweeping over the top of the mt and the fog clouds which were broken into patches were runing at a lightning speede and when one of these clouds would strike the mt all would be shut in with fog for perhaps 2 or 3 seconds when it would pass and opin a view to the west of dazzling Oring sunset over the extent of the whole western horrison this could be injoyed from 2 to 3 seconds more when the enveloping fog would come again to save the brain going crazy."

Phelps added an interesting observation concerning the rising and setting of the sun as viewed from Marcy. In Stoddard's version, he said, "The sun appears over the Green Mountains, in July, eight minutes before sunrise by the almanac, and is in sight, seventeen minutes after sundown."

One of the most awesome scenes Phelps witnessed from Marcy was recorded by Stoddard this way: "A thunder storm in the night is an awful sight from the summit of Tahawus. I once saw one at near midnight, approaching from the west, when it was all below me, and could look on the top of the cloud and see the streaks of lightning darting in every direction; it appeared like a mountain of serpents writhing in every conceivable manner."

The description of the route that Stoddard included in *The Adirondacks Illustrated* indicates that it was an unusual one, particularly as it "struck" the "John's Brook trail that goes down to Keene Flats near its centre." Sandra Weber speculated that Phelps led the Stoddard party "on a bit of a 'random scoot' up Panther Gorge and onto the side of Haystack... then... to the upper end of the gorge, where they joined the Johns Brook trail..." A study of a topographical map which shows the contours of the gorge makes it evident that there is only one way to do so: to go up the steep upper reaches of the stream that passes down into the gorge at its head. After a challenging climb, 600 vertical feet in a quarter mile, one could achieve a relatively flat area and soon reach the course of the present Phelps Trail to Marcy, about where the trail from Haystack joins it.

In 1985, on the occasion of the centennial of the Forest Preserve, Jim Goodwin (#24) led Barbara Hale (#713), Ed Hale (#714), Nina Webb, and Robbie Ticknor from the Lower Ausable Lake and via the Carry to the Upper Ausable Lake and the Warden's Camp to begin a trek to Marcy along Phelps' original route... "A six-hour climb – with three-and-a-half of those hours spent on the 1.3-mile bushwhack up Marcy's rock-scarred flank."[35]

Ed Hale wrote about the trip for the *Watertown Daily Times* (July 22, 1985):

"Did Old Mountain Phelps carry a rope?" a climber asks as the rock slide angles to 40 degrees with only nut-sized knobs and no cracks.

"Sure," Mr. Goodwin replies, "but Mary Cook... refused to use it."

Near the top of the white slide, Mr. Goodwin leads the party into the cripplebrush to reach an older slab with sloughing rock which stretches still higher towards Marcy's summit.

"Old Mountain Phelps is up there laughing at us," Mrs. Webb says.

After the rock slides, progress slows in the dense balsams. Mr. Goodwin searches for solid terrain beneath the thicket in which a hiker could drop out of sight.

He finds lines of least frustration – avoiding concealed cliffs and hidden holes, finding occasional islands of rock to change the pace.

Hale reveals that Jim whistled "in the brush... for assurance... so others can follow his lead." Six hours after they had started for Marcy, they stopped "upon a patch of green beneath the summit" to enjoy their lunch. Later, upon the peak they posed for a commemorative photograph with a homemade banner: "ATIS Mt. Marcy Expedition Via Original Route," etc. A hiker from Ottawa, one of many people atop the peak that day, had heard that the group had bushwhacked up it from the gorge. She surmised that they "must have used compasses." She was told, "No, we had Jim Goodwin." The return to the Ausable Club's facilities was accomplished along the marked trail. When Jim Goodwin led the Forest Preserve Centennial expedition, he was 75 years old. The trip marked the 188th time he had climbed Marcy.

Goodwin told Ed Hale that Phelps' original trail "was abandoned in 1873 when Verplanck Colvin cut what's essentially the present southeast trail for his surveyors" because he felt that the Phelps route was too rugged for "his surveyors to get instruments up there." Phelps was one of the men who cut the new route for Colvin and his "surveyors."

In 1872, Colvin and his men first approached Marcy by a circuitous route. Their journey began on September 2 at Port Henry. They proceeded to Plattsburgh "by steamer," went on to Wilmington, and climbed up Whiteface as far as the "'Rustic Lodge'… a log shanty… occupying [*his*] camping ground of 1869." The next morning they climbed to the summit of Whiteface, calculated its height, and measured angles to other peaks. They were back in Wilmington on September 6 and moved on to Lake Placid that night. On September 9, they departed from North Elba and headed to Indian Pass. On the 10th, Colvin visited Wallface Ponds and climbed Wallface Mountain. He and his men went through Indian Pass on the 11th and arrived at "the deserted iron-works at Adirondack village" that afternoon. On the 12th, at "mid-day," they departed for Marcy via the Calamity Pond route to Lake Colden, at which they arrived "a little after dark." A rain storm that evening made the Opalescent River "a furious torrent," and they were obliged to remain in their "bark wigwams" on the north shore of the river on the 13th. Colvin wrote, "The morning of the fourteenth was also stormy, but upon the return" of a man who had been sent back to the deserted village for provisions, "immediate preparations were made for the ascent of Mt. Marcy."

> We were early upon the trail, but, with the heavy theodolite and fragile barometers, made a slow march. The weather continued so unfavorable, and consequently the probability of our being able to accomplish the work was so slight, that even the guides, who had now acquired an interest in the survey, appeared discouraged. As hour after hour we ascended the foaming, rock-girt Opalescent river toward its source, the weather became colder and the thick clouds more disheartening.

Having achieved the summit in "late afternoon" by way, apparently, of the route that Emmons and Redfield had employed thirty-six years earlier, Colvin and his men were unable to proceed with measurements. They were "drenched with rain or cloud, that despite rubber covering had penetrated" their clothing, and they stood "shivering in the gray, icy mist that swept furiously over the summit."

> Benumbed with cold and unable to see for more than a few rods around, at the entreaties of the guides I reluctantly ordered an immediate descent, which was made upon the opposite or eastern side of the mountain.

The party halted, Colvin wrote in an extract of his report to the state legislature for 1872, about a mile from the summit, where they found "a level spot where water could be had." That spot was probably somewhere near the col between Marcy and Little Marcy. Because their fingers had become "so stiffened by cold," they were unable to "button the canvas" of their tent... "and the guides, after chopping some of the dwarfed timber for firewood, gave up in despair, and declared that we would 'freeze to death'" if they stayed where they were for the night. Consequently, another retreat began "down and across the great slide on Marcy... two miles" to the place where Colvin "had encamped" in 1871. "Meanwhile the rain did not cease to fall, and it was dusk when, trembling from fatigue and exposure, we stumbled into the old camp in Panther Gorge."

> The courage of our guides now returned. The timber was here large and good, and soon the echoing sound of chopping was heard, and the white chips flew from the trunks of the dead, dry, spruce trees. Huge logs of spruce and hard wood were quickly roaring and blazing, and we steaming before the fire in our soaked clothing.
>
> All were so exhausted that, directly after supper, we wrapped our heavy army blankets round us, and fell asleep.
>
> In the middle of the night the penetrating cold aroused us, and shouting for the guides to renew the fire, I saw with delight that the long storm had broken, for the sky was clear and the stars sparkled in the blue firmament. With the warmth of the fire came slumber again, only broken by daylight.

That morning, September 15th, revealed that the party had been joined in the night by a "noble deer-hound" which "evidently, in following his prey" had become lost. Colvin remarked, "He was only too glad to join himself to human company." The dog followed the surveyor and his party when they "again ascended Mt. Marcy."

Upon the peak, "barometric work immediately commenced," the theodolite – "probably the first ever placed" on the mountain – was erected, and "triangulation proceeded without an instant being taken for rest or refreshment during the day." The party remained atop the mountain through the night. Colvin made observations of *"Polaris* and *Alioth"* to lay out the "true astronomical meridian," and his men "kindled a beacon fire and burned magnesium ribbon" in an attempt to alert "other signal stations" to respond so that the team could measure "the great angles" by those "means," but they received no response. The "measuring" continued the following day, the 16th of September, until a "severe storm" set in. Colvin reported, "...the tent was struck, the camp broken up. Taking with me one guide, I descended the south side of Mt. Marcy, with the intention of climbing and barometrically measuring Skylight Mountain and Gray Peak, and to visit a little lake lying in the chasm between the mountains."

Colvin and the guide walked down in a "cloud... so dense that we could see nothing a hundred yards distant, yet we were able to reach the Gray Peak and measure it." He continued, "About 4 p.m. we stood on the shores of the little lake, in a deplorable plight, our boots full of water and clothing torn and dripping." The trip up Skylight was abandoned but the visit to the pond, previously known as Lake Perkins, Colvin said, was "a red-letter point" of the survey, "for we found it, as I had long surmised, not flowing to the Ausable, as has been represented, but to the Hudson river – an inaccuracy of the maps, which is perhaps the best proof that we were the first to ever really visit it." Colvin, initially, did not claim to have "discovered" the pond.[36] However, in his *Report of the Topographical Survey of the Adirondack Wilderness of New York for the Year 1873,* he took the liberty of renaming it "Tear-of-the-clouds." In 1872 he calculated its elevation at 4,326 feet above sea level[37] and commented, "It is, apparently, the *summit water* of the State, and the loftiest known and true *high* source of the Hudson river."

After making his brief observations at Lake Tear, Colvin and his guide, "followed the outlet of *Summit Water*... and made a hazardous descent through the ravine of Feldspar brook, reaching the shore of the Opalescent river about dark. They went on to Lake Colden that night.

Colvin and his men returned to Panther Gorge from the Upper Ausable Lake, via "Bartlett mountain" on August 23, 1873, and climbed Marcy again the following day apparently by way of the old trail up the slides on the southeast side of the mountain. The surveyor wrote, "Although it was extremely clear and bright, a furious gale from the west swept the summit... and it was impossible to use the theodolite. The heavy tripod, indeed, was blown from the summit down the ledge where we were sheltered." Consequently, work that afternoon was suspended early, 5 p.m., and the party made its descent "down the rock slope, two miles, into the deep gorge," and their camp within it. They went back up Marcy the following day, "carrying with labor all the instruments." During that day, Colvin calculated the mountain's height to be 5,402.65 feet above "the level of mean tide in the Hudson river."

> It was nearly dark when we hastily packed our instruments and commenced to descend, and we now added to our previous adventures the first descent of Mount Marcy in the night. Down the ledges and the oozy "slide," path of an avalanche, we groped our way, and once in the forest, lighting our lanterns, we went easily down to our camp.

After twice climbing Haystack, the "Matterhorn of the Adirondacks," on August 26th and 27th, Colvin "devoted" the 28th to climbing Mount Skylight. Although he neglected to mention the fact in his 1873 report, Colvin and his guide, Bill Nye, went to Skylight after ascending Marcy via the old route up the slides. After completing measurements and observations from the top of Skylight, they descended to the level of Mount Redfield, which, Colvin wrote, "I have named... in honor of the discoverer of Mount Marcy." Then he and his guide proceeded "toward a marsh which lies on the high plateau at the foot" of Redfield. They were, he wrote, "The first to reach" it: "Moss Lake." Colvin calculated its elevation at 4,312 feet above sea level. He returned directly to Lake Tear, "hastening as night approached," crossing "the plateau northward to the little summit lake," and remeasured its elevation, finding it to be, as he had previously calculated, higher than Moss Pond by 14 feet.

At Lake Tear, Colvin wrote,

> We here selected the route for a new trail over the mountains which would avoid the necessity of climbing Mount Marcy. We explored the low pass between the head of the inlet of Lake-Tear-of-the-clouds and the Ausable water, and found it an easy and perfectly feasible route. We descended rapidly along a rill that hurried, leap on leap, swiftly down to Marcy brook, and were in camp before dark, notwithstanding prophecies that we would have to make a night march of it.

On the 29th of August, 1873, the survey party again ascended Marcy with their "baggage and camp equipage," again by way of the old route, up the slides. The following year, Russell Carson wrote, "Old Mountain Phelps, Levi Lamb, and George Sawyer" cut the trail from Panther Gorge to Four Corners "and a short trail was cut from the pass to the top of Marcy." That, essentially is the route to Marcy from Panther Gorge used today from both Elk Lake and the Upper Ausable Lake. Carson wrote, "About this time, Phelps also built a bark shanty in the pass at the trail junctions, afterward *[after the short trail to Skylight's summit was cut]* called the "Four Corners," which was the forerunner of the several open camps which have been dear to the hearts of two generations of mountain climbers under the name of "Junction Camp." A lean-to, with a fabulous view of Marcy, was placed close by Four Corners in the 1920s but it was removed in the 1970s. Since then, Junction Camp, has

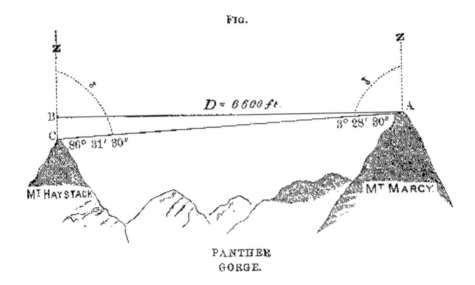

PANTHER GORGE.

The distance (D) between the mountain peaks here shown, as determined by triangulation, is 6,600 feet.† The difference of height between peaks (A to B being a line of true level) of course equals B C. The zenith of each station is shown by Z and Z′, but as the measurements were by reciprocal vertical angles taken on each peak the side B C can be easily computed (correcting the observed angles for refraction,)* as follows :

$$\sin C : \sin A :: A B : B C$$

Then we obtain —

$$\sin C\ (86° 31′ 30″) = \log.\quad 9.999201$$
$$\sin A\ (3° 28′ 30″) = \log.\quad 8.782565$$
$$A B\ (6{,}600) = \log.\quad 3.819544$$

Using Co. Ar. of C (0.000799) we have the log. of B C = 2.602908 and we obtain 400.781 feet. The observations are corrected for the elevation of axis of instrument and

Apparent difference in height.............	= 400.781 feet.
Correction for curvature...............	= 1.042 "
Mt. Marcy above Mt. Haystack.........	= 401.823 "
Same by mercurial barometer mean of two hundred selected observations.	= 396.570 "
	5.253 "

* The local co-efficient of refraction is yet to be precisely determined. The measurement of Bald Peak and Mount Dix, etc., by spirit level, as a test, is under consideration.
† Only graphically as yet.

A page from Colvin's *Report on the Topographical Survey of the Adirondack Wilderness for the Year 1873*

faded from memory. Carson did not know exactly when the trail from Junction Camp to the Opalescent was constructed, but he surmised that it had also been in 1874. That seemed likely as Colvin wrote, in the conclusion to his 1873 report, "The new passes and routes for trails across the mountains which we have explored will be found to greatly facilitate travel, especially the route by Lake Tear, the *summit-water,* at the south of Mount Marcy, which renders the climbing of the peak unnecessary to those merely desirous of crossing the range." However, Sandra Weber reports that the trail from Panther Gorge to Lake Tear and the one up Marcy were cut by Phelps, Lamb, and Phelps' son, Ed, in June of 1875. That trail, basically the one still in use from Four Corners, passed close by Schofield Cobble, the "rocky hump on the south side" of Marcy "between timberline and the summit and overlooking Junction Camp." Carson named the "cobble" after Peter F. Schofield, "a man whose Adirondack service has been noteworthy[38] and whose Adirondack experience in the early days was extensive." In *Peaks and People,* Carson included two extensive quotes by Schofield concerning weather phenomena on Marcy.

Weber also states that, after building a shanty between Skylight and Marcy, the two Phelpses and Lamb "decided to start cutting the trail down Feldspar Brook." She writes, "They cleared the route to within about two hundred yards of the Opalescent valley and the old trail, when the booming of thunder was heard over McIntyre and Wallface. With that warning, they stopped work and returned to camp." When the cutting was completed is not now known, but the trail was soon in use by hikers who started their treks from the deserted village of Adirondac. It completely replaced the old route that had continued past the Feldspar and had remained next to the Opalescent. It has been used ever since as the short route to Marcy with approaches from the Upper Works via Calamity Pond, from Lake Colden, and from Avalanche Camp via Lake Arnold.

After completing "topographical work" on Marcy, August 29, 1873, Colvin and his men "descended on the west side of the mountain." He wrote, "At morning we had sipped the head waters of the Ausable, an affluent of the St. Lawrence; now we quenched our thirst at the milky cataracts of the Opalescent river, the chill mountain torrent head of the Hudson." They reached Lake Colden, he wrote, "before dark," but he did not indicate whether they had done so or not by way of the Feldspar Brook.

The last calculation Colvin made of Marcy's height on August 29 was 5,382.95 feet above sea level. It wasn't until October 1875 that the survey began its work to accurately measure Marcy's height by means of leveling – physically extending a line of linear measurements from bench mark to bench mark ("station" to "station") from Lake Champlain (99.311 feet, according to Colvin) at Westport to the summit.

On his way to the mountain from the Upper Ausable Lake on October 19, 1875, Colvin decided to "essay a new route to escape the unnecessary ascent" of Bartlett Mountain. He passed "the flank of the mountain" and entered "the defile beyond it" to "reach the foot of Marcy by a continuous slope." Colvin's "new" route is still in use today. By the end of that day, the leveling party was "barely six miles" from Marcy's summit.

On October 22nd, Colvin made "a swift march to the summit of Marcy, in order to pick out the route for the leveling party and to read the self-registering thermometer" he had left on the summit on August 29, 1873. The ascent was made following the "new trail" to Junction Camp and the side trail to the summit, partially covered with snow. Above timberline he and his guide saw "hundreds of snow birds *(Plectorphanes)*"[39] which "rose fluttering at *[their]* approach" and "two eagles rising from the gulf at the east, soared past *[them]* majestically, unmindful of revolver shots." Uncovering a thermometer from a crevice where it had rested for more than two years, Colvin found that the lowest temperature it had recorded was 23 degrees below zero Fahrenheit... "far from being as low" as he had expected. He concluded that during the past two winters snow had covered the device and had insulated it from temperatures far more extreme. Also, to his disappointment, Colvin found that "signalling devices" that had been left on the summit had been "entirely destroyed," probably by the elements, but in the years to come, sometimes, hikers used wood from the Marcy signal tower to start fires with which to boil water for their "teas."

A curious observation Colvin recorded for that day is this:

> The view from the summit was superb, a great sea of mountains extending in every direction as far as eye could reach – broken here and there by the glimmer of water – sparkling lakes, among which, far in the south-west, I was surprised to see again a lake that I had observed from this peak in 1869, and which had not been visible to us since, so that its existence, even, had become almost doubtful. The fast descending sun threw its rays in an oblique manner upon the distant water and showed its bays and islands in bright relief against the dark back ground, and I regretted that the theodolite had not yet reached the summit, to enable me to obtain at least the direction of this singular and unrecognized lake. Its present appearance was undoubtedly caused by the remarkable vertical refraction which I have occasionally noticed in this region, thus refracting lakes or summits into view, otherwise just hidden by intervening mountains.[40]

Colvin was enough of a naturalist to make note of some other wildlife he observed during his expeditions. In 1873, he reported finding "some very small and beautiful white bivalve shells upon the bottom" of Moss Pond. On October 23, 1875, he observed "the ascent of a number of ravens[41] out of... *[Panther]* gorge... rising over the brink of the cliffs... uttering harsh discordant croaks." In 1876, he spotted "embryo frogs" in Lake Tear-of-the-Clouds and collected "a few minute shells" (two varieties of bivalves) from the pond. He also reported snipe[42] "seemed" to have made the shores of the pond "their summer home" that year.

On October 30th, the leveling party was unable to proceed, "the mountains wrapped in dense fog streaming down into the deep gorge, ghostlike over the black yet icy ledges or slide on the inclosing peaks. The black cliffs of Haystack are grim with monstrous yellowish icicles."

On October 31st, the survey crew awoke, "after a cold, shivering night, to find the earth covered with a deep fall of snow." That afternoon four men attempted to reach the summit "but found a violent hurricane prevailing, and, just above the timber line, were fairly blown from their feet, near the upper ledges, and deemed themselves fortunate to escape without loss of life or limb."

On November 1st, two of his guides scaled the icy dome "to bring away the theodolite" which Colvin had stored high on the peak. "The wind swept the summit at an estimated rate of seventy miles an hour, and it was intensely cold, but by creeping around under the shelter of the ledges they managed to reach the caché – now almost inaccessible with ice and snow – and brought away in safety the two boxes and tripod. The cold was so intense that one of the men froze both of his ears. The temperature at midday is below zero." The leveling work had stopped on "the icy shore of Lake Tear of the Clouds."

November 2nd was a "wild blustering winter day." The wind blew snow into the open camp (lean-to) and the men ate a dinner "in the midst of drifting snow mixed with ashes and smoke from the camp fire."

Wednesday, November 3rd, dawned "bright and clear" and the men hurried "to re-ascend Marcy, now deeply drifted with snow, and aglare with ice." Just below timberline, Colvin took "personal charge" of the leveling work. He calculated the elevation of timberline on the Lake Tear slope at 4,890 feet above sea level. By evening the measuring work had reached within 200 vertical feet of the summit before darkness compelled Colvin and his men, "worn out with exposure and exhaustion" to make their way down, "slipping and falling constantly from very weariness" back to their camp at Lake Tear.

On November 4th, Colvin reported, "The steep rocks are glary with ice, and we are compelled to move with caution. A single fall would destroy the instrument, and render impossible the completion of the measurement of Marcy." Braving the elements – "somewhat cloudy... colder than yesterday..." a storm approaching – the men "worked with steadiness, but with suppressed excitement and in silence."

Colvin wrote that he "was compelled to run the line around the side of the mountain, to escape the influence of the gale" and that he had to compensate for the "great dome" rock's "horizontal gravitation," its pull on the liquid in the tube of the transit's level.

> A dense fog, or frost, now enveloped us – the sun-light illuminating it with mysterious splendor – the sun itself brightening or darkening as the frosty vapor increased or decreased above us, while all around bright minute frost crystals danced to and fro in the air... Without rest, without food, we worked; eagerly, fiercely, determinedly on all day, and at length as evening approached we could see our goal just above us, and at 4:50 p.m. I placed the level on the summit of Marcy, adjusted it once more, and took the last observation on the graduated rod, which stood upon the copper-bolt *[No. 1, placed in 1872]* marking the trigonometrical station. Another permanent bench-mark (No. 111) was cut in the stone of the summit there; and then the party broke out spontaneously into *hurrahs!* But their voices and revolver shots sounded weak and faint in that thin, frosty atmosphere, and in the increasing duskiness, the men with moustaches, and eyebrows, and clothing white with frost – the instruments also frost encrusted – had a wild and singular appearance, in consonance with the place, season and occasion.
>
> The height of Mount Marcy was found to be
> 5,344.311 feet
> above mean tide level in the Hudson.

Farrand Benedict, employing only barometers, had calculated the elevation of the summit twenty-four years earlier at 5,344.69 feet – a difference of less than five inches.

"Joy," Colvin wrote, "reigned in the camp" that night. The next day most of the men began the return to the Upper Ausable Lake, but Colvin "determined to make a forced march with one guide to the south, westward of Mt. Skylight, to explore the Cliff mountain pass," through which, early in the twentieth century, a lumber road was constructed, much of it corduroy, to reach Buckley's lumber camp[43] at Uphill Brook. They later returned to Lake Tear on the Feldspar trail which had been rendered difficult to follow because the snow "had – in falling – frozen on the western side of every tree, so that the line marked upon the trees, of which we hoped to here avail ourselves, was hidden, and only visible when passed." Nonetheless, they reached Lake Tear at dusk and went on in the near darkness to Panther Gorge. The next day, as they made their way back to the Upper Ausable Lake, Colvin reported, "all snow disappeared on the southern exposures of the hills, and the crisp leaves made it seem like autumn again," but his adventures of 1875 were not yet at an end. Only with difficulty were Colvin and his men able to launch a boat upon the Lower Ausable Lake. Eventually, its progress came to a halt as its forward progress, was, at last, completely stopped by the ice upon the lake. They had to drag the boat up onto the ice and pull it like a sled to the lake's outlet, all the while fearful that it and they might break through. Fortunately, they "effected the passage in safety... drew the boat on shore..." and by "a rapid march, at dark... entered the settlement of Keene."

Marcy became the keystone of Colvin's survey, its height a "constant" and "standard" which he employed in calculating altitudes and positions of other geographical features of the region. The chief surveyor returned to the mountain in August 1876, ascending the peak from the deserted village of Adirondac, Lake Colden, the Opalescent and the "new" trail to Lake Tear-of-the-Clouds. He reached the summit on the 9th, and returned to it on the 10th, hoping, both days, to detect signals, flashes from heliotropes, set up on other mountains. Due to "smoke or haze," he was unable to discern any on the 9th but managed to spot flashes from Dix and Whiteface on the 10th. He most wanted to detect the signal from Mount Emmons (the peak in Hamilton County that we call Blue Mountain), but could not spot it the 9th, 10th, or 11th, and so gave up the effort, and retreated from the mountain after dark on the 11th. On the 17th, he was upon St. Regis Mountain, from which his guides began to clear timber which obstructed "the view in many directions." One of his guides suggested that they collect the dead and fallen brush and trees in heaps and burn it:

> This was accordingly commenced, but to our confusion and alarm in a very few moments the fire proved the master, and spreading with a fearful roar, sweeping up into the dead tree tops, caused us to beat a most hasty and ignominious retreat, barely escaping with our instruments down the ledges before the torrent of flames swept across the summit and wrapped it all in fierce conflagration. As night came on the scene became one of wild sublimity. From our camp, where we watched with anxiety, we looked up out of the darkness at the sea of flame. Now it reached the brink of the cliff above, and soon the tall trees became columns of live coals, till burned away at the base they would bend, totter and fall down the cliff like bars of white hot iron, carrying the flames down into fresh ground, where the peat-like soil – dry as tinder – instantly caught the place and spread the conflagration.

One of the guides assured Colvin that "fire on a mountain summit burns but a little way down, the draft of air being against it," but "all night the fire raged." Rock, "deprived of its water of crystallization by the fervent heat," exploded. Colvin later wrote, *"August 18th* showed the correctness of the old hunter's theory. The fierce fire had already consumed every thing upon the crest of the mountain... and now burned but feebly beneath the ledges surrounding the peak." Colvin and his men set up his instruments on the summit, the smoke dispersed, and the surveyor was thereafter able to discern the signals on Whiteface, Marcy and McIntyre and, later, "in the dim distance southward, the position of Mount Emmons."

He was back atop Marcy, again via Upper Ausable Lake and his trail to Lake Tear, on August 27th ("too late to attempt any thing on the summit") and the 28th, but his signal receiving work was again frustrated by "the 'smoke,' the singular, dense, reddish vapor (the *höhenrauch*[44])" which had settled over the region and had made "even the form of Mt. Emmons" impossible to see. The haze continued on the 29th and on the 30th, which "was not quite so hazy." Colvin was not about to give up. He wrote, "I shall remain here... until I obtain the Mt. Emmons signal, come what may, for the closing of the angle between Emmons and St. Regis is vital."

August 31st: "The atmosphere smoky and hazy beyond all our experience..."

September 1st: "We were awakened by a low, distant rumbling of thunder, which we hail with joy, hoping a rain to clear away the fearful haze..." But only a shower came, "insufficient to clear the atmosphere."

September 2nd: "All last night it rained," Colvin wrote. "I was kept awake by anxious joy, listening to the spattering rain and occasional distant thunder, hoping that this would suffice to clear the air. But at morning the wind is furious, blowing at a rate of a mile a minute... The wild blasts sweep through the cold gorge, and we seek the shelter of our camp and blankets."

September 3rd: "The gale last night was terrific. Trees were uprooted and our bark shanty stripped of its covering. At sunrise the wind had greatly subsided." The party "hastened to the summit" and found all "the most distant peaks" were distinctly visible. They spotted the signals on Hurricane, Dix, Whiteface, McIntyre (Algonquin), at the head of the Beaver River, and, at 9 a.m., "the bright flash of the heliotrope signal on Mt. Emmons."

On August 2, 1877, Colvin again departed for Marcy from Keene Valley by way of the Upper Ausable Lake. The following day was a Sunday, and, he wrote, "it was our good fortune to have religious services conducted by a reverend friend" who had accompanied him and his guides to the lake. "The guides ranged logs for seats, and under a bright sky in this remote but sheltered forest glade, deep-carpeted with rich green mosses and rare ferns, arose the mingled voices, offering thanks for all the blessings that we had received." The next morning, August 4, Colvin's men, a thousand feet below Marcy's summit, "procured" timber for a "permanent signal" they would erect atop the mountain the week that followed. Colvin, went to the summit each day, watching for signals from other mountains. He wrote:

> While I wearily watched at the theodolite, day by day, the guides had, with infinite labor, brought the timbers for the signal. Along the tortuous trail, up through the dense dwarf forest, up over ledges and the open rock of the peak, above wooded line they labored, a single timber at times taking a day's work, for three powerful guides, to bring to the summit.

The men drilled holes for iron ring bolts which were placed in them to help secure the four great legs of the structure. When they went to pour molten lead into one of the holes as an adhesive to hold a ring bolt, "as though the hole had contained water, the melted lead was blown forth with violence; one of the men narrowly escaping being blinded by it." Thereafter, the men first heated the bolts and inserted them in the other holes before adding the lead to them.

The construction of the tower was completed August 10th. It was supplied with a "new form of revolving reflector placed upon the top." The retreat from the mountain began the same day, most of the men carrying the equipment back to the Upper Ausable Lake and Colvin, "with one aide," heading, back over Marcy from their Lake Tear camp, to "explore the region between Marcy and the Gothics."

> Down over open rock; down over the elastic beds of creeping trees, we entered at length the dense mass of the taller trees – centenarians five feet high – and fought our way through them until the trees grew tall enough to admit of scrambling underneath. Thus, at length, we reached a marsh or meadow, like many of those far up upon the side of Marcy, and found this to be another divide between the waters of the Hudson and the Saint Lawrence.
>
> Crossing this marsh, we entered the forest northward, and skirting a nameless mountain, saw below us a deep gorge where the first rills joined to form John's brook. Before descending into this gorge we took our course by the sun, and with severe labor climbed again the opposite slope of the chasm, entering a dense and silent forest which showed no trace of ever having been visited by man. Here we disturbed a bear which we heard gallop away crushing the underbrush before him. At length in a deep valley at the foot of Basin mountain, we halted for lunch where a dyke projected from the foot of the mountain like a wall across the head of the defile.

Colvin and his "aide" proceeded, "scaled cliffs and wooded slopes, and soon found" themselves "in the dwarfed timber once more." They reached Basin's summit at 2 p.m., and, after placing "a small reconnaissance signal" on the peak, retreated quickly as a storm soon enveloped the mountain. Colvin wrote, "Lightning above and lightning below the storm swept down, a heavy rain drenched the summit, and we were compelled to seek shelter under a ledge in the dwarfed forest just below the crest." After the storm passed, he returned to the summit, "secured" a few observations, and made some sketches... before "lengthening shadows warned us to descend." As they proceeded "eastward," they found their way "barred by lofty cliffs," but, "fortunately," Colvin "found a short small cavern or enclosed stair-like passage," by which they were able to "pass down through the front of the cliff" to a place where they could "descend with ease." By evening, they were back at the Upper Ausable Lake.

Colvin would return to Marcy numerous times during the remaining years of the survey, but his great adventures on the mountain were at an end. However, his assistant and longtime companion Mills Blake, who accompanied Colvin on many of the early ascents of Marcy but whose name does not appear in any of the accounts so far mentioned, lived at the summit, in a tent, and engaged in "measuring angles" from September 10th to October 17th, 1883. Carson, who met Blake after Colvin had died, wrote, "The long sojourn, so late in the season, was a severe experience and striking proof of the zeal for the work and devotion to duty that inspired Colvin and his aides. A violent storm on the 25th of September drove the party from the top, but the next day they were back, repairing the damage done by the wind, drying out their blankets and the contents of the tent, and continuing their work." Demonstrating that the mountain continued, all the while, to attract recreational climbers, Carson mentions, "Mr. Blake's diary shows that in the thirty-seven days, they had visits from four parties of tourists. On October 4th, W. Scott Brown of Elizabethtown, Scott D. M. Goodwin of Albany, Henry Tracy of Keeseville, Assistant Rush, and two rodmen arrived to stay overnight, making eight on the summit that night and taxing the little tent and the supply chest to their limit. On the second, the snowdrifts on top were five feet deep, and the spring, about one hundred feet below the summit, was frozen over and covered with four feet of snow."

Carson also reports that the first winter ascent of the mountain, March 18, 1893, "was made by Benjamin Pond and J. W. Otis" two men "working for the Ausable Club while stationed at the Inlet Camp on the Upper Ausable Lake."[45] Carson was told that they had "talked indefinitely" about "attempting the mountain on snowshoes," but had not determined to do so until that "clear and cold" morning arrived:

> Taking nothing that was not essential, not even lunch, they snowshoed across the lake, around the toe of Bartlett Mountain, and up Marcy Brook to the foot of Panther Gorge. Thence up the side of Skylight to the Junction Camp and then on to Marcy. About a thousand feet below the top they were obliged to remove their snowshoes, and when they reached the timberline they found the dome so encrusted with ice that it was necessary to chop out steps with an axe... Descending, they slid part of the way on their snowshoes. It was after dark when they returned to the camp, ravenously hungry but so tired that they were unable to eat.

The next recorded winter ascent was made in February 1899 by Gifford Pinchot,[46] accompanied, most of the way, by C. Grant LaFarge,[47] who wrote an account of the trip, "A Winter Ascent of Tahawus," which was published in *Outing* magazine in April 1900. LaFarge went with Pinchot to the Tahawus Club at the Upper Works because he "wanted some fresh air and a chance to use the old snowshoes that had laid away for three years." Pinchot, LaFarge explained, "was going to look at the McIntyre Iron Company's tract." They had inquired "as to the practicability" of making "an ascent of Tahawus on snowshoes," and they were told, "it could be done... from Lake Colden... [I]f we got a good, clear, still day we ought to have no difficulty... [but] such weather was rare... On the whole the impression conveyed was that we might try it if we wished."

Carson, in his account of the trip in *Peaks and People,* suggested that it was "unpremeditated," but LaFarge wrote that though "it would be pleasanter to let it wait, say until June... we then and there resolved to go up to the camp on Lake Colden as soon as possible... [and] allowed that project *[climbing Marcy]* to subside... each of us, I think, quite convinced that the other was not going to let him fail to have a try at it." After they had arrived at the auxiliary headquarters of the Tahawus Club at the Lower Works and tramped about on snowshoes in the afternoon, LaFarge wrote, "I knew, as we crunched our way homeward through the twilight and the gathering cold, that not to stand upon its lofty summit and survey the splendid panorama was a mistake not to be made."

Two days later, LaFarge and Pinchot "set out for *[Lake]* Colden. LaFarge carried only a camera with him. Guides, ahead of them, carried all of their supplies. They made their way to the Upper Works, Calamity Pond, the Flowed Lands,[48] and Lake Colden, stopping along the way so that Pinchot could examine trees and take photographs of them with his Kodak. A fierce wind obliterated the snowshoe tracks ahead of them and "*[g]*rowing darkness and the driving clouds of snow-dust made it impossible to have aught but a sense of the steep mountain walls rising close about" them "in the gloom..." They found the club's cabin, "nestling under the base of McIntyre" and "concealed among the overspreading trees... *[b]*uried deep in curling drifts..." and "lit by a roaring fire in the broad chimney, and once within, little cared for the howling wind outside." At that point, an attempt to climb Marcy seemed unlikely. In fact, after they had fallen "heavily upon the hot supper in a way which you have got to go to the woods to know," they "discussed the next day's plans." LaFarge wrote, "As well as I can remember, there was no word of climbing Tahawus – in fact, the conditions of weather seemed to preclude the attempt – but our canvass of the surroundings in every direction indicated that we should take the Tahawus trail, to see those woods still untouched by the axe, of which we had heard, and through which led that trail to the top of the mountain." They were not about to let the chance of climbing the mountain slip away; however, the prospects appeared dim the next morning with "the gale... still raging, and the cold bitter; the sun shining faintly through the minute snow crystals with which the air was laden."

LaFarge described following the trail with two guides up the Opalescent and plunging into "the unbroken dense timber" along the way on snow that was "both deep and soft," but, he noted, they were out of the wind. He marveled at the "immaculate beauty of the snow itself and its many wonderful forms; the hushed silence, the many records of the feet of passing animals and of birds, which reveal themselves now as never at any other time; the sweet notes of friendly chickadees; the varied colors and textures of the tree-trunks and sumptuous richness of the evergreens, and the air that is like new life." Their "hearty exercise" took them higher. The snow grew deeper. They occasionally lost the trail: "*[H]*ere was good evidence that these winter solitudes were not often invaded, for it was marked only by a summer blase *[sic],* and this was often concealed by the depth of the snow."

The four men reached Lake Tear-of-the-Clouds at noon. After kindling a fire, they melted snow to create water with which to brew some tea, which they consumed, and they ate partially thawed doughnuts. Refreshed, LaFarge heard "a brief exclamation from Pinchot, indicating that in his opinion it would be no great task to go on to the end." LaFarge "instantly assented," and they were soon ready to proceed.

As they resumed their climb, the "walking was bad, as the incline was quite steep and the snow heavy, and the little fir trees grew so close together as greatly to impede our movements," but LaFarge "welcomed the exertion" because he "found" that while they had been resting he had let his feet "get cold." They worked their way through "[q]ueer little mis-shapen dwarfs, gnarled and perverted, struggling to maintain their kind in this forsaken place." One of the guides, "who wore very long snowshoes... meant for open country... announced that the difficulty of their management and the painful condition of his feet necessitated his turning back." He went back to their "tea" place to keep the fire going there. Soon the other three "came to the end of the timber," where they encountered a "steep bank, rising above our heads... formed by the edge of the snow-cap reaching down over the matted tops of dwarf spruce." After winding a scarf about his head and the lower part of his face, LaFarge, "with a series of wild plunges... scrambled up" the bank and discovered that "the snow above was a kind of crust over the tops of the trees and was coated with shell-ice, just strong enough not to break under the spread of the snow-shoes and so slippery as to make control of them impossible."

> There was only one thing to do – fall down; and this I did and took off my snowshoes. Pinchot had got ahead but came back to help me. The guide who was near, shouting to make himself heard in the awful wind, complained that he had a sort of numb feeling in his leg, and when we told him to go back, he turned and disappeared in the direction whence we had come. Then I struggled on – it was only about a hundred yards or so, but I was thankful it was no more. The crust would bear me up for a few paces, and then give way and down I would sink to the waist in the tangled mass of thick-set branches. The wind caught the big snow-shoes and tugged at them with vindictive fury, and the thought of the predicament the loss of them would entail filled one with a kind of angry terror. When we reached firm ground, we first sought safety for the snow-shoes and found the strong, crooked top of a fir tree peeping above the snow, to which we tied them securely.
>
> The way now led straight up-hill and mighty unpleasant it looked – what we could see of it, that is, for the wind was no more to be faced than a battery of charging razors; and to stand upright in it was more than we cared to attempt. The ridge up which we were crawling on all fours was in large part smooth ice, with only occasional patches of snow or little projecting tips of rock to afford hold for hands and knees. We worked our way slowly and painfully, gaining one of them after another, and when the more furious gusts of the ever opposing wind would descend upon us like malignant fiends, we lay prone at full length and buried our faces in our folded arms, that we might breathe; and hoped not to be dislodged from that precarious holding, for close upon our right hand the mountain fell steeply away to what seemed to be a precipice, and between us and that dreadful brink was no obstacle to a descent into the abyss. The cold was such as I had not ever imagined... it cut and choked and hurt with maddening cruelty. All view of the world below us was cut off by the dense curtain of drift, and all that we could see was the treacherous slope to which we clung, vanishing dizzily down into a gray-white nothingness.

LaFarge, whose feet, "if not actually frozen" were "at least frostbitten" decided, just two hundred feet from the summit, that he "could no longer stand the cold... which was benumbing" his entire body. He was obliged "to give it up" and return alone to the place where they had left their snowshoes, but Pinchot continued up. LaFarge, sheltered in a notch, probably on the summit side of Schofield Cobble, saw Pinchot, "still creeping upward with many pauses, until finally he disappeared over a shoulder at the top." He "seemed to be gone a long time," but, after a while, LaFarge saw him again, making his descent. They were soon reunited and back at Lake Tear by 2:30 p.m. They returned to the cabin at Lake Colden "before dark." Pinchot had taken his camera to the summit and had snapped a picture there: of the signal tower, devoid of heliotrope, that Colvin's survey had left there, upon the summit rock. The tower would eventually fall victim to the elements and its vandalism by hikers who used its wood for fires they built in the lee of the rock and nearby ledges. Colvin's reports were no longer published. His survey was at its end. The same month that LaFarge's story was published in *Outing,* Colvin lost his job, his position as superintendent of the Adirondack Survey eliminated by the Governor of New York, Theodore Roosevelt. A year and a half later, destiny would reach out to Roosevelt within a hundred yards of the spot where his friends, Gifford Pinchot and C. Grant LaFarge, had rested and grown cold before they had begun the final leg of their climb of Mount Marcy... on the eve of the Blizzard of 1899.

Vice President Roosevelt had been at Isle la Motte in Lake Champlain on September 6, 1901, when he received word that President McKinley had been shot at the Pan American Exposition being held in Buffalo. He quickly made arrangements to go to Buffalo from Burlington, Vermont, and arrived there by special train September 7. During the time he was there, the President's recovery from his injury appeared likely, so much so that Roosevelt said he was "absolutely sure" McKinley would recover. Consequently, the evening of September 10, Roosevelt left Buffalo and thereafter proceeded by way of Albany by train to North Creek, where he arrived on the 11th. He went on, by buckboard, to the Lower Works headquarters of the Tahawus Club, where he was met by his wife, Edith, and with her went on to the Upper Works, where he and his family stayed at the MacNaughton Cottage.

After hearing on Thursday, September 12, that the President's condition had improved, Mr. and Mrs. Roosevelt with their two daughters and three of their sons – along with a governess, James MacNaughton,[49] and brothers Beverley and Herman Robinson – headed into the woods. Supported by several guides, the party went by way of Calamity Pond to the Flowed Lands and on to two cabins at Lake Colden where they spent the night.

In *A History of the Adirondacks,* Alfred Donaldson continued the story, relating that Mrs. Roosevelt, the children, and the governess, Miss Young, on the morning of September 13 returned to the MacNaughton Cottage at the Upper Works. Vice President Roosevelt, MacNaughton, the Robinson brothers, and guide Noah LaCasse started for Mount Marcy:

> They left Lake Colden at 9 a.m. and by noon had reached the summit of the mountain. They remained there about fifteen minutes only, and then descended a few hundred feet to the shelf of land that holds Lake Tear-of-the-Clouds, where they rested and ate lunch. While chatting and looking around, they saw a hurrying guide emerge from the woods below. A few moments later this man, Harrison Hall, handed Mr. Roosevelt a telegram which told him that President McKinley's condition had suddenly changed for the worse.
>
> This was at half-past one. The party immediately hurried down the mountain and reached the club-house at half-past five. Finding no further news there, Mr. Roosevelt reluctantly consented to spend the night, but made arrangements to leave at the earliest possible moment in the morning. At eleven o'clock that night, however, Mr. MacNaughton brought him another message saying that the President was dying. Without a moment's hesitation Mr. Roosevelt declared his intention of starting immediately for Buffalo, and asked for a conveyance. At this his friends seconded by the guides, urged him to wait till daylight. The roads were so rough and treacherous as to be considered impassable of a dark night, and this night was of the darkest. The men

around the club were not the kind to balk at any ordinary risk, but none of them cared to be the driver in this one. Being informed of this, Mr. Roosevelt said he would take a lantern and go afoot. This threat, backed by preparatory action, induced one of the guides, Dave Hunter, to volunteer as a driver. A little later the start was made in a now historic night ride from one of the most isolated spots in the wilderness to the nearest railway station at North Creek, forty miles away.

Three relays – three drivers, three teams of horses – were required to transport Roosevelt to North Creek, where he arrived to board a special train at 4:39 a.m. September 14, 1901. While the Vice President was on his way to North Creek, somewhere along the road (28N) between Tahawus and Minerva, at 2 o'clock in the morning, McKinley had died and Roosevelt had succeeded to the Presidency of the United States. Roosevelt did not learn of the President's death until he reached North Creek. There, his secretary, William Loeb, Jr., told him of McKinley's passing.[50]

In 1867, according to Stoddard and other late nineteenth century writers, "an avalanche of loose rocks and earth swept downward from" Mount Colden, "and carrying all before it plunged into the sleeping" Avalanche Lake, "nearly dividing it in two." The avalanche, Stoddard reported, "[W]here it started it is but eight or ten feet broad and as many deep, but increasing in volume as it descended, it tore its way through the soft rock until, at the bottom, the track is 75 feet wide and 40 or 50 deep." Stoddard continued, "Here in 1868 occurred a pleasant little episode in which 'Bill Nye took a hand'... William B. Nye, a noted guide and hunter of North Elba."

Stoddard, quoting Nye, went on to tell the famous "Hitch Up, Matilda!" story, which is recounted in this book in Barbara Harris's chapter about Nye Mountain. Nye, with his home not far from Lake Placid, became the preeminent Marcy guide from North Elba. He was noted for taking visitors on the round trip, through Indian Pass to the "deserted" village of Adirondac at the Upper Works, up the Calamity Brook trail to Lake Colden, up Marcy, back down the Opalescent, and out to North Elba through Avalanche Pass by way, of course, of Avalanche Lake.

Colvin visited Avalanche Lake and went through Avalanche Pass in 1869, the same year he first climbed Mount Marcy. He must have considered the hike through the pass difficult, for in 1873 he pioneered a route between Lake Colden and North Elba through "Caribou Pass," to the northwest of the peak now known as Avalanche Mountain. The present trail that takes hikers to Avalanche Lake from Marcy Dam was probably originally laid out by Nye, who in his later years worked for Henry Van Hoevenberg, the erstwhile inventor who established Adirondack Lodge at Heart Lake.

The story of Van Hoevenberg, Mr. Van as he is still fondly called, is a mix of fact and fancy, some of which was devised by Mr. Van himself. He told of leaving New York City in 1877, suffering from "aggravated hay fever," visiting the Ausable lakes, where his malady "left" him, and taking a mountain "walk" with a young lady he had met at the Upper Ausable Lake, Josephine Scofield. She was suffering from consumption (tuberculosis) and apparently experienced a miraculous recovery from that disease's ravages while camping on the Upper Ausable Lake. Van Hoevenberg's legend holds that the couple climbed Mount Marcy, that Mr. Van pledged his love to Miss Scofield, and that together, as they surveyed the view spread before them from the summit, picked out a site for their wedded home: on the shore of a heart-shaped pond which was then known as Clear Lake. Van Hoevenberg later claimed that he walked from Marcy to the pond. Later, after their vacations had drawn to a close, the happy couple returned to New York, Miss Scofield took ill again, left the city for her home in Toronto, stopped at Niagara Falls, walked out to the brink of the Horseshoe Falls... and was never seen again. Mr. Van returned to the Adirondacks in 1878, bought 640 acres of land around Heart Lake, named the little crag above the pond Mt. Jo (after Josephine), and began construction of his log hotel – not his honeymoon cottage – Adirondack Lodge.

The story of Henry and Josephine has been told many times, with many variations.[51] Donaldson tells it well, but incompletely, in *A History of the Adirondacks*. Historians have traced the story of Josephine (or Jane) Scofield (Schofield) and Henry Van Hoevenberg as best they can, but the bulk of the legend appears to be romantic fabrication. Donaldson accepted the original story and wrote that Mr. Van had returned "to the woods, having resolved to carry out alone, as a form of memorial, the general scheme that had been planned." He described the "original" Adirondack Lodge:

> The exterior of the house was formed of giant spruces, many of them measuring over two feet in the lower courses. The main building had a frontage of eighty-five feet and was thirty-six feet deep and three stories high, with a rear wing of almost equal size. A very high, built-in observation tower rose above the gabled roof, and broad piazzas stretched on every side. The interior was inlaid with every refinement of rustic work that skill and ingenuity could devise. It also contained every comfort and sanitary convenience that the times afforded, and was one of the first Adirondack hotels to offer bath-rooms to its guests.

The lodge opened to the public in the summer of 1880 "and for fifteen years enjoyed a quiet but steady popularity... largely due," Donaldson wrote, "to the personality of the owner" who an "indefatigable tramper himself... opened and kept open over fifty miles of wood trails, diverging from the lodge to the many points of scenic beauty in the neighborhood." Those trails, cut and brushed out by Bill Nye and other woodsmen, were wide and well marked. The Marcy trail, "the shortest route" to the highest peak, passed by what Mr. Van called "Crystal Falls." Nye had named it Wallace Falls after guidebook writer Edwin R. Wallace. Today we call it, in a most uninspired manner, Indian Falls. With the comfort of his guests in mind, Van Hoevenberg had shelters, "camps," built along his trails, including the Tahawus Cabin which was erected on the plateau below Mount Marcy's summit. The Van Hoevenberg Trail to Mount Marcy, particularly after the establishment of the Lake Placid Club, became a major route to the peak. Altered several times over the past 130 years, it is now the most traveled route to Marcy's summit.

In 1895, Mr. Van lost his lodge, a consequence of, Donaldson wrote, "litigation with some of his patents." The property passed through several owners but Mr. Van was retained as innkeeper for at least one year, probably two. Records indicate that the lodge failed to open in 1898. It was operated in 1899 and 1900 by W. W. Pierce. In September of 1900 the property was purchased by the Lake Placid Club, and Mr. Van returned to it as the lodge manager in 1901. He remained until the great fire of 1903. Donaldson told the story of his last day:

> On June 3d, the fatal day, there was no one there but a gang of workmen. Mr. Van had been off camping for the night and scouting for danger. He returned home in the belief that none was near. Hardly had he entered the house, however, when a telephone call for help came from South Meadows, a mile away to the east. The fires were there and headed for the lodge. Horses and men were at once despatched to the rescue, but were soon forced to turn back before rapidly advancing smoke and flames.

Mr. Van, meanwhile, had mounted his seventy-foot outlook tower, and tried to peer over the smoke-smothered tree-tops. He could just see the flare of inevitable doom surging down from Mount Jo. He was being hemmed in by two fires. He saw that the lodge was doomed and that his own escape was already problematical. He called to his men to help him carry down his large telescope and place it in a boat, which he pushed out into the lake. Then he threw the table silver into shallow water. Next he brought out the unfinished model of... his latest invention... and placed it on a rock in the clearing. Finally, he emptied the stable of horses, and locked the doors. These things done, he turned his thoughts to escape.

Van Hoevenberg and "his men" then began their retreat from the fire, up the Indian Pass Trail from the lodge, but they were not far along before one of the men, Frank Williams, "discovered that Mr. Van had disappeared." Williams ran back to the lodge "and there found the captain determined to go down with his ship." Donaldson continued, "Mr. Van drew a revolver and bid Williams begone. The latter sat down and refused to budge without his employer. This restored reason to the fanatic. He hastily gathered a few things and consented to go. The two men started to run. They were none too soon. The flames were already leaping across their path." Donaldson concluded his account with this line: "The Adirondack Lodge had passed into the Land of Things that Were."

During the decade that followed, the Lake Placid Club maintained control over Mr. Van's former property; lumbermen and hikers returned to the area. The hiking trails in the immediate vicinity of the lodge had been destroyed by the fire. The lower section of the Marcy trail cut by Nye was a ruin, but by 1904, the route to Marcy via Lake Arnold had been opened. Mr. Van's original trail to Mount Marcy, by way of Indian Falls and Plateau, was not restored until 1919.

In 1911 three skiers went from South Meadows to Marcy by way of Marcy Dam.[52] Their trip was recorded, according to William H. White in an article, "Mount Marcy – Winter 1911 – A First Ascent on Skis," published in the January 1984 (Vol. XLVIII, No. 1) *Adirondac*, "solely by old glass plate slides found in the Archives of the Adirondack Research Center at Union College in Schenectady."[53] The photographer was John S. Apperson, Jr.[54] of Schenectady, a General Electric engineer. That much seemed certain. However, much else was uncertain. White wrote that Apperson's companions on the trip were Irving Langmuir,[55] a skiing enthusiast who also worked at G.E., and another man whose identity "has been lost in the passage of time." White also wrote, "We know that they got to Indian Falls as we have a view of one skier at the *[lumber]* camp with Marcy in the background." Someone at some time wrote the names "Apperson, Canivet,[56] and Paskey" on the envelope containing the photographs kept at the research center and that pencilled inscription led to the speculation that, perhaps, Langmuir had not been a member of the party. In his *Wild Snow – 54 Classic Ski and Snowboard Descents of North America* (American Alpine Club, 1998), Louis W. Dawson credited Apperson, Canivet, and "Passkey" with the "first recorded ski descent of Marcy." Thus Langmuir, a Nobel Prize laureate and the first of the great Adirondack skiers, had lost the credit ascribed to him by White. However, recent research by Richard E. Tucker[57] has revealed that three skiers joined Apperson on the trip: Jean Canivet, Max Paaske, and Irving Langmuir.

Sandra Weber, who performed research at the center in preparing her book, *Mount Marcy, The High Peak of New York,* found that "closer inspection of the photos" showed the skiers' route was not by way of the Van Hoevenberg trail but by way of "Lake Colden and then past Lake Tear to the summit." In the Apperson Papers at the research library, she found a letter by Apperson to Orlando Beede (February 1922) which affirmed that contention.

**A member of the Apperson party at a camp –
possibly the Tahawus Club camp on Lake Colden**

The photograph which shows one of the skiers atop a snowbank at roof level at a camp with "Marcy in the background" was not taken at Indian Falls. Christine Bourjade (#4967W) speculated that it had been taken at the Tahawus Club cabin on Lake Colden, the one at which Pinchot and LaFarge had stayed during their winter adventure in 1899. Anne Knox, the club's historian, has confirmed Christine's identification of the building.

The actual "first" ascent (or descent) of Marcy on skis was reportedly made in February 1910 when a "man" on Norwegian skis joined a party of four snowshoers making the journey to the summit from the Upper Ausable Lake. Who that skier was is not known today.[58]

Herb Clark, Bob and George Marshall began several of their early hiking expeditions from Lake Placid, where they got off the train from Saranac Lake and from whence they proceeded by foot to South Meadows or the grounds of Adirondak Loj, as it became known under the auspices of Melvil Dewey's Lake Placid Club. George Marshall in an essay, "Approach to the Mountains," mentioned that, "just before leaving the road" (today's Route 73), they "looked with happy anticipation across the flower-studded Plains of Abraham to the high mountains, dominated by Tahawus and MacIntyre and cut dramatically by Avalanche and Indian Passes. These, with their encircling wild country, were our objectives."

He continued,

> We thought of Emmons and Redfield and their first ascents of the highest peaks four generations before, of Alfred Street and his purple-worded enthusiasm for Indian Pass, and of Verplanck Colvin who explored, surveyed and loved these mountains more than anyone before or since. These men were here when the wilderness spread far beyond its present bounds and before tragically large portions of the mountains were lumbered and burnt...
>
> The pack baskets which Bob and I carried on our second trip to South Meadows were not too heavy, but they must have held us down pretty well. When we took them off, where the South

Meadows Road turns to the east, something seemed to be missing. When we crossed the branch of the Ausable River and left the Heart Lake road to climb the then trailless Mt. Jo, we seemed to float to the top. We were like balloons freed of their ballast.

The descent was quite a different matter... we picked our way with care through fire slash...[59]

In "The High Peaks of the Adirondacks" (1922), Robert Marshall frequently lamented the signs of fire and lumbering that he, George, and Herb Clark had encountered during their ascents of the peaks. However, he made no mention of such damage in his description of Marcy. He wrote that it had "six important trails up it," including the now abandoned one which ran from "Lake Sanford through the pass between Redfield and Cliff Mountains," reaching the Opalescent at Uphill Brook. The view from Marcy, Marshall wrote, "is not so fine as from several other peaks, yet it is beautiful enough to suit the most exacting. The view I like the best is over the Lake Tear Notch toward those three magnificently wooded mountains, Allen, Skylight and Redfield." After mentioning, "merely to list them," the views over "the Gothics, down John's Brook Valley, and towards MacIntyre," Marshall concluded, "Marcy is the only mountain in the Adirondacks from which all the 4,000 foot peaks can be seen." He was not correct. Grace Peak (East Dix) cannot be seen from Marcy's summit. Neither can Couchsachraga: the Panther ridge hides it from Marcy's view, but, of course, it isn't 4,000 feet in elevation either. When Marshall wrote the pamphlet about the High Peaks, he had not yet climbed Couchie. He had not yet been urged to do so by Russell Carson, who upon studying the topographical maps available at the time, decided that Couchie had a highest contour elevation of 4,000 feet.

Bob Marshall returned numerous times to the High Peaks during his short life – he died at age 38. On July 15, 1932, on Marcy he met conservationist Paul Schaefer,[60] whom John S. Apperson, Jr. had sent with movie camera and film to the High Peaks to record fire and lumbering damage. Schaefer first encountered Herb Clark, who was awaiting the arrival of Marshall, who was that day engaged in a marathon hike, attempting to climb as many peaks as he could in a single day. The chance meeting helped spur something greater than marathon hiking. The two men conversed over their lunches. They found they had a common interest: the integrity of wilderness. Schaefer told Marshall about new threats the Adirondack Park faced – the possibility of cabins being built on state lands, the "stripping" of Mount Adams by lumbermen – and a recent disaster: a fire which had burned the forest from the Opalescent to the summit of North River Mountain. Before he bounded away from Marcy's summit, Marshall, who had already advocated the organization of a group that would "fight for the wilderness," told Schaefer, "We simply must band together, all of us who love the wilderness. We must fight together – wherever and whenever the wilderness is attacked." He meant it. In 1935, Schaefer received an invitation to join the Wilderness Society which had been organized by Marshall and seven other individuals who vowed to fight to protect wilderness lands everywhere in this country.

Grace Hudowalski, a founding member of the Adirondack Forty-Sixers and its historian for more than 50 years, wrote about Mount Marcy in the March-April 1953 edition of *Ad-i-ron-dac* (Vol. XVII, No. 2). She wrote about Redfield, Emmons, Hoffman, Colvin, Old Mountain Phelps, Theodore Roosevelt, Pinchot and LaFarge – "the great and the near great" who took "their respective places in Marcy's kaleidoscope" before turning to her "personal impressions" of the mountain. She had a story to tell unlike that of any other climber and, at the same time, just like those of thousands of others. It concerned her first trip up Marcy in 1922, a story related by Suzanne Lance in "The History of the Adirondack Forty-Sixers." Grace was sixteen years old at the time. She didn't return to the High Peaks until after she married and began to accompany her husband and the young people that he and the Reverend Ernest Ryder introduced to Adirondack climbing, but the memory of that first climb stayed with her always. "Walk softly and reverently... Do your share and a little more... Be cheerful..." were bits of advice her father gave her before she embarked upon that trip. He also told her, "It's not important whether you reach the top of the mountain, but it is important how you make the climb." Grace never forgot those words and shared them, lovingly, with others.

Another hiker whose influence was tremendous upon Adirondack hikers of the twentieth century, Jim Goodwin, was only nine years old when he first climbed Marcy in the company of his father, and a group of his father's friends. Their route from Interbrook Lodge, below today's Garden parking lot, was by way of a tote road, now the Southside Trail, to Mel Hathaway's hermitage, now the site of Johns Brook Lodge. The year was 1919. Lumbering had devastated the Johns Brook valley in previous years and had virtually destroyed the Phelps Trail which had been cut, according to Russell Carson, by Ed Phelps and Seth Dibble in 1871 as far as the head of Panther Gorge. Carson wrote, in *Peaks and People,* that the "Johns Brook trail now has two options." (It still does.) "The old way is by Slant Rock, a steep, muddy path that seems as long and tedious coming down as it does going up." (Though it may still seem "long and tedious" coming down from Marcy, thanks in large measure to ADK trail crews, it is no longer muddy, most of the time.)

Carson continued:

> In 1920, State Forester Arthur S. Hopkins[61] laid out a new route from Bushnell Falls going in a southwesterly direction around the western side of Little Marcy and intersecting the Van Hoevenberg Trail , by which it continues to the top. Passing, as it does, by an easy grade through a beautiful stand of virgin timber, this has become one of the most popular approaches to Tahawus. It has been suggested that this trail be called the Hopkins trail in honour of its originator. Indeed, this suggestion might appropriately be carried a step further to include giving the name Hopkins Hump to the subordinate peak by which the trail gets to Marcy. This would be a splendid compliment to a man whose Adirondack service in modern times has helped bring to public attention the fact that the Adirondack Mountains are not inaccessible, and has also taught the uninitiated how to get to the principal peaks. Hopkins Hump is 4720 feet high but does not have enough of a rise on all sides to be ranked as an individual mountain. In 1893 it was designated "No Name Mountain" in the field notes of D. M. Arnold, who was running the lines of township 48, Totten and Crossfield Purchase, for the Adirondack Mountain Reserve. Through a misunderstanding it later was called "No Man's Mountain." It has also been called Little Marcy. But none of these are map names, and no confusion will follow if the name Hopkins Hump is adopted.

Carson's influence was such that the trail that Hopkins laid out as a short cut for his state Division of Lands and Forests survey crew is now, indeed, the Hopkins Trail, from Bushnell Falls to its junction with the Van Hoevenberg Trail. However, "No Name Mountain," now measured at 1,446 meters (4,744 feet) is now, on the map, Little Marcy. The Phelps Trail, which Jim Goodwin followed to Marcy, also joins the Van Hoevenberg Trail for the final climb up Marcy. It originally began below the bridge on Intervale Road to the Garden. The Hopkins Trail originally began at the Garden. Carson's contention that the Hopkins Trail had "become one of the most popular approaches" is no longer true, perhaps because it differs very little in terms of mileage from the Phelps Trail, because it seems less direct, and because it ascends to the Van Hoevenberg Trail along a line high above the Johns Brook and affords very few vistas along its course. Orra Phelps described the trail in the first ADK *Guide to Adirondack Trails, Northeastern Section* (1934). She wrote, "The trail still follows the stream but is high above it... climbing is steep, and the grade increases somewhat with elevation, but soon one is high enough to get glimpses out into the valley." Jim Goodwin's son, Tony, in the current *Guide to Adirondack Trails: High Peaks Region*, remarks that the Hopkins Trail's "grades are generally easier than those of the Phelps Trail, but it is quite wet near its junction with the Van Hoevenberg trail." He makes no mention of "glimpses into the valley," but he does write that the trail, after it joins the Van Hoevenberg one "passes the former site of the Hopkins Lean-to" a short distance from the site of the former Plateau Lean-to.

Jim Goodwin recalls that, on his first trip to Marcy, the group hiked along the "abandoned" Phelps Trail over AMR land to Slant Rock, where they stopped for lunch, and then climbed, without packs from that point, to the summit. Within a year of the time Grace Hudowalski climbed the mountain, Jimmy had begun to guide others up mountains, often camping at Slant Rock on the way to Marcy. By the end of the century, he had climbed Marcy 196 times. He told Sharp Swan that, as a "boy guide," working for three dollars a day, he "used to sell people the idea of a beautiful trip going up Marcy in the middle of the day, climbing Skylight and returning through Panther Gorge to Slant Rock, where the trip began. In those days, Panther Gorge was just a beautiful trip. It was sort of a miniature Yosemite Valley."

In 1928, the president of the Adirondack Mountain Club, Pirie MacDonald, donated money with which to build what Henry Van Hoevenberg had previously hoped to erect: a stone shelter atop Marcy. That summer, work crews mixed mortar and placed stones gathered from the summit to construct the shelter on the south side of the summit rock. Although hardware, bags of cement, and other construction materials had to be hauled all the way to the work site, water – for the crew, for a horse employed to do some of the hauling, and for mixing the mortar – was obtained from the same spring that had quenched the thirst of Benson Lossing and the members of his hiking party in 1859, when they had found atop the mountain its first stone shelter.

Jim Goodwin also told Sharp Swan about spending the night in the shelter, Christmas Eve in 1935. He and a friend climbed to the summit from Adirondak Loj through "deep, powdery snow" that "made breaking the trail with skis difficult," but along the way they picked up enough firewood so that when they arrived at the shelter they could keep the stone building warm during their overnight stay.

Sharp continued the story:

> Even though the temperature that night dipped to twenty degrees below in Keene Valley, some four thousand feet lower than their stone shelter, inside the small compartment the woodstove and three llama wool sleeping bags stuffed inside one another kept Jim warm. Luckily the evening was a calm one, allowing them to bundle up in the warmest clothes and make a dash for the summit. From the highest point in New York the lights of Lake Placid were clear and bright to the north, but after only a few minutes, the cold bit through their clothes and drove them back inside their stone shelter.
>
> That night, while they slept, Jim said he never heard Santa Claus or his reindeer fly over, but the following morning old Saint Nick had left them a present neither one would ever forget. Outside their warm shelter lay a sea of clouds with Dix, Haystack, and the Range appearing as

islands rising above the ocean. Jim said, "It looked as if you could take a boat and paddle over to Haystack and onto Dix."[62]

On November 24, 1950, the day before the Big Blow swept through the High Peaks, Forty-Sixer Treasurer A. G. "Ditt" Dittmar (#31) and his wife Mary (#29) were returning from a hike through Avalanche Pass when, between Marcy Dam and Adirondak Loj, they encountered two Explorer Scouts from Gouverneur "who said that they were planning to camp at Marcy Dam and then climb Marcy the next day." Ditt wrote, "We gave them a map and bid them good luck – but it was the luck they needed the most. I thought about them the next day and wondered if they would get out alive."

Later, Ditt discovered their names in a register and wrote to one of them, Robert DeLong, "to see how they had made out."

DeLong reported:

> ... We started up following blue markers on what appeared to be a ski trail. However, we turned off about one quarter mile up and headed for Indian Falls. We were both worried about falling trees, for when a particularly large gust would come along, a pine or a spruce, upwards of 50-60 feet high, would come crashing down. Indian Falls was particularly beautiful for it was sheathed in ice... After reaching Plateau leanto we decided to try to go on. Once out on the rocks I was a bit scared. I guess John was too. We held a conference behind a rock to escape the wind and the flying corn snow which had the effect of BB shot on one's face. John was all set to turn back. I went on alone, but John soon joined me. We made progress by running from rock to rock. Once when I stood partially erect, the wind caught me and actually carried me about twenty feet... Luckily I tripped and the wind swept by me.
>
> I remember telling John that we could build a fire in the shelter, which I thought was the size of a small room. Crawling in the window, for we couldn't open the iron door against the wind, we found a "closet" with about a foot of snow. This really disappointed us, as did the view which was about 50 feet "downward" (one couldn't look into the wind due to the flying snow.) I changed mittens and we started down. My hat... I had it tied down with the hood of my ski jacket but the force of the wind tore it off. The descent was rapid but without incident 'til we reached the junction of the ski trail and our trail. John and I were bending over a pool of water drinking when "crack!" a limb broke. John made the quickest move I have ever seen him make when he jumped up and dove for shelter...[63]

By the early 1960s the shelter atop Marcy had suffered the ravages of time and blatant disregard. Its iron doors drooped upon their hinges, its windows were broken. Its two rooms, both of which had once contained woodstoves and bunks, were uninhabitable, littered with rubbish and stinking of urine. The structure was finally razed by the state in 1968.

During the weekend of May 24, 1974, members of various wilderness organizations, including the 46ers, participated in Clean-Up Days and removed garbage and litter from lean-to sites on the approaches to Mount Marcy. "The History of the Adirondack Forty-Sixers" in this book relates the results of that early stewardship effort made by club members. Elsewhere in the club history, and in Christine Bourjade's chapter about the Upper Range, the remarkable story of Dr. Edwin H. Ketchledge (#507) is told. Ketch organized efforts to reseed the vulnerable alpine summits. He also was instrumental in organizing the Summit Stewards program which has done much to protect the fragile, alpine-like summits and to educate the public about them. The Forty-Sixers helped fund the program in its early years; today the program is supported by the Adirondack 46R Conservation Trust which was established by Grace Hudowalski.

Heaven Up-h'isted-ness!

Marcy's history is a rich one. Its stories are many, too many to be recounted in any one book, but Sandra Weber has done a masterful job revealing the mountain's history in her *Mount Marcy, The High Peak of New York* (2001). She writes about other early trips to the mountain; other winter "adventures"; the impact of too many hikers beginning in the 1960s; lost hikers, injuries, and deaths; land purchases; Henry James's hiking experiences; the proposal, after World War I, to establish the area of Mount Marcy as Victory Mountain Park, a memorial to the war's dead; and Ranger Pete Fish (#1396).[64] Her book is a valuable edition to anyone's collection of High Peaks literature and history. Earlier in this book, in her history of the Forty-Sixers, Suzanne Lance writes about the centennial of the first ascent of Marcy, an event in which many early 46ers participated, and one which, years before cell phones were even imagined, a generator was hauled, in part by a horse, to Marcy's summit so that the ceremonial proceedings that day could be broadcast throughout the state by radio.

Grace Hudowalski once said that every mountain is different and that each one means something different to the people who have climbed them. Each of us – those who have climbed the mountain – has a Marcy story. Many of us have numerous Marcy stories. Marcy is part of our history. We are part of Marcy's history.

P. F. (Fay) Loope (#4) by the end of 1948 had climbed Marcy sixty-five times. He recorded some of his stories of the mountain in a piece, "Moods of Marcy," published in the January-February 1949 issue (Vol. XIII, No. 1) of *Ad-i-ron-dac*. In that essay, he wrote, "One does not really know a mountain until he has stood on it in sunshine and in storm; in rain and in snow; in the summer haze of dog days and in the glistening crystals of a sub-zero day; in noonday sun and in inky blackness; in evening's fading light and in the glow of a morning sun still hidden below the horizon."

He continued, "To know a mountain in these and other conditions is to really know it and love it. It is never twice alike. The sky, the clouds, the atmosphere, the day, the air, the wind, the snow, the many other things combine to make it always different."

Loope went on to describe Marcy, on one occasion, seeming "cold and unfriendly"; on another, after dark, with "air so clear that every star is twinkling and they all seem startlingly near." He wrote,

> The snow field on the east side of Marcy[65] is sometimes painted red by the rising sun. One's shadow cast upon it is green... The first red glow of the morning sun and the last rays of the setting sun painting the snow-capped peaks is a sight long to be remembered. This color when seen from the high altitudes is much brighter than when viewed from the valleys. Never do we see these colors in summer...
>
> The frost formations which the clouds build out on the windward side of all projecting objects on the mountain top in freezing weather are another interesting phenomenon. Rocks... all objects protruding above the surface develop ice formations... sometimes six or eight inches in thickness. The frost flowers formed on a still, cold, cloudy night are even more interesting. These thin, leaf-like formations are very delicate and are never alike... They are short-lived, vanishing in the sun or the first high wind or snow.

"Twice," Loope wrote, "I have seen the White Mountains from its summit in winter – never in summer."

In her "Marcy Kaleidoscope," Grace Hudowalski also wrote about climbing Marcy (August 1939) to see the sunrise from its summit:

> Leaving the Loj at 1:30 a.m., our way was lighted by a magnificent display of the Aurora Borealis. Climbing that night was fun until we reached Plateau. The cone of Marcy was enveloped

in mist and the air was cold and damp. By the time we reached timberline the mist was so dense that cairns were hard to find even with strong flashlights and the leader dared not move from the line of vision of the person behind who stayed in sight of the last cairn. And then, without warning, we were there against the ledge and the bronze centennial marker. We put on every item of clothing... and huddled together for warmth, taking an occasional sip of coffee from our thermos bottles.

All of a sudden – as wind blew mist away – the day began! Tinted in shades of palest pink to deepest rose, the eastern skyline appeared. Sun dogs stretched themselves out until there were six vari-colored lavender-purple rays. Then, towering over Giant-of-the-Valley, came the sun, a huge bursting ball of flaming gold!

All around and beneath us great waves of soapy low-lying clouds lapped against Marcy's peak completely hiding all other heights. We were "cleaving the sky." Gradually Skylight, Redfield, the McIntyres, Haystack came above the cloud waves like submerged rocks on a wave-tossed sea. And, as we watched Gray Peak appear, we saw on the rose-tinted clouds over it, the shadow of Marcy.

Near the end of her essay, Grace wrote,

There have been many notable ascents of the High Peak of Essex in my life. Each one was different and each one marked taking someone new to the summit and sharing with him that "heaven uph'istedness" feeling which Old Mountain Phelps spoke of...

Climbers will always aspire to Marcy. Why? "Because it's there" and it's the highest in the area. "How" will they "make the climb?" Again and again, we hope, to capture some new mood of the High Peak of Essex, Mount Marcy, Cleaver of the Sky – the rooftop of the Empire State.

On a summer's day, Marcy sometimes hosts hundreds of people, but there are occasions when you can be alone atop the mountain, alone upon the anorthosite, among the lichen, near alpine flora (boreal bent grass, Bigelow's sedge, dwarf willow, black crowberry, etc.).[66] You can be alone, atop Marcy, except for a red eft resting below the summit rock; alone except for a meadow vole hiding beneath the scrub in a crevice on the slope towards Gray Peak; alone except for a white-throated sparrow, a dark-eyed junco, a yellow-rumped warbler, a Bicknell's thrush foraging nearby; alone except for a peregrine falcon or ravens soaring above Panther Gorge; alone except for the air, the sky, the clouds, the stars, the universe all around you as you achieve "heaven up-h'isted-ness" on that storied, ancient peak.

Endnotes

1. Russell M. L. Carson was convinced that Spafford's gazetteer applied the name "Giant of the Valley" to a lesser peak near what was, in 1813, the village of Pleasant Valley – now Elizabethtown. In *Peaks and People of the Adirondacks* he suggested that the name (Giant of the Valley) "belonged to a mountain one mile southeast of the courthouse at Pleasant Valley." *The Modern Babes in the Woods, or Summerings in the Wilderness,* by H. Perry Smith (1872) included E. R. Wallace's "Guide to the Adirondacks," which contained a description of Giant which maintained "This mountain or culmination of mountains has borne no name until recently, when several individuals christened it the 'Giant of the Valley' though this title properly belongs, and was first applied, to Cobble Hill." However, since Giant may be seen clearly from numerous locations in the Champlain Valley, from whence it appears to be one of the region's most prominent peaks, the mountain was well known long before Wallace wrote his guide. It is therefore likely that Wallace and Carson were mistaken and that the name was actually applied to the high peak.

2. The Peruvian Mountains, as the Adirondacks were then known, were rumored to possess considerable mineral wealth. In fact, the name "Peruvian" is said to have been applied to the mountains because they potentially contained precious metals similar to those of Peru. The supposed discovery of silver in the area of Nye Mountain is told in this book's chapter about Nye mountain.

3. Many years later, a Mrs. Morrison loaned the "Holt family papers" to Carson. In a manuscript, "More About Harvey Holt" by Holt's daughter, Nettie Holt Whitney (1925), Whitney wrote that Holt and Cheney "were the first to cut a trail up this side *(Keene Valley side)* of Marcy, which was in 1836, to accommodate their hunting expeditions." Philip G. Terrie, Jr., in his "Editor's Introduction" to the 1973 edition of Carson's *Peaks and People of the Adirondacks* (Glens Falls, N.Y.: The Adirondack Mountain Club), agreed with George Marshall that "the date for the cutting... is dubious." Terrie pointed out that Holt and Cheney "were working at the McIntyre settlement that year" and that Mrs. Whitney "had not even been born in 1836... she may easily have erred by as much as several years" in assigning the date. It remains curious, however, that Redfield made note of both "Cheney's Camp" and "Holt's Camp" in his field notes. Cheney had likely previously camped at Lake Colden, almost definitely in 1836 and perhaps previous to that year. Holt may, indeed, have camped previously at "Holt's Camp," also, perhaps, in 1836. Charles Fenno Hoffman wrote, after his 1837 attempt to climb Marcy, "So far as I learned, it is only lately that curiosity has prompted those who have passed a great part of their lives in the neighborhood to make the ascent." Thus, it is possible that Holt had previously been to the top of Marcy, but there is no proof that he had.

Terrie, in "The First Ascent of Mt. Marcy, Who Made the Climb?" *(Adirondac,* December 1973, pgs. 121-122, 132-133) speculated, concerning the first ascent, that it was "not certain that John Cheney, Harvey Holt, or any of the other woodsmen actually reached the summit on August 5, 1837." However, Terrie concluded, based upon Charles Fenno Hoffman's having credited John Cheney with uttering the famous "It makes a man feel what it is to have all creation under his feet" quote, that Cheney was a member of "the final assault party." It was Terrie who determined that the plaque atop Marcy, placed there in 1937, credited too many men with having made the first ascent. His research led him to conclude that William Redfield, Ebenezer Emmons, James Hall, John Torrey, Charles C. Ingham, and David Henderson were members of the party and that in addition to Cheney and Holt, the only other very likely member of the party was Ebenezer Emmons, Jr. "Beyond that everything is speculation." In the same edition of *Adirondac,* Terrie suggested, "in the interest of historical accuracy" the ADK "should see that the plaque is removed." He concluded, "The mountain itself certainly does not care by whom or when it was first ascended."

4. Carson, *Peaks and People of the Adirondacks* (Garden City, New York: Doubleday, Doran & Company, Inc., 1928), pg. 55.

5. James Hall, who was born in Massachusetts, was an 1832 graduate of Rensselaer Polytechnic Institute, where he studied geology under Amos Eaton and Ebenezer Emmons. He received his masters degree in 1833 and remained at Rensselaer to teach chemistry and later geology. In 1836 he became assistant geologist for Ebenezer Emmons, chief of the Second District of the state survey. His initial assignment was to study iron deposits in the Adirondack Mountains. In 1837, the survey was reorganized and Hall was put in charge of the Fourth District, in western New York. After the survey ended in 1841, Hall was named the state's first paleontologist and published (1843) *Geology of New York, Part IV.* That volume was "received with much acclaim and became a classic in the field." At Albany, he constructed a laboratory which became a center for the training of geologists and paleontologists. The building, the James Hall Office, still exists and is a National Historic Landmark. In 1850 he participated in a geological survey of northern Michigan and Wisconsin and discovered the first fossil reefs ever found in North America. He later became the state geologist for Iowa (1855-1858) and Wisconsin (1857-1860). In 1866 he became the director of New York's Museum of Natural History in Albany, and in 1893 he was appointed the State Geologist of New York. His publications included *The Paleontology of New York* (thirteen volumes - 1847-1894), 30 other books, and more than 200 papers. He was a founding member of the National Academy of Sciences, a founder of the International Geologic Congress, a member of the Geological Society of London, a

correspondent of the French Academy of Sciences, and the first president of the Geological Society of America. He died in 1898 and is buried in the Albany Rural Cemetery. A residence hall at RPI in Troy is named after him.

6. Charles Cromwell Ingham, who was born in Ireland in 1797, studied art at the Royal Dublin Academy and emigrated to the United States in 1816 or 1817. He took up residence in New York City, where he was the founder of the National Academy of Design and gained renown as a portrait painter, particularly of women and children. He died in New York on December 10, 1863. Among his works were his Adirondack landscapes, a portrait of Mrs. David Colden (1830) and portraits of David Henderson, DeWitt Clinton, the Marquis de Lafayette, and Major General Winfield Scott.

7. John Torrey was born in New York in 1796. He studied botany, mineralogy, and chemistry under the tutelage of Amos Eaton and, in 1815, took up the study of medicine. After becoming a doctor (1818), he published *Catalogue of Plants Growing Spontaneously within Thirty Miles of the City of New York* (1819), and in 1824 he published *Flora of the Northern and Middle States*. He began teaching chemistry and geology at the United States Military Academy at West Point in 1824 and became professor of chemistry and botany at the College of Physicians and Surgeons in New York in 1827. He remained in that position until 1855 and served concurrently as professor of chemistry and natural history at Princeton (1830-1854). He was appointed New York State Botanist in 1836 and published his *Flora of New York* in 1843. With the assistance of one of his students, Asa Gray, Torrey published the early portions of *Flora of North America (1838-1843)*. In 1853 he became the chief assayer for the United States Assay Office.

Torrey, who is regarded as the first professional botanist in the New World, advocated the "natural system" of classification of plants and was the first botanist to describe a carnivorous plant, *Darlingtonia*. He has several plants named after him, including Torrey nutmeg, found in Florida, and Torrey pine, found in southern California. Also, a peak in Colorado is named for him. He climbed that mountain when he was 76 years old. Golf enthusiasts are probably familiar with a famous course which rests atop cliffs descending to the Pacific Ocean in San Diego, California: Torrey Pines. The city also is home to Torrey Pines State Reservation.

8. Many soldiers of the war traveled north from Troy along what was called the Great Northern Turnpike. Today's Route 9 follows much of the course of the turnpike through Essex County and, from it, War of 1812 soldiers would have been able to see many of the peaks of the eastern portion of the High Peaks.

9. Sandra Weber, *Mount Marcy, The High Peak of New York,* (Fleischmanns, New York: Purple Mountain Press, 2001), pg. 44.

10. In 1846, the Union included the Louisiana Purchase but not, officially, the territory that was ceded to the United States from Mexico at the conclusion of the Mexican War. Headley was aware that New Hampshire's Mount Washington was higher in elevation, but he was not aware of other peaks in the "White Hills" and the Appalachians of North Carolina and Tennessee that were also higher. Mount Mitchell, the highest mountain in the East, was first officially measured just before the Civil War, during a survey of the state of North Carolina headed by Ebenezer Emmons.

11. Joel Tyler Headley (1813-1897), a graduate of Union College and Auburn Theological Seminary, was an ordained minister, newspaper writer (associate editor of the New York *Tribune* for one year), and author who traveled in Europe in 1842 and wrote early travel books, *Letters from Italy* (1846) and *The Alps, and the Rhine* (1848 - dedicated to E. C. Benedict). He became "the most prolific American popular historian of the nineteenth century" and was author of thirty books (biographies, histories, and travel books) during his life. *Napoleon and His Marshalls* (1846) went through fifty editions. *Washington and His Generals* (1847) was another of his popular books. *The Great Riots of New York 1712 to 1873* is often cited by modern historians. Headley was a member of the New York State Assembly (1855) and New York's Secretary of State (1856-57). Other books by Headley included *History of the War of 1812, Sacred Mountains, Grant and Sherman,* and *Life of Farragut*. Edgar Alan Poe may have based his story "The Cask of Amontillado" (1846) on Headley's story, "A Man Built in a Wall" (1844).

12. Charles Rockwell Lanman (1819-1895) was a painter, art critic, author, government official, librarian, and traveller. His early life included newspaper work in Michigan and Ohio before he joined the editorial staff of the *New York Express*. He studied art under Asher B. Durand, was a friend of poet William Cullen Bryant and artist Thomas Cole, and became an elected associate of the National Academy of Design in 1846. He served as librarian for the United States War Department, the House of Representatives, and the Washington City library. He was also head of the returns office in the U.S. Interior Department; private secretary to Senator Daniel Webster; American secretary to the Japanese legation; and assistant assessor for the District of Columbia. Among his published works were the *Dictionary of the United States Congress* (1859), a biography of Daniel Webster, and accounts of his own travels and explorations in the United States, including *Adventures in the Wilds of the United States*. He also counted among his acquaintances Charles Dickens and Washington Irving, who called him "the picturesque explorer of our country." In writing about the work of Cole and Durand, Lanman helped define the Hudson River School of painting, particularly the "holy feeling" experienced by the artists when surrounded by nature.

13. Anyone who has ever attempted to sleep upon spruce bows will likely surmise that Lanman and his companions actually chose the foliage of some other evergreen for their bedding.

14. Thomas Cole, the famous Hudson River School painter (1801-1848), visited McIntyre (Adirondac) in 1846. In 1847 he painted *Mount Marcy from the Opalescent,* but Sandra Weber in *Mount Marcy, The High Peak of New York,* reports that "the scene is not an accurate rendition of any real location" and says that it is "unclear" whether or not "Cole ever climbed along the Opalescent, let alone up Marcy." It should be noted, however, that Cole was known for his "imaginative" landscapes as opposed to the "actual views" created by other artists such as Durand.

15. David Parsons Holton (1812-1883) was a medical doctor, school teacher, and an early proponent of phonotypy, the practice of transcribing speech sounds by means of phonetic symbols that was championed early on by, among others, Andrew Comstock (1795-1864), Isaac Pitman (1813-1897), and Alexander John Ellis. Phonotypy developed into the phonetic symbols used today for shorthand and, in dictionaries, to indicate pronunciation, sound, and inflection. Holton traded his medical practice and property in New York City with Dr. Waitstill Ranney, who had a practice in Westport, New York, and moved to the Lake Champlain town in 1843. From Westport, Holton conducted his new practice throughout that town, Moriah, Essex, Elizabethtown, and Jay, and also served as Westport's superintendent of public schools. He was soon appointed county Superintendent of Common Schools, turned his medical practice over to another doctor, and "devoted" himself full time to "the improvement of" Essex County's "one hundred and sixty-nine schools." In his "Reminiscences," Dr. Holton wrote about conducting lectures in all of the schools of the county and that "among the exercises which occupied us during a part of those evening sessions, was that of analyzing and classifying the sounds of spoken language, and practicing in concert the pronunciation of the vocal elements, thus enunciating the several steps of progression in speaking of a word or of a sentence." In the fall of 1847, he left Westport and returned to New York City. He devoted most of the rest of his life to promotion of causes such as advancement of agriculture and the welfare of orphans. Interested in genealogy, he was later a founder of the New York Genealogical and Biographical Society (1869).

16. Orlando Kellogg (1809 - 1865) was a lawyer and resident of Elizabethtown who served as Surrogate of Essex County (1840-1844). In 1847 he was elected to the United States House of Representatives and served until 1849. During that time he became a friend of Abraham Lincoln of Illinois. He resumed his law practice in Elizabethtown in 1849. He was a delegate to the Republican national convention in 1860 and returned to Congress in 1861. Back in Washington, he resumed his friendship with Lincoln, then President. He died in Elizabethtown in August 1865 and is buried there in Riverside Cemetery.

17. Augustus Cincinnatus Hand (1803-1878) was born at Shoreham, Vermont. After completing his study of law at Litchfield, Connecticut, he moved to Elizabethtown and opened his practice there. He was appointed Surrogate of Essex County, served in the United States House of Representatives

(1839-1841) and the New York State Senate (1845-1847). He was elected to the New York Supreme Court in 1845 and served as a member of that court and the state Court of Appeals until 1855, when he resumed his law practice in Elizabethtown. He was a delegate at the Democratic Party national convention in 1868. He is also buried at Riverside Cemetery in Elizabethtown.

18. Byron Pond was an Elizabethtown native, lawyer, county judge, and surrogate of Essex County.

19. Wendell Lansing, who was born at Perryville, N.Y., moved to Union Village (now Greenwich) in 1829. He published a paper there called the *Champion* and then started the *Banner*. He married there and had three children including a son, Abram, who later owned and edited the *Plattsburgh Sentinel*. In 1839 Wendell Lansing moved to Keeseville, where he started the *Essex County Republican* and later published the *Northern Standard*.

20. Archibald McIntyre was the founder of the Iron Works, the man for whom the McIntyre Range was named.

21. Andrew Comstock (1795-1864), author of the *Rhythmical Reader* (1832) and *A Treatise on Phonology, Comprising a Perfect Alphabet for the English Language* (1846).

22. Richard Henry Dana (1815-1882) suspended his college education at Harvard to go to sea as a common sailor in 1834. *Two Years Before the Mast* (1841) details the voyage and provides accounts of life in California before the Gold Rush. Upon returning to Massachusetts, Dana completed his education, studied law, and became a leader of the American Bar Association and an expert on maritime law. He was an advocate for the rights of sailors and an antislavery activist. He helped found the Free Soil Party in 1848 and was a member of the Massachusetts state legislature (1867-1868). He died in Rome, Italy, in 1882. He published his account of his visit to the Adirondacks, based upon his diary entries, twenty years after his climb of Mount Marcy. The highlight of the trip, in retrospect, occurred – after his return through Indian Pass to North Elba – when he met John Brown, who was to become infamous a decade later (1859) for his raid on the Federal Arsenal at Harper's Ferry, Virginia.

23. Sandra Weber provides details about McEntee and Tubby's climb in a chapter, "Trips Up the Opalescent" in her *Mount Marcy: The High Peak of New York*. Jervis McEntee (1828-1891), Joseph Tubby (1821-1896) and Tubby's son Josiah traveled through the region in June and July 1851. McEntee kept a diary, and in it he described hunting, fishing, and climbing Mount Marcy with a guide named Puffer.

24. Thomas Addison Richards (1820-1900), whose family emigrated to the United States in 1831, was a Hudson River School painter and the first director (1858) of the School of Design for Women at Cooper Union in New York City and, beginning in 1867, taught art at New York University. His illustrations appeared in the books he wrote and in publications such as *Harper's*.

25. Weber speculates that the climb reported by Richards occurred in 1853. However, in his *The Romance of American Landscape* (1854), the London-born painter, illustrator, and author wrote about the area of the Saranac lakes, not about a trip to Mount Marcy. In "A Tramp in the Woods" (pg. 242), he allowed one of his companions, a Mr. Brownoker, to tell a story of a "devil of a tramp" he once "had with a friend through the woods to the Adirondack" (the iron works). The character Brownoker mentions the "many varied glimpses of the great walls of the Indian Pass" he supposedly obtained from the shores of lakes Henderson and Sandford *[sic]* and says, "The soaring crown of Tahanous *[sic]*, or Mount Marcy as it is sometimes vulgarly called, we reached from this centre *(the village of Adirondac)*." It seems likely that, because Richards allows a character to tell the story of the trip to Adirondac and because that account reveals no details of the trip to the summit of "Tahanous," that Richards did not venture there before he published *Romance of American Landscape*. In *Appleton's Illustrated Hand-Book of American Travel,* Richards recommended the climb up Marcy, but there is no evidence that he had made it himself. His account of his supposed trip, described in *Harper's Monthly* (September 1859), seems more a flight of fancy than a true account of a trip up the mountain. It is difficult to credit Richards or any member of the party he allegedly accompanied with actually having made the climb. An illustration Richards executed to accompany his *Harper's* article, "The Ascent of

Mount Marcy," shows gentlemen assisting three ladies along the trail and a fourth, bearing a standard, in their vanguard. The distaff members wear full Victorian dress, albeit their skirts are hiked up a bit. Weber asks, "Since no other women had ever climbed Marcy, why invent such a scene?" Why indeed? We can only speculate. What seems definite is that Richards spun much fiction into his travel accounts.

26. Weber writes, in *Mount Marcy,* that the *Essex County Republican* reported that Cook was "the first woman that ever stood upon" Marcy's summit but that in its next issue the report was made that the previous information had been incorrect: "Miss Cook was not the first woman to ascend Tahawus. She was the second." These reports were made in 1870, at least a decade after some woman, we cannot be certain who she was, was the first of her gender to reach the top of Marcy.

27. The Adirondack Iron and Steel Company was originally formed in 1839 for the purpose of acquiring the McIntyre mine. It was reorganized under the same name in 1850. Its shareholders included Archibald McIntyre, Archibald Robertson, and the estate of David Henderson, as well as Dr. James MacNaughton and Dudley S. Gregory – father of a son, George, who married Henderson's daughter Margaret, and Elizabeth, who married Henderson's son Archie. *(The MacIntyre Mine - From Failure to Fortune,* by Harold K. Hochschild, Blue Mountain Lake, NY: Adirondack Museum, 1962).

28. A cupola furnace resembled a blast furnace but was of a much smaller size. A puddling furnace was one that converted pig iron (smelted, crude iron which was poured off into forms to make standard size bars, "pigs," into wrought iron) by heating and frequently stirring the molten iron in a reverberatory furnace (one with a roof designed to reflect heat back upon the material being worked). The iron produced was of a lesser quality than that produced by the Bessemer process. The pigs produced were transported to Jersey City, where they were remelted and refined, principally, to make steel eating utensils.

29. Dixon began making graphite products in 1827, including lead pencils, stove polish, and lubricants. He discovered that graphite crucibles withstood high temperatures, and established a crucible steel works in Jersey City in 1850. He also experimented with photography and photolithography and devised a technique for printing bank notes in color to prevent counterfeiting.

30. Theodore R. Davis (1841-1894) was a popular illustrator for such periodicals as *Frank Leslie's Magazine* and *Harper's Weekly* in the later half of the nineteenth century. He is most famous for his views of battles of the Civil War, which he prepared for *Harper's*. He served on the staff of General John A. Logan during the siege of Vicksburg and marched to the sea with General Sherman. His most famous illustrations include one of the fight between the *Monitor* and the *Merrimac* and one of the impeachment trial of Andrew Jackson. He was wounded at the battles of Shiloh and Antietam and apparently thwarted amputation of his legs, according to his obituary in the *New York Times,* by sleeping "with pistols under his pillow" and daring his doctors "to touch him." He largely recovered from his injuries, retired to Asbury Park, New Jersey, and provided the designs for the White House china employed during the Rutherford B. Hayes administration. When he climbed Mount Marcy in 1858, Davis was already an established artist. He also became a "prolific writer for the New-York daily newspapers."

31. Frederick Stanton Perkins (1832 -1899) was born in Oneida County, New York, but moved with his family to Burlington, Wisconsin, when he was four years old. Wisconsin would be his home for the remainder of his life. However, in 1853, he travelled to New York City and began a two-year study of art under Jasper Cropsey. In 1857, while visiting the Wyoming Valley of Pennsylvania, he began collecting Native American artifacts and eventually amassed the country's largest collection of stone and copper implements devised by the people who originally occupied the lands of our country. He worked in Wisconsin as a farmer and, briefly, as a portrait painter, but archaeology and his collection of artifacts became his great passion. When he visited the Adirondacks and stayed at Keene Valley in 1857, Perkins climbed with Old Mountain Phelps and purportedly helped name Saddleback, Basin, and Skylight mountains. In 1858 Perkins brought Mary Cook with him to Keene Valley and climbed Marcy with her and Phelps. Perhaps, when they were atop the mountain, August 19, and

built the shelter Lossing found, Phelps also christened the small pond below the summit and easily seen from it, Lake Perkins. It, of course, was later renamed: Lake Tear-of-the-Clouds.

32. Street had been preceded to Avalanche Lake by Robert Clark and Alexander Ralph, who, in 1850, climbed Colden by way of the Trap Dyke. See Tim Singer's chapter about Mount Colden for more information.

33. Professor Smith (1815-1877) was a theologian born in Portland, Maine, and a graduate of Bowdoin College (1834). He studied to become a Presbyterian minister at Andover Academy and eventually, in 1855, became professor of systematic theology at Union Theological Seminary. Little is known about his excursion into Panther Gorge, most likely in the company of Old Mountain Phelps, in 1865.

34. The essay, essentially the same, appeared under the name "A Character Study" in Warner's *In the Wilderness* (Boston: Houghton, Osgood & Company, 1878).

35. This and other quotes about the hike are from "Climbers Follow Ghost Up Mt. Marcy," by Ed Hale, pgs. 8-11 in the December 1985 (Vol. XLIX, No. 10) of *Adirondac*. The climb was made in July.

36. In his 1897 *Report to the Superintendent of the State Land Survey of the State of New York,* Colvin claimed (Pg. 448) to have "discovered" Lake Tear-of-the-Clouds in 1869.

37. In 1875, Colvin corrected the elevation of Lake Tear, finding it to be 4,321.963 feet above sea level, just nine feet higher than Moss Pond. The most recent topographical map of the Mount Marcy region (1979) shows Lake Tear to be about 1,315 meters above sea level and Moss Pond to be about 1,295 meters above sea level, a difference of about 65 feet.

38. Schofield climbed in the Adirondacks in the 1870s and was an important proponent of the Adirondack Forest Preserve. He served on the New York Board of Trade and Transportation's and the Brooklyn Constitution Club's forest committees whose reports (largely written by Schofield) recommended that the state purchase additional forest lands. Donaldson in his *History of the Adirondacks* writes that the reports "were widely distributed and read, and did much to enlighten and align public sentiment in favor of forest-preservation." Schofield wrote a Junction Camp "sketch" which today is preserved within the Donaldson Collection at the Saranac Lake library.

39. Now *Plectróphenax nivális,* the snow bunting. It would be considered highly unusual today to see those birds near Marcy's summit. They are usually found in the winter months in fields at lower elevations.

40. It is not possible today to determine with authority what lake it was; however, given his reference to it lying in the southwest and "its bays and islands," it is likely Newcomb Lake. That light can be bent over a relatively short distance to reveal otherwise hidden features such as mountain peaks and bodies of water is a Colvin pronouncement unsupported by science.

41. Ravens were nearly extirpated from all of New York by the beginning of the twentieth century. From 1914 to 1950 only ten sightings of the birds were reported in the entire state. Their return began in the late 1960s, and today, they are relatively common in the Adirondack Park.

42. Wilson's Snipe *(Gallinago delicata)* used to be widely hunted in the fall, and their population was greatly reduced by the early twentieth century. Though still not common, snipe may still find their way to Lake Tear-of-the-Clouds.

43. The log buildings at Buckley's camp were put up by Finch, Pruyn and Company before the First World War. They were intentionally burned to the ground in June 1922, after which the *Essex County Republican* noted, "The buildings will be missed by those who go to Mt. Marcy. They had been occupied by a large number of mountain climbers and were ideal for the purpose." Later in the decade a lean-to was constructed at the site.

44. *Höhenrauch,* a German word, is roughly equivalent to today's English portmanteau word *smog* (combining *smoke* and *fog*). Colvin was familiar with "smog" observed in Europe, the result of the burning of the upper organic layers of drained bogs in northern Germany, usually in the late spring, over a period of up to seven years for each section of bog that was in the process of being converted to arable land. The höhenrauch ("high smoke"), as it moved through the atmosphere, dimmed the

sun over lands downwind and was seen as haze as far away as the Alps, Hungary, and southern France.

45. Otis was a forester and the game warden for the Adirondack Mountain Reserve (AMR). Pond was an AMR employee.

46. Pinchot, who was born in Simsbury, Connecticut, in 1865, graduated from Yale College in 1889. He did postgraduate study at the French national forestry school for a year and, upon his return to the United States, became one of this country's first foresters. He worked as a resident forester for Vanderbilt's Biltmore Forest Estate for three years. He became head of the Division of Forestry of the United States in 1898. In 1900 he founded the Yale University School of Forestry and served as a professor at the school from 1903 to 1936.

47. Christopher Grant LaFarge (1862-1938) was the son of a famed American artist John LaFarge. He was a partner in the Heins & LaFarge architectural firm of New York and worked on such projects as the Cathedral of Saint John the Divine, New York's Fourth Presbyterian Church (now the Annunciation Greek Orthodox Church), Brooklyn's Reformed Episcopal Church of the Reconciliation (now a Masonic lodge), buildings of the Bronx Zoo, St. Anthony Hall at Yale University, Houghton Memorial Chapel at Wellesley College, the Chapel of the Most Holy Trinity at the United States Military Academy at West Point, the Cathedral of St. James in Seattle (the roof of which collapsed under the weight of snow in 1916), and New York City subway stations, notably the original one at City Hall. LaFarge was also illustrator of a book by Elsie Clews Parson, *American Indian Life*.

48. The Flowed Lands (Flowed Land) was created following the death of David Henderson to divert water from the upper Opalescent River to the Calamity Brook. A dam was placed on the Opalescent, and water backed up by the dam created the flooded land. When the water reached above the level of a channel cut to connect the flooded land to the Calamity Brook, it flowed down the brook and thus supplied a more dependable flow of water to the McIntyre mine's furnaces. The dam which created the Flowed Land was damaged by a flood in 1979, and it was partially breached in 1984 by the DEC. Now the Opalescent receives nearly all of the flow from its upper reaches and Lake Colden, and the Calamity Brook's flow has been considerably reduced.

49. MacNaughton was the president of the Tahawus Club. The 3,990+ foot peak that was once thought to have a highest contour level of 4,000 feet may be named for him or, perhaps, his father.

50. Sandra Weber presents a full account of this story, complete with a number of interesting variations, in her chapter, "Roosevelt's Ride" in *Mount Marcy, The High Peak of New York*, pgs. 129-136.

51. See Sandra Weber's "Heart Lake," pgs. 96-97 in *Mount Marcy* and in two chapters – "The Legend of 1877" and "Miss J. J. Schofield" – in *The Finest Square Mile, Mount Jo and Heart Lake* (Fleischmanns, NY: Purple Mountain Press, 1998).

52. The original Marcy Dam was constructed to provide an impoundment for water to carry logs in the spring down the Marcy Brook to the Ausable River and down that river to Au Sable Forks, where the logs were used for pulp wood by the J. & J. Rogers Company. Today's dam is a recent structure. The pond which it holds back has been a popular camping spot since the early 1930s. At that time there was but one lean-to near the pond and, in the summer, a tent which served as an interior ranger's headquarters. Today, as many as 50,000 people visit Marcy Dam each year. The dam, now considered a "non-conforming" structure, may one day be removed. A curious positive result of the 1903 fire which burned the area around the dam and created the meadow that surrounds the pond: it became a perfect habitat for the Philadelphia vireo *(Vireo philadelphicus)*, a bird which can still be spotted (and heard) in that vicinity during the summer months. Chickadees, with little fear of people, may be fed by hand at the dam in the winter.

53. The research library is now housed in the former home of Paul Schaefer in Niskayuna, New York. See Note #60 below.

54. Apperson (1882-1963) was an engineer who worked at G.E. in Schenectady for 47 years. His friend, Irving Langmuir, introduced him to skiing. "Appie," according to his *Wikipedia* biography, "is best known for his important role in the continuing protection of the Adirondack Preserve." He was a charter member of the Adirondack Mountain Club. He also became the mentor and a close friend

of Adirondack legend Paul Schaefer. Louis W. Dawson in his *54 Classic Ski and Snowboard Descents of North America* (American Alpine Club, 1998) writes that Apperson made the first ski descents of Basin and Saddleback in 1918 and that he had "scores" of other "firsts" but disliked publicity and did not record his trips." See Christine Bourjade's chapter, "The Upper Range," in this book for more information about Apperson.

55. Langmuir (1881-1957) was a chemist and physicist noted in the history of science for his 1919 article "The Arrangement of Electrons in Atoms and Molecules." He worked at G.E. in Schenectady from 1909 to 1950, and there, among other things, invented the gas-filled incandescent lamp (with a tightly coiled tungsten filament in a bulb filled with inert gas) which served to light the world for most of the twentieth century. He won the 1932 Nobel Prize in Chemistry for his work in "surface chemistry." He attended schools in this country and in Paris, was a graduate of the Columbia University School of Mines (1903), earned his Ph.D. (1906) at Göttingen, Germany, and did postgraduate work in chemistry also in Germany. Dawson (see note #54) writes that while he was living in Germany, Langmuir was a pioneer skier in the northeastern Alps. *Wikipedia* notes that Langmuir was "one of the first scientists to work with plasmas and was the first to call these ionized gases by that name, because they reminded him of blood plasma." Electron density waves found in plasmas are known as Langmuir waves. A device used to measure temperature and density in plasma physics is known as the Langmuir probe. He contributed to atomic theory and helped define our modern concepts of valence shells and isotopes. Langmuir turned his attention to atmospheric science in the late 1930s. During World War II he worked to improve sonar systems for the detection of enemy submarines, developed protective smoke screens for naval vessels, worked on methods for de-icing aircraft wings, and, ultimately developed the iodide method of cloud seeding. The house in which Langmuir lived for many years in Schenectady is a National Historic Landmark. After he died in 1957, Irving Langmuir's obituary appeared on the front page of the *New York Times*. See Christine Bourjade's chapter, "The Upper Range," in this book for more information about Langmuir.

56. Canivet was a Schenectady resident who worked with Apperson at G.E. He was born in 1887 and died in 1925. Information about Max Paaske is lacking. Christine Bourjade reports that he was also an associate of Apperson at G.E.

57. Tucker, a facilities engineer with G.E., has been actively researching the history of Adirondack rock climbing and skiing for more than a decade. He is currently writing a history of Adirondack skiing and has prepared the "Adirondack Chronology" which appears on the Protect the Adirondacks! (formerly called the Association for the Protection of the Adirondacks) website.

58. See "Winter Adventures," pg. 179, in Sandra Weber's *Mount Marcy*.

59. George Marshall, "Approach to the Mountains" in *Ad-i-ron-dac,* March-April 1955 (Vol. XIX, No. 2), pg. 25.

60. Schaefer (1908-1996) was born in Rotterdam, New York, and grew up in Schenectady. He spent the summers of his youth at Bakers Mills, where members of his family still go. After quitting school at age 14, Schaefer learned carpentry and later became a builder and restorer of early American homes and Adirondack camps. Like Bob and George Marshall, he greatly admired Verplanck Colvin and his accounts of his adventures in the Adirondacks as well as his advocacy for wilderness preservation. After meeting John S. Apperson, Jr., he became an ardent conservationist. In an article in the New York State *Conservationist,* Dave Gibson and Ken Rimany wrote that with "Apperson as an Adirondack mentor, and Bob Marshall and later Howard Zahniser of the Wilderness Society as national partners, Paul assembled and led the broadest, most effective coalition of advocates for the Adirondack wilderness ever assembled, influencing everyone from governors, to labor unions, to sportsmen, to garden clubs. An eternal optimist, he inspired all he met to get involved in their Adirondack Park and its legacy." Gibson and Rimany credit Schaefer with influencing "the Adirondack policies of nine Governors and countless commissioners and legislators." For fifty years he served as an officer of the Association for the Protection of the Adirondacks. He was recognized in 1998, in *Audubon* magazine, as one of the nation's top conservationists of the twentieth century. Quotes attributed to Schaefer are from "Bob Marshall, Mount Marcy, and – the Wilderness" published in the Summer 1966 edition of *The Living Wilderness*.

61. Hopkins, who was the Assistant Director of Lands and Forests for the state Conservation Department, was active in the activities of the ADK and the Forty-Sixers of Troy. He made the first recorded ascent of Cliff Mountain (1921). He and Ranger Clinton West constructed the first trail up Colden (1923) from Lake Colden. He was the speaker atop Mount Esther in 1939 when the Esther centennial plaque was placed there. His pamphlet, "Trails to Mount Marcy," published by the Conservation Department, was the inspiration for thousands of hikes to the peak.

62. Sharp Swan, "Roots, Boots and Routes" in *Of the Summits, of the Forests* (1991), pgs. 87, 94-95.

63. From "Marcy in the Hurricane," by Robert DeLong and A. G. Dittmar, pg. 54 in the May/June 1951 (Vol. XV, No. 3) *Ad-i-ron-dac*.

64. As of August 28, 2008, former Ranger Pete Fish had climbed Marcy 700 times. In a letter he wrote for the Fall 2008 *Peeks,* with tongue in cheek firmly, he said that when asked why he climbed Marcy so often, he either looked mystical and used the old response, "Because it's there," or explained, "more honestly... because I am old and keep forgetting that I have been there before." Pete calculated that 700 hikes to Marcy's summit required 10,360 miles of walking and a total vertical ascent of 409 miles. Along the way to and from Marcy, picking up litter and stopping to converse with (and educate) other hikers, Pete has long been a one-man trail maintenance crew and a profound and effective steward of the High Peaks.

65. The snow field, Christine Bourjade explains, is a "band shaped gulley on the Haystack side just below the summit" where snow swept from the mountain's cone accumulates. Skiers, she says, "access the snow field from the Skylight side, ski down, and somewhat contour around the summit to rejoin the Mr. Van Trail, climb Marcy again," and repeat the process until "it's time to ski back to the Loj." She reports that the snow field's depth often reaches 40 feet. The snow remains, beckoning skiers, until the end of June. It has achieved a degree of fame which attracts avid skiers from all over the Northeast and elsewhere.

66. The flora of Mount Marcy have been catalogued by state Botanist Charles H. Peck in Colvin's *Seventh Annual Report* (1880), his "Plants of North Elba" in the *Bulletin of the New York State Museum* (1899), and by Dr. Orra Phelps, Dr. Edwin H. Ketchledge, Michael DiNunzio, and others more recently. Because several of the species found near Marcy's summit are exceedingly rare, hikers should walk and sit only on bare, open rock on the mountain.

Notes About Summit Elevation Figures

The mountain elevation figures which appear at the beginning of each High Peak description in this book are based upon metric measurements of the mountains recorded on United States Geological Survey maps released during 1978 and 1979. Thirty-two of the forty-six High Peaks are shown on those maps as having elevations rounded to the nearest full meter. For instance, Mount Marcy's elevation is recorded as 1,629 meters above sea level. Converted to feet, Mount Marcy's elevation is 5,344 feet.

Fourteen of the forty-six High Peaks are shown on the maps without exact elevations. Those elevations must be approximated with reference to the highest recorded contour lines near their summits. In this book, a "c" (for "contour") is appended to the metric elevation of each of the fourteen, and a "+" follows the English measurement equivalent indicated within parentheses following the metric elevation. The "foot" figures are approximations based on a number of differing factors. In most cases, the "+" following the "foot" figure indicates that the actual elevation may be as little as a single foot or as much as 32 feet greater than the figure listed. For a complete explanation of the mountain elevations, see Appendix B (Pages 304-306) in *Of the Summits, of the Forests* (The Adirondack Forty-Sixers, 1991).

MOUNTAIN IMAGES

DOUGLAS ARNOLD (#4693W)

Mount Marcy, New York State's highest peak, from Skylight summit
Read about Mount Marcy on pages 155 to 208.

GEORGE SLOAN (#2651W)

From Haystack, Marcy looming over Panther Gorge

KEVIN B. MACKENZIE (#5430)

Blake's Peak and the rest of the Colvin ridge as seen from Nippletop
Douglas Arnold writes about Blake's Peak and Colvin on pages 482 to 494.

PHIL CORELL (#224W)

Wright Peak and its distinctive slides
Sean O'Donnell recounts climbs up both slides on pages 372 to 374.

MOUNTAIN IMAGES

BYRON HAYNES (#699)

Lower Wolf Jaw summit
Mary Lou Recor describes the naming of Lower Wolf Jaw on page 533.

KEVIN B. MACKENZIE (#5430)

The massive slides on Giant's east side as seen from Rocky Peak Ridge
Chuck Gibson writes about Giant and Rocky Peak Ridge on pages 419 to 432.

SEAN O'DONNELL (#5120W)
Alpine bog along the ridge between Rocky Peak and Rocky Peak Ridge

KEVIN B. MACKENZIE (#5430)
Whiteface summit Castle
Tim Tefft writes about Whiteface
on pages 539 to 556.

KEVIN B. MACKENZIE (#5430)
Indian Head above Lower Ausable Lake
Read about Indian Head in the legend
of "Adota of Tahawi" on page 498.

Mountain Images

KEVIN B. MACKENZIE (#5430)

MacIntyre Range in early spring from Indian Falls
Sean O'Donnell writes about the MacIntyre Range on pages 345 to 390.

KENNETH MARCINOWSKI, SR. (#4240)

Painted trillium (*Trillium undulatum*) bloom around Adirondack Loj in May

ANTON M. SOLOMON (#3626W)

Hardwood forest trail in the Sewards
John Sharp Swan writes about the Seward Range on pages 287 to 326.

1 - Closed gentian (*Gentiana linearis*) on Haystack summit
2 - Bog laurel (*Kalmia polifolia*) on Marcy's alpine meadow
3 - Patch of the Forty-Sixers of Troy, designed by Ed Hudowalski (#6) in 1937

ALEX RADMANOVICH (#4968W)   SUZANNE LANCE (#1802W)

ANTON M. SOLOMON (#3626W)

SUZANNE LANCE (#1802W)   BYRON HAYNES (#699)

4 - Yellow pond lily colony with Gothics in background
5 - Diapensia (*Diapensia lapponica*) on Marcy's alpine summit
6 - Vegetation along Allen herdpath

1 - Pink lady's slipper (*Cypripedium acaule*)
2 - Bluebead lily (*Clintonia borealis*)
3 - Spring view from Marcy Dam walkway

ALEX RADMANOVICH (#4968W)

ALEX RADMANOVICH (#4968W)

SEAN O'DONNELL (#5120W)

GEORGE SLOAN (#2651W)

ALEX RADMANOVICH (#4968W)

4 - Emblem redesigned by Ed Hudowalski (#6) in 1948
5 - Pitcher plant (*Sarracenia purpurea*)
6 - Hobblebush (*Viburnum lantanoides*)

SEAN O'DONNELL (#5120W)

Alpine garden on summit of Rocky Peak Ridge

BYRON HAYNES (#699)

Upper Range from Pyramid
Christine Bourjade writes about the Upper Range on pages 500 to 529.

Mountain Images

CHRISTINE BOURJADE (#4967W)

Sawteeth from Upper Ausable Lake
Read about this mountain on page 478.

SEAN O'DONNELL (#5120W)

Adirondack sunrise from Skylight

CHRISTINE BOURJADE (#4967W)

Mount Colden seen from the Flowed Lands
The story of Mount Colden is told by Tim Singer on pages 231 to 243.

SEAN O'DONNELL (#5120W)

The lush, moss-covered Herbert Brook, named after Herb Clark (#1), leads climbers to Mount Marshall's summit.

Mountain Images

KENNETH MARCINOWSKI, SR. (#4240)

Fairy Ladder Falls
Described on page 489.

GEORGE SLOAN (#2651W)

Johns Brook above Slant Rock
Slant Rock is described on page 510

DANIEL EAGAN (#4466)

Dix (left) and Macomb (extreme right) from Elk Lake
Daniel Eagan recounts the stories of the Dix Range on pages 433 to 464.

1 - Rose twisted-stalk (*Streptopus roseus*)
2 - Wood anemone (*Anemone quinquefolia*)
3 - Lake Marie Louise with Rocky Peak Ridge summit beyond, see page 431.

ALEX RADMANOVICH (#4968W)

ALEX RADMANOVICH (#4968W)

SEAN O'DONNELL (#5120W)

ANTON M. SOLOMON (#3626W)

ANTON M. SOLOMON (#3626W)

4 - A deer keeps an eye on passing climbers.
5 - Opalescent Flume between Uphill Lean-to and Lake Colden

Mountain Images

CHRISTINE BOURJADE (#4967W)

Snow cornice on Gothics north side trail
Read about this mountain on page 530.

BYRON HAYNES (#699)

The trail to Saddleback's summit ascends the mountain's intimidating cliffs.

GEORGE SLOAN (#2651W)

Santanoni from "Times Square"
Phil Corell tells the story of the Santanoni Range on pages 269 to 286.

SEAN O'DONNELL (#5120W)

The abundance of deer's hair sedge on Algonquin pays tribute to the alpine summit vegetation restoration project spearheaded by Edwin H. "Ketch" Ketchledge. See pages 80-83 and 527-528.

Mountain Images

SUZANNE LANCE (#1802W)
Great Slide (right) and Zipper Slide (left) on East Dix (Grace Peak)

PHIL CORELL (#224W)
Typical Range Trail scrambling

PHIL CORELL (#224W)
One of many ladders that aid hikers in the High Peaks

Blowdown is part of the High Peaks climbing experience. Above, the devastating effect of a May 2009 microburst on a section of the Calkins Creek Fire Road near Latham Pond. As shown in insert a DEC trail crew cleared the trail shortly after.

Lower Range and Johns Brook valley from the Giant Ridge Trail

Skylight
Height: 4th – 1,501 meters (4,925 feet)

Gray Peak
Height: 7th – 1,471 meters (4,826 feet)

By John Konowitz, Jr.

Tucked deep in the shadows of majestic Mount Marcy, Gray Peak and Skylight were two of the last major mountains in the northeastern United States to be climbed.

In the valleys below the three mountains lie the highest sources of the mighty Hudson River. Starting as droplets and running off the sides of the peaks are numerous streams that flow into Moss Pond and Lake Tear-of-the-Clouds. Not only do those ponds have outlets which flow into the Hudson, but also from their shores there are spectacular views of Mount Marcy.

There are four major routes to Skylight and Gray, two of which go over Mount Marcy. The Van Hoevenberg Trail from Adirondak Loj goes past Indian Falls and over Marcy to Gray and Skylight. From Lake Tear-of-the-Clouds you can follow the Feldspar Brook and the Opalescent River to Lake Colden and return to the Loj through Avalanche Pass or head up the Lake Arnold Trail to Avalanche Camp and Marcy Dam and out.

The trail from the Garden along Johns Brook also goes over Marcy to Gray and Skylight. You can return to the Keene Valley area by dropping down into the spectacular Panther Gorge and climb up and over Haystack on the way out.

From Tahawus, following the Opalescent to its source at Lake Tear, you can cross the Feldspar Brook, the stream which flows from New York's highest pond. With a single step, you can span the source of the Hudson – which later becomes more than five miles in width near Croton-on-Hudson before it flows on to the Atlantic Ocean, 310 miles from Lake Tear.

The Elk Lake-Marcy Trail is not a highly traveled route, but it provides some tremendous views of Skylight, Haystack, and Marcy. The author and Peter Levine (#1160), approached Mount Marcy from the Elk Lake Trail on a warm and sunny Sunday in July and saw only two other people along the way from Elk Lake to Four Corners.[1]

Verplanck Colvin was the first man known to summit Gray and Skylight, almost forty years after the Emmons party first ascended Mount Marcy. Old Mountain Phelps and Frederick Perkins, while on Marcy in 1857, named Skylight because a rock projection they saw upon its summit looked to them like a dormer window on a house. Gray Peak was named about 1869 for the noted 19th century botanist Asa Gray. Russell Carson reported in *Peaks and People of the Adirondacks* that Mel Trumbull believed the name was "bestowed by

John Torrey

New York Professor J. A. Lintner,[2] who spent time that summer *(1869)* in the vicinity of Mount Marcy."

A native New Yorker, Gray was born November 18, 1810, in Sauquoit, Oneida County. He attended Fairfield Academy in Herkimer County and graduated in 1831 from the Fairfield College of Physicians and Surgeons, but he never practiced medicine. Gray had, as early as 1830, begun exchanging plants with John Torrey, America's first professional botanist. He began teaching at Hamilton College during the summer of 1834, and he made a plant collecting trip with Torrey in New Jersey in 1834, just two years before Torrey was appointed New York State Botanist and three years before Torrey joined the first party ever to ascend Mount Marcy.

Gray finished his first botanical textbook, *Elements of Botany*, in 1836 and was appointed the University of Michigan's first professor of botany in 1838. In 1841, he began working on his *Botanical Text-Book,* which, following its publication in 1842, became a standard text, as did his *Manual of the Botany of the Northern United States* (1847). Gray's manual has been updated continuously over the course of 160 years and is still a primary botanical reference book.

Asa Gray

With Torrey, between 1838 and 1843, Gray created the monumental work *Flora of North America,* and in 1842 he was appointed professor of botany at Harvard University. There he remained until 1873. He corresponded with Charles Darwin, supplied Darwin with evidence supporting his theory of evolution, and became that scientist's greatest advocate and critic in the United States. He was a founder (1863) of the National Academy of Sciences, was president of the American Academy of Arts and Sciences for ten years, and was a regent of the Smithsonian Institute for fourteen years. Before his death (January 30, 1888) he donated his large library and his impressive collection of plant specimens to Harvard. In 1900, he was elected to the national Hall of Fame.[3] Whether or not Asa Gray ever saw the mountain which bears his name on the shoulder of Mount Marcy is not known, but it is known that in helping John Torrey collect specimens for the *Flora of North America*, Gray worked in the southern Adirondacks.

On September 16, 1872, Colvin and his guide, Bill Nye, descended from Mount Marcy over Gray Peak to explore the area around Lake Tear.[4] Colvin's description of that trip, in his manuscript, "The Discovery of the Sources of the Hudson," doesn't sound much different than what a bushwhacking hiker might find today:

Down we plunged, down through the dense thickets of dwarfed balsam, whose dead limbs, claw like spikes clutched our clothing as though determined to resist all exploration. Our rubber coats were speedily torn to ribbons, our other clothing gripped, ripped, and torn, and the icy drizzle of the clouds penetrated everything and chilled us despite our labour. Suddenly, precipitous ledges barred our way; the fog prevented our availing ourselves even of the best routes. The dwarf trees we grasped to aid us to descend pierced our hands with their sharp spines. Here as we hung halfway down, the whimper of the hound above us called us to aid him also, and frequently, poor thing, since he would come, he learned that tails will serve for handles. Once, in some ravine, the next labour was to climb from it again, and finally when the side of Marcy seemed to lose its downward slope, and rose up in all sorts of rock masses, separated by rifts and walled ravines and holes, we found ourselves quite lost in the dense fog, and all uncertain which way to go to find our Gray Mountain... Fearful was the denseness of the balsam chaparral. This mountain crest appeared almost impregnable, so strangely dense its pygmy forest, whose outer surfaces of dead boughs like bayonets, as weathered and gray as was the frequent outcropping rock, showed to what the mountain owed its colour. At length we reached a summit....

And now from Gray Peak we have a downward work, and must search for and reach, that remote unvisited lake which we have so long hoped to see... the way southward the valley lies, which we must enter and explore, and plunging from the crest, we fight another, and descending battle with bristling chaparral. So steep the mountainside descends that the dwarfed timber of the crest, thus taken in flank, is soon pierced and left behind, above, but ledges and slippery rocks make every footstep dangerous. Hanging by roots, slipping, sliding, and leaping, down we go. Now, occasionally, we reach a pleasant glade, deep with the thickest richest velvety green moss, such as may be seen in Labrador. It rises to our boot tops and we stride through it as through snow. The trees, though no longer dwarfed, are but pygmy trees ten or twelve feet in height, all gray and lichen grown and ancient. Lo! This one scarce five feet in height, we cut into and count a hundred annual rings of woody growth.

They eventually made their way to the pond and discovered that it flowed to the Hudson River and not to the Ausable and St. Lawrence rivers as originally thought: "First seen as we then saw it, dark and dripping with the moisture of the heavens, it seemed in its minuteness and its prettiness, a veritable Tear-of-the-Clouds, the summit water as I named it." As hard as it is to believe, the source of the Hudson was discovered almost fifty years after the source of the Columbia River on the West Coast.

Marcy from Moss Pond

Almost a year later, on August 28, 1873, Colvin, Old Mountain Phelps, State Botanist Charles Peck, and guide Roderick McKenzie made the first ascent of Skylight. Upon descending, they were the first people to reach Moss Pond, which, today, is still a beautifully secluded gem amidst the almost impregnable thicket between Skylight and Redfield.

During the dry summer of 1994 the author and another hiker were able to walk out to the middle of the pond on their journey from Redfield to Skylight and enjoy the scarcely seen view of an Alps-like Marcy. On another hot, dry trip the author and Bob Hudak (#1721) heard a trickle of water as they bushwhacked through Colvin's impregnable chaparral. Reaching down into the recesses to an underground stream they were startled to find a pink retractable plastic drinking cup. That pretty much assured them that they had not been the first to happily stumble upon the elegant and timely thirst-quenching spring.

Ed Hudowalski took this photograph of Skylight's cairn when it was first built.

A "legend," created by the Rev. Ernest Ryder (#7), has it that if you carry a rock up Skylight and place it on the pile at the summit you will enjoy good weather. The huge cairn on Skylight's peak attests to the power (and promise) of the legend.

From the summit, on a clear day, the view is expansive, with 30 of the 46 high peaks appearing. Two of the more impressive views are of the towering dome of Mount Marcy, with green lichen on the rocks shining in the sun, and the wild precipitous chasm of Panther Gorge as you look from Skylight towards its dizzying depths. The alpine meadow on the rocky top of Skylight is as beautiful as any you will find in the Adirondacks.

Clyde H. Smith produced an essay about Skylight's flora, "Mountaintop Treasures" in his book, *The Adirondacks*, in 1976.[5] After mentioning that the mountain's "rocky top is like a plateau and encompasses several acres above timberline," he wrote,

> Scattered clumps of stunted evergreens mingle with grassy patches and miniature bogs among loose boulders and open ledges... the sedge meadows, heath rush, snowbanks, and wind-exposed areas are communities that support plant growth. The Alpine plants here are unique in this region, thriving only on summits where the harsh conditions are similar to those of their habitual terrain in the Arctic. Flowers are tiny and delicate, and most have a very short blooming period. The best time to see their colorful display is usually between mid-May and late June.

Smith wrote of climbing Skylight in hopes of capturing photographic images of some of the mountain's plants and blooms. His time to do so was limited by an approaching thunder storm, but he found and took pictures of Lapland rosebay – "dazzling magenta... quaking in the wind"; diapensia – with "cushions of thickly clustered minute leaves"; Labrador tea – "scattered all over, their... white blossoms bobbing like ping-pong balls in the breeze"; cotton grass – "a grasslike sedge... easily recognizable because of its cottony seed heads"; and – "the most delicate treasure or all, the fragile flowers of alpine azalea" with "pink blossoms, which are about the size of a matchhead" standing "upright on transparent red stalks."

He also wrote about one of Skylight's botanical communities in particular:

A mountaintop bog may be no bigger than a teacup, or it may be hundreds of feet across. The important thing is that the bog supports life, most often on a miniature scale. For example, the wrens egg cranberry grows as a baby vine with flowers not much bigger than a pinhead and shaped like a shooting star. It really takes close examination to find these minute plants camouflaged among tussocks of grass.

With the storm upon him – his photographic session abbreviated – Smith "raced below treeline as a blinding flash of lightning streaked through the air followed by a clap of thunder." He sought refuge, a few minutes later, in the Four Corners Lean-to that had sheltered hundreds of hikers before him. Many of them had probably carried rocks to the cairn atop Skylight in hopes of avoiding being there in such a storm. Smith made no mention of carrying one himself to the top.

The trail to the top of Skylight from Four Corners was built by Old Mountain Phelps and John Moore around 1875. It is the shortest trail in the Adirondacks that departs from another trail and ascends to a High Peaks summit.

Gray Peak summit register canister. Joe Turon (#1016) took the photo.

The path to Gray's summit begins where the Feldspar Brook issues from Lake Tear-of-the-Clouds. Today the path is lightly maintained by Forty-Sixer volunteers. Ascending some of the ledges along that route requires a bit of scrambling, but the way to go is obvious. A short distance before the summit, hikers seeking views will find a rocky lookout from which Moss Pond may be seen.

For many years, Gray's herdpath extended beyond the summit rock and along its highest ridge to a point from which the prospect of Marcy is magnificent. In the past, some bushwhackers continued along the rude path to the wild col between the two peaks and, trampling through the scrub growth, made their way to Marcy's summit. Today, with protection of Marcy's fragile alpine species in mind, responsible hikers have given up that route, have returned to Lake Tear and Four Corners, and have followed the official trail to the top of the state. The "Walk Softly" wilderness ethic that the Forty-Sixers have adopted dictates that, when we climb the High Peaks, we stay on official trails and Wilderness Paths. The deterioration and destruction of the alpine meadows on Marcy, Algonquin, and other above timberline peaks has been considerably stemmed in recent years because more people have confined their travel to approved routes and have trod, whenever possible, only on bare rock on the high summits.

Skylight and Marcy can be seen from the Northway, at about mile marker 71. In the spring and early fall, when they are snow covered, they really stand out and seem to beckon those of us who are drawn to or have been drawn to the source of the Hudson and the peaks which nestle close to the dome of the state's highest peak.

Endnotes

1. Four Corners derives its name from the fact that four trails intersect at that point: the one to and from Skylight, the one to and from Marcy, the one to and from Panther Gorge, and the one along the Feldspar Brook to and from the Opalescent River. The trails diverge from one another at angles close to 90°, 180°, and 270°.

2. About 1853, Joseph Albert Lintner (1822-1898) of Schoharie, New York, became interested in the study and collection of insects. He was a manufacturer of woolen goods at Utica in 1860 when he secured a position in the zoological department of the New York State Museum in Albany. He devoted the next dozen years of his life to his work at the museum and devoted much of his time to entomological research. He became the state entomologist in 1881. It is likely that he and Asa Gray were acquaintances.

3. The Hall of Fame for Great Americans is located on New York University's former Bronx campus, now that of Bronx Community College. It opened in 1901 atop a bluff, New York City's highest point, above the Harlem River. Bronze busts of the honorees and plaques identifying the inductees are housed within a neo-classical colonnade. Only 98 Americans have been named to the hall, but none since 1976. Those named in that year have yet to have their busts added to it.

4. In his report of his survey activities for the year 1872, Colvin wrote about making a "visit" to a "little lake lying in the chasm" between Gray and Skylight on September 16. He also referred to it as a "little pond" and a "red-letter point in this survey" as he determined that its outlet flowed not to the Ausable but to the Hudson. He then surmised that it was "the *summit water* of the State... the loftiest known and true *high* pond source of the Hudson river." In his *Report of the Topographical Survey of the Adirondack Wilderness of New York for the Year 1873,* pg. 37, he first referred to it as "Tear-of-the-Clouds" when reporting about his visit, with Nye, to the pond following their ascent of Skylight and visit to Moss Pond.

5. Clyde H. Smith (1931 - 2008) was a free-lance photographer and avid outdoorsman who lived the last thirty years of his life near Wadhams in Essex County. Born in Gorham, New Hampshire, he lived for a number of years with his parents atop that state's Mt. Cardigan, where his father manned the fire tower. According to his obituary in the Plattsburgh *Press-Republican,* "As a small boy Clyde hiked down and back up the mountain to go to school every day, nurturing a love for the mountains that remained with him all his life." He graduated from high school in Spruce Pine, North Carolina, and spent summers at Camp Mowglis on Newfound Lake in New Hampshire. There he was a camper, counselor, and trip master. Majoring in forestry, he attended the University of New Hampshire before he enlisted in the United States Air Force during the Korean Conflict and served as an architectural draftsman. After his discharge from the Air Force, he moved to South Burlington, Vermont, and took up a career as an architect before turning his attention to photography. His photographs appeared in numerous publications, including *Adirondack Life, Audubon, Skiing, Vermont Life,* and *Yankee,* and he helped produce twenty-one books that included his images. *The Adirondacks* was published by Viking Press in 1976. "Mountaintop Treasures" appears on pages 38-40 of that book.

About the Author

John Konowitz has ascended all of the 46 high peaks several times. His love for the mountains began when, as a boy, he hiked with his father and other counselors of Camp Pok-O-Moonshine in Willsboro. He completed his 46 on Mount Emmons in 1968. As a teacher and coach at the AuSable Valley School District, he was never far from the mountains he loves, and frequently returned to the peaks. After he became the head men's basketball coach at SUNY New Paltz and, later, at SUNY Cortland, John continued to work as an advisor at the Pok-O-MacCready Camps, and he continued to climb and explore the mountains of the region. An insurance and investments counselor today, Konowitz and his wife Judy spend summers at their camp on Fern Lake and still climb as often as possible.

MOUNT COLDEN
Height: 11th – 1,437 meters (4,715 feet)
By Tim Singer (#1038)

With two marked trails, two approaches by rock slide, and several other routes for the imaginative "random scooter," Mount Colden provides a variety of opportunities for those in search of a challenge, a traverse, or a straightforward hike.

Sandwiched between 5,000-footers, Colden appears aloof, a mountain without a range. James Kobak III (#1791W), who has more than 20 full rounds of the 46 to his credit, says, "What makes Colden cool is that it kind of stands alone, right in the middle of it all. The giants of Marcy and Algonquin stand shoulder to shoulder with it, yet it is content to be by itself."

Compared to its higher neighbors, Mount Colden "is perhaps even more interesting with the extensive slides and unique large dike on its west side."[1] And how many mountains in the Adirondacks provide an unobstructed view from summit to base? That is what Colden provides. From its highest point one can peer straight down to Avalanche Lake, with its famous "Hitch-up-Matildas" bridging vertical cliffs above thin, cold strips of water.

According to Alfred B. Street, the Indians called Colden *Ou-no-war-lah,* meaning "Scalp Mountain."[2] If only that name, based on the mountain's physical appearance had endured… However, the naming of nature's places in the Adirondacks "tends to be uninspired."[3] Dozens of Long Lakes, Bear Mountains, and Buck Ponds are evidence of the lack of imagination; but more than lacking in inspiration, the naming of places is a lot like politics: filled with confusion, patronage, and struggle for recognition.

The name *Colden* was the first European name, but not the only one, given to the mountain. But the name *Colden* has been derided. David C. Colden was a New York businessman and one-time chairman of the board of selectmen of Jersey City, New Jersey.[4] In New York, he played host to Charles Dickens, the celebrated British author, and William C. Macready, one of the nineteenth century's most revered actors.[5] Prominent both politically and socially in the metropolitan area, Colden made but two visits to the Adirondack high peaks.

One of those trips occurred in August 1836. Colden, a financial backer of the McIntyre Iron Works,[6] accompanied the company's manager, David Henderson, to the iron works on the Opalescent River. During a period of eight days, a party of company executives, employees, scientists, guides and friends explored the region around the "works," braving rainy conditions, a midsummer frost, and even an encounter with a pack of wolves.[7]

Much was accomplished during that pioneering mission, including the first recorded visits to the lakes known as Avalanche and Colden. It is also a matter of history that during the exploration, William C. Redfield made a discovery of no small significance. In his field notes, published in 1838, Redfield wrote as follows:

"Lake Colden" by Benson Lossing

Friday, August 19th. At noon the weather broke away and Messrs. McMartin, McIntyre, and Hall went up by the Lake *(Colden)* to the gap beyond. Myself and Mr. Henderson with one of the men proceeded up the main or east branch about two miles southeasterly (general course) from the encampment... From this point I mounted a hill about 150 feet on the south bank and saw a third high peak bearing N. 80 or 85 east – bearing of the mountain east side of Lake Colden forgotten – but was surmounted by a beautiful dome of rock the whole apparently of difficult ascent.[8]

This has been regarded as the "first known notice of Mount Marcy."[9] Though one must assume that the mountain had previously been sighted from more distant points, before Redfield took note of it, it had not been presumed New York's highest peak.

David C. Colden was a member of the 1836 party but, by all accounts, he was not crucial to either the research or exploration involved. Instead, apparently, he spent much of his "vacation" hunting and fishing. It was due to his stature, his association and friendship with David Henderson, and, perhaps, his character that Mr. Redfield, not long after the exploration, named Mount Colden in his honor.

It was a nice yet controversial gesture. "The story goes that the owners of the Iron Works were peeved at the naming of a mountain on their preserve without their permission."[10] So it was that, in 1837, Ebenezer Emmons re-christened the peak *Mount McMartin* in honor of Judge Duncan McMartin, an entrepreneur and a partner in the iron works who made his home at North Broadalbin in Fulton County.[11] Some of the funds McMartin used to support the iron works were garnered from a lottery that Archibald McIntyre, David Henderson, and he ran in the state of New Jersey.[12]

To add to the confusion, not long after naming Colden, Mr. Redfield changed his mind. "The mountain on the easterly side of Lake Colden," Redfield wrote in 1837, "had received the name Mt. McMartin in honor of Judge Duncan McMartin."[13] Redfield had clearly yielded to the wishes of the proprietors of the iron works and, possibly in doing so, acknowledged the designation as a memorial tribute to McMartin, who had recently died.

While in 1837 the mountain's name had apparently been settled, maps, texts and scientific chronicles continued to inspire confusion. For many decades, both names were used, depending on one's source or preference. Not until late in the nineteenth century did McMartin all but give way to Colden.

All of the confusion, the debate, was perhaps best summarized and best simplified by none other than Orson "Old Mountain" Phelps:

> The next oldest naming I can learn of was by McIntyre's, Henderson's and Colden's party, accompanied by Redfield, and John Cheney and Harvey Holt for guides, they held a consultation and decided to leave Tahawus alone with its very appropriate Indian name, and take the next highest for the venerable McIntyre. Mr. Henderson had already had one mountain and a lake named for him so he was counted out. Next came their friend Colden, and they decided to give him a mountain and a lake and named Mt. Colden and Lake Colden in honor of him.
>
> By some misunderstanding of writings, probably Mt. Colden had gotten put down on some of the maps as Mt. McMartin. This could be proven a mistake if there were not two living witnesses that were present at the naming of them, namely John Cheney and Harvey Holt, who both say it was named Mt. Colden before the name Mt. McMartin was ever heard of; and then the fact that as many as four different mountains are called McMartin shows that some one is mistaken about it.[14]

And Colden it shall remain. McMartin would have been a worthy and more appropriate pick. He was a northern New Yorker, important to the history of the region. His roots and heritage lasted into the twenty-first century. One Arthur Crocker, who passed away in January 2005, was a summer resident of Newcomb, a "foremost leader" in the Adirondack environmental movement, and the grandson of Christine McMartin, a direct descendant of Duncan McMartin.[15]

Nevertheless, Russell Carson, who aggressively and passionately advocated the naming of mountains for fitting individuals (i.e., Donaldson and Emmons), called the naming of the peak deplorable.[16]

While the early explorers of the region were quibbling over the name of the peak, they apparently didn't bother to take the time to climb it.

At the time of the historic 1837 expedition, during which he climbed Marcy, Algonquin and Nippletop, Professor Emmons did climb some 1,500 feet up Colden's Trap Dyke, but he did not continue to the summit. In his *Geology of New York, Part II, Comprising the Survey of the Second Geological District*, Emmons was first to write about Colden's best known feature:

> The dyke, which is the most remarkable object of this place, cuts through the mountain nearly from top to bottom. At its base, where it rises up from Avalanche lake, a deep gorge has been formed by the action of a small stream, which rises some distance up the present gorge, probably

Great Trap Dyke at Avalanche Lake.

From Ebenezer Emmons'
Geology of New York, Part II, Comprising the Survey of the Second Geological District

in several, small springs. Its depth is about one hundred feet, and it is bounded by perpendicular walls of naked rock, with numerous clefts, however, which permit small shrubs to take root and grow. At the lower part of the mountain, the width of this gorge or chasm is about eighty feet, which is the width of the dyke, the whole of which is removed up to the walls upon each side. The materials which have been swept out of this gorge are in confused heaps below, and help to fill up the chasm between the mountains, in which the Avalanche lake is situated. Besides the immense quantity of materials from the dyke, consisting of rocks, earth and trees, a great slide, extending also from the top to the base of the mountain, contributes largely to the loose materials in this narrow pass. Great quantities of apparently pulverized vegetable matter are deposited in this lake, at least along the shores. That part of the gorge nearest the lake is steep and difficult of ascent, and also the deepest; while in ascending the more distant part, the inclination is found to be less, but the space above is crowded with large rocks which have been moved from their beds, some of which are fifty feet in length, and all have commenced their journey to the region below.

Upon the west side of Avalanche lake, Mount McIntyre rises in a mural precipice of one or two hundred feet; in the face of which, the dyke which bisects the opposite mountain distinctly appears. After going up three or four hundred feet of this latter mountain, the dyke can be traced up by the eye to near the summit of Mount McIntyre, by two parallel cracks or fissures, which appear from this distance about two feet wide. Upon this mountain there is a great deficiency of water, and there is no stream pouring down upon this face of it; and from this cause, the dyke is not broken up as on the opposite side. A small stream flowing into the cracks and fissures would break up this mass entirely; while freezing and expanding would first separate, and then force down the masses into the chasm below.

The dyke consists of the rock denominated sienite, or hornblende and granular feldspar. In the midst of the Sandford ore bed, the same rock appears, and which I found in three or four places, through the great mass of the mountain in which this ore occurs is the ordinary hypersthene rock.

The view which I have given of this dyke is strictly a map, or it is a perfect transcript of it as it was when the view was taken; but great changes are taking place from year to year, and a view which is literally correct to-day may not be so to-morrow. One half of the mural precipice which appears in the sketch, may tumble down in an instant.

The honor for the first recorded ascent of the mountain goes to two nephews of David Henderson, both employees of the McIntyre Iron Works: Robert Clark and Alexander Ralph,[17] who was one of the last managers of the mining operation before it closed in 1857. His name has since been lost to history. For Clark, originally from Scotland, Colden and the iron works, for which he served as a clerk, were just stops along the way to a distinguished book and map publishing career in Cincinnati and western Ohio.

If you discount the romantic (and possibly apocryphal) tale of Esther McComb's accidental ascent of the peak that bears her name (see the chapter about Esther in this book), then the Clark-Ralph 1850 climb up Colden, via the Trap Dyke, truly is the first high peak summit attained "for the sheer joy of climbing." All prior first ascents of record (Giant, Dix, Big Slide, Whiteface, Marcy, Algonquin, Nippletop) were performed by individuals engaged in scientific research or political boundary survey work.

Alfred B. Street described Colden as "the most savage mountain, by far, of the Adirondacks, – the very wild-cat of mountains."[18] His assessment seems overly dramatic today. The Colden of the twenty-first century appears downright inviting: accessible, interesting, picturesque.

Trails approach the summit from opposite sides. The Lake Colden trail, constructed in 1923 by state forester Arthur S. Hopkins, is beautifully open, yet steep in grade. "The trail up from Lake Colden is brutal," says contemporary hiker Jody Edwards (#1618). "It's a great footpath, but is just relentless in its elevation increase – no breaks – not steep enough to rocket you to the top like the slides, but steep enough to be one of the most unforgiving 'normal' ascents."

Approaching from the northeast, the Lake Arnold route is both shorter and more gradual, if not any more favorable. This approach, constructed in 1966, is named the "L. Morgan Porter Trail" in honor of the long-time chairman of the Adirondack Mountain Club guidebook committee. Porter spent countless hours with a measuring wheel, trekking more than a thousand miles while ascertaining accurate distances along trails in the Adirondack high peak region. To get to the start of the trail which bears his name, hikers usually have to ascend the one and one-half miles from Avalanche Camp to Lake Arnold up "Heartbreak Hill," a trek which provides a cardiovascular workout up a relentless stretch of trail that is "difficult over loose basketball-sized anorthositic rocks and many boulders. It is very rocky, annoying terrain and an excellent opportunity to sprain an ankle."[19]

A hiker reported of Lake Arnold and Mount Colden on an Internet website as follows: "It's a bug infested mud hole with a bad trail. But the views from Colden are unbeatable. Well worth the mud." Equally as fine is the view from the north (false) peak of Colden, which the Lake Arnold trail passes directly over.

According to the original edition of the Adirondack Mountain Club's *Guide to Adirondack Trails, Northeastern Section* (1934), a "new trail" had been cut from Lake Arnold to Colden, but that route, which ascended to the col between the north peak and the mountain's summit, was destroyed during the Big Blow of 1950. With the completion of the L. Morgan Porter trail in 1966, an eastern approach built after the Big Blow fell out of favor. That route, which left the trail to Feldspar Brook about two thirds of a mile south of Lake Arnold, also ascended to the col between the north and main peaks, but the extra distance traveled from Avalanche Camp and the greater vertical ascent made it, for most hikers, a much less desirable trip.

The mountain's earliest trail was laid up the north ridge by the Adirondack Camp and Trail Club. Built in the early 1920s, it began an eighth of a mile south of Avalanche Camp along the trail to Avalanche Pass. No trace of that trail has been seen since the 1950 "hurricane," however, a new slide created by Hurricane Floyd in September 1999 provides a bushwhack and technical route up the same ridge.

Another of Colden's recent slides is a wonder both to view and to climb. Created by the great sculptor Nature in 1990, the slide's bare rock descends the south face from a point just below the summit ridge and falls all the way to the blue trail near Feldspar Brook. The approach to its base is long, but convenient, and the rewards of climbing the slide come with each step upward as surrounding mountains come into view, while the summit of Colden, always in sight, nears ever so slowly.

This photograph by Seneca Ray Stoddard
shows how the Trap Dyke appeared in the late nineteenth century.

Then there's the Trap Dyke. It is nothing short of the greatest marvel, the most talked-about climb, one of the most interesting features in all the Adirondacks. Geologists believe that over a billion years ago molten rock flowed into a fissure which split the anorthosite which now forms the dyke's walls. Much of the newer rock eventually eroded to form the deep cavern that is now the dyke. "The ascent today up the gorge and thence onto the slide above offers perhaps the most enjoyable alpine-like climbing in the Adirondacks,"[20] writes Jim Goodwin (#24), who, along with Edward Stanley, made the first recorded winter ascent of the Trap Dyke in December 1935.

Ed Palen (#710) owner of Adirondack Rock and River, a rock and ice climbing school in Keene, has been leading trips to the Trap Dyke for over 20 years. "Running a guide service in the Adirondacks, I try to push wilderness climbing as much as possible. So with this in mind, the Trap Dyke is by far and away the most popular and our most requested back country ascent in the region. Only New Hampshire has scrambles that can rival it."

Pressed into explaining why the Trap Dyke is so special, Palen is quick to rattle off the reasons:

1. It is located in one of the most stunning settings in the East, with a relatively short, scenic approach;
2. It's a route that leads to a spectacular summit, necessary for any true classic;
3. It includes rock scrambling and slide climbing (as opposed to trailed hiking), offering a more challenging, open and varied climbing experience;
4. While the route is considered to be semi-technical in nature, the climbing is straight forward enough that just about anyone in good physical condition can attempt it;
5. The dyke has an interesting history with the first ascent being done in 1850 by employees of the McIntyre mine; and
6. The route is every bit as much a classic line in the winter as well as the summer, although a bit more serious in the winter.

The Trap Dyke route has been the site of one death and several major accidents over the years. All were in the winter and involved avalanches or falls on the icy, upper slide section.

Additionally, the summer has served up incidents, with the dyke being the scene for more rescues than any other Adirondack climbing or hiking route. Two occurred in 2004. Climbers sometimes head out onto the upper slide section too early from the dyke (what knowledgeable climbers call the "first exit") and freeze due to fear, unable to proceed up or go back down. Those who thus are stuck have to be helped to safety. Graphic stories abound, worthy of a *National Geographic* documentary or an "Adrenaline Series" publication. More to the point, some episodes are downright "Colvinesque" – in the tradition of a climb Verplanck Colvin made down the dyke on September 18, 1872. In his report to the state legislature the next year, Colvin wrote simply, "Of the dangers of the descent, finished at a quarter to eleven at night, I will not speak."[21] He did not elaborate. Ed Palen does:

My own experiences include a rescue in the late fall of a stranded climber. The rescue was typical. We were driven into Marcy Dam, hiked to the lake, were rowed across to the dyke and then climbed up to the stuck individual. It was late October, and the dyke was covered with verglass (thin ice) everywhere. Each night it iced over and each day it melted and was climbable. Because we arrived at 10 p.m. the dyke was icy and scary. We chipped ice for foot and handholds and slowly climbed up with headlamps. The stranded climber had headed out too soon at the first exit and got scared. He had been waiting there for eight hours. When we left the dyke and headed out to him onto the slide, there was no ice and the climbing was easier. We went above him, made an anchor, lowered him a rope and harness, tied him in, and lowered him into the dyke. From there we rappelled with him to the bottom, and the DEC took over with blankets and hot liquids. This taught me that the dyke can be relatively easy in normal conditions or deadly in the late fall/early winter when verglass covers the rock.

Palen concluded that when the ice is thin, crampons don't work, yet boots will slip. Another one of his experiences involved an avalanche on the upper dyke (before the normal, second exit onto the slide):

> The time I was avalanched was in February. I felt the slope had a chance of avalanching; so I kept our team well to the side and probed with my axe to intentionally trigger the slope. The slab of snow in the whole dyke *whoomphed*, and the break occurred high above us. The avalanching snow moved in slow motion, but, even with us to the side, it covered us up to our chests. The brunt of the snow slid past and on down to the lake. (We made sure no one was below us.) I realized from this episode just how right conditions are in the dyke for avalanches to occur. I gained a ton of respect for that climb in winter and don't even consider climbing it within a few days of a new snowfall. At least two broken legs have occurred in the dyke due to parties getting avalanched there.

Danger lurks on any exposed mountain, not just Colden, and can occur on, above, or below cliffs; and as is so often the case in the Adirondacks, weather can precipitate disaster and injury.

On July 27, 1978, Gretchen Weeks, 22, of Brighton, Michigan, embarked on a camping trip to the High Peaks, accompanied by her mother Barbara, 46, of West Falls.

Making their way around Avalanche Lake and dropping their gear at the base of the Trap Dyke, Gretchen and Mrs. Weeks decided to make the steep technical climb to the summit of Colden. As the *Lake Placid News* reported the following week:

> Within a short time, they found themselves in the midst of an afternoon thunderstorm. Once the storm had passed, they returned to the base of the Trap Dyke and set up their two-man nylon tent on a point of land to the right of the dyke, close to the shores of Avalanche Lake.
>
> "We had climbed into our sleeping bags and had the stove burning inside the tent," said Gretchen. "Outside, dusk was beginning to turn to dark. There was a strange sound. Suddenly the tent fell on us and Mom cried out in pain.
>
> "Something had hit my right arm but I could move. I struggled to the bottom of the collapsed tent and found my knife in my boot and cut my way out of the tent. It was then I saw the dead white birch tree resting on top of Mom. It was about ten inches thick and 25 feet long.
>
> "It was then I panicked. Mom told me to get myself together so I could be of help. She thought her pelvis was broken, and maybe a leg and some ribs. She was in great pain.
>
> "We planned what to do. The first aid kit had some codeine in it. I gave her some and then headed for the ranger station at Lake Colden (about one and a half miles away). I hated to leave her alone."

Bushwhacking through the mud, twigs, and wet leaves, Gretchen found herself disoriented. Eventually, the batteries in her flashlight died. In order to return to her tent as easily as possible, Gretchen swam across the lake to the peninsula campsite. After searching for and finding another flashlight while comforting her mother, she then swam back – a distance of some 300-400 feet – to the outlet of Avalanche Lake.

Again, the flashlight batteries did not last. Following several wrong turns along the trail to Lake Colden, Gretchen eventually reached the ranger's cabin. The *Lake Placid News* picks up the story:

> This particular night, the interior station not only contained help in the form of Charlie Nolan (caretaker) and a telephone and radio to contact the outside world, but the three-man high peaks trail crew that had been working in the area all week.

It was nearly 11:00 p.m. when Gretchen reached the cabin. George Viscome of Lake Placid, the crew's foreman, Jay Catalano of Saranac Lake and Steve Fogel of Willsboro, who were bunking upstairs in the ranger's cabin, were not yet asleep. When they heard Gretchen ask for help as she entered the cabin, they dressed and came down.

As Gretchen told them what happened, the three trail crew members began gathering equipment – a cross cut saw, ax, sleeping bag, a wool jacket, ponchos, a first aid kit and flashlights.

Over the next 12 hours, Charlie Nolan, the trail crew, and Gretchen removed the tree and administered to Barbara Weeks as best they could, using advanced wilderness skills but admittedly very basic medical technique. With clouds low in Avalanche Pass, a helicopter rescue appeared unlikely, yet late in the morning, conditions briefly allowed it. Using the sleeping bag as a stretcher and with Gretchen holding her mother's hand, the group lifted Mrs. Weeks onto the helicopter's litter. Within minutes, she was at Lake Placid Memorial Hospital.

Diagnosed with a severely fractured pelvis along with internal bleeding, Barbara Weeks spent the next three days in intensive care and received eight pints of blood. Several surgeries over the next few years allowed her to live a normal, if not one hundred percent mobile life. Now in her 70s, she "can't climb mountains anymore, nor do I do wilderness camping, but I still love mountains and the woods. I will always be a mountain lover and a tree hugger."

Thirty years later, both mother and daughter still deal with the psychological aspects of their ordeal. "Gretchen has, at times, felt guilty for urging me to go with her on that trip," wrote Barbara in 2008. "I was the only one available at the time and our family has a rule. 'Do not go into the wilderness alone.' She thinks that if I stayed home, the tree would not have 'got' me, but I see it this way: If she had gone alone and the tree fell on her, there would have been no one there to get rescue and she might very well have died. Not on my watch, if I can help it. To me she was a hero, because they had to replace most of my blood when I got to Placid Hospital. Without her trip to the Ranger Cabin over a dark, dangerous route, I might have bled out."

Her daughter (now Gretchen Weeks Brough) counters, "My family has always called what I did that night 'heroism', and maybe it qualifies. All I ever see when I look back on it is the things I did wrong. But a hero is never a hero in her own eyes. I just did what I had to do to keep my mother. At the end of the day, that's all that matters."

The major lesson Gretchen learned from the experience is one all hikers, climbers, and campers should heed: "My parents raised their children to be competent and self-reliant, and the family backpacking and climbing trips we took every summer were part of that. So we were by no means strangers to the Adirondack interior; but wilderness is still wilderness, and nature doesn't care how experienced you are. In the blink of an eye, the forest can fall on you with the bland indifference of a rock rolling over a bug."

Shortly after the incident, Gretchen began dating George Viscome, the foreman of the trail crew that assisted in her mother's rescue. The romance did not last, but their shared experience and a love for the mountains have led them to remain friends to this day.

"Thank God for that interior cabin," Gretchen Weeks said back in 1978. "What would I have done without it? Thank God the trail crew was at the cabin. If we had to get help from all the campers in the area, it would have been hours before we got back to Mom."[22]

Today, while only the Lake Colden interior outpost is manned year round – and the likelihood that a well equipped trail crew would happen to be nearby – the 1978 rescue of Barbara Weeks seems, indeed, miraculous. It is hoped, if not expected, that all who venture into the wilderness are self-reliant and prepared for emergencies, because help is rarely so readily available.

Peter Wollenberg (#918), a Virginia native who spent childhood summers in the Adirondacks, fell in love with the mountains and eventually chose to attend college at the University of Vermont. On April 7, 1977, the UVM Outing Club concluded a week-long trip into the High Peaks with a climb up Colden. The eight-person team split into two groups. Three of the members took the trail. Wollenberg joined "four other adventuresome souls," and, furnished with crampons and ice axes, began the ascent of the Trap Dyke.

> The day was beautiful and not too cold as our party made its way up the dyke. The lower slope was relatively gentle, but the upper sections required some step cutting by the leader. We weren't using ropes, but it didn't seem particularly necessary. We ascended to the top in perhaps three or four hours. We met the rest of the party up there and ate lunch, enjoying the spectacular scenery in the direction of Algonquin and Marcy.
>
> After lunch, our leader offered to take any and all adventuresome souls down the Trap Dyke so that some of us could use our newly learned glissading skills.

Again, five chose the dyke and three chose the trail, "which in hindsight was a better option."

> We had decided to remove our crampons because they can be, at best, a hindrance when glissading and, at worst, a serious hazard if you catch your heel and started tumbling. That wasn't bad logic until we hit the steeper and now icier section. Those with hard mountaineering boots fared much better at step kicking and footing than those of us with "mouse boots" (winter Korean army boots) on. No edging whatsoever in those things.
>
> I was trying to follow the footsteps that were being kicked and cut into the particularly steep section we were traversing. I made it about two thirds of the way across when I lost my footing. I started to slide and immediately went into an ice axe arrest. The axe stayed, I slipped off the head, and the lanyard around my wrist *came untied at the axe.*
>
> I glanced down as I started sliding rapidly down the slope toward the far wall of the Trap Dyke. My exact thought at the moment was: 'Oh, This is IT!'
>
> Some undetermined time later, I was lying still on my back listening, as I recall, to water running somewhere. Then I became aware of people shouting at me.
>
> Members of the party, led by my friend Dan, helped to stabilize me with ropes to make sure I didn't go anywhere further. The leader, John, was dazed from his own tumble down the icy slope after he tried to grab me and stop my slide. In retrospect, he may have slowed me down enough and prevented me from hitting the far wall of the Trap Dyke.
>
> Dan went for help at Ranger Charlie's (Nolan) cabin not far away. He told us later that the phone didn't work, but they were able to raise help with a radio.
>
> Late in the afternoon as it was getting dark, I heard the sound and saw the shape of a helicopter. The chopper hovered overhead as I was bundled into a basket stretcher then lifted into the chopper. John was also lifted into the chopper, and we were quickly on our way to Lake Placid Memorial Hospital.

In the emergency room, Wollenberg was treated for a dislocated elbow. The following week, he was back at school, arm in a sling for another month. "Physical therapy brought back almost all of the range of motion, but to this day, I can't quite touch my right shoulder with my right hand."

While a climb *down* the Trap Dyke is rare[23] and, possibly, ill-advised, the ordeal was largely the result of an accident, as opposed to ignorance or ill-preparedness. "The accident didn't put a dent into my love of hiking, winter climbing, or even ice climbing," wrote Wollenberg in 2004. "My love of the Adirondacks certainly hasn't diminished either in the nearly 30 years since that incident."

Peter's "great adventure" and subsequent attitude are testament to the dangers of climbing, the love of climbing, and, through experience, a respect accorded to the mountains.

When Jon Krakauer and others wrote of the harrowing 1996 season on Mt. Everest, it served not so much as a cautionary tale as it did an intrigue, even a lure. In the Adirondacks, the elevation, not to mention the stakes, is decidedly lower, yet, despite tales of woe, the mountains remain alluring. "I love the way Colden displays itself from Route 73 (near Lake Placid)," writes Jody Edwards. "It shows off its slides with no pretensions – they are an amazing visual feast to the tourist and, to the hiker, an insufferable taunt that says 'you know you want to climb me' and 'climb me if you can.'"

Mt. Colden stands alone and, because of this, it stands out. When a hiker sets out to climb it, regardless of route, he or she is probably climbing *only* Colden. Who would climb Nye without also attempting Street? Who wants to ascend Donaldson without taking in Emmons and Seward?

Unless you are in a serious "peak-bagging" mode, a climb up Colden is just that: a climb up a single mountain. However, on that climb you can...
- take your time while marveling at Avalanche Pass...
- go the extra distance in reaching the great south slide...
- withstand, as one hiker did in 1976, driving rain and record winds only to arrive at the summit, his 46th peak, just as the eye of Hurricane Belle was approaching...[24]
- trod on fresh snow and follow the even fresher tracks of a snowshoe hare along the exact route of the trail up the mountain, an unforgettable experience three hikers shared in the spring of 1992...[25]
- witness a touching January memorial when a son scattered his mother's ashes among the snow and spruce trees on the summit...[26]
- become stranded, stuck on a 50-foot ledge, while helpless climbing companions rush home for help before returning, ropes in hand and stronger in numbers, to return to the site where a dog was wagging its tail. The canine was Otis, a white Shepherd-husky-terrier mix belonging to members of the famous "Ski to Die" Club. The fateful location on the slides of Colden is known to this day as "Otis Gully"...[27]

Jim Kobak has climbed Colden more than thirty times. When asked what he thinks about the mountain, he simply says, "All I really know about Colden is that I can't wait to climb it again."

Endnotes

1. A *dyke* (or *dike*) is, according to *Webster's New International Dictionary of the English Language*, second edition (Merriam-Webster, 1954), "a tabular body of igneous rock that has been injected while molten into a fissure; – so called originally in Scotland, where such rock resisted erosion and stood above the adjacent country in a manner suggestive of a wall." *Trap* is defined by the same dictionary as "any of various dark-colored, fine-grained igneous rocks, including esp. basalt, amygdaloid, etc." In the case of the Colden Trap Dyke, the rock that was injected into the large fissure which is exposed on the side of the mountain was and is more prone to erosion and thus has been largely removed by the forces of nature. The resulting "walls" on its sides are therefore made of the harder, more

resistant anorthosite which makes up the bulk of the mountains of the High Peaks. "Dyke" appears to be the preferred spelling when used to name the feature on Mount Colden, but some writers have employed "dike." In an effort to achieve a degree of consistency, the word is spelled as "dyke" throughout this chapter except for this instance when the word "dike" is employed as it was in the material quoted from the *Guide to Adirondack Trails,* Adirondack Mountain Club (edited by Tony Goodwin), 12th edition, pg. 145.

2. Alfred Billings Street, *The Indian Pass, Source of the Hudson* (New York: Hurd and Houghton Publishers; Cambridge: Riverside Press, 1869), pg. xv.

3. Jim Bailey, "Places in the Heart," *Of The Summits, of the Forests* (Morrisonville, NY: The Adirondack Forty-Sixers), pg. 114.

4. Russell M. L. Carson, *Peaks and People of the Adirondacks,* (reprint of 1927 Doubleday, Page and Company edition; Glens Falls: The Adirondack Mountain Club, 1973), pg. 39.

5. Carson, pg. 47.

6. Originally named Adirondack Iron and Steel Company, it was also known as the McIntyre Iron Works. The original village, now known as the Upper Works was first called McIntyre or McIntyre's Village and later Adirondac. The Lower Works, which became the site of the National Lead Company's titanium mining operation in the twentieth century, was known as Tahawus.

7. The exploration party into the high peaks included, at various times, Archibald McIntyre, Duncan McMartin and David Henderson, proprietors and developers of the iron works; David C. Colden, Abraham Van Santvoord and William C. Redfield, potential investors; James Hall, state geologist; and "woodsmen" John Cheney and Harvey Holt.

8. Carson, pg. 43, quoting Redfield's article about the expedition as published in the *American Journal of Science and Arts* (1838).

9. Carson, pg. 43, footnote.

10. Edward A. Harmes, "The Forty-Six Peaks," *The Adirondack High Peaks and the Forty-Sixers* (Adirondack, NY: The Adirondack Forty-Sixers, 1970), pg. 37.

11. Carson, pg. 46.

12. http://www.openlens.us/articles/tahawus/Adirondack.asp; A Brief History of Mining Operations in Tahawus, NY.

13. Carson, pg. 46.

14. Orson Schofield Phelps, "The Adirondack Mountains," edited by Bill Healy in *The High Peaks of Essex - The Adirondack Mountains of Orson Schofield Phelps,* (Fleischmanns, NY: Purple Mountain Press, 1992), pg. 15.

15. http://www.protectadks.org/e-news_002_01_cfp.html

16. Carson, pg. 47.

17. Carson, pg. 48.

18. Street, *op. cit.,* pg. 63.

19. http://www.adirondackjourney.com/Colden.htm

20. Jim Goodwin, "The Forty Six Peaks," *Of The Summits, of the Forests* (Morrisonville, NY: The Adirondack Forty-Sixers), pg. 49.

21. Verplanck Colvin, *Report on the Topographical Survey of the Adirondack Wilderness of New York for the Year 1873* (Albany: Weed, Parsons and Company, Printers, 1874), pg. 278.

22. Material drawn from the *Lake Placid News,* August 3, 1978, and interviews with Gretchen Weeks, Barbara Weeks, George Viscome, Jan. 2008.

23. In a story she related for the CD *Mountain Tales by Grace,* Grace Hudowalski told of descending from Colden by way of the Trap Dyke in the 1930s with Louise Goark (#14) and Clarence Craver (#15). Though the group had little difficulty making the trip down, apparently some other hikers did not believe that they had actually descended the mountain by that route.

24. Ken Herz (#1334) completed his 46 in August 1976, after two prior unsuccessful attempts to achieve the summit. He was led by Sharp Swan (#566W). Herz recalled that "following a cold, rainy, miserable climb, we got to the top and the rain and wind completely stopped." Hurricane Belle hit the

eastern United States between August 6 and 10, 1976, killing 12 and causing $24 million in damages, mainly in North Carolina, Connecticut, New Jersey, Vermont, and New York. It is unclear whether Herz's party experienced the eye of the hurricane or an abating of the storm.

25. The author was hiking with Wally Young (#491) and Mike Horwich (#3094) April 16, 1992. Six inches of fresh snow covered the tracks of any previous hikers. Several hundred yards above Lake Arnold, the animal's tracks joined the trail and continued up the marked route to a point just below the false peak.

26. Reported by Jim Kobak (#1791W).

27. *Adirondack Life,* February 2008.

View from the Trap Dyke taken
by Ed Hudowalski about 1940

About the Author

Tim Singer, 46er #1038, is a professional television sports commentator and producer who lives with his wife Augusta Wilson (#5315) in Shelburne, Vermont. A graduate of SUNY Plattsburgh, he also has long been associated, presently as program director, with the Pok-O-MacCready Camps in Willsboro. He completed his first of four rounds of the forty-six on Gray Peak on August 5, 1974. His first ascent was that of Colden on August 12, 1967, when he was eight years old.

CLIFF MOUNTAIN
Height: 44th – 1,202 meters (3,944 feet)
By Tom Wheeler (#3356W)

Ed Hudowalski crossing Twin Brook on the way to Cliff in 1937

There are few of the 46 peaks which have been considered as inconsequential as Cliff Mountain. Indeed, Russell Carson in *Peaks and People of the Adirondacks* dignifies the peak with the book's shortest chapter: two short paragraphs consisting of but six sentences.

Cliff is one of four peaks which the second series of USGS surveys, released in the middle of the twentieth century, showed to fall below four thousand feet. Even in that small group, it lacks status. While Couchsachraga is much shorter, it has the greater notoriety because of its remoteness and its association with the hermit Noah Rondeau. Blake is of rugged ascent and is associated with Colvin's loyal assistant, Mills Blake. Nye has gained notoriety both for its lack of views and its association in the past with intertwining herdpaths. Lowly Cliff has often been, for many hikers, simply a climbing afterthought following an ascent of Redfield.

The mountain is named after a line of cliffs, which now often go unseen by the hiker, along its southeast edge. The Lake Sanford-Marcy trail that once regularly provided views of those cliffs was abandoned twenty-five years ago.

Carson's chapter on Cliff is so succinct that we may as well quote it in full:

> According to Mills Blake, Cliff Mountain was named by Verplanck Colvin. Blake has in his possession a sketch drawn by Mr. Colvin about 1872 showing the mountain by this name. No earlier use of this explanatory, characteristic name is known. Its first appearance in print is probably that in Colvin's 1874-79 report.
>
> The first recorded ascent of Cliff Mountain was on June 17, 1921, by Arthur S. Hopkins while running the north line of Township 45, Totten and Crossfield Purchase. Hopkins qualifies his claim to the record by stating one of his timber cruising parties perhaps reached the top in 1917.

That's it. Moreover, when the ADK reprinted *Peaks and People* in 1973 with a 56-page "Editor's Introduction" by Philip Terrie, supplementing and correcting Carson's work, not a single word is devoted to the "chapter" on Cliff. Finally, when George and Robert Marshall set out with Herbert Clark to climb all of the 4,000-foot mountains in the Adirondacks, they apparently failed to notice that the USGS maps of the time showed Cliff with a contour at the 4,000-foot level. The result was that there is no mention of the mountain in Robert Marshall's "The High Peaks of the Adirondacks."

Verplanck Colvin's first mention of Cliff is in an introductory essay for his third report. He states, "Subsequently, by way of the Panther gorge and Mt. Marcy, a winter exploration was made of the region lying southward and around the slopes of Mt. Redfield. On this short expedition, the Cliff Mountain pass was at length visited and explored, the return being made along the icy shores of the Opalescent river."[1]

Fortunately he later provided us with a more elaborate description of that trip, which, while it did not include an ascent of the mountain, provides a glimpse into the character of Colvin and a graphic description of Cliff.

In 1875 Colvin determined to measure precisely the height of Mount Marcy by beginning at a known elevation at Westport on Lake Champlain and measuring the increase in altitude by spirit levels from that point forty miles to the summit of Mount Marcy. Because of delays in receiving state appropriations, he was unable to leave Albany until September 30 and did not commence the work until late that evening. The tedious and meticulous work continued until November 4, when at 4:50 p.m. the final measurement was taken on the summit of Marcy. He returned with his crew that night to a camp in Panther Gorge. The next day, Colvin wrote, "the storm having ceased, though the snow was knee deep, as it was bright and clear, though cold, I determined to make a forced march with one guide to the south, westward to Mount Skylight, to explore the Cliff mountain pass, a wild gorge to the west of Mt. Redfield."

Colvin proceeded up to what we would call Four Corners and crossed over the ice-covered Lake Tear-of-the-Clouds. His description continued:

> [D]iverging to the eastward, plunged into the trackless waste of semi-dwarfed forest in a southerly direction, passing to the eastward of the Pinnacle *[sic]* peaks, through a wild and unknown forest without mark or sign to guide us, save occasional glimpses of the sun. The fresh snow was here so deep and the boughs of the evergreens so heavily laden with it, that it was with difficulty we got along... By the time we reached the side of Mt. Redfield our boots were frozen on our feet and our clothing icy. After a perilous descent on some of the slides of Uphill brook, we diverged upon the side of Redfield, and about noon reached a point far up on the western cliffs of that peak which afforded a grand view into the pass between us and Cliff mountain.
>
> Opposite us arose the black and singularly rounded and embossed front of Cliff mountain, apparently a mass of hypersthene rock, crowned above the sloping brink of its precipice with a dense half-dwarfed forest of balsam and spruce trees, below which on the incline of the brink, sheets and patches of bright green and red mosses (sphagnum) extended, maintaining foothold where snow had ceased to stay.
>
> Two or three hundred feet below us the grim cliffs drew together at the summit of the pass, but away southward the slopes descended into a blue abyss of forest... Turning northward, we descended, amid cliffs, to the divide in the defile, where I took barometrical observations synchronous with those taken by an assistant at a benchmark near Marcy, the first use of our new line of levels. From these observations, the height of the pass has been computed at 3,550 above tide. *[Colvin then descended toward the Opalescent and ascended back to Lake Tear by following the Feldspar brook.]*[2]

It is apparent that Colvin had a great curiosity about the pass, and his description makes it clear that it was his first view of it. His reference to it in the introductory sentence as a "wild gorge" and already as Cliff Mountain pass, suggests that others had previously described the pass to him. It also suggests that Colvin did not name the mountain, as Carson suggested, but simply applied a common name to it. This is not inconsistent with Blake's statement to Carson that he had seen the name on an earlier sketch map.

Colvin himself discussed his naming of mountains in an earlier essay attached to his second report: "At different points, however, in the progress of the angular work, important peaks, rising even to altitudes above 4,000 feet, have been found, to maps hitherto unnamed and unlocated. It became necessary to give to each some title by which it might be known upon the field books, and referred to in measurements. Wherever the Indians, guides, or hunters had names for such peaks, even though grotesque, I have adopted them; and indeed, in all the nomenclature of the region all important popular names have been adhered to, even when taste would have led to a change."[3] As a final argument, it would appear that Colvin otherwise, primarily named mountains in the high peaks area after people: Wright, Seymour, Redfield, Street, and Adams, for example.

Colvin's second report also gives some indication as to why the pass between Cliff and Redfield was of such interest to him. In Appendix A he discussed establishing a new trail: "The route for the new trail over the mountains, which I selected, runs directly from the old Panther Gorge Camp, up the deep valley and over the slight divide to the summit water, Lake Tear-of-the-Clouds, where the wood and water are good and a bark wigwam will be constructed... Leaving this lakelet, the future trail will either descend to the Opalescent and Lake Colden, or by a new subordinate pass, discovered west of Mount Redfield, will reach the 'White lily' trail."[4]

An examination of the USGS map of the region will show, south of Allen mountain, "White Lily Pond," which drains into the Boreas ponds. The earliest USGS maps (the Santanoni and Mount Marcy quadrangles) from about 1900, show a trail leading from Sanford Lake, up the south branch of the Opalescent River, over a low pass, and descending to White Lily Pond.[5] That, no doubt, is the trail to which Colvin referred. A trail through the Cliff-Redfield pass proceeding south along the Opalescent would intersect with that trail and provide access to Upper and Lower Works. The existence of the trail suggests that the area was well known to others before Colvin. They, probably, had often seen the cliffs for which Cliff is named.

There is spectacular scenery on all sides of Cliff Mountain. In addition to the cliffs on the side toward Redfield, beautiful cascades and waterfalls on the Opalescent grace the north side of the mountain from Uphill Lean-to to Lake Colden. Robert Wickham, in *Friendly Adirondack Peaks,* wrote, "[The] Opalescent River is the most beautiful stream in the Adirondacks. Both above and below Flowed Land its gorges, flumes, and falls, and its clear water, revealing, reflecting, heightening the varying iridescent colors – blue, green, bronze - of the smooth worn rock of its bed leaving nothing to be desired for beauty in a mountain stream."[6]

Cliff is bounded on the west by the Flowed Lands. (Some omit the "s" on "Lands," but both the ADK and the DEC use the plural.) In order to provide additional flow into Calamity Brook for the iron works, the Opalescent was dammed there and a channel built to divert the stream. The "calamity" by which David Henderson fell dead to a fatal pistol shot occurred during an exploration of the possibility of creating the additional flow. Despite his death the project continued and was completed about 1854.[7] When the dam was in place, all reports indicate that the resulting lake with surrounding mountains was incredibly beautiful. However, some one hundred and twenty-five years after its construction, the dam failed. "The former dam at Flowed Lands was seriously damaged by flood in 1979 and intentionally breached in 1984 [by the DEC] for safety reasons. Stream flow soon reverted to the natural channel and the former impoundment site naturally revegetated itself and beavers returned to the stream channel to create new dams."[8]

Photograph of Colden from the Flowed Lands

The Flowed Lands provides the backdrop for a number of campsites and lean-tos. Among the outstanding features is a knob of land with a secluded lean-to and behind it tiny Livingston Pond. Just to the north of that site, Cliff is notched by a stream whose north side is hemmed by steep cliffs but whose south side provided, especially before Hurricane Floyd, a very practical route directly up Cliff to a point near the summit. That route was not often used until the mid 1990s, when it became a relatively popular winter route. Hurricane Floyd created significant new obstacles along it.

The Hanging Spear Falls trail leads between the Flowed Lands and the former Twin Brook Lean-to site along the Opalescent. (This was sometimes referred to as the East River trail.) The trail along the Opalescent is very near the route first taken by William Redfield on his first trip to the Adirondacks in 1836:

> On the morning of the 18th, we resumed the ascent of the stream in its bed, in full view of two mountains from between which the stream emerges. About two miles from our camp, we entered the more precipitous part of the gorge through which the river descends. Our advance here became more difficult and somewhat dangerous. After ascending falls and rapids, seemingly innumerable, we came to an imposing cascade, closely pent between two steep mountains, and falling about eighty feet into a deep chasm, the walls of which are as precipitous as those of Niagara, and more secluded.[9]

This is Hanging Spear Falls, one of the most imposing and spectacular cascades in the Adirondacks.

There are some who have bushwhacked up Cliff from near the falls. The usual route for the ascent of Cliff, however, is from the Uphill Brook Lean-to area, proceeding down the abandoned Twin Brook trail and then up the mountain just before its cliffs would present a serious obstacle to the hiker. The route is precipitous and often involves pulling oneself up its steep sections. Because of the steepness and the wear on the vegetation and limited soils, the route has sustained significant degradation over the years. The present herdpath to the peak reaches a broad summit ridge after a time, but at some distance from the true summit. The path then follows along the ridge, on the north summit, before it descends to a col between the two peaks and ascends again to reach the true summit.

Another route was more popular before the abandonment of the Twin Brook Trail, especially for those approaching the mountain from the Upper Works. Today, from the Uphill Brook Lean-to, it requires proceeding much further down the Twin Brook Trail, well past the height of land. Where there is a significant rubble slide, the hiker may ascend to the notch between Cliff's true summit and its false summit. It appears that this route and the route directly from the Flowed Lands lead from opposite sides of the mountain to the same notch.

Because of the damage caused by hikers along the former, common route to Cliff from the area of the Uphill Brook Lean-to, in the spring of 2007, a new approach avoiding the wet area begins along the Wilderness Path to Redfield, opposite a side trail to the lean-to or about 120 yards west of the Uphill Brook crossing. The Cliff path diverges from the Redfield one approximately a tenth of a mile from the lean-to and, cutting to the west for about a hundred yards, joins the course of the former herdpath above the area that formerly was so muddy. The remainder of the path, Christine Bourjade (#4967W) reports, is an "almost pleasant climb in dry conditions." She says, "The now closed section has recovered and is a pretty meadow in mid-summer." She adds that the cliffs "are still steep and the ridge walk still meanders," but Cliff now has a single, approved route to its summit.[10]

Arthur S. Hopkins participated in the "Esther McComb" memorial ceremony in 1939. He tore his pants during the hike to Esther's summit. He climbed Cliff in 1921.

As Carson mentioned, the first recorded ascent of Cliff Mountain was on June 17, 1921, by Arthur S. Hopkins. His ascent was no doubt connected to the state purchase of the lands for the forest preserve.

The first recognized winter ascent of Cliff was by Howard Kasch (#79) and Warren Langdon (#65) in February 1948. They spent the following night at Twin Brook Lean-to in temperatures that reached 40 degrees below zero.[11]

Those who have climbed Cliff or have hiked around the mountain and observed the spectacular scenery which surrounds it know that it deserves greater recognition than it has previously received in print.

Endnotes

1. Verplanck Colvin, *Seventh Annual Report of the Topographical Survey of the Adirondack Region of New York,* 1879, pg. 15. (This book contains the reports for the years 1874-78 and is often characterized as the "Third Report" as no separate reports were done for the intervening years.)

2. *Ibid.*, pgs. 101-103.

3. Colvin, Verplanck *Topographical Survey of the Adirondack Wilderness: Second Report,* 1874, pg. 133.
4. *Ibid.,* pg. 167.
5. A reference in E. R. Wallace's 1872 *Descriptive Guide to the Adirondacks* suggests that this trail then led to the Upper Ausable Lake.
6. Robert Wickham, *Friendly Adirondack Peaks, 1924* (privately published), pg. 83.
7. This is the date given by Barbara McMartin in *Discover the High Peaks.*
8. DEC High Peaks Unit Management Plan, March 1999, pg. 162.
9. William Redfield, "Some Accounts of two visits to the Mountains in Essex County, New York, in the years 1836 and 1837; with a sketch of the northern Sources of the Hudson" published in (Silliman's) *The American Journal of Science and Arts,* Vol. XXXIII, No. 2, January 1838, New Haven, pg. 305.
10. Information based upon notes supplied by Christine Bourjade in January 2009.
11. Katherine (Kay) T. Flickinger in "Climbing the Forty-Six on Snow and Ice" in *The Adirondack Forty Sixers,* 1958, pg. 92.

MOUNT REDFIELD
Height: 14th – 1,404 meters (4,606 feet)
By Tom Wheeler (#3356W)

Verplanck Colvin named Mount Redfield for William C. Redfield. In his first report about his Adirondack survey to the state legislature, Colvin wrote, "The appropriateness of the new names Mt. Redfield, Mt. Street, and Mt. Adams given to summits heretofore unnamed, will be appreciated by those familiar with the written history of the region."[1] A year later (1874), in his second report, Colvin stated, "As we descended Skylight, we reached the level of the peak which I have named Mount Redfield, in honor of the discoverer of Mount Marcy."[2] In a separate article in that report, "Triangulation," he discussed the naming of various mountains, including Mount Redfield:

> The peak which I have named Mt. Redfield lies to the south and west of Mt. Skylight... It is named in honor of William C. Redfield, whose services to science have been so various and valuable, and who was also one of the earliest explorers of this region. It is he who first described Mt. Marcy, calling it the "High Peak of Essex," and by his energy and enthusiasm the first expedition to the summit was organized. It was he who claimed the Opalescent to be the true head of the Hudson – and passing the streams which descended from Lake Tear without discovering it – held that the loftiest source of the Hudson river was in the mountain meadow or marsh... [T]he labors of Prof. Redfield seem to me to demand the recognition which I have given them in the mountain so near the scene of those early explorations. It is remarkable that like Mts. Haystack and Skylight, this peak should have so long escaped notice, though possessing an altitude of 4,688 above tide.[3]

Redfield deserved the honor. Not only did his observations lead to the first ascent of Mount Marcy during the expedition he helped lead with Ebenezer Emmons, but Redfield was one of the outstanding minds of his time. William C. Redfield was, in the early nineteenth century, the embodiment of an energy of observation and enthusiasm that generated the first great period of American science.

He was born in Middletown, Connecticut, on March 26, 1789. At the age of thirteen, upon the death of his father, he was apprenticed to John Pierce, a saddle and harness maker. At the end of his apprenticeship he walked seven hundred miles to visit his mother in Ohio. Since his formal schooling ended at an early age, he educated himself through reading and study. He became a successful businessman, an entrepreneur who established a steam navigation company for transportation on the Hudson River between New York and Albany.

Accidents on early steamboats, often involving fire and explosion, were numerous and often deadly. To avoid loss of his shipments, Redfield employed barges which were towed by steamboats up and down the river. Thus he could advertise, "Passengers on board the safety barges will not be in the least exposed to any accident by reason of the fire or steam on board the steamboats. The noise of the machinery, the trembling of the boat, the heat from the furnace, boilers and kitchen, and everything which may be considered unpleasant on board a steamboat are entirely avoided."[4] The Swiftsure Transportation Line, which he headed until his death, was a great success.

Redfield, foreseeing the potential of the railroad, in 1829 published a pamphlet proposing a network of railroads from the Hudson to the Mississippi, and he was instrumental in the development of early railroads in Connecticut and New York. However, he is best remembered today for his contributions to science. Although hundreds of hikers climb the mountain named for him each year, very few are aware that Redfield was a geologist and a meteorologist. He is credited with having discovered the cyclonic nature of hurricanes. After noting the different directions trees fell during the "Great Gale," a storm which struck Massachusetts and Connecticut on September 3, 1821, he expounded his theory of cyclone hurricane winds in articles published in the *American Journal of Science and Arts* in 1831 and 1833. Thereafter, he was at the center of what is known in the history of meteorology as the "American Storm Controversy." J. R. Fleming in his *Guide to Historical Records in the Atmospheric Sciences,* writes that "Hotly debated issues *[of the controversy]* included the cause of storms, their phenomenology, and the proper methodology for investigating them" and says that the "controversy stimulated the development of an observational 'meteorological crusade' by the American Philosophical Society, the Franklin Institute, the Army Medical Department, the Navy Department, and the Smithsonian Institution which transformed meteorological theory and practice."[5]

The explanation of the nature of these storms was of tremendous interest to mariners. Redfield was soon the author of articles published in the United States Naval Magazine and in the London Nautical Magazine providing advice to sailors concerning hurricanes, optimal strategies for avoiding the centers of the storm, and correcting long-standing naval doctrine. His meteorological advice was published in the standard guide for mariners, *Blunt's American Coastal Pilot,* for the succeeding forty years.

Marcus Benjamin, in a history of American meteorology, writes, "During the decade in which the Smithsonian Institution came into formal existence three distinguished American meteorologists – perhaps the three most distinguished that this country has ever known – were actively studying the phenomena of storms. These men were Redfield, Espy, and Loomis."[6] As a result of his central role in the study of storms, Redfield is recognized today as one of the fathers of American meteorology.

The 1837 exploration of Mount Marcy was a scientific expedition which included Redfield, John Torrey, Ebenezer Emmons – each a preeminent scientist – and James Hall, who would become one. Torrey wrote *A Flora of the State of New York* (1843) and, with Asa Gray, the monumental *A Flora of North America* (1838–43). Hall and Emmons were geologists. All four were original members of the American Association for the Advancement of Science

(AAAS), and three of them – Redfield (1848), Torrey (1852), and Hall (1853) – became presidents of that association. At an 1838 meeting of the New York Board of Geologists at Emmons' home in Albany, plans were made to create a national organization. This resulted in the founding in 1840 of the Association of American Geologists. In 1842 that organization was expanded to become the Association of American Geologist and Naturalists; and at a meeting in 1847, acting upon a proposal by Redfield, that organization voted to reconstitute itself as the AAAS. At its first meeting, held in 1848, the AAAS elected Redfield as its first president.

Another leading New York scientific society was the Lyceum of Natural History which, founded in 1817, evolved into the New York Academy of Science. Torrey was one of its original members (at age 21) and served as its president (1824-26, 1838). It appears that Redfield and Torrey were good friends. Redfield joined the Lyceum in 1837 and served as both First Vice President (1852-53) and Second Vice President (1847-51).[7]

To illustrate how little was known of the Adirondack region in the early 1800s consider this quotation from Spafford's *Gazetteer of New York,* published in 1813:

> It only remains now to notice the Mountainous country around Lake George and to the west of Lake Champlain, called the Peruvian Mountains; which furnish the northern sources of the Hudson and form the height of land which separates the waters of the Hudson from the St. Lawrence. The greatest altitude of any part of this tract is found in some summits in Essex County. The highest of these is probably that called Whiteface in the Town of Jay, which commands a view of Montreal, at the distance of near 80 miles. The height of this mountain is little short of 3000 feet from the level of Lake Champlain.

Archibald McIntyre, owner of the iron mining operations located at Adirondac, invited Redfield to visit the area in 1836. The motivation for doing so was probably a commercial one. Investment was needed, perhaps a railroad as well. It appears that McIntyre had hopes that Redfield and his associates might "take hold of our Iron Concern, and make the most of it for themselves and us."[8]

At the same time, Emmons had received an appointment to perform a geological survey of the region of New York north of the Mohawk, the area forming the Second Geological District. Based upon his experience in 1836, Redfield organized a return trip to the area in 1837. Afterwards, he wrote the definitive description of the trips in his article "Some Accounts of two visits to the Mountains in Essex County, New York, in the years 1836 and 1837; with a sketch of the northern Sources of the Hudson," published in (Silliman's) *The American Journal of Science and Arts,* Vol. XXXIII, No. 2, January 1838. The article was of such interest that it was republished in *Family Magazine,* which provided a broader public access to the information.

During the initial visit in 1836 Redfield went from the mines with McIntyre, David Henderson, David Colden, and James Hall (who at the time was an assistant to Ebenezer Emmons in the geological survey of New York) to the area of Lake Colden. What exactly the arrangements were for the 1836 trip are a matter of some conjecture, although Redfield's field notes indicate that he already had a relationship with Emmons. He wrote: "Wednesday, Aug. 10... Find Mr. H and Mr. C our departure delayed by the non-arrival of Mr. McIntyre, Mr. Hall, and Prof Emmons and must wait until tomorrow. Conclude to start for Lake George and meet them at Ticonderoga."

His article "Some Accounts" demonstrates his wide ranging curiosity and his interest in scientific description:

On the evening of the 13th of August we were entertained with a brilliant exhibition of the Aurora Borealis which between seven and eight p.m. shot upward in rapid and luminous coruscations from the northern half of the horizon.

To travel in view of the log fences and fallen trees of a thickly wooded country affords a favorable opportunity to observe the specific spiral direction which is found in the woody fibre of the stems of forest trees... The spiral is towards the left... against the sun... This coincides with the direction of rotation in our great storms.

The beaches of the river on which we now traveled by means of frequent fording are composed of small laboritic rock, and small opalescent specimens not infrequently showed their beautiful colors in the bed of the stream. *[This is the stream that we now know of as the Opalescent.]*

Since we leave it to other chapters to describe Marcy, Colden, and Algonquin, we will simply refer to one more event which occurred on August 19, 1836:

Myself and Mr. Henderson with one of the men proceeded up the main or east branch about 2 miles south easterly from the general encampment *[on Lake Colden]*. We found this route sufficiently practicable and the river running in a continued rapid, with succession of picturesque falls of great interest... Besides these there is one fall or rapids of about 100 feet in 30 or 40 rods and the whole stream descends in the 2 miles by our estimates, 550 feet - perhaps much more and continues to be rapid at our highest point of ascent. From this point I mounted a hill about 150 feet in the south bank and saw a third high peak bearing N. 90 or 85 East... surmounted by a beautiful dome of rock the whole apparently of difficult ascent. *[Field notes of Redfield]*

Before returning to camp, the writer ascended a neighboring ridge for the purpose of obtaining a view of the remarkable elevated valley from which the Hudson here issues. From this point a mountain peak was discovered which obviously exceeds in elevation the peaks which had hitherto engaged our attention." *[Some Accounts]*

Of course, the mountain he observed was Marcy. It is, however, a matter of speculation as to where, exactly, Redfield made his observation of the mountain. The fact that it lies south of the river at a point where it is still a rapids suggests that the observation was made from a shoulder of Cliff mountain. If it was farther upstream, perhaps it was from a shoulder of the mountain which bears his name.[9]

It is not often recognized that Redfield's claim of first discovery was not universally accepted. For example, Winslow Watson writes of the Adirondacks in 1852 as follows:

Their highest peaks are visible from Burlington... The idea, however, is inaccurate that this tract had not been explored until a recent date, or that these mountains were unknown, until a late discovery. All these scenes have been, for many years, familiar to innumerable hunters, pioneers, and surveyors. Most of these prominent summits are visible through a wide territory (which has been occupied for half a century) not in the obscurity of distance, but in the full exhibition of their majesty and glory.[10]

Although there is no evidence to indicate that Colvin climbed to the summit of Redfield, he was on the mountain at least twice and made the first measurement of its altitude. On August 28, 1873, he climbed and measured the height of Skylight (its first ascent). He then descended toward Mt. Redfield, and when level with its summit measured its height to be 4,688 feet. He descended towards a pond which he described: "The little pool is margined and embanked with luxuriant and deep sphagnous moss, and we named it Moss Lake."[11] He barometrically measured the altitude of the "lake" at 4,312 feet and then felt it necessary to return quickly to Lake Tear-of-the-Clouds to make a measurement of its height for comparison. He did not proceed to the summit of Redfield on that occasion because barometric measurement depends on no significant change in atmospheric pressure between two readings. In order to make a direct comparison of the heights of the two ponds, he had to calculate the altitudes as quickly as possible. His measurements placed Lake Tear fourteen feet higher in elevation than Moss Lake (now Moss Pond). Although others have speculated that he may have ascended to the summit of Redfield that day, his narrative does not indicate that he did. On the contrary, his account makes it quite clear that he left immediately for Lake Tear after visiting Moss Pond.

Colvin's second visit to Mount Redfield was on November 6, 1875. His description of that visit to the mountain is set forth in the discussion of Cliff Mountain and appears to indicate that he traversed a shoulder of Redfield rather than ascending it. In summarizing the second trip, Colvin referred to an exploration "around the slopes of Mt. Redfield."[12]

Colvin's second report includes a large panoramic illustration entitled "The Heart of the Adirondacks" (Plate 5) which from a southern vantage point shows the landscape from Boreas mountain to the Wolf Jaws. Labeled in the drawing is Mt. Redfield (and "Mt. Allyn").

When Bob Marshall wrote about climbing Redfield with his brother George and Herbert Clark, he noted the pristine nature of the woods in the area of the mountain. The trio followed the route from Uphill Brook and turned right at the first major tributary – the route most hikers have used since the early 1970s. Marshall wrote, "As we tramped along through the glorious unmarred woods which covered the mountain, we certainly felt grateful to the State for having purchased this land just in time to save it from the lumbering operations."[13] The area in the immediate vicinity of Redfield was never logged because of its timely acquisition by the state, but it was a close call. Just south of the Uphill Brook Lean-to was the site of a nineteenth century logging camp at Buckley's Clearing. The old Lake Sanford-Marcy trail from that site was once known as the "Buckley tote road." According to the DEC's High Peaks Unit Management Plan, Buckley's Clearing is one of the twenty most important historic sites in the High Peaks.

Up until 1916, most of the state purchase of lands for the Forest Preserve was through acquisition at tax sales. In November of that year, the voters approved a bond issue which included 7.5 million dollars for the purchase of lands for the Forest Preserve in the Adirondacks and Catskills. As a result, more than 75,000 acres of land were acquired in the High Peaks region during the next ten years. The state, for the first time, expropriated important lands from unwilling sellers if necessary. Because of opposition from the Tahawus Club and the McIntyre Iron Company, the state had to use that authority to purchase the 5,000-acre Lake Colden Gore, which included lands from Indian Pass to Cliff Mountain and parts of Redfield. An early issue of *High Spots* notes, "With the completion of the purchase of Mt. Marcy, just announced, the State comes into possession of all or part of forty of the forty two 'high peaks' listed in Robert Marshall's account... The acquisition of the following high peaks has been approved, and as soon as negotiations are completed these also will become State land: Skylight, Redfield..."[14]

When Marshall climbed the peak, the condition of the forest on Redfield presented stark contrast to the conditions observed on many other peaks. The Adirondack region had been devastated by two terrible years of forest fires, 1903 – when 406,000 acres burned – and 1908, when 292,000 acres burned.[15] In 1913 another fire struck Giant and Rocky Peak Ridge.

Lumbering had become more mechanized, and industrial methods of logging had permitted more remote sections to be logged. Finch Pruyn and Company had logged to within a mile and a half of Lake Tear-of-the-Clouds. They had used sleds guided by cables as well as dry chutes to bring logs down from the high peaks. They also logged on Colden above Avalanche Pass. Other lumber companies were logging in the peaks around Keene Valley, the Cold River country, and the Sewards.

Finch Pruyn had purchased timber rights which would have resulted in logging additional areas of the high peaks belonging to the McIntyre Iron Company and the Adirondack Mountain Reserve. Fortunately, purchase of lands by the state ended the logging operations before they reached the upper slopes of Redfield. Finch Pruyn made claim against the state for their loss of timber by reason of the sale and received $750,000 to resolve the claim.

Lumbering left extensive areas of slash which made recreational use of a mountain far less appealing. Marshall's description of his experience on Redfield contrasted sharply with his description of hiking a logged or burned mountain. For example about Phelps he wrote, "I never enjoyed climbing a mountain less. There were hours of pushing through terrible fire slash, working up slides and walking logs."[16] That condition persisted for some years later. In a 1931 article in *High Spots,* Kim Hart describes why a trail up Phelps is undesirable: "Phelps has a good view, but the foreground is very slashy, a fact that detracts considerably. This slash will decay after a while with the result that Phelps will become one of the best mountains. Since nobody could enjoy climbing the mountain now, on account of slash, a trail is unadvisable."[17] By contrast, Marshall writes of Redfield (and Allen, Herbert, Seymour, and Macomb), "These are the most beautiful of the trailless mountains left. If they are reserved forever as absolutely wild forest lands, those preferring trailless peaks will always have five to meet their needs."[18]

The first recognized ascent of Redfield was by Ed Phelps in 1894.

The *Ad-i-ron-dac* for January 1952 has an article by Paul Van Dyke describing the first winter ascent of the mountain. Van Dyke, Gil Barker, and Bob Collins (#923) of the Cornell Outing Club climbed it December 29-30, 1949. They proceeded from Adirondak Loj on large "pickerel" snow shoes and later camped at Uphill Brook Lean-to. That night the temperature fell to 17 degrees below zero at the Loj. Van Dyke wrote, "Usually we would remove extra wool shirts as the exertion of trail work warmed us up, but that day even bushwhacking up the steeply wooded side of Mount Redfield under thirty to thirty-five pound packs did not make us sweaty. Using crampons as well as snowshoes, we reached the summit by eleven-thirty... The brush was thick and traveling on the big pickerel snowshoes was very difficult." From the summit of Redfield the three men descended toward Skylight, climbed Skylight, and returned to the Loj over Mount Marcy.

Van Dyke later became the first director of the Adirondack Mountain Club's Winter Mountaineering School, which published the *Adirondack Winter Mountaineering Manual* in 1957. To this day the manual provides relevant advice for climbing the High Peaks in wintertime. The somewhat sobering dedication of the manual is to two individuals who lost their lives climbing the Adirondacks in winter.

The summit of Redfield is about a mile west southwest of the summit of Skylight. There have been three primary routes for ascending it. Occasionally it has been climbed by proceeding along the long ridge between it and Skylight. Colvin clearly descended from Skylight along that ridge during his visit to Moss Pond, just three hundred fifty feet in elevation below Redfield's summit. The disadvantage of that route is that the ridge has very thick cripplebrush.[19] Another route developed from the height of land lying between Cliff and Redfield along the old Lake Sanford-Marcy "yellow" trail. However a blowdown wind event in the mid 1970s and closing of the trail between the old Twin Brook Lean-to and the Uphill Brook Lean-to about 1980 made that route less inviting and it eventually disappeared. The third route, following Uphill Brook and one of its significant tributaries, is both straightforward and scenic. It is very near this area that the 46ers established the designated Wilderness Path after adoption of the High Peaks Unit Management Plan.

The summit of Redfield is forested, but has several viewpoints, including an excellent view toward Allen and a vista of the south.

Endnotes

1. Verplanck Colvin, *Report of the Topographical Survey of the Adirondack Wilderness of New York,* 1873, pgs. 40-41. That the name was quickly accepted is confirmed by the references to the name in Colvin's further reports and other sources of the 1870s. For example, Street, Redfield, and Allen are all specifically identified in maps of the towns of North Elba, Keene, and North Hudson in O. W. Gray & Sons, *New Topographical Atlas of Essex County,* published in 1876.
2. Verplanck Colvin, *Topographical Survey of the Adirondack Wilderness: Second Report,* 1874, pg. 37.
3. *Ibid.,* pgs. 134-135.
4. Fred Erving Dayton, *Steamboat Days,* Chapter 4, quoting company advertisement.
5. J. R. Fleming, *Guide to Historical Records in the Atmospheric Sciences,* Revised Edition, 1997.
6. Marcus Benjamin, "Meteorology," published on the web by the National Oceanic and Atmospheric Administration: http://www.history.noaa.gov/stories_tales/meteorology.htm
7. Redfield's son, John Howard Redfield (who illustrated Redfield's article in the *Journal of Science and Arts* with a map based on his father's field notes) was also a prominent member of the Lyceum for many years and an original member of the AAAS.
8. Letter from Archibald McIntyre to Duncan McMartin, Nov. 15, 1836. There is no documentation that anything came of this.
9. Sources for this section include the following:
Recollections of John Howard Redfield (privately published 1900).
Excerpts from a manuscript of William C. Redfield on the Hudson Region transcribed by Russell M. L. Carson, from the certified copy of Mills Blake, April 4, 1926; thereafter transcribed by Grace Hudowalski from Carson's copy, June 8, 1940 [referred to as "field notes of Redfield"].
Russell M. L. Carson, "Mount Redfield was named for William C. Redfield," reprinted from *The Cloud Splitter,* Albany Chapter, ADK, October-November 1940.
Herman LeRoy Fairchild, *History of the New York Academy of Sciences,* 1887.
Sally Gregory Koblestedt, *The Formation of the American Scientific Community,* 1976.
10. Winslow C. Watson, "Report on Survey of Essex County" contained in *Transactions of the New York State Agricultural Society,* 1852.
11. Verplanck Colvin, *Topographical Survey of the Adirondack Wilderness: Second Report,* 1874, pgs. 37-38.
12. Verplanck Colvin, *Seventh Annual Report of the Topographical Survey of the Adirondack Region of New York,* 1879, pg. 15.
13. Robert Marshall, "High Peaks of the Adirondacks," ADK, 1922, pg. 22.
14. *High Spots,* Vol. 1, No. 4 (1923), pg. 2.
15. These are the figures given by Barbara McMartin in *The Great Forests of the Adirondacks,* 1994. Norman Van Valkenburgh in 1968 gave figures of 464,189 for 1903; 346,953 for 1908, and 50,349 for 1913. H. M. Suter in his report for the United States Department of Agriculture wrote that "between April 20, and June 8, 1903 over 600,000 acres of timberland in northern New York were burned over." Suter, *Forest Fires in the Adirondack in 1903,* page 5. His tables show a total of 637,350 acres burned. It was during the 1903 fires that the original Adirondack Lodge burned. The lodge is now known as *Adirondak Loj* – the curious spelling being a legacy of Melvil Dewey's simplified spelling

system. Dewey was the founder of the Lake Placid Club, which purchased the Loj property from W. W. Pierce of Plattsburgh in 1900.
16. Marshall, pg. 32.
17. *High Spots,* Vol. VIII, No. 2 (1931), pg. 27.
18. *Ibid.,* pg. 28.
19. Cripplebrush is seemingly impenetrable vegetation, usually a tangle of balsam fir.

ALLEN MOUNTAIN
Height: 25th – 1,325 meters (4,347 feet)
By Tom Wheeler (#3356W)

Allen Mountain's remoteness makes it one of the more challenging of the forty-six high peaks. Allen, which lies south of the terminus of the Great Range, connects along an irregular ridge to Skylight Mountain. The route most commonly followed to Allen's base, because the nearest roads which approach the mountain are private and closed to hikers, is a hike of over four miles from the former site of the Twin Brook Lean-to, a point which is itself five miles along the Opalescent River trail from the former Mount Adams parking lot near the Upper Works. The distance is even longer if one chooses the difficult bushwhack to the summit from the Elk Lake-Marcy Trail. That approach has never developed a herdpath, and adding to the challenge of Allen is the fact that both routes may become blocked by blowdown.

Allen Mountain received its name about 1869. The definitive account of the naming is found in Russell Carson's *Peaks and People of the Adirondacks.* Carson was at first baffled in attempting to discover the source of the name, but his research eventually uncovered not only the origin of the name but also the fact that, at the time he was doing his research, its namesake was still alive. He was able to obtain very complete details concerning the naming of the peak. It appears that it was named for Frederick B. Allen, an Episcopal minister. A number of years after the peak received its name, Allen's daughter, Mrs. B. Preston Clark, employed Charles Beede (a son-in-law of Old Mountain Phelps) as a guide. In a letter to Carson, she wrote, "In speaking of Allen Mountain, he told me that it had been named after a Rev. Mr. Allen who was one of the men who used to camp on the Upper Ausable Lake with that group of fine men – Rev. Joseph Twichell, Charles Dudley Warner, Horace Bushnell, and others. Mr. Twichell was my father's most intimate friend, and I have so often heard of those years when these men went camping together there."

Carson wrote that Allen was camping with the "Rev. Joseph Twichell, Charles Dudley Warner, and Dr. Horace Bushnell... on the Upper Ausable Lake on August 20, 1869, when a great cloudburst occurred."

He continued...

> An interesting letter from Mr. Allen to the writer tells of that storm: ..."The rain continued to increase and lasted all day. It fell in such torrents our tents afforded us little protection. We all adjourned to a small shed with shingled roof which proved the driest spot that could be found... This great rain has been made memorable because it caused the great avalanche on

Avalanche Lake... [T]he surface of the Upper Ausable Lake, which is over a mile long and perhaps half a mile wide, rose over thirty inches."

Mel Trumbull, one of the guides with the party, recalls that it was proposed that a name be given as a reminder of the storm, and that Dr. Twichell, who was Mr. Allen's closest friend, immediately pointed to a nameless peak and suggested that it be called "Allen Mountain." Mr. Allen was not present at the time.

Old Mountain Phelps wrote a variant of Carson's story. In his essay about Phelps, "A Character Study," published in 1878 in the book *In the Wilderness,* Charles Dudley Warner writes, "He has been bitten by the literary 'git-up.' Justly regarding most of the Adirondack literature as a 'perfect fizzle,' he has himself projected a work and written much of the natural history of the region." Phelps' manuscript was not published in his time, but it survived and was ultimately brought to the attention of Bill Healy, who, in 1990, published the work under the title *The High Peaks of Essex, The Adirondack Mountains of Old Mountain Phelps.* That book contains both an edited version and a manuscript version of the Phelps essay. A reading of the manuscript reveals that Phelps was given to imprecision. Nonetheless, he appears to confirm the casual nature of the naming of the mountain. He writes, "To the south are a range of mountains running south to the White Lily pond and on the west of Mt. Marcy Brook, in this group is Mt. Allen a Mt. some 4500 ft high. It was named by Phelps the guide in honor of two sportsmen of the name of Allen."[1]

Allen himself indicated that he remembered nothing of the naming of the mountain for him. In a letter to a Mr. Ayres dated March 13, 1923, he writes,

> A gentleman at Glens Falls, N.Y., has been investigating the early history of the larger Adirondack Mountains. This is a summary he makes of the mountain named for me, by the early guides when I camped out.
>
> I never climbed the mountain but it has been on the maps for many years.

To illustrate an article he wrote for the July/August 1959 *Ad-i-ron-dac,* Warder Cadbury included two sketches made by the Rev. Allen. One is of Lower Ausable Lake and the other of Gothics. Cadbury wrote,

> He was born in Boston in 1840, and... was for many years at Trinity Church in Boston... Before his death in 1925, he was superintendent of the Episcopal Mission and a pioneer in the development of children's playgrounds as a means of preventing juvenile delinquency. In the summer of 1869 through 1871 he came to the Adirondacks for the fishing and recreation, carrying in his pocket small sketch books which he filled with delightful pencilled landscapes and portraits. Through the kindness of his daughter, photocopies of about 40 of these pictures are now at the Adirondack Museum....
>
> One of Allen's best pictures is a portrait of the famous guide, Old Mountain Phelps, and he has preserved a characteristic anecdote of that grand old man. Once when Allen and his friends complained to Phelps that he had placed their camp in a spot where they could not get a good view of the Gothics across the Ausable Lake, Phelps replied, "That's the reason I put the camp here. Some kinds scenery you don't want staring you in the face all the while. You want to row out on purpose to see it."[2]

It should be noted that, according to Cadbury, Allen himself was never fully convinced that the mountain was named for him. He quoted Allen's son as saying, "My father himself was also skeptical about Allen Mountain... Yet Mr. Russell Carson has vouched for the fact."[3]

Allen's sketches have appeared as illustrations in several publications, including, notably, *Guide-Boat Days and Ways,* by Kenneth Durant.[4]

The first depiction of Allen Mountain appeared not long after the mountain was named. Verplanck Colvin's large panoramic sketch, "The Heart of the Adirondacks," appears in his report of the Adirondack Survey for the year 1873. One of the peaks in the drawing is labeled "Mount Allyn." The peak is recognizably the mountain as we know it today. About the drawing Colvin states, "My sketch shows the core of region or section which should be forever preserved in its natural wilderness condition as a forest park or timber reserve for the benefit of the people of the State of New York... The names of the great mountains will be found above them, and it is hoped that this will prevent errors in nomenclature in the future. The sheer rocks and glaring slides upon the mountain sides are shown in the drawing and afford a good idea of the wildness of this range, the crest of our state."[5]

That the name (Allen) was quickly accepted is confirmed by the references to the name in Colvin's report and other sources of the 1870s. For example, Street, Redfield, and Allen are all specifically identified in maps published in 1876 of the Towns of North Elba, Keene, and North Hudson.[6]

The remoteness of Allen and the distance of its summit from the nearest trail have made it the subject of awed respect among hikers. Indeed, the first recorded ascent of the mountain, August 19, 1921, by Robert and George Marshall and their guide Herbert Clark, took place more than fifty years after the mountain was named. Robert Marshall described the mountain:

> This is in great contrast to the last mountain [Rocky Peak Ridge], being wooded with virgin timber and showing no trace of human interference. We climbed it from Redfield, crossing the broad South Valley of the Opalescent, from where there was an easy ascent to the wooded summit. This is quite pointed but, unfortunately, there are not many ledges. However, we found two spots from which we got good views. From the one we could see a semi-circle of forested mountains and valleys from Marcy to Boreas. What I liked best about the view was the profile of Panther Gorge, looking near the bottom like a bucket, so straight were the slides. The view of the Gothic Range was very fine. From the other spot we could see only one view, but it was worth the whole climb. It was of the Opalescent Valley, backed by dark green Redfield.[7]

There has never been a marked trail to the summit of Allen. However, about 1930, the Trails Committee of ADK, chaired by Arthur S. Hopkins, made a proposal for "A Great Trail Circle" in the High Peaks. The proposal was ambitious in scope. The trail was to begin in Keene Valley, connect with the W. A. White trail leading to Lower Wolf Jaw; proceed along the Great Range to Marcy, descend Marcy to Skylight Notch (Four Corners), and climb Skylight. However, then imagination took hold. From Skylight, the trail was to follow the connecting ridge to Allen and, from Allen, cross to Pinnacle at the end of the Colvin-Blake ridge. From the summit of Colvin the route would have proceeded to the summit of Nippletop and thence to Dix, returning via St. Huberts to Keene Valley. Hopkins suggested that since the trail would primarily cross state lands and require the consent of only two landowners for its construction, "[i]t would therefore seem that there should be no serious obstacle in the way of this project except that of securing the necessary funds or an adequate amount of volunteer labor to complete the job." He suggested that work could begin during 1930 and be a major activity of the ADK in 1931.[8]

The trail was never built, but it is unclear whether this was the result of the intervention of the Great Depression or the development of countervailing interests within ADK. Very

Grace and Ed Hudowalski on Allen in the late 1930s

soon after the Hopkins proposal appeared several articles printed in *High Spots* suggested leaving some peaks without trails. The first, by Kim Hart, discussed the desirability of a range of options for different hikers. He wrote that while many hikers prefer trails, "[t]he mountaineers who have so far received next to no consideration are those fond of scouting their own trails through unknown forests. Since this group is comparatively small, it by no means requires any large portion of the woods; nevertheless it is still large enough to deserve a few mountains, valleys, streams, and ponds." His proposal divided the mountains in the High Peaks into various different classes, one of which was to be reserved for that special group. "Class E," he wrote, "consists of five peaks, namely Redfield, Herbert, Seymour, Allen, and Macomb. These are the most beautiful trailless mountains left. If they are reserved forever as absolutely wild forest lands, those preferring trailless peaks will always have five to meet their needs. No better use can be found for any one of these peaks which are all remote."[9]

Similar views arguing for leaving some areas untouched were contained in an article by Robert Marshall, who described an ascent of Lost Pond Mountain with Herbert Clark up Roaring Brook. Marshall wrote, "There is a small group which desires the joy of getting back where even trails cease and where man may live intimately with the purely primitive... One may also do what Herb Clark and I did the other day when we turned our backs on both roads and trails and followed the torrent of Roaring Brook to its source on the high slopes of Lost Pond Mountain... Indeed for all we could observe... Northern New York was an aboriginal wilderness."[10]

The common approach to Allen from the area of the Upper Works takes the hiker from the location of the McIntyre Iron Works of the 1830s to 1850s, through areas no doubt hunted by the legendary guide Cheney, and past scenes demonstrating by contrast the impact of intense modern mining and logging.

For many years trails along the Opalescent started at Sanford Lake. Early a route to Marcy started there. The general path of that route was from the area of the iron mines to the Opalescent River, to the junction of the Opalescent with Upper and Lower Twin Brook (the Twin Brook Lean-to site), up Upper Twin Brook, through the pass between Cliff and Redfield, and to an intersection with the trail from Lake Colden to Marcy. That junction is one tenth of a mile past Buckley's Clearing, site of a former lumber camp.

At the Twin Brook Lean-to site, a trail split off and continued along the Opalescent to Hanging Spear Falls and the Flowed Lands, where it joined the Calamity Brook trail. That trail, which closely follows the route Redfield took to Lake Colden on his first visit to the area in 1836, is much longer if one is going to Marcy.

However, few trails in the Adirondacks have undergone as many changes as the trail which once led from Lake Sanford to Mount Marcy. Since much of the route to Allen still follows a portion of that trail, its history is outlined in this chapter, although it could as easily have been described in the chapters about Cliff, Redfield, or even Marcy

The first reference to a route to Marcy from the Sanford Lake area through the Cliff-Redfield pass was in Colvin's second report. In Appendix A, he wrote, "The route for the new trail over the mountains, which I selected, runs directly from the old Panther Gorge Camp, up the deep valley and over the slight divide to the summit water, Lake Tear-of-the-Clouds, where the wood and water are good and a bark wigwam will be constructed... Leaving this lakelet, the future trail will either descend to the Opalescent and Lake Colden, or by a new subordinate pass, discovered west of Mount Redfield, will reach the 'White lily' trail."[11]

Logging operations as early as the 1880s resulted in a tote road being built through the Cliff-Redfield pass and a lumber camp being established along the Opalescent on the north side of the pass. The 1885 Forest Commission Report indicates that in the area of Tahawus,

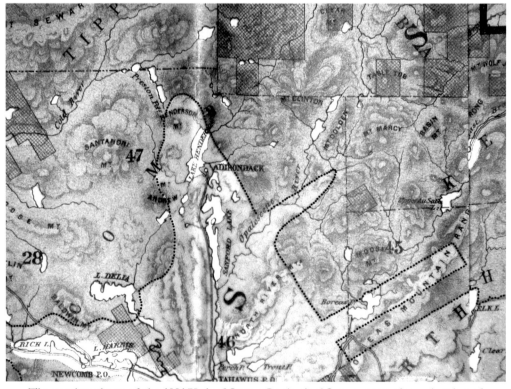

The section above of the 1891 United States Geological Survey map shows lumbered areas within the thick dotted line (added) around Newcomb, Lake Sanford, and extending up the Opalescent and into the Cliff-Redfield col.

the Adirondack Club sold "the timber on sections not lumbered to Finch Pruyn."[12] In 1891, the Forest Commission published a "Map of the Great Forest of Northern New York showing the forest area and Boundaries (in blue) of the Proposed Adirondack Park."[13] The map shows areas of virgin forest in dark green and, in a lighter green, forest "where merchantable softwoods have been removed." An examination of the map shows a thin wedge of the light green color up the Cliff-Redfield pass to the Opalescent at Buckley's Clearing.

The route through the pass, known as the Buckley tote road, led from the clearing, over the pass and down Upper Twin Brook, to the Opalescent and along the Opalescent for a considerable distance. Today's trail still follows sections of that tote road.

The 1891 report also provides information about hiker use of the area: "The Adirondack Club which owns or controls over 120,000 acres in this vicinity has its headquarters here [the deserted village or Upper Works] using, for this purpose, the old boarding-house... the rules of the club, however, limiting the accommodation of travelers to one night's stay... Lake Sanford, a mile or so south of the club house, is a narrow lake four miles wide, but with no particular attractions."[14] The report discussed climbing Mount Marcy from Lake Sanford, but it referred only to the trail from Calamity Brook.

In a letter to the Forest Commission published in the 1893 report, the president of the Adirondack Club reported that logging by Finch Pruyn & Co. of their lands commenced in 1881. He indicated that "on the Marcy slopes, the more recent operations of the axeman are plain." He continued, "The trails leading through the Indian Pass and Avalanche Pass from Adirondack Lodge bring tourists frequently to the clubhouse at the Upper Works where they receive good accommodations for a limited time... The old deserted village, the iron dam, and the abandoned furnaces now overgrown with grass and bushes, have always attracted tourists to the locality."[15]

About 1897, the Adirondack Club dissolved and was shortly replaced by the Tahawus Club, which was less accommodating to tourists. Most of the lands were sold to Finch Pruyn, but 10,874 acres remained with the iron company. That tract was sold to the National Lead Company in 1941.[16]

About 1912 the Conservation Commission began, more aggressively, to establish and mark trails, place trailhead signs, and set up lean-tos.[17] At the same time, as a result of the devastation of forest fires in 1903 and 1908, the state had begun building and manning fire towers and had increased patrols. A camp or lean-to in the vicinity of Buckley's clearing may have been established by the state before 1922, for T. Morris Longstreth refers to "Buckley Camp erected by the State" in his *The Lake Placid Tramper's Guide*.[18] He makes no reference to a route from "Buckley Camp" to Sanford Lake, but the map attached to his book shows a road leading from Sanford Lake to the Buckley Camp site. By contrast, neither tote road nor trail is shown through the pass on the USGS map from the turn of the century. However, that map shows the trail to Lake Colden by way of Hanging Spear Falls.

There is little doubt that the Lake Sanford-Marcy route was soon marked as an official trail. O'Kane's *Trails and Summits of the Adirondacks,* published in 1928, gives a full description of the trail from Lake Sanford through "the divide between Mount Redfield and Cliff Mountain and... down the waters of the Upper Twin Brook." O'Kane notes a signboard at the trailhead indicating the beginning of trails for Mount Marcy. He also gives more detail about Uphill Brook Lean-to. He writes, "Near the junction of the Opalescent River and Uphill Brook there is a shelter known as Uphill Brook Camp, built through the generosity of... President Edward A. Woods of the Camp and Trail Club. It is open to the public."[19]

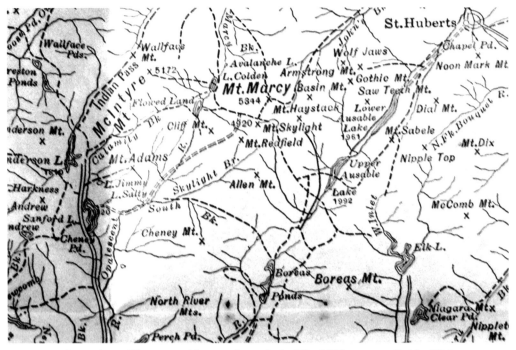

A portion of Longstreth's map from *Lake Placid Trampers Guide,* 1922

The Conservation Commission demonstrated its commitment to recreational use of the mountain trails through its publication of a series of "Recreation Circulars." In 1920, Arthur S. Hopkins wrote "Trails to Mount Marcy" for the Conservation Department. That pamphlet contains a description of the Sanford Lake to Marcy trail. It notes that the trail for its entire length from Lake Sanford "as far as Buckley's follows an old tote road." There is also a note that the trail passes over private lands and that the easement for public use confines its use to foot travel only.[20]

The Adirondack Mountain Club issued its first trail guide to the High Peaks region in 1934. It describes the Lake Sanford-Marcy Trail, starting at the bridge across Lake Sanford, following "a good logging road for miles," passing the Sanford Iron Mines after three quarters of a mile, and after a further quarter mile turning into the woods. It notes that it was 7¾ miles to Buckley's Clearing.[21] The 1941 second edition of the guide reports that there was an open camp at Twin Brook, at the junction with the trail leading to Hanging Spear Falls.

The 1945 edition of the trail guide shows the dramatic changes resulting from reopening of the mines at Tahawus. During World War II, the need for titanium resulted in the reopening and major expansion of mining operations in the Tahawus-Upper Works area and the construction of a railroad from North Creek to the mine. The operations resulted in a residential boom in the area, with the small village of Tahawus filling with miners. The result on the trailhead was dramatic. "Sanford Lake is a roaring mining community quite different from the ghost town of a few years ago, and is hardly recognizable to the hiker whose last visit was prior to 1942."[22] A like description is given in the guide book editions for 1947 and 1950.

While the 1934 guide makes no mention of the trailless peaks, by 1941 very general directions are given for climbing the 21 untrailed summits. The descriptions are based on an article written by Grace Hudowalski and C. Howard Nash and first published in the 1939

ADK yearbook. The route described for Allen would be followed for years: "While one can push through from the Elk Lake Trail, it is easier to go in to Lake Sanford, past the old iron works, and along the Opalescent River. Three and a half miles up this trail, cross the river about 75 yards below the junction of the Opalescent River and Dudley Brook, the present site of a lumber camp." By a series of lumber roads, one finally reaches the Skylight Brook and then Allen Brook, where the ascent of the mountain begins.[23]

The 1956 High Peaks guide notes that a new parking lot and trailhead had been established east of the bridge over Lake Sanford in 1954. A slight rerouting of the first half mile of the trail through woods had also been accomplished. L. Morgan Porter, the editor of the 1956 guidebook, was a stickler for detail. For example, he wrote that Buckley's Clearing "though much overgrown" is at 8.07 miles and the intersection with the trail from Lake Colden at 8.19 miles.[24]

The 1962 edition of the guidebook noted, "As this goes to press, news has been received that Tahawus Village is to be moved and the present site added to the mine area, extensive ore deposits having been discovered under the village." The 1971 guidebook reported, "Across the bridge is the mining area of the Titanium Division of the National Lead Company. The village of Tahawus was moved to Newcomb in 1965 after rich deposits were discovered under the site. The whole area is now a desert of mine tailings."[25] The head for the Opalescent-Twin Brook trail had been moved three miles north to the location of the old Mount Adams trailhead.[26]

The new trail passed two small but picturesque ponds, Lake Jimmy and Lake Sally, first named by the owners of the long abandoned iron works. The first map to show the ponds is found in Emmons' final *Report of the Geological Survey for the Second Geological District,* published in 1842. Lake Sally is identified just as it is today. However, what we know as Lake Jimmy is labeled as "L. Hamish," a designation which comports with the Scottish background of the early operator of the mines, David Henderson. (Of course, both MacMartin and MacIntyre, who were the principals in the mine, were of Scots descent as well). The name's transformation over time to "Lake Jimmy" seems logical as Hamish is the Scottish for James. In any event, by 1876 the name "Lake Jimmy" appears on the town map.[27] The "Jimmy" and "Sally" for whom the ponds were named appear to have been lost to history.

Concerns about the condition of the trail beyond Twin Brook Lean-to are reflected in the guidebook description by 1962: "The climbing becomes quite treacherous, especially in wet weather due to slanting, slippery corduroys... [At 7.69 m.] the climbing becomes steady up a rocky, eroded trail."[28]

No doubt in part because of the poor nature of the trail, in 1980, the DEC announced a decision to abandon the section of trail from Uphill Brook Lean-to through the Cliff-Redfield pass. Notice of the closure appeared as an editor's note in the 1980 Tenth Edition ADK *High Peaks Guide*: "Since both the East River and the Buckley Tote Road trails terminate within one mile and a half of each other, the DEC decided in 1980 to abandon the Buckley Tote Road and to no longer maintain the trail from Twin Brook Lean-to to Uphill Lean-to."[29] In 1989, Barbara McMartin wrote, "The abandoned route... can still be followed but with difficulty. Blowdowns have not been cleared, but detours are manageable... There is an extensive stretch of side-sloping and very slippery corduroy."[30]

At about the same time, hikers hoping to climb Allen from the west received bad news. Finch Pruyn & Co. notified the Adirondack Mountain Club that "persons who travel on their property to climb Allen Mountain will be subject to arrest" although enforcement was to be deferred until the ADK could notify its members. A notice published in the October 1980 *Adirondac* contained the following language:

The formerly popular approach to Allen via Marcy Trail from Lake Sanford by way of the Opalescent River is now closed to the public by the owners of the property in this area. Hence, routes to Allen involve fighting cripplebrush and blowdown along the ridge from Skylight or climbing from Elk Lake-Marcy Trail. The latter route is best made from the flat area N. of the Adirondack Mountain Reserve boundary line, descending to Marcy Brook, and heading along the slopes of Allen to the upper reaches of Sand Brook where a route leads to the summit through relatively little blowdown.[31]

Various reasons have been given for the closing of the popular route used by hikers. One may speculate that it resulted in part from the increased conflicts within the park focused on the creation of the Adirondack Park Agency. James A. Goodwin indicated that "In 1980 the Finch Pruyn Company closed their lands to the public, except on established state trails, because lessees of hunting camps complained of higher rent when the public paid nothing to use their lands."[32] The draft High Peaks Unit Management Plan issued in December 1994 described the closure as being the result of "User conflicts [which] arose when hikers did not respect private posted land and strayed away from designated trail corridors, built fires, or camped illegally."[33] The final High Peaks Unit Management Plan issued in December 1999 included additional language: "Routes leading to Allen and Santanoni Mountains were closed when users did not respect private posted land, hunted illegally on these lands, strayed from designated routes, built campfires, or camped on the property."[34]

Efforts were initiated by the Forty-Sixers to alleviate the problems created by the closure. The effort was ultimately successful due to the reputations and persuasive abilities of James and Tony Goodwin.

James Goodwin described his role as follows:

Though for a year his predecessor rebuffed me, in 1981 I was fortunate enough to find the company's new forester, Dick Nason, in a cordial and cooperative mood... Dick gave us permission to flag out a route to Allen along Lower Twin Brook that reached state land without passing any hunting camps. The next hurdle was permission from DEC to continue that flagging on to join the old route to Allen. The initial response to my letter requesting permission to mark this route was a letter to the effect of "we're sorry you are having trouble completing your 46, perhaps you could try these other routes" and helpfully enclosing photocopies of my own descriptions from the High Peaks guide. Further contact clarified the real nature of my request and permission was granted – thus avoiding miles of side hill bush whacking on state land.

In fact, approval was not quite as smooth as James Goodwin indicated. It took several years of effort by him, with the support of the 46ers, to finally achieve success. Fortunately he had a well positioned ally in his son, Tony, who was third vice president of the Adirondack Mountain Club. Tony was able to obtain the backing of the ADK and of its somewhat preservationist Conservation Committee for the proposed route. In an article in the September 1982 *Adirondac,* ADK Conservation Committee chair David Newhouse announced a decision made in June of that year approving the plan "in response to a request from 3rd Vice President James Goodwin" [sic]. The approval reflected a discussion of a number of issues sensitive to the more preservationist members of the club. In particular, it was concluded that the proposed route did not encroach on any significant trailless area, and it served the purposes of preserving access, maintaining good relationships with neighboring landowners, and preventing the creation of new herdpaths on the unspoiled north and east flank of Allen.[35]

As a result of the efforts of the Goodwins, a meeting was held on April 18, 1983, at Ray Brook with representatives of the DEC, Finch Pruyn, the 46ers, and the ADK. The 46er proposal was approved, and the marking of the trail by the Goodwins and the 46ers took place shortly thereafter.

Exceptionally dry weather in the summer of 1999 turned the Adirondacks into a tinderbox. By the beginning of September, green leaves were curling on deciduous trees. On September 2, a hiker started a small campfire on the trail to Bear's Den on a shoulder of Noonmark. Failure to completely put it out resulted in a forest fire which took several days to contain. It destroyed more than eighty acres of forest. One of the consequences of the dry conditions throughout the Adirondacks was that the soil had much weaker binding characteristics than it normally would have had. Root balls around trees weighed less and had less hold. The drought was brought to an abrupt end by the remnants of powerful Hurricane Floyd on September 17. Floyd dumped as much as six inches of rain on the Adirondacks and had strong winds which funneled through the southern Adirondacks. New slides were formed on the shoulder of Wright; off Colden, blocking Avalanche Pass; and on other high peaks. Tens of thousands of trees with weak root balls fell in the southern High Peaks. The devastation blocked trails from the Dix range across an arc to the Upper Works. Trails and paths to Allen, Cliff, and Redfield were closed. It was a year before reestablishment of a path to Allen.

The route, reestablished, from the former Twin Brook Lean-to site leads, after many miles, to the base of the mountain and a beautiful glen alongside Allen brook. The brook descends along a series of picturesque waterfalls to the glen, which is a perfect spot for a hiker who wishes to rest and prepare for the serious climbing ahead. Although one has already hiked more than seven miles, there are still over seventeen hundred vertical feet to ascend. The ascent is often along a slide and is sometimes quite steep before the herdpath turns to the summit which, as Marshall noted, is wooded. However, one can find views.

While the vast majority of hikers have climbed Allen along the route from the former Twin Brook Lean-to site, there are other approaches to Allen Mountain that have been used by hikers over the years.

Allen may be climbed from Skylight. Lyle Raymond (#182), with a companion, Lyle Hongo, after camping at Feldspar Lean-to the previous evening, climbed Skylight and left that summit at 10:30 a.m. for Allen. Along the way, they went through an open area before beginning a very steep ascent. Raymond wrote,

> It was our desire to pass along the northerly side of the ridge... keeping above the blowdown along Skylight Brook and below the blowdown along the ridge top... Our journey along the east ridge of Skylight was a complete success. Blowdown was negligible, the whole traverse being through heavy forest... The first half of the traverse was a long, gradual downgrade; then it changed to a gradually steepening upgrade with the side of the ridge (at right angles to our course) becoming rapidly steeper. We skirted the fringes of the blowdown area below us, and when the terrain suddenly angled sharply upward, we realized we were on the north shoulder of Allen. Bearing left, we negotiated a series of ledges without difficulty and shortly sighted the register at 1 p.m.

The return trip was less of a success: "We retraced our route to Skylight Brook. Here we made our first error of the day, by not returning over Skylight." Instead they attempted to avoid that bushwhack by proceeding east. Forced to their right by the terrain and blowdown, they finally intersected the Elk Lake-Marcy Trail not far from the Panther Gorge Lean-to and did not reach Lake Tear until 7:30 p.m.[36]

Another alternative route is approaching from the Elk Lake-Marcy Trail. That route goes through a low, swampy area which drains into the Upper Ausable Lake. Thus, it is best not to leave the trail until it reaches higher ground. One should proceed generally west, crossing Marcy Brook and then continue to Sand Brook. That brook descends almost directly from Allen's summit.

A variation of this route was described by Louis B. Puffer (#50).[37] He snowshoed up Allen in the spring of 1941 from St. Huberts. He wrote,

> For a long time we had figuratively speaking had our eyes on Allen Mountain, perhaps because it seemed to be about the most remote and inaccessible of the high peaks... We finally decided on a route up the Ausable Lakes – a route passable only in winter to those intending to hike all the way... At eight we left the car at St. Huberts on the long trek up the valley... Lower Ausable Lake, with the towering mountain walls seemed longer than it should, even tho the snowshoeing was good and our packs not too heavy... While the Lower Lake may be more beautiful in itself, the views from the upper one, especially of the Great Range, seemed to us much lovelier. From here Haystack really looked like one, with a white cover...
>
> We pushed up the narrow, crooked inlet a mile or more and then struck off thru the woods to the right, making no effort to find or follow any trail. The going, especially through the marsh near the inlet, was not too good at first but it was easy to see that in summer it would have been terrible, as we reached higher ground it improved. About three in the afternoon we reached Marcy Brook [and made camp]... The morning of April first brought a threat of snow, but after breakfast we crossed the brook and started up the northeast shoulder of Allen – the one between Marcy Brook and Sand Brook – without any expectation of reaching the top. The snowshoeing was perfect, the climbing was not hard, and the snowstorm only a sprinkle; so we kept on until we suddenly discovered that we were on the top of the ridge at the north end of the summit cone. Then of course it would not do to turn back and after a stiff six hundred foot climb we reached our goal. The weather had almost cleared and with no leaves on the hardwoods and about seven feet of snow under foot, the views especially toward the north and northeast, were grand indeed."[38]

Despite the weather conditions, the ascent by Puffer and his companions did not "qualify" as a winter climb. Credit for the first winter ascent is instead given to a group from Rensselaer Polytechnic Institute for an ascent they made on January 30, 1950.[39]

Endnotes

1. Bill Healy, *The High Peaks of Essex, The Adirondack Mountains of Old Mountain Phelps* (Fleischmanns, NY: Purple Mountain Press, 1992), pg. 86.
2. Warder Cadbury, untitled article in *Ad-i-ron-dac,* July-August 1959, pgs. 72, 73.
3. *Ibid.,* pg. 73.
4. Kenneth Durant, *Guide-Boat Days and Ways* (Adirondack Museum, 1963). The seven full-page sketches are primarily guide-boat scenes and are found before pgs. 23, 65 (with a view of Ampersand Mountain), 107, 153 (showing Gothics from Upper Ausable Lake), 173, 215, and 251.
5. Verplanck Colvin, *Topographical Survey of the Adirondack Wilderness: Second Report,* 1874. The illustration is Plate 5, found at pg. 31; the discussion is found in Appendix A, pg. 166.
6. O. W. Gray & Sons, *New Topographical Atlas of Essex County,* 1876, pg. 73.
7. Robert Marshall, "The High Peaks of the Adirondacks," (Albany: Adirondack Mountain Club, 1922), pgs. 29-30.
8. Arthur S. Hopkins, "A Great Circle Trail, Forty Miles over the High Peaks" in *High Spots,* 1929, pgs, 2-3.
9. Kim Hart, "A Plan for Trail Development," *High Spots* (ADK), Vol. VIII, No. 2, 1931, pgs. 27-29.

10. Robert Marshall, "The Perilous Plight of the Adirondack Wilderness." *High Spots* (ADK), Vol. IX, No. 4, October 1932, pg. 3.

11. Verplanck Colvin, *op cit.*, pg. 167.

12. *Report of the First New York State Forest Commission,* 1885, pg. 97.

13. The area within the Adirondack Park has forever thereafter been referred to as "within the blue line."

14. *New York State Forest Commission Report,* 1891, pg. 164. Pages 106-194 are an article entitled "The Adirondack Park."

15. *New York State Forest Commission Report,* 1893, pgs. 159-160. The Adirondack Club was formed in 1877. Title to the land was held by the Adirondack Iron and Steel Company, successors to the original developers.

16. Arthur H. Masten, *The Story of Adirondac,* 1923; Adirondack Museum edition with introduction and notes by William K. Verner, 1968, pg. 179.

17. See, *e.g., Conservation Commission Annual Report,* 1918, pgs. 98-99.

18. On page 47, while giving instructions on how to bushwhack up Colden, for which there was apparently no trail.

19. Walter Collins O'Kane, *Trails and Summits of the Adirondacks,* pgs. 77 and 90-91.

20. Arthur S. Hopkins, *The Trails to Marcy,* pgs. 16 and 17. The booklet was Recreation Circular 8 and was published in numerous editions over the years. The page numbers refer to the 1939 edition.

21. Orra Phelps, *Guide to Adirondack Trails Northeastern Section* (Albany, NY: The Adirondack Mountain Club, 1934), pgs. 48-49.

22. Orra Phelps and A. T. Shorey, *Guide to Adirondack Trails Northeastern Section* (Adirondack Mountain Club, 1945), pg. 46.

23. Grace Hudowalski and C. Howard Nash, "21 Trailless Peaks," *High Spots, The Yearbook of the Adirondack Mountain Club 1939,* pgs. 13-26; Allen, pgs. 22-23.

24. L. Morgan Porter, *Guide to Adirondack Trails High Peak Region* (The Adirondack Mountain Club, 1956).

25. Production at the mines ceased in 1989. In October 2003, the great majority of the National Lead (by then NL Industries) property was acquired by the Open Space Institute and in February 2008 the state purchased the property from the institute. A portion of the property was to be maintained as sustainable forests. As much as 6,000 acres was expected to be transferred to the state for eventual inclusion in the High Peaks Wilderness. In order to preserve the Mount Adams fire tower, the Open Space Institute has retained ownership of a single acre containing the tower.

26. The summit of Mount Adams which can be reached by a side trail provides magnificent views from its fire tower which was built in 1912.

27. O. W. Gray & Sons, *New Topographical Atlas of Essex County,* 1876, pg. 72.

28. L. Morgan Porter, *Guide to Adirondack Trails High Peak Region,* (Gabriels, NY: The Adirondack Mountain Club, Inc., 1962), pages B5-4. Subsequent guidebooks repeat this language.

29. Lawrence Cotter and James Goodwin, *Guide to Adirondack Trails High Peak Region,* 10th edition, 1980, pg. B5-5.

30. Barbara McMartin, *Discover the Adirondack High Peaks,* 1999, pg. 121.

31. *Adirondac,* October 1980, pg. 119.

32. James A. Goodwin, *And Gladly Guide* (undated, but published 2003), pg. 120.

33. *Ibid.,* pg. 100.

34. *Ibid.,* pg. 85.

35. David Newhouse, "ADK Action on Trails," *Adirondac,* September 1982, pg. 23.

36. Lyle Raymond, "Allen from Skylight," *Adirondac,* September-October 1961, pg. 90.

37. Louis B. Puffer was an active volunteer with the Green Mountain Club. Puffer Shelter, on the Long Trail north of Bolton Mountain, is named for him.

38. Louis B. Puffer, "Good Old Web Feet," *High Spots ADK Yearbook,* January 1942, pg. 20-21.

39. Katherine (Kay) T. Flickinger, "Climbing the Forty-Six on Snow and Ice," *The Adirondack Forty Sixers* (Albany, NY: The Adirondack Forty-Sixers, 1958), pg. 96.

About the Author

Tom Wheeler (#3356W) is both a Winter 46er and a 111er (#282). He is married to Eileen Wheeler (#2543W) and 111er (#365). His son Matthew is 46er #3711 and 111er #307. Tom is an attorney with offices in Potsdam, where he served as village justice for 19 years. He now resides in the town of Canton. He served in various offices in the Adirondack Mountain Club and was its president for three years beginning in December 2002. A recent board member and vice president of the 46ers, he is currently the organization's president. His hobbies, in addition to hiking, include collecting rare books (often about the Adirondack region) and birding. Many of the sources he cites in the "Mountain Profiles" of Cliff, Redfield, and Allen are from his own collection.

Noah John Rondeau's Cold River Hermitage

Santanoni, Panther, and Couchsachraga
By Phil Corell (#224W)

Following the destruction caused by the Big Blow of 1950, interest in climbing the forty-six High Peaks of the Adirondacks grew slowly during the remainder of that decade, but the number of 46er finishes began to steadily increase after 1960. Access to the region improved with the construction of the Adirondack Northway, more people began to pursue recreation in the outdoors, and some who turned to climbing the Adirondack High Peaks began to focus on the goal of becoming 46ers. For many of them, the Santanoni Range became the final challenge in their pursuit.

Unlike the conditions we find today in the Santanoni range, in the early 1960s there were few herdpaths to follow, and route-finding was difficult. In addition, the storm of November 1950 had left waves of blowdown on the trailless peaks. Travel was also hindered by new growth sprouting from between the fallen timber. Progress was often measured in terms of hours rather than minutes.

Another impact on the area came from the development of summer camps for young people. Youth from metropolitan areas and foreign countries traveled to the Adirondacks to live with their peers in challenging outdoor settings. Many of the camps employed the mountains and lakes as integral aspects of their programs. As of the spring of 2008, the Pok-O-MacCready Camps in Willsboro could boast that more than 300 of their campers and counselors had become 46ers. Many of them had been members of groups which, as they were preparing to climb the Santanonis, were told stories about the remote area in the southern High Peaks, the huge mining complex they would pass, dump trucks that dwarfed normal vehicles, a hermit who had lived in the woods year round, and the difficulties they would encounter: blowdown and cripplebrush.

In 1960 a group of teenagers from Camp Pok-O-Moonshine was attempting a climb of Couchsachraga Mountain from the Ouluska Lean-to, a shelter near the site of the former home of the hermit Noah John Rondeau on a bluff above the Cold River. The accepted route to Couchsachraga at that time involved a bushwhack along streams draining the northern side of the Panther-Couchsachraga ridge. After completing a 13-mile pack into the lean-to, the group had their first tour of the "city" of Cold River although its "mayor," Noah John, had departed the site some ten years earlier. The remains of several teepees of notched logs, small buildings, and a garden gone wild stimulated their curiosity.

On the day of the climb, the leader set a firm turn around time of 3 p.m.

Much of the day was spent finding the approach to the mountain and following various streams toward the summit ridge. At the appointed turn around time the group could sense the summit was near, but, despite the protests of the boys on the trip, their leader held firm and the group turned and headed down. Just after dark, with the batteries of their two flashlights fading, they stumbled onto the marked trail which led to the lean-to. They realized then that, had they not turned back, they would have most certainly spent the night in bivouac. Their leader had made a wise decision.

Although unsuccessful in achieving their goal during that trip, the group did determine the best way to avoid the famous Cold River swamp by following logging roads built during the post-storm clean up.

Grace Hudowalski in her *Mountain Tales* CD describes the concern early climbers had about that swamp. She, the Dittmars and Helen Menz (#42) received help from the Hermit in locating a route around that obstacle.

Few climbers from the "new generation" of 46ers have ever ventured to the Cold River or fought their way through the fabled Ouluska Pass; and, sadly, the only obvious remnants today of the Hermit's Cold River City are elsewhere: at the Adirondack Museum at Blue Mountain Lake. Hurricane Floyd and subsequent wind storms have rendered Ouluska Pass nearly impassable.

During the summer of 1961, Jim "Beetle" Bailey (#233)[1] led another group of Pok-O-Moonshine campers attempting to reach the summits of Santanoni and Panther. In the late 1950s and early 1960s a formal trail up Santanoni, although not maintained, was still in existence. Leaving the blue trail from the Santanoni parking lot to Duck Hole, the trail to Santanoni's summit ascended 2,000 feet in two miles. The group saw a bicycle which had been left resting against a tree at the trail junction, and just as they crested the Santanoni ridge, they met a hiker who, at the time, was in his sixties, Charles Brayton. Brayton had been a Pok-O-Moonshine camper in 1914 and needed Panther and Couchsachraga to finish his 46. The day was overcast with a light drizzle, but the Poko boys hoped that the clouds would lift. Brayton decided to join them and re-climb Santanoni.

As they signed the Santanoni register a sobering realization came over the party. Still in the book, from October 10, 1958, was the signature of Howard P. Gilroy of Schenectady. He had written that it was "Cloudy – Not raining yet." The next entry, that of October 19, was written by a member of a search party: "2nd trip in two days looking for lost hiker H. P. Gilroy. Twenty-five others did not sign on top looking for same... no one should travel alone!"

The Poko group atop Santanoni in 1961 was there with rain coming down and visibility limited, and Jim made the wise but "unpopular" decision to turn back. Four members of the group would remain "45ers" until the following summer. Brayton returned to hiking the next spring and become Forty-Sixer #219.

When neither Gilroy nor his body was found, a rumor circulated that he had been involved in an insurance scam and, later, it was said that he had been found in Buffalo living under an assumed name. However, in June of 1988 his remains were at last located in the Panther Brook valley. A forensic examination of his bones indicated that he had broken a leg, probably explaining why he had been unable to extricate himself from the mountain and indicating that he had probably died of exposure. The warning written years before should not be forgotten: "no one should travel alone!"

The bicycle at the trail junction that the Poko boys had seen had been left there by Gilroy. No one in recent years has even considered the Duck Hole trail, often a mire of old corduroy and mud, suitable for bicycles.

The Mountains

Due to their remoteness, the mountains of the Santanoni Range are often the final peaks climbed by those seeking to become 46ers. Prior to 2008 the accepted legal route to the three peaks left the blue trail by a beaver dam near the Bradley Pond lean-to. The original trail, which went directly to the summit of Santanoni, began at a junction with the Duck Hole Trail (blue trail) on the Santanoni Brook about a half mile south of Bradley Pond. It roughly followed the original path taken by Verplanck Colvin during his survey of the area. The 1934 Adirondack Mountain Club trail guide noted, "Allow more than the usual time for the very steep and difficult climbing on this trail." With the Open Space Institute's purchase of the side of Santanoni, the former route is once more open for use.

Finch Pruyn donated 1805 acres south of the Santanoni height of land to the state in 1955, but the company maintained control of the lands through which the trail passed. The 46ers' first Trailmaster, Jim Goodwin (#24), was responsible for scouting and developing a legal route after Finch Pruyn chose to close the Santanoni trail in 1979 because it passed over lands they were leasing to a hunting club. Jim worked with Finch Pruyn, the Department of Environmental Conservation, the Adirondack Mountain Club, and the Forty-Sixers to have a legal route approved. In 1981 Dick Nason, property manager for Finch Pruyn, had a crew clear the property line from the blue trail to the ridge from Panther. From that point Jim and a Forty-Sixer work crew flagged the route to Panther Brook, and after the route was established, the flagging was removed.

In the winter 1981-1982 issue of *Adirondack Peeks,* Jim warned hikers about a problem that Finch Pruyn loggers created. After the 46er flagging crew had left, company workers returned to mark the boundary line in yellow paint. They marked the end of their line at the top of a cliff. A number of hikers who followed the blazed line missed the flagging heading to the left to Panther Brook and climbed to the top of the cliff. Most who reached the cliff proceeded briefly up the ridge before turning back. The Forty-Sixers received angry notes from a number of climbers who assumed the organization had marked the line which they had followed as a path. The Finch Pruyn crew cut off the trees at knee height and left them where they fell. Eventually the route was cleaned out, a path developed, and the flagging was removed, but even today, because alternate routes have developed, the section of trail from the shore of Bradley Pond to the cairn on Panther Brook can confuse hikers.

The work of the Finch Pruyn crew also opened access to Bradley Pond, which had become difficult to reach after the Big Blow of 1950. In August of 1992 two 46ers, Andrew Canning (#2245) and Brian Roddiger (#3256) were walking in from Tahawus to climb the Santanonis. They were hiking next to the brook on the blue trail near the junction with the abandoned Santanoni trail when they noticed unusual marks on the ground. As they rounded a bend in the trail, they overtook a middle-aged man who had been dragging a metal rowboat. He was obviously tired as he sat next to it at the side of the trail. He seemed surprised when Canning and Roddiger asked what he was doing. He said that he was going to go fishing in Bradley Pond – a somewhat astounding notion: The pond is small, muddy, shallow and, given its elevation, probably devoid of fish due to the effects of acid rain. He offered the two all the money in his pocket if they would carry his boat the rest of the way. They decided that $13 would provide "refreshment" that night and agreed to do so. Later, on the way out from their hike, they looked for the fisherman and for the boat but saw neither.

The lore of Santanoni mystery grew that day. Did that fisherman catch anything in Bradley Pond? Whatever happened to the boat? Did he drag it back down the trail? Did he find other hikers to help him haul it away?

The route that Jim Goodwin and the 46ers established has become the path of choice to "Times Square" – a name which developed in the 1970s for the intersection of the herdpaths on Panther ridge. The gain in elevation is much more gradual than was the climb of the old Santanoni trail, and views of Mt. Henderson and the High Peaks open to hikers as they ascend the "new" route.

Santanoni, Panther, and Couchsachraga are considerably easier to climb today than they were during the decade after the Big Blow of 1950. In fact, most hikers in their quests to become 46ers now climb all three in a single day, but such was not the case in the past. The Adirondack Mountain Club's *Guide to Adirondack Trails, Seventh Edition* (1962) contained this advice in the description of the climb to Santanoni:

> Allow more than the usual time for very steep and difficult climbing and note the route carefully through the blowdowns for the return trip. Do not try to include the other two Santanoni peaks (Panther and Couchsachraga) with this peak in a one day trip. This was quite an ordeal before 1950, but since the "hurricane" it would be sheer folly to try it.[2]

The same trail guide, in its section on the "Trailless Peaks," told its readers this about today's route from Times Square to Couchsachraga: "The traverse of the ridge between Couchsachraga and Panther Peak is a difficult trip, being complicated by heavy blowdown, and is not recommended." Concerning the route to Panther, the trail guide was less cautionary. The recommended route to Panther was basically the one which hikers use today, but it began south of Bradley Pond. The trail guide mentioned an alternate approach – "to climb Santanoni first and then traverse the ridge to Panther" – but concluded that that route was "a longer and more difficult trip than a look at the map would suggest."

Before the 1950 storm created horrific blowdown in the area, in an article which appeared in a 1947 edition of *Ad-i-ron-dac*, Robert Denniston (#40) asked, "Can it be done in a day?" He wrote about a trip – an attempt to climb all three – he had taken in August 1946 with four campers from Camp Lincoln. After leaving Duck Hole Lean-to at 7 a.m. his group spent four hours in reaching the summit of Santanoni and less than two hours in achieving Panther. They continued their hike to "Couchie," an ordeal which required another two and a half hours. Then, because it was late in the day, they decided to head for Noah John Rondeau's camp on the Cold River and take the Northville-Placid Trail back to Duck Hole. They reached the trail at 8:20 p.m. and, in fading light, slogged the remaining five miles to their lean-to at Duck Hole, arriving at 10:30.

In the May/June 1956 issue of *Ad-i-ron-dac*, Rudy Strobel (#98) described his trip up the three Santanonis to complete his 46. In the early years of the gravel road that initiated the approach to Santanoni, because large chunks of stone had not yet been packed down into the road bed, hikers found the footing difficult and uneven. Rudy hiked the nearly five miles to the Santanoni Lean-to (now called Bradley Pond Lean-to). He described following, from a small sign, an indistinct trail to the summit of Santanoni the next day. He wrote, "Before the storm of November 25, 1950, Santanoni had a marked trail as I found many of the old markers. I also found traces of log steps that someone had laboriously set into the lower sections of the trail... As I approached the top of Santanoni, I ran into the thick spruces mentioned in the current ADK Guide."

Upon returning to the lean-to he encountered another group from Camp Lincoln – six boys and a counselor. The hikers decided to join forces the next day for an attempt on

Panther and Couchsachraga, Rudy's 46th peak. Leaving from the lean-to at 7:45 a.m., the group headed almost due west. Rudy wrote, "The first hour out from the lean-to was through the worst blowdowns I have seen in the Adirondacks. It was worse than that encountered on Allen, Seward, Donaldson, and Emmons." After reaching the summit of Panther at noon, Rudy and the Camp Lincoln group began their trip to Couchsachraga an hour later. Rudy explained, "Apparently the foliage misled us as we found that at least a half dozen minor bumps lie between Panther and Couchsachraga." They reached the summit at 5 p.m. The group had already agreed to return via Rondeau's and the Cold River. The thought of attempting the trip back to Panther was out of the question. Arriving at the Hermit's camp at dusk, they continued on to the Cold River Lean-tos, which they reached at 11 p.m., and there they spent the night. "We ate the last of our lunch and eventually started a fire as it got quite chilly without the comfort of our bedding rolls." The group arrived back at their camp the next day, twenty-four hours after they had started. They shared their final meal at the National Lead Company's cafeteria at Tahawus before heading for home.

In the next issue of *Ad-i-ron-dac*, Arthur Davis (#134) reported, "The descent from the summit (of Panther) to the Duck Hole Trail at Bradley Pond, perhaps a short two miles, took me three hours and ten minutes, with no stops except for getting stuck in, on, and under the endless log jams."

Between November 1950 and the late 1960s very few hikers even contemplated attempting to climb all three Santanonis in a single day.

The Newcomb area, south of the Santanonis, offers a vista of the range. Anyone driving through the town should stop at the rest area along Route 28N. There the panorama of the High Peaks to the north is a sight worth seeing. From Newcomb, a visitor can begin a five-mile hike, ski, or snowshoe to the Camp Santanoni historical site. The former Great Camp was constructed in the 1880s by Robert C. Pruyn, an Albany banker. The extant cedar buildings linked by huge porches are currently being repaired and preserved. Santanoni dominates the view from the far side of the lake as one approaches the camp on the road. Near the road's entrance at Newcomb, visitors go by a series of farm buildings and fields, a complex which, in its heyday, provided all the food for the family as well as employment for a number of area people.

In 1953 the Melvin family of Syracuse purchased the property. In 1971, Douglas Legg, an eight-year-old grandson of the owners, wandered away from the lodge. Neither he nor his body was ever located despite an extensive search instituted by state agencies and local volunteers. In February 1972 the state of New York took title to the Santanoni Preserve through the agency of the Nature Conservancy, which had purchased the property from the Melvin family.

The Newcomb area also boasts access to another feature of the Santanoni Range. In September 1985, following torrential rains, a new slide appeared on the side of Santanoni along the course of the Ermine Brook. Viewed from the Santanoni Preserve and the Moose Pond area, the slide appears to snake its way down from a ridge south of the main peak. An expedition to it may be begun from the road to the Santanoni Camp. Follow the road from the preserve's entrance gate, go 4.5 miles, and proceed at that point on the road to Moose Pond. There, just out of sight of the pond, a horse trail leaves the road on the right. It circles around the east side of the pond and, in another 1.4 miles, crosses Ermine Brook before continuing north to the Cold River Horse Trail. The brook provides access to the slide.

Those who have made the trip warn that to continue from the slide's headwall to Santanoni's summit is a journey meant only for those who have plenty of time and a desire to push through the three-quarters of a mile of thick scrub and blowdown. For most, the 16-mile round trip required to reach the top of the slide and the return to Newcomb is a sufficient challenge.

Also worth mention is the state's Visitor Interpretive Center, also located in Newcomb. The facility offers both historical and natural interpretations of the area. A network of trails and exhibits is available at the site.

MOUNT SANTANONI
Height: 13th – 1,404 meters (4,606 feet)

French Canadians converted the Saint Regis and Abenaki Indians to Christianity, and Saint Anthony became their patron saint. Thus most authorities attribute the name *Santanoni* to a corruption of the words *Saint Anthony* by the Indians. The name as we know it made its first appearance on a map of the region published in 1838 by William C. Redfield. Theodore R. Davis, an artist and writer, and David Hunter, a fifteen-year-old, were the first to climb the peak in 1866. Six years later, Hunter and Hank Parker guided Verplanck Colvin to the top. The trail built to Santanoni by the Tahawus Club in 1895 was approximately the same as the one that Hunter and Parker cut for Colvin. Hunter was the caretaker for the Tahawus Club for many years.

In his "Extract from the Report of 1872" Colvin described his first ascent of Santanoni that September:

> On the twenty-fifth we proceeded to Tahawus settlement, about ten miles distant, and secured packmen for the sub-expeditions.
>
> Starting from Tahawus on the following morning, we reached the iron-works about noon on our way to Mt. Santanoni, which was to be one of the triangulation stations. In the evening we made a brush camp and passed a comfortable night. Next day (27th) we were early traversing the woods, (there was no trail nor were there choppings on the trees for guidance,) and following a small stream which came from the lofty crest, continued to ascend. The open character of the gorge we climbed, enabled me to apply my method of approximate measurement, by barometer and level, of inferior mountains, to several summits, as hereafter more particularly described, from which the height of Andrew mountain is found to be [3,216] feet, and North River mountain [3,758] feet.
>
> We reached the summit of Santanoni about mid-day. Singularly enough, the weather, which for a day or two past had been threatening, was now moderately fair, and permitted the angular observations to be made very complete. Mt. Marcy, so often shrouded in the clouds, stood grandly out, a sharp, gray cone. The positions of various lakes and their islands were determined, and especially the lower end of Long lake, which, like a great river, lay stretched before us in the west. Late in the afternoon the work was stopped by heavy clouds, but not until the necessary angles had been measured, the barometrical observations (showing its height to be [4644] feet) finished, and five reconnaissance maps of topography completed. The sun was setting as we left the crest and forced our way down through the dwarf balsam and spruce trees on the flanks of the mountain. We had left all our heavy baggage in cáche a mile from the summit, beside the gorge up which we had climbed. For sake of food, camp-fire and blankets we hurried down in search of the gorge, and in about an hour found it, and commenced its descent just at dark. At

length, very tired, we found our supplies, and by the light of a torch the guides cut night wood and built a hut of balsam boughs, the sound of the axe echoing desolately in the dark forest.

During the night the clouds disappeared, the stars shone out and a furious, cold wind swept over the woods.[3]

Colvin's words provide a modern reader with a sense of the untracked wilderness through which he traveled. Attaining the summit with the technical gear necessary to conduct his research was no easy task, and the surveyor's tendency to remain late upon a summit making observations and then having to scurry back to his camp in darkness made his expeditions exciting to many who read the reports about the survey. Those reports, avidly read by Robert Marshall, who spent summers at Saranac Lake, in part motivated him to follow some of Colvin's footsteps through the wilderness.

In his 1922 booklet, "The High Peaks of the Adirondacks," Marshall recorded view ratings that he, his brother George, and their guide Herb Clark had devised. They rated the view from Santanoni as the second best view in the High Peaks.

The trio climbed to the summit via the ridge from Panther Peak, which they had ascended from the dam on the Cold River. Robert wrote, "The view from Santanoni was worth far more than it cost us to reach the top – worth any trouble, in fact, for only Haystack do I consider finer. Whichever way you look, it is very impressive. Santanoni is in the heart of the wilderness, dividing the mountain from the lake region." Subsequent mining operations at Tahawus were to affect the view rating for the peak. In 1988, a poll of 46ers revealed that Santanoni's "view rating" had dropped to ninth.

Interestingly Marshall's brief prose sketch concerning Santanoni states, "There is no trail up this mountain, although lumber roads run well up it from the Tahawus side." Apparently he did not know about the trail which had been cut by the Tahawus Club. Walter O'Kane's *Trails and Summits of the Adirondacks,* published in 1928 states, "While there is a trail to the summit, it is not an easy trip and should not be undertaken by any one unfamiliar with woods travel."

In a description of a trip he took up Santanoni in the early 1920s, Robert Wickham wrote the following in *Friendly Adirondack Peaks* (1924): "On the floor of the open camp, at one end, was a good bed of fresh balsam; at the other end were a table, benches, some cooking utensils, and a small supply of sugar, flour and butter, left by recent occupants. We cooked unleavened bread in the fry pan and some slices of bacon over a fire in the built-up stone fireplace..."

What Wickham described was a scene repeated over and over again throughout the High Peaks at least until the late 1960s. Hikers camping at lean-tos then could still find food "treasures" left by previous groups. Particularly fortuitous finds – for some – included such items as a can of stew or beans, sometimes even fresh eggs. Leaving food for others or cutting fresh balsam boughs for the bed of a lean-to for the next group was considered good etiquette in those times. With the huge increase in hikers and the closing of lean-to garbage pits, the former, accepted practices had to change.

Wickham described leaving Duck Hole one day and heading up the valley in the direction of Bradley Pond to camp. The next day his party reached the northeast peak of Panther by 11 in the morning. On the summit he found a tin cartridge box sealed with adhesive tape and marked "register." It held the names of five climbers, two from August 5, 1921, and three others from August 21, 1921: Robert and George Marshall and Herb Clark. Wickham and his group fought their way through thick mountain balsam along the ridge, onward to Santanoni.

They saw signs of an old survey line that had been cut many years before but found it of little benefit. They also found several white cloth game preserve signs tacked to trees along the way, and Wickham told of pressing water out of moss in an attempt to secure liquid to slake their thirst – a practice the author, as a young boy, remembers well from his first climb up the back side of Couchsachraga.

Upon reaching the summit, Wickham and his party were awed by what they saw. He wrote, "Applying the standard as to beauty of views I find myself agreeing with Marshall that the views from Santanoni are excelled, of a certainty, only by those from Haystack, possibly by those from Nipple Top… Santanoni stands detached, in the midst of vast woods, with no other mountains close to him – an outpost between the big range and the lake country. The immensity of the region impresses one more from Santanoni than from any other peak."

Wickham, like O'Kane, located what had eluded the Marshalls and Clark: the trail from the Tahawus Club. He wrote, "We discovered a trail leading down to the east, toward Santanoni Brook, and were afterwards informed this trail followed down the brook, coming out on the road leading north from Tahawus Post Office to Tahawus Club." Ignoring the trail but not wishing to re-trace their path to Panther, the group bushwhacked along a northeasterly course over two ridges and emerged just north of Bradley Pond. Wickham makes no mention of having actually passed the pond even though their route most certainly would have taken them close to it.

Jim Goodwin has mentioned that the junction, where the old trail reached the summit ridge of Santanoni, was always difficult to see due to low scrub and dwarf balsam. This remains the case today.

Grace Hudowalski made an interesting observation in her CD, *Mountain Tales*. She accompanied Margery Ludlow (#27) on her 46er finishing climb of the Santanonis in 1941. Grace describes climbing – half way up the Santanoni trail – on steps constructed by the Civilian Conservation Corps during the Great Depression. Those steps were on a section of the old Tahawus Club trail, which was the accepted route for climbing the mountain before the Big Blow of 1950 swept the area. Goodwin recalls that a group of Boy Scouts from Newcomb was responsible for reopening the trail several years after the storm. For years after that repair, climbers could spot one-inch-diameter aluminum disks, painted red, that the Scouts had placed periodically along the route. They have disappeared due to the loss of trees or the thoughtlessness of souvenir hunters. Somewhere along the course of that old trail a few of the disks may now lie in the forest duff.

One of Santanoni's most enduring mysteries – mentioned earlier – concerned the 1958 disappearance of Howard P. Gilroy, who, after arriving in the Adirondacks on a bus at Schroon Lake, had ridden his folding bicycle to the hamlet of Tahawus and had stayed an evening at the hamlet's YMCA before he set out, on the bicycle, for Santanoni. When he didn't return to pick up gear he had left at the YMCA, authorities were notified and a search for him began. Despite the efforts of National Lead Company personnel and volunteers, the only discovery was Gilroy's bicycle hidden in the woods. The night before Gilroy had been reported missing, rain and gale-force winds had whipped the area, uprooting trees and cutting off power.

The mystery of Gilroy's disappearance deepened when it was discovered that Howard P. Gilroy was not the missing hiker's real name. He was, in fact, 59-year-old Leslie A. Wiggs of Schenectady; however, members of the Schenectady Chapter of the Adirondack Mountain Club who had climbed with him only knew him as Howard Gilroy. It was reported that he hiked alone quite often and was not one for idle conversation on the trail, especially about himself. He did not usually carry a canteen and seldom drank while hiking. He did carry on his belt a little pouch which contained something like gorp and occasionally snacked on it. He was also known to have carried a camera with him on his trips to the mountains.

Wiggs-Gilroy's father, who lived in Norfolk, Virginia, offered a $500 reward for information leading to the discovery of his son's whereabouts, but he did not live long enough to learn what had happened to his son. In June 1988 human remains and a camera[4] were found by two Connecticut hikers in a gorge between Santanoni and Panther Peak. The remains were later identified as those of Leslie Wiggs. Possibly the gorge where the remains and camera were discovered was the same one that Verplanck Colvin had written about in 1872 – next to which he had left "cáché" of his "heavy baggage."

The Adirondack peaks change their appearance with the seasons. In summer, climbers work their way to Santanoni through low scrub, their legs often scratched and bleeding. From the summit they can enjoy an expansive, panoramic view, but they are still hemmed in by the growth that covers the summit ridge almost entirely. Winter climbers who reach the corniced summit ridge consider it one of the most beautiful sights in the High Peaks. The white outline of the ridge fixed against the blue sky offers them the finest winter photo opportunities imaginable. Only the tops of the balsams poke above the deep drifts. They know that they must remain on the broken path. Huge amounts of snow collect along the flanks of the summit ridge each winter.

Panther Mountain
Height: 18th – 1,354 meters (4,442 feet)

Panther is an old and common name in the Adirondacks, as the naming of topographic features after animals seems always to have occurred. The mention of a Panther Mountain in the area of Tahawus is first noted in an 1840 pamphlet which described ore veins in the area, but the peak initially called Panther is the mountain we now refer to as Mount Henderson.[5] The United States Geological Survey "Santanoni Quadrangle" map of 1901, published in 1904, contains the earliest known identification of the Panther Peak that 46ers climb.

Credit for the first ascent went to Daniel Lynch, an Adirondack land surveyor from Minerva, who in 1904 ran a line over the tops of Santanoni, Panther, and Henderson. Reference to no earlier climb can be found.

In the Marshalls-Clark view ratings Panther Peak was considered to have the tenth best view and was grouped with the likes of Skylight and Gothics. Robert and George Marshall and Herb Clark first climbed Panther on the same day they climbed Santanoni. Robert wrote the following about it in "The High Peaks of the Adirondacks":

> By mounting a tree we found Panther Peak, and a thirty minute desperate struggle with the mountain balsam brought us to the summit. We dreaded the mile and a half of balsam between us and Santanoni, but somebody had cut a rough trail between the two peaks, which made the going less difficult.

The "rough trail" probably followed the survey line which had been cut in 1904 by Daniel Lynch.

Ed Hudowalski on the Panther Brook

It seems that, before the November 1950 storm made the area around Bradley Pond virtually impassable, most climbers who went to Panther did so along the long ridge between it and Santanoni after first climbing Santanoni by way of the old Tahawus Club trail to that peak. Although the Adirondack Mountain Club's seventh edition trail guide (1962) recommended climbing Panther from Bradley Pond, by the early 1960s the accepted route was the one from Santanoni. That approach remained the preferred one until Finch Pruyn closed off access to the Santanoni trail, which, as of 2008, is open once again.

With the large increase in the numbers of people doing winter climbing, Panther has become a popular destination, particularly since access to the 4,000-foot "Times Square" junction has been made easier by the Panther Brook approach. In winter, a short walk from the junction, Panther's snow-covered dome offers beautiful views.

Prior to its removal, the summit register canister on Panther eluded many a winter hiker. In summer it was at eye level in a small clearing, but in winter only the tops of trees near the canister poked from the surface of the snow. The maze of trails on top of the ridge has also misled many a climber seeking Panther's summit.

COUCHSACHRAGA MOUNTAIN
Height: 46th – 1,156 meters (3,793 feet)

Robert Marshall's 1922 descriptions published in "The High Peaks of the Adirondacks" concerned only 42 High Peaks. Couchsachraga ("Couchie") was not considered to be over 4,000 feet and no mention of it was made. Subsequently added to the list, it was first climbed by Robert and George Marshall and Herb Clark in 1924. Considered to be 4,000 feet in elevation at that time, Couchie's elevation was reduced by the 1954 USGS survey. The most diminutive of the original forty-six high peaks, according to the USGS 7.5 by 15 minute "Santanoni Peak" map released in 1979, it is 1,156 meters (3,793 feet) in elevation. Consider, too, that Couchie is one of only two 46er peaks which cannot be seen from Mount Marcy.[6]

The Marshalls originally rated its view as #32, better than that of Rocky Peak and similar to Big Slide, Seymour, Marshall, and Donaldson. Many present day climbers wouldn't be so kind.

Interestingly the name Couchsachraga was first given to Mount Emmons in the Seward Range and the Marshalls initially called the present Couchsachraga, Cold River Mountain. They later felt that the summit should bear its present name.

"Couchsachraga" is an ancient Indian name for the region we know as the Adirondack wilderness, translated to mean "the great and dismal wilderness" and designated by European map makers as "the beaver hunting grounds of the Five Nations." In the 1700s the British Governor of the Province of New York, Pownall, stated that the "Couchsachraga," located in the valley between the Seward and Santanoni ranges, was one of the four great hunting grounds of the Iroquois.

In 1940 a committee of 46ers comprised of Orville C. Gowie, C. Howard Nash, and Grace L. Hudowalski petitioned the state Board of Geographic Names to permanently name Blake's Peak, Mount Marshall, and Couchsachraga Mountain. Thanks to their efforts these peaks bear their current names. As support for the naming of Couchsachraga they cited the desire to perpetuate the original Native American name for the area and Governor Pownall's report of 1766 referring to the area as the "Couchsachraga."

During the early years of recreational climbing, most hikers attempting Couchsachraga used the Cold River approach. Although, later, some climbers employed the ridge from Panther to reach Couchie, the effects of the Big Blow of 1950 again obliged aspiring 46ers to approach the peak from the Cold River side. After that storm, with state approval, a timber salvaging operation began in the Cold River area. That necessitated upgrading the access road and constructing buildings near the salvage site. In the late 1960s those buildings were burned by the Department of Environmental Conservation. The logging roads have since been turned into the horse trail system that exists in that area.

During the late 1960s and early 1970s, as the number of climbers increased, the present herd path from the Panther ridge developed into the accepted approach to Couchie from Times Square. Before it did, the trek from the Panther ridge to Couchsachraga often took hours to complete.

Noah John Rondeau: The Hermit of Cold River

The approach to Couchsachraga from the Cold River required a 13-mile hike from Corey's, past Ward Brook Lean-to and Mountain Pond. After hikers had reached the Cold River, they had to negotiate their way past a swamp and a confusion of streams.

Many early 46ers were befriended by Noah John Rondeau, the self proclaimed "Mayor" of Cold River. Noah John ran away from home in his early teens and had only an eighth grade education. However, he was well read, interested in astronomy, and a proficient violin player. He lived for a time at Corey's and there learned the ways of the woods from an Abenaki Indian, Daniel Emmett. He hunted and ran a trap line but soon had run-ins with the local Conservation Department officers.

Familiar with the Cold River area through his hunting and guiding, during the winter of 1929 he began his self-imposed exile there as a year-round hermit. For more than 20 years Rondeau stayed in the woods, living off the land and making one trip a year, around Christmas time, to the outside world. Occasionally acquaintances would take canned goods, supplies, and mail to him at his hermitage. His longest continuous stay there was 381 days. Because he was living on land belonging to the Santa Clara Lumber Company, with their permission, the Conservation Department couldn't force him out or curtail his hunting on that property.

He constructed his "village" on top of a bluff at a site where there had been a dam on the Cold River. The village consisted of a "Town Hall," a "Hall of Records," and several twelve-foot high teepees of notched logs. In winter he lived in the log "Town Hall," which he heated with a stove fashioned from a 55-gallon drum. The logs which comprised the teepees were notched at two-foot intervals so that Noah John could quickly break them with the butt of his axe to feed his fires. When the weather grew warmer, he would move to one of the teepees where he could use the smoke of a fire to drive away the bugs – a technique that was used in lean-tos by campers when fires were permitted in the High Peaks.

Early 46ers such as Ditt and Mary Dittmar and Ed and Grace Hudowalski became the hermit's good friends. With Noah John's help, hikers could avoid the bothersome swamp and negotiate the maze of streams coming out of the Panther-Couchsachraga drainage. Mary Dittmar's sister, Helen Menz, described an experience with Noah John in 1940. She, Mary (#29) and a friend, Ruth Prince (#43) hiked to "Cold River City" with the intention of staying a night there before climbing Couchsachraga. Noah John welcomed the three young ladies to his hermitage, but he was concerned that they might have difficulty completing their hike to the top of Couchie. The next day he offered to guide them across the swamp. Soon he was leading them up the mountain, and, later, Helen took a picture of him on the summit. Helen and the Dittmars made annual trips to the Cold River

Noah John at Cold River

to visit the hermit. Grace Hudowalski often told of the times she carried a birthday cake to him in her arms the 13 miles from Corey's to Cold River.

Although he lived as a hermit, Noah John loved people and enjoyed the company he received. He was famous for stashing food and supplies along his trap lines and the paths he followed through the woods. As he walked them, he might stop and retrieve a jar of coffee or some sugar hidden in a stump.

Rondeau was a skilled marksman with both a rifle and long bow. Unfortunately, however, his hunting and trapping became a source of conflict with local Conservation officers. During his years in the woods, he had several run-ins with "the law" and once spent time in a local jail. One popular tale about Noah John concerns a Conservation officer's accusation that Rondeau had shot at him. Supposedly, in defense of the hermit, a number of his friends testified that Noah John was an outstanding shot and that if he had truly tried to shoot the officer, he would have killed him. The account goes on to say that the charges against Noah John were dropped; however, the story has never been fully verified.

Rondeau's life was to change in 1947 when he was "discovered" by representatives of the New York Sportsman's Show. He was flown out of the woods by helicopter with some of his possessions and appeared in New York City. Soon he was on radio and television, and he was the subject of many newspaper articles. His celebrity lasted almost three years. Then, "old news" and disappointed, he returned to his camp on the Cold River in 1950.

Again his life, and that of all Adirondack climbers, was soon to change. When Rondeau left the woods he usually took a "short cut" through Ouluska Pass on his way to Corey's. Logging roads which then existed shaved several miles from the walk around Seymour past Mountain Pond. He chose November 25, 1950, as the day to leave the woods for one of his annual visits to civilization. That was the day the Big Blow began. State officials, reacting to the damage wrought in the area of the Sewards and the Cold River by the storm thereafter, "closed" the woods. Noah John's life as the "Hermit of Cold River" was over.

Through sheer luck and determination that day, Noah John had made it to Ampersand Camp, his normal mid-point on the trip out. He was "trapped" there for several days before crews could open the road and allow him to continue his trip to Corey's. At the time of the storm Rondeau was 67. He lived until he was 84 and died on August 24, 1967, at the Lake Placid Hospital. Part of his "city" is on display in the Adirondack Museum in Blue Mountain Lake. Hikers in the 1960s and early 1970s could see remnants of his camp – Rondeau's buildings and several teepees on the bluff at the head of Ouluska Pass. Still, at that time, snow peas grew in an area where Noah John had had a garden. He had raised carrots, onions, turnips, and potatoes as well.

The Tahawus Mine Site

No climber can venture to the Santanonis via the former site of Tahawus without being struck immediately by the impact and scope of the mining operation which took place there. Questions arise when viewing the MacIntyre Furnace, the abandoned village of Adirondac, or the huge mining complex at Tahawus. Little did the Native American trapper Lewis Elijah Benedict know what he was setting in motion when, for "$1.50 and a plug of tobacco," he led David Henderson through Indian Pass to the location of a rich vein of iron ore in 1826.

Lossing's view of the village of Adirondac after the MacIntyre Mine closed

Soon a claim was staked by Archibald McIntyre, Duncan McMartin, and David Henderson; the "village" of McIntyre (later known as Adirondac) was born; and the mining of iron ore began. During its peak operation in the late 1840s more than 400 men extracted 50 tons of ore and produced 14 tons of iron daily at the site. In 1854 the furnace, which remains today as one of the best preserved ones of the Antebellum period, was constructed. However, a chain of events closed the operation in 1857. Transportation of materials to and from the site was costly and time consuming. The furnace demanded an almost insatiable supply of wood for charcoal, the location of the ores relative to the furnace was problematic, and the operation suffered from constant water power problems.

The quest for more water led to one of the region's best known tragedies. In 1845, David Henderson, along with his son and a guide, John Cheney, decided to scout the area north of Adirondac for potential sources of greater water power. While visiting what we know now as Calamity Pond, Henderson set down a gun, one which belonged to Cheney. It accidentally discharged, and its projectile struck Henderson. He died a few minutes later. A monument, commemorating Henderson, stands along the trail today. Calamity Pond, Calamity Brook, and the nearby Calamity Mountain all remind us of his tragic death.

In 1854 the Saratoga and Sackets Harbor Railroad surveyed the right of way between the existing end of the line in North Creek and the site of the blast furnace. Funding for the construction of the rail line never came through. Consequently the site remained difficult to access. Another concern was an impurity found in the ore. That turned out to be a mineral from which, later, titanium could be extracted, and that "impurity" led to the mine's rebirth in the 1940s. A spring run-off in 1856 destroyed the dams along the Opalescent and crippled the supply of water power to the site. The impact of those events spelled the end of iron mining at both the Upper Works and the Lower Works the next year.

In his *The Adirondacks: Illustrated* (1874), Seneca Ray Stoddard described a visit to what was then left of the village of Adirondac:

The preserved 1854 blast furnace

> Just above the head of Lake Sanford is the "new forge," the huge building itself in a dilapidated condition, but the great stone furnace, forty feet square at its base, stands firm and solid as when made; a few rods beyond this is the ruined village, where a scence [sic] of utter desolation met our view.
>
> Nearly a quarter of a century has passed away since the busy hum of industry sounded here; where once was heard the crash of machinery and the joyous shouts of children at play, is now the shrill bark of the fox or the whir of the startled partridge, in place of the music of voices, all was silence, solemn and ghostly. Over the mountains and middle ground hung a dark funereal pall of cloud across which the setting sun cast bars of ashen light; they fell on the nearer buildings bringing out their unseemly scars in ghastly relief and lay in strips across the grass grown street which led away into the shadow. On either side once stood neat cottages and pleasant homes, now stained and blackened by time; broken windows, doors unhinged, falling roofs, rotting sills and crumbling foundations, pointed to the ruin that must surely come. At the head of the street was the old furnace, a part of one chimney still standing, and another shattered by the thunder bolt lay in ruins at its feet. The waterwheel – emblem of departed power – lay motionless, save as piece by piece it fell away. Huge blocks of iron, piles of rusty ore, coal bursting from the crumbling kilns, great shafts broken and bent, rotting timbers, stones and rubbish lay in one common grave, over which loving nature had thrown a shroud of creeping vines.

Stoddard went on to describe a boarding house and the village's school house – its bell suspended from a tree. He wrote of the demise of the iron works: "In the death of Mr. Henderson the motive power was removed, and it was allowed to run down, work gradually ceased, and three years after his death the upper works were abandoned."

During the 1870s the area was to generate an interest in recreation. In 1876 the Preston Ponds Club, later known as the Adirondack Club, was formed. The club, the first fish and game club established in the Adirondacks, was renamed the Tahawus Club in 1901. That same year, Vice President Theodore Roosevelt, who was hiking up Mount Marcy and staying with his family at the Tahawus Club near the "abandoned village" of Adirondac, received news that President McKinley, victim of an assassin in Buffalo, was dying. From Adirondac, he began his overnight trip to the train station at North Creek, where he learned that McKinley was dead and he had become President.

The former iron mining site at the Lower Works was to be changed by World War II. When the war began, most of our country's titanium – used then, in particular, as a pigment for white paint – came from overseas. Paint supplied to the United States Navy required titanium – which could be produced from the "impurity" which had made the production of iron difficult at the time of the McIntyre mine's operation. In 1940 the federal government had the state bypass the "forever wild" clause of its constitution. Thereafter more than 1,500 workers were sent into the region to build a 30-mile highway, a village for miners, and the entire refining plant. The new Tahawus - village, mine, and refinery – was built in less than a year's time.

High tension lines had to be brought through the mountains to power the operation. Facing the same transportation concerns that plagued the earlier mining effort, the government completed a twenty-nine mile rail link between the refining plant and North Creek in 1944. In 1963 the discovery of a rich vein of ore at Tahawus led to the dismantling of the "town" and its move to Newcomb. An entire mountain of ore was later removed from the site.

A recession and declining demand for domestic titanium began in the 1970s. In 1982 a strike by United States Steel workers in Sayreville, New Jersey, where the ore was being processed, closed the mine. One hundred ten Tahawus workers were laid off. In 1983 the Delaware and Hudson Railroad fell into bankruptcy and shut down rail service. National Lead (NL Industries) purchased the rail line to preserve the value of the property and continued to run loads of previously refined ore out from the site until 1989, when, finally, the company's operations at Tahawus came to an end. Access to the pit mine and buildings was blocked and caretakers patrolled the area.[7]

The Tahawus mining area underwent a major transition in May of 2003 when the Open Space Institute (OSI) reached an agreement to purchase approximately 9,600 acres from NL Industries. NL retained title to the 1627 acres that comprised the site of the former titanium mine. OSI divided the purchased land into seven separate parcels, four sub-divisions. In March 2008 Joe Martens, president of the Open Space Institute, reported that 6,813 acres, the northern tract designated "Forest Preserve," had been sold to the state. That tract includes Mount Adams, Preston Ponds, and Henderson Lake.

Martens also reported that, subject to a conservation easement, 2,979 acres, the southern tract, was sold as "Working Forest" to Finch Pruyn which, in turn, sold it to the Nature Conservancy (which purchased all of Finch Pruyn's holdings in the Adirondack Park). The Nature Conservancy has plans to sell the tract for timber harvesting, but the conservation easement secured by the OSI will be conveyed to the state so that the land may be used by the public. The OSI obtained an additional 2,000 acres of land from Finch Pruyn when it sold the southern tract to the company. Included in that acreage was the east flank of Santanoni Mountain, including the land upon which the old Santanoni trail ascended to that peak's summit. The trail had been closed to the public for more than a quarter century. The OSI plans to convey title to the property to the state but has granted permission for public use of the land and hiker access to the old trail.

Four parcels of land which total 260 acres will be retained by the OSI as "Historic Resource" areas. The structures existing on those parcels will be maintained, including the "Upper Works" (originally McIntyre and later known as Adirondac), the 1854 blast furnace, the summit of Mt. Adams (including its fire tower, which will be rehabilitated), the observer's cabin at the base of Mt. Adams, and the cabin on Upper Preston Pond.

Additionally, the OSI, Martens reports, has completed the stabilization of the MacNaughton Cottage with foundation and roof work and replacement of all decayed structural material and completed the first phase of stabilization work on the 1854 blast furnace. Trees and shrubs growing on the structure were removed, brickwork on the roof has been repaired, and a plexiglass cover has been installed to stop water infiltration. The OSI plans to replace the furnace's mortar and rebuild its four brick archways.

Chuck Vandrie, a historical preservation specialist with the Department of Environmental Conservation, reports that the state museum has surveyed the area around the village of Adirondac and has identified other points of historical significance.

The Masten House, a building which was used by NL Industries as a corporate retreat on 46 acres of land, may soon be leased to the SUNY College of Environmental Science and Foresty for use as a northern forest conservation education and training facility.

The majority of the mine buildings at the Tahawus site have been demolished, but at the time of this publication the NL office and garage remain as does a house near the landing strip on the property. Thus the second great mining era in the heart of the Adirondack wilderness, begun during World War II, has come to a close and much of the area will eventually be reclaimed by nature.

In June of 2007 a second major land transaction concluded with the purchase of 161,000 acres of Finch Pruyn land by the Nature Conservancy for $110 million. More than a third of that land (57,699 acres) is earmarked for sale to the state to be added to the Forest Preserve. Another 73,627 acres will be protected as a working forest with a state-held conservation easement that will require sustainable forestry and provide public access to certain tracts.

The aspect of the transaction which has a major impact on the High Peaks is an additional 1,715 acres which will eventually pass into the Forest Preserve. That parcel includes the hunting clubs which currently control access to Allen Mountain. The announced timetable by the Nature Conservancy provides that the clubs will have exclusive use of the land for the first three years. They will have exclusive use of the land during the next two years only during the hunting and fishing seasons. During the last five years of the transition, the clubs would be required to share the use of the lands with the public, and at the end of the ten-year period the land will become part of the Forest Preserve. All structures existing upon it will then be removed or demolished.

Completion of the Tahawus Tract sale has opened a vast new area for outdoor recreation. Already many have taken canoes into Duck Hole via Henderson Lake and the portage to Preston Ponds. Skiers have raved about the breathtaking views from the middle of those lakes that were previously closed to the public. The relatively short climb of Mt. Adams allows views of the surrounding area from the wooded summit area that would be lost without maintaining the tower. Meanwhile the efforts of the OSI and the DEC have allowed for the preservation and selective stabilization in the village of Adirondac, the McIntyre Furnace, the tower on Mount Adams and the observer's cabin. This is an exciting time for the Santanoni/Tahawus area.

Fortunately a grant arranged by the Adirondack Museum in Blue Mountain Lake allowed Bruce Seely, in the summer of 1978, to research and document the McIntyre Furnace. Seely's research appeared in an article he published in a 1981 issue of the *Journal of the Society for Industrial Archeology*. Included in that piece were diagrams, photos, and explanations of the furnace's workings and history. The furnace, which is located next to the road from Tahawus to the Upper Works (Adirondac), is now listed on the National Register of Historic Places, and thus a portion of the McIntyre mining operation's history has been preserved.

From the summit of Santanoni one may look down at the huge National Lead Company site and see the enormity of the mining operation that took place there. Driving to the Santanoni trailhead, one passes huge piles of waste rock and ore which still dwarf the buildings which remain at the site.

Logging in the Region

Extensive logging took place with the start of mining in the area. The need for charcoal to fuel the furnaces created a huge demand. Hundreds of acres of forest were cleared by the workers as the mining operation grew. Also, as previously mentioned, the Santa Clara Company logged on the Cold River side of the Santanoni Range, and Finch Pruyn worked the Tahawus side of the mountains.

Many of the tote roads and skidways built by and for loggers became trails or access routes to the mountains of the area. In his book, *Friendly Adirondack Peaks*, Robert Wickham advised potential hikers to be cautious when following those "snake paths." They often led unwary trampers astray. Lumbermen would venture away from established skidways to find prime trees to be cut. Once felled, the trees were cut into 14-foot lengths with the contractor's mark placed on the end and a metal spike driven into each log. Horses would then hook onto the spike and "snake" the logs to the nearest skidway. Hikers using a skidway as a path would often stray onto a "snake path" which would suddenly dead end and leave them, potentially, lost and confused. Most, however, found their way to the summits of Santanoni, Panther, and Couchsachraga – the three high peaks of the fabled Santanoni Range.

Endnotes

1. Jim "Beetle" Bailey served as president of the Forty-Sixers from 1966 to 1969.

2. Adirondack Mountain Club, *Guide to Adirondack Trails – High Peak Region and Northville-Placid Trail, Seventh Edition,* (Gabriels, New York: Adirondack Mountain Club, 1962), pg. B5-18.

3. Verplanck Colvin, *Report on the Topographical Survey of the Adirondack Wilderness of New York, For the Year 1873,* (Albany: Weed, Parsons and Company, Printers, 1874), pgs. 279-280.

4. Reports concerning the discovery of Gilroy/Wiggins' body and camera did not reveal whether or not any film that the camera might have contained was salvageable.

5. Mount Henderson was named for David Henderson, an administrator of the McIntyre Iron Works in the mid-1800s, whose fame was assured by his tragic death on the shore of Calamity Pond in 1845.

6. The other peak which cannot be seen from Marcy is East Dix.

7. The author remembers taking his sons to the viewing area by the edge of the pit in the early 1980s. Over 300 feet down, the trucks on the floor looked like Tonka toys. Samples of the magnetite were in a box for visitors to take. Now the pit has completely filled with water and become a large, deep pond.

About the Author

Phil Corell was born in New York City and raised in Mt. Kisco, New York. His introduction to the Adirondack high peaks began in 1956, when, as a ten-year-old, he first attended Camp Pok-O-Moonshine in Willsboro. Phil completed his first round of the 46 in the summer of 1962 and continued his involvement with the Pok-O-MacCready Camps for the next fifty years. His winter hiking began in high school when he traveled to the Adirondacks over vacations to climb with former camp counselor and 46er President Jim Bailey.

Despite wrestling at Franklin and Marshall College, Phil found time during vacations to continue his winter climbs. He completed his first winter round in 1985 and has continued to actively climb. After graduation he began his thirty-three year career at Saranac Central School, initially as an elementary teacher. He retired in 2001 as Pupil Personnel Director and Director of Special Education.

His wife of 35 years, Mary, and both his sons, Jay and Mark, are also 46ers. The boys finished their first rounds in 1987 at the ages of 9 and 11. Both are multi-round 46ers, and Mark finished his Winter 46 while in college. While the boys were growing up, Phil was active in coaching and officiating wrestling, working with Scouting, and teaching Wilderness Recreation courses at Plattsburgh State University.

Phil served four terms as 46er president, thirty-five years on the staff of the Outdoor Leadership Workshop, and is currently the club's treasurer. His most gratifying memories during the past fifty plus years of climbing are the family and friends with whom he has shared his experiences in the mountains.

The Seward Range
By John Sharp Swan, Jr. (#566W)

The Seward Range rises above one of the most remote and beautiful areas in the High Peaks. In 1840, University of Vermont Professor Farrand N. Benedict wrote, "During the whole distance down Long Lake, Mount Seward is the most conspicuous object in view. It is not, however, an insulated peak, but a cluster of mountains which, as a whole, present a very imposing appearance." The most elevated peak of the cluster, Mount Seward, though only 4,331 feet in elevation, stands out in particular; however, for years, its prominence as seen from Long Lake and Tupper Lake belied its lesser elevation. In 1837 Professor Ebenezer Emmons estimated the height of Seward to be 5,100 feet. It was not until 1870, when Verplanck Colvin climbed Seward with his guide Alvah Dunning, that its actual height was determined to be considerably less than 5,000 feet.[1]

Hemmed by four major rivers – the Ampersand, Raquette, Cold, and Moose – the Seward Range has remained relatively secluded – wild and remote – for most of its existence, easy access to it blocked by Ampersand Mountain and the Sawtooth and Santanoni ranges. Nonetheless, for almost two centuries, places such as Ampersand Lake, Ouluska Pass, Duck Hole, and Follensby Pond have lured people to the region over which the mountains of the range tower. Beautiful waterfalls, balanced boulders the size of small houses, and hidden canyons waiting to be explored lie below the peaks. The Sewards are also a range steeped in history.

When the Civil War came to America, political rivals William H. Seward and Horatio Seymour chose different paths as they attempted to bring the rebellious southern states back into the Union. Today the Adirondack peaks named for them are separated by the wild Ouluska Pass.

For twenty years Ebenezer Emmons was at odds with other geologists – including two who had been with him on the first ascent of Mount Marcy – concerning theories he developed following his discovery of a fossil. One of his detractors enjoyed camping in the shadow of the mountain that would eventually be named Mount Emmons.

Enfeebled and suffering from tuberculosis, Alfred L. Donaldson went to the village of Saranac Lake to die, but, "taking the cure" there, he survived another 28 years and lived long enough to write what many scholars regard as the definitive history of the Adirondacks. Mount Donaldson, of course, is named for him.

The Sewards are also a mountain range which has witnessed drastic change. Although it has been 80 years since the last timber was cut and sledded off the mountains, the woods are still decades, if not centuries, from recovering from logging by the Santa Clara Lumber Company. The men who originally hunted and fished in the region once marveled at the beauty of the tall trees and open woods surrounding the Seward Range. That forest has disappeared, but travelers who were willing to expend the effort to reach the region before the Civil War saw those woods in their primitive state.

The Philosophers Camp

Ten members of the Saturday Night Club who were guided down the beautiful Raquette River along the western edge of the Seward Range in 1858 were among the few who saw the area of the Seward Range in its purest state. William Stillman, an artist in the group, wrote that the Raquette "was a deep mysterious stream meandering through unbroken forest, walled up on either side in green shade, the trees of centuries leaning over to welcome and shelter the voyager."[2]

During the month of August, the ten men camped at Follensby Pond[3] in the shadow of Mount Emmons. At the pond, they swam and fished and hunted, and they explored the region which few other men had seen. Towering pines, some rising more than 200 feet, dominated the forest near the pond. Large native trout were one easy fly-cast away, and there was plenty of game to hunt.[4]

The ten men – no ordinary tourists – had come to the Adirondacks to get away from the stresses of urban life and the tensions of the time. Some of the most celebrated intellectuals of their day, the group included, in addition to Stillman, the poet and essayist Ralph Waldo Emerson and poet James Russell Lowell. Henry Wadsworth Longfellow, America's preeminent poet, had been invited to accompany the others, but he demurred. He reportedly asked, "Is it true that Emerson is going to take a gun?" and concluded, "Then somebody will get shot." Beautiful old growth maples which shaded the campsite inspired the intellectuals to call it Camp Maple, but their guides quickly renamed it the "Philosophers Camp."[5]

During their journey to the camp, the Philosophers, when they arrived there, had been greeted by the excited citizens of the village of Keeseville. At first the luminaries were impressed and thrilled that so many "country backwoodsmen" had come out to see them. Leading the local people was a man who, holding a portrait of Louis Agassiz, compared its image to the visages of the members of the group. When Agassiz was at last recognized, the man pointed and said, "Yes, it's him," and with that the whole town quickly gathered around the Swiss-born Harvard professor – the most renowned scientist of his day. Stillman noted, with wry humor, that the people of Keeseville had come out to see "Agassiz and his friends."[6]

Although many people knew Louis Agassiz as a naturalist, as a geologist he was considered revolutionary. In 1840, he had published a study on glaciers, *Étude sur les Glaciérs,* which contained theories that shook the geological world and put him at odds with other geologists, including Ebenezer Emmons, who believed that the planet's geological formations could be explained by a great flood such as the one described in the Bible. Emmons and Agassiz would eventually become embroiled in a public dispute that would leave the geological community bitter and divided. It becomes ironic, therefore, that Ebenezer Emmons' name would be applied to a mountain in a region that Agassiz found fascinating.[7]

The Philosophers enjoyed their stay at Follensby Pond so much that they agreed to return the following year and decided to spend $600 for 22,500 acres around Ampersand Pond, at the base of Seward Mountain. Stillman, who visited that pond for the first time in 1859, wrote, "It was certainly the most beautiful site I have ever seen in the Adirondack country. Virgin Forest... the tall pines standing in their ranks along the shores of a little lake that lay in the middle of the estate, encircled by mountains, except on one side where the lake found its outlet and the mountains were clothed to their summits in primeval woods." It was there that the Philosophers built a club house, but their pleasures at Ampersand came to an end just two years later, when the Civil War broke out. Two of the original company died during the war and, for the remaining members of the group, the forest site lost much of its allure. Within a few years the club house began to decay and, thereafter, the site was allowed to return to its original wooded state.[8]

The primeval forest that the Philosophers had stood in awe of before the Civil War came under attack by the 1870s. Twenty-five years after Stillman and the rest of the Boston philosophers had created Camp Maple, the painter, led by his original guide, Steve Martin, returned to the site. He hardly recognized it. All of the timber had been cut, a forest fire started by a nearby lumber camp had blackened the woods, and the trout had been replaced in the pond by an alien species: Northern Pike.[9]

At first the cutting of timber – mostly of giant pines and spruces – took place only on the perimeter of the Seward Range, along the Raquette. Gradually, however, the lumbermen moved closer to the mountains. In recent years several logging research enthusiasts have discovered a few of the towering pines that the Philosophers, especially Emerson, wrote about. Most had been blown over or were standing dead. The girth of those giants was so great that it took two members of the research group, reaching around the bases of the trees, to be able to touch each other's hands. Two pines, which the logging research group named the "Sentinels," stood watch over the entrance to the Boulder Brook area. When the researchers last saw them, though, they each had been sheared off at about thirty feet above the ground. At the time of logging operations, due to their height and the denuded area around them, the "Sentinels" must have been visible for miles up and down the valley.

In addition, while ambling in woods the researchers discovered a stack of cut, old-growth pine trees rotting away where they were piled after the Big Blow of 1950. The stack had survived for decades because of the sheer size of the logs. To the lumberjacks of the 1950s who came by them, the enormous trees were too tempting to pass. It was only after they were cut down and stacked that the loggers realized that the logs were too big to transport. There they rest, gradually returning to the earth, a memorial to a time when the Philosophers fished, hunted and wandered within an unspoiled wilderness.

Santa Clara Lumber Company

Carved out of the wilderness, the village of Tupper Lake was home to only 17 families in 1889, but the logging industry made it a boom town in 1890. Work and money and a railroad that was pushed to the middle of nowhere made Tupper Lake the third most populated town in Franklin County. A Potsdam surveyor described the hectic scene of April 1890: "The people there have all gone crazy. They seem to think that they are going to have a city immediately... all the surrounding woodland is all surveyed and laid out into streets and lots."[10]

Nearby, in 1889, the Santa Clara Lumber Company had purchased 39,000 acres in the southeastern corner of Franklin County for $4.50 an acre, the going rate for land with old-growth forest on it. In the center of that property was Ampersand Pond and the forest which Stillman had described – "clothed to the summits with primeval forest" – the forest in which the Philosophers had camped. The lumber company sold the property to New York State almost thirty-five years later for $19 an acre *after* it had been almost completely stripped of its timber to the very tops of the "summits."[11]

Not even the remoteness and high broken ground around the Seward Range could protect the forest. Although Santa Clara was one of the first lumber companies in America to reforest its lands with thousands of saplings, it was also incredibly proficient in harvesting the timber on the land. With innovative techniques, the company logged some of the roughest, rockiest and most remote terrain in the Adirondacks. Throughout the period of its operations in the area, the Santa Clara Lumber Company used mechanical advantage to take timber off of the Seward Range.

Some of the innovations included a steam engine that pulled horses up the slopes on a sled to the loading areas and a large, heavy braking spool used to lower heavy log sleds down the mountains.¹² When that brake failed, killing two horses in Ouluska Pass, the company's men modified another, more mobile device called the Barienger Brake. That machine increased the safety as well as efficiency of the sleds plying the steep terrain.¹³

During its reign in the Seward Range the Santa Clara Lumber Company controlled the flow of the major rivers and cut large spruce trees as high up as 3,800 feet on slopes as steep as 45 degrees. It built hundreds of miles of roads and some incredibly elaborate bridges – some hundreds of feet long – all to get their timber to market. It even set a world record at its mill in Tupper Lake for the number of logs sawed in a single day. The Santa Clara company brought off millions of board feet of timber from their land.

The president and owner of the Santa Clara Lumber Company, Ferris J. Meigs was the first from his company to explore the newly purchased land in 1889. He wrote about it as follows:

> No white man, except Gene Bruce [*one of Ferris Meigs' logging superintendents*], as far as anyone knew, had ever traversed that unbroken virgin forest between Ampersand and Preston Ponds. Bruce had gone through a year or so before. And what a forest it was, so largely comprised of spruce, that the other species were rare by comparison. The soft humus, the moss, the blackness, relieved and intensified by the occasional shaft of sunlight, the brilliant water of the streams, rushing over the rocks and pebbles in virgin purity; the sweet, pungent fragrance of the conifers, all made for a great satisfaction. It was a wonderful trip.

The Philosophers would not have appreciated that Ferris Meigs, who was awed by the beauty of the area, added, "some of these acres yielded 66 cord per acre."¹⁴

Though Meigs was the president of the company, the man who ran the woods operation was Fred LeBoeuf. Born in 1865, a French Canadian, LeBoeuf took to the forest at an early age after performing poorly in school. He had a great memory for details and numbers, but he found it almost impossible to read or write, a fact that he desperately tried to hide his whole life. In the woods and away from books LeBoeuf thrived, rising through the ranks from the lowest position in the lumber camps as chore boy, to skid chief, to lumber camp supervisor, and, finally, to woods supervisor. Meigs wrote that LeBoeuf "became the foundation rock of the company." He was "honest, loyal, hard working... a remarkable handler of men, he was capable and fearless in every emergency." As a self-taught engineer, LeBoeuf "could lay out the tote and logging roads in that rocky, mountainous, heavy wooded terrain with the greatest accuracy and skill, judging levels, direction and location with uncanny ability." It was not until generations later – long after Fred LeBoeuf died in 1935 – that some of his family members understood why he could neither read nor write: some of them were diagnosed with dyslexia.¹⁵

While Meigs and LeBoeuf were the chief administrators of the Santa Clara Lumber Company, the real back bones of the company were the lumberjacks. In a time before heavy machinery, everything had to be bulled by men with horses and hand tools such as peaveys. Dynamite was the only aid they had to clear new roads of stumps and rocks as well as the log jams on the river drives. The lumberjacks, mostly French Canadians, labored long hours in the woods, doing all of the back-breaking work to cut down the trees in the late summer and fall. They worked in the freezing temperatures, deep snows and high altitudes loading up the sleds to get the timber down to the banking grounds by the rivers that were sometimes more than five miles away. The river drivers, who performed the most dangerous job of logging, then conducted the timber down the cold, swollen rivers to the sawmills in the spring. The process, from cutting the trees to getting the timber to the mills in Tupper Lake, including the time it took to make the roads and build the lumber camps, required more than a year.

Each five-man lumberjack crew worked to cut and skid the logs a couple of hundred yards to loading ramps near the sled roads. When the company started taking down timber they used a revolutionary cutting device: the two-man saw, a piece of equipment that did as much to change the lumber industry as the chain saw would decades later. Before the early 1890s, a lumberjack chopping down a tree and cutting it into uniquely Adirondack 13-foot lengths, averaged 70 trees a day. With the introduction of the two-man saw, production increased to 160 trees a day for each two-man team.[16] A lumberjack was paid about $2 a day for his work; the precise amount depended upon the number of logs stacked on the loading ramps. However, each lumberjack had to pay a dollar back to the company for room and board.[17]

Though the Philosophers made note of the towering pines of the area, pine trees actually made up a very small percentage of the forest. What Santa Clara wanted most were the tall, straight, old-growth spruce trees. Some spruce stumps that logging researchers have found are more than three feet in diameter. Even at the higher altitudes, above 3,000 feet, where the heights of the trees were greatly diminished due to their environment, it was not uncommon to find stumps as well as live spruce trees over two feet in diameter.

Peppered throughout the region, about a mile apart and in close proximity to the timber that was being cut, were the Santa Clara lumber camps. In Township 27 alone, in which the Seward Range lies, there were at least 30 camps; however, usually, only a couple of lumber camps operated at a time. At the peak of its operations, though, while it logged along the Cold River, Santa Clara had a small army of men living in eight camps. They were usually constructed with what the lumber jacks considered worthless timber – cedar or hardwoods – and built to last only a couple of seasons. Able to house up to 50 men and a dozen horses, the camps were usually lice-infested, but the infestations were somewhat controlled by spraying the bunks with kerosene. If logs were on site, a camp could be built in 15 days by a good ten-man crew. Most of the materials used to build the cabins was found in the forest. The only sawn wood that needed to be transported into the interior was for the roof sheathing and the floor boards. A thin layer of tarpaper secured to the roof with nails was employed to keep the buildings dry. Incredibly, each camp had its own telephone, enabling it to communicate with the outside world. The provisions, approximately 1,200 pounds of supplies each day, were transported to the camps by sleds or tote wagons that cut deep ruts into the soil. The ruts can still be found meandering through the woods.[18]

Santa Clara's headquarters during the years they logged along the Raquette River was at Axton Landing. Originally known as Axetown, that headquarters was abandoned when the timber in the area ran out. Thereafter, Santa Clara moved the headquarters deep into the interior, to a site which still bears the name of the head camp, Number Four. That camp, just eight tenths of a mile from the present Ward Brook Lean-to, boasted twelve buildings and was the main transfer point for goods coming in from the main office at Tupper Lake. For more than fifteen years Number Four was a bustling community from which men, horses, and supplies moved in and out of the Seward Range.

At Number Four in April 1914, a man died in the men's building when, in a drunken brawl, he hit his head on the edge of a bed. Woods Supervisor Fred LeBoeuf, who absolutely forbid possession or consumption of alcohol in any of the Santa Clara camps, must have been mortified when he heard the news. However, if the large number of whiskey bottles that logging researchers have found is any indication, the lumberjacks drank plenty of alcohol.[19]

By 1925, the last logs had been pulled off the west side of Seward and Donaldson and the few remaining lumberjacks left to cut timber in other dwindling old growth forests. In their wake, the loggers left behind hundreds of miles of roads, lumber camps in various stages of decay, and lumberjack paraphernalia everywhere, most of which was considered worthless at the time.

Today one can still gain a glimpse into the life of the men who worked in the woods of the Seward Range eighty-five years ago. A hiker might find galvanized buckets, barrel hoops, or dozens of broken and splintered Barienger brake wheels. The forest is reclaiming now what was hers in the large field that once surrounded Santa Clara's headquarters at Number Four. The sounds and smells of the once-vibrant community are gone. The rectangular mounds that indicate where buildings once stood, in a few years, will disappear. Soon only historians and a few astute hikers will be the only ones who will know that the site was once that of a thriving lumberjack community.

There is one other clue that the hiker might discern. Sometime after the last lumberjack left Number Four, Frank Eldred, the former chief clerk at that camp, went back there with his wife and planted some Scotch Pines in the clearing that surrounded the camp. The non-native species is easy to distinguish from the indigenous trees because of the red color of its bark, which appears to be continually shedding. If you are ever passing by the two lean-tos at Number Four on the way to Duck Hole and you find yourself looking at the strange out-of-place trees, think of Frank Eldred, Fred LeBoeuf, Ferris J. Meigs, and the many sturdy lumberjacks of the Santa Clara Lumber Company. As long as the trees live, they will remind us of the brief time that the company thrived in the woods around the Sewards.[20]

Noah John Rondeau

Noah John Rondeau presenting a bouquet of flowers to Mary Dittmar with Ditt Dittmar at her side. The photo was taken (time release) in the early 1940s by Ditt.

As soon as the Santa Clara Lumber Company discontinued its operations in the Seward Range, a middle-aged man looking for a way to avoid the problems of civilization stepped into the void. On a bluff overlooking the Cold River, the barber-turned-hermit, Noah John Rondeau, set up his own small village in a perfect spot. Not only were there building materials on site from the abandoned lumbercamp, but there was also a dam, appropriately called the

Mary Dittmar with Noah on a trout fishing expedition

"Big Dam," over which Rondeau could easily cross the river in winter or when the river was running high. There was another advantage: the site was on private land surrounded by property owned by New York State. At the time, fortunately for Rondeau, the Santa Clara Lumber Company was involved in a boundary dispute with the state, and that dispute was not settled until after the lumber company had already sold the majority of its land holdings to the state. When the courts ruled in favor of Santa Clara, the company found itself still in possession of a slice of land half a mile wide and approximately nine miles long. That parcel would not be added to the state's holdings until the 1950s. It was on that property that Rondeau set up his hermitage. Had not Santa Clara owned the land, Rondeau would not have been able to construct his tiny village, and he would not have been later "discovered" there by 46ers who were on their way to climb Couchsachraga. The stories of the "discoverers" – including 46er Historian Grace Hudowalski and 46er Treasurer Adolph "Ditt" Dittmar – are too numerous to recount here fully, but they have been preserved.[21]

Life for Noah John Rondeau in the woods was not always as free and easy as it appeared to be to the hikers who visited him in the summer. Most of the impressions we have of the hermit were recorded when the trout were plentiful, his snow pea and vegetable garden was overflowing, and he had been genuinely happy to entertain guests. Being a hermit seventeen miles from Corey's was a full-time occupation. There was always firewood to be cut, trap lines to run on both sides of the Cold River, and a larder to be stocked. (Noah John had several run-ins with officers of the state Conservation Department as they attempted to prove that he took deer out of season.) When deep snows made walking difficult and his cupboards were almost bare, Rondeau often had to eat the same thing day after day. Life as a hermit was difficult and demanding..

The Big Blow of November 25, 1950, knocked down thousands of trees in the area near where Noah had taken up his residency. Because of the fire hazard associated with so many downed trees, the Conservation Department closed the region for five years. Noah John, not allowed to reside at his village, thereafter lived with his sister in Au Sable Forks and later moved to Wilmington, New York. There he built a replica of his Cold River hermitage and,

**Mary Dittmar, Ruth Prince King, in back, and Helen Menz
with Noah John Rondeau on Couchsachraga in 1942**

until his death in 1967, eked out a meager living by playing the part of the hermit he had actually been.

In the late 1940s Noah had his "fifteen minutes of fame." A celebrity of sorts, he visited sportsmen shows and was interviewed on the radio. Everyone it seemed wanted to see the "Hermit of the Cold River," and for a short time his appearance brought him a small amount of money, more than he had ever had his entire life. After his fame waned, Noah clung to his hermit image, signing autographs, "Noah John Rondeau, Adirondack Hermit." He could be seen out in front of a gas station in Au Sable Forks posing for pictures next to a large kettle which hung from a tripod, mimicking the one at his hermitage. Under it was a sign: "Hermit Fund." He had received donations in his kettle previously at sportsman shows.[22]

While he was camping at Indian Falls in September 1951, Chris Fearon met the hermit, who had been engaged to guide a client up the Upper Range. Fearon heard Rondeau's high squeaky voice before he saw the barely five-foot tall bearded man. "Hard times! Oh these are hard times," Noah said, referring to a drizzle that was soaking the area. It was a phrase that he liked to use whenever he knew other people found a situation uncomfortable. He sported new Bean boots, a leather jacket, and a packbasket, acquisitions made possible by the modest windfall which had come to him after being invited to the sportsmen shows. The hermit and his client camped next to Fearon that night.[23]

In subsequent years Fearon went to visit Rondeau at his sister's home in Au Sable Forks. After a "chaw" about the government, the sportsmen shows, and the possibility of publishing the hermit's diary, Fearon invited Noah John to eat at one of the local restaurants, a place that the old hermit liked to go to for lunch. There, Noah John insisted that they sit at a particular table near one of the two large picture windows in the front of the restaurant. He overruled Fearon's table choice, explaining, "That would spoil the show." Fearon, who did not know what Rondeau meant, sat down with his back to the window. Later, he did not remember what he ordered, but he certainly recalled what Noah John had: an open faced roast beef sandwich covered with hot steamy gravy. When the sandwich arrived, Noah John pushed his eating utensils aside, picked up a handful of meat, and brought it to his mouth. "The gravy smeared over his hands and collected on his beard," Fearon said, and he asked why Noah did not use his fork and knife. "That would spoil the show," Noah John replied. Fearon continued to ask questions about the hermit's life while Noah John ate, and the hermit responded with gestures while covering his chin, beard, and the table with gravy and meat. At the end of the meal, Noah John said, "Well, it has been another successful show! I can't let my public down, now can I? Turn around and just look." There, behind Fearon, was a crowd of kids, some of them pressing their noses against the glass, clapping and smiling at the "show" that the "Hermit of Cold River" had put on. Noah John stood up and modestly bowed to his fans. "I try to come down every day," Rondeau said, "and they always gather around to watch the wild man from the woods eat. Of course, I eat with a knife and fork when I am home with my sister. This hermit show is for my public."[24]

Fearon walked Noah back to his sister's home, and there, by his car, he took a photograph of Noah – a picture that he still has in his scrapbook. Noah signed two postcards, "Noah John Rondeau; Adirondack Hermit" and gave them to him.[25]

Today Rondeau's former hermitage is somewhat a mecca to people who travel to the Cold River region or hike the Northville-Placid Trail. Over the years the site has diminished. The one remaining building has almost completely rotted into the ground. Even though Noah John's ashes were supposed to be cast around his hermitage, and he was buried in Lake Placid instead, his hermitage remains a revered place. In May 2000, on a tree on the bluff where Noah John Rondeau once held sway over Cold River City, two hikers bolted a plaque inscribed with a tribute: *Noah John Rondeau, Adirondack Hermit; The Last of the Last*. They did so of their own volition, without the consent of the Department of Environmental Conservation. Noah John, who was a "creative writer" and knew something about defying authority would have approved the installation of the plaque.

MOUNT SEWARD
Height: 26th – 1,320c meters (4,331+ feet)

When the Republican Convention convened in Chicago in 1860, party members throughout the nation expected New York Senator William H. Seward to carry the nomination for President. Horace Greeley, abolitionist and editor of the *New York Tribune*, telegraphed his office, "The conviction is that the opposition to Governor Seward cannot be concentrated on any other candidate and that he will be nominated." Seward had been the spokesman and front man of the Republicans since the party's inception in 1854, and he had been patiently awaiting the nomination, but it was not to come. In one of the greatest upsets in the history of American politics, from behind the scenes, another man snatched the nomination just when it was within Seward's grasp. With the country at the brink of civil war, that man, who historians continually rank as our greatest president, was Abraham Lincoln.[26]

Of Welsh and Irish descent, William Henry Seward was born on May 16, 1801, in Florida, New York, near the Pennsylvania and New Jersey border. Known to his family members as Henry, the red-headed Seward was raised by a domineering father, Samuel Sweeney Seward (1768-1849). A doctor, Samuel was also a merchant and owned a fleet of sloops that plied the Hudson between Newburgh and ports south. Believing that it would prepare him for the real world, he criticized and pushed his son relentlessly.[27]

William Henry Seward

Henry entered Union College at the age of fifteen, but after his father refused to pay what he thought were frivolous expenses, such as a tailor bill, at eighteen years of age, the younger Seward rebelled, dropped out of college, and accepted a teaching job in Georgia. When his father learned that his son had moved to the Deep South, six months later he had him brought back to New York and school. William Henry Seward graduated from college in 1820.[28]

In an era that did not necessitate going to law school to become a lawyer, Seward passed the bar in 1822 and became a partner of Elijah Miller in Auburn, New York. Confident "that he would be back all too soon," his father gave him fifty dollars so that he could move there, but William Henry never returned. He considered Auburn his home for the rest of his life.[29]

Whether by design by his partner or simply true love, Seward married Frances Miller, the daughter of his associate on October 20, 1824. Together they had five children of their own and raised a nephew who had been orphaned in early childhood.[30]

Though his father had been a judge and served in the state assembly, when Seward showed interest in taking up politics, Samuel, fearing that public service would interfere with Henry's practice, advised him against entering the field. Eventually, however, the elder Seward was very proud of his fourth child and came to see eye-to-eye with him on politics. He lived long enough to see his son become Governor of New York and a United States Senator.[31]

In the late 1820s, thanks in part to the mysterious murder of the author of a book revealing the secrets of the Masonic Order, there was a backlash in newspapers and a protest movement by poor farmers of western New York against that "aristocratic" fraternity. Some of the most powerful and famous men in American politics – George Washington, Thomas Jefferson, Andrew Jackson, and New York's Governor DeWitt Clinton – were members of the fraternity. When citizens learned of a cover-up of the crime by sheriffs and judges who happened to be Masons, they burned some of their lodges and created a political party solely dedicated to the overthrow of the fraternity.[32]

Seward, who throughout his life championed justice and the underprivileged, took up the Anti-Mason platform. Although, like many other political organizations of that era, the Anti-Masonic party was short-lived, during his association with the party, Seward met one of its chief spokesmen, the young editor of the Albany *Evening Journal*, Thurlow Weed. Leader of the opposition to the Democratic Party, Weed was a great political strategist. Though he never attained high office, he wielded considerable political influence, first in New York and, later, in the nation, and he championed Seward. The two became so closely allied that Seward once said, "Seward is Weed and Weed is Seward. What I do Weed approves. What he says, I endorse. We are one."[33]

An eloquent speaker and writer, Seward won election to the state Senate on the Anti-Masonic ticket in 1830. He was one of the youngest state senators, but as the influence of the party began to wane, he lost his reelection bid four years later, and though he had looked forward to returning to his law practice and his family, he found himself thrust back onto the political stage by Weed, who engineered his nomination for Governor by the newly organized Whig Party. Running against the formidable Democratic party and their nominee Governor William L. Marcy, he lost the 1834 election by more than 10,000 votes.[34]

The men who made up New York's political machine in the antebellum period were among the most prominent in America. With a population which exceeded that of any other state by more than a million, New York was the most powerful state in the country. She ranked first in terms of industrial output and New York City served as the nation's financial center. The governors and senators of New York helped lead the nation: men like Seward, William Learned Marcy, Horatio Seymour, Silas Wright, and John A. Dix. Seward was to become one of the most powerful of all.

After he lost his gubernatorial bid to Marcy in 1834, Seward returned to his law practice, establishing himself as a competent lawyer and achieving a modest degree of wealth. Following the Panic of 1837, one of the worst depressions in the eighteenth century, the Democratic Party fell into disfavor and Seward was again nominated for Governor to run against the three-term incumbent Marcy. "A perfect tornado" swept him (with a plurality of more than 10,000 votes) and his fellow Whigs into office in 1838. The Whigs won 101 of the 128 state assembly seats.[35]

Seward was ushered into the capital at Albany by a one hundred cannon salute and for two terms fought for several issues that would make his running for a third term untenable. Believing that internal improvements were of primary importance, Seward saw canals, turnpikes, and the newly invented railroad as ways to augment the wealth of the state and speed communications between New York's communities. He encouraged and promoted the surveys of the state, including, of course, the one which was exploring the Adirondacks in hopes of finding resources ready to exploit. The Erie Canal and its subsidiary branches usually brought millions of dollars to the state coffers, but because of the depression, when Seward was in office, state debt climbed from $16 million in 1838 to $27 million in 1842.[36]

By 1842, with the state debt mounting and his opposition growing, Seward, knowing that he could not win a third term, decided to return to private life. For the next six years he labored to replenish his law firm's bank accounts. He worked as a patent lawyer and argued some very public cases involving the issue of slavery. He also was an advocate for rights for Irish immigrants.[37]

By 1848 Seward was at the forefront of the slavery debate. He jumped back into the political ring and was elected to the United States Senate in 1848 and won reelection in 1854. In the Senate, he opposed the expansion of slavery into the new territories, and the nation listened in 1850 as he aligned himself with the Abolitionists. Speaking of a "higher law," beyond the reach of the Constitution, he said that God would not allow slavery to exist. In 1859 he predicted in his famous "irrepressible conflict" speech that the nation would either have to choose between free or slave labor. By that time he was the nation's most widely recognized anti-slavery politician.[38]

The sectional conflict between the North and the South gave birth to the Republican Party in 1854 when anti-slavery factions of the Democratic and Whig parties combined with other splinter groups. In a well timed and executed abandonment, Weed and Seward broke from the Whig Party and immediately assumed leadership of the new party. In 1856, when the Republicans were poised to nominate their first national candidate, Seward hoped that he would be that person, but Weed realized that the timing was wrong: that a first candidate of the fledgling party could not win election. He told Seward to be patient, that he would be nominated the next time, 1860. John C. Frémont, the first Republican candidate, was easily defeated. Four years later Seward was ready to be his party's candidate.[39]

HEAVEN UP-H'ISTED-NESS!

Hundreds of electors from every state in the troubled Union descended on Chicago in May of 1860 for the Republican National Convention. Unlike the other national parties, which spanned all corners of the United States, the Republicans were an entirely northern party, one with a very vocal minority, the abolitionists, making up part of their membership. That alarmed many Southerners. However, in reality, most Republicans only wanted to stop the spread of slavery – to reserve the territories for free labor – not to affect slavery where it existed already. Part of the perception problem for the Republicans rested with Seward. Weed had tried to turn the Senator's speeches away from the abolitionist point of view, but that strategy came late, just months before the convention. The South was so nervous about Seward and his message that a price was put on his head.[40]

Unbeknownst to Seward, forces were lining up against him at the convention. Oddly, the abolitionist editor of the *New York Tribune*, Horace Greeley, was among a group of men with political clout who worked to prevent his nomination. Weed had offended those men in previous elections when he pushed their nominees aside to put forth his own candidates. Furthermore, Seward's radical stance proved to be an insurmountable hurdle for some delegates, particularly from the western and central states, and Seward's support of the Irish over the years hurt him in key states such as Pennsylvania and Indiana, where the anti-Catholic and anti-foreigner party, the No-Nothings, were strong.[41] Eventually a clamor arose within the convention: "Any one other than Seward."[42]

From behind the scenes came the dark horse, Abraham Lincoln. On the third ballot he won the nomination and, while Greeley smiled, Weed buried his hands in his face, tears running down his cheeks. New Yorkers were incensed and the local Adirondack newspaper the *Elizabethtown Post* reported that "the nomination [of Lincoln] is a gross insult to the great republican party" and "never had a candidate been forward with so little claim."[43]

Disappointed, Seward nonetheless attempted to hide his dissatisfaction. During the fall, putting on a brave face, he made an extensive tour of the states of the Northwest and campaigned for Lincoln. Every once in a while, however, he let his guard down and his disappointment showed through. One time he quipped to a Georgian, "Somebody from Virginia offered $20,000 reward for my head, to be given to the south, but the Republican Convention at Chicago gave it over to you without compensation." Another time when someone spoke to Seward about being overlooked for a position, he said, "Disappointment! You speak of disappointment. To me, who was justly entitled to the Republican nomination for the presidency, and who had to stand aside and see it given to a little Illinois lawyer. You speak to me of disappointment!"[44]

Lincoln only received 40 percent of the popular vote, but because there were four parties contending in the election and the Democratic Party had split over the slavery issue, the Republicans won. The South saw the Republican election as the final straw. Although Lincoln reiterated many times, especially in his inaugural address, that he had no intention of abolishing slavery where it existed, it did not seem to matter. He warned the South that "No state, upon its own mere action, can lawfully get out of the Union" and he advised the slave states: "In your hands and not in mine is the momentous issue of civil war." The South, however, had made up its mind, and South Carolina seceded from the Union on December 20, 1860, ten other states thereafter withdrew, and the Civil War began.[45]

Because Seward had worked hard for Lincoln during the election campaign, he was rewarded with the prestigious position of Secretary of State in the new administration. He arrived to take up his cabinet post in Washington, D.C. with his habitual black cigar. His once fiery red hair had turned gray and it now looked "rusty," but as Secretary of State he would reach the apex of his career.[46]

Seward, it was assumed, would be the real president. Lincoln had served only briefly as a representative in the late 1840s and, even though he was considered a brilliant debater, he had no practical knowledge about running a government. Nonetheless, he proved to be a strong leader – one with vision, intuition and drive. In the beginning the relationship between the two men was a cool one. Eventually, however, after he exerted his leadership, the President befriended Seward and continually went to him, seeking council and editorial input for such important documents as the Emancipation Proclamation and the Gettysburg Address. By 1863 Seward was able to tell diarist George Templeton Strong that Lincoln was "the best and wisest man" he had ever known.[47]

Washington, at that time, was the most fortified city in the world. It was encircled by twenty miles of impenetrable intersecting trenches and sixty heavily armed forts. Seward, who usually ended his day at the State Department at four in the afternoon, would occasionally ask Lincoln to accompany him on carriage rides to visit some of the outlying forts. The two men seemed to enjoy each other's company, but they must have been an interesting couple to see as they road through the streets of the capital: Lincoln was a foot taller than Seward and with the added height of his stove pipe hat, he must have appeared disproportionately taller than the Secretary of State. In the evenings, Lincoln would visit the Secretary at his home, and there the two men "would talk for hours, Seward leaning back on his easy chair, smoking his cigar, and Lincoln resting his long legs on the fireplace fender."[48]

The greatest of Seward's war objectives was to keep the southern states isolated and prevent other countries, particularly France and England, from recognizing the Confederacy. Such recognition might have been fatal to the Union cause. During the Revolutionary War, France's recognition of the young United States had spelled the end of British rule in the colonies. The Confederacy hoped that a similar end might come in their war against the North. Recognition by either France or England would bring international legitimacy to the Confederacy, boost morale, and enable the South to negotiate military and commercial treaties while encouraging foreign investment. Then the blockade around the southern states by the United States Navy could be raised and allow a flood of arms and munitions to enter the South while the warehouses stocked with cotton could open their doors and pour that commodity back to Europe.[49]

As Secretary of State, Seward's greatest challenge came at the beginning of the war. In November of 1861, Union Captain Charles Wilkes fired two warning shots across the bow of the unarmed British mail packet, *Trent*. He then boarded the craft and took off two Confederate commissioners bound for Europe. To a nation starved for good news after the Union defeats at Bull Run and Balls Bluff, Wilkes became an instant hero. Everywhere toasts were raised to the captain's daring. The British, on the other hand, were infuriated. The Prime Minister declared to his cabinet ministers, "You may stand for this but damned if I will." Great Britain demanded an apology and the immediate release of the Confederates imprisoned in Boston. Some of the King's troops were mobilized to show that they meant business. Throughout Great Britain the cry for war went up.[50]

Seward locked himself in his office to study international law for two days and emerged, as Lincoln said, "armed to the muzzle with the subject." The Secretary of State explained that since Captain Wilkes had boarded the *Trent* without authorization, the United States was not responsible for his actions and therefore not obliged to apologize. The British had been trampling American rights, boarding ships without provocation, since before the War of 1812. They had ignored the pleas of the United States to desist for decades. Seward would let the two commissioners go since Great Britain was finally acknowledging the rights of neutral vessels. He had tweaked the nose of the British Lion while saving face and preventing another war, and his handling of the "Trent Affair" is considered one of his most brilliant actions.[51]

Despite a rough beginning, the Civil War went well enough to prevent England and France from recognizing the Confederacy. After Lincoln issued the Emancipation Proclamation (which Seward helped to draft), no foreign nation would dare recognize the South because doing so would be tantamount to approving slavery. Lincoln had changed the direction of the war: from exclusively bringing the South back into the Union to freeing the slaves.[52]

Throughout the conflict Seward handled foreign affairs masterfully. In addition to keeping France and England neutral, he prevented several extremely powerful ships called the Laird Rams from entering the sea lanes to destroy Union shipping. When France set up a puppet regime in Mexico, an obvious violation of the Monroe Doctrine, Seward, with the intent of saving precious manpower and energy, delayed ousting the government until after the war. Overall, his tenure as Secretary of State was judicious, adept and effective.[53]

Richmond fell to Union forces on April 3, 1865 and two days later Abraham Lincoln, riding in a carriage, entered the burned out capital of the dying Confederacy. On that same day, Seward was injured in a carriage accident, fracturing his jaw and breaking an arm. Wearing a neck brace to keep his jaw shut, he could only speak mumbled words to visitors. That brace would eventually help save his life.[54]

On the night of Friday, April 14, 1865, Good Friday, a man with a long overcoat appeared at the door of Seward's home to deliver medicine to him. He was denied entrance but pushed past the servant at the door. When Seward's son Frederick tried to intervene, the man pointed a gun several inches from his head and pulled the trigger. The gun misfired. He then clubbed Frederick – splitting his head open and almost killing him – and brandishing a knife, climbed the stairs to the bedroom where he began slashing Seward. The Secretary was stabbed four times before being wrestled away from his attacker by an army nurse, Seward's daughter, and another son. The man ran away yelling, "I am mad." At first it was believed that the wounds would be fatal; however, fortunately for Seward, his neck brace had prevented a fatal penetration of the knife.[55]

At the same time that Seward was attacked, John Wilkes Booth fired his derringer into the back of President Lincoln's head at Ford's Theater in Washington. The city, which had been joyously celebrating the surrender of Robert E. Lee's Confederate Army, was thrown into chaos and alarm. Both Booth and Seward's assailant, Lewis Powell, were eventually caught and hanged at the Old Arsenal Penitentiary. Vice-President Andrew Johnson assumed the Presidency and asked the recovering Seward to remain in the new administration as Secretary of State.[56]

It would take Seward months to recuperate from the attack, but he never fully recovered. The stress of nursing both her husband and her son back to health led to the death of his wife, Frances, only six weeks after the "night of horrors." When Seward's daughter Fanny began taking over her mother's duties, she fell desperately ill with tuberculosis and died just short of her twenty-second birthday. The *Washington Republican* reported that "the assassin's blows passed by the father and son and fell fatally on the mother and daughter." Seward was heartbroken.[57]

During his years in Johnson's cabinet Seward pursued the expansion of the United States. He sought to acquire lands in the Danish West Indies, annex Hawaii, and bring the Dominican Republic into the Untied States. However, the purchase of 586,400 square miles of land from Russia in 1867 for $7.2 million became his crowning, expansionist achievement. Seward named the territory after the prominent peninsula, Alaska, but some Americans believed they had a better name for the frozen tundra that the Secretary had purchased: "Seward's Folly."

It would not be until decades later, when the "Gold Rush" of 1896 began, that the wisdom of Seward's purchase would be realized.[58]

His years as a cabinet member in the Johnson Administration became frustrating ones. Now that the Civil War was over, Seward believed that the South should be allowed back into the Union under more conciliatory terms than the Radical Republicans were willing to allow. Both Lincoln and Johnson advocated Seward's policy, and President Johnson vetoed numerous Reconstruction bills sponsored by the Republicans. Seward wrote some of the important veto messages. Disappointed with the shift in attitudes of the Republican Party – a party that he had helped create and one over which he had formally wielded so much influence – at the end of his term in March of 1869 Seward retired from public life. Despite the grievous injuries suffered from the assassination attempt and an increasing paralysis that overtook him, he went with some of his family members on a world tour. He returned home to Auburn in the fall of 1871 and died a year later, October 10, 1872. Thurlow Weed, his lifelong friend and pallbearer at his funeral, wept openly as Seward's casket was lowered into his grave.[59]

Naming of Mount Seward

Seward had been in office as Governor for only a year in 1840 when the name Mount Seward first appears in a letter from Farrand Benedict, an assistant on the geological survey to Ebenezer Emmons. The first New York State Geological Survey had been created by Governor Marcy in 1836, but when he was defeated by Seward for reelection of 1838, the survey came under the purview of the new administration. Seward supported the project so enthusiastically that it became known as the "Seward Survey." As Emmons had done for Marcy in 1837, Mount Seward in 1840 was named for the sitting governor, in this case, for the man who sustained their survey.[60]

MOUNT DONALDSON
Height: 34th – 1,252 meters (4,108 feet)

Dr. Edward Livingston Trudeau, the most famous tuberculosis doctor in the nation, walked into the room where the future Adirondack historian Alfred Lee Donaldson lay on a bed. The twenty-nine year-old Donaldson had come to Saranac Lake in February of 1895 after being diagnosed with the dreaded disease sometimes called "consumption." Normally the prognosis would have been considered a death sentence. Tuberculosis was the greatest killer of adults between the ages of 20 and 40 in the United States, and, at the end of the nineteenth century, one out of every seven people world-wide died of the disease. Fully one quarter of all of the deaths in Europe in the eighteenth century were attributed to the "white plague," and by the late 1880s, 450 people a day in the United States died of the disease.[61]

Consumption began with night sweats. Intermittent coughing, which followed, eventually became persistent and constant. It raised phlegm or blood-streaked sputum and ultimately pure blood. There would be the daily fevers, chronic fatigue, and the inevitable weight loss. A person's lungs were literally dissolving and their body was being consumed. Death came from drowning in one's own bodily fluids, through starvation, or by metastasis to other organs that forced them to shut down.[62]

The high strung and nervous Dr. Trudeau walked into the room and quickly sat on the bed next to Donaldson. Even though the outside temperature was about twenty degrees below zero, Trudeau wore no overcoat, only a sweater. The fur cap pulled down over his ears was speckled with snow, and ice had formed on his mustache. Donaldson said that he had expected an elderly, portly doctor whose demeanor would suggest there was really nothing that could be done – medical treatment futile. Instead, after listening to Donaldson's lungs, the long and lean Dr. Trudeau declared, "You have a chance. I can't do much for you, but I can tell you what to do for yourself." Thanks to the work of Trudeau and the other doctors in Saranac Lake, Donaldson would live for more than a quarter century more.[63]

Trudeau's regimen for TB sufferers was different from the norm. Instead of treating patients the usual way – wrapping them in bedclothes, shutting the windows, and leaving them in dark rooms – Trudeau, who suffered from tuberculosis himself, prescribed a new treatment. Having come to the Adirondacks to die, he found instead that he regained a great measure of his health. The cold, dry, fresh air, lots of rest, and moderate exercise coupled with three generous meals a day had worked wonders. Though, in reality, he cured very few patients, his treatments nonetheless prolonged lives and made productive citizens of thousands of men and women who migrated to Saranac Lake village for treatment of the disease.[64]

By the early twentieth century, Saranac Lake had become the "City of the Sick." Thousands of people diagnosed with tuberculosis left their homes and loved ones to go to the sanatoriums (derived from the Latin word *sanare,* meaning to heal) and smaller "cure" cottages that sprung up around the village. Since it was common knowledge that the disease was easily spread through the air, being diagnosed with TB was tantamount to having the plague, and tubercular invalids became "untouchables." However, at Saranac Lake, an infected person was not an outcast. The town grew into a TB colony, its daily life revolving around the disease. The activities of the village stopped between two and four in the afternoon, while patients in the village took the "cure." During rain or shine, cold weather or summer warmth, invalids wrapped in blankets could be seen resting on their open porches. By 1920 the village boasted six major sanatoriums and 150 cure cottages; and as the country embraced Trudeau's ideas, the number of sanatoriums around the country increased from 100 in 1900 to nearly 400 ten years later. A magazine solely dedicated to tuberculosis patients, the *Journal of the Outdoor Life,* was published, and a brisk business was done selling gear and cure paraphernalia to the invalid population. After 1944, when the first antibiotic was found to be an effective cure for consumption, Saranac Lake began to revert to its previous state: that of a sleepy Adirondack town.[65]

When Alfred L. Donaldson finished the two-volume *A History of the Adirondacks* in 1921, he had completed a work that had been ten years in the making. It immediately became the definitive work on the history of the people and events of the Adirondack region. Three editions were published in the next 55 years. Adirondack author T. Morris Longstreth, a friend and contemporary of Donaldson, wrote; "Mr. Donaldson has here done the rarest of things – a work not attempted before and that need not be attempted again." Along the way toward completing his history, Donaldson received many words of encouragement, and A. W. Durkee spoke for his generation as well as ours when he wrote as follows in 1920:

> It is a pleasure to know that you are doing what I have always wished someone would do, to preserve the record of so many items that will soon be unobtainable by reason of the death of the last remaining few of the old lovers of the wilderness. The modern Adirondacks will never have the grip on people's imagination, as have the old Adirondacks.[66]

Through his research, Donaldson, amongst a myriad of other discoveries, uncovered the word *Couch-sa-ra-ge,* gave us the Philosophers, and was the first historian to reveal that Native Americans never named the highest mountain in New York *Tahawus.* His sketches of "Old Mountain" Phelps, Alvah Dunning, and Paul Smith are priceless gems, full of information which would have been lost had he not talked to people who had known those icons. Interviewing hundreds, if not thousands of people, he collected valuable information about the region. Nearing the end of his research, he would write, "Indeed, I have probably the most complete collection of Adirondackana in existence, comprising, so far as I know every book, pamphlet, and magazine article that has anything of interest concerning these mountains."[67]

Born into a wealthy banking family in 1866, Donaldson spent most of his youth studying literature and music, particularly the violin, in France and Germany. Though his father wanted him to attend Yale University, he chose instead to go abroad and study in Berlin, Munich, Paris, and Hanover. As a sixteen-year-old, he met composer Richard Wagner, who inspired him to continue his study of the violin; however, he never became a professional musician, but he enjoyed music throughout his life. Even when his strength began to wane, rendering the playing of his violin an impossibility, he still took great pleasure listening to classical compositions on his Victrola.[68]

Upon returning to New York City in 1890, he went to work in his father's bank. For five years he worked in the city, but, he later wrote, "too much alluring fiddling at night, followed by strenuous office confinement by day gradually undermined my always delicate health." Diagnosed with tuberculosis in 1895, he said he was "banished to Saranac Lake." For almost thirty more years, until his death, that village was his home and a community that he thoroughly enjoyed. Despite living with a life-threatening condition, he wrote to a friend in 1919 that he still had so much disdain for New York City that he "would not live there again if I had my health and a million dollars."[69]

Once under the care of Dr. Trudeau, and living in the crisp Adirondack air, Donaldson regained some of his health. Loving the Adirondack Mountains and knowing that the possibility for a complete cure was slim, he dove into life in the tight-knit community. With the help of his father and two fellow tubercular sufferers, he created the Adirondack National Bank, one of the first financial institutions in the mountains. Working with other Saranac Lake men, he also helped establish a savings and loan company and a telephone company. In 1902, at the age of 36, he fell in love and married another TB sufferer, Elizabeth Sherwood Hollingsworth of New York. They would have no children.[70]

For a man in such frail health, he maintained a dangerously hectic pace, becoming a village trustee for three years and president for two. However, in 1910 he suffered a relapse which obliged him to withdraw from his business pursuits. Fortunately those businesses thrived, and he was able to step aside with an ample income.[71]

While the relapse had drained some of Donaldson's precious energy, Trudeau taught all of his patients, in the face of an uncertain outcome, to be cheerful and positive. Self-pity and despair were not tolerated in the community. Donaldson adhered to the doctor's teaching, and his personal physician, Dr. S. F. Blanchet, wrote, "There was no bitterness in his nature. The whole spirit of the man was tuned to the things in his life that seemed lovely to him; out of each minute, each hour, each day, he tried to make a perfect thing, and with all who came close to him, he shared his joy in life."[72]

In May 1912, Donaldson's life changed again. Stephen Chalmers, a close friend and author, went to the Saranac Lake Library seeking answers to some questions he had concerning the history of the Adirondacks. After being told that no history of the region existed, he marched out the door and went around the corner to Donaldson's house. There, Chalmers told Donaldson that a book on the history of the Adirondacks needed to be written and that he was the perfect man for the job: Donaldson had the literary skills – having written several books – the wealth, time, interest, drive, persistence, organization, love of the mountains, and the personality to interview the people necessary to produce a book. Before Chalmers' arrival that day, Donaldson had been "collecting old books and records concerning the region, and he had already begun jotting down facts and stories that the guides told me. He said, however, that he had never thought of writing the history."[73]

Donaldson feigned a reluctance to take on the job, but he was actually elated by the proposal. Finally consenting to attempt it, he began the daunting task of collecting the history of the Adirondacks. His weak condition prevented him from leaving his home on Church Street in Saranac Lake to do anything other than the easiest of tasks. In fact, close to the time that he began his research he wrote, "I am handicapped somewhat by not being able to travel and having to get everything by correspondence. Moreover, my limited strength compels me to work very leisurely." When some of his contacts suggested that he go to them, he had to explain why he could not. To John Agar, who wanted him to go see the Indian Carry between Stony Creek and Upper Saranac only eleven miles away, he wrote, "I appreciate your offer to meet me at the Inn and show me the new lay of the land, but unfortunately I am debarred by limited lung capacity from any tramping of long trips. I had my fill of both in the early days, however, and I remember the old carry very well."[74]

At home he typed hundreds of letters through which he interviewed Adirondack personalities such as William Durant of the Adirondack Railroad Company and the common stage coach drivers who plied the dirt roads between Bartlett's Hotel on Round Pond (now known as Middle Saranac) and Keeseville. He wrote to the anti-Semitic and peculiar Melvin Dewey, president of the Lake Placid Club and originator of the Dewey Decimal System, and Dewey sent back an invitation to dinner written in his "Simple Speling" language: "Won't yu cum ovr most eni day & dyn with us?"[75]

Reclusive Verplanck Colvin, Superintendent of the Adirondack Survey (1872-1900), refused to be interviewed. Donaldson, exasperated, explained, "I have written to him, but my letters have never been answered. I have had friends in Albany try to see him on my behalf, but he has always refused them admissions to his house."[76]

At first Donaldson believed his book would take only a few years to write. To Mr. Herreshoff, whom he interviewed in 1913 concerning his chapter on early settlers of John Brown's Tract, he expressed the hope that "you and Mr. Eaton will not be surprised or disappointed if it takes me a year or two longer to complete and bring out my book." He confessed that "the undertaking is rather more than I thought, and grown in detail as I progress." The book, which contained 44 chapters, would not be complete until the fall of 1921.[77]

As he wrote, Donaldson was always aware that he might not live to realize the completion of the project. Consequently, he kept his notes and research well organized so that, in the event anything happened to him, his "material" would be "in such shape that a literary executor" could complete whatever he was unable to finish.[78]

His desire to complete his research may have actually helped him prolong his life. It certainly provided him with purpose during his waning years. Writing from his house in Saranac Lake or at his summer cabin a few miles away on Lake Kiwassa, he cherished the work. His attitude is particularly evident when he wrote on January 8, 1919, "I myself... shall reach another miles-stone tomorrow – my 53 [birthday] and for the last 23 years of my life I have enjoyed the purest luxury of invalidism – something which I find very few know how to enjoy. I work morning, noon and night at my history." He told an interviewer, "[It] is delightful work that [is] just suited to my tastes and circumstances."[79]

There were bound to be dead ends and letters returned to him that read, "I have only a few papers and some hear-say testimony... regretting that I am unable to aid you in your quest." Also he had to limit the scope of his work. When a historian from the southern Adirondacks suggested a few topics that he might consider including in the history, Donaldson responded, frankly, that "there is nothing of particular historical interest connected with these localities whose development, I gather, has been rather humdrum, uneventful and limited."[80]

While Donaldson did most of the correspondence himself, either by writing directly or having contacts stop by his residence, he did receive quite a bit of help from others who did the leg work that he could not. He hired James Macmillan at 50 cents an hour to do research at the New York State Library in Albany, but most of his assistance came from volunteers who enjoyed helping him in his endeavor. His good friend and publicist Henry Harper was the most influential of them.[81]

An ardent Adirondack historian himself, Harper collected a substantial library of information concerning the region and helped with all aspects of the research. "I hope your house is portable," Donaldson joked, "for the bare walls, it strikes me, will soon be the only thing that you haven't sent me." Dividing his time between New York and a cabin on Long Lake, Harper wrote to Donaldson more than 75 times. Each letter was filled with inquires, encouragements, suggestions, and proposed revisions. Harper made his own historical discoveries, and Donaldson wrote to a friend that he "continues to be the most wonderful god-father to the undertaking." Indeed, Donaldson was grateful for all the work Harper did for him. When Harper found some unique information about the great Totten and Crossfield land purchase Donaldson gleefully wrote, "I haven't been so pleased over anything in a long time... And as I sat ruminating on the new find and anticipating the joys of a new trail, I realized how infinitely much of added scope and interest my book will owe to you, and how day by day you are making it more and more 'our' book. Ultimately, I know, I shall feel ashamed to subscribe my name to it alone."[82]

The two men enjoyed each other's correspondence. Donaldson even confided, "It seems like the good old times once more to sit in my big chair in the library window, sipping coffee, smoking my morning cigar and reading one of your jolly letters again." However, they disagreed about Verplanck Colvin.[83]

After reading his reports, Donaldson felt that Colvin deserved more recognition for conceiving the idea of an Adirondack Park and, he thought, "purely as a surveyor he was excellent, and his capacity for detail has always impressed me as being stupendous." Harper, who had met Colvin several times, felt that he was nothing more than a power hungry politician, not someone who cared about the Adirondacks. Harper suggested that Donaldson find an independent, knowledgeable source to settle their dispute; so Donaldson wrote Irving Morris, one time Chief Clerk of the State Engineers Department whose survey crews had labored closely with Colvin during his work in the Adirondacks.[84]

In a letter marked "Confidential," Morris, acknowledged Colvin's significant role in helping to establish a Forest Preserve, but he pulled no punches when he added, "the scientific value of the surveys which he made, however, is very small." According to the engineers who had been with Colvin, "the manner in which the work was laid out and conducted was so haphazard and faulty that it was impossible to secure lasting results." When the legislature abolished the survey in 1900 and the State Engineers entered Colvin's offices, they found in them a mass of notebooks, "possibly thousands – piled in the rooms without method or system, but simply thrown on the floor and piled up." Morris reported that three engineers had spent nearly a week's time going through the records and, after all that time, "they were unable to use a single record in Mr. Colvin's office." As far as his well received published survey reports were concerned, Morris said that "[t]hey read more like a history of a camping outfit than a report of an engineering survey."[85]

Morris counseled Donaldson, "[I]t would seem unnecessary and inadvisable to criticize Mr. Colvin in the book you are about to write" and "if I was in your place, I would not feel justified in praising him in any way." In Donaldson's history, 639 pages, excluding the appendices and indexes, only four pages are devoted to Colvin.[86]

Confidential conversations that Donaldson dared not employ led to insights into the character of Old Mountain Phelps. "I knew him personally and have quite a stock of stories of him," Keene Valley resident Jennie Scanlon wrote. "I am afraid the bits which I know of him are not what you care to incorporate in the book... Between you and me and I only dare to whisper it, Mr. Phelps was a much over stated man. If Charles Dudley Warner and Stoddard had not taken him up and boomed him, he would never become famous."[87]

By 1915 Donaldson had gathered enough history to finish several chapters and he was anxious to have the public read them. Entitled *Chapters of Adirondack History*, they were published in the local newspaper, and the author asked that readers offer "suggestions, criticism and corrections" to "help to make the ultimate publication in book form fuller and more accurate." He also sent portions of the text – chapters and, even, single paragraphs – to anyone willing to check and confirm the details. To A. W. Durkee, who knew the Adirondack entrepreneur Paul Smith, he wrote; "[T]he important point about your reading the chapter is to find out whether it satisfies one who knew Paul so long and so intimately. And I want you to be perfectly frank about it. I'm not sensitive about my writing, and I'm honestly out for any suggestions that will improve what I've done."[88]

Donaldson's papers are full of corrections supplied by his correspondents. Harper was especially critical, and Donaldson always deferred to his friend. "I'll write it over," he said. "I will make the alterations you suggest, for I think that they are good ones." It is obvious from Donaldson's papers that he checked and rechecked his sources. In the margins of his notes, today's researchers may find several "This does not tally with the facts."[89]

One can only be impressed with the scope of Donaldson's research, his diligence in checking facts, his persistence in pursuing leads, his attention to detail. Over the years, however, other historians have been critical of *A History of the Adirondacks,* saying that it contains "sometimes dubious and usually poorly documented information." That assertion denigrates the work of the author. He did incredible service to the history of the Adirondacks by compiling information that undoubtedly would have otherwise been lost forever. More than eighty years after its initial publication, Donaldson's work remains the foundation of Adirondack history.[90]

Even though he lacked the energy to play some of his favorite games, billiards or, even, chess, Donaldson seemed always optimistic. By the middle of 1919 he was close to finishing the book. He wrote, "I have only two or three uncompleted chapters now." He was trying to find a publisher and he was selecting the thirty-two illustrations that the history would contain. In February of 1920, responding to an inquiry about the book, he said "if I am spared, I hope to finish the work this year." [91]

A History of the Adirondacks was published in two volumes in 1921 by the Century Company of New York. Exhausted upon its completion, Donaldson had composed the first comprehensive history of the region he loved. Two years later he was laid to rest in Lake Placid. In his will, he bequeathed his entire Adirondack collection to the Saranac Free Library, establishing it as one of the premier Adirondack research libraries.[92]

The Naming of Donaldson

In 1924, largely due to the efforts of High Peaks historian Russell Carson and the Adirondack Mountain Club, the 4,215-foot mountain (the 1924 elevation) just south of the larger Seward Mountain was named Mount Donaldson. In August of that year Carson, Herb Clark, and George Marshall along with a good friend of Carson's, Charles West, decided to climb the newly christened mountain. They could not think of a better way to honor Alfred Donaldson than to climb his mountain.[93]

Carson and Donaldson had begun a lively and extremely friendly correspondence with each other in 1922, eventually exchanging family photographs and niceties, as Carson began his research for his book, *Peaks and People of the Adirondacks,* which would be published in 1927. Since Donaldson was the eminent authority on the Adirondacks, Carson sought his advice and knowledge. Donaldson was happy to oblige, reading Carson's mountain sketches and directing Carson to people who might help him clear up some research problems. Carson's obvious enthusiasm for his subject impressed Donaldson, and, for more than a year, he eagerly watched the High Peaks historian as he traveled down historical avenues that Donaldson had not visited.

During the winter of 1923, as he began his research concerning Mount Colvin, Carson found people who actually praised the reclusive, old surveyor, Verplanck Colvin. Donaldson warned him to take the tributes with a grain of salt, for most people thought poorly of the man and "in my chapter, I was forced, as you may recall, to damn him with rather faint praise." Carson's diligence in tracking down historical leads directed him to Mills Blake, Colvin's valued assistant and companion during the Adirondack Survey, who still lived in Colvin's Albany home. Eventually Carson would be so impressed with Blake that he and friends would suggest that the mountain just south of Mount Colvin be named Blake's Peak. However, in 1923, Mills Blake was virtually unknown.[94]

Donaldson was excited about Carson's contact with Blake and wrote to Carson, "your visit with Mr. Blake makes me wish more than ever that I had discovered him when I was writing my history, especially if, as you say, most of Colvin's papers and records are in his possession."[95] The more Carson did research about Colvin, the more he was steered to a different conclusion about the eccentric surveyor. In Donaldson's letters, at the end of October 1923, there were only a few hints that indicated that Donaldson's strength was waning, and Carson had no idea that in fewer than two weeks Donaldson would be dead. In those last weeks, Donaldson also seemed to be drawing a different conclusion about Colvin than the one he had arrived at while researching his history of the Adirondacks. In his last letter to Carson he expressed his new view:

> It is also very gratifying to hear some pleasant things about Mr. Colvin, for I happened to discover no one who had deciphered the finer and more human side of the character. What you have brought to light only confirms my conviction that there are two sides not only to everything but to everybody, and if we only seek long enough, we will at some time discover the good that is more or less in every character. Personally, I have always admired Mr. Colvin's work and enthusiasm for these mountains. And I have felt more or less surprised that the public estimate of his career was so deeply tinged with criticism as I found it.[96]

Donaldson's death came as a shock to Carson and cut short some of the research on which they were working together. Even though the two men never met and only corresponded by mail, in the short time that they did so, Donaldson and Carson became good friends, and it is obvious that the two men thoroughly enjoyed corresponding with each other about Adirondack history. Within weeks after Donaldson's death, Carson resolved to name a mountain after the Adirondack historian. Appropriately, that mountain in the Seward Range could, reportedly, be seen from Donaldson's summer cottage on Kiwassa Lake.

Clark led the way over from the top of Seward. At fifty-four, he was still lean as a greyhound and quick through the dense trees. He and Marshall had been to Donaldson several years earlier, while climbing the mountain with George's brother Bob on the way to becoming the first 46ers. They had christened it, for lack of a better name, North Seward.

Clark became entangled in the thick "cripplebrush" (a word created by the guide) along the ridge that led to the summit of Donaldson, and Marshall said that he "always wondered whether this was one of the few times Herb made a mistake, or whether he was just initiating Russ." Carson, who was forty and weighed about 200 pounds, had only climbed a few mountains previously. For him the climb was a strenuous one. On the summit the group signed a register to be left behind for fellow climbers and broke off a balsam sprig from a tree before they headed out of the woods and back to Saranac Lake.[97]

Russell Carson, Herb Clark, and Charlie West on Donaldson on August 11, 1924

At 30 Church Street, the hikers presented the balsam sprig from the top of the mountain to Elizabeth Donaldson. She had lived with her husband in that home for twenty-three years, ten of them while he compiled *A History of the Adirondacks*.[98]

MOUNT EMMONS
Height: 40th – 1,231 meters (4,039 feet)

In 1836, Democrat Governor William Learned Marcy appointed four geologists to survey the minerals and geological resources of the state.[99] While documenting the resources in upstate New York, Ebenezer Emmons, head geologist of the Second District, found a unique fossilized trilobite, the oldest fossil in the world at that time, and felt that the new find could be the basis of a new subdivision in the geological timeline. The discovery would begin the "war of the geologists." In reality, that war was a lop-sided affair, with the majority of the scientific community lining up against Emmons. From 1842 until the final year of his life in 1863, Ebenezer Emmons struggled against men who ridiculed his observations. In 1857, after fifteen years of frustration, he wrote that "their stout and unscrupulous denials of the correctness of my position carried all geologists with them and left me to struggle alone and single-handed." Both James Hall, who was Emmons' first assistant during the geological survey, and William C. Redfield, who was with Emmons on the first ascent of Marcy in 1837, as well as other prominent American geologists, turned against him.[100]

Ebenezer Emmons, the son of a minister, was born in 1800 and raised in the Berkshire Mountains of western Massachusetts. In 1814, he entered Williams College and began a relationship with that institution that would last for the rest of his life. He graduated a star pupil in 1818 and began his professional career as a physician, but in 1826 he embarked on a new career, first teaching chemistry and then geology and mineralogy at his alma mater.[101]

It was a time of changing geological theories. The science was less than a hundred years old, and theories about the formation of the earth were just beginning to emerge. Fossils were recognized as markers of geological history by the middle of the eighteenth century, but as late as the 1820s dinosaurs[102] were thought to have been gigantic lizards that once inhabited the earth. Over the short course of their science's existence, geologists had formulated theories about the earth's development and knew the basics of how rocks were created. They had a good understanding of the ages of rocks based on either the fossils found within rock strata or the lack thereof. They also had developed a geological timeline which included some of the names for geological ages with which modern geologists are familiar: Pre-Cambrian, Cambrian, and Mesozoic.[103]

While Ebenezer Emmons understood the contemporary theory of how the earth had formed, he was, nonetheless, a diluvialist – a person who believed that the world, at one time, had been covered completely with water and that most of the formations on the surface of the earth could be explained by the power of waves and water. His observations had led him to write "Tidal waves, normal oceanic currents, and river currents with their burdens of detritus [loose stone and matter], have ever exerted their powerful agency in distributing the waste materials of continents, and in constructing the fossiliferous mountains of the globe."[104]

Diluvialist theory was in accord with the Old Testament story of Noah's Ark and the great flood. Emmons was very religious and saw the hand of God everywhere in his surroundings. His daughter once wrote that the Emmons family started Sunday service on Saturday evening, and it was considered a sin to laugh until Monday morning. Despite this, Emmons' scientific background made it impossible for him to take at face value that life and the world had been created in seven days. In 1848 he asked, *"[I]s it possible that twenty four hours difference in the ages of two animals should make such a wide difference in the disposition of their* remains that... the remains of the first should be entombed thousands of feet below the last?"[105]

Emmons hypothesized that eskers, kames, and other positive relief features of the landscape of the planet had been caused by the actions of waves. Erratics – rocks and boulders carried to and deposited at sites sometimes hundreds of miles from their sources – posed a problem for the geologist, one that he was able to resolve through rationalization and imagination. He hypothesized that the erratics had floated in icebergs until warmer temperatures had released them, and then they had dropped to the bottom of the ocean floor. Such erratics were eventually found on the summits of some of the mountains – Marcy and Algonquin included – that rose high above the sea.[106]

Louis Agassiz, the naturalist who arrived at the Philosophers Camp in 1857, was the author of a revolutionary book about glaciers and their forces. His *Étude sur les Glaciérs,* written in 1840, brought him into direct conflict with Emmons. While living in a cabin close to ice flows in Switzerland, Agassiz had noticed scars that glaciers had left on the surface of the earth. He also observed that the rivers of ice had deposited huge boulders miles away from their sources, pushed debris into mounds, made positive relief features such as eskers and kames, and created scraped and polished U-shaped valleys. He noticed such features far from known glaciers and believed that the rivers of ice had once flowed beyond their then limited influence. He hypothesized that the whole world had been, at one time, covered with ice that had wiped out every living thing on the planet. His "Ice Age" theory, coupled with another scientist's observation that the sun was cooling, led to the development of a doomsday scenario which, for twenty years after the Civil War, made some people believe that the world would again be encased in ice... in their lifetime. Agassiz traveled as far as Brazil to find evidence in support of his theories, and although some of his assumptions were fundamentally wrong, his ideas and observations shattered the "great flood" theory of geologists like Emmons.[107]

When Ebenezer Emmons was appointed New York's Chief Geologist and took on the assignment to survey the 10,000 square miles of the Second District, the state's northernmost section, he chose James Hall (1811-1898) to assist with the daunting task of documenting all the minerals of the district. Hall, the son of a miller from near Boston, was recommended for the position because of his knowledge of iron ore. Both he and Emmons had studied geology at the Rensselaer School in Troy, New York, under the famous teacher Amos Eaton. Troy was the birthplace of American geology and it was a mecca for anyone who intended to study minerals and paleontology. After graduating from Rensselaer in 1832, Hall taught at his alma mater. He was there when Emmons asked him to assist with the survey, but Emmons later criticized his assistant, saying that during the survey, Hall "made many blunders," including misidentifying rock samples.[108]

Ebenezer Emmons

In subsequent years, the relationship between the two men became very bitter. There is an unsubstantiated rumor that Hall never repaid $400 that he borrowed from Emmons, which for the average person in 1840, who only made $129 a year, amounted to a considerable sum. The default may have been the source of the rift that eventually separated the two.[109]

Hall would stay with Emmons for little more than a year before being promoted, at age twenty-five, to the post of Chief Geologist of the Fourth District. He also became the State Geologist and State Paleontologist and remained in those positions until his death in 1898. With a new assistant, Emmons combed his district for minerals over the next five years and produced a much quoted annual report.[110]

During the first year of the survey, from two different locations, Emmons and Hall had spotted a conspicuously tall mountain which they both believed demanded exploration. The following year, on August 5, 1837, Emmons, Hall, and a group of men from the iron mines at the village of McIntyre (later known as Adirondac) climbed to the summit of the unnamed and previously unclimbed mountain. The group also included the scientist William C. Redfield. He noted that the route they had taken to the summit had not been without danger. On the previous night, they had been visited by a panther, whose growls could be heard as it circled their shelter, just beyond the light of their campfire.[111]

Using barometers, Emmons and Redfield calculated the height of the mountain to be 5,467 feet; just 123 feet greater than that recorded by modern means. Even though the temperatures hovered under fifty degrees, the group spent five hours on top. Hall, perhaps sensing the significance of the moment, took the time to write a letter from the summit. He wrote, "From this mountain we have one of the grandest views imaginable... Some of these mountains are clothed in evergreen, others are laid bare by slides leaving a crest of naked rocks. Innumerable little lakes and streams are seen in all directions." Charles Ingham, an artist who was a member of the party, nearly fainted along the way and appears to have only rested from the ordeal of the climb. He did not make a sketch or paint while on the summit.[112]

On top, Emmons and the eleven other people in the group determined a name for the mountain. "This privilege [of naming mountains] belongs by common consent to the first explorers," Emmons wrote. "A more appropriate name could not be conferred on the highest summit of this group than Mount Marcy." The namesake, William Learned Marcy, was the governor of the most populated, economically advanced, and most powerful state in the union. It seemed appropriate, at the time, to name the mountain after Marcy, a personal friend of Emmons who had pushed the state legislature to provide the $104,000 in funding for the survey. Emmons and the others resting on the summit that day believed that Marcy deserved the honor, but Emmons also realized that some people might criticize the selection. He went on to name Dix Mountain after the standing Secretary of State and, later, Seward Mountain after the governor who succeeded Marcy. He noted that disapproval of the naming of Marcy would be "of but little consequences."[113]

For the group of men who were the first to venture to the top of Mount Marcy, their seven-day journey into the wilderness ended back in the village of McIntyre after they had also been the first to climb Mount McIntyre, the second highest mountain in the state, now known as Algonquin Peak. Before the exploration of the region was complete that summer, Emmons would also make the first recorded ascent of Nippletop.[114]

Emmons' salary was allocated both for his field work and for the compilation of his findings. In his 1837 report, submitted in February 1838, he mentioned naming the state's highest mountain after Governor Marcy. In the report he also suggested a name for the cluster of mountains explored the previous summer. "I proposed," Emmons wrote, "to call the Adirondack Group a name by which a well known tribe of Indians who once hunted here may be commemorated." While "Adirondack" conjures up pleasant images of wilderness and beautiful sheets of water, it is not clear what Emmons' source for the name was. There was never a Native American tribe known as Adirondack, as Emmons claimed, nor was the tribe, as Emmons wrote, "well known." Over the years, it has become apparent that the name was derived from an Iroquois derisive term for the Algonquins. Loosely translated as "bark eaters," the Iroquois word was used in ridicule of their neighbors to the north. The Iroquois maintained that the Algonquins often did not have sufficient stores to see them through the winter and were therefore obliged to eat bark in order to survive.[115]

Emmons' suggestion for the name of the mountain range came at a time when some white men were actively romanticizing and idealizing Native American culture. They dubbed waterfalls, rivers, peaks, and mountain ranges with names which supposedly had been applied to them by Native Americans, but, actually, were of their own invention. Just a month after Emmons climbed Marcy, poet and writer Charles Fenno Hoffman set out on a failed attempt to climb the peak and later wrote, in a letter which appeared in the *New York Mirror,* that Marcy, as he had seen it from Lake Sanford had been "sheathed in snow" and that "soaring as it did far above" the adjacent peaks and "seeming to pierce, as it were, the blue sky which curtained them, the poetick Indian epithet of TAH-A-WUS, *He splits the sky,* was hardly extravagant to characterize its particular grandeur."[116] Some who read Hoffman's account assumed that Native Americans had applied the name *Tahawus* to the "High Peak of Essex." For more than eighty years, until historian Alfred L. Donaldson discovered otherwise, people believed that Tahawus was the original Native American name for the mountain. In reality, Emmons' name for the highest mountain in New York, Mount Marcy, came first. There is no recorded Native American name for it.[117]

Emmons' discovery of a fossilized trilobite in Washington County near Greenwich, New York, was to set the geological world on edge. The fossilized trilobite, an ancient ancestor of the horseshoe crab, was unlike any fossil previously discovered and, at the time, was considered the oldest fossil to have been found. The find, coupled with its placement in a body of rocks, called into question the established geological timeline. Emmons noted the fossilized animals and vegetation lying in the rock formations and designated them as having been the products of what he called the "Taconic System." He then set out to demonstrate that his hypothesis was correct.[118]

His theories triggered a firestorm of criticism. The alteration of the established geological timeline was something few geologists were willing to accept without substantial evidence. At first this criticism was respectful and congenial, but when it became obvious that Emmons stood by his claims and after he revealed new evidence to support them, the reaction from the geological community became nasty. James Hall was his most outspoken critic during the ensuing years. He doubted that Emmons' trilobite was anything new and suggested that Emmons was an incompetent geologist. Emmons wrote, "I never treated Mr. James Hall unkindly in my life. I was the instrument who secured his appointment as paleontologist by [G]overnor Marcy." He continued, "He has with great zeal denounced me... and run his statements to prove the error of the Taconic system over forty pages."[119]

On March 7, 1851, that zeal came to a head when Emmons took the stand as a key witness in a libel case tried in Albany. In 1849, James Hall had enlisted the help of the Philosophers Camp's Louis Agassiz to denounce, in the press, a new geological chart "corrected and approved" by Ebenezer Emmons. Of course, Emmons had included in the chart his Taconic System. Map maker James T. Foster had sued Hall and Agassiz for libel damages in the amount of $40,000 and $20,000 respectively. During the procedure, *Foster v. Agassiz,* Hall schooled Agassiz' lawyers concerning the details of the theoretical Taconic System. He hoped to ruin Emmons and his system. A procession of expert witnesses dismantled Emmons' theories and publicly humiliated him. Foster lost the Agassiz case and dropped the one against Hall. Soon thereafter, Hall published his own commercially successful geological chart, one that eliminated the Taconic System.[120]

If Hall and the other geologists believed that the trial would once and forever put an end to Emmons and his theories, they were mistaken. In his mid-fifties, Emmons could have bowed out and retired from the field of geology, but, instead, he began a new career. He took his cause beyond the easy reach of Hall and the others by accepting a job as the State Geologist of North Carolina which was conducting an ongoing survey of its natural resources. Still, his steadfast belief that his theories were correct, even in the face of unrelenting derision in geological journals, made him a pariah in the geological community. His specimens at New York's Museum of Natural History were removed and the curators avoided him each time he entered the museum. Whenever a new curator took over the position, Emmons carped, "I suppose like the others you will not speak to me or recognize my position of state geologist." He wrote that on some of his trips from North Carolina home to Albany, an assistant to James Hall, a Mr. Meek, "was afraid of making a call at my house lest Hall might hear of it" and was offered the position as assistant only if "he [Meek] agreed that he would have nothing to do with Emmons."[121]

In North Carolina, Emmons took to his new career with renewed energy and drive. His vigor and geological curiosity never wavered, even when testing his Taconic System theories, and he continued to reinforce and expand those theories. He continued his fight by writing a text book on American geology in 1855. If he could not persuade his colleagues, then he would influence the next generation of geologists. Believing that, eventually, his theories would be accepted, he declared, "I shall floor them."[122]

In 1856, he disagreed with another man with whom he had climbed Mount Marcy in 1837, William C. Redfield, about the classification of a fossilized fish. Redfield's theories were backed by other state geologists and Louis Agassiz. Again, Emmons stood alone against the American geological community.[123]

Hall would, perhaps, have been a better choice for the position of Chief Geologist of North Carolina Survey due to his sympathies for the South. Emmons was out of place there in the years just before the Civil War began. He complained, "I am so perfectly afloat in political feeling that I am nearly useless. I have to be cautious in my words but I can't conceal my union feelings... It is not safe for a northern man to register his name on the books of the hotel as a native even of N.Y. There is more tyranny in S.C. than in Austria." To a colleague he wrote, "I cannot but look with great fear upon the results of agitation, and it unfits me to work."[124]

Just before the war broke out, Emmons seemed to make headway with his Taconic System theories. To combat the American alliance against him, he elicited the help of Europeans. Surmising that the world's geological formations had all been shaped under similar circumstances, he believed that there should be observable similarities between the North American continent and the European one. He believed that the key to victory was with geologists outside the influence of James Hall.[125]

On September 2, 1860, Ebenezer Emmons left his home in Albany for what would be the final time and headed back to North Carolina to continue his work as State Geologist there. Although the tensions of an imminent civil war should have been an ominous sign to him, Emmons felt obliged to return to the South, and when South Carolina seceded from the Union three months later and war broke out in April of 1861, he found himself stranded below the Mason-Dixon Line with no way to return north through Confederate lines.[126]

In the succeeding months, some European geologists saw promise in the Taconic theories and began to support him, but Emmons was completely unaware of the turn of events. His supporters, however, were ecstatic that he was finally being vindicated. "I do so want to communicate the news to our honest and good friend Emmons!" wrote geologist Colonel E. Jewett in January of 1862. "But [he] is not to be corresponded with and [he is] sealed up with the Rebellion. When he comes back (should) we not get up an ovation for him and let mankind know his worth and merit?" Emmons would never hear that "ovation." Although his wife was able to make her way through lines and more than likely showed her husband the letters backing his theories, Ebenezer Emmons was ill. On October 3, 1863, with his wife and son by his side, he died. His body was brought north and buried in Albany. In an ultimate irony, when James Hall died in 1898, he was buried next to Emmons.[127]

The eminent Adirondack historian Russell Carson wrote in 1927 that Emmons "lived to see his theories vindicated," but most modern geologists, unless they have studied the history of geology, have never heard of the Taconic System. Although Emmons spent the last twenty years of his life trying to convince the geological community of the validity of his theories, after he died it was the European geologists who eventually disproved his ideas. While Emmons had actually discovered a new and unique trilobite, the Taconic System that he derived from the discovery was too loosely defined. Because Emmons included rocks in the system that were from much more recent geological periods, his theory was dismissed.[128]

The Taconic System, as a geological model, exists today only as a footnote in the history of geology. Emmons was wrong about the Taconic System, but his contributions to the history of the Adirondacks were enormous. Not only did he discover massive resources for the State of New York in the region, he also may be credited with revealing the area to the world. Within weeks of the release of his published article on the first ascent of Marcy, the first of many tourists arrived to experience the beauty of the mountains.[129]

The Naming of Mount Emmons

The name, *Mount Emmons,* was originally applied to a mountain near Raquette Lake, but because the local population insisted on calling it by their name for it, Blue Mountain, Mount Emmons ceased to be. In 1927 Russell Carson proposed that the southernmost peak of the Seward Range, originally named South Seward by the Marshall Brothers and Herb Clark when they first climbed it in 1925, be named after Ebenezer Emmons. By June of 1942, the New York State Board on Geographic Names had approved the designation, and in 1952 the name Mount Emmons appeared for the first time on the United States Geological Survey's Ampersand Quadrangle.[130]

First Ascent of Seward, Donaldson, and Emmons

The first ascents of Seward, Donaldson and Emmons are usually credited to Verplanck Colvin and the hermit of Raquette Lake, Alvah Dunning. In October 1870, Colvin, only 23 at the time, hired the older man to guide him up the previously unclimbed Mount Seward. With piercing hazel eyes and a hook nose, Dunning was a character who believed that the world was flat. Colvin was a self-centered, self-promoter who would become superintendent of the Adirondack Survey (1872-1900). Their trip up Seward and Colvin's well publicized record of the ascent would help to make the surveyor's name well known in New York State. Even the governor quoted a passage from Colvin's report about the climb in his annual message to the state.[131]

The days were short and the nights cold when they climbed Seward that October. Colvin and Dunning should have easily made it to the summit and back in one day. The distance was only seven miles as the crow flies as they walked through an old-growth forest. However, due to their late start, they were forced to bivouac somewhere on the ridge near the summit of Seward. Dunning played his role of guide by giving up a wool blanket to Colvin and "kept himself warm by chopping firewood" all night.[132]

The two men are officially the first people to ever step on the summit of Seward, and they are also credited with the first ascents of Donaldson and Emmons; however, Colvin's vague description of the climb up Seward makes it impossible to determine whether or not they actually made the summit of either of the other two peaks, especially Emmons.

It is important to remember that it was not until the 1920s, when Bob Marshall noticed that Donaldson and Emmons met his criteria for high peaks that were more than 4,000 feet in elevation, that the two were considered separate peaks on the Seward Mountain ridge. Colvin desperately wanted to be the first person to climb such a prominent and important Adirondack mountain and would have taken the most expedient and easy route to Seward's summit. He probably would not have bothered going over what he considered some insignificant bumps along his route. Climbing to Seward, he and Dunning would have achieved the ridge near the summit of Donaldson, and they might have wandered over that peak, but in order to climb Emmons, they would have had to deliberately turn south, away from Seward. Of the dozens of routes the pair could have taken, there is really only one that would have passed close to the summit of Emmons. Even that one would have required that they deliberately turn from that route to climb to the summit.

Therefore, credit for the first ascent of Emmons more than likely belongs to the Marshall Brothers and their guide Herb Clark. Those three, in 1925, were the first hikers to climb the isolated peak intentionally. By that late date, however, Emmons was surrounded by at least six defunct logging camps, built as high up as the 3,200 foot level. Sled roads radiated from the camps to within a quarter of a mile of the summit. It is not inconceivable that some energetic lumberjack on a Sunday day off took the time to climb the peak just for the fun of it.

There is some evidence suggesting that other people climbed Seward previous to the ascent of Colvin and Dunning. The famous Adirondack guide and hunter John Cheney claimed to have climbed Seward around 1850 while tracking a moose through the Cold River region. However, it is unlikely that Cheney climbed the mountain while pursuing his prey. The thick cripplebrush that crowded the top of Seward would have probably dissuaded both the moose and the hunter from heading up and over the summit.[133]

George Marshall also wrote that Arnold Guyot and his nephew, Ernest Sandoz, may have climbed Seward as early as 1863, seven years prior to Seward and Dunning's ascent. Guyot was a good friend of Louis Agassiz, having spent some time studying glaciers in Europe and helping to formulate Agassiz's theories for the *Étude sur les Glaciérs*. At the urging of his friend, Guyot left Europe and came to lecture at Harvard before taking a permanent position at Princeton. His young nephew, in addition to being a good hiking companion, also was a superb artist who drew pictures and devised maps for some of his uncle's books. Agassiz's stay at the Philosophers Camp only four years before must have influenced Guyot and brought him to the region.[134]

Colvin knew of the earlier claim of first ascent but dismissed it. It is not clear from the vague description of the climb whether Guyot achieved the summit of Seward or neighboring Seymour. He and his nephew are, however, entitled to the honor for the first ascent of one or the other, but we will probably never know which they actually climbed.[135]

From the summit of Seward today's hikers proceed to Donaldson and Emmons along a well defined path that has remained fairly constant since its development in the 1960s. Originally the trail passed below the crest of the ridge to avoid terrific blowdown caused by the Big Blow of 1950. Today, long after the fallen timber has rotted away and the second growth has finally reached a reasonable height, the path still follows that same indirect, circuitous route below the ridge, now avoiding phantom blowdown.

Mount Seymour
Height: 36th – 1,247 meters (4,091 feet)

On the fourth ballot, when it came time for the chairman of the North Carolina delegation to cast all nine of his delegates' votes, he surprised everyone at the 1868 Democratic Convention in New York City by announcing that "the great state of North Carolina" had cast all of its votes in favor of Horatio Seymour.[136]

Seymour had been the man that the Democratic Party looked to when it needed a nationally known public figure to lead the way. Before the convention, he had tried to diffuse any movement to make him the Presidential candidate by unequivocally telling the press, not once but two times, that he would not accept the nomination. However, when the chairman of the North Carolina delegation evoked his name, the convention erupted with applause, and the people in the galleries rose to their feet and began yelling "Horatio Seymour! Horatio Seymour!" Future New

Horatio Seymour

York Governor Samuel J. Tilden,[137] banged his gavel and announced that if the gallery did not quiet down he would have the people in it removed by force if necessary.[138]

After calm settled on the convention, Seymour stepped to the podium, as he had previously, and again declined the nomination. He said, "I am grateful for any expression of kindness. It must be distinctly understood, it is impossible, consistently with my position, to allow my name to be mentioned in this convention against my protest. The clerk will proceed with the call." For a fourth time, Horatio Seymour had expressed his determination not to be his party's nominee.[139]

During the next four days no candidate was able to amass the required 211 votes for the nomination. The convention appeared deadlocked. However, during the roll call for the twenty-third ballot, Civil War General Alexander McCook of Ohio surprised everyone by standing up and casting all 21 of his state's votes for Seymour, "a man whom the Presidency has sought, but who has not sought the Presidency." The hall resonated with enthusiasm: "Three cheers for Horatio Seymour!" Seymour spoke yet again and declared once more that he was not a candidate. He then left the hot and smoky hall to get some fresh air. His absence noted, Clement Vallandigham called upon the delegates to nominate the former Governor of New York, unanimously, as their choice for the Presidency. Every delegate voted for Seymour, the final vote cast by Tilden, the chairman of the New York delegation. Seymour had won the nomination without knowing it, but would he accept it? Surely he would not decline it again. In what Seymour called "the biggest mistake of my life," one of the most reluctant candidates in the history of American politics soon thereafter accepted the nomination to run as the Democratic candidate for President against the popular Union General Ulysses S. Grant.[140]

Born on May 31, 1810, at Pompey Hill in Onondaga County, a third generation New Yorker, Seymour was named after his father's oldest brother, a man who was to become a United States Senator from Vermont (1821-33). His father, who was a banker and served for a time as mayor of Utica, suffered occasionally from fits of depression. Horatio Seymour, one of six children in the family, grew up to become an incredibly honest and ethical man. He was six feet tall, had a straight nose, long sideburns that accentuated his lean face, large hazel eyes, and a balding head. He was slender of figure and "liked to work in his hayfields or go on long trips to the Adirondack Mountains."[141]

After attending Union College in Schenectady he was admitted to the bar in 1832, and after one year in practice, at age 23, he was asked by the newly elected Democratic Governor William L. Marcy to serve as his military secretary. He accepted that appointment and remained in the post until 1839, when Marcy left office. The relationship between the two men continued until Marcy's death in 1857. Seymour considered him his closest political friend. In 1835, on his own birthday, Seymour married Mary Bleecker, the youngest daughter of a wealthy landowning Dutch family from the Utica area. Although they were devoted to each other their entire lives, they were never able to have children.[142]

After the Panic of 1837, Seymour's father, believing that he was financially ruined, committed suicide. At that time, suicide, in addition to being emotionally devastating to a family, carried a stigma almost impossible to erase. Horatio had seen the effects of depression on his father and vowed that he would live his life peacefully and without stress, but that was a resolution, because of the demands placed upon him by the Democratic Party, that he was never able to fully realize.[143]

After the Whigs and William H. Seward swept away all opposition and turned the Democrats out of office after the Panic of 1837, Seymour, in 1841, reluctantly decided to run for a seat in the state assembly in order to help oust the majority party from power. The political pendulum had begun its swing back in favor of the Democrats, thanks in part to reckless spending by the Whigs on canal projects. Seymour won the seat and remained in it for the next five years, during which time he became chairman of the Committee of Canals. Because of countrywide attention to the Erie Canal, that position propelled him into the national limelight.[144]

After being elected Speaker of the Assembly, because of bickering among his fellow state Democrats, he decided to retire in 1846 to his newly built home in Utica. There, relaxing in front of the cozy fireplace in his library, he vowed never to return to politics, but he had a propensity for doing what he considered to be right and the political demands put on him by the Democratic Party made it impossible for him to stay away from the political arena. Time and again Horatio Seymour did what his party asked of him. He ran for Governor five times: in 1850, 1852, 1854, 1862 and 1864, and won the post twice: in 1852 and 1862.[145]

At the urging of Marcy, Seymour made the run in 1850, but before he ran, he complained "[I]t is a very great sacrifice for me to be a candidate." After losing, he remarked, privately,

"I am relieved to be in the minority, and out of power" and added, "I could not be persuaded again to give up the comfort and respectability of private life." Only Governor George Clinton was ever nominated for governor more times than Horatio Seymour.[146]

Seymour was not a mudslinging politician. He believed that "a man should seek office on his character and person." When the temperance movement swept the eastern United States in 1853, Seymour, known to many as the "teetotaling Episcopalian," refused to be caught up in it. He said, "[A]ll experience shows that temperance, like other virtues, is not produced by lawmakers, but by the influences of education, morality and religion. Men may be persuaded... they cannot be compelled to adopt habits of temperance." He was branded a drunkard and a panderer to the liquor interest and, because of his convictions, lost the election of 1854 by 300 votes... out of a half a million cast.[147]

Throughout his life Seymour loved to camp and trek in the Adirondacks. It was after his 1854 defeat that he took his much celebrated trip down the Raquette River (September 1855). His party consisted of seven people, including an acquaintance from his days as governor, a sixty-year-old spinster, Amelia Murray. Seymour invited her along at the last moment. Her pluck and adventurous attitude belied her station in life: she usually resided in Buckingham Palace and was maid of honor to Queen Victoria. Three years before the Boston philosophers made their historic trip down the Raquette, for ten days, Seymour and his company traveled by guide boat down the river a distance of more than one hundred miles. On the water and on foot, they passed through the remote Adirondack wilderness. They feasted on trout and potatoes garnished with such "high pleasantries," concocted by the English Lady, as wild berry pudding and lemon in their tea, before nearly running out of food. Murray acknowledged that "Mr. Seymour's patience and good humor never gave way." Forty years later the route they followed would be peppered at every crossing, carry, and lake with hotels, trains and shelters. Of the governors who have High Peaks named for them, Seymour is the only one to have actually traveled through the heart of the region.[148]

The 1850s were an incredibly volatile time. The slavery issue tore the nation apart and because of polarization between the North and the South only weak presidents, until Lincoln was elected, could win the Presidency. Presidents Fillmore, Pierce and Buchanan rose to the post simply because anyone with conviction either for or against slavery could not win election. At a time when the nation needed strong leadership in the face of the approaching crisis, the United States elected only indecisive and feeble leaders.[149]

Seymour and other Northerners in the Democratic Party believed that slavery would eventually die due to the flood of cheap immigrant labor coming to America from all over the world. The new Republican Party, born in 1854, pressed hard to halt slavery at every turn and put pressure on the South to end its support of human bondage. Abolitionists within the party who advocated the forcible release of slaves from their masters alarmed many Southerners and put them on the defensive. To those Southerners, the election of Abraham Lincoln in 1860 was the final straw. They believed that the Republican President would attempt to end slavery, and following his election, the southern states began to secede from the Union.[150]

When the Civil War began in April 1861, Horatio Seymour was one of the Republican Party's harshest critics. He supported Lincoln's resolve to bring the South back into the Union, but he opposed the federal government's strong-arm tactics. When Lincoln jailed, without due process, hundreds of citizens of the Border States for criticizing the Republican administration, Seymour, historically a staunch defender of individual rights, was outraged. "I deny that this rebellion can suspend a single right of the citizens of the loyal states," he declared, and he added "I denounce the doctrine that civil war in the south takes away from the loyal north the benefits of one principal of civil liberty."[151]

The war proceeded badly for the Union through the autumn of 1862, and Lincoln called for 75,000 additional troops to try and put down the rebellion. In the east, General Robert E. Lee and his Army of Northern Virginia thwarted every attempt by the Union Army of the Potomac to capture Richmond, the capital of the Confederacy. By that time it was evident that the conflict would be long, brutal, and bloody. With public disenchantment with Lincoln, his policies, and the running of the war, the Democratic Party stood a good chance of winning in gubernatorial elections that year, and, once again, Seymour was asked to run for Governor in New York. "I did what I could to avoid the nomination," Seymour wrote, "but I was forced on." He said, that he wanted "a strong compact party that can defy violence and keep the fanatics in check."[152]

He won that election, but before he delivered his inaugural address the following January, Lincoln extended an olive branch to him. The President wrote, "I, for the time being, am at the head of a nation in great peril, and you are at the head of the greatest state in the Nation." Lincoln sought Seymour's support, but Seymour was not easily appeased. In his inaugural address and thereafter through other pronouncements, he expressed his outrage at the trampling of rights guaranteed by the Constitution. He regarded the Emancipation Proclamation and the Draft Act as unconstitutional. The constant changing of generals at the head of the nation's largest army and the thousands of dead Union soldiers brought home in coffins led Seymour to become a leading proponent of a negotiated peace with the South. He believed that the southern states could be brought back into the Union under honorable terms. Some people believed that Seymour's peace stance undermined morale in the North and gave hope to the South.[153]

The two years that Seymour served as Governor during the Civil War were trying ones for the two political parties. "If we could hang Seymour we would save ten thousand men," wrote a Republican. Despite being looked upon by many Republicans as the most detestable of all the Democratic Governors, Seymour's state's contributions to the war effort were enormous. Horatio Seymour loved his country and put forth every effort to fill up the thinning ranks of the armies and raise money to quell the rebellion. New York enlisted 115,000 more soldiers than any other state did. The state could boast that it raised 200 regiments and that 464,701 of its men joined the army and navy. It also provided the greatest amount of supplies and gave the most money, and its citizens bought the largest number of war bonds for the effort. More than forty generals hailed from the Empire State and the most famous Union Ironclad, the *Monitor*, her iron armor plating forged from Adirondack ore, was built and launched from the Navy Yards in Brooklyn.[154]

New York also absorbed the greatest amount of debt of all the states, giving out over $43,000,000 in enlistment bounties. Her citizens paid the most taxes and gave the most to relief organizations. New York also paid dearly for her contributions. More New Yorker volunteers died, either on the battlefield or from disease, than did citizens of any other state – nearly one fifth of the 260,000 Union fatalities during the war.[155]

In the fall of 1864 Seymour again reluctantly accepted his party's nomination to run for another term as governor, but by then the war was progressing better for the Union. General William Sherman had captured Atlanta, Georgia, one of the biggest prizes in the South. Grant was knocking at the door of Richmond, and General Phillip Sheridan had razed the Shenandoah Valley while winning several spectacular battles. Seymour, clinging to the forlorn hope that a negotiated peace was still a possibility, was defeated at the polls.[156]

During the three years which followed the surrender of the Confederacy in April 1865, the North began the reconstruction of the South and readmitted all but three states to the Union.

In the national election of 1868, for the first time since 1860, the South would again be represented in an election. Despite having declined the nomination for President five times, saying "I have not the slightest desire to occupy the White House; there is too much trouble and responsibility, and no peace," Seymour was again pressed into service to run against Grant in the election. The race was unlike any other that Seymour had experienced. He was not prepared for the viciousness of the campaign as Grant's men smeared his good name and dug up everything in his past and used that information against him. Employing half-truths and outright lies, Grant's political thugs made an issue out of Seymour's father's suicide, saying that only an insane man could do such an act and therefore Seymour had to be insane as well. Seymour's stand against the temperance bill of 1853 was, to Grant's supporters, evidence that he was a drunkard and a puppet of the liquor interests, and his war record was evidence that he had been a Southern sympathizer.[157]

Seymour's sister was incensed by the political abuses. Few politicians in the nineteenth century had ever experienced such an onslaught, and she cried out to her brother, "Why don't you do something about this? Why don't you deny the charges?" Confident that his record spoke for itself, Seymour answered, "Time will take care of that."[158]

In terms of the popular vote Seymour did very well in the November election, only losing by 300,000 votes out of 6,000,000 cast, and the citizens of three states had not been allowed to vote, one of them the most populous state in the South, Virginia. Seymour carried his home state, New York, and neighboring New Jersey, but he received only 80 Electoral College votes while Grant's total was 214.[159]

Even though Seymour called running for President his "biggest mistake," he remained active in politics the rest of his life. He was nominated for governor a sixth time, in 1876, while asleep in bed, but had the state convention reconvene so that the delegates could select another candidate. He also declined to be a candidate for the Senate, but helped other candidates in their campaigns for office, like Samuel J. Tilden in his nearly successful run for the Presidency in 1876. Seymour's passion for politics never waned as he grew older, more feeble, and suffered increasing deafness. Even though his doctor had warned him against delivering a speech on a cold November day in 1880 for Presidential nominee Winfield Hancock, Seymour disobeyed, saying "I must go; for I cannot abandon my friends in their hour of need, even if I die in consequence." He was to live six more years and die, on February 12, 1886, at his home on the Mohawk River. For more than 50 years his wife Mary had been by his side. Without him, she lasted only twenty more days. Appropriately they were buried together in the same grave.[160]

First Ascent of Seymour

The first ascent of Seymour may have been by Verplanck Colvin and his guides David Hunter and Hank Parker on October 1, 1872... or it might have been made by Arnold Guyot and Ernest Sandoz in 1863. Both groups were aiming for the summit of the more prominent peak, Seward, but apparently missed in the thick clouds that obscured the mountain tops. It is unclear from the vague description written by Guyot whether or not he actually made the summit of Seymour or had indeed reached the summit of Seward. George Marshall believed that Guyot was the first to climb Seward. In an unpublished article, "Arnold Guyot and Ernest Sandoz in the Adirondacks and the Seward Range," he defended their right to first honors. In any case, either the team of Guyot and Sandoz or Colvin and his guides should be given credit for climbing Seymour first.[161]

Though Colvin, in 1873, applied the name *Seymour* to a mountain in the Sawtooth Range, just north of the present Seymour, it was somehow transferred to the peak just east of

Mount Seward. At that time both Colvin and Seymour were members of the Adirondack State Park Commission, with Seymour serving as the commission's president. Though the Park Commission was of no real consequence to the development of the Park, it was instrumental in establishing the Adirondack Survey and making Verplanck Colvin its superintendent. There can be no doubt that the famous politician deserved the recognition but, perhaps, the timing of the naming is suspect. Colvin might have been inspired to name the mountain *Seymour* in order to "pay" the politician for having assisted him in receiving his appointment. Seymour would be the last New York governor to have a High Peak named in his honor.[162]

Seymour at this time (2010) has only a non-maintained herd path to its summit. The route has changed little since it was first developed, but a portion of it used to follow a large slide on the north side of the mountain. Over the years that

Ed Hudowalski and Ernest Ryder on Seymour

slide has grown in; vegetation now covers what was once a gorgeous path to the summit. A herd path developed along the west side of the slide, but because of the steepness of the terrain it has now become one of the worst – eroded and muddy – trails in the Adirondacks.

Conclusion

Long after we are gone, the names bestowed on Mounts Seward, Seymour, Donaldson, and Emmons will stand as testaments and memorials to three men who believed in the righteousness of their causes and one who believed that Adirondack history had to be preserved. Mount Seward and Seymour are dedicated to two political figures, William H. Seward and Horatio Seymour, who gained national prominence during the volatile antebellum era and helped the Union through the dark years of the Civil War, although their philosophies differed considerably. Ebenezer Emmons brought the word *Adirondack* into our vocabulary, defended his Taconic System until his final days, and was honored with his permanent memorial, Mount Emmons, thanks to historian Russell Carson. Mount Donaldson is dedicated to historian Alfred L. Donaldson, who, despite having a life threatening disease, managed through herculean efforts to produce the consummate book on Adirondack history.

The remnants of the Santa Clara Lumber Company are quickly disappearing in the Seward Range. For 30 years the innovative lumber company, led in the field by Fred LeBoeuf, was able to take timber off of the steepest, roughest ground in the High Peaks. After 80 years the woods are finally healing. The forest that the Philosophers knew has vanished, but eventually, thanks to the remoteness of the Seward Range, future generations will again experience the beauty that the Philosophers knew.

Endnotes

Seward Range

1. Verplanck Colvin, "Mountain Measuring," *The Adirondack Reader,* Paul Jamieson, ed. (Glens Falls: Adirondack Mountain Club, 1982), pg. 394.

The Philosophers Camp

2. Alfred L. Donaldson, *The History of the Adirondacks* (Fleischmanns: Purple Mountain Press, 2 vols., 1921), Vol. I, pg. 394.

3. Follensby Pond was named after the first hermit of the area, Captain Folingsby. He lived and died near the pond some twenty years before the establishment of the Philosophers Camp.

4. Donaldson, Vol. I, pgs. 175-176.

5. *Ibid.*

6. Paul Jamieson, *Adirondack Pilgrimage* (Glens Falls: ADK Mountain Club, 1986), pg. 81.

7. *Ibid.,* pg. 132.

8. Donaldson, Vol. I, pg. 188; William J. Stillman, "Philosophers Camp," *The Adirondack Reader,* Paul Jamieson, ed., pg. 76.

9. Jamieson, *Pilgrimage,* pg. 94.

Santa Clara Lumber Company

10. *Town of Altamont Centennial, 1890-1990* (published in Tupper Lake, 1990), pg. 5.

11. Barbara McMartin, *The Great Forest of the Adirondacks* (Utica: North Country Books, 1994), pg. 97.

12. The brakes were hauled up the mountains by hitches of as many as eight horses.

13. Frank Reed, *Lumberjack Sky Pilot* (Old Forge: North Country Books, 1965), pg. 47.

14. Ferris J. Meigs, photostatic copy of *Santa Clara Lumber Company* found in Tupper Lake Library, pg. 66.

15. *Ibid.,* pg. 66.

16. Although Meigs wrote that all his Santa Clara crews cut their timber into 13-foot lengths, logging researchers have found quite a few 16-foot logs lying in a back bay away from the main channel of the river and abandoned along the side of a sled road.

17. Meigs, pgs. 42-43; Harold K. Hochschild, *Lumberjacks and Rivermen in the Central Adirondacks 1850-1950* (Blue Mountain Lake: Adirondack Museum, 1962), pgs. 40-50.

18. Nelson C. Brown, John Wiley and Sons, *Logging* (New York, 1934), pg. 66; *Ibid.,* pg. 294; Meigs, pg. 28.

19. *Tupper Lake Free Press,* Tupper Lake, N.Y., April 1914.

20. Interview with Chris Fearon, January 8, 2006.

Noah John Rondeau

21. Meigs, pgs. 62-63.

22. - 25. Interview with Gabreille Caffe, Spanish Fort, Alabama, April 1996.

Mount Seward

26. David M. Ellis, *et al., A History of New York* (Ithaca: Cornell University, 1957), pg. 239.

27. Dexter Perkins, Dumas Malone, eds., *Dictionary of American Biography,* American Council of Learned Societies (New York: Charles Scribner's and Sons, 1935), Vol. 16, pg. 615.

28. Park D. Goist, "William H. Seward and His Father," *New York History* (Cooperstown: New York State Historical Association), April 1963, Vol. 44, pg. 130.

29. Thornton K. Lothrop, *William H. Seward* (Boston and New York: Houghton Mifflin and Co., 1899), pg. 5.

30. Frederick Bancroft, *Life of Seward* (New York and London: Harper and Brothers, 1900, 2 volumes), Vol. I, pg. 12.

31. Goist, pg. 137.
32. Ellis, *et al.,* pg. 212.
33. Edward Everett Hale, Jr., *William H. Seward* (Philadelphia: George W. Jacobs, 1910), pg. 112; David H. Donald, *We Are Lincoln Men* (New York: Simon and Schuster, 2003), pg. 151.
34. Milton M. Klein, *The Empire State* (Ithaca and London: Cornell University Press, 2001), pg. 379.
35. *Ibid.*
36. Ellis, *et al.,* pg. 218.
37. Dexter Perkins, Dumas Malone, eds., *op. cit.,* pg. 616.
38. *Ibid.,* pg. 617.
39. Doris K. Goodwin, *Team of Rivals* (New York: Simon and Schuster, 2005), pg. 187.
40. Joseph J. McCadden, "Governor Seward's Friendship with Bishop Hughes," *New York History* (Cooperstown: New York State Historical Association), January 1966, Vol. 46, No. 1, pg. 181.
41. They were named the No Nothings because when someone outside the party asked them to explain their platform, they replied that they "knew nothing."
42. McCadden, pg. 181.
43. *Elizabethtown Post,* Elizabethtown, N.Y., May 24, 1860.
44. Donald, pg. 147.
45. Joseph J. Thorndike, ed., *The American Heritage New Illustrated History of the United States* (New York: Dell Publishing Co., 1963, 18 volume set), Vol. 5, *The American Civil War,* pg. 43.
46. Donald, pg. 171.
47. *Ibid.,* pg. 156.
48. Patricia L. Faust, ed., *Encyclopedia of the Civil War* (New York: Harper and Row, 1986), pg. 804; Donald, pg. 169.
49. James M. McPherson, *Crossroads of Freedom, Antietam* (Oxford: Oxford University Press, 2002), pg. 37.
50. Shelby Foote, *Civil War, A Narrative* (New York: Random House, 1958, 3 vol. set), Vol. I, pg. 157.
51. Donald, pg. 162.
52. McPherson, *op. cit.,* pg. 143.
53. Dexter Perkins, Dumas Malone, eds., pgs. 619-620.
54. Goodwin, *op cit.,* pg. 737.
55. James L. Swanson and Daniel R. Weinberg, *Lincoln's Assassins* (Arena Editions, 2001), pg. 12.
56. *Ibid.*
57. Goodwin, pg. 751.
58. Frederick W. Seward, *Reminiscences of a War-Time Statesman and Diplomat* (New York: G. P. Putnam's Sons, 1916), pg. 364.
59. Goodwin, pg. 751.

Naming of Seward

60. "Seward Surveys" (http:www.mez.harvard,edu/Department/Inventpaleo/Trenton/Intro/geologyPage/caseof (2004), pgs. 1-2.

Donaldson

61. Donaldson, Vol. I, pg. 243; "Tuberculosis: The People's Plague," http://www.adirondackhistory.org/newtb/one.html, (2000), pg. 1.
62. *Ibid.,* "The People's Plague."
63. Donaldson, Vol. I, pg. 243.
64. *Ibid.,* pg. 247.
65. "Tuberculosis: The Wilderness Cure," http:www.adirondackhistory. org/newtb/four.html, (2000), pg. 2.
66. Alfred Lee Donaldson Papers, 4 sets of letters in boxes, letter to A.W. Durkee, Box 1, (Letter #45), Feb. 8, 1920, Saranac Free Library, William Chapman White Memorial Room, Saranac Lake, N.Y.
67. Donaldson Papers, Box 1, Durkee (#43), February 11, 1920.

68. Donaldson, Vol. I, pg. vii.
69. *Ibid.,* Donaldson Papers, Box 1, Henry Harper (#155), January 2, 1919.
70. Donaldson, Vol. I, pg. vii-viii.
71. *Ibid.,* pg. ix.
72. J. F. O'Neill, "Alfred Lee Donaldson, Historian of the Adirondacks," *Journal of the Outdoor Life*, Vol. XXI, No. 11, Nov. 1924, pg. 673.
73. Donaldson Papers, Box 2, Mr. Herreshoff (#185), December 1913.
74. *Ibid.*
75. Donaldson Papers, Box 1, Melvin Dewey (#31), March 19, 1921.
76. Donaldson Papers, Box 2, H. H. Hall (#83), April 18, 1918.
77. Donaldson Papers, Herreshoff (#185).
78. *Ibid.*
79. Donaldson Papers, Box 2, Dr. Arpad Gerster (#75), January 3, 1919; Donaldson Papers, Herreshoff (#185).
80. Donaldson Papers, Box 2, Macomb Foster (#68), January 27, 1919; Donaldson Papers, Box 2, Herbert Lloyd (#250), October 24, 1919.
81. Donaldson Papers, Box 2, James McMillan (#262), November 22, 1913.
82. Donaldson Papers, Box 2, Harper (#152), December 28, 1918; Donaldson Papers, Box 2, Harper (#155), January 2, 1919.
83. Donaldson Papers, Box 2, Harper (#148), December 1918.
84. Donaldson Papers, Box 2, Harper (#170), December 17, 1918.
85. Donaldson Papers, Box 2, Irving Morris (#313b), February 15, 1919.
86. *Ibid.,* (#313b).
87. Donaldson Papers, Box 2, Jennie Scanlon (#348), Dec. 1918.
88. Donaldson Papers, Box 2, Herreshoff (#216), November 5, 1915; Donaldson Papers, Durkee (#43).
89. Donaldson Papers, Box 2, Harper (#171), May 14, 1919.
90. Russell M. L. Carson, Phillip G. Terrie, ed., *Peaks and People of the Adirondacks*, (Adirondack Mountain Club, 1973), pg. xxvii.
91. Donaldson Papers, Box 2, Harper (#164), April 1919; Donaldson Papers, Durkee (#43).
92. "Library Given Rare Adirondack Records," copy in vertical file under Donaldson in Saranac Free Library, William Chapman White Memorial Room, Saranac Lake, N.Y. Only date indicated was 1924 and no other source written on document.

Naming of Donaldson

93. Carson, pg. xxiv.
94. Alfred Lee Donaldson Papers, letter to Russell M. L Carson, March 31, 1923, Adirondack Museum, Blue Mountain Lake, N.Y.
95. *Ibid.,* June 9, 1923.
96. *Ibid.,* October 23, 1923.
97. Carson, pg. xxv.
98. *Ibid.,* pg. xxiv.

Emmons

99. Between 1830 and 1860 there were fifty-six state and federal surveys in the 33 states. The country and the states wanted to assess their land with an eye toward harnessing the resources that they found.
100. Ebenezer Emmons to President Hopkins of Williams College, October 22, 1857, Williamsiana Collection, Williams College, Williamstown, Massachusetts.
101. M. Hopkins, "Sketch of Dr. Emmons," *Williams Quarterly*, Vol. XI, Oct.-Nov. 1864, pgs. 260-261.
102. The word *dinosaur* was not coined until 1842.
103. "The Dinosauria," http://www.ucmp.berkeley.edu/diapsids/dinosaur.html, pg. 1.

104. Ebenezer Emmons, *American Geology*, (Albany: Sprague and Co., 1855), Vol. I, pg. 28.
105. Ebenezer Emmons, "Notice of Scientific Expedition to Nova Scotia", *Geological Review*, 1848, pg. 26.
106. Jamieson, *"Pilgrimage,"* pg. 131.
107. Robert Macfarlane, *Mountain of the Minds*, (New York: Vintage Books, 2004), pgs. 124-125.
108. "James Hall (1811-1898)," http:www.mez.harvard.edu/Department/Inventpaleo/Trenton/Intro/geologyPage/caseof, (2004), pgs. 4-7; Jules Marcou, "Biographical Notice of Ebenezer Emmons," *The American Geologist*, June 1891, pg. 10.
109. Sandra Weber, *Mount Marcy*, (Fleischmanns: Purple Mountain Press, 2001), pg. 25; Robert W. Fogel and Stanley L. Engerman, *Time on a Cross*, (Boston-Toronto: Little, Brown and Co., 1974), pg. 248.
110. "James Hall (1811-1898)."
111. Weber, pg. 30.
112. James Hall, Letter to Editor, Mount Marcy, Essex County, August 5, 1837, *Albany Daily Advertiser*, (August 15, 1837).
113. Ebenezer Emmons, "First Ascent of Marcy," Paul Jamieson, ed., *Adirondack Reader*, pg. 393.
114. Carson, pg. 34, pg. 194.
115. Ebenezer Emmons, "First Ascent of Marcy," Paul Jamieson, ed., *Adirondack Reader*, pg. 393; Carson, pg. 59.
116. Charles Fenno Hoffman, "Scenes at the Sources of the Hudson," *The New York Mirror*, October 21, 1837.
117. Carson, pg. 59.
118. Markes E. Johnson, "The Second Career of Ebenezer Emmons", *Abstracts with Programs-Geological Society of America*, January 1980, Vol. 12, No. 4, pg. 144.
119. Marcou, pg. 10.
120. Johnson, pg. 144.
121. *Ibid.*, pgs. 144-146.
122. Marcou, pg. 8.
123. Hopkins, pg. 265.
124. Johnson, pg. 160.
125. Marcou, pg. 15.
126. Johnson, pg. 162.
127. Marcou, pg. 9.
128. *Ibid.*, pg. 13.
129. Carson, pg. 245; Interview with Dr. Markes Johnson, Williams College, May 18, 2005.
130. Carson, pg. 242.

First Ascent of Seward, Donaldson, Emmons
131. Verplanck Colvin, "Seward," Paul Jamieson, ed., *Adirondack Reader*, pg. 394.
132. Jamieson, ed., *Adirondack Reader*, pg. 397.
133. The author once spotted a moose fairly high on the side of Emmons and tracked it to about 3,000 feet before turning back. It seemed to be heading over the shoulder of Emmons and the steep, rough, thick terrain did not appear to hinder its movements; Carson, pg. liii.
134. "Guyot, Arnold [Henri]," http://etcweb1.princeton.edu/campusWWW/Campanion/guyot arnold.html.
135. Carson, pg. liii-liv.

Seymour
136. Stewart Mitchell, *Horatio Seymour* (Cambridge: Harvard Press, 1938), pgs. 423-424.
137. Samuel J. Tilden was the great great uncle of the author.
138. Mitchell, pg. 423.
139. *Ibid.*, pg. 424.
140. *Ibid.*, pgs. 429-430.

141. Stewart Mitchell, "Seymour," Dumas Malone, ed., *Dictionary of American Biography*, (New York: Charles Scribner's Sons, 1935), pg. 6; Irving Stone, *They Also Ran*, (Garden City: Doubleday, Doran and Co., 1945), pg. 268.

142. Mitchell, "Seymour," pg. 7.

143. Stone, pg. 270.

144. Mitchell, "Seymour," pg. 7.

145. Stone, pg. 273.

146. *Ibid.*, pg. 274.

147. *Ibid.*, pg. 274; A. C. Ravitz, "Harold Frederick's Venerable Copperhead," *New York History*, (Cooperstown: N.Y. State Historical Association), January 1960, Vol. 41, No. 1, pg. 35.

148. Mitchell, pg. 176; Hon. Amelia Murray, "Letters from the United States, Cuba and Canada," *Adirondack Reader,* Jamieson, ed., pg. 241.

149. "Historical Rankings of United States Presidents," http://en.wikipedia.org/wiki/Historical_rankings_of_United_States_Presidents, (2006).

150. Thorndike, ed., *op. cit.,* Vol. 5, pg. 43.

151. Stone, pg. 277.

152. Allan Nevins, *War for the Union 1862-1863*, (New York: Konecky and Konecky, 1960), pg. 144; Stone, pg. 276.

153. William B. Hesseltine, *Lincoln and his War Governors*, (New York: Alfred A Knopf, 1948), pg. 286.

154. Ellis, *et al., A History of New York*, (Ithaca: Cornell University, 1957), pg. 338.

155. *Ibid.*, pg. 338.

156. Milton M. Klein, *The Empire State*, (Ithaca and London: Cornell University Press, 2001), pg. 431.

157. Mitchell, "Seymour," pg. 9; Stone, pg. 266.

158. Stone, pg. 267.

159. *Ibid.*

160. *Ibid.,* pg. 281; Proceedings of the Senate and Assembly of the State of New York, *In Memoriam. Horatio Seymour*, (Albany: Weed, Parsons and Co., 1886), pg. 22.

First Ascent and Naming of Mount Seymour

161. Carson, pg. liv.

162. *Ibid.,* pg. 214.

About the Author

Born in Syracuse, New York, while his father was at graduate school, Sharp followed his parents up to their Adirondack children's camp, Pok-O-MacCready, when he was only ten days old. He eventually worked his way out of diapers and into the ranks of "Poko" as camper, counselor, section head, and headmaster of the boys camp and now its fourth generation director.

Sharp graduated from Westminster College in Fulton, Missouri, with a history degree and a passion for the American Civil War. He has spent a substantial amount of time during the past twenty years in the Seward Range looking for the last vestiges of the Santa Clara Lumber Company (1889-1926) and serves on the board of the Adirondack Center Museum in Elizabethtown, New York.

Sharp became a 46er on Marshall in 1969 and, because he was only 14 at the time, had root beer instead of champagne to celebrate that occasion. In subsequent years, he has completed more than twenty-five rounds of the 46, each time finishing on Marshall. He has been a cook group leader at the 46er Outdoor Leadership Workshop since 1979 and has attended both National Outdoor Leadership School (NOLS) and Outward Bound.

Sharp resides in the lovely and historic hamlet of Essex and has three grown children. In the off-season, when not at Poko, he is a partner in and president of Cloudsplitter Carpentry, LLC.

STREET MOUNTAIN
Height: 32nd – 1,260c meters (4,134+ feet)
By Barbara Harris (#2824W)

"Nature is man's teacher. She unfolds her treasurers to his search, unseals his eye, illumes his mind, and purifies his heart; an influence breathes from all the sights and sounds of her existence."

– ***Alfred Billings Street***

Street and Nye are like map and compass[1] – they go together – but why are they referred to as "Street and Nye" when many hikers go up Nye first and then Street? "Maybe because of Street's height," Jim Goodwin (#24) surmises. Ditt Dittmar (#31) said he always climbed Street and then Nye "in that succession all six or more times, from Rocky Falls." Helen Menz (#42), when asked why replied, "Maybe it's easier to say." Four out of five times that she climbed them, she went up Nye first. Now a Wilderness Path from the Indian Pass Brook leads hikers to a col on the ridge between Street and Nye, and there the informal trail splits. At that point because Nye is closer than Street, most who aspire to reach both summits, usually go to Nye first, Street later. However, "Street and Nye" the mountains remain. Somehow we can't bring ourselves to say "Nye and Street."

The first human impressions upon Street's summit, so far as anyone knows, were made by the boots of Herb Clark and brothers George and Robert Marshall. They climbed Street first and then went on to Nye on June 27, 1921, and thus became the first hikers to climb the peaks, "Street and Nye," in the North Elba Mountains. Robert Marshall, a year later, wrote that they "ascended... from the tote road leading to Indian Pass. The climb was long but there were no very steep places. The top is flat, and for the last half hour we hardly rose at all. The summit is also heavily wooded so that, aside from glimpses toward Nye, Heart Pond and MacIntyre, we saw nothing."[2]

Verplanck Colvin named the mountain in 1872 for Alfred Billings Street. Born on December 18, 1811, in Poughkeepsie, Street was a man of many talents. He was a poet, a lawyer, an editor, an author, a critic, and director of the New York State Library (1848 to 1862), and state Law Librarian (1862 to 1868). He was associated with the State Library at Albany from the time he became its director in 1848 until he died in 1881.

In his book about his service in the Civil War, *Three Years with the Adirondack Regiment*, Major John L. Cunningham included an incident he witnessed which reveals something of Street's character:

> Law School students spent much time in the State Library... Alfred B. Street... was somewhat irritable and easily annoyed. One cold winter day he noticed a couple of students with their feet raised against the edge of a marble-topped radiator. He approached them with some wrapping

paper and said, in sarcastic kindliness: "Young men, if you will drop your feet I'll put a paper over the hot marble so you won't burn your shoes. You are away from home and I'd like to be a mother to you." Of course the feet came down and remained down. He was really angry and had some reason for it in the careless thoughtlessness of these students... I did not consider him so much the "grouch" that most of the students did.

Alfred Billings Street

At the age of 15, Street began writing poems, some of which were published by William Cullen Bryant in the *Evening Post*. He attended Dutchess County Academy and, after graduating from that institution, studied law with his father at Monticello. He was admitted to the bar in 1835 and worked in his father's office in Monticello until he moved in 1839 to Albany, where he set up a law office and practiced the profession for several more years. On November 3, 1841, he married Elizabeth Weed of Albany, and they had one son, Alfred W. Street. From 1843 to 1844 he was editor of the *Northern Light*, a literary journal sponsored by a group of prominent Albany citizens headed by John Adams Dix, for whom Dix Mountain is named. Street presented many of his poems before the literary societies of colleges in New York state. He was a member of Phi Beta Kappa and various literary societies and, in the nineteenth century, was one of America's best known poets. He found some of his themes in the forests, mountains, and the lakes of New York. His best known works, however, are the historical poems *The Burning of Schenectady* (1842) and *Frontenac* (1849). He also wrote *Woods and Waters: or, The Saranacs and Racket* (1860), which contains an account of a trip he made to the summit of Whiteface in 1858.

Street's second prose work about the Adirondack region, *The Indian Pass* (1869), recounts his adventures in September 1868 with his son and two guides, Loyal A. Merrill and 18-year-old Robert Scott Blinn. The party started at North Elba and walked through Indian Pass to the Upper Works before proceeding to Lake Colden, Marcy, Panther Gorge, the Ausable Lakes, and Keene Flats (Keene Valley). Thereafter Street made his second ascent of Whiteface. With two other guides, Street, his son, and an artist, Homer Martin, concluded the adventures of *The Indian Pass* with an ill-fated attempt to go to the "Gorge of the Dial," (Hunters Pass) from "Mud Pond" (Elk Lake).

When leaving the junction with Nye and turning southwest to hike to Street Mountain, today's hikers walk through what was destruction created in 1999 by Hurricane Floyd's winds. The hike is made relatively easy because of the work of the 46er trail crew. (See the Nye Mountain chapter for more discussion of that work). Nature's wrath, which destroyed so much, also created something new: views of Algonquin and Wright that had not existed before. Enjoy them now, for in a few years Mother Nature will enclose the flanks of the Wilderness Path with growth that will, before long, obscure the vista.

The hike from the junction to Street's summit is only six tenths of a mile. It is quick and enjoyable because of the Wilderness Path, which avoids, to the north, a swamp along which a multi-branching and ever expanding herdpath used to lead hikers into mud holes. When climbing up the boulders under the summit, you will find bunchberry, wood sorrel, and Clintonia. On the summit look at least 15 feet up a tree for a sign identifying the peak.

There is no view to be found from the summit rock; however, there are spots nearby from which marvelous views are available. The more stunning of the two is found along the first herdpath to the east. Follow that path for a minute, but take care when advancing to the furthermost rock as you must leap over a deep crevasse to reach it. The vista opens there and includes Giant, Basin, the McIntyres, the Santanonis, even the Sewards, if you stretch your neck. To find the second view, return to the summit rock and proceed straight ahead for another minute. You will arrive at a spot at which you might feel you can reach out and touch Algonquin. Lost Pond Peak is literally right in front of you. At your feet, some of the groundcover is goldthread. In the spring you will be greeted by singing warblers on the summit trees.

Something you won't find on the trailless peaks, including Street, are the canisters that used to be on them. The High Peaks Wilderness Area Unit Management Plan of the New York State Department of Environmental Conservation deemed them non-conforming structures under the Adirondack Park State Land Master Plan and required their removal in July 1999. Many climbers enjoyed signing their names and entering comments in the log books that the canisters sheltered. Many, too, enjoyed reading the messages entered by others. Suzanne Lance discusses the canister "issue" in her "History of the Adirondack Forty-Sixers" at the beginning of this book. Consequently that information is not repeated here, but it was a bittersweet decision to remove the canisters as "our tradition of mountain stewardship made the choice clear," that the canisters had to go.[3]

In the 1940s it was unusual for hikers to meet on the trailless peaks. On September 7, 1940, quietly celebrating his completion of the forty-six peaks, Jim Goodwin was alone atop Street eating his lunch, but he wasn't alone for long. Soon he heard voices of other people coming up the mountain. A few minutes later, Grace Hudowalski (#9) and Ed Hudowalski (#6) arrived with Franklin Wilson, Jr. (#25) who, as he reached the summit, also became a Forty-Sixer. Jim later commented, "To become a 46er and have the Hudowalskis celebrate with me was a unique experience. No one knew about the great view from Street that day."[4]

On another day, a nice one sixty-four years later, people atop Street had to wait turns to take in the views from the two spots mentioned earlier. There were 20 hikers on the summit at one time.

A little known fact about Street is that its rock contains enough iron ore to render a compass useless. In April 1988, Suzanne Lance (#1802W) led her new then non-46er husband George Sloan (now #2651W) up Street and Nye. (They were on their honeymoon.) Before they departed from Street, they decided not to retrace their snowshoe tracks the way they had ascended but, instead, to drop off Street and angle back to their trail farther down the flank of the mountain. Suzanne pointed through the trees in the direction she said they had to go. George, who had been a Boy Scout, pulled out his compass. Its needle indicated that they had to go the opposite direction. There, on Street, George and Suzanne had their first argument as a married couple. Suzanne prevailed. She later wrote, "My new husband displayed great faith in his new wife by disregarding his compass reading and following me down the mountain and back to the Loj. Had we gone his way we would have wound up at Wanika Falls."[5]

Fifty years earlier, Bill Lance, Suzanne's father, had been on a hike with Ed Hudowalski that took them to Street and Nye. On the ridge Bill's boot heel came off and he thereafter had to walk on his toes because, otherwise, the little nails which protruded from the exposed heel would catch on the ground over which he walked. While stepping over a downed tree, he scraped the nails on it, leaving a mark. Ed was navigating their route to the peak with his compass. They walked for a while and, before long, were about to step over another downed tree when they noticed the nail-marks which had been etched the first time they had stepped over it. They had walked in a compass-guided, straight-line circle. Suzanne remarked, "They surmised that there must have been some ore on the Street/Nye ridge that interfered with compass readings."[6] Family lore had preserved that assumption, which Suzanne recalled a half century later and thus was able to avoid an unnecessary and inconvenient honeymoon trip to Wanika Falls.

If you have ever looked closely at the ADK's map, "Trails of the Adirondack High Peaks Region," you may have noted that the summit of Street is indicated with a curious notation: "Flag 2." Tony Goodwin surmises that when survey work was taking place in 1941 for the map that would include Street, surveyors probably placed a flag on the summit which, through triangulation measurements helped to determine the mountain's height. A hole was drilled in the rock upon the summit and the flag was supported on a staff that was inserted into the hole. Flag 2 could be seen from Marcy, Algonquin, and Cascade – other "bases" for the High Peaks survey. Once Street's elevation was determined (4,166 feet at that time), other elevations could be calculated through triangulation using "Flag 2" as a point of reference. Though the flag has long been gone, the notation of its former location remains on the popular map of the area.[7]

Rocky Falls on Indian Pass Brook, with its too-close-to-the-water lean-to but refreshing swimming hole below the lower falls, was once a starting point for climbing Street. The DEC is continuing to do routine maintenance on the lean-to, but when it needs to be replaced, it will be relocated at least 100 feet from the brook.[8] By the early 1970s, when more hikers were attempting the 46 than ever before, the bushwhack up Street from Rocky Falls fell out of favor and the routes, which later proliferated, from the brook where the Old Nye Ski Trail crossed it, became the standard herdpaths to both summits. Although Rocky Falls is closer to Street's summit than the Old Nye Ski Trail, treks to the summit were often long and challenging. Thick stands of balsam and spruce made navigation difficult and many a seasoned hiker recalls, not particularly fondly, having to surmount numerous "false peaks" along the way to the top.

Rain, a "heavy" snowstorm, and more rain in mid May 1976 forced a hiking party from the Gordon Cornwell Seminary of South Hamilton, Massachusetts, to remain for three days on the side of Street. The group was well equipped – with tents, sleeping bags, food, cooking gear, parkas, "good boots" – but the week-long trek that had been planned as the culmination of the seminary's "Wilderness Experience and Christian Maturity" class was thwarted from completing its ambitious expedition by miserable weather. They had planned to climb Street and Nye, descend to the west by a bushwhack route to Moose Pond, proceed southwest to Mountain Pond, go from there to Preston Ponds and then on to Henderson Lake, climb Mount Marshall, and return to Adirondak Loj along the Indian Pass Trail. They had also planned to spend the final full day of their week-long expedition engaged in rock climbing on Mount Jo before returning to the seminary. All that they actually accomplished was a climb of Street.

Photo of Rocky Falls by Barbara Harris

The group of fifteen had left from the Loj on Sunday, May 16, and had camped along the Indian Pass Brook before proceeding to the summit of Street, which they reached – a day behind schedule – at noon on Tuesday, May 18. That was when rain began to fall. The expedition's leader, Dr. George Ensworth, decided that the members of the party had to "get away from the wet and cold." So the hikers descended between a quarter and a half mile to the southeast and, at about 3,500 feet in elevation, set up camp. Dr. Ensworth later told *Plattsburgh Press-Republican* reporter Melissa Hale, "That night it turned to ice. Then it began snowing."[9] The group remained in their camp until Thursday, May 20, when, at last, the members began a long and slow retreat to Adirondak Loj.

Several things were unusual about the expedition and its members: the group was equipped with radio equipment; the DEC was involved in monitoring its progress and condition through radio contact; and three of the members of the group were not seminary students or instructors.[10] They were Secret Service agents who had been assigned to accompany one of the group during its expedition: Michael Ford, son of the President of the United States.

Conservation Officers Gary Mulverhill, David Scudder, Harold Karaka, Charles Reynolds, and Lieutenant George Firth departed from the Loj at 8 o'clock in the morning and went into the woods from the Indian Pass Trail to meet the group as it slogged its way out through wet and mud and blowdown. The instructors, Secret Service men, and seminary students had endured a "strenuous" hike out which Dr. Ensworth said included traversing a "burned area" through which they had had to go "over logs for five hours." By the time they met up with Dr. Ensworth and his group, about three miles from Adirondak Loj, the DEC officers were as wet as the members of the expedition, but the officers were not wearing blue jeans as some of the expedition's members were. The officers assisted some of the cold, wet, and "fatigued" members of the group – "the most faltered steps hikers" – by carrying their packs back to the hiker's building (High Peaks Information Center) on the Loj property late in the afternoon, and inside that facility the group enjoyed the warmth of the fireplace and hot drinks served up by David Tate and Michael Hoffman. The DEC men had not been aware that Ford was a member of the group until he approached them at the hiker's building, thanked them for their help, and identified himself. Tate and Hoffman weren't told that Michael was a member of the group until long after the students, instructors, and Secret Service agents had departed again for Massachusetts.

Dr. Ensworth told reporters that the expedition had accomplished its goals of "students testing... themselves in handling stress... understanding and insight into how the wilderness experience relates to the Christian experience... training so the seminary students could in turn take church groups on wilderness camping trips." He said that they had been aware of the danger the group faced from the potential of hypothermia, that they had been "equipped to respond to such an eventuality," and that the students had been "affected positively by the whole thing." Yet some had worn down parkas and denim trousers during the trip.

Wallface and Indian Pass Trail

Wallface, the 1,000-foot cliff at the head of Indian Pass, once thought to be unclimbable, now challenges technical climbers with twenty major routes. John Case of Keene Valley pioneered the first. Jim Goodwin, Fritz Wiessner, and Peter Gabriel worked out the other three.[11] Still only the experienced should attempt climbing the precipice.

Alfred Street in *The Indian Pass* described the "gorge" below the massive bastion of Wallface from an outlook on its north side:

> Down, down, close under me and at either hand, fell the sheer precipice on the brow of which I was perched, plunging... into the black abyss, so black, so deep, it seemed as if the earth had yawned and stood with sable throat to swallow me. The indescribable crawl of the nerves, felt only in the most dangerous situations, thrilled my whole system. I had the insane desire, the almost irresistible impulse, to throw myself headlong into the chasm. Merrill tore a large stone from the cliff and hurled it. So deep the chasm that gravitation seemed suspended, for, notwithstanding its weight, the stone wavered like a wounded bird ere, plunging below, it was lost to the eye. No sound of its smiting the floor of the gorge followed. The distance was too great to allow the echo to be heard.
>
> Immediately to our right, the picturesque profile of the wall, where it soared from the thousand feet of our level a half thousand more into the sky, looked grim and threatening, the outlines twisted into the semi-likeness of a man, or rather the whole likeness of a grinning demon.

Street, whose style was both Romantic and Gothic, continued:

> At last, the wild picture being ingrained, or rather sunk like an intaglio into my memory, there to remain forever, we prepared to descend. And first, to withdraw from our dangerous and precarious perch! Leaving one pendent branch to clutch another, unclasping our foothold from one crevice to insert it quickly in a second, we turned round, and drew ourselves cautiously upward until we reached again the level brow of the precipice. Fighting through the ghastly labyrinth of the "slash" *[blowdown]*, we plunged downward toward the gorge. Down, down the steep side of the rocky wall, pendulumizing (excuse the word) ourselves over the chasm, and scrambling down the ravine...

Street's party later camped for the night, but the poet, at midnight, was awoken "by a terrific storm of thunder and lightning, accompanied by bursts of blasts that shook the

Indian Pass was one of New York's scenic wonders in the 19th century. Above is an etching of Charles C. Ingham's view of it, "Adirondack Pass."

scene almost like an earthquake" in the place, he said, the Indians called the He-no-do-aw-da, the Path of the Thunderer. He devoted five pages of his chapter about Indian Pass to his description of the storm and its thunders, which he imagined to be the voices of McIntyre and Wallface in lofty contention for supremacy. He began:

> I found the two mountains in furious altercation, one answering the other, as if about to engage in mortal strife. As I listened, the sounds shaped themselves into words.
> "Ho!" roared the towering McIntyre, "why am I thus disturbed! Cease that voice of thine, O Wallface, or dread my wrath."
> "Ho, ho!" thundered Wallface in his turn, "dost thou threaten? Cease that voice of thine, thy silly clamor, or dread *my* wrath."
> "What!" said the mighty McIntyre, and as he spoke an angry glare of lightning kindled all his awful form that was offered to my gaze, playing around his head as if he were darting red glances at his foe: "this, slave, to me – me, who could crush thee with my might as my slides crush the rocks in their pathway?"
> "Thou crush me, proud mountain – me, whose craggy breastplate hath dashed back a thousand storms, and against which centuries have gnawed in vain! Thou crush me! ho, ho, silly thing, thou provokest me to laughter!" and a blast thundered from Wallface that seemed to make him shake like the pine-tree in the wind...

In the middle of the nineteenth century the pass was considered one of the most "awesome" wonders of the state of New York. Today it receives far fewer visitors than does Cascade Mountain, which, when Indian Pass was at the height of its Romantic popularity, probably had yet to be climbed.

Indian Pass was the supposed destination of a hiker, Thomas Carleton of Skaneateles, during the Columbus Day weekend of October 1993. He had told his wife, before he departed from home, that he might hike in the Indian Pass area, but where he actually went has never been determined.

He began his solo expedition when the weather was warm, but a cold snap soon dropped the temperature to 25 degrees and snow flurries were in the air. Carleton's wife reported that he had not taken a tent with him as he had been hoping to occupy a lean-to. Nor had he carried a cooking stove. However, he was an experienced hiker and was otherwise well equipped for his three-day excursion – perhaps too "well" equipped. A friend had advised him to carry a gun as a precaution in case he met up with a rabid animal. Reportedly, Carleton took a gun along with him.

Following the long weekend, when her husband did not return home, Mrs. Carleton notified the DEC and a search for the missing man began. However, from the start, the search was hampered. Carleton's car was parked at Adirondak Loj, but he had not signed any one of the three trail registers on Loj property. For two weeks thereafter, volunteers and DEC Rangers searched for the missing man. A bloodhound was brought in to help with the effort. Helicopters combed the area from above. Late in the month, authorities heard from a couple from Ithaca who had seen the missing man's photograph in a news report about his disappearance. They had been hiking along the Indian Pass Trail on October 9 and had, they were certain, seen Carleton at Scott's Clearing.

Speculation suggested that Carleton, a state prison system psychologist, had intentionally disappeared. However, it was reported that he had shown no signs of depression or despondency. Ranger Pete Fish, who interviewed Mrs. Carleton, was assured that "He *[had]* too much going on to quit."[12]

The formal search for Carleton ended October 19, 1993. To this day, he has not been found, but more than a decade after he disappeared, hikers on MacNaughton happened upon camping gear which, according to Peter Bronski in his book *At the Mercy of the Mountains: True Stories of Survival and Tragedy in New York's Adirondacks,* forest rangers confirmed had belonged to Carleton.[13]

From the Indian Pass Trail, between Rocky Falls and Summit Rock, today's explorers can follow a trail that will lead them to Scott's Pond (named for Robert Scott) and the Wallface Ponds. Verplanck Colvin wrote about the ponds and Wallface when he visited the area in September 1872:

> We were in hopes of finding some little lakes, known as "Scott's ponds" which, though doubted by some who had been unable to find them – Mr. Scott, their discoverer, having only seen them in winter, as level, snow-covered openings in the forest – were said to exist upon the top of Wallface, and which were probably the highest sources of the Ausable river. After a toilsome climb up the steep gorge of the river, wetted by aid of rope-like roots, we reached less difficult ground, where the stream divided into a number of smaller brooks. These streams had probably been the means of bewildering previous searchers for the ponds; lack of woodcraft leading them to waste time in exploring to their source all the numerous brooks. Pushing forward we passed the clear, cold, spring-like streams, following, without hesitation, the more tepid and discolored water of one branch, which tasted like that derived from a pond or bog. Advancing in this manner, I caught the first glimpse of open water, which proved to be the largest of these high mountain ponds. It was small and apparently shallow. Several brooks enter it; one coming from two level moss-swamps which, in barometer, was found to be [3091] feet, or higher than either Lakes Colden or Avalanche.

Colvin continued to the "western side of Wallface, where the brooks trend to the Raquette, through Cold river, but finding nothing of importance returned" and "had the fortune to stumble upon another lake, whose shores it is probable had never been previously visited by man." He found its altitude to be 3,168 feet and wrote that it was "a wild, unearthly place." He proceeded to the top of Wallface Mountain, determined its elevation to be 3,893 feet, and, with the aid of an assistant at "the station in the abyss at the foot of the precipice," calculated that the Wallface cliff was 1,319 feet in height.[14]

Between the ponds that Colvin explored and the summit of Street there is another body of water snuggled beneath a horseshoe-shaped ridge that has come to be known as Lost Pond Peak. Lost Pond rests at about 3,700 feet in elevation. It is the source of a stream called Roaring Brook that, joined by another stream which descends from the southwestern flank of Street, flows into Duck Hole and the Preston Ponds on its way to Henderson Lake and the Hudson River.

Among Lost Pond's earliest visitors (June 20, 1920) were Herb Clark and brothers George and Bob Marshall. They had not intended to make a trip to the pond but, the day before, while they were camped at South Meadow, they met a lumberjack, Ed Young, who arranged to meet with the trio the following day at the lumber camp at "Mud Preston" (Scott's Clearing on the Indian Pass Trail) the next day. There, while rain was teeming outside, the Marshalls and Clark met with Young inside a shanty near the dam that contained the pond that existed then at the clearing. Ed told the three about Lost Pond. After the downpour subsided, Herb, Bob, and George set out for the pond along a blazed line which Young had cut for his own pleasure a few days before.

George Marshall later wrote, "The way to Lost Pond was superlatively beautiful... ascending through a deep coniferous forest... at times between high rocks... across a little marsh where the ground was covered with a profusion of spring wild flowers and thick moss... carpets of goldthread... along the brook, buckbean." They crossed a ridge and discovered the pond, "one of the most beautiful and wildest spots we had ever seen." They returned to the Indian Pass Trail by way of a different route, which took them by the Wallface Ponds and enjoyed "their rare beauty."[15]

Lost Pond Peak beckons some hikers from Street or from the summits of the McIntyres. Herb Clark and George Marshall climbed it on August 1, 1929, when they were attempting to return to Lost Pond, which, George wrote, was "well named."[16] Tom Wheeler (#3356W) was with a small group of hikers who ascended the peak in September 1996. He remembers "the beautiful waterfalls... on the stream that runs down from the col between Street" and the peak which is about 3,800 feet in elevation. John Winkler (#1279), who has bushwhacked all 46 peaks, writes in his book, *A Bushwhacker's View of the Adirondacks* about Lost Pond Peak: "This completely trailless mountain has one of the best views... if it were a 46er peak I'm certain the view rating would be in the top ten."

MacNaughton Mountain

From Wallface Ponds you may wish to proceed southwest to MacNaughton Mountain, named for James MacNaughton, grandson of Archibald McIntyre, the principal organizer of the Adirondack Iron Works. MacNaughton mountain was not on the original list of peaks thought to be 4,000 feet or more in elevation, but as a result of the USGS survey of the High Peaks region conducted after World War II, MacNaughton was elevated in stature (just as Nye, Cliff, Blake, and Couchsachraga were reduced). The 1953 Santanoni quadrangle map showed MacNaughton to have two peaks that were at the 4,000-foot contour level. Thereafter, a good many 46ers climbed it and a canister containing a log book was placed on the northernmost peak of the mountain's three summits. The club did not require anyone to climb the mountain to achieve 46er status, but the club's official "Climbing the Adirondack

46" check list indicated that "most" members climbed it. MacNaughton, even from Wallface Ponds – a nine hundred-foot ascent, has always been a difficult climb, often a taxing one through cripplebrush and blowdown. However, even MacNaughton has herdpaths upon it today and, alas, when the mountain was remeasured in the early 1970s it was found to be 1,214 meters in elevation – 17 feet shy of 4,000 feet.[17] Still, though it offers only limited views, MacNaughton remains an interesting, remote mountain, and it is higher than Couchsachraga, Cliff, Nye, and, possibly, Blake.

George Marshall might approve of MacNaughton's diminished status for he once wrote, "I hope the range from MacNaughton to Nye will forever remain trailless and wild… I consider trailless cross-country travel in the Adirondacks, whether to the summit of a mountain or to a far away pond, the most delightful form of recreation I know."[18]

Endnotes

1. Former Ranger Pete Fish (#1396) often speaks of a map and compass as being a "mapandcompass" because, for a hiker trying to find his way in the wilderness, one cannot be used without the other. Because "Street and Nye" are so close to one another, almost always climbed during a single trip, and set in the minds of most 46ers as a closely matched pair, they are, in effect, "StreetandNye."

2. Robert Marshall, "The High Peaks of the Adirondacks" (Albany: Adirondack Mountain Club, 1922), pg. 31.

3. *Adirondack Peeks,* Spring/Summer 2001, pgs. 17-18.

4. Interview with Jim Goodwin, October 22, 2004.

5. Email from Suzanne Lance.

6. *Ibid.*

7. Phone conversation of October 27, 2004, with Tony Goodwin.

8. Kristofer Alberga, Supervising Forester, Division of Lands & Forests, Region 5, New York State DEC, phone conversation.

9. Details concerning the ordeal of the Gordon Cornwell Seminary's expedition are derived from *The Lake Placid News* of Thursday, May 27, 1976 ("President's Son Finds Mountain No Easy Street," by Gary Spencer) and the *Plattsburgh Press-Republican* of Wednesday, May 26, 1976 ("A Time for Testing," by Melissa Hale). Fourteen inches of snow fell in the Lake Placid area during the night of May 18/19, 1976.

10. Two other members of the expedition were also not seminarians or faculty members at Gordon Cornwell. They were an Outward Bound instructor, Gerald Hartis, and a Wheaton College outdoor program instructor, Paul Mitchell.

11. "Rock Climbing is Fun." *Ad-i-ron-dac,* March/April 1947.

12. Information derived from the *Plattsburgh Press Republican* newspapers of October 1993.

13. Letter from Captain John C. Streiff, Regional Ranger - Region 5 - to Barbara Harris. Also, Peter Bronski, *At the Mercy of the Mountains: True Stories and Tragedy in New York's Adirondacks* (The Lyons Press, 2008).

14. Verplanck Colvin, *Report of the Topographical Survey of the Adirondack Wilderness of New York for the Year 1873* (Albany, NY: Weed, Parsons and Company, 1874), Appendix D, pg. 275

15. George Marshall, "Lost Pond" in *Cloudsplitter,* June 1941, pgs. 2-3.

16. *Ibid.*

17. *Of the Summits, of the Forests* (Morrisonville, NY: Adirondack Forty-Sixers, 1991), "End Notes," pgs. 305, 328.

18. George Marshall, *op. cit.*

NYE MOUNTAIN
Height: 45th – 1,180c meters (3,871+ feet)
By Barbara Harris (#2824W)

"If you're lucky enough to be in the mountains, you're lucky enough." [1]

Nye Mountain was named about 1873 by Adirondack map maker Dr. William Watson Ely[2] for Verplanck Colvin's favorite guide, William "Bill" Nye.[3]

Nye, in 1853, built a farmhouse along the West Branch of the Ausable River in North Elba. That building, recently a bed and breakfast, the Ski-T Farmhouse at 22 River Road near the Olympic ski jumps, has terrific views. After living in the farmhouse for only a couple of years, Nye sold it; and after it had had a succession of other owners, the building was purchased by the Lake Placid Club. It had a new life as a clubhouse and little restaurant for Lake Placid's winter colony. There, during the 1932 Winter Olympics, spectators sat in a charming, old-fashioned tea room, relaxed, and enjoyed hot coffee and doughnuts.[4]

A cross country ski trail, used during the 1932 Olympics, ran from Adirondak Loj to Lake Placid. Part of the route followed a lumber road which, coincidentally, passed over the northeast ridge of Nye Mountain. Today, a portion of the route to the mountain still follows the Old Nye Ski Trail, and hikers who follow it still sometimes come across relics, such as stove parts, of a lumber camp that once existed along it. The Big Blow of 1950 obliterated most of the old ski trail, and forest growth since has obscured much of the route it followed.

Bill Nye was born in Berlin, Vermont, in 1816, the only child of his father's first wife. In 1835 he went to sea aboard a whaler bound for the Indian Ocean, but after what he considered to have been too little shore leave, he returned home to work the farm. Next he moved to Charleston, South Carolina, and ran two sailing vessels in Charleston Harbor and on the Ashley River before returning to sea for three and a half years as first mate of a brigantine. Upon returning to New England, he took up farming yet again before he headed west to St. Louis in 1848 to join a survey expedition led by Colonel John C. Frémont and guided by Kit Carson, but he came down with a "fever and ague" and was soon back in Vermont. In the spring of 1851 he arrived at North Elba. There, on the Ausable River, he established a sawmill, but he sold it in 1855, when finally he discovered his true calling: guiding.

Bill Nye's nineteenth century fame was associated with the story of the Hitch-up Matildas. In 1868 bachelor Bill, a six foot tall, strong, and modest man, guided a Mr. and Mrs. Fielding and their "handsome as a picture" niece Dolly, who stirred in Bill a feeling that he had perhaps made a mistake in living alone so long. He guided the three on a trek through Indian Pass to the iron works at Adirondac and back over Mount Marcy to North Elba via Avalanche Lake and Avalanche Pass. Along the side of the lake, their return to civilization was seemingly blocked by a high wall of rock which descended directly into the water.

The classic account of the incident, supposedly in Nye's words, was first published by Seneca Ray Stoddard in his *The Adirondacks Illustrated* (1874):

> I said I could carry them or I could build a raft, but to build a raft would take too much time while I could carry them past in a few minutes. Provisions were getting short and time set to be at North Elba, so Mr. Fielding says, "Well, Matilda, what say you? Will you be carried over, or shall we make a raft?" Mrs. Fielding says: "If Mr. Nye can do it, and thinks it safe, I will be carried over, to save time." "Well, Dolly, what do *you say?*" "Oh, if Mr. Nye can carry aunt over he can

Stoddard's illustration of Hitch up Matilda!

me, of course; I think it would be a novelty." Mr. Fielding says: "Well, we have concluded to be carried over, if you can do it safely." I said "perfectly safe: I have carried a man across that weighed 180 pounds, and a nervous fellow, at that." I waded across and back to see if there had been any change in the bottom since I was there before. When in the deepest place the water is nearly up to my arms for a step or two; I had nothing with me then. When I got back Mrs. Fielding said she did not see how I was going to carry them across and keep them out of the water. I said "I will show you; who is going to ride first?" Mr. F said "it was politeness to see the ladies safe first: so *Matilda* must make the first trip;" *she* would "let the politeness go, and would like to see Mr. F. go over first," but he said "she had agreed to ride if I said it was safe; *now* he wanted to see her do it;" "and *so I will!*" said she; "how am I to do it?" I set down with my back against a rock that came nearly to the top of my shoulders, told her to step on the rock, put one foot over one side of my neck, the other over the other side, and sit down. *That* was what she did not feel inclined to do, and was going to climb on with both feet on one side, but her husband told her to "throw away her delicacy, and do as I told her," reminding her of her word, which was enough; she finally sat down very carefully, so far down on my back that I could not carry her, I told her it wouldn't do, and at last she got on and I waded in.

"Hurrah! there they go!" "Cling tight, Matilda!" shouted the young lady and the husband in the same breath. "Hold your horse, aunt!" laughed Dolly. "Your reputation as a rider is at stake: three cheers for aunt Mazeppa! – I mean aunt Matty; novel, isn't it? Unique and pleasing; you beat Rarey,[5] auntie, that's what you do!"

I had just barely got into the deep water, steadying myself with one hand against the rocks and holding on to her feet with the other, when, in spite of all I could do, she managed to work half way down my back.

"Hitch up, Matilda! *hitch up,* Matilda! why *don't* you hitch up?" screamed Mr. Fielding, and I could hear him dancing around among the rocks and stones, while I thought Dolly would have died laughing, and the more he yelled, "hitch *up,*" the more *she* hitched *down,* and I began to think I would have to change ends, or she would get wet: but by leaning way over forward, I managed to get her across safe and dry. Then, "how was she to get off?" I said, "I will show you." So I bent down until her feet touched the ground, and she just walked off over my head, the two on the other side laughing and shouting all the time.

Dolly, when it was her turn to cross, "let" her aunt and uncle "see that all the money spent at riding schools hadn't been thrown away in *her* case."[6] Nye told her that she had to "sit straight as a major general," and, apparently, she did. Then, as the guide reported, "The rest was easy enough, rather more in my line too, and we got back all right." Since the time Stoddard's guidebook first told the story, a number of bridges have been built across the span where the Fielding incident took place. Each bridge has had the same name: "Hitch Up, Matilda."

Nye, who spent a lot of time in the woods, wrote once about his first experience with a catamount (mountain lion). In 1852, while boarding with Nelson Blinn of North Elba, he headed one day to Indian Pass to hunt deer. He saw plenty of tracks, all seeming to indicate that the deer were on the run. Then he spotted tracks that told him why: the imprints of wolves. He wrote, "I hadn't gone far when I saw a fresh panther track. Not being used to that kind of game, I thought best to let him alone and look after the deer. When it was time to go home, I thought I would take my track back… I had not gone far before I saw a panther track, he had crossed mine… When I got within a mile or so of the clearing *(of the Blinn house)* it began to grow dark. Then I heard one of the most unearthly screams; it appeared to be about forty rods to my right in the tops of the trees. It started my hat up some, but it did not fall off… He followed me to the edge of the woods, keeping about the same distance from me, and every little while he would cheer me on with one of those yells."[7]

In September 1872, as he guided Verplanck Colvin, Bill led the way to the summit of Gray Peak in a pea-soup fog by reckoning their position from the sound of the echoes of their shouts which bounced off Marcy and Skylight. They also made an important discovery that day when they determined that Lake Tear-of-the-Clouds, previously known as Perkins Pond or the Summit Water, does not drain to the Ausable River but is the highest pond source of the Hudson. Colvin employed Nye a number of times during the years of his Adirondack Survey, and Henry Van Hoevenberg held him in such high esteem that he awarded him the contract for blazing and building the many trails that emanated from Adirondack Lodge,[8] including the first one from the lodge to Marcy's summit. With his own money Bill had already built (about 1865) the first trail from Lake Placid to Whiteface.[9]

There isn't "gold in them thar hills," but there is a story of lost silver on Nye Mountain. According to the tale, William Scott, late in returning from a hunting trip, was forced to take shelter for a night under a rock overhang. When he awoke in the morning, he was surprised to see a vein of silver imbedded in the rock above him. Unfortunately, when he attempted to find the place again, he was unable to do so. About fifty years later, Nye and Scott's son, Robert, attempting to retrace William's half-century-old steps, determined that the silver must have been somewhere at the base of Nye Mountain. Together they did not find the vein under which the elder Scott had bivouacked. However, legend has it that Bill alone found it and that once a year he was seen setting out for the family homestead in Vermont with a very heavy packbasket on his back.[10]

In the spring Bill used to run a sugar works on the John Brown farm across the river from his cabin.[11] A friend of the abolitionist of Harper's Ferry fame, Nye wrote of the return of John Brown's body following his execution in 1859:

> When John Brown's body was brought to North Elba, Mrs. Brown requested me to have it carried upstairs and put in shape for the public to view… A few days after he was buried she gave me the collar that they took from around his neck before they put the rope around. I kept the collar until after the war ended, then I let my half-sister (Mrs. Sarah Pratt of Berlin) take it to keep it for me, and she laid it away so carefully that she has not been able to find it.[12]

In 1880 Bill returned to Berlin, Vermont, to live in a room above the woodshed on the Pratt farm, to hunt, and to fish. He died in a fire, apparently sparked by an overturned candle in his room, in February 1893. John Brown's collar was probably also lost in the fire that consumed the Pratt home, barns and outbuildings.[13]

There have been a number of plane crashes in the Adirondack Mountains, one of which occurred near Nye. The remains of the plane rest on the side of the mountain's 3,100-foot western shoulder. On the snowy night of December 25, 1978, a Piper Navajo private airplane crashed at that spot while on instrument approach to the airport at Lake Clear. Three men and a dog perished. A second dog walked away and was found ten days later rummaging through the garbage at the Lawrence Maxwell residence on Bear Cub Road in Lake Placid. The wreckage, however, went undiscovered until April 30, 1979, when a Civil Air Patrol crew on a training mission finally spotted it.

Two rangers were lowered from a helicopter to the top of the shoulder, and they used chainsaws to clear a path several hundred yards down through timber and heavy blowdown to the place where the plane had slammed into the face of a cliff five months earlier. The bodies of the dead men were carried to the top of the western shoulder so that they could be removed by helicopter. All three men had been killed instantly when the plane crashed.[14]

No longer the "Bermuda Triangle" of the trailless High Peaks – so called because people attempting to climb Street and Nye sometimes became disoriented and lost – the initial approach to the two peaks is now a single Wilderness Path established by the Adirondack Forty-Sixers with the approval of the New York State Department of Environmental Conservation on September 11 and 12, 1998. Wilderness Paths have been laid out to reduce the impact of hikers on the old "trailless" peaks.[15] Former alternate routes are blocked or obscured. The hope is that new paths will preserve the experience of following unmarked trails. Blowdown deemed to spur hikers to take alternate routes has been cleared away; however, if blowdown is merely an inconvenience, it has been left in place. Some tripping of feet, one experienced hiker says, "may keep you on your toes."

While working on the Wilderness Path for Street and Nye one weekend, those who helped with the project first heard the story of the Nye Wolf. One of the crew returned to camp with a pant leg shredded. He claimed that he had been attacked by a creature – half spirit, half beast. He said that although the Nye Wolf was "magical, it was not very swift." He said that it liked to eat hikers, but it was rarely fast enough to catch one. However, what it lacked in speed, it made up for in cunning. Before the trail rehabilitation, Street and Nye had been known for their confusing multiplicity of herdpaths. Those, the work party learned, were created by the Nye Wolf. Hikers became lost, disoriented, and tired as they tried to follow the many paths. A few tired ones, the story teller maintained, became easy prey for the wolf. The 46er trail work volunteer who was "attacked" claimed the Nye Wolf had become enraged when he discovered that his traps were being removed. With the work complete and the confusing old herdpaths blocked and obliterated, the spirit beast now must search a much wider area for lost hikers he may devour.[16]

After all of the work of the 46er trail crew, on September 16, 1999, Hurricane Floyd roared through the High Peaks, and, due to damage to the Wilderness Paths on them, Street and Nye once again seemed to encourage "random scoots," as Old Mountain (Orson Schofield) Phelps referred to bushwhacking. Fallen trees looked like giant matchsticks thrown through the wilderness and piled on top of one another. The Wilderness Paths had to be reestablished. On June 17, 2000, Forty-Sixers worked during thunderstorms and amidst swarms of blackflies to clear a route through the Floyd damage. One of the places where one may appreciate the challenge they faced and see the magnitude of the clearing job they did lies above the junction where the paths to Nye and Street diverge. On the way to Street, today's hikers walk through what was a mass of destruction. Nature's wrath, which destroyed so much, also created something new: At that spot there now is a view of Algonquin and Wright that had not been there before.

On June 16, 2001, the 46ers did some major rock stabilization work along a muddy section by the brook before it turns towards Nye. It allows hikers to walk along a single narrow path rather than the former constantly widening swath many had been creating while attempting to avoid the mud. If hikers remain on the rocks as they follow the path, the mud will dry and the area along its sides will renew with vegetation.

Since 2004, Trailless Peak Adopters Pete Hickey (#3202W) and his son Jean René Hickey (#3824) have been checking the condition of the Wilderness Path each spring and fall and have been maintaining it. With its new path, Nye probably won't confuse hikers as much as it once did. There was a time when the Last Chance Ranch was visited by weary hikers who had lost their way, either going to or returning from Nye. Eventually they followed the Indian Pass Brook downstream, and more than a few of them concluded their confused rambles when they emerged from their misplacement at the ranch.

There is now an outlook along the route to Nye at about the 3,200-foot level. There you can stand on a boulder and look to the southeast to see Mount Jo, Heart Lake (formerly called Clear Pond/Clear Lake)[17] and, directly in front, the magnificent high peaks.

Mount Jo was named after Josephine Scofield of Brooklyn, New York. With Henry Van Hoevenberg, known affectionately as Mr. Van, she climbed Marcy in 1877, and, according to tradition, they selected, from that high vantage point, the site of their future home. They chose a tiny lake that looked to them to be heart-shaped and immediately named the mountain rising from its shore Mount Jo, in her honor.[18] They did not realize that Alfred B. Street had named it the Bear, around 1865, and had written a poem about the little mountain beside the pond.[19] Josephine, it is said, chose the spot where the Adirondack Lodge was built, but she never saw it as she died soon after she had been to Marcy with Mr. Van.

On the Adirondak Loj Road in the town of North Elba,[20] on the way to Heart Lake, you can see, to the west, across the Plains of Abraham,[21] the five bumps of Nye, which Grace Hudowalski (#9) said she always went over when climbing the mountain in order to assure herself that she had, indeed, been on Nye's summit. To the south are Street and Indian Pass with the 1,000-foot vertical cliff of Wallface Mountain on its western flank. The cliff is one of the highest east of the Mississippi River.

On the Old Nye Ski Trail, at its junction with the "Garden Trail to Mt. Jo," in the center of a rock, one may find a silver bolt. On one of its sides it reads, "19 L P CLUB," and the other side, "22 S.N.Y." The bolt marks a corner of the boundary between state land and Adirondack Mountain Club property, formerly owned by the Lake Placid (LP) Club. On a tree nearby an ADK sign advises hikers: "Trail Not Maintained Beyond This Point." At that point those venturing towards the Indian Pass Brook and Street and Nye come under the jurisdiction of Department of Environmental Conservation rules and regulations from the High Peaks Unit Management Plan. Among them is this one:

Warning: The DEC considers the unauthorized placement of flagging to mark a trail to be littering. The blazing or painting of trees or rocks is considered defacing state property. Both actions are subject to prosecution and resulting in significant fines.

During a rainy summer when walking towards Indian Pass Brook you may find the Death Angel, a mushroom of the species *Amanita,* near the bases of hemlock and cedar trees. Look at it, but don't touch it: when ingested, it is deadly. Closer to the brook the cedars are quite large because they were spared the lumberjack's axe. They are close to 300 years old and, according to Ed Ketchledge (#507), some of them could be as much as 500 years old.[22] Just past an old lumber camp that the Wilderness Path passes through, step lightly as the Indian Cucumber Root that grows there is becoming rare.[23] On the flat just before the Street/Nye junction are many Indian Pipe. Mary Chiltosky, in her book *Cherokee Plants,* writes, "The Great Spirit turned the old men into grayish flowers we now call 'Indian Pipe' and he made them grow where friends and relatives have quarreled."[24] Judging by the multitude of Indian Pipe at that location, there must have been a few discussions, when the maze of herdpaths were there, as to which was the correct path to follow.

The 1953 survey upon which most recent trail maps have been based used to indicate that the most northerly peak of Nye was the mountain's summit. However, the most recent trail map (2004) included with the 13th edition of the Adirondack Mountain Club's High Peaks Region trail guide shows the Wilderness Path to Nye ending on the southern summit that 46ers recognize. The 3,895-foot contour line has been removed on the revised map for the northern peak.[25]

The mountain was once thought to be 4,160 feet in height. Herbert Clark (#1) and brothers George (#2) and Robert Marshall (#3) were first to climb it, on June 27, 1921. They included the mountain in their expeditions because it was shown on maps based upon surveys of the 1890s to be that altitude. The survey of the 1940s reduced it to 3,895 feet, but keeping with 46er tradition it will never lose its original status. Another survey concluded in the 1970s further reduced Nye's height to a contour elevation of 1,180 meters, and thus the precise height of the mountain is difficult to determine. Its highest point is probably about 3,870 feet. The latest ADK trail guide has it listed as fiftieth in height of the High Peaks region.

On Nye's cozy summit you will find a red disk on a tree. You will also find, without much difficulty, that the summit affords no view of other peaks. However, if you head north northwest to a small boulder and play "King of the Mountain" atop it, you can see some of the Sawtooth Mountains.

In addition to the route to Nye from Indian Pass Brook, there is another interesting but longer approach to it from Wanika Falls on the Northville–Lake Placid Trail. Early in the ascent, the hiker, staying in the streambed above the falls, may admire numerous, beautiful cascades. What seems a perfect walk through the woods abruptly ends, however, when you have to leave the stream. After the "Big Blow of 1950," Jim Goodwin (#24) led groups in and out from Nye along the Wanika Falls route in order to avoid the blowdown on the Heart Lake approach. He was accompanied by some Boy Scouts on one trip. They stayed in the streambed until they reached its source: a little pond below the ridge between Street and Nye. Looking up to the ridge that day when they reached the pond, they could see a group of hikers from Camp Pok-O-Moonshine. They were having a difficult time making progress. The Poko trip leader believed it the logical thing to do: to stay on the ridge. Jim had his group stay below it, and they beat the summer camp group to the summit.[26]

Endnotes

1. The quote is from a slate sign that hangs proudly in the author's home.
2. Dr. Ely (1812-1879) made the first recorded ascent of Ampersand Mountain in 1872. He also constructed that peak's first trail in an unconventional way: by starting at the summit and following a compass route down its north side to Round Lake. He would later clear Ampersand's summit for better views and erect a 9-foot long shanty with an open southeastern front. Verplanck Colvin credited Dr. Ely with naming Ampersand Mountain and honored him by designating the mountain's

western 3,110-foot peak Mount Ely. (Information from "Dr. Ely and His Adirondack Map," by George Marshall, *The Ad-i-ron-dac,* May/June 1954. Courtesy of the Adirondack Museum.)

3. Russell Carson – personal letter of June 2, 1923, to Alfred Donaldson. Courtesy of the Adirondack Museum. It has also been suggested that the mountain was named by Colvin in 1872.

4. "History of Ski T Farmhouse" by Mary MacKenzie, February 1999; courtesy of Carolyn Wiggin.

5. Mazeppa and Rarey are, today, obscure allusions. Voltaire wrote an apparently true story about a Polish nobleman, Mazeppa, in his *History of Charles XII, King of Sweden.* Mazeppa became page to Polish King John Casimir, was well educated, and, as a young man, had an affair with the wife of another nobleman. Voltaire wrote, "When the husband discovered it, he had him tied stark naked on the back of a wild horse and let him loose... The horse, which came from the Ukraine, returned there, carrying Mazeppa, half-dead from fatigue and hunger. Some peasants succoured him, and he remained among them for a long time, distinguishing himself in several expeditions against the Tartars. His superior learning gave him great prestige among the Cossacks; finally, his daily-increasing reputation forced the tsar to make him prince of the Ukraine." A Byron poem (1818) about Mazeppa's excruciating ride to the Ukraine was popular in the nineteenth century. John Rarey (1827–1866) had a world-wide reputation as a tamer of wild horses. He has been called the original "Horse Whisperer."

6. S. R. Stoddard, *The Adirondacks Illustrated* (Albany, NY: Van Benhuysen & Sons, 1874), pgs. 130-133. Dolly's riding instructors would have taught her that proper ladies rode "side-saddle." In the case of the "Hitch Up Matilda," she straddled the back of her "beast of burden."

7. *Plattsburgh Press-Republican,* March 22, 1890.

8. The original structure on the shore of Heart Lake was "Adirondack Lodge." After the Lake Placid Club assumed control of the property, Melvil Dewey's simplified spelling for the site was "Adirondak Loj." That is the spelling for the building still in use today.

9. *Adirondack Life,* Spring 1974, pgs. 11, 46.

10. *Plattsburgh Press-Republican,* March 22, 1890.

11. *The Conservationist,* February/March 1969, pg. 29.

12. *Adirondack Life,* Spring 1974, pgs. 46, 47.

13. *Ibid.*

14. *The Adirondack Daily Enterprise,* April 30, 1979.

15. The designation "trailless" has been somewhat a misnomer since the late 1960s and early 1970s for the twenty-one 46er peaks which do not have formal trails maintained by the Forty-Sixers, the Adirondack Trail Improvement Society, the Adirondack Mountain Club's chapters, or the DEC. Popular routes up the "trailless" peaks developed into well defined herdpaths, a few of which were, and are, so well defined that marking them with colored discs might be considered superfluous. Except after disruptions such as Hurricane Floyd (which affected formal trails as well), most of the herdpaths have been as easy to navigate as many marked trails. The Wilderness Paths – marked only where considered necessary – are (or will be) as easy to follow as the herdpaths were.

16. Pete Hickey email.

17. Clear Lake was renamed Heart Lake to avoid confusion with Lake Clear Junction north of Saranac Lake. Sandra Weber, *The Finest Square Mile - Mount Jo and Heart Lake* (Fleischmanns, NY: Purple Mountain Press, 1998), pg. 78.

18. Alfred Donaldson, *A History of the Adirondacks* (New York: The Century Co., 1921), Vol. II, pg. 25; and Sandra Weber, *The Finest Square Mile,* pg. 32.

19. Weber, *The Finest Square Mile,* pg. 18.

20. North Elba had a population of about 210 people in the 1840s. The United States Post Office determined to give the settlement its own post office. According to Mary MacKenzie, the late historian of the town of North Elba and the village of Lake Placid, the name probably derived from the old Elba ironworks, and the "North" was added to avoid confusion with Elba in Genesee County (*The Plains of Abraham – A History of North Elba and Lake Placid,* 2007, pg. 13). The hamlet may have been named after the Mediterranean island of Elba at about the time Napoleon was in exile there.

21. The "Plains of Abraham" is, roughly, the area north and south of Route 73 from Adirondack [sic] Loj Road to Bear Cub Road in the town of North Elba. Much of the property, at one time, belonged to abolitionist Gerrit Smith, who encouraged free black Americans to settle on his land and who enticed John Brown of Harper's Ferry fame and notoriety to establish a homestead on a portion of it in 1849, the same year the town of North Elba was established. For a time, a settlement (1840 - c. 1860) known as Timbuctoo, a community of free blacks existed in the neighborhood of the hamlet of North Elba, near the point where the vista of the mountains, from Colden to Street and Nye, opens to the modern day motorist on Route 73. Novelist Russell Banks has a short story, "The Plains of Abraham," in his volume *The Angel on the Roof.* His *Cloudsplitter,* a historical fiction, tells about John Brown, the Plains of Abraham, and Timbuctoo. According to H. P. Smith's *History of Essex County (1885),* the area derived its name from its "poor sandy soil," such as would have been encountered in the Middle East by the Biblical Abraham. Potatoes, wheat, and, in recent years, soy beans, have been grown on the plains.

22. Interview with Dr. Edwin Ketchledge, August 22, 2004.

23. Anne McGrath, *Wildflowers of the Adirondacks* (Manhattan, KS: EarthWords, 2000), pg. 75.

24. Internet - "Wildflowers of North Carolina." The story is told by Mary Chiltosky in her *Cherokee Plants and Their Uses: A 400 Year History* (Sylvia, NC: Herald Publishing Company, 1975).

25. Tony Goodwin email, October 2004. Some copies of the 13th edition of the trail guide do not contain the updated map. If the map contains a notation, "Reprinted with revision 2004," it is the latest, corrected one. Left over maps were placed in 13th edition books until all were used. The 2004 revised maps were enclosed with the others.

26. Jim Goodwin interview, October 22, 2004.

About the Author

Barb Harris, 46er #2824W, is a Mary Kay sales director. While in high school, she moved with her Air Force family to the Adirondacks from the Ozarks Mountains of Arkansas in 1962. She graduated from Peru Central School, where she met and married her husband Gary Harris. They live in Plattsburgh and have two grown sons, Michael and Dean, and two granddaughters, Amanda and Kristin. Barb, in 1988, after reading Russell Carson's *Peaks and People of the Adirondacks,* hit the trail every available weekend and finished her first of five rounds of the 46 (two in winter) on Haystack, September 21, 1990. More mountain ranges calling from the east led to the NE 111 finish on Carrigain in the White Mountains on July 10, 1997. A new discovery of love for backpacking found the Northville/Lake Placid trail completion on August 31, 1999. A ten-year odyssey of climbing the Adirondack Top 100 Mountains was happily gratified on October 13, 2003, on North River Mountain. A busy 2004 completed the Firetower Challenge on Belfry in July and also found the All Season of the 46 accomplished on Haystack on a glorious October 13th. After climbing the first round of the 46 the next patch was the 46 hours of trail work. She was on the executive board of the Adirondack Forty-Sixers as director, vice-president and president from 2000-2003, and she currently serves on the Grace Peak Committee and on the board of the 46R Conservation Trust. Barb has earned an award from the Forty-Sixers for 146 hours of trail work, and she has received the club's Founders Award. After successfully climbing Street in 1990, she never wanted to go back again and mess with her success of getting through the "Bermuda Triangle." She has now been back to visit Street and Nye eight times.

THE MACINTYRE RANGE
By Sean O'Donnell (#5120W)

The MacIntyres from Indian Falls

    The MacIntyres represent a classic Adirondack mountain range. Often called the region's noblest group of mountains, the range stands alone, has definitive start and finish points, runs in a virtual straight compass line, and is isolated on all sides by steep valleys, pristine lakes, and stupendous mountain passes. Along its northern crest is an impressive crown of bare summits, while its long southern spine offers some of most wild and densely forested peaks and slopes in the Adirondacks.

    The twenty mile hike to circumnavigate the MacIntyre Range is a walk through history, complete with sights that spark the soul and light fire to the adventurer in all of us: two awe-inspiring mountain passes; the Hitch-up Matildas that allow passage through the cliff-encased Avalanche Lake; the ghost town of Adirondac, the site of ore extraction that helped usher America into the Steel Age; the enormous boulders that create an obstacle course in Indian Pass; the massive eight hundred-foot tall sheer face of Wallface Mountain towering above; the luxuriance and fertile lushness of a climb along Herbert Brook, where one can find nearly every shade of green. The full spectrum of beauty, history, and wonder that greeted the first explorers, scientists, artists, and industrialists who explored the area still inspires all those who hike in, through, up, and around this mightiest of mountain ranges: The MacIntyres.

Heaven Up-h'isted-ness!

The MacIntyres as seen from Mount Colden

Algonquin Peak
Height: 2nd — 1,559 meters (5,115 feet)

For years I had seen the Adirondacks from the air and roads. Only the other day did I have a chance to hike part of their 700 miles of trails. I now know why so many people love this sanctuary and call it one of America's treasures... the forty-six peaks that are 4,000 feet or higher, the 200 lakes, the hardwoods and conifers that fill the valleys, the pure cold streams, the alpine flora of the barrens – these are among the great wonders of the world... Conservationists the country over should visit the Adirondacks to learn from the men and women who guard this wonderland how they can bring their own wilderness areas under the constitutional protection.

These words, written by United States Supreme Court Justice William O. Douglas, have great meaning to anyone who has hiked in the High Peaks, for they ring true with what so many of us hold dear. Our revered playground is a special place. In 1962, Justice Douglas climbed to the top of Algonquin with Orra "Doc" Phelps (#47). Throughout his life, Justice Douglas was an ardent hiker and champion of wilderness and conservation. That perfect day in June, Douglas accompanied Doc Phelps, Dr. Marian Biesemeyer, Herb Allen, and Landon Rockwell to celebrate the first hike of Orra's tenure as the Adirondack Mountain Club's first Ranger-Naturalist. Assuming the role that would serve as a model for the summit stewards, Doc did not disappoint those on hand for the trek.

Rockwell, former chairman of the Department of History at Hamilton College, summarized the trip in the July 1962 *Adirondac*. He described Orra waving her hand to and fro, as she cited both Latin and English names of plants along the lower trail to Algonquin. Cornus, oxalis, goldthread, Clinton's lily, wild sarsaparilla, and twisted stalk. Phelps' niece, Mary Arakelian, also described the hike in her book *Doc: Orra A. Phelps, M.D.* (2001).

Orra Phelps was spotting flowers, mosses, almost everything that grew – and confirming the Justice's own quick identification of his old friends. And then they were showing him new friends – Marcy, Colden, Skylight, Gothics and the rest – Eleanor Friend pointing out the Ranger's cabin on Lake Colden and taking pictures, Justice Douglas taking pictures and making notes, Herb Allen telling the Justice about the 1950 hurricane... Brad Whiting making out Lake Champlain.

The trail was in impeccable shape, for to ensure that Justice Douglas would see the Adirondacks at their best, Orra had led a clean-up crew from the Adirondak Loj up to the summit the very day before. All told the day was the perfect showcase for the High Peaks, the magic of the experience, and the views, both trailside and out over the other magnificent peaks of the neighboring mountains.

Trips like these paved the way for the success of the mission of the new ADK Conservation Committee, which Orra spearheaded until 1972. She also created the ADK Nature Museum with Dr. Arthur E. Newkirk. It was based in a tent on the shores of Heart Lake. Orra kept her reference and working materials in the trunk of her car.

Soon the region's top botanists were stationed at the base of the MacIntyre Range. They began documenting and planning the conservation efforts that would save the rare summit vegetation from its near extinction due to hikers unwittingly trampling over the plants as they wandered across the great open summits. Phelps and Newkirk welcomed people like Dr. Mildred Faust, Ruth Schottman, Dr. Nancy Slack, and Dr. Edwin H. Ketchledge, who were instrumental in conducting plant inventories and documenting the rare summit plants which were also found in the arctic alpine zones of the world. On a 1963 trip to Alaska, Orra marveled at finding the same plants she had found in only one spot before, atop the highest summits of the High Peaks. This was the impetus for the summit stewardship program, which is dedicated to saving these rare summit oases, remnants from the last great ice age.

Interestingly enough, this stewardship started many years before when these rare plants were identified and published in books and scientific articles of the day. Nathanial Bartlett Sylvester mentioned them in his 1877 book *Historical Sketches of Northern New York and the Adirondack Wilderness*. After listing the highest peaks and their Indian names, he added that near the summits there lived many rare arctic plants. Among them were the mountain golden-rod, the *Arenaria groenlandica*, (Greenland sandroot), and the *Potentilla tridentata*, (white cinquefoil).

In 1990, the summit steward program was officially launched as a cooperative effort of the ADK, the Nature Conservancy, and the New York State Department of Environmental Conservation. The summits of Wright, Iroquois, and more extensively Algonquin, which had been trampled bare by hikers' footsteps, have shown tremendous regrowth of many species thanks to this program. A steward is almost always stationed atop Algonquin from May to October. Collectively the stewards have educated literally tens of thousands of hikers about the fragility of the summit area, the variety of species struggling to survive there, and the importance of treading carefully across these oases of rare arctic alpine life in order to protect and preserve them. Many listen and understand, and every trip across the high ridge shows proof of this as the once endangered species now flourish. Early summer brings the first blooms, and fall shows the mountaintops at their most colorful as the leaves of these miniature plants mimic their cousins on the lower slopes by bursting into rich autumnal colors.

He-no-ga, "The Home of the Thunderer," was the name given to Algonquin by the Iroquois, or so legend has it. As we have come to discover, there are many "interpretations" to the naming of mountains and the claims of responsibility and origin. One has to wonder if Charles Broadhead uttered He-no-ga when he made the first documented climb in the MacIntyres in 1797. While surveying the southern boundary of the Old Military Tract, as he stood on or near the sub-summit now bearing the name Boundary Peak, he must have gazed upward at the behemoth of rock towering above him. Could one look upon such a lofty prominence and not feel compelled to call forth its name? Or be inspired to make one up on the spot?

As the true origin of the name He-no-ga and the inklings of thought from Broadhead during his climb float just out of verifiable reach, so too does any evidence of Broadhead climbing the wide open and thoroughly inviting route to the summit of Algonquin. Would this hardy surveyor have scaled the rock slabs up to the summit to look down on everywhere his travels below had taken him? There may be no evidence to say he did, but there's also no evidence he didn't. And don't even bother to ask your typical 46er whether the summit lure would have been a draw big enough to entice a quick climb.

Fast forward forty years and the mountain finally got its first officially recognized name. In fact, when Ebenezer Emmons, Chief Geologist for the northern district of the Geological Survey of New York, and his Marcy first ascent crew were happily doling out names to all the peaks around them, they christened the entire eight mile long range as Mount McIntyre. It was a fitting and generous moniker, for the man they were honoring was of great stature at both the state and local levels.

Archibald McIntyre (1772-1858) served as New York State Comptroller from 1805 to 1821 (the longest tenure ever in New York), State Senator of the Fourth District from 1821 to 1826, and as a member of the planning board for the Erie Canal. In 1810, McIntyre founded the North Elba iron works on the AuSable River near the "Plains of Abraham." Bounded by today's bustling Route 73 and Adirondack *[sic]* Loj Road, the area bears little resemblance to the small and wild community it was in the 1820s when a narrow and circuitous path kept the valley secluded. The Plains of Abraham, which spilled into obscurity when McIntyre abandoned his North Elba works for Tahawus, later became a haven for free African Americans.

Emmons lead another High Peak first ascent on August 8, 1837, three days after his fabled Mount Marcy expedition. This time the mountain was McIntyre, and fittingly, Archibald McIntyre was part of the group – in legend only. Just as there were inaccuracies in the official list of members of the Marcy climbing party, as author Russell Carson later pointed out in his book *Peaks and People of the Adirondacks*, so were there questions as to whether or not McIntrye was on the first recorded ascent of the mountain. McIntyre wrote a letter to James Hall the day before the climb from his office at the Tahawus iron works. The argument is strong that he could not have trudged in and up the mountain in the time frame of the Emmons climb. James Hall is credited with the first mention of the name of Mount McIntyre a week later in his article published in the *Albany Daily Advertiser* on August 15, 1837. [Author's Note: The name *MacIntyre* was originally spelled the same as the name of the man the mountain was named after— Archibald *McIntyre*. *MacIntyre* conforms to the current USGS topological map spelling of the range. For the sake of historical accuracy, I have used the "period" spelling when referring to the mountain.]

William C. Redfield recorded the expedition in his essay "Two Visits to the Mountains of Essex County, 1836 and 1837," which was published in 1838. In the essay, Redfield doesn't list the members of the party who climbed the mountain, but the expedition that left Albany on July 28. That group consisted of Messrs. McIntyre, Henderson, Hall (who was geologist of the western district of the state), together with Prof. Torrey, Prof. Emmons, Messrs. Ingham and Strong of New York, Miller of Princeton, and Emmons, Jr. of Williamstown. Yes, this list, along with the guides John Cheney and Harvey Holt, are the same names on the plaque that sits atop Mount Marcy. Just as there are claims questioning the veracity of who really climbed Marcy that day, so too is there no certainty as to the exact membership of the group that first climbed Mount McIntyre.

Redfield may have neglected to mention any of the party by name, but he gave a description of the climb that mirrors what one would see if one were to climb the mountain today. The ascent, most likely led by seasoned guide John Cheney, left from an encampment along Lake

In a photograph from Grace Hudowalski's collection, her husband Ed is at right atop Wright Peak. Rising above in the background is Algonquin Peak.

Colden and followed the small stream that borders the present day trail. Up the drainage they climbed. Though short of a mile in distance, they found it necessarily difficult. When they hit the lower reaches of the belt of dwarf forest, the main peak finally appeared, rising to their right, with its "steep acclivity" of naked rock running from the ground underneath their feet to the summit.

> Wishing to shorten our route, we here unwisely abandoned the remaining bed of the ravine, and sustaining ourselves by the slight inequalities of surface which have resulted from unequal decomposition, we succeeded in crossing the apparently smooth face of the rock by an oblique ascent to the right, and once more obtained footing in the woody cover of the mountain. But the continued steepness of the acclivity, and the seemingly impervious growth of low evergreens on this more sheltered side, where their horizontal and greatly elongated branches were perplexingly intermingled, greatly retarded our progress. Having surmounted this region we put forth with alacrity, and at 1 P.M. reached the summit.

Sounds like a typical Adirondack bushwhack!

With storm clouds approaching from the west, the summit party did not linger. Redfield felt the view was similar to Marcy, though now affording views down on to many of the lakes in the direction of Saranac that the mountain itself blocked from Marcy's vantage. Most striking was the great dike on Colden, with the parallel attraction of the whitened path of a slide that had recently descended into Avalanche Lake. The views of Wallface were distinct, as were the sparkling surfaces of Lake Champlain and the Saranac Waters. Redfield also noted, "Mount McIntyre is also intersected by dikes, which cross it at the lowest points of depression between its several peaks, and the more rapid erosion and displacement of these dikes has apparently produced the principle ravines in its sides."

After identifying the same rock formations and plant life as they found on Marcy, and surmising that great cracks and fissures near the summit must have been caused by earthquakes, they took a quick barometric measurement, and did rough triangulation measurements of nearby mountains. Redfield figured there must have been close to ten peaks at or near the five thousand foot level, and perhaps two dozen that surpassed the highest elevation of the Catskill group.

The party descended into Indian Pass, supposedly after rough weather pushed them off the summit, but Redfield made it sound as if the plan had been to return to the small mining settlements at McIntyre (also known as Adirondac) by way of the great Notch beneath Wallface. Whatever the case, they descended into the "valley of the Au Sable" by way of one of the many steep ravines on the western side of Algonquin. John Winkler (#1279), who may be the only modern hiker to climb all of the forty-six High Peaks by means of strictly bushwhack routes, speaks of following a drainage up through steep gorges and over thirty-seven waterfalls on his ascent of Algonquin—perhaps the same route the original party traversed. Pictures from aerial flights show the ravines to be incredibly narrow, surrounded by boulders and rock outcroppings sometimes a hundred feet high.

Jack Colby, a member of the 46ers of Troy on Algonquin in 1932. In the background are Colden and Marcy.

Redfield's party made camp at the base of the mountain, spending a stormy night alongside the growing stream they had followed. Daybreak opened with copious rainfall, which accompanied them as they proceeded up into Indian Pass the following day on their return. Redfield mentioned "this extraordinary pass … excites the admiration of every beholder." Most interesting was the circumnavigation of Lake Henderson at the end of the journey. "It is not many months since our woodsman, Cheney, with no other means of offense than his axe and pistol, followed and killed a large panther on the western borders of this lake."

The Emmons route became the first blazed trail up to the MacIntyre Ridge when Verplanck Colvin, Superintendent of the Adirondack Survey, and his triangulation crews ascended McIntyre some forty years later. However when they descended, they brought the name McIntyre with them. The ubiquitous Colvin had renamed the mountain Algonquin. He felt the peak deserved to be the standard bearer of the area's original inhabitants, the Algonquin Indians, who surrounded the High Peaks and most of New England from early in the first millennium until the great war with the Iroquois in the mid-sixteenth century.

In his colorfully written guide book of 1928, *Trails and Summits of the Adirondacks*, Walter Collins O'Kane gives great and timeless descriptions of the two trails still in use today. The "popular" trail from Heart Lake and the Adirondack Lodge (note the spelling used by O'Kane; this was also before there was a High Peaks Information Center) was cut by Henry Van

Hoevenberg in 1881, and follows virtually the same route as it does 125 years later. However O'Kane's recount tells of walking through areas ravaged by the fires in the early twentieth century. The route followed old logging roads, and yellow discs, and passed the same streams we navigate today. In the lower sections where today's hikers are surrounded by a lovely birch forest, O'Kane saw an area recovering from extensive logging. Today it takes a walk of some three and a half miles up the mountain before one enters an area of pristine woods touched neither by fire nor lumbermen.

O'Kane also gives a great description of the trail that starts from Lake Colden. This is the same trail that was used by the Emmons and Colvin parties. Officially opened in 1901, it began near the fire-ranger's cabin on Lake Colden. If one was to stay at the bottom of the lake near the Opalescent, like Emmons, Stoddard, and Colvin used to, one would have crossed the dam and ascended a ladder over a short cliff on the western end—just as one does today, nearly a hundred years later. Following the blue discs, one is literally walking in the footsteps of history all the way to the summit of Algonquin above. From the summit O'Kane takes seven entire paragraphs to point out all the mountains visible from the open rocks of Algonquin. He doesn't miss a single High Peak, and impressively recognizes the Green Mountain summits of Grant, Roosevelt, Wilson, and Breadloaf. It's amazing to think one could climb the mountain tomorrow with O'Kane's guidebook from 1928 and easily pick out every major peak in both New York and Vermont!

IROQUOIS PEAK
Height: 6th – 1,478 meters (4,849 feet)

Interestingly enough, the Iroquois tribe, who vanquished the Algonquin, was commemorated with its own summit, just south of the highest peak of the MacIntyre Range. Separating the two is a smaller bump given its own name, Boundary Peak. Long has this "referee" between the two great summits been the center of debates as to the origin of its name in relationship to any actual boundary or territory line between the two Indian nations. Since the Indian nations were not much for surveying and building walls, this argument is impossible to maintain. The name was most likely symbolic and never meant to imply an actual boundary.

But since that hasn't stopped the arguments before, there is no reason not to explore this matter for the sake of entertainment. When Verplanck Colvin decided every significant peak in the MacIntyre Range deserved its own name, he decided the native tribes should be represented. What better place than what Colvin felt was one of the noblest of Adirondack mountain ranges. As the Iroquois were the second dominant tribe in the area, Colvin gave the name to the second highest peak in the range. Originally he had decided to name the mountain Mount Clinton in honor of Governor DeWitt Clinton, but during his 1873 naming spree his record-keeping was not organized and much confusion surrounded the names of the peaks south of Algonquin.

In 1880, Colvin cleared up the mess with a definitive map and notation where each peak name rightfully belonged. Clinton was the southernmost summit, and Iroquois the rocky summit at the end of the high ridge from Algonquin. In his statement pertaining to the naming of "Mount Iroquois" and "Mount Algonquin," he laid out reasons including his determination that the boundary lines between the two nations actually passed between the two peaks. Carson, in his book *Peaks and People of the Adirondacks*, noted that "an investigation, which has had the aid of Mr. Peter Nelson, Assistant State Historian, has failed to show a historical foundation for the existence of such a line." It did, however, show the boundary line that Colvin used as being exactly the same as the northern survey line of the Totten and Crossfield Purchase, which was in fact a sale of Mohawk Nation land (a member of the Iroquois Confederacy) originally brokered by Joseph Totten and Stephen Crossfield, both ship carpenters for the City of New York, on behalf of the British Crown.

So, there may not have been any correlation to an Algonquin-Iroquois boundary of hunting lands, but Iroquois Peak does indeed fall within the northern edge of the tract of land held and conveyed by the Mohawks. The boundaries between the two Indian nations were in a state of constant flux during those days. Although there were attempts to further prove Colvin's claims by running an east/west line from established points outside the mountains, the transitory nature of these points made an exact and certifiable boundary line through the mountains impossible to determine. One fact remains without question. The Algonquin held and hunted the lands north of the High Peaks, while the Iroquois owned claim to the lands to the south. Since they rarely, if ever, ventured up the mountains of the Adirondacks, this symbolic Boundary Peak does a nice job of keeping the history and relative proximity of the two tribes alive.

There are no documented climbs of Iroquois between the 1837 climb of nearby Algonquin and October 1883 when William H. Brown made the first verifiable ascent to erect a signal for the Colvin survey. Colvin gave a height for the peak in his 1873 report. Although he was on Algonquin and Boundary, no one has been able to find notes of him actually climbing through the scrub to the summit of Iroquois. Brown supposedly cut a trail on his way to Iroquois, something Bob and George Marshall found no evidence of during their ascent of the peak in 1919. What they did find was, "To get to this peak you must tug, tussle, push and batter your way through as dense a mass of mountain balsam as ever grew. Progress is measured by inches. If you are strong and persevering you may finally get through what as the bird flies is only a mile, but as the man travels seems like ten."

To the Marshalls the struggle was worth it, as they rated the view above that of Algonquin itself. Being further down the ridge, Iroquois' summit affords a better perspective of both Indian and Avalanche Passes, with more of the massive cliffs of Wallface visible. And below is the third of the four great passes of the MacIntyre Range, Algonquin Pass (Today the DEC and several guidebooks refer to this pass as Cold Brook Pass in an attempt to eliminate any confusion about its location.), appearing almost directly below the peculiar prominence with many names, including the prevailing "Shepherd's Tooth." After the walk through the dense obstacle course across the ridge, with its omnipresent MacIntyre mud, the best part of Iroquois is enjoying the summit in near or total solitude, after venturing over from Algonquin and its almost constant crowds.

Since Iroquois is in a straight line with little elevation gain from the junction with the Lake Colden trail, a herd path to its summit developed quickly after the Marshalls established the notion of climbing all the High Peaks. Somewhere between a true trailed summit and trailless peak, it did host a canister and logbook at various times. Carolyn Schaefer, on her 1954 women's trip to Iroquois and the naming that day of Shepherd's Tooth, wrote about signing the logbook on Iroquois. However, the first official logbook (Iroquois Book 1) welcomed hikers from August 12, 1967 through July 9, 1969. By the late 1970s, the logbooks of Iroquois disappeared, much sooner than those on the other trailless peaks. There was an adorable attempt to resurrect the logbook tradition in 1995 when someone placed a two ounce (yes, that's a 2 oz.!) micro-sized hotel room service jelly container on the summit. It attracted several scraps of paper, but was short lived.

> August 12, 1967. This can is dedicated to the 3 Iroquois Indians killed by Samuel de Champlain on the banks of Lake Champlain in the year 1609. Weather cloudy, but with holes: Climbers who placed this first canister up: David Archer — #318, Gail O'Brien — #291, Wally Dog O'Brien – (left blank), Peter Goodwin — #240.

So read the first official inscription in Iroquois Book 1. Many 46ers miss the logbooks, which were officially removed from the trailless peak summits by the club in 2001 in order to comply with state regulations. There are often wonderful entries in them—from the witty and inspirational, to tales of sheer horror about reaching the summit. Three entries from Iroquois Book 9 on August 19, 1975 provide examples:

> Barbara Alden Hayward (Little Ones Tennis Champ) A little windy for a tennis court, but a great place anyway. (Maybe a weather station)
> Robert Hayward – Hi Grace! I am disappointed there are no Bugs!!!

> Jeff Roecker – hiked around Algonquin so I could save it for last 46r. Flew a kite from Algonquin before we left and can see it now.

> Lyn Ratcliff – Escorting Jeff R. Carried a 24 lb. Watermelon from the lodge. Will celebrate on Algonquin. There are 4,362,551 blueberries. Good pie!

WRIGHT PEAK

Height: 16th – 1,398 meters (4,587 feet)

"The office should seek the man, not man the office" **– Silas Wright**

Jokingly referred to as the windiest place on Earth, Wright Peak is the northern high peak of the MacIntyre Range, sitting at a height just beneath the middle ridge from Iroquois to Algonquin. The mountain appeared on maps and in text under the names McIntyre North Peak, Mount Wright, Wright's Peak, and finally by the name it is called today, Wright Peak. We learn from his report of 1873 that in that same year Verplanck Colvin was responsible for naming the mountain. He called it Mount Wright.

> To the peak next north of Mount McIntyre, I have given the name Mount Wright, after Governor Silas Wright, who was indeed a representative of the northern region, and whose own St. Lawrence County may be looked upon from the summit of this vast granite monument.

Although smaller in stature than its larger and more popular neighbor, the mighty Algonquin Peak, Wright Peak has numerous features providing it with its own unique charm. It is the highest mountain in the Adirondacks (aside from Whiteface) with a dedicated downhill ski trail cut to just below the summit. It can be climbed virtually to its top by means of a slide, and its summit boasts the rare designation of being an arctic alpine zone. Upon its summit there also lies one of the most sobering reminders of America's vigil against the Communist threat during the Cold War.

In 1837, as fabled guide John Cheney was leading Ebenezer Emmons and a small party up the flanks of Mount McIntyre, the eventual namesake of the range's most northern peak, Silas Wright Jr., was serving in the United States Senate. Born in Amherst, Mass. on May 24, 1795, he moved with his father to Wyebridge, Vt., in 1796. He attended and graduated from Middlebury College in 1815, and moved to Sandy Hill, Washington County, N.Y., in 1816 where he studied law. He was admitted to the bar in 1819 and commenced practice in Canton, St. Lawrence County, N.Y.

He began what would become a prodigious political career almost immediately, serving as surrogate of St. Lawrence County 1821-1824. He ascended to the New York State Senate, serving from 1824 to 1827. In 1827 he issued a report to the senate outlining the Democratic financial policies and abolitionist support with which he was identified throughout his life, and which he subsequently enforced as political measures. While in the state senate he opposed the advancement of his bitter political rival, DeWitt Clinton, an amusing fact since the southern peak in the MacIntyre Range was known as Mount Clinton unofficially for many years before being certified Mount Marshall. So even on the MacIntyre Range, Wright ended up having the last word over his rival.

Silas Wright

Wright was appointed brigadier general of the State militia in 1827, and elected to the Twentieth Congress of the United States serving from March 4, 1827 to February 16, 1829. During his short tenure there he voted for several controversial measures, including protective tariffs. The protective tariff of 1828 was favored by bankers, merchants, and manufacturers in the North, and strongly supported by the new western states. It expanded on a series of tariffs that were designed to fast track America's emerging manufacturing sector. However, the agrarian-based South was in opposition and called it the Tariff of Abominations, for it increased prices of the goods on which they depended. The tariff further deepened the gestating North/South divide.

Wright was comptroller of the State of New York, 1829-1833; elected to the United States Senate in 1833 as a Jacksonian (later Democrat) to fill the vacancy caused by the resignation of William L. Marcy; reelected in 1837 and served until November 26, 1844, when he resigned, having been elected governor of New York.

As a United States Senator he again made his presence known. As a member of the committee on finance he was involved in a number of legislative initiatives relating to U.S. government fiscal policies. He supported a bill that allowed the use of force to enforce tariff laws. He voted in favor of Henry Clay's tariff compromise bill of 1833 and then in

1842 voted to rescind the provisions of that bill. He defended President Jackson's removal of federal government deposits from the Bank of the United States and opposed Daniel Webster's efforts to re-charter that institution. Wright opposed the distribution among the states of surplus Federal revenues and supported the independent treasury scheme of Martin Van Buren. While Wright was against slavery he was also against inciting war to abolish it, remaining true to his statement, "Wrong acts never serve a good cause." He was also heavily involved in the political debate and strategy over the annexation of Texas.

Silas Wright may seem as ambitious a politician as any, however that was far from the truth, for he was just a simple man of great integrity with a desire to serve the public and his party. The higher he ascended, the trickier the minefield of politics he was forced to navigate. High politics of the era were not the realm of men of great integrity! In the end, Wright spent most of his time fighting his own success, even when he couldn't decline his way out of it. He was reluctant to run for re-election to the Senate in 1843, but colleagues convinced him not to allow a Whig the opportunity to gain the seat. So for his party he ran, and won. Partisan politics were as acrimonious as ever during his return to the Senate. However, President Tyler made an overture of cooperation by crossing party lines to offer Wright a seat on the Supreme Court. Tempted he certainly was, but he eventually declined the offer.

The Supreme Court was the first of a series of declinations from Wright. His good friend Martin Van Buren struggled for the presidential nomination in 1844. Van Buren circulated a letter stating his intention that if he failed to secure the bid, he would support Wright for the office of president and instruct his supporters to cast their votes for the Senator. Wright stubbornly refused to accept any such plan. He did not want the presidency, nor did he want to risk any appearance of being involved in a conspiracy to defeat Van Buren so he could gain the nomination.

James K. Polk, a former Speaker of the U.S. House of Representatives and governor of Tennessee, finally won the Democratic presidential nomination. Silas Wright easily won the vice presidential nomination. Wright learned of his victory by a new invention, the telegraph. He immediately wired back declining the nomination. A series of telegraph messages were exchanged, but Wright maintained his refusal, and the nomination was given to George Dallas of Pennsylvania. The perception that he turned down both the presidential nomination and the vice presidential nomination out of a matter of integrity and loyalty to his personal and political friend Van Buren only made Wright more popular than ever.

This brought incredible pressure on Wright to run for governor of New York, a position he had previously declined. Even his close friend Van Buren argued that Wright should run. Van Buren pointed out that Wright's refusal to run might reflect poorly on Polk. Wright's presence on the ticket would help Polk carry New York. Wright still asked his supporters not to nominate him, but he won the nomination anyway. Wright was not happy about winning the nomination, and secretly hoped that he would lose the general election to the Whig candidate, Millard Fillmore. On winning this nomination, Wright said, "never has any incident in my public life been so much against my feelings and judgment." To his great surprise and disappointment, Wright defeated Fillmore and became governor of New York. He won with just 50.5 percent of the vote. Millard Fillmore, an illustrious contemporary of Wright, later became the thirteenth President of the United States.

Wright could finally retire from politics, even if it was not voluntarily, when he lost his re-election bid for governor in 1847. He retired to his farm in rural Canton, which he enjoyed running. He worked the earth with sleeves rolled up and hands-on involvement. He gave up alcohol entirely after a lifetime of extremely heavy drinking. The physical exertion, the summer heat, and maybe even his sudden abstinence proved to be too much for Wright. Having left the governorship in January, that same summer he suffered two mild heart attacks, and on August 27, 1847, he succumbed to a third one. Despite Wright's aversion for politics in his later years, he instituted many important policies, especially in the area of banking and finance. In 1882 the first fifty dollar Gold Certificate was issued with a portrait of Silas Wright. The reverse was printed in orange ink and featured a Bald Eagle perched atop an American flag.

Returning from the political arena to the mountains, we'll venture back in time to August of 1893 and one of the earliest documented climbs of then trailless Mount Wright. Local guide Charles Wood led state botanist Professor Charles H. Peck to the summit during a study of the plants of North Elba. After fighting through the cripplebrush, or krummultz zone, an impenetrable tangle of intertwined branches of dwarf balsam and stunted black spruce, they would have broken out on to the western rock ledges and their pockets of wildflowers, grasses, sedges, and arctic alpine varietals.

Later, when the Marshalls climbed Wright with Herbert Clark, a trail had as yet not been cut and the trio bushwhacked up "from the MacIntyre Trail where it crosses a ravine about three-quarters of the way up." They encountered some scrubby balsam on the route up and chose to descend straight down the drainage to MacIntyre Falls. They were lucky and dodged the balsam on the return. The Marshalls were likely among the only, if not *the* only visitors to Wright during the early and mid 1920s, for there are few references of others climbing it. In his guidebook published in 1928, *Trails and Summits of the Adirondacks*, Walter Collins O'Kane gives a splendid ten page description of the two trails to Algonquin, but neglects to mention anything of interest atop Wright.

It wasn't until news spread of the Marshall's conquest of all the four thousand foot tall peaks that hiker interest began to grow past the usual, well-trodden trails. In 1922 the Adirondack Mountain Club published Robert Marshall's pamphlet, "The High Peaks of the Adirondacks." In large part it was the book's descriptions of climbs like Wright Peak, the list of summit view ratings, and the sheer joy Bob expressed in his discoveries that attracted hikers to the region eager to follow in his footsteps. Bob's small book is often credited with spawning a new phenomenon that was given what some considered to be the disparaging name of "peakbagging." The first trail to Wright's summit was cut in the early 1930s, as mentioned in the 1934 *Guide to Adirondack Trails, Northeastern Section*, published by the Adirondack Mountain Club. The description was a brief four lines, yet encouraged the hiker to seek out the open and rocky peak with splendid views.

With its close proximity to the busy portal of Heart Lake, Wright is one of the most popular destinations in the mountains today. An open summit, remains of a wrecked Cold War era bomber just below, and wonderful spring wildflowers and fall foliage make this a special peak. One never knows what one will find there. On a fall colors hike in 2005, the author journeyed over Algonquin to Iroquois and saved Wright for the last stop of the day:

> Late afternoon gave me the summit to myself and treated me with a rare wildlife sight. As I neared the great summit bulb of rock, movement in the brush at the base alerted me that a good size animal was also enjoying the warm Indian summer weather as well. To my surprise, and delight, I chanced upon the rare mountaintop presence of a mature grazing porcupine. Ten feet below the 4,560-foot summit, the old fellow was soaking up the late day sun and enjoying a snack of bilberry leaves.

MOUNT MARSHALL
Height: 24th – 1,330c meters (4,363+ feet)

On June 26, 1921, the Marshall brothers and Herb Clark made the first documented climb of Mount Marshall, and most likely the first ascension period. "On the whole mountain we could not see a single trace of the presence of any human being, not even an old blaze on a tree," noted Bob in his book "The High Peaks of the Adirondacks." Their route took them down off Iroquois (though at the time they believed they were actually traversing to a mountain named Iroquois), over the fabled prominence they had named Catamount Roost, and into Algonquin Pass. The pass, between the peaks of what we now call Iroquois and Marshall, was then another wild un-navigated realm, and "almost as remarkable as Indian Pass."

The trio was duly impressed with the adventure, feeling the mountain was probably the wildest in the Adirondacks. From the pass the group tramped up through the most luxuriant woods they had ever seen. Densely wooded at the summit, it took but a little exploring to find ledges that revealed surprisingly good views. How else could the team have afforded the summit a view rating of twelfth best in the mountains? From the vantage points they found views back toward the cliffs of Iroquois, down on to the Scott Ponds Plateau, and along the length of Marshall's southern reaches all the way to Santanoni. Most impressive of all was a birdseye glimpse of Wallface from almost directly above it. The topper was the view the modern climber knows best—the sweeping panorama from the southwest side of the summit that stretches from the scarred western side of Mount Colden, across and past Mount Marcy all the way to Mount Adams. It is truly one of the best in the region.

With the exploits of the Marshall team, the secluded and undisturbed Mount Marshall slowly began welcoming a host of eager suitors. Lost may be the completely unspoiled nature of the climb experienced by this first team, but the mountain has never lost any of its charm. The approach up Herbert Brook is as sublime a hiking route as there is in the Adirondacks. Lush and verdant as a rainforest, at times you are surrounded by plants and mosses in a hundred shades of green. The brook spills over cascades, runs across long slabs, and winds through and around moss covered boulders. Numerous waterfalls accent the journey, and a special one high up near the source of the brook is framed by a backdrop of pure bright green moss. One can only imagine the superlatives Bob Marshall would have used to described it, but his trek down the mountain was into Indian Pass and not down this brook which so many would eventually travel.

Bob Marshall may have been the first to climb the mountain, but his name was the last of many to land on its shoulders. The following procession of names given to this peak over the years is as serpentine as piecing together a puzzle. The peak, originally just the southern sub peak of the massif known simply as Mount McIntyre, was first separated and named in 1873 by Colvin during his vast naming and re-naming spree. Sort of. His papers and sketches showed that he named our Iroquois Peak of today, Mount Clinton for DeWitt Clinton. He also threw about the name of Mount Iroquois, presumably the first name of Mount Marshall, just as the Marshalls themselves called it. South McIntyre was also bandied about and this confusion continued until 1880 when Colvin decided to set the record straight. He settled on a progression of Algonquin, Boundary, Iroquois, and finally Mount Clinton.

So, the first semi-official name assigned to the mountain was Mount Clinton. The problem was, while Colvin had roughly sketched crude maps showing the assignments, he had never submitted them for inclusion on state or national sanctioned maps. So the confusion continued. With no one climbing these lesser peaks of the MacIntyre Range after Colvin's teams completed his surveys, they attracted little attention. By the time the Marshalls began climbing, Mount Clinton had all but fallen from local usage. To them, the last of the MacIntyre summits (now Marshall) was called Iroquois, and so they actually named what they believed to be an un-named peak (now Iroquois) Mount Herbert, after their beloved guide. When Bob included it in his book, the names initially stuck.

When Carson turned his attention to these names in his book *Peaks and People*, his investigations revealed the mistakes. Like everyone else, he took it upon himself to do a little naming. After he determined the proper location of "Mount Iroquois," he felt it was too important a name to be displaced. So he offered his own solution. "Therefore, as the final step in clearing up the naming muddle, the author is taking the liberty of transposing the name 'Herbert Peak' to the 4,411-foot peak that was Marshall's Iroquois, but in fact was nameless." Not even the diligent Carson had retrieved Colvin's initial name for the peak of Mount Clinton, and now a new name was pushed forward, albeit with strong supporting arguments.

Carson reminded the reader in his text of the naming of other mountains for the region's great guides of the early days. He felt strongly that the mountains they explored should become monuments to these strongest of guides: Mount Phelps, in the Keene Valley region for Orson "Old Mountain" Phelps; Nye Mountain in North Elba for Bill Nye; and the fortress-like sentinel of Cheney Cobble in Newcomb for the earliest and most illustrious guide of them all, John Cheney. To Carson it was only fitting that a mountain be named for the great guide from Saranac, Herbert K. Clark. And a High Peak it should be, since Clark had the great distinction of being one of the first to climb them all. When the Adirondack Forty-Sixers club officially formed, Clark received the designation of 46er #1.

For years, the champion oarsman of Saranac Lake, this strongest of hikers, was the quintessential Adirondack guide. He was a master woodsman and taught the art of woodcraft to the Marshall boys when they were youngsters playing on the shores and in the woods around Saranac. Carson felt he was the greatest climber he had ever known. "On a mountain, he was a marvel of speed, especially if the going was rough, and even when past fifty he could outdistance almost any younger man with ease." How many of us today marvel at some of our "more experienced" companions who seem to leave us gasping for air in their wake.

Carson laid out an outstanding case for his audacious re-naming. He followed his "Herbert Peak," with the re-naming of a peak as a monument for the Marshall brothers—one in the Dix Range, about as far from the MacIntyres as you can get. Although Colvin had designated the name for the peak the Marshalls themselves called "Middle Dix" and "Little Dix" (Hough Peak), as the very fitting "Cone Mountain," Carson had only found it referenced in the surveyor's notes and sketches, and never in print or on published maps. "Therefore, the writer has no compunctions for ignoring all its former names and calling the peak 'Mount Marshall' in honour of Robert and George Marshall." Again he followed his claim up with compelling arguments for the naming. Most of those arguments would be used later in the eventual official naming of today's Mount Marshall.

"View from Herbert"

Getting mountains named "officially" is about as arduous as you would imagine it to be. Over the years, mapmakers usually had the discretion to name natural features based on previous references, local usage, and land ownership. Often capricious mapmakers and surveyors would change names from one issue of a map to the next. As the federal government undertook more surveys and implemented a more regimented approach to the naming of features, names again changed.

The shocking, premature death of Robert Marshall in 1939 spurred the 46ers of Troy (the precursor to the present club) to petition the state and federal boards of geographic names to officially name Mount Marshall after Bob. At the same time they submitted requests for the permanent naming of Blake's Peak and Couchsachraga, whose names had been omitted from the 1932 map. The club could not, however, include Herbert Peak in their petition as a recently passed state regulation prohibited the naming of any natural object for a living person – and Herb Clark was still alive.

Theodore Anthony, an attorney from Newburgh, and a member of the Adirondack Mountain Club, had originally objected to Russ Carson's unauthorized names for several of the High Peaks that appeared in his book *Peaks and People of the Adirondacks* in the 1920s. Anthony conducted a campaign against the names that Carson had proposed. Having failed to garner public sentiment against

"Up Herbert Brook"

Carson's peak names, in particular the name Mount Marshall, he then turned to the legal system and lobbied strongly for the regulation prohibiting naming natural features for living people. (For additional information on the 46ers' peak naming petition effort, see the "Activities of the Forty-Sixers of Troy" section of the history chapter.)

On October 15, 1940, the 46ers of Troy petitioned the state Board of Geographic Names for the official naming of Blake's Peak, Couchsachraga, and Mount Marshall. After submitting their petition, the 46ers were informed that the mountain they referred to as Mount Marshall had officially been named Hough Peak (after Dr. Franklin B. Hough, who was known as the "father of American forestry") in June, 1937, as part of the state's Fifty Years of Conservation Celebration. Club members were then forced to identify another High Peak to bear the name of Mount Marshall. After much debate the peak they chose was the mountain they referred to as Herbert. Since Herb Clark was alive they were legally blocked from petitioning for a peak named in his honor. So to get a Mount Marshall, the club had to displace Herbert Peak.

Despite receiving notification in June 1942 that the name designation of Mount Marshall had been approved, the 1953 topographical map listed the mountain's name as Mount Clinton. Perplexed and defeated by the unexpected name designation, it took the 46ers a number of years to prepare and resubmit another round of petitions to state and federal naming boards. Finally in December 1972 the U.S. Board on Geographic Names approved the name of Mount Marshall for the southwestern most peak of the MacIntyre Range.

As a tribute to the first 46er, and the guide who made the first round of all the High Peaks possible, the 46ers called the sublime brook that leads to the summit of Mount Marshall, Herbert Brook. Though first discovered by Grace Hudowalski and her party of hikers on an ascent of the mountain, it has proved to be a fitting tribute for Clark. Just as he led the Marshalls up the forty-six High Peaks so does Herbert Brook lead hikers to the summit of Mount Marshall.

Interestingly enough, the first logbook — "Ointment Can Logbook #1" – also celebrates Clark. Sammy Benedix, Agnes W. Benedix, Priscilla Chipman, and Peggy Keating placed the first canister, and perhaps first in the mountains, atop what they called Herbert Peak – 4,411 feet. "The four undersigned members of the N.Y. Chapter of the A.M.C. reached this point @11:35 A.M. on Sunday, August 4, 1946." That August saw two parties (one of six hikers, the other of seven) reach the summit, and September welcomed the Cornell Outing Club during the era's famous Intercollegiate Outing Club Association (IOCA) weeks. The next entry wasn't until July 4 of the following year! These first logbook entries usually were just a date and list of the climbers, but finally it took a college kid to start the tradition of spicing things up.

> September 13th, 1947 – IOCA College Week.
> The mountains proud we see in time come under;
> And earth, for age, we see in time decay. – G. Fletcher (1601)

The next entry from George Koch, of the LSUOC, a rival college outing club, added playfully: "But we got here first!" This first "Ointment Can" book measured a scant two by three inches but lasted nine years! The entrants were a who's who of the early Forty-Sixers, as well as hikers never heard from again. On August 20, 1955, Carolyn Schaefer closed out the book with "…#27. 4 hours from Cold Brook. In 1954, we spent 8 hours from Flowed Lands." Five years after it tore through the High Peaks, the Big Blow of 1950 was still playing havoc with hikers venturing up the trailless peaks! In fact, it was nearly two years before another entry hit the logbook. "First up since the Big Blowdown. It's rough going! – The Hartmanns, 8/14/52." Once again, the logbooks proved to be one of the best written histories of the conditions on the mountains themselves.

The Tooth, The Wart, or The Roost?

One of the MacIntyre Range's most visible and striking features is a small protuberance of rock on the southern slopes of Iroquois. From all points south of Colden, this little prominence is so clear and pronounced it has demanded a name of its own. From the Flowed Lands, along the flumes of Uphill Brook, from Skylight, Redfield, Cliff, and even distant summits like Basin, this feature adds one more pyramidal tooth to the entire MacIntyre Range profile. It seems fitting that the name Shepherd's Tooth is the title most commonly used today for the bump. In 1954, while the men of the Zahniser and Schaefer families were on a fishing trip, the women decided to climb Iroquois. When they inadvertently ended up on the tiny peak beneath Iroquois' summit, they named it. They never could have guessed that their moniker would become part of the High Peaks lexicon. Or could they?

Perhaps they even helped their cause. Members of the families went back to the summit and placed a canister, that contained a letter explaining their naming of the sub-peak, as well as an "order" form to send to them to receive a special patch they had made of a small "boomerang" with the name "Shepherd's Tooth" around it. For those who made the trek down the southern rock faces of Iroquois and fought through a few minutes of insufferably dense scrub, the reward was this new "merit badge." Even today one can see the occasional patch adorning a hiker's pack, next to their 46er patch, winter rocker, and other earned badges.

Those who found the canister, and mailed in the form to receive the badge were not disappointed. Not only did they receive a patch, but they also received a special Shepherd's Tooth High Peaks Edition Map, and a letter reprising bits of the original 1954 climb, as well as the continuing effort to keep the name alive and the patches flowing. Carolyn Schaefer (#104) began the tradition when she led the all women's hike that day in 1954, and ordered the first batch of one hundred patches for her Skyline Outfitters store in Keene ten years later in 1964. Here is some of her account of the climb, which originally was intended to be a traverse of both Iroquois and Herbert (Marshall).

> …We decided to climb Iroquois and look over the situation from above. It was a women's expedition, all the boys having gone fishing. One of us had never been up Iroquois and the others would be guides, and perhaps get her interested in becoming a Forty-Sixer. As we stood on top signing our names in the register, we looked over at Herbert. 'It is a long way over there, but what's that little peak in between? It's early in the day; let's see if we can get to that.'
>
> We went down at the end of Iroquois, tangling our hair in the spruce branches, getting down on our hands and knees to crawl beneath them, dropped down to the col and found a corner to ascend the little peak, the only place we could see that was possible. The top was like a little meadow and we sat down to eat our crackers and cheese. 'Where are the tin cans and bottles and candy wrappers? There aren't any around. Wonder how many people come over here?' We took out the map. Elevation 4500'. No name for this little bump.
>
> We could name it and leave our names in a water bottle under some rocks. Now what shall we call it?' After much deliberation and no decision someone suggested our last names. But they were German and didn't sound right next to Indian names. Our German student commented

that Schaefer meant 'shepherd' and Zahniser meant 'iron tooth'. 'And it looks like a tooth, sitting up here in the sky, and you can just imagine a mountain sheep standing here looking down on the surrounding forest.' We found a pencil stub in a knapsack, and a candy wrapper wasn't hard to find. After burying our container and thinking we might soon be back with a better one, we made our way back from the newly named 'Shepherd's Tooth'.

In the same era, the terrific writer, environmental activist, and Professor Emeritus of English at St. Lawrence University Paul F. Jamieson (#146) wrote eloquently about the remarkable little rock cobble. After climbing Algonquin Peak to start his quest to climb the 46 High Peaks in 1934, he was nearing the end of the list in the mid 1950s. In his book *Adirondack Pilgrimage*, Jamieson writes about his long distance relationship with the little peak. As many of us have been captivated by the little bump, so too was Jamieson. Once you know where to look, any glance at the MacIntyres from any viewpoint within miles of the Range always leads one to search for it. You will first spot Algonquin, then the ridge to Iroquois and invariable look for and say, "Ah, you can see Shepherd's Tooth as well!"

But for Jamieson, there was no moniker "Shepherd's Tooth," yet. Also, the name originally applied by the Marshalls and bandied about by the earliest 46ers seemed to have slipped out of usage. So, Jamieson called upon his readings of the classics to help define the knob. In his chapter called "The Wart of Iroquois," he explains that from the Opalescent, this peculiar bump "appears to be completely wooded and has often reminded me of the wart of the nose of Chaucer's miller:

> Upon the cop upon his nose he hade
> A werte, and theron stood a toft of herys

No doubt that was the first time words from Chaucer's *The Canterbury Tales* had ever been the inspiration to describe a feature in the Adirondacks! The obscurity of the reference, as well as the less than lyrical quality to the name, made it unattractive to all but a few 46ers who from time to time argued that Jamieson had been first to give the feature its name. Jamieson wrote of a trek in the mid 1950s from Iroquois to Algonquin Pass and on to Marshall. Part of his commitment to the route was to be able to inspect his "wart" up close.

His description was of a day, timeless to all who hike in the mountains—when fog envelopes the peaks and brings in a wildness that stretches back a thousand eons, shutting out views of any sign of man, and grounding the airplane, the one vehicle that has the means to intrude upon any area and moment of solitude. In the milky, gray, cold and inhospitable day, the route off Iroquois led him into a sea of the densest cripplebush imaginable and all thoughts of Chaucer, his miller's nose, and the unique knob were sidelined to the rigors and concentration of navigation. And then the wart came to find him.

> Suddenly a huge shape loomed up over the tops of the balsam. It looked like the prow of a ship bearing down, or rather up, on us, not thirty yards away. In the mist it looked spectral, like the bark of the Flying Dutchman or Noah's ark come to rest and petrified on Iroquois rather than Ararat.

It was in that moment of wonder that Jamieson felt the bump to be un-climbable. One does not scale a phantom, period. And in the swirling mist, with yet another mountain to climb on the day's agenda, Jamieson and his partner said goodbye and descended into Algonquin Pass. The "Wart of Iroquois" was indeed a fitting and colorful name, and it may have been coined before "Shepherd's Tooth," but neither, in fact, can lay claim to first naming rights.

That honor remains from the day of the first documented climb of the knob, by the illustrious trio of Bob, George, and Herb.

In 1918, while atop Herbert (Iroquois), the Marshall boys surely looked down on the bump during their survey of a route to Iroquois (Marshall). Fond of stories and the lore of the hills from before their time (some stories belonging to verifiable fact and others to probable whimsy), they often talked about what great animals they would like to have seen. The catamount was clearly a favorite. Tales of walking up on a feeding catamount, or seeing one scamper up among the thickets to finally rest upon a lookout of open rock were often told. Understanding the great cats, and how they have the habit of searching out high outcrops of rock as survey perches, one only needs to stand on the knob to understand why the brothers named the rock as they did.

On their trip to Marshall from Iroquois in June of 1921, the boys climbed to the top of the nub and agreed that it surely must have been—at some time and perhaps for centuries on end—the catamount's favorite roost. It has a commanding bird's eye view down to the shores of Lake Colden, the Opalescent River, and the area of the Flowed Lands, all of which would have been full of game. There was never any mention of the boys spying one of the great mammals themselves, as the species had been eradicated from the state by that time. But they had named the bump not with the present in mind, but with the wild past in mind. They named it in honor of the region's greatest of hunters, and the crow's nest he would have called home: Catamount Roost.

Whatever unofficial name one chooses to call it, there are few who would argue that it truly is one of the great "little" features that makes the Adirondacks special. In his 1992 book, *Into the Adirondacks*, Jim Poulette (#2729) writes about a special afternoon he spent there. "Many people get closer to themselves, to their instinctual inner knowing, when surrounded by the earth's natural elements. Shepherd's Tooth was our place." Yes, the grand summits will always draw the gaze, but the small distinguishing marks are what give the mountains we love their character. The scars and slides, angles and bumps, and striking features like Shepard's... well, whatever you want to call it.

Indian Pass – Da-Yoh-Je-Ga-Go

Indian Pass. One of the most sublime miles in the Northeast! This stupendous gorge, nestled in the crooked debris at the bottom of an ancient swath of destruction, lies directly at the base of the western flanks of Mount Marshall, a mere few hundred feet from the base of the adjacent sheer cliffs of the clean-scraped Wallface Mountain. These awe-inspiring vertical cliffs are the tallest and most dramatic on the East Coast, featuring numerous challenging rock climbing routes like the fabled Mental Blocks.

The debris field is an impressive graveyard of house-sized boulders which turn the trail into an obstacle course winding up ladders and stone staircases, around crevasses and through caves, and right underneath towering overhangs. From Summit Rock one can gaze in wonder at the full breadth of Wallface's wide expanse of sheer rock directly in front and above. Turning left, one can follow the course of the south flowing branch of Indian Pass Brook as it winds toward Henderson Lake, spilling into the Hudson River, and ultimately coursing past Manhattan as it dumps into the Atlantic Ocean.

This is Indian Pass, much as it has stood for the last several thousand years since the retreat of the great Laurentian Glacier. From the very first visits of the "white civilized man" in the early nineteenth century, Indian Pass became a fascination and lure for anyone travelling to the area. But let's venture further back in time, sometime after the Ice Age yet before the Abenaki scout Lewis Elijah led David Henderson on a three day journey from North Elba through the pass to the mother lode of ore at Tahawus, all for a dollar and a half and a plug of tobacco.

Before the Europeans reached the shores of America, Native Americans roamed the lands, but the High Peaks region was not a desirable place to settle and there is no proof that anyone actually lived in the area. There were tribes nearby though. The Algonquin lived along the shores of Lake Champlain (or whatever they called the lake before its renaming by Samuel de Champlain) and unconfirmed reports had the tribe establishing inland settlements along the upper reaches of the Hudson River.

The Mohawks lived further south in the Mohawk River Valley and the Adirondack foothills. One of the seasonal practices was for hunting parties to leave the settled areas in the fall and hunt until early winter before the rivers froze. They would have likely hunted within close proximity to the Hudson River and followed it up to its source. One of the hunting routes ran through Indian Pass connecting the fields of North Elba and the headwaters of the rivers flowing into Lake Champlain to the headwaters of the forest branches of the Hudson: a true Indian Pass.

The Indians had several names for their awesomely rugged, yet breathtakingly beautiful trail. *Otne-yar-heh*—"Stonish Giants"; *Ga-nos-gwah*—"Giants clothed with stone"; *Da-yoh-je-ga-go*—"The place where the storm clouds meet in battle with the great serpent"; and *He-no-do-aw-da*—"The Path of the Thunderer," are the colorful and evocative names.

This Indian trail had been in use long before Lewis Elijah's time, which is why David Henderson referred to it as The Indian Pass in his October 14, 1826, letter to Archibald McIntyre describing his arduous journey from the Plains of Abraham, north of the pass, to the discovery site of iron ore deposits far below the southern exit of the pass in Tahawus and Upper Works. At some point the pass was supposedly renamed Adirondack Pass, perhaps for tourist purposes, but the name never stuck, and reverted to the more meaningful Indian Pass.

After David Henderson's famous trek, and the establishment of the Tahawus mines, easy access to the pass opened up the floodgates of explorers, surveyors, and romantics. It is interesting to note that Henderson was the first to envision exploiting the pass for mass tourism. In a March 27, 1837, letter to McIntyre, Henderson wrote: "The territory is getting so much notice that I verily believe were a railroad to be made from the lake and a large public house erected it would become a fashionable resort for the summer months—the notch being the greatest curiosity in the country next to falls of Niagara. If Niagara be the prince of waterfalls the other exhibits the prince of precipices."

In recent years the towns of Newcomb and North Elba fancied chopping a snowmobile trail through the pass for recreation and tourist dollars, but the logistics and pressure against such projects have doomed such ventures. Likewise, Henderson's proposal almost two centuries ago was rejected, and the hiker has been the benefactor. The pass remains as unspoiled and rugged as it has been for the last ten millennia.

Surprisingly, those early days were some of the busiest for Indian Pass. How could they not be? The accounts of visits to the pass flooded back to civilization and they all echoed a similar sentiment: sheer awe. The fabled scientist Ebenezer Emmons expostulated at length in his reports to the state about the pass for he was so taken by it. "I should not have occupied so much space of describing merely a natural curiosity, were it not for the fact that probably in this country there is no object of the kind on a scale so vast and imposing as this."

The arrival of the Romantic poets and writers added a lyricism to the descriptive passages. Alfred Billings Street eloquently summed up his first impression:

> A shudder shook my frame. My eyes swam, my brain grew dizzy. After a few moments of thus bracing my system and recovering from the first sickening shock, I again looked. What a sight! Horrible and yet sublimely beautiful—no, not beautiful; scarce an element of beauty there—all grandeur and terror.

Obviously these Romantics had spent a good deal of their lives sipping tea in Victorian parlours, but we do feel the power of Indian Pass through their words. The writer Charles Fenno Hoffman called the pass "one of the most savage and stupendous among the many wild and imposing scenes at the source of the Hudson." His guide on that trip was the famous John Cheney, for whom Cheney Cobble in the North River Range is named. For Cheney, Indian Pass was simply, "Church." Indeed.

Visual artists were also drawn to this attraction. Great landscape painters brought their sketch pads, easels, and palettes to the pass. Thomas Cole, the father of the Hudson River School, led the surge in the first half of the century, and painted a highly charged and heroic painting in 1847: *Indian Pass—Tahawus*. The only problem with the painting is that it was a highly stylized and fictitious piece, depicting a native Indian (there were none locally at that point) by a stream with a large conical rendering of Mount Marcy looming in the background. Of course Marcy cannot be seen from Indian Pass, and it also has some close next-door neighbors like Skylight, Gray, and Haystack and many others sharing the skyline. The painting is quite stunning nevertheless.

If Cole's *Indian Pass—Tahawus* is fun to inspect for its inaccuracies, then Charles Cromwell Ingham's 1837 painting *The Great Adirondack [Indian] Pass, Painted on the Spot* represents the opposite. For indeed, Ingham painted his masterful work of pastoral realism right from the perch atop Summit Rock, or Lookout Point as it was then called. Ingham's painting is truly as fine a piece of Adirondack artwork as has ever been produced, and takes you instantly to a summer afternoon aboard Summit Rock.

Seneca Ray Stoddard, one of the most influential photographers of the era, was drawn to Indian Pass as well. His sketch of the pass heading into the boulder field after that first mesmerizing glance of Wallface, and his travelogue depiction of his voyage make up a whole chapter in his *The Adirondacks Illustrated* from 1874. Reading the account of his Indian Pass journey—his delightful attention to detail—is like dusting off the memory of your own first tramp through there. As ancient as the pass is, it is also timeless. His closing words not only reflect his love of the pass, but echo what most 46ers cherish, and hold dearly, about all of our favorite hikes.

> Does it pay to go through Indian Pass? I answer a thousand times yes. It costs a little extra exertion, but the experiences and emotions of the day come back in a flood of happy recollections, and the soul is lifted a little higher and made better by a visit to that grand old mountain ruin.

Tragedy at 4,580 Feet

A little after midnight, on January 16, 1962, the city of Watertown, New York was strafed with a bombing run by the 380th Bomb Wing stationed at Plattsburgh Air Force Base. The delivery vehicle was a B-47 Bomber, a multimillion dollar warplane, and the bombs were electronic blips being judged by the radar unit at nearby Camp Drum (now called Fort Drum). The run was a success, and Watertown was ablaze in imaginary flames. The plane radioed in asking permission to take another bombing run, and then return back to Plattsburgh via an alternate flight path.

Their alternate flight path ended in the High Peaks' greatest man-made disaster.

After their radio communiqué at 2:00 a.m., the B-47 vanished into the thin January air, a mighty and disturbing feat for a craft spanning 116 feet in width, 108 feet in length, and standing a towering 28 feet tall. At a hefty 80 tons, this was no lightweight of the skies. With a cruising speed of over 550 MPH and a flight range of 4,000 miles, the area where the plane could have ended up encompassed the square mileage of the entire Adirondack Park.

The plane was officially listed as missing at 8:00 a.m. There had been no word from the four-man crew comprised of First Lieutenant Rodney D. Bloomgren, 26, of Jamestown, N.Y., commander; First Lieutenant Melvin Spencer, 28, of Tuscaloosa, Alabama, co-pilot; First Lieutenant Albert W. Kandetski Jr., 25, of Sunnyvale, California, navigator; and Airman First Class Kenneth R. Jensen of El Cajon, California, observer. A call went out requesting information from anyone who may have witnessed a low flying plane or explosion, and the responses started pouring in.

A reported blast in the hilly farmlands southeast of Watertown led nowhere, as did the sighting of an object resembling a fuselage spotted from the air near Barnes Corners in Lewis County. The latter turned out to be a mangled and gnarled tree trunk. Near Potsdam, a woman reported flares lighting up the night skies, and another report spoke of a whining plane heading into Lake Ontario. Massena had an explosion, Colton had a jet burst into flames, Lyon Mountain was belching fire and smoke, and even Sunset Lake in Vermont had tire skid marks leading to a massive hole in the ice.

These erroneous reports led to one of the largest civilian and military searches in the history of Upstate New York. It resulted in a wild goose chase through snow and bitter cold temperatures. None of the reported sightings was even close. By January 20th, a full four days after the disappearance, a fleet of over fifty planes including a massive, specially modified C-54 transport from Goose Bay, Labrador, was scouring the remote Adirondacks, desperately looking for the wreckage. Even the Royal Canadian Air Force searched areas along the Saint Lawrence River. The crewmen of the B-47 were trained for disaster and equipped with survival gear, but time was running out.

It was on Sunday, January 21, when the news finally came in. The plane, or what was left of it, had been found. A National Guard pilot had spotted a wing and three parachutes resting on the northeast slope of Algonquin Peak. Across Wright Peak was strewn the majority of the plane wreckage, with much scattered across the saddle between them. The parachutes brought a sense of optimism, and urgency, to the rescue teams being helicoptered down onto frozen Heart Lake. New York State Department of Conservation Rangers, New York State Troopers, an Air Force team, and other volunteers gathered and plotted their mission, all the while looking up at a whirling maelstrom surrounding the summits of the entire MacIntyre Range. Helicopter reconnaissance was out of the question.

At 4:00 p.m. a team of five local, hand-picked men started up the mountain leading the search and rescue. Three dogsled teams followed to retrieve any wreckage they found along the way. At 8:30 p.m., the lead team was stopped in its tracks by the blinding ice and snow of the blizzard conditions raging above treeline. Subzero temperatures and 60 MPH winds drove the teams back in a retreat through biting sleet and near-zero visibility conditions.

Monday came and the teams set out once more. They went from a quiet winter's day in the valleys below to another roaring nightmare of swirling snow, so thick one could barely see the man next in line. Again the teams were forced back to camp. However, a pair of expert local woodsmen and climbers, Bill Frenette (#216) and Garfield Jones (#220), set out on an independent search that same Monday at 3:30 a.m.

Knowing the wind patterns of the range, they ascended Wright via the ski trail, and were able to make it atop the peak without encountering the devastating winds until the last fifty feet below the summit. They spotted the wreckage and followed a path of debris down the southeastern side of the mountain from the summit down to near the 3,000-foot level. The impact of the metal had stripped the trees bare and the wreckage was driven deep into the earth by incredible force.

Air Force officials estimated the plane was flying in a direct path toward Mount Marcy when it slammed into Wright, thirty-five feet below the summit. The plane hit at about a seventy degree angle, head-on, and both plane and occupants disintegrated on contact in the terrific blast. Identification of the men (this being before the age of DNA analysis), was virtually impossible, though all the remains that could be found were helicoptered back to Plattsburgh.

The teams tried to establish a base camp atop the peak, but continuing bad weather forced the men off the mountain. On January 29 the search and salvage was called off, as nothing further could be gained until later in the spring. Investigators determined the low level training run had not allowed the crew to use navigational aids, and that bad weather, turbulence, and probably a failure of the plane's altimeter, were all contributing factors to the crash.

In July of 1962, Albert Kandetski's father planted four red spruce trees in a rectangular bower near treeline on Wright Peak as a memorial to his son and the other crewmen. In 1965, a bronze plaque was erected by the 820th Combat Support Group, one of several auxiliary groups that supported the 380th Bomb Wing, at the approximate point of impact just off Wright's summit. Near this marker are pieces of debris from the aircraft still to this day, including aircraft-grade aluminum parts that shine untarnished from the ill-fated summit to the heavens above.

Some years later a second bronze marker was erected at the back of the MacIntyre Falls campsite. A short herdpath leads away from the open camping rings through the woods to the site of this secluded monument. Some rumors attribute this seemingly arbitrary placement to the team running out of daylight, and choosing a spot near where they stopped along the trail. Others say the Air Force preferred to give the airmen a quiet, out of the way memorial.

The crash may have been the most horrific in the High Peaks, but it exemplified the bravery, determination, and courage of the park rangers, Air Force, Civil Air Patrol, State Troopers, Army, National Guard, and hearty civilian volunteers who braved the worst imaginable winter conditions to scour an inhospitable mountain summit in search of the fallen. Man at his most selfless.

A Tale of Survival in Algonquin Pass

In the 1960s the MacIntyre Range saw yet another plane crash. However this one ended with a dramatic life saving rescue. Many factors contributed to this miracle, not the least of which were luck and timing. The date was August 9, 1969, a night of fair weather and moderate summer temperatures. These two factors eliminated a whole host of secondary problems, for weather and exposure often contribute to fatalities among survivors of the initial impact.

F. Peter Simmons, a relatively inexperienced pilot, left the Islip airport on Long Island (New York) for a solo night flight up to the Adirondack Regional Airport in Lake Clear. He was flying home to his family camp on Big Tupper Lake, and family members were waiting to pick him up at the airport. He never arrived. His Cherokee 140 found a different runway on which to touch down.

When Simmons' plane became ensnared in a downdraft as he flew over the High Peaks region, he was forced to use every lesson he had learned in flight school and from his 350 hours of flight experience. He knew he was going down and could not stop his descent so he pulled the Cherokee's nose up and dropped his airspeed down to 65 MPH. Sensing impact, he switched the master and the mags off. The last thing he remembered was a slight thump from one of the wings, as if it clipped a branch. Then fate took over.

His plane had missed the rocky flanks of Iroquois by a scant few hundred yards on one side, and the slopes of Mount Marshall on the other. As if guided by pure luck, the plane came down in the flat of Algonquin Pass, just as the slope turns downward toward Lake Colden. To help matters more, the plane was less than a hundred feet off the only trail in that area of the forest.

The Cherokee was not equipped with a shoulder harness and Simmons paid a heavy price for it. The impact threw him forward into the instrument panel, shattering his cheekbone, fracturing his skull, crushing his left eye socket, and breaking his lower jaw. A leg, ankle, and wrist also broke in the crash. He was in rough shape and going nowhere. To compound matters, the Cherokee was not carrying a crash-locator beacon.

Campers down by the lakes below had heard the impact and told Forest Ranger Gary Hodgson about it. He called the State Police to offer his services and give the Civil Air Patrol (CAP) a possible search parameter. The CAP sent twenty-seven planes up over the area and at 4:45 p.m. on August 10, some fifteen hours after the crash, the fuselage of the Cherokee was spotted from the air. However the pilot incorrectly identified the crash site as being Mount Marcy and it wasn't until 6 p.m. that another pilot gave a correct detailed description of the landing site.

Hodgson, Marcy Dam caretaker Al Jordan, and a dozen other rescuers including five state troopers, assembled at Marcy Dam and set out for the crash at 6:45 p.m. Around 8:40 p.m., just as dusk was settling around them, they found the Cherokee and Simmons inside. Incredibly, the Cherokee was fairly intact, resting at about 3,800 feet.

Jordan and Hodgson treated Simmons for shock, placing him inside a sleeping bag and lighting a lantern for heat. The next morning, some thirty-two hours after the crash landing, Simmons was airlifted out by the Conservation Department's helicopter. Dr. Herbert Bergamini and Dr. E. Addis Munyan stabilized Simmons until he was safely delivered to Lake Placid Hospital by 9:00 a.m.

This was the first, and only, rescue in the Adirondacks by the Civil Air Patrol. Simmons recovery was slow and intensive, but there are few days that go by when he doesn't feel a debt of gratitude to all the people who helped save his life—from the campers who helped guide the initial search, to the CAP for pinpointing his location, to the rescuers for securing and stabilizing him, and to the airlift and doctors who put him back together. Many people worked together to save a life stranded on the MacIntyre Range. Simmons has repeatedly shown his appreciation by throwing summer parties in recognition of those who saved his life that fateful August night.

An Ancient Pass, An Abandoned Path, A Gem of an Adirondack Bushwhack

Standing on Marcy Dam, the eye is treated to a wondrous composition of the scarred towering flanks of Mount Colden dropping nearly straight down into the cleft of Avalanche Pass. To the right, the long shoulder of Algonquin reaches toward the same pass, yet smack in the middle is the inconspicuous bump that makes the whole picture complete. Though one of the Adirondacks' hundred highest peaks, in its setting among giants, Avalanche Mountain (once called Caribou Mountain) does seem to cower in diminutive reverence.

But without this special little bump, there would be no spectacular Avalanche Pass, or no Hitch-up Matildas to navigate across the dark deep of Avalanche Lake. This seemingly benign, rounded lump of a mountain as viewed from the dam turns into a rampart of sheer cliff for that one glorious mile of rugged terrain between Avalanche Camp and the end of Avalanche Lake. Nearly impossible to scale, it serves its purpose well as a loyal inducer of Adirondack awe and wonder.

Quiet wonder lies here, too, on this overlooked peak shrouded beneath the presence of its popular neighbors. A favorite bushwhack of hearty 46ers since the early days, the northern routes to the summit offer spectacular views of Colden's many slides, and a bird's eye view of Avalanche Mountain's imposing eastern summit slides. From the wooded summit, some poking around will reward the hiker with a fantastic up-close perspective of Colden's powerful western face, and the enormity of the MacIntyre Range's massive girth stretching from Wright Peak through Iroquois.

The gem of all views is the sublime vantage down on to Lake Colden, Flowed Lands, and the ridge of Calamity Mountain with Mount Adams behind it. This is the mirror image of the same fantastic view of Avalanche Mountain itself that one sees standing on the shore of Flowed Lands, or on the dam at the end of Lake Colden.

If the summit was open like Summit Rock, or Roostercomb, indeed there would be a well-beaten path and summer crowds. And that path would likely lead through one of the rare forgotten Adirondack passes: Caribou Pass. Caribou Pass? This rarely mentioned cleft might have slipped away if it were not for old hiking accounts and its continued inclusion on the USGS topographic maps. Yet its history runs as deep as many of the other great passes.

But again, what is Caribou Pass? Chances are you have looked right through it without even knowing, for this pass is hidden in plain view in that magnificent panorama from Marcy Dam. Look to Avalanche Mountain, then to the notch it forms at the base of Algonquin's shoulder. There you have the pass, and the long drainage leading right up into it, beckoning to be explored.

After a rugged trip through Avalanche Pass in 1869, Verplanck Colvin decided there had to be a better way to lug his heavy equipment from North Elba to Lake Colden. In September of 1873 he explored the next pass over.

> Deep in the defile we were surprised to find a rich little oasis meadow of 'blue-joint' grass, which, thick and rank, rose to our elbows. It was full of paths made by deer, and cozy beds from which they had only risen at our approach. A discussion which ensued as we climbed the mountain side in regard to the American reindeer or caraboo [sic], was the occasion of our naming the new pass after an animal which once inhabited the region, but which is now, probably, here extinct.

Although he was wrong about the existence of caribou in the area, Colvin had found an easier way to reach the Opalescent. The trail was informally adopted and appeared on an 1876 map of Essex County. It didn't last long, for Henry Van Hoevenberg came along and improved the Avalanche Pass trail, and soon built his own namesake trail to Marcy. The early 1900s saw the pass opened again, but this time by loggers cutting roads straight up to the height of land in the pass.

Little sign of those roads remain, and the top of the pass shares the same attribute as many of the other passes in the area. From Caribou Pass one can walk to either side of the cleft and see streams flowing toward opposing destinies. Along the northern slopes, the streams flow toward the Saint Lawrence and on the southern side the waters flow into the Hudson and ultimately run past New York Harbor.

It was up the northern drainage and along Caribou Pass Brook that a small party, including the author of this chapter, made a trek into Caribou Pass on June 25, 2005. The brook was typical of Adirondack brooks with cascades, flumes, and several waterfalls splashing over boulders and one lovely twelve foot falls filling up its own little swimming pool below. Hints of an approaching pass cropped up time and again in the form of cliffs and sheer walls, and striking dry gorges that must burst into life during the spring melt and runoff from massive Algonquin above. Here is a description of that hike.

> As blue sky began dipping on the horizon and the terrain began to level, we crossed an ancient log bridge over the highest reaches of the brook. We had retraced the footsteps of adventurers, survey teams, and working foresters and arrived at the top of the pass. As our first steps into the pass opened into a small plateau of scraggly spruce and balsam, the impression was underwhelming. The area was more like a typical summit for the lower Adirondack mountains and not a noble pass.
>
> It was when we pushed deeper into the pass that we found the magic. Hidden by this tangle of struggling trees was the western side of the pass. Looking in that direction, all we could see was a dark gray shadow. Something loomed in that darkness, and after a minute's tramp we found it. The quintessential element of any pass. The sheer cliff wall. Unlike the broken and jagged cliffs of Avalanche and Indian Passes, the wall flanking Caribou Pass is smooth like the rampart of a fortress. It forms an impenetrable barrier to Algonquin's eastern side, running hundreds of feet wide and reaching heights of between twenty and fifty feet of near ninety degree vertical rise.
>
> We followed the wall to the far end of the pass, where the whole mass began sliding down to the south and found an opening that afforded us a view through the shoulders of Avalanche and Algonquin of Calamity Mountain. This was the tease of better views from above and so we abandoned the quiet pass and climbed the steep and thick western side of Avalanche Mountain to gain the summit. All the while we found places to turn around and admire the impressive wall of rock, and increasing views of Algonquin, then Boundary, and finally Iroquois and Wright Peaks above.

Although the pass now is home to pine martens, dragonflies, and birds like Bicknell's Thrush, Caribou Pass became home to the fictional hero in T. Morris Longstreth's *Mac of Placid* (1920). In the book, Mac had run amok with a throng of whiskey-fueled loggers and had escaped a wild drunken brawl by hiding in a cave in Caribou Pass.

> The cave was a chance find of mine on a wild-bee hunt, he said, and few others knew about it, as those who traveled the trails (meaning a dozen or so a year) preferred that through Avalanche Pass. A great slab of granite had fallen from a higher ledge and caught upon two boulders. With

Colden, left, and Avalanche, right, before Marcy Dam was rebuilt in the 1930s

such portals and backed by the solid cliff it was impervious to all the elements, and roomy as you'd want.

In 1946, Ed and Grace Hudowalski explored the area after being entranced with the view from Marcy Dam and wrote about it. "We resolved suddenly, one day last August, to bushwhack up Caribou Pass, climb Avalanche Mountain, and descend into Avalanche Pass." Easier said than done! Or as some climbers would say, two out of three ain't bad. The first objective was deemed fairly easy and pleasurable. "Caribou Pass is not as spectacular as some of the other passes. It is, however, interesting and gives one a feeling of wild remoteness."

The second objective was met after "about a 25 minute scramble up a steep slope, over some small cliffs, and through thick balsam and scrub hardwoods." Some things haven't changed! With no views from the summit, they pushed on toward Avalanche Pass.

> This side of the mountain is very steep and made up of tier upon tier of cliffs and ledges, most of them hidden from view by trees. From these ledges, covered thickly with blooming sheep laurel, very striking views unfolded of Mount Colden and its trap dyke, of Cliff and Redfield Mountains, and of Lake Colden and the Flowed Lands. The view of the trap dyke is particularly impressive as one looks directly down into it for its entire length.

The views may have been impressive, but so too was the route. Ed spoke of inching down steep chimneys, and sliding down trees which happened to grow conveniently close enough to the sheer cliffs they were navigating. After several hours of this fun, the going became sheer perpendicular: "Seeing as how we could not go down, we started back – *upwards!*"

Soon the party encountered a chimney, which led them to a dyke. "This dyke—later we learned it wasn't a dyke but a 'fault'—was the exact replica of the dyke on Colden except much smaller. Its floor was covered luxuriantly with moss, ferns, and wood sorrel." Ed added, "It was so lovely that we had to stop often and admire the quiet wild beauty of it." Ed Hudowalski loved his "random scoots," and one can almost hear his simple prompt, "Try it!"

From Colvin's first exploration in 1873, to the logging of the early twentieth century, to Ed and Grace's jaunt in 1946, and finally to a twenty-first century bushwhack, this pass and mountain have been explored and exploited. They continue to offer a unique experience in the middle of the High Peaks for those who desire to seek them out.

The Wrong Slide to Wright Peak

Among the most striking and inviting features of the Adirondack High Peaks are the slides. Slides are the barren areas left behind by the giant swathes of destruction wreaked upon the mountainside by a landslide. The Adirondacks are full of slides. The combination of steep slopes, thin layers of soil above hardened bedrock, and the right weather conditions work together to create the perfect environment for these short but monumental moments of utter destruction. Just as the soil of a potted houseplant will pull away from the pot when it is dry, so too does the soil in the mountains. It lifts slightly off the smooth bedrock beneath, and when heavy bursts of rain hit after a dry spell, there is more moisture than the soil can absorb. Water slips in and runs down the bedrock, further loosening the grip between soil and surface. At the same time the soil that is absorbing the heavy rain gathers weight. When the soil can hang on no longer, down it all comes under the firm hand of gravity. Left behind is a clean and direct route up the mountainside.

Almost every mountain range in the High Peaks region has at least one slide. Some individual mountains have several, and a few appear to be nothing but a series of slides. Best of all, several of these slides top out near a mountain's summit. Giant, Dix, Nippletop, Gothics, Santanoni, and Emmons, to name a few, have all been climbed via their slides. In the MacIntyre Range, Marshall, Algonquin, and Wright all have prominent slides. But Wright Peak has the most climbable slide route to its summit of the three. Wright Peak has slides on its eastern shoulders, and its northeast and southeast faces. From Marcy Dam, the northeast slides jump right out at you, but are relatively short and start and end in the middle of the mountain, well below the summit ridge. From most summits to the south of Wright, and especially from the North Peak of Colden and from Algonquin, the twin parallel slides of the southeast face are clearly visible.

The longer and westernmost slide is the Wright Slide, or the 1938 Slide. It was a heavy September downpour after a dry August that caused a long ribbon of mountain to descend to the valley below. Alton Clint West, the Lake Colden Ranger, noticed the new slide from the top of Indian Falls. Soon thereafter, he climbed with Dr. Orra Phelps to inspect the new slide and both were awestruck by the forces of nature that caused the teardrop-shaped scouring of mountainside. Four hundred feet wide at the base, and nearly one half mile long in length, it was a sight to behold. Not as wide or long is the smaller slide next door, standing to the east by several hundred feet. This slide, whose origin and date remain a mystery, is informally called the Wrong Slide. If you were to stand on Algonquin and look at the twin slides you would understand why.

The Wright Slide starts further up the Wright Brook Valley, and heads far up the mountainside within striking range of the summit. The Wrong Slide does not. In fact, no one would look at it as a desirable route to the summit. The slide ends several hundred feet below the summit ridge and a good quarter mile away from it. But how thick can it really be between the slide and the summit? On August 11, 2004, several climbers, including this author, were "lucky" enough to find out.

> Of course, our objective for the day's climb had been the 1938 Wright Slide. The same one climbed by West and Phelps, and the one written about by Barbara McMartin in her *Discover the Adirondack High Peaks*. It had not only been climbed countless times over the years, but one in our party had climbed it several times already and had written a terrific piece about it in the 46er magazine, *Peeks*. The title was 'A Matter of Luck.'

We had read and listened to previous hiking accounts, knew where to look on Marcy Brook for the confluence with Wright Brook, were prepared for the slow two mile bushwhack up the valley drainage, and should have been on the slide within a couple of hours. Wright Brook flowed into Marcy Brook right where we expected it to, the crossing went smoothly, and our progress up Wright Brook was slow, due to slippery rocks, trips up and down the banks, and plenty of time spent in and out of the brook. But the cascades and waters flowing over long green slabs were musical and sublime, and a deep gorge near the bottom of the brook was a treat we hadn't expected.

No need to rush through treasures like these. And so we didn't. We just kept heading upstream and occasionally tuned in to our intrepid guide's instrument of direction. A GPS? Altimeter? No, not even a simple map and compass. We were being led by the slow ticking hands of a watch! At around two hours and fifteen minutes, we would supposedly be at our point to head into the woods. A small tributary would be our confirmation for the open route and promise of the Wright Slide just above.

The clock hit two hours and close enough to fifteen minutes, a trickling drainage came in from the northern side of the valley, and we all shrugged and said let's get climbing. So up we went. Thicker into the tangles of dense hobblebush, sod holes, and the occasional shin busting blowdown we ventured. Up a little. No sign of the bright shining beacon of bare rock. Over a little, for perhaps we were off line. This became a bit of a game. Up and over, all the while searching for our large granitic needle in a spruce stack. Progress slowed, and just as we took a break to pull the pine needles out of our shirts, one in the party, who had scouted ahead, called back with good news. He had found the slide.

We squeezed through the scraggly brush of the debris field, over to the invisible beacon of our scout's voice and popped out at the bottom of a slide. But there was no celebration, for we had all looked at the reconnaissance photos and knew about the Wrong Slide, and that we did not want to go up it. So, which slide had we arrived at? Well, reasoned the two in our party who had explored the Wrong Slide, it had to be the Wright Slide for the Wrong Slide had the distinction of being home to an unmistakable landmark. One of the wings of the B-47 Bomber that crashed atop Wright Peak in 1962 had come to rest on the slide. Looking up, there was no sign of any B-47 wings. Good enough. Besides, the path of least resistance was better than trudging through more brush looking for what might prove to be a non-existent nearby slide.

The slide was a mix of smooth rock, the occasional scrub brush, and small rivulets of water dribbling down its face. Moderate steepness to begin with gave way to a few sections that had us scrambling hand over hand. Behind us the views emerged. What started as a large portrait of Mount Colden blossomed magically with the addition of Mount Marcy over Colden's northern shoulder. The slide's steepness increased and chased the trip leader into the scrub at the far side, while the fearless one in the group clambered right up the middle. The last two culprits stayed close to the near side, one hand within reach of the spruce and dwarf balsams that would be a safety net.

In short order the slide evaporated beneath them and they found themselves on a small ledge at the top. The view down the slide into the valley below was almost as nice as the appearance of a herdpath at the top. They rejoiced, believing they had climbed the right slide after all. Strangest of all was the welcome mat of a flattened piece of airplane tire at the entrance of the herdpath. With this bit of good news the group plopped back down on the ledge for lunch, and to drink in the new and improved vista which now included Basin, Saddleback, and Gothics. Directly in front and towering above was Algonquin, with its thin northeastern ribbon slide hundreds of feet long twinkling from the falling flow of high alpine waters.

Lunch went down with smiles, laughter, and the occasional gasp of awe at the unique vantages of the familiar mountains around them. Truly one of the great joys of venturing off trail are the amazing views and new angles. This lunch spot offered some of the best. Sitting at the top of a seldom visited slide with the impressive Colden right next door, with a narrow valley snaking downhill beneath, the distant melody of rushing water, and nary another human presence or voice reminded the group what made hiking the High Peaks such a special endeavor.

And then the fun began. Packs hoisted, the bushwhackers ventured across the makeshift welcome mat and came to an instant standstill. What had at first appeared to be a herdpath was no more than an indentation in the brush. Spreading out and searching confirmed the obvious that they had tried hard to ignore. With no signs of human life, and no open rocks of a summit beckoning above, they were indeed at the top of the Wrong Slide. From that vantage all they could make out was the steep and thick slope above. Yet, at this point in such a journey, it was in for a penny, in for a pound. So into the thickest of the thick they dove. The electronics guru checked her GPS and announced the summit was just over one quarter of a mile away.

Thick, impenetrable, sharp, littered with sod traps, slimy logs, boulders and ledges to scramble over, our route provided all of these in stocked abundance. The group traversed slowly uphill, past numerous pieces of B-47 wreckage, and pushed and pulled and wrenched their way onward. Progress became measured in feet and minutes, and there were plenty of both.

We couldn't have rushed if we wanted to, and despite the tangle and scrapes and bruising terrain, our goal of the summit, and the nice open rock it promised, crept closer. It took an hour and a half to gain the summit ridge. Fifteen minutes later we clambered up on to a large glacial erratic to survey our progress. Through the thick jumble of cripplebush the semblance of a summit appeared a few hundred feet to the west. And to the east was the thickest stand of spruce and balsam we had ever seen. Most were of the standing dead variety, immovable and perpetually hungry for human flesh.

It was also the route we had just survived, albeit having fed some of those soldiers, those guardians of the mountainside, along the way. A breath later and my aches and pains disappeared. The growing vista that began at the bottom of the slide had come into full bloom. We were now looking down on Phelps, Tabletop, and little TR Mountain in the foreground. Behind this mass of near peaks rose the entire Great Range, save Haystack. Giant, Rocky Peak Ridge, and Green gave way to distant views of the Vermont peaks spread out across the Long Trail. Swinging toward the north the view crossed over Big Slide, Cascade, Porter, and Pitchoff. The Jay and Sentinel Ranges and Whiteface filled out the remainder of the view and gave us the impetus we needed to forge ahead on the last leg of the climb.

Two full hours since we had finished our lunch and dove into the gnarliest of thickets, we stumbled across the summit of Wright Peak. Not what we had in mind when we began, but we persevered and now had a war story to entertain our friends and lean-to companions with. For the roughest bushwhacks need to be shared with people who appreciate the tough and rumble of close quarters navigation. Call it therapy!

Avalanche Pass, Avalanche Lake, and Lake Colden

A stupendous gorge, the sheer walls of Avalanche Mountain, a hidden sliver of a lake, and one of the largest high altitude lakes in the state lie stacked upon one another in the narrow valley separating the imposing western flank of Mount Colden and the eastern side of the

On the Hitch-Up Matilda of the 1930s

MacIntyres. Each magnificent in their own right, together they form a nature lover's hat trick, and are the perfect way to end an exploration of any of the mountains towering above. The trail, known as the Avalanche Pass to Lake Colden run, is one of the most popular in the region and never fails to impress.

Of the three attractions, Lake Colden was probably the first discovered by the white man. The old Indian route through Indian Pass was the chief means of getting from the headwaters of the Hudson to North Elba, though one might be right to assume Avalanche Pass was probably surveyed as far as Avalanche Lake. As Colvin found during his surveys, the pass and lake were not friendly to travelers laden with supplies, which is probably why Indian Pass, no easy route in its own right, was preferred. The establishment of the McIntyre Mine and the small village of Adirondac naturally brought geologists and survey teams to the southern door of the High Peaks. In 1827, Major Reuben Sanford and Judge John Richards ventured in to survey a parcel of land known as the Gore, east of Township 47. This parcel extended into Indian Pass, over the MacIntyre range, along the valley of Calamity Brook, and down over Mount Adams and Lakes Jimmy and Sally.

It is possible that Sanford and Richards may have ventured up to Lake Colden during their survey in that year. However, when surveying the Gore around Lake Colden in 1833, they discovered Avalanche Lake. David Henderson writes of his attempt in late summer of that same year to "… continue on to a very narrow pond between two immense precipices in the adjoining great mountain—which Judge Richards & Mr. Sanford told us, is the greatest curiosity they ever saw." Henderson had followed the East River (Opalescent River) and discovered Hanging Spear Falls. The day was wet, and the route full of scrambles and rock hops. They only got as far as the area we know now as Flowed Lands. The group returned via the easier route along Calamity Brook.

In 1836, when Redfield and company ventured up to Lake Colden for the first time, they also went via the East River. His party encountered traces of wolves and deer, moose, and "… at the inlet of Lake Sanford, the fresh and yet undried footsteps of a panther, which apparently had just crossed the inlet." The company had employed three woodsmen who made their nightly stays more comfortable. "A comfortable hut, of poles and spruce bark, was soon constructed by the exertions of our dexterous woodsman …" The route they traveled is the same as the Hanging Spear Falls trail of today, however where today's trail is well situated up and away from the Opalescent, on this trip the party

> … entered the more precipitous part of the gorge through which the river descends. Our advance here became more difficult and somewhat dangerous. After ascending falls and rapids, seemingly

innumerable, we came about noon to an imposing cascade, closely pent between two steep mountains, and falling about eighty feet into a deep chasm, the walls of which are as precipitous as those of Niagara, and more secluded.

After conquering the Hanging Spear Falls portion, it was only several hours later that the party, after having crossed the Upper Still Water (Flowed Lands), found a beautiful lake, of about a mile in extent. "This lake, to which our party afterwards gave the name of Lake Colden, is situated between two mountain peaks which rise in lofty grandeur on either hand." Redfield was keen to document his account and gave a vivid description of wildlife at its most natural, and visceral, in his text. His description illustrates how the mountains were on a daily basis before the intrusion of man.

> Previous to reaching the outlet, we had noticed on the margin of the river, fresh tracks of the wolf and also of the deer, both apparently made at the fullest speed, and on turning a point we came upon the warm and mangled remains of a fine deer, which had fallen a sacrifice to the wolves; the latter having been driven from their repast by our unwelcome approach. There appeared to have been two of the aggressive party, one of which, by lying in wait, had probably intercepted the deer in his course to the lake, and they had nearly devoured their victim in apparently a short space of time.

The 1836 trip that earned Lake Colden its name, and eventually the mountain above it as well, was a case in point of being in the right place at the right time. When Henderson ventured up to the mine, he brought David Colden and Abraham Van Santvoord with him. They were all good friends, but more importantly, Colden and Van Santvoord were successful businessmen and Henderson hoped to interest them in the property. Perhaps he named the lake after his friend to entice his investment in the area. Or, perhaps because David Colden was the type of man one would name things after. A grandson of Governor General Cadwallader Colden, he was an ambitious man of social prominence. Charles Dickens, on his first visit to America, had a letter of introduction from the English actor William Charles Macready to Colden, and was entertained by him.

In a March 22, 1842 letter to Macready, Dickens wrote: "David Colden is as good a fellow as ever lived, and I am deeply in love with his wife; indeed, we have received the greatest and most earnest and zealous kindness from the whole family, and quite love them all." It must have been the clean American air. Colden made an impression on John Cheney as well, though the respect was mutual. After one of his visits with Cheney as guide, Colden sent Cheney a rifle with a silver plate on it that read: "To that Mighty Hunter John Cheney of Adirondack from David C. Colden." The title Colden gave to Cheney stuck and was used by many writers in later descriptions of him.

The 1836 trip also produced a second naming of a lake. On August 19, the party split into two. Henderson, Cheney, and Redfield followed the course of the main stream of the Hudson up toward its source, while McIntyre, Duncan McMartin, and James Hall went up to explore the narrow valley at the northern end of Lake Colden. Cheney's party stirred up the quarters of a family of panthers along the way, to "the great discomfort of Cheney's valorous dog." McIntyre's party found the wondrous lake referred to by Sanford and Richards. "Immense slides or avalanches had been precipitated into this lake from the steep face of the mountain, which induced the party to bestow upon it the name of Avalanche Lake."

When Colvin visited the area in 1872, he recorded, aside from many new names, several firsts of his own. At the time Lakes Colden and Avalanche were thought to be the highest bodies of water east of the Rocky Mountains. He dispelled that, first by finding Scott Ponds to be several hundred feet higher in elevation, and then several days later discovered and verified the altitude of Summit Water, which he wrote about as being a "tear of the clouds." He not only gave Lake Tear-of-the-Clouds its name, but also established it as the highest source of the Hudson River. Colvin was also the first to navigate the waters of Lakes Colden and Avalanche. He writes about the maiden voyages in his 1873 *Report of the Topographical Survey*.

> The following day, which was one of rain and heavy clouds, I launched and tested the canoe—named the *Discovery*—being the first boat of any kind placed on Lake Colden, and was surprised at the shallowness of the lake. The boat was transported to Avalanche Lake, on which also no boat of any kind had ever floated, and I had the pleasure of the first sail upon that gloomy water. The canoe, though narrow, carried three men with ease—and more when balanced with outriggers—and it enabled me to make soundings in different parts of the lake, and to examine the geological structure of the cliff walls, which fall directly into the water. This, with barometrical leveling, engaged us to so late an hour that we had again to stumble along the trail in the dark, back to camp at Lake Colden. The canoe remains at Avalanche Lake, and will render the Avalanche pass more convenient to travelers.

The Other Hidden Gems

The wonderful thing about a huge mountain massif like MacIntyre is the plethora of hidden jewels in her craggy crown: sublime alpine gardens in their spring glory; numerous open bumps and perches with their unique vantages; secluded waterfalls and mountain tarns where the dragonflies rule. All of these treasures, some off trail, some on trail, and some off, *off* trail, are what have inspired and enthralled the visitors to and natives of this region since man first set foot upon its soil and bedrock. Seeking out, stumbling upon, and relishing these treasures is one of an Adirondack explorer's favorite things to do.

A small cobble is located at roughly 2.9 miles where the Algonquin trail from Adirondack Loj hooks to the left and begins the last climb before the Wright intersection. It has been called The Cobble and Englehard Peak by the "Pok-O Crew," summer campers from the Pok-O-MacCready Camps. Yet, it is most often referred to as Wrong Peak. Whatever the name, this chunk of rock is a beauty. From the collection of herd paths leading to it from the main trail, all of which lead to a short but rather itchy climb, this peak gets its fair share of visitors. But seldom is one visited while enjoying its vistas. Snacking on lunch, you will need several pairs of hands to count the trampers en route to the nearby summits of Wright and Algonquin, yet usually not one digit to count those who brave the scratchy cripplebrush or steep ledges to gain the little summit.

A mere fifty feet or so from the trail, the eighty-foot eastern cliff face is an impressive and virtually unscalable obstacle. The typical course to follow is a ledge scramble to the southern end of the wall, or a rugged tussle with very dense foliage to gain the weathered herd path some fifty feet beyond. With its vast flat expanse of rock for a summit, the views from this little peak are indeed worthy of the same praise bestowed upon its taller relatives nearby. One looks up almost directly at the conical summit of Wright Peak above. Algonquin's crown sits like a shrunken head atop a massive girth of mountain shoulder. The shoulder and small western knob, or sub peak known as Little Algonquin or Little MacIntyre, block out the southern views toward Iroquois, Marshall, Indian Pass, and Wallface.

However, the panorama that opens up just past the little sub peak is a wondrous one hundred and eighty degree vista of the nearby mountains of MacNaughton, Lost Pond Peak, Street and Nye. Beneath them lies what was known in Colvin's time as the Valley of the Au Sable. The view continues across Indian Pass Brook to Mount Jo, now more diminutive than ever, with a commanding view of the valley all the way to Lake Placid, where the town gives way to the mountain group of Mackenzie, Moose, and finally Whiteface. The Sentinels and Pitchoff merge with Cascade, Porter, and Big Slide, creating an imposing perimeter for the Plains of Abraham or the large tracts known as North and South Meadows. This small summit also boasts of having a thriving community of alpine vegetation including a tangled mass of cripplebrush, numerous wild blueberry bushes, and a lovely creeping stand of black crowberry.

Less than a half mile away from Wrong Peak lies another gem on the western flanks of the range. It has been called Little Algonquin by some, Little MacIntyre by others, and is basically overlooked by most everyone else. By the end of this description, a fitting name will be bestowed upon this gem, with the same presumptions taken by Carson and Colvin. For once upon an afternoon the peak was first climbed by a trio who deserve their own recognition, and this little peak would be the perfect one. But first, the account of the visit to her on October 5, 2006.

The trip began as I tried to find information on the little summit from anyone who may have visited her at some point. Easier said than done, for it seemed only the smallest handful of people had ever been there. John Winkler (#1279) was one, and was happy to provide whatever details he could remember from his several trips, all of which were made a decade or so earlier. Winkler had traversed to the bump on a contour from the Wright spur trail intersection on the Algonquin trail. The going had been tight, slow, scratchy, but that's what all of his off trail hikes, which number in the hundreds, were like. He had built a cairn on the summit and left stamped postcards for people to send to him with their tales of climbing the little peak. None ever arrived. So, John was very supportive of my trip and my reconnaissance of his canister and postcards! The problem was finding someone to go with me. It wasn't until I contacted Spencer Morrissey (#5320W) for information and got back a 'Never been, when are we going?' email that I knew the trip was on.

Initially, we decided our approach would follow Winkler's route from the Wright spur, but a reconnaissance trip to Wrong Peak in mid September changed that. I determined a route straight from Wrong would run almost to the little summit through deciduous forest slopes and avoid a ridge full of tight and unforgiving spruce. My only concern was the echoes of tumbling water reverberating out of the drainage between the two ridges. Somewhere down below I just knew we would run into something. However the semblance of an old logging road just below Wrong convinced me I must have been looking at the perfect route. As with most inclinations off trail, sometimes you are right, sometimes wrong, and oftentimes both.

The old logging road turned out to be a phantom path that disintegrated into a logjam of blowdown and watery drainages. If you didn't get cracked in the shin by a hidden log, you nearly lost your leg as it slipped into a hole hidden by a thin sheath of moss. The going was slow, painful, and not the best psychological start to an unknown bushwhack route. Twenty minutes later we ran across the stream I had feared to be an impassable chasm, and naturally the tide took a turn for the better. Well, the upper portion was indeed a chasm, but we had arrived at the bottom of it, where the brook tumbled harmlessly downhill over comforting flumes and gentle waterfalls. Coming straight off Wright and Algonquin above, a stream had found its way through a natural channel as perfect as a concrete overflow valve on a hydroelectric dam.

Two twenty-foot walls, in perfect parallel symmetry, form the gateway for an impressive broken ladder waterfall. At the top of the chimney the flow navigates around a huge boulder, wedged and suspended some fifty feet above the small pool at the bottom and exits to these great stone gates. Few waterfalls can match it for the uniqueness of its almost perfectly tailored construction. After marveling at the sight, we began the short but steep climb to the secluded peak above. The woods were welcoming and the going was smooth in most spots. As with any open higher summit, the crown was ringed with a stand of balsam and spruce that made for several minutes of struggle. Effort that was rewarded with a delightful ledge of alpine vegetation, a scattering of large rectangular erratics standing guard on her eastern flank, and after one last climb, a large open summit full of colorful fall colors and sweeping views.

Unlike Shepherd's Tooth, where you are propped up on the side of Iroquois, atop this particular knob you are set a good half-mile away from the main mountainside. This allows for a sweeping perspective of the entire range. Wright, Algonquin, Boundary, Iroquois, and finally Marshall all are laid out in front of you. Impressive are the glistening slides on the side of Algonquin, and the bird's eye view down on the closest of the steep ravines that scour the range's western flanks. These features almost look like channels running from high up near the ridgelines all the way into the valley below. There is an even wider array of arctic alpine plant life here than on either Wrong Peak, or Shepherd's Tooth. Clumps of sedges and grasses, in their golden fall hue, contrasted with the bright red of the mountain blueberry bushes, but most striking of all was the amount of bright yellow dwarf larches. They were found in large glowing swaths along the very top of the peak, as well as strewn across the southern and western slopes.

This wonderful little oasis, so seldom visited it shows virtually no signs of human intrusion, was once the subject of a day's botanical exploration. During her tenure as Ranger-Naturalist, Orra Phelps led many trips and bushwhacks, and one such trip included Dick Andrus and Dr. Ed Ketchledge. Their destination was Algonquin's northwest knob. The trip brought out Orra's medical background, for the two men had developed terrible headaches during the steep scramble. Orra felt the culprit was carbon dioxide, and that the men were not ridding their lungs of it due to breathing short and shallow breaths during the climb. Her prescription was for occasional breaks for deep breathing and two aspirins once the trip was done.

Sure enough, it worked. While back at the Loj reflecting on the hike, they joked over what the unnamed peak should be called. Dick's Peak, Orra's Knob, and Ketch's Point became the three choices, yet the arguments were for fun only and never amounted to anything. Since this trip was the first documented climb of the prominence, and by three of the region's most distinguished naturalists, the author felt inclined to issue a decree from the very summit on his own journey there, half a century later.

> … this little bump should be named for these three and their first documented ascent of it. Since they were instrumental in the stewardship projects that have saved, reclaimed, and illuminated numerous areas atop the High Peaks, it seems fitting the name should commemorate both themselves and their efforts. 'Steward's Cobble' feels just about perfect.

The first bumps on the northern side of MacIntyre offer some wonderful exploring opportunities as well. The two bumps to the north of Wright, collectively know as The Whale, both have numerous open rock ledges that offer superb views. The highest point of The Whale is a ledge that literally looks down across a dozen smaller ledges to the southern end of Marcy Pond and sweeps south until it runs into Wright Peak. From the ledge you get a bird's eye view down on the twin northeastern slides, best known for the deadly avalanche of 2000 that killed one skier. The area between has commanding views down valleys heading to Avalanche Pass and Indian Falls and Pelkey Basin. TR and Phelps Mountain are in the foreground, with a background sweep from Big Slide to Marcy and Colden. One day, while bushwhacking from The Whale toward Whale's Tail, the author and Christine Bourjade (#4967W) ran into a well-trodden bear path that headed straight in the direction of Marcy Dam. The weathered nature of the path along with a buffet of food and drink for any ursine, explained the bear troubles in the area in recent years.

On the southern terminus of the range, one enters the wildest reaches of the MacIntyre massif. The numerous sub-peaks of Mount Marshall extend all the way to the shores of Lake Henderson, with more than a dozen distinct bumps for the climbing. In the midst of these distant bumps sit the two main slides on Mount Marshall. The slide visible from Mount Adams, or the western slide, is an older slide. It runs at a manageable twenty-degree grade and offers excellent views back at Adams and also of the North River Range. The eastern slide is much steeper and newer, estimated to have fallen in the 1970s or early 1980s, and provides nice views of Henderson Lake and Santanoni Peak. To gain the true summit from either slide adds several hours to a climb of Marshall, as one must traverse a mighty distance through the thickest stands of cripplebrush imaginable.

David Henderson documented an early exploration of these southern McIntyre slides in a letter to Archibald McIntyre on June 15, 1844.

> Cheney and I went over the mountain east of the Notch (Indian Pass) and then on to the wing of Mount McIntyre, for the purpose of coming down a ravine which I had often noticed from Lake Henderson and which runs down in a *straight* line from the top of the mountain. We found a stream running down this ravine, which empties into the stream from the Notch. The wild and abrupt scenery in this gorge equaled anything I ever saw—the stream running for over a mile upon a *steep* inclined plane of smooth solid rock, and from 50 to 100 feet wide.

Winter on the MacIntyre Range

Thanks to its full spectrum of terrain, the mountains of the range hold many tricks and treats for the winter enthusiast. There are few people to summit Wright Peak in winter who have not returned telling tales of hurricane force winds and clinging to the summit like a canary in a vacuum cleaner. And stories of early season trailbreaking attempts up Mount Marshall often end in resignation and defeat. When the high winter winds blow, Algonquin closes up shop and its summit becomes as impenetrable as any mountain across the globe.

And yet when the perfect bluebird winter day comes along, the winter climber ascends through a glittering sugar frosted landscape to stride across one of his or her favorite places on earth. The lure of this magical kingdom—whether it be basking in the glow of the rare windless sun drenched day or fighting through unconsolidated snow, a billowing headwind and the biting sting of sideways snow—has been a draw for mountaineers for over a century.

Small groups had been exploring the High Peaks area in winter since the late nineteenth century. The arrival of a group known as the Sno Birds at the Lake Placid Club for the 1904 Christmas holidays began a healthy progression of activity on the High Peaks. They began their play on nearby Whiteface, snowshoeing and then skiing to the summit, and slowly forged on into the interior peaks of the region. Few records exist of winter climbs of the MacIntyre Range from these early times. The first documented ascent is a February 1923 climb of Algonquin by the Marshall brothers and Herb Clark. One would surmise that if Marcy was climbed in the 1890s, surely some adventurer would have climbed the even shorter route up to Algonquin from the Adirondack Loj—possibly even Henry Van Hoevenberg himself.

Reports are conclusive though that by the end of the 1920s Algonquin was being snowshoed regularly and had joined the ranks of Whiteface and Marcy as having been conquered on skis. The article "Winter Ascent of Mount McIntyre" in *Mountain Magazine*, published by the Associated Outdoor Clubs of America, appeared in 1928 with several photographs taken by Russell Carson. This climbing party consisted of Arthur S. Hopkins of the Conservation Department, Albany N.Y., Thomas B. Gilchrist, of Bronxville, N.Y., and Alexander W. Miller, Robert C. Carter, and Russell M. L. Carson of Glens Falls, N.Y.

The group had decided to spend the Lincoln's Birthday weekend at the Adirondak Loj, which had reopened under the ownership of the Adirondack Mountain Club on December 26, 1927. The route from Glens Falls was a long one, for automobiles had to travel via Schroon Lake, Elizabethtown, and through Wilmington Notch to get to Lake Placid. From there it was a chilly twelve mile ride aboard a three-seat sleigh pulled by a team of horses across the Plains of Abraham to the Adirondak Loj, which was described as "the last word in roughing it easy."

The Loj had been built to combine rustic charm and the new comforts of the day, including furnace heat, electric lights, unlimited hot water, shower baths, a commodious drying room for wet clothing, and plenty of lounging chairs. A roaring log fire awaited their arrival and a plain but delicious hot meal put the warmth back in their bodies. In the great room they looked over the maps and decided a nice easy snowshoe hike to Indian Pass or Avalanche Lake would be the program for the next day. The morning of February 10 arrived with moderate temperatures and blue skies and the party found the lure of a mountain climb irresistible.

They unanimously decided they would try "old McIntyre." At 7:55 a.m. the group left the Loj and headed up an unbroken trail, but snow conditions afforded quick travel. Once altitude was reached the snow depths increased and occasionally swallowed up the trail markers. Only once along the climb did they have trouble following the trail and for the most part "enjoyed an easy pleasant walk through the snow laden forests until we reached timber line. Here the crust was hard and icy and all progress was balked until we put on creepers."

The snowshoes of the time were without the standard claws of today. These "creepers" would be lashed on under the ball of the foot with rawhide thongs when climbing above treeline on icy slopes. They provided enough bite and, aided with the stability of walking staffs, the group continued in a slow and steady climb, reaching the summit at 2:20 p.m. Not a bad time considering the trailbreaking effort, wooden and rawhide snowshoes, and strapped-on traction devices! Despite pleasant temperatures on the summit, the clouds had dropped a shroud on the mountaintop, affording them only a brief glimpse of Marcy and Colden, and making their decision to leave twenty minutes later an easy one.

The highlight of their descent is one every winter climber can relate to: "Coming down we could often sit on the tails of our snowshoes and slide a hundred or more feet at a time." (It's nice to know the very first winter climbs in the High Peaks enjoyed the simple pleasure of the butt slide.) Their winter equipment consisted of warm caps and woolen mittens, flannel shirts, sweaters, mackinaws and several woolen socks under ordinary snowshoeing moccasins. For most of the climb they carried their sweaters, for the exertion made them so warm.

For the whole group, and especially Carson, this was their first winter ascent. Especially impressive was the fact that one had never worn a pair of snowshoes and another had never climbed a high peak.

If skiing began in earnest on the MacIntyre Range in the 1920s, it exploded in the 1930s. Downhill skiing was growing in popularity and ski enthusiast Hal Burton began the hard preliminary work of designing a ski trail up to the summit of Wright Peak. Burton went on to author the 1971 book *Ski Troops*, about the 10th Mountain Division. Ultimately designed by Otto Schniebs and Robert St. Louis, the trail was cut in 1938. Otto was one of the ski pioneers of the day, having emigrated to America in 1928 after serving as a former mountain trooper in Germany's WWI army. Schniebs became the ski instructor for the influential Appalachian Mountain Club. From 1930 to 1936, he headed the ski program at Dartmouth College, making him a key figure in popularizing stem turns on these shores. The first certification course for amateur instructors was held in 1933 by the U.S. Eastern Amateur Ski Association at Dartmouth College under the direction of Otto Schniebs. Nineteen candidates showed up, and only eleven passed. In 1936 he took over ski instruction at the Lake Placid Club, and made famous his mantra: "Skiing is not a sport, it is a way of life."

To call the Wright Peak ski trail a success would be a great understatement, for in its very first season of use more than 2,000 individual trips were recorded by the ski instructor of the Adirondak Loj. The trail topped out some fifty feet of vertical elevation below the summit, but surely some of the skiers, such as Burton or Otto, who also owned and ran two ski schools in the vicinity, would have climbed the last few feet to the summit. Any confirmation of a summit ascent at this time though has long since disappeared. In fact, in his book *Ski Troops*, Burton lamented the introduction in the 1940s of mechanized means of ascending mountains in order to ski down them. Because of this, he said, "… The thrill of accomplishment in having climbed a mountain, accompanied by a long rest on the summit to savor the scenery, disappeared forever from skiing."

However, in this same winter of 1938, Helen Menz (#42) climbed over Algonquin and across to Iroquois and back with a group of friends. A decade later, on February 1, 1948, Kimball Hart and Kay Flickinger (#41) made this same journey on skis. Hart became chairman of the ADK Winter Activities Committee and decided he would encourage college-age groups to climb the High Peaks in winter. He set up competitions among college outing clubs and awarded trophies to honor their achievements. Now climbing the Winter 46, or earning the big "W" as it is also known, began in earnest.

With the lure of presumably unclimbed winter ascents before them and the glory of hoisting trophies overhead after laying down such a claim, the following winter of 1948-49 saw a proliferation of college teams. The number of mountains unclimbed in winter began to fall. The RPI team climbed Marshall on December 21 to open the winter season and recorded the first winter climb to that summit. Hart created a special "V-Badge" as the ADK Winter Mountaineering emblem, given to anyone who had climbed five High Peaks in winter. As applications came in for the badge, the ADK discovered that it wasn't just the college kids out there climbing in winter. This new sport had taken hold.

Cotton Kills – A Case of Hypothermia

The mountains are always a dangerous place. Combine intense physical exertion and the resulting fatigue with loose rocks, slippery roots, steep slabs, precarious ledges, and swift flowing brooks and you have a recipe for any disaster waiting to happen. If the temperature drops, which in the mountains can occur in all twelve months of the calendar, the stakes rise dramatically. The human body has an optimal range at which it functions best. Go outside the range and ordinary tasks and functions become more difficult. At a core body temperature of 95 degrees, hypothermia starts to set in. Warning signs include uncontrollable shivering, memory loss, disorientation, incoherence, slurred speech, drowsiness, and exhaustion. When the body dips to eighty degrees unconsciousness occurs, and below seventy-eight degrees, the heart usually stops.

Hypothermia has its share of accomplices when chilling the human body. Outside ambient temperature may be the starting point, but wind-chill and skin moisture conduction are also contributing factors. Wind literally sucks the heat off the human body and carries it away. Moisture against the skin causes conduction where heat is drawn from the skin in contact with the water to aid in evaporation. Combine these two with the exertion of hiking and the result can be dangerous.

On a long winter hike, the average prepared hiker spends his time dipping back and forth along thin thresholds. Stop and you get cold. Stay cold and you start to shiver and lose feeling in your fingers. The answer is to make stops short, add extra layers of clothing when at rest and shed those layers when under exertion, and gobble down food at regular intervals. Eating enough food and staying hydrated help you maintain internal core temperature. Wearing a base layer of clothing that wicks moisture away from the skin and an outer shell that protects against wind-chill, rain and snow also help retain body heat. The key factor is movement. Stay moving and you usually stay warm. But if you are forced to stop, and have not equipped yourself with the gear and knowledge to combat the elements, then you open the door for hypothermia, "killer of the unprepared."

The catch phrase "Cotton Kills" is the poster slogan for hypothermia. Cotton fiber is not waterproof, does not insulate when wet, and completely absorbs liquid. In summer this combination can keep the body cool by drawing heat off the skin through conduction. In cooler weather, however, cotton's particular properties pose a special danger. The saturated cotton fibers pull from the skin the heat that the body needs to prevent a drop in core temperature.

In the fall of 1974, on Thanksgiving Day, a pair of hikers arrived at the Upper Works parking lot for a backpacking trip through Indian Pass, over Algonquin Pass, and down to Lake Colden. Steven L. Collier, 23, and Patrick J. Eagan, 27, were about to embark on a trip that neither had envisioned as they loaded their packs and got under way for Henderson Lean-to at the far southern end of Indian Pass. Steven was excited to start his first backpacking trip and had arrived with a new pack, sleeping bag, foam sleeping pad, and down jacket. All good equipment. His choice of clothing was less than adequate—cotton long johns, cotton blue jeans, a cotton flannel shirt, wool socks, and summer hiking boots—and would prove to be a deadly choice.

The night at the lean-to was cold with a dusting of snow. They had joined another group of five with the same destination for the following day. After a breakfast of tea and oatmeal the two were on their way into Indian Pass. For some reason they decided not to bring water, and managed their thirst with a small flask of brandy. They shoved off at 9:30 a.m. and three hours later reached Summit Rock. Having conquered the first goal of the day, they enjoyed a lunch of rolls, cheese, deviled ham and a mouthful of brandy each. Thirty minutes later they dropped down out of the pass toward the Cold Brook trail junction. At this point the trip was running smoothly and everything was in order. The next stop came at the junction for the trail that would lead them up through the high pass between Mount Marshall and Iroquois Peak.

It was 2:15 p.m. when they began the climb to Algonquin Pass. They started "playing leapfrog" with their lean-to companions on the climb up. Snow had started falling and Patrick pushed ahead into the deeper snow, breaking trail for the pair. Patrick remembers thinking Steven was "absolutely normal" as they began the new leg, and figured his hiking partner was right behind him. Time was becoming a factor as Patrick wanted to make the height of land before taking a break. The unconsolidated snow wore on both of them and soon Steven was falling behind.

Patrick forged ahead and made the pass ahead of everyone else. He flung his pack to the ground and sat down on it and waited. The first person up was from the other party. He looked concerned and told Patrick that his companion, Steven, wasn't doing so well. Steven was exhibiting classic hypothermic symptoms of disorientation and confusion. The other hiker felt Steven "… had adopted the I-don't-care-if-I-make-it attitude. And that's not a good attitude to have up here." Indeed it was not. Patrick went back down the trail to find his exhausted friend. He helped him back up to the pass, fed him a piece of cheese, and gave him a short breather.

With snow twelve to eighteen inches deep in the pass, oncoming darkness and cold, and his friend in rough shape, Patrick got Steven back up and started leading him toward the safety of the Colden Lake lean-tos or Ranger Outpost. The other group had opened a nice trail, the climbing was over, and the going was good … for Patrick. For Steven, however, the debilitating effects of hypothermia were taking their toll. Unbeknownst to either of them, Steven's core temperature had most likely dropped below 90 degrees thanks to lack of water, consumption of alcohol, albeit minor, and his layers of cotton clothing literally sucking the heat out of his body.

"The thing that struck me," Patrick said, "was that he couldn't walk more than ten paces without falling"—classic symptoms of someone in the later stages of hypothermia, yet neither would recognize it. Steven just wanted to stop, while Patrick felt they needed to push down to the lake and the ranger cabin. The more Steven tried to walk, the more he fell. Once he went through the thin ice on the brook, wetting his boots, socks, and pant legs. By then his falls in the snow had thoroughly soaked his cotton layers. He had lost his hat, so now the lion's share of his body heat was being lost to radiation. When he finally could go no further, Patrick made the decision that probably sealed his fate. Despite having dry and warm clothes, two sleeping bags, and a tent in their packs, he thought he was close enough to the lake so that the time spent getting Steven into a bivouac would be better spent getting help.

One hiker couldn't think for himself, and the other just didn't have the knowledge of first aid or understand the gravity of the situation. It was a deadly combination that would be compounded when Patrick arrived at the lake expecting his situation would prompt a diligent and determined rescue. This hope would not be realized. And so Steven sat in the snow. He was now wearing an Eddie Bauer down jacket, the only change to his attire since he stopped. He was still without a hat on his head, and his socks and boots were full of water slowly freezing around his feet. His pack and a second down jacket, warm clothing, sleeping pad, two empty water bottles, and sleeping pad were within arm's reach. He had everything he needed to save his life except an understanding of the situation.

Patrick rushed into the Ranger Outpost at just after 7 p.m. There was Charlie Nolan, caretaker of the interior outpost. Unfortunately, while Charlie managed the upkeep of the ranger station, he was no ranger. In fact, there were no rangers in the area. Charlie sent Patrick out to one of the lean-tos looking for "a chap I've known for some time." Arthur Reidel was that chap, an M.I.T. graduate with decent mountain experience. Arthur went about getting a rescue party together. In his lean-to was a bunch of photography majors from R.I.T. They just shrugged when he asked them to help in the search.

"Their sensitive camera gear was covered with snow and ice. That didn't impress me," was Arthur's recollection. He didn't push them, knowing they would probably not be much help. He ran up to the next lean-to and explained the problem to a dark mass of sleeping bags. No one stirred. Sound asleep already at eight o'clock? The next lean-to offered the same result. He shouted into the darkness that someone was probably dying and he needed help. They either didn't hear him or chose not to respond. "Fortunately at Beaver Point there were decent people." At the second lean-to at Beaver Point, out of five people, two rallied to the cause and joined the rescue.

The four rescuers, Reidel, Eagan, and newcomers Dexter Dimarco and George Herman, both of Pennsylvania, gathered at the Ranger Station. Charlie had prepared a thermos of hot tea, which they brought along with a Coleman lantern, and the snow boat. The snow boat was a six-foot fiberglass rescue sled. The time of their departure? 8:30 p.m. An hour and a half to rally a rescue for a man dying on the side of a mountain! Forty-five minutes later they reached Steven in light winds and a temperature of sixteen degrees. He was barely conscious, in shock, with a shallow pulse confirming the late stages of hypothermia. All of the factors of the evening had conspired against Steven.

After a futile attempt to get some hot tea in Steven, the rescue team decided it would have been difficult to warm him effectively on the spot, and that a dash back to the cabin on Lake Colden was the best choice of plans. Finally, after almost three hours of sitting in below freezing temperatures in layer upon layer of wet cotton, Steven was put inside a down sleeping bag. Arthur's explanation of the assessment, under the duress of the situation was: "The thought was that the best thing for him was to get him down as fast as possible. We weren't sure what shape he was in. When I went up, I thought I'd dump some tea in him, stand him up, and march him down. It didn't turn out that way…"

The trip down was hell. It was steep, and the group broke through the ice covering the stream on many occasions. About fifteen minutes from the ranger cabin they checked and found that Steven had stopped breathing. They picked up the pace, but by the time they had him inside his pulse was gone, and his heart had stopped. Mouth to mouth resuscitation and cardiac massage came too little too late. "But he was dead. There was just no two ways about it." Steven Collier, on his first backpacking trip, had died fifteen minutes from the Ranger Cabin on the lowest slopes of the MacIntyres. But his fate had been sealed long before that moment.

The next day when Ranger Gary K. Hodgson, an experienced search and rescuer, and Investigator R. H. Garrand of the State Police arrived by helicopter all they could do was confirm the obvious. As Hodgson noted, "This was the first death I've been involved with that is definitely hypothermia. It's like reading it in a textbook – the sequence of fatigue, confusion, and dehydration. It falls into a pattern."

They all agreed it was the combination of factors that conspired against Steven. Had he been wearing all wool clothing he likely would have survived. Had he been changed into warm and dry clothing, even if it had been cotton clothing, at the top of the pass and sheltered in a sleeping bag or two and tent, he probably would have survived. Lack of water, coupled with alcohol consumption didn't help. An uncovered head, and the delay in reaching him with a rescue party, greatly exacerbated the situation. All of these issues, in hindsight, could have been addressed and could have saved the man's life.

This story, when published in the Fall 1974 issue of *Adirondack Peeks*, came with an introduction that it was printed with the intention of serving as a case study to educate winter hikers about the dangers and symptoms of hypothermia. As was illustrated, two factors contributed to the tragedy. First, the victim was unprepared for the conditions, and second, his hiking partner and well-meaning rescue team lacked an understanding of the stages of hypothermia.

Although cotton clothing, the chief culprit in Steven's death, has all but disappeared from the winter hiker's wardrobe, hypothermia still poses a serious risk to all who venture out in the winter. The exertion of climbing amplifies all the other factors inherent to hypothermia.

The death of Steven marked the second death from hypothermia in less than a month. In October of that same year a young Canadian man had become disoriented while descending Algonquin and had gotten lost on the northern slopes of the mountain. He was found, frozen inside his cotton clothing on the far side of Indian Pass Brook near the base of Nye Mountain. These two deaths prompted efforts by the DEC to post warnings about winter dangers, and the assignment of rangers to the High Peak interior area. Hypothermia education also became more of a focus in educational classes and training for camp counselors and directors. All hikers must be able to recognize the symptoms of hypothermia as well as know the steps necessary to safeguard oneself, and more importantly, others against this potential killer.

In 1981, there was another winter adventure on Algonquin Peak that easily could have ended in death. But sometimes luck compensates for the lack of preparedness, and defeats the icy grip of winter. On January 3 of that year, hikers Michael Boxer, 19, and Steven Sygman, 21, both of Brooklyn, got caught in whiteout conditions atop Algonquin and became disoriented in the near zero visibility. They picked the wrong day to hike, and the wrong night to bivouac on the second highest mountain in the state. The day was forecast to never reach zero degrees, and that night found the temperature plunging to minus forty.

Goals should never replace common sense, yet Boxer was determined to reach the summit of Algonquin. Four other friends from Brooklyn College did their best to persuade Boxer to postpone his attempt, but were unsuccessful. For Boxer, the lure of a summit conquest in the trying conditions of winter at its most extreme was too strong to resist. He was going no matter what, and of the remaining five, only Sygman decided to join him. The difference between these hikers and the previous cases described above was of proper clothing, but also the time of year.

It is often said the deadliest time in the mountains is late in the fall, when the valleys are still green, and yet the mountains are under full transformation to a landscape of ice and snow. Fair weather three-season hikers, who would usually never consider hiking in winter, often attempt a last hike of the season before turning to pursuits like reading and downhill skiing. At these times, they often make the mistake of wearing and carrying their three-season clothing and gear. The full-fledged winter hiker, on the other hand, wears clothes that sit in his closet all summer. He or she is prepared for this time of year, when hiking becomes a close cousin to all-out mountaineering when such choices are mandatory. Cotton kills, especially in late fall, whereas wool saves lives, even on the coldest nights of the year.

Boxer and Sygman were in the mountains to hike under full winter conditions, and headed off toward Algonquin dressed for the part. They carried food for two days, a stove, and an

Ensolite pad to sit on while they ate lunch. What they didn't bring was a map and compass. In whiteout conditions, north can become south, east can become west, and a person easily can become lost. This is exactly what happened to the pair. Thinking they would return following their tracks, they struggled up through the maelstrom to top out on Algonquin. Unfortunately for them, the second they lifted their feet out of the snow, the swirling winds filled in their tracks with snow. Up that high, amongst the drifted, "teacupped" snow, tracks become part of a white jigsaw puzzle where every windswept wave and crest may be mistaken for a hiker's last track.

Lost, following one phantom trail after another, the pair decided to head toward treeline and hoped to find the break indicating the trail. What they found was the start of a streambed, or drainage. It sure looked like a trail and it was heading down out of the worst of the winds and cold, so they followed it. With no compass they had no way of knowing that they were heading due west toward Indian Pass. The western side of Algonquin became a sea of snow, with spruce traps sucking the hikers into holes up to their armpits. The struggle didn't last long. Knowing they were lost and in trouble, they found shelter in an impression in the mountain and dug in for the night. While wet from fighting through the snow, their wool and synthetic clothing was still trapping heat and providing valuable insulation.

The pair helped their cause immediately by firing up their stove and drinking hot chocolate. They also warmed up some jello. The stove ran out of fuel, but every little bit of warmth added to the body was doing a heap of good. The problem that could have potentially killed them came when Boxer, who had broken through the ice and whose feet found the water below, decided to take off his wet boots. Within minutes, his wet boots froze solid, and he had no way of getting his feet back inside them. The rangers who participated in the rescue felt this probably would have killed them had the following day's search party not found them.

Boxer's foolish decision became apparent almost immediately. With the insulating factor of the boots removed, he slipped the liners of his mittens over his frigid toes. They only slowed the inevitable loss of heat. He became disoriented, incoherent, and began shivering—the telltale signs of hypothermia. He had also trapped the two of them in their tiny hole. Where could he go with mittens for boots? The pair had summitted with crampons and had not carried snowshoes. In addition they had left behind their tent and sleeping bags. They were going nowhere, except further into the slow icy grip of the killer of the unprepared.

By now, the rangers of the High Peaks were well acquainted with hypothermia and winter rescues. The next morning dawned bright and sunny, with no wind. This was wonderful luck that easily trumped the bone-chilling outside temperature of twenty-five degrees below zero. Good visibility and low winds meant the DEC helicopter could fly. Time and fortune shifted onto the hikers sides, but they still had to be found. That proved easier than expected, for Ranger Hodgson theorized correctly: "They will most likely be found on the west side of Algonquin, the Indian Pass side. They probably started down my favorite stream. If they follow it, they will come out by Scott's Clearing Lean-to on the Indian Pass trail."

Ranger Hodgson sent three summit rangers — Nancy Proctor, Jeff Brown, and Bill Rudge — with ranger Joe Rupp, fully equipped for the rescue effort, down the Indian Pass trail toward the stream. From above, ranger Pete Fish led a sweep of the summits of Wright and Algonquin, but it was Hodgson's seasoned thinking that zeroed in on the hikers. Flying in the helicopter, accompanied by rangers Bob Bissonette and Dave Ames, Hodgson directed the pilot right to the western side of Algonquin. Sure enough, the three spotted tracks leading off the summit and down the stream bed. Ironically, as they swept down the ravine looking for signs of the hikers, they passed right over Sygman and Boxer, who were waving a piece of yellow material. The helicopter never saw them, despite the pair being in an open area.

Returning with the helicopter to the open western flanks of Algonquin, the three rangers decided it would be best, and easiest, to descend following the tracks. Bissonette operated the winch and lowered the other two rangers eighty feet to the ground near the treeline below. Within minutes the rangers found the stranded hikers, with the helicopter following overhead. All four were airlifted from the mountainside, and ten minutes later the helicopter touched down on the pad at Saranac Lake Hospital. Dr. Edward Hixson was waiting and immediately submerged Boxer's feet in whirlpool baths at body temperature for half an hour. At the time, Hixson found the hikers' body temperatures to be just below normal in the 96-degree range. The men's clothing had done its job and insulated them properly. Had they been dressed in cotton clothes the men would have died before daybreak.

Without the helicopter rescue, though, Boxer and Sygman, who at 4 a.m. that night removed his boots as well, would have almost surely lost their toes. Boxer had signs of frostbite on all ten, while Sygman showed signs on two. "Never take your boots off in situations like that," Dr. Hixson said as he left the hospital. "You can walk with your feet frozen in your boots, once you take them off you're trapped."

Even with all their judgment and execution mistakes, these last two men survived because the layers of wool and synthetic clothes surrounding them provided warmth under adverse conditions. It is the new synthetic and old wool layers that insulate when wet and breathe excess moisture away from the body that will ultimately save your life, even when all else appears dead set against you. If only there was a shelf in the store that stocked common sense, humility, and reason.

Hypothermia has killed people in every month of the year, and everyone should have knowledge of the causes, symptoms, and remedies for avoiding and attending to this killer of the unprepared. Most local first aid classes, and any decent first aid manual, will provide enough of an overview to dramatically increase survival odds. Veteran High Peaks ranger Pete Fish has done a fine job over the decades spreading the message among 46ers that "cotton kills." There will always be something left behind when packing for a hike— a "I should have taken this," or "I could have done that." By being more prepared as opposed to less, and maintaining a cautious and healthy respect for the mountains and their unpredictable weather, we all can do our part to make sure that stories like those above remain the case studies of the past, and not the news stories of the present.

Avalanches Don't Happen in the Adirondacks. Do They?

With all the mountain ranges scarred by scores of slides, one would think the Adirondacks would be one big danger zone of avalanches. They are. And they aren't. The truth is most of the biggest slides are far from hiking trails, and don't attract the attention of many people. Hikers climb on trails that are rarely in danger. Cross country skiers generally traverse lanes across lakes and through more gentle rolling terrain. Even ice climbers tend to stick to the traditional waterfalls and ice routes. Reports of trouble are few and far between. Backcountry skiers venture closest to the danger, but they have skied on countless slides for decades without being swept away. Avalanches were "never on the radar" as being a danger. That all ended on February 19, 2000. The region was finally hit by a lethal avalanche.

Ninety percent of avalanches occur on open slopes between thirty and forty-five degrees. The most dangerous pitch appears to be thirty-seven or thirty-eight degrees, which is right at the high end of the average "skiable" Adirondack slide, and right in the range of an avalanche. Most of the potential triggers—heavy snowfall, prolonged periods of extreme cold, high winds, periods of rapid warming, and rainfall—happen with routine regularity in the High Peaks region. So, why the lack of deadly avalanches? Most likely it is because the number of skiers who could potentially trigger slides remains relatively low. In the last several decades there just haven't been that many hardcore backcountry skiers. Aside from the Ski to Die Club, an informal group of intrepid skiers who have visited virtually every slide in the High Peaks since their founding in 1974, few others follow in their freshly carved tracks. Maybe it has been just dumb luck that no one has set off an avalanche. Or perhaps the skiers were doing everything right without really thinking about it.

Numerous newspapers reported accounts of the February 2000 avalanche. In those articles, Mark Meschinelli, one of the founders of the Ski to Die Club, described his approach to skiing slides. He said that he thought the slides in the Adirondacks rarely aligned with all the factors to create avalanche danger, and that the potential for an avalanche was relatively low. Also an ice climber, he had many years of experience and felt he could assess the danger more by paying attention to the weather than by probing and assessing a cross-section of snow. He also skied most slides from the safer vantage point of the edges rather than by carving turns across the middle. That, along with trusting his gut, was his greatest defense against avalanches. Meschinelli identified long stretches of unusual cold, followed by heavy snowfall as the worst two ingredients for triggering an avalanche. In early February of 2000, just such a cold spell set in on the High Peaks.

Later that month, after several storms dumped large amounts of fresh snow on top of the area, a handful of skiers set their sights on two new slides on Wright Peak. The September before, Hurricane Floyd hit the area and dealt the largest blow of destruction since the Big Blow of 1950. The storm had caused two brand new slides on the northeast slopes of Wright, one narrow, and one wide. Ron Konowitz (#487) had been eyeing both all winter. Ron, an avid skier, had skied virtually every skiable slide in the area. Earlier that season, Ron had made several trips down the narrow slide, but noticed the wider slide was having trouble holding snow. Ron, and his wife, Lauren, however did cross it the week before, and Lauren recalls hearing "weird hollow sounds" underneath them.

The morning of February 19, new snowfall and dreams of fresh tracks had Ron and Lauren planning an exploration of the slide. Since there had never been a serious avalanche in the High Peaks, the danger never crossed their minds. They met two other friends, Rohan Roy and Christina Ford, at the Adirondak Loj, and prepared for their day outdoors on the slopes of a new slide. In came two more skiers and friends of the group, Toma Vracarich and Russ Cook. They were easily convinced to join the group, which soon made its way toward Marcy Dam under brilliant blue skies and pleasant temperatures in the mid twenties—perfect weather for skiing the benign slides of the Adirondacks.

After a perfect run down the narrow slide, they relaxed in the sun and enjoyed a quiet lunch away from people and cars and any signs of man. They also got excited when Rohan completed a run down the wide slide through the trees nearby. In newspaper accounts Ron remembered, "He was hootin' and hollerin. So we went up." As simple as that. Ron made a ski cut on the slide, and noticed no settling, cracks, or sloughing of snow. "It looked like a perfect slope with perfect powder. There was probably two and a half feet of fresh powder on top of it."

Ron, Lauren, Russ, and Toma looked down from the top. Ron went first, skiing down about a hundred feet and stopping, still high up on the slide. Lauren skied down and joined him, while Russ could only make a few turns before one of his skis broke. Toma went last, and on about his third turn the floor fell out. Either he fell, or the avalanche had opened up underneath him. A loud hollow sound boomed and the others below could feel the whole slope settling. As Ron recalled vividly, "The whole thing cracked, like 300 feet wide, right where he was ... I remember seeing pieces of slab like ice in a river; it was coming towards us in waves. It was this huge concussion. It was like snow coming off a metal roof: It starts slow and starts picking up speed. I remember looking over at Lauren and reaching toward her, and then I got sucked under the snow; it was like a trap door, and I got dropped straight in."

The ride for Ron was fast and brutal. All the precautions of removing skis and packs, and all the recommended survival actions raced through his mind, but there was nothing he could do but hang on for the ride. The first push buried him, but then a second wave "pushed me over some kind of lip, and I went over a couple more drops and then all of a sudden I was launched into the air. I was flying through the air sideways and I was like, 'Wow! The sun.' I was out of the snow. And I landed on my side. My skis were gone, my pack was gone, my poles were gone, my jacket was all ripped, my clothing was all ripped."

Ron was battered and bruised, and the only person not trapped in the snow. Rohan had been watching the group's run from just above the fracture line and saw the whole thing. He watched the forces of nature strip bare the entire slide and suck his friends along with it. He skied the remaining ice and bare rock down to Ron and together they began searching for the others. Ron was yelling out for his wife, and he called down to people at Marcy Dam. The two scoured the area, looking for people or equipment. They heard a weak cry for help. Rohan rushed down into the trees of the debris field and found Russ, hurt but okay. One down, and two to go.

Lauren was lucky to be wearing a red anorak that day, for it got pulled up off her and the smallest piece of it poked through the snow. This was also down in the debris field right across from where Rohan had located Russ. Rohan probed the area beneath the anorak with his ski and hit Lauren's body. He quickly dug out her face, and to his relief found her still breathing. He called out for Ron who came and had a different reaction. His wife was badly battered, with blood all over the white snow. He fought his fears and started digging her out from the rock-hard snow that occurs after avalanche snow sets. Chrissy Ford had been on the narrow slide, and the avalanche happened so fast she didn't even see it. Now she joined the search effort, and went back up the slope with Rohan to search for Toma.

It was forty-five minutes before Ron completed digging out Lauren from the cement-like snow, and still no sign of Toma. Without an avalanche beacon, the kind worn by all skiers out in the western United States where avalanches occur with some frequency, it was like searching for a needle in a haystack. Even three hours after the slide occurred, as a helicopter lifted the survivors to safety, the scores of rangers and other recruits had yet to find the lost member of the party. It took them until nearly six o'clock that evening to find Toma. The coroner figured he died on impact, and there would have been nothing that could have been done for him had he been located sooner.

The accident changed the course of preparedness for most backcountry skiers, guides, and rangers. The innocence of the Adirondack backcountry skiing experience was lost. Several veteran skiers would be forever changed by the experience, and yet the numbers of skiers venturing out to tackle the slides continues to grow. Equipment is better, the Internet provides instant reports of fresh descents, and every year seems to usher in a new extreme sport. One can only hope that the factors don't align again any time soon as they did that perfect "bluebird day" in February of 2000... and that another streak of good luck holds for many years to come.

Bibliography

American National Biography, Dictionary of American Biography: A Life of Silas Wright, 1795-1847. New York: O'Donnell, W. C. Jr., 1913.

Arakelian, Mary. *Doc: Orra A. Phelps, M.D. Adirondack Naturalist and Mountaineer.* Utica, NY: North Country Books, 2001.

Carson, Russell, M. L. *Peaks and People of the Adirondacks.* Adirondack Mountain Club, 1927 and 1973.

DiNunzio, Michael G. *Adirondack Wildguide: A Natural History of the Adirondack Park.* Lake George, NY: Adirondack Mountain Club, 1984.

Donaldson, Alfred L. *History of the Adirondacks, Vol 1 & 2.* New York: The Century Company, 1921.

Glover, James, M. *A Wilderness Original: The Life of Bob Marshall.* Seattle, WA: Mountaineers Books, 1986.

Guide to Adirondack Trails, 5th and 8th editions. Adirondack Mountain Club, 1950, 1972.

Jamieson, Paul. *Adirondack Pilgrimage.* Lake George, NY: Adirondack Mountain Club, 1986.

Jamieson, Paul. *The Adirondack Reader.* Lake George, NY: Adirondack Mountain Club, 1982.

Keller, J. E. *Adirondack Wilderness.* Syracuse, NY: Syracuse University Press, 1980.

Marshall, Robert. "The High Peaks of the Adirondacks." Adirondack Mountain Club, 1922.

Masten, Arthur H. *The Story of Adirondac.* Syracuse University Press, 1968.

O'Kane, Walter Collins. *Trails and Summits of the Adirondacks.* New York: Houghton Mifflin Co., 1928.

Phelps, Orson Schofield, Healy, Bill (editor). *The High Peaks of Essex: The Adirondack Mountains of Orson Schofield Phelps.* Purple Mountain Press, 1992.

Poulette, Jim. *Into the Adirondacks.* North Country Books, 1994.

Redfield, W. C. "Some accounts of two visits to the Mountains in Essex County, NY…." *American Journal of Science and Arts, Vol XXXIII.* New Haven, CT: B. L. Hamlen, 1838.

Schaefer, Paul (editor). *Adirondack Explorations: Nature Writings by Verplanck Colvin.* Syracuse University Press, 2000.

Slack, Nancy G. & Bell, Allison, W. *85 Acres: A Field Guide to the Adirondack Alpine Summits.* Utica, NY: North Country Books, 1993.

Stoddard, Seneca Ray. *The Adirondacks Illustrated.* S. R. Stoddard, 1874.

Sylvester, Nathanial Bartlett. *Historical Sketches of Northern New York and the Adirondack Wilderness.* 1877.

Weston, Harold. *Freedom in the Wilds, a Saga of the Adirondacks.* Adirondack Trail Improvement Society, 1971.

Wickham, Robert S. *Friendly Adirondack Peaks.* Binghamton, NY, 1924.

Wilson, Grant James and Fiske, John (editors). *Appleton's Cyclopedia of American Biography.* New York: D. Appleton and Company, 1887-1889.

About the Author

The Birth of a Forty Sixer: At age twelve and in summer camp, Sean O'Donnell was "dragged" up his first High Peak (Mount Marcy) through endless drizzle and view-engulfing fog. It was one of his worst outdoor experiences. The following year he was forced into the High Peaks again. The trip wound through Avalanche Pass, hopped across the Hitch-Up Matildas of Avalanche Lake, and after a serene night on Lake Colden, climbed Algonquin Peak via the steep and magnificent original Eastern Emmons route of the first documented ascent in 1837. It was one of his best outdoor experiences. He hasn't stopped hiking since.

MOUNT PHELPS
Height: 31st – 1,268 meters (4,160 feet)
By Ron Konowitz (#487)

Russell M. L. Carson wrote in *Peaks and People of the Adirondacks* (1927):

> It is a misfortune, amounting almost to an injustice, that the name of Old Mountain Phelps, the great Keene Valley guide, who himself named so many of the mountains was given to an unimportant peak in North Elba on the opposite side of the range from the locality where he achieved fame... To Phelps, "Mercy," as he called it, was the chief mountain of the globe, and his love for it amounted to worship. Probably no guide in all Adirondack history loved the peaks and his profession as he did. Such a man richly deserved one of the finest peaks named in his honour.

Carson went on to explain that Little Marcy (which Carson hoped to have renamed as Hopkins Hump), near the head of Johns Brook, was named for Phelps by Verplanck Colvin about 1870, but "Who transferred the name, we do not know, but in some unexplainable way it was moved to a peak of little prominence northwest of Tabletop, called by the North Elba folk 'South Meadow Mountain.' While the original Mount Phelps was not of first magnitude, its proximity to Phelps's beloved Marcy made it a far more fitting peak to bear his name."

Carson's brief chapter concerning Mount Phelps concludes with this paragraph:

> Mount Phelps is not often climbed – another reason why it is not a happy choice to bear the name of the man whose lifelong hobby was mountain climbing and who was the first to popularize mountaineering in the Adirondacks. It has no trail, but there are old lumber roads almost to the summit.

In "The High Peaks of the Adirondacks," Bob Marshall provided two other names for Mount Phelps – Little Tabletop and North Tabletop – and produced a list of the "view ratings" for all of the mountains he discussed in the pamphlet published in 1922. The list was a "composite" one based upon the ratings made by Herb Clark, George Marshall, and Bob. Phelps ranked #40 out of 42. The only mountains which the three rated as having lesser views were Street and Nye. Carson, in *Peaks and People,* published a second list, "Rating of Views from Adirondack Peaks 4,000 Feet or Over by Robert and George Marshall, May 26, 1926." In that list Phelps was #38 out of 46 – a considerable improvement for Phelps's rating. The peaks with lesser ratings were East Dix, Porter, Emmons, Cliff, Esther, South Dix, Street, and Nye. Why the Marshalls (and Clark) considered the view from Phelps to be inferior is easily explained: the ruin wrought upon the landscape by logging and by fires. Here is what Bob wrote about Phelps in 1922:

MOUNT PHELPS

I climbed this mountain one dark afternoon from South Meadows. I never enjoyed climbing a mountain so little. There were hours of pushing through terrible fire slash, working up slides and walking logs. Fortunately, old lumber roads led up as far as South Meadows Mountain.[1]

A view over miles of ugly slash toward Heart Pond and a glimpse through the second growth toward Marcy Brook are all one can see from the summit.

Much has changed over the past 100 years in the area of Phelps and the areas that may be viewed from it. The slash is gone. Only keen observers can discern where fires and loggers ravaged the peaks. In 1988, Forty-Sixers who responded to a questionnaire, gave Phelps a "composite" view rating of 24.

Was Carson justified in considering the naming of the peak such a misfortune?

Orson "Old Mountain" Phelps

Phelps himself, when standing atop "Mercy," often saw it, but, apparently he did not know of it as South Meadow Mountain. In the "Adirondack Mountains" an original manuscript by Phelps that was transcribed by Bill Healy for his *The High Peaks of Essex: The Adirondack Mountains of Orson Schofield Phelps,*[2] the famed guide described the view from Marcy and included a description of the area that could be seen "farther east" where "you have the same wild look near by bringing in Flat top Mt in the second range from this we fall abrutly down to the South Meadows and the eastern part of N Elba..." Sweeping from Mount Phelps, east towards Howard Mountain, and then south and west towards what today is called Tabletop there is a high horseshoe shaped ridge with seven peaks including the two which 46ers climb. All are above 4,000 feet in elevation. The ridge – Tabletop to Mount Phelps – clearly visible due north from "Mercy" – was what Old Mountain Phelps designated "Flat top Mt."

What we now call Mount Phelps was first climbed in 1904 by Charles Wood, chief timber cruiser for the J. & J. Rogers Company. It was never climbed by Old Mountain Phelps. His domain was Keene Flats (Keene Valley) and the area of the Ausable Lakes, where, on Upper Ausable, he had his "guides camp."

Charles Dudley Warner, in a sketch originally published as "The Primitive Man" in the *Atlantic Monthly* and later as "A Character Study" in his volume of essays *In the Wilderness* (1878), wrote of the guide as follows:

> He was a true citizen of the wilderness. Thoreau would have liked him, as he liked Indians and woodchucks, and the smell of pine-forests; and, if Old Phelps has seen Thoreau, he would probably have said to him, "Why on airth, Mr. Thoreau, don't you live accordin' to your preachin'?" You might be misled by the shaggy suggestion of Old Phelps's given name – Orson[3] – into the notion that he was a mighty hunter, with the fierce spirit of the Berserkers[4] in his veins. Nothing could be farther from the truth. The hirsute and grisly sound of Orson expresses only his entire affinity with the untamed and the natural, and uncouth but gentle passion for the freedom and wildness of the forest. Orson Phelps has only those unconventional and humourous qualities of the bear which make the animal so beloved in literature; and one

does not think of Old Phelps so much as a lover of nature, – to use the sentimental slang of the period, – as a part of nature itself.

Phelps was born at Wethersfield, Vermont, May 6, 1816,[5] the same year that witnessed the births of fellow famed guides Bill Nye and Alvah Dunning. He moved with his father, a surveyor, to the Schroon Lake area about 1830 and worked for a time at the Adirondack Iron Works at Adirondac before settling at Keene Flats.

Seneca Ray Stoddard in his 1876 edition of *The Adirondacks Illustrated* said of Phelps, "He doesn't aspire to much as a hunter, but claims to have caught more trout than any other man in the country."

Stoddard continued:

> In 1844 he was with Mr. Henderson at Adirondack, soon after which he married and settled in Keene Flats, and in 1849 made his first trip to the top of Marcy, passing out over Haystack around the head of Panther Gorge and to the summit, descending near where the main trail now runs, being the first man to get to the top from the east;[6] he afterward cut what is now known as the Bartlett mountain trail, and soon guided two ladies up, which was considered quite a feat for them to perform and a feather in his cap, as it had been considered impracticable until then. He also marked trails to the top of Hopkins' Peak, the Giant, up Johns Brook to Marcy, and several others; has made a valuable map of the country around, is a prized and regular contributor to a local paper, and has written a voluminous treatise on the Adirondack lakes and mountains, trees, birds, beasts, etc., which shows the close observer and enthusiastic student of nature, and which will contain much valuable information when, as is promised, it is given to the public.[7]

With Phelps as his guide, Stoddard ascended Mount Marcy, a climb which, according to Stoddard, was most often "made" from the Upper Ausable Lake "near its outlet, passing over Bartlett Mountain to Marcy Brook, three and a half miles distant; then up toward the west or through Panther Gorge..."

Warner wrote, "Old Phelps was the discoverer of the beauties and sublimities of the mountains and when city strangers broke into the region, he monopolized the appreciation of these delights and wonder of nature." He loved his "random scoots" and "regular walks," and his reverence for the mountains and outrageous tales made him a most sought after guide.

Phil Gallos writes in his book, *By Foot in the Adirondacks,*[8] "It must have been quite a scene when this child of nature sat on a log by a fire and discussed history and philosophy with a well known writer *(Warner),* a president of Yale *(Dr. Noah Porter),* and two noted theologians *(the Reverends Horace Bushnell and Joseph Hopkins Twichell).*

As Stoddard mentioned, Phelps wrote a column for the *Essex County Republican* called "Speckerlations," which contained both poetry and prose penned with his "quaint" phraseology. He also served as Verplanck Colvin's chief guide in the 1870s but later relinquished the job to his son, Ed, himself a very accomplished Upper Lake guide who worked for the surveyor for 20 years.

Old Mountain Phelps died on April 14, 1905, at the age of 88. He is buried in the Estes family cemetery in Keene Valley.

Mount Phelps remained trailless until 1967. Up until that time the Van Hoevenberg Trail up Mount Marcy crossed the Phelps Brook and headed up to Indian Falls past Phelps Lean-to. That popular camping spot offered great swimming holes, clear cold cooking and drinking water, a wonderful stone fireplace for a roaring fire, and the babbling brook to soothe campers to sleep. "A Good Woodsman leaves dry wood and food for the next camper" was a sign of the times. Unfortunately, the well used lean-to sat a little too close to Phelps Brook and was removed by the DEC in the 1980s. Today you can follow a drainage ditch that leads down to a small grassy meadow where the lean-to was located. An old, 24-inch diameter cedar log with steps notched into it and a railing still attached marks the beginning of the old trail to Indian Falls from the lean-to.

Prior to 1967, the popular route up Phelps followed the Van Hoevenberg Trail and then an old logging road, located between Phelps and Tabletop, to a point high up on the south side of the mountain. The cutting of the official hiking trail was somewhat controversial. More than a few 46ers wanted Phelps to remain trailless, but others preferred a single, marked trail to several herd paths which were then developing on the mountain. Suzanne Lance tells more about the controversy in her club history earlier in this volume.

The present trail up Phelps leaves the Van Hoevenberg Trail approximately one quarter mile above the old lean-to site. It climbs up and south through mature birch trees and small balsam firs. It swings a hard left to follow a flat, old lumber road before cutting a 90 degree right turn and heading due east up a mostly steep pitch which involves some brief rock scrambling.

At that point, a glacial erratic split in half provides an interesting habitat for a variety of mosses and brings to some hikers memories of filling metal canteens with water from dripping mosses on hot August days.

Soon the trail reaches the ridge line and becomes a solid granite path from which occasional spectacular views of the MacIntyres and Mount Colden can be seen. Suddenly, the dome of Mount Marcy – the "Pleasure Dome" – in all its glory appears and dominates one's vision. Old Mountain Phelps, attaining that height, would have been pleased with the view.

Balsam firs and spruce, supported by six to twelve inches of soil, now dominate the mountaintop forest. Still, a few of the larger trees that once stood sentinel on the peak remain. The peak is often battered by straight line winds that rush to it through Avalanche Pass and hit its west side – flat out – at about 3,500 feet, and that is what they have done: flattened out the forest on the flank of the mountain that affords the views to the south.

The last stretch of the trail to the summit is truly spectacular, providing great views amid healthy, small firs and spruce trees with lots of new lime green lichen growth on them. They are waiting it out – forest succession – until the next big wind topples the trees which have grown tall and vulnerable.

The summit of Mount Phelps offers views of most of the eastern High Peaks Wilderness, and it is interesting to note that, from the summit, if you look to the east, you can see Beede Road in Keene Valley. That is the road on which Orson Schofield Phelps once lived and it is the road along which the cemetery lies in which he rests today.

Phil Gallos wrote, "Phelps loved the wilderness like nothing else, like the only thing that was lasting and real in this world. To him every mountain and every brook and every lake was a special personal friend, and the great forest was the spirit which gave life to all."

Alfred L. Donaldson, in his chapter about Old Mountain Phelps in *A History of the Adirondacks,* includes this about the guide:

> He was prone to nickname the natural wonders that he loved best. Mount Marcy he always called "Mercy." He held it to be the stateliest peak, commanding the finest view in the world. People would sometimes speak of the Alps or the Himalayas as having mountainous merit. But such idle talk annoyed him, and he would squelch it with a sneer. "I callerlate you hain't never been atop o' Mercy," he would say, and turn away in disgust.

The Reverend Ernest R. Ryder and Ed Hudowalski on top of Phelps.
Fire swept over the peak in 1903. Its view remained wide open for decades thereafter.

Though Old Mountain Phelps never climbed the mountain which bears his name, if you look out upon the vast expanse of wilderness which you can see from the summit of Mount Phelps, you realize that Phelps is, in fact, an apt and appropriate name for the peak which celebrates one of the greatest guides and greatest characters in Adirondack history. If Phelps were with you atop the mountain that bears his name, he might just "callerlate" that it provides a fine view of the peaks he climbed and loved, particularly, due south as the raven flies, his beloved "Mercy."

Endnotes

1. This reference to South Meadow Mountain is curious as Carson asserted that Mount Phelps was originally known by that name. It is likely that the mountain to which Marshall refers is a lesser peak to the north of Phelps, directly above the area known as South Meadow.

2. Bill Healy, *The High Peaks of Essex: The Adirondack Mountains of Orson Schofield Phelps,* (Fleischmanns, NY: Purple Mountain Press, 1992). Healy's "Introduction" provides insightful information about Phelps and his manuscript about the High Peaks. The volume also contains Phelps's obituary as it appeared in the *Utica Post-Dispatch* on May 15, 1905.

3. *Orson* is Latin, for *bear*. An old French story concerns a child, Orson, who was raised in a forest by a bear.

4. Berserkers were legendary Norsemen who wore coats of bearskin *(bearsark)* and were said to have gone into battle in trances of fury.

5. Since the early part of the twentieth century capable historians have written that Phelps was born in 1817 and that he died in April 1905 at the age of 88. However, since he was born in May and died in April, he could not have been 88 at the time of his death. Scofield (Schofield) family genealogists give 1816 as the year of his birth. His father, born in Connecticut, was Orin Phelps. His mother, a native of Vermont, was Ruth Scofield.

6. There is some doubt as to whether or not Phelps was the first to climb Marcy from the Keene Valley side.

7. At least in part, the manuscript by Phelps that was transcribed and published by Bill Healy in 1992 was likely the one to which Stoddard refers. In *Adirondacks Illustrated,* Stoddard published a cleansed version of some of what Healy later transcribed.

8. Phil Gallos, *By Foot in the Adirondacks,* (Saranac Lake, NY: Adirondack Publishing Company, Inc., 1972).

TABLETOP
Height: 20th – 1,345 meters (4,413 feet)
By Ron Konowitz (#487)

Old Mountain Phelps made reference to the mountain now known as Tabletop in his manuscript, *The Adirondack Mountains,*[1] and Verplanck Colvin included it in a reconnaissance map he made about 1872, but both men called the mountain Flat Top. It was first labeled Tabletop, suggestive of its appearance when viewed from other nearby peaks, in Gray's *Atlas of Essex County* in 1876. The name *Table Top* appears on the 1902 U.S. Geological Survey map of the Mt. Marcy Quadrangle (based upon surveys of 1891-92), but the designation in print sweeps northeast from present day Tabletop and includes two other peaks between today's summit and that of Howard Mountain.

Tabletop formed a portion of the boundary of the lands once owned by the Adirondack Mountain Reserve (AMR), property which had been purchased by the Ausable Club. In 1900, the club owned just over 40,000 acres of land, including Indian Falls, Lake Arnold, Tabletop, and Marcy. Officials of the AMR signed contracts with the J. & J. Rogers Company to harvest timber along the north Marcy Brook around Indian Falls, and soon thereafter a 15-foot wide fire line was cut in a southeasterly direction to help stem any possible forest fire from spreading to AMR lands in the Johns Brook Valley. That line passed close by the summit of Tabletop.

Negotiations for state acquisition of Mount Marcy, Indian Falls, and Tabletop began in 1917 with major fund raising headed by the Association for the Protection of the Adirondacks. Anticipating the sale and ownership by the state, the Victory Mountain Committee was established, and it proposed calling the great tract within the High Peaks region Victory Mountain Park in commemoration of the victory of the United States and its allies in the Great War (World War I). Although Victory Mountain Park was never realized, purchase of the tract was. When it became official on February 9, 1923, it included the areas already mentioned as well as the entire Johns Brook Valley and the north slopes of the peaks of the Great Range from Haystack to Lower Wolf Jaw. At that time the holdings of the AMR were reduced to just over 16,000 acres. We are truly fortunate today that the land acquired had been purchased by the AMR, which preserved it, and that the AMR sold it to the state for the benefit of all.

Robert Marshall in his Adirondack Mountain Club pamphlet of 1922, "The High Peaks of the Adirondacks," wrote as follows about Tabletop:

> About six miles from Keene Valley the trail up Marcy divides. One part keeps to John's Brook. The other leaves it and gradually works its way up Tabletop and from there goes up Marcy, joining the Heart Pond Trail.[2]

Tabletop, as its name implies, is very flat, and in addition is heavily wooded on top. As a result, one can see nothing from it. About the only worth-while view can be had from just off the trail a short way below the summit. Here one can look down the John's Brook Valley to Keene Valley.

After reading that description, we are left to wonder today whether or not Herb Clark and the Marshall Brothers actually climbed the mountain we know as Tabletop. The trail described, which begins along the Johns Brook about 1.6 miles from Johns Brook Lodge (JBL) and across the brook from the Bushnell Falls Lean-tos, does not "work its way up Tabletop." Following a branch of the Johns Brook, it ascends to a rather flat area, the Plateau, at an elevation of about 4,350 feet just to the north northwest of Little Marcy. About a half a mile back towards Bushnell Falls the trail comes closest to Tabletop, but it is still about a mile away from the summit. Jim Goodwin, who climbed Marcy in the 1920s, says that there never was a trail up Tabletop.

The original Adirondack Mountain Club *Guide to Adirondack Trails, Northeastern Section* (1934), edited by Orra Phelps, described the trail taken by the Marshalls and Clark:

Where the trail divides take right fork – trail marked with yellow discs. For ¾ m. the grade is easy and leads through splendid spruce and white birch. The trail still follows the stream but is high above it. The next mile of climbing is steep, and the grade increases somewhat with elevation, but soon one is high enough to get glimpses out into the valley. After climbing 1400 ft. in less than 2 m. from the junction, the trail becomes nearly level and for ¼ m. winds through the thick spruces, and suddenly comes out onto a trail, marked with blue discs. This is the Heart Lake-Marcy Trail[2] which is followed (to the left) from this point *(to Marcy)*.

The junction of the "trail marked with yellow discs" and the trail "marked with blue discs" is about one quarter mile from the summit of Little Marcy (4,765 feet) to the southeast. Tabletop is about a mile and a half away due north. Climbing to the top over a false peak along the way would have been rather difficult. So, is it possible that Clark and the Marshalls climbed Little Marcy by mistake and not Tabletop?

Since both Marshalls returned to climb in the area long after they first ascended all of the High Peaks, if they had been mistaken in 1920, they certainly would have corrected their mistake. After all, they had corrected a climbing error earlier, after they determined in 1924 that they had not previously been atop Emmons when they thought they had been in 1921. As a result, Clark and the Marshalls did not become 46ers until June 10, 1925, almost a year after they had thought they had finished climbing all of the then 4,000-foot peaks on Cliff (June 26, 1924).

In "The High Peaks of the Adirondacks," Bob Marshall also wrote, "Of the forty-two high peaks *(Blake's Peak, Couchsachraga, Gray Peak, and Cliff were not included in the original listing of the High Peaks)* only fourteen have trails up them." The hand drawn map by Marshall included with the 1922 pamphlet shows "Roads & Trails." The map shows – or his text indicates – trails that went to or over the following summits: Marcy, Haystack, Basin, Saddleback, "Gothic," Colvin, Dix, Giant, MacIntyre (Algonquin), Skylight, Seward, Big Slide, Whiteface, and Tabletop.

The trail passing over the summit of Tabletop is clearly marked on Marshall's map, but also clear in a table in the pamphlet is the elevation of the mountain, then, according to the 1902 Marcy Quadrangle, 4,400 feet. A study of the map also makes it clear that Clark and the Marshalls did not follow the route of the "trail marked with yellow discs."[3] They must have departed from it relatively early on in the going, diverging from it, probably on the fire line mentioned earlier. According to Carson, "A broad lane about fifteen feet wide, which has been cut in a southeasterly direction from the summit of Tabletop, gave a clue to the first known ascent" of the mountain, credited to Rogers Company timber cruiser Jim Suitor, who was in charge of cutting the fire lane in 1911.[4] It probably also gives a clue as to the identity of the "trail" described by Marshall. A line cut "southeasterly" from the summit would, if cut long enough, have met the trail described in the 1934 Adirondack Mountain Club guide. Thus a possible route to the summit is relatively easy to explain. It would have been fairly fresh, easy to discern and follow in 1920. Sharp Swan (#566W) reports that Grace Hudowalski (#9) said that the old "lane" was an easy route to the summit. Sharp has a 1942 aerial photograph which clearly shows the lane. It would have been possible before the Big Blow of November 1950 to have employed the lane as a route to Tabletop.

Still, we have to wonder about the route from Tabletop's summit to the "Heart Pond Trail." Marshall's map indicates that the route from Tabletop to the trail went, generally, south southwest and had its junction with the "Heart Pond Trail" just about where the 1934 "trail marked with yellow discs" did. Was that route also the way of the "broad lane"? Carson maintained that the lane had been cut in a "southeasterly direction" from the summit, but he also mentioned that the lane had been cut to fulfill a condition of a sale of timber, by the AMR, to the J. & J. Rogers Company. "Part of this purchase," he writes, "was that the purchaser should make a fire line around the cutting." If that is true, the lane must have extended from the summit in two directions. If it did, it may very well have gone to the south southwest. Marshall, in "The High Peaks of the Adirondacks," mentions "six important trails" up Mount Marcy. He nearly dismisses the "Heart Pond" trail. He writes, "From the north there is also a trail, very muddy and running mostly through slash." The slash had to have been the result of the great fire of 1903 which destroyed much of the Van Hoevenberg Trail from Heart Lake. The Marshalls and Herb Clark avoided that route by climbing Tabletop from the Johns Brook Valley instead of from Indian Falls.

Long after the Marshalls and Clark climbed Tabletop the most common approach to the peak was from the old Lake Placid Club ski lodge, now the Adirondack Mountain Club's Adirondak Loj.[5] In the 1960s, the old Marcy Dam trailhead at Heart Lake, now in the midst of the Adirondak Loj camping area, sported a canteen: a small building with a fold-down window counter at which hikers could purchase everything from chocolate bars to "D" batteries for their Army surplus flashlights. Carrying your Army packboard, with a duffle bag tied with clothesline to hooks along the sides of the board, and employing a towel over your shoulders to pad the canvas straps, you could hike the two-plus miles to Marcy Dam. Once there, you could pick from one of many lean-tos at which to rest or camp or continue on to Indian Falls to stay right on the Marcy Brook in one of two lean-tos. From Indian Falls, you could see high on Wright Peak, when the sun shone, the glint of the metal of a wing of an airplane, the B-47 that crashed into the peak in 1962.

The trip up Tabletop began upstream from your lean-to. You had to navigate through a maze of herd paths, often muddy, and, if you were a skilled route finder, or lucky, you might reach the summit within two hour's time. As you progressed from Indian Falls, some of the herdpaths petered out and disappeared. An old 46er tells of climbing the mountain with a summer camp group on a hot August afternoon in 1962. After their path dissolved into scrub and gnarled spruce, those hikers found themselves amidst dense blowdown, a reminder of the destruction created by the Big Blow of November 1950. They had to "crawl up and over gray, skeletal remains of fallen spruces, climb atop them, scrambled under them." The old timer says, "I don't believe we actually stood on *terra firma*, just below the summit for over an hour. Sometimes, the ground was ten or twelve feet below us as we stepped and jumped from one trunk to another in the midst of the tangle of giant pick-up sticks."

Heaven Up-h'isted-ness!

Near Indian Falls one night, another hiker heard something "crashing" through the underbrush fifty feet from the Van Hoevenberg Trail. The "crasher," it turned out, was Fred Hunt (#593W), who signed in at summit registers as Cat Eyes. The first nighttime 46er, Cat Eyes that night was continuing his own private search for a hiker, Steven Thomas, who disappeared while climbing Mount Marcy earlier that year, 1976.

Indian Falls was the site of a large lumber camp early in the twentieth century, that of the J. & J. Rogers Company. Lumber roads used for sledding out the logs to Marcy Dam left from Indian Falls both towards another large camp at Avalanche Camp and a lesser known camp between Tabletop and Phelps. A portion of the latter road later became the Mount Marcy Ski Trail.

Anyone who has ever had the pleasure of descending that old ski trail in six to twelve inches of untouched powder on backcountry skis knows what it is to feel something akin to "heaven up-h'isted-ness."

During the 1930s the trail was widened to accommodate an increasing number of wilderness skiers descending from the upper slopes of Marcy. Tony Goodwin (#211) in his *Northern Adirondack Ski Tours* (1981) wrote about the trail:

> In 1936, the Adirondack Mountain Club made several improvements on this trail so that it would be more suitable for skiing. These improvements included widening the trail to at least 10 feet all the way to Plateau and cutting an entirely new route from Phelps Lean-to above Marcy Dam to Indian Falls. The present hiking trail follows much of this route, but there is still nearly a mile of separate trail. This ski trail may not look anything like the wide swathes on an ordinary downhill ski area, but the separate route and the widening make all the difference in making the descent fun rather than just possible.

Several old ski jumps constructed in the 1980s by Willie Janeway (#1846) of the Adirondack Mountain Club Trail Crew can still be found on the 50-meter hill section today, but the old 50-meter-long ski bridge has since been dismantled.

Prior to 1973, two trails led to Mount Marcy from Marcy Dam. One was the wide ski trail; the other was the separate, narrow hiking trail. The two rarely crossed. With the advent of ski lifts and a decline in backcountry skiing in the 1960s, the DEC decided to close the old hiking trails on Mount Marcy and Wright Peak and reroute them to follow the ski trails. However, during the last two decades, a dramatic increase in the popularity of backcountry skiing has devotees thinking that it is time to reestablish the old hiking trails and set aside the ski trails solely, in winter, for skiers. Since the 1973 trail closure, skiers and snowshoers have had to share the same trail to Mount Marcy. While each group usually tries to be mindful of the other, some feel that it's only a matter of time before a collision, which might leave both a skier and a snowshoer seriously injured, will take place along the trail.

Each January, a group of old friends gathers at Camp Peggy O'Brien to hike, play cards, and share tales of "epic hikes." Jim Kobak (#1791W) and Ed Bunk (#3052W) decided one winter to go into the Johns Brook area a day early, attempt to complete the "Circle of Doom," and arrive back at O'Brien in time to surprise their just arriving friends. Leaving JBL in the wee hours, the pair bushwhacked up Phelps from the Klondike Notch trail and proceeded to Tabletop and Marcy. Jim was fighting the flu; consequently, on Marcy they had to abandon their quest. Later, in the summer, Kobak, Bunk, and Jason Fiegl (#4953) and Zoë, a dog, completed the circle from the Garden. They were on Phelps for sunrise and then moved on to Tabletop, Marcy, Haystack, Basin, Saddleback, and Gothics before witnessing sunset on Armstrong. They continued over Upper and Lower Wolf Jaws and closed the circle at the Garden at midnight, having hiked about 29 miles and having completed a total ascent of about 13,000 feet.

Today, hikers follow a maintained but unmarked "Wilderness Path" cut with DEC approval by the Forty-Sixers to the summit of Tabletop. It departs from the Van Hoevenberg Trail just below Indian Falls at a point where a large rock cairn and sign have been placed. The sign reads, "Unmarked Route to Tabletop Mt." Some miss the former challenge of negotiating the multitude of "secret doorways" leading to the summit canister. Some, too, miss the canister which contained the register with its notes written by the mountain's climbers. They often reported that the herd path had been muddy and confusing and that the climb had been frustrating, difficult. Many veterans, repeat climbers, thought the route was simply fun. The new route has helped stem damage to the mountain wrought by hikers, many of whom had climbed the mountain in order to become 46ers. The Wilderness Path – although it has, in effect, made attaining Tabletop's summit less challenging than it was – demonstrates that the Forty-Sixers are concerned about the mountains its members climb and that they are determined to preserve the peaks and the paths that lead to them and do as little harm, along the way, as they can. The days when most "trailless peaks" were scarred with deep and muddy herdpaths are over, and they should never return so long as responsible hikers and their organizations respect the mountains and help maintain the Wilderness Paths.

Hiking the relatively short path, you can find beautiful lime green mosses scattered among the balsam and spruces. The trail is steep in places, but it affords occasional great views back towards Colden and the MacIntyre Range. After reaching the ridge, you have only a short trek to reach the south summit. If you continue another fifty yards, you can find excellent views of Marcy and the Upper Range.

By far the best time of year to climb Tabletop is in the late winter, when a fresh blanket of snow covers the peaks and the deep frozen base of snow allows you to stand high and look in all directions before pointing your skis down to make quick turns through snow-covered patches of buried blowdown to Indian Falls.

Endnotes

1. Phelps's manuscript appears in Bill Healy's *The High Peaks of Essex - The Adirondack Mountains of Orson Schofield Phelps,* 1992.
2. The Van Hoevenberg Trail.
3. The trail with the "yellow discs" was laid out by state Forester Arthur S. Hopkins in 1920. It is now known as the Hopkins Trail.
4. In his chapter about Tabletop, Carson mentions Charles Broadhead, the surveyor who ran a 1797 line over the side of Tabletop, and D. M. Arnold "of Ticonderoga, a surveyor well along in years" who "was employed in 1893 by W. Scott Brown to run the boundary lines of Township 48, Totten and Crossfield Purchase," which was owned by the AMR. According to Carson, "Arnold told Brown that he had named the mountain *(Tabletop)* in 1866 when he was running a line from Lake Champlain through to Cold River." Carson suggests that "there is no reason to believe that the early surveyors went to the true summit," but he quotes Broadhead's field notes "in reference to crossing the Tabletop range": "Top the mountain – very rough, chief of the timber fallen down by the wind – the greatest part of this mountain is covered with snow 12 inches deep (7 June)." The reference to the "Top of mountain" may suggest to some that Broadhead did achieve the summit, but the line he ran, and the line Arnold ran, both pass over the Tabletop ridge about a half a mile to the northeast of the summit.

5. There were several ski trails in the Heart Lake area in the 1940s, including the Mount Jo Rimrock Trail, which was the site of the Kate Smith trophy ski race contest between the women's national teams of Canada and the United States. The race was named in honor of the popular radio singing star who had a home in Lake Placid. In 1953, A. T. Shorey, another Adirondack Mountain Club guide book editor, handmarked trails, sites of structures including lean-tos, names of brooks and other features on a copy of the 1946 reprint of the United States Geological Survey Marcy Quadrangle (1902). He labeled Mount Phelps, Indian Falls, and the yellow trail from Bushnell Falls to Plateau. He indicated a trail that ascended what was later to be named Howard Mountain and drew an arrow pointing southwest from the 3,905-foot peak. What the arrow indicated is now unclear, but it points almost directly to the ridge of three summits which terminates at the peak of Tabletop. Also on Shorey's map: the Wright Peak Ski Trail, the Mount Marcy Ski Trail, the Mount Jo Rimrock Ski Trail, and the Whale's Tail Ski Trail.

BIG SLIDE
Height: 28th – 1,290c meters (4,232+ feet)
By Ron Konowitz (#487)

In *Peaks and People of the Adirondacks,* Russell M. L. Carson wrote that Big Slide was named either from a great slide that descended from the mountain in 1830 on the Johns Brook side or a later one on the South Meadow slope, about 1856. Carson explained:

> The slide of 1830 began near the top, in the town of Keene, and carried a generous piece of that town down the mountain and deposited it in the town of North Elba. The older Keene Valley guides claim that Otis Estes, an old-time resident, named Big Slide about 1856. While the coincidence of that date, with the date of the slide on the South Meadow side of the mountain, might indicate that the name came from the younger slide, it seems very likely that the older slide inspired the name. A Keene Valley native would have been more apt to name the mountain for the slide on the Keene Valley lateral.

Carson credited surveyor John Richards with the first ascent of Big Slide while he was running a line in 1812 of Township 12 in the Old Military Tract. The east line of that township (now Keene) is only about 100 yards from the top of the mountain. Thus, if Carson is correct, Big Slide was the fourth high peak of the Adirondacks to be climbed.

In his chapter about the mountain, Carson places "Big Slide as the fourth high Adirondack peak to be climbed," but in his "Table of First Recorded Ascents of the Forty-Six Highest Adirondack Peaks" he lists Big Slide as the third to be climbed, after Giant of the Valley and "Dix's" Peak. The reason for the discrepancy: Carson listed Whiteface as the fourth to have been climbed (1814), also by John Richards, but in a footnote commented that Whiteface was known "to have been climbed earlier" but the names of the climbers and dates were lacking.

Carson told of an "old trail" up Big Slide that had "disappeared... cut about 1900 by M. E. Luck, proprietor of a hotel on Johns Brook. That trail was discussed by Jim Goodwin in *Of the Summits, of the Forests* (1991). He wrote:

> Guy Terry, a guest at Interbrook Lodge, then located on the Johns Brook road, had constructed a popular trail to Big Slide from the top of Railroad Notch... In later years, however, thick growth

after the 1903 forest fire and a lack of maintenance made the notch trail difficult to follow. The trail from the notch to Big Slide fell from use, and for a number of years thereafter, until the route from the south was built, Big Slide had no viable trail.

That explains why Bob Marshall wrote of Big Slide as he did in "The High Peaks of the Adirondacks" (1922):

> I understand there is a trail up this mountain from Keene Valley. We climbed it through a primeval forest from the head of South Meadows Brook. Even if there had been no view, the woods alone were worth the climb.
> The top of the mountain has been only partially cleared. One gets a very fine, uninterrupted view toward the Gothic Range just across John's Brook Valley, and Marcy, Colden and MacIntyre. On the other side through the trees there are glimpses of the view toward Placid.

By the time Bob and George Marshall and Herb Clark climbed Big Slide, the trail from Railroad Notch must have fallen into disuse.

Today, a favored route to Big Slide is the one from the Garden parking area which passes over the Brothers, formerly Twin Mountain. With spectacular views and some interesting rock scrambling along the way, the route to Big Slide over the Brothers makes for a classic Adirondack hike.

The trail, cut originally by Cecil Parker to advance his guiding of Keene Valley summer residents for blueberry picking outings on the Brothers, was extended in 1910 by Guy Terry. It went to Railroad Notch and joined the original trail cut from Interbrook Lodge.

The first views from the trail up the Brothers occur after approximately three quarters of a mile of climbing. After that point you bob and weave through forests and along open rock ledges until you reach the First Brother. Just below its summit, kids are often thrilled with a giant "cave." At the top, a 360-degree panorama is achieved and you can sense the spirits of Keene Valley climbers who cherished the First Brother and the valley below.

A short steep rock scramble leads to the Second Brother. From it, the trail moves through a birch forest to the Third Brother before it descends into a thick balsam/spruce forest, through which it passes on its way to a junction with the trail leading to Big Slide's summit from Johns Brook Lodge.

The Garden, where today's hikers begin their treks up and over the Brothers, was once a real garden, planted by Alfred Wells around 1910. Constant raids upon it by bands of adolescent deer and rowdy raccoons eventually led to its abandonment. A right of way was later granted to the site, and a parking lot was established there, at the end of Johns Brook Road. However, most of the early foot traffic up the Johns Brook Valley was by way of the Southside Trail, originally a lumber road, because the present trail to state Department of Environmental Conservation's ranger headquarters and Johns Brook Lodge (JBL) was, at that time, overgrown and difficult to follow. The Johns (John's) Brook, by the way, was named either for a Captain Johns or John Gibbs, who arrived to settle in Keene Valley in the early 1800s. Gibbs had been a captain in the Massachusetts militia during the Revolution. Peggy O'Brien (#560) speculated that "Captain Johns" may have been "a familiar use of a first name" and that the two names applied to the same man, the same "Captain,"[1] whose 600 acres of property was near the mouth of the brook near the present day Mountaineer in the hamlet of Keene Valley.

The Railroad Notch trail from Keene Flats (Keene Valley) to North Elba, constructed before the Civil War, passed between Big Slide and Porter Mountain. (Imagine what the

Cascade Lakes would be like today if that early road had remained the main route to North Elba's Lake Placid.) The road through the notch was named for its builder, a man named Biddlecome. Alfred L. Donaldson in *A History of the Adirondacks* described it:

> It follows Slide Brook to the South Meadows Brook, and comes out near Adirondack Lodge, although it seems probable that originally it came out nearer the Plains of Abraham, for it became the highway to that spot and Keene Valley. A horse and wagon could get through in summer, jumpers[2] were pulled over it in winter, and riders on horseback went over it at all times. It was used as a bridle-path as late as 1840...
>
> This Biddlecome Road was soon given a more picturesque name. It was in spots, of course, exceedingly narrow and rough, and some traveler, after coming over it, remarked that he had gotten through, but that "it was tight nipping."[3] This at once became a designation for the road or its worst parts, and for many years people spoke of coming or going "through Tight-Nipping."

The name of the pass through which the road went, recalls that the route was, in the mid-nineteenth century, proposed for use by a railroad that might have been built from Lake Champlain to Ogdensburg on the St. Lawrence River; however, the railroad was never built. Its proposed course between Keene Valley and North Elba is preserved on some older maps with the now curious name Railroad Notch.

In recent years, overflow Garden parking concerns led the Town of Keene to create a new parking area at the south end of Marcy Field, charge a parking fee, and provide a shuttle bus to transport hikers and their gear to the Garden, manned by an attendant. Since its inception in the 1990s, the attendant has been Eloise Endicott, daughter of Bill Endicott (#80), who completed his Forty-six on Emmons in 1950. He was the president of the club 1953-1956.

A large lumber camp for the J. & J. Rogers Company was formerly located in the area of the present ranger outpost along the main trail from the Garden to John Brooks Lodge. Other lumber camp buildings were in the area of the present day Johns Brook Lodge. Crews clear-cut trees on the Brothers and as far up as the base of the cliffs on Big Slide in 1921. Soon after the Adirondack Mountain Reserve (AMR) sold its land in the Johns Brook Valley to the state, the J. & J. Rogers Company, while pulp prices were falling, sold its valley holdings as well.

Johns Brook Lodge (JBL) was built in 1924 and 1925 on the site of the old J. & J. Rogers Company backwoods office which had been taken over by an old guide, Mel Hathaway, after he had been evicted from AMR property near the Upper Ausable Lake for violating Ausable Club hunting restrictions. Hathaway, sometimes called a hermit and sometimes called a squatter, was again evicted, and he reluctantly left the woods to spend his final years living with his daughter in Syracuse. It is said that he sometimes notched blazes on telephone poles when he ventured out from his daughter's house, so that he could later find his way back to it.

Scouted in 1925, the very direct trail from JBL to Big Slide was cut in 1927 by John Myers and members of the Adirondack Mountain Club. The shortest of Big Slide's three paths, it starts on the Slide Mountain Brook, passes along through a beautiful birch forest, and ascends the lower portion of the 1830 slide, now mostly grown in. Much of the route is along former J. & J. Rogers Company lumber roads, also grown in.

The longest and least traveled route up Big Slide begins at JBL and, following the Klondike Notch Trail, an old tote road, it arrives at a junction with the Yard Mountain trail cut in the 1930s by A. T. Shorey. A small, new sign nailed to a 4x4 reads "Yard 1.2, Big Slide 2.7."

Following that trail is like taking steps back in time. Needles of conifers cover the rarely hiked trail, and occasional areas of blowdown open up views of the Range Trail. You find old, rusty metal trail markers and might spot bobcat tracks along the way. Near the summit there is a grassy meadow where in late summer you can find raspberries. Atop Yard, an old sign nailed to a tree, perhaps by former JBL caretaker Spencer Cram or Bob Denniston or Peggy O'Brien reads, "ADK Mtn. Club Trail to Klondike Notch 1.25, Johns Brook Lodge 1.53."

From the summit of Yard[4] to the summit of Big Slide you will find evidence of 1999's Hurricane Floyd. Old growth trees were leveled and, as a result, new views opened up. Areas which now receive more sunlight than they did previously support new plant life.

In an article printed in 1973 in *Adirondack Life,* Clyde Smith discussed the merits of skiing and snowshoeing, using a trip up Big Slide as his outdoor field testing. After ascending with climbing skins upon his skis, he wrote, "At first I didn't do badly; but Adirondack trails are narrow, so narrow in fact that you can't do a snowplow, much less turn to stop."

What Clyde wrote a quarter century ago remains true: Adirondack trails are narrow, but there are, sometimes, great, open forests alongside the trails and along the flanks of some of the mountains. That is true of Big Slide and of Phelps. Big Slide also makes a wonderful winter climb. Although the Brothers approach can be icy, both that trail and the one from JBL afford sun and views through the leafless hardwoods, and there are lots of great skiing opportunities.

Another feature of Big Slide is that it provides opportunity for Class IV rock climbing. One cliff named "The Courthouse" by Ed Palen (#710) and former Essex County District Attorney Ron Briggs is on the south shoulder of the Fourth Brother. Another cliff that lures technical climbers is the more prominent slab just below the summit. It offers both incredibly scenic and challenging climbs. In 1953, world renowned mountaineer Fritz Wiessner[5] and George Austin were the first to climb the slab's steep face. In the 1960s the Penn State Outing Club, with rock climbing book author, artist Trudy B. Healy (#148), climbed the slab and completed it with a more direct and difficult, unprotected finish.

The classic route on Big Slide, however, remains "Slide Rules," climbed in 1980 by Don Mellor and Andy Helms.

In August of 1966, a group of young Camp Pok-O-Moonshine hikers spent two days climbing the Range Trail in a driving rain. They braved hail on Haystack and, throughout the trek northeast along the Range, never found a view from any of the summits they passed over. On the morning of the final day of the expedition the counselor in charge proposed a climb of Big Slide, but only three of his ten campers volunteered to go. Again, rain and clouds soaked and enshrouded the hikers as they reached another summit. However, as they hastily gulped down peanut butter and jelly sandwiches, the rain subsided. Then, after they had begun their descent, a small "porthole" of blue appeared in the sky. "Maybe," suggested John Konowitz, the counselor, "we should climb back to the summit." They did, and for the first time in their lives, Ed Palen, Steve Passamande, and the author took in the spectacular view of the Range Trail and beyond from the summit of Big Slide. It was a view to be remembered and cherished for a lifetime.

Endnotes

1. Peggy wrote about "Johns Brook" in the May 1982 (Vol. XLVI, No. 4) issue of *Adirondac,* pgs. 18-19.
2. Jumpers were log sleds.
3. "Nipping," originally referred to tightly squeezing or compressing an object between two surfaces.
4. Yard on older U.S. Geological Survey maps is listed as being 4,018 feet in elevation. Because the drop in elevation between it and Big Slide is only about 200 feet, it is not considered a separate 4,000-foot peak.
5. Fritz Wiessner (1900-1988) was a friend of John Case and Jim Goodwin. Born in Dresden, Germany, he started climbing with his father in the Alps before World War I. Before immigrating to New York in 1929, he had already established himself as a preeminent rock climber. He is credited with numerous first ascents including, many in the Gunks, one of Wallface Mountain, and another of Wyoming's Devil's Tower. He was also a pioneer of technical climbing in the Gunks. In 1939, he led an American expedition to within 700 feet of the summit of K2 in the Himalayas, having turned back, reportedly, because a Sherpa guide was disinclined to offend his gods "by being on the summit in the darkness." A skilled skier, Wiessner served as a technical advisor to the United States Army's 10th Mountain Division during World War II. He remained an active climber into his eighties.

About the Author

Ron Konowitz (#487) began hiking and spending summers in the Adirondacks during the late 1950s at Camp Pok-O-Moonshine, where his parents worked. One of his childhood heroes was then 46er President Jim Bailey (#233), who in addition to being a Poko counselor was also a good friend of his parents. Camp Director Jack Swan (#267) and the many 46er staff members led Ron on incredible hikes in the High Peaks. He finished his first round in 1968 on Emmons. He has since hiked over 20 rounds.

Ron began learning about Adirondack winters in 1972 when he moved to the mountains full time. In 1978 he accepted a position, offered by then School Board President and former 46er President Bill Endicott (#80) to teach 5th Grade at Keene Central School. Since then many of his students have become 46ers. In 1989 Ron and Ed Palen (#710) started the Keene Kids Climbing Club. Ron has guided for the Adirondack Mountain Club, Rock and River Guide Service, and the Mountaineer. He has been involved in search and rescue for over thirty years. He is currently the Wilderness Rescue Coordinator for the Keene Valley Fire Department.

Ron has served as a director of the 46ers. He is also a member of the Grace Peak Committee as well as an advisor to the 46er Conservation Trust. He is a presenter on back country emergencies for the 46er Outdoor Leadership Workshop. He helped with the start of the summit rehabilitation program by carrying grass seed and lime to the summits of Algonquin and Marcy and served as a volunteer steward. He has helped maintain the Marcy and Wright Peak Ski Trails as part of the adopt a resource agreement with the ADK Ski Touring Council. Ron was recently honored with a 46er Founders Award.

Ron started skiing the High Peaks in 1976. In 1996 he became the first person to climb on skis and then descend on skis all 46 peaks. Standing atop Allen on March 12, 1996, with childhood Poko hiking friend Sharp Swan (#566W) and Teresa Cheetham Palen, he felt a deep sense of satisfaction and realized how Camp Pok-O-Moonshine and the 46ers of Troy had directed his life towards that very spiritual moment. Ron had kept this goal of skiing the 46 Peaks to himself and a small group of friends. Sharp suggested that he somehow document the achievement; so a two-paragraph letter about the achievement was written and sent to Grace.

As a child, Ron had always been in awe of Grace Hudowalski (#9). As an adult, he and Grace became friends, but Ron was still in awe of her. In the summer of 1996 Grace invited Ron to the Boulders for dinner. He had always enjoyed visiting and trading stories of mountain adventures with Grace, but that night was to be exceptional. Grace had also invited hikers extraordinaire Ed Bunk (#3052W), Wayne Ratowski (#3036W), and Mimi Moulton (#3148). After a wonderful dinner augmented with great tales, Grace announced a toast to Ron's ski round. She asked Ed Bunk to reach in the corner cabinet and bring out the bottle of Cherry Herring. It was quite dusty and the cork, which had not been extracted in many years, was very dry. Following some very formal toasts, someone asked Grace when that bottle had last been opened. Grace replied, "Well, my husband Ed passed away in 1966. Cherry Herring was always our favorite after dinner drink." Ron was totally humbled. Grace had chosen the occasion some 30 years after Ed's death to reopen that bottle. She had given Ron a special moment to be forever remembered, just as she had done for so many others during her lifetime.

CASCADE MOUNTAIN
Height: 35th – 1,249 meters (4,098 feet)
By Gretel H. Schueller

"Peerless Placid has long been known as the 'Gem of the Adirondacks.' Many places offer as their natural attraction a single lake, bit of forest, or mountain. Some have two of these features. Placid has all three at their best," boasted Seneca Ray Stoddard in his 1907 edition of *The Adirondacks Illustrated*. There's no doubt that Stoddard's prolific guidebooks tempted throngs of tourists to venture into the mountain town and its surroundings.

Today, Stoddard's legacy is evident. In 2004, about 1.8 million people visited the Lake Placid area, according to the Lake Placid/Essex County Tourism Bureau. On a typical fall foliage weekend, some 7,000 cars roar into the Lake Placid area. Between Lake Placid and Keene Valley, many of them, like a long metallic ribbon, are parked along Route 73, and from them hikers flock to Cascade Mountain. In 1995, the number of visitors registered at the Cascade trailhead totaled 15,266. In recent years, the number has neared 20,000.

Cascade Mountain's first recorded ascent appears to have been by a trapper named Lon Pierce when he shot a bear caught in a trap on the summit in 1872. While bear sightings on Cascade's brow are now a rarity, the people following Pierce's path to the summit are anything but.

The road from Keene to Lake Placid along the Cascade Lakes is one of the most scenic stretches of highway in the Adirondacks. The scenery does not stop with the roadside vistas; it continues from the trailhead to Cascade (and Porter) by Upper Cascade Lake.

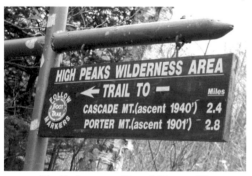

Trail sign on side of Route 73

Cascade Mountain is considered the easiest climb of the High Peaks, and in measure beyond the level of effort it requires, it offers an impressive 360-degree view. It is a 2.4-mile hike to the rock summit, which provides eye-widening views of the High Peaks area. Marcy, Haystack, Algonquin, Giant, and Lake Placid can all be seen. The Olympic ski jumps poke above the trees nearby, and if you venture to the northwest ledge, you can see Upper Cascade Lake below. The only drawback is Cascade's popularity. As one veteran climber scoffed, "Everybody does Cascade." According to the DEC, groups with as many as 300 hikers have been documented on its slopes. Nonetheless, it is a good initiation to the Adirondack Mountains.

If mountains had psychiatric disorders, Cascade would most likely be the victim of multiple personalities. Over the years, Cascade has carried numerous names and looks. Its former identity, Long Pond Mountain, most likely originated from the narrow stretch of waters now

CASCADE MOUNTAIN

Cascade as seen from Route 73

called Cascade Lakes. Earlier, the mountain held the more obscure moniker of Shining Peak. Physical modifications predate Cascade's name changes. The big slide on Cascade Mountain, which made two lakes of one, occurred long before the region was settled. In addition, the slide uncovered a few geologic treasures: notably, very large scapolite and hornblende crystals and blue calcite. In 1994, the family of Spencer Cram of Keene donated a sizeable collection of Adirondack material, including "gems" scapolite, and horneblende crystals from the Cascade Slide to the mineral collection of the New York State Museum in Albany.

From akermanite to wollastonite (an ingredient in billiard balls, electrical panels, and automotive parts), at least 11 minerals, some quite rare, are found on the Cascade Slide. It is a geologist's dream, a mineralogical delight, and the destination for dozens of geology field trips every year. Other minerals present include red garnet, forsterite, magnetite, quartz, and titanite. (Note that it is illegal to collect minerals on state land in the Adirondack Park.)

> At Edmonds' Ponds [Cascade Lakes] the primitive limestone has been bared by a slide on the Keene summit on the southeast side of the ponds. It lies in the upper part of the slide in a vein from twenty to forty feet in width.
> – *History of Essex County,* 1885, by H. P. Smith

The picnic day-use area between the two lakes is an ideal starting point for a geological journey into the past. Walk up to the remains of the dam at the base of Cascade Falls, and from there climb the gully to the east of the falls. Many of the rocks along the way are loose and the way is steep. Once you're above the falls, head west to the stream that supplies the waterfall. In the streambed, minuscule variations in crystalline structures hint at the sort of physical and chemical reactions that took place long ago. For example, xenoliths and streaks of marble surrounded by anorthosite are evidence of the enormous pressures – 7.4 kbar, enough to squeeze rocks into new ones – and searing temperatures of at least 750 degrees

Celsius that once existed here. Examinations of the minerals indicate that they must have formed underneath as much as 15 miles of overlying rock. The exact timing of the deep-earth cookery is still a matter of debate among geologists. However, there is general agreement that the rocks making up the Adirondack region are among the oldest on the planet, around one billion years old.

Cascade Mountain also reveals its birth on a larger scale. About 18,000 years ago, leviathan glaciers pummeled the mountain. A result of serious glacial scouring, Cascade boasts a cirque, a hollow depression that looks as if someone took an ice-cream scoop to the mountain's side. Cascade's two lakes also have glaciation to thank for the fault zone that now hold their 48 acres of water.

Once the glaciers melted away, lichen, mosses, ferns, and sedges were the first life forms to colonize the landscape. (In fact, the channel along Cascade Falls is still home to a fragile array of those early plants, including slender cliff-brake, berry bublet ferns, and Braun's fern.) Then the trees returned and, eventually, so did the people.

One of the first people to offer food and shelter to visitors in the region was Robert G. Scott. In 1850, he built what eventually became a well-known stopping-place on the Cascade Road. More elaborate lodgings soon followed. Cashing in on the allure of the secluded spot, the Cascade Lake House stood on the fill, or talus, of Cascade Slide, between the upper and lower lakes. Nicaner and Ellen Goff Miller built the initial portion of the hotel, a three-story, barn-like structure which accommodated 50 in 1878. Guests could fish, boat, hike, play tennis on an enclosed court, and bowl on the resort's alley. The Millers renamed the lakes after the falls that "cascaded" between them. The mountain joined the lakes, previously called Edmonds' Ponds (after a Keene family), and before that, Long Pond, in the rechristening. From the hotel, a steep path once rose to the summit of Cascade, but no evidence of it exists today. Robert Marshall described an attempt to retrace the trail in his 1922 pamphlet, "The High Peaks of the Adirondacks":

> There used to be a trail up this mountain from Cascade Lake but, like many other Adirondack trails shown on the map, it is no more. We followed the general course of the old trail but saw no trace of it. Lower down the going was very steep, and we had to crawl and pull ourselves along the rocks. Higher up this steepness largely disappeared, and a fire slash was substituted.[1]

In 1883, the Millers sold the lakeside hotel to W. F. Weston and J. H. Otis. Under the new management, "it became a roomy structure, remodeled and enlarged to three times its former capacity for the season of 1888," wrote Bryant F. Tolles Jr. in *Resort Hotels of the Adirondacks*.[2] The 150-guest structure even boasted its own post office, Cascadeville, albeit only seasonally. In the 1894 edition of his guide, Edwin Wallace provided a rave review:

> The mountain-hostel... is now an imposing edifice, possessing every modern appliance for comfort and elegance... the spacious parlor with its fine piano... massive and ornamental fireplaces. Pure running water is... from the rocky heights of the cascades. The waitresses are neat and rosy-cheeked country maidens. The hostelry is considerably patronized by artists and devotees of nature, who delight in the wild sublimity of the surrounding scenery.[3]

The Cascade Lake House served stagecoach travelers *en route* to Lake Placid. In its heyday, the hotel claimed the distinction, at 2,045 feet, of occupying one of the most elevated positions of any hotel in the Adirondack Mountains. After 1905, however, the hotel gradually declined under several owners. Eventually, in 1923, it – along with 1,440 acres of land, including the two lakes and two mountains – was sold to the Lake Placid Club. At summer's end in 1927, the hotel closed its doors for good. Blasting for the improved state road, Route

73, through Cascade Pass in the 1930s damaged the hotel, and it was soon thereafter torn down. In 1951, the club sold all of the property to the state. Today, all that remains of the Cascade Lake House are its foundation slabs.

The Mount Porter House also known as Watch Rock Hotel, west of Keene Valley between the Johns and Slide brooks, had a shorter life. That late-Victorian, four-story hotel existed only three years before fire damaged it, and on December 18, 1891, the building was torn down. Built by James Holt and the Hurley brothers, the hotel occupied a spectacular site at an elevation of 1,900 feet on the right side of today's Johns Brook Lane about a quarter mile from the Garden. According to guidebook publisher Charles Possons, that hotel could accommodate up to 150 people "in a modern manner."

Outdoor enthusiasts still stream to the area, and many of them climb Cascade up one of the most popular of the High Peaks trails. Despite its heavy use, however, Cascade's trail is in fine shape. It follows a route laid out in 1974 by the Algonquin Chapter of ADK to replace an old trail that was steep and badly eroded. At the trailhead, ferns and bunchberry abound. In summer, bladder campion, flowering raspberry, meadow rue, and cow vetch bloom in sunny spots along the lower reaches of the route. Trail crews have arranged rocks to make the ascent easy and to forestall the effects of erosion. The well maintained trail – one of the best examples of trail engineering in the Adirondacks – offers a moderate grade despite an elevation gain of 1,940 feet in only 2.4 miles. In memory of Landon "Rocky" Rockwell, who was an avid hiker and part-time resident of Keene Valley, the Rockwell Memorial Project is an annual Albany Chapter of the ADK day of trail maintenance on the Cascade trail. Volunteers work to clean out waterbars, build and install new ones, and harden the trail.

Marked with red trail disks, the trail follows a ridge line all the way from Route 73, with three short steep sections between gradual uphill sections. Paper birch are common at the beginning. As the trail nears the summit, spruce dominate. Near the rocky top, all trees, stunted, form patches of elfin woods. Cairns above the tree line and panoramic views of Pitchoff, Porter, Marcy, and other peaks mark the last push to the summit.

Even though the Cascade ridge is at a high elevation, no alpine vegetation has been documented on the mountain. Researchers suspect the reason: the effect of past fires. During the summer and fall of 1903, six hundred thousand acres of forest burned in the Adirondacks. Piles of dry logging slash, a 72-day drought, and high winds fueled fires which raged over Cascade, Porter, Mt. Van Hoevenberg, Big Slide, Dix, and on the north slopes of Mt. Marcy. Fall rains and moderating temperatures finally helped to extinguish them. The scenario repeated itself in 1908 and 1909, when an additional 300,000 acres burned. Prompted by the devastation, the state's forest fire detection and fire fighting force was enlarged and updated. Reform of lumbering practices, such as enactment of the "top lopping law" to reduce logging slash, also played a significant role in reducing the occurrence and spread of fires.

The 1903 fire's legacy on Cascade's slopes is evident in the abundance of paper birch, opportunists that moved in after old spruce and fir turned to char. Of course, fires were not the only culprit of tree clearing. To fuel the manufacture of charcoal iron, it is estimated that between 200,000 and 250,000 acres of Adirondack-Lake Champlain valley forests were cleared, according to Barbara McMartin in her book, *The Great Forest of the Adirondacks*.[4] To make a ton of iron required as much as five hundred bushels of charcoal; and maple, birch, and beech made the best charcoal. Charcoal kilns sprouted up across the North Country. Much of the forest around Cascade went to fuel the J. & J. Rogers Company's four forges in Jay.

An 1881 article in the *New York Times,* by "An Old Adirondacker," described the scene. The Cascade Pass, the author wrote, was once lined with "a most lovely and picturesque forest, filled with ferns and shrubbery, and presenting the muscular trunk of the beech, the white boil of the birch, the trembling poplar, the tall pine, regular spruce, and spreading hemlock." That landscape had become "a blackened mass of burned trees and scorched or shriveled shrubbery, desolate, grim, forbidding, with nothing but ashes and tangled black trunks and branches. The charm is all gone from the opening of this pretty pass. It appears that Mr. Weston, ex-member of the assembly from Keene, had opened some ironworks in the valley and must have some charcoal, and so desolated this whole region. The value of the 'stumpage,' it was estimated – that is, the whole return from this horrible destruction – was only $1 per acre to the owner."

Perhaps the forest is more resilient than we think. Ten years later, the same landscape appeared less ravaged. McMartin provides the account of a traveler to the Cascade Lakes in 1891:

> Similarly, along the road west from Keene there were reports of large areas "which have been cleared by charcoal burners, but which are rapidly recovering their growth. Beyond and west of Cascade Lake... are some abandoned charcoal kilns, and here everything was cut but now the land is covered with extensive second growth."[5]

Pitchoff

Crowds of hikers ascend Cascade, forgetting the shorter, gem-filled trip to Pitchoff, just on the other side of Route 73 from the main parking lot for Cascade. One group of outdoor enthusiasts, however, has recognized its allure: On just about any summer afternoon, rock climbers are sure to be clinging to the cliffs of Pitchoff.

In an essay in the anthology *Rooted in Rock,*[6] Alex Shoumatoff tells of "an old Indian," Henry Nolat, "who lived in a one-room shanty at the foot of Pitchoff until he died a few years ago. Nolat had long streaming hair and knew the mushrooms, and he used to go up on Pitchoff and cut the inner bark of black ashes into strips of bast that he wove into pack baskets, which is one of our indigenous Adirondack crafts."

Hiking Pitchoff is a lesson in divine detail, of using all five senses to explore its features – like the tiny waterfall, delicately trickling between moss-dappled rocks. One could easily miss it. Yet the waterfall, like the velveteen carpets of moss and ashy curls of bark that cling to yellow birch, remind us that even the grandest project depends on the success of the smallest parts. Each discovery moves you forward along the trail, unearthing more detail. The path of discovery is much like Pitchoff itself – not a straightforward mountain but a series of small, connected summits.

If you have two cars, you can also hike the full length of the roughly five-mile trail along Pitchoff's narrow ridge. Its two trailheads, 2.6 miles apart, are both on Route 73.

The western trailhead is directly opposite the trail to Cascade. The trail, marked by red disks, gains about 1,500 feet in elevation, most through a birch forest. The first overlook seems like a tempting diving board into Upper Cascade Lake below. This will be the first of many impressive rocky outcrops you will achieve as you climb. You'll be rewarded with great views in all directions: Cascade, Porter, Algonquin, Marcy, and Colden. Paper birches are the pioneers of a forest. In fact, they were the first hardwoods to return to the region about 9,000 years ago, after the retreat of the glaciers. They are sun lovers and are the first trees to appear in abandoned cropland or pastures – or in the case of Pitchoff, into forest openings made bare by extensive logging and fire. Keep your nose tuned to the occasional clump of sweet-smelling balsam. It's a big change from Robert Marshall's 1922 description of Pitchoff as "bare and burned."

Higher up, things shrink in an effort to shield themselves from trunk-snapping winds, snow packs, and other extreme tempers of North Country weather. A stunted, twisted forest of balsam-fir marks the final leg of the ascent.

About 1.6 miles from the western trailhead, you'll see the Balanced Rocks, a group of reddish boulders perched on rocky ledges. The boulder embellishments continue to the top. Two boulders positioned by a long-gone glacier are poised on the summit as well. Indeed, the mammoth slabs of rock perch precariously, as if dropped from the hand of some giant onto the open peak. In his *Indian Pass,* Alfred Street writes that "Big Pitch-off Mountain" derived its name from a "leaning rock of 500 feet at the northeast corner of its crest."[7]

There are many stories written in the stones of the area. Take, for example, the unusual carved rock along Route 73, overlooking Upper Cascade Lake. At one time, a stagecoach line ran through the pass to Lake Placid. During road maintenance in the 1930s, the crew found a large rock that had tumbled down the side of Pitchoff. They decided to keep the rock in a small drive-off area (on your right, past Upper Cascade Lake heading toward Lake Placid) and create a monument to those stagecoach days. Donald Roger, then a highway department district engineer, contacted Fred Carnes, owner of the Carnes Granite Company in Au Sable Forks. A plan was made: Lewis Brown of Chazy drew the sketch of a horse-drawn stagecoach; then Wilfred Carnes used the region's first portable sandblasting machine to carve it into the rock. Stagecoach Rock, as it is now known, is best seen when wet.

Owl's Head

In contrast to Cascade Mountain, Owl's Head is a quiet and rather gentle neighbor. As author Barbara McMartin puts it, "This is a small peak with big views."[8] Heading east on Route 73, about a mile past the Cascade Lakes, turn right onto Owl's Head Road. The trail starts on the corner, where the road swings sharply right, opposite a private sign; there is no trail sign. On a summer evening, songs from wood and hermit thrushes vibrate through the woods. Perhaps they are eagerly anticipating the generous harvests of blueberries that will soon be appearing. Despite its short length (just a little over a mile round trip) and proximity to the main road, the walk to the crest of Owl's Head easily ranks near the top for beautiful views that start quickly and keep going.

The trail ascends through forest, but soon the views begin. The first rock ledge looks east and south. As you continue, the forest thins and allows you peeks of mountains. Climb over boulders to more rocky ledges, all with panoramas. A moderate climb follows across bare rock. Within minutes, the trail winds around to the rocky summit of Owl's Head, with its full-circle vista.

Aside from easily-earned views, soothing bird songs, and blueberry treats, Owl's Head also offers the climber nearly a dozen finger and hand cracks of moderate difficulty. Intellectually challenging without causing muscular meltdown, it's a good place to reflect on tougher climbs while enjoying the backdrop of Hurricane and Cascade in the distance.

Overall, Cascade Mountain and its neighbors see a lot of climbers – of rock and ice. Here, the quintessential climbing routes of the Adirondacks are clustered. The north face of Pitchoff carries a generous collection of loosely connected slabs, including the especially popular roadside Chimney Cliff and the scenic Barkeater Cliff (perhaps after a presumed translation of *Adirondack* or the Barkeater Inn at the foot of the road). Chimney Cliff, with its easy access from Route 73 and abundance of moderate to difficult routes, draws many technical climbers. The multiple crack and face lines on the rock, conspicuously lichen-free, confirm that.

The slabs of Pitchoff, worn away by hands and feet, are made of a coarse-grained rock, foliated with twisting, alternating bands of light and dark. They remind hikers and climbers alike of the turbulent origins of these mountains. Called syenite gneiss, this rock was born of earth's most primal, powerful forces. From deep within its gut, the planet brandished pressure and heat that squeezed, buckled, warped, and reformed the stone into new shapes with new chemistry.

Cascade Pass and the Cascade Lakes

In the winter, claim veteran ice climbers, Cascade Pass is one of the most accessible spots in the East. That's when those geologically grand slopes above the Cascade Lakes drip with ice and entice bearers of ice picks and crampons. In 1997, the waters bore witness to another violent force; that one, however, was not geologic. On August 19, 1997, Jeanine Glanda was found dead in her Ford Explorer at the bottom of Upper Cascade Lake. Her estranged husband, former Lake Placid resident Jeffrey Glanda, was eventually convicted of the murder-for-hire killing and sentenced to two life terms in prison without parole. The motive: money, in the form of three life insurance policies. Glanda is currently incarcerated at Attica Correctional Facility. "He will leave prison in a box," Essex County District Attorney Ronald Briggs told the Ottoway News Service.

Today, wedged within a narrow valley, the two lakes belie little of the past. Their tranquil surfaces reflect mirror images of the tamarack, white pine, and sugar maples lining their shores. Lower Cascade Lake – long, narrow, and relatively shallow – connects by a small brook to Upper Cascade – round and deep.

The waters were once the source of plenty of big fish stories, such as this one reported in 1906 in the *New York Times*. Professor Myron R. Van Ness, principal of Lake Placid High School, and his wife went fishing one June day:

> …but Mrs. Van Ness could not land the fish nibbling at her hook. Finally she got an excellent bite. When she tried to reel in, however, the fish fought furiously. The professor went to her assistance, and after a long fight they managed to tire the fish out. He floated to the surface and they got a glimpse of a lake trout fully two feet long… Giving a gasp as if in a death struggle, the big fish opened his mouth and out popped a smaller one, limp and nearly dead, but with the hook firmly in its jaws. With a disgusted swish of the tail, the big fish turned and sank beneath the surface.

However, the lakes no longer boast the biological riches they once did. The state's largest population of the round whitefish *(Prosopium cylindraceum)*, neither white nor round, makes its home in the lakes. Signs posted at the lakes warn anglers of the presence of the endangered native. Round whitefish, one of the original inhabitants of the cold North Country waters after the last glaciers melted, currently survive in only six other lakes. In 1906, in contrast, the silvery-bronze, oval-shaped fish swam in the waters of 68 lakes. Known as "frostfish," they were historically widespread in the Adirondacks. Acid rain and competition from nonnative species, such as yellow perch and smallmouth bass, are the main reasons for their decline.

As a result, Upper and Lower Cascade Lakes are the focus of an ongoing study. "There has long been concern about environmental implications of heavy road salt and sand applications in the Cascade Lakes watershed," explained Clarkson University Professor of Biology Tom Langen. "However, winter weather is exceptionally severe along this stretch of highway, and local residents and other road users are justifiably concerned that any changes in winter road management not reduce road safety."[9]

Road salt seeps into soil and water. At high concentrations it stresses plants and animals – as evidenced by heavy die-backs of white birch, scotch and white pine trees between the road and the lakes. During a sampling, Langen and his team found concentrations of sodium chloride in the lakes that are 100 times higher than non-roadside Adirondack waters, and the concentrations appear to be increasing. The team's goal is to evaluate whether current winter maintenance practices are causing long-term damage and whether alternative methods of snow removal might be more appropriate.

When surveyed in 1951, Upper Cascade Lake was home to round whitefish, brown trout, lake trout, brook trout, white sucker, pumpkinseed, lake chub, creek chub, and common shiner; but in 1984, another survey found only one round whitefish, along with brown trout, splake, brook trout, white sucker, lake chub, and golden shiner (nonnative). A year later, fearing that splake were preying on the endangered species, stocking came to an end. Brook trout stocking, however, continues in both lakes.

Left over from stocking efforts by the Lake Placid Club before 1951, brown trout nose about in Lower Cascade Lake, reproducing naturally. Round whitefish are also faring better in Lower Cascade Lake. In 1970, due to the healthy levels of round whitefish surveyed, about 10,000 eggs were transferred to the Brandon Hatchery. Fry from those eggs were stocked into Cat Pond on the Rockefeller estate in Franklin County. (Those fish survive in Cat Pond.) The following year marked another successful collection of eggs. Trap netting of spawning fish in 1992 established that the species is thriving in Lower Cascade Lake.

One of Cascade's non-aquatic natives is making a rebound as well. The northern raven, which had not been common in the Adirondacks since the 1800s, now actively nest on cliffs near Upper Cascade Lake. Look up and you might just see them, soaring over the valleys.

Endnotes

1. Robert Marshall, "The High Peaks of the Adirondacks," (Adirondack Mountain Club, 1922), pg. 35.

2. Bryant F. Tolles Jr., *Resort Hotels of the Adirondacks*, (University Press of New England, 2003), pg. 172.

3. Edwin Wallace, *Descriptive Guide to the Adirondacks,* published by the author, 1884, pages 319-320.

4. Barbara McMartin, *The Great Forest of the Adirondacks*, (Utica: North Country Books, 1994), pg. 36.

5. *Ibid.,* pg. 37.

6. *Rooted in Rock, New Adirondack Writing: 1975-2000,* Jim Gould, editor, (Syracuse University Press, 2001), pg. 344.

7. Alfred Billings Street, *The Indian Pass, Source of the Hudson,* (Riverside Press, 1869), page xviii.

8. Barbara McMartin, *50 Hikes in the Adirondacks: Short Walks, Day Trips, and Backpacks Throughout the Park,* 4th edition, (Countryman Press, 2003), pg. 172.

9. Tom Langen interview, personal communication.

PORTER MOUNTAIN
Height: 38th – 1,240c meters (4,068+ feet)
By Gretel H. Schueller

Porter is the under-appreciated stepchild of the 46 Adirondack High Peaks. Hikers looking for an easy climb typically turn to Cascade Mountain – occasionally adding Porter only as an afterthought. Most diehards prefer the revered, more distinguished elevations of Marcy or Algonquin.

Recent hiker entries at the DEC Cascade trailhead register attest:

"Views were nice, but the summit is not as open as Cascade. Would definitely suggest bagging both while you're up there."

"A bit disappointing after hitting Cascade a few minutes earlier. My advice is do Porter first, and then Cascade."

"The only thing that makes this summit worth the time is that is counts as one of the 46 High Peaks. Mostly tree covered with a few views toward Cascade."

Nevertheless, hiking Porter is a better alternative to the anthill that Cascade usually turns into late in the day. On a September afternoon in 2002, for example, more than 70 groups had registered at Cascade, and people were still streaming to its summit.

Those who choose to travel the path less traveled are up for some rewards. The summit of Porter is little more than a narrow, bedrock ledge, but hikers enjoy greater solitude there and look over at the crowds on Cascade. They also have impressive views from the top, even though Porter is not bald. Granted, the vista is more limited by trees, compared to that of Cascade, but a peek of the 5,344-foot Mount Marcy more than compensates. The trip up offers several treats too, including some nice meadows and evidence of the 1903 fire. Porter also has one of the longer summit ridges of the 46: about two thousand meters long and only a few meters wide in places. Its long ridge stretches from near Keene Valley almost to Cascade Pass, with numerous humps and bumps along it.

Originally called West Mountain, because it shoots up in the west of the valley between Keene and Keene Valley, the mountain was renamed in honor of Dr. Noah Porter after he made the first recorded ascent of the peak with guide Ed Phelps (son of Old Mountain Phelps) in the summer of 1875. Because there was no trail, Porter, a Keene summer resident, paid Phelps to mark a route and that inspired a suggestion that the mountain's name be changed. According to Russell M. L. Carson, author of *Peaks and People of the Adirondacks,* Porter's "popularity in Keene Valley was such that there was no opposition, and the name was quickly adopted."[1]

Noah Porter

Porter, whose first visit to the Keene area was in 1872 or 1873, was the 11th president of Yale University (1871-86). The Connecticut-native was also an early and vocal spokesperson for the preservation of the Keene Valley area. Carson said, "Those who knew Dr. Porter recall him as a good woodsman and an untiring walker and oarsman."[2]

In his book, *A History of the Adirondacks*, Alfred L. Donaldson describes one of the doctor's last outings in the mountains. "His favorite lake was the Upper Ausable, and when his waning strength warned him that he had camped upon its shore for the last time, he asked his guide, Melville Trumbull, to row him around it on a farewell tour. Pausing here and there to glimpse some well-loved vista, the doctor sat in silent contemplation, while the tears welled in his eyes. The old guide said it was the saddest thing he ever saw."[3]

Fire and lumbering destroyed the trail that Ed Phelps cut on Porter in 1875, but today three trails lead the way to its summit. The most trafficked and the shortest is the connector via the Cascade trailhead. The two other routes leave from the Keene Valley side. One, passing through a large stand of beech trees, ascends from the parking lot known as the Garden. That route, which goes over Little Porter, has the most moderate grade, but parking near the trailhead can be difficult. The third trail ranks as the best – and often tastiest. With access to it from the Keene Valley Airport via the Ridge Trail, it is the longest and steepest route to Porter's peak, but it is also the most rewarding – especially in late August if ripe berries are your wish. The hike to the summit of Porter crosses the aptly named Blueberry Mountain, passes through spruce forests, mounts steeply at a ravine, and continues along a beautiful ridge with easy grades before finally passing two fine ledge lookouts a short distance from the summit.

Blueberry Mountain alone is a worthwhile hike, about five miles round trip. The trip to Porter via Blueberry, while steep in spots, is a must-do for anyone who likes solitude. A combination of brooks, open areas, flat rock climbing, and beautiful foliage along the way provides much to see and experience in a single trip. Nailed to the occasional tree are round yellow Department of Environmental Conservation disks that show the way. The markers are particularly helpful in autumn, when the path is blanketed with leaves and sometimes difficult to discern. The Schenectady Chapter of the ADK maintains the trail as well as the one to Porter from the Garden via Little Porter.

From the airport the grade is moderate at first as the trail winds around hills and moves through lumbered woods until a brook crossing at 1.2 miles. The grassy glades in that area are a legacy of the devastating 1903 fire, which sparked near Lake Placid – most likely from a train. It was a bad year for trees overall: 643 forest fires ravaged more than 464,000 acres of land in the Adirondacks and Catskills. Dry weather and high winds fanned the flames. Gusting winds carried sparks to other locations before fire fighters could extinguish the original fires. For seven weeks, from April 20 to June 8, the infernos burned. The Forest, Fish, and Game Commission estimated the value of the timber destroyed in the 1903 Adirondack fires at $669,000.[4]

Almost two decades after the fires, much of the damage was still apparent. Robert Marshall in his 1922 pamphlet "The High Peaks of the Adirondacks" described his hike along the route to Porter: "Fire had burned up most of the slash, which helped make the going easy... The view was much like that from Cascade, but even slashier. It was rather sickening to see the burned land on all sides."[5]

Time has healed the damage. For the next half mile, the trail turns steep and rocky. The reward is several open ledges, which provide good views of Keene Valley and Hurricane. The path takes hikers past granite boulders topped with velvet carpets of moss, reminders that the region is one of unique and varied geology. The bedrock that makes up the Adirondacks belongs to the Grenville Province, a vast stretch of rock that reaches into much of eastern Canada, born from material about a billion years old. The mountains themselves, however, were not formed until ten million years ago – so recent in geologic terms that Porter, along with the rest of the Adirondacks, is still increasing in elevation.

Alternating between flat and steep sections, the trail arrives (after a 1,900-foot ascent) at the summit of Blueberry Mountain. The broad western summit (3,050 feet) is open, except for a large boulder. The glaciers that carved the Adirondacks' distinctive topography covered the area 18,000 years ago. The boulder, known as a glacial erratic, is evidence of those earth-moving mammoths of ice. With the glaciers long gone, the views are now of Giant and Hurricane mountains. The panorama and the solitude here tend to encourage hikers to linger at the top.

Another 2.1 miles will take you to the summit of Porter – and through spruce forest. The going soon gets steep, but arriving at the ridge, the trail grows easier and continues through groves of gnarled spruce and lichen-covered granite to a point just shy of the summit. On the top, you immediately forget what it took to get there in the first place.

ADK member Fred Schroeder (#1114) recalls a recent fall hike up Porter via Blueberry:

> It has one of the prettiest ascent trails, thanks to the Schenectady Chapter, with its constantly changing aspect of mature, adolescent, and pubescent woods, with an occasional stream and half-point view thrown in. Then the top, although slightly wooded, has this magnificent panoramic view of just about anything worth seeing in the high peaks. On this day, the colors were just emerging except in the valleys that showed deep red. The descent was something else – challenging as we picked our way down the precipitous route to Blueberry and then rewarded by that magical open plateau with its stunning views of Keene Valley. It was a long exhausting trip for some of us but worth it.[6]

Autumn, may in fact, be Porter's best time: the voracious black flies and mosquitoes are gone, the humidity is low, the crisp air offers views that can extend for miles, and the foliage, of course, is spectacular. Maples, beech, and birches burst in a kaleidoscope of scarlet and gold, in quiet contrast to the verdure of spruce and fir.

Endnotes

1. Russell M. L. Carson, *Peaks and People of the Adirondacks,* (Doubleday, Doran & Company, Inc., 1928), pgs. 184-185.

2. *Ibid.,* pg. 185.

3. Alfred L. Donaldson, *A History of the Adirondacks,* (The Century Company, 1921), Vol. II, pg. 46.

4. Taking into account a century's worth of inflation, the timber destroyed by today's reckoning would have been valued in excess of $100,000,000.

5. Robert Marshall "The High Peaks of the Adirondacks," (Adirondack Mountain Club, 1922), pg. 36.

6. *Cloudsplitter,* Vol. 68, No. 1 (January-February 2005). The hike mentioned was accomplished in September 2004.

About the Author

Journalist Gretel H. Schueller writes about science and the environment. Her articles have appeared in such magazines as *Audubon, Discover, Hooked on the Outdoors, National Wildlife, New Scientist, Popular Science,* and *SKI* – and her writing has taken her from the North Slope of Alaska to Midway Atoll in the Pacific Ocean. Before becoming a freelancer, she held editorial positions at several national magazines, including *Audubon.* She has written two children's books about science. Currently, she is working on a book about food and the gods of Greece. She also teaches journalism at the State University of New York in Plattsburgh. One of these days she hopes to hike all 46 peaks. She lives in Essex, New York.

GIANT
Height: 12th – 1,410 meters (4,626 feet)
By Chuck Gibson (#251)

Giant is a mountain of superlatives. "Massive" and "sprawling," according to Laura and Guy Waterman,[1] Giant boasts the High Peaks' earliest ascent, its highest waterfall, its most storied slides, some of its most spectacular trails, and the area's first retreat for intellectuals. A summer morning spent ascending the palisades of stone known as the Giant Ridge Trail, with its ever expanding views, delivers a shot of heaven up-h'isted-ness that ranks with the best.

In fact, the Giant Ridge Trail is one of the more recent of Giant's paths, constructed in nine days by Jim Goodwin and two colleagues in 1955. The route connected two trails already in place: the one up the Nubble and the trail from Roaring Brook Falls. The Ridge Trail has since been renamed the Zander Scott Trail in memory of Alexander Scott, an Adirondack Trail Improvement Society (ATIS) counselor and trail crew member who was killed in a plane crash in Alaska shortly after his graduation from Princeton University in 1992. The trail, which ascends Giant from Route 73, has become the most popular route up Giant. It is also the shortest in terms of mileage and ascent.

A day on the Zander Scott Trail begins in the shadowy fastness of the Chapel Pond Pass. There you are hemmed in by a glorious array of cliffs well known to rock climbers, their belaying calls often hanging in the morning air. The cliffs have also been historically hospitable to peregrine falcons; however, no nests of those raptors have been discovered on the cliffs since 1998.

The trail ascends steeply until it reaches its first outlook on a cliff top which looms over the inky splotch of Chapel Pond far below. Round Mountain shows off its rock-rent though denominating shape and the Lower Range heaves into view as well. Transfixed, you pause at the outlook to let the view soak in before, reluctantly, returning to the trail. And then, always surprising, quickly, Giant's Washbowl appears.

Verplanck Colvin made a special trip to the Washbowl on October 8, 1875, to check out the unique spot. He, like you, first toiled up that steep slope... "sufficiently dangerous to be exciting"... until reaching the cliff top view mentioned already. "From this advantageous though dangerous position," he wrote, "we could look down upon the lake that we had left *[Chapel Pond]* and the gray cliffs which descended vertically to the black waters."

Continuing, Colvin crossed "a peculiar ridge densely wooded with evergreens" and in another instant "stood on the rocky shores of a beautiful lake of clear blue water nestled amid the upper ridges of this grand old mountain, the veritable Giant's Basin, or wash-bowl, as the guide preferred to call it."

Colvin found the pond's odd outlet at its south end: "a dry channel, elevated a few feet above the water level of the lake, while stretched across it here and there were green, mouldy logs, high and dry, as left by some ancient freshet." In other words, he had found it an outlet for the Washbowl only in times of high water. Its real outlet may well be hidden, beneath the pond's surface. At the other (north) end "a small springy bog was stamped into mire by the deer, which evidently found this an undisturbed retreat."

Undisturbed no more, the Washbowl usually echoes to voices and now, to keep up with modernity, even boasts its own climbing wall: Banana Belt. Colvin, before returning to Keene Valley by dark, lingered at the Washbowl and measured its length to be precisely 781.29 feet. He had already climbed Giant, two years before via Hopkins.

Harold Weston remembered catching ten-inch speckled trout in the pond in 1915 but lamented that "soon the Washbowl may become nothing more than a frog hole as grasses and weeds encroach from each end." It is not now a particularly robust body of water. The Giant Mountain Unit Management Plan figures its area at 4.2 acres and its maximum depth to be 23 feet. Geologically it is known as a kettle pond, formed by a huge block of ice a few thousand years ago. It supports a few brook (speckled) trout.

The back cover of Weston's book, *Freedom in the Wilderness,* has an interesting tale about a trip to the Washbowl taken in the winter of 1921. After eating lunch at "an old lean-to there," Weston decided "to try a short cut down the steep slopes of Chapel Pond Cliffs where the soft snow had blown off and most of the surface was iced over." A photo shows Chapel Pond far below, through burned trees (from the fire of 1913) and, on the ice, a dark spot is discernible where men were cutting ice and transferring it to a horse-drawn sledge. Those men later told Weston that when they saw and heard a dark object moving down the cliffs, they assumed it was a bear come out of hibernation. No one hiked in the winter then.

From the Washbowl, the trail begins an ever-steepening ascent to a series of ledges. Along the way, above the Nubble junction, is a section of trail improved during the summers of 2005, 2006, and 2007 by ATIS and ADK crews that worked under contract for the ATIS. Switchbacks and steps have replaced the old, rough, eroded trail, and drainage ditches have been installed to prevent most erosion.[2] Once on the ledges, expansive views open up. Noonmark pokes over Round, and the whole Range cuts a skyline to the south. The slot of Hunters Pass soon becomes entirely visible – reminding Barbara McMartin[3] of a "gunsight" – and a mysterious pond appears to the south. It is Twin Pond, companion to Round Pond, passed on the way to Dix. You now gaze down to the Washbowl as before you gazed down to Chapel Pond. *Déjà* view.

Before the 1903 fire destroyed it, a short-lived trail emerged onto the ledges after having ascended them from the valley to the north. In that valley, between Giant and Rocky Peak Ridge, the trail had famously negotiated a flume by means of ramps and ladders and passed by the Dipper, Giant's only other body of water.

Two major fires ravaged Giant – in 1903 and 1913. The 1903 fire, coming from the south, burned all of Rocky Peak Ridge and swept over the south shoulder of Giant. The 1913 fire laid siege to the same area and threatened to finish the job. Weston recalled viewing that blaze from a site near Chapel Pond, the heat being too intense to reach the pond itself. "Shrouds of smoke darkened the sky, increasing the dramatic effect of the light from the flames on the cliffs above the pond. Some trees were breaking off and falling to plummet down into the water... It seemed like a scene from Dante's *Inferno.*" Back in St. Huberts, Weston's mother was "assembling a few cherished possessions in a small steamer trunk" and the leaders of the Ausable Club were planning evacuation. Meanwhile, a contingent of Plattsburgh soldiers, called in by President Wilson, had cut a fire line up Giant and along

Giant as it appeared from Rocky Peak's fire-scarred summit in the 1930s

the summit ridge. The line held, rain fell, and most of the west side of Giant was saved. The Ridge Trail actually traverses the northern limit of the flames. It was no wonder that no one had built a trail along it earlier, before birch had applied their beneficent and healing touch to the terrain. On the slab of Giant's summit rock, a reminder of the effort to stem the fire remains, but it is fading with the passing years. Look for it and you will find, carved into the stone, the graffiti of the soldiers who cut the fire line: "Co. B. 3 Infantry."

Much of the forest, including even the soil, had been burned down to bare rock. By the beginning of the 46er era, in the early 1920s, the damage definitely diminished the attraction of both Giant and Rocky Peak Ridge. "Were this view (from Giant's summit)," Robert Marshall wrote, "unmarred by fire scars, there could not be a more beautiful one."

Tony Goodwin argues, "Today the views are among the finest – in part *because* of the very same fire. With the blackened stumps gone and the valleys now a lush green, the many remaining open ledges provide an annual show of colors. Such is the irony of natural forces that what may seem disastrous in one era can seem more beautiful perhaps than the original in another."

The Zander Scott Trail reaches a junction with the Roaring Brook Trail at about 3,900 feet in elevation. The latter trail is much older, cut around 1874 by Orlando Beede, whose father built the Beede Heights Hotel, precursor to the Ausable Clubhouse. That trail could therefore be considered a trail cut for the tourist trade. Incredibly, it was a bridle path. Horses and their riders were able to go as far as a spring 350 vertical feet below Giant's summit, within easy striking distance of the top on foot. The current Roaring Brook Trail's switchbacks along its way to the top of Roaring Brook Falls are reminders of this amazing history. It is probably safe to say that no horse could make it now.

The falls are one of the Adirondacks' highest and *the* highest in the High Peaks. They remain a jaw-dropping sight for car-bound tourists below on Route 73. Two separate drops contribute to the effect. Overall height estimates in the nineteenth century ranged widely from 200 feet (Seneca Ray Stoddard)[4] to 400 feet (Wallace Bruce).[5] The current figure comes in at about 325 feet, only 25 feet lower than T Lake Falls,[6] considered the Adirondacks' tallest. Whatever the height, the last word belongs to Stoddard: "It isn't much besides spray when it reaches the bottom."

Geologically, the falls are an indication of a "hanging valley," so called because the cataract "hangs" over a valley, in this case Keene Valley. The bowl-like valley above the falls is called a glacial cirque and actually held a glacier up until a few thousand years ago. The vicinity of the falls is much enhanced by groves of old-growth hemlock with trees dating back to the sixteenth century. The overall effect today from Route 73 is not much different from Stoddard's day, when he noted the falls as "a thread of silver as seen in glimpses through the trees."

The rock wall behind the falls was considerably widened and scoured by the events of June 29, 1963. Near the end of a hot and muggy afternoon, a deluge hit the slopes of Giant, with possibly as much as six inches falling near Giant's summit. That downpour on the mountain created a layer of lubrication between smooth slabs of bedrock and saturated soil. Suddenly huge sections of earth, rocks, and trees began to slip. The slides converged in the streambed above the falls and slid down more, damming and bursting and picking up steam. The slurry ran over the falls and buried a number of cars on the road below. Miraculously, no one was hurt, but, before the cars could be dug out the next day, some of the people who had been in them had to be rescued.

Nancy Lee, who has a camp near the base of the falls, tells of her house starting to shake. When she ran out with her husband, Day, she saw a surge of muddy water swiftly swirling through her trees, soon depositing five feet of silt on her driveway. What had been Route 73 was suddenly a roaring river, filled with huge boulders and peeled logs. There was "a sickly sweetish smell of stripped logs as at a sawmill." Day, donning waders, was the first to reach the marooned cars. The first thing he noticed was a Volkswagen jammed with a family of five, all hoping the extra weight would keep the car from sliding into the river. While Day watched, the car next to the Volkswagen slid into the river.

That night, the Lees hosted eighteen people in their home. Some were to become lifelong friends.[7]

Nancy's daughter, Pamela Cranston, a poet, writes of that day: "We never know when the Brown River of big moments will come crashing upon us. Life wields the harrower's blade when we least expect it – forcing us to grow or die standing still."

The next day things looked better: "Our small band of survivors huddled together, dried our sodden clothes by the stoked fire, and told our stories over and over: how the beer in the ice chest was found, the wire spectacles surfaced, all unscathed. Dazed but grateful to be alive, we partied into the night, turning our fear into festival."[8]

Far above the human drama, the falls was facing its own crisis. It had slowed to a trickle. Upstream, Roaring Brook had breached a small ridge and escaped into the next watershed north, Putnam Brook. Two New York State rangers, John Hickey and Bill Petty, decided to restore the flow of the falls, and a crew of four men, working for ten days, constructed a series of log cribs to block the stream's escape and guide it back into its historic bed. Fortunately, their rescue mission was a success. The log cribs are still visible a little above the spot where the present Roaring Brook Trail crosses its namesake stream. However, a lean-to which had been built by Camp Dudley near the brink of the falls on the right bank of the brook had been destroyed when the mountain washed over it. It was not replaced.

The slides that were scoured that late June day in 1963 markedly altered the west face of Giant. Created were six new ones: the Bottle, the Question Mark, Diagonal, Eagle, Finger, and Tulip. They were quickly named and soon climbed. The Bottle was scaled on July 13, by the first group to venture to the mountain after the slides were created. One of the members of that group, boys from Camp Pok-O-Moonshine, remembers the "sickly sweetish smell" as well and recalls that the mountain had been closed to climbers during the two-week period following the deluge. "There wasn't," he says, "a living thing anywhere along the brook below the point where we crossed over to the new Bottle slide. All was rock – light gray in color, almost white – boulders, gravels, sands, and broken, twisted and denuded timber."

William James

Putnam Brook, which briefly burgeoned with the waters of the Roaring Brook, figures into the story of Giant as well. Near the end of it, at the base of the mountain, the well known Putnam Camp was created in 1875. Four men – among them most famously the philosopher William James – decided to purchase land there from Smith Beede, whose son Orlando had constructed the Roaring Brook Trail a year earlier. They constructed a cabin, called the Shanty, which served them until the following year, when they purchased Beede's farmhouse and some additional land. Putnam Camp today still includes Beede's farmhouse, its focal point, and other buildings that were built over the years. One of them, the Stoop, features walls that literally open up to magnificent views. Putnam Camp, one of the great Adirondack institutions, welcomed intellectuals to Keene Valley.

The camp's Adirondack precursor would have to have been the Philosophers Camp, convened by Ralph Waldo Emerson at Follensby Pond in 1858. Sharp Swan writes about that experiment in backwoods living in his chapter of this book about the Seward Range. Richard Plunz, Keene Valley historian, writes that Putnam Camp should be considered "the logical successor to the ideals that Emerson and *[William]* Stillman had imbued in the Philosophers Camp experience, tempered by the intervening decades of enormous cultural change in both the cities and Adirondacks alike."

In fact, Putnam Camp, with its simplicity combined with intellectual rigor, could be said to hearken all the way back to Henry David Thoreau's cabin on Walden Pond at Concord, Massachusetts. Remarkably, too, Emerson's son, Edward, was a frequent visitor at Putnam Camp. However, as a second generation of Transcendentalism jumped New Hampshire and Vermont and settled at the foot of Giant, a strain of whimsy was introduced. For example, Emerson is well remembered for constructing – out of such flotsam as tin cans and stovepipe – a suit of armor that still stands in the dining room.

Other famous visitors included Sigmund Freud and Carl Jung in September 1909. They had been invited by James Putnam, one of the original owners, after Freud lectured in Massachusetts. Freud was entranced by this New World curiosity and enjoyed especially discovering a porcupine (dead), an animal he had longed to see for some time. That desire had perhaps been prompted by Schopenhauer's notion that porcupines were constantly congregating (for warmth) and likewise separating (in pain) until an equilibrium was reached. Freud saw this as a metaphor for human interaction and, since there were no porcupines in Europe, he had been anxious to see one. Meanwhile... Jung climbed Haystack.[9]

Freud and Jung, 1909

The relationship of another original camp owner, William James, with the Adirondacks was a profound one. He honeymooned at Putnam Camp in 1878 but sold his interest in the camp in 1880 as he gravitated more towards Glenmore, another intellectual retreat which was organized in 1879 near Hurricane at the other end of the valley. However, James returned often to Putnam Camp for many years. He could not interest his novelist brother Henry in Keene Valley, and their sister Alice dismissed this "bosom of nature" as "just about as much of a humbug as I always knew it was."[10]

William James, founder of American psychology and, perhaps, America's greatest philosopher, was well aware of the "peculiar sources of joy" to be found in tramping the Adirondacks. In a letter he described his sensory longing, "the smell of the spruce, the feel of the moss, the sound of the cataract, the bath in its waters, the divine outlook from the cliff or hill-top over the unbroken forest." Perhaps no other well known American before Bob Marshall so well understood that strange euphoria familiar to 46ers: "Mountain climbing itself – its sheer exhilarations, the conquest of summits and the outlook from great heights – had for him its thrilling appeal."

Putnam Camp certainly encouraged a rarified intellectual atmosphere. One frequent visitor was Felix Adler, founder of the Ethical Cultural Society as well as the ATIS. His daughter recalled, "As a small girl I remember finding the long philosophical dialogues that my father and Professor James would enter into on mountain climbs very tedious. Halfway up a steep spruce slope under the summit of Giant, we children would have to take off our rucksacks, sit down patiently, and wait while the two elders would discuss at length the 'ego and the me' or the categorical imperatives of Kant: bees buzzed around us, and blueberries and the distant rocky top, the realities of life as we conceived them, beckoned us. My father would stand on the trail stroking his beard as he worked at some difficult thought, and James would state, 'Ah, Adler, I believe I have you there.'"[11]

The voluminous Putnam Camp logbooks provide fascinating reading. A reader, opening one of them practically at random, can be transported back to episodes such as this about a night ascent in July 1912:

> All ready for Giant, looking in the light of the candles which they carried like a procession of spooks, the long file left the camp and wound its way up the mountain. The night was damp and still. Every now and then a drop of water fell from the green leaves above to the dry leaves below, and the agile toad could be heard leaping out of danger. Before long we discovered that night besides being damp and still, was hot as well. By the time we crossed the brook all sweaters were off and most tongues were out. Here the going became worse. Shouts of "root," "rock," "high step," "log on right," etc. rent the darkness. At half-way rock most of the party rested but Barbara, who had to be down by six, kept on, escorted by the Doormouse [sic].

In such fanciful activities did the Putnam Campers push the hiking envelope almost a century ago.

The very first trail on Giant was constructed by the venerable Old Mountain Phelps from Keene Valley by way of Hopkins in 1866. You can still get a sense of the trail by parking at the new Rooster Comb lot and ascending the Ranney Trail to Hopkins and continuing on to Giant. Such an excursion makes for a long day, but, as a direct route from Keene Valley, it is sensible and scenic. Named for Erastus Hopkins[12] – a Presbyterian minister who held a pulpit in Troy and, later, a Massachusetts legislator – Hopkins is an excellent destination by itself.

The same general route, via Hopkins, was used by Colvin on August 13, 1873, as he made his first ascent of Giant. His party reached the summit of Hopkins at 12:30 in the afternoon, and Colvin later wrote, "The dark evergreen forest crowding itself for standing room upon the precipitous sides of the well-named Giant Mt. behind us – the peaceful snowy clouds and azure sky above – afford a contrast which made the view from this point extremely beautiful." The view is still beautiful and, arguably, because of the intimate beeline view up the Ausable Lakes valley, for example, Giant's equal or better.

Colvin finished his altitude measurements on Hopkins by 3:30 and continued to toil upward toward the big one. Apparently Phelps' trail, cut out seven years earlier, had not received much traffic. Colvin and his men found the going between the two peaks very difficult: "Windfalls of timber, dense thickets, descents and ascents along a broken ridge rendered progress slow, especially of the guide carrying the theodolite[13] packed in a box upon his back."

Reaching the summit of Giant at 7 p.m., Colvin described the somewhat desolate view, no doubt filtered through his realization that daylight was fading quickly: "At our feet, cliffs a thousand feet in height fell away to a gray map-like picture, as chill and silent as a world deserted and left vacant. The sun left some crimson streaks upon the western clouds – only sufficient to make more mournful the somberness of the rest – the multitude of peaks seemed a myriad of gray domes and ridges, sunk together in one common slumber to last forever."

Old Mountain Phelps, about the same time (1873), described the summit as "covered with scrub balsam 10 to 15 feet high so the view has to be taken where there are openings." His description and that of Colvin make it clear that Giant has always had views, but, five years later, Colvin ordered some men to go back to the summit and clear the crest for a signal tower. That work created the mostly open top we know today.

Colvin's description touches on a peculiar feature of Giant. The prospect from it instills a pervasive sense of removal from the central mass of the High Peaks. Although 38 of the 46 peaks may be seen from Giant (second only to Marcy in that respect), most of them as seen from Giant seem to rise upon a distant horizon. Bob Marshall thus described the view as being "of the same type as the Whiteface one," and he went on to explain that "there is a very good general view of the great ranges to the west. But they are too far off for their individual merits to stand out." You gaze out from Giant with almost the feeling that you are approaching the High Peaks proper within an airplane. Orientation here is entirely westward, but by wading through some very earthbound krummholz, you find views to the east towards the Champlain lowlands and Vermont.

Phelps agreed with this general assessment. He rapturously described the view from Giant westward (even having the mountains speak for themselves à la Street), but he dismissed the view eastward as "lumbered over and mostly burned, which gives it a desolate look." The connection between logged and burned lands was not coincidental. Logging led to burning. A 1916 map showed that while roughly fifty percent of the Giant Mountain Wilderness had been logged by that time, only one percent of the logged area had escaped fire.

Colvin, meanwhile, found himself, not uncharacteristically, on a mountaintop at dusk. Scorning the advice of his long-suffering guides, he began a descent:

> Off the trail – in darkness – descending cliffs – across holes and chasms – on dead fallen limbs – feeling, not seeing, we made our way down to water, a narrow swift rill shooting down over the rocks and precipices. Refreshed and invigorated by water – cold and pure – the only drink which the Creator, in his wisdom, has provided for man and beast – we resolved to continue the descent; and hideous hours passed away as we crept down amid dangers which we often suddenly felt when it was almost too late…

Such suffering was second nature to Colvin, and only four nights later he instigated a similar dangerous descent from Dix, "rendering the previous night-descent of Giant inferior in danger." Furthermore, unlike the escape from the summit of Dix, during which Colvin and his men spent the night halfway down on a cliff top, his descent of Giant proved successful. The party reached Keene Flats (Keene Valley) at midnight.

Climbing Giant can actually feel like ascending towards the moon. The Ridge Trail climbs 3,000 feet in 2.9 miles, the equivalent, for example, of doing Poke-O-Moonshine three times. There is a sense of a giant stone stairway to the stars, a petrified escalator. One early unknown party wrote a song about an upward trip:

> As we go climbing toward the moon, boys
> As we go climbing toward the moon
> Way up above the valley people
> As we go climbing toward the moon.
>
> And when we reached the summit,
> Our spirits were not cowed,
> Although we were enveloped
> In a black and stormy cloud.

The protagonists of that ditty go on to describe two enjoyable nights in a lean-to that used to exist just north of the summit. From it, they watched the moon "a-smiling down." That lean-to was a fixture of Giant's top in the old days, sometimes even stocked with ATIS blankets. It escaped both fires only to succumb, eventually, to time.

Weston remembered a stay there in 1923 with his new bride. "The camp had been taken over as a summer resort," he wrote, "by two obstinate, seemingly arthritic porcupines; no matter how often you drove them out, they would slowly and silently lumber back just as soon as they thought you were asleep and then try to curl up like affectionate kittens on part of your blanket."

Giant's summit was reached before any other of the 46. A contingent of British soldiers under the command of Lord Jeffrey Amherst might have been atop the mountain in the 1750s.[14] That may sound preposterous, but, remember, Giant's iconic shape is visible from a large portion of Lake Champlain, the preferred corridor of travel from Canada to Manhattan in the 18th century. Who knows what sailor, soldier, or settler might have studied with interest the huge dome to the west, as modern tourists do from the Essex-Charlotte Ferry. From Giant's lofty summit, observers would have been able to spot enemies afloat on the lake. However, how they would have quickly communicated their intelligence remains a mystery. Historians, therefore, have credited Charles Broadhead, a surveyor, with the mountain's first ascent – on June 2, 1797. Thus Giant was climbed before a number of other notable peaks of the Northeast such as Maine's Katahdin (1804) or New Hampshire's Mount Adams (circa 1820).

Broadhead approached Giant along what is still the mountain's most arduous route – from the east. He was marking the southern line of the Old Military Tract, 665,000 acres of land now within the present counties of Clinton, Essex, and Franklin. It was set off, officially, in 1781 by the State of New York "for raising two regiments for the defense of this State on bounties of unappropriated lands." The law concerning the tract was rewritten in 1787 with the intent that the "unappropriated lands" within it were to be sold to raise funds for the state's coffers. The 1787 measure passed by the state legislature also ordered the survey of the boundaries of the tract.

After ascending the ridges below present-day Bald Peak, Broadhead reached the Giant Mountain Wilderness Area's other Roaring Brook – the one which flows from the mountain's northeast cirque. At that point the terrain assumed its more rugged character and Broadhead often had to take his line around cliffs. At the 4,000-foot level he encountered two feet of snow, but he eventually crested the summit ridge 300 yards north of the top. Historians assumed he checked out the highest point. Russell Carson reported, "The line passes close to the true summit and it is very likely that Broadhead [sic] went to the top to make a reconnaissance. Arthur S. Hopkins [of the state Conservation Department] has been over Broadhead's line, and it is his opinion that Broadhead is entitled to the record of the first ascent."

Broadhead continued straight down the other side of the mountain ("descending steep rocks, no Timber"). No doubt, Giant's west cirque was even then wracked with slides. Eventually he reached the "Leavel Land" at the base of the mountain and continued on, after crossing the Ausable River. He had much farther to go. He marked his line up by the Wolf Jaws, past Tabletop (also snowy), and eventually topped Boundary (forty years before Algonquin was first climbed). He proceeded all the way to the vicinity of Wallface. Broadhead's surveying exploits have remained little known but for his mention in Carson's book and his fuller treatment in Laura and Guy Waterman's *Forest and Crag*.

Most would consider Giant well named: its huge bulk being legendary. Its older, more lofty and complete name – Giant of the Valley – is said to have originated on its eastern side as a nod to one or more of its ascending bumps as seen from Pleasant Valley, south of Elizabethtown. Horatio Spafford's *Gazetteer of the State of New York* (1813) placed the name on one such knob. However, Old Mountain Phelps maintained that the mountain was named by Professor Arnold Guyot, the famous geologist, who made his first ascent of an Adirondack peak, one of the Sewards, in 1863. Phelps claimed that Guyot saw a slide on the southwest side of the mountain that resembled a "monstrous figure of a giant." Anyone who has studied Adirondack slides can well imagine it, but Phelps' assertion about the naming of the mountain is the only one which credits Guyot.

The experience of climbing Giant is enhanced by climbing it by way of its other trail, cut in 1968. It approaches the mountain from the east and ascends via Owl Head – which has no "apostrophe s" to distinguish it from other like-named peaks. Owl Head is an excellent destination for a day hike with children or for those who wish a short and different Adirondack experience. The climb – until reaching its rocky climax – is a mostly gentle woods walk, and the view it affords is a beautiful one of forest and crag. Giant and its little known east cirque loom to the west.

Owl Head may have been crossed by the original trail from the east, cut in 1927. That route, which began at Elizabethtown's Kilkenny Lodge – which could be reached "by walking across the golf course" *[Cobble Hill Golf Course]* – went over West Cobble (west of Cobble Hill). By 1934, it had fallen into disfavor as indicated by the trail description contained in the ADK's first *Guide to Adirondack Trails, Northeastern Section:*

> ...it has not been cut out in several years. It is a long route, about 9 m., but interesting because of the many views offered from the ridge. It is also difficult because of the loss of 1000 ft. elevation which must be climbed again and because of the uncertainties of the trail – windfalls,

underbrush and loss of markers. It should be undertaken only by the experienced, and these should provide themselves with a map and compass and be prepared for difficulties.

On the current trail – maintained by the 46ers – from Route 9N, you proceed from Owl Head to High Bank, a mysterious sandy rampart (probably a glacial deposit) high above the Roaring Brook. Barbara McMartin remarked that the scenery as viewed from High Bank reminded her of the Rockies. Beyond, before it continues on to the top, the trail winds up to the only lean-to in the Giant Mountain Wilderness Area (GMWA).

That lone "open camp" provides a key to understanding, in part, the 2004 Giant Wilderness Unit Management Plan. The current thinking is summarized:

> Historically the DEC has taken a minimalist approach to the GMWA. This is likely due in large part to the concentration in use and facilities in the High Peaks Wilderness Area (HPWA). Had the Department invested significant resources in developing the GMWA it is likely the overuse situation that exists in the nearby HPWA would be mirrored in this unit.

The "minimalist approach" has been a boon for Giant. While the High Peaks proper, already in state ownership, were being heavily developed with lean-tos and trails in the 1920s and 1930s, much of the Giant region remained in private hands and escaped "back country infrastructure" improvement. Another reason for the lack of lean-tos on Giant mentioned in the plan is the "ease to most interior locations in a single day's walk."

The 21st century plan calls for no more lean-tos. The strategy should be seen as a conscious attempt to keep Giant as a sort of day hiker's alternative to the High Peaks Wilderness, without the latter's messy campsites and lived-in flavor. At a place such as High Bank, you realize, with a sort of shock of appreciation, that this is exactly the right way to preserve the wonderful experience of climbing Giant.

Endnotes

1. Laura and Guy Waterman, *Forest and Crag, A History of Hiking, Trail Blazing, and Adventure in the Northeast Mountains* (Boston: Appalachian Mountain Club, 1989), pg. xxx.

2. Tony Goodwin reports that funding for the work to improve the trail above the Washbowl "came from donations made to ATIS in memory of Alexandra (Sandy) Scott, who died of cancer in 2002." She was the mother of Zander Scott. Goodwin continues, "The Scott family have been summer residents of Keene Valley and members of ATIS for many years… It was Zander's connection with the (ATIS) trail crew that led to using some of the funds contributed in his memory to make the earlier improvements below the Washbowl in 1992."

3. Barbara McMartin (1931-2005), between 1972 and 2005, wrote 25 books about the Adirondacks. Among them was one familiar to many 46ers: *Discover the Adirondack High Peaks* (Woodstock, VT: Backcountry Publications, 1989). Contributing to that guidebook's descriptions were Lee Brenning, Phil Gallos, Don Greene (#1949), Edwin H. Ketchledge (#507), Gary Koch (#1137W), and Willard Reed (#1316). She was also author of ten other guidebooks in her *Discover* series and was author of *The Adirondack Park, A Wildlands Quilt* (Syracuse, NY: Syracuse University Press, 2000); *Hides, Hemlocks and Adirondack History* (Utica, NY: North Country Books, 1992); and *The Great Forest of the Adirondacks* (Utica, NY: North Country Books, 1994) as well as a series of pamphlets, *Citizen's Guides,* for the Adirondack Park Agency. She served as the vice-president of the Adirondack Mountain Club and the Association for the Protection of the Adirondacks; chaired the Adirondack Park Centennial in 1992; and served on the New York State Department of Environmental Conservation's High Peaks Advisory Committee (1974-1978) and its Forest Preserve Advisory Committee (1979 to 2003), the last six years as chairman. She was a recipient of the Adirondack Museum's Founder's Day Award and the Adirondack Council's Adirondack Communicator and Adirondack Heritage awards.

4. Stoddard in his *The Adirondacks Illustrated* (1876 edition) quoted Old Mountain Phelps as he and the guide considered the prospect open to them from the "summit of a small hill behind the house of 'the Widow Beede'" located between the Ausable River and Roaring Brook. Phelps pointed out the falls: "See that bare rock near Smith Beede's? There are Roaring Brook Falls, the highest in the mountains; nearly 200 feet sheer fall at one leap..."

5. Bruce, in his *The Hudson* (1894), wrote, "...we visited Roaring Brook Falls, some four hundred feet high, a very beautiful waterfall in the evening twilight." Bruce's book was republished in 1907 as *The Hudson, Three Centuries of History, Romance, and Invention.*

6. T Lake Falls is located along the outlet stream of T Lake, located west of the north end of Piseco Lake in the town of Arietta, Hamilton County. The falls is estimated to fall, in a single leap, between 300 and 600 feet. No precise measurement of it has been recorded. The Hudson River Gorge's spectacular O. K. Slip Falls plunges only 250 feet.

7. "In Memory of the Great Flood," from *News, Notes and Nonsense,* Ausable Club publication, 2002.

8. Pamela Cranston, *Coming to Treeline* (St. Huberts Press, Oakland, CA, 2005).

9. George Gifford, Jr., M.D., "Freud and the Porcupine," *Harvard Medical Bulletin,* March/April 1972.

10. Quoted Jean Strouse in *Alice James, A Biography* (Houghton Mifflin, Boston, 1980).

11. Quoted by Josephine Goldmaple in "An Adirondack Friendship," *Atlantic,* September 1934.

12. According to Carson, Hopkins began making visits to Keene Valley "about 1860 and soon became acquainted with... Old Mountain Phelps." Hopkins occasionally went with Phelps to the Upper Ausable Lake and once told the guide that he believed Resagone, an Italian word meaning "the king's great saw," might be an appropriate name for the mountain they passed along the way, Sawteeth. The name was adopted in a transmuted form, Resagonia, for a while in the St. Huberts and Keene Valley area but ultimately fell out of favor. It is likely that Phelps named Hopkins for the minister, for whom he had a great deal of respect.

13. A theodolite is a surveyor's instrument, which when set upon a tripod is used to measure horizontal and vertical angles. Colvin's had been made to order upon his own specifications. It was carried from point to point in a large, often cumbersome wooden box that was carried by one of Colvin's "woodmen," strapped upon his back like a pack basket.

14. Weston even suggested that a portion of General Burgoyne's British army passed through Chapel Pond Pass in 1777 – a notion which historians would adamantly reject.

ROCKY PEAK RIDGE
Height: 23rd – 1,336 meters (4,383 feet)
By Chuck Gibson (#251)

Even though Rocky Peak Ridge is the easternmost of the High Peaks, it has a Western flavor. There's a whisper of Wasatch or Wyoming in its endless scale, rangy ridges, spectacular vistas, and lone prairie summit. Its wide-open spaces and (relatively) meager history evoke the American frontier. A 1974 *Adirondack Life* profile reveals the allure: "Rocky Peak Ridge is neither steeped in tradition nor lavished with natural beauty, but its barrenness gives it a certain mystery, a quality of remoteness and isolation." And even though slightly lower than Giant, Rocky is the more challenging climb.

One hiker's first memory of Rocky Peak Ridge is a vivid one. Imagine a ten-year-old boy ascending Giant one July morning with his grandparents. He[1] was burning to grab peaks. The night before, grandparents and grandson had camped at the top of Roaring Brook Falls,

Rocky Peak Ridge, as seen from Giant in the 1930s

a pleasant activity then, now obviously verboten. That was long ago – at the tail end of the pack basket and blanket roll era. Giant would (hopefully) be his seventh High Peak, but having heard the enticing juxtaposition "Giant and Rocky," he longed to bag #8 as well. However, his grandparents were skeptical. Giant and a few others – especially Marcy – were familiar, but Rocky Peak Ridge? What was the world coming to? There was no need to climb such a peak. Besides, where was it? None of them knew.

Once on Giant's summit, they looked around for a nearby bump to climb, hopefully down a short ridge. But... that couldn't be it – way over there – could it? It looked so far away... and enormous. Ah, yes, that was it. Rocky Peak Ridge had been spotted and the young peakbagger was soon pleading with his grandparents to be allowed to go to it.

His grandparents, apprehensive, if not appalled at the prospect, furrowed their brows and conferred before reluctantly giving their assent: He could go – but it would have to be alone. They would worry and wait. Pleased and a bit more subdued, he bade them farewell and slowly began to pick his way down the herdpath through spruce and scarps of stone. The unexpected scale of the massif ahead was scary – and thrilling. He was walking towards an unknown mountain and would either conquer it, disappear, or (melodramatically) die. An early jolt of existentialism like electricity shot through his young body, and he has never forgotten that moment.

Soon, when he was almost out of earshot, he heard his grandparents calling. They had reconsidered. He had to climb all the way back and rejoin them. Rocky Peak Ridge would have to wait for another day.

So in spite of Rocky Peak Ridge's historical reputation as Giant's disappointing appendage (or worse), his experience has always confirmed the opposite: that Rocky Peak Ridge is a big separate mountain, definitely worthy of attention. Those who climb Rocky Peak Ridge from New Russia already know its considerable bulk and sublimities. The spectacular trail, cut in 1968, opened a whole new consideration of Rocky Peak Ridge and helped take the mountain out of Giant's shadow.

Now, it seems, it is a peak on everybody's A-list. Consider these raves:

> "Nowhere else in the Adirondacks can you experience such vast openness as you hike mile after mile among grand vistas." *(Barbara McMartin)*

"Probably the best hike in all of the Adirondacks." *(Tony Goodwin)*
"As close to heaven as I'll ever get." *(Gary Randorf)*

With the New Russia trail, Rocky Peak Ridge came into its own.

The trail's hefty ascent is as legendary as its views. Part of the reason is that the trail passes over many bumps – thereby ramping up its cumulative climbing – but another factor is that the trip begins at such a low elevation, 600 feet, at the lowest trailhead in the High Peaks. The altitude difference between base and summit, 3,700 feet, is quite remarkable.[2]

Rocky Peak Ridge has always been linked to Giant, sometimes even being referred to as the "Giant's Wife."[3] They certainly faced the 1903 and 1913 conflagrations together, Rocky Peak Ridge taking the direct hit from the south and acting almost as a firewall to prevent irreparable damage to Giant, not to mention Keene Valley… probably not the first time a wife has protected her husband. The fires left the area a wasteland, often burning even the soil down to bare and blackened rock.

Rocky Peak Ridge, after the fires, was not an impressive sight to the new, fledgling 46er generation. Early commentators were withering:

"A badly burned and ragged mountain" that was "hardly worth the trouble." *(Bob Marshall)*
"A barren looking mountain, desolate and alone." *(Grace Hudowalski)*
"A grim, desolate mountain, all ugly bare rock and slash." *(Russell Carson)*

The first 46er book (1958) got personal, describing this Wife as "denuded of forest jewels" and "hardly a fitting consort for her companion of the west." It has been speculated that its grim features were so forbidding that no one dared bestow a human name on the peak for fear of insulting the namesake.

Nevertheless, the name of the mountain has evolved. First called Bald Mountain or Bald Peak, its name was changed (legend goes) to Rocky Peak Ridge by Bill Laverty, a lodge owner and trail builder from New Russia. The name makes sense since, as Grace Hudowalski points out, the top "is composed of several rocky peaks," memorable to all who have climbed over them. Calling the mountain Rocky Peak Ridge, instead of the oft-abbreviated Rocky Peak, recognizes this salient topographical fact.

Nestled among the "rocky peaks" of the "ridge" lies a delightful pond, notable for being the state's third-highest body of water. In fact, no less an authority as Bob Marshall called it *the* highest of its size, when he made a quick stop at it on August 10, 1921. Its sky surface, speckled with rocks, appears almost a mirage to the modern day hiker toiling up the notoriously dry East Trail from New Russia. Lake Marie Louise is named in honor of a hiking girl who roamed this high country in the 1880s. Her father, Thomas P. Wickes, bestowed the name. The attachment between water and daughter was lifelong, and eventually, following her request, Dr. Alphonso Goff of Keene scattered her ashes there from an airplane in the late 1950s.

Early trails on Rocky Peak Ridge were constructed from both directions. Laverty, around 1880, pushed a trail up from New Russia. Guides Ed Phelps and Charlie Beede (directed by Thomas Wickes) cut a trail from Giant about 1905. The first ascent of record was by two New Russia guides, Fred Patterson and Sam Dunning, in 1878. However, after the devastating conflagrations of the early twentieth century, Rocky Peak Ridge was bereft of trailed approach. For many years, before 1968, it was considered trailless and had its own canister.[4]

Since the construction of the East Trail, Rocky Peak Ridge has never been the same. That trail has no rival in the Adirondacks when it comes to offering up ever-changing views. "One of the most spectacular trips in the mountains," crowed the second 46er book (1972).

Dismissed as grim and desolate by early writers, Rocky Peak Ridge has rebounded with its forests. A brief Internet search reveals that many feel the mountain has still not yet received the praise that it is due. One posting is even provocatively titled "Better than Giant?" The rehabilitation of Rocky Peak Ridge's reputation is in full swing. A true Cinderella peak, transformed in a few generations from ugly stepsister to belle of the ball, Rocky Peak Ridge deserves to step into the limelight. Such is the healing power of the Adirondacks.

Endnotes

1. The 10-year-old would become the author of this "Mountain Profile," Charles (Chuck) Gibson, Jr. In August 1957 he climbed his first peak, Marcy. He finished on truly trailless Couchsachraga on July 23, 1963, at the age of 13.

2. Because the trail from New Russia to Rocky Peak Ridge climbs several subordinate peaks along the way and drops to lower elevations between them, the total ascent for a climb of the mountain is approximately 5,200 feet.

3. As late as 1937 an ADK map showing trails of the Mount Marcy region showed Rocky Peak Ridge as "Giant's Wife." The map was published in the *Bulletin of the Adirondack Mountain Club* (Vol. 2, No. 3), May 1938.

4. The East Trail continues to Giant from Rocky Peak Ridge's summit following, for the most part, the herdpath that the author was about to follow from the Giant to its "wife" when he was ten years old. Along its route up Giant it skirts the side of the landmark slide that identifies the larger mountain from points to the east. The huge slide was scoured as a consequence of the same deluge that created the "new" slides on Giant's western cirque in June 1963. The slide on the side facing Rocky Peak Ridge is considered the largest in the eastern United States. Rocky Peak Ridge's summit log was removed after the East Trail was completed.

For more discussion of the herdpath which later was marked as the trail between Rocky Peak Ridge and Giant, see Suzanne Lance's "History of the Adirondack Forty-Sixers" in this book.

About the Author

Chuck Gibson finished on Couchsachraga when he was 13 and has kept hiking in the Adirondacks ever since. Originally from Iowa, Chuck moved to the North Country in 1975 and has worked as a teacher, job counselor, social worker, and poet. For many years he lived in Wadhams, by the waterfall. His daughters, Shannon and Kerry, now work (and occasionally hike) in Oregon. For eight years he's been Director of Literacy Volunteers of Essex/Franklin Counties, a nonprofit service based in Port Henry. His new wife Ann, whom he met on top of Cascade, now shares his life.

THE DIX RANGE
By Daniel Eagan (#4666)

The Dix Range dominates the southeastern Adirondack High Peaks. Its two major arms include five mountains over four thousand feet in elevation: Dix, Hough, South Dix, East Dix, and Macomb. The range rises from the southeast edge of the Boquet River valley and the east edge of the Elk Lake valley.

Hunters Pass, one of the highest of the Adirondack notches and one of the last to be explored, lies at the foot of Dix Mountain. The pass marks the boundary between two watersheds. The North Fork of the Boquet River flows northeast from it to Lake Champlain and eventually the St. Lawrence, while the inlet to Elk Lake flows south to the Hudson. Other streams flowing from the Dix Range include Lillian, Slide, West Mill, and Lindsay brooks. Among the ponds are Round, Twin, Dial, Lillypad, Rhododendron, Cranberry, Dix, and Moss.

There are two major trails into the area, both dating from the 1870s, as well as several well-defined herdpaths and the remains of woods roads.

The distinctive profiles of Dix and conical Hough are among the easiest mountains for travelers to identify. From the east, the range can be seen from the shores of Lake Champlain and the summits of the central Green Mountains. From the west, the majestic slides on Dix, as well as its signature Beckhorn, are a dominant view on the road from Keene to Keene Valley.

Dix presents one broad shoulder streaked with slides to the Boquet River valley to the north. Another shoulder extends south, dropping gradually until it rises to the wooded summit of Hough Peak. Dropping to the hogback "Pough," then to a col, the range continues up over the three distinct summits of Macomb Mountain, gradually descending over Sunrise Mountain and other, nameless peaks that skirt the private land of the Elk Lake Preserve. At the col before Macomb, a second ridge extends northeast over South and East Dix, Spotted Mountain, Elizabethtown #4, and several minor humps until it reaches Route 73.

The Dix Range is within the Dix Mountain Wilderness Area, one of the least trailed and used wilderness areas in the High Peaks region. Bounded on two sides by large, private preserves, and on two others by major highways, the area is protected from casual visitors. The lack of marked trails and trailheads with services deters some potential hikers. Those who do try to summit the area's peaks face daunting approaches as well as some of the most demanding ascents in the High Peaks.

One of the most dramatic views of Dix is from its neighbor, Nippletop. From there, the slides on Dix, and its summit, are a forbidding sight. However, the views from the Dixes are equally impressive. Apart from glimpses of the Adirondack Northway from East Dix, and indications of buildings on Elk Lake from Macomb, the views from the peaks are of total wilderness: forests, water, and most of the other High Peaks.

Dix Mountain.   Photo by Ken Marcinowski

DIX MOUNTAIN
Height: 9th – 1,470c meters (4,823+ feet)

Dix Mountain has the distinction of being the second High Peak to have been climbed. While running a line that separated the town of Keene from the town of North Hudson, a surveyor named Rykert summited Dix in 1807. His survey established the northern line of Township 49 and the southern line of Township 48 of the Totten and Crossfield Purchase. All references state that Rykert's first name is unknown, but it is still interesting to speculate about his identity, and we can still imagine the difficulty of his climb, miles from any road, through bogs and virgin forest, up slides and through krummholz, until he reached a summit that revealed an awful solitude.

According to Russell M. L. Carson, Professor Ebenezer Emmons named Dix, apparently during his ascent of Marcy. The name first appears in print in *Assembly Document No. 161, February 1, 1837.*[1] At the time, John A. Dix was New York's Secretary of State.

John A. Dix

Born in New Hampshire, July 24, 1798, Dix enjoyed a privileged youth and, at the age of fourteen, entered the army during the War of 1812. On leaving the service, he became a lawyer and journalist in Washington, married Catharine Morgan, the daughter of a Congressman, and moved with her to Cooperstown in 1828. His hard work and good reputation led to political appointments, and as Secretary of State from 1833-39 he proposed the first attempt at a statewide geological survey. He also founded a scientific and literary magazine, *Northern Lights*, abandoning it in 1843 to take his ailing wife to Europe.

Elected to the U.S. Senate in 1845, Dix became a committed abolitionist, a position that later drove him from politics for a decade. During that time, he worked as president of two railroads and resumed his law practice in

New York City. In 1860, he was asked to rescue the postal system from bankruptcy. He performed that work so well that at the close of the Buchanan administration, he was appointed Secretary of the Treasury, a critical position as Southern states were seceding, and financing for the Union fell into doubt. Dix's steps to secure the nation's assets – including the mint in New Orleans – led to his penning a line that served as a rallying call during the Civil War: "If anyone attempts to haul down the American flag, shoot him on the spot." Lincoln subsequently commissioned Dix a major general. As Commander of the Department of the East, he helped suppress the New York City draft riots. After the war, he served as minister to France, and, at the age of seventy-five, was elected governor of New York.[2]

Some complained that Dix did not deserve to have a high peak named after him. Travel writer Charles Lanman seemed especially angry, alluding to "the folly of a certain state geologist, in attempting to name the prominent peaks of the Adirondac Mountains after a brotherhood of living men... if this business is not supremely ridiculous, I must confess that I do not know the meaning of that word. A pretty idea, indeed, to scatter to the winds the ancient poetry of the poor Indian, and perpetuate in its place the names of living politicians."[3] Russell Carson noted that, like Governor Marcy, Dix never visited the Adirondack Mountains (he got as far as Lake George), but he spoke often of the importance of the mountains to the state's interests, and, as governor, urged the passage of legislation to preserve Adirondack land.

During an era when graft and corruption were rampant, Dix was regarded as an absolutely trustworthy politician. His honor and probity, never in doubt, were the main reasons why he, a Democrat, was nominated by the Republican party to serve as governor. His unimpeachable career, rugged authority, and lifetime of service to the country make him an excellent namesake for one of the most noble of the Adirondack peaks. In addition, in 1850 he published *A Winter in Madeira; and a Summer in Spain and Florence*, a collection of travel essays so popular that it went through five editions. That work was a precursor to the post Civil War boom of travel books.

A more difficult question is what the correct name of the mountain is. Emmons referred to it as "Dix's Peak," a designation that persisted through Colvin's surveys. In 1895, however, the Marcy quadrangle listed simply "Dix Mt." (It's "Dix Mtn." on the 1953 and 1973 quads and "Dix Mtn" on the ADK High Peaks maps.)

Carson credits Emmons with the first ascent of Nippletop and believes the scientist camped in the Gorge of the Dial the night before (August 30, 1837). It is surprising that the professor had little to say then about Dix. When he climbed Nippletop, the mountain looming across the gorge would have been the most prominent feature of the surrounding area. That makes the inflated altitude he gave for it all the more puzzling. (As Carson notes, the measurement Emmons took of Dix by theodolite from an inn at West Moriah was off by almost four hundred feet.)

The area was not visited much in the 1830s. The absence of reliable roads may have been the main reason Township 49 remained unexplored much later than the other parts of the High Peaks region.[4] Even by 1933, W. D. Mulholland was writing hopefully in *High Spots* that the "new Chapel Pond highway" would be completed soon.[5] In the early days, visitors to the Dix Range were determined ones.

The main route from Elizabethtown to Keene Flats (the early name for Keene Valley) was close to today's Route 9N. Nineteenth century maps show a rough road from Keene Flats up to Chapel Pond, as well as a road to the Ausable Lakes.

In the early twentieth century a story emerged that an old "Military Road" had once led from Keene to Schroon Lake by way of Chapel Pond Pass. Keene Valley artist Harold

Weston insisted that General Burgoyne and his troops used it during the Revolution, but according to a letter printed in the *Elizabethtown Post* (December 6, 1900) the "old Keene" or "old Military" road was used during the War of 1812. The letter, probably penned by Adirondack Mountain Reserve superintendent Walter Scott Brown, maintained that the "'army encamped through the winter' in log barracks, when it passed the county *[Essex]* on its way to Albany after the battle of Plattsburgh *[September 11, 1814]*..." Ed Palen (#710) recently concluded that the construction of the road was commissioned by the state in 1811.[6] It can still be spotted in sections. Its course took it from Chapel Pond, over a hill 2,000 feet in elevation, across the outlet of Twin Pond, and to a "plateau" upon which the log barracks were purportedly built, and, after passing Lily Pad Pond and "Upper" Moss Pond, joined the old Schroon-Elizabethtown state road, the equivalent of today's Route 9.

South of the Dix Range, a road led from Cedar Point (Port Henry) on Lake Champlain through Moriah and across the state road near today's North Hudson Cemetery. It then wound through the drainage of West Mill Brook before following Niagara Brook to Clear Pond. Work on the road started soon after iron ore was discovered at McIntyre (Adirondac). The road doesn't appear on Burr's 1829 map (neither does Clear Pond or Elk Lake); the 1839 version shows it as a "cross road," i.e., one level up from a path, and not recommended for travel on horseback.

In his book *Clear Pond* (1991), Roger Mitchell includes testimony that the Cedar Point road was a "disappointment" and "abominable."[7] In *Wild Scenes in the Forest and Prairie* (1839), Charles Fenno Hoffman said it took several hours to travel eight miles by wagon from the state road to Clear Pond.

More than any other factor, poor roads limited economic growth in the area. In fact, the ultimate failure of the Adirondack Iron Works can be attributed directly to transportation woes. Once reliable roads were built from Schroon to Elizabethtown, and from there to Keene Valley, the area was open to tourists.

No matter how difficult it was to travel into the Elk Lake and Boquet River valleys, it seems improbable that no one climbed any of the mountains in the range in the years after Rykert. Even just to scout lumber, or while hunting and trapping, someone must have struggled up one of the many slides to a summit ridge. Wouldn't the early residents of Keene Flats have challenged each other to the top of Dix? And with more amateur sportsmen arriving each season, wouldn't guides have staked out routes for hunting and fishing? Unfortunately for historians, climbing without a purpose, just to reach a summit, in those days may have been considered too frivolous to record.

Israel Johnson, a veteran of the War of 1812 and an amateur inventor, moved to Clear Pond around 1830 and ultimately cleared about 100 acres for his farm and sawmills.[8] His was the only house between Schroon and the McIntyre Iron Works; consequently, it served as a rough inn for travellers. Emmons may have stayed with him while on his way to Adirondac in 1838. His *Natural History of New York* (published 1842) includes an engraving of "Nipple Top, Dix's Peak, and McCombe's Mountain" drawn from the shores of Clear Pond.[9] Joel T. Headley, author of *Adirondack; or Life in the Woods* (1849), passed by Johnson's property on his way to the iron works. However, Winslow Watson's 1853 *General View* of Essex County makes no mention of Dix, Mud Pond, Clear Pond, or Hunters Pass, even while singling out Indian Pass and the Wilmington Notch as "Natural Curiosities."

Alfred Billings Street, a fabulist of the first order, tried to reach Hunters Pass after a trip through Indian Pass in 1869. Because the guide he had hired, Elijah Simmonds, had "taken sick," Street set out on the journey with his son and two other guides. The plan was to approach the Gorge from the south, traveling on a dirt road from Fenton's Tavern on the Cedar Point Road to Clear Pond. On reaching the pond, Street promptly got lost, crossing and recrossing Niagara Brook instead of following the road from Clear Pond to Elk Lake. In fact, it took Street two days to get to Elk Lake. The author exclaimed about the utter isolation of the savage wilderness around him, and referred dramatically to panthers, wolves, and other wildlife. When he finally was within sight of "the three terrific slides that gash the north flank of Dix's Peak," Street offered a fourteen-stanza poem about a forest shanty (or lean-to). He and his party then returned to Fenton's for dinner.[10]

A closer reading of Street's account reveals that his guides found a corduroy road near Clear Pond, which he correctly identifies as the Cedar Point road. The party spent a night in the shanty that they found by Clear Pond and made use of a boat that had been left there. Apart from the lumber road to Elk Lake, Street eventually found other evidence of man, including mink traps and a raft. He should have found a lot more. Israel Johnson's improvements couldn't have disappeared in twenty-five years; indeed, Street refers to "quite a farm cleared at the pond, but I looked in vain for the customary homestead"[11] – not surprising since he missed the broad road to Elk Lake as well. The area was far from "almost totally unknown."

Street credits guide and trapper Elijah Simmonds, going to it from Elk Lake, with summiting Nippletop. Here are Street's words for the guide's first glimpse of Hunters Pass: "What was this thing at his left, soaring close from his feet up, dizzily up, until it seemed to clutch the heavens. It was a terrible wall, a horrible precipice rising sheer from the ground, here glistening in naked, cracked, scooped-out rock..." Elijah then climbed Nippletop (which Street bowdlerized as Dial). Looking back at Dix, he saw it "smoothed over with gold, as though a glittering yellow mantle was cast over it. It rounded down to the Gorge, north, four thousand feet, – rearing one thousand feet higher a crest like the front of a lion; then falling gradually toward its southern termination to where it rose again in a sharpened peak like the haunch of the same animal, until the vast mass declined in a more easy slope to Macomb's Mountain at the south." Street quotes Elijah as saying that "The top of the ridge at the south rises as sharp almost as a knife. It isn't more than a foot wide, and slopes down each side in a rocky precipice covered with small spruces."[12]

This may be the first close-up description in print of the summit of Dix, and it seems reasonably accurate today, apart from the exaggerated narrowness of the Beckhorn ridge. Still, Elijah loses some credibility when he claims that the view from Dix is "grand, but the same as from the Dial."

In a letter to the *Albany Evening Journal* on August 26, 1871, Verplanck Colvin wrote that he first climbed Dix in 1870, when he and State Botanist Charles H. Peck cut a trail up its shoulder.[13] Actually, the two found their way to the top alone, then returned down a trail blazed and cleared by their "toiling" guides, "the first complete trail up the mountain." Colvin didn't note his actual route, although he ended up overlooking the "Gorge of the Dial." Their shortest path would have paralleled the current trail up to the Beckhorn, although it is possible that Colvin and Peck started out near Clear Pond and hiked over the entire ridge. In Colvin's letter, he mentioned visiting "Johnson's Clear Pond" the day before ascending Dix.

That same year, Orlando Beede, son of Keene Valley innkeeper Smith Beede, cut a trail up Dix from St. Huberts. His route went between Noonmark and Round Mountain, across the Boquet valley, then up the river itself almost to the height of land marking Hunters Pass. Beede's trail then struck south to the summit of Dix. According to Carson, the trail followed a trapper's line "which James J. Storrow used when he ascended Dix in June, 1870, guided by Hiram Holt."[14]

Holt was a noted Keene Valley guide. James Jackson Storrow, who was very likely the first to climb most of the peaks of the Great Range, was born in 1837 to a wealthy Boston

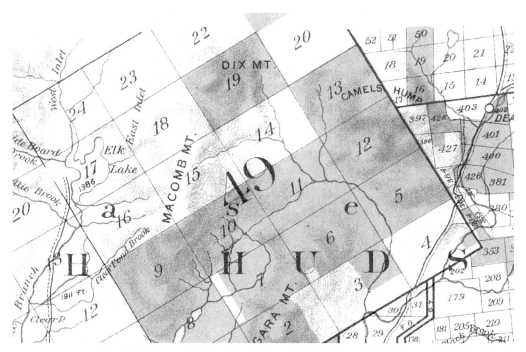

The USGS map of 1895 shows "Dix Mt." and "Macomb Mt." but not the other three major peaks of the range.

family. One biographer wrote that, "Though naturally quiet and studious, all his life he loved the outdoors... Storrow allowed himself little diversion, though he had a wide range of general interests. Even on mountain-climbing expeditions he often spent much time in thought."[15] Storrow would become one of the country's most famous lawyers after he and Chauncy Smith successfully defended Bell Telephone in a series of patent infringement cases. He and his descendents were also noted philanthropists who funded the Boston Symphony and the Boys and Girls Clubs of America. Storrow himself bequeathed funds to purchase Franconia Notch in New Hampshire, helping save the area from development.

Colvin was back on Dix in the summer of 1873 to plant Bolt Number 10 on the summit before crossing Nippletop and Elk Pass to Mount Colvin. To a cautious hiker, his description of the expedition, which began at St. Huberts, is a little alarming. He started later than planned on August 16, "leaving behind us trails and marked trees," although he was following the route of Beede's trail if not actually using it. Colvin reached and then followed the Boquet River "through this pathless forest, which was, however, everywhere tracked by the foot-prints of wild beast; now fording the stream to escape precipitous climbing, now clambering up over the huge rocks in its bed, over and amid which the clear water fell foaming."[16] He and his men camped at Hunters Pass that night.

The surveyor described starting up Dix on the morning of the seventeenth through sheer wilderness. "Here there was no sign, but instead, paths stamped by the footprints of deer, panther and bear showed us where these creatures had found spots amid the cliffs which they could climb, and availing ourselves of these runways, we slowly toiled upward." Was it professional jealousy that made Colvin neglect to mention the work Beede had done just two years earlier or was Colvin trying to impress the state legislature with his dedication to completing an accurate survey? Perhaps he was lost, but... "After struggling through dense thickets of spruce and balsam, at half-past one in the afternoon we reached the summit of Mount Dix. It was wonderfully clear, not a cloud to be seen."

Colvin mentioned Bald Peak, Hurricane, the Crown Point lighthouse, Clear Pond, Elk Lake, the Boreas range, and Haystack and Marcy when describing the views. He filled twelve pages in his "large theodolite book" with measurements, drew four reconnaissance maps, and took forty-six barometrical observations. (He couldn't resist a dig at Emmons for computing the wrong altitude of 5,200 feet, although his own was off by sixty feet.)

As Colvin worked, one can picture his guides and workmen nervously eyeing their surroundings by the waning light of a sun sinking over Elk Lake. When the self-taught surveyor finally looked up from his instruments and realized the time, it was too late to descend safely. No one had brought any emergency gear. Out of water, they had to head down until they found some. Colvin later wrote, "[S]oon we became entangled amid ledges, slides and cavernous rocks that rendered the previous night-descent of the Giant inferior in danger. In the darkness, clinging by roots, aiding each other from ledge to ledge, and guiding with special care the footsteps of those carrying the theodolite, etc., we finally found ourselves slipping on the edge of rocks draped in cold, wet, sphagnous moss." After locating water a little lower, Colvin led his men to the very edge of a cliff, where he finally decided it was time to bivouac.

We've all probably encountered the same sort of recklessly gung-ho hiker, one who insists on continuing ahead despite the rain, gloom, lack of trail, etc. It's reassuring to learn that someone like Colvin had to struggle with trees, roots, rocks, and slides the same way we do and that he, too, ran out of water and got lost and complained about the weather. Less comforting are his accounts of tearing up mounds of moss to make bedding or chopping down and burning trees whenever he stopped for the night.

In his defense, Colvin was funded – or not – by the whim of state legislators, and he no doubt found it necessary to exaggerate both the danger of his work and the remoteness of the area, and there's no denying the hardships he endured. He spent almost a month camped below the summit of Dix in July and August of 1880 (at one point taking observations from the summit of Macomb), describing it as a time of almost unremitting rain and thunderstorms.

By 1880, Keene Flats had become a legitimate tourist destination. Most visitors arrived via Elizabethtown, but Harold Weston writes that there was a "dangerous winding road through Chapel Pond Pass. There were three or four places where the road crossed sand slides with a deep ravine below. My mother recalled coming to Beede House that way in 1886 with a four-horse double-decked stagecoach. At those places where the road was crumbling away, the driver, cracking his whip to get past the danger sooner, shouted to his frightened passengers 'Lean to the hill!'"[17]

E. R. Wallace's 1875 Adirondack travelogue describes Clear Pond and Elk Lake as tourist destinations as well. "Rufus Fiske's secluded 'Lake-side Inn,' at Clear Pond, can accommodate about 40 visitors. John Moore, at his charming sylvan resort at Mud Pond, can provide for an equal number."[18] Wallace wrote that Moore and Samuel Sanders, financed by locals, built a bridle path to the foot of Marcy, following the route similar to today's Elk Lake-Marcy Trail. Wallace goes on to write, "The opening of a good trail to the top of Dix's Peak, 3 m N. E. of Mud Pond, is also due to the enterprise of the same parties. The prospect enjoyed from the summit is one of the very grandest that any of the range presents and is richly worth the exertion acquired for its attainment."[19]

Wallace may have hiked the area himself, or he may have relied on Street's earlier descriptions. More likely, he listened to guides. Either way, he offered this description of Hunters Pass:

This imposing ravine is bounded by the stupendous walls of Dix's Peak on the S. E. side and those of Dial or Nipple Top on the other. These mountains are classed among the loftiest of the Adirondack Range, and here the perpendicular declivity of their sides, stretching away for a distance of half a mile, attains an altitude of from 200 to 500 ft. "Its walls," says the veteran hunter Elijah Simons *[sic]*, "are not as high as those of the Indian Pass, in sheer ascent, but they are still as green as God made them, and have not been desolated by fires as have the sides of Wallface and McIntyre.

The travelogue composer concluded, "Nature seldom displays a more amazing spectacle of gloomy, savage, solitary grandeur."[20]

The area was by that time so domesticated that Wallace could supply distances and times for the routes from Keene Valley to Dix, Elk Lake, and Round Pond. He helpfully pointed out that from Clear Pond, it was a short jump first to Fenton's Tavern and then the estimable Russell Root's. "'Root's!' Who among Adirondack tourists is unfamiliar with this time-honored name? Perfectly home-like in all its appointments, this old established 'Sportsman's retreat' affords a most agreeable resting place for the weary traveler; 25 or 30 guests are furnished with pleasant rooms, and supplies are procured at 'Root's Store.'"[21]

Wallace continued producing guides until the end of the century. He revised some details, such as the names of the innkeepers, but his descriptions of the area essentially remained intact. One notable change: he quickly adopted the name Elk Lake, given by Colvin in 1873 to replace Mud Pond.[22]

Other written accounts of Hunters Pass are strikingly similar to each other. *The Military and Civil History of the County of Essex*, written in 1869 by Winslow Watson, notes that the pass "can now only be reached by the severest toil of several miles (but the feat has been achieved by brave and delicate woman) and when this is accomplished, the dense forest, the masses of rocks and their mosses, and their debris gathered for ages, renders the gorge almost impenetrable."[23] Watson was apparently quoting the *Elizabethtown Post*, but compare his description to that in *A Descriptive and Historical Guide to the Valley of Lake Champlain and the Adirondacks* (1871), credited to Andrew Williams: "The scene can now only be reached by the severest toil of several miles, (but the feat has been achieved by a brave and delicate woman,) and when this is accomplished, the dense forest, the masses of rocks, their mosses and their debris, gathered for ages, render the gorge almost impenetrable."[24]

The same *Descriptive and Historical Guide* includes a map "constructed" by W. W. Ely, M.D., which shows a bridle path leading west of Elk Lake to the western shores of the Upper Ausable Lake, where it intersects with another bridle path. Remarkably it went over the Pinnacle Ridge, then southeast, skirting Nippletop and Dix, and back to Clear Pond. Anyone who tried to ride a horse over that route is probably still missing.

Old Mountain Phelps wrote an idiosyncratic description of Dix that most likely dates from the same period (the 1870s):

> Dix peak desends rapidly south to the mountain incircled basin of Mud pond. In passing from Dix S.E. to MaComb Mt there is a verry singular formation a sharp ridg connects them running at right angles with Dix and MaComb it must be as steep as 70 degrees both ways and so narrow it would take a well ballanced head to pa∫s it the Macomb Mt is a high ridg east of mud pond is and much rent by Avalanches on the west side and a ma∫s of broken mts on the east extending to Schroon River
>
> Dix peak is 5,000 ft high and has something of a trail from Mud pond to the top of it cleared by John Moors. The Town line of Keene and North Hudson passes over its summit.[25]

Phelps is credited with giving the Beckhorn its distinctive name, which even then required explanation for most readers. Anvils are so foreign in today's world that even when defined the name is as good as meaningless.[26] Some hikers today think the Beckhorn better resembles the profile of a claw hammer or the business end of a pry bar, but Phelps could be an intriguing stylist. To him, the summit of Dix was a "sharp, narrow, curved, uneven ridge covered with balsam brush from two to four feet high, and as thick as hair on a spaniel dog; a look at it reminds one of a look at an old poor cow doubled up to lick her hip, and for a man to travel it with a knapsack on would be like ants taking [a] big egg and traveling the cow's back." [27]

In 1885, the state created the Adirondack Forest Preserve, but it was a largely ineffective way of protecting the environment. The land on either side of the Dix Range was owned by lumbermen or speculators who were waiting either to work the area themselves or to sell if lumber prices rose. When William G. Neilson and other investors formed the Adirondack Mountain Reserve (AMR) in 1887, the entire area faced the risk of clear-cutting. Neilson and his partners sought to protect the land around the Ausable Lakes, buying Township 48 of the Totten and Crossfield Purchase from George Thomas of the Thomas and Armstrong Lumber Company of Plattsburgh. Their holdings included most of the Boquet River valley, stretching to the flanks of Dix Mountain and south almost to Elk Lake.

Near the end of the nineteenth century, members of the AMR built a second trail to Dix which paralleled the current Henry Goddard Leach Trail up the shoulder of Noonmark before dropping into the Noonmark/Bear Den col. The path then followed Gravestone Brook until it joined the old Dix trail near Dial Pond. The trail was damaged so heavily by the fire of 1903 that it was thereafter abandoned.

It may be hard today to grasp how thoroughly the land around Dix was lumbered. The AMR leased its Boquet land to lumber companies, such as J. & J. Rogers, using the money it earned to retire its debt. In 1891, Finch Pruyn and Company bought most of the land around Elk Lake from Phoebe Bloomingdale. While cutting on the slopes of Macomb and Dix, all the way up to Hunters Pass, the company leased the land immediately around the lake to various innkeepers.[28]

What trees weren't cut by the hundreds of men working for Finch Pruyn, J. & J. Rogers, and other companies burned in the raging fires of 1903 and 1913. The first conflagration destroyed the entire Boquet River valley. Writing in *Up the Lake Road*, Edith Pilcher noted that the worst of many 1903 Adirondack fires "started on the east side of Dix, leap-frogged across the Bouquet Valley to Noonmark, and then spread eastward over the summit of Round Mountain."[29] The fires spread east and west, reaching Chapel Pond and the summit of Bear Den. Twenty-five thousand cords of pulpwood, cut, stacked, and ready to be removed by J. & J. Rogers, were lost as well.

Eyewitness accounts tell of desperate conditions. William G. Neilson wrote, "A tornado of fire, borne by a great south wind, came from Macomb, climbed Dix, and swept over Noonmark... a roaring mass of flames that could be heard for miles." In a letter, George Moffat wrote about "a flame-colored pillar of smoke, awful to behold."[30] The fire continued until rains arrived on June 8. Neilson's grandchildren, who maintain a family camp in St. Huberts, have saved his fire-fighting memorabilia, including breakable glass globes filled with inert gas, used for fires inside buildings, and coiled canvas hoses worn like backpacks. These, attached to wooden hand pumps stationed on a lake shore, could shoot a stream of water fifty feet.

In *High Spots* almost thirty years later, ADK member Francis Bayle described how the 1903 fire affected the road through the Chapel Pond Pass. Once a dirt path bounded by lush green branches and leaping brooks, the forest was "bare, blackened poles standing up from the soil-free rocks."[31] The sun baked the dirt, and brooks were reduced to feeble trickles.

Artist Harold Weston wrote of three lumberjack camps – in the Dix valley, the notch of Noonmark, and in the Chapel Pond Pass – built to handle the detritus of the fire. "The north side of Noonmark was almost completely burnt except for a small patch of spruce trees just below the top."[32] Weston also described the wooden troughs built "to slide the five-foot lengths of the dead tree trunks down to the notch… [O]nce in a while a log would get going too fast and jump the tracks. The peeled saplings of this log chute could be plainly seen from the porch of the Inn like a shining monorail zooming down the side of Noonmark to a point well below the notch."[33]

Weston climbed Dix some years later, using the old trail through the Noonmark notch. He later wrote, "My brother and I got lost and then shown up, for thinking we could travel in an unfamiliar area without help of compass. This was in the summer of 1911. Together with an Exeter classmate of mine we went over Dix via the ATIS trail, not very well kept up but far better than the obscure track down to Elk Lake, where we spent the night at the Lodge."[34] A month later, the artist contracted polio. It took him years to build up the strength to hike the mountains again.

In September 1913 fire, a result of lightning on the northern slope of Dix, hit the valley again. Weston wrote,

> It was a most dramatic sight with smoke clouds billowing up from the Bouquet Valley like boiling thunderclouds well below you. At that time it was not a crown fire and there was too much smoke to see any flames… The heat was so great that we stopped in the shelter of a knoll before the dirt road slipped down near the [Chapel] pond, and at that we had to shelter our faces from the heat. Clouds of smoke darkened the sky, increasing the dramatic effect of the light from the flames on the cliffs above the pond. Some trees were breaking off and falling to plummet down into the water. Suddenly, sharp but deep reverberations sounded above the crackling and roaring of the fire. They were explosions of rock, deprived of its water by crystallization on account of the intense heat. These explosions blew off small pieces of hot rock which sent up little clouds of steam as they hit the water.[35]

A 1916 Conservation Department map indicates that about forty-three percent of the Dix Mountain Wilderness Area burned in the fires.[36]

Weston also related a hair-raising tale of a young Norwegian nanny named Ingrid, who climbed Dix solo in 1922. The trail by that time was in a state of disrepair, overgrown in many sections with raspberry brambles. Ingrid reached the summit safely but got lost on her return. For a mile stretch, the trail followed one of the corduroy woods roads built across the Boquet valley after the fire of 1903. She missed an unmarked turn-off through thick raspberry bushes, ended up too far down the valley, and tried to short-cut her way back over Round Mountain. Late that afternoon she spotted the dirt road by Chapel Pond and headed that way. About halfway there, Ingrid slid down a rock face to a ledge covered with blueberry bushes. As Weston noted, that was her second mistake: "When bushwhacking you should never slide or jump down before making fairly sure you can climb up again. Once on the blueberry ledge Ingrid discovered that this maybe hundred-foot-long sloping shelf on the mountain's side ended in a drop-off at least fifty feet into the black depths of Chapel Pond."[37]

Unable to climb back up the slippery rock, Ingrid ate her fill of blueberries and settled down to sleep. Scraping noises above woke her at dawn. Ingrid thought rescuers were coming to help her and called out. "Only then did she see the big black bear who had come skidding down the rock funnel to get his breakfast of blueberries. He seemed more startled than she, swung around, distended his sharp nails to get traction and had no trouble scrambling up the steep granite slope with more speed than you would imagine possible."[38] Later that day Ingrid was able to attract the attention of a chauffeur on the road far below. She was finally rescued by four guides, two of whom lowered her by rope to the pond.

The Marshall brothers and Herb Clark climbed Dix and Hough in 1920. Robert Marshall described the route from St. Huberts as "the hardest mountain trail I know of in the Adirondacks."[39] He also complained that the fires had "spoiled" the views to the north and east.

In a privately published book, Robert S. Wickham gave a charming description of climbing Dix in 1923 with his son. They started out from the Ausable Club golf course, went through the Noonmark notch, passed abandoned lumber camps, and crossed the North Fork of the Boquet River. Wickham complained about "very bad going through down, burned timber and small, thick, second growth birch and poplar saplings."[40] Rather than follow the trail through bad slash, they bushwhacked up the slope of Dix about five hundred feet and then crossed over to Hunters Pass.

> Packing through was difficult. We went very slowly – we had to. Down timber, piled up rock masses, tumbled about, moss covered, into which your foot would disappear, then your ankle, to be followed by your leg, and finally by your knee, into some hidden crevice. The packs tugged and swung on our backs. We sat down many times, both by and without choice. In time we reached the height of land... and could look down the valley to Elk Lake lying amidst light green timber, the black topped soft wood having been cut out. The rocky sides of Dix on the one side, the steep, balsam covered sides of the Nipple Top range on the other, and the piled up confusion of the floor of the pass itself gave us as much wild beauty as we could wish for...[41]

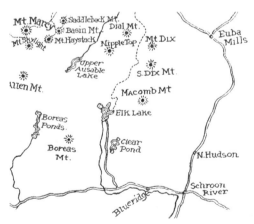

Portion of map from Robert S. Wickham's book, *Friendly Adirondack Peaks*

Descending towards Elk Lake, they first reached a draw road (bigger than a tote road, but not quite a woods road), then an abandoned lumber camp. The road broadened as they continued on to a larger lumber camp at the site of the Dix Pond clearing. They camped that night a mile further, by East Inlet, where they caught twenty-seven small trout.

Like Weston, Wickham and his son found the lumber chutes fascinating. He described the one on Nippletop at length before addressing his climb up Dix. They had intended to follow the old trail from East Inlet to a saddle between Dix and Hough, but lumbering had "eliminated" it. They set out due east from the larger lumber camp, following traces of the trail, which invariably vanished. Most Forty-Sixers will sympathize with his description of their eventual bushwhack up Dix: "When we would come to a down, weathered dead log, climb up on it, and walk its slippery length for thirty or forty feet above tops and bushes, we would feel elated over our progress and hope we could step over on to another and continue – only to have our hopes dashed to bush at its end. After much floundering about we finally gave up trying to trace and follow the trail and began to toil straight up."[42]

While eating lunch, Wickham and his son discovered that they were sitting near the trail, which they followed to the summit. "Dix made us humble and respectful. We got down on our knees to him many times – he forced us to do so. In five and a half hours we had conquered him, the hardest climb we had yet had, although we had ascended but twenty-six hundred feet."[43]

After a description of the views, Wickham turned his attention to the rocks beneath his feet:

> On the summit we found a cylindrical brass cut about five inches long with a screw in a swiveled socket to fasten its cover on, the cover, however, being missing – maybe taken thoughtlessly by someone as a souvenir – a rusty, tin, tobacco box cover screwed down in the place where the brass cover should be, the cup bearing on its outside surface the raised initials, 'A.M.C.' In the cup were a bit of a pencil and many scraps of paper containing names and dates of visitations there. The first date we noticed was August 17, 1910. One scrap of paper under the date of June 9, 1920, informed us that Herb Clark and Bob Marshall climbed Dix and South Peak on that day and that the latter was stung by a hornet on South Peak where the hornets were written of as being thick and of hot temper. We did not see any.[44]

Wickham and his son descended the same trail, then continued along the ridge to a brook. There they found another timber chute, and followed it down to the "boulevard" near the shore of Elk Lake. It is very likely that they were on the same tote road that many others have used as a route down Lillian Brook. They reached the Elk Lake House in time for dinner.

Five years after Wickham's book was published, Walter Collins O'Kane wrote *Trails and Summits of the Adirondacks*, one in his series of influential guidebooks to the mountains of the Northeast. He described the St. Huberts trail to Dix as starting up the hill from the baseball grounds of the Ausable Club (near the site of today's hiker parking lots). O'Kane noted that the trail passed two abandoned lumber camps before crossing the North Fork of the Boquet and pointed out further evidence of lumbering before reaching the summit.

Still, the fires and wind storms that had torn through Elk Lake and Boquet River valleys had nearly ruined the Dix Range trail system. For many hikers, they were among the worst trails in the Adirondacks.

In 1932, partly to retire a bank loan, the Adirondack Mountain Reserve sold 4,700 acres in the Boquet River watershed to the state for about $26,000.[45] A year later, contributing editor William D. Mulholland wrote in *High Spots* that, "The recent acquisition by the State of lands of the Adirondack Mt. Reserve in the watershed of the north fork of the Boquet River places on State land and opens to the public two old and interesting trails – one from St. Huberts to Dix and a branch from this trail to Noonmark. The direct trail to Dix bears blue markers and starts near the old St. Huberts baseball diamond while the branch trail to Noonmark is designated with red trail markers."[46] Mulholland also noted that a trail from Round Pond to Dix would be cut.

Two years later, A. T. Shorey, who worked for the Conservation Department and later chaired the ADK guidebook committee, wrote an article called "The Great Circle Trail" for *High Spots*. In it, he described an itinerary for an eight-day, forty-mile circuit from Keene Valley over the Great Range and down to Elk Lake. From Panther Gorge, "It would be well to continue on to Elk Lake and put up for the night and possible two nights with brother Davis at his Elk Lake Lodge."[47] On the eighth day, the route led either over Colvin via

Pinnacle, or through Hunters Pass. "Whichever route you elect, pray for dry weather," Shorey advised. (He also recommended proceeding from Colvin to Nippletop, where "you are now confronted with a problem – namely, to get down the east slope of Nippletop into Hunters Pass.")

Shorey's alternate route gives a good idea of the conditions facing hikers in the 1930s:

> The other route from Elk Lake is via the tote road up the east side of the lake and around the west slope of McComb, then north-west across two brooks (no trail about a half mile), down the north side of the second brook to and along the east side of Dix Pond (not on map) to the East Inlet tote road; then north on tote road through a beautiful valley hemmed in by cliffs on both sides, till the road peters out at the last shanty clearing; then the route is close under the ledges of Nippletop to the head of the Pass, a wild and cluttered up half mile. There will probably be a white string stretched over this route before many weeks to guide the C.C.C. boys who are expected to build a trail. This string will also show the route from the head of the pass to the intersection of the trail up Dix from St. Huberts. At St. Huberts the Great Circle trail, somewhat bent in places, comes to an end.

With characteristic understatement, Shorey noted that, "This is a trip for Adirondackers, not easy chair tourists."

That same year, 1935, the long-promised new highway by Chapel Pond had yet to be completed. But *High Spots* reported that, "Some work was done on the Elk Lake - Dix Trail late in the fall by Civilian Conservation Corps (CCC) forces from the Minerva Camp." They continued work in the spring, finishing the trail up to Hunters Pass."[48]

During and after World War II, the area received little attention. The ADK's 1950 *Guide to Adirondack Trails* gave a straightforward description of the route from St. Huberts to Dix that is largely the same today. In travelling from Elk Lake, the guidebook noted, the trail followed "an old wood road" to Slide Brook, where there was a small shanty clearing.[49] "Beyond the clearing the route is a log road for 1 m." After the Dix Pond, the trail "passes two more shanty clearings" before reaching the Beckhorn trail, "Best used for descent." They are the same clearings noted by Wickham and his contemporaries; they are still discernible today. An inset map of the "Elk Lake Region" shows a woods road crossing Lillian Brook on its way up towards Hough, while one for the "Bouquet Valley Region" shows "Trailless Routes" to the Dix Range along both forks of the Boquet River.

The author, presumably A. T. Shorey, enthused about the hikes, which are "most interesting" and "unsurpassed for beauty."[50] "An old hunters' and fishermen's trail begins on the high bank of a tree filled excavation on the side of the road just south of the Bouquet bridge." The guidebook suggested ascending Spotted Mountain from the South Fork and then continuing over "several humps" to East Dix, South Dix, Macomb, and down the new slide.

The guidebook explained how to proceed from the North Fork, cross by Lillypad Pond on an "unmarked trail," and proceed to the slides on the east side of Dix. "Select your slide and climb it to the summit," the book advised, adding that returning via the trail to St. Huberts is "a 'random scoot' for a champion."

Anne Biesemeyer Bailey (#163) recalls that the Big Blow of 1950 caused so much damage that some areas of the High Peaks were closed for five years. When she tried to climb Macomb and the trailless Dixes with her friends and guide Mary Schaefer, they were forced to spend the night "high on the ridge of East Dix."[51]

At that time, and through the 1960s, the DEC was responsible for the upkeep of trails of the Dix Range. Under Jim Goodwin's leadership, ATIS trail crews did what they could in the area, but they necessarily concentrated on paths on AMR property. Similarly, the owners of the Elk Lake Lodge took care of the paths on their land. The state trails once again fell into disrepair.

In the first issue of *Adirondack Peeks* (Fall/Winter 1963-1964), Forty-Sixers expressed concern over rumors that the Conservation Department was planning to cut trails from the North Fork of the Boquet up Hough, over the Dixes, and down to Schroon Lake. Dick Babcock (#115) wrote an editorial asking that the trailless Dixes be protected from trails.

In her book *From the Black Forest to Tibet: One Woman's Mountains* (1993), Trudy Healy (#148) described a challenging hike up Dix in 1963, "perhaps the roughest and steepest trail in the High Peaks."[52] At one point she slipped:

> I heard it crack as I skidded by my leg.
> "I broke my leg," I told Karen as I lay on the ground, looking up at my daughter.
> "Nonsense, Mama!" Karen declared. "If anything it's just sprained."
> "Sprains don't go CRRACK! Karen!"
> Actually, lying there, it didn't hurt, so I got up. Ouch! Can't stand on that leg: what do I do now?
> ... [H]ere I was, high up on Dix, five miles from the highway... one thing saved me: instead of sneakers like usually, I had worn L. L. Bean boots, that came pretty high up on the leg. By that time it was badly swollen, so the boot acted like a walking cast. I... limped along at a pretty fair pace – one mile per hour...
> When we finally got down, Karen drove me to the Keene Valley Hospital where much to my disgust I was kept overnight. They couldn't put a cast on because of the swelling.

In describing the St. Huberts trail to Dix, the eighth edition of the ADK's *Guide to Adirondack Trails* (1972) notes the same large boulder and lumber clearings that O'Kane cited almost fifty years earlier. From Elk Lake, the guidebook stated, that lumbering on private land continued until 1962. The start of the Dix trail, once a tote road, had been "bulldozed out for the recent lumbering."[53]

In 1978, the Forty-Sixers began maintaining the Dix trail from Round Pond. The Elk Lake Lodge is responsible for private trails on their land, but the Forty-Sixers have assumed responsibility for the Elk Lake-Dix trail. Trail crews have replaced the bridges across Lillian and Slide brooks. The old herdpath to the Macomb slide has been replaced by a Wilderness Path laid out by Trailmasters Len Grubbs (#2541W) and Bill Johnson (#3874W).[54] That path, looked after by members of the Forty-Sixers, continues from Macomb to the Beckhorn on Dix and includes the old herdpath from South Dix to East Dix. Other herdpaths in other areas have become more pronounced. One up the North Fork of the Boquet River is marked on the latest ADK High Peaks Trail map. From that path, the East Dix slide is easily reached.

Responsibility today for the trails to the Dix Range depends in large part on the 46ers, who schedule four or five trail crew trips a year in the area. They head out in May and June to clear blowdown from the Dix-Round Pond and Elk Lake trails and, in the summer, work on side-cutting and trail hardening. A dozen or more trees can fall across a trail after a major storm, all of which must be cut and removed by hand. Berry and viburnum shoots grow at a phenomenal rate and must be pruned back by hand. Both of the trails cross extensive sections that can be flooded. In on-going projects, 46er volunteers "harden" the flooded areas with rocks and gravel retrieved from streambeds.

As much as Dix endures, it also changes, sometimes dramatically. At some point around August 12, 1993, new slides appeared on its north face after two days of heavy rain. Betsey Thomas-Train (#3516) climbed over the range on August 13. She wrote, "When we reached the Dix summit, the rain started to clear; so we assumed it was safe to go down as planned. The trail became a river of rushing water and then it was gone. We were up to our knees in mud, crawling over downed trees and debris, when we gradually realized what happened."[55]

The Dix-Round Pond Trail was closed until DEC workers could find a new route around the boulder field at the base of the slides. Don Mellor, author of *Climbing in the Adirondacks*, considers those slides among the best Class 3 climbs in the High Peaks. In the Fall/Winter 1997-98 issue of *Adirondack Peeks*, Stephanie McConaughy (#3230) gave a compelling account of climbing one of them:

> The slide itself is an amazingly clean, glistening white pocked with dark gray, and very grippy. The climbing is steep and unyielding. On several pitches, I measured the slope at 35 degrees. At about 3600 feet, you have to choose the right or left branch, going around an island of trees and vegetation that miraculously survived the onslaught of mud and water... As you reach the top of the island at about 3800 vertical feet, you can see two other slides off to the left that ascend to the ridge line southeast of the Dix summit... When we were near the top at about 4540 vertical feet, we... took a deep breath and plunged into a wall of cripplebush *[sic]*. Couchsachraga, and even Emmons, were blissful memories compared to this... [W]e ascended 250 feet in 30 minutes... and emerged on the trail, scratched and bleeding, 50 vertical feet below the summit.[56]

It has been close to a hundred years now since fire and lumbering last claimed the Boquet Valley and a similar passing of time since clear-cutting leveled the forests around Elk Lake. The woods have come back, passing from second growth to their current mix of hardwood and fir.

The raspberries that so bedeviled Ingrid are mostly gone, replaced by aspen and hobblebush. Across the Boquet and up the floor of the valley the forest shifts to more birch, white and yellow, their bark glowing in the slanted light of winter or in the subdued tints of sunrise and sunset. Ascending parallel to the slides the forest changes again to balsam and spruce. Mosses cluster near the trail, and buoyant bunchberry gathers around rocks and roots, offering a different and equally elegant appearance each succeeding season, from creamy blossom to holiday-red berry. On the summit, krummholz gives way to sedges and sandwort.

So far no one has been able to design an "easy" route up Dix. From Elk Lake, it is a 13.2-mile round trip on a trail that often resembles the tangle of boulders found at the bottom of a slide. That's when a passing shower hasn't transformed it into a smoothly flowing stream. Two "knolls" passed on the way in can be especially discouraging on the way out. The trail splits just after Dix Pond, with the Elk Lake trail continuing up through Hunters Pass on the route of an old woods road and the newer Beckhorn Trail taking an essentially vertical route to the Dix summit. The Hunters Pass option has its own vertical challenges until it junctions with the Dix-Round Pond trail.

Coming in from Route 73, the Dix-Round Pond trail climbs quickly to the campsites around beautiful Round Pond. It's another stiff climb to the junction with the Noonmark-Round Mountain trail. The route to Dix then takes a wide semi-circle around the drainage of Gravestone Brook before ambling along the North Fork of the Boquet to the Boquet River Lean-to. From there a gradual climb over rough ground leads to the bottom of a slide and a demanding ascent to the junction with the Elk Lake trail.

Even before Hurricane Floyd, ascending via Lillian Brook required determination. The downed and tangled trees forced hikers to crouch, stoop, and crawl up the streambed or, at times, just shoulder their way through clutching, grasping, resilient spruce boughs. Almost as if to taunt climbers, soft beds of sorrel line the banks of the brook. The Lillian Brook approach is now a Wilderness Path maintained by the 46ers.

Early guidebooks described the clear-cut and fire-damaged route from the northeast as easy, but as the forest has grown back the bushwhack has become more complex. On the far side of Macomb are stands of young balsam, massed shoulder to shoulder and just tall enough to block your view, just dense enough to scrape your arms raw, and, in season, covered with enough pollen to parch your throat and deplete your water supply.

As Guy and Laura Waterman have reported, the Dixes played a role in the development of the Forty-Sixers: "The Reverend [Ernest R.] Ryder and some of the parishioners, notably Edward C. Hudowalski, gradually raised their sights from casual mountain climbing to systematic peakbagging, completing the Marshall's forty-six on Dix in a dense fog on September 13, 1936."[57]

Dix demands toil and struggle, but rewards hikers with what may be the most satisfying of the High Peaks summits. Certainly Ryder and Hudowalski were satisfied. From Dix, they went on to found the Forty-Sixers of Troy.

HOUGH PEAK
Height: 21st – 1,344 meters (4,409 feet)

Hough Peak is a fairly sharp cone on a ridge extending southeast from the main summit of Dix. For a mountain in the shadow of more substantial summits, it has enjoyed a surprising number of names. Early writers referred to it as "Middle" or "Little Dix." Colvin sometimes called it "Cone Mountain." The Forty-Sixers of Troy campaigned to have it known as Marshall, after Forty-Sixer #3, Bob Marshall, but in 1937, it was named once and for all after Franklin Benjamin Hough, "the father of American forestry."

Hough was born in 1822 in Martinsburg, New York, the son of a doctor. After graduating from Union College (1843) and studying medicine at Western Reserve Medical College, he began practicing medicine in Somerville, New York (1848), and soon thereafter moved to Lowville, four miles from his birthplace. Although he served as regimental surgeon in the 97th New York Volunteers during the Civil War, he retired from medicine early in his career to concentrate on research and writing. He pioneered county histories in New York, wrote a well-regarded catalogue of plants as well as a study of Duryee's Brigade during the Civil War. He is most known today for his writings and speeches on forestry.[58]

Franklin Hough

Hough was superintendent of the first complete census of New York, in 1855, and of one in 1865. Comparing results between the two, he became alarmed at rapidly dwindling timber reserves. He campaigned for forest protection, and in August 1873 delivered one of the country's landmark conservation speeches, "On the Duty of Governments in the Preservations of Forests," before the American Association for the Advancement of Science.

Largely as a result of his speech (and after three years of lobbying by concerned scientists), the federal government established a Division of Forestry in the Department of Agriculture. Hough was named "special forestry agent" – the first federal expert on forestry – in 1876. The next year, he traveled close to 8,000 miles across the country researching what would become a four-volume *Report on Forestry*.

The physician and self-taught scientist must have had a prickly personality: his contemporaries used adjectives such as rough and uncouth to describe him. A widower, he was the sort of man who could woo Mariah Kilham, his second wife, by sending her a list of his mineral specimens. Three months before his wedding, he offered her this explanation of his character: "While some sought pleasure in walking the streets and visiting places of amusement, or pored over some classical author, or found in the social circle his happiness, I retired to the fields and groves or along the margin of some lake or river where I could study the works of nature in all their loveliness."[59]

Once he took up the cause of conservation, Hough was indefatigable in the defense of forests, calling for the protection of government lands and an end to land grants to railroads, homesteaders, and others. He was given co-author credit with Verplanck Colvin for the text of the *First Annual Report of the Commissioners of State Parks,* and he drafted the federal Forest Preserve Act. He was a key figure in the Division of Forestry but became a victim of politics and was replaced by a partisan appointee in 1883. He died in 1885, a month after the bill he had framed for the state of New York, the Forest Commission Act, had been approved by the legislature. That act created the Catskill and Adirondack Forest Preserves. Congress would eventually follow Hough's wishes and pass the Forest Reserve Act (1891). The USDA Forest Service today names Hough as the first in its line of Chiefs or Foresters.

Hough grew up within sight of what would become the Adirondack Park, and he clearly relished his time in the woods. In his autobiography he mentioned hiking twenty-five miles with a fifty-pound pack and, on another occasion, walking forty-five miles in a night. He loved history as well, and his meticulous research, respect for the past, and accomplished writing have been an inspiration for subsequent generations of historians. By taking a sober approach to conservation, backed by logic and statistics, he arguably accomplished as much as more emotional writers such as Colvin.

Still, the decision to name Middle Dix after Hough blind-sided some of the Forty-Sixers. Russell Carson had proposed Marshall for the mountain's name change in *Peaks and People* (he wanted the current Mount Marshall named after the Marshalls' guide Herbert Clark). The name appeared as *Marshall* on a New York State Conservation Commission map in 1927. However, many disputed the choice, in part because the Marshalls were still alive. The brothers themselves objected to the proposed name.

After Bob Marshall died, the Forty-Sixers of Troy petitioned the state (1940) to change Middle Dix to Marshall. To the surprise of Grace Hudowalski, chairman of the renaming committee, the name had already been changed to Hough. (See Suzanne Lance's "History of the Adirondack Forty-Sixers" for more information about the naming of Hough.)

Hudowalski questioned Carson about the matter. He replied, "I recall that I made a suggestion for naming some large forest tract for Dr. Franklin B. Hough, and I have a faint recollection that I heard or was consulted about an idea of naming a mountain for him. I did not know it had been done until your letter, and was not aware until today [October 26, 1940] that the name was on the U.S. Geological Survey map of the Mount Marcy Quadrangle."[60]

Carson went on to say, "The name Hough is a distinguished one, but it would be more appropriate for a forest monument. A side consideration is that I do not believe 1 [*one*]

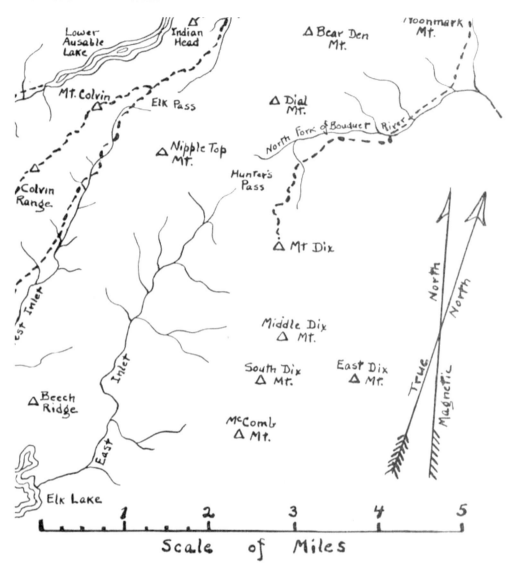

In Walter Collins O'Kane's *Trails and Summits of the Adirondacks*, 1929, the peak Robert Marshall had called Middle Dix appeared on the map that accompanied the book.

person out of a hundred knows how to pronounce the name correctly (Huff) today." Carson also discussed the differing philosophies of Colvin and Hough, attributing "the curious overlapping of Park and Preserve" to the "compromise of the ideals of the two men." However, the occasion for the renaming, a year-long anniversary in 1935 commemorating 50 Years of Conservation, was beyond dispute.

Two days later, Hudowalski contacted William G. Howard, director of the Division of Lands and Forests for what was then called the State of New York Conservation Department. He stated that Commissioner Lithgow Osborne recommended the name change, backed by the Adirondack Mountain Club – and Russell Carson. That same day, Hudowalski also wrote to Hugh M. Flick, the Secretary of the State Board on Geographic Names. In his reply, he wrote, "I have been informed by the United States Department of Interior, Board on Geographical Names that the name Hough Peak was accepted in June 1937 and that it was approved both by our State Board and the Federal Board."[61]

Hudowalski wrote about the name change in the *High Spots* yearbook for 1942:

> While it is unfortunate that this particular mountain was chosen to bear Dr. Hough's name, there is no doubt that he was a great man in many fields of endeavor, and especially was he outstanding in forest preservation. Surely his tireless efforts and notable results entitle him to a forest monument![62]

Like Dix and South Dix, Hough boasts a bowl-shaped cirque on its western flank, the result of glacial erosion. Its slopes turn from a typical northern boreal forest of spruce and balsam to mostly balsam, characterized as "sub-alpine," over 3,100 feet.

The Marshalls and Herb Clark are credited with first climbing Hough on August 13, 1921, although it is likely that others hiked over it from the Dix summit without realizing it was a peak that could be claimed. Bob Marshall described the summit as "by no means worth the trouble of climbing." He may have been discouraged after tackling the mountain from the east, from the headwaters of the South Fork of the Boquet River – quite possibly the most difficult approach to take today. Earlier that same day Bob, George, and Herb climbed Macomb, South Dix, and East Dix. They descended East Dix via a slide and crossed the charred floor of the Boquet valley before heading up Hough. They appeared to descend due west from the summit, "down what closely approaches a 1,500-foot precipice," according to Carson.

Forty-Sixer records are incomplete before 1956, but canister tallies in 1957 and 1958 show that fewer than forty people made it to the summit of Hough each year. The numbers increased dramatically after that, presumably because blowdown from the Big Blow of 1950 had finally been cleared. There were 110 climbers in 1959 who signed in, 183 five years later, and 459 by 1980. (The numbers are similar for Macomb, South Dix, and East Dix.)[63]

The first issue of *Adirondack Peeks* (Fall/Winter 1963-64) contained an editorial by Dick Babcock (#115) excoriating the Conservation Department for proposing a new trail from the North Fork of the Boquet "up Hough and over all the Dixes to Hoffman and down to Schroon Lake."[64] *Peeks* editor Trudy Healy (#148) complained that the trails would "take the challenge away from finding our own way up the trailless summits."

In December 1949, Paul Van Dyke, Gil Barker, and Bob Collins (#923) climbed Hough during a hike that included South Dix, East Dix, and Macomb. Almost fifty years later (1995), Trailmaster Len Grubbs (#2541W) described an endless series of spruce traps while climbing Hough: "Along the ridge [between Hough and South Dix] they attacked with a vengeance. Dave Hudda (#3018), who was in the lead, became the first victim. I watched as the trap opened, swallowing him. He was in up to his shoulders. A cascade of wet snow buried his snowshoes. He was immobile, helpless... We proceeded only a few steps before Wende Grubbs (#2542W) disappeared from sight, leaving behind a few flakes of snow that swirled above her dungeon."[65]

Today the mountain is a relatively easy walk of a mile from the summit of Dix, along a ridge that affords occasional views of the Elk Lake valley as well as the South Dix-East Dix ridge. The best views from the restricted summit are back to Dix. A small clearing near the site of the former canister is the setting for countless photographs of proud hikers who have added Hough to their lists.

Coming from the South Dix-Macomb col, Hough is more of an adventure. Hikers must first summit the onomatopoeic and rhyming Pough, a small hogback that can be dense with blowdown. (Pough is an informal name that is not recognized on maps.)

South Dix / Carson Peak
Height: 37th – 1,240c meters (4,068+ feet)
East Dix / Grace Peak
Height: 42nd – 1,221 meters (4,006 feet)

In a photo from the 1930s, well posed, Grace Hudowalski leads – right to left – Charlie Horn, Ernest Ryder, and Jack Colby to the summit of South Dix.

Extending on a ridge generally northeast from the main Dix range, South Dix /Carson Peak and East Dix /Grace Peak are the only two of the forty-six high peaks to have directional names, a circumstance that has been noted by writers and historians since the 1920s. In *Peaks and People of the Adirondacks,* Russell M. L. Carson reported that the mountains were named by Robert Marshall in his booklet "The High Peaks of the Adirondacks," and that had Marshall not called them "South Dix and East Dix in his booklet... they would still be nameless mountains." Carson commented, "The most interesting fact about these two mountains is that their names are not important enough to be retained and that they can be given distinctive titles, when the right occasion comes, without violation of old-established names."[66]

Perhaps in response to Carson's assertion, Stephen Davis set out in 1974 to change either South or East Dix to Davis Mountain, in honor of his grandfather, Albert Tatum Davis, a Saranac Lake forest surveyor who had died ten years earlier. In a letter she wrote to Ditt Dittmar about the issue, Grace Hudowalski mentioned that the DEC had already dedicated a plaque in memory of the surveyor at the Adirondack Center Museum in Elizabethtown.[67] She also wrote to Stephen Davis and explained that the Forty-Sixers of Troy had helped petition name changes for several High Peaks in the 1930s and 1940s, partly in response to the renaming of "Middle Dix" (Hough). About that effort, she wrote:

They included in their petition all the names Carson had in his book that were not permanent and wrote up their reasons which were accepted by the Department of Conservation, published in all papers by the State Board of Geographic Names and finally submitted to the National group. This was to prevent more switching.

Hence the statement in Carson's book... does not hold true today.[68]

In *Discover the Adirondack High Peaks* (1989), Barbara McMartin and her co-authors reported that, "There is a move afoot today to give East Dix the name Clark, for Herb Clark, who was the Marshalls' guide and companion."[69] One of the prime instigators was Patricia Collier (#971), who proposed the change to David Newhouse (#317), president of the Adirondack Mountain Club, in February 1986. That September, Newhouse named Collier chair of a special committee to investigate the proposed name change. "I would think that George Marshall's and the 46'rs support would be almost essential," Newhouse wrote.[70] That November, George Marshall wrote that, "I have long felt that one of the High Peaks should be named for Herb."[71] Marshall even thought that "Herbert," although informal, would be a better name than "Clark," used, by his count, for twenty-four other Adirondack names. A month later, the executive committee of the ADK voted to support the name change.

When Collier asked the Forty-Sixers to endorse the change, then-president Donald J. Hoffman (#1148) sought Grace's opinion. Citing a 1930s State Conservation Department "Map of the Mt. Marcy Region," she noted that only five High Peaks had no names at that time.[72] East Dix and South Dix were not among them. Consequently, at that time, Grace felt that the two peaks had been "permanently" named. Repeating the trouble the Forty-Sixers had with the naming process for mountains such as Hough and Marshall, she maintained that none of the High Peaks should have its name changed:

> I have no objection to the name of Herbert Clark being on a mountain, however, if a mountain is chosen, then it should not be a High Peak...
>
> I won't attempt to give special reasons why the 46 should retain their present names as it's well known they have been published in several books, guide books, maps, and on more than 40,000 *Climbing* folders which the Adirondack Forty-Sixers have distributed free...
>
> Even attempting to change the name of any of the 46 would only lead to considerable confusion and pity the poor historian who would have to explain this to thousands of hikers over the ensuing years![73]

Grace thought that Herbert Brook or the naming of one of the ADK Hundred Highest (in particular #49, Lost Pond Mountain) in Herb Clark's honor would be appropriate.

Hoffman wrote back to Collier in January 1987 denying the Forty-Sixers' support for her campaign. "Is it wise to change the name of a mountain that already has an official name?" he asked. "Is it justified to now make a change in this mountain's name? Grace mentions confusion arising. I think a good case could be made for a strong word ... chaos!!"[74]

Philip G. Terrie (#772), who edited the reissue of *Peaks and People*, didn't buy Grace's argument – "If people can change their names, then so can mountains." – but he also held back from completely agreeing with the proposal. "Is Herbert Clark more deserving than Harold Hochschild?[75] Should we save a peak for someone like Paul Schaefer, whose contribution to the Adirondacks is truly monumental?" Terrie also resisted naming another mountain after Clark. "Furthermore, I think that any geographical feature in the Adirondacks that does not currently have a name should never be named... the act of naming is an act of claiming, denoting a sense of ownership or mastery. It suggests the anthropocentric arrogance that has destroyed so much of the American wilderness."[76]

The November 21, 1987, issue of the *Adirondack Daily Enterprise* included an article by John Duquette calling for a mountain to be named after Clark,[77] but momentum for the campaign faded away.

Tim Tefft writes of the change in the 46er's view arrived at in the last ten years as follows:

> Although the 46ers had previously opposed the renaming of either East Dix or South Dix, based in large measure upon Grace's arguments, at the club's fall 2001 meeting, L. John VanNorden (#2110W) proposed naming a mountain after her. VanNorden and other members of the 46ers, citing Grace's more than sixty years of "forty-sixing," her love for the mountains, her longtime advocacy for the Adirondack Park and for the preservation of the High Peaks region, felt that a peak – a High Peak – should be named in her honor. Recalling that Russell Carson had maintained that both *South Dix* and *East Dix* were names "not important enough to be retained" and that they could be "given distinctive titles, when

Russell Carson negotiating a descent on a ladder

the right occasion" came along, members of the 46er executive committee began to consider the possibility of naming East Dix in honor of Grace and South Dix in honor of Russell Carson, the man who suggested the impermanence of the names in his 1920s history of the High Peaks.

Grace was present at the executive committee's fall 2002 meeting when Douglas Arnold (#4693W) was appointed head of the committee – the Grace Peak Committee – charged with conducting the campaign to rename South Dix in Carson's honor as *Carson Peak* and East Dix *Grace Peak*. Pursuing a suggestion made by Jennifer Runyon of the United States Board of Geographical Names, Arnold asked Grace directly what her opinion was concerning the proposed changes. She told him, "I always believed Carson deserved a peak." Regarding the proposal to name East Dix in her honor, she said, "It's a silly notion." Arnold reports that he responded that there were many 46ers who believed that the proposal was "not so silly," and that Grace's rejoinder was "Well, they are your mountains, too."

The 46ers, believing that Grace Hudowalski's and Russell Carson's roles in promoting and championing the High Peaks of the Adirondacks were of paramount significance, have officially sanctioned the efforts of the Grace Peak Committee. The committee has been actively promoting the renaming of the two peaks and has received endorsements from the Board of Directors of the Adirondack Mountain Club (ADK) and most of its chapters, town governments, civic organizations, and many individuals. The formal proposal was submitted to the New York State Committee on Geographical Names in March 2009, five years after Grace's death. The U.S. Board of Geographic Names has yet to consider the proposals; however, in recent years it has agreed to two new names for Adirondack peaks, TR Mountain and Goodman Mountain. Perhaps, within a few more years, two new names, those of Grace Peak and Carson Peak, will replace those of East Dix and South Dix. Climbing folders, maps, and other ephemera will have to be recreated and rewritten to reflect the changes, for, although Grace advocated permanence for the names of her beloved peaks, the Forty-Sixers believe the changes are appropriate. Over time, with the forces and beneficence of nature – with the frequent disregard of many people but the nurturing stewardship of others – the mountains have changed. They will continue to change. Change may also come – as it has before – to the roster of names of our storied summits.

In 1927, Carson wrote that the Marshalls were the first to summit East and South Dix, which they reported accomplishing on August 13, 1921. It was part of a marathon hike that started with Macomb and, after South and East, continued down to the valley floor and back up over Hough. Almost fifteen years after the devastating fires of 1913, the area was still charred ruins. The Marshalls did not rate the views from these peaks highly, and George later wrote, "We climbed these on what probably was our hardest Adirondack day."[78] About South Dix, Robert Marshall wrote that it had "one of the most desolate views I know of – nothing but burned wasted land on all sides."[79]

However, when S. R. Lockwood read Carson's book, he wrote the author a letter on November 20, 1927, stating that he and a friend accidentally climbed South Dix in 1913 while trying to summit Dix. (Lockwood said he got lost on new tote roads, built to remove downed trees in the aftermath of the fires.) George Marshall agreed a month later that Lockwood's claim was probably true.

To further confuse matters, Hans Steiniger wrote in an East Dix canister register that he was the first to climb the mountain, on August 10, 1917, and that he named it "Dragon Tooth." Steiniger was making a joke (and a pretty obscure one at that), but his entry was reprinted in the spring 1972, issue of *Adirondack Peeks*.[80] As a result, Steiniger's contention had to be refuted by Philip Terrie in the 1973 reissue of *Peaks and People*.

Like their names, East and South Dix are very often afterthoughts during longer treks. To a hiker trying to climb the Dix Range in a day, the mountains invariably sit directly before or after higher summits. If you can spot a second car, a direct route will start at Elk Lake, ascend Macomb, traverse the South and East range, then backtrack to the South Dix col prior to ascending the hogback before Hough, moving on to Dix, and heading to the second vehicle at the Ausable Club or the Round Pond trail parking area along Route 73. An alternative is to bushwhack up the Boquet River herdpath, ascend the slide on East Dix, then tackle the remaining four peaks – and return to a second car at either end of the trail from Elk Lake to the Ausable Club or the Round Pond trailhead.

If you were Trudy Healy, this might be too easy:

> The day before this was written, I went over the Dixes. Climbing Macomb, it is true, I didn't use the common approach, but avoided the lower, alder-infested reaches of the brook. An old lumber road angles up the hillside and brought me to the stream just below the base of the slides. I then followed the southern-most, old rock slab, because it is more interesting underfoot than the more popular, newer slides. (Of course, anyone who gets sick and tired of traipsing where everyone else traipsed before him, can break away when a spirit of adventure compels him. But if it's run-of-the-mill trips you want, by all means, use herd paths.) When I reached the Macomb summit ridge, I was wondering: should I avoid The Path and struggle along the side of the mountain? Good gosh, no! I'm not that much of a fool! Before The Path, I thought I was doing really well to get from Macomb to the summit of South Dix in thirty-five minutes. Yesterday, in spite of my advanced years, it took thirty, without even half trying. For speed records you just can't beat herd paths.[81]

John Winkler (#1279) wrote to *Peeks* about another route up East Dix. "Back in the early 70s when I first started climbing, I climbed East Dix by way of Spotted Mountain and up the ridge. At that time this was the conventional route." A few years later, he climbed via the slide, which he described then as "a total bushwhack," as the herdpath petered out near Spotted Mountain. In 1995, Winkler and Mike Whalen climbed the slide again. "We took the herd path along the South Fork of the Boquet and then bushwhacked (near Spotted) over to the North Fork." The herdpath by then went all the way to the slide. "To my amazement (I shouldn't be surprised) there is also a herd path parallel to the slide to use should the slide be slippery or icy. These paths were not here 20 years ago!"[82]

A hundred years ago, they were – or at least parts of them, according to the maps of the period. The 1901 Elizabethtown quad, based on an 1892 survey, shows a number of unmarked trails or woods roads: a path along the North Fork of the Boquet that angles south before fading away at Lillypad Pond; a path along the South Fork that skirts around Spotted Mountain on its way to the East Dix slides; one beside Lindsay Brook; and another along West Mill Brook, this one turning southwest in the route of the old Cedar Point road. The equivalent 1895 Mt. Marcy quad shows this last trail following the valley northwest of Camels Hump and Niagara Mountain until it climbs a thousand feet over the southern slopes of Sunrise Mountain to meet up with Clear Pond Inlet.

The "Bouquet Valley Region" map inserted into the 1950 ADK trail guide lists the paths along the two forks of the Boquet River as "Trailless Routes." The map, drawn by E. H. Leggett in 1945, has the North Fork path continuing south from Lilypad Pond to the South Fork, then crossing the floor of the valley to ascend Dix from the east. The South Fork path ascends Spotted Mountain on its way to East and South Dix. Remnants of the Lindsay Brook and West Mill Brook trails can be seen on the 1955 Elizabethtown quad, and, even up to 1964, some maps included woods roads along both forks of the Boquet and the Niagara Brook. The current ADK High Peaks trail map shows the old road along the North Fork of the Boquet as a "bushwhack route."[83]

The confusion between *Boquet* and *Bouquet* River can sometimes arise within the same sets of maps. No one has been able to supply a totally credible reason for the name. The wildflowers that grow along its banks could be a connection, but why this river and not any other? R. Pearsall Smith noted, "It is also said to have been named for Henry Boquet, an English officer; but the name appears on French maps previous to his residence in the country."[84] Winslow C. Watson refutes the Gen. Boquet attribution, primarily because he served in the west during the French and Indian War. Watson also rejects the idea that the river was named for flowers. "The most probable origin, I think, is the French word *baquet*, trough. This term would have been remarkably descriptive of the appearance of the stream below the falls."[85] Franklin B. Hough agrees with Watson: "(P)robably from the French 'boquet,' trough."[86] David H. Burr also used *Boquet* in his series of maps.

Nonetheless, Alfred L. Donaldson referred to the "Bouquet River" in his *History of the Adirondacks*. The 1901 Elizabethtown quad also has *Bouquet*, but the 1905 New York State Forest, Fish and Game Commission *Adirondack Map* has *Boquet* River. The 1950 *Guide to Adirondack Trails* has *Boquet* on one map and *Bouquet* on another. The current *Trails of the Adirondack High Peaks Region* prefers *Boquet*, but the U.S. Geological Survey metric maps stick with *Bouquet*. So it goes: Robert Marshall, Robert S. Wickham, and Walter Collins O'Kane all use *Bouquet*; Verplanck Colvin, E. R. Wallace, and Russell M. L. Carson, *Boquet*. You are likely to hear many more ways of pronouncing it.[87]

MACOMB MOUNTAIN
Height: 22nd – 1,338 meters (4,390 feet)

How and when Macomb, the southernmost of the High Peaks, was named has never been clearly determined. The name was settled at some point between the Battle of Plattsburgh (September 11, 1814) and the publication in 1842 of the *Natural History of New York*, which included a print by R. C. Taylor of "Nipple Top, Dix's Peak, and McCombe's Mountain." One early map lists a "McComb's Mountains," referring to the entire Adirondack area.[88] Russell Carson suggests that this name was gradually transferred to the current mountain, but then hints that people in the area knew better. For one thing, it would mean the mountain was named for Alexander Macomb, Senior, a somewhat unsavory speculator who was the man behind Macomb's Purchase. Born in Ireland, Macomb emigrated to Albany in 1755. He built up a small fortune trading furs and supplies in Detroit with his brother and a third partner. In New York City by 1785, Macomb and two Irish compatriots engineered a land scheme through which he was to lay claim to almost twelve percent of the entire state at pennies to the acre. The purchase included Herkimer, St. Lawrence, and Franklin counties in what would become the Adirondack Park, but the deal unraveled almost at once, with Macomb eventually spending time in jail.

General Macomb

Macomb's son, Alexander, Junior, was born in 1782 in Detroit and received a wealthy child's upbringing. He entered the military at the age of sixteen, trained at West Point, rose through the ranks in the Corps of Engineers, and by 1814 was a brigadier general assigned to the Lake Champlain area. Given credit for defeating the British at the Battle of Plattsburgh that September, Macomb was hailed a hero and promoted to major general. He served in Detroit until 1821, when he became chief of the engineer department in Washington, D.C., and ultimately the commander-in-chief of the army. Among other things, he was responsible for eliminating daily whisky rations and instituting pensions for soldiers and their widows. He died in Washington in 1841 and was honored in memorials throughout the country.[89]

No matter how grateful locals may have been over his part in the Battle of Plattsburgh, it cannot be proven that the mountain was named for him. Military scholars believe that Thomas Macdonough actually played the decisive role in the victory. Commanding a fleet of four warships and ten gunboats – which at the time made up the entire United States fleet on the lake – Macdonough engaged superior British forces on September 11 near Cumberland Head outside Plattsburgh. Macdonough and his sailors routed the enemy in a daring, head-on encounter. The British land troops were so discouraged that they gave up almost immediately. Some historians believe that the battle essentially ended the war, as the defeat left Great Britain with no grounds to claim United States territory during peace settlements at Ghent.

Commodore Macdonough, who went on to an exemplary naval career, was captain of the *U.S. Constitution*, "Old Ironsides," when he died of heart failure in 1827.[90] Colvin, for one, thought he was as important a figure as Macomb and named "the loftiest peak in the Jay Range" after him. (On the "Sketch Showing the Region Under Survey" in the *Seventh Annual Topographical Survey*, Colvin marked a "Mt. McDonough" directly west of the town of Willsboro. In the same edition, a "Progress Sketch of Primary Triangulation, 1878" shows "Mac

Early hikers on Macomb

Donough" to be directly north of Hurricane.)[91] A benchmark on the easternmost summit of Jay Mt. may have been what Colvin intended to call MacDonough. But like so many of his appellations, the name did not stick.

The first recorded ascent of Macomb was by Keene Valley guide Mel Trumbull and artist Alexander H. Wyant in 1872. Born in Elizabethtown, Trumbull joined the navy at fourteen. After his service he moved to Keene Valley and became a guide. His clients – including author Charles Dudley Warner and Yale University president Noah Porter – indicated how respected he was.[92] Trumbull had what ended up to be the last guide's camp on the Upper Ausable Lake, and he was famous for his stories, especially his late-night encounter with a hungry panther. It's not difficult to picture him, so familiar with the area, picking his way up Macomb for a fee. The presence of Wyant, whom writer Eliot Clark described as physically weak and by temperament dour and "not communicative," is a bit more surprising.[93]

Born in Ohio in 1836, Alexander Helwig Wyant started out as an apprentice to a harnessmaker, then became a sign painter. When he was twenty-one, he saw an exhibition of Hudson Valley painters and was so impressed that he moved to New York City to learn from painter George Inness. After studying in Germany and touring Europe, Wyant returned, in 1867, to New York City, where he opened a profitable studio. Influenced by Joseph Mallord William Turner and John Constable as well as American painters, Wyant painted romantic landscapes that were extremely popular.

The painter Roswell Shurtleff, who had been visiting the Adirondacks for years, lured Wyant to Keene Valley in 1869. Captivated by the area, Wyant returned frequently. He took many of his subjects from Keene Valley, but also roamed throughout the High Peaks. *The Flume, Opalescent River* is an especially dramatic painting, while no one familiar with the area could fail to recognize his version of *Noon Mark, Adirondacks*.

A year after he climbed Macomb, Wyant and landscape photographer Timothy O'Sullivan took part in an expedition under Lt. George Wheeler through Arizona and New Mexico. Wyant returned with a paralyzed right arm, apparently the result of a stroke, although the incident was covered up in official reports. Amazingly, Wyant taught himself to paint left-handed, and his subsequent work proved as successful as ever. In fact, some critics detected a new freedom in his brushwork.

Wyant built a summer home east of the Ausable River in 1875, and in the 1880s spent much of his time in Keene Valley with his wife and son. He died in New York City in 1892. His work never went out of vogue during his lifetime, and today it can be found in the collections of the Adirondack Museum, New York City's Metropolitan Museum of Art, and the National Gallery in Washington. On the market, his oils can bring up to $300,000.

The easiest route up Macomb for Trumbull and Wyant may have been from Elk Lake, where the guide could have sighted a path up the Slide Brook drainage. (The Slide Brook name appears on 1895 Marcy quad, but the slides that most ascend today occurred much later.) However, there was the Cedar Point Road from Clear Lake along Niagara Brook to West Mill Brook, still marked on the 1895 Marcy quads, and a woods road up the North Fork of the Boquet. That would have been a closer approach for the artist at least, although a longer hike that would have stretched over East and South Dix as well. In those days before Colvin's surveys, Wyant and Trumbull might not have realized that the unnamed South Dix and East Dix were worth claiming as first ascents.

It seems that Macomb was always accessible from the woods and tote roads from the north and east. The 1894 edition of E. R. Wallace's *Descriptive Guide* has this brief notice: "There is also a good trail from Elk Lake to the summit of Macomb Mt.; distance 3mi."[94] The same note appeared in the 1899 edition, but, as he noted, twenty years later Carson could find no trace of a trail.

Subsequent writers, such as Wickham and O'Kane, mention Macomb primarily in passing. The 1934 *Guide to Adirondack Trails* simply says that "Dix is a peak in a narrow range that extends S. over S. Dix to McComb Mt."[95] Writing in *High Spots* in 1935, A. T. Shorey described a "Great Circle Trail" which traversed the west slopes of "McComb" on its way to Hunters Pass. The Marshalls and Herb Clark ascended Macomb on logging roads from Elk Lake up to "a big slide."

The fires which devastated the Boquet River Valley and the area around Elk Lake had the paradoxical effect of making Macomb an easier climb. Jim Goodwin, who climbed the mountain in 1926, told Sharp Swan that the area was "nothing but grass."[96]

In *Of the Summits, of the Forests*, Goodwin described the "great series of slides" on Macomb that occurred in 1947, adding that "for a number of years, climbers of Macomb merely walked up the graveled swath to the foot of whatever slide they wished to choose to ascend to the mountain's south peak. Today's climbers make their way to the south peak slides through a poplar and birch second growth along the Slide Brook and a tributary from the south."[97]

The 1950 edition of the *Guide to Adirondack Trails* also describes "a tremendous new slide" that actually crossed the Elk Lake-Dix Trail within a few hundred feet of the Slide Brook clearing. It advised, "Go up this slide following its main stem nearly to the top where it becomes too steep for safety."[98]

The 1953 quad is the first to mark the results of the hurricanes of 1947 and 1950. It is interesting to see how the slide contracts and grows through each subsequent edition of the map. In March, 1975, avalanches swept down the main slide, according to a report by Roger Harris (#778W) to *Adirondack Peeks*. As mentioned elsewhere, Hurricane Floyd in 1999 had a devastating effect on the area, particularly the Lillian Brook drainage.

Information about winter ascents is sketchy, although Guy and Laura Waterman note that in December 1949 Paul Van Dyke, Gil Barker, and Bob Collins climbed Macomb as well as South Dix, East Dix, and Hough.

Of all the freedoms enjoyed by our forefathers, perhaps the one resorted to most often was Freedom of Spelling. A print in the Emmons book refers to "McCombe's Mountain." The 1895 Marcy quadrangle lists the mountain as "Mc.Comb Mt." The 1953 and 1967 quads have it as "McComb Mt." It's not until the 1979 Mount Marcy 25,000 scale metric topographic map that we find the correct "Macomb Mtn."

Endnotes
Dix

General information from the Dix Unit Management Plan, the various Verplanck Colvin surveys, Russell M. L. Carson's *Peaks and People*, and ADK Trail Guides.

1. Emmons's reasons for climbing Marcy had the same mercenary tinge that colored all early recorded exploration in the area. As John A. Dix noted when calling for the survey, the purpose behind the expedition was to uncover "mineralogical productions" – money-making minerals. (Paul Schneider, *The Adirondacks: A History of America's First Wilderness*, New York: Henry Holt, 1997, pg. 130.)

2. Dix biographical data from Allan Nevins, *Dictionary of American Biography*, Vol. III, Part 1, ed. Allen Johnson and Dumas Malone (New York: Charles Scribner's Sons, 1930, renewed 1959), pg. 325; Phyllis F. Field, *American National Biography*, Volume 6, ed. John A. Garraty, Mark C. Carnes (New York, Oxford: Oxford University Press: 1999), pg. 638.

3. Charles Lanman, *Adventures of an Angler in Canada, Nova Scotia and the United States* (London: Richard Bentley, 1848), pg. 91.

4. Arthur H. Masten, *The Story of Adirondac*, with an introduction and notes by William K. Verner (The Adirondack Museum/Syracuse University Press, 1968), pg. xvii.

5. W. D. Mulholland, ed., "Trail Notes," *High Spots*, Vol. 10, No. 4 (October 1933), pg. 22.

6. Ed Palen, "Routed in Rock," *Adirondack Life*, Vol. 35, No. 4, pg. 20. The letter, presumed to have been written by Brown, was republished in the February 1982 *Adirondac* (Vol. XLVI, No. 1), pgs. 6-7. Peggy O'Brien (#560) wrote that she and her brother, Jim Goodwin (#24), "had a fascinating time trying to follow the old road from the description..."

7. Roger Mitchell, *Clear Pond: The Reconstruction of a Life*, (Syracuse University Press, 1991), pg. 75.

8. In 1831, Johnson signed a contract for the land with Gerrit Smith, whose father Peter acquired it in tax sales, but lost it to Smith's agent Joseph Frost in 1846. Frost's daughters sold their inheritance to land speculator Orson Richards in 1870. He in turned deeded it to Dean Sage of Brooklyn in 1875. The land continued to change hands until it was acquired by the Glens Falls lumbering concern Finch, Pruyn and Company from Phoebe Bloomingdale in 1891.

9. The engraving printed in the report by Emmons was "from a sketch by R. C. Taylor."

10. Alfred B. Street, *The Indian Pass* (New York: Hurd and Houghton, 1869), pg. 181.

11. *Ibid.*, pg. 172.

12. *Ibid.*, pg. 183.

13. Russell M. L. Carson, *Peaks and People of the Adirondacks*, ed. Philip G. Terrie, Jr. (Glens Falls, NY: The Adirondack Mountain Club, 1973), pg. 88.

14. *Ibid.*, pg. 89.

15. Storrow biographical information from William Chauncy Langdon, *Dictionary of American Biography*, Volume IX, Part 2, ed. Dumas Malone (New York: Charles Scribner's Sons, 1935, renewed 1964), pg. 99; Federal Writers' Project of the Works Progress Administration, *New Hampshire: A Guide to the Granite State* (Boston: Houghton Mifflin, 1938), pg. 512.

16. Verplanck Colvin, *State of New York Report on the Topographical Survey of the Adirondack Wilderness of New York for the Year 1873* (Albany: Weed, Parsons and Company, 1874), pg. 28.

17. Harold Weston, *Freedom in the Wilds: A Saga of the Adirondacks* (St. Huberts, NY: Adirondack Trail Improvement Society, 1971), pg. 42.

18. E. R. Wallace, *Descriptive Guide to the Adirondacks and Handbook of Travel to Saratoga Springs, Schroon Lake, Lakes Luzerne, George, and Champlain, The Ausable Chasm, the Thousand Islands, Massena Springs and Trenton Falls* (New York, Syracuse: The American News Company, 1875), pg. 163.

19. *Ibid.*

20. *Ibid.*, pg. 164.

21. *Ibid.*, pg. 162.

22. A few years later, in his essay "A Wilderness Romance," Charles Dudley Warner was critical of the name change. He wrote "people of grand intentions and weak vocabulary are trying to fix the name of Elk Lake" on Mud Pond.

23. Winslow C. Watson, *The Military and Civil History of the County of Essex, New York; and a general survey of its physical geography, its mines and minerals, and industrial pursuits embracing An Account of the Northern Wilderness; and also the military annals of the fortresses of Crown Point and Ticonderoga* (Albany: J. Munsell, State Street, 1869), pg. 333.

24. [Andrew Williams], *A Descriptive and Historical Guide to the Valley of Lake Champlain and the Adirondacks* (Burlington, VT.: R. S. Styles' Steam Printing House, 1871), pg. 92.

25. Bill Healy, ed., *The Adirondack Mountains of Orson Schofield Phelps* (Fleischmanns, NY: Purple Mountain Press, 1992), pg. 83.

26. Don't look for *beckhorn* in a dictionary, because it's not an English word. At least it's not acknowledged in *Webster's Third New International Dictionary, Random House Dictionary of the American Language*, or even the *Oxford English Dictionary*. "Beakhorn stake" shows up, however, as a small bench anvil having a horn on one side. *Beak horn* is found: as an anvil with a beak or point. Given Phelps's idiosyncratic spelling, he was probably aiming for 'bickern," originally an anvil with two projecting taper ends, and later the term for the taper itself. The *OED* traces this back to the seventeenth century and cites Sir John Talbot Dillon's 1781 *Travels through Spain*: "They have no other word in the Spanish language for a bickhorn, or a bench vice, than *Vigornia*."

27. Healy, pg. 23.

28. One of the inns, the Elk Lake House, wrote Robert S. Wickham, "was built of peeled spruce logs years ago, and artistically built, by Pell Jones, its guardian angel." Wickham offered a vivid description of Pell's laziness: "Seventeen summers ago [1906] on returning from our first Marcy climb Little Squaw and I had found Pell down in his small potato patch digging worms, sitting in a rocking chair to do it, moving the chair about with him as he changed position to dig." (Robert S. Wickham, *Friendly Adirondack Peaks* ((privately printed, 1924)), pg. 182.)

29. Edith Pilcher, *Up the Lake Road* (St. Huberts: The Adirondack Mountain Reserve, 1987), pg. 88.

30. *Ibid.*, pg. 89.

31. Francis L. Bayle, "Forest Fires," Francis L. Bayle. *High Spots*, Vol. 7, No. 3 (September, 1930), pg. 4.

32. Weston, pg. 80.

33. *Ibid.*, pg. 81.

34. *Ibid.*, pg. 93.

35. *Ibid.*, pg. 95.

36. See "The Fire Protection Map of 1916," Jerry Jenkins with Andy Keal, *The Adirondack Atlas* (Syracuse University Press & The Adirondack Museum, 2004), pg. 105.

37. Weston, pg. 136.

38. *Ibid.*, pg. 137.

39. Robert Marshall, "The High Peaks of the Adirondacks," (The Adirondack Mountain Club, 1922), page 15.

40. Wickham, pg. 153.

41. *Ibid.*, pg. 156.

42. *Ibid.*, pg. 174.

43. *Ibid.*

44. *Ibid.*, pg. 177.

45. Henry L. DeForest, President, *Adirondack Mountain Reserve President's Report 1932*. Pamphlet dated August 20, 1932.

46. W. D. Mulholland, ed., "Trail Notes," *High Spots*, Vol. 10, No. 4 (October, 1933), pg. 22.

47. A. T. Shorey, "The Great Circle Trail," *High Spots*, Vol. 12, No. 3 (July, 1935), pg. 5.

48. W. D. Mulholland, ed., "Trail Notes," *High Spots*, Vol. 13, No. 1 (January, 1936), pg. 13. The Civilian Conservation Corps was organized under President Franklin Roosevelt's New Deal legislation,

the Emergency Conservation Work Act, in 1933. The CCC employed young men who lived in camps, wore uniforms, and lived under a system of discipline similar to that of the military. Camps were established throughout the United States. Among the camps in the Adirondacks were ones at Lake Placid (1933-1941), Newcomb (1933, 1935-1941), Tahawus (1933), and the one mentioned, at Minerva (1935-1936).

49. *Guide to Adirondack Trails*, 1950 Edition (Albany, NY: Adirondack Mountain Club, 1950), pg. 49.

50. *Ibid.*, pg. 86.

51. Anne Biesemeyer Bailey, "A Keene Valley Childhood," *Adirondack Peeks*, Vol. 41, No. 2 (Fall, 2004), pg. 8.

52. "From the Black Forest to Tibet: One Woman's Mountains," *Adirondack Peeks*, Vol. 20, No. 1 (Spring/Summer 1993), pg. 2.

53. *Guide to Adirondack Trails*, Eighth Edition (Glens Falls, NY: Adirondack Mountain Club, 1972), pg. B4-6.

54. As of 2008, Wendy Grubbs (#2542W) and her husband were maintaining the Wilderness Path from the Dix Trail up and over Macomb to the col between that mountain and South Dix. Brian Hoody (#4410W) was taking care of the paths on South Dix and East Dix. Christine Bourjade (#4967W), Alex Radmonovich (#4968W), and Gary Koch (#1137W) were working on the Lillian Brook fork and the remainder of the path along the range's ridge as far as the Beckhorn.

55. Stephanie McConaughy, "Loving the North Slide on Dix," *Adirondack Peeks*, Vol. 34, No. 2 (Fall/Winter, 1997/98), pg. 11.

56. *Ibid.*, pg. 12.

57. Laura and Guy Waterman, *Forest and Crag* (Boston: Appalachian Mountain Club Books, 2003), pg. 517.

Hough

58. Hough biographical information from Henry S. Graves, *Dictionary of American Biography*, ed. Dumas Malone (New York: Charles Scribner's Sons, 1932, renewed 1960), Vol. V, Part 1, pg. 250; Neal S. Burdick, "Fathers of the Forest Preserve," *A Century Wild: Essays Commemorating the Centennial of the Adirondack Forest Preserve*, ed. Neal S. Burdick (Saranac Lake: The Chauncy Press, 1985), pg. 106; Vivian G. Smith, ed., *With Hand and Heart: The Courtship Letters of Franklin B. Hough and Mariah Kilham* (Utica, NY: North Country Books, 1993).

59. Smith, *With Hand and Heart...*, pg. 26.

60. Russell M. L. Carson to Grace Hudowalski, October 26, 1940.

61. Hugh M. Flick to Grace Hudowalski, November 1, 1940.

62. Grace L. Hudowalski, "A Major Peak Gets a New Name," *High Spots: January 1942 Adirondack Mountain Club Year Book* (New York: Adirondack Mountain Club), pg. 26.

63. Chuck Bennett, "Usage Survey of Untrailed Peaks in the Adirondacks," *Adirondack Peeks*, Vol. 23, No. 1 (Spring/Summer, 1986), pg. 2.

64. Reprinted in *Adirondack Peeks*, Vol. 31, No. 1 (Spring/Summer 1994), pg. 14.

65. Len Grubbs, "Hough, Puff and the Spruce Critter," *Adirondack Peeks*, Vol. 32, No. 1 (Spring/Summer 1995), pg. 12.

South Dix/Carson Peak and East Dix/Grace Peak

66. Russell M. L. Carson, *Peaks and People of the Adirondacks*, ed. Philip G. Terrie, Jr. (Glens Falls, NY: Adirondack Mountain Club, 1973), pg. 223.

67. Grace L. Hudowalski to Ditt Dittmar, April 20, 1974.

68. Grace L. Hudowalski to Stephen Davis, April 20, 1974.

69. Barbara McMartin and Bill Ingersoll, with Lee M. Brenning, Phil Gallos, Don Greene, E. H. Ketchledge, Gary Koch, and Willard Reed, *Discover the Adirondack High Peaks* (Canada Lake, NY: Lake View Press, 2001), pg. 147.

70. David Newhouse to Patricia Collier, September 11, 1986.

71. George Marshall to Patricia Collier, November 24, 1986.

72. The peaks that were not labeled on the map (1930) "compiled" by Hopkins "from Forest, Boundary, and U.S.G.S. Surveys," were Blake's Peak, Couchsachraga, Emmons, and Hough (Middle Dix). Whiteface and Esther did not appear on the map either, both being north of the area covered. Hopkins' map also labeled today's Marshall as MacIntyre.

73. Grace Hudowalski to Donald J. Hoffman, January 12, 1987.

74. Don Hoffman to Patricia Collier, January 19, 1987.

75. Harold K. Hochschild (1892-1981) was a student and patron of the Adirondacks who wrote *Township 34: A History with Digressions of an Adirondack Township in Hamilton County in the State of New York* (self-published, 1952). From that volume, the Adirondack Museum at Blue Mountain Lake published brief extracts, among them *The MacIntyre Mine – From Failure to Fortune* (Blue Mountain Lake, Adirondack Museum, 1962). Hochschild was president of the American Metal Company, now AMAX, Inc., was the founder of the Adirondack Museum, and was chairman of the New York State commission which created the Adirondack Park Agency. His papers (1936-1971) are housed in the Adirondack and Catskill Research Library in Schenectady. His son, Adam, founder and editor of *Mother Jones* magazine, wrote about his relationship with his father in *Half Way Home: A Memoir of Father and Son,* 1986.

76. Philip G. Terrie to Patricia Collier, February 22, 1987.

77. John Duquette, "Herb Clark sensed right route to top," *Adirondack Daily Enterprise*, November 21, 1987.

78. George Marshall to Patricia Collier, November 24, 1986.

79. Robert Marshall, "The High Peaks of the Adirondacks," (Adirondack Mountain Club, 1922), pg. 34.

80. Unsigned, "History Corrected," *Adirondack Peeks*, Vol. 9, No. 1 (Spring, 1972), pg. 13.

81. Trudy Healy, "In Praise of Herd Paths," *Adirondack Peeks,* Vol. 5, No. 2 (Fall, 1968), pg. 15.

82. John E. Winkler, "East Dix Revisited." *Adirondack Peeks*, Vol. 33, No. 2 (Fall-Winter 1996/97), pg. 22.

83. Maps referred to include *Map of New York Exhibiting the Post Offices, Post Roads, Canals, Rail Roads, & c. By David H. Burr*, 1829, 1834 and 1839; *Mt. Marcy, N.Y.*, U.S. Geological Survey, 1895, 1953; *Elizabethtown, N.Y.*, U.S. Geological Survey, 1901, 1955; *Colton's Map of the New York Wilderness Compiled by W. W. Ely, M.D.*, 1869; *Map of the Adirondack Forest and Adjoining Territory Compiled from the Official Maps and Field Notes on file in the State Departments at Albany, N.Y.*, Forest, Fish and Game Commission, 1905; *Adirondack Map compiled by the Conservation Department of the State of New York*, 1964; *Elk Lake Region* and *Bouquet Valley Region*, E. H. Leggett, in *Guide to Adirondack Trails*, Adirondack Mountain Club, 1950; *Elizabethtown, New York*, U.S. Geological Survey, 1978; *Trails of the Adirondack High Peaks Region*, Adirondack Mountain Club, 2003.

84. R. Pearsal Smith, *Historical and Statistical Gazetteer of New York State* (Syracuse: R. Pearsall Smith, 1860), pg. 296, note.

85. Winslow C. Watson, *Pioneer History of the Champlain Valley* (Albany: J. Munsell, 1863), pg. 96, note. The falls mentioned are in Willsboro. Most rivers which flow into Lake Champlain were provided their names by people who passed their mouths or journeyed up them from the lake.

86. Franklin B. Hough, *Gazetteer of the State of New York* (Albany: Andrew Boyd, no date [1873]), pg. 288, note.

87. Many locals pronounce it *bo' kwet'*. More refined visitors to the area tend to pronounce it *bo' ket'*.

Macomb

88. Russell M. L. Carson spotted "McCombe" references in the 1824 edition of *Spafford's Gazetteer*, in David Burr's 1829 *Atlas of the State of New York*, and in the 1895 edition of E. R. Wallace's *Descriptive Guide to the Adirondacks (Land of the Thousand Lakes)*. See Carson, *Peaks and People of the Adirondacks*, ed. Philip G. Terrie, Jr. (Glens Falls, NY: The Adirondack Mountain Club, 1973), pg. 11.

89. Macomb biographical material from: Julius W. Pratt, *Dictionary of American Biography*, ed. Dumas Malone (New York: Charles Scribner's Sons, 1933, renewed 1961), Vol. VI, Part 2, pg. 155.

90. Macdonough biographical material from: Charles O. Paullin, *Dictionary of American Biography*, ed. Dumas Malone (New York: Charles Scribner's Sons, 1933, renewed 1961), Vol. VI, Part 2, pg. 19; Col. David G. Fitz-Enz, *The Final Invasion: Plattsburgh, the War of 1812's Most Decisive Battle* (New York: Cooper Square Press, 2001), pg. 193; Benjamin F. Feinberg, *Commodore Thomas Macdonough – The Man* (Battle of Plattsburgh Day Commission, 1958); Plattsburgh Centenary Commission, *Dedication of the Thomas Macdonough Memorial* (Plattsburgh, 1926).

91. Verplanck Colvin, *State of New York Seventh Annual Report on the Progress of the Topographical Survey of the Adirondack Region of New York, to the Year 1879* (Albany: Weed, Parsons & Company, 1880). The "Sketch Showing the Region under Survey" is "Adirondack Map No. 1," opposite page 1. "Progress Sketch of the Primary Triangulation, 1878" is "Map No. 5," opposite pg. 224. A map drawn by Katherine Elizabeth McClellan in her self-published 1898 pamphlet *Keene Valley "In the Heart of the Mountains"* shows a "McDonough" directly south of Jay Peak. In describing the views from Elizabethtown, *Posson's Guide to Lake George, Lake Champlain and Adirondacks, Ninth Edition* (Glens Falls, NY: Chas. H. Possons, 1891) notes, "To the north, Saddle Mountain and Mount MacDonough show themselves." (Pg. 219)

92. Charles Brumley, *Guides of the Adirondacks: A History* (Utica, NY: North Country Books, 1994), pg. 164.

93. Eliot Clark, *Alexander Wyant* (New York: privately printed, 1916), pg. 31.

94. E[dwin] R. Wallace, *Descriptive Guide to the Adirondacks (Land of the Thousand Lakes)*, (Syracuse: Watson Gill, 1894), pg. 342.

95. *Guide to Adirondack Trails, Northeastern Section* (Albany: Adirondack Mountain Club, 1934), pg. 34.

96. Sharp Swan, "Macomb in 1940," *Adirondack Peeks*, Vol. 30, No. 1 (Spring/Summer 1993), pg. 16.

97. Jim Goodwin, "Macomb," *Of the Summits, of the Forests* (Morrisonville, NY: The Adirondack Forty-Sixers, 1991), pg. 60.

98. *Guide to Adirondack Trails, 1950 Edition* (Albany, NY: The Adirondack Mountain Club, 1950), pg. 93.

About the Author

A member of the NE111, Daniel Eagan (#4666) is currently working on several other lists. He lives in New York City and is co-editor, with his wife Melissa (#4667), of *Adirondack Peeks*.

NIPPLETOP
Height: 15th – 1,400c meters (4,593+ feet)
DIAL
Height: 41st – 1,220c meters (4,003+ feet)
By Sally Hoy (#2924W)

A print from 1840: "Nippletop from Mud Pond"

In his *Report of the Topographical Survey of the Adirondack Wilderness of New York for the Year 1873*, Verplanck Colvin wrote about his work party's escape from the brink of a cliff following their nighttime descent from the summit of Dix:

> Daylight, August 18th, showed us the wildness of our situation, and the means of extrication; and, breakfastless, after dangers unnecessary to relate, we descended *[from a bivouac upon a "precipice" of Dix]* to the south portal of the Hunter's Pass upon a stream which flowing southward, out of the pass, formed one of the sources of the Hudson river. Turning northward, we entered the portals of the Hunter's Pass (the Gorge of the Dial), which so many have longed to explore and

Heaven Up-h'isted-ness!

NIPPLE TOP.   DIX'S PEAK.   MCCOMBE'S MOUNTAIN.

"View from Clear Pond, looking northeast, from a sketch by R. C. Taylor" – 1841
(From Ebenezer Emmons' report, *Geology of New York, Part II,
Comprising the Survey of the Second Geological District*)

endeavored in vain to reach, and ascended betwixt its walls of rock to its summit... The inclosing mountains rise over a thousand feet above, on either side, and the spectacle is grand and imposing. Descending northward, we were once more on the St. Lawrence river side of the mountain range. We had left camp for the ascent of Mount Dix, with the intention of returning that night, and now, fearing lest our friend left there should become alarmed at this continued absence, we marched as rapidly toward where we thought the camp might be as our exhaustion permitted, firing occasionally revolver shot signals to acquaint him with our approach, but more, perhaps, with the hope that he might prepare us a breakfast. We at length found camp and man all right. A heavy storm in the afternoon tried the value of our bark roof, and gave us opportunity for rest...

August 19th. Raining slightly and very threatening. Determined, nevertheless, to set out upon the ascent of Nipple Top mountain, on the eastern slopes of which we were encamped...

In the rain, and with fog surrounding them, the survey party followed a stream "till its course diverged from" their intended route to the summit. They "climbed steadily," and "at 1 P.M. thought" they were on the summit, but...

...having chopped down trees, and the clouds rolling away, we saw another summit farther south which we reached at 2 P.M., which proved to be the true crest. Dense white cloud enveloped us, but it was in rapid motion, and at intervals opened and showed glimpses of chasms and mountains. Suddenly it was swept away at the east and Mount Dix, scarred and savage rock, rose before us; beyond it the rolling country near Lake Champlain.

Colvin aptly described much of the difficulty involved in the surveying work that he, Mills Blake, and their workmen and guides performed in the Dial and Nippletop area. However, while the raw and harsh land at times showed its gruff side, Colvin managed to see its wonders as well:

> The gorgeous sunshine streaming on the distant cirro-cumulus clouds below, produced a rare effect. Suddenly, starting with surprise, our mingled shouts arose, for on the breast of the cloud each saw his own form, the head surrounded by a rich *anthelia,*[1] a circular glory of prismatic colors, the renowned "Ulloa's rings" which that philosopher beheld from the summit of the Pambamarca.[2] Not one of the mountain guides had ever seen or heard of such sight before. It was gone all too quickly, yet it seemed as though nature to-day were reveling in splendors, for the clouds vanishing in the wets, a sierra of mountain crags was uncurtained, torn rugged and wild, above all which rose Ta-ha-wus, "Cleaver of the clouds."
>
> ...late in the afternoon, we diverged into the bed of Gill Brook and made better progress, stopping at 5:45 PM at a beautiful little cascade in the stream, the Artist's Falls,[3] where the water pours in a clear sheet over a sloping rock into a crystal pool, to glide brightly away amid the great boulders below. Left a bench-mark (No. 62) on a rock determining its altitude to be 1937.947 feet above tide-level.

Colvin and his crew measured the height of Nippletop by using a barometer, a theodolite (a measuring device that consists of a telescope mounted on a swivel), and a stanhelio automatic signal located on Bald Peak near Westport on Lake Champlain. The initial measurement had been calculated from the summit of Dix ("by combined barometer and spirit level") on August 17. After Colvin and his crew found the "true crest" of Nippletop on the 19th, through *"direct* observations" he calculated the "height of Nipple Top" to be "4,656 feet above tide level." The 1953 survey put it at 4,600 feet but the survey conducted in the early 1970s failed to provide it with an exact height. Its highest contour was listed as 1,400 meters, making the summit's approximate height 4,593 feet above sea level.

Based upon his study of the report made to the New York State Assembly by Ebenezer Emmons in 1838, Russell M. L. Carson concluded that Emmons and the members of his survey party were the first men to climb Nippletop (August 30, 1837). Emmons made it clear that the survey party had camped in Hunters Pass, between Dix and Nippletop, the night before, and climbed to the top of Nippletop the next morning. Emmons, Carson wrote, "apparently did not make a barometrical measurement of Nippletop's height, but 'approximated it by leveling.'" That approximation was 4,900 feet.

Hunters Pass was once known as the Gorge of the Dial and was probably so named by Emmons who, in 1837, also may have given the name Dial to what is presently Nippletop. The name never took hold as anyone viewing the mountain from Elk Lake was quick to observe, as Old Mountain Phelps opined, "The name suggests itself." However, the rather frankly descriptive name for the mountain offended some Victorian sensibilities. According to one story, a young lady once recorded these words in her diary: "Climbed N.....top with the delightful Mr. Phelps." When her father inquired about the missing letters, she blushed and answered truthfully. He was mortified and began writing letters – to the superintendent of the town of Keene, to Phelps, to the governor of New York – demanding a name change so that others might be spared a similar assault upon their gentility. Charles Dudley Warner noted in his volume of essays about the Adirondacks, *In the Wilderness,* that "Nipple Top" was "a local name which neither the mountain nor the fastidious tourist" was able "to shake off." He added, "Indeed, so long as the mountain keeps its present shape as seen from the southern lowlands, it cannot get on without this name." According to tradition, Old Mountain Phelps transferred the name Dial to the peak just to the north along Nippletop's ridgeline.

With two other guides, Alfred Billings Street, his son, and an artist, Homer Martin, once attempted to go to the Gorge of the Dial, from "Mud Pond" (Elk Lake). Street reported in *The Indian Pass* that the guides were unfamiliar with the territory: "They did all that experienced woodmen could do, but they could not perform impossibilities, that is, scent out the trail as the hound scents the deer." Following lumber trails, the party lost its way between Clear Pond and Mud Pond: "Etchings of roads indeed lay about, but they only led to some chopping, and then ceased." Still they attempted to find the route to the Gorge:

> At length a path at the foot of the pond did present itself. How green and open and pleasant the little vista looked, inviting the step with an irresistible charm! And we entered. A sunny knoll was crossed, and we all congratulated ourselves that our troubles were over. Soon would the blue gleam of Mud Pond shine through the trees; and on we went. But the path began dwindling to a trail, and faint at that; broken corduroys over marshy spots became frequent. Wilder and wilder the trail grew; prostrate trees blocked, thickets covered it. The choking foliage twined at length so densely, that the broken spots in the mouldering corduroys could not be seen. And thus our progress became slow and painful. At last all traces of the track ceased in a tangled "wind slash"... But on we went. I felt confident we were lost, still I struggled forward, dashing the thickets aside to see where I could plant my feet in safety.

They continued along what they later discovered was the long abandoned Cedar Point Road[4] from the McIntyre Iron Works to Lake Champlain" until "the rainy dark fell" and they were forced to bivouac for the night. The next morning, abandoning the trip to the Gorge of the Dial, they returned to Clear Pond.

Charles Dudley Warner wrote about Hunters Pass in "A Wilderness Romance," one of his essays published in 1878 in *In the Wilderness*. He mentioned the "opening" between Dix and Nippletop, "the gate-posts of the pass into the southern country" from the north:

> It is the most elevated and one of the wildest of the mountain passes. Its summit is thirty-five hundred feet high. In former years it is presumed the hunters occasionally followed their game through; but latterly it is rare to find a guide who has been that way, and... tourists have not yet made it a runway. This seclusion is due not to any inherent difficulty of travel, but to the fact that it lies a little out of the way.
> When we went through it last summer; making our way into the jaws from the foot of the great slides on Dix, keeping along the ragged spurs of the mountain through the virgin forest. The pass is narrow, walled in on each side by precipices of granite, and blocked up with bowlders *[sic]* and fallen trees, and beset with pitfalls in the roads *[sic]* ingeniously covered with fair-seeming moss. When the climber occasionally loses sight of a leg in one of those treacherous holes, and feels a cold sensation in his foot, he learns that he has dipped into the sources of the Boquet, which emerges lower down into falls and rapids, and, recruited by creeping tributaries, goes brawling through the forest basin, and at last comes out an amiable and boat-bearing stream in the valley of Elizabeth Town. From the summit another rivulet trickles away to the south, and finds its way through a frightful tamarack swamp, and through woods scarred by ruthless lumbering, to Mud Pond, a quiet body of water, with a ghastly fringe of dead trees, upon which people of grand intentions and weak vocabulary are trying to fix the name of Elk Lake. The descent of the pass on that side is precipitous and exciting. The way is in the stream itself; and a considerable portion of the distance we swung ourselves down the faces of considerable falls, and tumbled down cascades. The descent, however, was made easy by the fact that it rained, and every footstep was yielding and slippery. Why sane people, often church-members respectably connected, will subject themselves to this sort of treatment, – be wet to the skin, bruised by the

rocks, and flung about among bushes and dead wood until the most necessary part of their apparel hangs in shreds, – is one of the delightful mysteries of these woods. I suspect that every man is at heart a roving animal, and likes, at intervals, to revert to the condition of the bear and the catamount.

Warner reported that there was no trail through Hunters Pass, "the least frequented portion of this wilderness," but he mentioned that there was "a well-beaten path a considerable portion of the way and wherever a path" was "possible." He imagined an earlier time, when the pass was a highway for a "whole caravan of animals who were continually going backwards and forwards, in the aimless, roaming way that beasts have, between Mud Pond and the Boquet Basin."

I think I can see now the procession of them between the heights of Dix and Nipple Top; the elk and the moose shambling along, cropping the twigs; the heavy bear lounging by with his exploring nose; the frightened deer trembling at every twig that snapped beneath his little hoofs, intent on the lily-pads of the pond; and the velvet-footed panther, *insouciant* and conscienceless, scenting the path with a curious glow in his eye, or crouching in an overhanging tree ready to drop into the procession at the right moment. Night and day, year after year, I see them going by, watched by the red fox and the comfortably clad sable, and grinned at by the black cat...[5]

Charles Dudley Warner

In the high style of the late Romantic period, Warner continued to wax eloquently about Hunters Pass before he intimated that his desire to explore it had been "stimulated by a legend related" by his guide and told to him "that night in the Mud Pond cabin." Warner noted that the story didn't "amount to much, – none of the guides' stories do, faithfully reported" – and he "should not have believed it if" he "had not had a good deal of leisure" on his "hands at the time, and been of a willing mind, and… in rather a starved condition as to any romance" in the region. He listened to the tale and repeated it with all of its details about a cave "high up among the precipices on the southeast side of Nipple Top," where, perhaps, "Spaniards" had mined and smelted silver. His guide had never been to the cave but, he said, his father had found it long after it had been abandoned. He had found a manufactured chair within it as well as a crow bar that must have been used to extract silver from veins found in the rock of the cavern… and he had removed from the back of the chair a "waistcoat… of foreign make and peculiar style… with buttons of silver!"[6]

Old Mountain Phelps served as Warner's guide when he climbed Nippletop in 1877 with a third hiker, "a chaplain." Their route was along the Gill Brook "and up one of its branches to the head of Caribou *(Elk)* Pass." Warner wrote that they climbed "about the first of September" during a dry spell that had lasted several weeks and had made the woods tinder dry.

The way, as we ascended, was not all through open woods; dense masses of firs were encountered, jagged spurs were to be crossed, and the going became at length so slow and toilsome that we took to the rocky bed of a stream, where bowlders and flumes and cascades offered us sufficient variety. The deeper we penetrated, the greater the sense of savageness and solitude; in the silence of these hidden places one seems to approach the beginning of things. We emerged from the defile into an open basin, formed by the curved side of the mountain, and stood silent before a waterfall coming down out of the sky in the centre of the curve... Fairy-Ladder Falls. It appears to have a height of something like a hundred and fifty feet, and the water falls obliquely across the face of the cliff from left to right in short steps, which in moonlight might seem like a veritable ladder for fairies... At the top we found the stream flowing over a broad bed of rock, like a street in the wilderness, slanting up still towards the sky, and bordered by low firs and balsams, and bowlders completely covered with moss. It was above the world and open to the sky.

Warner called the spot where he and Phelps and the "chaplain" stopped and rested for the night "Bridal Chamber Camp." There they "lay, as it were, on a shelf in the sky, with a basin of illimitable forests below... and dim mountain-passes in the far horizon." The following morning they "addressed" themselves to the climb. In "What Some People Call Pleasure," Warner described that trek:

> The arduous labor of scaling an Alpine peak has a compensating glory; but the dead lift of our bodies up Nipple-Top had no stimulus of this sort. It is simply hard work... The pleasure of such an ascent is difficult to explain... I do not object to the elevation of this mountain, nor to the uncommonly steep grade by which it attains it, but only to the other obstacles thrown in the way of the climber. All the slopes of Nipple-Top are hirsute and jagged to the last degree. Granite ledges interpose; granite bowlders seem to have been dumped over the sides with no more attempt at arrangement than in a rip-rap wall; the slashes and windfalls of a century present here and there... almost impenetrable... and the steep sides bristle with a mass of thick balsams, with dead, protruding spikes, as unyielding as iron stakes. The mountain has had its own way forever, and is as untamed as a wolf; or rather the elements, the frightful tempests, the frosts, the heavy snows, the coaxing sun, and the avalanches have had their way with it until its surface is in hopeless confusion. We made our way very slowly; and it was ten o'clock before we reached what appeared to be the summit, a ridge deeply covered with moss, low balsams, and blueberry bushes.
>
> I say, appeared to be; for we stood in thick fog or in the heart of clouds which limited our dim view to a radius of twenty feet. It was a warm and cheerful fog, stirred by little wind, but moving, shifting, and boiling as by its own volatile nature, rolling up black from below and dancing in silvery splendor overhead. As a fog it could not have been improved; as a medium for viewing the landscape it was a failure; and we lay down upon the Sybarite couch of moss... to await revelations.

They waited two hours, "without change, except an occasional hopeful lightness in the fog above" before the sun, for a moment appeared "spectral." It appeared again. They "caught sight of a patch of blue sky." A slight wind stirred, "and the fog boiled up from the valley caldrons thicker than ever. But the spell was broken."

> In a moment more Old Phelps was shouting, "The sun!" and before we could gain our feet there was a patch of sky overhead as big as a farm. "See! quick!" The old man was dancing like a lunatic. There was a rift in the vapor at our feet, down, down, three thousand feet into the forest abyss, and lo! lifting out of it yonder the tawny side of Dix, – the vision of a second, snatched away in the rolling fog. The play had just begun.

They turned to see "the gorge of Caribou Pass" before it became enshrouded again. Then they saw, afar, the "peaceful farms of the Ausable Valley... the plateau of North Elba and the sentinel mountains about the grave of John Brown." They waited longer to see Colvin "heaved up like an island out of the ocean" and still longer for Dix "to show its shapely peak and its glistening sides of rock gashed by avalanches." Warner wrote that the "spectacles to right and left, above and below, changed with incredible swiftness." It was a "glory of abyss and summit, of color and form and transformation... seldom granted to mortal eyes" which they viewed for an hour before "our vast mountain was revealed in all its bulk, its long spurs, its abysses and its savagery, and the great basins of wilderness with their shining lakes, and the giant peaks of the region, were one by one disclosed... and tranquil in the sunshine."

Because "moving about" on the mountain was "not a holiday pastime," instead of looking for the cave of lore, they set about trying "to discover a practicable mode of descent into the great wilderness basin" to the south. "It was enough," Warner wrote, "for us to have discovered the general whereabouts of the Spanish Cave, and we left the fixing of its exact position to future explorers." They descended by way of a "spur" – thick with balsams, "slashes of fallen timber, and every manner of woody chaos" – and a slope – "for a couple of thousand feet... formed of granite rocks all moss-covered," and "at short intervals" they "nearly went out of sight in holes under the treacherous carpeting." They passed through sections where "great trees were laid longitudinally and transversely and criss-cross over and among the rocks." They had had no water since breakfast and, because, at last, they could "hear the water running deep down among the rocks, but... could not come at it," their "thirst began to be that of Tantalus." Finally, before they "reached the bottom of Caribou Pass, the water burst out from the rocks in a clear stream that was as cold as ice." They followed the stream and soon "struck the roaring brook that issues from the Pass to the south... not an easy bed for anything except water to descend... and before" they "reached the level reaches, where the stream flows with a murmurous noise through open woods," one member of the party (Old Phelps) began to show signs of exhaustion." They still had "six or seven miles" to go.

"What Some People Call Pleasure" tells the rest of the story.

Colvin's 1873 approach to Nippletop had been from the east where no established path exists today. His party descended to Elk Pass and, as mentioned in Douglas Arnold's account of Blake's Peak, camped that night above the stepped cascade that Colvin named Fairy Ladder Falls. He also christened a shallow pond near his camp Lycopodium Pond for the ground cover that adorned its shoreline: club moss.[7]

A hike up Dial and Nippletop can be like a walk through an outdoor classroom where one can learn about plants just by observing them and reading about them in a good reference book. Many plants that grow in the area are edible. The shamrock-like leaves of the wood sorrel *(Oxalis acetosella)* that carpet the forest floor are rich in Vitamin C. Blueberries, rich in anti-oxidants, are found dotting the Elk Pass ponds. Bilberry *(Vaccinium myrtilloides)*, found higher up on Nippletop, can be steeped in some water and sugar with lemon peel and baked in a tart. The stem of a striped maple *(Acer pensylvinicium)*, named for its green and white stripes, might make a great walking stick, but, of course, no trees on Adirondack Mountain Reserve property or on state park land should ever be cut for such a purpose. Many striped maples can be found in clearings created by loggers. They don't grow too big or live too long, but deer like them. They can be found on the side of Bear Den above the Lake Road.

Jewelweed *(Impatiens capensis)* can be used to treat poison ivy. Crush the plant's tender stems and with them rub the juice produced directly onto the rash or, even, an irritating bug bite. Many people find that the irritation will disappear within a day or two. Coincidentally, jewelweed (also known as spotted touch-me-not) often grows close by poison ivy (because both plants can thrive in similar micro-habitats). Some poison ivy can be found along the Lake Road not far from the Ausable Club.

Other plants and shrubs of interest found in the area include bouncing betty, flat top asters, goldenrod, hawkweed or devil's paintbrush, red berried hobblebush (the one that hog ties the unsuspecting hiker), clintonia (named after Governor DeWitt Clinton), bunchberry, mountain laurel, and British soldiers.

A lovely plant that is seen along the path next to the ponds in Elk Pass is the closed gentian *(Gentiana linearis)*. Bearing blue, bottle-shaped flowers about an inch and a half long, closed gentian grows to about two feet in height. It has adapted well to wet areas.

Indian pipes are in abundance on the steep slope of Nippletop above Elk Pass. Their white color reminds us that they have no chlorophyll and do not carry on photosynthesis. Their food comes from the soil in which they grow. Lichens abound as well and are a good indication of air quality. Native Americans used various lichens as diapers, dyes, and dressings for wounds.

Most hikers go to Nippletop and Dial from the Ausable Club at St. Huberts. After signing in just before the AMR gate and beginning the walk up the Lake Road, many will turn onto the Henry Goddard Leach[8] Trail, about three quarters of a mile from the gate. That trail, marked with yellow DEC discs, goes up a shoulder of Noonmark and passes over Bear Den to Dial and Nippletop beyond. Hikers who wish to return by way of a different route (and most hikers do) descend from Nippletop to Elk Pass and return to the Lake Road by way of the Colvin Trail. Others pursue the route in reverse, going up Nippletop first from Elk Pass and returning to the Lake Road over Dial, Bear Den, and the shoulder of Noonmark. The round trip is about fourteen and a half miles from the parking lot next to Route 73 and back.

Since the days of the Marshall brothers and Herb Clark, many who climb Nippletop, the fifteenth highest peak of the 46, have considered the view from it among the finest in the Adirondacks. Mount Dix, with its "scarred and savage rock" as Colvin described it, seems so close it would be tempting to leap to its side. Other prominences which may be seen in all their glory on clear days are Mount Colvin, Blake's Peak, the Pinnacle Ridge, the Great Range, Mount Marcy, Allen Mountain and, back to the east: Giant. If you have the misfortune to be shrouded in fog and clouds atop Nippletop as Jennifer Hoy was on a fall day several years ago, be sure to return another day. A clear day's view is a hiker's reward remembered.

If slide climbing is of interest, Nippletop has one that is rated 5.1 in difficulty. To get to it, head south out of Elk Pass and stay on the east side of the drainage. The slide will appear on the left (east). It is about 0.85 miles in length and rises over 1,500 feet with pitches ranging from 33 degrees to 45 degrees. A website, www.summitpost.com, warns: "A fall would be deadly since it is steep; there is nothing to stop you on the way down." The website also recommends staying away during the wet season. In winter the slide might easily spawn an avalanche. Mel Trumbull, a guide who once had a camp at Upper Ausable Lake long ago told Jim Goodwin that Nippletop (then trailless) could be climbed via the slide leading up and out of the Elk Pass. Trumbull called the route, "more'n feasible." In the mid 1920s Jim and Peggy Goodwin (later O'Brien) found a herd path through the pass. They believed it was a remnant of a trail that had been used by Elk Lake loggers of earlier days. Jim and Peggy soon found the slide and followed it to Nippletop's summit.

Dial, 41st in height, was first climbed in 1884 by Ed Phelps and Ed Beede, Keene Valley guides. Its summit elevation is estimated at about 4,003 feet.

Which of Dial's two principal peaks is its true summit has long been a question, North Dial or South Dial? Maps don't actually provide those names for the two peaks, but Barbara McMartin in her *Discover the Adirondack High Peaks* wrote that South Dial is "a wooded hummock so undistinguished you probably won't know you have reached it, even if it is the official Forty-sixer Dial peak."[9] She noted that there "is a wonderful ledge" near the summit of North Dial from which Colvin, Allen, Skylight, Haystack, Marcy, the Great Range, Big Slide, Porter, Cascade, and Whiteface may be viewed. The 1979 metric Mount Marcy U.S. Geological Survey map clearly places the name "Dial" on the north summit, but both it and the south summit top out just above the 1,220 contour level. There simply is no practical way to determine, even in this era of GPS devices, which is the higher of the two. However, it might make sense to transfer "official" status to the north peak because it provides such a stunning view.[10] It certainly is a nicer place to stop for lunch or to enjoy a trailside snack and study the rock that makes up the ledge. It contains crystals of garnet, which industry employs as an abrasive. Other notable rocks are gneiss, intrusive granite and gabbro, plus iron ore, graphite, pyrite, and zinc.

If you follow the Henry Goddard Leach Trail from Nippletop to the two Dials and head from them back to the Lake Road, you pass over Bear Den and then ascend a shoulder of Noonmark.[11] A sign once posted there explained, "In 1999 a fire started by a campfire on the western shoulder of Noonmark burned 90 acres before the rains from Hurricane Floyd extinguished it. This campfire was inappropriately built on organic soil which caused it to burn laterally outside the fire ring and, not fully extinguished by the campers, may have smoldered several days." Right after the incident, one could see that the trees left standing indicated which way the fire had traveled up the mountain: they were all charred on one side. Today, raspberry bushes galore and other pioneer plants and shrubs have begun to fill the emptiness and stabilize the area which in time (several centuries) will return to is former state. Remaining today are reminders of the fire: barrenness, charred pieces of wood, and stumps bleached white by the sun. Despite the appearance, the views of the high peaks opened by the devastation are awesome from the burned over area. From it the hiker can see the slides on Dix, the Great Range, and the valley below. A major forest fire in 1903 burned toward Noonmark from North Hudson before rain finally quelled the flames just before they reached the Ausable Club property on the other side of Noonmark.

Those who hike to the mountains by way of Adirondack Mountain Reserve property from the Ausable Club must respect the AMR's rules. No fires are allowed. No one may camp on the property. Dogs cannot go on the property, either. Only club members and their guests may fish the streams. No one may hunt on the property. Hikers are required to stay on the marked trails until they reach state land.

The AMR property is a wildlife refuge, but before the corporation purchased its lands, the area around the Ausable Lakes was used extensively by guides and their clients, fishermen, hunters and trappers. Wildlife in the area in the mid-nineteenth century was plentiful. Verplanck Colvin, on occasion, was able to climb up and down mountains because his guides could follow the paths "of deer, bear, and panther." Those paths "showed us where these creatures found spots around the cliffs."

Wesley Otis was the original game warden whose job it was to protect the AMR lands and guard against the poaching of local hunters. This was not an enviable job as many of the locals were related to him in some way or another and many of them had long hunted on the property before the AMR assumed title to it. When Otis retired, LaGrand Hale replaced him as warden.

Early one fall morning in 1912, Rob Otis (the son of Wesley Otis) and Frank Heald went out hunting. They shot a couple of nice bucks and dressed them on the spot. While they were sitting on a log and having a smoke, they spotted a very large bear and, of course, they shot it. They later returned to Rob's home with the trophy, apparently the largest bear ever taken in the area. Folks from the neighborhood appeared at Rob's wanting so see the prize... even LaGrand Hale, the AMR warden. He asked no questions, but he left suspicious and decided to conduct some detective work to see if he could determine whether or not the bear had been taken on AMR property.

To Hale, because the bear was so large, it was evident that Otis and Heald could not have dragged it out of the woods without help. So he walked up the Lake Road looking for signs of a wagon or some other vehicle having been on it at about the time the bear had been shot. He came upon the tracks of wheels but found no impressions of horseshoes. Later that day, however, he appeared at Rob's home and there he placed a very large bear's heart on the picket fence. Hale had found the entrails of the bear, and he wanted his friends to know that he had found the place where the bear had been shot, illegally: on AMR property.

How had Otis and Heald taken the carcass from the woods? They borrowed a two-wheeled sulky from Spencer Nye's livery and, under cover of darkness, went up to where they had left the bear. "By tipping the phils high in the air, the men were able to lash the animal to the framework. When the phils were brought back to horizontal, the bear became suspended between the wheels and it was down hill from there back to Rob's house."

Later, it is said, "the boys" skinned that bear and sold the hide to a club member for a good sum of money.[12]

Just before Alfred Street embarked upon his failed attempt to pass through the Gorge of the Dial in 1868, the guide he had hired to conduct his party, Elijah Simmonds,[13] "was taken sick." Consequently, Street had had to rely on two other guides unfamiliar with the gorge, which, he said, had only been visited by Elijah and his brother William. Simmonds, Street asserted, was "the most noted and trustworthy hunter and trapper of the region" and "was perfectly familiar" with the gorge's "locality."

Simmonds told Street about a "trapping excursion" he had made "one autumn" that had "brought him to Mud Pond. Seeing the opening between the mountains *[Dix and "Dial"]*, he was seized with a desire to know what existed there." In a boat, he went to "the head of the pond and struck into the woods." He followed no trail. "He crossed an intervening point and ridge, and for three long miles, he battled the forest, gradually ascending." The "ground became more abrupt" and he continued up "a half mile" before his route "became a steep break-neck ascent." Thereafter, he "clambered" upward, "catching branch, rock, and sapling. For twenty or thirty rods he thus dragged himself, when suddenly he reached level ground": the top of the pass.

Street blossomed with Romantic extravagance in describing what, apparently, Simmonds was first to see:

> What was the towering thing at his left, soaring close from his feet up, dizzily up, until it seemed to clutch the heavens. It was a terrific wall, a horrible precipice rising sheer from the ground, here glistening in naked, cracked, scooped-out rock; there dark with shaggy spruces (nearly the only foliage) – clutching the seams, tottering on the ledges, and stooping as if to tumble headlong from the narrow and sickening platforms. Up, up went the awful wall, stretching on, on, in a northerly direction for two miles, – a mile farther than the Indian Pass. Who would

suppose, while viewing with astonished eye this famous pass, that here, lurking in its ambush, existed a gorge which almost equaled the rocky wonder, – here, unknown and unsuspected! and he looked with utter amazement...

The Dial *[Nippletop]* wall rises from one thousand to fifteen hundred feet... A fringe of foliage trembles from the summit of the wall and down the sheer descent as much foliage as rock is discernible...

Fire had not swept the Gorge as at the *[Indian]* Pass; the foliage was consequently fresh and green, and all as Nature had left it as its birth. And what a fearful forge... had fashioned it! What sublime period saw it wrought in all its grandeur. No wonder Elijah's mind shrank appalled at the sight as it rose, rank above rank of trees, until the eye seemed as if it would never scale the summit.

Simmonds, Street wrote, "paced the mighty object of Nature... let his eye rove over a mighty ocean of woods," and "then ascended the Dial to kindle a bonfire on its globe."

Simmonds approached Nippletop from the northeast – possibly following the route that the Emmons party had in 1837. He began his ascent along the course of a stream – a tributary of the North Fork of the Boquet River that joins the brook flowing north from Hunters Pass about three quarters of a mile north of the top of the pass. He began the climb at 4 in the afternoon and reached the summit as "the dilated sun was sinking behind the peak of old Tahawus... reddened by the lustre." He was able to see Haystack, the Wolf Jaws. He "traced the South Branch of the Boquet... to its junction with the North Branch... and thence the river's northeast path toward Lake Champlain," but, Street wrote, "the grandest sight was Dix's Peak. It's enormous bulk rose so near, it seemed as if he could toss a bullet against its side. It was smoothed over with gold as though a glittering yellow mantle was cast over it..."

"The top of the ridge at the south rises as sharp almost as a knife," continued Elijah. "It isn't more than a foot wide, and slopes each side in a rocky precipice covered with small spruces. It is a quarter of a mile too."

"How did you pass over it, Elijah?"

"As you ride a horse," answered Elijah. "It wants a steady head to cross over it, for if you should slip"...

But to return to the kindling *[of]* the fire on the top of the Dial. He did so, and then descended as rapidly as possible to see the effect.

A pyramid of fire flamed from the dome, flooding it with crimson splendor, and touched the Gorge in spots, speckling the bottom like huge fireflies. It must have been a strange spectacle that weird pyramid...

Street's account of the bonfire and its effect ended there. Legend says that its glow could be seen from Keene Valley. No forest fire resulted, at least any that has been recorded. Apparently Simmonds' bonfire consumed itself and did not spread except through the fantastic account left to us by Alfred Billings Street.

Endnotes

1. *Anthelia* is the plural of *anthelion* – a term from Greek literally meaning "anti-sun." Merriam-Webster says that it is "a rare species of halo" also known as a counter sun. More particularly, it is the "brightish-white spot on the parhelic circle opposite the sun."

2. Pambamarca is an eroded stratovolcano in the northern Andes of Ecuador. The area was explored by Antonio de Ulloa (1716-1795). In 1735, he became a member of the French Geodesic

Mission, a scientific expedition under the auspices of the French Academy of Sciences sent to what was then Peru to measure a degree of meridian at the equator. While in Peru (1736-1744), he and fellow Spaniard Jorge Juan discovered the element platinum. In 1745, he sailed for Spain, but the ship in which he traveled was captured by the British, and he was taken as a prisoner to England. He made contact with fellow scientists in England, was made a fellow of the Royal Society, was able to gain his release, and returned to Spain, where he published (1748) an account of his adventures in *A Voyage to South America*. In Spain, he served on "various important scientific commissions" and established the first museum of natural history, the first metallurgical laboratory in Spain, and an astronomical observatory at Cadiz. He returned to South America to serve as governor (1758-1764) of Huancavelica (one of the departments of Peru), where he also managed a quicksilver mine. In 1766 he was appointed the governor of West Louisiana but was forced by French colonists to abandon the post by the French colonists of New Orleans during the Creole revolt of 1768. For the remainder of his life he served as a Spanish naval officer. His description of the meteorological phenomenon twice referenced by Verplanck Colvin in his survey reports was first published in his *Relación histórica del viaje á la América Meridional* (1784), a book which contains much information about South America's geography, inhabitants, and natural history.

Ulloa's halo, as it is sometimes called, may be seen if an observer, usually upon a mountain, is surrounded by fog just before it unfolds enough to reveal the sun. If he then looks in the opposite direction, he may see a fogbow: "a faint white, circular arc or complete ring of light" in the antisolar position... "usually in the form of a separate outer ring around an anticorona." (Tricker, *An Introduction to Meteorological Optics*, 1970, pgs. 192–193). When Colvin and his men observed Ulloa's rings, their bodies projected shadows upon the nearby fog and the "halos" were seen upon the margins of those shadows.

That Colvin was familiar with Antonio de Ulloa's observation of a "fogbow" indicates the breadth of the surveyor's scientific study.

3. The location of Artist's Falls along the Gill Brook has, apparently, been forgotten; however, should someone find the "bench-mark (No. 62)" placed by Colvin nearby it, it may be found again. It should be about four tenths of a mile along the Colvin Trail from its beginning on the Lake Road. Tony Goodwin notes that "Artist's Falls" appears on today's maps; however, it seems that Colvin's "Artist's Falls" were somewhere above the cascade currently bearing the name.

4. Cedar Point is now Port Henry. The road mentioned was constructed (1830-1831) from Cedar Point to a road that still runs from just below the outlet of Sanford Lake to the Upper Works. The Cedar Point Road went west from Lake Champlain to what is now the hamlet of North Hudson, along what is basically the route of the present day Blue Ridge Road, north along the course of today's Elk Lake Road, and, near Lake Clear, west through the forest to a bridge across the Hudson River below Sanford Lake. Douglas Ayres, Jr. recounts the history of the road in "The Ore Haul Road," which was published in the February 1983 edition of *Adirondac* (Vol. XLVII, No. 10), pgs. 6-9. The road was used by members of the group which first climbed Mount Marcy. They traveled from Lake Champlain via Clear Pond and from there proceeded to the McIntyre. The road was kept open year round as best as possible as it served to link the iron mine with Lake Champlain, the Lake Champlain Canal, and, ultimately, via the Hudson, Jersey City, New Jersey. Following the abandonment of the iron works in 1858 the road from Sanford Lake to Clear Pond was rapidly reclaimed by the forest through which it passed.

5. Black cat is another name for *Martes pennanti,* often called the Adirondack fisher.

6. The story of Spaniards and silver has also been told concerning Pharaoh Mountain near Schroon Lake.

7. The yellow powder of lycopod spores has been called "vegetable sulfur." Highly flammable, it was used in the early days of photography as flash powder and for stage lighting. The spores, which ignite with quite an explosion, were also used for fireworks. In the Middle Ages they were employed as a diuretic in the treatment of kidney stones. During the seventeenth century they were prescribed to treat everything from dysentery to gout, from rheumatism to psoriasis. Homeopaths prescribe the spores today for digestive problems.

8. A member of the AMR, Leach was editor of a periodical, *The Forum,* from 1923 to 1940 and president of the ATIS (1927-1937).

9. Barbara McMartin, *Discover the Adirondack High Peaks* (Woodstock, Vermont: Backcountry Publications, 1989), pg. 186.

10. Tony Goodwin points out that the question as to the high point of Dial "shouldn't be a discussion at all." He says that matter came into question with the publication of the Sixth Edition of the *ADK Guide to Trails* "in 1957 when Morgan Porter had been working from a preliminary version of the Marcy quadrangle that apparently showed the elevation of 'North' Dial to be less than 4,000 feet. The published version of the Marcy quadrangle, however, showed Dial as 4,020 feet and this fact was noted as a footnote in the Seventh through Tenth editions without ever bothering to correct the basic text in the guide." Tony, editor of the Eleventh Edition, attempted to end the confusion by "declaring that 'South' Dial was just a part of the ridge to Nippletop" since "North Dial" and "South Dial" were "the same height on both the older and newer maps and 'North' Dial was clearly the more prominent summit."

11. Russell M. L. Carson in *Peaks and People of the Adirondacks* wrote that Noonmark was known as Dial before and after Alfred Street attempted to transplant that name to Nippletop. The artist R. M. Shurtleff apparently thought Noonmark a better name for the mountain as, according to tradition, the sun in its course across the sky, from a vantage at Beede's Heights (now the Ausable Club), was directly above the mountain at noon. This was before standard time zones were adopted in the United States at the close of the nineteenth century. Noon before then was when the sun, as viewed from anywhere, reached the midpoint of its daylight journey, the midpoint being the meridiem (hence a.m. - *ante meridiem*, for before noon, and p.m. – *post meridiem* for after noon). Old Mountain Phelps is credited with transferring the name Dial to its present location between Bear Den and Nippletop. Whether the transfer was from Noonmark or Nippletop remains a matter of speculation.

12. In www.adkrealty.com/hunters.html.

13. Street spelled Simmonds *Simons.*

About the Author

Sally Hoy, who was born in Rochester, was introduced to camping and skiing almost before she could walk. She got her first taste of the Adirondack Mountains on a climb up Snowy Mountain with her dad while camping at Lewey Lake in the early 1950s. Thereafter, she says, she was hooked. It would be long after she started her own family, however, before climbing the High Peaks became a reality. In July of 1991 she and her 13-year-old daughter, Kate, became 46ers on Iroquois Peak. To help celebrate, her husband Tom went along bearing gifts and cracked a couple of ribs on the way. Their sons became avid outdoorsmen, too. Adam became an Eagle Scout while Robert made the Junior Olympic cross country ski team.

Sally is also a Winter 46er, having finished on Iroquois as well. Other climbing credits include the 111 highest in the Northeast, the Northville-Lake Placid Trail, the Fire Tower Challenge, the Long Trail, and some 14,000 footers in Colorado.

Sally taught nursery school and later retired as a reading teacher from the Warrensburg Central School District. She is past president of the Glens Falls/Saratoga chapter of ADK and of the Glens Falls Symphony Orchestra and was treasurer of the Bill Koch Ski League, a Cub Scout den leader, and a Brownie leader. She has served as director and vice president of the 46ers and a committee member of the Adirondack 46er Conservation Trust. She has enjoyed the camaraderie of trail work, recalling having once moved an outhouse near Feldsbar Brook. She has volunteered for the Glens Falls Medical Mission to Guatemala and served as a Life Line installer.

Sally has two grandsons. At age two, David completed his first fire tower. His little brother is not far behind. She remarks that they are members of another generation of mountain stewards in the making.

SAWTEETH MOUNTAIN
Height: 33rd – 1,260c meters (4,134+ feet)
By Douglas Arnold (#4693W)

Bob and George Marshall and Herb Clark's rating of sixteenth for the view from the summit of Sawteeth is deceiving. In his 1922 booklet "The High Peaks of the Adirondacks," Bob wrote, "We had been told that Sawteeth was so heavily wooded on top a person was a fool to climb it. The first part of the statement was certainly true, but there were also ledges. From these, on the way up we got two superb views, one toward the wooded Armstrong, the other toward bare Gothic. But the best view was reserved for the summit. This was looking over the Great Basin, finest stretch of primeval forest in the State, toward Allen, Skylight, Haystack, Marcy and Basin, all heavily wooded save where some great slide had left a streak. If I were asked to name the most beautiful single view in the Adirondacks, I would be inclined to place this grand prospect first."

The following description is transcribed from a 46er log book:

March 4th, 2000: A short sprint to the real summit reinforces my reasons for declaring Sawteeth my favorite peak. There in front of us is a magnificent bowl of snow, trees and rock. The crystal white porcelain is etched to expose the images of the Ga-nos-gwah. The Iroquois caretakers of this land called these peaks Ga-nos-gwah or "Giants clothed with stone." These Goliaths now bear the names Pyramid, Gothics, Saddleback, Basin, Marcy (Tahawus) and Haystack. They form the jagged rim of this priceless goblet. The deep azure blue sky contrasts with the glimmering chalice. We gorge on the fruit that fills this tureen, forged when man was only a twinkle in our Father's eye. I feel I can reach out and touch the jagged edge. My mind cannot resist envisioning the act.

At the beginning of a trip to Sawteeth Mountain be sure to pause for a moment at the Ausable Club's golf course and discover the reason the mountain is so named. Glimpses of the "Great Saw" come from between the cottages. Exposed are the teeth backlit by the sky. The extraordinary view reveals the honing glacial action that rasped the teeth. Upon your return, look again. The sun will be low and you will likely catch a glint off the sharpened points.

Russell M. L. Carson, who wrote *Peaks and People of the Adirondacks,* was a stickler for detail. He found that the mountain had been labeled "Resagonia" on a local map, and, after years of research concluded that that name had been suggested for the mountain by the Reverend Erastus Hopkins of Northampton, Massachusetts. Carson credited Ed Phelps, "who furnished the faint clue," as well as W. Scott Brown, the Rev. H. H. Pittman of the Church of the Good Shepherd in Elizabethtown, and Dr. L. Clark Seelye of Northampton, Massachusetts, for providing him with information which helped him piece together the story of the naming of the peak.

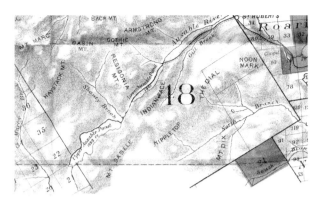

Sawteeth was "Resigonia" and Colvin was "Sabele" on the 1895 U.S.G.S. map.

Hopkins, who summered in Keene Valley for a number of seasons around 1860, suggested the name to Old Mountain Phelps, who, apparently, enjoyed using it. He said that Hopkins had told him that the name in Italian meant "the king's great saw." A mountain with a similar saw-like profile which rises above Italy's Lake Como is named Resagone. The name applied to Sawteeth was apparently a corruption of the Italian word, but Carson remarked, "Hopkins's definition of the name was forgotten in the course of sixty-five years, and a tradition supplanted it that Resagonia was an Indian word." By the time Carson was doing his research about the high peaks of the Adirondacks, "the pretentious foreign name" had "never succeeded in pushing the characteristic Yankee name off the peak."

The first recorded ascent of Sawteeth is credited to Newell Martin about 1875. Martin, a graduate of Yale, enjoyed climbing the cliffs of Sawteeth above Lower Ausable Lake as did John C. Case and Jim Goodwin (#24) in the 1920s and 30s. Carson wrote at length about Martin in his chapter about Sawteeth in *Peaks and People of the Adirondacks*:

> There *[at Yale]* he introduced the art of steeple-climbing, which for a time became a favorite outdoor sport at New Haven. He first came to the Adirondacks while an undergraduate, and soon earned the reputation of being the most venturesome amateur climber of his day. His preference was for "walking up the hills" off from the trails and at steep places. He and Charlie Beede are said to be the first to climb Gothic by the way of the present trail from St. Hubert's,[1] and they came down the great slide... Martin also climbed Mount Colvin where it rises steeply from the ice caves on the Lower Lake.[2]

The first trail to Sawteeth, now referred to as the "Scenic Trail," leaves from the Lower Ausable bridge and crosses the Cascade Brook just below Rainbow Falls. Strewn with huge boulders that have fallen from the steep cliffs above, it passes along the northwest shore of the lake before beginning the ascent of the first tooth of the saw.

White-lettered green signs mark the trail's breathtaking lookouts. After checking out the first one, just 250 feet above the lake, you will come to the second, next to St. Bernard's Rock. If, after passing it, you turn around and look, you may discern the profile of a dog of that species. An even more spectacular view can be obtained from Lookout Rock, just off the main trail at about 1.8 miles from its start. A short spur trail climbs to it. Lower Ausable Lake is revealed in its entirety 1,600 feet below. The main trail proceeds, and takes you up a ladder just below a fourth lookout which affords a view of Upper Ausable Lake before it proceeds over Sawteeth's southeast summit and down into a col, "Rifle Notch," which can be seen from vantage points across the valley. From them the "notch" appears like the rear portion of a rifle sight. When viewed from Saint Huberts it is seen as a knife-like cut in the skyline. Ascending to the summit you pass the junction to the Warden Camp Trail descending to the left.

Sawteeth's summit is heavily forested and surprisingly flat but it offers one of the great views obtainable in the Adirondacks from the summit lookout rock above the "Great Basin."

Heaven Up-h'isted-ness!

Far below is the valley of the Shanty Brook. The "Great Basin" is the entire valley below, from the flanks of Sawteeth and Gothics to Basin.

The second trail to Sawteeth, the Alfred E. Weld Trail, passes by Rainbow Falls. A short side trail leads to the base of the falls where you can see that the streambed follows a six-foot wide diabase dike which has eroded through the anorthosite. As the water drops approximately 150 feet from above, in the late morning hours of summer, sunlight filters through the cascade to create prismatic displays. At one time the cascade, one of the most spectacular in the Adirondacks, was known as Corinne Falls.

The Weld Trail, intended to guide climbers to Pyramid Peak and Gothics, was cut in 1966. It is named in honor of the father of former Massachusetts Governor William Floyd Weld, whose family owns a camp on Upper Ausable Lake.

The Adirondack Trail Improvement Society (ATIS), with funds donated by the Weld family, asked Jim Goodwin to use his knowledge of the area to plan a new route to Gothics. The membership of the ATIS had thought to build a trail to Gothics from Upper Ausable Lake following the Shanty Brook, bypassing Sawteeth. Jim was convinced, however, that the best trail to Gothics would be up into the col between Pyramid and Sawteeth, over Pyramid, and on to Gothics. Once that trail was completed, Jim cut the side trail to the summit of Sawteeth.

Jim's close friend, Trudy Healy (#148), was upset at the cutting of the new route. She felt that Pyramid provided perhaps the most spectacular view in the Adirondacks and should remain trailless. She scolded Jim and predicted that, in no time at all, people would be up there playing their radios. She was right. News that the trail had been cut quickly spread. A short time after it opened, Jim was cutting the extension trail to Sawteeth when he was visited by a friend who reported that he had run into a man on Pyramid playing a radio.

Trudy was right, too, that the view from Pyramid is breathtaking. When you climb over the summit and into the col you feel as if you are standing on mother nature's knife edge. One gaze upward leaves you in awe. The slides of Gothics plunge to the right. The impressive slides of Saddleback and Basin, in the near distance, plummet to the left.

The side trail that Jim cut to Sawteeth is short and direct. In his youth, in the 1920s, he and his sister Peggy tirelessly explored the mountains. They had climbed Sawteeth from the watershed above Rainbow Falls but had achieved the summit via a slide. Bob Marshall also used the old slide to climb Sawteeth. He wrote, "We followed the old Gothic trail by Rainbow Falls to where it crossed the first big slide on Sawteeth. We followed this up a way and then cut directly for the summit." Today the A. E. Weld Trail crosses the base of the slide but second growth has all but obscured it from view.

An article, "The Back Way to Sawteeth," by Adolph G. "Ditt" Dittmar (#31) in the November/December 1949 issue of *Ad-i-ron-dac* described the route, but his trip was from Gothics via Pyramid. He indicated that a faint trail could be seen from Gothics to Pyramid, but after that there was no trail. He wrote, "Soon a cut beside the cliffs will be found. Follow it down. Ferns through a fairly open forest will make the going very easy to the col... We sat down to rest here and remarked that we were at a point just about as remote from trails and civilization as one can get in the Adirondacks."

About achieving the summit he wrote, "In an unbelievably short time you will find yourself at the lookout at the end of the Ausable Lakes trail on the summit of Sawteeth. Look back and hold your breath! Yes, you did come down that! How fortunate that you skirted those cliffs!"

Dittmar completed the trip a second time with his wife Mary (#29), on July 24, 1950, as she completed her second round of the 46.

The third approach to Sawteeth, from the north end of Upper Ausable Lake, starts near the Warden's Camp. That trail crosses Shanty Brook and proceeds up the more moderate western slopes of Sawteeth. Along the way look for a trail junction on the right for the Tammy Stowe Loop which leads to views from cliffs and ledges that overlook the upper lake.

Standing on today's dam at the end of Lower Ausable Lake, a hiker on the way to Sawteeth can imagine the glacier, thousands of feet thick, that scoured the valley the Ausable Lakes occupy. Geologists theorize that at one time the two lakes might have been one and that alluvial deposits from Shanty Brook eventually divided it. The

Ditt Dittmar on Sawteeth

evidence is not clear, but from the dam, even an amateur geologist can see a glacial moraine to the left and behind the boathouse. It is the steep gravel bank that forms the last hill before the lake. It is possible that the moraine once dammed the north end of the lake and that it prevented glacial runoff from escaping into the Ausable River watershed. Instead, the water would have flowed in the opposite direction, toward the Boreas Ponds and eventually to the Hudson River.

The work to build the first dam at the end of the lower lake, to provide the motive power for a saw mill operated by David Hale, began in 1855. However, the dam was breached by flood waters in 1856. Heavy rains created a slide on Gothics and a rush of water which swept down the Rainbow Brook. It carried away the dam and, downstream – from Keene Valley to Jay – it swept away bridges and homes along the course of the Ausable River. The freshet continued all the way to Au Sable Forks and Keeseville. Six people drowned in the flood, and the loss of property and livestock was such that Keene area citizens sued the state. Trial testimony concerning those suits is contained in the collection of the Keene Valley Library. The courts eventually ruled that the state was not liable for the damages because the freshet was an "Act of God."

The dam, larger and stronger, was rebuilt at the lower lake outlet and the saw mill resumed operations in 1857. The level of the lake, backed up by the dam, was fifteen feet higher than it had been before. For almost a century and a half, the dam existed as it had been built, although it was repaired and refitted several times during the intervening years. However, its foundation logs, below the water line and protected therefore from rot, were not replaced. That foundation survived until the dam was rebuilt in the winter of 2003/2004. The Adirondack Mountain Reserve (AMR), owners of the property, built the new dam with a keen eye towards the original's historical significance. Its design was only slightly altered so that it might better withstand the punishment of spring melts that often send huge chunks of

At "Sawteeth Ledge" in the 1930s

ice crashing over the verge. The original sluice gate was preserved and incorporated into the new dam.

Guides began to escort adventurous people to the Ausable Lakes just before the Civil War. Seneca Ray Stoddard listed 13 serving the Keene Flats (Keene Valley) area in 1876.[3] By 1881, Wallace's guide to the Adirondacks listed the names of 28 who worked out of Keene Valley and the "Ausable Ponds." Twelve of them built camps, often just "open camps" (lean-tos), on Upper Ausable Lake. They built their own boats to shuttle guests back and forth across both lakes. The Carry Trail between the lakes even then was employed as a portage route. Sylvanus Well,[4] who owned the property at that time, welcomed the guides and their guests as long as they didn't cut live trees, were cautious with their fires, and refrained from logging.

Endnotes

1. That trail is the one described as "Gothics from the Lake Road" in the ADK's *Guide to Adirondack Trails: High Peaks Region*. The trail was the first cut to the top of Gothics in 1886.
2. A slide of huge boulders along the side of Mount Colvin created a deep underground cavern. Snow buildup inside the cavern never completely melts. In the summer, the water near the "caves" is usually five degrees colder than the rest of the lake – an attraction for trout.
3. Stoddard's list included the names of Orson "Old Mountain" Phelps, Ed Phelps, Harvey Holt, Smith Beede, Orlando Beede, and Mel Trumbull.
4. Well was a state canal commissioner and lumberman. Construction of the original dam cost $1,416.15.

MOUNT COLVIN
Height: 39th – 1,240c meters (4,068+ feet)
By Douglas Arnold (#4693W)

There can be no doubt that the man this mountain commemorates was worthy of the honor. No one disputes that Verplanck Colvin's greatest contribution to New York state was his survey of the Adirondack Wilderness. Moreover, he insisted the mission should include recording the resources of the region and documenting the exploitation of the wilderness that he had come to love. He helped lead the fight for legislation to protect it from further abuse. Nina Webb in her *Footsteps Through the Adirondacks, The Verplanck Colvin Story* wrote that when he was on the summit of Mount Seward "on October 17, 1870, Colvin[1] had seen with his own eyes the extent of the lumbermen's destruction. He was horrified and came down all fired up about the importance of protecting the forests from such devastation."[2] His account was read at the Albany Institute, and as a result came to the attention of many important state officials. His "eloquent, earnest, and profuse"[3] argument for the creation of an Adirondack Park was soon thereafter published in the *Annual Report of the New York State Museum*. In part, he wrote as follows:

The Adirondack wilderness contains the springs which are the sources of our principal rivers, and the feeders of the canals. Each summer the water supply for these rivers and canals is lessened... The immediate cause has been the chopping and burning off of vast tracts of forest in the wilderness, which have hitherto sheltered from the sun's heat and evaporation the deep and lingering snows, the brooks and rivulets, and the thick, soaking sphagnous moss which, at times knee-deep, half water and half plant, forms hanging lakes upon the mountain sides; throwing out constantly a chilly atmosphere which condenses to clouds the warm vapor of the winds, and still reacting, resolves them into rain. It is impossible for those who have not visited this region to realize the abundance, luxuriance and depth which these peaty mosses – the true source of our rivers – attain under the shade of those dark northern evergreen forests... With the destruction of the forests, these mosses dry, wither and disappear; with them vanishes the cold, condensing atmosphere which forms the clouds... The remedy for this is an Adirondack Park or timber preserve... The interests of commerce and navigation demand that these forests should be preserved; and for posterity should be set aside, this Adirondack region, as a park for New York.

Verplanck Colvin

Two years later, in 1872, Colvin was appointed to serve as a member and the secretary of a "commission of State parks for the State of New York." Three of the other members of the seven-man commission were Congressman William Wheeler,[4] former Governor Horatio Seymour,[5] and Franklin B. Hough.[6] Colvin was author of the short-lived commission's only annual report, which advocated the protection of forest lands considered vital to the conservation of the state's water resources. Governor John A. Dix[7] received the report, but no action was taken at that time concerning the commission's recommendations. Colvin had already spent several years and large sums of his own money researching the assets of the Adirondacks.

Colvin, who lobbied for the position, was appointed Superintendent of the Adirondack Survey in the spring of 1872 and was (eventually) provided with funding, one thousand dollars, intended to help him complete "a survey of the Adirondack wilderness of New York, and a map thereof." It was a job he would keep for twenty-eight years, until 1900 when, at last, his position was abolished by Governor Theodore Roosevelt. In the meantime, Colvin had taken on a second survey – that of state land holdings in the Adirondack region – and had produced a host of topographical survey reports for the legislature, drawn numerous maps, created charts and pen and ink mountain views, and tramped through the region again and again, sometimes funding the survey with his own money, often working "in the field" late into the fall, and constantly championing the region and striving to protect it from "wanton destruction." However, Colvin never completed the survey; he never produced "the map thereof." Maps of the region were produced by the United States Geological Survey, however, shortly after Colvin was forced into retirement at the beginning of the twentieth century.

Colvin's scientific contributions usually go unheralded. His knowledge of maps, map making, surveying, and geography combined with his unique practical understanding of mountain terrain led him to discover a general law of symmetry regarding mountain slopes. He recognized that there is a relationship between the parabolic curves inherent in gneissoid and granitic mountain slopes. That observation allowed cartographers, supplied with basic information – such as the base, height and distance – to calculate the proportions between contour lines accurately and plot them on maps. Colvin's observations also enable geologists to study the scratches and curves in rock leading to and from valleys and interpret the direction of glacial movement through them.

After his crushing release from his position with the state, Colvin returned to Albany, where he had been born January 4, 1847. He became somewhat a recluse in his family homestead where he surrounded himself with his many field notebooks, sketches, charts, unfinished maps, and survey instruments. In 1916, he was seriously injured when he slipped on ice and fell while running to catch a trolley car. He suffered a concussion. Nina Webb wrote about his physical and mental deterioration thereafter:

> He became a hermit in his own house, cared for by Mills Blake... Although it seems logical to say that Colvin's decline was directly related to his fall, the bitterness and despair he felt at being so rudely treated by the state were major contributors to his emotional collapse.
>
> As Colvin's condition worsened, Mills did all he could to help. It was agony for him to watch the once proud and hardy man waste away, and to realize that the keen intellect was dimming with each passing day...
>
> The effects of Colvin's concussion lingered on. It soon became obvious that his mental problems were not going to be temporary. Signs of paranoia appeared. Colvin was losing his wits.[8]

Clara Dennis, his neighbor and friend, maintained that Colvin's reclusive living, poor nourishment, and long hours of study over many years prevented him from recovering. In January 1919 he was committed to Albany Hospital where he was held for three weeks in the "mental ward," before being declared a lunatic by a court.

Webb wrote of him, after he was transferred to the Marshall Infirmary in Troy on February 22, 1919:

> Verplanck Colvin, brilliant engineer, scientist, inventor, and artist, was consigned to the fetid atmosphere of a mental institution. In a dark ward whose windows were barred, he was hidden away from the sweet smells of the Adirondack woods he loved so much. And there, deprived of the sights and sounds of gentle winds, rainbows, and glorious sunsets, he went downhill very quickly...
>
> Colvin's dreary life continued for another fifteen months. Finally, on May 28, 1920, his dark eyes closed for the last time. Death came at 7:30 in the evening, at the end of a lovely sunny day. It was the time of day when Colvin, in his prime, might have been resting on a mountaintop, sketching the beauty of an Adirondack sunset.
>
> Devoid of barometers, blankets, and transits, Verplanck Colvin had climbed his final mountain. Stilled forever was the enthusiastic, educated voice that had urged the creation of the Forest Preserve and the Adirondack Park...[9]

He was 73 years old.

There are numerous publications through which one can learn more about Colvin's life, including Webb's excellent biography, Russell M. L. Carson's brief account of his life in *Peaks and People of the Adirondacks,* and his own reports to the state legislature. Those reports had significant impact, particularly the early ones which revealed the High Peaks region to numerous readers. They helped inspire the creation of both the state Forest Preserve (1885) and the Adirondack Park (1892), and they directly influenced two young men. George

Marshall later wrote about the discovery of those reports at the Marshall summer cabin at Knollwood on Lower Saranac Lake:

> For years the reddish-brown reports of the *Topographical Survey of the Adirondack Wilderness* were obscured in shadow at the bottom of the bookcase until one day Bob discovered them. Immediately he became enthralled by these accounts of the explorations of Verplanck Colvin and Mills Blake. Their adventures were not in distant Himalayas or Rockies, but were among the mountains which surrounded us. The heroes of these explorations were not the contemporaries of Columbus or Daniel Boone, but of our father. This opened our eyes to new possibilities and, when soon thereafter Bob read Longstreth's *The Adirondacks,* we determined to penetrate those mountains, which previously had been accepted as a scenic backdrop along the skyline across the lake, and see what lay beyond.[10]

Thus the adventure of 46ing, now shared by thousands, began, inspired in large measure by Verplanck Colvin.

Colvin made seven first accents of the 46 high peaks,[11] including that of the mountain which bears his name; however, there was controversy, which persisted for many years, concerning the peak's name.

Colvin and his crew made an ascent of Mount Hurricane near Elizabethtown on July 22, 1873. Included in the party were the Reverend Dr. Theodore L. Cuyler of Brooklyn, survey assistant Mills Blake, and a local guide, Elijah Simmonds. While taking measurements, Colvin periodically asked Simmonds if he knew the name of the particular summit he was sighting. Simmonds peered through the scope of the theodolite trained on one of the mountains and responded that he thought it was nameless. Carson, who heard this story from Mills Blake, reported it in his *Peaks and People of the Adirondacks:*

> Then Dr. Cuyler spoke, "Let me name that mountain." On Mr. Colvin assenting, Dr. Cuyler said, "I name it 'Mount Colvin.'" Colvin does not refer to this incident in his 1873 Report, but in a later report states that Mount Colvin was named by Dr. Cuyler in an article in the New York *Independent* in 1876.[12]

Colvin originally credited the naming of the peak to "the guides." He described the peak's first ascent in his *Report of the Topographical Survey of the Adirondack Wilderness of New York for the Year 1873:*

> Rousing the men early on the 20th *[August 1873]*... we commenced our climb to the summit of the next mountain eastward, which the guides had named Mount Colvin. The knowledge that it was a mountain heretofore unascended, unmeasured and – prominent as it was – unknown to any map, made the ascent the more interesting. The indications of game were naturally abundant; the rocks and ledges geologically interesting; and, judging by the outlook from inferior summits, the view from the top could not fail to be superior... and reaching at length the height, its last approach a cliff almost impregnable, we drew ourselves up over the verge to find a seat upon a throne that seemed the central seat of the mountain amphitheatre. Deep in the chasm at our feet was the lower Ausable lake, each indentation of its shore sharply marked as on a map; beyond it the Gothic mountains rose, carved with wild and fantastic forms on the white rock, swept clear by avalanches and decked with scanty patches of stunted evergreens. Everywhere below were lakes and mountains so different from all maps, yet so immovably true. There was too little time to satisfy us. Here was golden sunshine, a balmy air and a wealth of work before us...

Colvin that day calculated the height of the mountain to be 4,142 "feet above tide level."

Although Colvin had been told that the mountain was nameless in 1873, according to Carson, its name "would have stood without opposition if a quarrel had not developed between Colvin and R. M. Shurtleff"[13] over a trivial matter. In the 1880s when the controversy regarding the name brewed, few disputed that Old Mountain Phelps had previously called the mountain "Sabille or Sabele" for the Indian, Sabael (Elijah Lewis),[14] who discovered the iron ore at Adirondac (now the Upper Works) and led the David Henderson party to it from North Elba in 1826.

Carson related the story of the incident which led to the quarrel and its eventual outcome:

> A number of years after Mount Colvin was named, Colvin and his party camped on the Upper Ausable Lake, occupying one of two open camps[15] built close together with the open ends facing, so that one fire would warm both. In this camp they found a jack,[16] which they rigged up. While they were there, Shurtleff and Orlando Beede arrived to occupy the other camp. After dark Colvin went up the inlet with Old Mountain Phelps, to jack a deer. He shot at one, but it escaped, although he thought he had wounded it. After Colvin came in, Shurtleff and Beede took the jack. They came back so soon with a deer that Colvin suspected that Shurtleff had found the deer which he had shot. Colvin said nothing at the time, but several years later Shurtleff and Colvin met at Lake George. There Colvin accused Shurtleff of stealing his deer and a quarrel ensued. Shurtleff was bitter about the matter and determined to do away with the name "Mount Colvin." He had a number of trail signs painted bearing the name "Mount Sebille," and he put these up on the Mount Colvin trail. The name "Colvin" had been generally adopted, however, and these signs led to a great deal of confusion. Later, Shurtleff realized that the quarrel was petty and he dropped his opposition to the name "Mount Colvin."

Carson went on to mention that the name "Sebille" had gained a degree of acceptance during the time the signs were in place and wrote that "the mountain continues to be known by both names." That may have been true in the 1920s, but "Sebille" now is just a memory, a historical footnote.

Colvin's ego may, in part, have been the reason the controversy arose. In fact, while Carson was researching the naming of the high peaks, he received a couple of letters requesting that he restore the name "Sabele" to Mount Colvin. He once wrote that Colvin "was a remarkable, knowledgeable, complex man who had many faults. His ego was a part of his leadership and determination to answer the question. Without it he could not have had the successes he amassed. His constant questioning of supposed facts drove him to find the truth in everything he did from his calculations to his understanding of the need to protect the wilderness called the Adirondacks." He expanded upon that theme in *Peaks and People* when he wrote, "Colvin's main faults were an unfortunate egotism and carelessness about details in writing up his reports. The main criticism that has been heard from the men who knew him was that he was inclined to take the attitude of 'big I, little you,' which cost him many friends."

Over time, however, Carson came to believe that Colvin was more than a man of determined pursuit. In a letter to Alfred Donaldson, author of the two-volume *History of the Adirondacks,* Carson recounted a visit he enjoyed with Colvin's longtime friend and associate Mills Blake. When he met with Blake and Clara Dennis, who helped care for the surveyor in his declining years, he learned that Colvin had been a charitable individual. Mrs. Dennis told him that after Colvin's death, person after person had testified "with tears in their eyes" to his helping them when they were in need. In his letter to Donaldson, Carson wrote, " You are probably much amused by now at my having lost my head in hero worship of Mr. Colvin. That is hardly the case however. I am enthusiastic, and yesterday was an extremely interesting day, but yet I have not entirely lost my sense of proportion and still recognize Colvin's faults and weaknesses, to realize that he was a very remarkable man and a man of wonderful knowledge."

Mount Colvin and Blake's Peak

Mount Colvin and Blake's Peak are usually approached from the Adirondack Mountain Reserve's Lake Road along the Gill Brook. The scenic Gill Brook Trail which leads to the Mount Colvin trailhead offers many breathtaking views of flumes and cascading waterfalls. Closer to Lower Ausable Lake a second trail to Colvin bypasses the boulders and rocks found along the other trail along the brook. A third trail leaves the road at the height of land above the boathouse. Climbers can also approach the peaks from the opposite direction, from the Elk Lake-Mount Marcy Trail and, hiking over the Pinnacle Ridge, ascend Blake's Peak first and then Mount Colvin.

From below Elk Pass the trail to Mount Colvin climbs a very steep ridge before it crests a knob and descends into a col just below the summit which can be seen above, but one more steep climb must be made. Upon achieving the height, don't miss the summit trail to the right. A brief clamber places the hiker on the summit rock which provides stunning views of both lakes and the Great Range beyond. To the northwest the outlooks of Sawteeth go relatively unnoticed as the massive slides of Gothics dominate the view.

Lower Ausable Lake, almost 1,600 feet below the summit, was the scene of one of Colvin's most harrowing adventures in the fall of 1875. In his *Seventh Annual Report on the Progress of the Topographical Survey of the Adirondack Region of New York to the Year 1879,* he told of his survey work from Keene Valley, through the valley of the Ausable Lakes, on to the summit of Mount Marcy and beyond. On the 4th of November he determined the height of Mount Marcy to be "5,344.311 feet above mean tide level in the Hudson." On the 5th, "while some of the party were engaged in transporting baggage and instruments back along the trail to the Au Sable – the storm having ceased, though the snow was knee deep – as it was bright and clear, though cold," he decided to "make a forced march with one guide to the south, westward of Mt. Skylight, to explore the Cliff mountain pass, a wild gorge to the west of Mt. Redfield." He later returned to Panther Gorge by way of the Opalescent River, the Feldspar Brook, and Lake Tear-of-the-Clouds.

On November 6, Colvin and the men who had remained with him at Panther Gorge started out of the mountains:

> The whole party marched under knapsacks and presented a picturesque appearance winding along the trail. The day was bright and pleasant, and a short distance down the gorge we observed abundant tracks of numerous smaller animals in the snow, squirrels, rabbits, etc.; but the snow soon became less and less deep, and to our surprise as we descended from the gorge to our old camp near the south-east end of Bartlett mountain, all snow disappeared on the southern exposures of the hills, and the crisp leaves under foot made it seem like autumn again. One of our guides here met us on the trail with the alarming news that the river inlet of the upper Au Sable lake was frozen, and that we must march through the woods directly to the lake. Reached the shore before dark and were compelled to break a passage through the ice for the boat to reach the open water. Brought the party, instruments and baggage through in safety and camped near the outlet.
>
> The morning of the 7th showed the shore ice so much increased during the night, that it was evident an immediate retreat was necessary, in order to pass the cliff-walled and dangerous lower Au Sable lake. Cut our way again with one boat across the ice in the lower end of the upper lake, and, leaving the boat, set out, burdened with baggage, for the lower Au Sable.

Colvin's party "under heavy packs" arrived forty-five minutes later at the head of the lower lake which...

> ...was a sheet of ice, too thick to break a passage with boat, apparently too thin to hold a man, while the black rocks on either side – combed with ice – forbade escape along the shore. More provoking, our light boat left here for this probable semi-sled use had been taken by some guileless hunter who left a huge clumsy craft upturned upon the shore instead. We had no time to hesitate. Our provisions exhausted, and we must move on. Loading our baggage into the heavy boat left us, we launched it upon the first thin ice of the marshy inlet, and the whole party entering the craft we endeavored to fight our way along, chopping ice or breaking it by sliding the boat up upon the surface and breaking it down. At length the ice refused to yield, and cautiously stepping from the boat, the water rising above the ice we drew the boat up, and turned it into a sled; then led by one of the guides, who far ahead selected a safe route on firm ice, we drew our uncouth craft along the frozen lake. In this manner we slowly made our way northward, at the rate of a mile an hour, having frequently to diverge on account of thin ice. On either side the gloomy cliffs, inclosing this wild lake, arose in savage sublimity, rendered more stern by the masses of ice and avalanche of snow, which leaping the cliffs filled the chasms to the very shore of the lake.

Colvin, his men, his instruments, and their "baggage," safely reached the lake's outlet at three o'clock that afternoon and, by "rapid march, at dark... entered the settlement of Keene, and were once more within the limits of civilization." The "grass was still green and the weather pleasant" and Colvin saw some "'rabbits,' or great northern hares, brought in by a hunter... not changed into the white winter coat, as those near Marcy had long since done."

On another occasion, members of the survey team were returning from Boreas Mountain when they arrived at the head of the lower lake and found it covered with a thin layer of ice. They had started across, without their boats, when it became apparent that safe passage was impossible. They headed for the north shore, but as the first of them reached it, Mills Blake fell into the lake. He pushed through the last of the ice to the shore and then thrust the end of a cedar branch back to their guide, Ed Phelps, who was in trouble behind him. If you study a topographic map of the area where the men went ashore, you soon realize that they had no choice but to proceed up the side of Sawteeth Mountain in order to work their way back to the outlet of the lower lake. They endured the arduous trek and, in the dark, reached one of the notches on the mountain's side. The climb up, through, and down from that notch to the dam at the end of the lake took four and a half hours. Blake and Phelps and the other members of the team didn't reach Keene Valley until eleven o'clock that night.

Colvin's summit rock tells a story of its own. It is fitting that evidence of the man that the mountain is named for remains upon it. At your feet, embedded in the rock, is an original survey marker and the guy-rings that Verplanck Colvin had drilled into the rock during his survey, more than one hundred thirty-five years ago. Other mountains still sport Colvin rings and markers, but many of his markers have disappeared, ripped from mountain rock by seekers of souvenirs. The reminders of the surveyor, scientist, and champion of wilderness preservation remain atop his monument precisely where he left them.

Fairy Ladder Falls

One of the most interesting of High Peaks waterfalls can be found high on the Gill Brook but away from the Colvin trail. The stepped cascade, Fairy Ladder Falls, is best approached

(a short bushwhack east and downward) from just below the junction of the Colvin Trail and the Elk Pass Trail. Colvin and his men discovered it and the surveyor named it on August 19, 1873, after they had made a rapid descent from the summit of Nippletop. They had left that peak relatively early – 5:30 in the afternoon – and had had time to reach "the bottom of Elk Pass" and "erect a shanty of boughs." Colvin wrote, "The camp was in an open grove fronting an unknown waterfall, which from its silvery spray and step-like form I named *Fairy Ladder Falls,* the height of the foot of which I found to be 3,111 feet above tide."

Few hikers today venture to Fairy Ladder Falls. The cascade remains secluded, lovely, and, perhaps, enchanted. A visit to it will, in a sense, take you back to Colvin's time.

Fairy Ladder Falls – photo by Douglas Arnold

Endnotes

1. Pronounced *'Käl* (as in college) *-vin* (as in vintage). Albany's Colvin Avenue is named for his family.

2. Nina Webb, *Footsteps Through the Adirondacks, The Verplanck Colvin Story* (Utica: North Country Books, 2002), copyright 1996 by Nina Webb, pg. 33.

3. *Ibid.*

4. Wheeler, whose home was in Malone, would go on to become Vice President of the United States (1877-1881).

5. For more on Horatio Seymour, for whom the high peak in the Seward Range is named, see Sharp Swan's chapter about Seymour.

6. For more on Franklin B. Hough, for whom the high peak in the Dix Range is named, see Daniel Eagan's chapter about Hough.

7. For more on John A. Dix, for whom the highest peak of the Dix Range was named, see Daniel Eagan's chapter about Dix.

8. Webb, pg. 157.

9. Webb, pgs. 159-160.

10. George Marshall, "Adirondacks to Alaska, A Biographical Sketch of Robert Marshall," *The Ad-i-ron-dac* (Vol. XV, No. 3 - May-June 1951), pg. 44.

11. Carson lists Colvin's first ascents, all with guides and most with members of his survey parties, as those of Mount Emmons, Mount Donaldson, Mount Seward, Gray Peak, Skylight, Upper Wolf Jaw, and Mount Colvin. The Seward record is disputed. With Colvin on Mount Colvin in 1873 were his assistant Mills Blake, Charles H. Peck, Old Mountain Phelps, Eli Chase, and Henry Reed (the last three serving as guides and workmen).

12. Carson was unable to find any article by Dr. Cuyler in the *Independent,* but he did find one by Cuyler in the July 24, 1873, edition of the Elizabethtown *Post* which reported the name of the mountain as Colvin.

13. Roswell Morse Shurtleff (1838-1915) was a well known artist of the second half of the nineteenth century.

14. Elijah Lewis was the Indian who led David Henderson and his party to the iron ore deposit at Adirondac. His father was a well known Abenaki. Jim Goodwin reported in *Of the Summits, of the Forests* that Old Mountain Phelps had named the mountain "after Sabael, the Indian whose son, Elijah Lewis" led Henderson. The father, Sabael, was reportedly twelve years old when he followed the British army to Quebec's Plains of Abraham. The Reverend John Todd spent some time with Sabael at Indian Lake and wrote about him in "Summer Gleanings" (1852): "The old man was in battle at Quebec, when Wolfe fell and the city was taken. His father was a kind of chief or brave, and he was his father's cook. He knows that he was then twelve years old. The Battle took place in 1759, consequently he must now be one hundred and one years old." Todd wrote that Sabael had a son, "Lige" or (also) "Lewis Elijah" Benedict. Russell Carson wrote of the older man, Sabael, in his newspaper column, "The Foot Path," in March 1929. He said that Sabael was the first human being known to have explored the Adirondack wilderness. When the ATIS put up the signs for the trail to the mountain, the name was spelled *Sebille*.

15. Lean-tos.

16. A jack light for attracting fish or for hunting game at night.

BLAKE'S PEAK
Height: 43rd – 1,210c meters (3,970+ feet)
By Douglas Arnold (#4693W)

Russell M. L. Carson wrote in *Peaks and People of the Adirondacks* that he and several of Mills Blake's friends[1] conceived the naming of Blake's Peak in 1924 to honor the man who had lived in the shadow of his lifelong friend Verplanck Colvin. Carson's suggestion to name the high peak adjacent to Mount Colvin for Blake met with favor, and in 1925 Arthur S. Hopkins put the name on the Conservation Commission's base map.

Blake trained as an attorney, but because the drudgery of indoor work did not agree with him, he asked to join his friend on the Adirondack Survey. Colvin hired him and made him his chief clerk and assistant. Second-in-command and in charge of the Division of Levels, his duties included recording data, assisting in the coordination of crews, leading crews to remote sighting locations, hiring guides, ordering supplies, backpacking supplies and surveying equipment, and completing numerous other tasks that Colvin wished him to perform. When Colvin needed assurance that a task be done and done well, he relied on Mills Blake. One of his assignments was to record theodolite data. In 1883, while he was posted on Mount Marcy from September 10 to October 17, he endured cold rain, snow, and hurricane force winds in order to record that data.

Mills Blake

The survey required many men to accomplish its work. Colvin hired and fired lots of good men, but one man was indispensable and stuck with Colvin throughout the quarter century of the effort: Mills Blake.

While he was conducting his research for his history of the High Peaks of the Adirondacks, Russell Carson conducted correspondence with Blake and made several attempts to meet with him in Albany. Finally, he gained Blake's confidence and was invited to visit him at the Elms, the Colvin homestead on Western Avenue in Albany. The house was being rented, but its wing still contained Colvin's life's work. Blake took Carson into the room that had been the "Office of the Adirondack Survey." Carson wrote to Alfred Donaldson about the visit. He commented, "I wish I had the gift of writing that I could draw a picture of the place for you as it impressed me... It would have been a gold mine of information... Perhaps the most interesting thing was Colvin's first map, showing many things by erasures and additions and alterations which do not show on his published maps but furnish interesting side lights to any one who knows a little about his work."

Prior to Colvin's death in 1920, Blake had worked and lived with his friend at the Elms, but at the time Carson first visited him, he was living with the Dennis family on a side street across from the Colvin homestead, where, while the survey was being conducted, the two devoted countless hours, during the winters, recording and writing the survey reports and planning work that lay ahead. The remaining time they spent in the Adirondack wilderness.

Carson, after he also met Clara Dennis, Colvin's longtime housekeeper, told Donaldson, "Mrs. Dennis said the two men loved each other and that their devotion was beautiful. Neither had married, and both were free to come and go as they chose and they devoted their lives to the work they loved and they had many happy years together in it."

On March 15, 1926, Blake wrote to Carson to inform him that the Colvin homestead had been sold. George Marshall, also alerted to the sale, became concerned about the survey records and went to Albany, where he found Blake as he was pulling a child's wagon loaded with books from the Colvin homestead to his living quarters at the Dennis home. The books were unbound Colvin reports. Marshall helped with the move and then went with Blake to the Elms, up to the second floor and into the survey office. He was awestruck by the priceless collection of instruments, minerals, fossils, artifacts, unpublished reports, and sketches that the room contained. Stunned by the extent of the historical record that he saw, he wrote to Carson and said, "I was never so tempted to commit theft in my life."

Mills Blake had been upset over the sale of the homestead. He believed Colvin had wanted the estate to be used as an educational institution instead of being sold, as it had been, to serve as the new site of the Lutheran Church of Albany. After years of dispute, a court concluded that a diligent search had failed to discover what monies Colvin had wanted to put in trust, that he had failed to appoint trustees to administer any such trust, and that the sale of the property had been proper.

In 1930, Blake died. Colvin's heirs sold the remainder of his library. However, tradition holds that Colvin, after he had been dismissed from state service by Theodore Roosevelt in 1900, had "stuffed a lot of his surveying records and reports into cardboard cartons and piled them up on his back porch."[2] Nina Webb in her book about Colvin, *Footsteps Through the Adirondacks,* recorded the rest of that story:

> There they stayed until he died. Not too much time passed before some state employees gave in to their temptation to retrieve the valuable materials on their own. One day, after making sure that nobody was in the house, they went to the porch and snatched the boxes away. How fortunate for all of us that they made that daring raid, because the contents of the cartons make up the core of New York State's Colvin Collection.[3]

Those records remain today with the New York State Department of Conservation in Albany.

Verplanck Colvin, before he died, had provided a final resting spot for his friend, and even today an unmarked stone remains next to Colvin's in the Coeyman's cemetery in Albany County. For reasons unclear to this day, Colvin's heirs would not allow Blake to be interred there. Instead, through the generosity of the Dennis family, he was laid to rest a few miles away in their family plot.

After Carson published his book in 1928, solidifying the name Mount Colvin, a controversy regarding a geographical name "rule" erupted. Colvin had passed away in 1920 but Mills

Blake was still living when *Peaks and People* was published and Blake's Peak had appeared on the 1925 map included with Arthur S. Hopkins' "Trails to Marcy" pamphlet. The complicating factor was the rule adopted in 1890 by the United States Geological Survey that said, "Names of living persons should be applied *[to geographical features]* very rarely, and only those of great eminence should thus be honored." The concern, though expressed, ultimately did not affect Blake's Peak, and it wasn't until 1947 that the "rule" was emended and formalized by the federal Board of Geographical Names. Today, honorees must be deceased at least five years before consideration of applying their names to geographical features can be considered.

Carson wrote an article detailing some of his thoughts about the naming of mountains in the October 1940 *Cloud Splitter*. Although he was writing about Mount Redfield, his first paragraph might still apply to the naming of other peaks. He wrote,

> While mountains are the handiwork of the Great Creator of the Universe, mountain names when not the heart work, are apt to be the sad headaches rather than the good headwork of men. Too seldom is mountain nomenclature inspired by sentimental logic; and too frequently, especially in the Adirondacks, are its derivations far removed from personal relationships of men to mountains, or to any appropriate fitness. It then degenerates to the stupid egotism that gives names to mountains that have only remote or long-range connection with the names... When the name and the hill do not fit according to popular judgment or prejudice opinion, the devil is to pay: but when a mountain and its name are in harmony with each other, infinite is in tune with the finite and nature lovers rejoice.

After *Peaks and People* was published, a New York City attorney, Theodore V. W. Anthony, opposed Carson's naming of Mount Marshall (previously Middle Dix and now Hough). Anthony later expanded his opposition to include any mountain that Carson had named for honorees who were still alive. Blake and the Marshall brothers were the only honorees alive at the time the book was published. In a letter, dated May 28, 1928, to the Adirondack Mountain Club, Anthony maintained that the naming of Blake's Peak was improper. He went on to suggest that it be named, instead, after John Jay, Chief Justice of the United States (1789-1795) and Governor of New York (1795-1801). He was apparently unaware that a range of mountains (and one of that range's peaks) in the town of Jay had already been named for the famous New Yorker.

The Conservation Department was drawn into the dispute. W. G. Howard of the department sent a letter to Carson on September 25, 1935, to explain that Bob Marshall had requested his name be removed from Middle Dix. However, Marshall had urged that Blake's Peak become official. Howard said that he would be glad to support the naming with the endorsement of the Conservation Department. Carson responded that he would formalize the request, but it wasn't until after the 46ers of Troy took up the challenge in 1941 that the peak was officially named (June 26, 1942).

Carson was right. Mountains should be named for people who had direct associations with them. Blake's Peak is an appropriate designation for the mountain close by its partner upon the map, Mount Colvin.

According to Carson, Blake's Peak[4] was first climbed about 1874 by Ed Phelps and "a man named Miller." Most 46ers climb it and Mount Colvin during a single trip. The trail to Blake starts not twenty feet from Colvin's summit. It is likely you will summit Colvin again on your return from Blake to return to the Ausable Club at St. Huberts. However, you can approach Blake from the Pinnacle along the Boreas Range from the Elk Lake-Marcy Trail or approach both peaks from a trail which ascends from the Carry Trail between the Ausable Lakes. Most 46ers choose to climb Colvin first and then Blake from one of the routes that begin along the Gill Brook.

Leaving Colvin's summit and heading towards Blake's Peak, before descending into the col, stop at the lookout a few hundred yards south along the ridge. It too provides a fabulous view to the west. As you proceed, you will descend to the col between the collegial peaks. There you will find the junction where the trail from Carry joins the Colvin-Blake trail.

Climbing again, to the summit of Blake, you'll soon discover why the Marshalls rated Blake's Peak's view 37th. The summit today provides no view, but if you proceed south towards the Pinnacle, you can find openings which reveal Elk Lake in the distance. Lookout Rock, three tenths of a mile from Blake's summit, reveals the upper lake. If you choose to continue on to the Pinnacle, be aware that there are connecting trails which lead to private camps along the Upper Lake. Those trails are closed to hikers who otherwise enjoy a great privilege of hiking to Colvin and Blake, in part, on trails which pass through AMR property.

The Pinnacle Ridge Trail

The Pinnacle Ridge Trail, which extends from Blake to Pinnacle, is one of the least frequented ridge routes in the High Peaks. From the Pinnacle, the trail descends rapidly to the northwest before it swings southwest to join the Elk Lake-Marcy Trail just to the south of Marcy Swamp. It is part of the Great Trail Circle proposed by the ADK soon after its founding in 1922. The "circle" was never actually built, but the trail along the Boreas Ridge (now known as the Pinnacle Ridge) had already been cut, originally to delineate AMR protected property from AMR land to the east in the Elk Lake watershed. The AMR sold timber rights to that land to David Hunter in 1916. William A. White marked the line, and George Morrison and Howard Brown cut it. A trail to the Pinnacle from Upper Ausable Lake had been cut, according to Carson, "as early as 1904."

The Pinnacle Ridge Trail is particularly interesting because it does not suffer from overuse. Walking it is a refreshing experience as it shows few signs of erosion brought on by the scouring of hikers' boots. It passes through tall deer grass and fern meadows that are blemished only slightly by a path that is sometimes indistinct. The trail provides occasional views into the Elk Lake drainage on one side and the Ausable Lake valley on the other. Along the way you will arrive at a short side trail that will lead you up a ladder and, up again, to a sign that reads "72 steps" to a view. If you count your steps, you will find that information rather accurate. When you reach 67 you will see Elk Lake framed by balsam trees. At 72 you will find a truly exceptional view of the Elk Lake area.

The Beede House and St. Hubert's Inn

Two hundred bushels of wheat was the purchase price in 1858, when Smith Beede bought 600 acres of land adjacent to the "Old Military Road" (today's Route 73) just north of Roaring Brook where it crosses the Beede Brook (now Putnam Brook). The tract extended from Beede Heights (now the Ausable Club) across the valley and up the western slopes of Giant Mountain. Beede cleared some of the land and grew potatoes and wheat amongst the tree stumps in fields now used as the Ausable Club's golf course. He built several small outbuildings and had little trouble filling them with guests who began to flock to the area after Murray's Rush[5] to the Adirondacks began in 1869.

In 1870, William G. Neilson is said to have built the first summer cottage, "Noonmark Lodge," on a lot he bought from Beede, and in 1876 Beede built a hotel that was 105 feet long and three stories in height. Beede's, as it was known, could accommodate 150 guests, but it proved so popular that Beede and his son Orlando expanded the facility in 1886. According to Alfred Donaldson in his *History of the Adirondacks,* it "still failed to meet the measure of its popularity. The Alp-like beauty of the spot, combined with its nearness to the twin Ausable Lakes, made it a mountain Mecca." In 1882 the Beedes sold a lot on the Beede Heights property to Dr. Felix Adler and in 1883 they sold others to William A. White and a Miss Hillard. The name Beede Heights gave way to a new one, Keene Heights.

During the summer of 1889 the newly formed Adirondack Mountain Reserve Corporation organized the Keene Heights Hotel Company and began negotiations to purchase the Beede House and the surrounding 600 acres. However, before the sale was finalized, the hotel, uninsured, was destroyed by fire (March 3, 1890). Concerned that the sale might be cancelled, the Beedes began rebuilding immediately, but, as the club was more interested in the land than the structure, the transaction was completed. The Keene Heights Hotel Company completed the construction of the classic Victorian era hotel within four months' time.

In the background: The St. Hubert's Inn.
In the foreground: the original AMR Lake Road gate.

A Mrs. Alderson felt the name Keene Heights Hotel was unattractive. While traveling in Europe she had been inspired by the story of a nobleman who, according to legend, was hunting on a Good Friday in about the year 695 when he came across a white stag with a crucifix hanging from its antlers. He was so moved that he became, as Saint Hubert, a protector of forest animals. Mrs. Alderson was so stirred by the legend that she insisted the new hotel bear the name St. Hubert's Inn. The nearby hamlet, formerly Keene Heights was later officially designated St. Huberts (no apostrophe) by the United States Post Office.

Over the next few years the St. Hubert's Inn struggled. It was much more elaborate than the Beede House had been, had fewer rooms for guests, and was more expensive to operate. With its financial difficulties and a decline in reservations following the 1903 forest fires, the inn was forced to close. The AMR's stockholders debated at length about purchasing it to serve as a private club. Some felt the survival of the AMR was more important than preserving the hotel. Eventually, however, a deal was struck and the AMR bought the inn. A new organization, the Ausable Lakes and Mountain Club (later shortened to the Ausable Club) reopened the hotel as its clubhouse in 1905. The AMR shareholders drafted a new constitution which provided that the shareholders were entitled to long-term lease agreements of the cottages and camps they built on the property. Some rules concerning the leases have changed over the years but today descendants of the original stockholders still retain rights at the Ausable Club as proprietary members.

From the Lake Road

Beyond the AMR gate on the Lake Road, trails flank the opposing banks of the Ausable River. The East River Trail meanders through some virgin timber that remains between the Gill Brook and the east bank of the Ausable. A second trail skirts the west bank of the river all the way to Lower Ausable Lake. Both trails offer tranquil walks through some of the most pristine woods in the Adirondacks. "Grandmother" trees survive in those woods thanks to the forest management of the AMR. The trails ramble alongside the river, make forays up steep banks to points above deep gorges, and they pass over rocks and ledges, many of which afford views. Walking those routes, hikers will find themselves absorbed by the cleansing wilderness. Frequent stops are necessary to admire nature's wonders. Climbers with mountain summit agendas seem to prefer walking the Lake Road. The trails along the river seem to require a slower pace and a less ambitious schedule.

There are five river crossings which may be reached from the Lake Road. The first can be found just before the AMR gate if you make a sharp right immediately before it. After passing the gate keeper's hut, you will cross a bridge. The trail to the right proceeds to the W. A. White Trail and eventually up the ridge to Lower Wolf Jaw. The trail to the left connects to the West River Trail.

A second crossing at 0.4 miles from the gate leads hikers to Cathedral Rocks and Pyramid Brook. The next trail that leaves from the Lake Road crosses the trussed, wooden Canyon Bridge. Most climbers heading to the Wolf Jaws' summits via the Wedge Brook Trail use that bridge.

The trail to Beaver Meadow Falls and Gothics departs from the Lake Road about 1.75 miles from the AMR gate. It proceeds over a fourth bridge which passes over the gorge of the Ausable River. Along the way, the Lost Overlook Trail goes to the south and west to dual outstanding views of the lakes and surrounding area. That side trail, according to Harold Weston, was originally cut by David Hale for a trap line.

The fifth and last bridge between the AMR gate and the lower lakes crosses the alluvial flats of the Cascade Brook just below the lake's dam. The view from the bridge is one of the best in the Adirondacks. The lower lake is walled by the slopes of Sawteeth and Colvin. Above the boat house, Indian Head looms. Just to the south are Fish Hawk Cliffs.

Along the Lake Road, about 1.1 miles from the gate and just before Thunder Bridge, a side trail leads to the Flume, where the Gill Brook descends through a deep gorge. Millions of years ago tension caused a crack to open in the surrounding anorthosite and molten magma filled the opening with minerals not as durable as the surrounding stone. More susceptible to erosion than the surrounding rock, the flow of water, freeze and thaw, has created the gap through which the brook now tumbles.

A story concerning the guide Mel Trumbull has its locus at the Flume. One night he was sent from the upper lake back to St. Huberts to deliver a note. It was late in the evening. He was carrying a lantern to light his way along the Lake Road when he heard a noise and spun around to investigate its source. Through the gloom of the night, reflected by the light of his lantern, he saw the yellow eyes of a panther. Quickening his pace, he ran as fast as the rocky and muddy road would allow. When he was alongside the Flume, holding up his lantern, he looked again for the panther. Seeing no eyes glowing from between the trees, he assumed the cat had abandoned its stalk. Relief filled Mel's mind. He relaxed. Then, an instant later, he heard a rustle of foliage and the scream of the cat. Mel dropped to the ground just as the panther leapt over him and fell into the depths of the Flume. Trumbull then jumped to his feet and fled down the road. He told the story of his lucky escape when he reached St. Huberts. The following morning, when he and others went to look for whatever remained of the panther, it could not be found. Perhaps a hungry, mad, and very wet cat escaped the depths and lived to hunt again.

Indian Head

Two other side trails from the Lake Road take hikers to spectacular lookouts above Lower Ausable Lake. Two trails – one from the height of land to the south of the Ausable Club's boathouse and the other from the Mount Colvin trail – ascend to the brow of Indian Head. The vista from Indian Head includes both lakes, Nippletop, Colvin, Sawteeth, and most of the peaks of the Great Range. The trail from the highest point on the Lake Road ascends via switchbacks to a short side trail that leads to the Gothic Window which provides a view of the eastern flank of Gothics. It proceeds via more switchbacks and a ladder before it arrives at a junction with trails that lead to Gill Brook and to Fish Hawk Cliffs. From the junction, hikers move on to Indian Head along the trail to the right which climbs up and over bare ledges. The brow of Indian Head can be a dangerous place. Be sure of your footing, especially if you venture to a ledge which looms directly over the boathouse 750 feet below.

Fish Hawk Cliffs can be reached from Indian Head or from the Colvin trail. The cliffs were likely named as they are because, at one time, they served as the aeries of ospreys (fish hawks). The cliffs, slightly lower in elevation than Indian Head, provide the best imaginable view of the cliffs of Indian Head... or Adota, an Indian whose visage has been preserved in stone. The legend was recounted by Grace Hudowalski.

Adota of Tahawi

For the June 1939 edition of the Albany Chapter of the Adirondack Mountain Club's *Cloud Splitter*, Grace Hudowalski wrote the following piece, "Adota of Tahawi," a "legend" set on the shore of Lower Ausable Lake:

Adota, Sachem of Tahawi, lived alone. He was a kind and gentle old chieftain, full of love and understanding for his people. In his more youthful days, he had been most aggressive and zealous – the greatest among many great warriors. Had he not guided his wild, warlike Tahawi well, so well that the Saranacs were forced to obey them?

But that was many, many moons ago before Adota (the bow) had grown old. Now his wigwam was the only one at "The Dark Cup" (Lower Ausable Lake) and it was pitched right beneath the sheltering brownish-red rock that jutted upward, shutting out the storms and wind that often threatened. The tribe of the Tahawi dwelt farther south in a village that bordered "The Lake of the White Water Lily" (Upper Ausable).

Adota was not a happy Sachem. His mind was too full of memories of his beloved family and especially of his dear grandson, O-jis-ta (the star) whom Adota had hoped would someday rule the Tahawi of the Couchsachrage. But O-jis-ta had been called to adorn the brow of Ha-wen-ne-yo and now Adota no longer cared to live.

One afternoon as the great Sachem sat by his wigwam looking into "The Dark Cup" and seeing reflected there dark clouds with sudden flashing lights so bright as to dazzle his eyes, he called his Tahawi to him. As he stood straight and stern before them, he spoke of great triumphs and they relived with him the glory of past days. He recalled to them "The Star" and they saw his shoulders bow as with a great weight and they sorrowed with him in his loneliness. Even as he spoke the streaks of lightning that came to the sky and the thunders that fell from the clouds lent a portentousness to the Sachem's frail old form.

In the grayness that surrounded the Tahawi they saw a radiant look come to the old chieftain's face; they saw Adota raise his hands as though beckoning to some far-away loved one; they heard his voice lifted in a mystical joyousness; they saw him fall backward! Adota had gone! And as he went the storm so increased that the tribe was forced to find shelter in the woods.

It was afterward, when the Storm Clouds spent themselves and "The Dark Cup" was calm that Kaiwa (the sky), the medicine man, called them again to the shores of "The Dark Cup" and pointed to the reddish-brown cliffs. There, outlined in the vivid strokes of an artist-sculptor, was the face of Adota of Tahawi, and resting on his breast was the papoose, O-jis-ta, both of them looking over their beloved tribe of Tahawi.

There beneath the rocks Adota was buried. Above him, stoical and wise, his likeness – a wondrous reminder, a fitting shrine to a great Sachem.

* *

Legends – while of doubtful certainty, and authenticity – play an important part in one's love for the Adirondacks of today, the Couchsachrage of yesterday. Should you go to the St. Hubert's region and walk down the road to the shores of the Lower Ausable, far above the lake you would see the rugged beauty of

Adota, more commonly known as "Old Indian Face." Early June is the month to visit this shrine of old legends. To the left of the road, just above the boathouse, is a clump of slender birches — alert, like watchful braves; worshipful — like white-robed choirs. Beneath these is a grassy plot — seldom walked on — and there one will find a profusion of pale blue forget-me-nots blooming in ethereal beauty. Who knows but this is really the resting place of *Adota of Tahawi?*

Endnotes

1. Robert Marshall and George Marshall; W. Scott Brown of Elizabethtown; Charles F. West, William B. Curtis, and Arthur F. West of Glens Falls.

2. Nina H. Webb, *Footsteps Through the Adirondacks, The Verplanck Colvin Story* (Utica: North Country Books, copyright 1996 by Nina H. Webb), pg. 173.

3. *Ibid.*, pgs. 173-174.

4. Over the years, Blake's Peak, the name the mountain was originally given, has been informally replaced by its more familiar abbreviated designation, *Blake*.

5. "Murray's Rush" refers to the impact that the Reverend William H. H. Murray's *Adventures in the Wilderness; or, Camp-Life in the Adirondacks* (Boston: Fields, Osgood, and Co., 1869) had on the region. Murray's somewhat exaggerated stories of his hunting and fishing adventures in the Adirondacks played a major role in stimulating tourist travel to the area. Briefly mentioning Whiteface and Marcy on a single page, the Boston clergyman did not otherwise write about the mountains in his famous book.

About the Author

Forty-sixer #4693W Douglas R. Arnold's adventure began at Lake Tear, where his father showed him "you can jump over the Hudson." That night the stars were so numerous and brilliant the pair could not discern the constellations. The next day, father and son climbed "The Cloudsplitter," Skylight, and Haystack, and the challenge to become 46ers had begun. Doug's father's career got in the way of continuing his quest, and the family moved, but for Doug the desire to become a 46er burned on. Many years later he made his way back to New York and realized his dream, but the desire to climb just burned even higher. Four years later he completed a "W"inter round, and now Doug unofficially counts the rounds mentoring his son, daughter, and friends, anyone who expresses a willingness to climb and discover what he has found in the High Peaks.

Doug is a 46er director and chairman of the Grace Peak Committee. He hopes to one day see East Dix re-named Grace Peak and South Dix re-named Carson Peak. He is a member of the ADK, has adopted and repaired two lean-tos on the Oswegatchie River, and does trail work for both the 46ers and the ADK.

THE UPPER RANGE
By Christine Bourjade (#4967W)

HAYSTACK
Height: 3rd – 1,512 meters (4,961 feet)

And if it be an act of philanthropy to preserve the masterpieces of art for the public good, it is equally commendable to seek to preserve the masterpieces of nature.

– *Robert W. de Forest*

With Orson "Old Mountain" Phelps during a four-week expedition, Verplanck Colvin's survey team cut the first trail up Haystack and reached its summit on August 26, 1873, from the Bartlett Ridge trail cut by Phelps in 1861. Colvin noted, "no trail, no mark of axe on tree, here indicated that man had ever ventured before even on the lower steeps of this proud mountain, though one or two have claimed course." The following day the surveyor made the first altitude measurements of Basin, Saddleback, and Gothics, "stupendous mountains, majestic landmarks of the State." For a while, Colvin considered Haystack above 5,000 feet in elevation, but, oddly, Ebenezer Emmons, who completed the first geological survey of the area in 1837, had made no mention of Haystack.

Colvin set a copper bolt on Haystack's summit while conversing across Panther Gorge with two assistants climbing the side of Marcy. Phelps, who called the state's highest peak "Mercy," later wrote, "Looking down from Haystack into Panther Gorge, we saw a pass greater than any other in the region. It was so narrow that Colvin could talk from the summit of Haystack to his men on the summit of Mercy over a vacuum 2,000 feet deep." Sound travels just the same 150 years later. Sean O'Donnell (#4223), who was on Haystack's summit on August 28, 2003, reported, "We could hear, clear as a bell, people laughing and talking atop Marcy."

Jim Goodwin describes Panther Gorge "as remaining a pleasant herdpath route, with its cliffs and waterfalls a miniature Yosemite Valley with a spectacular waterfall off Marcy and a magnificent open red spruce forest prior to the 1950 hurricane." E. R. Wallace in his *Guide to the Adirondacks* wrote about a particular attraction that could be found in Panther Gorge, "Panther Gorge Falls... situated" a mere 10 miles "from Keene Flats!" That cataract, possibly, is the "spectacular" mentioned by Goodwin, who said the route through Panther Gorge provided "a practical, glorious trip." In 1926, with two clients, he climbed Haystack from the gorge in a line pretty much between the summits of Marcy and Haystack.

The storm of November 25, 1950, inflicted considerable destruction within the gorge. Today, huge boulders up the headwall and ever widening beaver ponds make Goodwin's old route extremely difficult. Another difficulty: within the gorge at one point, a mere third of a mile climb involves 602 feet of ascent.

"Mount Haystack from Upper Ausable Inlet" by Verplanck Colvin
(From *Seventh Annual Report of the Progress of the Topographical Survey of the Adirondack Region of New York to the Year 1879*)

Psychologist and philosopher William James, who endured a sleepless night in Panther Gorge in 1898, wrote about his time there:

> I spent a good deal of it in the woods, where the streaming moonlight lit up things in a magical chequered play, and it seemed as if the Gods of all the nature mythologies were holding an indescribable meeting in my breast with the moral of the inner life… the intense significance of some sort, of the whole scene, if one could tell the significance, the intense inhuman remoteness of its inner life and yet the intense appeal of it; its everlasting freshness and its immemorial antiquity and decay; its utter Americanism and every sort of patriotic suggestiveness, and you, and my relation to you part and parcel of it all, and beaten up with it, so that memory and sensation all whirled inextricably together… It was one of the happiest lonesome nights of my existence and I understand now what a poet is.

In August 1849, Old Mountain Phelps led Almeron Oliver and George Estey from Elk Lake to Marcy, passing over Haystack on the way. Later Phelps wrote, "From the top of Bartlett Mountain I could see Haystack and mistook it for Mercy. I climbed Haystack and then from the top of it could see Mercy 200' higher." Upon reaching Marcy, Phelps and his two companions looked back to Haystack, capped by about 18.5 acres of alpine meadow, and Phelps remarked, "That mountain is a great stack of rock. It resembles a stack of hay." Haystack had been named.

Colvin called Haystack the "Matterhorn of the Adirondacks" and sketched a view of the peak as seen from the inlet of Upper Ausable Lake. In 1888, the overgrown Bartlett trail was cut out again, as was an old trail from Shanty Brook to Haystack.

In August 1949, the Forty-Sixers, joined by the Adirondack Mountain Club and others, conducted a service on Haystack's summit to commemorate the first ascent of the mountain (by Old Mountain Phelps). That celebration is described in Suzanne Lance's "History of the Adirondack Forty-Sixers" elsewhere in this book.

Heaven Up-h'isted-ness!

On the weekend of September 6-8, 1996, eleven women, each portraying a woman from the 1800s, climbed Haystack using an Upper Ausable Lake century-old lean-to as a base camp. The year was chosen in commemoration of the 75th anniversary of women acquiring the right to vote. Each participant had chosen a character either from within her own family or a well-known historical character, all having done some climbing in the Adirondacks more than 100 years before. All of their attire, the menus (sausage, flapjacks, etc.), and the shouldering of pack baskets was the result of the previous winter's historical research. The eight women in the group who made it to the summit were rewarded by magnificent views. The expedition enjoyed good weather until leaving Haystack as the approach of Hurricane Fran made the Lower Ausable Lake traverse more adventurous than they had anticipated.

Haystack was climbed on snowshoes, February 12, 1915, by Willis D. Wood, Frank Weld, George Bodman, and their guide, Pete Lamb. The previous day they had only made it part way up the mountain in deep snow and through uncooperative weather.

In 1911, John "Appy" Apperson was a member of a party that made the first ski ascent of Marcy. A few years later, Appy led the first ski up Mount Haystack, "steepest of all the Adirondack summits." In late February 1922, during another deep snow winter, the legendary Herman Smith "Jackrabbit" Johannsen teamed up with Dr. Irving Langmuir, Apperson, and a Schenectady group. After spending a night in Keene Valley, they skied up the Ausable Lakes and started, on the way to Haystack, up Bartlett Ridge. At the top of the ridge all, except Apperson and Johannsen, were exhausted and turned back. The two men who continued on reached tree line just before sunset and donned crampons to climb the last 300 feet to the summit. Night time descents and overnight bivouacs didn't bother those famous cross-country skiers. The winter ascent was quite a feat considering their wooden skis were likely eight to nine feet long and most skiers didn't use poles, instead relying on a technique still in use: crashing or grasping tree branches for balance during the descent. By 1980, "Skiing is a controlled fall" was one of the slogans of the Ski To Die Club, a High Peaks ski mountaineering group.

Years after some of his legendary ski ascents, while standing on top of Marcy on a beautiful end of February day, Johannsen reminisced about his Haystack climb:

> We stood there together on the top of Haystack and looked over here towards the setting sun. The sky was a wonderful rose. All the intervening peaks were basking in the sunset glow. High overhead rode the full moon which we knew would give us plenty of light as we picked our way down again. It was a sight neither of us would ever forget, for in that moment we saw the world below as though it was frozen in time. There were no past, no future, just the present. And it was unspeakably beautiful.

Jackrabbit was one of the ten founders of the Lake Placid Snow Birds Ski Club in 1903. By 1906, the organization had 1,400 members. In 1921, the club adopted the "Sno-Bird" as the emblem of its Winter Sports Association. A few years later, their offer to the state Conservation Department to cover the cost of building a lean-to between Haystack and Basin was accepted. That lean-to, built at the beginning of the Haystack Brook between Haystack and Basin and named for the ski club, sheltered hikers until 1976.

Harold White, who had earlier climbed Haystack on snowshoes from his family's Upper Ausable Lake camp, in a March 2, 1922, letter to Apperson expressed skepticism about a Haystack ski climb. He wrote, "I do not see how you got up Haystack on skis, as when I made the trip on snowshoes, I had to nail first one shoe and then the other to the crust in order to get up. At that time I think it would have been impossible on skis, and I came down altogether too fast, sitting on the snowshoes."

While commemorating the 1922 ski ascent, six members of the "Ski to Die" club went up Haystack from the east, up what they called the Johannsen Face. On March 13, 1993, they were hit by several feet of snow. That Saturday, a blizzard blanketed most of the East Coast, affecting twenty-six states and Canada. The ski out via the Johns Brook feeder below the Shorey Short Cut was a very slow affair and the journey didn't end until they reached the Ausable Inn in Keene Valley at 11 p.m.

In a March/April 1996 account, Ann Eastman recalled the ordeal:

> From Haystack summit ridge the east face funnels into Haystack Brook... although the terrain sounds gentle, winter reality is extreme: waterfall after huge frozen waterfall led us deeper into the streambed. The first skiers had a cushion of snow. But in passing through, they took mounds of snow with them, leaving sheer ice for the slower, more intimidated skiers like me... We caught the Haystack trail where it crosses the stream and decided to follow it to the pass between Haystack and Basin mountains. From there we could climb the Shorey Short Cut trail and connect with the Phelps Trail. Our reward for the steep climb to the col – we hoped – would be a packed trail for seven miles down Johns Brook Valley... The packed trail that we had hoped to find from Slant Rock was not there. Our expected rocket ride out became a marathon slog, so much we swore the trail was uphill, not downhill... At the Garden we found our car embedded in fresh powder. Extricating it was out of the question: we just skied down the road to Keene Valley.

Lincoln Barnett,[1] through *The Ancient Adirondacks* (Time-Life *The American Wilderness* series, 1974), helped bring the Adirondacks to national attention. In a section of the book, "Nature Walk/On Haystack Mountain," Barnett wrote about an October climb of Haystack by way of the carry between the Upper and Lower Ausable Lakes, the Bartlett Ridge Trail, the Haystack Brook Trail, the Range Trail, and the trail up and over Little Haystack to the mountain's summit. He described the trails, the climbing, the trees and plants along those trails. Concerning the last portion of the trek, from Little Haystack to Haystack, he wrote,

> Stone cairns guided us down a precipice that sometimes allowed no more than two or three inches for foot- and handholds. Shortly we found ourselves in the col confronting the ultimate peak. Before us we saw a less perpendicular approach glazed with the ice and snow of the night before, icicles dangling from ledges of weathered rock and glimmering in the lowering sun...
>
> We scrambled up over a succession of ledges upholstered with a springy jungle consisting of alpine plants with tangled branches and miniature leaves that exist only on the loftiest mountaintops of the High Peaks – Lapland rosebay, bearberry willow and a number of grasses...
>
> Each of the High Peaks offers its individual glories. From the summit of Marcy, for example, the Adirondacks fade into infinity like a great sea of blue, undulating swells. But the view from Haystack, by contrast, reveals the mountains in dramatic intimacy... to the west, the mural of Marcy above Panther Gorge; to the east, the stark geometry of Gothics, a mountain whose summit is virtually bare of forest cover.

About Haystack's summit rock, Barnett wrote, "In its crevices grew sedges and rushes, most notably a straw-colored rush called deer's hair... Here on the pinnacle of Haystack we were standing in the very heart of the Adirondack wilderness, seeing 27 of the major peaks marching across the horizon, their profiles chiseled by gorges and ravines, slide-scarred, blotched with the blue of lakes, bogs, and ponds."

The view from the third highest peak was rated number one by the first three Forty-sixers: the Marshall brothers and Herbert Clark. Robert Marshall, in "The High Peaks of the Adirondacks," wrote,

Everyone has his favorite mountain. My favorite is Haystack. Primarily because in the whole vast panorama visible from the mountain there is virtually no sign of civilization. Whichever way you look, save toward a small burned section near the Giant, there are the forests, the mountains, the ponds, just as they were before white man had ever set foot on America. It's a great thing these days to leave civilization for a while and return to nature. From Haystack you can look over thousands and thousands of acres, unblemished by the works of man, perfect as made by nature.

Of course there are views of overwhelming beauty. I know of no two finer prospects than the one over Panther Gorge toward Marcy, and the one over the rocky Gothics. But it is the sense of being in the center of a great wilderness which gives the greatest charm.

BASIN
Height: 8th – 1,471 meters (4,826 feet)
SADDLEBACK
Height: 17th – 1,380 meters (4,528 feet)

According to some accounts, Basin was named in 1857 by Orson Phelps and his friend the artist Frederick S. Perkins as they were standing on Marcy and looking at a striking "basin" between the steep peeled walls of Basin, Saddleback, Gothics, and Sawteeth's many shoulders. However, from Marcy's summit, one is unlikely to think of a basin while enjoying the view towards the mountain.

Perkins, who was from Wisconsin, spent his first of several summers in Keene Flats in 1852 painting and naming mountains with Phelps. On Phelps' maps, a mountain that could be Dix is indicated as Perkins Peak. Today, in spite of the old guide's efforts, no major land feature bears the artist's name.

Others attribute Basin's naming to Colvin, who completed the first recorded ascent of it on August 10, 1877, in the company of Ed Phelps (Orson's son). Colvin set an original triangulation bolt on Basin in 1876. However, it is believed that James Storrow, an avid bushwhacker, had climbed most if not all of the peaks of the Upper Range with his guide, Orlando Beede, several times during the previous decade.

According to Mel Trumbull, in 1868, long before Colvin's ascent, a well known artist, Alexander H. Wyant, had named the valley of Shanty Brook "Great Basin." (The Wolf Jaws are the result of his keen sense of observation, too). So, one can easily imagine Colvin standing atop Basin and finding the name for the mountain appropriate. The Haystack side, with its extended tall cliff, lined at its base by a mossy meadow, is aptly named the Basin amphitheater.

Early Forty-Sixer Nora Sproule descending a ladder on Basin

Jack Colby, Charlie Horn, Ed Hudowalski, Harry May, and Bill Lance going down Basin

The summit of Basin offers a front row seat for viewing Marcy and countless High Peaks. Robert Marshall wrote, "No words can describe a person's feeling as he looks over this enormous hollow and gets perhaps the finest view now possible of the type of forest which once covered all of the North woods region."

James M. Glover in his *A Wilderness Original, The Life of Bob Marshall,* quotes Bob's account of the details of the Haystack to Gothics portion of a marathon hike:

> From Haystack we descended 1900 feet into the saddle then climbed another 1900 feet to the summit of Basin in exactly one hour and three minutes... and by the time Gothics was reached Bob was ready with vital statistics. They had walked ten miles and 9,200 up and down feet from Panther Gorge in 4.5 hours... Back at camp in the Gorge they tallied the final numbers. They had climbed a total of 9,200 feet and descended the same amount. Bob calculated that this was equal to three and a half up-and-down miles, total horizontal miles numbered about twenty.

We certainly don't want to diminish the extraordinary accomplishment, but even today's sign at the foot of Little Haystack indicating the direction, distance and climbing a hiker may expect when heading to the next mountain along the Range doesn't exaggerate as much. It indicates that the climb to Basin's summit involves 1,734 feet of climbing. Even including the ups and downs over Little Haystack, going from Panther Gorge to Gothics involves 3,900 feet of climbing and 2,500 feet of descent over 4.5 miles. The Haystack-Basin col sits at an altitude of 3,825 feet, not 3,000 feet.

On the same 1857 day that Phelps and Perkins claimed to have baptized Basin, they reportedly also named Saddleback "Saddle Mountain," an apt name considering its appearance when viewed from Marcy. Nevertheless, the map which accompanied Seneca Ray Stoddard's 1874 *The Adirondacks Illustrated* labeled the mountain as Saddleback, which, according to some sources, is derived from the view of the mountain from the Keene Valley area. Mel Trumbull believed that Alexander H. Wyant named it Saddleback.

Saddleback's first ascent is sometimes credited to James J. Storrow and Orlando Beede (1870 or 1871), but, according to Russell M. L. Carson, in *Peaks and People of the Adirondacks,*

Newell Martin made the first recorded ascent (August 5, 1894). The fact that another hiker, Walter Lowrie, refuted vigorously Martin's claim but doesn't give himself any first ascents credits the James Storrow theory. Martin claimed that in August 1894 he beat Lowrie's record of the number of mountains, including Saddleback, climbed in the same day. That contention seems ample proof that Martin could not have been the first one to climb Saddleback. It is therefore a mystery as to why Carson maintained that Martin was the first person to climb the mountain.

Saddleback offers magnificent and dramatic views of its two immediate neighbors, Gothics and Basin. Up the last 500 feet to its summit, along the trail from the col to the east, Saddleback offers a unique and impressive view of the relentlessly steep "cables" trail leading to Gothics.

According to several publications John Apperson, with Irving Langmuir, ascended Basin and Saddleback on skis in 1927. However, Apperson's papers testify to the contrary and give ample credit to the Appalachian Mountain Club's Bemis Crew;[2] however, that group had a reputation for vastly embellishing their reports of their yearly 1920s winter climbing expeditions. Their records mention late 1920s climbs over the Great Range but all accounts are short of details. Better documented are climbs of Basin and Haystack by students from Yale and Kingswood universities during the 1948-1950 Christmas holidays.

The Adirondack Mountain Club's publication *Adirondac* of January/February 1964 tells of a New Year's 1928 party of five men (Jas. Christy Bell, William J. Dean, Lawrence I. Grinnell, Arnold W. Knauth, and William J. Parker) and two women (Anna and Marjorie Lord Strauss) who spent a few days at Johns Brook Lodge (JBL). The group of seven travelled by train in the company of fifty-nine convicts being transferred from Sing Sing to Dannemora prison. At Westport, at 4:40 a.m., the prisoners staged an escape attempt, but only one got away and the seven vacationers were in Keene Valley by dawn and at the lodge before noon. As happens occasionally in winter, it rained all afternoon, but the temperature dropped to 5°F below zero during the night. The next morning, intending to climb Gothics over a hard crust, the group had an easy time climbing to the lean-to in the col but "the icy roof of Gothics" made them turn towards Saddleback. Five of them went for Haystack the following day but found out that even on a perfect day, conditions above tree line were dramatically different. They noted that "Everest can hardly be more fiercely cold and uncomfortable. It was too late to try for Haystack summit itself, which was glittered with ice. The view was stunning."

In spite of the failed Haystack attempt, the group can most likely claim the first winter ascent of Saddleback. As he followed broken tracks all the way to the col, it could be that Jim Goodwin's ascent during the 1927-1928 Christmas holidays took place a day or two after the aforementioned group's. He was probably the first person to reach the true summit of Gothics in winter. Will Glover's 1915 winter ascent of Giant is another first winter climb wrongly attributed to Apperson in some publications. Author Henry I. Baldwin reported that during a July 1922 personal communication, Johannsen explained that Apperson had accompanied him "in part" to Marcy, McIntyre, Whiteface and Haystack.

To stimulate winter climbing, in 1948 the ADK winter activities committee with Kim Hart as chairman created three trophies to be awarded annually for outstanding accomplishments (climbing, skiing, camping, etc.) in the High Peaks during the winter months. A fourth was added in 1950: an individual award, the Winter Mountaineering Emblem (a V badge), which could be earned by anyone who climbed five Adirondack Peaks over 4,000 feet in elevation between December 21 and March 21. The club's Winter Camp on Johns Brook (five minutes from the lodge on the opposite side of the brook), by prior arrangement, could be opened and meals served there. If one chose to rough it, "the winter camp bed could be built of balsam boughs placed directly above the snow." Winter Camp was replaced later by today's Grace and Peggy O'Brien camps. First aid kits were placed along various trails in case of winter climbing emergencies and hikers were advised not to go up when temperatures were below minus 40°F. The Range and the back peaks of the Dix Range were considered the most hazardous in the 1950s.

On the Upper Range

After its creation in 1922, the Adirondack Mountain Club cleared 6.5 miles of new trails (up Short Job, up Big Slide, to Railroad Notch, from Upper Wolf Jaw to Armstrong and to the Gothic col coming up from Beaver Meadow Falls). Arthur S. Hopkins, then ADK Chairman, Committee on Camps, Trails and Shelters, had big plans one spring:

> The trail committee hopes, in addition to scout and construct a trail from Panther Gorge to the Ausable Lakes-Marcy Trail, thus giving a short cut to Johns Brook Lodge from the South. Other contemplated projects for this season are a trail from Slant Rock Trail to the top of Basin; from the Range Trail to the notch between Armstrong and Gothic, from the Range Trail to the notch between Armstrong and Upper Wolf Jaw. The completion of these trails will, with the existing ones, make it possible to climb any one of the mountains from Wolf Jaw to Marcy from Johns Brook Lodge and return without going over any other peak. It is hoped that the above trail program may be completed during the season of 1928 so that in 1929, the trail activities of the Club may be transferred to other regions, such as the Seward-Seymour area.

The herdpath connecting Panther Gorge to the Phelps Trail up into the col where one can choose either to climb towards Marcy or Haystack never became a trail. It was completely abandoned after the Big Blow of 1950. As for the rest of the plan, it remained wishful thinking.

The Orebed Trail, along the upper reaches of the brook of the same name, is slated for rerouting around a shoulder on the flank of Gothics to the east. The trail provides the quickest and easiest route to Saddleback and, once on the side of that mountain, tremendous views of Gothics. The summit ridge is mostly the mix of smallish firs and birches that usually dresses higher slopes. Nevertheless, the mountain's highest point, immediately above the infamous precipitous cliff that plummets down its west side, provides a breathtaking view of the slide-scared slopes of Basin. The precipice can be challenging, whether going up or down it. Many hikers have quailed at some point while attempting to reach its top from the pleasant Chicken Coop Brook col between Saddleback and Basin or in descending from the cliff's high perch. It often stirs within its climbers an alarming, queasy feeling. There are more dizzying challenges between the col and the top of Haystack. In fact, more so than anywhere else along an officially maintained route, the law of gravity is the hiker's nemesis on the Upper Range. Still we all proceed, our strength fueled by the surrounding beauty and our fear dissipated by the prospect of reaching yet another nest in the sky.

During an October 2004 interview, Tony Goodwin, who as part of his numerous activities, guides groups of young mountaineers, added, "The young hike mostly to socialize. Girls are afraid of ladders and bridges but boys trust structures. Since it's about paying attention to handholds and footing, Saddleback's rock face acts as an equalizer as the girls usually pay more attention and the mountains bring them together."

Bunchberry *(Cornus canadensis)* lights the trails from spring to fall and countless American toad *(Bufo americanus)* reluctantly let us by or stop us in our tracks. Chicken Coop and Basin Brook cols, respectively sitting, at 4,130 feet and 4,555 feet, present tiny flowering meadows carpeted with *Clintonia borealis* (bluebead lily) in late spring, but the mountains change: during the last few decades, and even the last few years, many new slides, probably a half dozen, have developed on the shoulders of Saddleback and Basin.

On Basin, next to the bolt placed in 1876 by Colvin, don't you feel like a bald eagle watching the world from its tree-top home or the peregrine falcon from its cliff-top aerie? As steep as climbing Basin is from either direction, you always feel safe and comfortable on the summit unless the weather is really miserable. You truly feel special on Basin, like children allowed to stay up late and feel big... for a little while. You play at being big and powerful, knowing all along that you are living a fairy tale: lucky to be up there. Basin demands a steep climb from both directions. The north side has a chute that will accelerate a descent noticeably when icy... and maybe not in the desired direction. Actually, while travelling between Saddleback and Haystack occasions abound to break an ankle as you have to constantly use everything on either side of the trail to get up or down countless ledges that come in a great variety of sizes and steepnesses. Even opting to climb or descend via a bushwhack along Chicken Coop or Basin Brook, you can't avoid all of the challenging portions of trail to reach Basin or Haystack.

From Basin's summit, Haystack looks like an easy climb. However, it is not so friendly a sight from the top of the Blue Connector trail from which its imposing mass makes it look like a self-assured giant, towering and elusive at the same time. You have come from so far and the mountain tells you, the conqueror of the day, to pause for a moment, catch your breath, befriend it in some way to get acquainted, to tread carefully and treat gently its gatekeeper, Little Haystack. The krummholz circling Little Haystack is impenetrable, giving one scared hiker no choice but to control his heart and get over it. Haystack is not that difficult a climb, even though rather steep on all sides, but you feel very exposed as just about all of the last half mile to the summit is above treeline. Little Haystack holds the key to Haystack's haven and, small in name only, it is a tough one to go by. In good weather the gatekeeper may let you by with a certain ease; in adverse conditions, you may be told, and not always very gently, to come back another day.

The Blue Connector is a calf muscle test, which at its height of land offers the first great views of Marcy. In winter, there are inevitably a few certainly athletic skiers in the Marcy snowfield making their rounds over and up and down around and back up, and down...

Standing tall with its dramatic views, Haystack always keeps us on edge and alert. The abyss of Panther Gorge, Marcy's imposing slopes, the Upper Ausable Lake so far below, and the rampart of Little Haystack make sure that we never cease, even for a second, to respect Haystack's authoritative pose. If the wind is sweeping the ridge, we cling onto an imaginary railing.

The Haystack Brook Trail is of an easier grade and the climb from Bartlett Ridge is extremely rewarding. In late July, above tree line, every shrub at one's feet is blooming and it is disconcerting to constantly have to choose while climbing what is best to admire – the distant or the close views, both so extraordinary.

The Johns Brook Valley

Most hikers who ascend the peaks of the Upper Range approach them from the Garden parking area. From the Garden to Johns Brook Lodge, whether on the main trail or the Southside Trail, many who aspire to climb Haystack, Basin, and Saddleback walk the Johns Brook Valley.

Two clusters of privately owned camps, well hidden within the trees and some way off the trails, surround Johns Brook Lodge. Most of those parcels were bought in the late 1890s or around the time of Arthur S. Hopkins' 1923-1924 survey. The owners have made a point of keeping the extraordinary "estates" within their families. The properties, surrounded by state land, vary in size from less than an acre to more than 30 acres, making for some 165 acres of privately owned land.

An essay by Jim Goodwin in the September 1982 edition of *Adirondac* reveals that extensive lumbering was done the last quarter of the nineteenth century and during the beginning of the twentieth century up to 4,000 feet in elevation, as high as the base of Big Slide's summit cliffs. Even the steep slopes of Mount Colden were cleared. Goodwin wrote, "Graded lumber roads led everywhere and lumber camp housing grew up everywhere." He remembers as a young boy (1920) visiting the Johns Brook Valley lumbering operations and even getting a ride on an empty rig all the way to the loading station located where the ranger cabin now stands. Logging in that area ended in the spring of 1921, and, in 1924, in most of the Ausable watershed. In 1920, a bond issue approved by the New York state legislature enabled the state to start buying large tracts of land from private owners to add to the forest preserve. Lumbering activities stopped half a mile above the present Johns Brook Lodge. Beyond that point, the Adirondack Mountain Reserve (AMR) had protected the forest from logging.

Jim wrote about the transition:

> Mel Hathaway's camp was burned in 1924 to make way for the construction of Johns Brook Lodge. A new era of history was coming to the Adirondacks because of the bond issue voted by the New York Legislature to add to the Forest Preserve much of the land in the High Peaks Region. With the purchase of this land by the State, the romance (and destruction) of the lumbering operations along with the backwoods life of people like Mel Hathaway were soon to give way to a massive invasion of the mountains from the population centers. With this influx would come the accompanying facilities such as Johns Brook Lodge, trails marked with formal signs and trail markers (instead of axe-cut blazes), plus numerous lean-to camps… *(The)* beginnings of the modern road system brought more hikers to the trails where cheaply bought surplus Army equipment made unguided trips possible.

Lean-tos

At 3,600 feet, Sno-Bird Lean-to, blessed with a privy offering "the best view in the Adirondacks," was built by the state on AMR land in the early 1920s with funds, as previously mentioned, provided by the Lake Placid Club's Sno-Birds. The lean-to was replaced and moved to the other side of the trail in 1969 and taken down by the AMR in 1976.[3] Sno-Bird was the fourth lean-to to be erected, Four Corners the first, in 1919. By 1924, fifteen had been built.

Harold Weston wrote about the first night he spent (October 1, 1923) in Sno-Bird:

> We had been told that the lean-to was "finished" and assumed that it meant it was in condition for hikers to spend the night there. We reached the camp towards dusk… the walls of the lean-to were finished, but on the floor of the camp, where some day a springy depth of Balsam boughs might presumably be found, the tops of the trees cut for the logs that made the walls were nailed about five inches apart above some rocks and muddy ground. Unfortunately, the person who lopped off branches was in a hurry and left sharp stubs sticking out in all directions composing a spurred corduroy bed for its first guests to repose upon. I may not mind hardships

of a kind, but I'm no guru with a yen to sleep on a bed of spikes. Hurriedly because it was getting dark and about to rain, I gathered as many evergreen branches as I could to form a two-foot wide base for a "mattress" of boughs at one end of the camp... In the meantime Faith was cooking supper over a very smoky fire made from the countless chips of all sizes from the camp logs, which of course had just been cut. The bedding proved as dismal as the fire, which constantly threatened to go out. Soon after we lay down, the firm spikes of the corduroy began to assert their manhood. Then, after we got a real fire going because it was getting colder, the wind shifted, smoke filled our end of the lean-to and we wished it would rain harder and put that fire out. Never on a mountain have I shivered and wept through a more miserable night.

Gothics Camp Lean-to, located in the Saddleback-Gothics col, was erected in 1925 and burned down in 1969. By 1963 its fairly new corrugated iron privy was "disgracefully ugly." Except for the view the lean-to provided of the side of Gothics, the site was never really adequate: campers had to descend about 300 feet to find water below the camp.

Hogback Lean-to, which stood on the Phelps Trail about a mile beyond Johns Brook Lodge, was removed in the early 1970s because its outhouse leached into Hogback Brook and there were no alternative locations for it farther from the brook due to the steepness of the terrain.

The 1947 and 1971 maps show three lean-tos in the vicinity of Bushnell Falls at the foot of Gooseberry Mountain, where Chicken Coop flows into Johns Brook. In 1926, a couple was stranded in the Chicken Coop Lean-to when a flash flood caught them. They were rescued by other hikers staying at JBL. That lean-to, on the south side of the brook, burned in the spring of 1963 and wasn't replaced. One of the two remaining has been moved 200 yards up the Hopkins Trail.

Slant Rock

In 1886, a scouting party decided to reopen the trail to Mount Marcy from Bushnell Falls. They did well all the way to Slant Rock, where the team failed not only to cross the brook (the famous rock was at that time protected by a dense forest) but also to notice that a branch of the brook was coming from the right (south). They followed the left curving brook along its north bank. They discovered their mistake somewhere between Basin and Shorey's Mountain and, discouraged, never returned to complete the job.

It could very well be that because of that (wrongly oriented) trail work, for many decades that route was the way to the Upper Range. On his first Marcy attempt via Johns Brook, Walter Lowrie, misled by that path, spent a night in the woods. Luckily, his companion, Harry Catell, was a young physician who carried a few opium pills in his pocket which greatly eased the pair's hunger and fear through the long hours of darkness. Lowrie later recalled having Slant Rock as an exclusive campsite for three years until James P. Atkinson[4] and Hugh Hodge discovered it too. According to Lowrie, Atkinson and Hodge were the strongest climbers of the era. He wrote, "Perhaps no one climbed further and more furiously than they." They rediscovered Slant Rock while bushwhacking down from Point Balk after a visit to Marcy. The slanted rock was already famous as it had long before been used by Old Mountain Phelps to shelter his guests while taking them along "his" trail to Marcy. Phelps figured that Slant Rock was a fragment fallen from the cliff of Colden Ridge. Lowrie, who wished that Point Balk be named after Phelps, recalled that the famous guide called the "hump" above Slant Rock "Colden Ridge" for in following that ridge one has to make a slight (not that short and easy though) descent to get on the slope of Colden. Phelps named it on his own map of the High Peaks as seen in a copy maintained in the Keene Valley Library archives.

In 1887, Atkinson's mother bought a small cottage neighboring Phelps' home, and the young man recalled spending a lot of time listening to the guide's "experiences and advice in woodlore." Reminiscing about life in the valley in the 1880s, Atkinson admired the old guide's son just as much: "Ed Phelps... knew direction intuitively. Someone once said that if you pick Ed up in his sleep and put him down in another part of the woods, on awakening he could head straight for home."

A lean-to facing the massive rock on its west side was eventually built. It has recently been rebuilt above and to the west of its namesake. The new location offers a good view of Bassinette (Basin's middle bump). On August 6, 1964, a Slant Rock camper had an unusual photo opportunity as a Conservation Department helicopter, flying material for lean-tos, crashed on Basin's foot near Slant Rock. Unharmed, the two-crew members walked out on their own after landing in a blowdown area. The crash had been due to engine failure. After necessary repairs were made, the helicopter was flown out under its own power. Apparently one can encounter and be impeded by blowdown any which way he chooses to travel through the Adirondacks.

Point Balk

In December 1968, after a late start (time being spent enjoying a big breakfast), a group of skiers, confident they could return to Adirondak Loj in the dark after climbing Marcy, encountered problems with their bindings and lost their map. As the temperature dropped (negative 25°F was recorded that night at Lake Colden), Dick Stepp and Steve Clautice decided to go north, hoping to intersect the Phelps Trail to Keene Valley. In doing so, they reached the "summit" of Point Balk, the impressive ledge standing 1,000 feet above Slant Rock. Not realizing where they were, they began descending. A few hours later, exhausted, "not sure how to get down Balk and not able to get back up," they decided to sleep half an hour in the last hole they had made falling down. When the sun came up, they saw the cliff below and decided to traverse. They climbed a tree from which they confused Haystack with Marcy, kept going on a northerly course, and at 8 a.m. reached the Hopkins Trail. By noon they were at Bushnell Falls. As they walked past the ranger cabin on Johns Brook, it was getting dark again. Out "a few demoralizing hours later," the duo climbed Algonquin after a couple of nights indoors.

The very few visitors to Point Balk "Peak" never fail to mention that the uncommonly challenging ascent is unlikely to make it a popular destination. In August 2004, Brian Yourdon (#5321W) and Spencer Morrissey (#5320W) climbed to the rocky prominence from the new lean-to near Slant-Rock. They enjoyed the views while zigzagging the rock ledges to gain access to the mostly wooded summit.

Upper Ausable Lake "Paradiso"

The road to the Lower Ausable Lake on the other side of the Great Range was laid out on August 24, 1887. In May of that year the Adirondack Mountain Reserve (AMR) had been organized and successfully subscribed enough funds to complete the purchase of their property, 28,000 acres, on May 17. Because, from "the earliest time," the land around the lakes had been treated as public property, it "was no easy task to convince the local community that the choice lay between a lumbered and burned district – which would have no charm for summer boarders – and a preserve maintained under reasonable restrictions. Trails and roads would be kept open to all who wished to enjoy the extraordinary beauties of the district and to retain them uninjured."

Charles Holt, a member of the famous guiding family, recounted that in 1875 "camping" on the Upper Ausable Lake was the thing of all others to be done. An 1875 edition of the *New York World* complained of problems due to overcrowding and of the more than occasional sudden deluge of rain that never fails to greet campers in the Adirondack mountains, but artists of the era united in saying that they had never seen anything in the Old World and in the New, more beautiful. The Upper Lake was even called "Paradiso" by summer visitors. By 1891, a new road had been constructed by the AMR "at great expense" and the cost of access was "a saddle horse for $.30, one horse and wagon for $.50, two horses and wagon $1.," etc.

Previous to the AMR purchase, the Thomas and Armstrong Lumber Company had owned the land and had given local guides permission to build semi-permanent camps on the Upper Ausable Lake. The company believed the guides' presence would discourage illegal lumbering and guard against forest fires. The camps, about two dozen of them, were built in the 1870s and 1880s. One who built much earlier and the first to do so was Old Mountain Phelps.

Seneca Ray Stoddard's account, in his 1874 guidebook *The Adirondacks Illustrated* of Phelps' accommodation (lean-to) by the "Upper Ausable Pond" painted the following picture of his camp:

> Camp Phelps is one of the most complete in its appointment and management of any shanty in the Adirondacks. The structure is of an elegant design, and built of magnificent logs cut and curved artistically with knots of various and unique pattern in bas relief. The main door is about 2.5 by 5 feet, swings outward, and is locked with a string; it contains an immense reception room, drawing room, private parlor and sleeping rooms en suite, with wardrobe sticking out all around the sides. The grand dining hall is situated on the lovely lawn, which is quite extensive, and splendidly furnished with hemlock extensions and stumps. This spacious structure is six by ten feet on the ground, and between four and five feet high, and is surmounted by a Yankee roof of troughs in two layers, the upper covering the crevices in the lower so as to exclude the rain, but far enough to give perfect ventilation. This *chef d'oeuvre* of architecture is first class in every respect, it is luxuriously upholstered throughout with spruce boughs, in the culinary department is a stupendous range which floods the drawing room with light, and, in short, it contains all the modern improvements, including hot and cold water, which is carried to every part of the establishment in pails. Here we gathered, ten in all beside two or three dogs, in a space about six by eight feet square and while the fire snapped and flickered, filling the shanty with dancing shadows, stories of hunting and fishing adventures were told that all were expected to believe...

After the AMR took over the land, only certain guides were permitted on the property. Hunting was prohibited and fishing was restricted to members and guests of the AMR. Hikers and campers on the property were required to have a guide who belonged to the Keene Valley Guides Association, which had been organized by the AMR. The guides adopted bicycles as a method of transportation to get to the lakes. By 1906, the AMR had begun buying the camps and dismantling them. At the same time, the organization ceased to authorize new guides. By 1907, the construction of closed camps began on the Upper Lake, and ownership of the old sites began passing into the hands of AMR members. Many of the guides shifted into guide-caretaker roles for the new owners. Today some of them are fourth generation descendants of the original guides.

Most AMR members were committed to keeping the forests in their natural state, and Robert de Forest,[5] an AMR president, was an ardent conservationist. Nevertheless during its first fifty years, the AMR financed many of its operations by selling lumbering rights in the peripheral area. The J. & J. Rogers Company was then the largest lumber contractor in the High Peaks. Between 1901 and 1918, the AMR signed several contracts with that company and a few others to cut timber from its lands.

Due to financial difficulties, the AMR at first opened acres of forest to logging in 1909 to pay for taxes, and to secure additional funds, proceeded with five large land sales – a total of 18,215 acres – to the state between 1921 and 1932. The tops of Haystack, Basin, and Saddleback remained within the AMR's boundaries until they were sold to the state in 1978. Today, the AMR's property boundary is, for the most part, along the 2,500-foot level above the lakes. About 7,000 acres of AMR property remain. Between 1958 and 1960, there was a controversy among members over a timber contract that had been let on Bartlett Ridge. The lumbering was averted after camp owners joined together to compensate the club for the loss of revenue that the cutting of the 130 acres would have yielded.

While preserving the original beauty of the Upper Range for their enjoyment, AMR members have done likewise for all of us. The slopes of Haystack, Basin, and Saddleback are among the rare few that have never been touched by man or fire. Even the hurricanes of 1952, 1995, and 1999 weren't as vicious on the slopes of the Upper Range as they were on other mountains of the region.

Ed Isham served as a guide (1905-1907) with Pete Lamb at the Ausable Lakes. After that he guided for the Taylors, Merle-Smiths, and MacIntoshes, owners of three camps in the Orebed section of Johns Brook. (Monroe Holt, a guide, had a camp even higher up the brook). In 1905, following Newell Martin's suggestions for the route, with Lamb, Ed Phelps, and Charlie Beede, Isham cut the Range Trail. Soon after, he cut a trail up Orebed Brook (then AMR property) to connect with the Range Trail in the Gothics-Saddleback notch. Following a line of blazes put in by Dr. Lowrie, Lamb and Holt had re-established the Johns Brook Trail to Marcy in 1903.

Either because of the guides or the variety of scenery in the 1800s, the path via the Upper Lake was often preferred to the Johns Brook route. Driving the development of new ways to reach the whole Range was the fact that the Upper Lake had become private property. Consequently hikers had to pay to use the road to the Lower Lake and were required to obtain a permit and hire a guide. In 1950, one could still arrange for a guide and boat to reach the Upper Ausable Lake.

Hiking has always been (and still is) a favorite activity of the Upper Lake residents and many of their visitors. The first trail up Marcy from the Upper Lake was cut in 1861 by Orson Phelps and other Keene Valley guides above Panther Gorge over Bartlett Ridge. That trail was superseded a dozen years later by an easier one hacked out by Verplanck Colvin's survey party. The Phelps Trail, named in memory of Old Mountain Phelps, was first blazed by his son Ed. Possibly the best guide of all time, Ed Phelps is credited with seven first ascents. Only the Marshalls and their guide, Herb Clark, have more first ascents to their credit: eight.

According to Adirondack Trail Improvement Society (ATIS) records, Thomas P. Wickes, a vacationer and New York lawyer, engineered the construction of the Beaver Meadow Trail to Gothics in 1886. Hosteller Norman Dibble cut the trail to Marcy via Slant Rock. It disappeared because of neglect and had to be recut in the 1890s. One of many ATIS trails was cut over the Range Trail from Haystack to Gothics. When completed, the route featured a fixed rope on the east side of Basin down a rock chute (now bypassed) and a wooden ladder up the steepest portion of Saddleback cliffs. The Blue Connector was built in 1919 and maintained by Ed Phelps until 1921.

Guide Books

In 1879, even surveyor Verplanck Colvin was surprised by the speed with which the tourism industry was developing in the Adirondacks, helped by the publication of several guidebooks (Stoddard in 1874 and E. R. Wallace in 1880). The first trail guides were published later, in the 1920s.

E. R. Wallace's *Descriptive Guide* went through numerous editions (1875, 1878, 1879, 1888, 1894, etc.). The 1878 edition mentions Bushnell Falls vaguely... being, maybe, 8 miles from Keene Flats. In the 1894 revised printing, the falls is "perfectly sequestered and fascinating."

Charles H. Possons' *Adirondack Guidebook*, published in 1893, mentioned, "Bartlett mountain is in the north, impending over the Ausable Pond, and marked by its sharp cone." We can be certain that the author is describing Haystack as seen from the Upper Lake. He is a bit off, as well, when describing the vegetation: "As the height increases, the Balsam becomes more and more dwarfed, but maintains the aspect and form of the perfect tree in miniature." Of the mosses, Posson wrote, "The foot often sinks ankle deep in the rich vegetation that mantles the rock in its soft and delicate hues, like a velvety carpet."

T. Morris Longstreth wrote two books about the Adirondacks. The first, a more general volume, *The Adirondacks,* published in 1919, was followed in 1922 by a pocket size booklet, *The Lake Placid Country, Trampers' Guide,* a trail guide with numerous suggestions for outings, with indications of distances and times required to complete hikes, and with a full description of the territory to be traversed. One of the booklet's four maps was for the Great Range. Longstreth raved about Haystack: "The view affords two of the greatest moments attainable in the Adirondacks, one when you stand on SW spur of the summit, as on the prow of a great ship... the other is to be had from the NW side, looking across at the gigantic precipices of Marcy, falling sheer for hundreds of feet into Panther Gorge, giving one the only savage and sublime impression to be had of the Cloud-Cleaver." Of the five pages about the Great Range, only three quick lines cover the Johns Brook access option: "Or it can be done by ascending the Johns Brook Trail... but this takes away from the continuity and dignity of the climb."

Robert S. Wickham's *Friendly Adirondack Peaks,* published in 1924, is written in a personal manner. The author, a lawyer from Binghamton who had climbed 21 of the High Peaks, pretended that most of his "reporting" was based upon his hikes over the mountains, including two overnight trips over the Great Range. Some of the details of the account of his Range Trail odyssey provide unintended comic relief. That it was windy on Haystack summit, we believe easily, but that from a Haystack Brook col overnight camp Whickham's party climbed 2,300(!) feet up to Haystack, went back down to collect their gear before climbing the 2,200(!) feet necessary to reach Basin's summit, and proceeded up Gothics without even noticing that Saddleback was in the way... is a stretch. To be fair, a couple of paragraphs later there is mention of the great views of Gothics from Saddleback's summit. Several days in the mountains eating "oatmeal flavored with salt" may have confused the author as to views and the amount of ascent, not to mention forgetting a mountain along the way.

Walter Collins O'Kane's 1928 *Trails and Summits of the Adirondacks,* is a small book that offered extensive descriptions of trails, views, scenery, history, etc. It is particularly attractive as it contains numerous photographs of the mountains and lakes taken almost a century ago. You learn that Basin had a rope on its northern shoulder and three ladders on its southern one to aid trampers and that Saddleback's westerly end was precipitous but "the rocks have convenient clefts and irregularities." It is clear that O'Kane was inspired by previously published guidebooks as he perpetuates some errors and goes on and on about the views in such an excessive way that you don't need to bring a map. Reading the appropriate chapter while on a particular summit will provide more information about the surroundings than you can absorb. Nevertheless, it is a pleasant and informative read.

Who's Who

Among the summer residents who visited Keene Valley, the Ausable Club, and Putnam Camp, near the base of Giant, were men well known elsewhere. Some were clergymen, some educators and men of letters. Some were artists. The names of several distinguished Keene Valley visitors and summer residents have been preserved upon the landscape and in the names of hiking trails of the area. Other men, including summer residents and some who have lived year-round in the region, were pioneers of High Peaks hiking and influential proponents of environmental protection. Brief biographies of some of the men whose influence was particularly strong in the area of the Upper Range follow:

Horace Bushnell

Horace Bushnell, for whom Bushnell Falls is named, is best known as the creator of America's first city public park, Bushnell Park in Hartford, Connecticut, and as the author of a dozen books.

The first of six children, Bushnell was born (April 14, 1802) into a family of hard working farmers who later ran a wool carding mill. His parents were both deeply religious and his mother, hoping that he would one day become a minister, quietly guided him in that direction. From 1823 to 1827, he attended Yale College and studied in the theological department. Upon graduation, he accepted a teaching position in Norwich, Connecticut. A year later he became associate editor of the *Journal of Commerce* in New York City. He liked neither job and in 1829 returned to New Haven to study law at Yale. In 1831, his law studies completed, he was ready for admission to the bar. Instead, finally realizing his mother's dream, he began preparing for the ministry, and in the fall of 1831 entered the Theological School of Yale. In 1832 he was ordained as a minister and, that summer, while conducting a Bible class, met his future wife. In February 1832 he was invited to preach at North Church in Hartford, where he remained until his resignation due to poor health in 1859. His relation with Yale, at which he had earned four degrees, continued to his death. In 1880, his daughter, Mary Bushnell Cheney, wrote a biography of her father. She had a son, Horace Bushnell Cheney (1868-1936), and a grandson of the same name (1889-1919) who once climbed Marcy in five and a half hours, beating Will Glover's best time.

In *The Puritan as Yankee, A Life of Horace Bushnell* (2002), Robert Bruce Mullin wrote,

> Bushnell has usually been recognized as the father of American theological liberalism, the great champion of Christian education, and the paradigmatic figure of nineteenth-century American Protestantism. The popularity of Bushnell as a subject may in part stem from the breadth of his interests. Ranging far beyond narrow theological questions, he offered opinions on race, language, the Civil War, immigration, city planning, etc. Whatever a researcher's interest might be, one can usually find a quotation from him to make a point. He was both a Yankee and a Puritan: a Yankee in his love of innovation, a Puritan in his abiding trust in the values he first learned as a child in Connecticut.

Burton P. Twichell, the son of the Rev. Joseph Twichell, a longtime Keene Valley summer visitor, recalled his parents' early days in the area when he spoke before Keene Valley's Village Historical Society in August 1938. Joseph left his children a voluminous journal in twelve notebooks. From that record, Burton drew considerable information.

The elder Twichell first visited the Adirondacks in 1855 and that is when and where he became intimate with "the beloved" Warners (of Hartford). For a number of summers the Twichell family rented a cottage on the Dunham Plateau, and, in 1875, being on the Upper

Lake with President Noah Porter of Yale, the Reverend Dr. Twichell took "the round trip around Marcy" and spent a night under the open sky on the summit rock of Indian Pass.

Dr. Horace Bushnell, Charles Dudley Warner, and Old Mountain Phelps were often mentioned by Dr. Twichell in his journal, and Burton confirmed that day that even though his family knew Bushnell from Hartford, "where he left the memory of a great preacher and a public spirited citizen whose vision turned the worst slum district into the beautiful Bushnell Park in the center of the city," Bushnell only spent two summers in Keene Valley. Horace took "The Round Trip" with Twichell but "after studying the available maps and the topography of the country, he decided that there was a better route than the customary one. His new route became there-after the established route." At that time Bushnell's health was failing. On the second day of the trip Joseph, worried his companion might die, suggested that they return to the Upper Lake. "We'll go on," answered Horace, "unless YOU give out. They went for three days, completing the trip as planned.

Bushnell's daughter wrote that in 1868 and 1869 her father summered in the Adirondacks, and much enjoyed the time he spent with Orson Phelps. She wrote, "Though an invalid, he walked, and climbed, and fished, after a fashion that would have exhausted many men of perfect health. Mount Marcy was not enough for him, and, with an old trapper as a guide he set forth for twice as tough a job, to climb the Giant of the Valley by an unknown route. Reaching the summit late in the day, Horace proposed a faster descent via the slides. The two old men proceeded to coast down the steep incline, clinging or catching as they might, here and there, by a bush or shrub and safely, but after dark, made it back home." Preparing to go fishing, he would spend hours working on a branch with his pocket knife to turn it into a pole that suited him, as he had no use for the "modern" rod and reel. Several of his biographers have suggested that in the last few years of his life, Dr. Bushnell's health problems were so numerous and severe that he could not have done any arduous climbing, such as were required for the Marcy and Giant trips, but Dr. Twichell and Mary Bushnell Cheney confirmed them. There is no doubt that he went to the pretty falls named after him, but, given the distance, not often.

As early as the 1840s, Dr. Bushnell's health problems had been of concern. He coughed up blood, the consequence of alternatively preaching and praying in frigid winter air and overheated churches, an occupational hazard for a clergyman. From July 1845 to May 1846 he visited England and the Continent. Upon his return, to better his condition, he took to traveling again around the country and to Cuba for months at a time, but he always wrote to his wife to let her know how much he missed her: "I can do nothing more than tell you how fondly my heart turns back to find rest in you." All the while, he reflected and mused on the questions of the supernatural and God's relationship to the world in his writings. In 1857, he published *Nature and the Supernatural,* which is considered his masterpiece. By 1859, his throat problems forced him to resign his full time pastorate.

As a social critic he was "an amateur" as he openly rejected the abolitionists, arguing that their measures threatened the unity of the nation even though he had earlier said that slavery had a destructive influence on republican character. He advocated letting slaves have a family and an education, arguing that once slaves began to be treated as moral and intellectual creatures, slavery was doomed to disappear peacefully. In the meantime, "Northerners must understand that slavery is an issue that Southerners themselves had to address and should continue to honor the lawfulness of the institution and their obligation to support their Southern countrymen in case of a slave revolt. One needed to allow the inevitable course of history to work its way." Anti-slavery activists, Bushnell believed, hurt the cause of emancipation.

He also held strong views on race. Mullin writes that Bushnell often spoke of "the vigor of the Saxon race and virtue," of his little confidence in the eventual success of the freed blacks and of "the Irish, an example of the inevitable decline of a lesser race when it comes in contact with a more advanced one. It is not true that they become an integral part of our nation to any considerable extent. They become extinct and such would, as well, be the fate of blacks when slavery ended." Later he had his doubts that slavery would be ended through the moral progress of humanity. By the mid 1850s, he had come to fear Southern aggression more than abolitionist excess and his anti-Southern rhetoric became strident as the Civil War approached. "God, " he later wrote, "brought the war to make America truly a nation and offer an answer to the slavery question. During the course of the conflict the Union slowly learned that God was the ultimate source of all authority. The war was but one great chapter in the law of sacrifice. The law of God taught that only through the shedding of blood could greatness be accomplished." One can't but wonder how he could be so indifferent to the pain and suffering the war generated, even though he later went on to visit all the great battlefields. Mullin explains that, in the following decade, professionalization suggested that only credentialed people should speak authoritatively on issues, making the world far less hospitable to tinkering amateurs like Bushnell, whose posthumously published *Women's Suffrage: The Reform Against Nature* did nothing to improve his authority on matters that counted. In it he rehashed and applied his unsettling theories on slavery and the abolitionists.

Dr. Bushnell's death on February 17, 1876, was noted across the nation. Just two days before his passing, Hartford had voted to name in his honor the park that he worked so hard to establish. That project was dear to Bushnell. With the Industrial Revolution, many people flocking to the cities were poor, creating slums, and he didn't want one to spring up in the center of Hartford, the capital of the state. Also, he didn't want the parcel of land in the center of the city, next to the train station, to make a bad impression on the visitors. The creation of the park displaced about 200 poor people, most of them Irish laborers and African Americans who were servants in Hartford's well-to-do households. The project was proposed on October 5, 1853, and was accepted the next month. The following January, voters endorsed the project by a three to one margin, and Hartford became the first city in America to spend public funds (in this case $105,000) to build a park. In 1861, a total of 1,100 trees, comprising 157 species, were planted in the 41-acre park.

It was Reverend J. Twichell who took Dr. Bushnell to "his" falls for an overnight stay. Upon his old companion's praying by the water, he "found every other feeling swallowed up in the thought that God was there." Twichell added that after that very first visit "the fan-shaped cascade, a gem of beauty, *[had been]* called ever since then Bushnell Falls." Charles Dudley Warner reported in his book *In the Wilderness* (1878) that "Orson *[Phelps]* prized most the friendship of Dr. Horace Bushnell, a very liberal individual, for whom Bushnell Falls are named. They talked by the hour upon all sorts of themes." Consequently, the naming of the falls, with the approval of Phelps and Twichell, was secured.

The falls are about seven miles from the centre of the Keene Valley. Hikers are well advised to keep going past the steep and rugged spur trail that leads down to the bottom of the falls. A little further, when Johns Brook water isn't too high, where it hugs the trail, it is much easier to take a left and follow the brook downstream along its western shore, or even closer, to reach the top of the pretty scenery and proceed carefully down through the woods on the west side of the brook. At the bottom of the falls, due to the steep banks on either side, one feels a bit claustrophobic and is not usually tempted to spend much time there relaxing. W. Lowrie recounts that reaching Bushnell Falls in 1887 was relatively easy as hunters and fishermen using the Johns Brook lower valley camps as a base didn't need to go much further to satisfy their objectives.

Joseph Hopkins Twichell

The Reverend Joseph Hopkins Twichell (1838–1918) was one of the earliest summer residents of Keene Valley, if not the first. Twichell and his family went to Keene Flats for vacation for the first time in 1866. They also summered at Elk Lake. Twichell was educated at Yale, where his contact with Horace Bushnell helped him to choose the ministry as his life's career. During the Civil War, from 1861 to 1864, Twichell served as a chaplain in the United States Army. His experience with life and death on, among others, the Gettysburg battlefield gave him "understanding where differences in theology counted little." Since their publication, his *Civil War Letters* have earned considerable praise. They are, according to novelist Russell Banks, "a moving reminder that the Civil War was fought by intellectuals and churchmen, too – non-combatants who displayed enormous courage at considerable sacrifice."

"Joe" went on to be a highly respected individual whose friendship was valued. Following Dr. Bushnell's recommendation he became pastor of the new Asylum Hill Congregational Church in Hartford. He held that position from 1865 to 1912, all the while introducing countless members of his community to the Adirondacks. His friendships with Bushnell, Charles Dudley Warner, Mark Twain, Harriet Beecher Stowe, Yung Wing, and countless other celebrities of the late nineteenth century largely contributed to the first wave of summer visitors to the Adirondacks and to his own status as an Adirondack "expert."

Mark Twain's long relationship with Twichell, whom he considered a friend and mentor, has been the study of many an academic. The two met in 1868. In 1994, a play exploring and detailing their lifelong friendship was presented in Salem, Indiana. Always the humorist, Twain called his friend's ministry the "Church of the Holy Speculators." A biography of Twichell by Leah Strong was published in 1966. Another, by Steve Courtney, was published in 2008.

It appears that the Reverend Twichell was a source of "Adirondack trivia" for many writers and, most significantly, for guidebook authors. He had many opportunities to baptize unnamed falls and mountains after friends; however, the favor was never returned: the expert fisherman and avid climber's name does not appear on any map.

For decades, the "Yale man" was actively involved in the growth of his alma mater, so much so that the university provided him a Doctor of Divinity degree after his retirement. It was Twichell who recalled the last of numerous visits by Noah Porter, president of Yale University, to the Upper Lake (1875). Where the cone of Haystack presides over the grand views of the Great Range, the doctor that season, Twichell wrote, parted "with a friend he might never see again."

The Twichells also introduced a mountaineering family, now year-round residents, to the area. Howard Goodwin, later a Hartford insurance executive, was a boyhood friend and a Yale roommate of Twichell's son Joe. At the age of 11, Goodwin first visited Keene Valley with his family in 1895. With his friend, Howard first climbed Marcy from the Peel Jones Lodge at Mud Pond (Elk Lake) in 1901, overnighting at Skylight Camp, a lean-to then located about a third of the way between the floor of Panther Gorge and Four Corners. In Joe's company again and staying at the Lake Placid camp of Dr. Charles D. Alton, he made his second ascent of Marcy in 1903 from Heart Lake, after the great fire that swept the area that year. Goodwin met and went on to marry Charlotte Alton in 1909. The young woman spent all of her summers at Under Cliff on the shore of the lake and later with her new husband established her own family as permanent summer residents in Keene Valley.

Howard's son Jim and one of his grandsons, Tony, would become Adirondack celebrities in their own right for their extraordinary accomplishments and devotion to the High Peaks.

William A. White

One of the three founders of the Adirondack Trail Improvement Society (ATIS), William A. White first visited St. Huberts in 1864, riding his horse from Albany after having had it shipped from Brooklyn where he was a furrier. He served as the first president of the ATIS from 1897 to 1927. Walter Lowrie was on the executive committee. In 1948, Harold Weston, a highly regarded artist, designed the ATIS logo.

An inveterate walker, when arriving for the summer, White often hiked from Westport to Keene Valley. Before building his house within the AMR boundary in 1886, he spent his summers in New Russia and reached St. Huberts by walking over Giant. Once his summer house had been built in St. Huberts, if the weather was right upon reaching Elizabethtown, he would let the rest of the family proceed by carriage while he would walk to St. Huberts via Giant. He liked the mountain so much that he personally paid for the construction of two lean-tos near the summit, enabling climbers to enjoy mountaintop camping. He also funded the opening of the long gone trail that lead directly from Route 73 to the Dipper and, with the help of C. Goldmark, he blazed the Range Trail in 1897. His "special walk" was along the trail over the Range, which he laid out with Pete Lamb (a guide). In a March 1922 letter to John Apperson he recalled, "I made my first ascent of Haystack going up with only a dog for company, without any trail, about twenty five years ago from St. Huberts and back in one day, which I think was rather a good day's work although not all equal to what you accomplished."

At age 80, William A. White made his last hike in the High Peaks, a trip up Marcy. His son Harold's favorite climb involved an early start from their camp at the Upper Lake, breakfast on Haystack, followed by lunch on Marcy, and a leisurely walk down the Marcy Brook Trail. Since the time the AMR was established, members of the White family have enjoyed camps on the Upper Lake.

A. T. Shorey

Graduating from college in 1901, A. T. Shorey (1882-1974) followed in his father's footsteps and entered the newspaper business, eventually becoming editor of the weekly edition of the *New York World,* which ceased publication during the Depression. He then went to work for the New York State Conservation Department where he fielded questions about state-owned trails and campsites, wrote articles on camping and hiking for the department's magazine *The Conservationist,* and wrote trail descriptions for distribution. He loved the outdoors and became an active member of the ADK in 1923. The Adirondacks were his passion, and he enjoyed leading outings to his favorite spots. Because he preferred bushwhacking, an excursion with Shorey could be exhausting. His "short cuts" became legendary. After a particularly difficult climb a group of tired Boy Scouts told of hearing the by-then-elderly Shorey mutter, "Can't understand why I feel stiff. Never happened to me before."

Chairman of the ADK guidebook committee, he edited the 1945, 1947, and 1950 editions of the club's *Guide to Adirondack Trails.* He was the first person to receive the Frederick J. Loeper Memorial Award given to a Senior Citizen for outstanding community service. His work with the American Red Cross and with the Boy and Girl Scouts is particularly mentioned in the citation.

The Shorey Short Cut, which runs from the Phelps Trail near Slant Rock to the Range Trail in the col between Basin and Haystack, involves a 250-foot climb. Great views can be found along the mossy trail which features interesting large boulders often capped by ghostly shaped trees. The 1950 edition of the *Guide to Adirondack Trails* described the path (without calling it Shorey's) as a *"sporty trail with views."* The trail, built in 1940 by Shorey, offers on its high point a wonderful view of Basin. At a farther lookout lies a "perfectly framed portrait" of Haystack and Little Haystack. However, the route fails to take one directly to the summit of Basin and just about everyone who has travelled the 1.1-miles has found it an ordeal.

Shorey obviously designed the short cut for the views it offers. The rugged path is not aptly named and probably would not be so maligned by hikers if the "short cut" part of its name were erased. Like most of the paths on the Upper Range, it is mostly a rocky trail upon which one is hard pressed to find an inch of soft underfooting. The views of Basin and its twin summit, Lion's Head, are unique and well worth the ascent of "Shorey's mountain." Nevertheless, before the 1950 Big Blow, knowledgeable hikers such as Jim Goodwin always took the more direct route from Slant Rock along the drainage.

Several decades ago, a *New Yorker* cartoon pictured two men in a canoe confounded on their way upstream by an enormous waterfall. A copy of the cartoon was and may still be hanging on the walls of Johns Brook Lodge. On the print, the character in the stern of the boat asks, "Know any more short cuts?" A guest couldn't resist adding another caption in the margin: "Dedicated to A. T. Shorey."

In 1956, with five senior Girl Scouts in his party, A. T. Shorey made his 50th and final ascent of Marcy. His legacy remains with his short cut and, perhaps, this sentence: "I would urge all hikers to hike with an inquiring mind as well as with educated feet."

Robert Balk

Point Balk, a northern shoulder of Little Marcy at about 4,350 feet of altitude above Slant Rock, is a tormented rock structure that rarely attracts climbers. It is named after Robert Balk (1899-1955).

Born in Estonia, Balk came to the United States in 1924 with a doctorate in geology from Breslau to assume a position as assistant in the department of geology at Columbia University. He was appointed, in May 1925, to map the geology of Newcomb Quadrangle, the greater part being in Essex County. "Primary Structure of the Adirondack Anorthosite," published March 1929, is one of the many articles Dr. Balk researched and wrote for the *Geological Society of America Bulletin*. He taught at Hunter College, 1928-1935, all the while pursuing independent field study on weekends and holidays. While an associate with the New York Geological Survey, he began an intensive study of the Adirondack Shield. Instead of establishing headquarters at some hotel or village as was the custom, he carried his food and lodging in a pack and camped on top of outcrops and at the foot of cliffs. As he was an expert climber, nothing escaped him, his specialty being the structural geology of igneous and metamorphic rocks.

After heading the geology department at Holyoke College (1935-1947), he worked as a professor at the University of Mexico until 1952. That year his wife, Christina Lochman Balk (1907-2006), accepted a position to teach and act as dean of women at the New Mexico Institute of Mining and Technology. By the time of his death, Robert Balk had become principal geologist of the New Mexico State Bureau of Mines. He died in the crash of a TWA plane on a New Mexico mountainside during a snowstorm on February 15, 1955. The wreck, scattered in a remote, narrow canyon 9,000 feet up in the Sandia Mountains, is still "intact" today. All aboard the plane, including fifteen other passengers, perished.

In 1989, Mrs. Balk, who had received her Ph. D. from that institution in 1933, gave most of his papers to Johns Hopkins University. She established a memorial fund for her husband, the income from which supports field work by graduate students of geology at the university.

Dr. Balk was remarkable for his eagerness to have his students go into the field and learn geology first hand. He was also distinguished by his strong support for women entering geology. He promoted the non-traditional choice for women in the 1940s and he prepared an outline of job possibilities to encourage women to enter the field.

Upon Dr. Balk's sudden death, Arthur E. Newkirk, president of the ADK, immediately embraced the suggestion of the members of the club to have Old Mountain Phelps' "Colden Ridge" named after the geologist. The number of days and nights he spent in the Adirondacks and in the Johns Brook Valley studying the origin of anorthosites made him the perfect namesake for that particularly interesting and imposing band of cliffs.

It is believed that Will Glover played a large part in the naming of Point Balk. Glover, like Dr. Balk, was an active member of the ADK, Keene Valley Chapter. The two men likely knew each other well, for they both spent much time in the woods during the 1930s and 1940s. Glover, who in the late 1940s had acted as a fire tower observer, was then working at the U.S.G.S. and it is well known that a commonly accepted name can make it onto a map when an update occurs and no other name has yet been applied to the land feature in question. In any case, it was a very discreet and short campaign as the only document requesting the appellation is the Newkirk letter asking the Keene Valley Chapter for its support of the naming. The name, Point Balk, appeared on maps within a few years.

The most accessible text about the Adirondacks written by Robert Balk is a forty-three page chapter entitled "The Geologic Story of the Mountains." It was included in the 1942 publication of *The Friendly Mountains, Green, White, and Adirondacks*. From the first few words, and in an immediately captivating way, Dr. Balk conveys his deep love and knowledge of the mountains:

> The Friendly Mountains are old. They seem wise, like aged folk wrapped in shawls of deep green, who, having experienced aeons of geologic past now contemplate their life through mists of time. These ranges have forgotten more experiences than the young alpine chains of the west have yet known. They have lived through so many millenniums that they can afford to be tolerant of the little humans that swarm over them like ants. These ranges are venerable... It has been said that when men and mountains come together great things take place. Certainly large ideas are born, and great questions posed.

Walter Lowrie and Newell Martin

Will Glover once commented that Walter Lowrie had the

> ...capacity either to traverse a trail or to journey through unbroken forest with an ease that seemingly was effortless; and with never a misstep or a stumble, plus the possession of a sense of direction that time and again brought us to our destination with the precision of filings drawn to a magnet.

A near drowning in the undertow of the surf at Spring Lake, New Jersey, shelved Lowrie's father's project for building a cottage there. Inspired by his wife, he went to the Adirondacks in 1887. The first year the family lived on the "Hartford Platter," in a house owned by Miss Dunham, Charles Dudley Warner and Joseph Twichell, the second house built by summer visitors in the Keene Valley. In 1888, following Old Mountain Phelps' advice on location, he built, near Phelps Falls a cottage on a five-acre parcel for which he paid $2,000. Later, Lowrie's father provided for Phelps and his wife by buying their home with the understanding that they could live in it the rest of their days.

Beginning at the age of 19, Walter Lowrie (1868-1959) climbed assiduously for more than a decade and explored the Great Range from the Johns Brook Valley and the Ausable Ponds. At times, he went up Johns Brook all the way to the Panther Gorge headwall, down to Panther Gorge, and up Bartlett Ridge to finally reach Haystack's summit before returning to Slant Rock via Little Haystack. He did so, usually, in record time. From 1887 on, Walter Lowrie climbed Haystack, Basin, and Saddleback numerous times, alone or with Malcolm MacLaren (who became head of the electrical engineering school at Princeton University). Occasionally, Walter hiked with the Rev. Twichell. He notably climbed Haystack in 1889 from the Johns Brook side.

He kept records of some of his hikes (1892, 1895, 1896, 1898) in a small paperback log book which provides detailed accounts (times, altitude, distances, and drawings of routes and mountains) of his adventures. His and others' records, most notably Jim Goodwin's, confirm that Panther Gorge contained a beautiful, open forest that was easily traversed, as were the ascents to the Range via the then-called Basin Brook (today a brook without a name below Shorey's Short Cut) and via Saddleback Brook (which is now Chicken Coop Brook). Furthermore, his comments and times suggest that a well defined herdpath crossed the whole length of the Range from Haystack to Gothics.

Lowrie would leave from his Keene Valley home, "Bonaventure," and adopt Slant Rock as a base camp. One can assume that Colvin, with his large team and considerable survey equipment, had cleared somewhat wide paths to Haystack and Basin in 1874. However, it is interesting to note that the trails to Haystack and Basin from the Upper Ausable Lake weren't indicated on maps in the first guidebooks as the guides and later the AMR may have discouraged the various authors from displaying them.

In a 1933 essay about mountain climbing in Keene Valley, Dr. Lowrie – by then rector of a New York City church and a noted theologian and interpreter of Kierkegaard – wrote that after 1887 the ever increasing summer visitors had nothing to do but climb and that is what they did, particularly with the short access via the AMR road and lakes and with the club rapidly opening new trails to all the mountains rising from the valley. One has to remember that the tourists of that era spent weeks, if not months, in the Keene Valley area.

Able to find his own way and carry his own pack, Lowrie wasn't very popular with most guides. He gave equally in return with disparaging remarks, not only about the laziness and incompetence of many a guide (Ed Phelps being the exception) but, as well, of the "guided" hikers who laid claims to achievements that he felt were his own. Lowrie credits the aging Old Mountain Phelps with guiding him through the mountains by way of precise descriptions but he didn't take well to a few other claims about "his" beloved mountains. To make his point, Lowrie may have discredited the accomplishments of others while convincing only himself that all who claimed to do as well or better than him in climbing either died or were forever incapacitated. However, he credited Harvard students from Putnam Camp with numerous "bushwhack" climbs along the Range. He wrote, "I used to encounter groups of them from time to time in every likely and unlikely place in the mountains."

As the years went by, some of the trek times Dr. Lowrie reported appeared to shorten significantly:

> We once started from Slant Rock and, with our camping accouterments (which proved a superfluous burden), went up Marcy, thence over Mt. Colden and down the slide to Avalanche Lake, then up the side of McIntyre to the peak called Iroquois, which was a sad mistake because the dwarf balsams between that and the summit (Algonquin) made the going very slow, and

that caused us to do another foolish thing, for we were so tired of trackless forest, having had no trail all day, that we gaily ran down to the Lodge, and then had to run all the way through Indian Pass to get to our destination, which was Iron Works, where we arrived at 10 o'clock at night, a good deal puzzled by the darkness during the last hours.

Lowrie maintained, "I am not boasting of the rapidity of our going, for I never set out to beat a record for time. That sport was cultivated by boys who came after me by several years."

Lowrie's little book, now property of the Keene Valley Library, detailed the same 1892 trip, with a notable difference: He and MacLaren left Slant Rock the morning of July 16th and after spending the night at Lake Colden, climbed Algonquin only and with great difficulty, as it took them about six hours to reach the summit. From there, a trail took them easily down to the Lodge and then on to the Upper Works where they spent the following night before returning home over Marcy on the 19th after spending the night of the 18th camping under Slant Rock.

Using Bushnell Falls and Slant Rock as base camps, Lowrie and MacLaren would climb Haystack (via Panther Gorge), Basin (1 hour 45 minutes via "Little Basin"), and Saddleback in record times. Jim Goodwin later did much the same up Chicken Coop (then called Saddleback Brook) or the brook up Basin's south shoulder which offered an open forest to Little Basin. To reach Haystack in the first few years, Lowrie chose to climb to the top of Panther Gorge and then down it to "slab up" Haystack's bare slides rather than go over Little Haystack. Increasing traffic soon created a more defined path as is evident by an August 20, 1898, account of a hike from Haystack to Gothics: the trek took a mere 8.5 hours from the Upper Ausable Lake to Keene Valley. Until a trail was cut over "Horse Hill" (today's Blue Connector) in 1919, hikers coming from Slant Rock had to climb down the Gorge, skirt the base of Haystack to "Little Brook," and from there climb straight to the summit to join the path from the Upper Ausable Lake via Bartlett Ridge. According to Lowrie, he made the climb from Panther Gorge's Little Brook to Haystack's summit in about 50 minutes.

In July 1892, Lowrie and MacLaren were likely the first adventurers to complete "the hike" in just 14 hours. Starting in Keene Valley at 5 a.m., they reached Marcy via Johns Brook at 10 a.m., took a 45-minute lunch break, followed Marcy's shoulders (not going down to Panther Gorge) and were atop Haystack at 11:45 a.m.. An hour later, they allowed themselves a 30-minute lunch break on Basin before taking an hour to climb Saddleback (2:15 p.m.). The next part of the trek was comparatively slow. They reached Gothics at 3:40 p.m. The duo took a 20-minute rest before heading down towards the Lake Road and reaching home by carriage at 7 p.m.

In claiming that he and a few others had climbed Saddleback long before Newell Martin's "first" recorded August 5, 1894, ascent, Dr. Lowrie is most likely right. Martin is also credited with the first recorded ascent of Sawteeth (1875).

Martin (1854-1941), who became a lawyer, completed "the hike" in 16 hours on August 5, 1894, but he had added Skylight to the list of summits. However, he had two guides carrying his gear, each for half the length of the journey, which took him over the Range in the other direction. Martin claimed there was no path to follow from Haystack to Gothics, but one is hard pressed to believe that the Haystack Brook trail disappeared altogether upon reaching the Basin-Haystack col.

Lowrie later claimed that Martin had so taxed himself completing "the hike" that he was unable to climb again. However, contrary to Lowrie's assertion, Martin recovered from his hike.

Charles Holt reported that Newell, son of President Martin of the Imperial College of Peking, China, and a Yale graduate, used the Lambs' camp on Upper Ausable Lake as a base as early as 1873. He had quite a reputation and the guides looked at him with mixed feelings of awe and admiration: "He is the dare-devilest devil that I ever have seen. He's uncommon. He doesn't seem to care any more for his life than a row of pins."

Lowrie particularly resented Russell Carson's assertion, in *Peaks and People of the Adirondacks*, that Martin's August 5, 1894, ascent of Saddleback was the first on record. He staunchly maintained that he had climbed the mountain several times ("one of my ascents was the most notorious") but that countless other climbers had as well... and long before Martin. Lowrie's little book gives a detailed account of a 9-hour 20-minute July 7, 1892, climb of Saddleback with MacLaren and of going home over Gothics down to the Lake Road.

Letters published in *Ad-i-ron-dac* concerning Lowrie's assertions are riveting. All correspondents agreed that Lowrie exaggerated the state of health of Newell and others who completed hikes similar to his own, but no one supported Carson's conclusion about Newell's first ascent, and that omission endorsed Lowrie's claims that the Range had been walked many times before 1894. In fact, Carson had seemingly contradicted the Martin claim in another chapter of *Peaks and People*. He wrote that James J. Storrow, later a well known patent lawyer from Boston, spent the summers of 1869-1871 climbing in the area, including a trek made with guide Orlando Beede that included climbs of the peaks of the Upper Range. Thus Saddleback had been climbed a quarter century before Martin had first reached its summit.

In the late 1800s there were many tales about the prodigious climbing and walking feats of the young Lowrie, one of the first members of the ATIS. In the late 1930s, while staying at JBL with his wife, Dr. Lowrie, then 70, made the ascent to Marcy and returned to the ADK facility the same afternoon.

William Glover

In September 1901, guided by Dr. Lowrie and Ed Isham, thirteen-year-old William Glover (1888-1981) made his first High Peaks ascents – Marcy from the Upper Ausable Lake with an overnight stay in Panther Gorge under the roof of the then-called Skylight Lean-to. He did not know, while standing on Marcy, that at the same moment Vice President Theodore Roosevelt was proceeding towards the top of the state and about to turn back after being told that President McKinley, victim of an assassin at Buffalo, was dying. Glover would later comment, "The sensation produced in anyone who gains for the first time the summit of Marcy is something never to be erased from one's memory."

Lowrie chose to descend from Marcy by heading northeast and partly dropping down into Panther Gorge following a path described by the young William as "among mammoth boulders covered with a luxuriant growth of soft moss a rich green hue" and soon after lead the group "in a scramble over a rock slide up Haystack's slope almost directly to the summit of the peak." The descent was down the "perfect" trail that had been constructed from the Upper Ausable Lake to Haystack via Haystack Brook.

Glover made his last day hike to Marcy the year of his 80th birthday. Decades earlier, even though he strongly believed that climbing for records was the wrong approach, he had written to George Marshall, "OK, so how many times did I make it to the top of Tahawus?

...All I know is, that that trip was more or less a weekly occurrence during the vacation days of my college period. Put it down if you will, as not to exceed one hundred, if one has to be mathematical about such things."

An always active member of the Keene Valley Chapter of the ADK, Glover occasionally contributed to *Ad-i-ron-dac*. In the July-August 1957 edition, he fondly reminisced about his winter climbs at the beginning of the century. After Christmas 1914, he took an eleven-hour train ride, in a sleeper, to Westport followed by a four-hour sleigh ride to Keene Valley. The next sunny day, borrowing a pair of snowshoes, he climbed Hopkins and was rewarded by an acute headache for not wearing sunglasses and "a sense of amazement and fascination" that he hadn't foreseen either. A couple of days later, Noonmark proved a much more difficult climb as he didn't follow the trail while ascending the peak. Nevertheless Glover was soon back:

> The following March (1915) marked the acquisition of my car, a 1911 Cutting, known jocularly as the Coffee Grinder, by essaying an expedition to the Valley from New Haven with my roommate Bill Dannehower. Naturally the snow-capped peaks constituted a temptation of irresistible proportions. After acquiring two sets of snowshoes we proceeded up the Ranney Trail to Hopkins to use the connecting route which some years earlier I had put in company with Fritz Comstock. This ran from just below the peak, along the slope of Green Mountain, to the North ridge of Giant and thence to the top. The lack of snow at lower elevation and its packed state higher made our traverse exceptionally simple. On our arrival at the top, we found the lean-to which then stood there, completely blocked by drifting snow but a bit of excavating by means of our footwear made an entrance and behind the snow wall we ate our lunch in comparative warmth.

In part because of World War I, Glover did not return to the Adirondacks for twenty years. When Glover, with his son Bill and daughter Ruth, camped overnight at a friend's cabin along Orebed Brook on February 22, 1938, crusty conditions allowed father, daughter and son to make the summit of Big Slide. Glover commented, "We didn't even use creepers." Overnighting at the MacIntosh camp just before Christmas that year, they climbed the West Peak of Gothics. Glover, during the previous summer, had acquired a ten-acre property along one of Johns Brook's beautiful succession of pools and slabs about a mile below JBL and accessible only via the Old Johns Brook logging road. From that property, a few days after Christmas, he made it alone to Upper Wolf Jaw, possibly a first winter ascent of that peak. In March 1939, with son Bill and two skiers, guests of the Orebed cabin owner, Saddleback's summit was reached. During the 1940 Christmas holidays at his cabin, it rained four days but on the fifth day the temperature dropped and a couple of inches of snow fell. Consequently, having "observed what might be termed bankers' hours, 10 a.m., for my departure" for Basin, he surmounted the last lookout a short distance from the peak as it was now 2 p.m. and time to return to camp."

A graduate of Yale, trained as an attorney and admitted to the bar of the state of California, following the family tradition he spent most of his summers in Keene Valley. Today, close relatives enjoy houses in the valley and the camp by Johns Brook at the foot of both Jaws. All remember that climbing was a big part of Glover's summers. While at the end of the day he enjoyed his mother's hospitality,[6] he continuously climbed all of the peaks one can approach on foot from the Keene Valley, particularly the heights of the Great Range. He accessed them every way he could, but he rarely, if ever, boasted about any of his climbs.

Adrian Edmonds, a well known Keene Valley real estate developer (Adrian's Acres), recalls that when he was a small boy "it was a local custom to hold a contest each summer to determine who could go up Marcy from the hamlet and return in the shortest time. Glover was always the undisputed champion of this event." Much later, Glover was often seen, with Bill and Ruth in tow, his six-foot, five-inch frame bearing a heavy pack, walking up Market Street. Glover would arrive in early May and stay until mid October.

John Apperson and Irving Langmuir

John "Appy" Apperson (1878-1963) and Irving Langmuir (1881-1957) formed the Forest Preserve Association in 1934. They had met in 1910 and from then on together climbed many of the High Peaks on skis when not practicing skate-sailing on Lake George. Both worked at General Electric in Schenectady for decades, were ADK members, and summered on Lake George. Through his career at G.E., Dr. Langmuir, a physicist and a chemist, received 22 awards, 15 honorary degrees, 63 patents, and the 1932 Nobel Prize in chemistry for his discoveries and investigations in surface chemistry. Langmuir even pioneered cloud-seeding as a way to control rainfall, an idea that came to him while hiking on stormy Mount Washington in 1946. Mount Langmuir in Alaska and a college at SUNY Stony Brook, NY, are named for him.

Apperson, even though he wasn't an engineer *per se,* had the title of "Engineering General" at G.E. and under Langmuir's aegis managed to keep the job for decades in spite of occasional problems with his managers. When the Adirondack Mountain Club was formed in 1922, he became one of about 200 prominent people in the state who became charter members. He wanted the public land kept public, and wild, so that it could be enjoyed in its natural state. He was a longtime active member of the ADK's conservation committee. As his great mountaineering reputation helped him achieve his "environmental" goals, he never felt the need to reveal that his skiing ability was average at best and that some of his reported climbing exploits were pure fiction. However, an honest man, he preserved the truth in plain sight among his private notes and papers, often in hand-signed letters.

Among other successes, Apperson's forces prevailed over the Tahawus Club regarding the right of the state to buy lakes and shorelines, not just the high slopes around them. He prevented the state from building a series of lodges throughout the Forest Preserve and managed to have 1.5 million acres of land added to the park. His boat, *Article VII, Section 7,*[7] is on display at the Adirondack Museum at Blue Mountain Lake.

In the 1930s, Apperson was a very active member, with Louis Marshall,[8] of the Association for the Protection of the Adirondacks. The association was founded in 1901 by large estate and game park owners (J. P. Morgan, W. G. Rockefeller, W. C. Whitney, W. S. Webb, A. L. White, A. G. Vanderbilt, etc.) whose self-interests coincided with the public interest. They successfully opposed an amendment that would have allowed state lands to become potential timber-production until the park boundaries were extended by more than 1,500,000 acres.

An Albany *Times-Union* article by Barnett (Barney) Fowler published on January 29, 1961, described Apperson as follows:

> A modest man, whose life has been spent in a ferocious quest for the public good, is one of those men who represents the hard core battlers who for years fought to acquaint not only the public with the benefits of the outdoors, but legislature and legislatures as well. Tongue Mountain at Lake George, once privately owned, is State property today mainly due to the efforts of Apperson and those with whom he worked. French Point is State land today due to his subscription campaign and his success in convincing G.E., his employer, to sell the land at more than a reasonable cost... One of the examples of Apperson's devotion to the public welfare was his outright gift of the 14 acre Dome Island, a striking formation.

Ed Ketchledge (#507)

With an undergraduate degree in forest management, Dr. Edwin H. Ketchledge went on to receive his masters degree and Ph.D., specializing in the botany of the High Peaks region. He once commented, "Bonding with the natural world, I focused my interest in my mountains when I saw the erosion that was occurring in those alpine summits while pursuing my own graduate work. I became independent in my work when I did my masters. I was studying with no intention of climbing the 46. I saw the changes occurring; that is when I began to organize, seeing the raw earth exposed. Climbing I would see more and more black. I started working with my volunteers in 1955."

After joining the faculty of Syracuse University, Dr. Ed took up the study of the ecology of his favorite mountains. In 1964, with support from the United States Forest Service, he decided to inventory the status of trails and to outline steps to correct ecological damage. To complete his research work he visited most of the peaks and finally climbed them all to become a 46er. During his years as president of the club, 1975 to 1978, the Forty-Sixers took on its present conservation, stewardship, and trail maintenance efforts in coordination with the DEC.

During the 1971 hiking season, several teams under Dr. Ed went to work restoring vegetation on peaks and trails. Jack Swan (#267) and his camp group took care of the section from Sno-Bird to Basin's summit while others were on Skylight, Wright, Gothics, Algonquin, Cascade, and other peaks. At the same time, experimentation was done on Colden's summit to find out which kind of temporary grass would be best for retaining soil and allowing the native vegetation to regain its territory. Hiker tramping didn't hamper the germination and growth of the seedlings. The work even indirectly benefited wildlife as snowshoe hares enjoyed a new menu item.

In 1972, work was concentrated on Dix, Colden, Wright and Algonquin. Dr. Ed was always dismayed by the low number of volunteers but the few obtained extraordinary results. Today, the summit vegetation on most of the mountains above tree line is luxuriant and offers the hiker incomparable and unique scenery in between the snow seasons. It was hard work carrying up 400 pounds of lime, 400 of fertilizer, and 80 of seeds during the 1972 season. That year, on Dix, Dr. Ed told of getting a boost noticing that after six years the native alpine species had started to re-establish themselves. Nevertheless, he was disappointed that of the 50 volunteers, only a dozen were 46ers. By 1975, Dr. Ed's next step to complete the work was the judicious placement of rocks, directing alpine summit hiker traffic over one well marked trail. Temporary grass stabilizes the soil which in due time allows the natural mosses, lichens, and alpine plants to take over, and they do because they are dominant. It is a highly effective but very slow process.

Ketch, who has said that his deepest concern is a "higher sense of natural ethics," has commented about hiking... "the power not to...— in order to preserve the beauty of the Alpine meadow for the generations to come. Nine out of ten hikers are stupid, just stupid. We shouldn't even stay on the summits, just a very short visit. It's not a playground. Seeds are brought by the wind, not even one should be touched. I don't worry much when it is frozen and there is snow, but the rest of the time keep them on the damn trail and keep them off the vegetation."

Dr. Ed stresses that because summit vegetation is very exposed, we cannot underestimate the effect of the suddenness of environmental changes. The 85 acres comprising the Adirondack summit meadows covered by true arctic plants are, he says, "islands of history." The rare mountain flowers found are all remnants of the last ice age, forming a 10,000-year-old museum.

Diapensia mounds, often 2 feet in diameter could be forty years old, the sculpted Paper Birches are well into their seventies, and a majority of the over 100 different flowering plants and shrubs are young adults in their 30's. Black Spruce, Balsam Fir and dozens of moss and lichen species also grow on Adirondack alpine summits. Black Spruce will live up to 200 years and frequently grows where no other tree will survive, resulting in a variety of shapes and sizes. Under some of the harshest winter conditions, their exposed sides may be brown and bare of needles but the leeward side remains green. Needles persist an average of seven years on spruce and balsam. Interestingly, where the ranges of red and black spruce overlap, they interbreed, producing natural hybrids that have characteristics of both. Identifying them can be tricky, but if a spruce is in or around a bog, it is black; if it is on an upland site, it is red; if it's in between it could be either, or more likely a hybrid. Fir are fast growers but short-lived compared to the patient Red Spruce that can reach 400 years. Nowadays, this species suffers a lot of die-back under the influence of acid fog and air pollution. As well, their shallow root system makes them prone to blowdown and they are vulnerable to forest fires due to their high resin content.

Dr. Ed's legacy is five decades of dedication, knowledge, understanding, and efficient problem solving. The alpine vegetation has been restored to a large extent and a majority of hikers treat the summits they are so happy to visit with due respect. Under Ketch's leadership, the 46ers became a club fully "dedicated to environmental protection, to education for proper usage of wilderness areas, and to participation in work projects in cooperation with the DEC to achieve those objectives." Several non-profit conservation organizations, most notably the ADK, banded together to implement a summit stewardship program. In June 1990, Al Nejmeh and Peter Zika, after a June training session at Adirondak Loj, led by Forest Ranger Peter Fish and Dr. Ketchledge,[9] were the very first to take on the new jobs explaining the fragility and the significance of the alpine plant community to summit visitors.

We can conclude just as did the author of the August 9, 1950, editorial in the *New York Times:* "At summer's end the vacationers leave the Forest Preserve, but the mountains remain, rising new from each morning mist, painted freshly by every evening sunset. In a world where a man finds little permanent he can always fix on his mountains, forever unchanging yesterday, today and tomorrow. He may go but they remain. He can return, sure that he will find them as he left them, untouched by man, scarce touched by time."

Endnotes

1. Lincoln Kinnear Barnett (1909-1979) was a *Life* magazine staff writer, war correspondent, and editor. Among his other books were *The World We Live In; The Wonders of Life on Earth;* and *The Universe and Dr. Einstein.* At the time he wrote *The Ancient Adirondacks,* he was a resident of Westport, New York.

2. The Bemis Crew, snowshoers and skiers, mostly from Boston – a few from New York – became an informal winter mountaineering organization in February 1923 when a group of about twenty individuals spent a week at the Inn Unique in Crawford Notch, New Hampshire. The inn was otherwise known as the Bemis Place, after Dr. Samuel Bemis (1793-1881), a Boston dentist who became one of the first photographers in the United States (March 1840). Bemis once owned much of the area around Crawford Notch.

3. Seven other lean-tos above 3,500 feet were also removed following the implementation of APA regulations.

4. An 1892 graduate of Princeton, Atkinson eventually became the chief chemist of the New York City Department of Health. After discovering bacterial growth was considerably reduced at temperatures below 50°F, he mandated that milk be kept with ice until delivered to the consumer.

5. Robert W. de Forest was president of the Metropolitan Museum of Art and president of the Adirondack Mountain Reserve (AMR) from 1906 to 1931. He was also an original member of the Tahawus Club (organized as the Adirondack Club at the site of the McIntyre Iron Works in 1877).

6. Helen Wardell, Glover's mother, kept a private journal in which she provided details about the family trip of September 1881 from New York City to Keene Flats. It took all of one day to get to Albany and the night was spent in a noisy guest house. They left at 7:40 a.m. for Ticonderoga, where they embarked on a boat that landed at Westport at 3:15 p.m. From there they rode on a three-seated wagon that took them to their destination by 9:50 p.m. after a 6.5-hour trip over very rough roads. A few days later, having reached the Upper Ausable Lake the previous afternoon, she joined a party which reached Marcy's summit in 5.5 hours. The party spent the following night camping in Panther Gorge before returning to the Upper Lake camp. The guides (Blinn and Trumbull) were well prepared to ease the muscle pain of the climbers as Helen Wardell's menu description hints: "After a supper of beef tea and brandy, I retired and the guides told panther and bear stories around the bright camp fire for two hours, the moon rising full in the heavens. It was fine!"

7. On January 1, 1895, the "Forever Wild" clause (Article VII, Section 7 of the Constitution of the State of New York) went into effect.

8. Father of Bob and George and one of the original proponents of Article VII, Section 7 of the state constitution when it was considered before a convention in 1894.

9. Dr. Edwin H. Ketchledge died at his home in Potsdam, New York, on June 30, 2010.

The following contributed valuable help and showed great patience assisting the author of this chapter: Inge Aiken; Phil Corell; Pat Galeski, Keene Valley Library Archives; Susie Doolittle and Margaret Gibbs, Elizabethtown Historical Library; Tony Goodwin; James Goodwin; Tom Haskins; Gavin Isham; Bill Johnson; Dr. Edwin Ketchledge; Gary Koch; Suzanne Lance; Andrea Maters, Editor; Adirondack Mountain Club (ADK) library, Lake George; Jerold Pepper, Adirondack Museum, Blue Mountain Lake, Archive Library; Patti Prindle, the Association for Protections of the Adirondacks Archive Library; Anton Solomon; Julie and Breck Turner of With Pipe and Book, Lake Placid; and the late John E. Winkler, the only person to ascend all 46 peaks by way of bushwhack routes.

About the Author

Christine Bourjade (#4967W) somehow graduated from getting lost in the woods of France, where she was born in 1952, to completing several winter and summer rounds a handful of decades later. For more than 20 years she and her husband Alex Radmanovich (#4968W) have successfully run their own PR firm in Montreal, Canada, and raised their daughter, Lyla, who has climbed three High Peaks, at last count. When it came time to climb the New York State 100 highest, Alex said, "No way." Luckily, plenty of friends were willing to join Christine in the madness and even Alex went along for North River Mt. and Cheney Cobble in the winter. Living part time in New Russia, NY, Christine, a correspondent for the 46ers, has found time to do considerable trail work with her good friends and hiking companions Gary Koch (#1137W) and the late Ed Bunk (#3052W), as well as numerous requisitioned volunteers.

The Lower Range
By Mary Lou Recor (#2214W)

Gothics
Height: 10th – 1,443 meters (4,734 feet)

Verplanck Colvin was on top of Haystack Mountain on August 27, 1873, when he first calculated the height of "Gothic mountain... never previously measured... 4,744 feet." He noted in his report to the state legislature for 1873 that Haystack, Basin, and Gothics were "stupendous mountains – majestic landmarks of the State," but, he added, they had "remained unknown to surveys, though all three are superior in altitude to the famous Mt. Seward." Perhaps it was on that August afternoon that Colvin first decided that he would, one day, climb the "Gothic Mountain." However, his ascent was delayed. He later reported that the next year, 1874, was marked by legislative indifference and a "Reduction of Appropriations" which made it impossible for him to return to work in the mountains.

Another year passed. Colvin, stuck in his office in Albany, must have been aching to renew his adventures in the mountains. He must have dreamed of his return for an expedition to reach the top of the Gothic mountain.

However, the 1875 legislative appropriation, Colvin wrote, "was so small as to make it impossible to enter upon extended field-work." Nearly "two-thirds of the amount being required" for continuation of the Adirondack Survey, he reported, was spent "for the office map-work in Albany and Washington, and the re-equipment" of survey teams. "It was late in September... when the duties of the office, and the repairs of instruments and camp equipments, rendered it possible to take the field; but it was not until the 29th of the month that the necessary funds were received."

Colvin left Albany on September 30, 1875, with a "leveling party" which he "directed to extend a line of datums from Westport on Lake Champlain, forty miles backward into the wilderness to the summit of Mount Marcy." That day he and his men traveled to Ticonderoga by railroad and proceeded to Westport on a "steamer." By October 3rd, he was ready to set out for Keene "to take up the exploration of those branches of the Upper Ausable, hitherto unexplored, to search for certain elevated and unmapped ponds, and to carry a reconnaissance along the crest of the Gothic Mountains and into the passes immediately northward and southward of Mt. Marcy."

After spending several days at Elizabethtown involved with details of the datum line to Mt. Marcy, on October 6th, Colvin was satisfied that the "leveling party" was "pressing forward and finely with their work... in the thorough and systematic manner necessary." He left them, and "crossing the mountains westward," descended "into the valley of the AuSable." After a brief stop in Keene, he proceeded on October 7th, to Keene Valley, where he hired two guides, Ed Phelps and Roderick McKenzie. He went back to Keene to meet with the

Late nineteenth century view of "them Gothics" by Seneca Ray Stoddard. According to Old Mountain Phelps: "Ain't the kinder scenery you want to hog down."

leveling party and later "drove back alone in the crisp, frosty moonlight night to the head of Keene Valley." On October 8th, Colvin and Phelps climbed from Chapel Pond to Giant's Washbowl, and on the 9th, he set out with Phelps and McKenzie "for the exploration of the region to the north-eastward of Marcy, including the Gothic mountains."

The three men followed the Johns Brook upstream into the mountains and camped in a clearing along the Slide Brook near the beginning of today's trail to Big Slide, three tenths of a mile from Johns Brook Lodge. They climbed high on the side of "Slide Mountain" on the 10th, in a cold, drizzling storm, to the "edge of the cloud" and then sat and waited for the weather to clear so that they might obtain a view of the "Gothic mountains," but "the clouds drifted by, hour after hour, and at length, disheartened and chilled" they "returned to camp, dispirited, but not discouraged."

A "cold frosty night" was followed by "another stormy morning," but after observing that the barometer "was rising," Colvin decided to begin the climb of Gothics. After the three had had breakfast and packed up their gear, "the clouds cleared away from the mountains to the eastward – showing the peaks, however, all capped with snow." They set out for them "at once." By his account, they followed a stream for a bit, then passed through ever-thickening woods to the base of a slide, which they climbed. Finding themselves nearer the Wolf Jaws than their intended destination, they bulled their way through cripplebrush to the top of the ridge.

Colvin wrote, "Following the ridge, we made our way as rapidly as possible toward the southward, and soon became involved in an almost impenetrable windslash of fallen timber; and in working around this impediment along the tops of precipices, grasping icy limbs and roots for support, made a perilous passage." As they neared the summit, one of his guides "was overbalanced by his heavy knapsack and for a moment hung suspended feet upward over the verge, but with prompt aid escaped with the loss of his bowie knife." Undeterred, they pressed onward to the summit where Colvin noted:

Deep in the basin to the eastward lay a dark, narrow pool – black as ebony between its even darker walls of rock – the lower Ausable Lake; further south the Upper lake, like a bright jewel set in the gorgeous autumnal forest; and southward, still other ponds and lakes; while to the westward and northward a portion of the Saranac waters, and the bright surface of Lake Placid showed themselves, and above or beyond them, all the black, frost-crested mountain billows – revealed from this station in strangely different contour – with new passes, new gorges and new chasms.

Oddly, although Colvin mentions a view of the Upper Ausable Lake, the 1979 edition of the Adirondack Mountain Club high peaks guide, while crediting Gothics with views of 30 mountains, states that the Upper Lake is not visible. Perhaps Colvin's "bright jewel" was seen from another vantage point elsewhere along the summit ridge.[1]

The three, descending along the "icy ridge" in fading light, "were struck with horror. On every side yawned icy precipices, showing more grim and dreadful in the fast increasing darkness; and the elder guide (McKenzie) attempting to pass along below the crest, where some ice clad stems of the Labrador tea (*Ledum latifolium*) alone offered assistance to the hand, was suddenly suspended over the edge of a cliff – where, a thousand feet below, the clouds were drifting – and rescued himself by the sheer strength of his muscular arms." Today, where Colvin and his two guides spent a second chilly night, sheltered by a small clump of trees on the face of the mountain, with sheets of ice crashing down around them, Labrador tea still grows, eking out its hardy existence with the equally tenacious mountain sandwort.

Although Colvin's climb of Gothics is the first recorded ascent, Russell M. L. Carson in *Peaks and People of the Adirondacks* assigns the honor, "about 1870-71," to James J. Storrow and his guide, Orlando Beede. In the book *Of the Summits, of the Forests,* longtime Keene Valley resident and Adirondack guide Jim Goodwin also speculates that the renowned Boston patent lawyer, Storrow, and his favorite guide, Beede, were the first to reach the summit, but their ascent was never recorded. Carson was convinced that Storrow and Beede "had climbed all the peaks over which the Range Trail now passes" before the end of September 1871. He also noted that brothers Bob and George Marshall, to commemorate the climb of Gothics by Storrow and Beede, suggested that the col between Gothics and Saddleback be named "Storrow Pass" and that the one between Gothics and Sawteeth be named "Beede Pass."

Orson Schofield "Old Mountain" Phelps, father of Ed Phelps, is usually credited with the naming of Gothics in 1857 when he and Milwaukee painter Frederick S. Perkins stood atop Mount Marcy, gazing over at the cathedral-like grandeur of the Gothic slides. However, Philip Terrie in his editor's introduction to the 1973 edition of *Peaks and People of the Adirondacks* notes that the name "Gothics" as applied to the mountain appears in a poem by North Elba resident Dillon C. Osgood in 1850. From their vantage on Marcy, Phelps and Perkins would have seen the many rock faces that give Gothics its distinctive character, described by Don Mellor in his *Climbing in the Adirondacks: A Guide to Rock and Ice Routes in the Adirondack Park* as "the ominous but alluring slabs which gird the peak," a rock climber's dream. Although George and Bob Marshall, second and third to climb the 46 high peaks, ranked the view from Gothics #14, James R. Burnside in his 1996 book *Exploring the 46 Adirondack High Peaks* ranks Gothics #1. Old Mountain Phelps, from a camp on the Upper Ausable Lake, was said to have remarked, "Them Gothics ain't the kinder scenery you want to hog down."

Lower Wolf Jaw
Height: 30th – 1,272 meters (4,173 feet)

Upper Wolf Jaw
Height: 29th – 1,281 meters (4,203 feet)

Without necessarily intending to, Colvin, McKenzie and Ed Phelps became the first to achieve the summit of Upper Wolf Jaw that day in October 1875 when they were destined for Gothics. They did not, however, by Colvin's account, turn to the northeast for Lower Wolf Jaw. According to Guy and Laura Waterman in *Forest and Crag,* Ed Phelps was first on that summit, also in 1875. However, in *Of the Summits, of the Forests,* Jim Goodwin again speculates that the first ascent may have been accomplished by James Storrow and Orlando Beede.

In a manuscript, unpublished in his lifetime, Old Mountain Phelps takes credit for naming the "Wolfjaws," although he says the name was suggested by Alfred Billings Street in his book *The Indian Pass* (1869). That same year, artist Arthur H. Wyant, camping for ten days on Noonmark, created a painting of the Wolf Jaws. His guide, Mel Trumbull, credited Wyant with conferring the descriptive name – the two serrate summits and intervening notch bringing to mind the open jaws of a wolf.

Armstrong
Height: 19th – 1,350c meters (4,429+ feet)

However Gothics and the Wolf Jaws were named, the naming of Armstrong by Almon Thomas for his friend and business partner, Thomas Armstrong, is not in dispute.

Ironically, lumberman Almon Thomas's ties to the Adirondacks were stronger than those of attorney Thomas Armstrong. Thomas was born of modest means in Kingsbury, New York, and began his career by measuring logs in the employ of Charles Harris. He moved in 1847 to Plattsburgh, where he was hired by F. J. Barnard & Son of Albany to supervise their operations in the woods around Lower Saranac Lake. In 1852, he bought a half interest in the property and was instrumental in opening the Saranac River as a highway for log drives. By the time he formed the partnership with Armstrong in the 1860s, having bought, operated, and sold several mills and factories in Plattsburgh and Keeseville, he was a man of considerable means.

Thomas Armstrong, born in Ireland in December 1821, following his father's death, immigrated with his mother to Montreal, Quebec, in 1830. At thirteen, he went to work in Grand Isle, Vermont, and later studied law in Burlington before opening a practice in Champlain, New York. He enjoyed a reputation as one of the most successful attorneys in Clinton County and, in 1850, was appointed district attorney. In testimony after his death, his mother-in-law claimed she never knew him "to get the worst end of a bargain; he was shrewd and even up to the time of his death was able to drive a good bargain." He served as a lieutenant colonel in the 153rd Regiment, New York State Volunteers, during the Civil War, from 1862 until 1863, when he resigned. It was in Plattsburgh that he met and formed the partnership with Almon Thomas, buying 30,000 acres of timberland in Township 48, which included among other high peaks, Gothics, Armstrong and the Wolf Jaws. According to Russell Carson in *Peaks and People of the Adirondacks,* Thomas immortalized his friend in 1869 when he conferred the name "Armstrong" on the 4,000-foot mountain northeast of Gothics, formerly known locally as "Mountain Brook Hump."

Both Thomas and Armstrong lived out their lives in Plattsburgh, with Thomas dying there in 1894 and Armstrong on December 31, 1895. Armstrong was found dead in his room over A. McHattie's store in Plattsburgh on New Year's Day 1896. Unfortunately, his story did not end at that point. While he accomplished much in his life, including having a mountain named for him, he had another, sadder, darker side. In February and March of 1896, the Plattsburgh *Sentinel* reported about a legal dispute involving his will... wills, possibly. He was said to have left the bulk of his considerable estate to Union College in Schenectady. The court heard testimony concerning Armstrong's erratic behavior (he was prone to late night wanderings), his paranoia (he accused his stepdaughter of trying to poison him), and his obsession with his invalid wife (he spent days searching local cemeteries for the perfect plot for her final rest).

Ed Phelps and New York lawyer Thomas Wickes, an avid trail builder, claim the first ascent of Armstrong in 1875.

At the northwestern end of the Range, rising out of Keene Valley, sits a triangle of smaller, but no less rugged, mountains: Hedgehog, Rooster Comb, and Snow. According to Jim Goodwin, the name Hedgehog is odd for an Adirondack peak, as the hedgehog is a spiny mammal native to Eurasia and Africa, not North America, and it should not be confused with the prickly porcupine.[2] Rooster Comb was changed from Cock's Comb to accommodate more sensitive tastes. The smallest of the three, Snow Mountain, with its short ascents and open-ledge views, was named for Joseph Snow, the first to own the land at its base.

The AMR

When Thomas and Armstrong bought Township 48 from lumberman Sylvanus Wells in 1866, they also acquired property inhabited by David Heald, later Hale, who had been living on Lower Ausable Lake for twelve years. He also owned a small farm at the site of the current Adirondack Mountain Reserve gate. Wells hired Heald in 1854 to build a sawmill and dam near the outlet of the lower lake. Although the land around the lakes was posted against trespass, many local guides were permitted to build camps on the Upper Lake and conduct their business guiding well-to-do summer residents.

In 1886, businessman and Keene Valley summer resident William G. Neilson learned that Thomas and Armstrong planned to sell their interest in Township 48, which included the Ausable Lakes, to lumber interests. He so loved the natural beauty of the area that he sought financial help from friends and associates in Philadelphia to buy the township and create a nature preserve. By the spring of 1887, he had formed a company called the Adirondack Mountain Reserve (AMR) and purchased approximately 25,000 acres of prime Adirondack land. The company's mission was not only to protect the land around the Ausable Lakes but also to make it self-sufficient through mining, lumbering, and the selling and leasing of real estate. The first year, they improved the road to the lakes, making it passable by wagon. They built the St. Hubert's Inn, later reorganized as the Ausable Club, in 1890. The golf course, which affords a spectacular view across to the Giant of the Valley, was laid out in 1907.

The AMR continued to expand its holdings by buying and selling property until the years following World War I brought difficult financial times for the organization. To raise money and still protect some of the most environmentally fragile acreage in the Adirondacks, in 1923 the AMR sold, among other parcels, Mount Marcy, Johns Brook, and the northern slopes of the Lower Range to New York State, retaining the summits of the Great Range, from Haystack to Lower Wolf Jaw. In 1978, facing an ever increasing tax burden that threatened the future of the AMR, they sold the remaining summits above 2,500 feet to the state. Today, the boundary is marked by signs posted on the trails leading south off the ridge.

The ATIS

Beaver Meadow Falls

For trampers, bird watchers, strollers, mountain climbers, and those wishing to commune with nature, AMR stewardship has meant fairly easy access to some of the most spectacular terrain in the Adirondacks. In 1897, the AMR made the wilderness even more accessible when they formed the Adirondack Trail Improvement Society (ATIS) to build and maintain trails in Keene Valley, St. Huberts, and the Ausable Lakes area. According to Russell Carson in *Peaks and People of the Adirondacks,* Thomas Wickes laid out the Gothics Trail, which passes near the soul-inspiring Beaver Meadow Falls, as early as 1886. The ATIS built both the W. A. White Trail, named for a founding member and president (from 1897 to 1927), and the Wedge Brook Trail in 1928, which passes by the pleasing Wedge Brook Cascades. The most recent trail, and arguably the most scenic, was built in 1966 by Jim and Tony Goodwin and Burns Foster, grandson of an AMR member. Named for Alfred E. Weld, the AMR member who financed the project, it includes a short side trip to the 150-foot drop of iridescent Rainbow Falls and a steep, rugged climb over precipitous Pyramid Peak.

The Johns Brook Valley and the ADK

For the guides of the late 1800s, AMR stewardship and the building of trails meant the beginning of the end of their way of life. Although they were allowed to maintain their camps on the Upper Lake, the AMR imposed bans on hunting and the building of new camps as well as restrictions on fishing. Unwilling to live by the new rules, guide Mel Hathaway packed his belongings and moved almost directly north on the other side of the Lower Range to the Johns Brook Valley, where he took up residence in the former business office of the J. & J. Rogers Company of Au Sable Forks. His tenancy, however, did not last long.

J. & J. Rogers began logging in the Johns Brook Valley at about the same time Colvin first climbed Gothics. According to longtime Keene Valley resident Tony Goodwin, the brook was probably named for John Gibbs who owned the land at the confluence of Johns Brook and the Ausable River, although the commonness of the name "John" makes attribution difficult. Because the water flow was unreliable, Johns Brook could not be used for driving logs. Consequently, Rogers built a tote road along the south bank of the brook. According to Jim Goodwin in his memoir *And Gladly Guide, Reflections on a Life in the Mountains,* "At the height of the lumbering operations, modern four-wheel drive vehicles could easily have driven to the present site of Johns Brook Lodge."

By 1923, Rogers had mostly clear cut the valley of saleable timber and decided to sell the land along Johns Brook rather than wait twenty to thirty years for a new profitable crop. For the fledgling Adirondack Mountain Club (ADK), that decision could not have come at a better time.

The burro Nubbins and the Johns Brook Lodge hut crew of 1946: Tris Coffin, Mary Dittmar, and Ditt Dittmar. Note that the Lower Range could be seen from JBL.

The founders of ADK had among their organizational goals a desire to cut trails and to build permanent camps in the Adirondacks. The agreement they made with J. & J. Rogers included a gift of 15.5 acres along Johns Brook and a $15,000 mortgage. Forty-Sixer #2 George Marshall, ADK Conservation Chair A. S. Houghton, and state Supervisor of Forests Clifford Pettis selected the site for the lodge: the former Rogers office and home to Mel Hathaway. Naturally, the septuagenarian hermit was not anxious to move again. He rejected the ADK's offer to relocate his homestead to another site and, after much negotiation, opted instead to leave his beloved valley to live with his daughter in Syracuse.

Trails

In 1924, the ADK began moving materials to the lodge site via the Rogers tote road, soon to be the Southside Trail, and Johns Brook Lodge opened for business in July 1925. This also marked the beginning of serious trail building in the region with the Range Trail from Gothics to Armstrong in 1926, the Woodsfall Trail to Wolf Jaws Notch in 1927, the trail between Upper Wolf Jaw and Armstrong in 1928, and the reopening of the Phelps Trail from the Garden parking area to Johns Brook Lodge in 1931, a project necessitated by frequent flooding of the Southside Trail. In 1949, the ATIS ceded maintenance of the Range Trail from Gothics to Armstrong and the Wolf Jaw Connector to the club.

The Orebed Brook Trail follows the route of an old logging tote road to the col between Gothics and Saddleback. The ADK maintained a lean-to at the col until it burned in 1969. From that site, the Range Trail climbs steeply up Gothics over an open rock face, with cables bolted into the gneiss to aid the squeamish hiker. The ADK's 1950 guidebook described this section: "The cable here gives assistance where most needed. Care should be exercised in using the cable which may have frayed strands. A drop of 700 ft. in a ¼ mile precipitates one into the col between Gothics and Saddleback."

The aluminum cables became brittle over time and individual strands frayed and broke. Because hikers often cut their hands while hanging on, the DEC deemed the cables dangerous and removed them. For a time, discussion centered around whether or not to replace them. Since the cables tended to keep hikers on the designated trail, the DEC decided to replace them but with steel instead of aluminum. On September 11, 2005, Pete (#3202W) and J. R. Hickey (#3824), Johns Brook Interior Outpost Caretaker Dan Robinson and Assistant Ranger Liz Grades hoisted 80 pound packs of cable and garden hose at the outpost and headed toward Gothics. They planned to quickly install the cables, thread them through the rubber hose – to make them less slippery and easier to grab onto – then finish the day feasting on camp-cooked green chili enchiladas. According to Pete, "It didn't take long to install the cables, but when it came to threading them through the hose, it went great for the first 5 feet or so, but then friction took over. It took much longer to thread one section of hose than it did installing the cables. After one was done, we decided that it wasn't a good idea. Maybe if we had some kind of lubricant, it would have worked, but it would have taken several days to do it the way we were doing it. At the end, we were moving it a half inch at a time." The enchiladas were delicious.

The ADK also cut a trail up Short Job, not far from Johns Brook Lodge, to a lookout which offers a panoramic view of the major peaks of the Lower Range.

Camp Grace, Winter Camp, and Camp O'Brien

In 1929, Keene Valley guide Homer Brown sold property to the ADK along the south side of Johns Brook, including two hunting camps, Camp Grace (named for his wife) and Thistle Dhu ("This'll do"), which became Winter Camp. Up to that time, most activities at Johns Brook Lodge centered on the short summer season, although that didn't stop one hardy, but ill-advised, crew from spending a frigid, miserable night in the new lodge. All that changed in 1932 when Lake Placid hosted the Olympics and winter recreation became *de rigueur*. The ADK responded by insulating Thistle Dhu to create "Winter Camp." The original Grace Camp burned in 1967, was rebuilt to accommodate winter use in 1968, and was moved away from the brook to its current location in 1991.[3]

When Peggy O'Brien, sister of Jim Goodwin, took over as chair of the Johns Brook Lodge Committee in 1965, the lodge was suffering from years of genteel neglect and rodent infestation. During her tenure, she oversaw the cleaning and renovation of the lodge and installation of appliances. She wrote the JBL manual which is still in use. To recognize her years of service, the ADK built the current Camp Peggy O'Brien, away from the brook, in 1989 to replace Winter Camp which they removed a year later. In addition to the main lodge and two camps, the ADK owns the Henry Young Crew Cabin a short distance from the lodge, named for a former ADK president and used to accommodate field staff. In the winter the cabin is used as a warming hut maintained by ADK volunteers who have a radio to contact the Department of Environmental Conservation (DEC) in case of an emergency. All climbers are welcomed with warm beverages and heat.

The Johns Brook Valley is also home to a DEC cabin at the site of a ramp used by J. & J. Rogers to load logs on sledges for transportation to Keene Flats. According to Jim Goodwin, the DEC built the cabin in the 1950s, probably 1955, and now staffs it with a caretaker in summer. The suspension bridge behind the cabin was closed for several years because it had suffered a broken steel girder. The refurbished bridge opened again in 2008. One mile below the bridge is the ADK Keene Valley Chapter lean-to and the "Little Flume" where generations of Adirondackers have cooled off on hot summer afternoons.

Were Verplanck Colvin, Ed Phelps, and Roderick McKenzie to stand atop Gothics today, their view would not be much different from that of 1875, thanks to the prescient stewardship of the Adirondack Mountain Reserve, the Adirondack Mountain Club, and New York State. They would still find patches of hardy Labrador tea clinging to the sparse soil, see over to the precipitous rock faces of syenite gneiss on Pyramid Peak, look down on the man-made structures at the outlet of the Lower Ausable Lake and, despite a half century of logging, be awed by the beauty of acres of wild, unbroken forest.

Endnotes

1. Indeed, Upper Ausable Lake is fully visible from elsewhere along Gothics' summit ridge.
2. Porcupines were often called hedgehogs in America by its early English settlers, and there are still people who regularly call porcupines hedgehogs in this country. The name *porcupine* came to us, most likely from French Canada. Derived from Old French and Provençal, it literally means "hog with spines."
3. The moving of Camp Grace (Grace Camp) was a project that used both a helicopter and strong backs. Bob Grimm (#3020W) explains: "The current Grace Camp was built after the original burned... It was then relocated ... in 1991 to its current location. Building material and construction tools were flown in by helicopter at the annual JBL airlift in late April. The work was done in the first week of May, 'by hand.' The only power tool was a rented electric generator to run a skill saw, the generator was then carried out for return to the rental company. At the following JBL work weekend (Mothers Day), the inside was totally renovated. The following spring the front porch was added and the privy moved up the hill also."

Acknowledgments

For research on the lives of Almon Thomas and Thomas Armstrong: James G. Bailey (#233), City of Plattsburgh Historian.

For research assistance on the history of the Adirondack Mountain Club: Jack Freeman (#1327W), ADK volunteer.

For assistance on the history of trail building and Adirondack Mountain Club activity in the Johns Brook Valley: Jim and Tony Goodwin.

About the Author

Mary Lou Recor, 46er #2214W, began volunteering with the 46ers by working with the trail crew. She became club secretary by winning a coin toss and subsequently served as director, vice president, and president (2003-2006). The Northville Lake Placid Trail introduced her to long-distance hiking. Consequently she spends more time sleeping in a tent and less time climbing the Adirondack High Peaks. She also volunteers with Vermont's Green Mountain Club as outing leader and guidebook editor. She lives in Colchester, Vermont.

WHITEFACE MOUNTAIN
Height: 5th – 1,483 meters (4,865 feet)
By Tim Tefft (#616)

In his 1876 edition of *The Adirondacks Illustrated,* Seneca Ray Stoddard wrote that on "the topmost part" of Whiteface, "firmly attached to the rock," he and his companions "found the card of the chief of the Adirondack Survey, a metallic disk with this inscription: 'Whiteface Mountain, Station No. 2. Verplanck Colvin, S. N. Y. Adirondack Survey, 1872.'" Stoddard continued, "All around, the surface of the rock was scarred and chiseled with the names of former visitors while on one, cut deep and clear were the words, 'Thanks be to God for the mountains!' and every heart joined with that grand old mountain peak in saying, 'thanks be to God for the mountains.'"

Numerous other inscriptions, a few of which may still be seen, covered the summit rocks of Whiteface in the late nineteenth century; most of them consisting of dates and the initials of people who had reached the top of "The Northern Sentinel." The inscriptions were carved and scratched into the stone. Mount Marcy bore similar graffiti at that time, but Whiteface was the most frequently climbed high peak of the Adirondacks and probably had been subject to the impact of "tourists" more than the "High Peak of Essex."

Native Americans passing along the Lake Champlain Valley long before Europeans arrived upon the continent were surely familiar with Whiteface, which according to tradition, in the language of the Algonquins, was called *Wa-ho-par-te-nie* – supposedly meaning "it is white."

Russell M. L. Carson in *Peaks and People of the Adirondacks* wrote that Whiteface was also called *Thei-a-no-guen,* "white head," a name also applied by Canadian Indians to the famous Mohawk chief of the eighteenth century known by whites as King Hendrick. Supposedly, too, it was called *Ou-no-war-lah,* a Mohawk word which allegedly meant "scalp mountain," a presumed reference to the appearance of the slide on the southwest flank of the mountain, as if it had been created by a giant scalping knife sliced down the mountain's side. Alfred B. Street attributed the same Indian name to Mount Colden, and it may be surmised that if the name had been applied to Colden, it would have been because that mountain has long been scarred with slides which might have appeared to have been similarly created.

Ebenezer Emmons, who climbed Whiteface in 1836, wrote that the mountain received its name "from the circumstance of a slide having on one side, laid bare the rock, which has a grayish white appearance." Emmons made mention again of the naming of the mountain in the *Geology of New York, Part II, Comprising the Survey of the Second Geological District,* 1842. He wrote that the mountain had "received its name from a slide which is known to have taken place about thirty-five years ago; it commenced within a few rods of the summit, and swept the entire length of the western slope" – the side of the mountain as viewed from Lake Placid. E. R. Wallace, in his *Descriptive Guide to the Adirondacks,* 1888, wrote that the slide had occurred "about 100 years" before.

Heaven Up-h'isted-ness!

In *A History of the Adirondacks* (1921), Alfred L. Donaldson said that the "name is said to come from a slide which occurred early in the last century and left a glare of naked rock from the summit part-way down one side of the mountain *[the Lake Placid side]*. Harvey Moody *[1808-1890]*, the old guide, placed the date of this about 1830, and said it was witnessed by an early resident of North Elba, Uncle Joe Estes, who was roofing his barn at the time. He heard a tremendous roar and rumble, and looking up, saw smoke and dust rising from the mountain. As they cleared away, a fresh and glittering scar became visible."

Donaldson continued, "There may have been a slide at this time, but not the one that gave a name to the mountain, for it was known as Whiteface many years before." In fact, because slides occur on many of the high peaks at a rate of several a century, it is highly likely that slides have appeared on the southwest flank of Whiteface with a fair degree of frequency over the last 5,000 years. For instance, on Labor Day in 1971, a new slide appeared on the Lake Placid side of the mountain. A three-day's steady rain and a four-inch downpour loosened a thin layer of soil near the summit. It flowed off the rocky upper level of the mountain and avalanched a wide, white swath. However, Stoddard in the 1895 edition of his Adirondack guidebook suggested that the slide's appearance which might have led to the naming of the mountain, whenever it might have occurred, had nothing to do with the moniker attached to it. He wrote, "Early in autumn and late in spring, it wears its white hood of snow, that obviously earned for it its name of 'Whiteface' from the Indian."

Thus there are two contending possibilities for the naming of the mountain which Carson considered to have been the first high peak to receive a name. Certainly, in late spring and early fall, when snow caps the peak but leaves its lower sides bare, the mountain appears to have a white "face" laid back and gazing towards the sky.

Geologists theorize that the basic rock of the High Peaks, anorthosite, formed deep below the surface of the earth approximately 1.2 billion years ago when, perhaps as deep as 25 kilometers below the surface, magma intruded up through rifts in earlier rock that had covered the area. A portion of the deepest anorthosite, rich in Labradorite crystals and coarsely grained, eventually, through thrust faulting, was "shoved over" some of the upper portion of anorthosite, and, with continued uplift and the erosion of the strata which had earlier covered the surface, emerged in the area which is now dominated by Mount Marcy. The original upper anorthosite emerged north of Basin. Whiteface Mountain's summit reveals some of that other rock: gabbroic anorthosite. It is a lighter colored rock than the anorthosite of the Marcy area, and when it is exposed by a landslide, it appears whiter than the anorthosite found on Marcy. So, too, the rocks atop Whiteface, containing fewer dark crystals than the stone of Marcy, are "whiter."

Russell M. L. Carson speculated that a surveyor, John Richards, climbed to the summit in 1814 when he "ran the east line of the Whiteface Mountain Tract, which is on the easterly line of Township 11, Old Military Tract." Carson noted that Richards' field notes in reference to the mountain made mention that "no vegetation grows on the top of this remarkable hill," and Carson said that the surveyor's "comments indicate that he made the short trip from the line to the top, which would require only fifteen or twenty minutes of easy travel over rock." Carson also noted that it was likely that the mountain had been climbed even before Richards was on or near its summit.

Settlement in the area of Wilmington, North Elba, and St. Armand – the towns which lie at the base of Whiteface and Esther – began in the 1790s. By 1810 the hamlet now called Wilmington had been established in what was then the town of Jay.

When he published his *Gazetteer of the State of New York* in 1813, Horatio Gates Spafford wrote a description of the Adirondacks, which were then known as the Peruvian Mountains because of their supposed mineral wealth. He said that the mountains attained their "greatest altitude... in some summits of Essex County." "The highest of these," he wrote, "is probably that called Whiteface in the Town of Jay which commands a view of Montreal, at the distance of near 80 miles." Historians have speculated that his report concerning the view from the summit (on an exceptionally clear day) means that someone had been to the top of the mountain before 1813, but there is no historic record to indicate who might have been the first to ascend the peak.

It should be noted, though, that Jacques Cartier had looked south from Hocheloga (now Montreal) in 1535 and had seen the mountains of northern New York. Undoubtedly he saw what we call Whiteface. The mountain can be seen from other points at great distance... from the valley of the St. Lawrence River to the Lake Champlain Valley, along the ridges of the Green Mountains, and, even, from the top of Mount Washington in New Hampshire. The latter peak was climbed by Darby Field in the company of "Indians" in 1642, and it had a hiking trail to its peak before 1816. Whiteface, in New York,[1] was the first of the high peaks of the Adirondacks to have an established trail to its summit, about 1860, but it was visited by several well known explorers of the region before that trail was built.

James Hall

Ebenezer Emmons made the first officially recorded ascent on September 20, 1836, in the company of Professor James Hall. They were engaged in the preliminary field work for the state geological survey of the area. According to Carson, "Emmons had suspected that there was an error in Spafford's statement of its measurement." That measurement was a "little short of 3000 feet from the level of Lake Champlain," as Spafford reported it in his discussion of the mountains of New York State. However, in his description of the town of Jay, Spafford wrote that the "noted cobble" was "about 2600 feet in height." He actually had not made an attempt to measure the height of the mountain himself but had relied on "correspondents" for his information. Lake Champlain is, on average, 93 feet above sea level. Thus, by Spafford's reckoning, Whiteface was about 3,100 feet in altitude above sea level. However, since no reference to the "base" for the estimate contained in the town of Jay description is given, one has to wonder what that base was. Possibly it was Lake Placid, which is approximately 1,850 feet in elevation. By today's measuring, Whiteface rises 3,000 feet above the level of that lake. Therefore, the figures contained in Spafford's *Gazetteer* are not necessarily as grossly inaccurate as has been previously assumed.

Using a barometer, Emmons calculated the height of Whiteface to be 4,855 feet – a remarkably accurate estimate – ten feet less than the figure assumed for the mountain's altitude today. According to Carson, the height determined by Emmons was "important at the time, for it corrected the popular fallacy that the highest peak of the Catskills was 1,200 feet higher than Whiteface, which up to that time had been called the highest peak of the Peruvian or McComb's Mountains."

From Whiteface, Emmons and Hall could see the higher peaks to the south, then "all nameless, unmeasured, and never ascended," and the Williams College professor of geology knew then that Whiteface was higher than any of the Catskill peaks but not the highest peak of the Adirondacks.

Verplanck Colvin first went up Whiteface in 1869, before he began work on his epic "Topographical Survey of the Adirondack Wilderness of New York." He returned in September 1872 with a mountain barometer with which to calculate the height of the peak, and on September 3rd climbed from Wilmington and "shortly after dark reached 'Rustic Lodge'… a log shanty…" occupying his "camping ground of 1869." Colvin reported that "the night was wintry, and the morning of the 4th showed the forest whitened with snow and ice. The altitude of the Rustic Lodge, as taken with barometer, is [4,116] feet." If Colvin's measure of the altitude of the log shanty was reasonably correct, it was probably located about where the Wilmington Trail lean-to once stood.

Colvin spent two days on Whiteface in 1872, part of the time waiting for clouds to clear so that he could measure angles and make his observations. He was delighted when "after a few dismal hours… the snow-white vapor lifted and suddenly we saw the rugged mountain crests, dark passes, blue gleaming lakes and sparkling ponds," but "more time was fretted away in waiting than consumed in work." Two "signal flags" and the survey's "No. 2" copper bolt were placed at the highest point on the summit by his workmen. Colvin, by comparing his barometric readings from the summit with synchronous readings recorded by an assistant at Wilmington, calculated the mountain's height to be 4,918 "English feet above the sea." Professor Emmons' 1836 estimate was actually more accurate, but Colvin would determine the summit's altitude more precisely in the years ahead.

On September 1, 1876, from the "notch" between Marcy and Gray Peak, the surveyor was able to make observations from which he concluded that Whiteface was "at least four hundred and fifty feet… lower than Mt. Marcy" – less than 4,894 feet above sea level – but in order to be more precise about the height of Whiteface, he was determined to measure it by having his men ascend it, from the known level of Lake Placid, all the way up, with a leveling rod. That work began in mid-September 1878. At sunrise on October 11, Colvin and some of his guides and workmen ascended the mountain on horseback from Wilmington. He reported that they "reached at dark the log camp a quarter of a mile below the summit" and that the next morning, the summit "was hidden in the clouds, which swept around our cabin and hid every thing beyond a radius of fifty to a hundred feet." Because observations from the summit would have been impossible at that time, he and his men "busied" themselves "with the construction of a stone fire-place within the log cabin, as the cold was beginning to be severe." The party slept "comfortably" that night and "at morning ascended the peak."

Anxious to determine the progress of the men working with the leveling rod up from Lake Placid, Colvin that morning (October 13) fired his revolver "as a signal," and it was "quickly answered from far down the ledges on the south-western front of the mountain and faint shouts and hurrahs below showed where the leveling party were slowly measuring their way upward along the steep, avalanche-swept path of the 'Great Slide,' along which the trail descended to Lake Placid."

After instructing the men with him to begin construction of a platform at the summit signal station (from 1872), Colvin "descended the 'slide,' clinging to the low, flattened limbs of the dwarfed trees, to prevent being suddenly precipitated down the steep incline." He reported that he "came upon the leveling party, measuring step by step up the steep ledges, sufficiently difficult to climb without any incumbrance" at a place "half a thousand feet below the summit." Colvin later returned to the summit to begin "the triangulation northward," and at "nightfall the leveling party descended to their tents westward."

The following day, "the work of both parties was resumed," and while Colvin "measured and repeated the important angles which would carry the nice determination of distances, latitudes and longitudes, westward into Franklin county, the leveling party crept upward toward the summit." At noon, Colvin took the final leveling measure which determined the mountain's precise height – which he later reported to be 4,871.655 feet above sea level.

Colvin remained on Whiteface, continuing his observations until October 27, when, at last, satisfied that "all the necessary angles had been observed," he ordered "the baggage transported back to Wilmington." In the midst of what he described as a severe storm, he, an assistant, and a guide, "burdened with knapsacks and instruments, made a hazardous descent of the icy slide" towards Lake Placid. "The trail below," he later wrote, "was found difficult owing to fallen timber brought down by the recent tornado, and it was near night when we reached Lake Placid."

That trail had been in existence for perhaps as many as a dozen years when Colvin descended it in 1878. In an article which appeared in a 1928 edition of the *Lake Placid News,* longtime guide Ellsworth Hayes (1848-1936) reported that the Lake Placid route to the summit of Whiteface was cut by his famous colleague Bill Nye about 1865. Alfred Billings Street made his first ascent of the mountain in 1858 in a pathless manner along virtually the same route. His guide was Dauphin Thompson, a young man from North Elba who, in 1859, went with one of his brothers, William, to join John Brown in his raid on the federal arsenal at Harper's Ferry, Virginia. There, in the arsenal's "engine room" Dauphin died. He was bayoneted by a United States Marine.[2]

Dauphin Thompson

Street described his ascent of Whiteface with a companion and Thompson in his *Woods and Waters: or, The Saranacs and Racket* (1860). The three began their excursion from J. V. Nash's hotel on today's Mirror Lake, then Bennett's Pond. They crossed over to Paradox Pond *(Paradox Bay)* and, from there, after Thompson "drew a boat from a thicket," crossed Lake Placid "toward Whiteface, the mountain all the while lifting his proud cone higher and higher until the summit smote the blue of the morning." Very likely, it was from today's Whiteface Landing that the three began their "three-mile ascent" at "seven in the morning."

Street wrote, "Path there was none." Early on, the ascent, he said, "was neither steep nor toilsome. Soon, however, it became obstructed by large rocks, which we clambered up, inserting our feet in the crevices, or resting them upon the mossy points and notches, and clinging to the knotted roots or branches of the firs and hemlocks."

At one point along their route, they descended to the "margin of a headlong brook" and saw, above them, " a milk-white water-fall" as it "hurled itself over frowning ledges, and foamed past and down a wild ravine until lost in leafy gloom." Street named it "the stream of the White Falls." He wrote, "The ascent now became more and more precipitous. Dead trunks blocked our way, crumbling into brown, damp flakes almost at the touch of our climbing feet; immense masses of roots erect, with corresponding hollows, thickets almost impenetrable, mossy cavities in which we plunged waist-deep, underbrush that clung around our feet like serpents, and low boughs forcing us to stoop for passage." Thus the state librarian and accomplished poet wrote one of the first accurate accounts of an Adirondack bushwhack with obstacles which "interrupted" the trekkers' progress. He also wrote about the moss they encountered, which "spread its piled velvet over almost every object – the coiling root, the mouldering log, the runnel cradled deep in the dingle, and the ledges on the levels of our way." Street's adventure had only just begun.

He wrote that suddenly "the green gloom opened into broad sunlight, and, looking out and down in that direction, I instinctively recoiled, with thrilling nerves. There, its edge within three paces, frowned a terrific chasm, cloven thousands of feet down, down through the breast of the mountain." He saw, half way down the gorge, "a floating atom" which he supposed was "an eagle tacking up the side."

Nineteenth century engraving: "Ascent of Whiteface"

"Shuddering from terror, and yet fascinated" by the "wild grandeur of the scene," he soon heard a "whoop" from Thompson ahead of him and then continued his ascent, which, he wrote, "became harder and harder, from the increasing steepness and the density of the underbrush, as well as the barricade of branches through which" they "plunged, twisting aside and breaking off limbs for passage. Frequent halts were... made, generally beside some cool, clear spring, oozing out from moist roots and mossy clefts, for deep and most delicious draughts."

"Now and then," he wrote, "a dead pine or hemlock, fallen from above, would bridge some deep ravine, offering an upward path along its broad breast and jagged points."

After another hour of "clambering," the three "broke through a dense thicket, and a startling sight met" their eyes. It was a "slant plunge of rock, perfectly smooth and sloping steeply to a sheer precipice" which lay "directly" in their path. Thompson said, "This is the Little Slide." He, to Street's professed amazement "and no little dread... planted his foot upon it with the evident intention of crossing."

"You don't mean to say that our course lies over that place!" said I.
"Sarten," returned he, "right crost."

"There's no right about it," returned I, "and hang me if I go!"

"No other way," responded the other coolly *(sic)*, and advancing toward the middle. "There aint no dannger as I knows on. These spots o' moss is the dandy to git us crost."

"They are, eh! Suppose those spots of moss should slip, where would we go then? Down that precipice as sure as we're alive! There isn't a crack in that slide – and slide it is, sure enough! – as big as a knife-blade, to squeeze a finger in, and it's as smooth as a new-washed dinner plate except the moss!"

"No dannger and no other way," returned the lad, treading over the shining surface unconcernedly as if on his cabin floor. "We can't go below it, that's sarten and we can't git above it as I knows on; at least without tuggin' and scratchin' and scrabbin' wuss than a bear climbin' a tree with a twenty pound trap on his paw. Folly me, and we'll git crost, I'll be bound."

Many a climber must, at some time, have felt as Street did that morning on the side of Whiteface. "Folly, sure enough!" he said just before he made clear his reservations about the entire enterprise: "The greatest folly is in coming here at all! climbing this savage and nearly inaccessible mountain with a hare-brained boy! Why," he continued, "that rock is like a steeple, and smooth as a looking-glass," but "finding no help for it," he said that he "stepped upon the rock, and, with my frame tingling, moved cautiously along the slope, looking steadily before me, with my companion at my right." He reached the other side and noted that he "inwardly" vowed "never again to commit such insanity." He would, however, have to cross the slide again during the descent later that day.

From the far side of the little slide, the trio continued upward, "now doubly painful" because, Street said, the mountain had become "almost perpendicular." They pulled themselves "up by branches, hanging to roots, scrambling through clefts and over ledges, until, bursting through a barrier of close underbrush," they "found" themselves "on the brink of a long, slanting pathway of granite": the "Great Slide." Street wrote, "Down it pointed, and up, up, up it sloped, a stony ladder, grey and glistening, up to the very summit which now stood boldly out against the sky." He continued as follows:

Although not nearly so steep nor so perilous, to all appearance, as the Little Slide, the thought of ascending it produced a new crawling of the nerves. I knew it must be four thousand feet in air, and that all around were tremendous chasms and dizzy precipices, over which, by one slip of the foot, I might be hurled. But the guide's figure, sharply relieved against the sky as he travelled upward, called me on, with my comrade by my side. The steepness hardly allowed us an upright position; huge boulders blocked our path; springs spread an oily, slippery ooze over the bare granite. My soles, too, from the polishing of the dead leaves and pine-needles, had become like glass, and my tread, consequently, was not sure.

But I persevered. The scene behind us was but a glimpse of a distant region, narrow and vague. On either side, the close forest stood up to the very edges.

We had been half an hour on the Slide, and still were toiling up, up – the grey path slippery and blocked with boulders as before, when we came to a bed of pebbles and broken rock, which often rolled from under our tread, and went rattling down the Slide. A little way above stood the summit – a high rampart of rock. Suddenly we turned from the Slide into a slight track winding upward, and went along a rocky platform or gallery, jutting from the sides of the rampart. Glancing to the left, I shuddered at the dizzy chasm below, and grasped a bush instinctively. A few more winding steps to the right, and I stood upon the summit.

A deliciously cool wind was flowing over the peak, as if the air was stirred by a mighty fan.

I threw myself beside my companion upon the ground; I drew in with delight the nectarean air; my heated pulses grew calm, and the dews of my long struggle with the mountain dried upon my forehead.

From the peak, soon thereafter, Street saw "a most grand and enchanting prospect" which included Lake Placid, "studded with emerald island-gems" to the south; "a cultivated region, meadows and grain-fields, the roofs of Wilmington, and the two villages of Jay" to the northeast; and, to the east, in the words of Dauphin Thompson, "The Green Mountains, in old Varmount."

> Southward rose the Adirondack range, breaking the sky with its pointed peaks. A single cloud stood over Tahawus like a plume – the only sign of life between me and it, being the smooth, bright fields of North Elba; and I exulted in the feeling that I had conquered a height little inferior, if at all, to his imperial crest.

Briefly Street took notice of a "little meek-eyed blossom, struggling through the ungenial moss" at his feet and listened as Thompson discussed an obviously incorrect notion of "a heap o' ... fools" that there was a pond atop the mountain. The three men remained on the summit for two hours before beginning their descent by the route they had followed during their ascent. The climb had taken them seven hours. The trip down to "the welcome waters of Lake Placid, crimson... in the last lustre of sunset" required but four hours.

About a decade later, Street returned to the summit of Whiteface. His second ascent was made along a much less formidable route: one, according to El Hayes, that had been cut by an "old guide" Andrew Hickock in 1860. Laura and Guy Waterman in their book, *Forest and Crag* (Boston: Appalachian Mountain Club, 1989) wrote that Hickock had built that "first formal trail" of the Adirondacks "by 1859." Street, in *The Indian Pass* (New York, Hurd and Houghton, 1869), said that Hickock "had cut a road nearly straight to the crest. In fact," he continued, "it is so steep on account of its straightness, that the only wonder is he did not tumble over backward while performing his task."

Street and his guides and Hickock started up the mountain at "four o'clock in the afternoon." They passed "a rough field or two in the rear of Hickock's dwelling, and crossing the Ausable River by a wooden bridge, entered a smooth, grassy glade of the forest at the foot of the Titan. Up the ascending track (here a broad one) we went in single file."

"Soon," Street reported, "there was a white flashing among the leaves, with a pleasant rumble crumbling on the ear; a mountain-stream leaping down among its green rocks, bearing tidings in the foam of its descent, as to the steepness of its birthplace. No name had yet been affixed to the torrent, but, as I saw it glittering in its craggy home, I named it 'The White Ribbon.'"

On the group went as the sun set and twilight was followed by the rising of the moon. Street said that there was "No turning, but straight upward with continuous strain. Straight as the honey-bee's flight, or the robin's." Further he commented, "Evidently, Hickock fastened his eye to the top, and to the top he went (as well as he could), 'straight as a string.'"

> "You think this here mite o'ground steep, don't you?" said Hickock, as I slipped, in clambering up an ascent blunt as a lynx's snout.
> "Well, it's no more to be named at the same time o' day with a spot up thereaway, than a puff-ball with a pipping apple!"
> That spot haunted Hickock.
> "It is rather steep here, isn't it?" said he.
> "Ah – ah – ah – yes, confoundedly so!" panted I...
>
> By and by I saw an ascent like a grenadier's cap.
> "We don't go up that place, Hickock, surely!"
> "That's just the place we do go up! Why, that's the place I've been tellin' you of!"

Street did "claw up" that spot and thought, "by Jove," that at the top of it he had achieved the mountain's summit. However, "it was only a clearing with a shanty lurking in a deep hollow." While the guides – probably Loyal A. Merrill and Robert Blinn – cut "shanty-wood" for a fire, the poet contemplated a trip by moonlight to the summit, but after a "wild-wood supper" and taking shelter in the shanty, he was soon in the "Land of Dreams."

Hickock's shanty was probably located near the site later occupied by a lean-to below the Whiteface Memorial Highway's Wilmington Turn retaining wall. It was the first such structure built for the use of "tourists" on a mountain in the Adirondacks, but it was very primitive compared to two hotels which had been built at the top of New Hampshire's Mount Washington in the 1850s. By the middle of that decade, Mount Washington had a trail to its summit wide enough to accommodate wagons.

The next morning, which dawned with clouds and threatened rain, the party started upward again, passing "through the rapidly diminishing trees," and eventually emerging "upon the bare summit, – a long ridge running northeasterly, with a sudden dropping of the prospect." They ascended the ridge, "a steep, widening, but low cone, with a spacious area at the top, and the pinnacle was won!"

Street noted that on the summit, "In a hollow of the rocks, stone walls had been rudely built, with boards laid on top – a mountain shanty." Of the view he wrote, "At first, all is one vast stretch of mist, an ocean over which are thickly scattered mountain-tops like islands," for he and his party were above the clouds which shrouded the valleys of the Ausable and the Saranac. He continued, "A magnificent prospect indeed, with the vapor lending it vagueness and mystery. Such might have been chaos, ere 'the Spirit of God moved upon the waters.'" Soon, however, the mist rose, the sun appeared, "And see! a multitude of pinnacles with one peak soaring over all, rosy in the sunrise! Aha! Tahawus, kinging it over his realm as usual!" He also mentioned seeing Lake Placid, "the portal of the Indian Pass," McIntyre, Keene Valley at the "feet of the Ausable Mountains," and "the lake of Corlear" (Lake Champlain) as well as the Saranac Lakes, the Raquette River, and both Big Tupper and Little Tupper lakes.

As the "brief sunlight faded" and rain began to fall, the party started down the mountain, to the clearing of the shanty and then down the precipitous "Hickock's Chuckle." Street wrote, "I went down by digging my heels in, and sliding down, with my eyes shut, trusting to faith. Hickock went down with four strides and a half, the half scattering a mud puddle all over my blue hunting-shirt."

> Down, down, down! At last I concluded to slip all control over my person, and "let it go." I have an indistinct recollection of being wafted down an enormous descent until I heard a rumbling... "The White Ribbon."

A short time later the party reached the stream along which they had the afternoon before begun their ascent, and before the day was over, having left Hickock at his home, Street and his guides were traveling by wagon west, through "Whiteface Clove" or "Wilmington Notch" on their way to Scott's at North Elba.

As Street was celebrating Whiteface in the turgid sublime prose of *Woods and Waters*, the eruption of the Civil War put recreation in the Adirondacks on hold, but the mountain was not forgotten. James Russell Lowell, who had seen Whiteface in 1858 on his journeys to and from the Philosophers Camp *[see Sharp Swan's chapter about the Seward Range]* was called upon to create a poem at war's end, "Ode Recited at the Commemoration of the Living and Dead Soldiers of Harvard University, July 21, 1865." In it, referencing the preservation of the

Union, he exorted, "... from every mountain-peak/ Let beacon-fire to answering beacon speak,/ Katahdin tell Monadnock, Whiteface he,/ And so leap on in light from sea to sea,/ Till the glad news be sent/ Across a kindling continent,/ Making earth feel more firm and air breathe braver: 'Be proud! for she is saved, and all have helped to save her!...'"

Seneca Ray Stoddard, in the early editions of his *The Adirondacks Illustrated,* described an excursion he made in the fall of 1873 to the top of "Old Whiteface" along a "Pony Trail" from Wilmington. "George Weston..." Stoddard wrote, "cut a road to the top of the mountain and built a little house up there." He "soon lost all *his* money and sold out to Sidney Weston," the proprietor of the Whiteface Mountain House who accompanied Stoddard and "the Professor" to the crest of the pinnacle "for the grandest mountain view to be had in the Adirondacks."

Horses and Riders on Whiteface
From *The Adirondacks Illustrated,* **1873**

Stoddard noted that they began their trip "at nine in the morning, with the thermometer at 48." They traveled on a wagon for the first two miles of the excursion and, on horse back, "proceeded up the bridle path toward the summit, traveling about a mile westerly then turning toward the south," at which point they "entered the standing timber and began the ascent in earnest." This was the same path by which Colvin was to ascend Whiteface in 1878.

Carson presumed the date for the construction of the pony trail to have been "about 1872 or a little later," but El Hayes, who "was in charge of this trail for the Hotel Whiteface in the summer of 1871," believed that it had been built "about 1870."[3] Hayes mentioned "a cabin below the summit" where he "kept supplies for overnight guests including a brand new 'spy glass.'"

Stoddard wrote about passing over "an open space called 'Lookout Point,' half way to the summit." There he and the members of his party "scraped whole handfuls" of blueberries from bushes which "grew thick... in ten minutes gathering all we cared for." Lookout Point was probably the minor peak we call Lookout Mountain:

> Then we resumed our course and pressed upward through the dark woods, scrambling up the steep path where great rocks alternated with pools of black muck in a semi-liquid state, trodden and mixed by horses' feet, and we wondered that horses could climb such places with a hundred and fifty to two hundred pounds of humanity on their back; but Baldwin *(one of the guides on the trip)* said to his knowledge not an accident further than being lost for a night, ever happened on the mountain. We reached the shanty, three-fourths of a mile from the summit, a little past noon, and here occurred a desperate encounter between three men on the one side and six slices of bread and butter, supported by other fixtures, on the other, which resulted in their total defeat and destruction.

"The shanty," wrote Stoddard, "is in a small clearing, at the highest point where wood and water can be obtained, has log sides, with a roof, part canvass, part bark. Within is a parlor and cook stove; along one side, raised a little above the floor, a platform that looked as though it might do service as Brigham Young's family bedstead, was covered with spruce and

SUMMIT OF WHITEFACE MOUNTAIN.

From *The Adirondacks Illustrated*

hemlock branches, and blankets. A sort of cross between a stairway and ladder led up to the ladies' dormitory under the sharp roof, through which the stars could peep in places. Here, in the bed which was over nearly the entire floor, 'permiscus like,' we could discover signs of the tender feeling with which the fair sex was regarded – in the springy moss and fine leaves which had been stripped from the hemlock branches, on which the lords of creation slept down below. The pipe from the stove in the lower room, where the fire can be kept roaring all night, passed up through this one, and altogether it was a cosy, jolly, fun-provoking place to be in, where, as our guide remarked, 'if there was any fun in a fellow it was going to show itself.' We, in imitation of others before us who had written their names in every conceivable and reachable place in the building, registered and proceeded on our way to the summit."

The guide, Baldwin, told Stoddard that hundreds of people rode to the top of Whiteface each year. He mentioned the family of a doctor from Buffalo who ascended the peak on four "very valuable" horses. The doctor's wife, Baldwin said, "a woman that would weigh two hundred," was placed on the "finest one of the lot and started, and I felt bad for I knew something would happen, and they rode those horses to the very top and just turned around and... rode down again without getting a scratch!"

Women, Baldwin said, managed to "keep the horses' backs... like a man, of course, and it makes me laugh to see them sometimes when they find that they've got to go in that way. So modest when they start, some of them, that they are dreadfully afraid of showing their *feet*, but they soon get over that and come down with colors flying." Baldwin said that Mrs. W. H. H. "Adirondack" Murray had set the fashion herself. Stoddard said, "It is needless to add that the Turkish costume is considered the most appropriate for this style of amusement."

In his guide book, Stoddard discussed the view from the summit of the mountain thoroughly and even mentioned a "mere speck – the home and resting-place of old John Brown" at North Elba.

The fourth early trail up Whiteface was one cut by Russell and Samuel French from Franklin Falls. Sandra Weber, in her *The Lure of Esther Mountain, Matriarch of the Adirondack High Peaks,* writes that the French trail was built in 1872.[4] It was wide enough to accommodate a wagon for the first four and a half miles of its route and thereafter a walking path continued two more miles to the summit and passed along its route, near the peak, another rude shelter that Russell French had built. What was then known as the "Old French Trail" was still in use in the 1930s, long after the trail from Lake Placid had been rerouted to avoid the precipitous slides of the mountain's southwest cirque and long after Hickock's "straight as a string" route from Wilmington had ceased to exist. In the *Guide to Adirondack Trails, Northeastern Section,* edited by future Forty-Sixer Dr. Orra Phelps (#47) and published by the Adirondack Mountain Club at Albany in 1934, the trail was fully described. Included in the description were the trail's several junctions with a cross country ski route that then looped around the base of Whiteface and its then new crossings of the Whiteface Veterans Memorial Highway. By the 1950s the trail was no longer in use. Today, its beginning, at a point four miles northwest of Wilmington on the road to Franklin Falls, is on privately owned and posted property.

Winslow C. Watson in his *Military and Civil History of the County of Essex, New York* (1869) spoke glowingly of Whiteface, saying, "This peak from its rare and admirable proportions, its bald summit, solitary isolation, and the vast preeminence of its height above surrounding objects, is a beautiful and conspicuous landmark, over a wide horizon." He continued, "A few years since it presented a spectacle of unequaled sublimity. In the heat and drought of midsummer, the combustible materials upon its summit were fired by accident or design, and during one whole night the conflagration raged, exhibiting to the gaze of hundreds, almost the splendor and awfulness of a volcanic eruption in its wild vehemence."

Fires were frequent in the Adirondacks in the nineteenth century. Much of the area near Wallface was burned before 1860. With the advance of the lumber companies in search of hardwoods for charcoal and, later, most any tree, but particularly spruce, for pulpwood, slash left behind, dry seasons, and, sometimes, sparks given off by the wheels of trains on rails, led to fires which rampaged through large tracts of forest. Particularly devastating was the great fire which swept through North Elba and portions of the town of Keene in 1903. Five years later, after other fires devastated other mountains, the state's Forest, Fish and Game Commission (precursor of the Conservation Department and the Department of Environmental Conservation) decided that fires had to be spotted, reported, and put down before they could spread over wide areas. Consequently, during the summer of 1909, the commission established its first two forest fire observation posts in the Adirondacks – one on Mount Morris near Tupper Lake and the other atop Whiteface.

Initially, the observation post on Whiteface was a tent upon a platform at the summit. The observers who manned the station were linked by telephone directly to the village of Lake Placid. Thirty-eight fires were spotted and reported by the observers that first summer, but a difficulty was quickly noted: the men manning the station often had "to contend with... a hazy or smoky atmosphere" and on many an occasion "the mountains were shut in by clouds." The district manager of the fire district thereafter recommended that future observation posts, which were to be placed atop towers, should be spaced "not over fifteen miles apart."

Eventually there were 49 fire towers in the Adirondack Park. The one on Whiteface, which replaced the temporary tent shelter, was ready for the 1915 season. Sam Cheetham, who was born at Hartford, Connecticut, contracted tuberculosis and moved to Saranac Lake – where he could see Whiteface Mountain. Even though at the time of his initial convalescence he was able to climb stairs only on his hands and knees, he vowed to climb the mountain someday. On June 6, 1915, he did. He was the peak's first fire tower observer. In 1972, the mountain's last fire tower was dismantled and removed to Blue Mountain Lake, where it stands today at the Adirondack Museum.

The mountain, as already noted, had been the site of other structures, including two of Colvin's summit signals, the second built directly upon the summit above the drill hole which had held his No. 2 survey bolt. He noted in his 1897 report that the bolt had "been removed... probably taken by some tourist as a souvenir." Iron ring bolts "and some small holes in which the feet of the tripod of the theodolites" *(which he had employed to make his triangulation observations)* had been set were also still to be found around the summit rock in the early twentieth century. The signal tower was removed, much of it used for fire wood, soon after 1900.

In 1909, not far from the fire observers' tent platform, a new structure also was raised on Whiteface: The *Elizabethtown Post,* in the third week of August reported the construction:

> Already the only mountain in the Adirondacks equipped with a telephone service, Whiteface has this week assumed additional distinction through the opening on its summit of an embryo "tip-top" house. Ashley Maynard, of Wilmington a guide for many years in this vicinity, has erected a very comfortable log camp near the summit of the peak, and the mountain climbers are rejoicing accordingly, for now they can not only telephone their safe arrival back to their friends in Lake Placid and elsewhere but they can make a stay of several days and nights on the summit if they desire.

After the construction of the "castle" at the head of the parking area on the Whiteface Veterans Memorial Highway, a pay telephone was installed there, and climbers and tourists thereafter were able to communicate with the world below. Today, with cell phones ubiquitous, calls are made even from the summit rock.

Russell Carson remarked in *Peaks and People of the Adirondacks* (1927) that "an automobile road to the top of Whiteface" had been proposed. He wrote, "Mount Washington, in the White Mountains, in addition to its trails, has

The shelter on Whiteface was still in place when Russell Carson (middle) and Herb Clark (right) posed for this picture.

both an auto road and railroad. Its summit has been desecrated and made filthy by careless picnickers, who, having attained the summit without effort, were unappreciative and indifferent about leaving it in such a condition that others who came after them might enjoy the pleasure that an undefiled mountain top affords. A few spots should be left for those who enjoy the out-of-doors on foot." He hoped that the road to the top would not be built.

Mount Washington's carriage road was completed in 1861, its cog railroad opened in 1869, and in 1899 a Stanley Locomobile climbed the mountain on the carriage road. By 1911, that route had become an "auto road." The voters of the state of New York, in November 1927, approved an amendment to the "Forever Wild" clause of the state constitution which allowed the building of the Whiteface highway as a memorial to the men who had fought the Great War (World War I). Governor Franklin D. Roosevelt "turned the first shovelful of earth to begin the building" of the highway on September 11, 1929, and "actual construction was started on Christmas Day, 1931." Through the depth of the Depression, construction of the roadway from Wilmington to the parking area "273 vertical feet" below the summit went on, but only during the clement weather after the winter of 1931-32. The "Castle" at the head of the parking area, the "summit shelter," the elevator to the summit and its approach tunnel, the fifth-of-a-mile walkway up the northwest arête, and the toll house at Lake Stevens were also built as part of the massive project, one of the most ambitious of the time. The cost was $1,250,000.[5]

When the highway opened to traffic on July 20, 1935, the first vehicle to pass the toll gate was a 50-year-old horse-drawn stagecoach that had once carried mail between Port Kent and Paul Smiths.[6] Franklin D. Roosevelt, whose father, James, had been an original member of the Tahawus Club, returned to Wilmington on September 14, 1935, to dedicate the completed highway as a "Memorial to the World War Dead of New York State, in the presence of a throng assembled at the summit."[7]

People who drove up Whiteface walking to the summit in the 1930s

Actually, the ceremony took place in the area where the Castle would later be built. The President, who had suffered from polio, was, of course, unable to walk to the top of the mountain, and the 424-foot-long elevator access tunnel and "modern electric elevator, through the heart of the rock summit" had not yet been built. A photograph of the occasion shows the President standing in the midst of the "throng" behind a lectern bearing the great seal of the United States. A large balsam fir had been brought to the site for the dedication and numerous others flanked the retaining wall that overlooks Lake Placid. Three years later, the Castle, the tunnel and elevator, and the summit house were completed, and in 1952 an electric light was installed on top of the summit structure as an "eternal flame" to shine through the night in memory of veterans who sacrificed their lives for the country. The highway was rededicated in 1985 by Governor Mario Cuomo as a memorial to the veterans of all of America's wars since the Revolution.

Whiteface was already the most frequently photographed mountain in the Adirondacks, especially as viewed from the village of Lake Placid. After tourists began to ascend it via the highway, it became the mountain from which the most photographs are taken. A vast variety of souvenir items from patches and pennants to plates and cups have also been produced, many of them bought by those who have climbed to the top after going up the highway in cars. The road is usually open, depending upon weather conditions, from mid-May to mid-October. Originally the "toll" was one dollar per car's passenger, with a "half rate for children under twelve." The toll, now inflated,[8] has purchased passage to the peak for as many as six million people. On one day alone, before 1940, more than 3,000 people went to the summit.

Whiteface was not the scene of activity during the 1932 Winter Olympics, because the games did not include alpine events, but the cross country ski loop around the base of the mountain was developed about that time. It is described in the 1934 *Guide to Adirondack Trails*. A few pioneering skiers apparently followed that trail to the old French trail from Franklin Falls to ascend Whiteface in winter, but the first recorded ski ascent of the mountain was that of a Norwegian scientist, author, explorer, and winter sports enthusiast, Fridtjof Nansen. He skied up and down Whiteface in 1912.

The first commercial ski area in the Adirondacks was also built on Whiteface. After voters agreed to amend the state constitution to allow for the construction of ski trails on Whiteface (but not on the side of the mountain above Lake Placid) in November 1941, Whiteface boasted just a year later that it was the largest ski area in New York, but the construction of the ski area at Marble Mountain actually began after World War II. The primary area was accessed from the memorial highway at today's Atmospheric Sciences Research Center, and skiers were carried on the backs of trucks and Sno-Cats to the upper level on the east flank of the mountain near the Wilmington Turn. The *Adirondack Record - Elizabethtown Post* reported at Thanksgiving time in 1952 that, with two feet of snow at the top of the mountain, "preparations" were "practically complete for the opening of the skiing season and that the "network of trails at both the 2,400 foot and 4,400 foot levels" had been "cleared of debris and the grass base clipped, leaving a smooth surface for skiing." At that time the Marble Mountain T-bar took skiers to the head of four trails, and five rope tows "near the summit of the big peak," had been "readied for use." The operation was reasonably successful in the late 1940s, but a few winters of sparse snow led to the construction, beginning in 1956, of the newer area on the east flank southwest of Wilmington. Governor W. Averell Harriman,[9] during the 1958 dedication of the new Whiteface Mountain Ski Center, rode the "first" chairlift up the mountain. The lift broke down and left the Governor suspended in mid-air for more than an hour and a half.

The alpine events of the 1980 Winter Olympics were run at the center, which has maintained for more than thirty years that it has the greatest vertical drop (3,430 feet) of any ski area in the eastern United States. The natural slides high on the mountain's southeast side – described by the Olympic Regional Development Authority (which runs the ski area) as "35 acres of expert extreme adventure terrain" – are rarely opened to skiers "due to safety hazards," but with modern, upgraded snow making capability (190 guns, more than 30 miles of pipe), when conditions are good, Whiteface Mountain has lots of terrain for skiers and snowboarders.

Work began in August 2007 to open additional ski terrain on the southeast flank of Lookout Mountain. The new trails (three of which are rated for expert skiers) cover 6.5 miles and bring the resort area's total skiable length very close to the maximum size allowed by state law, 25 miles. The new trails opened during the 2008-2009 ski season.

The skier who approaches the entrance to the ski center today from Lake Placid passes along state highway 86 through Wilmington Notch, a pass created by ancient glaciers and the West Branch of the Ausable River. In the nineteenth century, a stage coach road from Au Sable Forks to Saranac Lake passed through the notch, which the writers of the time considered to be a feature of nature surpassed in sublimity only by Indian Pass. Further on, going towards the entrance to the ski center, one passes High Falls Gorge, a tourist destination which features walkways along and bridges over the West Branch. The river's most spectacular waterfall is within the confines of the attraction.

The Wilmington Road in the 1930s

About two miles west of Wilmington, right next to the memorial highway and a half mile before the toll house, is the nation's oldest theme park, Santa's Workshop at North Pole. Designed by Arto Monaco (a former cartoonist for Walt Disney and later developer of Upper Jay's Land of Makebelieve and inventor of the game Otello), Santa's Workshop was operated by Julian Reiss and Harold Fortune. It opened to the public in 1949 and had its heyday in the 1950s and 1960s. In 1954, between June and November, 230,000 children and 470,000 adults visited the attraction. At times, the parking area at North Pole was so packed that traffic up the memorial highway to the site was at a standstill all the way down to Wilmington. The theme park fell on hard times in the 1990s and was sold. It failed to open one year, but by 2004 it was back in business.

Heaven Up-h'isted-ness!

An interesting meteorological phenomenon has been witnessed on Whiteface a number of times. According to Carson, Peter F. Schofield saw a startling phenomenon, "Ulloa's Rings," from the summit of the mountain during the summer of 1872. Schofield "suggested the euphonious title, 'The Spectre of the Adirondacks' for the ghostly visitor." Carson quoted Schofield as follows:

> At the time I was viewing this unique and interesting spectacle, the rising sun was shining from an unclouded sky, and just below the crest of the mountain was a huge bank of vapour lacking the closer texture of a cloud. Standing between this and a brilliant sun, my shadow, projected upon this background of vapour, was also surrounded and set off by an elongated, oval halo of prismatic hues. This latter effect was due, of course, to the penetration of the vapour drops by the sun's rays, to the reflection and refraction of these and their final decomposition into their prismatic colours displayed in this rainbow-like exhibit. As I walked along the crest of the mountain, this aerial companion keeping abreast of me imitated my every gesture and movement until, with the breaking up and dissipation of the vapour, it melted away into thin air.

Verplanck Colvin, in his 1879 report to the state legislature, wrote of witnessing the phenomenon on several occasions during his stay atop Whiteface the year before. He said, "It seemed not to be quite the same as that observed by Ulloa, being more brilliant, and differing in the color of one band. The center of the anthelia was roseate, the first ring pale purplish blue, the second yellow followed by a narrow band of green, beyond this a yellowish red band was succeeded by one of a deep, darkish red tint, after which the blue again appeared, the *green*, then yellow and red." He continued, "Cast against the surface of a dense frost-cloud this strange appearance excited awe and admiration; while the dim figure of the observer, with arms extended, appeared reproduced at the centre of the anthelia, like a shadowy cross standing upon the faint, ghost-like figure of the mountain."

Colvin also noted that the phenomenon differed that day from other instances of it which he had witnessed "in that several persons could at times see themselves together reproduced in shadowy form at the centre of the bow." He included a plate depicting "Ulloa's Rings" in his *Seventh Report*. The picture shows a person, presumably Colvin himself, standing atop the mountain's summit rock with arms outstretched. The "ghost-like figure" appears above and beyond him surrounded by the bands of color Colvin had detailed in his text.

Post card view of Whiteface from Lake Placid

As early as 1910, groups of young men and their counselors from Camp Pok-O-Moonshine began making regular ascents of Whiteface. They walked all the way from the camp on Long Pond in Willsboro, through the towns of Lewis and Jay, to Wilmington to reach the base of the mountain. After following the course of the old Weston trail to the summit, they descended the Lake Placid trail to Whiteface Landing and took a boat to the village of Lake Placid, where they often went to the movies as a special treat before they continued their three or four-day trip through North Elba to Marcy Dam, up and over Mount Marcy, and down to Keene Valley before returning to the camp. When good roads and motor vehicles became available in the 1930s the tradition of those "Marcy" trips ended, but the camp's interest in sending out hiking expeditions continued. In the late 1950s the tradition was renewed when another group of boys and counselors recreated the trip and walked all the way to Keene Valley via Whiteface and Marcy. Since that time, every six years or so, the trips have been renewed.

The adventure shared by all who have climbed the Forty-Six began, in a sense, on August 1, 1918, when two teenaged brothers, Robert and George Marshall; a friend, Carl Poser; and their guide, Herbert Clark, reached the top of Whiteface. It was the first 4,000-foot peak climbed by the four. The Marshalls and Clark would go on to climb all forty-six. They completed their adventure on Mount Emmons on June 10, 1925. The Forty-Sixers did not organize as a club – the Forty-Sixers of Troy – until 1937; and the organization did not become the Adirondack Forty-Sixers until 1948, the year when the Marshalls and Clark were recognized as the first Forty-Sixers, with Clark as Number 1, George as Number 2, and Robert as Number 3.

Herbert Malcolm (#5) could claim the earliest ascent of Whiteface by any club member. He climbed the peak in 1907. The first club member to finish his Forty-Six on the peak was John Alexander (#78) in November 1949. Since that time the peak has witnessed many other "finishes."

When he climbed Whiteface in 1836, Ebenezer Emmons observed the flora of the peak, and he wrote in his 1842 *Geology of the Second District* that the mountain had "a greater extent of surface upon its top than any other mountain of the northern counties; and hence, as a botanical field," it would "exceed the other summits for yielding a harvest of alpine plants." Bearberry willow, deer's hair sedge, mountain sandwort, Lapland rosebay, map lichen, three-toothed cinquefoil, alpine goldenrod, Boott's rattlesnake root, dwarf birch, black crowberry, snowberry, and diapensia, among other alpine zone plants may be found above tree-line on Whiteface; but the mountain has been disturbed, more than obviously, by the presence and activities of man. The summit has been visited by millions of people. It is nearly crowded with its stone summit shelter, its television and cellular phone masts, and its three-story, cedar-shake covered, round atmospheric research observatory. The mountain has witnessed more human impact than any other in the Adirondacks.

Former Forty-Sixer President Edwin Ketchledge (#507) did much to help preserve the alpine plant community at the summit. In the late 1990s, with the help of volunteers, including other Forty-Sixers, he used stones from around the summit to define areas where tourists and hikers should not walk when they are enjoying the views from the mountain. Niches where fragile summit vegetation was growing or could expand its growth were defined and stabilized. In a short period of time, some portions of the summit, which might have been trampled and destroyed, were preserved.

"Ketch" was also involved in turning the walkway from the Castle to the summit into a nature walk, with interpretive signs explaining the geological features and some of the flora seen along the way. Further, he organized the Whiteface Mountain Preservation and Resource Association, an educational corporation which was intended to "provide the public with information and interpretation" of the memorial highway "and its environs" as well as to continue to employ the mountain's existing resources, artifacts, and natural objects for the education of the people. With the help of volunteers, the association established an interpretive center in the toll house building at Lake Stevens, but that facility is now unmanned. Support for the project lapsed and Ketch was unable to reinvigorate it without a greater commitment of funding and support from the Olympic Regional Development Authority.

Dr. Ketchledge believed that a greater effort must be made to educate people about the impact they have on the natural environment. He said that an opportunity to do so is being missed. The state of New York, with the help of volunteers, could do much to develop an "outdoor laboratory" which could "dramatically convey some sense of the natural history of the Adirondacks" and the impact upon it by humans. He felt that such education is extremely important and that there is no better place – as along the highway and at the summit and the interpretive center – anywhere in the state to provide such an education.

The mountain indeed exhibits, dramatically, the impact of humans on the natural environment – from concrete and asphalt to cedar shakes and cell phones. More subtle is the presence, at the Wilmington Turn, across the highway from the Wilmington Trail, in summer, of common buttercup *(Ranunculus acris)*. We are tempted to regard the European weed with more than disdain when we spot it at a place little more than a quarter of a mile below the summit of a major Adirondack peak. What right does that invader have there? Then again, we might ask, "What right do we have?"

Above the Wilmington Turn, as the hiker's route ascends through clumps of dwarfed balsam fir and mountain alder, an herb, about 12 inches in height, with coarsely-toothed leaves may be seen along the trail. It accompanies the hiker nearly to the summit and, in late August, bears small, irregular white flowers striped with purple lines. Below, in a crack in the highway's asphalt, the herb also has emerged and blossomed in the company of diapensia. What is it? Eyebright *(Euphrasia americana)*. It is a plant and flower found more commonly at much lower elevations, alongside roads and in uncultivated fields nearby. It has found a niche on Whiteface and now it flourishes there. If we think about it, we realize that it has as much claim to be on Whiteface as any of the rest of us do.

Whiteface is truly one of the most remarkable mountains in the Adirondacks, one of the most remarkable in the world. It is rich in history, and its story still unfolds. The next time you reach its summit, before anyone already on top can ask you if you "climbed all the way," take a moment to think, to shout, or to whisper the message the mountain bore not so very long ago – "Thanks be to God for the Mountains." There is much for which to be thankful.

Endnotes

1. There is also a Whiteface Mountain in New Hampshire (4,010 feet in elevation) and one in Vermont (3,715 feet).

2. Dauphin Thompson was a neighbor of the fiery abolitionist. One of his brothers, Henry, married Brown's daughter, Ruth. His sister Isabella was the wife of Brown's son, Watson.

3. Philip G. Terrie, Jr., editor, *Peaks and People of the Adirondacks* (by Russell M. L. Carson) (Reprint: Glens Falls, NY: Adirondack Mountain Club, 1973), pg. xxxix.

4. Sandra Weber, *The Lure of Esther Mountain, Matriarch of the Adirondack High Peaks* (Fleischmanns, NY, Purple Mountain Press, 1995), pg. 33.

5. Quotes in this paragraph are from an early "Whiteface Mountain Memorial Highway" brochure, circa 1940.

6. Steven Englehart (executive director of Adirondack Architectural Heritage) in a "Narrative Statement of Significance" prepared as documentation for application for National Historic Registry of the Whiteface Veterans Memorial Highway Complex, reveals that the stage, driven by William Lamb, only went about half way up the roadway because, after a stone lodged in the hoof of one of the horses, Lamb decided that continuing the trip would put that horse at risk. Other details revealed by Englehart, one of whose sources for information was Doug Wolfe ("of the Atmospheric Sciences Research Center and an excellent local historian"), follow:

   a. The idea for an auto road to the summit was suggested by George Stevens of Lake Placid's Stevens House soon after 1900.

b. The Delaware and Hudson Railroad company once had on its drawing boards a plan for a cog railroad from Whiteface Landing to the summit.

c. An eighty-foot high tower, intended to honor veterans, was once planned for the summit.

d. Louis Marshall, father of George and Robert, was a principal opponent of the highway's construction.

e. The Pardee family of Philadelphia owned the summit before deeding it to the state to allow for the construction of the memorial highway and its facilities atop the mountain.

f. Lake Stevens, at the toll house, was created by damming the Whiteface Brook. The pond is named after Curtis and J. Hubert Stevens, winners of bobsledding medals at the 1932 Winter Olympics.

g. Lowell Thomas made a live, national radio broadcast from the summit.

h. Construction of the "tourist" trail to the summit from the castle in 1935 took only four weeks.

7. "Whiteface Mountain Memorial Highway" brochure, circa 1940.

8. The toll in 2009 was $9 for each vehicle's driver and $5 for each passenger – kids under six years of age, free.

9. (William) Averell Harriman was the son of Edward H. Harriman, who, like a Horatio Alger Jr. hero, worked his way up from a position as an office boy in a Wall Street financial concern to being the president of the Union Pacific Railroad and one of the most powerful men in the United States. Averell was chairman of the board of the Merchant Shipbuilding Corporation (1917-25) and a longtime chairman of the Union Pacific Railroad. He coordinated the Lend Lease program during World War II (1941-43), served as United States Ambassador to Russia (1943-46), was Ambassador to Great Britain (1946), Secretary of Commerce (1946-48), and Governor of New York (1955-58). He was an avid skier and developed Sun Valley, Idaho, in the mid 1930s.

MOUNT ESTHER
Height: 27th – 1,292 meters (4,239 feet)
By Tim Tefft (#616)

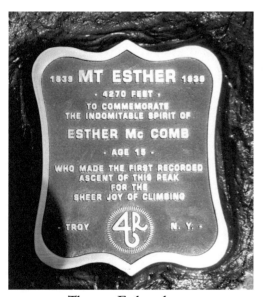

The new Esther plaque

On Sunday, July 30, 1939, a group of about twenty hikers bushwhacked their way to the summit of Esther Mountain. There they gathered to commemorate the centennial anniversary of what they thought was the peak's first ascent – one made accidentally in 1839 by a fifteen-year-old girl, Esther McComb. The celebration had been organized by two of the founders of the Forty-Sixers of Troy, Ed and Grace Hudowalski.

Grace, that afternoon, opened the ceremony atop Esther Mountain with comments about her interest in the mountain, and others in the group spoke briefly before Eleanor "Nell" Plum, chairman of the Albany Chapter of the Adirondack Mountain Club, unveiled (by removing a bandana from it) a bronze plaque which had been cemented to the rock of the mountain top by Ed Hudowalski. The plaque, which had been made by Margery Nash Ludlow of Troy, contained this inscription devised by Grace:

> 1839   MT ESTHER   1939
> – 4270 FEET –
> TO COMMEMORATE
> THE INDOMITABLE SPIRIT OF
> ESTHER Mc COMB
> – AGE 15 –
> WHO MADE THE FIRST RECORDED
> ASCENT OF THIS PEAK
> FOR THE
> SHEER JOY OF CLIMBING
> TROY   46R   N.Y.

Arthur S. Hopkins, assistant director of the Lands and Forests division of the New York Department of Conservation, who had suffered a significant rip to his trousers during his ascent of the mountain, spoke briefly; and the ceremony closed with the singing of "To Esther McComb." The words had been written by Clarence Craver and Grace:

> O, Esther, Spirit-brave!
> O, Maid! Undaunted, true!
> We pay our homage and respect
> Upon this mount to you!
>
> Not for renown or fame,
> You climbed this rugged peak;
> But for the joy of drinking in
> The virgin beauty deep.
>
> Long may thy spirit flame
> In hearts of everyone!
> Long may thy deed inspire, O Maid,
> Who climb here just for fun!

More than 40 years later, because the cement which held the plaque to the summit rock had begun to crumble, Ed Ketchledge reset it. A few years later it was removed and thought missing until it was recovered, cleaned, and set in place again during a 150th anniversary of the climb made in 1839 by Esther McComb.

Clarence Craver, a member of the 46ers of Troy, went on to become Forty-Sixer #15 on Mount Seymour in August 1939. Nell Plum became Forty-Sixer #26 on Allen Mountain on September 14, 1941; and Margery Ludlow became a Forty-Sixer #27 nine days later, September 23, 1941, on Couchsachraga. Nell and Margery were the fifth and sixth women to become Forty-Sixers.

Esther McComb was the only woman reputed to have made a first ascent of an Adirondack mountain, and Esther Mountain is the only High Peak named after a woman... long thought to have been Esther McComb. However, the story of the naming of Esther Mountain is not so certain anymore.

MOUNT ESTHER

Esther as seen from the Wilmington Trail

One of the great heroines of the Bible's Old Testament is Esther, the beloved Jewish queen of the Persian King Ahasuerus (Xerxes). She stood by her people and, with great courage, interceded with the king on their behalf and helped deliver them from potential slavery and destruction. The victory of the Jews over their enemies throughout Ahasuerus's provinces when Esther was their queen is remembered still and celebrated annually during the festival known as Purim. The brave woman who risked her life to save her people is the namesake of every woman since named Esther, and she may well be the woman for whom Esther Mountain was actually named.

But exactly when the mountain was named, and by whom it was named, is not now known.

In the early 1920s, when he was writing his historical sketches about the High Peaks for the members of the Glens Falls Rotary Club, Russell M. L. Carson had the greatest difficulty creating his piece about Esther Mountain because no one with whom he had corresponded, no book or document he read, could tell him how the mountain had received its name, but when he published his expanded sketches in *Peaks and People of the Adirondacks* (1927), Carson told the story of Esther McComb and Esther Mountain:

> Esther Mountain, which is northerly of Whiteface, is the farthest north of the major Adirondack peaks. Its northern slope descends to the road between Wilmington and Franklin Falls. In 1839, a family by the name of McComb lived on this road at the foot of the mountain. Esther McComb, a fifteen-year-old daughter, had an ambition to climb Whiteface, but her parents were unwilling. Disregarding their wishes, one day Esther started out, alone, to make the climb. She reached the top of the mountain now bearing her name, but became lost before getting to Whiteface. A searching party was out all night and found her the next morning. Her mother jokingly called the mountain Esther because of the occurrence, but the name was taken up and has remained.

Carson reported that he had obtained his information about Esther McComb and Esther Mountain's naming from Charles Beede, Keene Valley guide and son-in-law of Orson "Old Mountain" Phelps. Beede had heard the tale in 1923 from 88-year-old Wallace Goodspeed, a former guide who had conducted hiking parties up Whiteface in the nineteenth century. Goodspeed had told Beede that he had heard the story when he lived as a boy in the town of St. Armand near the supposed home of the McComb family.

After the story appeared in *Peaks and People,* it took on a life of its own. The tale was repeated, appeared in abbreviated form in Adirondack Mountain Club trail guides, and was elsewhere embellished. It became a part of the lore of the mountains. Even Robert Marshall, Forty-Sixer #3 and founder of the Wilderness Society, endorsed it. In a letter he wrote[1] in 1939 to Grace Hudowalski, Marshall suggested the forming of a group to climb Esther

Mountain "to commemorate Esther McComb and her remarkable initiative which resulted in the only first ascent of a high Adirondack peak by a woman and the first mountain to be climbed for the reason which instigates practically all Adirondack mountain climbing nowadays." That instigation: climbing "just for fun."

But Esther McComb probably never existed. The story told by Wallace Goodspeed to Charles Beede; passed on to Russell Carson by Beede; published by Carson; and broadcast by the Forty-Sixers and the Adirondack Mountain Club probably is not true.

Sandra Weber (#5227) in her 1995 *The Lure of Esther Mountain, Matriarch of the Adirondack High Peaks,* presented information about her search through historic records for Esther McComb. She was unable to find her.

Sandra reported that Carson had been told by other guides with whom he had corresponded that they did not know how Esther Mountain had received its name. Some had not even heard of the mountain before. One guide told him that the mountain was called Stores, and Bob Marshall reported that he had heard from a roommate at Harvard Forest College a story about a man from near Bloomingdale who had attempted to have the mountain's name changed from Esther to Estes, after the name of a man for whom the mountain had "really been named."[2] Although no evidence exists that the mountain had ever been named Estes, at one time a man known as Uncle Joe Estes had lived in the area.

No one in the area north and northwest of the mountain was ever named McComb either.

Weber did determine that a family named Combs had lived in the town of St. Armand on the flank of the mountain in 1858, when a J. H. French map of Essex County was published. That map also was the first document known which shows the peak, "Mt. Esther."[3] Unfortunately, even though Wallace Goodspeed might have incorrectly recalled the name of the family, the Thomas Combs family did not live in St. Armand or anywhere within view of Esther in 1839. They did not settle in that town until 1855. No records have been discovered which indicate that Thomas and Harriet Combs had a daughter named Esther either. The New York State Census of 1855 listed the family as having four daughters: Emily, 16; Ann, 15; Abigail, 10; and Harriet, 7. However, the parents were both 49 years of age in 1855 and very well may have had older daughters who no longer lived with them.[4]

Even if they did have a daughter named Esther, it is unlikely that she ever attempted to climb Whiteface from St. Armand. It is unlikely, as well, that she climbed from Wilmington. In 1839 the Combs family lived in the town of Lewis, and in 1850 they lived in the town of Essex. There was no Esther McComb or Combs living anywhere near Esther Mountain in 1839.

Sandra Weber discovered that Russell Carson wrote a letter on November 11, 1923, to one of his informants, Scott Brown, and told him the story he had heard from Charlie Beede. In that letter Carson reported the family name as *Macomb* and the date of the first ascent as 1849. Weber reports that elsewhere in Carson's notes "the name Macomb is crossed out and changed to Combs,"[5] but why the name was printed in *Peaks and People* as McComb and why the date of the supposed first ascent was given as 1839 is unexplained.

Because corroborating evidence is entirely lacking to support Wallace Goodspeed's 1923 story, it appears that the story of Esther McComb and her ascent of Esther Mountain is a tale spun by the then eighty-eight-year-old Goodspeed, who, if the incident had taken place in 1849, would have been eleven years old and likely have known the girl who lost her way to Whiteface.

Sandra Weber looked into other candidates, other women named Esther who might have climbed the mountain, but there is no compelling evidence to transfer the honor of first ascent to any of them. Consequently, no one today can say with any authority who deserves the credit. Nor can anyone state positively how the mountain got the name it had on the

1858 J. H. French map and in an 1865 volume, *Opening of the Adirondacks,* by an anonymous author.

Carson's account of the mountain's history says that a trail was built to its summit in 1866 by Russell French, the proprietor of a hotel on the plank road in St. Armand. The *Peaks and People* narrative about Esther Mountain concludes, "Charles Beede recalls going up the mountain by this trail when he was a boy, but does not know when it passed out of existence." However, no other evidence has ever been presented that that trail actually existed.

Sandra Weber reported in *The Lure of Esther Mountain* that "Russ and Sam French established a four-and-one-half-mile wagon trail up Whiteface Mountain from St. Armand"[6] in 1872. That trail offered the "easiest ascent of Whiteface,"[7] and its route may be seen on Seneca Ray Stoddard's *Map of the Adirondack Wilderness,* 1884, and the first United States Geological Survey map of the area, 1898. That trail was still in existence in 1934 when it was described in the Adirondack Mountain Club's first *Guide to Adirondack Trails*. If Russ French actually made a trail to Esther, it apparently did not remain in existence very long. Weber writes, "French's trail to the summit of Esther Mountain is not shown on any maps, probably because Whiteface quickly became a more popular destination."[8] However, Whiteface had long been a popular destination before French's trail to Esther Mountain was supposedly built.

Verplanck Colvin's reports about Whiteface Mountain in the 1870s make no mention of Esther Mountain or of any trail up Whiteface from French's Hotel. In his *Seventh Annual Report on the Progress of the Topographical Survey of the Adirondack Region of New York, to the Year 1879,* Colvin described a trip he made with some members of his survey crew up Whiteface on October 11, 1878. He reported that the trip "was not accomplished… without adventure, for in ascending the steep trail up the mountain next northward from Whiteface, one of the heavily loaded pack horses caught his foot in a root, slipped and fell headlong over a steep place, fortunately striking upon his back, which was well protected by sacks of flour and other provisions. The horse was extricated without injury, but the provisions were badly mixed. As the crest lacked a name, we now called it Pack-horse mountain."

Even though Esther Mountain is the most prominent peak "next northward from Whiteface," Pack-horse Mountain was probably what is today called Lookout Mountain, which Colvin probably ascended on a fairly well established trail which had been cut from Wilmington to Whiteface about 1860. The trail from that village to the summit of Whiteface shown on Seneca Ray Stoddard's 1883 map of the Adirondack Wilderness is probably that trail. Its route is similar to that of today's Wilmington Trail. It seems unlikely that Colvin would have made his own trail and more unlikely that the trail would have deviated from a course to its destination by passing over Esther. Colvin's sketch map of the Adirondack region which was included with the printed edition of his *Seventh Annual Report* does not label Pack-horse Mountain. Thus, the higher peak to the north, Esther, probably was not Pack-horse Mountain.

In 1934 Esther was a trailless peak, but the Whiteface Memorial Highway was under construction in that year. At one point, the auto route passed within a half a mile of Esther's summit, but in the 1930s that short ascent was blocked by a tangle of old growth balsam fir and red spruce. In fact, the bushwhack to Esther from the Wilmington Trail, the preferred route, was also difficult at that time. Esther was truly trailless then. However in the late 1940s it became an easy climb for hikers along a cross country ski trail from Lookout Mountain. It was treated as a trailed peak in the Adirondack Mountain Club's trail guides published in 1957 and 1962. The club's maps of trails of the *High Peak Region* which were prepared in 1956 and 1962 show the trail to Esther from Lookout, and hikers of that era remember that Esther was not a particularly challenging climb. However, after skiing came to an end at Marble Mountain and at the "upper level" on Whiteface in 1958, the old ski trails began to grow in, slowly but surely. Still, the 1972 eighth edition of the *Guide to Adirondack Trails* says, "This major peak used to be numbered among the trailless peaks, making the aspiring 46er bushwhack through the thick cripplebrush to reach the summit..." but the "advent of a ski trail running N along the ridge from the Wilmington Trail to Whiteface has made the ascent relatively simple."

By the time the club's ninth edition of the trail guide was published (1977), the ski trail had filled with new-growth firs, spruce and other trees. The tenth edition (1980) moved Esther to the "Peaks Without Maintained Trails - The Trailless Peaks" section and explained, "the ski trails once cut to its summit are now so overgrown that they are presently somewhat difficult to follow – showing that nature 'reclaims its own' rapidly when man does not interfere by maintaining trails."

Gradually, over the years since the mid-1970s, Esther Mountain has been visited by thousands of hikers, thousands of 46ers, and it no longer can be regarded as "trailless." It may be approached from the Wilmington Reservoir on the trail which begins its ascent along White Brook and crests the ridge of Marble Mountain near the top of the old Whiteface Mountain Ski Center T-bar route. Hikers also often begin their expeditions to Esther at the former ski center's lodge area, presently the headquarters of the Atmospheric Research Center. Their route up Marble Mountain, for the most part, follows that of the former lift, passing, on the upward way, the cement piers which once supported the lift's superstructure.

In the late spring the area where the Marble Mountain route and the Wilmington Trail intersect is an ideal place to see a host of pink moccasin flowers. The birch trees of that area, beneath which the orchids grow, demonstrate that the land there was impacted by the activities of man: initially, in the nineteenth century and early twentieth century, by the lumbering of the J. and J. Rogers Company and later by the builders of the original Whiteface Mountain ski area, once the largest such resort in New York State.

In fact, from the top of Marble Mountain to the flank of Lookout Mountain over which the Wilmington Trail climbs, the route which hikers follow today was once used much more frequently for descents than it was for ascents. The Whiteface ski center which opened in 1948 had its "school slope" with rope tow; slalom course; and four trails accessible from the T-bar lift on the side of Marble Mountain, but good skiing conditions were infrequent on that eastern exposure during the first years of the center's operation. Consequently an auxiliary set of runs, at the "upper level," was established high on Whiteface Mountain near the wall which hikers approach before they reach the "Wilmington Turn" of the memorial highway about four tenths of a mile from that mountain's summit. The upper level once featured a snack bar, two rope tows, four downhill runs, several cross country ski trails, and, atop Lookout Mountain, a comfortable, insulated "shelter."

Hikers today pass an old toboggan storage shed a short distance before the Wilmington Trail turns on the plateau-like flank of Lookout to head to Whiteface. Also, after the trail turns again to head upwards to the highway's wall, the present trail follows the route of one of the two upper level rope tows past the former site of the Whiteface-Wilmington Lean-to. From that lean-to area, the skiers of the late 1940s and early 1950s could head directly to the shelter on Lookout Mountain and proceed from there, usually on Nordic skis, to the top of Esther Mountain. Today's trail from the old shelter site to the top of Esther follows the route of that old ski trail almost precisely.

The Forty-Sixers removed blowdown and closed an alternate herdpath on the route to Esther in 2004 and recommended that a bridge be built over a perpetually muddy mire in the col between Lookout and the ridge leading up to the peak. The state Department of Environmental Conservation (DEC) approved the improvement but, Trailmaster Len Grubbs reported, "had no funding for the project. The Forty-Sixers, recognizing the value of the project, provided the funding for the material so the work could move forward."

In the spring of 2007, the DEC purchased cedar logs for cribbing, planks, and nails and had those materials flown to the site. Several weeks later, on June 24, a volunteer Forty-Sixer trail crew began the construction of the bridge. Len wrote later, "We found the drop site within a few feet of the construction site, a great relief for us since it limited the distance we had to haul the heavy timbers. The work progressed rapidly, without a hitch, and by mid-afternoon, a sixty-foot bog bridge spanned the swamp."

The shelter on Lookout was formerly the starting point for the once popular "inferno race." The participants followed the Wilmington Trail downhill to the top of Marble Mountain and then sped down that mountain to a finish line at the base of its T-bar lift. The racers and other skiers who descended from the upper level to the base did not have to ski up the Wilmington Trail. They were carried to the upper level on the backs of trucks or Sno Cats that dropped them off at the snack bar on the flank of Esther.

Esther's lower flanks have been busy with activity for most of the last 150 years. The J. and J. Rogers Company owned property in St. Armand and Wilmington around Esther Mountain from which they obtained timber, initially for conversion into charcoal for the operation of their iron works and, after 1893, for the production of pulp for their paper mill at Au Sable Forks. During the 1920s the company began to sell its holdings to New York State. The peaks of Esther and Lookout were purchased in June 1921. By 1930, the Rogers Company had divested itself of all of its holdings in the area of Whiteface and Esther. Left behind were the remains of old charcoal kilns, a man-made pond, and at least two log flumes which once were used to send pulpwood down to the Ausable River.

Construction of the Whiteface Mountain Memorial Highway began on Christmas Day in 1931, and the first auto tourists ascended the highway in the summer of 1935. Most of the occupants of the thousands of cars that went up the highway that first season were entirely unaware that they did so on the shoulders of Esther Mountain.

Today the Atmospheric Sciences Research Center maintains weather instruments on the side of the mountain, and other scientists have studied the phenomena of red spruce decline on Esther and "waves" of balsam fir die-back which can be clearly seen from Whiteface. The mountain remains an active site for scientific research and it continues, each year, to attract hundreds of hikers, many of whom aspire to become 46ers.

For many years, at her summer home near Adirondack on Schroon Lake, Grace Hudowalski had on her porch a summit register canister which had once been fastened to a tree at the top of Esther. Esther Mountain meant a lot to her. After reading Russell Carson's *Peaks and People* and after having determined that she would climb the 46 peaks, Grace decided that Esther Mountain would be her finishing peak. Thus it was that she became 46er #9 on Esther Mountain on August 26, 1937. She was the first woman to complete the 46 and the first 46er to finish on Esther. She championed and celebrated Esther McComb... but it is possible, just possible, that the first woman to climb the mountain "just for fun" was Grace herself.

Endnotes

1. Sandra Weber, *The Lure of Esther Mountain, Matriarch of the Adirondack High Peaks* (Fleischmanns, NY, 1995), pg. 52. Sandra's book provides much other information about the history of Esther Mountain. It is a "must read" for Forty-Sixers.

2. *Ibid.*, pg. 49.

3. *Ibid.*, pgs. 26-27.

4. One more daughter has recently been rediscovered: Rosetta Combs, "daughter of Thomas and Harriet Combs" of "Essex County, New York" married Ransome N. Kenney, and moved with him to Holton, Michigan. According to *A Portrait and Biographical Record of Muskegon and Ottawa Counties* (Michigan) published in 1893, Rosetta Combs married Kenney about 40 years earlier (1853). A Kenney family genealogy speculates that she was born in 1830. She would have been in her twenties at the time of her marriage. Since the oldest Combs daughter listed in the 1855 New York Census, overseen by Franklin B. Hough, was sixteen years old and therefore born about 1839, it is highly likely that Thomas and Harriet had other children born between 1830 and 1839. It is therefore still possible that one of them may have been named Esther.

5. Weber, pg. 48.

6. *Ibid.,,* pg. 33.

7. *Ibid.*, pg. 34.

8. *Ibid.*

The Membership Roster of the Adirondack Forty-Sixers

Prepared by Mike Becker (#1889W)

Heaven Up-h'isted-ness!

The membership roster of the Adirondack Forty-Sixers follows. Note that a "W" following a member's number indicates "Winter" Forty-Sixer status. Note, too, that mountain names have been simplified so as to preserve space in the membership list:

	Member	First Ascent	Forty-sixth Peak
1	Herbert K. Clark	Whiteface (8/1/18)	Emmons (6/10/25)
2	George Marshall	Whiteface (8/1/18)	Emmons (6/10/25)
3	Robert Marshall	Whiteface (8/1/18)	Emmons (6/10/25)
4	P. F. Loope	Marcy (5/27)	Rocky Peak (9/33)
5	Herbert L. Malcolm	Whiteface (10/07)	Couchsachraga (6/8/35)
6	Edward C. Hudowalski	Marcy (7/32)	Dix (9/13/36)
7	Ernest R. Ryder	Whiteface (8/11)	Dix (9/13/36)
8	Orville C. Gowie	Marcy (7/32)	Couchsachraga (8/25/37)
9	Grace L. Hudowalski	Marcy (8/22)	Esther (8/26/37)
10	C. H. Nash	Marcy (2/37)	Allen (8/28/37)
11	Charles W. Horn	Marcy (6/31)	Marshall (9/37)
12	Henry H. Arthur	Nippletop (9/34)	Couchsachraga (9/16/37)
13	Paul H. Arthur	Marcy (1929)	Couchsachraga (9/16/37)
14	Louise A. Goark	Colden (8/34)	Panther (8/38)
15	Clarence R. Craver	Street (7/34)	Seymour (8/39)
16	Alice Waterhouse	Unknown	Sawteeth (10/8/39)
17	Ramon L. Hall	Marcy (10/12/30)	Macomb (10/14/39)
18	Edward A. Harmes	Whiteface (7/31/32)	Couchsachraga (7/19/40)
19	John M. Harmes	Whiteface (7/31/32)	Couchsachraga (7/19/40)
20	Edward B. Clements	Marcy (9/35)	Allen (8/11/40)
21	Rudolph Clements	Marcy (9/35)	Allen (8/11/40)
22	Nora L. Sproule	Armstrong (1936)	Emmons (8/11/40)
23	Eugene L. Bamforth	Algonquin (7/23/36)	Esther (8/18/40)
24	James A. Goodwin	Giant (7/19)	Street (9/7/40)
25	Franklin H. Wilson, Jr.	Marcy (7/35)	Street (9/7/40)
26	Eleanor M. Plum	Marcy (5/32)	Allen (9/14/41)
27	Margery N. Ludlow	Giant (1936)	Couchsachraga (9/23/41)
28	Frank C. Johnston	Dix (8/1/37)	Marshall (9/27/41)
29	Mary C. Dittmar	Marcy (6/23/32)	Redfield (9/6/42)
30	Elizabeth W. Little	Marcy (5/30/31)	Redfield (9/6/42)
31	Adolph G. Dittmar	Marcy (8/13/38)	Seymour (7/11/45)
32	Robert P. Jutson	Algonquin (7/4/34)	Esther (8/20/46)
33	Werner O. Bachli	Lower Wolf Jaw (10/42)	Panther (9/1/46)
34	Agnes W. Benedix	Giant (1945)	Phelps (9/2/46)
35	Jessie A. Benedix	Giant (1945)	Phelps (9/2/46)
36	Priscilla Chipman	Nippletop (8/40)	Phelps (9/2/46)
37	Margaret Keating	Dix (8/45)	Phelps (9/2/46)
38	Philip A. Macklin	Algonquin (8/7/37)	Nippletop (9/5/46)
39	Richard L. Macklin	Marcy (7/4/37)	Nippletop (9/5/46)
40	Robert Denniston	Marcy (7/38)	Allen (9/7/46)
41	Katherine Dockstader	Marcy (9/16/34)	Allen (9/7/46)
42	Helen C. Menz	Marcy (6/23/32)	Allen (9/13/46)
43	Ruth P. King	Marshall (7/40)	Esther (9/25/46)
44	Charles V. Trapp, Sr.	Marcy (9/2/45)	Seymour (10/13/46)
45	Charles V. Trapp, Jr.	Marcy (9/2/45)	Seymour (10/13/46)
46	George F. Trapp	Marcy (9/2/45)	Seymour (10/13/46)
47	Orra A. Phelps	Marcy (1924)	Allen (9/13/47)
48	Roy Snyder	Algonquin (6/37)	Hough (9/28/47)
49	Roy O. Buchanan	Algonquin (6/27)	Couchsachraga (10/7/47)
50	Louis B. Puffer	Marcy (1920)	Couchsachraga (10/7/47)
51	Howard F. Brown	Whiteface (7/30/39)	Seymour (10/12/47)
52	Dorothy O. Haeussler	Allen (9/14/41)	Seymour (10/12/47)
53	Louis H. Knapp	Whiteface (7/30/39)	Seymour (10/12/47)
54	Charles R. Hine	Marcy (7/41)	Esther (5/30/48)
55	Frank J. Oliver	Algonquin (9/24)	Seymour (7/29/48)

The Membership Roster of the Adirondack Forty-Sixers

	Member	First Ascent	Forty-sixth Peak
56	Paul E. Oliver	Haystack (7/46)	Seymour (7/29/48)
57	Peter Oliver	Algonquin (8/44)	Big Slide (7/30/48)
58	J. Daniel McKenzie	Whiteface (7/16/48)	Wright (8/7/48)
59	Lillian G. McKenzie	Whiteface (7/16/48)	Wright (8/7/48)
60	Chrissie Wendell (dog)	Giant (8/39)	Sawteeth (9/3/48)
61	David Wendell	Algonquin (1935)	Sawteeth (9/3/48)
62	Richard H. Wendell	Algonquin (1935)	Sawteeth (9/3/48)
63	Roland M. Wendell	Algonquin (1935)	Sawteeth (9/3/48)
64	Ted W. Dietze	Giant (7/45)	Allen (9/11/48)
65	Warren R. Langdon	Giant (7/45)	Allen (9/11/48)
66	Carrington Howard, Jr.	Seymour (8/2/44)	Couchsachraga (9/16/48)
67	Ralph J. Frank	Marcy (7/1921)	Esther (11/6/48)
68	David P. Farrington	Marcy (8/36)	Allen (11/27/48)
69	L. Morgan Porter	Whiteface (9/12/21)	Phelps (7/23/49)
70	Paul F. Boller	Marcy (1925)	Marshall (7/29/49)
71	William C. Patterson	Whiteface (8/41)	Seymour (8/1/49)
72	Peter A. Ward	Marcy (8/25/40)	Esther (8/13/49)
73	Linton Stone	Marcy (9/5/28)	Panther (8/20/49)
74	F. L. Peter Stone	Marcy (6/45)	Panther (8/20/49)
75	Joseph Gross	Lower Wolf Jaw (1945)	Colden (9/11/49)
76	David C. Hart	Colden (8/36)	Esther (9/13/49)
77	Roy C. Feber	Wright (5/48)	Sawteeth (11/12/49)
78	John C. Alexander	Blake (7/26/47)	Whiteface (11/19/49)
79	Howard Kasch	Rocky Peak (5/30/47)	Dix (5/30/50)
80	William E. Endicott	Whiteface (1930)	Emmons (9/3/50)
81	Manfred M. Hein	Porter (11/27/47)	Emmons (9/3/50)
82	Elisabeth L. Biester	Big Slide (8/39)	Seymour (9/13/50)
83	Paul G. Lauffer	Big Slide (9/1928)	Seymour (9/13/50)
84	William J. McRoberts	Colvin (5/24/47)	Whiteface (9/30/50)
85	Ruth T. Riford	Marcy (8/27/30)	Couchsachraga (9/30/50)
86	William J. Hentschel	Marcy (5/28/38)	Allen (10/14/50)
87	Phyllis A. Antonsen	Macomb (7/10/48)	Nye (11/19/50)
88	Elsa J. Turmelle	Upper Wolf Jaw (8/46)	Hough (9/4/52)
89	James H. Nye	Marcy (7/2/32)	Macomb (10/9/52)
90W	Harry K. Eldridge	Cascade (7/42)	Macomb (8/53)
91	Carl H. Crandall	Colden (9/42)	Couchsachraga (9/1/53)
92W	Edgar B. Bean	Colvin (8/1/53)	Seymour (3/13/55)
93	Floyd G. Moore	Algonquin (8/30/52)	Seymour (3/13/55)
94	John F. Siau	Giant (9/10/49)	Santanoni (4/3/55)
95	Clifford D. Walker, Jr.	Algonquin (10/52)	Allen (4/9/55)
96	Herbert C. Allen, Jr.	Marcy (1924)	Allen (4/9/55)
97	Stanley C. Conrad	Marcy (5/30/48)	Emmons (7/3/55)
98	Rudolph W. Strobel	Algonquin (1935)	Couchsachraga (8/9/55)
99	Allen T. Braswell	Unknown	Panther (8/25/55)
100	Robert K. Gilchriest	Marcy (6/50)	Panther (8/28/55)
101	Duane H. Nash, III	Whiteface (7/25)	Allen (8/29/55)
102	Edgar Wachenheim, III	Cascade (7/50)	Santanoni (8/31/55)
103W	N. Clark Gittinger	Macomb (5/16/53)	Sawteeth (10/29/55)
104	Carolyn Schaefer	Marcy (9/31)	Hough (8/17/56)
105	Mary Schaefer	Marcy (8/50)	Hough (8/17/56)
106	Monica S. Neville	Marcy (8/50)	Hough (8/17/56)
107	Nancy R. Johnson	Algonquin (9/3/47)	Couchsachraga (8/23/56)
108	Edward Foley	Colvin (7/52)	Allen (8/25/56)
109	J. Thomas Nash	Colden (9/7/48)	East Dix (8/27/56)
110	Evelyn S. Greene	Marcy (8/16/50)	East Dix (8/27/56)
111	Francis A. Schaefer	Marcy (8/16/50)	East Dix (8/27/56)
112	Michael Jarecki	Couchsachraga (9/4/45)	Gray (8/29/56)
113	Barbara B. Thoren	Gothics (7/49)	Santanoni (9/3/56)
114	Laurence Babcock	Gothics (7/49)	Santanoni (9/3/56)
115	Richard T. Babcock	Whiteface (1925)	Santanoni (9/3/56)
116	Willis A. Smarup	Giant (9/29/41)	Rocky Peak (10/13/56)
117	Robert B. Mitchell, Jr.	Marcy (5/30/36)	Seymour (10/28/56)

Heaven Up-h'isted-ness!

	Member	First Ascent	Forty-sixth Peak
118W	Richard M. Chrenko	Giant (1/6/55)	Emmons (5/25/57)
119	Peter Welles	Algonquin (8/49)	Sawteeth (7/21/57)
120	Tim Welles	Marcy (8/49)	Sawteeth (7/21/57)
121	William R. Schultz, Jr.	Marcy (7/51)	Nye (7/6/57)
122	Arthur Laemmel	Marcy (7/31/46)	Allen (8/9/57)
123	Lee Tomlinson	Marcy (5/48)	Emmons (8/11/57)
124	Daniel D. Stepnewski	Colden (7/5/52)	Couchsachraga (8/17/57)
125	Roger S. Loud	Cascade (7/42)	Allen (8/19/57)
126	A. Edward Blackmar	Colden (8/34)	Allen (8/26/57)
127	Haynes Kelly	Marcy (7/54)	Allen (8/26/57)
128	Phillip G. Ostrom	Haystack (7/56)	Allen (8/26/57)
129	James E. O'Brien	Porter (8/50)	Santanoni (8/29/57)
130	Normand L. Reynolds	Colden (1949)	Santanoni (8/29/57)
131	George Zwick	Big Slide (7/2/55)	Skylight (9/1/57)
132	Emmett C. Laird	Marcy (8/10/54)	Allen (9/7/57)
133	George D. Trent	Marcy (9/2/51)	Allen (9/7/57)
134	Arthur K. Davis	Whiteface (9/13/41)	Seymour (9/7/57)
135	Clarence Spangenberger	Algonquin (9/29/50)	Marshall (10/14/57)
136	Kathleen Spangenberger	Algonquin (9/29/50)	Marshall (10/14/57)
137	Howard C. Fleming	Whiteface (7/35)	Couchsachraga (7/6/58)
138	Arthur G. Beach	Basin (10/4/53)	Marshall (7/8/58)
139	Marcus G. Howard	Algonquin (8/12/44)	Esther (7/11/58)
140	Carroll M. Hodge	Nippletop (7/19/56)	Whiteface (7/30/58)
141	Hugh L. Polk	Big Slide (8/50)	Whiteface (7/30/58)
142	Eleanor G. Leavitt	Marcy (7/2/51)	Marshall (8/10/58)
143	William H. Leavitt	Marcy (7/2/51)	Marshall (8/10/58)
144	Lance Seberhagen	Algonquin (7/55)	Cliff (8/12/58)
145	Peter T. Smith	Giant (7/30/52)	Nye (8/15/58)
146	Paul F. Jamieson	Algonquin (7/34)	East Dix (8/19/58)
147	Franklin C. Elder	Marcy (5/10/55)	Allen (8/23/58)
148	Trudy B. Healy	Gothics (7/17/52)	Redfield (8/26/58)
149	Karen Howell	Cascade (7/28/53)	Hough (8/27/58)
150	Thomas E. Healy	Cascade (7/28/53)	Hough (8/27/58)
151	Adelaide M. Putnam	Giant (1914)	Emmons (8/28/58)
152	Richard T. Ernenwein	Algonquin (8/7/46)	Seymour (8/28/58)
153	Marguerite Kingsbury	Algonquin (9/46)	Tabletop (9/9/58)
154	S. Anne Parker	Marcy (10/2/51)	Tabletop (9/9/58)
155	Don Dickinson	Marcy (7/4/55)	Allen (9/27/58)
156	Robert A. Starbuck	Marcy (6/33)	Blake (6/13/59)
157W	Elwin C. Bigelow	East Dix (5/56)	Skylight (7/4/59)
158	Sandra Healy	Cascade (1955)	Panther (8/1/59)
159	Charles P. Fenimore, Jr.	Cascade (8/15/53)	Donaldson (8/8/59)
160	Charles L. Loucks	Algonquin (8/13/52)	Dix (8/13/59)
161	Dorothy C. Babcock	Dix (9/1/39)	Wright (8/20/59)
162	Clinton H. Miller, Jr.	Marcy (8/22)	Hough (8/21/59)
163	Anne B. Bailey	Cascade (7/48)	Santanoni (8/22/59)
164	Michael G. Healy	Wright (8/26/54)	East Dix (8/27/59)
165	Leslie R. Borland, Jr.	Marcy (1947)	Couchsachraga (8/29/59)
166	Norman Ganter	Cascade (1955)	Rocky Peak (9/1/59)
167	Howard C. Buschman, III	Algonquin (7/23/52)	Marshall (9/4/59)
168	R. Bruce Starbuck	Marcy (9/55)	Seymour (9/4/59)
169	Matthew Hale, Jr.	Giant (8/49)	Whiteface (9/10/59)
170	Charles P. Fenimore, Sr.	Cascade (8/15/53)	Couchsachraga (9/12/59)
171	Robert H. Johnson	Giant (5/47)	Couchsachraga (9/12/59)
172	Henry N. Germond	Algonquin (5/26/51)	Whiteface (9/19/59)
173	Katherine E. Germond	Algonquin (5/26/51)	Whiteface (9/19/59)
174	David D. Porter	Saddleback (6/55)	Couchsachraga (9/20/59)
175	Wayne Wiitanen	Big Slide (8/23/59)	Cascade (9/23/59)
176	Eleanor A. Friend	Dix (7/46)	Sawteeth (10/25/59)
177	William A. Penn	Marcy (1956)	Dix (11/7/59)
178	Eric R. Cronkhite	Upper Wolf Jaw (12/54)	Allen (11/7/59)
179	Gillett Welles, Jr.	Marcy (1942)	Nye (8/29/59)

The Membership Roster of the Adirondack Forty-Sixers

	Member	First Ascent	Forty-sixth Peak
180	Richard H. Haile	Macomb (5/16/53)	Seymour (4/2/60)
181	Myron Egtvedt	Marcy (8/21/54)	Whiteface (5/5/60)
182	Lyle S. Raymond, Jr.	Algonquin (8/38)	Allen (6/11/60)
183W	James W. Collins	Wright (3/28/59)	Skylight (7/16/60)
184	Donald Hinman	Algonquin (7/35)	Emmons (7/24/60)
185	J. Reed Hinman	Colden (7/49)	Emmons (7/24/60)
186	Karen O. Fraser	Cascade (7/53)	Redfield (8/9/60)
187	Stephanie D. Bugden	Dial (10/38)	Dix (8/13/60)
188	J. Tansley Hohmann, Jr.	Algonquin (8/52)	Seymour (8/19/60)
189	John W. Nields, Jr.	Gothics (8/48)	Seymour (8/26/60)
190	Elizabeth J. Nields	Giant (8/50)	Marcy (8/28/60)
191	Lance Wickens	Wright (8/53)	Santanoni (8/28/60)
192	Peter Beisswenger	Marcy (8/56)	Esther (9/15/60)
193	Polly H. Bancroft	Cascade (8/21/55)	Seymour (10/8/60)
194	Curt Beebe	Rocky Peak (12/58)	Whiteface (11/60)
195	Bruce D. Beck	Macomb (8/8/59)	Rocky Peak (2/12/61)
196	Donald M. Burness	Marcy (7/14/42)	Nye (5/21/61)
197	Neil S. Moon	Marcy (9/1/40)	Nye (5/21/61)
198	Laura W. Moon	Marcy (9/1/40)	Sawteeth (6/4/61)
199	Jules Bystrak	Marcy (8/17/34)	Couchsachraga (6/27/61)
200	J. Henry Bystrak	Dix (8/21/47)	Couchsachraga (6/27/61)
201	David R. Dittmar	Wright (5/31/55)	Hough (7/8/61)
202	Carolyn M. Douty	Porter (6/3/56)	Hough (7/8/61)
203	William F. Menz, Jr.	Porter (6/3/56)	Hough (7/8/61)
204	Joseph P. Kazlowski	Whiteface (8/53)	Sawteeth (7/22/61)
205	Terry Kazlowski (dog)	Algonquin (6/54)	Sawteeth (7/22/61)
206	Richard V. Upjohn	Giant (8/3/52)	Esther (8/12/61)
207	Peggy Hohmann	Algonquin (8/51)	Nye (8/17/61)
208	Arthur M. Thompson	Cascade (7/53)	Marshall (8/18/61)
209	Timothy Y. Hayward	Giant (9/49)	Gray (8/27/61)
210	Ronald J. Hongo	Algonquin (7/18/54)	Haystack (9/1/61)
211	James A. Goodwin, Jr.	Cascade (8/20/55)	Rocky Peak (9/2/61)
212	Wintrop A. Rockwell	Gothics (7/25/55)	Rocky Peak (9/2/61)
213	Jonathan W. Miller	Phelps (8/58)	Cliff (9/3/61)
214	Howard F. Sargent	Dix (10/54)	Gray (9/3/61)
215	George H. Wahl, Jr.	Algonquin (8/51)	Hough (9/5/61)
216	William C. Frenette	Whiteface (9/46)	Haystack (10/7/61)
217	Jane F. Croft	Marcy (7/4/58)	Marshall (10/14/61)
218	Judith A. Sherman	Marcy (9/54)	Marshall (10/14/61)
219	Charles L. Brayton	Whiteface (8/14)	Couchsachraga (5/27/62)
220	Garfield Jones	Algonquin (7/38)	Couchsachraga (6/17/62)
221	Robert A. Banks	Marcy (9/2/56)	Couchsachraga (6/17/62)
222	Robert W. Livingston	Cascade (7/25/52)	Allen (6/17/62)
223	Ole Borchsenius	Marcy (8/51)	Panther (7/18/62)
224W	Philip B. Corell	Giant (7/56)	Panther (7/18/62)
225	Mark Gibson	Marcy (8/55)	Panther (7/18/62)
226	Gary Kukura	Dial (6/58)	Panther (7/18/62)
227	Warren A. Wilber	Street (5/30/53)	Couchsachraga (7/22/62)
228	Peter H. Owens	Giant (7/14/60)	Couchsachraga (7/25/62)
229	Lawrence E. Cotter	Cascade (8/16/55)	Santanoni (8/6/62)
230	Alfred W. Latham, Jr.	Giant (7/59)	Whiteface (8/13/62)
231	Herbert McAneny	Marcy (8/17)	Couchsachraga (8/17/62)
232	Laura F. Nields	Cascade (1955)	South Dix (8/24/62)
233	James G. Bailey	Giant (7/56)	Emmons (8/25/62)
234	John Schuller	Giant (1954)	Panther (8/29/62)
235	Henry S. Brooks	Cascade (7/57)	Seward (8/29/62)
236	James C. Frauenthal	Algonquin (8/1/56)	Seward (8/29/62)
237	Stephen C. Frauenthal	Whiteface (7/15/55)	Seward (8/29/62)
238	Charles Simonds	Phelps (8/57)	Seward (8/29/62)
239	Philip S. Hill, III	Algonquin (7/59)	Allen (8/30/62)
240	Peter Goodwin	Giant (1956)	Santanoni (8/31/62)
241	Dessie Neville	Cascade (8/58)	Porter (8/31/62)

Heaven Up-h'isted-ness!

	Member	First Ascent	Forty-sixth Peak
242	Mary Cheney	Gothics (7/57)	Porter (8/31/62)
243	James Dickinson	Cascade (6/28/58)	Marshall (9/1/62)
244W	Donald E. McMullen	Whiteface (8/23/57)	Blake (9/1/62)
245	Thomas E. McMullen	Marcy (7/20/49)	Blake (9/1/62)
246	Robert H. Friis	Gothics (7/27/60)	Big Slide (9/22/62)
247	Frederick B. Smith	Marcy (7/56)	Sawteeth (9/23/62)
248	Jay Hohmann	Colvin (8/16/57)	Couchsachraga (10/15/62)
249	Robert L. Carson	Marcy (9/20/52)	Nye (6/8/63)
250	John E. Wilcox	Marcy (3/19/60)	Emmons (6/13/63)
251	Charles Gibson, Jr.	Marcy (8/57)	Couchsachraga (7/23/63)
252	Patricia Fee	Cascade (5/30/52)	East Dix (7/30/63)
253	Dorothy T. Tyo	Whiteface (10/24/53)	East Dix (7/30/63)
254	Winthrop Brown	Cascade (7/9/62)	Seward (7/31/63)
255	Dominick A. DeLisa	Marcy (8/54)	Couchsachraga (8/3/63)
256	Patricia C. DeLisa	Algonquin (10/59)	Couchsachraga (8/3/63)
257	David Wakefield	Algonquin (7/12/60)	East Dix (8/6/63)
258	Suzanne Atkinson	Giant (7/15/58)	Santanoni (8/17/63)
259	Barbara S. DeSilets	Giant (1958)	Panther (8/17/63)
260	O'Donnell L. Boyce	Giant (7/59)	Couchsachraga (8/20/63)
261	Jan Farfalla	Tabletop (8/18/56)	Colden (8/22/63)
262	Bruce M. Munson	Marcy (8/6/57)	Allen (8/26/63)
263	Robert C. Peet	Giant (8/3/51)	Iroquois (8/26/63)
264	Nancy C. Howarth	Esther (7/59)	Allen (8/28/63)
265	Thomas W. Kensler	Blake (8/20/59)	Dix (8/31/63)
266	Frederick Burton	Lower Wolf Jaw (8/9/61)	Wright (8/31/63)
267	Jack S. Swan	Algonquin (8/14/46)	Big Slide (9/1/63)
268	Virginia M. Hentschel	Colden (9/16/43)	Skylight (9/1/63)
269	Frederick W. Grahame	Haystack (8/7/54)	Emmons (9/1/63)
270	Eva Nagy	Marcy (8/5/60)	Emmons (9/1/63)
271	Paul Nagy	Marcy (8/5/60)	Emmons (9/1/63)
272	Edwin G. Smith	Marcy (8/18/35)	Emmons (9/1/63)
273	Marion F. Fresn	Marcy (7/31)	Couchsachraga (9/1/63)
274	Charles Buschman	Giant (7/14/56)	Whiteface (9/3/63)
275	Susan H. Rickard	Dial (10/17/57)	Allen (9/5/63)
276	Henry L. Young	Algonquin (9/10/24)	Seymour (10/3/63)
277W	Guy Huse	Haystack (9/5/59)	Couchsachraga (3/15/64)
278	Wayne C. Taft	Saddleback (11/17/57)	Couchsachraga (3/15/64)
279	Russell P. Van Korb	Cascade (8/58)	Couchsachraga (6/13/64)
280	Reginald Gilliam, Jr.	Cascade (7/55)	Emmons (8/5/64)
281	Ralph A. Cioffi	Marcy (5/30/57)	Seymour (8/12/64)
282	Frank E. Pluhar	Marcy (5/30/57)	Seymour (8/12/64)
283	Donald M. Wallace	Big Slide (10/56)	Dial (8/16/64)
284	George E. Reed, Jr.	Cascade (7/59)	Panther (8/20/64)
285	Arthur E. Kopp	Marcy (8/30/59)	Marshall (8/24/64)
286	John R. Henry II	Haystack (8/8/53)	Allen (8/28/64)
287	Robert J. Weissinger	Nippletop (10/56)	Seymour (8/30/64)
288	Jon F. Stevens	Wright (8/31/58)	Sawteeth (8/31/64)
289	Arthur J. Rose, III	Phelps (8/4/60)	Santanoni (9/3/64)
290	George K. McClelland	Cascade (7/21/61)	Colden (9/4/64)
291	Vincent McClelland	Cascade (7/21/61)	Colden (9/4/64)
292	Nulsen B. Smith	Giant (1959)	Colden (9/4/64)
293	Edwin P. Holt	Phelps (3/9/63)	Whiteface (9/5/64)
294	Mary M. Spofford	Algonquin (12/59)	Whiteface (9/5/64)
295	Jeffrey B. Byrne	Cascade (9/9/60)	East Dix (9/6/64)
296	Jonathan B. Hooker	Algonquin (1961)	East Dix (9/6/64)
297	George B. Harrold	Marcy (9/4/53)	Whiteface (9/6/64)
298	Warren J. McLane	Marcy (9/6/43)	Emmons (9/6/64)
299	Christopher G. O'Brien	Marcy (7/21/61)	Giant (9/7/64)
300	John E. Stannard	Wright (1/1/63)	Couchsachraga (9/8/64)
301	Carl H. Herzog	Marcy (10/13/56)	Allen (9/13/64)
302	Robert Lewis	Cascade (7/58)	Allen (9/26/64)
303	Charles G. Gardner	Marcy (10/12/51)	Redfield (10/10/64)

The Membership Roster of the Adirondack Forty-Sixers

	MEMBER	FIRST ASCENT	FORTY-SIXTH PEAK
304	Austra R. McLane	Colden (7/29/61)	Allen (10/17/64)
305	T. Michael Huston	Wright (9/15/61)	Rocky Peak (11/21/64)
306	Frederick R. Dettmer	Lower Wolf Jaw (7/62)	Allen (8/6/64)
307	Ulysses E. Lutz	Marcy (7/21/37)	Couchsachraga (8/11/64)
308	Daniel M. Silin	Cascade (1955)	Hough (6/7/65)
309	Jonathan J. Adams	Cascade (8/60)	Panther (6/15/65)
310	Armand Catelli	Marcy (10/52)	Couchsachraga (7/4/65)
311	Deborah Kaslowski	Porter (8/13/61)	Allen (7/20/65)
312	Geraldine F. Chittick	Colvin (9/1/52)	Nye (7/22/65)
313	Alan H. Hunt	Marcy (7/5/41)	Nye (7/22/65)
314	Philip T. Allen	Algonquin (8/22/57)	Whiteface (7/24/65)
315	Jonathan G. Daunt	Cascade (7/61)	Marshall (7/29/65)
316	William H. Localio	Algonquin (8/55)	Emmons (7/30/65)
317	David L. Newhouse	Dix (7/46)	Couchsachraga (8/4/65)
318	David Archer	Cascade (8/60)	Iroquois (8/10/65)
319	Didi M. Kearsley	Porter (7/6/64)	Macomb (8/12/65)
320	James R. Pugh	Cascade (7/5/65)	Macomb (8/12/65)
321	Frances Uptegrove	Tabletop (8/10/64)	Macomb (8/12/65)
322	Steven M. Kilby	Lower Wolf Jaw (1958)	Phelps (8/12/65)
323	Victor S. Sacco	Colden (7/14/57)	Panther (8/15/65)
324	Thomas W. Wyckoff	Esther (7/30/59)	Sawteeth (8/15/65)
325	David Lee	Giant (1960)	Hough (8/21/65)
326	Ian J. Joseph	Algonquin (7/61)	Lower Wolf Jaw (8/22/65)
327	Robert B. Koegel	Cascade (7/7/64)	Seymour (8/23/65)
328	Jeffrey Riklin	Big Slide (7/6/61)	Marshall (8/23/65)
329	David W. McEniry	Cascade (7/7/64)	Emmons (8/23/65)
330	David H. Battle	Cascade (7/6/64)	Seymour (8/25/65)
331	James M. Altman	Cascade (7/11/61)	Sawteeth (8/28/65)
332	Samuel O. Tilton	Marcy (8/18/58)	Macomb (8/28/65)
333	Jere M. Wickens	Cascade (7/11/61)	Iroquois (8/30/65)
334	Peter C. Munson	Macomb (7/60)	Allen (8/31/65)
335	Jamie Wickens	Algonquin (8/58)	Couchsachraga (9/3/65)
336	James R. Richer	Algonquin (8/58)	Marshall (9/3/65)
337	Bertha Dotterer	Marcy (9/51)	East Dix (9/4/65)
338	Susan D. Jarrell	Marcy (1961)	Emmons (9/5/65)
339	Maitland C. DeSormo	Algonquin (7/28/53)	Redfield (9/5/65)
340	John D. Shugrue	Wright (1950)	Whiteface (9/5/65)
341	Elizabeth B. Williams	Algonquin (1930)	Colden (9/7/65)
342W	David A. Vermilyea	Marcy (7/42)	Rocky Peak (11/2/65)
343	David B. Everett	Colden (1960)	Panther (9/1/65)
344	Will D. Merritt	Wright (4/19/57)	Marcy (3/19/66)
345	Edwin R. Scotcher	Marcy (8/49)	Blake (5/28/66)
346	Fred Fraser	Santanoni (9/55)	Couchsachraga (5/29/66)
347	Paul W. Weld	Algonquin (1936)	Emmons (6/25/66)
348	Marion E. Holmes	Marcy (1940)	Couchsachraga (7/3/66)
349	Elsie W. Triebig	Marcy (7/4/57)	Couchsachraga (7/3/66)
350	W. Beveridge Kendall	Saddleback (9/12/58)	Gray (7/3/66)
351	Eric D. Kuhn	Cascade (7/11/64)	Sawteeth (7/16/66)
352	Ralph T. Shuey	Colden (7/11/64)	Couchsachraga (7/16/66)
353	Charles Gibson, Sr.	Marcy (1928)	Marshall (7/22/66)
354	David P. Hyson	Haystack (6/59)	Phelps (7/31/66)
355	Marcia M. McClellan	Cascade (7/48)	Emmons (8/2/66)
356	Norman A. Greist	Colden (9/33)	Macomb (8/7/66)
357	John S. McIntosh	Marcy (11/9/57)	Allen (8/16/66)
358	Ray L. Donahue	Marcy (10/11/62)	Couchsachraga (8/16/66)
359	John Happel	Whiteface (8/35)	Couchsachraga (8/16/66)
360	Culver S. Tefft	Macomb (8/61)	Redfield (8/18/66)
361	Walter Gray	Cascade (6/13/64)	Santanoni (8/20/66)
362	Manuel Aven	Marcy (6/61)	Emmons (8/20/66)
363	Peter Aven	Marcy (6/61)	Emmons (8/20/66)
364	J. Vernon Lamb, Jr.	Marcy (1940)	Algonquin (8/20/66)
365	J. Vernon Lamb, III	Wright (9/62)	Algonquin (8/20/66)

Heaven Up-h'isted-ness!

	Member	First Ascent	Forty-sixth Peak
366	Tracy Lamb	Wright (9/62)	Algonquin (8/20/66)
367	Winifred Lamb	Sawteeth (10/17/65)	Algonquin (8/20/66)
368	Shirley Pytlak	Phelps (1960)	Colvin (8/20/66)
369	Richard S. Frank	Whiteface (7/64)	Allen (8/21/66)
370	James E. Gedney	Wright (7/7/64)	Allen (8/21/66)
371	David E. Harvey	Colvin (7/63)	Allen (8/21/66)
372	John A. Hartog	Lower Wolf Jaw (8/64)	Marshall (8/21/66)
373	Linda A. Oppenheimer	Cascade (7/61)	Marshall (8/21/66)
374	Paul Makara	Cascade (1956)	Marshall (8/22/66)
375	William L. Murphy	Wright (8/1/59)	Allen (8/24/66)
376	Samuel Hoar, Jr.	Cascade (1960)	Phelps (8/26/66)
377	Charles A. Bookman	Cascade (7/55)	Rocky Peak (8/27/66)
378	John M. Harvey	Algonquin (7/60)	Seymour (8/66)
379	James W. Page	Marcy (1956)	Sawteeth (9/1/66)
380	Jay Sulzberser	Algonquin (12/18/65)	Marcy (9/5/66)
381	Brian P. Higgins	Marcy (1962)	Couchsachraga (9/7/66)
382	Daniel Bonbright	Cascade (8/52)	Haystack (9/9/66)
383	Neva B. McMullen	Marcy (7/20/49)	East Dix (9/10/66)
384W	James H. Boomer	Algonquin (8/5/58)	Sawteeth (9/10/66)
385	Dennis O'Leary	Marcy (7/23/66)	Seymour (9/10/66)
386	Frederick Q. Gemmill, Jr.	Marcy (1958)	Couchsachraga (9/18/66)
387	Raymond B. Fields	Marcy (9/49)	Redfield (9/18/66)
388	Mimi Frenette	Cascade (8/5/65)	Allen (9/18/66)
389	Virginia Frenette	Phelps (12/64)	Allen (9/18/66)
390	Harry F. Jackson, Jr.	Marcy (8/29/57)	Allen (9/25/66)
391	Harry F. Jackson, Sr.	Marcy (9/16/55)	Allen (9/25/66)
392	Howard L. Steinman	Marcy (8/2/46)	Sawteeth (10/8/66)
393	Kirk L. Burness	Colden (7/26/59)	Tabletop (10/9/66)
394	John R. Hobson	Marcy (10/12/37)	Dix (10/30/66)
395	Richard Hunkins	Cascade (1940)	Redfield (10/30/66)
396	Richard T. Nelson	Big Slide (4/16/65)	Rocky Peak (12/10/66)
397	Dudley A. Gilbert	Dix (5/31/63)	Couchsachraga (5/28/67)
398	Richard Jablonowski	Marcy (9/63)	Whiteface (6/3/67)
399	Hilda H. Young	Saddleback (8/1/64)	Couchsachraga (6/10/67)
400	John P. Harrington	Colden (1956)	Dial (6/11/67)
401	Nelson H. Dunn	Marcy (8/17/64)	Marshall (6/18/67)
402W	Evan T. Bergen	Gothics (11/16/63)	Emmons (6/18/67)
403	John E. Palmer	Marcy (7/4/41)	Allen (6/24/67)
404	George Gibian	Marshall (5/30/63)	Blake (7/1/67)
405	Alan E. McIntosh	Giant (7/61)	Allen (7/11/67)
406	John Wall	Skylight (7/12/65)	Cliff (7/13/67)
407	Roger H. Sweeney	Haystack (7/57)	Allen (7/19/67)
408	David Bixby	Skylight (1960)	Allen (7/19/67)
409	John H. Donohue	Skylight (7/13/65)	Allen (7/19/67)
410	Mark Dumont	Cascade (1958)	Donaldson (7/21/67)
411	Robert G. Rowan	Colden (7/62)	Allen (7/23/67)
412	Dudley T. Marple	Gothics (9/58)	Seymour (7/29/67)
413	Nathan B. Marple, IV	Gothics (10/54)	Seymour (7/29/67)
414	Burton D. Wilson	Colden (10/61)	Marcy (7/29/67)
415	Eugene H. Staiger	Colden (7/3/64)	Rocky Peak (7/29/67)
416	Roger J. Breeding	Algonquin (8/28/65)	Seymour (7/31/67)
417	Scott McClelland	Cascade (1961)	Panther (8/8/67)
418	Stanley Solomon	Cascade (10/62)	Allen (8/8/67)
419	Robert Demuth	Santanoni (8/61)	Esther (8/10/67)
420	David R. Markham	Dix (8/62)	Nye (8/12/67)
421	Philip L. Holstein	Cascade (1965)	Sawteeth (8/13/67)
422	Christopher A. Stokes	Marcy (8/60)	Redfield (8/14/67)
423	Burns Foster	Haystack (1960)	Panther (8/18/67)
424	David L. DeCourcy	Phelps (7/15/64)	Rocky Peak (8/18/67)
425	Stuart R. Rickey	Cascade (7/64)	Rocky Peak (8/18/67)
426	Gregory F. Todd	Cascade (7/6/64)	Sawteeth (8/20/67)
427	Thomas Elkind	Porter (1962)	Allen (8/21/67)

The Membership Roster of the Adirondack Forty-Sixers

	Member	First Ascent	Forty-sixth Peak
428	James D. Gundell	Cascade (8/19/65)	Allen (8/22/67)
429	Katherine J. Moos	Cascade (7/63)	Saddleback (8/22/67)
430	James Dumont	Cascade (7/65)	Saddleback (8/22/67)
431	Christopher Bluhm	Basin (7/63)	Colden (8/22/67)
432	Susan Healy	Cascade (8/16/58)	Allen (8/22/67)
433	Steven B. Healy	Cascade (9/3/60)	Allen (8/22/67)
434	Newell E. Mitchell	Upper Wolf Jaw (9/10/55)	Sawteeth (8/26/67)
435	Timothy F. Boomer	Algonquin (8/5/58)	Allen (8/26/67)
436	Gail H. Chandler	Cascade (7/11/62)	Couchsachraga (8/26/67)
437	Ann J. Peet	Cascade (8/56)	Skylight (8/26/67)
438	Jeffrey B. Storer	Giant (7/65)	Couchsachraga (8/30/67)
439	Gregory C. Gardner	Cascade (8/27/58)	Big Slide (9/1/67)
440	Brooks F. Rogers	Giant (8/26/64)	Marshall (9/3/67)
441	Byron R. Thoman	Marcy (8/31/63)	Iroquois (9/3/67)
442	Barbara T. Sprenkle	Whiteface (8/39)	Couchsachraga (9/5/67)
443	Robert L. Sprenkle	Whiteface (8/39)	Couchsachraga (9/5/67)
444	Todd W. Sprenkle	Marcy (8/58)	Couchsachraga (9/5/67)
445	Jeanette F. Jones	Big Slide (10/5/63)	Cliff (9/9/67)
446	Norman C. Jones	Big Slide (10/5/63)	Cliff (9/9/67)
447	Daniel M. Chase	Cascade (1952)	Cliff (9/9/67)
448	Clyde Babb	Lower Wolf Jaw (8/21/66)	Sawteeth (9/15/67)
449	Karin S. Constant	Lower Wolf Jaw (8/21/66)	Sawteeth (9/15/67)
450W	George M. Rosenberry, Jr.	Giant (8/57)	Nye (9/16/67)
451	Thomas V. Lamb	Cascade (6/5/66)	Colden (9/17/67)
452	Helen L. Dunn	Marcy (8/17/64)	Blake (10/7/67)
453	Samuel J. Prichard	Skylight (1930)	Blake (10/7/67)
454	David Hunkins	Nye (1961)	Marcy (10/7/67)
455	Anthony Briggs	Big Slide (5/6/67)	Phelps (10/7/67)
456	David D. Boyce	Algonquin (5/23/63)	Donaldson (10/14/67)
457	Elsie Myers	Algonquin (5/23/63)	Donaldson (10/14/67)
458	Harold K. Boyce	Algonquin (5/23/63)	Donaldson (10/14/67)
459	Linda L. Boyce	Algonquin (5/23/63)	Donaldson (10/14/67)
460	Wynne H. Cotton	Gothics (8/1/64)	Donaldson (10/14/67)
461	Kingsley D. Maynard	Street (5/30/63)	Tabletop (5/30/68)
462	Lewis Buchholz, Jr.	Marcy (7/65)	Couchsachraga (5/31/68)
463	Brian C. Kullman	Marcy (8/60)	Couchsachraga (6/3/68)
464	Michael Garratt	Cascade (10/12/60)	Allen (6/21/68)
465	James C. Dittmar	Wright (5/31/62)	Seymour (6/26/68)
466	Fred R. Bryce	Saddleback (9/26/49)	Allen (7/4/68)
467	Becky Warner	Cascade (7/6/64)	Gray (7/12/68)
468	Charlotte W. Fletcher	Wright (7/60)	Nye (7/14/68)
469	Janet Webb	Marcy (8/34)	Nye (7/14/68)
470	Betty A. Church	Big Slide (7/3/67)	Panther (7/16/68)
471	Richard E. Church	Big Slide (7/3/67)	Panther (7/16/68)
472	Richard L. Goldin	Lower Wolf Jaw (9/1/62)	Marshall (7/20/68)
473	Winslow A. Robbins, Jr.	Big Slide (7/12/65)	Whiteface (7/20/68)
474	John P. Morgan, III	Cascade (9/61)	Sawteeth (7/29/68)
475	Mark Gibian	Dial (7/20/63)	Marshall (7/31/68)
476	Peter Gibian	Dial (7/20/63)	Marshall (7/31/68)
477	Stephen B. Gibian	Dial (7/20/63)	Marshall (7/31/68)
478	Harold A. Jensen	Marcy (7/13/63)	Allen (8/2/68)
479	George J. Sherwin, Jr.	Lower Wolf Jaw (8/16/66)	Allen (8/2/68)
480	Kenneth E. Bassler	Marcy (8/6/63)	Couchsachraga (8/4/68)
481	George H. Spring	Saddleback (8/5/61)	Couchsachraga (8/4/68)
482	Jon I. Lieberman	Giant (7/14/65)	Whiteface (8/6/68)
483	Douglas Manchee	Colden (7/65)	Haystack (8/9/68)
484	Martha B. Day	Marcy (1935)	Cliff (8/11/68)
485	Peter S. Day	Marcy (9/10/54)	Cliff (8/11/68)
486	Rex J. Brusgal	Algonquin (8/12/61)	Panther (9/14/69)
487	Ronald T. Konowitz	Wright (1962)	Emmons (8/12/68)
488	Gary Kwok	Cascade (7/63)	Emmons (8/12/68)
489	Jeffrey Reel	Whiteface (1965)	Emmons (8/12/68)

HEAVEN UP-H'ISTED-NESS!

	MEMBER	FIRST ASCENT	FORTY-SIXTH PEAK
490	Jeffrey Scott	Cascade (7/62)	Emmons (8/12/68)
491	George W. Young, III	Sawteeth (8/65)	Emmons (8/12/68)
492	Robert C. Spencer, Jr.	Skylight (10/12/63)	Emmons (8/13/68)
493	Stephen Frederickson	Big Slide (7/65)	Emmons (8/13/68)
494	Quentin Orza	Giant (8/10/65)	Emmons (8/13/68)
495	Robert E. Bers	Algonquin (7/16/63)	Whiteface (8/15/68)
496	Jane DeLisa	Big Slide (8/61)	Hough (8/16/68)
497	Charles D. Cohn	Dix (7/11/66)	Whiteface (8/16/68)
498	Margaret S. Endicott	Gothics (9/39)	Couchsachraga (8/11/68)
499	Roxane C. Lowther	Porter (7/8/67)	Cascade (8/22/68)
500	Robert L. Gilchriest	Wright (1961)	Allen (8/23/68)
501	Estelle Freedman	Gothics (10/11/58)	Hough (8/25/68)
502	John Broderick	Cascade (1965)	Colden (8/28/68)
503	Donald Denette	Cascade (7/13/64)	Panther (8/28/68)
504	Helene P. Foley	Giant (8/53)	Colden (8/29/68)
505	Janny Peet	Cascade (8/21/59)	Colden (8/29/68)
506	Peter A. Mark	Phelps (8/1/60)	Couchsachraga (8/30/68)
507	Edwin H. Ketchledge	Marcy (6/21/49)	Couchsachraga (8/30/68)
508	C. Basil Dearborn, Jr.	Lower Wolf Jaw (7/62)	Emmons (8/31/68)
509	Alfred Obrist	Tabletop (3/3/65)	Sawteeth (9/1/68)
510	William N. Bryce	Dial (11/13/65)	Allen (9/4/68)
511	Carl E. Haischer	Marcy (9/1/30)	Rocky Peak (9/7/68)
512	John H. Lochhead	Algonquin (9/30/55)	Haystack (9/14/68)
513	Charles Linett	Marcy (9/4/66)	Couchsachraga (9/23/68)
514	Charles R. Braxton	Cascade (8/59)	Couchsachraga (9/28/68)
515	Richard Nicholas	Marcy (5/30/57)	Seymour (10/12/68)
516	Rodney P. Swartz	Marcy (9/62)	Basin (10/12/68)
517	Fred S. Blomshield	Giant (9/27/64)	Emmons (10/13/68)
518	John H. Blomshield	Skylight (10/12/63)	Emmons (10/13/68)
519	Merlin P. Harvey	Marcy (8/31/52)	Couchsachraga (7/5/68)
520	David G. Newcombe	Haystack (7/5/67)	Gray (8/23/68)
521	Forrest A. Rowland	Sawteeth (7/14/66)	Whiteface (8/28/68)
522	Edward Vervoort, Jr.	Cascade (12/28/63)	Couchsachraga (2/22/69)
523W	Richard M. Stetson	Giant (11/21/64)	Wright (3/16/69)
524	Harley L. Gardner	Marcy (7/27/65)	Dix (5/24/69)
525	Robert Gardner	Marcy (7/27/65)	Dix (5/24/69)
526	Donald Messick	Marcy (7/27/65)	Dix (5/24/69)
527	Thomas Scheideler	Marcy (7/27/65)	Dix (5/24/69)
528	Joseph E. Franklin	Basin (2/26/67)	Nye (6/10/69)
529	Donald N. McGregor	Macomb (5/28/67)	Couchsachraga (7/3/69)
530	Eric G. Wagner	Cascade (1943)	Allen (7/4/69)
531	Philip M. Garratt	Cascade (9/1/50)	Skylight (7/9/69)
532	James W. Emerson II	Marcy (9/63)	Couchsachraga (7/15/69)
533	Douglas N. Close	Phelps (8/63)	Rocky Peak (7/16/69)
534	John S. Manly	Cascade (7/20/61)	Iroquois (7/19/69)
535	Robert M. Shwab	Dix (7/15/66)	Cascade (7/22/69)
536	Glenn W. Fish	Redfield (11/25/66)	Cliff (7/23/69)
537	Harry Gamble	Marcy (1921)	Cliff (7/23/69)
538	Elizabeth W. Jensen	Algonquin (7/18/64)	Emmons (7/28/69)
539	Thomas R. MacKenzie	Lower Wolf Jaw (8/5/64)	Iroquois (8/1/69)
540	Thomas H. Martyn	Algonquin (9/58)	Lower Wolf Jaw (8/2/69)
541	William J. Nealon	Marcy (8/2/61)	Lower Wolf Jaw (8/5/69)
542	Marian E. Nealon	Marcy (8/2/61)	Gothics (8/5/69)
543	Gregory B. Kucera	Big Slide (7/62)	Saddleback (8/9/69)
544	A. James Raporte	Wright (7/63)	Emmons (8/14/69)
545	Russell S. Miller	Macomb (9/2/65)	Allen (8/12/69)
546	Stephen M. Zeller	Cascade (7/14/56)	Phelps (8/14/69)
547	Steven R. Pierson	Dix (8/62)	Marshall (8/16/69)
548	Charles S. Hoover	Saddleback (6/25/42)	Allen (8/15/69)
549	James Anderberg	Colden (6/66)	Nye (8/16/69)
550	Bart I. Brodsky	Phelps (7/11/67)	Nye (8/16/69)
551	James Cramer	Phelps (7/67)	Nye (8/16/69)

The Membership Roster of the Adirondack Forty-Sixers

	Member	First Ascent	Forty-sixth Peak
552	Thomas R. Field	Marcy (8/66)	Nye (8/16/69)
553	Howard K. Uniman	Marcy (7/66)	Nye (8/16/69)
554	Merli M. Kaplan	Porter (7/6/65)	Redfield (8/18/69)
555	Julie Chandler	Cascade (7/31/64)	Redfield (8/18/69)
556	Douglas L. Hoffmann	Lower Wolf Jaw (6/23/52)	Cliff (8/18/69)
557	David E. Moore, Jr.	Macomb (9/66)	Redfield (8/18/69)
558	David L. Woodcock	Cascade (7/9/64)	Allen (8/20/69)
559	Charlotte G. Craig	Giant (1921)	Panther (8/21/69)
560	Peggy G. O'Brien	Giant (1923)	Panther (8/21/69)
561	Brooke (Barbara) P. Dittmar	Lower Wolf Jaw (7/23/63)	Redfield (8/21/69)
562	Susan M. Paden	Phelps (5/30/64)	Redfield (8/21/69)
563	Elizabeth A. Dittmar	Lower Wolf Jaw (7/23/63)	Redfield (8/21/69)
564	Katharyn D. Carter	Whiteface (8/62)	Redfield (8/21/69)
565	Marion N. Fields	Giant (5/30/64)	Phelps (8/22/69)
566W	John S. Swan, Jr.	Wright (8/63)	Marshall (8/23/69)
567	Philip C. Wall	Algonquin (7/3/68)	Big Slide (8/28/69)
568	James G. DeLago	Cascade (7/65)	Sawteeth (8/69)
569	Spiro Kavarnos	Phelps (3/30/69)	Marcy (9/1/69)
570	Jonathan Meigs	Marcy (9/57)	Tabletop (9/1/69)
571	Patience W. Meigs	Marcy (9/57)	Santanoni (9/1/69)
572	Burton L. Louk	Marcy (8/9/60)	Marshall (9/4/69)
573	Norman E. Greig	Seymour (8/28/69)	Whiteface (9/5/69)
574	N. Rey Whetten	Giant (9/55)	Macomb (9/13/69)
575	Richard W. Boehme	Marcy (8/31/62)	Couchsachraga (9/20/69)
576W	Leon G. Barry	Santanoni (8/31/68)	Emmons (9/21/69)
577	Donald R. Krahmer	Marcy (6/52)	Seymour (9/21/69)
578	H. William Page, Jr.	Algonquin (8/15/64)	Couchsachraga (9/27/69)
579	Evelyn F. Perry	Haystack (7/8/58)	Whiteface (9/27/69)
580	George E. Saunders	Armstrong (8/58)	Rocky Peak (9/28/69)
581	James E. Daley	Marcy (8/31/62)	Haystack (10/4/69)
582	Henry E. Mazanek	Marcy (10/37)	Couchsachraga (10/11/69)
583	Robert L. Wall	Marcy (9/56)	Couchsachraga (10/11/69)
584	William B. Eighme	Marcy (8/3/65)	Whiteface (10/12/69)
585	Alfred R. Hartmann	Cascade (12/20/67)	Basin (10/18/69)
586	Sonja D. Hartmann	Dix (5/19/68)	Upper Wolf Jaw (10/19/69)
587	Edith G. Prest	Lower Wolf Jaw (7/48)	Cascade (10/26/69)
588	William M. Prest	Giant (9/59)	Cascade (10/26/69)
589	Richard F. Rose	Phelps (10/9/65)	Blake (11/16/69)
590	Bernard R. Mulcahy	Marcy (6/64)	Allen (8/2/68)
591	Peter Cottrell	Macomb (7/28/62)	Couchsachraga (2/22/70)
592	John McKenney	Marcy (11/64)	Allen (2/23/70)
593W	Fred M. Hunt	Marcy (6/29/69)	Allen (2/24/70)
594	George Elias	Giant (7/24/65)	Couchsachraga (5/18/70)
595	Joseph C. Buck	Porter (6/30/63)	Marshall (5/23/70)
596	Robert G. Henckel	Hough (5/29/67)	Street (5/23/70)
597	Stuart A. MacDuffie	Marcy (9/7/62)	Nye (5/24/70)
598	Virginia M. Cone	Marcy (9/39)	East Dix (5/30/70)
599	Robert Ainley	Marcy (1957)	Algonquin (5/30/70)
600	Charles F. Mowry	Colden (5/29/65)	Gray (5/31/70)
601	Edwin P. Russell	Colden (5/29/65)	Gray (5/31/70)
602	Frank Russell	Santanoni (5/28/66)	Wright (6/1/70)
603	Llewellyn Bromfield	Marcy (8/28/53)	Cliff (6/12/70)
604	Larry Pasti	Wright (10/15/67)	Iroquois (6/13/70)
605	Judy Cameron	Marcy (9/35)	Hough (6/23/70)
606	John E. Goulder	Cascade (1965)	Rocky Peak (6/24/70)
607	Werner Baum	Whiteface (Mid-50's)	Emmons (6/26/70)
608	Robert M. Gallivan	Lower Wolf Jaw (9/3/66)	Allen (7/3/70)
609	Stuart Miner	Porter (7/63)	Emmons (7/4/70)
610	Lawrence R. Sedgeley	Saddleback (2/22/63)	Allen (7/12/70)
611	Robert Rosenheck	Marcy (1958)	Couchsachraga (7/26/70)
612	John E. Radcliffe	Marcy (11/67)	Emmons (8/2/70)
613	Charlotte Hitchcock	Cascade (7/68)	Wright (8/3/70)

Heaven Up-h'isted-ness!

	Member	First Ascent	Forty-sixth Peak
614	Mark Friedman	Phelps (7/11/67)	Nye (8/6/70)
615	Scott Rovner	Marcy (7/68)	Nye (8/6/70)
616	Tim Tefft	Giant (1961)	Redfield (8/6/70)
617	Glen D. Chapman	Santanoni (8/65)	Couchsachraga (8/11/70)
618	Catherine Crosby	Sawteeth (7/69)	Couchsachraga (8/13/70)
619	Patricia A. Thomason	Whiteface (1963)	Couchsachraga (8/13/70)
620	Anne Martyn	Cascade (8/63)	Big Slide (8/14/70)
621	Charles H. Bennett	Giant (9/4/67)	Seymour (8/15/70)
622	Lillian Bull	Algonquin (2/22/69)	Seymour (8/15/70)
623	Elly Strode	Marcy (7/15/67)	Seymour (8/15/70)
624	David B. Chandler	Cascade (7/63)	Nye (8/15/70)
625	Robert Chandler	Algonquin (7/1/61)	Nye (8/15/70)
626	Evan M. Kurtz	Cascade (6/65)	Macomb (8/15/70)
627	Edmund R. Scott	Phelps (7/1/69)	Macomb (8/15/70)
628	Todd McDowell	Lower Wolf Jaw (7/8/69)	Big Slide (8/15/70)
629	Louis A. Budell	Upper Wolf Jaw (1/22/66)	Esther (8/15/70)
630	Peter B. Hall	Marcy (5/2/69)	Tabletop (8/16/70)
631	Edward Bielawski	Marcy (1929)	Colden (8/16/70)
632	Steven Ramras	Giant (7/4/66)	Iroquois (8/17/70)
633	Joshua Sacco	Algonquin (8/10/64)	Sawteeth (8/17/70)
634	Paul Bronfman	Cascade (7/66)	Gray (8/18/70)
635	Paul Theimer	Giant (7/21/67)	Gray (8/18/70)
636	David Dumont	Big Slide (7/18/68)	Sawteeth (8/18/70)
637	Christopher Hyson	Big Slide (8/66)	Esther (8/19/70)
638	Eugene J. Fellows	Cascade (5/24/69)	Donaldson (8/22/70)
639	William Ladue	Giant (1929)	Seymour (8/23/70)
640	Paul Allen	Cascade (7/61)	Big Slide (8/23/70)
641	Kenneth Pin	Sawteeth (8/16/64)	Skylight (8/24/70)
642	James Lattin	Cascade (7/13/68)	Porter (8/27/70)
643	Harold Stillman	Algonquin (7/1/70)	Marshall (8/24/70)
644W	Warren E. Reynolds	Wright (9/3/57)	Emmons (8/25/70)
645	Thomas A. Dunn	Big Slide (8/20/62)	Allen (8/26/70)
646	Jules Comeau	Lower Wolf Jaw (6/14/68)	Marshall (8/27/70)
647	Jamie Fellows	Cascade (5/24/69)	Nippletop (8/29/70)
648	Mary L. Kent	Marcy (8/63)	Allen (8/29/70)
649	Ralph D. Williams	Marcy (6/13/40)	Allen (8/30/70)
650	Al Heller	Wright (8/27/69)	Allen (8/30/70)
651	J. Wister Meigs	Algonquin (9/2/38)	Rocky Peak (9/1/70)
652	Steven D. Allen	Marcy (8/66)	Couchsachraga (9/1/70)
653	C. Converse Goddard	Big Slide (1933)	Hough (9/2/70)
654	G. Kent Keller	Lower Wolf Jaw (7/59)	Allen (9/3/70)
655	Laura Chapman	Santanoni (8/65)	Iroquois (9/5/70)
656	Henry M. Childs	Cascade (8/25/65)	Couchsachraga (9/5/70)
657	Warren E. McKay	Marcy (9/5/65)	Couchsachraga (9/6/70)
658	Pam C. Coe	Phelps (7/2/66)	Couchsachraga (9/6/70)
659	Walter M. Chapman	Marcy (8/64)	Couchsachraga (9/7/70)
660	Fred W. Chapman	Giant (9/8/68)	Redfield (9/7/70)
661	Dawna C. Fazio	Marcy (8/64)	Gray (9/8/70)
662	Philip N. Pitcher	Marcy (8/25/55)	Couchsachraga (9/8/70)
663	Ernest Riegel	Armstrong (1937)	Macomb (9/20/70)
664	Gail R. Helfer	Phelps (6/3/68)	Santanoni (9/20/70)
665	Walter L. Gregory	Marcy (10/3/65)	Hough (10/2/70)
666	Paul A. Rothman	Algonquin (6/22/68)	Marcy (10/3/70)
667	Charles F. Beach	Marcy (10/56)	Allen (10/10/70)
668	Anne M. Chapman	Giant (9/8/68)	Hough (11/6/70)
669	Harris G. Abbott	Marcy (1956)	Cliff (8/7/70)
670W	Guy Waterman	Wright (2/8/69)	Marcy (3/21/71)
671	Lou Palmer	Marcy (9/6/66)	Couchsachraga (3/29/71)
672	Zbigniew S. Kornecki	Wright (7/31/67)	Redfield (5/28/71)
673	Leslaw J. Kornecki	Wright (7/31/67)	Redfield (5/28/71)
674	Stanislaw L. Kornecki	Wright (7/31/67)	Redfield (5/28/71)
675	Otylia R. Kornecki	Wright (7/31/67)	Redfield (5/28/71)

The Membership Roster of the Adirondack Forty-Sixers

	Member	First Ascent	Forty-sixth Peak
676	Stanislaw J. Kornecki	Wright (7/31/67)	Redfield (5/28/71)
677	Warren P. Deland	Marcy (10/2/54)	Couchsachraga (5/30/71)
678	David Vogel	Algonquin (8/66)	Allen (6/7/71)
679	Bobo M. Vivitsky (dog)	Gothics (9/7/64)	Marshall (6/7/71)
680	Jack Vivitsky	Big Slide (9/2/64)	Marshall (6/7/71)
681	Kenneth Leibert	Colden (7/7/59)	Allen (6/8/71)
682	Clifton A. Bischoff	Colden (5/29/67)	Allen (6/17/71)
683	Richard L. Erenstone	Cascade (7/65)	Cliff (6/19/71)
684	Edwin R. Page	Giant (1952)	Allen (7/5/71)
685	John Butterworth, Jr.	Giant (7/12/66)	Whiteface (1971)
686	Paul Guth	Phelps (7/1/69)	Marshall (8/1/71)
687	Alec Mahrer	Phelps (7/8/67)	Marshall (8/1/71)
688	Kenneth Schwartz	Phelps (7/8/67)	Marshall (8/1/71)
689	Caleb W. Burchenal	Marcy (8/59)	Couchsachraga (8/1/71)
690	John B. Kaman	Cascade (7/65)	Seymour (8/4/71)
691	David Nuckols	Dix (7/6/68)	Haystack (8/6/71)
692	Paul Nuckols	Dix (7/6/68)	Haystack (8/6/71)
693	Robert C. Nuckols	Dix (7/6/68)	Haystack (8/6/71)
694	Margaret Krahmer	Nippletop (6/9/68)	Emmons (8/7/71)
695	Betty Hicks	Marcy (8/14/51)	Allen (8/12/71)
696	Todd Weber	Cascade (7/69)	Cliff (8/14/71)
697	Steven Resnick	Colden (7/65)	Allen (8/15/71)
698	Jacques Robitaille	Cascade (7/1/68)	Allen (8/15/71)
699	Byron Haynes	Marshall (8/67)	Whiteface (8/15/71)
700	Thomas J. Clark	Cascade (7/67)	Allen (8/16/71)
701	Claudette de Lamater	Phelps (9/8/68)	Couchsachraga (8/16/71)
702	Sparkles de Lamater	Phelps (9/8/68)	Couchsachraga (8/16/71)
703	Glen H. Schaffer	Cliff (8/3/69)	Couchsachraga (8/16/71)
704	John R. Shaffer	Cascade (9/14/68)	Couchsachraga (8/16/71)
705	Ruth S. Farrell	Marcy (8/20/68)	Couchsachraga (8/16/71)
706	Philip Bush	Giant (7/68)	Colden (8/16/71)
707	Richard P. Handler	Marcy (8/55)	Couchsachraga (8/17/71)
708	Dan Broadbooks	Algonquin (7/1/70)	Big Slide (8/17/71)
709	Donald J. Bouyea	Dial (7/67)	Sawteeth (8/18/71)
710	Edward M. Palen	Porter (7/64)	Nye (8/18/71)
711	William M. Allen, Jr.	Wright (6/26/62)	Whiteface (8/19/71)
712	James F. Donnelly	Marcy (7/7/67)	Emmons (8/20/71)
713	Barbara M. Hale	Marcy (8/5/67)	Sawteeth (8/22/71)
714	Edward Hale	Marcy (8/5/67)	Sawteeth (8/22/71)
715	Kirt J. Hall	Marcy (6/67)	Haystack (8/22/71)
716	Howard C. Ward	Marcy (8/19/64)	Haystack (8/22/71)
717	Michael Aven	Cascade (7/67)	Panther (8/22/71)
718	James Toub	Phelps (7/11/67)	Dix (8/22/71)
719	Robert J. Muhl	Algonquin (3/4/67)	Redfield (8/23/71)
720	Richard Upjohn	Cascade (8/31/63)	Haystack (8/24/71)
721	Freda Lawton	Marcy (8/5/55)	Couchsachraga (8/25/71)
722	William P. Sorren	Cascade (7/63)	Allen (8/27/71)
723	Charles J. Dittmar	Algonquin (9/6/40)	Phelps (8/30/71)
724	Audrey W. Ashley	Marcy (9/61)	Allen (8/30/71)
725	Charles A. Ashley	Marcy (9/61)	Allen (8/30/71)
726	Thomas B. McLemore	Marcy (8/62)	Emmons (8/30/71)
727	Robert Loyer	Cascade (1958)	Marshall (8/31/71)
728	Roger Loyer	Wright (1958)	Marshall (8/31/71)
729	Ann McConnalee	Algonquin (9/1/68)	Colden (9/1/71)
730	Ilona McConnalee	Algonquin (9/1/68)	Colden (9/1/71)
731	James McConnalee	Algonquin (9/1/68)	Colden (9/1/71)
732	Julie McConnalee	Algonquin (9/1/68)	Colden (9/1/71)
733	Karen McConnalee	Algonquin (9/1/68)	Colden (9/1/71)
734	Anne T. Jalali	Colvin (8/16/60)	Dix (9/1/71)
735	Eric Lorentzon	Algonquin (1965)	Couchsachraga (9/2/71)
736	Lars Lorentzon	Algonquin (1965)	Couchsachraga (9/2/71)
737	Barbara A. Griffith	Marcy (7/25/64)	Cascade (9/2/71)

HEAVEN UP-H'ISTED-NESS!

	MEMBER	FIRST ASCENT	FORTY-SIXTH PEAK
738	Walter M. Chapman	Gothics (10/10/42)	Armstrong (9/2/71)
739	Barbara V. Johnson	Cascade (8/62)	Haystack (9/3/71)
740	Mary Doherty	Algonquin (7/6/69)	Tabletop (9/4/71)
741	Michael E. Middleton	Lower Wolf Jaw (9/66)	Allen (9/4/71)
742	Stephen Middleton	Colden (9/65)	Allen (9/4/71)
743	Lewis Dalven	Dix (4/69)	Emmons (9/4/71)
744	Raymond Krahmer	Haystack (5/30/69)	Cliff (9/5/71)
745	Mary L. Baum	Cascade (9/6/65)	Whiteface (9/6/71)
746	Larry Riegel	Colden (1962)	Dial (9/18/71)
747	Otis B. Bacon	Marcy (9/61)	Couchsachraga (9/18/71)
748	David McLemore	Marcy (8/62)	Nippletop (9/18/71)
749	John C. Heald	Marcy (1965)	Couchsachraga (9/6/71)
750	Walter G. Herrod	Wright (9/61)	Nippletop (9/21/71)
751	Frederick Donnelly	Marcy (7/7/67)	Haystack (9/25/71)
752	Philip B. Clough	Algonquin (10/15/69)	Couchsachraga (9/25/71)
753	Gregory White	Marcy (7/20/68)	Colden (9/26/71)
754	J. Coleman White	Dix (9/30/67)	Colden (9/26/71)
755	Newell A. Briggs	Giant (6/22/68)	Marshall (9/26/71)
756	Ruth S. Briggs	Giant (6/22/68)	Marshall (9/26/71)
757	Glen A. Bjork	Marcy (9/10/68)	Emmons (10/1/71)
758	Laurie Feinberg	Cascade (10/13/68)	Basin (10/2/71)
759	William C. Hill	Cascade (10/13/68)	Basin (10/2/71)
760	Gary Klee	Marcy (10/24/50)	Couchsachraga (10/4/71)
761	Elizabeth R. Heins	Cascade (8/68)	Hough (10/7/71)
762	Jacob W. Heins	Cascade (8/68)	Hough (10/7/71)
763	William B. Lawson	Marcy (8/28/69)	Redfield (10/10/71)
764	Manfred Delia	Phelps (7/30/65)	Santanoni (10/10/71)
765	Tashiko D. Delia	Phelps (7/30/65)	Santanoni (10/10/71)
766W	Elsie E. Chrenko	Marcy (5/30/63)	Emmons (10/19/71)
767	James S. Bruce	Marcy (7/24/66)	Tabletop (10/23/71)
768	Richard Olmstead	Whiteface (7/20/67)	Emmons (10/24/71)
769	David Middleton	Giant (7/69)	Esther (10/24/71)
770	Henry A. Cox	Marcy (5/30/70)	Esther (10/28/71)
771	Michael P. Hannan	Cascade (9/68)	Colden (10/31/71)
772	Philip Terrie	Couchsachraga (7/66)	Esther (6/26/69)
773	Thomas Cohen	Cascade (7/6/69)	Cliff (8/14/71)
774	Nancy A. Bergen	Algonquin (10/22/66)	Street (3/4/72)
775	Thomas S. Caramia	Dix (9/20/69)	Allen (5/27/72)
776	Donald Federman	Tabletop (8/30/69)	Gray (5/28/72)
777	Brian Aveney	Lower Wolf Jaw (9/3/66)	Seymour (5/29/72)
778W	Roger L. Harris	Big Slide (9/69)	Emmons (6/5/72)
779	Craig P. Palmer	Giant (5/30/71)	Whiteface (6/10/72)
780	James Underwood	Dix (7/67)	Esther (6/17/72)
781	Sean Cridland	Algonquin (6/23/71)	Emmons (7/7/72)
782W	Richard Mallinson	East Dix (9/27/70)	Esther (7/11/72)
783	Howard H. Hansen	Lower Wolf Jaw (6/7/69)	Nye (7/12/72)
784	David G. Butterworth	Big Slide (7/17/67)	Colden (7/13/72)
785	Gary W. Baker	Cascade (7/61)	Allen (7/15/72)
786	Frank Stickler	Marcy (6/9/70)	Whiteface (7/16/72)
787	Bradford Perkins	Giant (7/6/67)	Gray (7/17/72)
788	Jonathan A. Hart	Marcy (8/62)	Allen (7/17/72)
789	Jacques Elliot	Marcy (8/16/58)	Allen (7/27/72)
790	John R. Easter	Marcy (1961)	Allen (7/27/72)
791	George C. Wheeler	Algonquin (8/30/66)	Couchsachraga (7/29/72)
792	Harold A. Lyons	Gothics (8/36)	Couchsachraga (8/3/72)
793	Richard Hornstein	Cascade (7/2/69)	Emmons (8/3/72)
794	David P. Stover	Saddleback (8/5/69)	Emmons (8/8/72)
795	John B. Stover	Saddleback (8/5/69)	Emmons (8/8/72)
796	Thomas Stover	Saddleback (8/5/69)	Emmons (8/8/72)
797	William Betlen	Phelps (8/65)	Marshall (8/8/72)
798	Scott Price	Cascade (7/65)	Panther (8/9/72)
799	Charles S. Grant	Marcy (8/57)	Marshall (8/10/72)

The Membership Roster of the Adirondack Forty-Sixers

	Member	First Ascent	Forty-sixth Peak
800	John Betlen	Phelps (8/65)	Rocky Peak (8/10/72)
801	Margaret S. Atkinson	Marcy (8/13/51)	Marshall (8/10/72)
802	Dorrice Sacco	Algonquin (7/59)	Colden (8/10/72)
803	Michael J. Urfirer	Cascade (1966)	Emmons (8/11/72)
804	Walter Espenlaub	Wright (12/30/65)	Couchsachraga (8/11/72)
805	John Minot	Cascade (8/16/64)	Couchsachraga (8/11/72)
806	Robert Freeland	Dix (1958)	Cascade (8/12/72)
807	Lucy Loomis	Gothics (7/63)	Couchsachraga (8/13/72)
808	Joan Jordan	Giant (7/22/68)	Dix (8/17/72)
809	Barkley Stagg	Marcy (9/68)	Allen (8/18/72)
810	Kimberly A. Bacon	Whiteface (1970)	Allen (8/19/72)
811	Dore Davis	Whiteface (1970)	Allen (8/19/72)
812	Karla Krassner	Marcy (1968)	Allen (8/19/72)
813	Thomas Harley	Giant (10/25/69)	Redfield (8/19/72)
814	Lucy P. Ashley	Gothics (7/26/69)	Cliff (8/19/72)
815	Gordon Skinner	Marcy (1938)	Nippletop (8/20/72)
816	Richard Mecklenborg	Lower Wolf Jaw (6/69)	Esther (8/21/72)
817	Debi Davis	Whiteface (8/20/69)	Santanoni (8/22/72)
818	Sandy Snyder	Whiteface (1971)	Panther (8/22/72)
819	Melissa H. Spencer	Marcy (8/5/67)	East Dix (8/26/72)
820	Marilyn Fancher	Cascade (7/58)	Nippletop (8/27/72)
821	Norman Fancher	Cascade (4/30/67)	Nippletop (8/27/72)
822	David H. Burnett	Colvin (10/8/66)	Allen (8/27/72)
823	Henry L. Woolsey	Big Slide (7/64)	Seymour (8/28/72)
824	Clifford Mossey	Marcy (9/11/60)	Cliff (8/30/72)
825	Paul Whittlesey	Santanoni (1960)	Couchsachraga (8/31/72)
826	Malcolm M. Byrne	Cascade (8/67)	Cliff (8/31/72)
827	Patricia Quinn	Colvin (7/17/71)	Cliff (8/31/72)
828	Brenda Wachmann	Giant (7/25/69)	Seymour (9/3/72)
829	Constantin Wachmann	Giant (7/25/69)	Seymour (9/3/72)
830	Dara Wachmann (dog)	Lower Wolf Jaw (9/6/70)	Seymour (9/3/72)
831	Eric Wachmann	Giant (7/25/69)	Seymour (9/3/72)
832	Marc Wachmann	Giant (7/25/69)	Seymour (9/3/72)
833	Thaisa A. Beach	Skylight (9/8/57)	Donaldson (9/3/72)
834	Peter Allen	Cascade (1959)	Colden (9/3/72)
835	Sandy Elder	Sawteeth (8/67)	Porter (9/3/72)
836	Robert Drexler	Haystack (7/21/68)	Nippletop (9/3/72)
837	Richard Brewster	Marcy (8/21/68)	Marshall (9/3/72)
838	George Lyons	Marcy (8/58)	Sawteeth (9/3/72)
839	Matthew L. Dumas	Big Slide (5/22/71)	Skylight (9/4/72)
840	Alden L. Dumas	Big Slide (5/22/71)	Skylight (9/4/72)
841	Stephen Delventhal	Marcy (7/28/70)	Seymour (9/7/72)
842	David H. Burchenal	Algonquin (1962)	Redfield (9/9/72)
843	Joan R. Burchenal	Giant (1934)	Redfield (9/9/72)
844	Joseph E. Burchenal	Cascade (8/66)	Redfield (9/9/72)
845	Joseph H. Burchenal	Giant (1947)	Redfield (9/9/72)
846	Nathan Church	Marcy (6/25/67)	Marshall (9/17/72)
847	Herbert D. Perten	Macomb (8/22/69)	Redfield (9/23/72)
848	James A. McHugh	Dial (8/7/71)	Phelps (9/30/72)
849	Lois Gnann	Marcy (9/1/68)	Allen (10/1/72)
850	Robert A. Heffley	Gothics (10/19/68)	Street (10/1/72)
851	Frederick J. Schnettler	Marcy (7/62)	Nye (10/6/72)
852	Ellen Frenette	Phelps (9/69)	Emmons (10/8/72)
853	Pamela Frenette	Phelps (9/69)	Emmons (10/8/72)
854	Helen Whitford	Whiteface (5/25/71)	Armstrong (10/12/72)
855	Gary MacKeown	Marcy (1949)	Phelps (10/14/72)
856	Robert MacKeown	Marcy (1949)	Phelps (10/14/72)
857	Walter Carstens	Marcy (9/28/64)	Marshall (10/14/72)
858	Jessie Rennie	Dix (9/20/70)	Cliff (10/21/72)
859	Moir Rennie	Dix (9/20/70)	Cliff (10/21/72)
860	Sarah Rennie	Dix (9/20/70)	Cliff (10/21/72)
861	William C. Borland	Marcy (4/16/66)	Whiteface (10/22/72)

Heaven Up-h'isted-ness!

	Member	First Ascent	Forty-sixth Peak
862	Harold Hayes	Marcy (10/17/68)	Macomb (10/27/72)
863	John C. Parsell	Marcy (7/39)	Nye (10/28/72)
864	Richard A. Bolte	Marcy (5/31/69)	Seymour (11/4/72)
865	John J. Leach	Santanoni (6/67)	Cascade (11/28/72)
866	Robert A. Papworth	Whiteface (1957)	Couchsachraga (8/72)
867	Timothy Ramsey	Algonquin (7/56)	Cliff (3/25/73)
868	Thomas J. Reagan	Algonquin (7/56)	Cliff (3/25/73)
869	George Farnell	Marcy (8/1/64)	Esther (3/31/73)
870	David O. Cooney	Algonquin (10/69)	Cliff (3/31/73)
871	Ronald E. Turbide	Algonquin (7/2/65)	Cliff (3/31/73)
872	David Reisner	Marcy (7/7/68)	Allen (4/14/73)
873	Gordon V. Parmelee	Marcy (9/25/70)	Nye (5/5/73)
874	Richard I. McCabe	Whiteface (4/7/68)	Haystack (5/20/73)
875	Dana Loud	Cascade (7/59)	Couchsachraga (5/26/73)
876	David Loud	Cascade (1967)	Santanoni (5/26/73)
877	Christopher Perley	Dix (12/5/70)	Dial (5/28/73)
878	Richard Perley	Dix (12/5/70)	Dial (5/28/73)
879	Peggy C. Enichen	Marcy (8/6/70)	Cliff (6/2/73)
880	William Enichen	Haystack (1969)	Cliff (6/2/73)
881	Robert J. Mack	Lower Wolf Jaw (12/2/72)	Street (6/16/73)
882	Trent Trahan	Marcy (7/68)	Colden (6/22/73)
883	Edmund Lynch	Giant (5/15/65)	Marshall (6/23/73)
884	Francis A. Combar	Marcy (10/55)	Marshall (6/24/73)
885	Anne B. Munro	Marcy (7/63)	Redfield (7/2/73)
886	Robert F. Munro	Marcy (7/63)	Redfield (7/2/73)
887	Gregory M. Amico	Marshall (7/20/70)	Marcy (7/2/73)
888	Perrin Babcock	Cascade (unknown)	Marshall (7/7/73)
889	Caroline Dawson	Cascade (10/23/71)	Santanoni (7/7/73)
890	James Dawson	Cascade (10/23/71)	Santanoni (7/7/73)
891	Jonathan Goodman	Haystack (8/53)	Redfield (7/7/73)
892	Michael Mahrer	Marcy (7/66)	Marshall (7/8/73)
893	Dean Wikoff	Cascade (8/25/60)	Emmons (7/12/73)
894	Stanley W. Ashley	Wright (7/22/62)	Dial (7/16/73)
895	John P. Childs	Algonquin (8/24/65)	Esther (7/22/73)
896	Donald P. Wiedmann	Cascade (8/20/64)	Allen (7/23/73)
897	Mildred A. Wiedmann	Cascade (8/20/64)	Allen (7/23/73)
898	Duffield Ashmead	Big Slide (7/17/67)	Marshall (7/24/73)
899	Michael Chase	Cascade (7/10/71)	Allen (7/26/73)
900	Barry Berman	Dix (7/4/73)	Allen (7/28/73)
901	John Catlett	Dix (7/4/73)	Allen (7/28/73)
902	Matthew Coleman	Dix (7/4/73)	Allen (7/28/73)
903	Kenneth Friend	Dix (7/4/73)	Allen (7/28/73)
904	Stephen Glade	Dix (7/4/73)	Allen (7/28/73)
905	Douglas Ipsen	Dix (7/4/73)	Allen (7/28/73)
906	David Lazar	Dix (7/4/73)	Allen (7/28/73)
907	Jeffrey Reinauer	Dix (7/4/73)	Allen (7/28/73)
908	Ann L. Myler	Marcy (9/62)	Allen (8/3/73)
909	Ernest Myler	Marcy (5/30/52)	Allen (8/3/73)
910	Timothy Myler	Marcy (5/30/52)	Allen (8/3/73)
911	Joseph R. Biegen	Upper Wolf Jaw (1965)	Cliff (8/4/73)
912	Craig McGowan	Marcy (1968)	Cliff (8/4/73)
913	Brian A. McHugh	Porter (5/27/72)	Skylight (8/5/73)
914W	Dorothy Myer	Marcy (1952)	Panther (8/5/73)
915	David Wilson	Cascade (7/65)	Redfield (8/6/73)
916	Nicholas Newlin	Cascade (7/8/70)	Panther (8/9/73)
917	James H. Tenbroeck	Cascade (7/65)	Seymour (8/10/73)
918	Peter Wollenberg	Giant (7/69)	Nippletop (8/12/73)
919	Ellen Kraly	Dial (7/69)	Panther (8/13/73)
920	Patricia Caplan	Cascade (1970)	Colvin (8/13/73)
921	John Pomerance	Cascade (7/67)	Hough (8/15/73)
922	Sean Quinn	Colvin (7/30/69)	Whiteface (8/16/73)
923	Robert J. Collins	Marcy (3/21/49)	Dial (8/19/73)

THE MEMBERSHIP ROSTER OF THE ADIRONDACK FORTY-SIXERS

	MEMBER	FIRST ASCENT	FORTY-SIXTH PEAK
924	John L. Gillam	Marcy (9/65)	Couchsachraga (8/19/73)
925	Emily D. Leist	Cascade (7/28/67)	Colden (8/20/73)
926	Seth D. Levy	Cascade (1966)	Rocky Peak (8/21/73)
927	John C. Landes	Algonquin (7/70)	Allen (8/23/73)
928	Kirk Farrington	Cascade (7/69)	Allen (8/23/73)
929	David Douglass	Big Slide (7/30/73)	Giant (8/23/73)
930	Richard Hinman	Colden (8/71)	Giant (8/23/73)
931	Russell Sachs	Macomb (6/72)	Giant (8/23/73)
932	J. M. Grant Fullman	Gothics (8/68)	Couchsachraga (8/24/73)
933	James R. Harrington	Seymour (7/1/65)	Rocky Peak (8/24/73)
934	John A. Harrington	Marcy (9/19/65)	Rocky Peak (8/24/73)
935	Thomas E. Dietz	Marcy (5/30/67)	Big Slide (8/25/73)
936	Harrison K. Caner	Giant (8/53)	Esther (8/25/73)
937	Edward C. Youger	Marcy (5/30/70)	Nye (8/26/73)
938	Charles S. Laughton	Marcy (9/68)	Wright (8/26/73)
939	Douglas C. Laughton	Marcy (9/68)	Wright (8/26/73)
940	C. Chandler Clarke	Marcy (7/25/64)	Haystack (8/26/73)
941	Deborah C. Doro	Marcy (7/25/64)	Haystack (8/26/73)
942	Charles N. Schwerin	Marcy (8/61)	Allen (8/27/73)
943	Ethel H. Campbell	Marcy (1965)	Panther (8/28/73)
944	James F. Campbell	Marcy (8/65)	Panther (8/28/73)
945	Jeffrey M. Campbell	Marcy (8/65)	Panther (8/28/73)
946	Robin Campbell	Marcy (8/65)	Panther (8/28/73)
947	Jennifer Nields	Cascade (8/63)	Dix (8/29/73)
948	Lila Nields	Giant (1923)	Dix (8/29/73)
949	Emilie Budd	Skylight (8/69)	Marshall (8/29/73)
950	Charles T. Hanson	Giant (7/11/71)	Couchsachraga (8/29/73)
951	David Carter	Cascade (7/58)	Panther (8/30/73)
952	Samuel Field	Colden (7/51)	Redfield (8/30/73)
953	Paul M. Boynton	Haystack (6/25/69)	Allen (9/2/73)
954	Tigger Loud (dog)	Phelps (4/71)	Sawteeth (9/2/73)
955	Keith W. Riche	Wright (5/29/71)	Allen (9/2/73)
956	Roger E. Martin	Porter (7/26/67)	Giant (9/2/73)
957	James Lawler	Marcy (8/25/72)	Iroquois (9/3/73)
958	Arthur G. Bandorick	Marcy (9/2/62)	Couchsachraga (9/3/73)
959	Alder Tanton	Whiteface (1925)	Panther (9/3/73)
960	Charles Rausch	Haystack (7/63)	Allen (9/6/73)
961	Kenneth Nolan	Marcy (6/72)	Allen (9/8/73)
962	Malcolm L. Slater	Giant (1945)	Big Slide (9/9/73)
963	Leland B. Deck	Tabletop (10/17/71)	Esther (9/15/73)
964	Rani V. Palo	Algonquin (8/25/59)	Allen (9/22/73)
965	William L. Cronan	Marcy (9/2/72)	Basin (9/23/73)
966	Glenna Loges	Marcy (9/2/72)	Basin (9/23/73)
967W	John A. Robertson, Jr.	Macomb (7/2/72)	Cliff (9/23/73)
968	Erica D. Elia	Cascade (8/65)	Iroquois (9/28/73)
969	Christopher Lacombe	Wright (6/27/68)	Marshall (9/30/73)
970	Ignatius Lacombe	Marcy (7/4/62)	Marshall (9/30/73)
971	Patricia Collier	Cascade (3/20/71)	Whiteface (9/30/73)
972	Robert C. Wiley	Marcy (6/34)	Whiteface (10/6/73)
973	Kim Biel	Marcy (10/25/70)	Marshall (10/6/73)
974	Bruce Watson	Marcy (10/25/70)	Marshall (10/6/73)
975	Priscilla Gibson	Colden (9/67)	Allen (10/7/73)
976	John E. Bigelow	Marcy (9/49)	Couchsachraga (10/7/73)
977	Patricia J. Collier	Big Slide (7/25/71)	Basin (10/7/73)
978	Paul Collier	Big Slide (7/25/71)	Basin (10/7/73)
979	Sandra C. King	Big Slide (7/25/71)	Basin (10/7/73)
980	Jay S. Stagg	Marcy (1966)	Nippletop (10/7/73)
981	John Collier	Big Slide (7/25/71)	Saddleback (10/7/73)
982	Marie L. Haberl	Giant (1961)	Colden (10/13/73)
983	William R. Aemet	Cascade (8/20/64)	Panther (10/13/73)
984	Douglas Farnell	Whiteface (7/21/61)	Esther (10/14/73)
985	Carol Davis	Gothics (8/17/71)	Dix (10/20/73)

Heaven Up-h'isted-ness!

	Member	First Ascent	Forty-sixth Peak
986	Nancy J. Morris	Algonquin (5/69)	Dix (10/20/73)
987	Margaret O'Grady	Gothics (8/17/71)	Dix (10/20/73)
988	Bruce Bandorick	Colden (9/5/65)	Dix (10/21/73)
989	Christopher Nickolson	Cascade (9/70)	Street (10/21/73)
990	John Yuill	Marcy (8/4/62)	Couchsachraga (10/28/73)
991	Gary Riebel	Gothics (6/70)	Colden (11/11/73)
992	Rollin Marshall	Wright (8/6/62)	Marshall (12/29/73)
993	John A. Kochalka	Cascade (10/24/70)	Redfield (5/30/73)
994	Thomas O. Wall	Marcy (1938)	Couchsachraga (7/28/73)
995	David Morse	Marcy (1949)	Haystack (8/12/73)
996	Peter Gilbert	Cascade (7/58)	Allen (8/27/73)
997	George Gronk	Cascade (6/20/73)	Wright (10/4/73)
998	Michael W. Craib	Cascade (2/69)	Porter (5/14/74)
999	Nathan L. Whetten	Phelps (10/15/67)	Couchsachraga (5/18/74)
1000	Timothy J. Whetten	Phelps (10/15/67)	Couchsachraga (5/18/74)
1001	Rebecca C. Kirkman	Big Slide (7/25/71)	Panther (5/18/74)
1002	Joyce M. Ewashko	Algonquin (9/5/71)	Panther (5/18/74)
1003	Jere H. Brophy	Marcy (1950)	Couchsachraga (5/24/74)
1004	James R. Edwards	Colden (5/30/69)	Seymour (5/25/74)
1005	Kurt Edwards	Algonquin (9/5/71)	Seymour (5/25/74)
1006	Thomas Russell	Colden (5/30/69)	Seymour (5/25/74)
1007	David M. Heffley	Gothics (10/68)	Cliff (5/26/74)
1008	Brian Seirup	Marcy (5/29/71)	Rocky Peak (5/27/74)
1009	Kenneth Flower	Algonquin (7/10/64)	Allen (6/8/74)
1010	Richard Seirup	Colden (7/20/72)	Street (6/22/74)
1011	Andrew Seirup	Colden (6/72)	Redfield (6/23/74)
1012	David Heinbockel	Wright (6/27/71)	Emmons (6/27/74)
1013	William Heinbockel	Wright (6/27/71)	Emmons (6/27/74)
1014	Karl Berner	Big Slide (10/31/70)	Allen (6/30/74)
1015	William Berner	Giant (10/12/69)	Allen (6/30/74)
1016	Joseph P. Turon	Cascade (6/21/70)	Allen (6/30/74)
1017	Andrew L. Edlin	Cascade (7/14/70)	Allen (7/5/74)
1018	William R. Connors	Cascade (7/68)	Emmons (7/5/74)
1019	Donna Maritato	Marcy (6/70)	Allen (7/13/74)
1020	Robert Grobe	Marcy (3/65)	Allen (7/13/74)
1021	David L. Gosda	Giant (1954)	Cliff (7/13/74)
1022	Leslie B. Foster	Cascade (9/27/69)	Couchsachraga (7/13/74)
1023	Craig Stagg	Marcy (1966)	Sawteeth (7/14/74)
1024	Richard Heimler	Algonquin (7/10/70)	Santanoni (7/17/74)
1025	Robert B. Hayward, Jr.	Whiteface (8/58)	Haystack (7/20/74)
1026	Frank Morrison	Whiteface (7/30)	Sawteeth (7/23/74)
1027	Jeffrey A. Scott	Giant (7/69)	Hough (7/27/74)
1028	Robert A. Forrest	Marcy (11/7/70)	Allen (7/29/74)
1029	Scott Reichard	Giant (9/16/72)	Allen (7/29/74)
1030	David Reisner	Giant (1931)	Colvin (7/29/74)
1031	David J. Holland	Phelps (6/29/71)	Emmons (7/30/74)
1032	John Lawler	Marcy (8/25/72)	Blake (8/1/74)
1033	Kevin Lawler	Santanoni (6/9/73)	Blake (8/1/74)
1034	Timothy R. Lawler	Marcy (8/25/72)	Blake (8/1/74)
1035	Eric Robitaille	Marcy (8/11/68)	Saddleback (8/1/74)
1036	Henry Gebel	Phelps (8/16/72)	Sawteeth (8/3/74)
1037	Asa E. Wall	Marcy (5/62)	Esther (8/3/74)
1038	Tim Singer	Colden (8/12/67)	Gray (8/5/74)
1039	Eric Bononi	Esther (7/8/74)	Street (8/6/74)
1040	Craig Bortz	Esther (7/8/74)	Street (8/6/74)
1041	Stephen A. Higgs	Esther (7/8/74)	Street (8/6/74)
1042	David T. Hurlock	Esther (7/8/74)	Street (8/6/74)
1043	Paul Morley	Esther (7/8/74)	Street (8/6/74)
1044	David L. Rachlis	Esther (7/8/74)	Street (8/6/74)
1045	Jay Rasmussen	Esther (7/8/74)	Street (8/6/74)
1046	John H. Reohr	Esther (7/8/74)	Street (8/6/74)
1047	Alan Rosinski	Esther (7/8/74)	Street (8/6/74)

THE MEMBERSHIP ROSTER OF THE ADIRONDACK FORTY-SIXERS

	MEMBER	FIRST ASCENT	FORTY-SIXTH PEAK
1048	Stephen Shaffer	Esther (7/8/74)	Street (8/6/74)
1049	Jack D. Stewart	Esther (7/8/74)	Street (8/6/74)
1050	Frederick B. Strolz	Esther (7/8/74)	Street (8/6/74)
1051	James Freeman	Macomb (7/10/71)	Basin (8/7/74)
1052	Ronald Turboyne	Seward (7/23/67)	Basin (8/7/74)
1053	Robert Gertner	Giant (7/19/69)	Couchsachraga (8/10/74)
1054	JoAnne Krahmer	Giant (8/22/70)	Phelps (8/10/74)
1055	John Baringer	Algonquin (1/12/72)	Seymour (8/11/74)
1056W	John Esper	Sawteeth (1/73)	Seymour (8/11/74)
1057	Michael H. Welles	Marcy (7/62)	Marshall (8/11/74)
1058	David Shapiro	Big Slide (1964)	Marshall (8/12/74)
1059	Joseph Apicella	Upper Wolf Jaw (8/67)	Esther (8/13/74)
1060	Arlene Rhodes	Algonquin (5/31/68)	Esther (8/13/74)
1061	Brian S. Rhodes	Algonquin (5/31/68)	Esther (8/13/74)
1062	Harold R. Rhodes	Upper Wolf Jaw (8/21/67)	Esther (8/13/74)
1063	Jan T. Toof	Marcy (7/62)	Cliff (8/14/74)
1064	Shui Kai Chin	Cascade (8/64)	Hough (8/14/74)
1065	Robert O'Mallay	Wright (8/70)	Allen (8/15/74)
1066	Eric Gardner	Phelps (8/21/70)	Sawteeth (8/15/74)
1067	Robert Gardner	Phelps (8/21/70)	Sawteeth (8/15/74)
1068	Robert V. Sypher	Algonquin (5/73)	Panther (8/15/74)
1069	Marc Huberman	Marcy (8/70)	Emmons (8/15/74)
1070	Bonnie H. Serlette	Porter (9/2/67)	Esther (8/16/74)
1071	Eleanor Harrington	Porter (9/2/67)	Esther (8/16/74)
1072	Kay H. Metcalf	Porter (9/2/67)	Esther (8/16/74)
1073	Wayne Harrington	Porter (9/2/67)	Esther (8/16/74)
1074	Wilfred D. Harrington	Porter (9/2/67)	Esther (8/16/74)
1075	Dale Harris	Cascade (1967)	Emmons (8/16/74)
1076	Arthur W. Jubin	Marcy (1939)	Emmons (8/16/74)
1077	Michael Riley	Lower Wolf Jaw (7/11/72)	Street (8/17/74)
1078	Timothy Riley	Colden (7/5/69)	Street (8/17/74)
1079	Douglas E. Bird	Esther (7/31/71)	Allen (8/18/74)
1080	George T. Bird	Esther (7/31/71)	Allen (8/18/74)
1081	John L. Holstead	Marcy (6/26/72)	Allen (8/18/74)
1082	Nicholas Miller	Cascade (10/1/66)	Couchsachraga (8/18/74)
1083	Paul S. Unger	Algonquin (7/70)	Allen (8/19/74)
1084	Ronald Woodward	Colvin (8/20/72)	Colden (8/20/74)
1085	Abby C. Stoner	Cascade (3/20/71)	Macomb (8/21/74)
1086	Horace F. Byrne	Giant (1924)	Couchsachraga (8/22/74)
1087	Richard Feathers	Marcy (8/15/70)	Whiteface (8/24/74)
1088	Frank Steciuk	Marcy (6/70)	Allen (8/25/74)
1089	Jeanne Steciuk	Marcy (6/70)	Allen (8/25/74)
1090	Paul Steciuk	Marcy (6/70)	Allen (8/25/74)
1091	Peter Steciuk	Marcy (6/70)	Allen (8/25/74)
1092	Robert Steciuk	Marcy (6/70)	Allen (8/25/74)
1093	Robert S. Steciuk	Marcy (6/70)	Allen (8/25/74)
1094	Lance Collins	Marcy (7/61)	Santanoni (8/26/74)
1095	Kenneth R. Zahara	Colden (6/28/70)	Allen (8/27/74)
1096	June V. Collins	Big Slide (6/30/50)	Blake (8/28/74)
1097	Brad Shiller	Cascade (7/70)	Skylight (8/28/74)
1098	Benjamin S. Davis	Haystack (7/28/70)	Macomb (8/29/74)
1099	Hugh R. Davis	Haystack (7/28/70)	Macomb (8/29/74)
1100	Jean S. Davis	Haystack (7/28/70)	Macomb (8/29/74)
1101	John S. Davis	Haystack (7/28/70)	Macomb (8/29/74)
1102	Marn D. Venner	Haystack (7/28/70)	Macomb (8/29/74)
1103	Charles Hewitt	Marcy (3/69)	Panther (8/30/74)
1104	Stephen J. Ratcliff	Algonquin (8/14/71)	Allen (8/31/74)
1105	Anthony W. Graff	Cascade (6/29/65)	Couchsachraga (8/31/74)
1106	Benjamin Greshin	Lower Wolf Jaw (10/23/70)	Basin (9/1/74)
1107	Robinson Foster	Cascade (7/70)	Colden (9/1/74)
1108	Gordon J. Shaw	Marcy (9/27)	Emmons (9/1/74)
1109	Brian Toms	Esther (11/2/69)	Marshall (9/2/74)

Heaven Up-h'isted-ness!

	Member	First Ascent	Forty-sixth Peak
1110	Harvey R. Dearstyne	Sawteeth (9/70)	Allen (9/7/74)
1111	George R. Coughlan	Wright (10/23/71)	Allen (9/7/74)
1112	Leary B. Ratcliff	Wright (10/19/69)	Iroquois (9/8/74)
1113	Pauline G. Dumas	Giant (9/26/71)	Esther (9/8/74)
1114	Fred Schroeder	Giant (1968)	Cliff (9/14/74)
1115	James H. Boyle	Colden (8/8/73)	Rocky Peak (9/15/74)
1116	W. F. Boyle	Colden (8/8/73)	Rocky Peak (9/15/74)
1117	John A. Beecroft	Big Slide (8/73)	Haystack (9/1/74)
1118	John Saville	Marcy (8/58)	Marshall (9/17/74)
1119	Rebecca White	Porter (9/14/68)	Emmons (9/17/74)
1120	Barbara Webster	Phelps (9/19/71)	Allen (9/22/74)
1121	Cardell Brown	Porter (7/15/72)	Whiteface (9/22/74)
1122	Stephen R. Crook	Marshall (8/29/70)	Sawteeth (9/24/74)
1123	Christopher Jones	Marcy (9/71)	Rocky Peak (9/29/74)
1124	William D. Jones	Marcy (9/71)	Rocky Peak (9/29/74)
1125	Donald N. Boink	Lower Wolf Jaw (1969)	Gothics (10/5/74)
1126	Kent Heacox	Panther (6/3/72)	Sawteeth (10/5/74)
1127	Judith H. Trimble	Wright (7/4/71)	Sawteeth (10/5/74)
1128	John L. Trimble	Marcy (8/66)	Sawteeth (10/5/74)
1129	Alan H. Ratcliff	Algonquin (8/14/71)	Colden (10/5/74)
1130	James D. Parkes	Skylight (10/27/69)	Seymour (10/6/74)
1131	William A. Smith	Saddleback (9/63)	Allen (10/12/74)
1132	Maurice J. Jones	Marcy (11/26/66)	Emmons (10/12/74)
1133	Ivan Kusinintz	Marcy (11/6/66)	Emmons (10/12/74)
1134	John Falk	Cascade (1952)	Couchsachraga (10/13/74)
1135	Frank Packard	Algonquin (8/21/66)	Couchsachraga (10/13/74)
1136	Thomas J. Jennsen	Phelps (12/68)	Redfield (10/13/74)
1137W	Gary W. Koch	Cascade (7/12/73)	Nye (10/13/74)
1138W	Charles Koburger	Allen (3/16/72)	Cascade (10/13/74)
1139	Robert Wagner	Dix (8/66)	Seymour (10/14/74)
1140	Robert L. Pakish	Phelps (6/10/72)	Whiteface (10/14/74)
1141	John W. Gilbert	Phelps (6/10/72)	Whiteface (10/14/74)
1142	Michael Bendura	Phelps (6/10/72)	Whiteface (10/14/74)
1143	Scott Bendura	Phelps (6/10/72)	Whiteface (10/14/74)
1144	David Gilbert	Phelps (6/10/72)	Whiteface (10/14/74)
1145	Jaime S. Greene	Phelps (6/10/72)	Whiteface (10/14/74)
1146	Paul Newton	Phelps (6/10/72)	Whiteface (10/14/74)
1147	Robert Pakish	Phelps (6/10/72)	Whiteface (10/14/74)
1148	Donald J. Hoffman	Marcy (9/9/72)	Cliff (10/19/74)
1149	Dale Reisner	Marcy (7/17/68)	Couchsachraga (10/19/74)
1150	Phyllis D. Robens	Giant (9/3/71)	Haystack (10/20/74)
1151	Schuss Robens (dog)	Giant (9/3/71)	Haystack (10/20/74)
1152	William N. Robens	Giant (9/3/71)	Haystack (10/20/74)
1153	Harold A. Wilson	Cascade (9/27/69)	Emmons (10/26/74)
1154	Eugene Brousseau	Marcy (6/27/71)	Couchsachraga (10/26/74)
1155	Eric Welles	Cascade (7/20/70)	Big Slide (10/27/74)
1156	Gillett Welles	Cascade (7/20/70)	Big Slide (10/27/74)
1157	Ralph Brown	Phelps (7/10/72)	Marshall (11/9/74)
1158	Harold Witting	Basin (9/65)	Esther (11/10/74)
1159	Charles D. Plavcan	Algonquin (6/9/57)	Cliff (7/14/73)
1160	Peter Levine	Giant (7/70)	Marshall (8/12/74)
1161	John F. Loeber	Phelps (8/68)	Haystack (9/15/74)
1162	Glenn L. Sommer	Allen (7/3/71)	Gothics (9/15/74)
1163	Steven Jesmore	Phelps (6/10/72)	Whiteface (10/14/74)
1164	William J. Smolin	Giant (10/14/73)	Esther (3/16/75)
1165	Kurt D. Trolenberg	Phelps (7/14/69)	Emmons (4/23/75)
1166	Jeff Snow	Lower Wolf Jaw (8/15/72)	Phelps (5/17/75)
1167	Paul Scheiner	Marcy (10/7/73)	Dial (5/17/75)
1168	Mark R. Scheiner	Porter (7/7/70)	Nye (5/25/75)
1169	Mark Baldwin	Cascade (5/26/73)	Street (5/25/75)
1170	John J. de Barbadillo	Colden (5/70)	Giant (5/26/75)
1171W	Chai-Kyou Mallinson	Marcy (5/20/71)	Seymour (5/31/75)

The Membership Roster of the Adirondack Forty-Sixers

	Member	First Ascent	Forty-sixth Peak
1172	Andrew Zatt	Porter (5/11/74)	Upper Wolf Jaw (6/7/75)
1173	Robert Zatt	Porter (5/11/74)	Upper Wolf Jaw (6/7/75)
1174	Samuel J. Klein	Marcy (8/52)	Emmons (6/15/75)
1175	Clifford G. Reno	Colvin (7/12/67)	Couchsachraga (6/21/75)
1176	Walter P. O'Connor	Wright (8/15/64)	Street (6/22/75)
1177	David Petit	Phelps (6/10/72)	Tabletop (6/26/75)
1178	Emily H. Boyle	Cascade (1969)	Whiteface (6/27/75)
1179W	Kathleen M. Gill	Marcy (10/60)	Cascade (6/28/75)
1180	James W. Schaller	Marcy (5/19/66)	Couchsachraga (7/5/75)
1181	Dorothea R. Thoman	Cascade (8/31/63)	Panther (7/5/75)
1182	David E. Stucki	Colden (9/6/70)	Emmons (7/5/75)
1183	Beulah M. Rapp	Porter (8/3/74)	Whiteface (7/5/75)
1184	Franklin W. Rapp	Porter (8/3/74)	Whiteface (7/5/75)
1185	Gerrit J. Hospers	Skylight (7/26/73)	Saddleback (7/7/75)
1186	P. David Taber	Skylight (10/12/69)	Tabletop (7/13/75)
1187	Andrew W. Wolfe	Cascade (7/70)	Allen (7/15/75)
1188	Marion Huxley	Marcy (8/18/68)	Santanoni (7/17/75)
1189	Rita J. Pettigrew	Marcy (8/18/68)	Santanoni (7/17/75)
1190	Stanley S. Selwach	Algonquin (8/21/70)	Marshall (7/19/75)
1191	Edward E. Selwach	Cascade (7/8/67)	Marshall (7/19/75)
1192	Michael G. Rawdon	Whiteface (5/26/72)	Redfield (7/26/75)
1193	Frank R. Peters	Phelps (9/9/72)	Marcy (7/26/75)
1194	David S. Thomas	Upper Wolf Jaw (1969)	Esther (7/26/75)
1195	Leonard Borucki	Cascade (8/31/69)	Marshall (7/26/75)
1196	Alma M. Gray	Macomb (5/65)	Seymour (7/27/75)
1197	Danny F. Lancor	Marcy (1962)	Couchsachraga (7/30/75)
1198	Robert P. Harris	Phelps (12/12/71)	Tabletop (8/2/75)
1199	Florence A. Brinkman	Phelps (9/7/73)	Gray (8/2/75)
1200	William R. Brinkman	Phelps (9/7/73)	Gray (8/2/75)
1201	Robert E. Baldwin	Cascade (5/26/73)	Redfield (8/3/75)
1202	William J. Burke	Marcy (9/16/73)	Redfield (8/3/75)
1203	Betty J. Burke	Marcy (9/16/73)	Redfield (8/3/75)
1204	Adam Greshin	Lower Wolf Jaw (10/23/70)	Hough (8/3/75)
1205	Mario A. Gonyea	Whiteface (7/2/73)	Allen (8/6/75)
1206	Timothy Nardiello	Haystack (1973)	Allen (8/6/75)
1207	David C. Quimbach	Whiteface (7/74)	Allen (8/6/75)
1208	Charles L. Crangle, Jr.	Marcy (8/68)	Emmons (8/6/75)
1209	Steven A. Huberman	Colden (7/71)	Seymour (8/8/75)
1210	Jay P. Edlin	Giant (7/23/70)	East Dix (8/9/75)
1211	Karel K. Czanderna	Marcy (10/6/73)	Gray (8/9/75)
1212	Donald B. Avery	Phelps (6/10/72)	Tabletop (8/15/75)
1213	Charles F. Beach, Jr.	Giant (5/29/67)	Allen (8/15/75)
1214	John Newton	Cascade (6/9/73)	Phelps (8/15/75)
1215	Stephen A. Morgan	Marcy (6/15/70)	Allen (8/17/75)
1216	John B. Doebrich	Marcy (8/14/58)	Emmons (8/18/75)
1217	Jeff Roecker	Colvin (11/10/72)	Algonquin (8/19/75)
1218	William P. Myers	Big Slide (7/17/72)	Couchsachraga (8/23/75)
1219	Richard Baum	Whiteface (8/26/72)	Redfield (8/24/75)
1220	George C. Schmit	Marcy (5/19/73)	Marshall (8/24/75)
1221	Stephen R. Upjohn	Blake (7/9/68)	Panther (8/25/75)
1222	Dexter E. Churchill	Colvin (3/16/74)	Cliff (8/25/75)
1223	Gregory Smith	Lower Wolf Jaw (10/11/73)	Couchsachraga (8/26/75)
1224	Herbert Burchell	Marcy (9/9/72)	Allen (8/26/75)
1225	Daniel Graff	Cascade (7/1/65)	Tabletop (8/29/75)
1226	Terry M. Dwyer	Marcy (8/69)	Allen (8/29/75)
1227	Bruce H. Braine	Colvin (8/68)	Redfield (8/29/75)
1228	Neil Van Dyke	Porter (7/67)	Redfield (8/30/75)
1229	Richard A. Stillman	Wright (8/63)	Iroquois (8/30/75)
1230	Christopher Colt	Cascade (1971)	Gray (8/30/75)
1231	Joseph Garrison	Wright (7/18/73)	Nippletop (8/30/75)
1232	Eloise Stover	Algonquin (8/22/70)	Emmons (8/31/75)
1233	James R. Stover	Marcy (8/8/71)	Emmons (8/31/75)

HEAVEN UP-H'ISTED-NESS!

	MEMBER	FIRST ASCENT	FORTY-SIXTH PEAK
1234	Janie L. Stover	Wright (8/22/70)	Emmons (8/31/75)
1235	John B. Stover, III	Algonquin (8/22/70)	Emmons (8/31/75)
1236	Peter H. Gucker	Sawteeth (8/68)	Blake (8/31/75)
1237	Richard M. Stevens	Marcy (9/6/70)	Blake (8/31/75)
1238	Caroline D. Lussi	Marcy (1946)	Emmons (9/2/75)
1239	Philip B. Weld	Algonquin (8/1929)	Emmons (9/6/75)
1240	Deborah Wilson	Cascade (6/28/70)	Allen (9/7/75)
1241	Beth Osterlitz	Sawteeth (9/6/70)	Seymour (9/7/75)
1242	Christopher Osterlitz	Sawteeth (9/6/70)	Seymour (9/7/75)
1243	John D. Osterlitz	Sawteeth (9/6/70)	Seymour (9/7/75)
1244	Mark J. Osterlitz	Sawteeth (9/6/70)	Seymour (9/7/75)
1245	Michael J. Osterlitz	Sawteeth (9/6/70)	Seymour (9/7/75)
1246	Sylvia Osterlitz	Sawteeth (9/6/70)	Seymour (9/7/75)
1247	David W. Sodaro	Lower Wolf Jaw (6/71)	Haystack (9/7/75)
1248	Gregory J. Sodaro	Algonquin (9/72)	Haystack (9/7/75)
1249	Joanne S. Urioste	Colden (2/69)	Couchsachraga (9/10/75)
1250	Robert W. Zeuner	Marcy (9/4/61)	Allen (9/13/75)
1251W	Samuel D. Steen	Colden (9/10/70)	Emmons (9/13/75)
1252	Craig Jackson	Cascade (8/2/69)	East Dix (9/13/75)
1253	Lauren Jackson	Cascade (8/2/69)	East Dix (9/13/75)
1254	Paul R. Jackson	Giant (8/14/68)	East Dix (9/13/75)
1255	Virginia R. Jackson	Giant (8/14/68)	East Dix (9/13/75)
1256	Clifford E. Smith	Marcy (10/12/69)	Cliff (9/13/75)
1257	Gary Smith	Marcy (10/12/69)	Cliff (9/13/75)
1258	Robert F. Clements	Giant (9/19/70)	Marshall (9/21/75)
1259	Tim Clements	Giant (9/19/70)	Marshall (9/21/75)
1260	George F. Goebel	Giant (9/19/70)	Marshall (9/21/75)
1261	Scott Goebel	Giant (9/19/70)	Marshall (9/21/75)
1262	Erwin Cymet	Algonquin (9/16/72)	Marshall (9/21/75)
1263	Peter J. Thomas	Cascade (4/28/73)	Marshall (9/21/75)
1264	Ernest Sachs, Jr.	Unknown (1924)	Emmons (9/27/75)
1265	John H. Greer	Marcy (6/4/66)	Marshall (9/27/75)
1266	David C. Skillman	Marcy (9/53)	Seymour (10/4/75)
1267	Frederick C. Neebe	Giant (9/1/51)	Couchsachraga (10/4/75)
1268	Albert F. Heitkamp	Marcy (8/51)	Esther (10/4/75)
1269	James R. Leverett	Algonquin (9/4/71)	Marshall (10/4/75)
1270	Eugene J. McCardle	Whiteface (5/17/75)	Allen (10/4/75)
1271	Michael L. Wearing	Algonquin (9/16/72)	Marshall (10/4/75)
1272	John A. Harrington	Marcy (9/16/65)	Hough (10/10/75)
1273	Albert A. Pozzi	Marcy (8/63)	Couchsachraga (10/11/75)
1274	William F. Davis	Algonquin (5/30/64)	Whiteface (10/11/75)
1275	Jack Bigelow	Colden (7/27/62)	Emmons (10/17/75)
1276	Joan Camay	Esther (9/30/75)	Giant (10/18/75)
1277	William A. Lasher	Marcy (8/6/63)	Iroquois (10/23/75)
1278	Joanna L. Lasher	Marcy (8/6/63)	Iroquois (10/23/75)
1279	John E. Winkler	Marcy (7/62)	Allen (10/26/75)
1280	Herbert J. Nemier	Algonquin (8/7/70)	Couchsachraga (10/27/75)
1281	Stephen Thompson	Haystack (8/10/71)	Couchsachraga (10/27/75)
1282	Alton P. Dieffenbach	Marcy (6/56)	Marshall (11/8/75)
1283	Anna H. Ulman	Basin (8/8/63)	Phelps (11/10/75)
1284	Robert G. Haas	Marcy (9/67)	Whiteface (11/22/75)
1285	Woodruff Carroll	Algonquin (1969)	Allen (6/1/75)
1286	Nancy G. Birdsall	Cascade (8/66)	Marshall (6/16/75)
1287	Glenn Clemens	Marcy (1/2/70)	Couchsachraga (6/30/75)
1288	Rick Letarte	Marcy (8/69)	Couchsachraga (6/30/75)
1289	Todd Cedarholm	Marcy (8/69)	Esther (7/2/75)
1290	Joseph L. Esch	Wright (1962)	Tabletop (8/75)
1291	Carl F. Beyer	Marcy (9/26/71)	Seymour (8/29/75)
1292	Richard R. Kast	Saddleback (7/19/69)	Allen (9/7/75)
1293	Bruce Rio	Phelps (6/10/72)	Upper Wolf Jaw (10/12/75)
1294	Homer H. Glascock	Upper Wolf Jaw (10/12/64)	Whiteface (11/8/75)
1295	James T. Townsend	Macomb (6/15/75)	Dix (5/9/76)

The Membership Roster of the Adirondack Forty-Sixers

	Member	First Ascent	Forty-sixth Peak
1296	Thomas J. Blum	Marcy (9/26/65)	Allen (5/15/76)
1297	Tony Belaskas	Marcy (9/26/65)	Allen (5/15/76)
1298	George L. Havens	Santanoni (10/13/67)	Tabletop (5/22/76)
1299	John Bewick, Jr.	Wright (6/3/72)	Esther (5/29/76)
1300	F. William Walker	Haystack (9/8/63)	Redfield (5/30/76)
1301	Robert D. Hofer	Big Slide (10/70)	Allen (5/31/76)
1302	John R. Goff	Giant (5/66)	Couchsachraga (6/13/76)
1303	Leo J. Sommer	Street (9/1/74)	Seymour (6/18/76)
1304	Lewis G. Hoffman	Marcy (6/62)	Couchsachraga (6/20/76)
1305	John C. Cheney	Whiteface (7/59)	Redfield (7/4/76)
1306	Victor Petit	Phelps (6/10/72)	Basin (7/10/76)
1307	Donald E. Reed	Phelps (6/10/72)	Panther (7/10/76)
1308	Rolando Miranda	Cascade (5/30/71)	Seymour (7/11/76)
1309	George H. Buttler, III	Sawteeth (9/26/65)	Emmons (7/17/76)
1310	Carlisle F. Lustenberger	Cascade (4/25/65)	Emmons (7/17/76)
1311	Thomas Ellis	Marcy (7/3/73)	Panther (7/17/76)
1312	Joseph P. Kubala	Marcy (6/17/68)	Giant (7/18/76)
1313	John V. Whitney	Colden (7/14/70)	Blake (7/23/76)
1314	Philip D. Lister	Porter (7/16/72)	Couchsachraga (7/23/76)
1315	John M. Groff	Dix (6/23/74)	Allen (7/29/76)
1316	Willard L. Reed	Algonquin (10/7/73)	Allen (7/25/76)
1317	Barbara Smith	Cascade (7/26/68)	Haystack (7/25/76)
1318	Bruce Smith	Cascade (7/26/68)	Haystack (7/25/76)
1319	David L. Smith	Cascade (7/26/68)	Haystack (7/25/76)
1320W	Douglas L. Smith	Cascade (7/26/68)	Haystack (7/25/76)
1321	Lois B. Smith	Cascade (7/26/68)	Haystack (7/25/76)
1322	Howard E. Grout	Marcy (5/30/51)	Seymour (7/31/76)
1323	Frank Trerise	Marcy (5/30/64)	Emmons (7/30/76)
1324	Robert Robinson	Whiteface (7/17/73)	Esther (7/31/76)
1325	Lauren S. Waite	Giant (7/64)	Saddleback (7/31/76)
1326	Peter A. Waite	Marcy (11/3/73)	Saddleback (7/31/76)
1327W	John P. Freeman	Porter (1/8/72)	Colden (8/1/76)
1328	Douglas DeBoer	Marcy (8/66)	Sawteeth (8/2/76)
1329	Frederick DeBoer	Algonquin (9/64)	Sawteeth (8/2/76)
1330	Dan Canning	Cascade (5/26/73)	Couchsachraga (8/2/76)
1331	Thomas W. Kopp	Cascade (8/30/69)	Couchsachraga (8/2/76)
1332	John E. Scheetz	Marcy (8/12/66)	Marshall (8/7/76)
1333	Werner R. Haag	Marcy (6/17/68)	Redfield (8/8/76)
1334	Kenneth Herz	Giant (7/69)	Colden (8/10/76)
1335	James B. Kobak, Jr.	Giant (7/57)	Marshall (8/11/76)
1336	Mark E. Vermilyea	Cascade (8/62)	Iroquois (8/12/76)
1337	Marcy Ulman	Colvin (7/2/71)	Saddleback (8/16/76)
1338W	Neal W. Andrews	Whiteface (7/72)	Couchsachraga (8/17/76)
1339	Barbara Wadsworth	Cascade (8/24/71)	Allen (8/21/76)
1340	Bruce C. Wadsworth	Algonquin (8/9/71)	Allen (8/21/76)
1341	Elizabeth Wadsworth	Cascade (8/24/71)	Allen (8/21/76)
1342	Peter Wadsworth	Cascade (8/24/71)	Allen (8/21/76)
1343	Robert H. Sokol	Marcy (9/19/71)	Allen (8/21/76)
1344	Charles F. Kratzat	Marcy (8/19/72)	Allen (8/21/76)
1345	Robert Kratzat	Marcy (8/19/72)	Allen (8/21/76)
1346	David T. Druckerman	Marcy (7/24/70)	Esther (8/21/76)
1347	Howard B. Druckerman	Marcy (7/24/70)	Esther (8/21/76)
1348	Martin Druckerman	Marcy (7/24/70)	Esther (8/21/76)
1349	Francis J. Whitney	Cascade (9/6/70)	Esther (8/21/76)
1350	Jane Whitney	Cascade (9/6/70)	Esther (8/21/76)
1351	Karen Whitney	Cascade (9/6/70)	Esther (8/21/76)
1352	Mark J. Whitney	Cascade (9/6/70)	Esther (8/21/76)
1353	Paul V. Whitney	Cascade (9/6/70)	Esther (8/21/76)
1354	George M. Amedore	Whiteface (10/69)	Redfield (8/22/76)
1355	Jean M. Granger	Whiteface (10/69)	Redfield (8/22/76)
1356	Robert D. Wiley, Jr.	Cascade (5/27/72)	Tabletop (8/23/76)
1357	Robert D. Wiley, Sr.	Cascade (5/27/72)	Tabletop (8/23/76)

Heaven Up-h'isted-ness!

	Member	First Ascent	Forty-sixth Peak
1358	Andrew Behrend	Porter (8/15/71)	Big Slide (8/23/76)
1359	Daniel S. Ruchkin	Whiteface (9/57)	Redfield (8/25/76)
1360	Richard F. Feathers	Marcy (8/15/70)	Whiteface (8/25/76)
1361	Stephen S. LeViness	Big Slide (8/6/73)	Esther (8/28/76)
1362	Leon T. Fortune	Marcy (9/2/68)	Tabletop (8/29/76)
1363	Bruce J. Zakalik	Marcy (8/25/73)	Basin (8/29/76)
1364	David Howlett	Macomb (8/71)	Esther (8/29/76)
1365	George R. Viscome	Marcy (1971)	Panther (8/31/76)
1366	Alexander L. Mackay	Lower Wolf Jaw (6/3/73)	Redfield (8/31/76)
1367	Donna J. Cole	Cascade (10/10/65)	Couchsachraga (9/2/76)
1368	Barbara A. Peters	Marcy (5/26/72)	Allen (9/3/76)
1369	Bruce G. Peters	Marcy (5/26/72)	Allen (9/3/76)
1370	Gary B. Sokol	Marcy (9/19/71)	Nippletop (9/3/76)
1371	Raymond M. Lally	Marcy (1966)	Marshall (9/4/76)
1372	Clark Hall, Jr.	Colden (8/4/73)	Nippletop (9/4/76)
1373	Mark Ellison	Gothics (7/17/75)	Esther (9/4/76)
1374	Henry F. Parker	Phelps (8/28/71)	Dial (9/4/76)
1375	Gisela Pikarsky	Lower Wolf Jaw (9/7/70)	Marshall (9/5/76)
1376	Jacob M. Pikarsky	Lower Wolf Jaw (9/7/70)	Marshall (9/5/76)
1377	Ronald J. Christen	Gray (8/2/75)	Emmons (9/5/76)
1378	Peter Gillespie	Marcy (1952)	Emmons (9/5/76)
1379	Chester Rosinski	Saddleback (7/29/62)	Emmons (9/5/76)
1380	Marilyn V. Gillespie	Cascade (5/20/75)	Emmons (9/5/76)
1381W	Bruce O. Brown	Giant (3/27/74)	Colvin (9/5/76)
1382	Robert C. Potter	Marcy (7/68)	Esther (9/5/76)
1383	Robert L. Greenberg	Marcy (8/71)	Gray (9/5/76)
1384	Neal McHugh	Porter (5/27/72)	Seymour (9/6/76)
1385	Dorothy S. Darlington	Cascade (5/64)	Emmons (9/6/76)
1386	Ruth Happel	Algonquin (9/2/66)	Emmons (9/6/76)
1387	Ronald A. Hartman	Cascade (9/23/73)	Esther (9/6/76)
1388	Randell F. Sample	Colden (5/10/75)	Couchsachraga (9/9/76)
1389	Betty Peckham	Phelps (10/4/70)	Marshall (9/11/76)
1390	John C. Kellogg	Marcy (8/53)	Macomb (9/12/76)
1391	Aubrey Kalbaugh	Upper Wolf Jaw (6/28/65)	Couchsachraga (9/8/76)
1392	Walter S. Hayes, Jr.	Dix (7/17/71)	Haystack (9/18/76)
1393	James W. Spring	Nippletop (10/9/64)	Haystack (9/18/76)
1394	Linda H. Combs	Giant (7/18/73)	Seymour (9/19/76)
1395	Peter F. Roland	Marcy (7/12/69)	Allen (9/19/76)
1396	C. Peter Fish	Marcy (8/59)	Seymour (9/23/76)
1397	Ellsworth R. Littler	Marcy (10/21/56)	Emmons (9/25/76)
1398	John Perten	Cliff (9/1/73)	Redfield (9/25/76)
1399W	Nola Royce	Giant (5/27/73)	Marshall (9/25/76)
1400	Sarah L. Warner	Algonquin (1970)	Marcy (9/25/76)
1401	Joseph Tennyson	Cascade (10/4/70)	Nippletop (9/26/76)
1402	Patsy J. Myers	Big Slide (7/27/72)	Gray (9/26/76)
1403	Gordon Boutelle	Marcy (8/19/66)	Marshall (10/2/76)
1404	Jenny Loud	Cascade (8/67)	Iroquois (10/2/76)
1405	Thomas R. Stanwood	Giant (9/10/74)	Colden (10/2/76)
1406	R. Inslee Clark, Jr.	Marcy (1955)	Allen (10/10/76)
1407	Eugene S. Daniel, III	Lower Wolf Jaw (6/21/75)	Allen (10/10/76)
1408	Carlton Eno	Marcy (10/4/68)	Emmons (10/11/76)
1409	James E. Rogers	Marcy (7/13/68)	Emmons (10/11/76)
1410	Roland J. Boucher	Marcy (8/51)	Seymour (10/12/76)
1411	Dallas E. Cain	Marcy (10/4/57)	Redfield (10/17/76)
1412	Anthony Ballato	Algonquin (7/20/74)	Allen (10/23/76)
1413	James Rand	Big Slide (9/26/72)	Seymour (8/29/75)
1414	Charles H. Blount	Marcy (8/45)	Couchsachraga (9/7/76)
1415	Robert Thomas	Dial (7/8/74)	Couchsachraga (4/30/77)
1416	Read Kingsbury	Marcy (8/25/70)	Whiteface (5/15/77)
1417	Eugene M. Weber	Wright (7/3/71)	Blake (5/21/77)
1418	William F. Krusell	Porter (8/4/68)	Basin (5/29/77)
1419	John S. Benjamin	Marcy (6/67)	Gray (5/29/77)

The Membership Roster of the Adirondack Forty-Sixers

	Member	First Ascent	Forty-sixth Peak
1420	Andrew R. Zahora	Wright (7/5/72)	Couchsachraga (5/29/77)
1421	Dean F. Ottaway	Upper Wolf Jaw (9/62)	Blake (5/30/77)
1422	William T. Turner, Jr.	Marcy (6/17/67)	Haystack (7/3/77)
1423	Donna G. Elliot	Marcy (9/58)	Iroquois (7/6/77)
1424	Beatrice Felin	Whiteface (7/7/73)	Couchsachraga (7/10/77)
1425	James J. Litynski	Marcy (8/16/68)	Marshall (7/16/77)
1426W	Alan M. Via	Marcy (5/72)	Phelps (7/17/77)
1427	William M. Calder	Whiteface (7/70)	Panther (7/22/77)
1428	Michael E. Goldman	Giant (7/73)	Allen (7/28/77)
1429	Joseph E. Schedlbauer	Big Slide (7/29/70)	Santanoni (7/28/77)
1430	Neil Hess	Algonquin (1975)	Haystack (8/3/77)
1431	Larry J. Yokell	Giant (3/3/66)	Seymour (8/8/77)
1432	Kathleen A. Slocum	Rocky Peak (9/75)	Big Slide (8/8/77)
1433	Judy Ross	Whiteface (1968)	Emmons (8/9/77)
1434	James Rinzler	Algonquin (6/77)	Street (8/9/77)
1435	Benjamin T. Davies	Cascade (10/6/67)	Couchsachraga (8/9/77)
1436	Daniel R. Gilbert	Basin (6/8/74)	Big Slide (8/12/77)
1437	Dean N. Arden	Giant (9/19/70)	Cascade (8/13/77)
1438	Eric Arden	Giant (9/19/70)	Cascade (8/13/77)
1439	Jonathan Blank	Redfield (9/23/72)	Marshall (8/18/77)
1440	Fred W. Ulrich	Algonquin (9/14/74)	Big Slide (8/20/77)
1441	Edwin G. Haley	Marcy (8/73)	Dix (8/21/77)
1442	Edward Lutz	Lower Wolf Jaw (7/32)	Emmons (8/27/77)
1443	Charles E. Brotherton	Marcy (9/3/32)	Basin (8/28/77)
1444	Helen M. Brotherton	Marcy (8/29/64)	Basin (8/28/77)
1445	Edward P. Moore, Jr.	Giant (7/57)	Tabletop (8/29/77)
1446	Peter Ruchkin	Cascade (8/12/71)	Haystack (9/1/77)
1447	Elizabeth Engelhard	Wright (7/5/76)	Panther (9/1/77)
1448	Robyn Churchill	Cascade (8/19/74)	Gray (9/1/77)
1449	Jerold N. Graff	Cascade (6/29/74)	Esther (9/2/77)
1450	Scott Van Allen	Dix (10/14/73)	Tabletop (9/4/77)
1451	Ronald D. Parshall	Marcy (10/7/74)	Esther (9/8/77)
1452	Thomas R. Lee	Algonquin (7/21/74)	Skylight (9/11/77)
1453	Christian G. Behr	Porter (6/3/72)	Esther (9/11/77)
1454	Christian M. Behr	Porter (6/3/72)	Esther (9/11/77)
1455	June F. Behr	Porter (6/3/72)	Esther (9/11/77)
1456	Roderick Forsman	Algonquin (9/2/72)	Cascade (9/18/77)
1457	David E. Bourque	Marcy (7/74)	Marshall (9/30/77)
1458	Scott R. Ebeling	Big Slide (9/1/69)	Wright (10/1/77)
1459	Calvin R. Woods	Marcy (10/7/67)	Nye (10/9/77)
1460	Robert F. Peterson	Allen (6/19/70)	Marcy (10/29/77)
1461	William R. Keeney	Wright (7/23/71)	Big Slide (8/16/76)
1462	Leonard S. Wnorowski	Marcy (9/24/70)	Emmons (7/3/77)
1463	Philip Cataldo	Colden (10/10/75)	Dix (8/21/77)
1464W	Ralph B. Gibbs	Lower Wolf Jaw (2/9/74)	Allen (3/18/78)
1465	John Andrews	Cascade (7/65)	Allen (5/27/78)
1466	Ernest C. Hinck, III	Colden (7/1/67)	Allen (5/28/78)
1467W	Ronald A. Hahn	Santanoni (2/15/76)	Esther (6/3/78)
1468W	Friedel Schunk	Algonquin (5/6/77)	Emmons (6/17/78)
1469	Kurt Nellhaus	Saddleback (8/5/61)	Couchsachraga (6/25/78)
1470	Michael Giacchette, Jr.	Giant (2/21/76)	Seymour (6/28/78)
1471	Michael Giacchette, Sr.	Giant (2/21/76)	Seymour (6/28/78)
1472	Steven Giacchette	Giant (2/21/76)	Seymour (6/28/78)
1473	Peter A. Hoyt	Gothics (8/42)	Allen (6/30/78)
1474	Robert H. Stevens	Algonquin (1965)	Allen (7/2/78)
1475	Andre Fortune	Marcy (9/2/68)	Couchsachraga (7/4/78)
1476	Charles B. Egbert	Big Slide (9/14/75)	Marshall (7/13/78)
1477	W. Marshall Prettyman	Marcy (10/28/73)	Marshall (7/13/78)
1478	Clarence W. Gehris	Algonquin (6/17/63)	Sawteeth (7/18/78)
1479	Steven N. Nadel	Cascade (7/68)	Couchsachraga (7/19/78)
1480	Merle D. Melvin	Marcy (8/41)	Emmons (7/22/78)
1481	Stephen Boheim	Marcy (8/24/67)	Colden (7/22/78)

Heaven Up-h'isted-ness!

	Member	First Ascent	Forty-sixth Peak
1482	Kerwin E. Tesdell	Dial (6/12/77)	Whiteface (7/25/78)
1483	Robert Helenek	Algonquin (8/13/73)	Allen (7/29/78)
1484	Robert R. Ottaviano	Marcy (8/71)	Allen (7/29/78)
1485	William G. Huber	Wright (8/25/75)	Iroquois (7/29/78)
1486	William J. Hoffman	Cascade (7/30/74)	Redfield (7/29/78)
1487	G. Ernest Anderson, Jr.	Wright (1937)	Couchsachraga (7/31/78)
1488	Steven A. Urfirer	Marcy (1971)	Colden (8/5/78)
1489	Daniel Burnett	Wright (7/28/68)	Macomb (8/5/78)
1490	Matthew Silverman	Giant (7/76)	Phelps (8/5/78)
1491	Robert Sherman	Gothics (7/31/75)	Lower Wolf Jaw (8/6/78)
1492	Gary Levine	Esther (7/28/72)	Couchsachraga (8/8/78)
1493	Craig Morrell	Cascade (7/73)	Couchsachraga (8/8/78)
1494	Jay Phillips	Algonquin (7/72)	Couchsachraga (8/8/78)
1495	John Wolfe	Giant (7/73)	Couchsachraga (8/8/78)
1496	Kenneth D. Robinson	Whiteface (7/73)	Allen (8/9/78)
1497	James G. Van Allen	Marshall (7/13/74)	Panther (8/11/78)
1498	Robert D. Holley	Colvin (6/69)	Seymour (8/13/78)
1499	Mark A. Pope	Seward (6/13/76)	Allen (8/14/78)
1500	Robert M. Browning	Allen (5/27/78)	Saddleback (8/15/78)
1501	James R. Lenney	Cascade (1/19/74)	Seymour (8/20/78)
1502	Jere W. Brophy	Wright (7/22/72)	Gothics (8/20/78)
1503	Don Creighton	Whiteface (8/48)	Couchsachraga (8/22/78)
1504	Amy D. Snyder	Giant (1969)	Rocky Peak (8/27/78)
1505	William J. Bobear	Marcy (9/17/72)	Allen (8/27/78)
1506	John Nicoll	Marcy (1969)	Allen (8/27/78)
1507	Mike Skreiner	Cascade (7/70)	Blake (9/2/78)
1508	John C. King	Colden (5/22/71)	Couchsachraga (9/3/78)
1509	Howard W. Bitzer	Marcy (7/9/71)	Marshall (9/3/78)
1510	Hynrich W. Wieschhoff	Marcy (1953)	Nye (9/3/78)
1511	Robert D. Braggins	Wright (9/29/68)	Big Slide (9/17/78)
1512	Paul Kaminski	Macomb (6/30/76)	Allen (9/18/78)
1513	S. P. Kaminski	Macomb (6/30/76)	Allen (9/18/78)
1514	Frank Mosch	Marcy (4/29/75)	Gray (9/21/78)
1515	Joseph J. Sliwa	Marcy (4/29/75)	Gray (9/21/78)
1516	Maurice Fortune	Wright (9/10/72)	Seymour (9/24/78)
1517	James A. Watson	Phelps (7/4/72)	Couchsachraga (9/25/78)
1518	Robert G. McKinney	Marcy (9/18/71)	Big Slide (9/30/78)
1519	Richard V. French	Marcy (9/18/71)	Hough (9/30/78)
1520	David Armstrong	Armstrong (10/22/73)	Redfield (9/30/78)
1521	Bryan Goodwin	Lower Wolf Jaw (10/4/73)	Redfield (9/30/78)
1522	William C. Guenther	Macomb (6/29/75)	Allen (10/4/78)
1523	Randy Quayle	Giant (1958)	Iroquois (10/7/78)
1524	Thomas Puleo	Esther (8/10/72)	Haystack (10/8/78)
1525	Gregg R. Wheeler	Porter (1/9/72)	Marcy (10/14/78)
1526	Frank Roth	Phelps (9/27/69)	Iroquois (10/22/78)
1527	Malcolm Archard	Giant (7/30/75)	Haystack (10/29/78)
1528W	William F. Coonradt	South Dix (2/16/75)	Redfield (3/16/79)
1529W	William A. Kozel	Wright (6/22/69)	Redfield (3/16/79)
1530	Peter Dady	Wright (1966)	Esther (4/28/79)
1531	Phillip Parker	Giant (7/77)	Couchsachraga (5/19/79)
1532	Paul F. Rohrbacher	Macomb (5/30/76)	Esther (5/26/79)
1533	Stanley A. Maughan	Redfield (4/16/74)	Santanoni (5/27/79)
1534	Christine Jordan	Skylight (8/68)	Armstrong (6/10/79)
1535	Paul S. Jacobs	Marcy (1972)	Esther (6/14/79)
1536	Harry Urban	Marcy (7/4/67)	East Dix (6/22/79)
1537	David K. Martin II	Marcy (7/23/70)	Couchsachraga (6/23/79)
1538	David K. Martin, Sr.	Marcy (7/23/70)	Couchsachraga (6/23/79)
1539	Willliam E. Schilling	Marcy (8/1/72)	Whiteface (7/6/79)
1540	Martin Neilhaus	Marcy (1963)	Emmons (7/15/79)
1541	William F. Trolenberg	Cascade (3/9/69)	Esther (7/22/79)
1542	Gordon Cawood	Marcy (6/30/68)	Couchsachraga (7/23/79)
1543	Helen S. Cawood	Marcy (6/30/68)	Couchsachraga (7/23/79)

THE MEMBERSHIP ROSTER OF THE ADIRONDACK FORTY-SIXERS

	MEMBER	FIRST ASCENT	FORTY-SIXTH PEAK
1544	David Abrevaya	Porter (7/77)	Rocky Peak (7/25/79)
1545	James Pruchniewski	Tabletop (5/24/75)	Redfield (7/29/79)
1546	Stephen Dubey	Haystack (8/6/78)	Allen (7/29/79)
1547	Christian Proteau	Cascade (1977)	Big Slide (8/3/79)
1548	Lenore M. Steinmetz	Colden (7/21/60)	Whiteface (8/4/79)
1549	Deborah S. Nagel	Seymour (7/1/78)	Whiteface (8/4/79)
1550W	James B. Wulf	Algonquin (5/27/78)	Whiteface (8/4/79)
1551	Stephen C. Wulf	Algonquin (5/27/78)	Whiteface (8/4/79)
1552	Ida M. Sainsbury	Marshall (10/4/75)	Tabletop (8/5/79)
1553	Douglas P. Aronson	Wright (7/13/74)	Marshall (8/7/79)
1554	Robert C. Rowland	Giant (6/75)	Whiteface (8/18/79)
1555	Elaine Z. Montgomery	Algonquin (6/6/71)	Tabletop (8/22/79)
1556	Robert S. Montgomery	Marcy (10/17/71)	Tabletop (8/22/79)
1557	Donald E. Seeger	Gothics (10/30/76)	Allen (8/22/79)
1558	Terry Zapf	Marcy (8/25/65)	Couchsachraga (8/22/79)
1559	Clayton F. Bush, Jr.	Marcy (1954)	Cliff (8/24/79)
1560	Cynthia B. Rice	Marcy (1964)	Cliff (8/24/79)
1561	Edmund C. Higgins	Skylight (7/69/)	Wright (8/24/79)
1562	William Lee	Wright (9/1/74)	Basin (8/25/79)
1563	Terry R. Morley	Wright (5/8/77)	Sawteeth (8/26/79)
1564	Ernest C. Friedow	Marcy (11/2/74)	Allen (8/26/79)
1565	Mark E. Blaska	Whiteface (7/29/71)	Gothics (8/26/79)
1566	Frank L. Pilar	Algonquin (12/13/75)	Sawteeth (8/28/79)
1567	John Benjamin, III	Santanoni (9/19/70)	Big Slide (9/2/79)
1568	Amy P. Davis	Porter (9/17/72)	Allen (9/2/79)
1569	W. David Phelps	Porter (9/17/72)	Allen (9/2/79)
1570	Arlene S. Bredenberg	Tabletop (10/73)	Allen (9/2/79)
1571W	John M. Kennedy	Macomb (7/3/77)	Allen (9/3/79)
1572	Fred G. Turnbull	Cascade (10/19/65)	Emmons (9/9/79)
1573	Carl G. Schleicher	Big Slide (4/30/77)	Esther (9/15/79)
1574	Fred Jordan	Giant (5/15/77)	Allen (9/15/79)
1575	Kenneth C. Roberts	Marcy (8/13/70)	Gray (9/16/79)
1576	John C. Webster	Wright (7/12/76)	Saddleback (9/16/79)
1577	Sonja K. Goodwin	Dix (1969)	Macomb (9/23/79)
1578	Walter W. Goodwin	Marcy (1956)	Hough (9/23/79)
1579	Joseph Bandhold	Marcy (11/3/74)	Haystack (9/26/79)
1580	John B. Hagner	Algonquin (8/15/74)	Rocky Peak (10/5/79)
1581	Michael R. Kelly	Cascade (7/54)	Hough (10/6/79)
1582	Donald W. McLaughlin	Marcy (10/65)	Allen (10/7/79)
1583	Thaddeus Dydych	Algonquin (10/23/75)	Redfield (10/8/79)
1584	Penelope M. Wiktorek	Giant (4/17/76)	Colden (10/13/79)
1585	Clayton L. Knapp	Marcy (10/14/71)	Wright (10/13/79)
1586	James S. Appleyard	Big Slide (10/22/77)	Dix (11/18/79)
1587	Hugh B. Hollowood	Whiteface (5/58)	Couchsachraga (8/20/76)
1588	H. Galen Parker	Algonquin (8/30/70)	Marcy (8/20/77)
1589	Allison Reisner	Marcy (7/67)	Allen (7/23/78)
1590	Fred Schmeizer	Marcy (7/4/69)	Redfield (7/20/79)
1591	David Schwartzberg	Cascade (8/73)	Seymour (8/9/79)
1592	David L. Losee	Marcy (5/29/67)	Nye (1/12/80)
1593W	Robert L. Fuss	Santanoni (1/9/77)	Giant (3/2/80)
1594	Antonio A. Grippo	Giant (1958)	Couchsachraga (5/23/80)
1595	Tom Dudones	Whiteface (4/16/70)	Allen (5/25/80)
1596	Thomas M. Dincecco	Marcy (8/6/69)	Redfield (5/25/80)
1597	Fred Cady	Giant (4/11/76)	Gray (5/25/80)
1598	Fred A. Merrihew	Giant (1938)	Couchsachraga (5/25/80)
1599	Kim K. Merrihew	Colden (8/67)	Couchsachraga (5/25/80)
1600	Paul F. Merrihew	Whiteface (7/70)	Couchsachraga (5/25/80)
1601	Richard A. Ayling	Marcy (6/2/76)	Emmons (5/27/80)
1602	Richard A. Hudson	Saddleback (8/31/69)	Couchsachraga (6/13/80)
1603W	Cheryl N. Esper	Big Slide (7/10/77)	Santanoni (6/20/80)
1604W	Richard E. Casler	Wright (9/12/76)	Emmons (6/28/80)
1605	James W. Cooper	Esther (6/11/77)	Marcy (6/28/80)

Heaven Up-h'isted-ness!

	Member	First Ascent	Forty-sixth Peak
1606	Harold J. Schuler	Santanoni (5/28/77)	Cliff (7/2/80)
1607	Edward M. Cleland	Algonquin (6/26/74)	Allen (7/3/80)
1608	Thomas C. Hay	Big Slide (8/19/74)	Couchsachraga (7/5/80)
1609	Keith D. Solomon	Esther (8/4/75)	Saddleback (7/6/80)
1610	Carol Kobak	Cascade (9/71)	Gray (7/7/80)
1611	Jon Wolfe	Cascade (6/26/75)	Marshall (7/11/80)
1612	Lauren E. Jordy	Tabletop (6/75)	Redfield (7/12/80)
1613	Richard H. Tromel	Marcy (8/17/45)	Marshall (7/18/80)
1614	Albert P. Rosen	Cliff (8/18/75)	Colden (7/20/80)
1615	Mark Silverman	Dix (7/75)	Dial (7/25/80)
1616	Steve Rizika	Cascade (7/8/76)	Allen (7/26/80)
1617	Glenn Figard	Marcy (5/75)	Nye (8/3/80)
1618	Gerald B. Edwards	Upper Wolf Jaw (8/24/74)	Big Slide (8/5/80)
1619	Steven Ziff	Algonquin (7/24/75)	Tabletop (8/9/80)
1620	Lee W. Trow	Marcy (9/5/72)	Couchsachraga (8/11/80)
1621	Don Trow	Marcy (9/5/72)	Couchsachraga (8/11/80)
1622	Hanns Streuli	Algonquin (4/14/68)	Rocky Peak (8/13/80)
1623	Tracy M. Bendura	Cascade (5/24/75)	Colden (8/13/80)
1624	Richard Frank	Cascade (7/10/76)	Giant (8/13/80)
1625	Todd G. Van Allen	Skylight (6/29/75)	Sawteeth (8/14/80)
1626	Henry M. Sondheimer	Cascade (7/56)	Allen (8/15/80)
1627	Kenneth A. Bruno, Jr.	Big Slide (6/70)	Panther (8/17/80)
1628	Kenneth A. Bruno, Sr.	Marcy (6/4/77)	Panther (8/17/80)
1629	J. Roger Hanlon	Cascade (8/18/76)	Rocky Peak (8/20/80)
1630	David A. Hill	Haystack (8/22/74)	Rocky Peak (8/20/80)
1631	Claire Sherred	Porter (7/70)	Haystack (8/20/80)
1632	John W. Bailey	Marcy (8/73)	Esther (8/21/80)
1633	Wanda M. Bailey	Marcy (8/73)	Esther (8/21/80)
1634	Evelyn E. Salinger	Giant (9/26/69)	Sawteeth (8/23/80)
1635	Gerhard L. Salinger	Giant (9/26/69)	Sawteeth (8/23/80)
1636	Elliot A. Kirschbaum	Skylight (9/7/64)	Seymour (8/24/80)
1637	Thomas W. Fox	Big Slide (6/29/80)	Allen (8/26/80)
1638	Samuel B. Hagner	Marcy (1938)	Esther (8/26/80)
1639	Jon E. Freckleton	Colden (7/7/78)	Couchsachraga (8/27/80)
1640	Jon K. Freckleton	Colden (7/7/78)	Couchsachraga (8/27/80)
1641	Melinda L. Freckleton	Colden (7/7/78)	Couchsachraga (8/27/80)
1642	Timothy G. Hunt	Big Slide (1968)	Allen (8/28/80)
1643	Charles S. Bolton	Sawteeth (8/69)	East Dix (8/28/80)
1644	John E. Moon	Marcy (10/8/72)	Rocky Peak (8/28/80)
1645	Eileen M. Keegan	Tabletop (2/17/77)	Emmons (8/31/80)
1646	Immanuel Braverman	Wright (8/60)	Tabletop (8/31/80)
1647W	Kip Patnode	Marcy (9/2/70)	East Dix (9/6/80)
1648	Eileen Bobear	Giant (5/26/74)	Basin (9/7/80)
1649	Dilys C. Hoyt	Giant (8/23/76)	Iroquois (9/14/80)
1650	Hudson Kronk	Saddleback (8/14/71)	Couchsachraga (9/19/80)
1651	Vernon I. Saunders	Tabletop (8/24/71)	Nippletop (9/21/80)
1652W	Norman J. Smith	Marcy (6/25/73)	Allen (9/24/80)
1653	Raymond F. Bell	Dix (1967)	Seymour (9/25/80)
1654	Franklin B. Clark	Colvin (7/63)	Cliff (9/26/80)
1655	Jo Ann Sopko	Giant (6/19/77)	Dix (9/27/80)
1656	Michele Lee	Wright (9/1/74)	Iroquois (9/27/80)
1657	Richard A. Larsen	Dix (7/3/75)	Phelps (10/4/80)
1658	Frank Bianco	Whiteface (9/79)	Big Slide (10/5/80)
1659	Joanne G. Welch	Cascade (10/27/72)	Big Slide (10/25/80)
1660	William Welch	Cascade (10/27/72)	Big Slide (10/25/80)
1661W	Kenneth M. Ryba	East Dix (6/24/79)	Marcy (11/9/80)
1662	Timothy J. Watters	Marcy (9/20/75)	Nye (12/6/80)
1663	Newton M. Perrins	Marcy (9/56)	Skylight (2/16/81)
1664	Cyril P. Novoselec	Macomb (10/68)	Santanoni (5/10/81)
1665	Kenneth E. French	Phelps (5/27/74)	Big Slide (5/23/81)
1666	Gerald L. Carges	Cascade (8/23/69)	Basin (5/23/81)
1667W	Elizabeth B. Heald	Marcy (11/26/76)	Redfield (5/24/81)

The Membership Roster of the Adirondack Forty-Sixers

	Member	First Ascent	Forty-sixth Peak
1668	Wendy L. Roberts	Big Slide (5/78)	Couchsachraga (5/31/81)
1669	Karin Fraser	Cascade (1974)	Whiteface (6/8/81)
1670	Steven V. Baumeister	Big Slide (12/71)	Allen (6/11/81)
1671	Jefferson Wagener	Whiteface (9/20/75)	Haystack (7/2/81)
1672	Jennifer Wagener	Whiteface (9/20/75)	Haystack (7/2/81)
1673	Jean L. Wagener	Whiteface (9/20/75)	Haystack (7/2/81)
1674	Jerrold Wagener	Whiteface (9/20/75)	Haystack (7/2/81)
1675	Warren A. Brainard	Whiteface (9/20/75)	Allen (7/11/81)
1676	James C. Davis	Giant (8/75)	Cascade (7/12/81)
1677	Alan C. Brown	Whiteface (8/13/78)	Couchsachraga (7/17/81)
1678	Michelle Brown	Whiteface (8/13/78)	Couchsachraga (7/17/81)
1679	Marion L. Russell	Sawteeth (7/4/78)	Esther (7/23/81)
1680	Adam Abrevaya	East Dix (7/78)	Marcy (7/28/81)
1681	Bruce B. O'Neill	Algonquin (1/81)	Whiteface (7/31/81)
1682	Thomas A. Armstrong	Whiteface (9/23/78)	Redfield (8/1/81)
1683	Michael Green	Cascade (7/77)	Lower Wolf Jaw (8/7/81)
1684	James N. Ianora	Lower Wolf Jaw (7/75)	Couchsachraga (8/8/81)
1685	Eugenia W. Pitts	Marcy (1954)	Esther (8/9/81)
1686	Joseph O. Campos	Marcy (6/11/68)	Rocky Peak (8/9/81)
1687	Alex Lehmann	Cascade (7/7/79)	Colden (8/10/81)
1688	Jack Diamond	Upper Wolf Jaw (6/12/67)	Allen (8/14/81)
1689	John A. Rayburn	Giant (7/16/77)	Cascade (8/15/81)
1690	Shunsako Sato	Street (7/79)	Cascade (8/15/81)
1691	Michael Oberding	Algonquin (7/21/75)	Esther (8/15/81)
1692	Timothy M. Rice	Giant (1963)	Redfield (8/17/81)
1693	Joseph E. Anselment	Lower Wolf Jaw (8/56)	Whiteface (8/17/81)
1694	Leif H. Savery	Giant (9/8/75)	Gray (8/18/81)
1695	Benjamin J. Burnside	Cascade (7/1/78)	Skylight (8/18/81)
1696	James R. Burnside	Cascade (9/23/67)	Skylight (8/18/81)
1697	William C. Donovan	Marcy (8/11/53)	Esther (8/19/81)
1698	Heidi M. Bush	Colden (8/67)	Lower Wolf Jaw (8/20/81)
1699	Jeffrey R. Jonathan	Wright (3/21/70)	Redfield (8/21/81)
1700	Robert Mound	Sawteeth (10/20/74)	Colden (8/22/81)
1701	Andrew Salinger	Cascade (7/20/72)	Skylight (8/24/81)
1702	Ike Siskind	Marcy (6/53)	Rocky Peak (8/27/81)
1703	Marilyn Siskind	Marcy (5/24/70)	Rocky Peak (8/27/81)
1704	Stanley J. Moore	Marcy (6/69)	Couchsachraga (9/2/81)
1705	Marion B. Elliott, Jr.	Giant (5/29/76)	Esther (9/5/81)
1706	Betty N. Elliott	Giant (5/29/76)	Esther (9/5/81)
1707W	Philip B. Heald	Allen (9/24/80)	Nye (9/6/81)
1708	Erik Hutt	Giant (4/78)	Redfield (9/6/81)
1709	Lori Hutt	Wright (5/78)	Redfield (9/6/81)
1710	Michael Hutt	Giant (4/78)	Redfield (9/6/81)
1711	Owen D. Hutt	Cascade (9/77)	Redfield (9/6/81)
1712	Betty L. Bailey	Colden (7/3/70)	Esther (9/12/81)
1713	Joseph W. Coughlin	Cascade (10/15/80)	Big Slide (9/13/81)
1714	Henry Greiner	Giant (5/7/76)	Emmons (9/13/81)
1715	Robert W. McElwain	Giant (7/27/79)	Santanoni (9/13/81)
1716	Thomas Speedy	Colden (10/66)	Couchsachraga (9/19/81)
1717	Bernard Mansbach	Cascade (7/5/70)	Redfield (9/20/81)
1718	Charles Churchill	Lower Wolf Jaw (7/25/80)	Allen (9/25/81)
1719	George Hoch	Marcy (10/1/77)	Big Slide (9/25/81)
1720	Richard R. Michaels	Gothics (6/14/74)	Couchsachraga (9/25/81)
1721	Robert F. Hudak	Marcy (9/66)	Couchsachraga (9/26/81)
1722	John R. Gratto	Giant (7/7/79)	Couchsachraga (9/26/81)
1723	Barry Waling	Whiteface (5/4/80)	Couchsachraga (9/26/81)
1724	Richard V. Newell	Marcy (8/63)	Whiteface (9/27/81)
1725	Perry Pollock	Colden (9/17/77)	Dial (10/3/81)
1726	William S. Pollock	Colden (9/17/77)	Dial (10/3/81)
1727	Charles A. DeGraff	Wright (10/5/74)	Cascade (10/3/81)
1728	Christopher N. Bell	Dix (7/77)	Big Slide (10/3/81)
1729	Frederick J. Jones	Algonquin (8/73)	Allen (10/10/81)

Heaven Up-h'isted-ness!

	Member	First Ascent	Forty-sixth Peak
1730	Steven Racette	Phelps (5/3/78)	Sawteeth (10/11/81)
1731	George K. Schlidge	Big Slide (10/10/70)	Blake (10/1/81)
1732	Gerald J. Gnann	Cascade (4/76)	Allen (10/11/81)
1733	Ronald Heftie	Whiteface (8/71)	Gray (10/14/81)
1734	John Schneider	Colden (8/7/75)	Whiteface (10/17/81)
1735	Darrell Helms	Lower Wolf Jaw (4/24/77)	Gray (11/1/81)
1736	Eileen Donovan	Allen (7/4/74)	Cliff (11/15/81)
1737	Lee Clark	Whiteface (10/74)	Allen (11/15/81)
1738	Michael P. Douglass	Algonquin (2/19/78)	Marcy (11/28/81)
1739	Mason M. Howlett	Haystack (8/72)	Wright (8/9/91)
1740	Randi A. Oriani	Wright (8/76)	Couchsachraga (8/15/81)
1741W	Donald O. Berens, Jr.	Colden (1/26/75)	Marshall (1/9/82)
1742W	Gary F. Mitchell	East Dix (8/2/75)	Allen (2/28/82)
1743W	Peter Selig	Saddleback (2/19/77)	Emmons (3/6/82)
1744W	Douglas H. Wall	Algonquin (3/71)	Haystack (3/6/82)
1745	Russell Ley	Marcy (6/76)	Street (5/22/82)
1746	Anthony N. Roscigno	Marcy (10/9/77)	Santanoni (5/28/82)
1747	Paul A. Wilkinson	Macomb (9/29/78)	Tabletop (6/6/82)
1748	James L. Costley	Macomb (9/29/78)	Tabletop (6/6/82)
1749	Steven B. Phillips	Porter (5/22/75)	Redfield (6/12/82)
1750	Karen H. Robbins	Lower Wolf Jaw (11/9/74)	Allen (6/12/82)
1751	Ellen Somers	Big Slide (6/72)	Redfield (6/12/82)
1752	Mary A. Crook	Marcy (9/1/79)	Haystack (6/13/82)
1753	Larry A. Crook	Marcy (9/1/79)	Haystack (6/13/82)
1754	Gilbert P. Smith	Giant (7/68)	Allen (6/25/82)
1755	Sally J. Livingston	Cascade (10/5/79)	Santanoni (7/3/82)
1756W	John R. Wiley	Algonquin (1964)	Seymour (7/5/82)
1757	Stephen W. Davis	Cascade (5/12/73)	Allen (7/9/82)
1758	Steven Struhl	Algonquin (7/1/70)	Haystack (7/18/82)
1759	Aurelia G. Bolton	Giant (1943)	Santanoni (7/20/82)
1760	Robert Caruso	Giant (10/74)	Couchsachraga (7/24/82)
1761	Tim Becker	Marcy (7/20/80)	Allen (8/1/82)
1762	Bernhard Ries	Phelps (7/13/81)	Big Slide (8/5/82)
1763	Asher E. Miller	Big Slide (1976)	Dial (8/6/82)
1764	Robert Brown	Marcy (8/26/76)	Colden (8/7/82)
1765	Thomas P. Otis	Marcy (8/26/76)	Colden (8/7/82)
1766	Raymond Shandorf	Marcy (8/26/76)	Colden (8/7/82)
1767	Sheila R. Hartman	Giant (9/29/75)	Gray (8/9/82)
1768	Dennis L. Nemhauser	Phelps (7/81)	Cascade (8/10/82)
1769	Adam Sobel	Algonquin (7/81)	East Dix (8/10/82)
1770	Ted Rupert	Marcy (6/76)	Allen (8/13/82)
1771	Dennis G. Martin	Algonquin (1/7/74)	Allen (8/14/82)
1772	David P. Weisser	Wright (8/77)	Allen (8/15/82)
1773	G. Barrett Rich	Marcy (7/48)	Whiteface (8/16/82)
1774	Chipp Van Allen	Big Slide (5/29/77)	Seymour (8/18/82)
1775	Jeremy H. Greshin	Phelps (8/14/72)	Redfield (8/19/82)
1776	Michael S. Mathras, Jr.	Marcy (8/26/76)	Esther (8/20/82)
1777	Larry E. Pringle	Marcy (8/26/76)	Esther (8/20/82)
1778	Richard E. Church, Jr.	Dix (10/74)	Esther (8/21/82)
1779	John Van Hook	Gothics (9/3/77)	Seymour (8/22/82)
1780	John J. Hayes	Phelps (3/18/72)	Haystack (8/23/82)
1781	George R. Packard	Marcy (1949)	Giant (8/24/82)
1782	Margaret B. Moore	Cascade (7/7/76)	Esther (8/26/82)
1783	Charles K. Skee	Skylight (5/70)	Allen (8/26/82)
1784	Donna M. Skee	Marcy (10/74)	Allen (8/26/82)
1785	John W. Conway	Macomb (7/12/75)	Santanoni (8/28/82)
1786	George Hrubenak, Jr.	Giant (6/6/77)	Emmons (8/28/82)
1787	Robert J. Hrubenak	Giant (9/7/80)	Emmons (8/28/82)
1788	Fred A. Johnson	Giant (9/7/80)	Emmons (8/28/82)
1789	Lewis Hall	Marcy (1964)	Colden (8/28/82)
1790	Hank Bickel	Marcy (7/7/79)	Seymour (8/29/82)
1791W	Jim Kobak	Cascade (1975)	Allen (9/1/82)

The Membership Roster of the Adirondack Forty-Sixers

	Member	First Ascent	Forty-sixth Peak
1792	Robert W. Bredenberg	Marcy (6/37)	Cliff (9/4/82)
1793	Robert A. Dorner	Marcy (7/14/78)	Cascade (9/5/82)
1794	Daniel M. Noeller	Dial (8/9/79)	Giant (9/5/82)
1795	Russell L. Wilt	Giant (7/3/66)	Cliff (9/6/82)
1796	David M. Greene	Giant (8/23/78)	Haystack (9/11/82)
1797	Mary B. Harris	Marcy (1963)	Haystack (9/11/82)
1798	Terry Harris	Dix (6/74)	Haystack (9/11/82)
1799	Linda N. Sloan	Giant (5/26/79)	Seymour (9/12/82)
1800	Walter Pauk	Colvin (9/29/73)	Street (9/13/82)
1801	David W. Lance	Cascade (1962)	Haystack (9/18/82)
1802W	Suzanne E. Lance	Cascade (1962)	Haystack (9/18/82)
1803	J. Ripley Allen	Marcy (6/68)	Allen (9/19/82)
1804	Donald A. Reynolds	Phelps (4/11/66)	Tabletop (9/19/82)
1805	Douglas S. Reynolds	Marcy (10/7/70)	Tabletop (9/19/82)
1806	David L. Tanner	Marcy (1/6/74)	Tabletop (9/24/82)
1807	James Sampson	Big Slide (10/11/68)	Colden (9/24/82)
1808	William B. Evans	Giant (8/57)	Algonquin (9/24/82)
1809	Richard A. Sederquist	Marcy (8/12/76)	Hough (9/24/82)
1810	Edward C. Swift	Cascade (7/30/77)	Dix (9/24/82)
1811W	Douglas C. Frackleton	Marcy (6/7/77)	Rocky Peak (9/24/82)
1812	Ronald B. Pelinski	Skylight (3/73)	Emmons (9/29/82)
1813	Richard L. Wilkins	Algonquin (8/42)	Emmons (9/29/82)
1814	Robert A. Vititow	Whiteface (9/23/78)	Seymour (10/2/82)
1815	Daniel Rosenthal	Cascade (1979)	East Dix (10/3/82)
1816	Michael A. Rosenthal	Marcy (1965)	East Dix (10/3/82)
1817	John Russell	Phelps (12/14/69)	Iroquois (10/3/82)
1818	Anthony Ulrich	Phelps (8/29/81)	Esther (10/9/82)
1819	Ferdinand Ulrich	Phelps (8/29/81)	Esther (10/9/82)
1820	Paul M. Schurman	Marcy (6/24/65)	Seymour (10/9/82)
1821	Todd C. Lawrence	Big Slide (7/76)	Whiteface (10/14/82)
1822W	Michael A. Bromberg	Lower Wolf Jaw (7/26/80)	Iroquois (10/17/82)
1823	Judy Seybold	Cascade (9/80)	Haystack (10/18/82)
1824	Richard C. Fox	Marcy (5/29/49)	Gray (10/23/82)
1825	David H. LeRoy	Algonquin (8/1/74)	Santanoni (10/23/82)
1826	Katherine S. Van Woert	Basin (1967)	Allen (10/24/82)
1827	Ned Van Woert	Basin (7/71)	Allen (10/24/82)
1828	Peter E. Shafran	Algonquin (11/79)	Esther (10/26/82)
1829	Mitchell B. Wemple	Basin (8/27/77)	Nye (11/7/82)
1830	William H. O'Hern	Marcy (1970)	Couchsachraga (11/11/82)
1831	David M. Howard, Jr.	Colden (8/70)	Allen (7/6/77)
1832	Richard J. Brown	Big Slide (6/20/75)	Couchsachraga (10/14/79)
1833	Raymond P. Foote	Marcy (1933)	Couchsachraga (10/14/79)
1834	Brooks S. Clark	Armstrong (8/75)	Redfield (7/31/82)
1835	Mark Jordan	Big Slide (7/77)	Giant (8/5/82)
1836	Christine F. Lussi	Cascade (1967)	Haystack (8/21/82)
1837	Arthur Lussi	Whiteface (1965)	Nye (8/23/82)
1838	Richard W. Hacker	Dial (6/12/76)	Blake (9/4/82)
1839	Glenn A. Johnson	Giant (5/26/80)	Rocky Peak (10/3/82)
1840	Serge Lussi	Whiteface (1952)	Skylight (1982)
1841	Randall S. Hay	Algonquin (10/9/76)	Cliff (12/29/82)
1842	John Hubbell	Giant (1958)	Gothics (1/21/83)
1843W	Diane D. Sawyer	Seward (1/2/82)	Dix (2/26/83)
1844W	Tom W. Sawyer	Seward (1/2/82)	Dix (2/26/83)
1845	Gwenne R. Rippon	Marcy (8/61)	Haystack (3/20/83)
1846	Willie Janeway	Haystack (1970)	Iroquois (4/1/83)
1847	Joseph A. Pollock	Gothics (5/78)	Santanoni (4/9/83)
1848W	Bret R. Schneider	Marcy (6/75)	Allen (5/21/83)
1849	Ronald E. Schneider	Marcy (6/75)	Allen (5/21/83)
1850	Ronald A. Metzger	Giant (7/2/78)	Wright (5/23/83)
1851	Victor T. Raguso	Marcy (7/66)	Wright (5/23/83)
1852	Cathy Haag	Cascade (7/4/75)	Marcy (5/28/83)
1853	Fred G. Haag	Cascade (7/4/75)	Marcy (5/28/83)

Heaven Up-h'isted-ness!

	Member	First Ascent	Forty-sixth Peak
1854	Richard N. Schaffer	Algonquin (7/74)	Redfield (6/11/83)
1855	Gary M. Smith	Giant (7/1/78)	Iroquois (6/22/83)
1856	Richard Briggs	Wright (1/31/76)	Allen (6/24/83)
1857	Harrison S. Forde, Jr.	Santanoni (4/10/76)	Marshall (6/24/83)
1858	William E. Hester	Santanoni (4/10/76)	Marshall (6/24/83)
1859	John Marino	Giant (9/23/79)	Emmons (6/28/83)
1860	D. Bruce Campbell	Porter (6/1/68)	Haystack (6/27/83)
1861	Jean M. Campbell	Porter (6/1/68)	Haystack (6/27/83)
1862	Mark C. Beauharnois	Skylight (6/25/79)	Allen (6/28/83)
1863	Daniel E. Wolfe	Porter (9/16/79)	Haystack (6/29/83)
1864	Jaime T. Buceta	Marcy (unknown)	Allen (7/2/83)
1865	Arthur E. Powers	Algonquin (8/14/60)	Emmons (7/2/83)
1866	George D. Tilroe	Giant (9/9/78)	Emmons (7/3/83)
1867	Catherine J. Casler	Wright (9/12/76)	Emmons (7/3/83)
1868	Katherine S. Hacker	Marcy (7/79)	Emmons (7/3/83)
1869	Edward S. Mash	Marcy (9/7/69)	Gray (7/9/83)
1870	Jill R. Borgstede	Marcy (1974)	Gray (7/9/83)
1871	William R. Borgstede	Marcy (1974)	Gray (7/9/83)
1872	Jan W. Burrows	Wright (6/80)	Marshall (7/16/83)
1873	Carl Waldbauer	Algonquin (8/68)	Marshall (7/17/83)
1874	David G. Ignall	Cascade (7/11/77)	Sawteeth (7/30/83)
1875	Douglas A. Watson	Phelps (7/4/72)	Couchsachraga (7/30/83)
1876	Philip M. Watson	Phelps (7/4/72)	Couchsachraga (7/30/83)
1877	Todd Greenwood	Porter (7/70)	Redfield (8/2/83)
1878	George Pilkey	Marcy (6/60)	Allen (8/4/83)
1879	Inger F. Maeland	Cascade (8/21/81)	Colden (8/6/83)
1880	Keith A. Nordlie	Cascade (8/21/81)	Colden (8/6/83)
1881	Julie R. Marcellus	Algonquin (8/7/77)	Rocky Peak (8/7/83)
1882	Steve Elliott	Big Slide (7/77)	Dix (8/10/83)
1883	Maxwell L. Tananbaum	Cascade (3/16/81)	Big Slide (8/13/83)
1884W	Daniel Esper	Marcy (6/2/74)	Emmons (8/14/83)
1885	Charles G. Mattery	Marcy (7/39)	Allen (8/17/83)
1886	Mark W. Livsey	Allen (6/81)	Saddleback (8/18/83)
1887	George A. Wieber	Giant (7/40)	Skylight (8/19/83)
1888	Rudy Macander	Algonquin (10/5/77)	Santanoni (8/20/83)
1889W	Michael J. Becker	Dix (8/80)	Allen (8/21/83)
1890	Matthew Macander	Seward (7/3/82)	Marcy (8/21/83)
1891	Louis J. Gillespie, III	Cascade (1967)	Allen (8/22/83)
1892	Edward J. Rowland	Big Slide (8/2/70)	Emmons (8/27/83)
1893	Alice K. Baslow	Marcy (9/15/74)	Sawteeth (8/28/83)
1894	Glenn Baslow	Marcy (9/15/74)	Sawteeth (8/28/83)
1895	Patricia B. Egnew	Marcy (9/15/74)	Sawteeth (8/28/83)
1896	Roy C. Baslow	Marcy (9/15/74)	Sawteeth (8/28/83)
1897	Edgar F. Kohler	Marcy (9/15/74)	Sawteeth (8/28/83)
1898	Flora F. Kohler	Marcy (9/15/74)	Sawteeth (8/28/83)
1899	Caroline L. Forfa	Algonquin (9/73)	Allen (8/29/83)
1900	George H. Forfa	Algonquin (9/73)	Allen (8/29/83)
1901	James Peter Chingos	Giant (8/23/80)	Haystack (9/3/83)
1902W	John D. Nye	Dix (8/67)	Couchsachraga (9/3/83)
1903	Lynn L. Atwell	Cascade (10/3/74)	Esther (9/4/83)
1904	Mary N. Kennedy	Algonquin (11/74)	Panther (9/4/83)
1905	John D. Schellberg	Tabletop (6/26/83)	Marcy (9/4/83)
1906W	Steve Mackey	Marcy (10/76)	Donaldson (9/4/83)
1907	Licia S. Mackey	Marcy (10/69)	Donaldson (9/4/83)
1908	Nancy L. Olsen	Marcy (6/12/62)	Cliff (9/4/83)
1909	Mark E. Swanson	Marcy (8/26/68)	Couchsachraga (9/5/83)
1910W	Larry Braun	Big Slide (10/8/72)	Blake (9/5/83)
1911	Edward Kennedy	Algonquin (11/10/78)	Iroquois (9/10/83)
1912	Kenneth Heitkamp	Giant (8/65)	Tabletop (9/10/83)
1913	Robert M. Krug	Cascade (1973)	Santanoni (9/11/83)
1914	Richard H. Tourin	Marcy (8/63)	Redfield (9/12/83)
1915	Alison C. Gourdinier	Algonquin (9/70)	Couchsachraga (9/16/83)

The Membership Roster of the Adirondack Forty-Sixers

	Member	First Ascent	Forty-sixth Peak
1916	Joanna R. Donk	Haystack (1948)	Couchsachraga (9/16/83)
1917	Thomas J. Kopp	Algonquin (9/80)	Sawteeth (9/17/83)
1918	Gail R. Smallwood	Algonquin (9/80)	Sawteeth (9/17/83)
1919	Edmund Roberts	Giant (10/72)	Cliff (9/17/83)
1920	Allen Scholl	Big Slide (9/28/81)	Hough (9/18/83)
1921	Steven D. Wilson	Algonquin (8/16/78)	Allen (9/23/83)
1922W	George E. Banks, IV	Marcy (7/24/82)	Esther (9/24/83)
1923	Vincent J. Aceto	Phelps (5/30/70)	Couchsachraga (9/24/83)
1924	William E. Mitchell	Marcy (5/23/80)	Allen (10/1/83)
1925	Noel T. Morris	Marcy (7/58)	Sawteeth (10/2/83)
1926	Brenda J. Newman	Phelps (6/28/83)	Couchsachraga (10/3/83)
1927	Robert A. Newman	Phelps (6/28/83)	Couchsachraga (10/3/83)
1928	John Benzoni	Marcy (1964)	Couchsachraga (10/4/83)
1929	Carol C. Carman	Giant (9/16/78)	Iroquois (10/7/83)
1930	Joseph E. Carman, Jr.	Giant (9/16/78)	Iroquois (10/7/83)
1931	John M. Reschovsky	Colden (9/16/78)	Haystack (10/9/83)
1932	David L. Glatstein	Giant (7/17/80)	Santanoni (10/9/83)
1933	Samuel L. Gordon, Sr.	Phelps (7/54)	Santanoni (10/9/83)
1934	Charles Bennett	Cascade (11/14/82)	Gray (10/9/83)
1935	James A. Hart, Sr.	Algonquin (9/26/81)	Gray (10/9/83)
1936	Jon R. Hart	Cascade (11/14/82)	Gray (10/9/83)
1937	Deborah Morris	Big Slide (7/73)	Skylight (10/10/83)
1938	Harry A. Allan	Upper Wolf Jaw (5/1/81)	Redfield (10/10/83)
1939W	Frederick H. Turner	Cascade (9/81)	Algonquin (10/16/83)
1940W	Phelps T. Turner	Cascade (9/81)	Algonquin (10/6/83)
1941	Phil Caswell	Panther (8/4/83)	Whiteface (10/16/83)
1942	Charles O. Porter	Giant (1963)	Emmons (10/17/83)
1943	Wynton T. Hotaling	Giant (8/21/82)	Allen (10/20/83)
1944	Susan Hunter	Giant (10/25/80)	Haystack (10/22/83)
1945	Elaine Boshart	Algonquin (1/19/82)	Lower Wolf Jaw (10/22/83)
1946	Joseph A. Sladewski	Lower Wolf Jaw (5/73)	Allen (10/23/83)
1947	Jay Wadsworth E.	Gothics (4/28/81)	Colden (10/30/83)
1948	Elinor S. Grayzel	Marcy (3/81)	Cascade (12/11/83)
1949	Don Greene	Phelps (9/11/59)	Wright (6/8/63)
1950W	Charlie Clough	Santanoni (1/9/77)	Couchsachraga (1/20/80)
1951	Peter A. Wells	Cascade (1973)	Gray (8/13/80)
1952	Joseph R. Bigalow	Giant (7/68)	Allen (6/25/82)
1953	David M. Swan	Wright (7/1/66)	Marcy (9/17/82)
1954W	Gary F. Noyes	Marcy (8/74)	Street (2/27/83)
1955W	Thomas W. Nylund	Big Slide (1/6/79)	Blake (3/20/83)
1956	Ruth Burday	Phelps (8/28/76)	Giant (8/5/83)
1957	Benjamin S. Rinzler	Santanoni (7/77)	Panther (8/23/83)
1958	Andrew Aceto	Whiteface (1970)	Couchsachraga (9/24/83)
1959	Bruce W. Shaffer	Giant (8/21/79)	Colden (10/16/83)
1960W	Jeanne G. Sternbergh	Big Slide (1/7/79)	Haystack (2/25/84)
1961W	Louis J. Sorriero	Santanoni (1/77)	Seward (3/17/84)
1962	Patrick Hooker	Nye (6/2/73)	Redfield (5/21/84)
1963	Peter Wilcox	Algonquin (6/77)	Allen (5/26/84)
1964	James E. Close	Marcy (8/67)	Allen (5/27/84)
1965W	Sue Eilers	Santanoni (3/28/75)	Couchsachraga (5/27/84)
1966	Jon J. McCloskey	Dix (12/5/73)	Colden (6/9/84)
1967	Floyd F. Noreault	Marcy (7/12/63)	Marshall (7/1/84)
1968	Linda L. Coulter	Phelps (1979)	Lower Wolf Jaw (7/4/84)
1969	Ira Smith	Marcy (11/47)	Whiteface (7/7/84)
1970	Carl H. Fredrickson	Whiteface (10/7/78)	Haystack (7/15/84)
1971	Nina Doebrich	Cascade (8/8/78)	Gray (7/20/84)
1972	Melissa R. Donnelly	Phelps (7/26/81)	Whiteface (7/21/84)
1973	Erin Donnelly	Phelps (7/26/81)	Whiteface (7/21/84)
1974	Margaret A. Donnelly	Phelps (7/26/81)	Whiteface (7/21/84)
1975	Marguerite Banks	Marshall (7/24/82)	Street (7/21/84)
1976	Jodyann W. Kravec	Whiteface (9/3/77)	Redfield (7/21/84)
1977	John E. Kravec	Whiteface (9/3/77)	Redfield (7/21/84)

HEAVEN UP-H'ISTED-NESS!

	MEMBER	FIRST ASCENT	FORTY-SIXTH PEAK
1978	Krishine Fraser	Cascade (1979)	Street (7/23/84)
1979	Paul Boulay	Marcy (3/81)	Whiteface (7/29/84)
1980	Richard W. Ziff	Wright (6/29/79)	Phelps (7/31/84)
1981	Marilyn Burday	Phelps (1976)	Haystack (8/1/84)
1982	James M. Powers	Algonquin (8/14/60)	Redfield (8/4/84)
1983	Jim Bonesteel	Nye (8/77)	Basin (8/4/84)
1984	Steven Levine	Algonquin (1983)	Macomb (8/8/84)
1985	Wally Jenkins	Giant (8/5/67)	Santanoni (8/11/84)
1986	Eric Mathieu	Giant (7/78)	Porter (8/11/84)
1987	Charles S. Hadsell	Gothics (9/5/82)	Whiteface (8/12/84)
1988	Loren G. Schaff	Giant (6/29/81)	Whiteface (8/12/84)
1989	Barry Needleman	Cascade (7/77)	Dix (8/12/84)
1990	Donna L. Rupert	Marcy (6/79)	Santanoni (8/14/84)
1991	Richard A. Long	Wright (9/25/82)	Iroquois (8/17/84)
1992	Suzanne S. Long	Wright (9/25/82)	Iroquois (8/17/84)
1993	Tracy J. Pierce	Big Slide (5/78)	Iroquois (8/17/84)
1994	Raymond P. Bouchard	Wright (3/11/72)	Dix (8/19/84)
1995	John O. Close	Giant (7/5/81)	Sawteeth (8/20/84)
1996	Sharon R. Rosenthal	Marcy (9/9/69)	East Dix (8/20/84)
1997	Sally S. Sturner	Algonquin (7/25/78)	Allen (8/21/84)
1998	Linda J. Biesemeyer	Cascade (9/76)	Esther (8/21/84)
1999	Peter Biesemeyer	Cascade (unknown)	Esther (8/21/84)
2000	Thomas McNelly	Upper Wolf Jaw (7/17/61)	Marshall (8/21/84)
2001	Martin Stone	Wright (8/81)	Haystack (8/22/84)
2002	James P. Alsina	Sawteeth (8/25/66)	Redfield (8/23/84)
2003W	Mary P. Bunch	Algonquin (6/77)	Marcy (8/25/84)
2004W	Michael L. Bunch	Algonquin (6/77)	Marcy (8/25/84)
2005	John R. Stellrecht	Colden (7/3/82)	Marcy (8/25/84)
2006	Sue Stellrecht	Colden (7/3/82)	Marcy (8/25/84)
2007W	Raymond B. Held	Phelps (6/5/83)	Colden (8/25/84)
2008	Rick Carter	Marcy (7/22/73)	Whiteface (8/26/84)
2009	Lorri Wetzel	Marcy (5/74)	Allen (8/26/84)
2010	James E. Frey	Giant (10/81)	Redfield (8/27/84)
2011	Christopher Peckham	Porter (8/3/71)	Nye (8/27/84)
2012	Cyril Treadway	Marcy (8/71)	Emmons (8/28/84)
2013	Amanda C. Welles	Marcy (10/13/74)	Sawteeth (8/29/84)
2014	Christina T. Welles	Marcy (10/13/74)	Sawteeth (8/29/84)
2015	Charles D. McCarthy	Wright (8/22/76)	Marshall (9/1/84)
2016	Fred Cook	Whiteface (1957)	Dial (9/2/84)
2017	Gilbert E. Dannenberg	Marcy (1953)	Nye (9/2/84)
2018	Dana C. Rohleder	Algonquin (8/78)	East Dix (9/2/84)
2019	Francis A. Stunzi	Cascade (8/30/80)	Whiteface (9/6/84)
2020	Walter W. Favro	Cascade (8/30/80)	Whiteface (9/6/84)
2021	Ross Martin	Cascade (8/30/80)	Whiteface (9/6/84)
2022	Michael Ruhm	Algonquin (8/71)	Seymour (9/8/84)
2023	Ralph Ferrusi	Marcy (9/71)	Allen (9/9/84)
2024	Mark E. Turner	Colden (8/67)	Gray (9/9/84)
2025	Robert B. Cave	Sawteeth (7/27/80)	Basin (9/10/84)
2026	Barbara Peckham	Cascade (8/3/71)	Allen (9/11/84)
2027W	John B. Graham	Lower Wolf Jaw (7/2/78)	Esther (9/15/84)
2028	John E. Muniak	Algonquin (5/81)	Tabletop (9/15/84)
2029	Peter M. Sullivan	Colden (8/11/73)	Marshall (9/15/84)
2030	Barbara C. Fox	Marcy (9/76)	Saddleback (9/21/84)
2031	William J. Crangle	Marcy (unknown)	Haystack (9/22/84)
2032	Linda Filarecki	Cascade (7/79)	Saddleback (9/22/84)
2033	Harry W. Angleson	Marcy (6/55)	Rocky Peak (9/23/84)
2034	Katrina Van Tassel	Santanoni (5/27/84)	Street (9/23/84)
2035	Katy Macander	Giant (7/18/82)	Marcy (9/23/84)
2036	Neil F. Woodworth	Giant (7/70)	Cascade (9/23/84)
2037	Teresa Drost	Phelps (8/18/81)	Haystack (9/23/84)
2038	Gary Drost	Phelps (8/18/81)	Haystack (9/23/84)
2039	Thomas A. Lynch	Big Slide (7/69)	Haystack (9/23/84)

THE MEMBERSHIP ROSTER OF THE ADIRONDACK FORTY-SIXERS

	MEMBER	FIRST ASCENT	FORTY-SIXTH PEAK
2040	Michael T. Durocher	Marcy (7/78)	Iroquois (9/29/84)
2041W	Robert A. Veino	Phelps (11/8/80)	Wright (9/29/84)
2042	Kenneth E. Kramer	Skylight (8/20/70)	Redfield (9/30/84)
2043	Howard F. Adriance	Skylight (7/4/75)	Tabletop (9/30/84)
2044	Robert T. Durbin	Sawteeth (8/31/74)	Allen (9/30/84)
2045	David C. Bailey	Big Slide (8/4/74)	Colden (9/30/84)
2046	John J. Telfer	Big Slide (1971)	Redfield (10/1/84)
2047W	Michael G. O'Reilly	Haystack (1976)	Santanoni (10/3/84)
2048	Kathie LaBombard	Phelps (5/19/79)	Dix (10/6/84)
2049	Keith LaBombard	Phelps (5/19/79)	Dix (10/6/84)
2050	Thomas J. LaBombard	Phelps (5/19/79)	Dix (10/6/84)
2051W	Mary L. Connolly	Giant (1/14/84)	Gothics (10/6/84)
2052	Philip Levy	Lower Wolf Jaw (7/30/72)	Allen (10/7/84)
2053	Cyrus B. Whitney	Algonquin (10/76)	Marcy (10/7/84)
2054	Herbert B. Haake	Whiteface (5/5/60)	Colden (10/13/84)
2055	Andrew W. Bates	Marcy (9/30/83)	Haystack (10/13/84)
2056	Bernice Zehr	Marcy (1975)	Haystack (10/13/84)
2057	Robert B. Moore	Whiteface (11/30/74)	Santanoni (10/14/84)
2058	Cindy S. Watson	Esther (8/80)	Marshall (10/14/84)
2059	Jim Watson	Colden (1972)	Marshall (10/14/84)
2060	Paul V. Wicker	Santanoni (5/16/82)	Marcy (10/28/84)
2061	Carol H. Van Dyke	Marcy (7/27/77)	Esther (11/9/84)
2062	Beverly W. Van Diver	Whiteface (10/78)	Allen (11/11/84)
2063	Bradford B. Van Diver	Marcy (8/66)	Allen (11/11/84)
2064W	Breck K. Turner	Redfield (7/30/67)	Sawteeth (11/18/84)
2065	Don B. Martin	Colden (9/48)	Sawteeth (9/7/70)
2066	Myrna S. Martin	Lower Wolf Jaw (7/19/65)	Sawteeth (9/7/70)
2067	Terry J. Martin	Marcy (8/14/65)	Sawteeth (9/7/70)
2068	Tris M. Dunn	Marcy (8/14/65)	Sawteeth (9/7/70)
2069W	Victor N. Hobden	Whiteface (1/18/70)	Emmons (3/1/74)
2070	L. Aldrich Cass	Wright (8/23/69)	Allen (9/2/79)
2071	George D. Waldman	Wright (8/23/69)	Allen (9/2/79)
2072	William G. Cranker	Marcy (8/25/66)	Couchsachraga (6/2/83)
2073	David A. Edward	Lower Wolf Jaw (11/77)	Tabletop (10/13/83)
2074	Leo DeBlois	Marcy (7/5/80)	Esther (10/15/83)
2075	Ernest Wester	Algonquin (6/44)	Esther (10/15/83)
2076	Glen A. Vandewinckel	Cascade (5/31/75)	Nye (7/13/84)
2077	Allen B. McRae	Upper Wolf Jaw (7/1/58)	Redfield (7/22/84)
2078	Mikel D. Schwabel	Colvin (10/80)	Whiteface (8/19/84)
2079	William DeBello	Giant (1981)	Allen (8/31/84)
2080	Jonathan Runge	Wright (9/8/74)	Cliff (10/1/84)
2081	Carl F. Runge	Algonquin (10/52)	Cliff (10/1/84)
2082	Timothy T. Beaman	Big Slide (6/70)	Nye (3/17/85)
2083	Paul A. Garsin	Panther (10/20/80)	Tabletop (4/28/85)
2084	Gerald E. Carr	Dial (10/21/79)	Seymour (5/11/85)
2085	John J. Eastlake	Saddleback (10/7/69)	Skylight (5/22/85)
2086	Dieter W. Gump	Marcy (8/45)	Haystack (5/25/85)
2087	Kirk R. Davis	Algonquin (10/76)	Santanoni (5/25/85)
2088	Gerald R. Rising	Lower Wolf Jaw (1968)	Cliff (5/26/85)
2089	Michael J. Perosolak	Marshall (9/80)	Allen (5/26/85)
2090	L. Joseph Ferrara	Marcy (4/23/78)	Santanoni (5/26/85)
2091	Stephen D. Clark	Wright (7/21/79)	Marshall (5/30/85)
2092	Fred Eckel	Dial (9/10/67)	Redfield (5/30/85)
2093	Kenneth Marriott	Big Slide (4/9/81)	Cliff (5/30/85)
2094	Michael P. Nadiak	Wright (6/27/80)	Allen (6/9/85)
2095	Bennett Hirsch	Cascade (7/26/76)	Allen (6/15/85)
2096W	Frank G. Sorbero	Marcy (5/17/81)	Whiteface (6/22/85)
2097	William B. Mather, Jr.	Algonquin (6/50)	Allen (6/26/85)
2098	Ian Harper	Marshall (8/79)	Blake (6/28/85)
2099	Susan C. Fisher	Sawteeth (7/9/83)	Marshall (6/29/85)
2100	Douglas J. Redosh	Big Slide (9/72)	Panther (7/3/85)
2101	Michael J. Fedor	Marcy (4/75)	Rocky Peak (7/4/85)

Heaven Up-h'isted-ness!

	Member	First Ascent	Forty-sixth Peak
2102	John L. Turner	Whiteface (7/46)	Sawteeth (7/5/85)
2103	Eric Bansbach	Dial (5/17/80)	Wright (7/5/85)
2104	Janet Allocca	Marcy (8/65)	Macomb (7/5/85)
2105	Linda L. Paquin	Giant (1975)	Marcy (7/7/85)
2106	Glenn A. Powers	Algonquin (8/14/60)	Tabletop (7/10/85)
2107	Constance Centrello	Big Slide (9/24/83)	Nippletop (7/13/85)
2108	Alan G. Woodard	Gothics (7/78)	Emmons (7/20/85)
2109	Matthew Lestina	Colden (8/1/73)	Allen (7/21/85)
2110W	L. John Van Norden	Algonquin (5/78)	Haystack (7/23/85)
2111	Dianna Strnisa	Algonquin (8/23/81)	Big Slide (7/27/85)
2112	David E. Turnbull	Big Slide (9/26/73)	Haystack (7/27/85)
2113	Judith F. Groff	Cascade (7/74)	Skylight (8/3/85)
2114	Michael D. Marvin	Marcy (8/13/73)	Seymour (8/4/85)
2115	Russell H. Marvin	Marcy (8/13/73)	Seymour (8/4/85)
2116	Matthew P. Hoffman	Cascade (1980)	Emmons (8/7/85)
2117	Keith Gardner	Porter (8/9/75)	Whiteface (8/8/85)
2118	Raymond Kozloski	Marcy (6/17/71)	Dial (8/8/85)
2119	Leon R. Millett	Redfield (8/10/80)	Cascade (8/9/85)
2120	Richard J. Pauley	Allen (6/7/80)	Colvin (8/10/85)
2121	Andrew Caplan	Cascade (7/79)	Colden (8/10/85)
2122	Ernest R. Alden	Santanoni (6/23/84)	Whiteface (8/18/85)
2123	Eric J. Forman	Marcy (7/81)	Allen (8/18/85)
2124	Howard J. Dash	Wright (7/9/83)	Whiteface (8/18/85)
2125	Dorothy Seagle	Saddleback (8/63)	Whiteface (8/18/85)
2126	John P. Seagle	Giant (1945)	Whiteface (8/18/85)
2127	Michael P. Blinn	Macomb (8/28/77)	Allen (8/19/85)
2128	Kristin Sturner	Cascade (8/31/78)	Haystack (8/21/85)
2129	Stewart E. Byrd	Colvin (8/73)	Whiteface (8/21/85)
2130W	Kurt Pfeffer	Giant (11/22/83)	Esther (8/22/85)
2131	Richard H. Swain	Giant (6/14/77)	Iroquois (8/23/85)
2132	Dan A. Nielsen	Dix (6/19/71)	Whiteface (8/24/85)
2133W	Duane J. Rabideau	Algonquin (6/14/76)	Big Slide (8/25/85)
2134	Bradford R. Jones	Wright (1979)	Blake (8/26/85)
2135	Donald J. Yanulavich	Marcy (8/19/75)	Allen (8/28/85)
2136	E. William Brosseau	Sawteeth (10/4/74)	Blake (8/31/85)
2137W	Philip Alonzo	Marcy (5/70)	Cliff (9/1/85)
2138	Michael A. O'Donnell	Marcy (10/13/80)	Allen (9/1/85)
2139W	David A. Pisaneschi	Giant (4/6/76)	Allen (9/1/85)
2140	Alan Sanders	Whiteface (1969)	Esther (9/1/85)
2141	Richard H. Welkley	Marcy (6/12/73)	Tabletop (9/2/85)
2142	Mary C. Pinkerton	Marcy (8/79)	Sawteeth (9/2/85)
2143	William C. Coffin	Marcy (1970)	Sawteeth (9/2/85)
2144	Andrew S. Rawdon	Marcy (8/12/72)	Redfield (9/2/85)
2145	Marie Macander	Big Slide (10/2/72)	Colden (9/3/85)
2146	Michelle Macander	Cascade (9/19/82)	Colden (9/3/85)
2147	Daniel S. Weld	Cascade (7/19/64)	Hough (9/3/85)
2148	Jane O'Connell	Algonquin (7/31/82)	Whiteface (9/5/85)
2149	William B. Martin	Algonquin (7/31/82)	Whiteface (9/5/85)
2150	Bruce G. Cole	Algonquin (1960)	Street (9/7/85)
2151	Joseph Urbanczyk	Macomb (10/2/82)	Marcy (9/7/85)
2152	George A. Christian	Marcy (11/2/68)	Seymour (9/8/85)
2153	David A. Newman	Algonquin (8/31/81)	Iroquois (9/14/85)
2154	Doris L. Crangle	Marcy (Mid-1950's)	Gothics (9/14/85)
2155	Donald E. Crook	Wright (9/15/79)	Colden (9/14/85)
2156	Hervey C. Forward	Phelps (4/6/82)	Colden (9/14/85)
2157	Patricia Baldwin	Algonquin (9/25/72)	Marshall (9/15/85)
2158	Theodore P. Wright, Jr.	Algonquin (8/62)	Couchsachraga (9/21/85)
2159	Carl R. Kantner	Seymour (7/26/80)	East Dix (9/21/85)
2160W	Michael Hopkins	Marcy (1975)	Whiteface (9/21/85)
2161	Anneliese H. Lawson	Marcy (8/28/69)	Santanoni (9/21/85)
2162	Martin B. Taylor	Giant (3/9/74)	Tabletop (9/22/85)
2163	Rocco Saccone, Jr.	Algonquin (1/5/71)	Whiteface (9/25/85)

The Membership Roster of the Adirondack Forty-Sixers

	Member	First Ascent	Forty-sixth Peak
2164	Rocco Saccone	Marcy (9/30/70)	Whiteface (9/25/85)
2165	Rita E. Cantor	Marcy (7/15/81)	Nye (9/27/85)
2166W	Stephen J. Dunn	Colden (9/19/83)	Nye (9/27/85)
2167	Bonnie M. Dunn	Gothics (10/11/81)	Nye (9/27/85)
2168	Emile Richard	Giant (5/11/85)	Nye (9/27/85)
2169	Donald J. Orr, Jr.	Lower Wolf Jaw (10/80)	Haystack (9/28/85)
2170	Barbara Konowitz	Gothics (5/79)	East Dix (9/29/85)
2171	Robert J. Dwyer	Phelps (7/18/81)	Nippletop (9/29/85)
2172	John B. Corrado	Algonquin (9/3/61)	Emmons (10/8/85)
2173	Norma Corrado	Algonquin (9/3/61)	Emmons (10/8/85)
2174	Christine V. Torey	Porter (8/7/82)	Big Slide (10/12/85)
2175	Robert Bastian	Wright (5/4/85)	Colden (10/12/85)
2176	Elizabeth Rose	Cascade (1970's)	Colden (10/12/85)
2177W	Stephen L. Stoner	Cascade (7/15/83)	Seymour (10/13/85)
2178	Thomas M. Canning	Big Slide (7/75)	Sawteeth (10/14/85)
2179	David B. Cox	Sawteeth (10/5/80)	Cascade (10/14/85)
2180W	Benjamin S. Tennyson	Cascade (9/25/72)	Santanoni (10/18/85)
2181	Mark G. Benz	Marcy (1964)	Esther (10/20/85)
2182	Christopher Cosgrove	Marcy (7/83)	Whiteface (10/20/85)
2183	Larry Blumberg	Marcy (9/76)	Tabletop (10/26/85)
2184	Richard F. Olsen	Marcy (9/71)	Tabletop (10/26/85)
2185	C. Edmund Samuelson	Marcy (9/71)	Tabletop (10/26/85)
2186	Richard Skinner	Marcy (10/22/83)	Marshall (10/27/85)
2187	Edward M. Pike	Whiteface (7/22/84)	Seymour (11/3/85)
2188	Scott Pike	Whiteface (7/22/84)	Seymour (11/3/85)
2189	Matthew Pommerville	Giant (9/26/81)	Emmons (11/3/85)
2190W	Victor D. Pommerville	Giant (9/26/81)	Emmons (11/3/85)
2191	Diane Crawford	Haystack (10/78)	Sawteeth (11/11/85)
2192	Sylvia Lazarnick	Colden (12/70)	Porter (11/16/85)
2193	Charlie Goodrich	Whiteface (3/31/84)	Phelps (11/16/85)
2194	Peter Ricci	Wright (5/28/83)	Phelps (11/16/85)
2195W	Gary J. Dietrich	Giant (9/18/82)	Sawteeth (12/22/85)
2196	George B. Wingate	Cascade (6/52)	Couchsachraga (9/2/64)
2197	Edythe W. Robbins	Colden (9/70)	Allen (9/16/73)
2198	Valida S. Cote	Algonquin (7/47)	Tabletop (8/1/74)
2199	Dick Baranello	Seward (7/17/82)	Tabletop (6/22/85)
2200	Elise A. Kessler	Marcy (1964)	Seymour (7/31/85)
2201	Hans T. Kessler	Marcy (1964)	Seymour (7/31/85)
2202	Jeff Gaillard	Esther (8/23/75)	Colden (8/17/85)
2203	Ronald T. Morris	Marcy (7/4/62)	Seymour (8/28/85)
2204	Kathryn F. Nolett	Cascade (7/26/76)	Rocky Peak (9/14/85)
2205	David A. Peckham	Marcy (7/13/71)	Seymour (9/14/85)
2206W	Neal W. Shapiro	Porter (1973)	Gray (11/2/85)
2207W	Robert H. Werner	Marcy (3/27/76)	Redfield (2/22/86)
2208W	William D. Crowe	Santanoni (1/77)	Couchsachraga (3/1/86)
2209	Neil T. Van Dresar	Marcy (6/75)	Haystack (3/22/86)
2210	Vickie J. Van Dresar	Macomb (6/12/82)	Haystack (3/22/86)
2211	Paul A. Sirtoli	Basin (7/76)	Blake (5/24/86)
2212	Scott G. Burns	Marcy (1972)	Santanoni (5/25/86)
2213	Thomas R. Berrian	Marcy (5/28/74)	Emmons (6/14/86)
2214W	Mary Lou Recor	Giant (6/11/83)	Donaldson (6/21/86)
2215	Bruce T. Martin	Haystack (8/71)	Couchsachraga (6/29/86)
2216	Jean D. Hardy	Marcy (9/51)	Seymour (6/30/86)
2217	Carolyn M. Kaczka	Cascade (5/10/84)	Seymour (6/30/86)
2218	Eugene E. Kaczka	Wright (5/27/84)	Seymour (6/30/86)
2219W	Stanley M. Anderson	Porter (3/1/86)	Allen (7/4/86)
2220	Gerald E. Clark	Phelps (6/30/77)	Whiteface (7/6/86)
2221	Brian Guyette	Phelps (6/30/77)	Whiteface (7/6/86)
2222	Pattye Hitchins	Dix (7/3/82)	Esther (7/6/86)
2223	Ellen S. DuBois	Dial (8/18/84)	Esther (7/6/86)
2224	Thomas C. DuBois	Dial (8/18/84)	Esther (7/6/86)
2225	Christine P. Leanza	Wright (5/15/76)	Haystack (7/8/86)

Heaven Up-h'isted-ness!

	Member	First Ascent	Forty-sixth Peak
2226	Charles A. Berghane, Jr.	Phelps (10/1/72)	Allen (7/10/86)
2227	William A. Warren	Phelps (10/1/72)	Allen (7/10/86)
2228	Craig W. Johnson	Marcy (8/75)	Colden (7/11/86)
2229	Kirk Luchtenberg	Marcy (8/20/81)	Whiteface (7/11/86)
2230	Malcolm H. Wentworth	Cascade (9/8/84)	Gray (7/12/86)
2231	Marcia M. Wentworth	Cascade (9/8/84)	Gray (7/12/86)
2232	Matt Fitzsimmons	Haystack (7/24/82)	Emmons (7/12/86)
2233	Joan A. Robertson	Algonquin (7/19/70)	Allen (7/13/86)
2234	Barbara Reeves-Ellington	Marcy (9/3/83)	Allen (7/19/86)
2235W	Richard Reeves-Ellington	Marcy (9/3/83)	Allen (7/19/86)
2236	Anthony G. Wahl, III	Wright (7/81)	Redfield (7/26/86)
2237	Thomas D. Martin	Algonquin (5/86)	Allen (7/26/86)
2238	Carolyn D. Dzaugis	Lower Wolf Jaw (8/20/80)	Allen (7/26/86)
2239	Harold G. Spetla, Jr.	Porter (2/21/83)	Allen (7/26/86)
2240	Lynn A. Seirup	Lower Wolf Jaw (5/72)	Santanoni (7/26/86)
2241	Barbara Traver	Skylight (8/7/85)	Iroquois (7/28/86)
2242	Ann Alton	Cascade (7/63)	Panther (7/29/86)
2243	John M. Robbins	Algonquin (4/7/68)	Marcy (7/30/86)
2244	Brian Cameros	Giant (8/82)	Seymour (8/1/86)
2245	Andrew G. Canning	Porter (9/18/82)	Panther (8/1/86)
2246	Donald J. Baird	Cliff (7/20/84)	Emmons (8/2/86)
2247	Peter M. Trent	Lower Wolf Jaw (8/13/79)	Whiteface (8/2/86)
2248	Todd R. Earl	Giant (7/23/82)	Rocky Peak (8/3/86)
2249	Gail MacKenzie	Algonquin (8/71)	Iroquois (8/5/86)
2250	Catherine Eich	Seward (7/18/86)	Whiteface (8/7/86)
2251	Alex Kopista	Seward (7/18/86)	Whiteface (8/7/86)
2252	David W. Birdsall	Giant (6/79)	Tabletop (8/8/86)
2253W	Robert D. Wilcox	Gothics (6/5/81)	Whiteface (8/9/86)
2254	Paula C. Lutz	Colden (9/5/81)	Tabletop (8/10/86)
2255	Edmond F. Cassot	Cascade (7/75)	Nippletop (8/10/86)
2256	Richard A. Armitage	Sawteeth (5/72)	Dial (8/10/86)
2257	Scott Grunstein	Algonquin (7/81)	Rocky Peak (8/10/86)
2258	Stephen J. Easter	Cascade (9/27/69)	Allen (8/13/86)
2259	Sofia Sterling	Cascade (4/22/84)	Whiteface (8/15/86)
2260	Daniel J. Englander	Cascade (7/79)	Seymour (8/16/86)
2261	Ian P. Yurdin	Cascade (8/16/80)	Whiteface (8/16/86)
2262	Darlene Held	Nippletop (7/8/84)	Colden (8/20/86)
2263	Sally Loomis	Cascade (8/18/76)	Armstrong (8/21/86)
2264	Ann R. Hanlon	Cascade (1976)	Armstrong (8/21/86)
2265	Calvin Dupuis	Marcy (9/4/77)	Sawteeth (8/22/86)
2266	Christopher Hume	Cascade (8/79)	Santanoni (8/22/86)
2267	Angus Whelchel	Algonquin (7/26/81)	Rocky Peak (8/23/86)
2268	Lynn W. Whelchel	Algonquin (7/26/81)	Rocky Peak (8/23/86)
2269	Timo W. Fitzinger	Cascade (8/17/79)	Whiteface (8/26/86)
2270	Robert E. James	Marcy (1948)	Couchsachraga (8/30/86)
2271	John C. Edwards	Marcy (7/81)	Panther (8/30/86)
2272	Kimberly Edwards	Marcy (7/81)	Panther (8/30/86)
2273	Sandra Edwards	Marcy (7/81)	Panther (8/30/86)
2274	Scott J. Edwards	Marcy (7/81)	Panther (8/20/86)
2275	Brian Miller	Saddleback (7/81)	Nippletop (8/30/86)
2276	Cory Cipriani	Gothics (9/26/81)	Emmons (8/31/86)
2277	Albert T. Trendell	Cascade (8/1/81)	Dial (9/6/86)
2278	Frank E. Trendell	Marcy (5/10/80)	Dial (9/6/86)
2279	David A. Ness	Marcy (1967)	Couchsachraga (9/9/86)
2280	Harold R. Mereau	Giant (6/79)	Colden (9/13/86)
2281	Richard L. Burkdorf	Lower Wolf Jaw (9/12/82)	Sawteeth (9/14/86)
2282	John G. Davis	Lower Wolf Jaw (9/12/82)	Sawteeth (9/14/86)
2283	Boyd Richards	Marcy (6/15/86)	Rocky Peak (9/19/86)
2284	Glenn Wolford	Cascade (5/28/76)	Iroquois (9/19/86)
2285	Matthew K. Riedesel	Marcy (7/23/85)	Whiteface (9/20/86)
2286	Joan M. Yungwirth	Algonquin (8/24/76)	Whiteface (9/20/86)
2287	Ryan Ripper	Cascade (5/30/82)	Marcy (9/21/86)

THE MEMBERSHIP ROSTER OF THE ADIRONDACK FORTY-SIXERS

	MEMBER	FIRST ASCENT	FORTY-SIXTH PEAK
2288	Timothy L. McFaul	Wright (9/79)	Iroquois (9/28/86)
2289	Daniel J. Nickerson	Cascade (11/7/77)	Iroquois (9/28/86)
2290	Mark L. DeCracker	Sawteeth (8/20/77)	Esther (9/28/86)
2291	Barbara H. Hansen	Cascade (6/29/85)	Marshall (9/29/86)
2292	Eric M. Hansen	Cascade (6/29/85)	Marshall (9/29/86)
2293	David F. Morse, Sr.	Lower Wolf Jaw (3/15/64)	Redfield (10/3/86)
2294	Michael T. Leahy	Marcy (8/18/84)	Skylight (10/4/86)
2295W	James Mosher	Giant (9/9/84)	Basin (10/5/86)
2296	Susan H. Earley	Giant (8/25/84)	Redfield (10/8/86)
2297	Robert V. Wiles	Wright (9/3/78)	Cliff (10/10/86)
2298	Doris O. Wiles	Wright (9/3/78)	Cliff (10/10/86)
2299	William Wilson	Big Slide (7/29/77)	Panther (10/10/86)
2300	John M. Daniels	Dix (7/25/81)	Colden (10/11/86)
2301	Sheila M. Daniels	Dix (7/25/81)	Colden (10/11/86)
2302	Roger A. Rienicker	Wright (10/16/76)	Big Slide (10/11/86)
2303	Timothy C. McEachern	Iroquois (8/11/82)	Tabletop (10/11/86)
2304W	James C. King	Phelps (7/7/71)	Marshall (10/12/86)
2305	Malinda B. Chapman	Cascade (9/71)	Cliff (10/12/86)
2306W	David Dresser	Giant (1982)	Allen (10/19/86)
2307	Dennis Rea	Marcy (10/75)	Allen (10/19/86)
2308	William J. Embler, Jr.	Giant (9/19/82)	Phelps (10/20/86)
2309	Christian Embler	Giant (9/19/82)	Phelps (10/20/86)
2310	James H. Graves	Wright (7/19/86)	Haystack (10/20/86)
2311	Nancy L. Marvin	Lower Wolf Jaw (8/16/53)	Allen (10/25/86)
2312	Margaret Haslam-Jones	Cascade (1969)	Panther (10/26/86)
2313	Tom Haslam-Jones	Algonquin (4/20/85)	Panther (10/26/86)
2314	Ann Lowery	Phelps (9/81)	Wright (11/8/86)
2315	Edward G. Janeway, Jr.	Giant (1942)	Nye (9/23/84)
2316	Eric C. Fullager	Big Slide (8/70)	Giant (10/15/84)
2317	David P. Graefe	Algonquin (10/11/75)	Sawteeth (5/11/86)
2318	David R. Johnson	Marcy (8/75)	Colden (7/27/86)
2319	Claude M. Janeway	Giant (1962)	Couchsachraga (7/30/86)
2320	Matthew Gibson	Cascade (7/79)	Rocky Peak (8/6/86)
2321	Warren Gunderson	Gothics (5/67)	Emmons (8/9/86)
2322	Anne M. Janeway	Haystack (1976)	Panther (8/13/86)
2323	Katrina Lussi	Cascade (11/12/74)	Rocky Peak (8/22/86)
2324	Michelle Hamilton	Marcy (6/3/81)	Sawteeth (9/13/86)
2325W	Ronald W. Navik	Big Slide (12/29/79)	Iroquois (1/17/87)
2326W	Gordon Robinson	Nye (4/71)	Saddleback (3/8/87)
2327	John H. Alexander	Marcy (7/29/85)	Cascade (4/4/87)
2328	Thomas M. Graefe	Dix (8/76)	Gray (5/2/87)
2329	William R. Martin	Marcy (7/74)	Iroquois (5/17/87)
2330	Daniel J. Lewis	Lower Wolf Jaw (4/4/81)	Marshall (5/23/87)
2331	John C. Coleman	Allen (6/15/85)	Phelps (5/24/87)
2332	Vincent N. DeFelice	Marcy (9/1/74)	Allen (5/25/87)
2333	Raymond N. Johnson	Phelps (7/13/69)	Cliff (5/25/87)
2334	Earl F. Colborn	Marcy (5/29/82)	Gothics (5/27/87)
2335	Bryan Cleaveland	Marcy (7/67)	Gray (5/30/87)
2336	Stephen A. Brown	Santanoni (7/4/75)	Street (6/13/87)
2337	Matthew D. Clough	Santanoni (8/75)	Haystack (6/13/87)
2338	Brian D. Hendrie	Marcy (6/72)	East Dix (6/14/87)
2339	John T. Fassett	Giant (1979)	Nye (6/20/87)
2340	Kenneth Zakluliewicz	Marcy (9/7/80)	Emmons (6/21/87)
2341	Frank J. Traver	Skylight (7/84)	Allen (6/21/87)
2342	John F. Snow	Giant (7/5/65)	Couchsachraga (6/26/87)
2343	Mary G. Corell	Porter (10/14/72)	Couchsachraga (7/5/87)
2344	John P. Corell	Porter (9/18/82)	Panther (7/5/87)
2345W	Mark E. Corell	Phelps (10/16/82)	Panther (7/5/87)
2346	Gerald J. Dobbs	Cascade (5/26/86)	Seymour (7/11/87)
2347W	Conrad Sidway	Algonquin (7/85)	Allen (7/11/87)
2348	Beverly E. Messmer	Armstrong (7/21/83)	Esther (7/15/87)
2349	Kevin D. Flynn	Haystack (1976)	Allen (7/18/87)

Heaven Up-h'isted-ness!

	Member	First Ascent	Forty-sixth Peak
2350	Katie G. Scalise	Haystack (7/18/77)	Allen (7/18/87)
2351	Bruce Caputo	Colden (1952)	Seymour (7/19/87)
2352	David T. Watson	Phelps (7/4/72)	Allen (7/24/87)
2353	Kenneth N. Coulter	Algonquin (1983)	Wright (7/25/87)
2354	Susan M. Jarvis	Cascade (11/9/85)	Marshall (7/25/87)
2355	Nancy D. Allen	Big Slide (9/14/85)	Marshall (7/25/87)
2356	Michael Rockford	Giant (1980)	Dial (7/27/87)
2357	Jason Dresser	Colvin (5/26/85)	Haystack (7/28/87)
2358	John S. Mercer	Colvin (8/15/79)	Wright (7/30/87)
2359	Debra A. O'Donnell	Phelps (9/23/84)	Colden (8/1/87)
2360	Scott L. Wunderlich	Phelps (7/76)	Redfield (8/2/87)
2361	Wayne A. Speed	Cascade (5/29/83)	Allen (8/2/87)
2362	Lisa Macander	Cascade (6/30/85)	Basin (8/2/87)
2363	Nicholas S. Boltash	Cascade (5/24/86)	Seymour (8/3/87)
2364	Edward Stone	Algonquin (8/3/81)	Skylight (8/5/87)
2365	Christopher J. Rall	Cascade (1985)	Porter (8/5/87)
2366	Neal Sondheimer	Wright (8/78)	Iroquois (8/6/87)
2367	Scott E. Lewis	Cascade (7/17/84)	Iroquois (8/6/87)
2368	Abby Wahl	Algonquin (8/82)	Seymour (8/7/87)
2369	Michael Vladeck	Haystack (1984)	Nye (8/7/87)
2370	Jay V. Summerson	Wright (6/16/81)	Couchsachraga (8/9/87)
2371	Paul Eschmann	Marcy (9/21/73)	Phelps (8/11/87)
2372	Edward J. Banovic	Giant (7/20/84)	Seymour (8/14/87)
2373	Karen Banovic	Giant (7/20/84)	Seymour (8/14/87)
2374	Margo Rabb	Algonquin (8/83)	Santanoni (8/14/87)
2375	Steve Hart	Macomb (5/28/82)	Santanoni (8/15/87)
2376	David C. Hubbard	Cascade (4/30/86)	Nippletop (8/17/87)
2377	Esther Hubbard	Cascade (4/30/86)	Nippletop (8/17/87)
2378	William Orecki	Marcy (8/21/80)	Allen (8/17/87)
2379	Walter S. Bailey	Big Slide (8/20/80)	Santanoni (8/18/87)
2380	Archibald R. Montgomery	Marcy (8/60)	Allen (8/19/87)
2381	Brian Rinker	Cascade (6/9/74)	Whiteface (8/21/87)
2382	Jeffrey Rinker	Cascade (6/9/74)	Whiteface (8/21/87)
2383	Mindaugas Jatulis	Marcy (5/24/73)	Allen (8/21/87)
2384	Roger K. Kauffman	Marcy (12/19/72)	Seymour (8/22/87)
2385	Kenneth Nicolai	Gothics (7/72)	Whiteface (8/22/87)
2386	Richard J. Strowger	Cascade (7/26/77)	Giant (8/22/87)
2387	Ryan J. Strowger	Cascade (7/26/77)	Giant (8/22/87)
2388	Christopher I. Simser	Dial (8/28/84)	Allen (8/23/87)
2389	Katherine W. Batson	Cascade (6/29/85)	Dix (8/23/87)
2390	Mary H. Theisen	Cascade (9/25/85)	Dix (8/23/87)
2391	Maggie Piekarski	Marcy (8/73)	Allen (8/24/87)
2392	Rigg Piekarski	Marcy (8/73)	Allen (8/24/87)
2393	Robert M. Lohman	Santanoni (1960)	Seymour (8/26/87)
2394	Thelma Lohman	Santanoni (1960)	Seymour (8/26/87)
2395	Lee W. Mather, Jr.	Giant (8/16/79)	Allen (8/26/87)
2396	Richard D. Bonk	Phelps (6/30/80)	Seymour (8/28/87)
2397	Bunny Goodwin	Giant (9/67)	Esther (8/30/87)
2398	Richard Ames	Marcy (8/73)	Esther (8/30/87)
2399	Stephanie L. Bayan	Marcy (1961)	Sawteeth (8/30/87)
2400	Joanna Gunderson	Giant (1960)	Santanoni (8/31/87)
2401	David H. Salinger	Giant (9/26/69)	Esther (9/5/87)
2402	Peter E. Salinger	Giant (9/25/69)	Esther (9/5/87)
2403	Richard A. Kaul	Lower Wolf Jaw (7/17/76)	Whiteface (9/5/87)
2404	Dennis W. Linnehan	Marcy (7/7/78)	Rocky Peak (9/6/87)
2405	Carol S. Maher	Dix (7/5/82)	Rocky Peak (9/6/87)
2406	Robert Maher, Jr.	Marcy (5/65)	Rocky Peak (9/6/87)
2407	Eric J. Davies	Wright (unknown)	Basin (9/6/87)
2408	Jon Speed	Cascade (5/29/83)	Emmons (9/6/87)
2409	Ira H. Orenstein	Marcy (8/26/74)	Big Slide (9/6/87)
2410	J. Davis Chapman	Algonquin (2/13/83)	Gray (9/6/87)
2411	Richard D. Clark	Giant (11/80)	Santanoni (9/6/87)

The Membership Roster of the Adirondack Forty-Sixers

	Member	First Ascent	Forty-sixth Peak
2412	Gary H. Odell	Phelps (5/5/85)	Macomb (9/7/87)
2413	Jeff Wright	Gray (9/20/85)	Rocky Peak (9/12/87)
2414	Fritz Koennecke	Tabletop (1/6/79)	Cascade (9/13/87)
2415	James E. Byrne	Big Slide (4/14/79)	Wright (9/19/87)
2416	Louis P. Fortin	Big Slide (7/22/81)	Whiteface (9/19/87)
2417	Mary J. Nabywaniec	Cascade (3/84)	Whiteface (9/19/87)
2418	Terrence Tyler	Marcy (4/12/81)	Whiteface (9/19/87)
2419	James P. Hanrahan	Algonquin (1985)	Hough (9/19/87)
2420	Jerry D. Gallagher	Marcy (1957)	Big Slide (9/19/87)
2421	Robert S. Cassady	Marcy (10/83)	Iroquois (9/20/87)
2422	Denis Roy	Marcy (1980)	Cliff (9/20/87)
2423	Sally W. Roy	Phelps (1983)	Cliff (9/20/87)
2424	Bill Van Rosendael	Gothics (7/83)	Redfield (9/20/87)
2425	Peter B. Cohen	Marcy (1964)	Gray (9/25/87)
2426	Ellen Daniels	Algonquin (9/3/79)	Rocky Peak (9/26/87)
2427	Jane G. Daniels	Upper Wolf Jaw (7/69)	Rocky Peak (9/26/87)
2428	Karen E. Daniels	Cascade (10/5/75)	Rocky Peak (9/26/87)
2429	Walter E. Daniels	Wright (10/68)	Rocky Peak (9/26/87)
2430W	Paul J. Brach	Phelps (8/25/84)	Basin (9/26/87)
2431	Stephen Speno	Algonquin (6/81)	Allen (9/27/87)
2432	Sally S. Spear	Giant (9/76)	Marcy (9/27/87)
2433	Michelle Y. Chauvin	Algonquin (8/23/80)	Esther (9/28/87)
2434	J. Honeywell	Cascade (8/23/77)	Blake (10/3/87)
2435	Marie A. Honeywell	Cascade (8/23/77)	Blake (10/3/87)
2436	Alan J. Rebernik	Gothics (1/1/87)	Whiteface (10/5/87)
2437	Frederick E. Powers	Whiteface (8/27/63)	Rocky Peak (10/9/87)
2438	Paul J. Hoyt	Marcy (8/78)	Esther (10/10/87)
2439	Pat Beaudet	Phelps (8/80)	Skylight (10/12/87)
2440	Jon Bassett	Emmons (8/28/80)	Haystack (10/12/87)
2441	Ted Snyder	Big Slide (11/79)	Basin (10/17/87)
2442	Robert J. Ceglerski	Marcy (8/20/81)	Lower Wolf Jaw (10/17/87)
2443	Brent A. William	Cascade (9/26/81)	Big Slide (10/17/87)
2444	Richard J. Moran	Marcy (9/17/83)	Dix (10/18/87)
2445	Gerald Carozza	Giant (9/8/79)	Haystack (10/18/87)
2446	Todd Carozza	Giant (9/8/79)	Haystack (10/18/87)
2447	Jeff Farbaniec	Wright (7/83)	Redfield (10/18/87)
2448	Edward R. Wunder	Algonquin (9/3/83)	Haystack (10/20/87)
2449	John W. Halpin	Wright (7/16/75)	Haystack (10/24/87)
2450	Bonnie B. Kelly	Algonquin (9/1/85)	Haystack (10/24/87)
2451	Carolyn R. Pfaffenbach	Cascade (9/26/82)	Haystack (10/24/87)
2452	Peter I. Pfaffenbach	Cascade (9/26/82)	Haystack (10/24/87)
2453	Jon C. Wetzel	Lower Wolf Jaw (9/19/82)	Gothics (11/1/87)
2454W	Matthew J. Cull	Marcy (7/27/83)	Allen (11/3/87)
2455	Maureen T. Dooley	Marcy (8/8/82)	Skylight (11/14/87)
2456	George P. Gottwald	Marcy (6/30/82)	Esther (11/22/87)
2457	Kenneth A. Kleinberg	Macomb (10/28/74)	Seymour (12/20/84)
2458	Cal Southwick	Marcy (8/78)	Tabletop (10/11/86)
2459	Jody Southwick	Marcy (8/78)	Tabletop (10/11/86)
2460	Thomas W. Hall	Marcy (7/65)	Iroquois (5/16/87)
2461	Robert J. Fox	Wright (7/80)	Esther (7/21/87)
2462	Eugene S. Daniell	Big Slide (8/29/81)	Marshall (8/24/87)
2463	Karen G. Daniell	Whiteface (5/26/84)	Marshall (8/24/87)
2464	Thomas D. Kiereck	Lower Wolf Jaw (7/17/76)	Whiteface (9/5/87)
2465	Gary T. Hilt	Marcy (9/14/85)	Colden (9/12/87)
2466	Wardwell Leonard	Upper Wolf Jaw (8/72)	Esther (9/25/87)
2467	George W. Wescott	Marcy (1967)	Haystack (3/2/88)
2468W	Don W. Rain	Macomb (7/3/77)	Marcy (3/5/88)
2469	Sharon Alger	Cascade (1969)	Big Slide (4/9/88)
2470	Gary A. Williams	Cascade (10/81)	Blake (5/14/88)
2471	David G. Ragnone	Marcy (6/28/78)	Sawteeth (5/15/88)
2472	Wayne R. Storms	Marcy (6/28/78)	Sawteeth (5/15/88)
2473	David Bach	Colden (10/12/85)	Dix (5/22/88)

Heaven Up-h'isted-ness!

	Member	First Ascent	Forty-sixth Peak
2474	James M. Coughlin	Marcy (1946)	Dix (5/22/88)
2475	Philip A. Smethurst	Marcy (11/11/80)	Emmons (5/28/88)
2476	Terrence Quinn	Marcy (6/77)	Tabletop (5/28/88)
2477	Mary Hallenbeck	Dial (11/72)	Skylight (5/29/88)
2478	George Hallenbeck	Marcy (9/10/70)	Skylight (5/29/88)
2479	Peggy-Jean Prest	Phelps (5/29/82)	Marcy (5/29/88)
2480	Catherine P. Prest	Phelps (5/29/82)	Marcy (5/29/88)
2481	Theresa Klauck	Giant (7/14/84)	Couchsachraga (6/4/88)
2482W	Steven Empie	Cascade (10/8/83)	Iroquois (6/4/88)
2483W	Brian E. Bongiovanni	Marcy (1981)	Wright (6/6/88)
2484	Arthur H. Robertson	Cascade (1971)	Gray (6/11/88)
2485	Joan Roschinsky	Cascade (6/28/84)	Allen (6/11/88)
2486	Joseph A. Roschinsky	Cascade (6/28/84)	Allen (6/11/88)
2487	Joseph T. Chilinski	Big Slide (3/7/70)	Giant (6/25/88)
2488	Charles M. Liddle, Jr.	Cascade (1978)	Phelps (7/2/88)
2489	Kenneth D. Lurvey	Wright (6/21/87)	Emmons (7/2/88)
2490	Steven R. Garstad	Saddleback (7/21/79)	Haystack (7/3/88)
2491	Lawrence G. Newman	Algonquin (8/31/81)	Santanoni (7/3/88)
2492	Steven Shraeder	Marcy (7/24/69)	Allen (7/12/88)
2493	Michael A. Kerker	Santanoni (8/7/77)	Panther (7/12/88)
2494	Abe T. Allen	Basin (6/22/67)	Allen (7/15/88)
2495	Linda M. Edwards	Lower Wolf Jaw (10/8/83)	Panther (7/15/88)
2496	John J. Longacker	Phelps (7/24/73)	Couchsachraga (7/16/88)
2497	John A. Grant	Marcy (8/30/87)	Basin (7/23/88)
2498	Larry Springsteen	Marcy (5/73)	Colden (7/29/88)
2499	David C. Roy	Cascade (7/77)	Lower Wolf Jaw (7/29/88)
2500	Jeff Thompson	Wright (6/21/87)	Whiteface (8/3/88)
2501	Richard E. Thompson	Wright (6/21/87)	Whiteface (8/3/88)
2502	William V. McKee	Sawteeth (7/27/80)	Emmons (8/4/88)
2503	Nicholas Brown	Cascade (7/84)	Street (8/5/88)
2504	Stella Green	Phelps (1/21/84)	Basin (8/6/88)
2505	Jefferson Wilson	Iroquois (1982)	Nippletop (8/7/88)
2506	William H. Hearne	Colden (10/11/75)	Big Slide (8/7/88)
2507	John P. Hume	Cascade (8/74)	Seymour (8/13/88)
2508	Clarence F. Hammond	Marcy (8/15/87)	Couchsachraga (8/13/88)
2509	Connor O'Rourke	Cascade (8/18/78)	Dix (8/14/88)
2510	James R. Fazio	Santanoni (7/3/76)	Colvin (8/16/88)
2511	John R. Marshall	Marcy (8/31/61)	Marshall (8/19/88)
2512	Kimberly L. Marshall	Cascade (4/17/82)	Marshall (8/19/88)
2513	Matthew J. Marshall	Cascade (4/17/82)	Marshall (8/19/88)
2514	Michael Marshall	Cascade (4/17/82)	Marshall (8/19/88)
2515	Sharon L. Marshall	Cascade (4/17/82)	Marshall (8/19/88)
2516	Arthur L. Johnson	Marcy (6/70)	Blake (8/19/88)
2517	Metod M. Milac	Marcy (7/64)	Sawteeth (8/20/88)
2518	David Naylor	Marcy (6/68)	Sawteeth (8/20/88)
2519	William C. Kimball	Lower Wolf Jaw (8/16/86)	Haystack (8/20/88)
2520	John Farrell	Marcy (6/83)	Haystack (8/20/88)
2521	John White	Cascade (8/20/81)	Whiteface (8/20/88)
2522	Thomas E. White	Cascade (8/20/81)	Whiteface (8/20/88)
2523	Ross D. Melvin	Cascade (10/30/71)	East Dix (8/22/88)
2524	Melissa Streuli	Cascade (8/26/82)	Big Slide (8/31/88)
2525	Alison M. Volpe	Cascade (7/82)	Colvin (8/1/88)
2526	David F. Dayger	Giant (7/18/83)	Sawteeth (9/3/88)
2527	Lynn L. Kingsley	Marshall (6/11/77)	Cliff (9/3/86)
2528	Brian Kavanaugh	Giant (6/1/70)	Allen (9/4/88)
2529	Anne P. Dennis	Haystack (1926)	Allen (9/4/88)
2530	Kathie A. Friedman	Marcy (8/82)	Whiteface (9/4/88)
2531	Herbert J. Coles	Marcy (5/31/68)	Cliff (9/4/88)
2532	Stephen P. Schwartz	Algonquin (6/84)	Marshall (9/5/88)
2533	Richard H. Bennett	Marcy (8/71)	Hough (9/6/88)
2534	June Fait	Cascade (8/23/76)	Allen (9/6/88)
2535	Jeffrey A. Rolling	Giant (4/25/87)	Redfield (9/8/88)

The Membership Roster of the Adirondack Forty-Sixers

	Member	First Ascent	Forty-sixth Peak
2536	Norine Rolling	Giant (4/25/87)	Redfield (9/8/88)
2537	Phillip McDougall	Tabletop (10/25/80)	Marshall (9/10/88)
2538	Alice H. Broberg	Marcy (11/11/76)	Panther (9/10/88)
2539	Fred S. Turnbull	Algonquin (8/15/75)	Redfield (9/11/88)
2540	Henry L. Welch	Big Slide (2/8/86)	Cliff (9/11/88)
2541W	Leonard H. Grubbs	Marcy (4/19/88)	Haystack (9/17/88)
2542W	Wende Grubbs	Big Slide (2/17/87)	Haystack (9/17/88)
2543W	Eileen W. Wheeler	Cascade (9/25/85)	Colden (9/17/88)
2544	Martin Graetz	Dix (8/28/60)	Basin (9/22/88)
2545	Richard V. Johnson	Lower Wolf Jaw (8/5/83)	Whiteface (9/23/88)
2546	Charlotte Adams	Big Slide (9/83)	Iroquois (9/24/88)
2547	Steven Adams	Big Slide (9/83)	Iroquois (9/24/88)
2548	Jim Gratto	Giant (7/74)	Haystack (9/25/88)
2549	Emil A. Klymkow	Marcy (9/1/85)	Colden (9/25/88)
2550	Connie Stone	Cascade (5/16/85)	Skylight (9/25/88)
2551	Vernon Potter	Marcy (6/27/87)	Hough (9/26/88)
2552	Ron Mason	Giant (4/18/81)	Marshall (9/28/88)
2553	Wayne B. Virkler	Marcy (5/30/65)	Iroquois (9/29/88)
2554	Nancy S. Virkler	Cascade (9/25/71)	Iroquois (9/29/88)
2555	Sheila Stahley	Gothics (7/79)	Phelps (10/1/88)
2556	Paul E. Newton	Phelps (6/10/72)	Street (10/1/88)
2557	Scott McIntyre	Marcy (1972)	Big Slide (10/1/88)
2558	Erik Zimmerman	Cascade (7/78)	Big Slide (10/1/88)
2559	Suzanne Fortin	Basin (8/28/82)	Dix (10/2/88)
2560	Charles Huhtanen	Giant (5/8/81)	Allen (10/9/88)
2561	David Mack	Giant (1980)	Allen (10/9/88)
2562	Richard H. Harvey	Big Slide (8/6/45)	Allen (10/9/88)
2563W	Jacqueline Parker	Giant (5/27/88)	Haystack (10/9/88)
2564W	Neil Parker	Nippletop (1/2/88)	Haystack (10/9/88)
2565	Bainbridge S. Davis	Big Slide (7/20/75)	Skylight (10/9/88)
2566	Bradley M. Waters	Cascade (5/30/70)	Blake (10/9/88)
2567	Robert W. Gross	Marcy (8/24/71)	Allen (10/15/88)
2568	Rosemary DiRenzo	Phelps (5/15/80)	Sawteeth (10/15/88)
2569	David DiRenzo	Phelps (5/15/80)	Sawteeth (10/15/88)
2570	William H. Downing	Porter (5/23/87)	Hough (10/15/88)
2571	Heather S. Downing	Porter (5/23/87)	Hough (10/15/88)
2572	Brian E. Sander	Giant (7/2/82)	Whiteface (10/15/88)
2573	G. Trent LaCroix	Algonquin (5/86)	Emmons (10/16/88)
2574	Charles Brumley	Rocky Peak (9/9/84)	Esther (10/16/88)
2575	James L. DeGolyer	Marcy (10/68)	Saddleback (10/16/88)
2576	Peter H. Rogers	Big Slide (8/21/65)	Marshall (8/16/78)
2577	John C. Norton	Marcy (7/72)	Santanoni (7/4/88)
2578	Lincoln H. Billings	Colden (9/4/78)	Marshall (7/8/88)
2579	Ian T. Brock	Algonquin (7/79)	Nippletop (8/28/88)
2580	George V. Grenier, Sr.	Marcy (9/72)	Gray (9/21/88)
2581	Helen M. Grenier	Marcy (9/72)	Gray (9/21/88)
2582	Rebecca Bates	Algonquin (6/78)	Esther (9/25/88)
2583W	Deane H. Morrison	Santanoni (12/31/79)	Basin (2/25/89)
2584	Jeffrey P. Drost	Porter (5/28/83)	Whiteface (2/26/89)
2585W	Caroline S. Lovelace	Wright (2/28/87)	Hough (3/19/89)
2586	Stuart McCarty II	Santanoni (10/74)	Big Slide (5/13/89)
2587	Debra W. Gilmore	Giant (4/85)	Rocky Peak (5/20/89)
2588	Daniel W. Gilmore	Marcy (8/70)	Rocky Peak (5/20/89)
2589	Laurence T. Cagle	Marcy (8/76)	Emmons (5/28/89)
2590	Anne M. James	Giant (10/13/85)	Lower Wolf Jaw (5/30/89)
2591	Sondra A. Tornga	Marcy (8/1/86)	Panther (6/2/89)
2592	Inge H. Pangburn	Marcy (9/71)	Santanoni (6/3/89)
2593	Charles E. Pangburn	Marcy (9/71)	Santanoni (6/3/89)
2594W	Craig Billie	Marcy (7/22/83)	Haystack (6/5/89)
2595	Brien R. Sheedy	Marcy (8/9/83)	Tabletop (6/8/89)
2596	Lorena K. Parks	Giant (9/21/86)	Big Slide (6/11/89)
2597	Eberhard Burkowski	Marcy (5/60)	Seymour (6/12/89)

Heaven Up-h'isted-ness!

	Member	First Ascent	Forty-sixth Peak
2598	Robert Witherbee	Lower Wolf Jaw (5/28/80)	Marshall (6/17/89)
2599	Ruth E. Schurman	Marcy (5/63)	Couchsachraga (6/29/89)
2600	Carolyn A. Bach	Algonquin (10/25/86)	Basin (7/1/89)
2601	Sophie R. DeLong	Porter (9/10/78)	Iroquois (7/3/89)
2602	Galen Pavone	Tabletop (10/16/82)	Cliff (7/11/89)
2603	Philip S. Keane	Wright (7/56)	Emmons (7/12/89)
2604	Robert S. McLean	Cascade (7/24/75)	Haystack (7/12/89)
2605	Jerome F. Milks	Sawteeth (6/27/89)	Allen (7/13/89)
2606	Peter Henner	Marcy (7/75)	Rocky Peak (7/15/89)
2607	Kenneth Chartier	Marshall (7/11/87)	Marcy (7/22/89)
2608	Andrea Chartier	Marshall (7/11/87)	Marcy (7/22/89)
2609	Joel Ponerantz	Marcy (8/82)	Marshall (7/22/89)
2610	George W. Dolch	Marcy (7/55)	Esther (7/25/89)
2611	Jane Baldwin	Marcy (7/24/77)	Cliff (7/29/89)
2612	Warren C. Baldwin	Marcy (7/24/77)	Cliff (7/29/89)
2613	Mara J. Miller	Cascade (10/2/82)	Esther (7/31/89)
2614	Richard A. Meade	Marcy (1983)	Seymour (7/31/89)
2615	Gerhard W. Weber	Cascade (8/22/81)	Marcy (8/4/89)
2616	C. William Meyer, Jr.	Marcy (1980)	Lower Wolf Jaw (8/6/89)
2617	F. Peter Tolcser	Giant (2/24/73)	Haystack (8/6/89)
2618W	John H. Swanson	Dial (5/20/89)	Big Slide (8/6/89)
2619	Joseph Halm	Dix (8/80)	Whiteface (8/10/89)
2620	Ted Shuster	Algonquin (8/84)	Whiteface (8/10/89)
2621	William J. Andrews	Phelps (10/13/84)	Whiteface (8/11/89)
2622	Steven Cottet	Phelps (10/13/84)	Whiteface (8/11/89)
2623	John S. Kinne	Phelps (10/13/84)	Whiteface (8/11/89)
2624	Peter W. Wood	Tabletop (6/11/81)	Whiteface (8/11/89)
2625	Steven A. Gapp	Phelps (1987)	Hough (8/11/89)
2626	Sabele F. Gray	Blake (8/8/67)	Big Slide (8/12/89)
2627	Francesca Husselbeck	Armstrong (6/71)	Seymour (8/12/89)
2628	A. William Clock	Giant (9/65)	Seymour (8/12/89)
2629	Robert D. Nash	Marcy (1950)	Allen (8/15/89)
2630	Malcolm P. Nash	Colden (7/15/50)	Panther (8/15/89)
2631	Elizabeth Cropper	Colden (1969)	Allen (8/16/89)
2632	William H. Cropper	Colden (1969)	Allen (8/16/89)
2633	Debbie Marcy	Colvin (10/86)	Dix (8/17/89)
2634	Pat M. Wilson	Cascade (1969)	Dix (8/17/89)
2635	Rebecca Breslow	Giant (7/86)	Tabletop (8/18/89)
2636	Jennifer L. Livingston	Cascade (7/5/82)	Tabletop (8/18/89)
2637	Elizabeth Sitnick	Wright (7/85)	Tabletop (8/18/89)
2638	David M. Kassel	Big Slide (8/3/66)	Panther (8/18/89)
2639	Brendan Buschman-Kelly	Colvin (8/85)	Rocky Peak (8/19/89)
2640	Mary F. Buschman-Kelly	Marcy (8/73)	Rocky Peak (8/19/89)
2641	Mary L. Buschman-Kelly	Sawteeth (8/84)	Rocky Peak (8/19/89)
2642	Eric M. Anderson	Porter (7/87)	Sawteeth (8/20/89)
2643	Gay A. Mayer	Wright (8/28/83)	Dix (8/22/89)
2644	Mary W. Mayer	Giant (8/17/71)	Dix (8/22/89)
2645	Terence Berinato	Gothics (4/3/64)	Phelps (8/24/89)
2646	Beth Buschman-Kelly	Big Slide (8/82)	Haystack (8/24/89)
2647	Jane D. Rosenbloom	Cascade (1952)	Rocky Peak (8/24/89)
2648W	Peter Bushnell	Marcy (8/10/82)	Santanoni (8/25/89)
2649	Jeaneen Dumers	Wright (10/83)	Iroquois (8/25/89)
2650	Joanne M. Tulip	Colden (9/82)	Iroquois (8/25/89)
2651W	George Sloan	Marcy (8/69)	Skylight (8/25/89)
2652	Michael J. Baczkowski	Marshall (10/2/82)	Allen (8/26/89)
2653	Ronald G. Book	Algonquin (5/19/79)	Allen (8/26/89)
2654	Lynn W. Farnham	Marcy (1965)	Couchsachraga (8/26/89)
2655	William J. Lyons	Basin (5/77)	Allen (8/26/89)
2656	Mildred F. Adriance	Marcy (7/4/63)	Whiteface (8/26/89)
2657	Laurance C. Martin	Gothics (8/25/67)	Dix (8/26/89)
2658	Louis H. Wunderlich	Marcy (8/62)	Gray (8/27/89)
2659W	Ellsworth King	Giant (10/3/83)	Tabletop (8/27/89)

The Membership Roster of the Adirondack Forty-Sixers

	Member	First Ascent	Forty-sixth Peak
2660W	Judith King	Giant (10/3/83)	Tabletop (8/27/89)
2661	Julie Turner	Marcy (7/73)	Haystack (8/27/89)
2662	Eileen Urtz	Marcy (8/5/80)	Tabletop (8/29/89)
2663	Donald S. Powell	Esther (9/17/80)	Blake (8/30/89)
2664	Jeffrey A. Gronauer	Cascade (6/19/88)	Allen (8/31/89)
2665	Calvin J. Crouch, Jr.	Algonquin (6/15/86)	Emmons (9/2/89)
2666	Jeffrey A. Sederquist	Marcy (8/12/76)	Hough (9/3/89)
2667	Aims Coney	Colden (1965)	Haystack (9/3/89)
2668	Michael Matthews	Wright (8/13/83)	Colden (9/4/89)
2669	Frances S. Baker	Cascade (8/81)	Allen (9/5/89)
2670	Claire S. Stratford	Big Slide (1970)	Allen (9/5/89)
2671	Richard A. Best	Dix (10/16/88)	Haystack (9/7/89)
2672	Wendy Best	Dix (10/16/88)	Haystack (9/7/89)
2673	Ben F. Lostracco	Cascade (9/26/82)	Whiteface (9/16/89)
2674	Sally A. Hardenburg	Phelps (5/24/87)	Wright (9/16/89)
2675	William W. Durkee	Street (9/20/79)	Upper Wolf Jaw (9/16/89)
2676	Barry F. Greene	Cascade (5/29/71)	Whiteface (9/16/89)
2677	William H. Peck	Algonquin (6/5/76)	Whiteface (9/16/89)
2678W	John T. Omohundro	Algonquin (8/74)	Whiteface (9/16/89)
2679W	Susan S. Omohundro	Algonquin (8/74)	Whiteface (9/16/89)
2680	Pierrette Hutt	Allen (8/29/87)	Seymour (9/17/89)
2681	Christopher DeGiovine	Phelps (10/19/83)	Rocky Peak (9/22/89)
2682	Richard R. Maggi	Marcy (9/21/82)	Cascade (9/24/89)
2683	Johanna W. Stenger	Gothics (9/20/80)	Dix (9/24/89)
2684	Lois Wells	Marcy (10/49)	Marshall (9/25/89)
2685	Nathaniel Wells	Marcy (1974)	Marshall (9/25/89)
2686	Marilyn Corson	Cascade (5/77)	Skylight (9/25/89)
2687	Matthew Kennedy	Big Slide (7/74)	Sawteeth (9/29/89)
2688	Richard A. Stevens	Cascade (7/12/86)	Basin (9/30/89)
2689	David Cote	Giant (4/27/84)	Whiteface (9/30/89)
2690	Leo F. Cote	Giant (4/27/84)	Whiteface (9/30/89)
2691	Janice M. Slyer	Giant (7/28/85)	Rocky Peak (9/30/89)
2692	Lyn Howard	Big Slide (5/31/86)	Dix (9/30/89)
2693	Bernard J. Yelle	Giant (7/4/84)	Iroquois (9/30/89)
2694	Daniel A. Ladue	Whiteface (6/15/71)	Seymour (10/1/89)
2695	Henry Edmonds	South Dix (7/19/86)	Haystack (10/3/89)
2696	John Wienclawski	Wright (9/30/81)	Allen (10/7/89)
2697	Robert L. McGee	Cascade (9/86)	Phelps (10/7/89)
2698	Matthew J. Pontiff	Lower Wolf Jaw (7/77)	Blake (10/7/89)
2699	Paul E. Pontiff	Lower Wolf Jaw (7/77)	Blake (10/7/89)
2700	Joyce A. McLean	Gothics (8/76)	Santanoni (10/7/89)
2701	William R. Schultz	Marcy (6/5/76)	Seymour (10/8/89)
2702	William H. Goss	Giant (8/2/86)	Tabletop (10/14/89)
2703	David Toole	Marcy (9/2/84)	Hough (10/14/89)
2704	Daniel F. Martin, Jr.	Panther (9/78)	Lower Wolf Jaw (10/15/89)
2705	Patricia Kongshavn	Marcy (7/58)	Marshall (10/21/89)
2706	Alan S. Sheren	Cascade (7/8/84)	Haystack (10/25/89)
2707	Molly S. Sheren	Cascade (7/8/84)	Haystack (10/25/89)
2708	Burton L. Marker	Marcy (10/8/83)	Skylight (10/28/88)
2709	Richard W. Moore	Cascade (1958)	Allen (10/29/89)
2710	Douglas Morse	Cascade (10/1/83)	Giant (10/29/89)
2711W	George M. Bush	Marcy (1958)	Big Slide (11/4/89)
2712	Emmi Wilson	Lower Wolf Jaw (1967)	Marshall (11/7/89)
2713	Diana T. Butterworth	Giant (1971)	Colden (9/2/78)
2714	J. Warner Butterworth	Marcy (8/53)	Colden (9/2/78)
2715	Edward G. Von Seggern	Marcy (12/59)	Iroquois (9/27/86)
2716	Robert A. Hintermister	Upper Wolf Jaw (8/12/35)	Gray (7/16/88)
2717	Carol Horzempa	Algonquin (8/78)	Gothics (8/27/88)
2718	David Lehman	Colvin (7/85)	Nye (8/13/89)
2719	Andrew C. Miller	Phelps (8/4/86)	Iroquois (8/16/89)
2720	Harriet K. Hovanec	Cascade (8/76)	Marshall (8/19/89)
2721	Donald E. Aubercht	Saddleback (5/77)	Allen (8/26/89)

Heaven Up-h'isted-ness!

	Member	First Ascent	Forty-sixth Peak
2722	Evelyn E. Marshall	Giant (10/83)	Marshall (10/21/89)
2723	George Marshall	Marcy (1956)	Marshall (10/21/89)
2724	Keith Martin	Marcy (1968)	Porter (2/4/90)
2725W	Robert Anderson	Wright (1/1/83)	Whiteface (3/10/90)
2726W	Arthur Martineau	Colvin (3/16/85)	Whiteface (3/10/90)
2727W	James T. Beck	Marcy (8/79)	Emmons (3/19/90)
2728W	Robert S. Spreter	Phelps (2/80)	Emmons (3/19/90)
2729	Jim Poulette	Marcy (8/11/64)	Esther (4/15/90)
2730	Derek Williams	Cascade (9/26/81)	Blake (5/19/90)
2731	Dana B. Westcott, Jr.	Giant (5/19/85)	Hough (5/19/90)
2732W	Thomas D. Pinkerton	Whiteface (1957)	Seymour (5/27/90)
2733	Timothy H. Edgar	Big Slide (4/7/81)	Emmons (5/27/90)
2734W	Seymour Ellis	Marcy (6/30/87)	Emmons (5/28/90)
2735	Dorothy Sehlmeyer	Algonquin (8/11/86)	Emmons (5/28/90)
2736	Christel B. Crane	Cascade (7/1/85)	Haystack (6/26/90)
2737	Jim Crane	Cascade (9/14/85)	Haystack (6/26/90)
2738	Nancy G. Slack	Algonquin (6/53)	Allen (6/26/90)
2739	Don Marshall	Big Slide (5/78)	Marshall (6/26/90)
2740	Ron Shaffer	Marcy (9/25/83)	Marshall (6/27/90)
2741	Caroline H. Ford	Cascade (1980)	Esther (7/2/90)
2742	Henry Halama	Marcy (1963)	Esther (7/2/90)
2743	David W. White	Phelps (9/23/72)	Santanoni (7/2/90)
2744	Tracy S. Malloy	Marcy (1975)	Allen (7/3/90)
2745	Brad E. Young	Lower Wolf Jaw (6/84)	Dial (7/4/90)
2746	Mary D. Young	Lower Wolf Jaw (6/84)	Dial (7/4/90)
2747	Homer Mitchell	Marcy (7/61)	Dix (7/6/90)
2748	Allan W. Prowten	Marcy (9/2/82)	Big Slide (7/7/90)
2749	Robert J. Osborne	Marcy (9/80)	Nye (7/7/90)
2750	Thomas E. Mallette	Marcy (7/76)	Panther (7/9/90)
2751	Mary Mallette	Marcy (7/76)	Panther (7/9/90)
2752	Devon A. Taylor	Seymour (8/12/85)	Emmons (7/12/90)
2753	Nancy E. Taylor	Seymour (8/12/85)	Emmons (7/12/90)
2754	David G. Welch	Wright (4/54)	Haystack (7/14/90)
2755	Michael J. O'Connor	Upper Wolf Jaw (5/81)	Gray (7/15/90)
2756	Karen M. Grattidge	Giant (5/77)	Marshall (7/15/90)
2757	Joan F. Mullen	Cascade (1965)	Sawteeth (7/16/90)
2758	Richard Levine	Giant (5/77)	Emmons (7/17/90)
2759W	Craig A. LeRoy	Giant (11/76)	Emmons (7/21/90)
2760	Michelle D. Marker	Phelps (9/26/87)	Giant (7/21/90)
2761	Warren H. Axtell	Algonquin (11/1/69)	Basin (7/25/90)
2762	Rudolf Kraus	Phelps (10/19/83)	Emmons (7/27/90)
2763	Jennifer N. Matthews	Colvin (5/22/87)	Marcy (7/27/90)
2764	Joe Pane	Phelps (10/6/83)	Skylight (7/28/90)
2765	Karen R. Pane	Cascade (10/6/85)	Skylight (7/28/90)
2766	Joan Scott	Cascade (5/14/88)	Seymour (7/29/90)
2767	David G. Christoffersen	Marcy (1974)	Allen (7/29/90)
2768	Norbert J. Woods	Marcy (1980)	Skylight (8/3/90)
2769	Susan S. Woods	Algonquin (7/85)	Skylight (8/3/90)
2770	Robert S. Stuart	Porter (5/16/86)	Santanoni (8/3/90)
2771	John H. Devine	Algonquin (7/21/74)	Couchsachraga (8/4/90)
2772	Lanny S. Wexler	Marcy (7/2/84)	Skylight (8/5/90)
2773	William Eldridge	Marcy (7/12/86)	Haystack (8/5/90)
2774	Steven A. Halasz	Colvin (1982)	Seymour (8/8/90)
2775	Estelle M. Hahn	Skylight (7/31/82)	Phelps (8/11/90)
2776	Roger C. Hahn	Porter (8/12/85)	Phelps (8/11/90)
2777	James E. Carr	Dial (6/77)	Esther (8/12/90)
2778	Kenneth M. Kaufman	Phelps (9/3/79)	Nippletop (8/12/90)
2779	Raymond Hare	Marcy (7/85)	Street (8/14/90)
2780	Annette B. Johnson	Sawteeth (8/22/83)	Seymour (8/14/90)
2781	Mark Sabath	Cascade (7/16/87)	Nippletop (8/18/90)
2782	Bradley R. Strowger	Cascade (6/20/81)	Rocky Peak (8/18/90)
2783	Richard Vertigan	Big Slide (10/22/73)	Street (8/19/90)

The Membership Roster of the Adirondack Forty-Sixers

	Member	First Ascent	Forty-sixth Peak
2784W	Carl W. Klinowski	Porter (5/22/88)	Redfield (8/19/90)
2785	Joseph J. Platzer	Wright (5/14/82)	Panther (8/19/90)
2786	Daryl Harmon	Dial (9/14/74)	Sawteeth (8/20/90)
2787	Janet Huwiler	Cascade (1981)	Colden (8/21/90)
2788	Betsy Stewart	Porter (7/8/86)	Colden (8/21/90)
2789	Elizabeth Greene	Giant (8/57)	Allen (8/21/90)
2790	Jim Adams	Marcy (8/5/79)	Santanoni (8/22/90)
2791	Christopher S. Hughes	Algonquin (6/85)	Emmons (8/23/90)
2792	David K. Hofer	Big Slide (6/19/81)	Whiteface (8/25/90)
2793W	Linda LaMarche	Porter (11/26/88)	Whiteface (8/26/90)
2794	Jeremy T. Loveday	Dial (5/25/85)	Whiteface (8/26/90)
2795	Thomas E. Loveday	Dial (5/25/85)	Whiteface (8/26/90)
2796	Stephen H. Brill	Upper Wolf Jaw (5/16/87)	Blake (8/28/90)
2797	Jane Misurelli	Algonquin (1982)	Allen (8/30/90)
2798	Albert Kuhn	Marcy (9/79)	Allen (8/30/90)
2799	Edward L. Walsh	Marcy (8/7/85)	Colden (8/31/90)
2800	Edward J. Walsh	Marcy (8/7/85)	Colden (8/31/90)
2801	Eric Freedman	Giant (4/86)	Allen (8/31/90)
2802	Ann S. Palen	Giant (9/3/86)	Skylight (8/31/90)
2803	Alfred Polvere	Colden (7/17/82)	Giant (9/1/90)
2804	Natalie Polvere	Colden (7/17/82)	Giant (9/1/90)
2805	Christopher Lautenberger	Colden (9/2/84)	Nye (9/1/90)
2806	Andrew Lautenberger	Cascade (8/13/85)	Nye (9/1/90)
2807	William Lautenberger	Marcy (10/5/63)	Nye (9/1/90)
2808	Harry Sokol	Haystack (8/19/64)	Emmons (9/2/90)
2809	Yetta Sokol	Saddleback (9/21/68)	Emmons (9/2/90)
2810	Brian L. Bailey	Marcy (5/28/88)	Couchsachraga (9/3/90)
2811	Michael A. Stroud	Marcy (5/28/88)	Couchsachraga (9/3/90)
2812	Thomas Brennan	Marcy (7/79)	Seymour (9/9/90)
2813	Robert B. Cave II	Seymour (5/27/83)	Phelps (9/14/90)
2814	Dennis McIlroy	Colden (10/9/83)	Redfield (9/15/90)
2815	Doreen Smethurst	Dial (9/26)	Saddleback (9/15/90)
2816	Margaret K. Malone	Cascade (1971)	Panther (9/15/90)
2817	Darwin Tubbs	Marcy (1960)	Colden (9/16/90)
2818	Thomas Tubbs	Marcy (10/2/62)	Colden (9/16/90)
2819	Rita D. Reed	Algonquin (1980)	Dix (9/16/90)
2820	Robert A. Reed	Colden (8/72)	Dix (9/16/90)
2821	Irvin C. Simser	Phelps (5/27/86)	Whiteface (9/17/90)
2822	Donald C. McClean	Wright (9/1/87)	Couchsachraga (9/19/90)
2823	John D. Ryan	Rocky Peak (7/22/87)	Couchsachraga (9/19/90)
2824W	Barbara Harris	Porter (11/26/88)	Haystack (9/21/90)
2825	Charles A. Nowell	Algonquin (7/30/88)	Whiteface (9/22/90)
2826	Leslie McGregor	Lower Wolf Jaw (10/76)	Wright (9/23/90)
2827	J. Gerard Dollar	Algonquin (8/74)	Big Slide (9/23/90)
2828	Burton L. Hotaling	Cascade (10/5/82)	Skylight (9/25/90)
2829	Steven J. Leonard	Sawteeth (2/26/86)	Seymour (9/29/90)
2830	Edmond Brown	Cascade (9/72)	Seymour (9/29/90)
2831	Christopher W. Mack	Phelps (5/4/85)	Whiteface (9/29/90)
2832	Dale W. Mack	Big Slide (4/12/85)	Whiteface (9/29/90)
2833	Craig W. Tuckett	Cascade (7/15/84)	Whiteface (9/29/90)
2834	Alexis Levitin	Cascade (9/22/84)	Emmons (9/29/90)
2835	Ken Morgan	Wright (7/2/81)	Whiteface (9/29/90)
2836	Char Ratner	Haystack (8/88)	Hough (9/29/90)
2837	Judy Shea	Santanoni (8/23/85)	Porter (10/3/90)
2838	Lorraine Fobare	Cascade (8/23/89)	Porter (10/3/90)
2839	Catherine M. Liberty	Cascade (9/19/87)	Porter (10/3/90)
2840	Guy L. Merrill	Giant (9/80)	Haystack (10/6/90)
2841	Edward M. Damm	Marcy (8/89)	Rocky Peak (10/6/90)
2842	Mark Hudson	Giant (6/12/82)	Whiteface (10/6/90)
2843	Susan J. O'Hanlon	Algonquin (6/9/84)	Basin (10/6/90)
2844	Douglas Furman	Wright (7/4/84)	Iroquois (10/7/90)
2845	Erik H. Martin	Cascade (1981)	Iroquois (10/7/90)

HEAVEN UP-H'ISTED-NESS!

	MEMBER	FIRST ASCENT	FORTY-SIXTH PEAK
2846	Joseph M. Jillisky	Marcy (9/25/72)	Marshall (10/7/90)
2847	Michael Johnson	Marcy (8/6/87)	Whiteface (10/7/90)
2848	Jacques Grimard	Algonquin (10/4/86)	Tabletop (10/7/90)
2849	Jack Townsend	Phelps (1985)	Whiteface (10/7/90)
2850	Shari Shevy	Marcy (1972)	Cliff (10/14/90)
2851	Richard J. Bloomshield	Skylight (10/12/63)	Allen (10/14/90)
2852W	David J. Meeker	Lower Wolf Jaw (7/6/82)	Sawteeth (10/14/90)
2853	Jay Meeker	Lower Wolf Jaw (7/6/82)	Sawteeth (10/14/90)
2854	Robert B. Meeker	Lower Wolf Jaw (7/6/82)	Sawteeth (10/14/90)
2855	John Jurczynski	Whiteface (10/75)	Esther (10/27/90)
2856	James W. Seiler	Tabletop (3/14/87)	Allen (10/17/90)
2857W	Margaret MacKellar	Wright (9/19/87)	Whiteface (10/27/90)
2858	Robert E. Fortin	Marcy (4/12/81)	Tabletop (11/3/90)
2859	Jon C. Henderson	Marcy (8/18/89)	Big Slide (11/17/90)
2860	Stephen J. Schneider	Cascade (7/70)	Tabletop (8/86)
2861	Joseph A. Parrinello	Phelps (7/70)	Haystack (6/87)
2862	Dirk M. DiGiorgio-Haag	Algonquin (8/12/71)	Colden (12/29/87)
2863	Peter W. Atchinson	Marcy (9/59)	Saddleback (10/16/88)
2864W	Craig A. Batley	Colvin (2/15/82)	Santanoni (3/12/89)
2865	Sandy Schmidt	Marcy (7/12/73)	Seymour (9/3/89)
2866	Dean W. Whitcher	Whiteface (8/75)	Rocky Peak (5/5/90)
2867	Brendan Gibson	Cascade (summer 1980)	Porter (7/25/90)
2868	Brian Gibson	Cascade (7/83)	Wright (8/7/90)
2869	Paul R. Kehler	Dial (10/23/71)	Allen (8/27/90)
2870	James R. Spinella	Giant (7/4/80)	Allen (9/1/90)
2871	Robert E. Green	Phelps (1/21/84)	Colden (9/3/90)
2872	Walter F. Evans, III	Cascade (7/21/79)	Whiteface (9/9/90)
2873	Adrian Sadowski	Colden (7/24/89)	Whiteface (9/16/90)
2874	Stephen A. Sadowski	Colden (7/24/89)	Whiteface (9/16/90)
2875	Stephen E. Sadowski	Colden (7/24/89)	Whiteface (9/16/90)
2876	Donald E. Gebhart	East Dix (8/17/84)	Santanoni (9/29/90)
2877	Joseph J. Moscatello	Marcy (8/18/72)	Emmons (9/29/90)
2878	Daniel Goss	Giant (8/2/86)	Whiteface (10/6/90)
2879W	Carol S. White	Marcy (7/27/89)	Emmons (11/3/90)
2880W	David S. White	Marcy (7/27/89)	Emmons (11/3/90)
2881W	David Keep	Cascade (12/27/87)	Basin (1/26/91)
2882W	Dennis P. Crispo	Lower Wolf Jaw (2/24/89)	Whiteface (2/24/91)
2883W	Nicholas Ringelberg	Algonquin (9/87)	Gray (3/6/91)
2884W	James Palleschi II	Marcy (1/1/78)	Santanoni (3/10/91)
2885	Brian Peddie	Big Slide (10/19/85)	Sawteeth (5/4/91)
2886	Douglas Peddie	Big Slide (10/19/85)	Sawteeth (5/4/91)
2887	Philip Schillaci	Upper Wolf Jaw (10/84)	Whiteface (5/5/91)
2888	Raymond Sims	Wright (10/17/86)	Whiteface (5/5/91)
2889	Brian Mendis	Marcy (9/71)	Gray (5/13/91)
2890	Robin Mendis	Macomb (10/74)	Gray (5/13/91)
2891	Robert F. Harris, Jr.	Rocky Peak (8/4/84)	Emmons (5/14/91)
2892	Joshua Benin	Haystack (5/77)	Allen (5/16/91)
2893	David E. Cochrane	Marcy (9/71)	Nippletop (5/25/91)
2894	Keith G. Silliman	Giant (7/2/88)	Marshall (5/29/91)
2895	Frank G. McHale	Cascade (3/13/77)	Cliff (5/31/91)
2896	Daniel P. Kessler	Marcy (8/68)	Emmons (6/14/91)
2897	Marty Sosville	Marcy (8/62)	Cascade (6/15/91)
2898W	Robert Zayhowski	Marcy (5/86)	Santanoni (6/22/91)
2899	William C. Holmes	Upper Wolf Jaw (8/83)	Haystack (6/23/91)
2900	Jeffrey P. Smith	Colden (5/71)	Whiteface (6/23/91)
2901	Brian T. Sullivan	Lower Wolf Jaw (9/17/88)	Seymour (6/29/91)
2902	Ronald W. Naylor	Porter (11/26/88)	Haystack (6/29/91)
2903	Henry C. Jenkins	Big Slide (6/22/85)	Esther (6/29/91)
2904	Renate Koble	Esther (9/1/90)	Santanoni (6/29/91)
2905	Anthony Amaral, Jr.	Esther (9/1/90)	Santanoni (6/29/91)
2906	Bruce D. Ransom	Cascade (12/6/86)	Marshall (7/2/91)
2907W	Steven G. Spelter	Rocky Peak (6/16/90)	Marshall (7/2/91)

The Membership Roster of the Adirondack Forty-Sixers

	Member	First Ascent	Forty-sixth Peak
2908	Billie Whittaker	Whiteface (1952)	Sawteeth (7/3/91)
2909	Burton A. Sturner	Giant (8/17/80)	Haystack (7/6/91)
2910W	Marian A. Zimmerman	Phelps (10/11/86)	Giant (7/6/91)
2911	Marcia S. Hanson	Marcy (1965)	Iroquois (7/7/91)
2912	Stephen H. Kamnitzer	Marcy (5/84)	Allen (7/10/91)
2913	Thomas G. Dinse	Algonquin (5/23/69)	Saddleback (7/10/91)
2914	William B. DeMeritt	Cascade (7/13/88)	Tabletop (7/11/91)
2915	Frank R. Gardner, IV	Haystack (10/86)	Skylight (7/13/91)
2916	Raymond P. Saracino	Gothics (8/85)	Skylight (7/13/91)
2917	Walter M. Medwid	Marcy (7/73)	Wright (7/14/91)
2918	Robert Weisman	Phelps (7/88)	Rocky Peak (7/17/91)
2919	Barbara C. Reuter	Colden (5/13/89)	Skylight (7/20/91)
2920	Amy Seirup-Pottbecker	Algonquin (summer 1977)	Street (7/20/91)
2921	John Seirup	Phelps (5/25/73)	Street (7/20/91)
2922	Robert C. Consadine	Marcy (8/26/82)	Street (7/21/91)
2923	Katherine R. Hoy	Marcy (7/18/86)	Iroquois (7/27/91)
2924W	Sarah B. Hoy	Marcy (7/18/86)	Iroquois (7/27/91)
2925	Karen Huxtable-Hooker	Colden (3/8/85)	Emmons (7/27/91)
2926	David B. Rich	Colden (6/69)	Santanoni (7/27/91)
2927	Jonathan P. Rich	Colden (6/69)	Santanoni (7/27/91)
2928	Albert J. Fiorella	Haystack (6/23/85)	Dix (7/30/91)
2929	Neal A. Hudders	Algonquin (7/28/88)	Marcy (7/30/91)
2930	David E. Lybarger	Algonquin (7/28/88)	Marcy (7/30/91)
2931	Jesse Ferraro	Phelps (7/86)	Rocky Peak (7/31/91)
2932	Bryan M. Caldwell	Cascade (7/88)	Seymour (8/2/91)
2933	Donald O. Truax	Cascade (7/9/89)	Allen (8/3/91)
2934	Lester DeVarnne	Gray (8/19/90)	Allen (8/3/91)
2935	Mary Alice Koeneke	Algonquin (8/27/88)	Panther (8/3/91)
2936	Gordon C. Theisen	Cascade (8/1/87)	Emmons (8/8/91)
2937	Ronald O. Wager	Porter (8/7/82)	Haystack (8/8/91)
2938	Joseph W. Haus	Macomb (7/29/89)	Whiteface (8/10/91)
2939	Thomas F. Haus	Seward (7/28/90)	Whiteface (8/10/91)
2940	Bryce E. Button	Wright (3/2/82)	Panther (8/10/91)
2941	D. Graham Holmes	Cascade (unknown)	Couchsachraga (8/11/91)
2942	William G. Keswick II	Wright (8/15/88)	Whiteface (8/11/91)
2943	William G. Keswick, III	Wright (8/15/88)	Whiteface (8/11/91)
2944	Matthew Elliott	Big Slide (8/86)	Colden (8/11/91)
2945	William Throop	Giant (summer 1964)	Big Slide (8/15/91)
2946	Robin W. Huntley	Giant (6/1/91)	Allen (8/16/91)
2947	Donald D. Redden	Wright (10/11/86)	Cascade (8/16/91)
2948	Steven D. Redden	Wright (10/11/86)	Cascade (8/16/91)
2949	Kevin M. Burns	Marcy (8/10/85)	Allen (8/17/91)
2950	Michael L. Burns	Marcy (8/10/85)	Allen (8/17/91)
2951	Ronald N. Comstock	Big Slide (9/4/82)	Saddleback (8/17/91)
2952	Barbara J. Hall	Lower Wolf Jaw (8/15/81)	Saddleback (8/17/91)
2953	Diann Dimick	Algonquin (8/13/86)	Seymour (8/20/91)
2954	Howard E. Dimick	Cascade (11/25/84)	Seymour (8/20/91)
2955	Stephen A. Nichols	Algonquin (8/6/86)	Skylight (8/22/91)
2956	Richard Moomaw	Marcy (10/12/85)	Allen (8/23/91)
2957	Louise Dumouchel	Algonquin (10/80)	Marshall (8/24/91)
2958	Louis Marcotte	Algonquin (10/80)	Marshall (8/24/91)
2959	Tabor Nathan Tefft	Cascade (7/19/63)	Redfield (8/24/91)
2960	Sergio C. Gonzalez	Porter (9/30/89)	Seymour (8/25/91)
2961	David M. Rutkowski	Giant (7/1/83)	Whiteface (8/25/91)
2962	Joseph Rutkowski	Phelps (9/3/83)	Whiteface (8/5/91)
2963	Randy Rockford	Marcy (7/84)	Colden (8/25/91)
2964	Andrew M. Nania	Cascade (8/17/88)	Cliff (8/30/91)
2965	Edward J. Frick	Wright (9/11/67)	Allen (8/30/91)
2966	John F. Graefe	Upper Wolf Jaw (8/76)	Allen (8/30/91)
2967	Alan E. Benjamin	Big Slide (8/25/86)	Whiteface (8/31/91)
2968	David Silfen	Marcy (8/72)	Redfield (8/31/91)
2969	Brian Lee	Lower Wolf Jaw (1966)	Redfield (9/1/91)

HEAVEN UP-H'ISTED-NESS!

	MEMBER	FIRST ASCENT	FORTY-SIXTH PEAK
2970W	John E. Bolton	Marcy (9/1/90)	Dix (9/1/91)
2971W	Marta J. Bolton	Marcy (9/1/90)	Dix (9/1/91)
2972	Gregory S. Willhoff	Colden (7/11/70)	Seymour (9/1/91)
2973	Roger S. Wigent	Wright (7/19/86)	Skylight (9/1/91)
2974	Margaret T. Lipscomb	Gothics (8/6/88)	Giant (9/1/91)
2975	Marilyn R. O'Connor	Cascade (5/22/87)	Whiteface (9/2/91)
2976	Timothy P. O'Connor	Cascade (5/22/87)	Whiteface (9/2/91)
2977	Betsy Richert	Cascade (spring 1984)	Basin (9/2/91)
2978	C. Leon Harris	Marcy (8/13/70)	Allen (9/6/91)
2979	Matthew Townsend	Giant (7/87)	Rocky Peak (9/6/91)
2980	Cathy Ament	Phelps (9/16/89)	Wright (9/7/91)
2981	Maurice J. Sheedy	Phelps (10/8/83)	Gothics (9/7/91)
2982	Thomas Lowe	Marcy (8/88)	Rocky Peak (9/7/91)
2983	Frederic DeMay	Giant (8/76)	Gray (9/8/91)
2984	Daniel J. DeMay	Cascade (5/76)	Marcy (9/8/91)
2985	David R. Killius	Algonquin (6/15/85)	Giant (9/8/91)
2986	Jennifer A. Killius	Colden (7/15/86)	Giant (9/8/91)
2987	James E. Brown	Cascade (5/5/90)	Esther (9/11/91)
2988	Kenneth R. Habeck	Whiteface (7/78)	Allen (9/14/91)
2989	John A. Kurowski	Macomb (5/13/88)	Gray (9/14/91)
2990	Becky Mosher	Giant (9/9/84)	Algonquin (9/14/91)
2991	Dietland Muller-Schwarze	Marcy (8/20/85)	Esther (9/14/91)
2992	Erik Schleicher	Cascade (7/4/86)	Redfield (9/15/91)
2993	Cole H. Hickland	Porter (4/26/87)	Macomb (9/15/91)
2994	Sheila Young	Marcy (8/69)	Colden (9/18/91)
2995	Perry O'Neil	Giant (5/29/91)	Esther (9/18/91)
2996	Jeffrey S. Harrison	Algonquin (5/28/80)	Hough (9/20/91)
2997	Todd Case	Marcy (6/1/88)	Haystack (9/21/91)
2998	Jeremy M. Walsh	Marcy (6/1/88)	Haystack (9/21/91)
2999	Joseph Mynio	Marcy (5/80)	Blake (9/21/91)
3000	Theresa A. Kennedy	Big Slide (9/74)	Whiteface (9/21/91)
3001	Lance Marchese	Lower Wolf Jaw (7/11/87)	Haystack (9/21/91)
3002	Matthew Kuhrt	Big Slide (7/17/89)	Sawteeth (9/22/91)
3003	Michael Kuhrt	Dix (5/26/90)	Sawteeth (9/22/91)
3004	Duane K. Gould	Saddleback (7/69)	Sawteeth (9/22/91)
3005	Arthur P. Yannotti	Algonquin (8/17/85)	Wright (9/28/91)
3006	Nancy J. Yannotti	Algonquin (8/17/85)	Wright (9/28/91)
3007	Michael G. Putter	Wright (5/80)	Cliff (9/28/91)
3008	Christopher J. Walsh	Marcy (8/7/85)	Colden (9/28/91)
3009	George F. Konopski	Big Slide (10/16/83)	Street (10/5/91)
3010	Anthony Zazula	Big Slide (7/88)	Giant (10/5/91)
3011	Kevin F. Johnston	Cascade (6/8/85)	Cliff (10/5/91)
3012	Joel Kamnitzer	Cascade (8/26/86)	East Dix (10/6/91)
3013	Robert Shellhouse	Gothics (7/78)	Esther (10/6/91)
3014	James M. DiGennaro	Whiteface (8/81)	Cascade (10/9/91)
3015W	Richard E. Mooers	Wright (6/63)	Allen (10/12/91)
3016	Richard G. Albro	Wright (10/1/82)	Big Slide (10/12/91)
3017	James Sausville	Algonquin (2/70)	Redfield (10/13/91)
3018	David Hudda	Marcy (10/74)	Cascade (10/13/91)
3019	Donald Kinnear	Marcy (7/12/79)	Iroquois (10/19/91)
3020	Gerald Herman	Gothics (10/18/87)	Allen (10/19/91)
3021	Kathy Herman	Gothics (10/18/87)	Allen (10/19/91)
3022	Phil Ryan	Marcy (7/10/60)	Dial (10/19/91)
3023W	Richard R. Luetters	Cascade (12/6/86)	Basin (10/19/91)
3024	Linda F. Kern	Phelps (4/10/88)	Saddleback (10/19/91)
3025	Richard D. Kieffer	Lower Wolf Jaw (11/24/83)	Marcy (10/20/91)
3026	Alex Ziemkiewicz	Wright (8/2/86)	Marcy (10/20/91)
3027W	Carl D. Rosenthal	Wright (12/8/90)	Emmons (10/20/91)
3028	Michael Monahan	Haystack (8/27/87)	Cascade (10/20/91)
3029	Susan Patterson	Cascade (6/20/73)	Cliff (10/23/91)
3030	David S. Bender	Algonquin (5/16/87)	Nippletop (10/26/91)
3031	Jerry F. Weimar	Algonquin (5/16/87)	Nippletop (10/26/91)

The Membership Roster of the Adirondack Forty-Sixers

	Member	First Ascent	Forty-sixth Peak
3032W	William McDonough	Marcy (7/90)	Seymour (10/26/91)
3033	Margit Kotorman	Marcy (5/25/88)	Skylight (10/26/91)
3034	Joseph P. Fuerst	Big Slide (10/83)	Redfield (10/26/91)
3035	Melanie A. Fuerst	Big Slide (10/83)	Redfield (10/26/91)
3036W	Wayne T. Ratowski	Tabletop (8/24/91)	Marcy (10/27/91)
3037	Johanne H. Hagar	Giant (12/1/88)	Colden (10/27/91)
3038	Herman G. Drollette	Wright (2/23/91)	Whiteface (11/2/91)
3039W	Alan C. Knight	Wright (9/15/90)	Sawteeth (11/20/91)
3040W	Robert F. Grimm	Phelps (1/16/71)	Colden (12/21/91)
3041	Randy G. Powell	Big Slide (2/12/87)	Santanoni (12/27/91)
3042	Roger M. Norton	Cascade (summer 1967)	Street (5/26/85)
3043	Joseph W. Robbins	Wright (7/12/76)	Santanoni (8/24/89)
3044	Scott J. Kelley	Marcy (fall 1979)	Sawteeth (9/8/90)
3045	Dan Appel	Algonquin (8/86)	Cascade (8/17/91)
3046	Brigitte H. Johnson	Cascade (10/4/84)	Gothics (9/2/91)
3047	Robert F. Huitt	Colden (6/1/90)	Redfield (9/5/91)
3048	Paul LaSalle	Marcy (9/14/85)	Lower Wolf Jaw (10/20/91)
3049	Stanley Frost	Whiteface (5/57)	Allen (10/29/91)
3050	Steven C. Frost	Marcy (7/78)	Allen (10/29/91)
3051W	Brian A. Borton	Algonquin (1/26/91)	Marshall (1/5/92)
3052W	Edward P. Bunk	Marcy (3/10/90)	Marshall (1/5/92)
3053W	Andrew Przyblyowicz	Cascade (1/5/85)	Colden (1/26/92)
3054W	John F. Sharp	Giant (2/14/81)	Allen (2/2/92)
3055W	Alton W. Smith	Marcy (12/29/86)	Allen (2/2/92)
3056W	George S. Putnam	Algonquin (2/25/84)	Blake (2/23/92)
3057	Ronald C. Sawyer	Haystack (9/27/87)	Whiteface (3/6/92)
3058W	Richard M. Rozanski	Marcy (9/30/79)	Allen (3/14/92)
3059	Colin F. Glascock	Giant (8/14/69)	Allen (5/11/92)
3060	Frank E. Dogil	Marcy (8/8/85)	Cliff (5/17/92)
3061	Jeffrey L. Landa	Phelps (5/26/73)	Esther (5/23/92)
3062	Bruce B. Ross	Macomb (5/27/89)	Wright (5/24/92)
3063	James E. Geary	Algonquin (3/52)	Phelps (5/28/92)
3064	David D. DiPalma	Giant (11/11/89)	Haystack (5/30/92)
3065	Blake A. Harrison	Giant (11/11/89)	Haystack (5/30/92)
3066	Christian R. Sonne	Porter (8/15/81)	Iroquois (6/12/92)
3067	Matthew Sonne	Porter (8/15/81)	Iroquois (6/12/92)
3068	Nicholas B. Sonne	Porter (8/15/81)	Iroquois (6/12/92)
3069	Peter C. Sonne	Porter (8/15/81)	Iroquois (6/12/92)
3070	Kristin Adomeit	Algonquin (7/19/76)	Colden (6/12/92)
3071	Frank E. Fee, Jr.	Marcy (6/24/86)	Dix (6/20/92)
3072	Joseph R. Steiniger	Marcy (7/6/70)	Santanoni (6/27/92)
3073	James R. Warfield	Allen (7/1/89)	Cliff (6/28/92)
3074	Mark T. Gunkel	Algonquin (6/20/79)	Couchsachraga (7/5/92)
3075	Peter Biddle	Cascade (summer 1967)	Panther (7/7/92)
3076	Joseph Schick	Colden (7/58)	Emmons (7/10/92)
3077	George A. Van Laethem	Marcy (6/70)	Santanoni (7/11/92)
3078	Morgan Shipway	Giant (summer 1957)	Redfield (7/12/92)
3079	Maggie H. Spencer	Porter (7/17/87)	Haystack (7/15/92)
3080	Ellen W. Ohnmacht	Giant (8/28/89)	Allen (7/16/92)
3081	Fred W. Ohnmacht	Giant (8/28/89)	Allen (7/16/92)
3082	Constantine Gletsos	Phelps (5/26/90)	Gray (7/18/92)
3083	Larry Figary	Marcy (8/89)	Colden (7/19/92)
3084	James C. Wolfe	Colden (8/85)	Sawteeth (7/19/92)
3085	Thomas Reinckens	Phelps (7/84)	Cascade (7/25/92)
3086	Carla Hunter	Cascade (5/19/91)	Sawteeth (7/25/92)
3087W	David W. Hunter	Cascade (5/19/91)	Sawteeth (7/25/92)
3088	Ernest D. Mahlke	Gothics (8/20/77)	Seymour (7/26/92)
3089	James E. Morris	Lower Wolf Jaw (7/17/76)	Marcy (7/28/92)
3090	Richard L. Ehli	Marcy (9/14/86)	Iroquois (7/29/92)
3091	Theophile P. Masterson	Giant (9/17/82)	Haystack (7/30/92)
3092	Douglas Livingston	Phelps (6/17/84)	Santanoni (8/4/92)
3093	William L. Webb	Wright (8/15/78)	Emmons (8/4/92)

Heaven Up-h'isted-ness!

	Member	First Ascent	Forty-sixth Peak
3094	Michael D. Horwich	Algonquin (7/7/90)	Tabletop (8/4/92)
3095	Damon Jespersen	Unknown	Rocky Peak (8/5/92)
3096	Jason Metakis	Big Slide (summer 1988)	Rocky Peak (8/5/92)
3097	Marc Metakis	Big Slide (summer 1988)	Rocky Peak (8/5/92)
3098	David Fader	Marcy (8/81)	Whiteface (8/5/92)
3099	Lauren Z. Fader	Phelps (7/3/82)	Whiteface (8/5/92)
3100	John D. Cogar	Marcy (8/67)	Allen (8/5/92)
3101	Marie K. Wade	Cascade (9/29/84)	Allen (8/7/92)
3102W	Joseph E. Srebro	Phelps (2/86)	Emmons (8/7/92)
3103	Jeffrey D. Scott	Dix (8/20/81)	Phelps (8/7/92)
3104	Matthew B. Scott	Dix (8/20/81)	Phelps (8/7/92)
3105	Shaun Elkin	Wright (8/86)	Street (8/8/92)
3106	Michael G. Lewis	Wright (7/86)	Street (8/8/92)
3107	Erich Shigley	Cascade (7/88)	Street (8/8/92)
3108W	Scott L. Rishel	Cascade (8/10/71)	Whiteface (8/8/92)
3109	Ellen Hubbard	Gothics (8/25/81)	Haystack (8/12/92)
3110	John C. Hubbard, Jr.	Gothics (8/25/81)	Haystack (8/12/92)
3111	Carrie Lewis	Algonquin (7/27/87)	Allen (8/14/92)
3112	Jerry A. Sinden	Cascade (8/20/88)	Haystack (8/15/92)
3113	Michael A. Sinden	Cascade (8/20/88)	Haystack (8/15/92)
3114	Jamie Wilson	Cascade (8/20/88)	Haystack (8/15/92)
3115	William E. Wilson	Cascade (8/20/88)	Haystack (8/15/92)
3116	Asa Thomas-Train	Algonquin (7/16/89)	Armstrong (8/21/92)
3117	Patrick Loud	Cascade (8/85)	Panther (8/21/92)
3118	Claire F. Schulman	Seymour (5/25/87)	Panther (8/21/92)
3119	Thor Smith	Whiteface (9/23/78)	Seymour (8/22/92)
3120	Stephen P. Kehler	Esther (8/20/90)	Panther (8/26/92)
3121	Timo Viitanen	Gothics (9/9/89)	Porter (8/28/92)
3122	Thomas E. Saxton	Marcy (8/22/76)	Allen (8/29/92)
3123	Steven Silverberg	Cascade (4/13/91)	Emmons (8/29/92)
3124	Mark Schaefer	Lower Wolf Jaw (11/9/75)	Allen (8/29/92)
3125	Alan Alterbaum	Phelps (10/80)	Haystack (8/30/92)
3126	Steven F. Kasper	Colden (5/18/91)	Whiteface (8/30/92)
3127	Annette Muller-Schwarze	Big Slide (7/27/85)	Sawteeth (8/30/92)
3128	Matthew Armstrong	Big Slide (8/20/86)	Emmons (8/31/92)
3129	Sara Pavone	Cascade (9/18/83)	Emmons (8/31/92)
3130	Claudia Hager	Tabletop (5/28/92)	Whiteface (9/3/92)
3131	Sandra K. Russell	Seymour (7/21/87)	Whiteface (9/3/92)
3132	Gary H. Cook	Marcy (9/7/74)	Sawteeth (9/5/92)
3133	Paul R. Galizia	Giant (1986)	Gray (9/5/92)
3134	David W. Stadel	Algonquin (8/24/85)	Iroquois (9/6/92)
3135	Heather K. Morse	Cascade (10/14/85)	Emmons (9/6/92)
3136	Maria A. Beurmann	Colden (5/14/77)	Haystack (9/6/92)
3137	Rosemarie Victor	Colden (6/2/62)	Allen (9/6/92)
3138	Jean C. Victor	Colden (6/2/62)	Allen (9/6/92)
3139	Kyle E. McGinn	Algonquin (8/8/90)	Whiteface (9/6/92)
3140	Edward J. McGinn	Cascade (8/5/90)	Whiteface (9/6/92)
3141	Robin Geller	Cascade (2/27/88)	Gothics (9/6/92)
3142	Ned B. Sudborough	Rocky Peak (7/27/86)	Saddleback (9/6/92)
3143	Jens Kurejensen	Algonquin (8/1/65)	Seymour (9/7/92)
3144	Edward D. Parsons, Jr.	Marcy (7/38)	Emmons (9/9/92)
3145	Craig J. Byrum	Macomb (9/6/88)	Colden (9/10/92)
3146	George Dietz	Marcy (4/86)	Allen (9/11/92)
3147	Robert E. Dunham	Cascade (10/9/83)	Seymour (9/12/92)
3148	Miriam A. Moulton	Algonquin (9/29/90)	Phelps (9/12/92)
3149	Amy Daley	Porter (10/90)	Santanoni (9/12/92)
3150	Sharon Bishop	Cascade (6/3/78)	Dix (9/12/92)
3151	Jeffrey D. Wilson	Cascade (7/14/90)	Marcy (9/13/92)
3152	Lane A. Sanders	Marcy (5/28/88)	Whiteface (9/13/92)
3153	Joanne S. Altre	Porter (5/24/90)	Colden (9/13/92)
3154	Peter J. Koltai	Big Slide (4/73)	Nye (9/17/92)
3155	Eric McAuley	Algonquin (1986)	Haystack (9/19/92)

The Membership Roster of the Adirondack Forty-Sixers

	Member	First Ascent	Forty-sixth Peak
3156	John G. Fraser, Jr.	Cascade (8/67)	Emmons (9/19/92)
3157	Daniel J. Kress	Allen (5/15/76)	Rocky Peak (9/19/92)
3158	Lindsey Leiser	Tabletop (6/15/91)	Allen (9/20/92)
3159	Carol Lynn Michelfelder	Cascade (1987)	Dix (9/20/92)
3160	James E. Michelfelder	Cascade (1987)	Dix (9/20/92)
3161	Mary Michelfelder	Cascade (1987)	Dix (9/20/92)
3162	William Michelfelder	Marcy (8/59)	Dix (9/20/92)
3163W	Charles J. Kolodzey	Cascade (7/90)	Whiteface (9/20/92)
3164	Thomas J. Scalzo	Cascade (11/7/90)	Whiteface (9/20/92)
3165	Meredith A. Parsons	Algonquin (7/86)	Colden (9/21/92)
3166W	Christine A. Dresser	Cascade (5/11/86)	Algonquin (9/27/92)
3167	Amy Fallone	Algonquin (8/31/91)	Cliff (10/3/92)
3168	Michael Fallone	Algonquin (8/31/91)	Cliff (10/3/92)
3169	Michael H. Dobner	Upper Wolf Jaw (1/12/85)	Dix (10/3/92)
3170	Harold E. Sandals	Marcy (8/73)	Giant (10/4/92)
3171	Varick J. Stringham, Jr.	Algonquin (9/27/86)	Seymour (10/5/92)
3172	David T. DelliQuadri	Marcy (10/50)	Blake (10/8/92)
3173	Joseph C. Reiners, Jr.	Marcy (4/52)	Allen (10/9/92)
3174	Donald H. MacMillan	Wright (1/75)	Hough (10/10/92)
3175	Lee Fanger	Algonquin (9/64)	Nippletop (10/10/92)
3176	Anne Lassell	Giant (5/87)	Whiteface (10/11/92)
3177W	Holly Sullivan	Big Slide (8/12/90)	Iroquois (10/12/92)
3178W	John Wimbush	Big Slide (8/12/90)	Iroquois (10/12/92)
3179W	Ann Spencer	Algonquin (summer 1972)	Iroquois (10/12/92)
3180W	Armond E. Spencer	Algonquin (summer 1972)	Iroquois (10/12/92)
3181W	Sam D. Jones	Algonquin (6/25/86)	Big Slide (10/18/92)
3182	Frederick B. Finley, IV	Cascade (5/25/91)	Porter (10/24/92)
3183	Frederick B. Finley, III	Cascade (5/25/91)	Porter (10/24/92)
3184	Karen R. Gorsch	Cascade (10/15/89)	Porter (10/24/92)
3185	Louis Kotorman	Marcy (5/25/88)	Big Slide (11/12/92)
3186W	Steven Siegard	Whiteface (summer 1972)	Armstrong (12/5/92)
3187W	Jonathan A. Esper	Porter (2/22/90)	Redfield (12/28/92)
3188	Raymond J. Zegger	Cascade (8/71)	Seymour (7/9/89)
3189W	Douglas E. Downs	Skylight (8/76)	Whiteface (7/14/91)
3190	Nancy R. Smith	Marcy (7/58)	Haystack (5/24/92)
3191	Larry Fisher	Colden (1956)	Hough (7/11/92)
3192	Rachel Brown	Cascade (4/13/91)	Haystack (8/8/92)
3193W	John J. Bennett	Cascade (6/85)	Tabletop (8/16/92)
3194	Jeremy H. Schneider	Big Slide (summer 1979)	Haystack (8/20/92)
3195	Paul J. Moran	Marcy (9/23/62)	Couchsachraga (8/21/92)
3196	Leslie Bostrom	Sawteeth (8/62)	Haystack (9/2/92)
3197	Robert H. Feathers	Phelps (8/28/75)	Whiteface (9/5/92)
3198	Robert R. Smith	Big Slide (9/89)	Whiteface (10/4/92)
3199	Soonja Smith	Big Slide (9/89)	Whiteface (10/4/92)
3200	Jean-Philippe Hickey	Algonquin (8/1/88)	Rocky Peak (10/30/92)
3201	Jean-Pierre Hickey	Algonquin (8/1/88)	Rocky Peak (10/30/92)
3202W	Peter Hickey	Marcy (8/69)	Rocky Peak (10/30/92)
3203	Alan Traino	Phelps (9/79)	Allen (11/7/92)
3204	Thomas deHaan	Algonquin (8/85)	Blake (1/1/93)
3205W	Gregory Wait	Skylight (8/78)	Emmons (1/10/93)
3206	Fred Soder	Gothics (11/78)	Whiteface (2/5/93)
3207W	John B. Nesbitt	Lower Wolf Jaw (1/5/85)	Basin (2/14/93)
3208W	Steven M. Parnes	Giant (6/87)	Marshall (2/28/93)
3209	Joseph Perrone	Giant (3/29/91)	Iroquois (5/1/93)
3210	Maria Ranucci Walsh	Giant (9/21/90)	Santanoni (5/8/93)
3211	Jonathan R. Metzger	Phelps (summer 1976)	Sawteeth (5/22/93)
3212	Mark Tatigian	Marcy (11/16/85)	Couchsachraga (5/23/93)
3213	Ruth B. Robinson	Wright (1/2/58)	East Dix (6/18/93)
3214W	Gordon Hobday	Marcy (10/61)	Allen (6/20/93)
3215	Jeffrey L. Erenstone	Cascade (7/25/81)	Haystack (6/23/93)
3216W	Robert Juravich	Giant (5/29/89)	Esther (6/24/93)
3217	Karyn L. Traphagen	Wright (7/22/73)	Marcy (6/26/93)

Heaven Up-h'isted-ness!

	Member	First Ascent	Forty-sixth Peak
3218	Mark W. Traphagen	Algonquin (7/17/86)	Marcy (6/26/93)
3219	Sarah J. Traphagen	Algonquin (7/17/86)	Marcy (6/26/93)
3220	Hannah Traphagen	Algonquin (7/17/86)	Marcy (6/26/93)
3221	R. Lloyd Murdoch	Cascade (8/81)	Whiteface (7/1/93)
3222	Joseph C. Gardner, Jr.	Colden (7/46)	Allen (7/3/93)
3223	Herbert W. Dorn	Marcy (10/70)	Seymour (7/7/93)
3224	James J. Taub	Skylight (10/11/81)	Sawteeth (7/10/93)
3225	Ethan Youngerman	Marcy (8/87)	Santanoni (7/10/93)
3226	Armand Minuti	Dix (10/6/62)	Colden (7/10/93)
3227	William J. McCarthy	Dial (Mid-1970's)	Wright (7/10/93)
3228	Kenneth L. Barker	Cascade (7/25/89)	Marcy (7/16/93)
3229	Peter L. Darling	Wright (6/2/90)	Marcy (7/16/93)
3230	Stephanie McConaughy	Algonquin (6/14/92)	Couchsachraga (7/17/93)
3231	Stewart H. McConaughy	Algonquin (6/14/92)	Couchsachraga (7/17/93)
3232	James F. Bullard	Phelps (7/16/85)	Whiteface (7/17/93)
3233	Susan Roberts	Big Slide (8/25/83)	Couchsachraga (7/17/93)
3234	Eleanor I. Crandall	Porter (5/2/92)	Haystack (7/21/93)
3235	Richard L. Johnson	Porter (5/2/92)	Haystack (7/21/93)
3236	Nicholas T. Smith	Cascade (7/14/89)	Saddleback (7/22/93)
3237	Barbara A. Spiak	Giant (10/87)	Haystack (7/24/93)
3238	Donald J. Spiak	Giant (10/87)	Haystack (7/24/93)
3239	Richard A. Meili, Sr.	Wright (9/63)	Panther (7/24/93)
3240W	Eric N. Bauer	Phelps (8/86)	Dix (7/26/93)
3241	Alan L. Zaur	Big Slide (1980)	Allen (7/27/93)
3242	Leon E. Allen	Phelps (9/28/91)	Hough (7/27/93)
3243	Gary S. Henning	Algonquin (6/24/90)	Big Slide (7/31/93)
3244	Judith L. Wilkins	Cascade (8/9/87)	Colden (8/2/93)
3245	Scott C. Churilla	Lower Wolf Jaw (7/87)	Cascade (8/2/93)
3246	Erik S. Hess	Colvin (7/89)	Marshall (8/5/93)
3247	Joan Hasselwander	Algonquin (8/28/86)	Saddleback (8/6/93)
3248	Esi Tremblay	Giant (8/26/86)	Saddleback (8/6/93)
3249	David Ludman	Cascade (7/8/90)	Tabletop (8/6/93)
3250	Jay P. Okun	Dix (7/91)	Sawteeth (8/7/93)
3251	Rowana J. Okun	Dix (7/91)	Sawteeth (8/7/93)
3252	Sandra M. Ballard	Cascade (7/21/86)	Redfield (8/7/93)
3253	William G. Ballard	Cascade (7/21/86)	Redfield (8/7/93)
3254	Erin Haskins	Cascade (11/29/89)	Lower Wolf Jaw (8/7/93)
3255W	Thomas L. Haskins	Santanoni (8/6/73)	Lower Wolf Jaw (8/7/93)
3256	Brian H. Roddiger	East Dix (6/16/91)	Nye (8/11/93)
3257	Steven Violin	Algonquin (8/3/89)	Marshall (8/12/93)
3258	William C. LaRocque	Phelps (4/29/91)	Haystack (8/14/93)
3259	David R. Naysmith	Marcy (11/9/79)	Redfield (8/14/93)
3260	Russell D. Naysmith	Marcy (11/9/79)	Redfield (8/14/93)
3261	Thomas Penders	Haystack (9/23/89)	Whiteface (8/14/93)
3262	Kenneth R. Perrotta	Phelps (4/84)	Basin (8/14/93)
3263W	Barbara Bave	Big Slide (7/79)	Colden (8/14/93)
3264	Sarah E. Johnson	Cascade (5/27/90)	Whiteface (8/14/93)
3265	Jay Magiera	Algonquin (7/6/90)	Whiteface (8/14/93)
3266	Renee E. Bolton	Phelps (10/13/91)	Dix (8/15/93)
3267	Jennifer L. Bolton	Algonquin (4/28/91)	Dix (8/15/93)
3268	Jo Ellen Eisener	Gothics (10/10/82)	Iroquois (8/16/93)
3269	Richard T. Furman	Marcy (8/69)	Iroquois (8/16/93)
3270	Arlene M. Scholer	Marcy (10/9/79)	Iroquois (8/16/93)
3271	David Thomas-Train	Giant (7/29/60)	Allen (8/16/93)
3272	Alan L. Cameros	Wright (10/6/84)	Skylight (8/16/93)
3273	Zachary Bookman	Big Slide (11/87)	Haystack (8/16/93)
3274	Edward C. Dewar	Dix (7/11/89)	Phelps (8/19/93)
3275	Nicholas M. Handler	Cascade (5/84)	Rocky Peak (8/20/93)
3276	Andrew J. Weiner	Macomb (8/87)	Dix (8/20/93)
3277	Edward C. Kisloski	Dix (7/11/89)	Cascade (8/21/93)
3278	Christopher M. Demers	Cascade (8/12/88)	Haystack (8/21/93)
3279	Leo J. Demers	Cascade (8/21/88)	Haystack (8/21/93)

The Membership Roster of the Adirondack Forty-Sixers

	Member	First Ascent	Forty-sixth Peak
3280	Carol A. White	Marcy (6/81)	Haystack (8/21/93)
3281	Rock E. White	Marcy (6/72)	Haystack (8/21/93)
3282	Leslie M. Handler	Algonquin (8.67)	Iroquois (8/22/93)
3283	Galen Crane	Wright (10/17/87)	Rocky Peak (8/23/93)
3284	Robert N. Crawford	Upper Wolf Jaw (8/1/86)	Nippletop (8/28/93)
3285	Paul La Barbera	Upper Wolf Jaw (8/1/86)	Nippletop (8/28/93)
3286	Michael E. Neaton	Wright (7/30/89)	Phelps (8/28/93)
3287	Robert W. Conklin	Dix (8/20/77)	Allen (8/28/93)
3288	George F. Mosey	Cascade (8/15/85)	Whiteface (8/28/93)
3289	Marcia C. Mosey	Cascade (8/15/85)	Whiteface (8/28/93)
3290	Bruce R. Davidson	Algonquin (1950)	Santanoni (8/29/93)
3291	Alan B. Davidson	Marcy (7/16/78)	Santanoni (8/29/93)
3292	Brian S. D'Amour	Phelps (8/23/86)	Tabletop (8/29/93)
3293	Daniel D'Amour	Phelps (8/23/86)	Tabletop (8/29/93)
3294	Jeffey D'Amour	Phelps (8/23/86)	Tabletop (8/29/93)
3295	Michael D'Amour	Phelps (8/23/86)	Tabletop (8/29/93)
3296	Karen C. Eagan	Cascade (10/91)	Whiteface (8/29/93)
3297	Terry Gottesman	Cascade (10/19/91)	Whiteface (8/29/93)
3298	Jonathan Tennant	Blake (6/6/92)	Allen (8/29/93)
3299W	Thomas M. Faulkner	Cascade (5/16/92)	Allen (8/29/93)
3300	Charles J. DiVecchio	Giant (8/12/86)	Allen (8/29/93)
3301	Andrew D. Zdrahal	Marcy (10/87)	Gray (8/29/93)
3302	Ivan Zdrahal	Marcy (10/87)	Gray (9/29/93)
3303	David C. Skee	Upper Wolf Jaw (9/2/79)	Whiteface (9/4/93)
3304	Janet L. Skee	Sawteeth (2/21/83)	Whiteface (9/4/93)
3305	Scott Regis	Phelps (9/81)	Allen (9/4/93)
3306	William J. Watson	Santanoni (4/10/82)	Emmons (9/5/93)
3307	Sandra A. LaPerche	Gothics (8/3/87)	Dix (9/5/93)
3308	Edwin C. LaPerche	Gothics (8/3/87)	Dix (9/5/93)
3309	Allen Grunthal	Wright (8/25/84)	Haystack (9/5/93)
3310	William S. Lundy	Marcy (5/75)	Iroquois (9/5/93)
3311	Eugene W. Bruce	Cascade (8/9/88)	Whiteface (9/5/93)
3312	Sandy Bruce	Cascade (8/9/88)	Whiteface (9/5/93)
3313	Sue Kalafut	Phelps (5/23/87)	Dix (9/5/93)
3314	Lisa L. Schroeder	Marcy (7/25/86)	Skylight (9/5/93)
3315	Allen J. Dybas	Marcy (7/25/86)	Skylight (9/5/93)
3316	Martha Precheur	Gothics (8/18/87)	Whiteface (9/5/93)
3317	Gary H. Stevens	Cascade (7/29/90)	Seymour (9/6/93)
3318	Nan E. Stevens	Cascade (5/20/90)	Seymour (9/6/93)
3319	Kate A. Welch	Cascade (1980)	Haystack (9/6/93)
3320	Laurie L. Unetich	Allen (8/29/87)	Seymour (9/11/93)
3321	David J. Unetich	Allen (8/29/87)	Seymour (9/11/93)
3322	Harold C. Jacobus	Colden (8/3/91)	Whiteface (9/11/93)
3323	Kevin Jacobus	Colden (8/3/91)	Whiteface (9/11/93)
3324	Joseph B. Holland, Jr.	Marcy (7/66)	Seymour (9/11/93)
3325	William A. Best, Jr.	Marcy (5/29/78)	Allen (9/12/93)
3326	Robert Stanyon	Giant (9/3/83)	Hough (9/13/93)
3327	Lynn McDermott	Phelps (5/25/83)	Basin (9/17/93)
3328	Keith Kinnally	Algonquin (Mid-1970's)	Cliff (9/17/93)
3329	Michael Kinnally	Cascade (10/6/84)	Cliff (9/17/93)
3330	Peter Kinnally	Algonquin (9/14/85)	Cliff (9/17/93)
3331	Mildred E. Gittinger	Haystack (5/17/58)	Basin (9/18/93)
3332	Lawrence M. Hokirk	Colvin (5/29/93)	Marcy (9/19/93)
3333	Stan Lukas	Macomb (9/9/90)	East Dix (9/19/93)
3334	James F. Quigley	Cascade (7/24/90)	Colden (9/25/93)
3335	Allan R. Walker	Cascade (7/24/90)	Colden (9/25/93)
3336	Robert A. Moore	Cascade (10/18/90)	Marcy (9/25/93)
3337	Marcie Kobak	Phelps (8/25/83)	Marshall (9/25/93)
3338	Kevin J. Campbell	Dix (3/3/91)	Whiteface (9/25/93)
3339	Marcia K. Daubney	Cascade (10/21/88)	Allen (9/25/93)
3340	Jerome P. Trenkler	Algonquin (8/17/91)	Gothics (9/25/93)
3341	Anthony C. Brankman	Giant (5/30/70)	Gothics (9/25/93)

Heaven Up-h'isted-ness!

	Member	First Ascent	Forty-sixth Peak
3342W	Joseph B. Bogardus	Algonquin (10/8/88)	Giant (9/25/93)
3343	John M. Stengel	Marcy (9/7/86)	Whiteface (9/25/93)
3344	Rick Robertson	Marcy (7/79)	Couchsachraga (9/25/93)
3345	Michael G. Cashin	Algonquin (9/30/89)	Whiteface (10/2/93)
3346	Eugene Reilly	Big Slide (8/29/81)	Whiteface (10/2/93)
3347	Todd E. Stevens	Marcy (7/6/91)	Allen (10/5/93)
3348	John Shattuck	Porter (6/13/93)	Whiteface (10/8/93)
3349	Robert T. Milne	Giant (fall 1986)	Couchsachraga (10/8/93)
3350	Paul Kreher	Algonquin (6/90)	Allen (10/8/93)
3351	Egerton Boyce	Gothics (5/14/88)	Whiteface (10/9/93)
3352	Mark Aubin	Phelps (6/25/92)	Whiteface (10/9/93)
3353	Randy K. Perkins	Phelps (6/25/92)	Whiteface (10/9/93)
3354	Jay A. Erlebacher	Phelps (7/15/72)	Whiteface (10/9/93)
3355	John T. Gagne	Nippletop (10/9/88)	Whiteface (10/10/93)
3356W	Thomas B. Wheeler	Cascade (5/14/93)	Redfield (10/11/93)
3357	Fred J. Lamb	Giant (7/17/87)	Whiteface (10/14/93)
3358	Charles W. Kellogg, III	Algonquin (9/7/74)	Hough (10/14/93)
3359	Gillian S. Kellogg	Algonquin (9/7/74)	Hough (10/14/93)
3360	Justin Hoffman	Rocky Peak (7/89)	Sawteeth (10/16/93)
3361	Robert W. Hoffman	Phelps (8/80)	Sawteeth (10/16/93)
3362	Peter K. Thomas	Big Slide (7/13/76)	Couchsachraga (10/16/93)
3363	Robert B. Hanna	Dix (1977)	Whiteface (10/16/93)
3364	Diana P. Liu	Macomb (9/29/84)	Giant (10/16/93)
3365	Douglas R. Hoffman	Cascade (8/10/91)	Haystack (10/24/93)
3366	Gregory Hoffman	Cascade (8/10/91)	Haystack (10/24/93)
3367	Catherine W. Hoffman	Rocky Peak (7/89)	Haystack (10/24/93)
3368	Peter Slocum	Lower Wolf Jaw (1958)	Street (10/24/93)
3369	John M. Willis	Macomb (10/2/89)	Haystack (11/27/93)
3370	G. Wayne McIlroy	Algonquin (3/11/89)	Colden (12/17/93)
3371	Michael Tomsho	Algonquin (7/4/91)	Big Slide (12/29/93)
3372	Richard Carter	Colvin (6/6/61)	Seymour (7/1/67)
3373	J. Christopher Beattie	Marcy (4/59)	Phelps (8/12/72)
3374	Clarence A. Bissonnette	Marcy (1928)	Cliff (summer 1976 or 77)
3375	Robert Z. Dadekian	Algonquin (4/85)	Seymour (3/7/92)
3376	Kevin Boland	Dix (1980)	Gray (9/5/92)
3377	Cristina A. Insler	Marcy (5/84)	Santanoni (7/5/93)
3378	Amy M. Kleppner	Big Slide (8/72)	Rocky Peak (7/14/93)
3379	David Nimmons	Phelps (8/2/86)	Allen (7/29/93)
3380	Paul Nimmons	Phelps (8/2/86)	Allen (7/29/93)
3381	Phyllis Nimmons	Phelps (8/2/86)	Allen (7/29/93)
3382	Bill Philo	Cascade (6/8/91)	Whiteface (8/8/93)
3383	Joan Mackenzie	Marcy (10/29/77)	Big Slide (9/12/93)
3384	Paul R. Cote	Marcy (9/14/85)	Panther (9/12/93)
3385	Douglas Trendell	Cascade (8/1/81)	Haystack (9/27/93)
3386	Barbara J. Remeczky	Marcy (6/25/86)	Allen (10/7/93)
3387	Timothy C. Petrie	Marcy (8/26/83)	Whiteface (10/16/93)
3388W	Benjym C. Ellithorpe	Gothics (1/8/88)	Redfield (3/16/94)
3389W	David R. Reich	Upper Wolf Jaw (1/28/89)	Couchsachraga (3/20/94)
3390W	William (Willis) Forster	Marcy (summer 1968)	Gray (3/20/94)
3391	Helen Czajkowski	Marcy (12/73)	Rocky Peak (5/15/94)
3392	James J. Mullen	Marcy (10/73)	Rocky Peak (5/15/94)
3393W	Samuel Q. Eddy	Marcy (10/6/90)	Whiteface (6/4/94)
3394	William E. Green	Marcy (10/6/90)	Whiteface (6/4/94)
3395	John R. Daubney	Cascade (10/21/88)	Redfield (6/18/94)
3396	Peter Hutchings	Macomb (7/11/87)	Marcy (6/25/94)
3397	Thomas R. Wood	Wright (9/17/66)	East Dix (6/25/94)
3398	Peter J. Hills	Cascade (10/20/84)	Emmons (6/25/94)
3399	Andrew W. Deans	Marcy (8/28/87)	Gray (6/26/94)
3400	William S. Deans	Marcy (8/28/87)	Gray (6/26/94)
3401	Mitchell C. Smith	Algonquin (5/6/88)	Haystack (6/26/94)
3402	Mike Hendricks	Dix (8/74)	Allen (7/2/94)
3403	Brian J. Woods	Cascade (8/10/91)	Colden (7/3/94)

The Membership Roster of the Adirondack Forty-Sixers

	Member	First Ascent	Forty-sixth Peak
3404	Christopher F. Woods	Cascade (8/10/91)	Colden (7/3/94)
3405	Frank J. Woods	Marcy (6/7/80)	Colden (7/3/94)
3406	F. William Baker	Marcy (8/25/68)	Emmons (7/11/94)
3407	Kitty Vondrak	Algonquin (6/11/89)	Marcy (7/13/94)
3408	Joanne Battah	Phelps (fall 1986)	Iroquois (7/16/94)
3409	Karen K. Brown	Cascade (7/17/87)	Whiteface (7/16/94)
3410	Chris Cipro	Lower Wolf Jaw (8/30/91)	Seymour (7/17/94)
3411	John N. Hamilton	Lower Wolf Jaw (8/30/91)	Seymour (7/17/94)
3412	Timothy J. Noble	Big Slide (7/4/74)	Dix (7/17/94)
3413	William J. Marzano	Cascade (10/81)	Big Slide (7/17/94)
3414	Sue G. Seacord	Marcy (4/74)	Allen (7/18/94)
3415	Eliza Scott	Big Slide (7/15/80)	Emmons (7/19/94)
3416	Frank E. Guilfoil	Gothics (9/21/91)	Emmons (7/21/94)
3417	Peg Masters	Big Slide (5/12/91)	Emmons (7/21/94)
3418	Jack Hallnan	Algonquin (6/1/63)	Sawteeth (7/21/94)
3419W	Dan D'Angelico	Rocky Peak (9/16/89)	Cliff (7/23/94)
3420	Nora Doebrich	Porter (7/14/86)	Emmons (7/26/94)
3421	David Casner	Algonquin (8/1/89)	Redfield (7/28/94)
3422	Katharine L. Reichert	Marcy (9/76)	Allen (7/30/94)
3423	Frank P. Messina, III	Whiteface (8/6/86)	Seymour (7/31/94)
3424	Frank P. Messina, Jr.	Whiteface (8/6/86)	Seymour (7/31/94)
3425	Rose M. Messina	Whiteface (8/6/86)	Seymour (7/31/94)
3426	Joseph P. Dulin, Jr.	Phelps (10/8/89)	Whiteface (7/31/94)
3427	Pamela K. Dulin	Phelps (10/8/89)	Whiteface (7/31/94)
3428	Luke C. Stein	Big Slide (7/90)	Santanoni (7/31/94)
3429	Jared Belinsky	Dix (7/88)	Wright (8/1/94)
3430	James C. Blosser	Lower Wolf Jaw (8/16/76)	Marshall (8/4/94)
3431	Daniel W. Check	Colden (7/20/88)	Sawteeth (8/5/94)
3432	Larry Meyer	Cascade (9/83)	Allen (8/6/94)
3433	Bruce Gardner	Nippletop (9/1/92)	Haystack (8/6/94)
3434	Jerry W. Sherman	Tabletop (9/23/90)	Haystack (8/6/94)
3435	Thomas D. Doeblin	Marcy (1980)	Allen (8/6/94)
3436	Brian Packard	Giant (8/15/88)	Nippletop (8/6/94)
3437	John Hess	Algonquin (8/82)	Marshall (8/6/94)
3438	Samuel J. Balin	Big Slide (1990)	Wright (8/7/94)
3439	John V. Hartzell	Giant (10/72)	Cliff (8/7/94)
3440	Darren Flusche	Marcy (9/1/90)	Rocky Peak (8/8/94)
3441	Grace Flusche	Marcy (9/1/90)	Rocky Peak (8/8/94)
3442	Mark Flusche	Marcy (9/1/90)	Rocky Peak (8/8/94)
3443	Michael Flusche	Marcy (9/1/90)	Rocky Peak (8/8/94)
3444	Robert R. Stevens	Wright (6/11/94)	Cascade (8/8/94)
3445	Margaret Hawthorn	Cascade (6/87)	Panther (8/10/94)
3446	Reid Block	Cascade (8/7/91)	Tabletop (8/10/94)
3447W	G. Robert Cooley	Marcy (1964)	Dix (8/11/94)
3448W	Linda Cooley	Marcy (summer 1968)	Dix (8/11/94)
3449W	Michael Cooley	Giant (8/5/91)	Dix (8/11/94)
3450W	Richard B. Cooley	Giant (8/5/91)	Dix (8/11/94)
3451	Jerry R. Westcott	Colden (7/25/65)	Dix (8/12/94)
3452	Joyce Westcott	Wright (7/29/74)	Dix (8/12/94)
3453	William Dodd	Marcy (1/1/76)	Emmons (8/12/94)
3454	Carsten D. Vogel	Whiteface (summer 1988)	Redfield (8/12/94)
3455	Patricia Rucker	Marcy (9/92)	Haystack (8/13/94)
3456W	David T. Young	Marcy (9/92)	Haystack (8/13/94)
3457	Seamus Hodgkinson	Marcy (7/82)	Esther (8/13/94)
3458	Linda Bogardus	Marcy (7/2/89)	Basin (8/13/94)
3459W	Howard Stoner	Gothics (8/1/92)	Colden (8/13/94)
3460	Dennis J. Klimowski	Dix (6/15/85)	Cliff (8/13/94)
3461	Terry O'Hara	Algonquin (3/3/89)	Colden (8/13/94)
3462	Dana Brooks	Porter (6/23/90)	Colden (8/13/94)
3463	Cathy Seufert	Basin (9/63)	Emmons (8/17/94)
3464	Skip Sturman	Skylight (summer 1961)	Iroquois (8/17/94)
3465	Gerald P. Case, Jr.	Marshall (5/26/90)	Colden (8/20/94)

Heaven Up-h'isted-ness!

	Member	First Ascent	Forty-sixth Peak
3466	John Thaxton	Wright (9/84)	Couchsachraga (8/20/94)
3467	Patricia H. Thaxton	Wright (9/84)	Couchsachraga (8/20/94)
3468	David Interlicchia	Marcy (7/20/91)	Whiteface (8/20/94)
3469	Derek Rutledge	Phelps (10/14/89)	Colden (8/20/94)
3470	Liz Stephenson	Dix (spring 1990)	Haystack (8/20/94)
3471	Jeffrey Bizik	Dix (spring 1990)	Haystack (8/20/94)
3472	Howard R. Bird	Whiteface (7/31/71)	Panther (8/20/94)
3473	Alice G. Sondheimer	Wright (1978)	Basin (8/22/94)
3474	Andrew V. Stengrevics	Dix (8/75)	Rocky Peak (8/24/94)
3475	Russell W. Roberts	Algonquin (8/31/86)	Wright (8/24/94)
3476	Edward E. Marks, Jr.	Giant (6/5/93)	Colden (8/26/94)
3477	Brian M. MacDonald	Macomb (6/24/91)	Emmons (8/26/94)
3478	Andrew I. Henderson	Phelps (6/25/90)	Emmons (8/26/94)
3479	Nathan Jenkins	Phelps (6/25/90)	Emmons (8/26/94)
3480	Peter J. Bednarek	Phelps (6/25/90)	Emmons (8/26/94)
3481	Charles Barrows	Macomb (6/24/91)	Emmons (8/26/94)
3482	Donald A. Capron	Giant (1/24/93)	Lower Wolf Jaw (8/27/94)
3483	Susan C. Damm	Phelps (5/12/90)	Big Slide (8/27/94)
3484	Jay Hotchkiss	Dix (8/71)	Colden (8/27/94)
3485	William L. Hunt	Marcy (summer 1980)	Allen (8/27/94)
3486	Sandra E. Reimer	Marcy (8/5/80)	Whiteface (8/27/94)
3487	Scott Bresett	Giant (5/25/91)	Whiteface (8/28/94)
3488	Timothy J. Bresett	Giant (5/25/91)	Whiteface (8/28/94)
3489	Donald Kirche	Cascade (9/72)	Cliff (8/29/94)
3490	Lawrence W. Jackson	Saddleback (8/25/88)	Allen (8/30/94)
3491	Paul F. Beyer	Porter (5/24/75)	Redfield (9/2/94)
3492	Rich Niegocki	Blake (3/31/92)	Seymour (9/3/94)
3493	Carol Thiel	Big Slide (7/24/90)	Haystack (9/3/94)
3494	Edward J. Sheldon	Colvin (8/3/91)	Rocky Peak (9/3/94)
3495	Wanda A. Davenport	Marcy (7/25/88)	Couchsachraga (9/3/94)
3496	Edward A. Bown	Nippletop (6/27/93)	Rocky Peak (9/4/94)
3497	David Bieri	Wright (8/87)	Cliff (9/4/94)
3498	Thomas Massoth	Marcy (9/28/85)	Colden (9/8/94)
3499	Larry A. Britt	Algonquin (7/7/89)	Allen (9/10/94)
3500	Robert Brand	Marcy (summer 1961)	Allen (9/10/94)
3501	Sarah Beattie	Cascade (6/9/85)	Phelps (9/11/94)
3502	Stephen R. O'Neil	Marcy (7/12/92)	Seymour (9/11/94)
3503	Donald J. Piegza	Marcy (7/12/92)	Seymour (9/11/94)
3504	Edward L. Smelko	Big Slide (10/8/90)	Allen (9/13/94)
3505	Michael Fletcher	Skylight (9/5/88)	Wright (9/16/94)
3506	Darryl Lancaster	Algonquin (10/25/78)	Wright (9/16/94)
3507W	Alan J. Bushnell	Phelps (8/28/92)	Whiteface (9/17/94)
3508	Phillip J. Schedlbauer	Marcy (9/73)	Blake (9/17/94)
3509	Douglas Young	Marcy (5/82)	Blake (9/17/94)
3510	Joseph A. Roth	Algonquin (10/74)	Whiteface (9/17/94)
3511	Kelly Daley	Marcy (8/90)	Marshall (9/17/94)
3512	Emily Adler	Marcy (7/1/89)	Emmons (9/18/94)
3513	Michael S. Adler	Marcy (7/1/89)	Emmons (9/18/94)
3514	Norman Sills	Lower Wolf Jaw (9/20/69)	Whiteface (9/18/94)
3515	Kevin Ryan	Marshall (8/17/91)	Colden (9/18/94)
3516	Betsey Thomas-Train	Wright (8/17/79)	Saddleback (9/18/94)
3517	Stephen F. Pecsek	Giant (8/13/78)	Marshall (9/21/94)
3518	Ron Schneider	Cascade (10/6/90)	Rocky Peak (9/22/94)
3519	Kathy C. Hutchings	Marcy (8/19/86)	Seymour (9/23/94)
3520	Keith M. Hutchings	Marcy (8/19/86)	Seymour (9/23/94)
3521	Jeffrey J. Sargent	Marcy (9/6/92)	Whiteface (9/24/94)
3522	Karyl Sargent	Marcy (9/6/92)	Whiteface (9/24/94)
3523	Marguerite Petit	Cascade (5/1/93)	Haystack (9/24/94)
3524	Brian Hart	Marcy (10/2/83)	Skylight (9/27/94)
3525W	Paul Dicresce	Big Slide (1/88)	Allen (9/30/94)
3526W	Joseph E. Poliquin	Haystack (7/17/92)	Allen (9/30/94)
3527	Granville C. Savidge	Cascade (10/7/90)	Iroquois (10/1/94)

The Membership Roster of the Adirondack Forty-Sixers

	Member	First Ascent	Forty-sixth Peak
3528	Sharon Pavone	Algonquin (6/29/84)	Cliff (10/1/94)
3529	Stephen Gratto	Giant (7/7/79)	Gothics (10/1/94)
3530	Marilee Urbanczyk	Phelps (2/12/82)	Haystack (10/1/94)
3531	Mitchell P. White	Giant (5/73)	Esther (10/2/94)
3532	Jeff Durocher	Cascade (6/92)	Whiteface (10/2/94)
3533	Pamela D. Keida	Cascade (7/85)	Basin (10/2/94)
3534	Sherri S. Martin	Cascade (7/12/84)	Basin (10/2/94)
3535	Jeb Wallace-Brodeur	Haystack (7/77)	Rocky Peak (10/4/94)
3536	James F. Guderian	Dix (9/15/85)	Haystack (10/8/94)
3537	Aaron Poulin	Marcy (10/89)	Saddleback (10/8/94)
3538	Ted M. Poulin	Haystack (8/83)	Saddleback (10/8/94)
3539	James Chambers	Cascade (4/21/90)	Colden (10/8/94)
3540	Heidi R. Roland	Seymour (10/27/82)	Haystack (10/9/94)
3541	Mary S. MacDonald	Esther (9/15/85)	Redfield (10/9/94)
3542	Sandy Bonanno	Cascade (5/21/88)	Whiteface (10/9/94)
3543	Nancie Battaglia	Algonquin (5/80)	Haystack (10/9/94)
3544	Trudy Welch	Marcy (7/16/88)	Santanoni (10/9/94)
3545	Todd A. Roberts	Dix (10/75)	Haystack (10/12/94)
3546	Len Cormier	Marcy (9/72)	Basin (10/13/94)
3547	Scott E. Punter	Whiteface (9/3/82)	Esther (10/15/94)
3548	Mark Woods	Giant (7/22/89)	Cascade (10/15/94)
3549	Robert J. Woods	Gothics (8/13/88)	Cascade (10/15/94)
3550	John E. Fitzgerald, Jr.	Marcy (7/73)	Esther (10/15/94)
3551	John F. Richey	Algonquin (5/4/91)	Esther (10/15/94)
3552	James D. Malumphy	Algonquin (11/89)	Cascade (10/15/94)
3553W	John N. Rutledge	Colden (7/57)	Phelps (10/16/94)
3554	Cindy Gretzinger	Algonquin (6/4/88)	Iroquois (10/16/94)
3555	Nick Gretzinger	Algonquin (6/4/88)	Iroquois (10/16/94)
3556	Robert W. Craver	Algonquin (8/23/75)	Sawteeth (10/16/94)
3557	Todd Stinson	Cascade (8/1/77)	Allen (10/17/94)
3558	Gregory R. Blomquist	Marcy (spring 1970)	Emmons (10/23/94)
3559	Lorri Willett-Thatcher	Giant (5/90)	Phelps (10/29/94)
3560	Sally McGuirk	Cascade (9/12/93)	Big Slide (10/30/94)
3561W	Daniel Poole	Phelps (3/17/92)	Blake (11/5/94)
3562	Gary J. Dempster	Algonquin (8/89)	Whiteface (11/11/94)
3563	Kathy Hudson	Gothics (8/1/88)	Armstrong (11/13/94)
3564	Susan Hendler	Phelps (7/26/90)	Marcy (12/3/94)
3565	Dominick LoSurdo	Marcy (9/6/91)	Seymour (12/11/94)
3566W	Dennis P. Weaver	Marcy (9/6/91)	Seymour (12/11/94)
3567	Philip G. Wolff	Marcy (8/28)	Nye (9/40)
3568	Brian A. Bronfman	Cascade (1973)	Street (10/8/77)
3569	John P. Gaffey	Marcy (6/15/83)	Haystack (11/7/86)
3570	Mark T. Lee	Marcy (10/71)	Santanoni (5/18/94)
3571	Michael J. Lewis	Macomb (6/22/91)	Big Slide (8/18/94)
3572	Arthur Mansfield	Algonquin (8/73)	Rocky Peak (8/24/94)
3573	Susan A. Earley	Phelps (8/19/90)	Emmons (9/2/94)
3574	Derek Koniz	Phelps (6/30/77)	Sawteeth (9/4/94)
3575	Keith J. Lyons	Phelps (8/70)	Blake (9/17/94)
3576	Margaret Jacobs	Wright (7/4/86)	Haystack (9/30/94)
3577	Mark D. Olson	Lower Wolf Jaw (6/13/87)	Allen (10/2/94)
3578	Suzanne B. Olson	Lower Wolf Jaw (6/13/87)	Allen (10/2/94)
3579	Lisa C. Wiebrecht	Cascade (unknown)	Whiteface (10/7/94)
3580	Lynsey M. Fitzgerald	Upper Wolf Jaw (6/6/92)	Esther (10/15/94)
3581	Thomas H. Petersen	Big Slide (6/8/91)	Gothics (4/15/95)
3582	William B. Widlund	Cascade (6/13/71)	Marshall (4/20/95)
3583	Christopher J. Dunkerley	Wright (fall 1992)	Gray (4/28/95)
3584W	Karl R. Johnson	Cascade (6/30/89)	Sawteeth (5/7/95)
3585	Gail Hoffman	Phelps (2/9/91)	Dix (5/13/95)
3586	Gyula Pech	Marcy (7/1/89)	Nippletop (5/20/95)
3587	Charles Spyra	Phelps (5/24/83)	Allen (5/20/95)
3588	Jean Holcomb	Whiteface (summer 1984)	Macomb (5/27/95)
3589W	Dick Daniels	Marcy (10/15/88)	Colden (5/28/95)

Heaven Up-h'isted-ness!

	Member	First Ascent	Forty-sixth Peak
3590	Ernest C. Laug	Big Slide (3/10/89)	Whiteface (5/29/95)
3591	Hanns C. Meissner	Marcy (7/62)	Allen (6/3/95)
3592	Garry Brettbach	Tabletop (5/24/75)	Street (6/3/95)
3593	Mark Styczynski	Algonquin (5/3/93)	Allen (6/5/95)
3594	Ernest Valera	Algonquin (6/14/92)	Big Slide (6/6/95)
3595	Arlene Valera	Algonquin (6/14/92)	Big Slide (6/6/95)
3596	James A. Taub	Marcy (8/31/78)	Hough (6/7/95)
3597	John Cobb	Phelps (1/15/94)	Rocky Peak (6/17/95)
3598	Gregory J. Bown	Nippletop (6/27/93)	Big Slide (6/24/95)
3599	Mary Anne E. Martone	Big Slide (4/30/95)	Cascade (6/26/95)
3600	Lori S. Lasher	Algonquin (6/10/90)	Allen (6/26/95)
3601	Tarrence Lasher	Marshall (6/21/75)	Allen (6/26/95)
3602	Joan Farrell	Cascade (10/75)	Skylight (7/1/95)
3603	Jean A. Leonhardt	Giant (7/28/92)	Gray (7/3/95)
3604	Robert Leonhardt	Giant (7/28/92)	Gray (7/3/95)
3605	Thomas F. Powers	Giant (7/28/85)	Whiteface (7/3/95)
3606	John H. Fennessey	Big Slide (8/27/85)	Iroquois (7/6/95)
3607	Nancy Brunet	Marcy (7/6/83)	Iroquois (7/7/95)
3608	David Karpeles	Algonquin (7/5/82)	Big Slide (7/8/95)
3609	Robert S. Karpeles	Phelps (10/10/87)	Big Slide (7/8/95)
3610	Arthur H. Graves	Wright (7/29/82)	Whiteface (7/9/95)
3611	William R. Jasewicz	Marcy (8/19/86)	Whiteface (7/11/95)
3612	Patrick D. Quinn	Marcy (10/60)	Emmons (7/12/95)
3613	Ronald C. Dombroski	Santanoni (7/73)	Esther (7/14/95)
3614	John T. Mainey	Giant (9/82)	Esther (7/14/95)
3615	Bob Mattice	Marcy (6/69)	Esther (7/14/95)
3616	Barbara A. Monsour	Marcy (6/8/93)	Haystack (7/15/95)
3617	Donald P. Smith	Marcy (6/8/93)	Haystack (7/15/95)
3618	Matthew R. Patrick	Giant (10/88)	Seymour (7/16/95)
3619	Courtney D. Young, Jr.	Haystack (8/64)	Couchsachraga (7/19/95)
3620	Waldo Hutchins, III	Giant (1940's)	Blake (7/20/95)
3621	David Larson	Big Slide (8/21/93)	Allen (7/22/95)
3622W	William T. Bechtel	Giant (9/72)	Whiteface (7/22/95)
3623	William Todd Bechtel	Giant (9/83)	Whiteface (7/22/95)
3624	Audra Rice	Macomb (7/91)	Whiteface (7/22/95)
3625	W. Randolph Franklin	Marcy (9/9/78)	Rocky Peak (7/22/95)
3626W	Anton M. Solomon	Cascade (7/18/93)	Hough (7/22/95)
3627	Stefan Palys	Whiteface (8/93)	Big Slide (7/24/95)
3628	Raymond J. Moreau	Cascade (5/28/92)	Hough (7/25/95)
3629	Robert A. Paradis	Cascade (5/28/92)	Hough (7/25/95)
3630	Edward F. Gabrosek	Marcy (7/25/73)	Tabletop (7/26/95)
3631	Robert T. Okolish	Haystack (8/9/71)	Tabletop (7/26/95)
3632	James Inskeep	Phelps (1/23/93)	Esther (7/27/95)
3633	Michael Gebhard	Marcy (summer 1983)	Gray (7/27/95)
3634	Charles A. Johnson	Marcy (9/77)	Esther (7/29/95)
3635	Brian L. Neumann	Algonquin (8/8/84)	Colden (7/29/95)
3636	Timothy C. Woods	Cascade (8/10/91)	Whiteface (7/29/95)
3637	Jeffrey P. Davidson	Street (7/18/93)	Whiteface (7/29/95)
3638	Kara Davidson	Street (7/18/93)	Whiteface (7/29/95)
3639	Mark E. Davidson	Street (7/18/93)	Whiteface (7/29/95)
3640	Mary H. Davidson	Street (7/18/93)	Whiteface (7/29/95)
3641	Michael S. Davidson	Street (7/18/93)	Whiteface (7/29/95)
3642W	Ron Lester	Giant (6/90)	Whiteface (7/29/95)
3643	Karen A. McKenney	Marcy (8/87)	Dix (7/29/95)
3644	Marilyn M. Schust	Algonquin (9/9/90)	Haystack (7/29/95)
3645	Dorlian A. Johnson	Marcy (6/3/89)	Whiteface (7/29/95)
3646	Charles A. Hoffer	Cascade (7/19/94)	Marcy (7/31/95)
3647	V. Lynn King Malerba	Cascade (7/19/94)	Marcy (7/31/95)
3648	William Astor	Big Slide (6/30/93)	Nye (8/2/95)
3649	Jon Strazza	Phelps (7/92)	Nye (8/2/95)
3650	Joao Pinto-Leite	Phelps (10/24/93)	Emmons (8/2/95)
3651	Cole L. Dinse	Cascade (7/12/88)	Whiteface (8/3/95)

The Membership Roster of the Adirondack Forty-Sixers

	Member	First Ascent	Forty-sixth Peak
3652	Barbara B. Whitman	Allen (8/2/75)	Couchsachraga (8/3/95)
3653	Bruce R. Roberts	Algonquin (7/10/82)	Iroquois (8/5/95)
3654	Ginny Schnipke	Algonquin (7/10/82)	Iroquois (8/5/95)
3655	Susan C. Elliott	Cascade (9/4/89)	Macomb (8/5/95)
3656	Stephen P. Elliott	Marcy (8/48)	Macomb (8/5/95)
3657	Ian S. Fairweather	Cascade (8/11/91)	Panther (8/5/95)
3658	Sanjai Parikh	Big Slide (10/91)	Panther (8/5/95)
3659	Joseph O. Grupp, Jr.	Marcy (8/69)	Colden (8/8/95)
3660	Jennifer Roth	Rocky Peak (7/88)	Esther (8/8/95)
3661	Jonathan D. Miller	Cascade (8/4/67)	Couchsachraga (8/8/95)
3662	David Nash	Big Slide (7/6/91)	Iroquois (8/9/95)
3663	David W. Knutsen	Whiteface (8/11/81)	Street (8/9/95)
3664	John Detwiler	Marcy (8/83)	Allen (8/10/95)
3665	Susan B. Queary	Colden (7/75)	Allen (8/12/95)
3666	Erik Schlimmer	Giant (10/94)	Emmons (8/12/95)
3667W	James Schneider	Phelps (9/26/92)	Seymour (8/13/95)
3668	Dale W. Harris	Wright (8/17/88)	Rocky Peak (8/16/95)
3669	Wade A. Harris	Wright (8/17/88)	Rocky Peak (8/16/95)
3670	John J. Ferro	Marcy (6/26/91)	Haystack (8/17/95)
3671	Greg Davis	Lower Wolf Jaw (3/15/83)	Giant (8/17/95)
3672	Darrell M. Smith	Lower Wolf Jaw (3/15/83)	Giant (8/17/95)
3673	Bruce E. Wyka	Phelps (2/28/82)	Porter (8/18/95)
3674	John Brennan	Big Slide (7/89)	Haystack (8/18/95)
3675	Daniel E. Brennan	Marcy (7/21/90)	Haystack (8/18/95)
3676	Jason G. Lillard	Phelps (unknown)	Dix (8/18/95)
3677	Richard A. Hull	Marcy (9/19/80)	Couchsachraga (8/18/95)
3678	Matthew L. Malkiewicz	Cascade (7/16/80)	Couchsachraga (8/18/95)
3679	Richard P. O'Connell	Wright (9/29/84)	Couchsachraga (8/18/95)
3680	Brian T. Schiffino	Armstrong (9/10/94)	Lower Wolf Jaw (8/19/95)
3681	James S. Carlson	Lower Wolf Jaw (5/17/92)	Haystack (8/19/95)
3682	Paul R. Finley	Lower Wolf Jaw (5/17/92)	Haystack (8/19/95)
3683	Lynn S. O'Brien	Marcy (6/7/79)	Whiteface (8/19/95)
3684	Don Clairmont	Rocky Peak (9/13/90)	Allen (8/20/95)
3685	Michele Sellingham	Porter (9/8/91)	Whiteface (8/20/95)
3686	Jennifer Nierman	Cascade (4/25/91)	Rocky Peak (8/20/95)
3687	Rhoda Bedell	Marcy (7/25/91)	Redfield (8/20/95)
3688	Leon Whitcomb, Sr.	Marcy (7/28/91)	Redfield (8/20/95)
3689	Herman S. Hoffman	Porter (7/4/91)	Redfield (8/20/95)
3690	Ernest L. Manchin	Wright (7/29/84)	Santanoni (8/21/95)
3691	Michael J. Walker	Marcy (9/19/85)	Santanoni (8/21/95)
3692	Joan E. Baldwin	Cascade (9/27/88)	Skylight (8/22/95)
3693	Mark J. Colligan	Algonquin (7/86)	Whiteface (8/26/95)
3694	James E. Bansbach	Colden (8/78)	Esther (8/26/95)
3695	Alan E. Benson	Cascade (7/24/84)	Gray (8/26/95)
3696	Kirsten R. Benson	Cascade (7/24/84)	Gray (8/26/95)
3697	Margaret Sheldon	Colvin (8/3/91)	Whiteface (8/26/95)
3698	Joanne Whitney	Haystack (8/74)	Whiteface (8/26/95)
3699	Diane Demetriou	Phelps (8/24/91)	Wright (8/26/95)
3700	Gabriel A. Holmes	Cascade (1984)	Santanoni (8/26/95)
3701	Ralph A. Julian	Cascade (5/22/93)	Couchsachraga (8/26/95)
3702	Michael R. Capuano	Big Slide (9/4/94)	Whiteface (8/26/95)
3703W	Donna M. Jerdo	Cascade (6/94)	Whiteface (8/26/95)
3704W	Stewart Jerdo	Cascade (6/94)	Whiteface (8/26/95)
3705	Joel Cadbury	Big Slide (7/83)	Tabletop (8/26/95)
3706	Jacob Brown II	Dix (8/10/82)	Whiteface (8/27/95)
3707	Shane W. Brown	Dix (8/10/82)	Whiteface (8/27/95)
3708	Daniel N. Johnson	Cascade (8/6/94)	Wright (8/27/95)
3709	Patricia W. Johnson	Cascade (8/6/94)	Wright (8/27/95)
3710	Joanne Scheibly	Marcy (unknown)	Skylight (8/29/95)
3711	Matthew T. Wheeler	Cascade (5/9/93)	Marshall (8/29/95)
3712	Terry A. Peters	Porter (8/12/91)	Whiteface (8/30/95)
3713	Jeffrey L. Newcomer	Marcy (9/10/94)	Panther (9/1/95)

Heaven Up-h'isted-ness!

	Member	First Ascent	Forty-sixth Peak
3714	Brian T. Fovel	Cascade (4/21/79)	Whiteface (9/1/95)
3715	Sherry Eborn-Fovel	Cascade (4/21/79)	Whiteface (9/1/95)
3716	Peter Benoit	Big Slide (11/10/77)	Iroquois (9/2/95)
3717	Brad M. Hurlbrut	Wright (summer 1992)	Esther (9/2/95)
3718	Muriel A. Hesler	Santanoni (8/24/76)	Haystack (9/2/95)
3719	Lynn M. Achee	Giant (10/11/86)	Allen (9/2/95)
3720	Daniel P. Flanigan	Algonquin (8/7/89)	Seward (9/2/95)
3721	Geoffrey C. Walsh	Esther (8/22/88)	Seward (9/2/95)
3722	George J. Walsh, III	Esther (8/22/88)	Seward (9/2/95)
3723	Matthew Walsh	Esther (8/22/88)	Seward (9/2/95)
3724	Wilma R. Cipolla	Wright (7/31/75)	Saddleback (9/2/95)
3725	Sanford S. Whittum	Seward (8/27/75)	Saddleback (9/2/95)
3726	Christopher K. Savastio	Colvin (summer 1983)	Haystack (9/3/95)
3727	Dana Fast	Marcy (9/88)	Skylight (9/3/95)
3728	John Sanderson	Marcy (7/85)	Giant (9/3/95)
3729	David P. Young	Colden (7/3/93)	Dix (9/4/95)
3730	Randy Glenn	Giant (7/1/90)	Whiteface (9/4/95)
3731	Raphael Holmes	Cascade (7/29/88)	Marcy (9/4/95)
3732	Kimberly B. Cheney	Cascade (1947)	Allen (9/6/95)
3733	John R. Moravek	Dix (6/18/86)	Couchsachraga (9/9/95)
3734	Ralph C. Green	Whiteface (5/24/78)	Cliff (9/9/95)
3735	Roger Huestis	Whiteface (7/92)	Skylight (9/9/95)
3736	Carol Burchett	Marcy (10/11/91)	Seymour (9/9/95)
3737	John Burchett	Marcy (10/11/91)	Seymour (9/9/95)
3738	Stephen M. Burchett	Marcy (10/11/91)	Seymour (9/9/95)
3739	Monica A. Haus	Cascade (10/14/90)	Whiteface (9/10/95)
3740	Laurence Vogel	Cascade (6/7/95)	Santanoni (9/15/95)
3741	Daniel F. Joynt	Algonquin (7/4/85)	Allen (9/16/95)
3742	Gael A. Lord	Algonquin (7/4/85)	Allen (9/16/95)
3743W	Ralph T. Keating	Algonquin (5/18/77)	Esther (9/16/95)
3744	Garrett Traver	Algonquin (1/78)	Redfield (9/16/95)
3745	Barbara A. Relles	Cascade (5/16/7?)	Allen (9/16/95)
3746	Howard M. Relles	Lower Wolf Jaw (11/2/75)	Allen (9/16/95)
3747	Cecelia V. Graves	Giant (6/29/91)	Whiteface (9/16/95)
3748	Bruce C. Graves	Giant (6/29/91)	Whiteface (9/16/95)
3749	Mary Angela Farber	Algonquin (8/88)	Whiteface (9/16/95)
3750	David T. Farber	Dix (5/29/93)	Whiteface (9/16/95)
3751	James R. Heckathorne	Algonquin (7/10/92)	Whiteface (9/16/95)
3752	Krysa Heckathorne	Algonquin (7/10/92)	Whiteface (9/16/95)
3753	Tom Hardes	Algonquin (7/4/86)	Marshall (9/16/95)
3754	Dwain M. White	Big Slide (8/57)	Street (9/16/95)
3755	David E. Radus	Marcy (9/7/91)	Haystack (9/16/95)
3756	Janet S. Kubli	Skylight (7/12/79)	Haystack (9/17/95)
3757	Allison C. Kozel	Cascade (8/30/87)	Colden (9/17/95)
3758	Joseph C. Rossi	Whiteface (1/8/95)	Marshall (9/18/95)
3759	Alan R. Fairbanks	Marcy (9/9/62)	Haystack (9/20/95)
3760	Elaine E. Fairbanks	Marcy (1955)	Haystack (9/20/95)
3761	James L. Severino	Phelps (11/17/90)	Panther (9/22/95)
3762	Scott Vonderheide	Marcy (7/13/93)	Phelps (9/23/95)
3763W	Leo Briand	Phelps (4/22/89)	Whiteface (9/23/95)
3764	Marjorie Allshouse	Colden (9/15/90)	Whiteface (9/23/95)
3765	Jeffrey R. Ritter	Algonquin (8/72)	Nippletop (9/23/95)
3766	Anna Herbert	Tabletop (6/89)	Armstrong (9/23/95)
3767	Mark W. Sullivan	Marcy (9/12/90)	Rocky Peak (9/24/95)
3768	Diana M. Cogan	Gothics (6/26/84)	Colden (9/24/95)
3769	Alexander G. Gonzalez	Giant (7/1975)	Marshall (9/24/95)
3770	Thomas U. Wallenhorst	Cascade (7/7/91)	Skylight (9/24/95)
3771	John F. Wallenhorst	Algonquin (7/25/92)	Skylight (9/24/95)
3772	James L. Morley	Upper Wolf Jaw (7/15/84)	Wright (9/24/95)
3773	Kevin C. Morley	Upper Wolf Jaw (7/15/84)	Wright (9/24/95)
3774	Thomas McGuire	Haystack (8/28/91)	Rocky Peak (9/24/95)
3775	Peggy DeArmond-Rogers	Marcy (7/7/84)	Panther (9/24/95)

THE MEMBERSHIP ROSTER OF THE ADIRONDACK FORTY-SIXERS

	MEMBER	FIRST ASCENT	FORTY-SIXTH PEAK
3776	John P. Greene	Wright (9/9/78)	Emmons (9/25/95)
3777	Margaret Freifeld	Marcy (1969)	Sawteeth (9/25/95)
3778	Michael M. Tersegno	Lower Wolf Jaw (9/6/88)	Couchsachraga (9/25/95)
3779	Richard J. Longo	Giant (5/12/92)	Skylight (9/25/95)
3780	Garfield P. Raymond	Giant (4/30/95)	Couchsachraga (9/26/95)
3781	Paul W. Osuch	Phelps (5/28/93)	Blake (9/27/95)
3782	Michael D. Stempek	Cascade (9/74)	Gothics (9/29/95)
3783	David T. Poyer	Marcy (9/16/89)	Skylight (9/30/95)
3784	Judith M. Harbison	Cascade (7/4/88)	Saddleback (9/30/95)
3785	Kenneth G. Harbison	Cascade (7/4/88)	Saddleback (9/30/95)
3786	Jean Quattrocchi	Big Slide (8/82)	Cascade (10/1/95)
3787	Joseph Ryan	Marcy (9/13/93)	East Dix (10/1/95)
3788	Doreen Curtin	Cascade (7/79)	Rocky Peak (10/1/95)
3789	Rachel Parent	Phelps (10/24/93)	Esther (10/1/95)
3790	Martin Franklin	Marcy (7/8/92)	Allen (10/1/95)
3791	Susan Franklin	Marcy (7/8/92)	Allen (10/1/95)
3792	Mark S. Nygard	Marcy (2/27/78)	Hough (10/4/95)
3793	Peter Finley	Lower Wolf Jaw (5/17/92)	Nippletop (10/7/95)
3794	Joseph R. Jordan, III	Algonquin (7/79)	Santanoni (10/7/95)
3795	Robert G. Frawley	Algonquin (9/1/71)	Allen (10/7/95)
3796	Owen McCarty	Marcy (5/85)	Street (10/7/95)
3797	Russ Guard	Cascade (4/20/90)	Haystack (10/8/95)
3798	David L. Rosebrook	Giant (10/6/90)	Haystack (10/8/95)
3799	Renier Scheening	Algonquin (9/84)	Haystack (10/8/95)
3800	James L. Brown	Giant (7/1/90)	Whiteface (10/8/95)
3801	James W. Brown, III	Giant (7/1/90)	Whiteface (10/8/95)
3802	Timothy A. Gerling	Esther (10/2/94)	Allen (10/8/95)
3803	Martha A. DeLarm	Cascade (6/7/92)	Sawteeth (10/8/95)
3804	Katherine S. Halloran	Marcy (8/64)	Sawteeth (10/8/95)
3805	Gary Wilson	Colden (9/17/83)	Nippletop (10/8/95)
3806W	Marguerite Munch-Weber	Tabletop (7/31/93)	Cliff (10/8/95)
3807	Cathrine Moore	Marcy (8/23/88)	Cliff (10/8/95)
3808	Thomas J. McNamara	Giant (9/6/86)	Santanoni (10/8/95)
3809	David A. Page	Dix (5/14/92)	Seymour (10/8/95)
3810	Timothy D. Kelley	Algonquin (1/13/90)	Blake (10/9/95)
3811	Peter E. Van de Water	Marcy (summer 1948)	Whiteface (10/9/95)
3812	Bryan S. Dawson	Algonquin (4/1/95)	Panther (10/9/95)
3813	Joan Ferguson	Giant (summer 1981)	Haystack (10/12/95)
3814	Joseph G. Busch	Phelps (9/28/92)	Haystack (10/12/95)
3815	James M. Coyne	Phelps (5/11/79)	Dix (10/13/95)
3816	Gregory Fullman	Lower Wolf Jaw (8/7/94)	Whiteface (10/14/95)
3817	Chris Huestis	Marcy (5/13/89)	Whiteface (10/14/95)
3818	Donald Towers	Marcy (9/8/84)	Allen (10/15/95)
3819	Nathan C. Towers	Colden (9/7/85)	Allen (10/16/95)
3820	John Bousman	Giant (7/18/54)	Redfield (10/20/95)
3821	Richard G. Kramer	Marcy (10/52)	Redfield (10/20/95)
3822	Thomas R. Folts	Wright (7/68)	Esther (10/25/95)
3823	Don Dozier	Marcy (10/86)	Esther (10/29/95)
3824	Jean-René Hickey	Phelps (5/23/90)	Marcy (10/29/95)
3825	David Koschnick	Porter (3/19/95)	Marcy (10/31/95)
3826	Jerry Wiley	Porter (3/19/95)	Marcy (10/31/95)
3827	David C. Glenn	Colvin (6/18/94)	Haystack (11/4/95)
3828	Lynn A. Davies	Cascade (9/90)	Haystack (11/4/95)
3829	Kathy Thew	Algonquin (7/10/93)	Haystack (11/4/95)
3830	Mark Novak	Giant (10/6/90)	Allen (11/11/95)
3831	Thomas Winterberger	Giant (10/90)	Allen (11/11/95)
3832	Anthony J. Quinn	Marcy (8/78)	Sawteeth (11/11/95)
3833	Bruce Wright	Giant (5/6/92)	Whiteface (9/27/92)
3834	William B. Mulfinger	Marcy (1968)	Hough (8/18/93)
3835	Gretchen A. Zierick	Colden (7/68)	South Dix (7/24/94)
3836	William A. Turner	Marcy (8/68)	Sawteeth (8/11/94)
3837	Steven Healey	Marcy (summer 1990)	Allen (9/5/94)

Heaven Up-h'isted-ness!

	Member	First Ascent	Forty-sixth Peak
3838	Charles S. Herne	Giant (8/8/87)	Whiteface (9/5/94)
3839	Thomas S. Bastian	Colden (10/12/85)	Wright (1/1/95)
3840	Richard J. Kraft	Algonquin (8/15/80)	Seymour (6/17/95)
3841	Joey Elton	Phelps (7/83)	Giant (8/5/95)
3842	Jeffrey S. Prime	Whiteface (10/5/64)	Basin (8/12/95)
3843	Nancy D. Haswell	Marcy (8/5/80)	Rocky Peak (8/13/95)
3844	Mary Jo Bowdoin	Marcy (10/8/83)	East Dix (8/26/95)
3845	Lisa Meissner	Lower Wolf Jaw (1975)	Haystack (9/2/95)
3846	Klaus E. Meissner	Marcy (1966)	Saddleback (9/2/95)
3847	Janine M. DuMond	Lower Wolf Jaw (7/82)	Emmons (9/4/95)
3848	Lara Anne DuMond	Whiteface (9/89)	Emmons (9/4/95)
3849	Alan Wechsler	Saddleback (9/15/84)	Allen (9/6/95)
3850	Joseph Moser	Wright (6/25/83)	Couchsachraga (9/20/95)
3851	L. James Standen	Wright (6/25/83)	Couchsachraga (9/20/95)
3852	John M. Bansbach	Haystack (8/81)	Wright (10/7/95)
3853	Barry A. Brown	Colden (9/80)	Emmons (10/9/95)
3854	John J. Fowler	Wright (5/9/92)	Haystack (11/24/95)
3855W	Alan K. Lamb	Lower Wolf Jaw (1/10/87)	Marshall (1/21/96)
3856	Raymond C. Van Orden	Wright (8/91)	Marshall (2/6/96)
3857	John S. Perkins	Wright (8/91)	Marshall (2/6/96)
3858W	Steven E. Herrmann	Wright (2/86)	Santanoni (3/10/96)
3859	Brian J. Reader	Cascade (6/10/94)	Gothics (4/5/96)
3860	Ronald L. Wilson	Giant (8/91)	Allen (4/28/96)
3861W	Tim Hay	Allen (5/27/78)	Haystack (5/25/96)
3862	Anthony Chan	Giant (7/4/95)	Seymour (5/25/96)
3863	Bruce A. LaPlant	Marcy (7/2/91)	Whiteface (5/26/96)
3864	Michael F. Lonergan	Dix (5/21/95)	Santanoni (5/26/96)
3865	Michael G. Buono	Seymour (10/82)	Nippletop (5/31/96)
3866	Deborah D. Keough	Marcy (10/12/72)	Skylight (6/1/96)
3867	Richard D. Mules	Dix (5/16/80)	Dial (6/1/96)
3868	John M. Shiel	Cascade (8/19/92)	Seymour (6/9/96)
3869W	Michael P. McLean	Giant (6/25/89)	Haystack (6/14/96)
3870	Pamela J. McLean	Giant (6/25/89)	Haystack (6/14/96)
3871	Thomas Mason	Colden (2/93)	Big Slide (6/6/96)
3872W	Maria B. Hosmer-Briggs	Big Slide (unknown)	Esther (6/16/96)
3873W	J. Michael Forsyth	Marcy (6/2/73)	Esther (6/16/96)
3874W	William J. Johnson	Cascade (10/14/84)	Colden (6/29/96)
3875W	Connie J. Morrison	Cascade (7/1/93)	Colden (6/29/96)
3876	Jeffrey Knapp	Marcy (5/26/81)	Esther (6/29/96)
3877	Alfred O. Peters	Upper Wolf Jaw (7/2/95)	Emmons (7/1/96)
3878	Joan Peters	Upper Wolf Jaw (7/2/95)	Emmons (7/1/96)
3879	Michael E. Promowicz	Marshall (7/18/93)	Colden (7/2/96)
3880	Brian H. Universal	Marshall (7/18/93)	Colden (7/2/96)
3881	Brigit Loud	Cascade (9/86)	Allen (7/4/96)
3882	Richard Hart	Algonquin (7/5/88)	Gray (7/7/96)
3883W	John Lange	Algonquin (10/83)	Giant (7/7/96)
3884	Danny W. Scott	Wright (5/14/77)	Gray (7/9/95)
3885	Ludlow Miller	Armstrong (8/78)	Whiteface (7/10/96)
3886	Kevin MacDonald	Gothics (6/28/93)	Emmons (7/11/96)
3887	Riley J. Graebner	Cascade (8/21/88)	Rocky Peak (7/14/96)
3888	Dianne Bennett	Algonquin (8/8/82)	Rocky Peak (7/14/96)
3889	William Graebner	Algonquin (8/8/82)	Rocky Peak (7/14/96)
3890	John P. Washburn	Marcy (6/20/92)	Tabletop (7/17/96)
3891	Peter C. Stein	Big Slide (6/91)	Rocky Peak (7/19/96)
3892	Cody Washburn	Marcy (6/20/92)	Tabletop (7/19/96)
3893	Michael K. Washburn	Marcy (6/20/92)	Tabletop (7/19/96)
3894	Karen Hibbard	Colden (5/18/85)	Iroquois (7/20/96)
3895	Todd R. Cohen	Porter (7/1/85)	Tabletop (7/21/96)
3896	Chris Durlacher	Cascade (9/5/91)	Dial (7/21/96)
3897	Robert C. Burchett	Marcy (10/11/91)	Panther (7/25/96)
3898	Evan Macosko	Cascade (7/10/92)	Marshall (7/26/96)
3899	Jake H. Black	Marcy (9/21/91)	Allen (7/27/96)

The Membership Roster of the Adirondack Forty-Sixers

	Member	First Ascent	Forty-sixth Peak
3900	Jim Black	Marcy (9/21/91)	Allen (7/27/96)
3901	Judy Black	Marcy (9/21/91)	Allen (7/27/96)
3902	Thomas M. Black	Marcy (9/21/91)	Allen (7/27/96)
3903	Daniel Granger	Cascade (8/82)	Whiteface (7/27/96)
3904	Charles W. Cammack, III	Lower Wolf Jaw (9/5/71)	Emmons (7/30/96)
3905	Michael Bear	Dix (7/95)	Whiteface (8/1/96)
3906	Christopher R. Faust	Giant (7/93)	Whiteface (8/1/96)
3907	Brian Gluck	Big Slide (6/94)	Whiteface (8/1/96)
3908	Kurt P. Hinterkopf	Lower Wolf Jaw (6/93)	Whiteface (8/1/96)
3909	Paul Lilley	Iroquois (7/94)	Whiteface (8/1/96)
3910	Micah Shaw	Giant (7/94)	Whiteface (8/1/96)
3911	Ryan Yeskoo	Giant (7/93)	Whiteface (8/1/96)
3912	Peter Lane	Upper Wolf Jaw (7/91)	Whiteface (8/1/96)
3913	Russell T. Vought	Marcy (6/91)	Whiteface (8/1/96)
3914	Shai S. Walker	Whiteface (7/93)	Santanoni (8/1/96)
3915	C. Thomas McCall	Algonquin (8/9/64)	Esther (8/3/96)
3916	Hilary A. Papineau	Sawteeth (7/5/94)	Santanoni (8/4/96)
3917	Philip H. Gitlen	Sawteeth (6/88)	Haystack (8/5/96)
3918	Samantha Galloway	Dial (7/89)	Skylight (8/5/96)
3919W	Daniel H. Herbert	Redfield (6/17/94)	Haystack (8/5/96)
3920	Dennis W. Broadwell	Wright (5/24/87)	Seymour (8/6/96)
3921	Nat Silver	Cliff (7/15/94)	Iroquois (8/6/96)
3922	Morgan Goodwin	Cascade (7/3/89)	Santanoni (8/6/96)
3923	Alex Lazar	Giant (7/93)	Basin (8/7/96)
3924	Matthew D. Fowler	Giant (summer 1992)	Sawteeth (8/7/96)
3925	Karen Robards	Big Slide (8/89)	East Dix (8/7/96)
3926	John Macauley	Porter (7/12/94)	Gothics (8/7/96)
3927	David P. Ransom	Lower Wolf Jaw (7/20/93)	Whiteface (8/7/96)
3928	Louise F. Ransom	Lower Wolf Jaw (7/20/93)	Whiteface (8/7/96)
3929	Travis W. Scott	Cascade (9/10/88)	Saddleback (8/10/96)
3930	Charles C. Weld	Wright (1959)	Street (8/10/96)
3931	Martha L. Townley	Cascade (10/86)	Whiteface (8/11/96)
3932	Kristen Whitbeck	Rocky Peak (5/12/90)	Allen (8/11/96)
3933	Harald Fuller-Bennett	Phelps (7/93)	Colden (8/12/96)
3934	Zach Youngerman	Marcy (8/92)	Rocky Peak (8/12/96)
3935	Gregory L. Lyons	Marcy (6/24/90)	Haystack (8/13/96)
3936	Nick Barrett	Cascade (1967)	Emmons (8/14/96)
3937	Adam Ruder	Cascade (7/92)	Allen (8/15/96)
3938	Corey J. Forett	Whiteface (5/5/94)	Dix (8/15/96)
3939	Dale J. LaClair	Whiteface (5/5/94)	Dix (8/15/96)
3940	Samuel James	Marcy (12/28/36)	Haystack (8/15/96)
3941	Adam Giroux	Phelps (6/94)	Marshall (8/15/96)
3942	Sharon Flanagan	Big Slide (9/3/94)	Allen (8/17/96)
3943W	Nerses Ohanian	East Dix (11/25/94)	Allen (8/17/96)
3944	Peter B. Howell	Porter (8/14/89)	Marcy (8/17/96)
3945	Olivia S. Dwyer	Giant (7/7/92)	Whiteface (8/17/96)
3946	Erica Heiman	Cascade (7/25/91)	Colvin (8/17/96)
3947	Keith S. Murray	Algonquin (7/88)	Marcy (8/17/96)
3948	Norma G. Murray	Cascade (9/13/91)	Marcy (8/17/96)
3949	Cindy D. Berberich	Wright (6/1/91)	Allen (8/17/96)
3950	Brenden Shiel	Nye (10/23/94)	Sawteeth (8/18/96)
3951	Suzanne Blood	Whiteface (11/75)	Phelps (8/18/96)
3952	William Blood	Giant (10/86)	Phelps (8/18/96)
3953	Christine B. Gold	Sawteeth (8/62)	Allen (8/19/96)
3954	Robert Thomas	Macomb (9/4/93)	Allen (8/19/96)
3955	Henry Frueh	Marcy (7/18/80)	Couchsachraga (8/19/96)
3956	James C. Brust	Sawteeth (8/86)	Whiteface (8/20/96)
3957	John C. Brust	Giant (7/49)	Whiteface (8/20/96)
3958	Irene A. Royce	Gothics (8/23/88)	Santanoni (8/21/96)
3959	Christopher Murray	Cascade (7/5/93)	Colden (8/22/96)
3960	Kevin Murray	Cascade (7/5/93)	Colden (8/22/96)
3961	Ruth M. Gais	Giant (7/61)	Marshall (8/22/96)

Heaven Up-h'isted-ness!

	Member	First Ascent	Forty-sixth Peak
3962	Benjamin Baum	Porter (7/7/93)	Iroquois (8/22/96)
3963	Jonathan S. Blackwell	Big Slide (7/27/91)	Iroquois (8/23/96)
3964	Walter B. Blackwell	Porter (5/19/91)	Iroquois (8/23/96)
3965	Donald E. Gjertson	Marcy (6/18/95)	Allen (8/23/96)
3966	Niels K. Gjertson	Marcy (6/18/95)	Allen (8/23/96)
3967	Lorraine C. Smith	Cascade (10/7/89)	Porter (8/23/96)
3968	Tristan D. Roberts	Cascade (8/29/88)	Street (8/24/96)
3969	Kenvyn Richards	Marcy (8/20/56)	Marshall (8/24/96)
3970	Erik Mash	Lower Wolf Jaw (6/12/76)	Esther (8/24/96)
3971	Stefan Mash	Giant (7/17/82)	Esther (8/24/96)
3972	Joshua M. Segal	Porter (7/7/93)	Rocky Peak (8/24/96)
3973	Jessica Stites	Cascade (7/91)	Colden (8/24/96)
3974	Richard J. Prestopnik	Giant (8/13/78)	Esther (8/25/96)
3975	Judy R. James	Algonquin (6/81)	Allen (8/25/96)
3976	Tim Martin	Gothics (10/80)	Esther (8/25/96)
3977	Orrin C. Stevens	Big Slide (10/6/89)	Esther (8/25/96)
3978	Larry Ebert	Dix (7/77)	Cascade (8/26/96)
3979	Dorothy D. Consadine	Gothics (8/1/87)	Panther (8/27/96)
3980	Bernard Canning	Cascade (9/87)	Redfield (8/27/96)
3981W	Scott Yakey	Cascade (9/87)	Redfield (8/27/96)
3982	Kelly Moody	Big Slide (10/1/94)	Hough (8/28/96)
3983	David I. Harvey	Cascade (6/62)	Whiteface (8/28/96)
3984	Zachary D. Harvey	Dix (9/1/91)	Whiteface (8/28/96)
3985	Albert G. Andrejcak	Seymour (9/2/78)	Sawteeth (8/30/96)
3986	Tate M. Connor	Allen (8/23/94)	Haystack (8/30/96)
3987	Roger Borgen	Lower Wolf Jaw (7/76)	Cliff (8/31/96)
3988	Irene A. Logan	Colden (5/28/94)	Emmons (8/31/96)
3989	Jordan Alterbaum	Cascade (9/1/89)	Whiteface (8/31/96)
3990	Debbie Price	Cascade (6/28/92)	Basin (8/31/96)
3991	Conor E. O'Brien	Porter (7/4/93)	Santanoni (8/31/96)
3992	Joseph Clark	Giant (8/76)	Whiteface (8/31/96)
3993	Robert S. McLaughlin	Algonquin (8/29/89)	Allen (9/2/96)
3994	Alison J. Richards	Macomb (6/23/95)	East Dix (9/2/96)
3995	Arthur Bufogle, Jr.	Giant (10/14/84)	Allen (9/5/96)
3996	Sterling Salter	Colvin (8/19/93)	Rocky Peak (9/7/96)
3997	Christopher J. Konowitz	Cascade (1974)	Rocky Peak (9/7/96)
3998	Mary Ellen Bloniarz	Gothics (9/22/88)	Whiteface (9/14/96)
3999	Maureen A. Worden	Giant (9/18/87)	Whiteface (9/14/96)
4000	Miles K. Moody	Wright (5/30/63)	Big Slide (9/15/96)
4001	Edward Cibulsky	Esther (9/17/87)	Saddleback (9/15/96)
4002	Stephen A. Morrissey	Cascade (9/29/82)	Emmons (9/19/96)
4003	Lonnie B. Rood	Giant (8/4/90)	Saddleback (9/20/96)
4004	Normand LaForest	Phelps (9/6/87)	Haystack (9/21/96)
4005	Floyd R. Welker	Lower Wolf Jaw (9/16/71)	Rocky Peak (9/21/96)
4006	Paul W. Poling	Colden (11/84)	Allen (9/21/96)
4007	John W. Sullivan	Colden (10/2/92)	Allen (9/21/96)
4008	John C. Lesher	Saddleback (9/28/91)	Allen (9/21/96)
4009	Joyce C. Cady	Iroquois (7/5/93)	Whiteface (9/21/96)
4010	Beth C. Burghardt	Cascade (8/22/92)	Whiteface (9/21/96)
4011	Frederick M. Burghardt	Cascade (8/22/92)	Whiteface (9/21/96)
4012	Susan Y. Leveillee	Cascade (4/13/89)	Marcy (9/21/96)
4013	Alane Vogel	Algonquin (8/22/91)	Gray (9/22/96)
4014	Bruce Rabsjohns	Algonquin (8/18/90)	Whiteface (9/28/96)
4015	Peter I. Howard	Cascade (9/79)	Colden (9/28/96)
4016	Rodrick J. Finley	Algonquin (8/75)	Seymour (9/28/96)
4017	Andrew M. Weibrecht	Cascade (8/89)	Haystack (9/29/96)
4018	Jonathan C. Weibrecht	Cascade (8/89)	Haystack (9/29/96)
4019	Megan Papineau	Sawteeth (7/15/94)	Haystack (9/29/96)
4020	John P. Custodio	Giant (7/20/92)	Allen (10/1/96)
4021W	Serge Theoret	Marcy (unknown)	Cliff (10/5/96)
4022	Kenneth C. Borgers	Whiteface (11/2/91)	Colden (10/5/96)
4023	Carl Anderson	Haystack (8/78)	Colden (10/5/96)

The Membership Roster of the Adirondack Forty-Sixers

	Member	First Ascent	Forty-sixth Peak
4024	Lawrence E. Fuller	Gray (8/27/88)	Colden (10/5/96)
4025W	Skip Young	Dix (7/77)	Hough (10/5/96)
4026	Michael Tarala	Colvin (8/81)	Esther (10/5/96)
4027	Mark C. Parrish	Haystack (7/10/79)	Gray (10/5/96)
4028	Reid Grayson	Rocky Peak (7/12/92)	Redfield (10/6/96)
4029	Jane Grayson	Rocky Peak (7/12/92)	Redfield (10/6/96)
4030	William F. DeCamp	Saddleback (1980)	Cascade (10/6/96)
4031	Kathy McAuley	Giant (10/15/89)	Hough (10/11/96)
4032	Kathleen M. Komar	Marcy (10/8/88)	Haystack (10/12/96)
4033	Thomas Anadio	Marcy (7/87)	Whiteface (10/12/96)
4034	Robert St. Dennis	Giant (9/16/91)	Whiteface (10/12/96)
4035	Thea Hoeth	Whiteface (8/23/91)	Gray (10/12/96)
4036	Barbara A. Bansbach	Cascade (10/12/80)	Haystack (10/12/96)
4037	Chelsea E. Faulkner	Algonquin (6/13/93)	Sawteeth (10/12/96)
4038	Michael Garneau	Haystack (6/15/96)	Street (10/13/96)
4039	Wendy R. Sayward	Marcy (1967)	Basin (10/13/96)
4040	Jim Lemmerman	Iroquois (8/19/93)	Whiteface (10/13/96)
4041	Craig A. Emblidge	Algonquin (5/23/76)	Basin (10/26/96)
4042	Alisa O'Hara	Big Slide (8/29/92)	Rocky Peak (10/26/96)
4043	Katie Balcke	Haystack (7/27/91)	Phelps (10/26/96)
4044	Thomas M. Rosato	Algonquin (8/29/91)	Seymour (10/27/96)
4045W	Robert Novick	Marcy (9/11/92)	Colden (10/27/96)
4046	Tom Kasenchak	Marcy (9/11/92)	Colden (10/27/96)
4047	George Tselekis	Marcy (10/11/81)	Dix (10/28/96)
4048	Stephen C. Ashline	Whiteface (5/5/94)	Giant (11/4/96)
4049W	Thomas W. Regan	Algonquin (7/4/95)	Haystack (11/6/96)
4050W	Linda L. Coldwell	Giant (6/14/95)	Seymour (11/7/96)
4051W	William B. Knoble	Gothics (11/76)	Seymour (11/7/96)
4052	John Borel	Marcy (8/13/73)	Esther (11/11/96)
4053	Edward R. Forse	Marcy (7/22/61)	Seymour (8/13/77)
4054	John W. Hall	Marcy (8/27/56)	Gray (9/22/85)
4055	Bruce Gafner	Colden (5/75)	Couchsachraga (9/3/91)
4056	Walter J. Smith	Colden (5/1/71)	Phelps (9/20/95)
4057	Susan Thomas	Haystack (9/3/94)	Allen (7/28/96)
4058	Christine S. Danker	Cascade (8/23/86)	Whiteface (8/17/96)
4059	Jillian Danker	Cascade (8/23/86)	Whiteface (8/17/96)
4060	Robert McKenzie	Marcy (7/17/82)	Whiteface (8/25/96)
4061	C. Michael Tuckett	Cascade (7/15/89)	Big Slide (9/9/96)
4062	Jason Turner	Marcy (6/92)	Whiteface (9/21/96)
4063	Larry G. Turner	Big Slide (1965)	Whiteface (9/21/96)
4064	Anthony Mullin	Phelps (12/31/84)	Sawteeth (9/29/96)
4065	Laura Mullin	Phelps (12/31/84)	Sawteeth (9/29/96)
4066	Jonathan A. French	Whiteface (unknown)	Algonquin (10/2/96)
4067	Bill Steinmetz	Giant (9/5/87)	Whiteface (10/12/96)
4068	Steven C. Sutton	Whiteface (5/69)	Allen (10/26/96)
4069W	Alain Chevrette	Marcy (11/95)	Saddleback (11/30/96)
4070	Michael H. Jacques	Algonquin (12/1/93)	Emmons (3/13/97)
4071W	Wilfred L. Desbiens	Cascade (12/22/94)	Big Slide (3/15/97)
4072W	Veto P. Napolitano	Phelps (1/88)	South Dix (3/16/97)
4073W	Rob Carlo	Lower Wolf Jaw (3/18/93)	Marshall (3/21/97)
4074	Kathy Mario	Wright (9/18/93)	Iroquois (5/26/97)
4075	Richard Rizzolo	Algonquin (9/30/73)	Whiteface (6/7/97)
4076	Jeffrey T. Tornyos	Wright (5/12/95)	Rocky Peak (6/9/97)
4077	Robert L. Forest	Cascade (9/2/91)	Emmons (6/20/97)
4078	James Testerink	Cascade (9/5/93)	Whiteface (6/28/97)
4079	Dirk J. Testerink	Cascade (9/5/93)	Whiteface (6/28/97)
4080	Shirley Testerink	Cascade (9/5/93)	Whiteface (6/28/97)
4081	Woody Bowler	Cascade (11/76)	Allen (7/3/97)
4082	Robert Bowler	Big Slide (9/15/85)	Allen (7/3/97)
4083	Carol Plant	Cascade (9/82)	Allen (7/5/97)
4084	Scott Plant	Marcy (9/68)	Allen (7/5/97)
4085	Brett A. Schildkraut	Wright (9/83)	Whiteface (7/5/97)

Heaven Up-h'isted-ness!

	Member	First Ascent	Forty-sixth Peak
4086	Howard Metzger	Algonquin (unknown)	Couchsachraga (7/6/97)
4087	Roland Ivers	Marcy (7/80)	Emmons (7/12/97)
4088	Peggy Wiltberger	Skylight (10/81)	Santanoni (7/12/97)
4089	Julia H. Macy	Whiteface (7/92)	Allen (7/16/97)
4090	Daniel L. Goerlich	Esther (5/25/92)	Couchsachraga (7/19/97)
4091W	James R. Weed II	Cascade (5/13/95)	Seymour (7/20/97)
4092	Jonathan Ellinger	Cascade (8/7/95)	Whiteface (7/22/97)
4093	Gregory P. Labas	Marcy (7/3/93)	Nippletop (7/22/97)
4094	David W. Carpenter	Big Slide (9/14/81)	Whiteface (7/22/97)
4095	David Durant	Big Slide (8/90)	Cascade (7/22/97)
4096	Jonathan W. Geller	Marcy (6/92)	Cascade (7/22/97)
4097	Bruce I. Isham	Esther (4/27/96)	Saddleback (7/26/97)
4098	Andrew W. Cullen	Nippletop (10/4/92)	Dial (8/1/97)
4099	Robert Reynolds	Marcy (summer 1978)	Marshall (8/2/97)
4100	Brian J. Bestle	Giant (7/21/90)	Marshall (8/2/97)
4101	Brian Castagnier	Giant (7/21/90)	Marshall (8/2/97)
4102	Karl J. Schafer	Giant (7/21/90)	Marshall (8/2/97)
4103	J. Zachary Stein	Porter (6/31/94)	Santanoni (8/2/97)
4104	Walter A. Johnson	Dix (9/4/94)	Allen (8/3/97)
4105	Karl L. Burkert	Marcy (10/95)	Esther (8/4/97)
4106	Martin S. Paris	Whiteface (fall 1974)	Seymour (8/8/97)
4107W	Glen Larson	Upper Wolf Jaw (unknown)	Allen (8/8/97)
4108	Ben Anderson	Phelps (7/94)	Dix (8/8/97)
4109	Mary Anderson	Marcy (1979)	Dix (8/8/97)
4110	Matthew T. Hogan	Cascade (8/2/85)	Skylight (8/9/97)
4111	Peter K. Hogan	Cascade (8/2/85)	Skylight (8/9/97)
4112	Ryan M. Hogan	Cascade (9/2/89)	Skylight (8/9/97)
4113	Bob Tschiderer	Marcy (8/85)	Street (8/11/97)
4114	Henry J. Gugumuck	Marcy (6/75)	Whiteface (8/12/97)
4115	Richard C. Gugumuck	Marcy (6/75)	Whiteface (8/12/97)
4116	William G. Reamer	Cascade (6/16/92)	Dix (8/12/97)
4117	Brian J. Trombley	Cascade (6/16/92)	Dix (8/12/97)
4118	Raheli Millman	Cascade (7/7/92)	Dial (8/14/97)
4119W	David M. Marcy	Marcy (2/13/92)	Skylight (8/15/97)
4120	Paul G. Brach	Marshall (1/14/85)	Allen (8/15/97)
4121W	John E. Kenny	Giant (9/3/83)	Emmons (8/16/97)
4122	Timothy H. Bertram	Cascade (7/29/89)	Whiteface (8/16/97)
4123	Gary B. Bertram	Cascade (7/29/89)	Whiteface (8/16/97)
4124	Robert D. Fields	Algonquin (4/72)	Allen (8/17/97)
4125	Bill Blaiklock	Cascade (8/66)	Rocky Peak (8/18/97)
4126	Robert L. Vogel	Cascade (8/68)	Colden (8/18/97)
4127	Deborah D. Gaddy	Marcy (10/5/84)	Santanoni (8/18/97)
4128	Michael D. Bourque	Porter (5/29/88)	Allen (8/20/97)
4129	Ann Stowe	Dix (9/83)	Emmons (8/20/97)
4130	Will Stowe	Big Slide (8/91)	Emmons (8/20/97)
4131	William A. Stowe	Marcy (1979)	Emmons (8/20/97)
4132	Nathaniel Lewis	Seward (7/25/97)	Whiteface (8/21/97)
4133	Eric J. Marcotte	Seward (7/25/97)	Whiteface (8/21/97)
4134	Justin Karlitz-Grodin	Seward (7/25/97)	Whiteface (8/21/97)
4135	Meredith H. Kerr	Seward (7/25/97)	Whiteface (8/21/97)
4136	Derek Srygley	Seward (7/25/97)	Whiteface (8/21/97)
4137	Jake Apkarian	Seward (7/25/97)	Whiteface (8/21/97)
4138	David Dunlop	Couchsachraga (7/25/97)	Whiteface (8/21/97)
4139	Max J. Keller	Nye (7/20/97)	Whiteface (8/21/97)
4140	Barbara A. Blum	Phelps (7/11/91)	Whiteface (8/22/97)
4141	Bernie Newton	Cascade (6/24/95)	Whiteface (8/22/97)
4142	Jane M. Nye	Marcy (1943)	Nye (8/23/97)
4143	Wright J. Frank	Giant (1983)	Whiteface (8/24/97)
4144	Daniel E. Perregaux	Phelps (summer 1985)	Whiteface (8/24/97)
4145	Johanne Vaudry	Tabletop (10/7/90)	Allen (8/24/97)
4146	Joseph E. Cavaluzzi	Giant (7/92)	Allen (8/26/97)
4147	Joseph M. Cavaluzzi	Giant (7/92)	Allen (8/26/97)

THE MEMBERSHIP ROSTER OF THE ADIRONDACK FORTY-SIXERS

	MEMBER	FIRST ASCENT	FORTY-SIXTH PEAK
4148	Darrin Everleth	Marcy (8/30/87)	Sawteeth (8/26/97)
4149	R. Jeffrey Green	Macomb (7/27/91)	Giant (8/26/97)
4150	Robert B. Adams	Giant (8/17/93)	Iroquois (8/26/97)
4151	John S. Lecky	Algonquin (summer 1971)	Iroquois (8/26/97)
4152	Victor R. Gold	Giant (8/82)	Saddleback (8/26/97)
4153	Bruno H. Baldacci	Rocky Peak (7/11/95)	Marcy (8/27/97)
4154	John H. Wells	Lower Wolf Jaw (8/57)	Couchsachraga (8/27/97)
4155	Jacquelyn C. Fields	Algonquin (4/72)	Rocky Peak (8/29/97)
4156W	James A. Barnshaw	Phelps (8/87)	Cliff (8/30/97)
4157	Josh Williams	Algonquin (5/7/94)	Sawteeth (8/30/97)
4158	Norman Williams	Algonquin (5/7/94)	Sawteeth (8/30/97)
4159	Nicholas Parent	Cascade (5/14/94)	Skylight (8/30/97)
4160W	David F. Scruggs, Jr.	Colden (9/2/88)	Iroquois (8/30/97)
4161	Michele Towers	Giant (10/5/88)	Allen (8/31/97)
4162	Richard Shiel	Cascade (8/19/92)	Cliff (8/31/97)
4163	Gary Adams	Cascade (7/82)	Santanoni (8/31/97)
4164	Mark E. Anderson	Marcy (8/85)	Dial (9/1/97)
4165	Douglas G. Egeland	Cascade (6/20/95)	Redfield (9/5/97)
4166	Emily Selleck	Marcy (8/56)	Dix (9/5/97)
4167	Jeff Selleck	Giant (8/84)	Dix (9/5/97)
4168	Jeffrey A. Hackett	Colden (7/90)	Panther (9/5/97)
4169	James G. Cayea	Colden (10/2/87)	Haystack (9/6/97)
4170	Ken Cayea	Colden (10/2/87)	Haystack (9/6/97)
4171	James E. Fluegel	Big Slide (5/19/89)	Haystack (9/6/97)
4172	George F. Michael	Colden (10/2/87)	Haystack (9/6/97)
4173	James Ross	Colden (10/2/87)	Haystack (9/6/97)
4174	Lawrence G. Estill	Marcy (6/57)	Haystack (9/6/97)
4175	Anthony J. Cavotta	Giant (7/2/91)	Skylight (9/6/97)
4176	James J. Chorman	Marcy (7/6/92)	Skylight (9/6/97)
4177	Jonathan T. Jefferson	Gothics (summer 1991)	Allen (9/7/97)
4178	Rodney Storms	Giant (5/77)	Allen (9/7/97)
4179	Ed Streeter	Cascade (5/19/95)	Colden (9/13/97)
4180	David C. Sorbello	Colden (5/95)	Street (9/13/97)
4181	Ann T. Murphy	Gothics (9/22/88)	Nippletop (9/13/97)
4182	Andrew Licht	Algonquin (9/89)	Whiteface (9/13/97)
4183	Kenneth D. Licht	Algonquin (9/89)	Whiteface (9/13/97)
4184	Steven A. Bailey	Phelps (6/30/84)	Dial (9/13/97)
4185	Simon Thomas-Train	Cascade (9/10/89)	Lower Wolf Jaw (9/14/97)
4186	John Schwarz	Phelps (12/28/86)	Rocky Peak (9/14/97)
4187	George L. Traver	Skylight (7/84)	Seymour (9/15/97)
4188	Barbara I. Thomas	Colden (8/21/93)	Haystack (9/16/97)
4189	Elwood R. Findholt	Algonquin (10/15/75)	Whiteface (9/16/97)
4190	Robert M. Macy, Jr.	Whiteface (9/91)	Dix (9/19/97)
4191	Martin A. Cohen	Marcy (7/25/88)	Colden (9/19/97)
4192	Peter J. Spyra	Cliff (5/20/85)	Emmons (9/20/97)
4193	Sheryl Larsen	Wright (7/26/90)	Colden (9/20/97)
4194	Gregory R. Stone II	Cascade (5/20/93)	Sawteeth (9/20/97)
4195	Michael Stone	Algonquin (8/16/93)	Sawteeth (9/20/97)
4196	Carol A. Reese	Big Slide (10/88)	Giant (9/21/97)
4197	Alan R. Kapitzke	Giant (9/28/96)	Allen (9/21/97)
4198	Edward Hauschild	Dix (4/26/91)	Saddleback (9/26/97)
4199	James F. Newton	Cascade (4/1/95)	Santanoni (9/27/97)
4200W	Janet M. Stein	Emmons (6/1/88)	Allen (9/27/97)
4201	Ann K. Ferris	Marcy (9/21/91)	Marshall (9/27/97)
4202	John H. Ferris	Marcy (9/21/91)	Marshall (9/27/97)
4203	Robert Hartman	Gothics (7/16/94)	Skylight (9/27/97)
4204	Jennifer A. Ciardelli	Wright (10/3/94)	Seymour (9/27/97)
4205	Brook Erenstone	Cascade (8/25/85)	Skylight (9/27/97)
4206	Denise Erenstone	Redfield (6/71)	Skylight (9/27/97)
4207	Carl H. Andrus	Marcy (10/60)	Dial (9/27/97)
4208	Richard H. Ruh, III	Dix (8/25/86)	Whiteface (9/27/97)
4209	Dorinna Ruh	Cascade (5/2/92)	Whiteface (9/27/97)

Heaven Up-h'isted-ness!

	Member	First Ascent	Forty-sixth Peak
4210	Robert H. Kind	Giant (7/23/88)	Phelps (9/28/97)
4211	Caleb Smith	Gothics (9/20/94)	Whiteface (9/28/97)
4212	Lisa T. Williams	Marcy (8/85)	Esther (9/28/97)
4213	Edward H. Goldstein	Cascade (7/2/93)	Street (10/2/97)
4214	Sam Carpenter	Marcy (9/94)	Saddleback (10/2/97)
4215	Mary H. Loe	Colden (1975)	Santanoni (10/4/97)
4216W	David Goldman	Dix (10/17/92)	Seymour (10/4/97)
4217	Rick Story	Seymour (5/29/93)	Big Slide (10/4/97)
4218	Marguerite Mooers	Cascade (1973)	Sawteeth (10/4/97)
4219	Amy S. Weinar	Gothics (8/91)	Esther (10/4/97)
4220	Edward Broderick	Marcy (9/1/91)	Dix (10/4/97)
4221	Jeffrey L. Helfer	Dix (7/92)	Seymour (10/5/97)
4222	Matthew Jones	Phelps (4/25/96)	Whiteface (10/5/97)
4223	Robert F. Rinkoff	Algonquin (9/14/91)	Iroquois (10/7/97)
4224	Carl F. Holtz	Marcy (9/19/97)	Gray (10/8/97)
4225	Fred R. Gachowski	Marcy (1987)	Allen (10/8/97)
4226	Cary T. Howard	Marcy (1983)	Whiteface (10/10/97)
4227W	Lorraine Turturro	Phelps (3/8/97)	Whiteface (10/10/97)
4228	Barbara Kearns	Giant (6/29/91)	Street (10/11/97)
4229W	Wendy Sanders	Dial (12/6/87)	Tabletop (10/11/97)
4230	Mark E. Muller	Marcy (unknown)	Haystack (10/11/97)
4231	Michael Daley	Big Slide (8/94)	Rocky Peak (10/11/97)
4232	Edward M. Sullivan	Cascade (4/20/96)	Redfield (10/11/97)
4233W	David Z. Graves	Cascade (6/91)	Rocky Peak (10/11/97)
4234	Ken Clayton	Giant (6/17/95)	Marcy (10/11/97)
4235	Darrell J. Scott	Marcy (5/30/71)	Big Slide (10/12/97)
4236	Harry J. Stuart	Cascade (1960)	Gray (10/12/97)
4237	Brenden J. Rillahan	Cascade (8/3/93)	Emmons (10/12/97)
4238	Jade Lemmerman	Phelps (6/3/95)	Giant (10/12/97)
4239	Bonnie A. Schaller	Phelps (9/13/75)	Redfield (10/12/97)
4240	Kenneth Marcinowski, Sr.	Cascade (5/14/94)	Skylight (10/12/97)
4241	Nilde G. Marcinowski	Cascade (5/14/94)	Skylight (10/12/97)
4242	Paul C. Capra	Cascade (8/84)	Porter (10/13/97)
4243	David L. Sheeran	Giant (9/90)	Cliff (10/13/97)
4244	Robert B. Hall	Algonquin (1975)	Iroquois (10/18/97)
4245	Sheila Matz	Nippletop (6/90)	Iroquois (10/18/97)
4246	Melody A. Mackenzie	Redfield (8/4/90)	Colden (10/19/97)
4247	David D. Manning	Lower Wolf Jaw (9/84)	Santanoni (10/25/97)
4248	Timothy J. Fox	Marcy (6/29/91)	Whiteface (10/30/97)
4249W	Kenneth A. Walker	Marcy (2/8/86)	Whiteface (12/30/97)
4250	Kathryn W. Brown	Cascade (8/17/58)	Marshall (5/27/78)
4251	Rick Taylor	Marcy (7/5/80)	Macomb (7/12/92)
4252	Sam Schatz	Giant (7/16/94)	Santanoni (8/2/97)
4253	Tom Czerwinski	Couchsachraga (7/25/97)	Whiteface (8/21/97)
4254	James R. Tiffin	Wright (8/18/93)	Big Slide (8/31/97)
4255	Paul D. Little	Algonquin (5/30/60)	Cliff (9/1/97)
4256	Keyser Helene	Marcy (5/23/92)	Allen (9/27/97)
4257	Ed Jowett	Colvin (6/95)	Panther (10/11/97)
4258W	Carl R. Howard	Colden (8/29/81)	Esther (2/7/98)
4259W	Patrick Farrell	Big Slide (1986)	Esther (2/16/98)
4260W	Mark Lowell	Cascade (7/24/94)	Allen (3/6/98)
4261W	Michael C. Phelps	Phelps (9/5/97)	Haystack (3/17/98)
4262W	John G. Jaeger	Giant (12/21/96)	Basin (3/21/98)
4263W	Wade Baxter	Wright (7/13/96)	Skylight (3/22/98)
4264	Andy Mills	Porter (8/26/94)	Redfield (5/8/98)
4265	Derek Standen	Wright (7/21/84)	Skylight (5/23/98)
4266	Jamel M. Torres	Colden (5/25/96)	Big Slide (5/24/98)
4267	Narciso R. Torres	Colden (5/25/96)	Big Slide (5/24/98)
4268W	Laura J. Stewart	Marcy (8/93)	Seymour (5/30/98)
4269	Jonathan Patla	Gothics (5/30/97)	Macomb (5/30/98)
4270W	Susan Kirk	Cascade (4/7/91)	Marshall (5/30/98)
4271	Hans L. Steiniger, Sr.	Algonquin (7/67)	Panther (5/31/98)

The Membership Roster of the Adirondack Forty-Sixers

	Member	First Ascent	Forty-sixth Peak
4272	Frank Bradley	Marcy (6/1/81)	Haystack (6/10/98)
4273W	Charles Leduc	Algonquin (9/6/93)	Blake (6/20/98)
4274	Matthew A. Sorrell	Cascade (6/92)	Whiteface (6/21/98)
4275W	Christopher Koebelin	Marcy (6/23/89)	Seymour (6/21/98)
4276	Harry C. Groome, III	Giant (1972)	Emmons (6/23/98)
4277	Robert S. Tomlinson	Marcy (1959)	Whiteface (6/23/98)
4278	John D. Fitzwater	Algonquin (8/13/82)	Esther (6/27/98)
4279	Alexander B. Trevor	Gothics (8/6/59)	Marshall (7/3/98)
4280	Mike Quindazzi	Macomb (5/14/98)	Cliff (7/11/98)
4281	Jim Fayette	Cascade (11/4/89)	Panther (7/11/98)
4282	David Schmidt	Marcy (7/13/93)	Whiteface (7/16/98)
4283	William P. Schmidt	Phelps (7/9/93)	Whiteface (7/16/98)
4284	David Klimtzak	Allen (8/18/90)	Haystack (7/18/98)
4285	Maria Klimtzak	Cascade (9/1/95)	Haystack (7/18/98)
4286	Benjamin N. Waber	Giant (7/7/95)	Allen (7/19/98)
4287	Dave Mattsen	Lower Wolf Jaw (5/25/74)	Redfield (7/21/98)
4288	Bob Mattsen	Lower Wolf Jaw (5/25/74)	Redfield (7/21/98)
4289	Jeff Merrill	Colden (8/17/95)	Whiteface (7/23/98)
4290	Nancy Sherman	Rocky Peak (10/15/94)	Big Slide (7/25/98)
4291	William T. Yates	Phelps (7/9/93)	Saddleback (7/25/98)
4292	Kurt D. Ramig	Lower Wolf Jaw (7/2/70)	Haystack (7/26/98)
4293	Brian Hood	Cascade (8/8/95)	Marshall (7/27/98)
4294	Paul C. Agnew	Marcy (1965)	Gray (7/27/98)
4295	John A. Henderson	Wright (9/24/92)	Colden (7/27/98)
4296	Matt Andresen	Big Slide (7/20/97)	Allen (7/28/98)
4297	Alvin Fertel	Wright (summer 1991)	Allen (7/28/98)
4298	Sherry E. Dobbs, Sr.	Marcy (7/4/85)	Seymour (7/28/98)
4299	Meredith S. Morrison	Cascade (7/1/93)	Haystack (7/29/98)
4300	Kathryn K. Stuart	Cascade (summer 1978)	Saddleback (7/30/98)
4301	Bernard Grossman	Big Slide (9/21/84)	Dix (7/31/98)
4302	Christine S. Grossman	Big Slide (9/21/84)	Dix (7/31/98)
4303	John L. McGinn	Cascade (8/5/90)	Skylight (7/31/98)
4304	Mike DiFabio	Gothics (7/16/94)	Street (8/1/98)
4305	Michael T. Hatfield	Cascade (9/21/91)	Allen (8/1/98)
4306	Mary E. Houck	Marcy (8/1/89)	Rocky Peak (8/3/98)
4307	Robert E. Livezey	Algonquin (9/10/71)	Seymour (8/3/98)
4308W	David Medd	Marcy (8/2/91)	Gray (8/4/98)
4309W	Josh Mandel	Marcy (12/30/91)	Gray (8/4/98)
4310	Phil Maher	Cascade (6/28/94)	Big Slide (8/4/98)
4311	Anthony S. Mangano, Jr.	Giant (1982)	Couchsachraga (8/4/98)
4312	Margaret Mangano	Big Slide (1991)	Couchsachraga (8/4/98)
4313	William G. Collins	Colvin (9/7/94)	Street (8/5/98)
4314	Elinor L. George	Algonquin (6/14/97)	Saddleback (8/5/98)
4315	Jamie L. Thornton	Big Slide (unknown)	Skylight (8/6/98)
4316	Nicholas Bennett	Cascade (5/30/93)	Marcy (8/6/98)
4317	Mary A. Welch	Lower Wolf Jaw (1969)	Colden (8/6/98)
4318	Bill Murphy	Marcy (9/11/77)	Seymour (8/9/98)
4319	Lincoln Fancher	Marcy (6/70)	Panther (8/12/98)
4320	Jenna Kay	Cascade (summer 1994)	Sawteeth (8/13/98)
4321	Chad E. McCauley	Algonquin (9/9/92)	Allen (8/14/98)
4322	Scott Gaffney	Cascade (9/91)	Whiteface (8/15/98)
4323	Andy Schneider	Cascade (7/17/93)	Hough (8/16/98)
4324	Brett Schneider	Algonquin (6/2/93)	Hough (8/16/98)
4325	Irma S. Graf	Phelps (9/1/81)	Emmons (8/16/98)
4326	Sheri Kreher	Gray (8/91)	Haystack (8/17/98)
4327	Albert A. Lewis	Marcy (7/89)	Santanoni (8/18/98)
4328	Cameron Webster	Lower Wolf Jaw (7/30/85)	Couchsachraga (8/20/98)
4329	Susie Nakatsu	Cascade (8/26/95)	Santanoni (8/20/98)
4330	Kanji Nakatsu	Cascade (8/26/95)	Santanoni (8/20/98)
4331	Glenn P. Milley	Redfield (5/28/83)	Marcy (8/20/98)
4332	Patrick Cotter	Giant (5/18/97)	Emmons (8/20/98)
4333	Lynda Bernays	Cascade (7/64)	Emmons (8/21/98)

HEAVEN UP-H'ISTED-NESS!

	MEMBER	FIRST ASCENT	FORTY-SIXTH PEAK
4334	Alex Fuller	Cascade (7/94)	Emmons (8/21/98)
4335	Carrie Sweredoski	Wright (9/9/88)	Whiteface (8/21/98)
4336	Darrell M. Sweredoski	Wright (9/9/88)	Whiteface (8/21/98)
4337	Michael J. Sweredoski	Wright (9/9/88)	Whiteface (8/21/98)
4338	Mark Rushton	Dix (8/26/95)	Haystack (8/22/98)
4339	Theodore F. Thomas	Cascade (7/3/71)	Colden (8/22/98)
4340	Pamela J. Duell	Cascade (9/19/93)	Marcy (8/22/98)
4341	Mildred Gordon	Algonquin (9/4/95)	Iroquois (8/22/98)
4342	Robert A. Gordon	Algonquin (9/4/95)	Iroquois (8/22/98)
4343	Allen Crowley	Marcy (5/29/94)	Allen (8/23/98)
4344	Dave Deisinger	Colden (6/26/92)	Esther (8/23/98)
4345	Richard J. Deisinger, Jr.	Haystack (9/18/93)	Esther (8/23/98)
4346	Noel J. Bylina	Big Slide (5/10/97)	Phelps (8/23/98)
4347	Imri Allen	Phelps (11/27/92)	Whiteface (8/23/98)
4348	Bill McEvily	Algonquin (7/23/86)	Cliff (8/27/98)
4349	Susan K. McEvily	Colvin (5/15/84)	Cliff (8/27/98)
4350	David Kaczka	Giant (7/4/84)	Cliff (8/27/98)
4351	Colleen Bush-Larose	Giant (1971)	Colden (8/27/98)
4352	Doug Miller	Algonquin (10/82)	Santanoni (8/28/98)
4353	Alan J. Bangel	Dial (8/27/92)	Marcy (8/28/98)
4354	Kim F. Suckow	Phelps (1986)	Allen (8/29/98)
4355	Aaron Wade	Whiteface (8/18/91)	Nippletop (8/30/98)
4356	Michael J. Wade	Whiteface (8/18/91)	Nippletop (8/30/98)
4357	Carmen L. Ross	Wright (4/28/96)	Whiteface (8/30/98)
4358	Michael W. Stone	Giant (7/22/92)	Allen (9/1/98)
4359	Rick Kohlman	Marcy (1974)	Sawteeth (9/2/98)
4360	Arthur J. Lomax	Porter (5/18/96)	Basin (9/2/98)
4361	Mary E. Lomax	Porter (5/28/96)	Basin (9/2/98)
4362	Jim English	Algonquin (7/12/88)	Marcy (9/4/98)
4363	Jim Adelson	Lower Wolf Jaw (7/16/72)	Santanoni (9/4/98)
4364	Len Erkila	Marcy (7/1/82)	Allen (9/5/98)
4365	Brian J. Reilly	Giant (10/30/94)	Wright (9/6/98)
4366W	Michael Lepore	Phelps (6/1/96)	Skylight (9/6/98)
4367	Diane L. Lawrence	Algonquin (2/82)	Iroquois (9/6/98)
4368	Charles S. Lawrence, III	Gothics (7/20/85)	Iroquois (9/6/98)
4369	Sandy Morley	Phelps (10/2/88)	Big Slide (9/6/98)
4370	Geoffrey Gegwich	Gothics (summer 1993)	Allen (9/6/98)
4371	Lawrence Rathman	Marcy (1964)	Gray (9/8/98)
4372	Justin Rathman	Cascade (7/5/93)	Marcy (9/8/98)
4373W	Matt Clark	Marcy (9/70)	Hough (9/10/98)
4374	Crist Dixon	Algonquin (7/11/95)	Haystack (9/10/98)
4375	N. Scott Seifert	Cascade (8/19/86)	Redfield (9/11/98)
4376	Richard Douglass	Phelps (1/31/96)	Seymour (9/12/98)
4377	Carrie Howard-Canning	Marcy (7/84)	Seymour (9/12/98)
4378	John Knight	Giant (12/28/96)	Panther (9/12/98)
4379	Michael Rickard	Cascade (5/26/93)	Street (9/12/98)
4380	Frederick C. Bloom	Algonquin (6/1/96)	Saddleback (9/12/98)
4381	William H. Scott	Phelps (7/73)	Tabletop (9/13/98)
4382	Douglas T. Manderville	Whiteface (2/9/91)	Tabletop (9/13/98)
4383	Janice L. Coffin	Porter (5/17/96)	Phelps (9/13/98)
4384	Adella E. Lamb	Porter (5/17/96)	Phelps (9/13/98)
4385	Edward Neveu	Marcy (7/94)	Panther (9/13/98)
4386	Wendy Neveu	Marcy (7/94)	Panther (9/13/98)
4387	Jeff Reardon	Lower Wolf Jaw (8/90)	Basin (9/16/98)
4388	Edwin C. Esleeck	Cascade (7/17/93)	Wright (9/19/98)
4389	Martha K. Honeywell	Cascade (7/93)	Wright (9/19/98)
4390	Ruth A. Jamke	Wright (7/2/95)	Basin (9/19/98)
4391W	Christopher S. Ward	Wright (7/2/95)	Basin (9/19/98)
4392	Adam Bloniarz	Marcy (7/12/94)	Colden (9/19/98)
4393	John R. Uchal	Marcy (11/94)	Basin (9/19/98)
4394	Geraldine Ames	Algonquin (5/25/94)	Gray (9/19/94)
4395	Gary J. Herbert	Haystack (5/93)	Allen (9/20/98)

The Membership Roster of the Adirondack Forty-Sixers

	Member	First Ascent	Forty-sixth Peak
4396	Tom Painting	Haystack (5/22/93)	Allen (9/20/98)
4397	Adam Kopp	Giant (10/2/94)	Nippletop (9/20/98)
4398	Robert Kopp	Giant (10/2/94)	Nippletop (9/20/98)
4399	Lynda L. Fortier	Wright (5/15/98)	Cliff (9/20/98)
4400	Kelly A. Gingras	Wright (5/15/98)	Cliff (9/20/98)
4401	Richard C. Lockwood	Giant (9/7/92)	Allen (9/20/98)
4402	Bill Zona	Giant (9/89)	Allen (9/20/98)
4403	David Warburton	Algonquin (10/9/95)	Iroquois (9/20/98)
4404	Mary Putnam	Big Slide (10/9/93)	Dix (9/23/98)
4405	Margaret Watrous	Colden (7/54)	Dix (9/23/98)
4406	Ethan Weibrecht	Cascade (1994)	Whiteface (9/25/98)
4407	Carl Gronlund	Basin (9/7/94)	Whiteface (9/25/98)
4408	John Lajoie	Wright (10/11/96)	Esther (9/26/98)
4409	Barbara Landree	Wright (7/10/93)	Sawteeth (9/26/98)
4410W	Brian Hoody	Algonquin (10/1/94)	Marcy (9/26/98)
4411	Douglas Pirnie	Marcy (1970)	Dix (9/30/98)
4412	Karen Pirnie	Marcy (7/83)	Dix (9/30/98)
4413	Vic Kraus	Marcy (1971)	Whiteface (10/2/98)
4414W	Phil Hazen	Marcy (5/29/94)	Seymour (10/3/98)
4415W	Stephen J. Barlow	Phelps (1966)	Whiteface (10/3/98)
4416	David A. Lowe	Algonquin (9/89)	Esther (10/3/98)
4417	Eileen A. Lowe	Giant (10/90)	Esther (10/3/98)
4418	John M. McNally	Cascade (7/14/96)	Whiteface (10/3/98)
4419	George C. Baranauskas	Cascade (9/3/89)	Phelps (10/4/98)
4420	Christine Gouwens	Giant (7/95)	Tabletop (10/4/98)
4421	Rachael Levitz	Cascade (fall 1995)	Tabletop (10/4/98)
4422	Robert Aspholm	Colden (8/79)	Hough (10/4/98)
4423	Clifton Young	Marcy (7/12/96)	Allen (10/5/98)
4424	Jay Gross	Marcy (summer 1978)	Rocky Peak (10/11/98)
4425	Beau Lemmerman	Cascade (9/16/95)	Whiteface (10/11/98)
4426	Ben Stanley	Cascade (7/93)	Street (10/11/98)
4427	Michael McTighe	Giant (10/92)	Couchsachraga (10/12/98)
4428	Karen Gursky	Cascade (8/6/94)	Rocky Peak (10/12/98)
4429	Thomas Hanchett	Cascade (8/6/94)	Rocky Peak (10/12/98)
4430	Anita Farber-Robertson	Armstrong (8/9/93)	Blake (10/12/98)
4431W	Edgar Robertson	Lower Wolf Jaw (8/9/93)	Blake (10/12/98)
4432	Ken Klauck	Gothics (9/26/87)	Rocky Peak (10/12/98)
4433	Steven J. Richer	Cascade (6/17/95)	Street (10/12/98)
4434	Scott B. Loeber	Big Slide (fall 1986)	Skylight (10/18/98)
4435W	Geoffrey L. Hartpence	Dix (7/13/98)	Panther (10/18/98)
4436	Dan Leonard	Dix (8/24/91)	Iroquois (10/24/98)
4437	Carl Wegner	Big Slide (5/9/93)	Iroquois (10/24/98)
4438	Rob Howland	Algonquin (5/27/96)	Colden (10/29/98)
4439	James, Jr. Higgins, Jr.	Cascade (6/24/90)	Allen (10/31/98)
4440	James, Jr. Higgins, Sr.	Phelps (1/19/85)	Allen (10/31/98)
4441	Charles Pfister	Marcy (1964)	East Dix (11/1/98)
4442	James M. McElroy	Dix (8/86)	Esther (11/4/98)
4443	Arthur Malary	Marcy (8/95)	Whiteface (11/5/98)
4444	Cal E. Litts	Marcy (9/16/95)	Big Slide (11/7/98)
4445W	Patti Schwankert	Phelps (2/3/96)	Colden (11/7/98)
4446	Patrick McCullough	Marcy (8/6/93)	Whiteface (12/12/98)
4447	James E. Tribol	Phelps (8/18/92)	Whiteface (8/22/98)
4448	Reginald G. Parker	Giant (summer 1977)	Sawteeth (8/14/94)
4449W	Charlie Sabatine	Algonquin (7/26/85)	Cliff (8/19/96)
4450W	Sara C. Sabatine	Algonquin (7/26/85)	Cliff (8/19/96)
4451	Patrick M. Taylor	Marcy (8/4/92)	Big Slide (8/9/97)
4452	John J. Wuillermin	Cascade (10/93)	Allen (10/4/97)
4453	Daniel J. Weinstein	Street (7/76)	Rocky Peak (5/25/98)
4454	Terri J. Korb	Colden (7/10/82)	Seymour (6/21/98)
4455	Brian Riley	Giant (7/7/92)	Armstrong (7/21/98)
4456	Harold M. Hatfield	Marcy (10/88)	Allen (8/1/98)
4457	Meaghan Swan	Wright (10/18/92)	Algonquin (8/4/98)

Heaven Up-h'isted-ness!

	Member	First Ascent	Forty-sixth Peak
4458	Joshua P. Cook	Esther (8/30/86)	Colden (8/16/98)
4459W	Rik Jordan	Algonquin (7/92)	Emmons (9/1/98)
4460	John T. Reilly	Marcy (7/13/64)	Emmons (9/5/98)
4461	Shirley E. Thomas	Cascade (8/29/87)	Allen (10/3/98)
4462	Jackson E. Thomas	Cascade (8/29/87)	Allen (10/3/98)
4463	Judith A. Strohmeyer	Cascade (7/14/96)	Whiteface (10/3/98)
4464	James R. Strohmeyer	Cascade (7/14/96)	Whiteface (10/3/98)
4465	Becky J. Pfaffenbach	Cascade (9/26/82)	Haystack (10/4/98)
4466	Jenny Pfaffenbach	Cascade (9/26/82)	Haystack (10/4/98)
4467	Steve Samel	Lower Wolf Jaw (7/25/70)	Haystack (10/17/98)
4468W	Nancy Copeland	Giant (unknown)	Allen (11/7/98)
4469W	Jacqueline Bave	Marcy (8/78)	Tabletop (1/23/99)
4470	Derek Clement	Phelps (9/93)	Iroquois (1/30/99)
4471	Evan Moppert	Cascade (10/2/94)	Colden (2/7/99)
4472	Ross Moppert	Cascade (10/2/94)	Colden (2/7/99)
4473W	Jerry Moppert	Cascade (10/2/94)	Colden (2/7/99)
4474	Peter P. Howard	Gothics (8/20/89)	Marshall (2/28/99)
4475W	George S. Vengrin	Wright (winter 1980)	Seymour (3/10/99)
4476W	Jadwiga Rosenthal	Wright (12/31/94)	Seward (3/13/99)
4477	David R. Smith	Marcy (8/1/85)	Sawteeth (3/19/99)
4478	Nina White	Cascade (4/30/94)	Phelps (3/20/99)
4479W	Jim McLaughlin	Phelps (6/3/94)	Cascade (5/1/99)
4480W	Jason Deluca	Lower Wolf Jaw (9/15/91)	Marcy (5/8/99)
4481	John Speer	Algonquin (8/17/96)	Street (5/18/99)
4482	Christine Reister	Giant (10/1/92)	Basin (5/21/99)
4483	Kate McCahill	Cascade (1990)	Rocky Peak (5/22/99)
4484W	Scott Case	Giant (6/22/91)	Allen (5/22/99)
4485W	Maureen O'Leary-Laskey	Algonquin (unknown)	Allen (5/22/99)
4486	Sue Virostek	Marcy (2/19/90)	Whiteface (5/23/99)
4487W	Edward Yaris	Basin (1/18/98)	Gray (5/23/99)
4488	Hsin Wang	Macomb (8/22/87)	Big Slide (5/24/99)
4489	Ray Burnham	Cascade (6/22/94)	Tabletop (5/31/99)
4490	Chris Mazdzer	Marcy (7/6/96)	Haystack (6/12/99)
4491	Edward Mazdzer	Cascade (5/16/87)	Haystack (6/12/99)
4492W	Robert Heins	Giant (9/69)	Phelps (6/19/99)
4493	Dennis Babin	Lower Wolf Jaw (11/27/98)	Marcy (6/19/99)
4494	Melissa Livsey	Cascade (7/81)	East Dix (6/24/99)
4495	Steven Harty	Cascade (7/79)	Emmons (6/26/99)
4496	James R. Covey	Phelps (4/17/93)	Allen (6/28/99)
4497	Tim Wilmot	Lower Wolf Jaw (8/4/89)	Santanoni (7/5/99)
4498	Gary Berman	Wright (7/8/94)	Whiteface (7/10/99)
4499	John Case	Cascade (11/17/90)	Gray (7/11/99)
4500	David E. Bronston	Marcy (8/31/74)	Allen (7/11/99)
4501	William G. Cox	Giant (1995)	Phelps (7/13/99)
4502	Erin Hammond	Lower Wolf Jaw (5/16/97)	Big Slide (7/14/99)
4503	Laura Quayle	Whiteface (1993)	Phelps (7/16/99)
4504W	Philip D. Wescott	Hough (9/26/70)	Big Slide (7/17/99)
4505	Paul Sonneborn	Esther (7/19/95)	Allen (7/17/99)
4506	Raymond B. Sergott	Marcy (8/27/93)	Seymour (7/18/99)
4507	Michael R. Sergott	Marcy (8/27/93)	Seymour (7/18/99)
4508	Robert J. Buzzelli	Marcy (7/85)	Cliff (7/18/99)
4509	Kate Durlacher	Cascade (1991)	Giant (7/18/99)
4510	Donald P. Riley	Cascade (6/8/97)	Allen (7/19/99)
4511	David W. Tam	Cascade (8/20/95)	Emmons (7/20/99)
4512	Carol C. Parker	Giant (12/4/77)	Rocky Peak (7/23/99)
4513	John D. Jennings	Marcy (6/25/90)	Haystack (7/25/99)
4514	Coleman Blakeslee	Porter (7/94)	Iroquois (7/25/99)
4515	Frederique Wion	East Dix (7/13/97)	Blake (7/27/99)
4516	Nick Ladanowski	Big Slide (7/10/93)	Basin (7/28/99)
4517	Theresa Schaf	Giant (7/19/92)	Basin (7/28/99)
4518	Daniel Dedrick	Seymour (7/19/98)	Colden (7/28/99)
4519	Ross Diamond	Cascade (9/90)	Seymour (7/30/99)

The Membership Roster of the Adirondack Forty-Sixers

	Member	First Ascent	Forty-sixth Peak
4520	Aaron Herman	Marcy (7/1/93)	Santanoni (7/30/99)
4521W	Ken Austin	Giant (7/19/95)	Santanoni (7/31/99)
4522	Michael Worden	Cascade (8/7/93)	Haystack (7/31/99)
4523	Janice Kennedy	Phelps (8/6/96)	Rocky Peak (8/2/99)
4524	Joanne Kennedy	Cascade (6/29/96)	Rocky Peak (8/2/99)
4525	Jean T. Ryan	Colden (7/7/97)	Rocky Peak (8/2/99)
4526	Luvie A. Tuller	Cascade (6/29/96)	Rocky Peak (8/2/99)
4527	Andrew P. Matson	Phelps (8/2/93)	Seymour (8/4/99)
4528	Adam Trent	Marcy (7/11/82)	Allen (8/4/99)
4529	Jeff Chase	Macomb (7/19/99)	Whiteface (8/5/99)
4530	Patrick Picard	Macomb (7/9/99)	Whiteface (8/5/99)
4531	Isaac M. Ray	Big Slide (7/12/96)	Whiteface (8/6/99)
4532	William R. Soloski	Cascade (unknown)	Allen (8/7/99)
4533	Michael Baker	Marcy (6/22/97)	Emmons (8/7/99)
4534	Ben Frank	Wright (7/30/95)	Seymour (8/8/99)
4535	Kyle Cresci	Wright (8/8/95)	Phelps (8/9/99)
4536	Rebecca Ryba	Marcy (8/4/95)	Skylight (8/9/99)
4537	John E. Traver	Lower Wolf Jaw (7/3/88)	Gray (8/10/99)
4538	John F. Moynihan, III	Dial (6/26/96)	Skylight (8/12/99)
4539	Colin R. Smith	Whiteface (6/12/93)	Skylight (8/12/99)
4540	Paul Mudar	Cascade (6/8/95)	Skylight (8/12/99)
4541W	Keith A. Horne	Marcy (8/17/93)	Allen (8/13/99)
4542	Andrew Wilcox	Cascade (7/12/95)	Iroquois (8/13/99)
4543	Stanley M. Bischoping	Porter (7/3/93)	Donaldson (8/13/99)
4544	John S. Hutchins	Cascade (8/64)	Esther (8/14/99)
4545	Doug Jenks	Cascade (6/9/73)	Dix (8/20/99)
4546	Dana A. Brown	Big Slide (8/72)	Couchsachraga (8/20/99)
4547	Richard Melton	Marcy (9/28/91)	Cascade (8/20/99)
4548	Dick Gaffney	Marcy (8/72)	Skylight (8/21/99)
4549	Samuel R. Hoar	Cascade (8/8/93)	Santanoni (8/21/99)
4550	Daniel Rancier	Wright (8/15/88)	Emmons (8/21/99)
4551	Ronald J. Neissen	Giant (9/6/94)	Seymour (8/22/99)
4552	Bert Dennett	Blake (7/10/65)	Santanoni (8/23/99)
4553	Maureen Geer	Cascade (7/8/96)	Allen (8/23/99)
4554	Douglas W. Correll	Cascade (unknown)	Seymour (8/26/99)
4555	Amanda Wang	Cascade (8/89)	Rocky Peak (8/26/99)
4556	Benjamin S. Hutchins	Cascade (8/93)	Rocky Peak (8/27/99)
4557	Heather H. Hutchins	Marcy (8/5/67)	Rocky Peak (8/27/99)
4558	George C. Thomas	Marcy (8/23/91)	Whiteface (8/28/99)
4559	Gary Kelpin	Marcy (8/23/91)	Whiteface (8/28/99)
4560	Jane C. Smalley	Marcy (6/93)	Wright (8/28/99)
4561	Randy Baker	Cascade (8/87)	Donaldson (8/28/99)
4562	Thomas E. Purtell	Marcy (5/28/86)	Blake (8/28/99)
4563	William Opperman	Saddleback (5/24/75)	Allen (8/29/99)
4564	Michael P. Lennon	Colden (9/1/90)	Big Slide (8/29/99)
4565	Michael L. Dunn, Jr.	Marcy (8/26/89)	Colden (8/29/99)
4566	Edward S. Slattery	Marcy (5/98)	Sawteeth (8/30/99)
4567	George Ferrigno	Algonquin (5/13/83)	Marshall (8/30/99)
4568	John F. Macek	Colden (8/6/94)	Marshall (9/1/99)
4569	Mary Quinn	Giant (10/12/91)	Big Slide (9/2/99)
4570	Robert J. Ring	Marcy (7/79)	Seymour (9/4/99)
4571	Jeffrey Perkins	Giant (7/82)	Marcy (9/4/99)
4572	Lucas Perkins	Wright (8/91)	Marcy (9/4/99)
4573	Richard J. Barth, Jr.	Marcy (8/13/73)	Sawteeth (9/4/99)
4574	Christopher J. Yarsevich	Algonquin (7/19/97)	Haystack (9/4/99)
4575	Mary Jane Shonn	Marcy (1960)	Panther (9/4/99)
4576	Daniel D. Shonn, Jr.	Giant (8/19/82)	Panther (9/4/99)
4577	Cynthia R. Carr	Phelps (4/15/98)	Marshall (9/5/99)
4578	Daniel L. Carr	Phelps (4/15/98)	Marshall (9/5/99)
4579	Richard J. Cirre	Marcy (8/30/94)	Haystack (9/7/99)
4580	Morris Davison	Cascade (6/22/94)	Rocky Peak (9/9/99)
4581	Charles A. Decker	Cascade (4/27/94)	Basin (9/9/99)

HEAVEN UP-H'ISTED-NESS!

	MEMBER	FIRST ASCENT	FORTY-SIXTH PEAK
4582	Justin Robbins	Big Slide (unknown)	Gray (9/11/99)
4583	Edward Svendsen	Marcy (8/93)	Haystack (9/12/99)
4584W	Erling Svendsen	Marcy (8/93)	Haystack (9/12/99)
4585	David Hanchette	Marcy (8/19/51)	Allen (9/12/99)
4586	Ronald P. Marquis	Tabletop (7/28/98)	Marcy (9/12/99)
4587	Heather Mackey	Algonquin (7/12/94)	Haystack (9/12/99)
4588	Robert L. Evans	Marcy (6/1/88)	Panther (9/12/99)
4589	Robert J. Wright	Cascade (5/6/95)	Hough (9/12/99)
4590	Thomas McMahon	Cascade (5/6/95)	Hough (9/12/99)
4591	Janet Sedlack	Giant (9/19/79)	Iroquois (9/18/99)
4592	Derek Ohanesian	Whiteface (8/13/98)	Colden (9/18/99)
4593	Janis Spilker	Cascade (8/5/91)	Whiteface (9/18/99)
4594	Robert L. Spilker	Cascade (8/91)	Whiteface (9/18/99)
4595	Herman Kreiley	Marcy (6/24/95)	Phelps (9/19/99)
4596	Dean W. Baker	Giant (9/18/79)	Marcy (9/19/99)
4597	Michael A. Higley	Algonquin (6/14/97)	Haystack (9/20/99)
4598	Carsten P. Warnes	Algonquin (6/14/97)	Haystack (9/20/99)
4599	Eric Peterson	Big Slide (6/19/94)	Giant (9/23/99)
4600	Linda M. Norris	Marcy (10/15/93)	Emmons (9/24/99)
4601	Charles W. Norris	Marcy (10/15/93)	Emmons (9/24/99)
4602	David Brault	Cascade (10/26/97)	Colden (9/24/99)
4603	Frank A. Denchick	Cascade (10/26/97)	Colden (9/24/99)
4604	Joseph H. Gervais	Big Slide (7/18/76)	Sawteeth (9/25/99)
4605	Paul M. Gervais	Giant (1993)	Sawteeth (9/25/99)
4606	David S. Carlson	Whiteface (7/52)	Saddleback (9/25/99)
4607W	Phil Seward	Marcy (7/74)	Rocky Peak (9/25/99)
4608	Curt Snyder	Cascade (10/6/96)	Marshall (9/26/99)
4609	Theresa Kaschak	Giant (6/20/98)	Colden (10/2/99)
4610	David McCahill	Cascade (6/7/95)	Haystack (10/2/99)
4611	Gerald Carter	Marcy (7/6/96)	Blake (10/2/99)
4612	Neil Carter	Marcy (1968)	Blake (10/2/99)
4613	Alan J. Redmer	Lower Wolf Jaw (6/29/95)	Couchsachraga (10/8/99)
4614	Michael J. Terenzetti	Algonquin (9/6/87)	Marcy (10/9/99)
4615	Betsy Laundrie	Cascade (9/23/93)	Haystack (10/10/99)
4616	Catherine Laundrie	Porter (2/28/93)	Haystack (10/10/99)
4617	Philip P. Fountain	Cascade (6/7/97)	Saddleback (10/12/99)
4618	Michael P. Gagnier	Lower Wolf Jaw (9/12/92)	Marshall (10/15/99)
4619	Nancy P. Flynn	Wright (6/1/86)	Couchsachraga (10/16/99)
4620	William E. Flynn, Jr.	Wright (6/1/86)	Couchsachraga (10/16/99)
4621	David E. Dietrich	Cascade (5/3/97)	Seward (10/16/99)
4622	Joel T. Marchewka	Cascade (10/26/96)	Whiteface (10/16/99)
4623	Chris Helmes	Upper Wolf Jaw (10/2/94)	Gray (10/16/99)
4624	Richard D. Crammond	Marcy (7/1/89)	Gray (10/17/99)
4625W	Brecken S. Esper	Cascade (3/31/99)	Cliff (10/28/99)
4626W	Josiah Z. Esper	Cascade (3/31/99)	Cliff (10/28/99)
4627W	Mario Demers	Algonquin (8/8/98)	Whiteface (10/30/99)
4628W	Lisa Bowdey	East Dix (6/16/96)	Cascade (11/6/99)
4629	Carolyn M. Brightly	Algonquin (2/14/98)	Allen (11/6/99)
4630	John F. Reynolds	Algonquin (2/14/98)	Allen (11/6/99)
4631W	John B. Waldman	Giant (9/7/98)	Emmons (11/27/99)
4632	Harry Carlson	Colden (8/2/97)	Whiteface (12/5/99)
4633	Larry M. Loeb	Marcy (1970)	Emmons (12/25/99)
4634	Dean Delano	Marcy (6/20/96)	Gray (9/11/99)
4635	Thomas J. Hunt	Dix (10/8/80)	Whiteface (1/1/00)
4636	J. Grant Esler	Phelps (10/91)	Blake (1/7/00)
4637	Marcella H. Esler	Algonquin (8/13/93)	Blake (1/7/00)
4638	Stephen C. Hallock	Algonquin (8/1/81)	Redfield (7/19/97)
4639	Jim Silberger	Marcy (9/74)	Iroquois (6/10/89)
4640	Thomas J. Baesl	Colden (6/72)	Marshall (8/16/92)
4641	Steven Youmatz	Dix (10/28/89)	Couchsachraga (10/28/95)
4642	Colette Meltzer	Phelps (8/86)	Sawteeth (5/25/97)
4643	Sara M. Meltzer	Phelps (8/86)	Giant (5/25/97)

The Membership Roster of the Adirondack Forty-Sixers

	Member	First Ascent	Forty-sixth Peak
4644	Greg Turner	Unknown	Nye (8/30/97)
4645	George Sogoian	Marcy (2/1/76)	Esther (12/5/98)
4646	Mark Allen	Marcy (9/17/91)	Whiteface (7/10/99)
4647	Alfred E. Barnes II	Sawteeth (7/27/80)	Giant (7/30/99)
4648	Charles Head	Iroquois (7/25/94)	Phelps (8/4/99)
4649	Michael Higgins	Whiteface (5/29/99)	Big Slide (9/1/99)
4650	Stephen R. Barth	Saddleback (7/82)	Sawteeth (9/4/99)
4651	Ronald Nohe	Colvin (7/5/92)	Whiteface (9/11/99)
4652	Allen R. Crawford, Jr.	Algonquin (9/82)	Couchsachraga (9/16/99)
4653	Kurt Peterson	Marcy (1981)	Giant (9/23/99)
4654	Terry Lawrence	Cascade (6/5/86)	Armstrong (10/3/99)
4655	Kathleen Larson	Big Slide (11/14/93)	Wright (10/9/99)
4656W	John McHugh	Lower Wolf Jaw (3/11/95)	Marcy (3/18/00)
4657	Roger Baglin	Marcy (1951)	Cascade (1/1/00)
4658W	Fred McHugh	Dix (2/15/97)	Marcy (3/18/00)
4659	Dave Burday	Colden (10/11/97)	Santanoni (4/15/00)
4660	Michael J. Huneke	Marcy (5/28/94)	Whiteface (5/28/00)
4661	Andy Morse	Marcy (5/18/96)	Allen (5/28/00)
4662	Luke G. Dutton	Marcy (7/3/97)	Allen (5/28/00)
4663	Gary L. Dutton	Marcy (7/3/97)	Allen (5/28/00)
4664	Daniel G. Dutton	Marcy (7/3/97)	Allen (5/28/00)
4665	William Adamczak	Algonquin (8/7/96)	Saddleback (5/29/00)
4666	Daniel Eagan	Cascade (9/18/96)	Phelps (5/30/00)
4667	Melissa Eagan	Cascade (9/18/96)	Phelps (5/30/00)
4668	Wayne Haddock	Colden (5/31/80)	Allen (6/2/00)
4669	E. Dewey Reinhardt	Porter (6/13/86)	Dix (6/23/00)
4670	Jerry Underwood	Marcy (8/91)	Allen (6/24/00)
4671	Jeremiah Reiner	Algonquin (7/23/97)	Colden (6/29/00)
4672W	Bill Boulette	Giant (9/4/98)	Nye (7/3/00)
4673	Pat Allen	Marcy (5/20/96)	Sawteeth (7/8/00)
4674	Bruce G. Goodale	Marcy (9/6/61)	Seymour (7/8/00)
4675	Michael J. Audino	Algonquin (9/10/82)	Emmons (7/8/00)
4676	Frederick A. Eames	Marcy (10/74)	Redfield (7/8/00)
4677	Andrew D. Herzog	Sawteeth (7/12/97)	Dix (7/10/00)
4678	Alexandre Brault	Skylight (7/11/98)	Santanoni (7/11/00)
4679	George Giokas	Giant (10/4/81)	Hough (7/15/00)
4680	Daniel P. Hulme	Iroquois (8/14/95)	Allen (7/16/00)
4681	Michael Zick	Marcy (7/20/93)	Saddleback (7/20/00)
4682	David Hellenga	Cascade (9/3/93)	Saddleback (7/20/00)
4683W	Tim Laskey	Giant (1/3/97)	Dial (7/22/00)
4684W	F. Beecher Graham	Cascade (1/16/99)	Marcy (7/24/00)
4685	Anthony L. Arioli	Whiteface (7/23/97)	Marshall (7/26/00)
4686	Drew Prozeller	Phelps (7/65)	Street (7/25/00)
4687	Marc Austein	Cascade (7/11/97)	Marshall (7/26/00)
4688W	Inge Aiken	Rocky Peak (12/98)	Allen (8/2/00)
4689	Eugene S. Beautz	Marcy (8/10/87)	East Dix (8/4/00)
4690	Deborah Patterson	Porter (5/31/97)	Skylight (8/5/00)
4691	John R. Conroy	Giant (10/5/91)	Allen (8/6/00)
4692	Paul R. Soderholm	Colden (6/8/74)	Whiteface (8/6/00)
4693W	Douglas R. Arnold	Marcy (summer 1966)	Allen (8/12/00)
4694	John Bradley	Marcy (8/83)	Allen (8/12/00)
4695	Jenny Gaskin	Giant (8/22/97)	Saddleback (8/12/00)
4696	Nelson J. Fadden	Cascade (8/29/93)	Skylight (8/12/00)
4697	Paul Gaskin	Giant (8/22/97)	Saddleback (8/12/00)
4698W	Wayne Ouderkirk	Giant (9/76)	Macomb (8/13/00)
4699	Kathy Adams	Skylight (8/5/93)	Seymour (8/13/00)
4700	Holly Green	Algonquin (7/89)	Cliff (8/13/00)
4701	Thomas A. Rogers	Haystack (7/95)	Skylight (8/13/00)
4702	Robert T. Rogers	Big Slide (7/95)	Skylight (8/13/00)
4703	John A. Kronstadt	Whiteface (7/61)	Seymour (8/15/00)
4704	L. Clarke Miller	Cascade (8/83)	Giant (8/15/00)
4705	Morris Earle, Jr.	Giant (1963)	Allen (8/15/00)

Heaven Up-h'isted-ness!

	Member	First Ascent	Forty-sixth Peak
4706	Ben Earle	Gothics (8/27/96)	Allen (8/15/00)
4707	Donald A. Reynolds, Jr.	Marcy (5/68)	Seymour (8/16/00)
4708	Josh Green	Cascade (7/15/94)	Macomb (8/18/00)
4709	Noa Kay	Cascade (summer 1991)	Colden (8/18/00)
4710	Gay Barton	Saddleback (9/16/93)	Allen (8/19/00)
4711	Margaret Shiel	Giant (8/21/92)	Haystack (8/19/00)
4712	Jean Maier Burks	Cascade (7/60)	Sawteeth (8/19/00)
4713	Robert Miron	Marcy (9/26/97)	Haystack (8/26/00)
4714	Grant R. Haynes	Algonquin (8/95)	Big Slide (8/22/00)
4715	Jacques Tessier	Cascade (8/31/97)	Haystack (8/26/00)
4716	Deborah Tessier	Cascade (8/31/97)	Haystack (8/26/00)
4717	Don Tolhurst	Algonquin (10/7/89)	Emmons (8/26/00)
4718	Karen Estill	Giant (7/90)	Emmons (8/26/00)
4719	Judy Sears	Big Slide (10/82)	Emmons (8/26/00)
4720	Joseph D. Cantales	Dial (7/7/97)	Rocky Peak (8/26/00)
4721	Debra Cantales	Algonquin (8/21/93)	Rocky Peak (8/26/00)
4722	Esther Hodge	Cascade (10/25/97)	Haystack (8/27/00)
4723	David Hodge	Cascade (10/25/97)	Haystack (8/27/00)
4724	Pete Sokolosky	Algonquin (9/3/97)	Whiteface (9/2/00)
4725	Joseph Allegra	Porter (8/26/93)	Street (9/3/00)
4726W	Timothy Kase	Cascade (6/92)	Whiteface (9/3/00)
4727	Jerry Rasmussen	Colden (8/1/80)	Haystack (9/6/00)
4728	Edward M. Meeks, III	Cascade (7/5/97)	Rocky Peak (9/8/00)
4729	Thomas A. Davidheiser	Lower Wolf Jaw (8/4/93)	Whiteface (9/9/00)
4730	Dick Cummings	Cascade (6/6/95)	Nye (9/9/00)
4731	Mark Hopper	Porter (8/9/97)	Skylight (9/10/00)
4732W	Edward Sheridan	Marcy (9/17/85)	Emmons (9/13/00)
4733	Charlene Zebley	Marcy (8/9/91)	Esther (9/14/00)
4734	Reginald Prouty	Skylight (7/23/95)	Allen (9/16/00)
4735	Jeremy Tyrrell	Rocky Peak (9/1/96)	Whiteface (9/17/00)
4736	Phil Tyrrell	Rocky Peak (9/1/96)	Whiteface (9/17/00)
4737	Nik Tyrrell	Rocky Peak (9/1/96)	Whiteface (9/17/00)
4738	Rocio Tyrrell	Rocky Peak (9/1/96)	Whiteface (9/17/00)
4739	Dean R. Tyrrell	Rocky Peak (9/1/96)	Whiteface (9/17/00)
4740	Ginger Dora	Cascade (8/15/92)	Allen (9/17/00)
4741	William Dora	Cascade (8/15/92)	Allen (9/17/00)
4742	Lawrence T. Lepak	Seward (1977)	Seymour (9/22/00)
4743	Roy Van Dusen	Big Slide (3/21/81)	Hough (9/23/00)
4744	Jennifer L. Silberger	Cascade (1/15/96)	Whiteface (9/30/00)
4745	Ronald W. Danforth	Giant (7/91)	Allen (9/24/00)
4746	Matthew Silberger	Phelps (7/20/76)	Whiteface (9/30/00)
4747	Deb Fedele	Gothics (9/28/62)	Big Slide (9/30/00)
4748	Peggy Whaley	Cascade (5/28/94)	Marcy (9/30/00)
4749	Don Morrison	Marcy (9/15/78)	Couchsachraga (9/30/00)
4750W	Matthew T. Conrick	Colden (1981)	Street (9/30/00)
4751	Andrew Bagatta	Marcy (5/28/93)	Rocky Peak (10/7/00)
4752W	Sidney S. Borthwick	Cliff (6/24/00)	Phelps (10/7/00)
4753	Hannah Babcock	Marcy (7/80)	Whiteface (10/8/00)
4754	Susan Babcock	Marcy (7/80)	Whiteface (10/8/00)
4755	William Yellott	Cascade (8/7/99)	Skylight (10/8/00)
4756	Joan Collins	Cascade (10/11/97)	Skylight (10/8/00)
4757	Jean T. Borgers	Whiteface (11/12/90)	Rocky Peak (10/14/00)
4758	Mike Whelsky	Cascade (5/5/97)	Porter (10/14/00)
4759	R. (Sherwood) Veith	Algonquin (9/2/95)	Whiteface (10/14/00)
4760	Normand LaTour	Colvin (12/4/99)	Cliff (10/15/00)
4761	Pam Kennedy	Wright (10/94)	Seymour (10/21/00)
4762	Margo Ross	Phelps (8/91)	Seymour (10/21/00)
4763	David M. Teegarden	South Dix (8/10/91)	Cliff (10/21/00)
4764	Travis King	Wright (1/23/98)	Cliff (10/22/00)
4765	Bruce Bertrand	Porter (7/11/00)	Marcy (10/25/00)
4766	Cara G. Baker	Algonquin (9/84)	Allen (10/26/00)
4767	George A. Tongue	Marcy (1960)	Whiteface (10/28/00)

THE MEMBERSHIP ROSTER OF THE ADIRONDACK FORTY-SIXERS

	MEMBER	FIRST ASCENT	FORTY-SIXTH PEAK
4768	Ron Wilson	Marcy (7/59)	East Dix (11/4/00)
4769	Alan W. Morse	Marcy (5/18/96)	Skylight (11/5/00)
4770	Anita Vigorito-Benoit	Rocky Peak (8/25/88)	Seymour (11/12/00)
4771	Charles H. Wilson	Colden (10/82)	Haystack (11/20/00)
4772W	John C. Schroeder	Marcy (5/25/86)	Emmons (6/10/90)
4773	Henry Faller	Whiteface (1965)	Hough (10/18/97)
4774	Glenn Bernardis	Colden (1989)	Rocky Peak (6/22/98)
4775	Jacob Lemieux	Giant (7/95)	Panther (8/4/98)
4776	Elliott D. S. Adams	Porter (5/94)	Whiteface (8/21/99)
4777	Kenneth C. Robbins	Phelps (9/29/95)	Dial (9/23/99)
4778	Emily E. Byrne	Algonquin (7/94)	Cascade (8/13/00)
4779	Thomas S. Jewett	Giant (1966)	Colden (8/16/00)
4780	James R. Mersfelder	Marcy (7/13/82)	Nippletop (8/26/00)
4781	Becky Tennyson	Porter (8/21/95)	Allen (9/14/00)
4782	John P. Lawrence	Cascade (9/15/96)	Wright (9/15/00)
4783	Carl Moon	Cascade (9/96)	Colden (9/30/00)
4784	Michael Mancini	Sawteeth (5/96)	Allen (9/30/00)
4785	Danny Berry	Phelps (7/1/89)	Hough (1/27/01)
4786W	Paul Lamar	Whiteface (12/28/96)	East Dix (2/3/01)
4787W	John C. Case	Phelps (1/20/96)	Couchsachraga (2/18/01)
4788W	Richard Preis	Marcy (10/26/96)	Macomb (2/24/01)
4789W	Elizabeth Moloff	Couchsachraga (9/19/98)	Tabletop (3/11/01)
4790W	Guy Garand	Marcy (1977)	Gray (3/19/01)
4791W	Harold Kruyk	Whiteface (9/90)	Emmons (5/31/01)
4792	Eric Marshall	Cascade (6/30/99)	Allen (6/13/01)
4793	Ralph M. Esposito	Algonquin (5/83)	Marshall (6/14/01)
4794	Geoffrey Bucks	Cascade (8/6/94)	Whiteface (6/24/01)
4795	Rodney R. Bucks	Cascade (8/6/94)	Whiteface (6/24/01)
4796	Douglas Copeley	Marcy (8/31/71)	Allen (6/26/01)
4797	Brianna Livsey	Cascade (7/96)	Colden (7/1/01)
4798	John F. Miller	Phelps (7/92)	Haystack (7/2/01)
4799	Michael Miller	Dix (8/92)	Haystack (7/2/01)
4800	Terrence J. Loeber	Algonquin (summer 1991)	Marcy (7/4/01)
4801	James W. Yates	Cascade (7/20/93)	Couchsachraga (7/6/01)
4802	Deborah Vercant	Cascade (8/6/92)	Haystack (7/6/01)
4803	Matthew Vercant	Cascade (8/6/92)	Haystack (7/6/01)
4804	Michael L. Vercant	Esther (8/20/94)	Haystack (7/6/01)
4805W	Jeannette Donlon	Giant (6/21/98)	Redfield (7/7/01)
4806	Kevin Rathgeber	Giant (6/21/98)	Redfield (7/7/01)
4807W	Eric Donlon	Cascade (11/22/98)	Redfield (7/8/01)
4808	Marilyn Davis	Big Slide (3/83)	Allen (7/9/01)
4809	Russell Squire	Phelps (7/94)	Whiteface (7/21/01)
4810	James R. Stine	Wright (7/66)	Cascade (7/21/01)
4811	Christopher Leonard	Lower Wolf Jaw (5/29/99)	Whiteface (7/21/01)
4812	Chris Crosby	Marcy (7/96)	Cliff (7/21/01)
4813	Peter Olszewski	Algonquin (1970)	Colden (7/23/01)
4814	Brook B. Leiphart	Marcy (9/87)	Haystack (7/23/01)
4815	Brennan Basler	Algonquin (9/27/97)	Allen (7/25/01)
4816	Jeremy Cleaveland	Seymour (7/16/00)	Marcy (7/25/01)
4817	G. Neil Roberts	Porter (1988)	Marcy (7/27/01)
4818	Don Messinger	Giant (9/88)	Saddleback (7/28/01)
4819	Paul W. Taylor	Giant (5/5/89)	Allen (7/28/01)
4820	Michael Ryba	Cascade (5/26/96)	Haystack (7/28/01)
4821	Ray Hudson	Algonquin (7/76)	Rocky Peak (8/1/01)
4822	Shelly D. Hudson	Giant (6/58)	Rocky Peak (8/1/01)
4823	Gordon McLaughlin	Santanoni (7/6/01)	Whiteface (8/2/01)
4824	Jason Andrews	Seymour (7/8/01)	Whiteface (8/2/01)
4825	Travis S. Earl	Couchsachraga (7/6/01)	Whiteface (8/2/01)
4826	Max Weber	Seymour (7/8/01)	Whiteface (8/2/01)
4827	Rich Mather	Seymour (7/8/01)	Whiteface (8/2/01)
4828	Timothy Bowyer	Seymour (7/8/01)	Whiteface (8/2/01)
4829	Lia Call	Santanoni (7/6/01)	Whiteface (8/2/01)

Heaven Up-h'isted-ness!

	Member	First Ascent	Forty-sixth Peak
4830	Michael Gilhooly	Giant (10/24/98)	Skylight (8/4/01)
4831	Sallie McGill	Giant (9/13/97)	Redfield (8/5/01)
4832W	Mike McGill	Giant (9/13/97)	Redfield (8/5/01)
4833	Ralph S. Ryndak	Marcy (9/92)	Iroquois (8/9/01)
4834	Caleb Balderston	Cascade (6/18/98)	Whiteface (8/10/01)
4835	William Hopkinson	Cascade (7/89)	Whiteface (8/11/01)
4836	Andrew Bernstein	Tabletop (7/5/97)	Allen (8/11/01)
4837W	Mike Davis	Marcy (5/29/99)	Allen (8/12/01)
4838	Alan F. Turner	Marcy (7/13/82)	Couchsachraga (8/13/00)
4839	William D. Shaffer	Whiteface (9/27/97)	Haystack (8/13/01)
4840	Peggy L. Shaffer	Whiteface (9/27/97)	Haystack (8/13/01)
4841	Mary Davis	Cascade (7/13/92)	Lower Wolf Jaw (8/13/01)
4842	Miranda Davis	Cascade (7/13/88)	Lower Wolf Jaw (8/13/01)
4843	Peter F. Galvani	Giant (8/25/97)	Seward (8/14/01)
4844W	Michael Fuller	Giant (8/23/00)	Skylight (8/14/01)
4845	John Wood	Cascade (9/2/66)	Couchsachraga (8/15/01)
4846	Pam Gleason	Cascade (8/18/98)	Haystack (8/15/01)
4847	Dorothy Reichardt	Cascade (8/23/84)	Allen (8/16/01)
4848	David I. Theodorowicz	Marcy (10/18/97)	Whiteface (8/18/01)
4849	Kevin J. Sheehan	Marcy (10/18/97)	Whiteface (8/18/01)
4850	Jake Hutchins	Cascade (7/94)	Dix (8/18/01)
4851	Sarah Fuller	Wright (8/95)	Skylight (8/24/01)
4852	Andy McGuffey	Giant (8/86)	Marshall (8/25/01)
4853W	Doreen Heer	Gothics (8/5/95)	East Dix (8/25/01)
4854	Bonnie Prushnok	Big Slide (7/31/99)	Phelps (8/25/01)
4855W	Arlene Stefanko	Gothics (6/93)	East Dix (8/25/01)
4856	John Thompson	Cascade (9/1/94)	Colden (8/29/01)
4857	Ismael C. Colon	Cascade (5/28/99)	Emmons (8/29/01)
4858	Bruce Caryl	Algonquin (10/6/90)	Esther (8/30/01)
4859W	William Cole	Macomb (9/70)	Nippletop (9/2/01)
4860	Lynn Hilpertshauser	Rocky Peak (10/3/98)	Redfield (9/2/01)
4861	Dana Roberts	Rocky Peak (10/3/98)	Redfield (9/2/01)
4862	Dave Roberts	Rocky Peak (10/3/98)	Redfield (9/2/01)
4863	Jean Swanson	Macomb (8/8/98)	Whiteface (9/2/01)
4864	Donald W. Roth	Phelps (7/94)	Whiteface (9/2/01)
4865	Amy Dillenback	Giant (8/26/99)	Panther (9/2/01)
4866	JoAnn Zueckert	Marcy (7/4/49)	East Dix (9/2/01)
4867	George A. Disney	Cascade (5/82)	Esther (9/3/01)
4868	Elizabeth Disney	Cascade (7/11/94)	Whiteface (9/3/01)
4869	Alexandra Disney	Cascade (7/11/94)	Whiteface (9/3/01)
4870	Doug Tinkler	Giant (7/25/98)	Rocky Peak (9/6/01)
4871	Eric P. Hochreiter	Marcy (10/4/97)	Haystack (9/7/01)
4872	Mike Costello	Big Slide (8/28/94)	Tabletop (9/8/01)
4873	Kenneth Hubert	Marcy (9/24/00)	Seymour (9/8/01)
4874	Ronald C. Allen	Giant (10/6/97)	Cliff (9/9/01)
4875	Robert Carney	Marcy (9/30/89)	Redfield (9/9/01)
4876	Nour-Eddine Radi	Whiteface (7/3/99)	Street (9/10/01)
4877	Lincoln Sunderland	Cascade (7/30/98)	Allen (9/11/01)
4878	Fenton Thompson	Lower Wolf Jaw (5/28/99)	Allen (9/11/01)
4879	Kevin Kearney	Cascade (7/30/98)	Allen (9/11/01)
4880	Bobby W. Roe	Cascade (9/19/99)	Rocky Peak (9/14/01)
4881	Ron Fortin	Cascade (8/10/96)	Redfield (9/15/01)
4882	Marjorie E. Burns	Cascade (8/10/96)	Redfield (9/15/01)
4883	Terry Hastings	Marcy (7/23/94)	Big Slide (9/15/01)
4884	Robert W. Goossen	Marcy (5/19/89)	Allen (9/15/01)
4885	Irving E. Stephens	Marcy (summer 1999)	Cliff (9/15/01)
4886	Stuart Bartram	Algonquin (9/21/89)	Dix (9/15/01)
4887	Bruce Cole	Porter (7/7/96)	Iroquois (9/15/01)
4888	Cindi L. Cole	Porter (7/7/96)	Iroquois (9/15/01)
4889W	Ellen M. Cronan	Cascade (10/22/99)	Colden (9/16/01)
4890	Peter Roland	Cascade (8/13/92)	Skylight (9/16/01)
4891	William S. Tuthill	Macomb (5/28/95)	Wright (9/20/01)

THE MEMBERSHIP ROSTER OF THE ADIRONDACK FORTY-SIXERS

	MEMBER	FIRST ASCENT	FORTY-SIXTH PEAK
4892	Joseph Murphy	Cascade (8/19/67)	Couchsachraga (9/20/01)
4893	Karin Topfer	Wright (6/6/97)	Allen (9/22/01)
4894	Christopher Lanthier	Cascade (2/20/97)	Allen (9/22/01)
4895	George C. Singer	Giant (7/3/63)	Saddleback (9/22/01)
4896	Christopher W. Waite	Cascade (8/22/93)	Saddleback (9/22/01)
4897	Lance D. Ruppert	Cascade (10/14/90)	Dix (9/23/01)
4898	Haley Ruppert	Cascade (10/14/90)	Dix (9/23/01)
4899	Natalie Ruppert	Cascade (10/14/90)	Dix (9/23/01)
4900	Gail S. Ruppert	Cascade (10/14/90)	Dix (9/23/01)
4901	Greg Ruppert	Cascade (10/14/90)	Dix (9/23/01)
4902	Rosemarie Trainer	Algonquin (summer 1985)	Seymour (9/26/01)
4903	William Eberhardt	Esther (5/31/80)	Rocky Peak (9/28/01)
4904	Bruce Feher	Marcy (6/68)	Allen (9/29/01)
4905	James R. Maughan	Giant (9/27/97)	Whiteface (9/29/01)
4906	Steven Plehn	Unknown	Marshall (10/3/01)
4907	Ed Homenick	Colden (9/22/84)	Seymour (10/5/01)
4908	Charlie Burks	Colden (7/17/97)	Haystack (10/6/01)
4909	Tammy Kelly	Wright (6/19/99)	Colden (10/6/01)
4910	Michael Kelly	Wright (6/19/99)	Colden (10/6/01)
4911	Mike Mamrosh	Marcy (5/98)	Colden (10/7/01)
4912	Matthew C. LaFlair	Porter (6/14/97)	Whiteface (10/7/01)
4913	Paul E. Newton	Porter (10/1/94)	Whiteface (10/7/01)
4914	Debra Reif	South Dix (6/26/99)	Marcy (10/8/01)
4915	Tracy A. Wood	Cascade (6/15/85)	Panther (10/12/01)
4916	Harold H. DuBois	Whiteface (7/66)	Marshall (10/13/01)
4917	Bethany Hammond	Gray (5/99)	Iroquois (10/14/01)
4918	Matt McQuilton	Giant (spring 1997)	Colden (10/14/01)
4919	Tom Kligerman	Haystack (10/2/76)	Couchsachraga (10/15/01)
4920	Kevin Rooney	Marcy (5/11/96)	Esther (10/17/01)
4921	Rose A. Harris	Algonquin (8/4/93)	Allen (10/20/01)
4922	Carl Stephens	Marcy (5/28/88)	Haystack (10/20/01)
4923	David Dalton	Wright (10/88)	East Dix (10/21/01)
4924	Claire Dalton	Cascade (6/2/89)	East Dix (10/21/01)
4925	Robert Michell	Lower Wolf Jaw (8/8/01)	Big Slide (10/27/01)
4926	Paul Belanger	Algonquin (4/23/96)	Allen (10/27/01)
4927	Jane C. Haskins	Giant (summer 1979)	Wright (11/3/01)
4928W	James R. Dean	Phelps (7/26/95)	Haystack (11/10/01)
4929	Nick Citro	Lower Wolf Jaw (8/25/95)	Street (11/19/01)
4930	Rich Citro	Lower Wolf Jaw (8/25/95)	Street (11/19/01)
4931W	Ronald Mackey W.	Dix (1975)	Seymour (12/1/01)
4932W	Daniel Lewicki	Marcy (5/27/73)	Emmons (12/1/01)
4933	Dave Coppock	Colden (5/90)	Whiteface (12/28/01)
4934	Steve Musica	Giant (3/15/98)	Seward (12/30/01)
4935	Dean A. Christian	Wright (1965)	Gray (11/3/94)
4936	Margaret A. Faucher	Giant (1981)	Blake (8/16/97)
4937	Marc C. Faucher	Giant (6/15/85)	Blake (8/16/97)
4938	Paul Maurice	Algonquin (7/88)	Allen (6/26/98)
4939	Timothy J. Lawliss	Marcy (8/77)	Seymour (9/30/99)
4940	Nathen Strack	Lower Wolf Jaw (9/6/93)	Dix (10/11/99)
4941	Gail Magoon	Lower Wolf Jaw (9/6/93)	Dix (10/11/99)
4942	Erik Smith	Allen (1992)	Couchsachraga (8/31/00)
4943	Rebecca Rogers	Marcy (5/1/94)	Allen (9/3/00)
4944	Emilie W. Gould	Marcy (1969)	Redfield (9/12/00)
4945	John Barron	Marcy (5/20/85)	Porter (6/30/01)
4946	Daniel J. Stine	Algonquin (8/84)	Cascade (7/21/01)
4947	Adam Lawrence	Seymour (7/15/00)	Marcy (7/25/01)
4948	Luke Saunders	Seymour (7/8/01)	Whiteface (8/2/01)
4949	Russell L. Boronow	Giant (6/92)	Whiteface (8/2/01)
4950	Mark Layton	Marcy (8/22/95)	Sawteeth (8/4/01)
4951	Russell W. Myers, Jr.	Wright (7/28/82)	Whiteface (8/5/01)
4952	Victor Yates	Whiteface (10/9/90)	Gray (8/10/01)
4953	Jason Fiegl	Whiteface (2/16/97)	Seward (8/26/01)

Heaven Up-h'isted-ness!

	Member	First Ascent	Forty-sixth Peak
4954	John Candra	Cascade (8/24/96)	Marcy (8/30/01)
4955	Vlasta Candra	Cascade (8/24/96)	Marcy (8/30/01)
4956	Jennifer R. Wilson	Cascade (4/30/94)	Allen (9/2/01)
4957	Cecelia Horne	Street (8/3/96)	Macomb (9/3/01)
4958	Dan Spence	Cascade (1984)	Allen (9/15/01)
4959W	Gloria G. Daly	Marcy (7/29/91)	Phelps (9/30/01)
4960	Richard H. Griffin	Algonquin (8/4/93)	Allen (10/20/01)
4961	David Adams	Whiteface (5/7/95)	Allen (10/21/01)
4962	Paul Adams	Whiteface (5/7/95)	Allen (10/21/01)
4963	Dean M. Giuliano	Wright (8/12/95)	Allen (12/8/01)
4964W	Anne Gwynne	Lower Wolf Jaw (3/11/95)	Haystack (3/9/02)
4965W	Emerson Ellett	Algonquin (2/16/92)	Hough (3/17/02)
4966W	James Schaad	Big Slide (8/3/87)	Whiteface (3/17/02)
4967W	Christine Bourjade	Giant (9/99)	Haystack (4/6/02)
4968W	Alex Radmanovich	Giant (9/99)	Haystack (4/6/02)
4969	Jerry Babcock	Cascade (3/17/01)	Seymour (5/11/02)
4970	Diane F. Grunthal	Big Slide (7/26/92)	Allen (5/25/02)
4971	Ray Masters	Marcy (6/66)	Emmons (6/1/02)
4972	Laurence A. Nafie	Rocky Peak (6/7/90)	Allen (6/15/02)
4973	William L. Parker	Giant (6/7/90)	Allen (6/15/02)
4974	Bruce R. McLaughlin	Giant (9/28/69)	Iroquois (6/20/02)
4975	Terrence LaPier	Marcy (3/72)	Couchsachraga (6/21/02)
4976	Chuck St. John	Giant (9/2/75)	Cliff (6/25/02)
4977	Kevin Miner	Lower Wolf Jaw (8/16/91)	Hough (6/29/02)
4978	Robert F. Guba	Iroquois (8/29/93)	Panther (7/1/02)
4979	John A. Tabaczynski	Iroquois (8/29/93)	Panther (7/1/02)
4980	Bruce Anderson	Algonquin (9/77)	Sawteeth (7/4/02)
4981	Daniel A. Nye	Giant (1997)	Redfield (7/5/02)
4982W	Andrea V. Wright	Marcy (6/91)	Couchsachraga (7/6/02)
4983	Mark Robbins	Phelps (10/80)	Haystack (7/11/02)
4984	Carol A. Ehleben	Algonquin (7/25/92)	Hough (7/17/02)
4985	Dennis J. Clarke	Cascade (8/10/99)	Skylight (7/17/02)
4986	Aaron Bilek	Big Slide (1997)	Seymour (7/18/02)
4987	Raymond A. Merkh, Jr.	Giant (7/19/83)	Whiteface (7/19/02)
4988	Robert J. Perry	Nippletop (9/17/78)	Sawteeth (7/20/02)
4989	Thomas E. Whitt	Macomb (7/6/75)	Nippletop (7/21/02)
4990	Mark A. V. Roberts	Giant (summer 1998)	Iroquois (7/21/02)
4991	Douglas R. MacFarland	Algonquin (9/18/93)	Tabletop (7/21/02)
4992	Tim Gibson	Big Slide (6/96)	Panther (7/23/02)
4993	Matthew W. Balaguer	Cascade (7/26/95)	Esther (7/26/02)
4994	Daryl A. Fuller	Cascade (8/79)	Whiteface (7/27/02)
4995	Michael L. Littler	Colden (8/31/80)	Whiteface (7/27/02)
4996	David Lester	Algonquin (6/23/96)	Allen (7/28/02)
4997	Anthony M. Spensieri	Giant (1985)	Big Slide (7/29/02)
4998	Megan McClelland	Cascade (8/20/98)	Santanoni (7/30/02)
4999	David S. Miller	Wright (9/81)	Skylight (7/31/02)
5000	Nicholas B. Miller	Algonquin (8/19/93)	Skylight (7/31/02)
5001	Dave Rogers	Colvin (7/3/01)	Whiteface (8/1/02)
5002	Ben Malcolmson	Seymour (7/7/02)	Whiteface (8/1/02)
5003	Rick Farran	Marcy (10/26/94)	Allen (8/1/02)
5004	Anne Mausolff	Marcy (9/85)	Allen (8/2/02)
5005	Edna Northrup	Marcy (1950)	Allen (8/2/02)
5006	Brendan Murphy	Cascade (7/31/99)	Haystack (8/2/02)
5007	Brian Murphy	Cascade (7/31/99)	Haystack (8/2/02)
5008W	Laurie Schweighardt	Phelps (1989)	Marcy (8/3/02)
5009	Beverly Roberts	Big Slide (5/30/98)	Colden (8/3/02)
5010	Noryce Burgey	Marcy (1980)	Haystack (8/3/02)
5011	Louise Lanthier	Cascade (6/18/01)	Haystack (8/3/02)
5012	Christopher Bonino	Cascade (8/3/91)	Whiteface (8/3/02)
5013	Paul Bonino	Algonquin (8/89)	Whiteface (8/3/02)
5014	Joyce Albro	Big Slide (5/30/98)	Colden (8/3/02)
5015	Coleman Goughary	Cascade (8/31/97)	Whiteface (8/4/02)

The Membership Roster of the Adirondack Forty-Sixers

	Member	First Ascent	Forty-sixth Peak
5016	Emily Goughary	Cascade (8/31/97)	Whiteface (8/4/02)
5017	Debra R. White	Cascade (8/31/97)	Whiteface (8/4/02)
5018	Annie R. Hart	Whiteface (6/20/98)	Skylight (8/4/02)
5019	Michael H. LaFlair, IV	Porter (6/14/97)	Whiteface (8/4/02)
5020	Brendan Richardson	Marcy (8/19/97)	Skylight (8/4/02)
5021	Julie Richardson	Whiteface (10/28/95)	Skylight (8/4/02)
5022	Forrest Van Dyke	Cascade (8/10/95)	Whiteface (8/6/02)
5023	Sarah Van Dyke	Cascade (8/10/95)	Whiteface (8/6/02)
5024	Gary F. Rockwell	Marcy (10/61)	Emmons (8/7/02)
5025	Michael E. Gorman	Whiteface (7/64)	Sawteeth (8/7/02)
5026	Pamela K. Fischer	Cascade (8/1/91)	Emmons (8/8/02)
5027	Robert F. Fischer	Algonquin (8/1/92)	Emmons (8/8/02)
5028	Miriam Goler	Dix (8/8/96)	East Dix (8/8/02)
5029	Paul F. Rabenold	Whiteface (6/15/92)	Haystack (8/8/02)
5030	Christopher D. Alvino	Skylight (8/12/92)	Giant (8/9/02)
5031	Noah M. Silver	Gothics (7/10/99)	Whiteface (8/10/02)
5032	Joel Dobson	Marcy (7/63)	Skylight (8/12/02)
5033	David A. Henderson	Santanoni (10/8/94)	Cascade (8/12/02)
5034	Rene Clarke	Cascade (9/17/97)	Marcy (8/13/02)
5035	Evan Haynes	Cascade (7/96)	Nippletop (8/14/02)
5036	Keith Heidecorn	Cascade (7/96)	Colden (8/15/02)
5037	Andrew Waber	Cascade (7/19/97)	Gray (8/15/02)
5038	Frank J. Graessle	Marcy (7/76)	Whiteface (8/16/02)
5039	Ted Sonneborn	Algonquin (6/19/98)	Allen (8/16/02)
5040	Travis Graves	Algonquin (7/28/98)	Rocky Peak (8/17/02)
5041W	Aileen M. Genett	Algonquin (9/99)	Whiteface (8/17/02)
5042	Jonathan L. St. Mary	Marcy (1958)	Sawteeth (8/17/02)
5043	Nicholas Cohen	Cascade (7/10/98)	Wright (8/17/02)
5044	Jack VanDerzee	Sawteeth (8/12/94)	Colvin (8/17/02)
5045	Kathy Sprowles	Cascade (7/20/97)	Whiteface (8/18/02)
5046	Mark Arrow	Whiteface (10/12/90)	Esther (8/18/02)
5047	Seth Arrow	Whiteface (10/12/90)	Esther (8/18/02)
5048	Matt Bresler	Colden (1996)	Marshall (8/19/02)
5049	Colin J. Walsh	Giant (6/12/99)	Haystack (8/19/02)
5050W	Joseph M. Walsh	Giant (6/12/99)	Haystack (8/19/02)
5051	Marian W. Walsh	Giant (6/12/99)	Haystack (8/19/02)
5052	Peter P. Walsh	Giant (6/12/99)	Haystack (8/19/02)
5053	Maija E. Benjamins	Dix (8/4/99)	Sawteeth (8/19/02)
5054	Steven Wolosoff	Dix (8/4/99)	Sawteeth (8/19/02)
5055	Liza Goodwin	Porter (1995)	Santanoni (8/20/02)
5056	John Devaney	Marcy (8/14/01)	Panther (8/21/02)
5057	Jeri L. Bousman	Cascade (6/61)	Basin (8/22/02)
5058	Patrick A. Clark	Algonquin (11/84)	Emmons (8/22/02)
5059	Stephen S. Oliver	Gothics (7/24/96)	Whiteface (8/24/02)
5060	Scott Shaw	Cascade (8/24/97)	Hough (8/24/02)
5061	Christy G. Adams	Lower Wolf Jaw (8/30/97)	Marcy (8/24/02)
5062	Alan Classen	Lower Wolf Jaw (8/30/97)	Marcy (8/24/02)
5063	David A. Knights	Upper Wolf Jaw (8/17/96)	Colvin (8/24/02)
5064	William Leitch	Giant (8/17/00)	Whiteface (8/24/02)
5065	Ariel Diggory	Skylight (7/90)	Seymour (8/25/02)
5066	Brad Paradis	Giant (7/9/92)	Porter (8/25/02)
5067	Mark Leader	Panther (1994)	Allen (8/26/02)
5068	Jeff Thompson	Whiteface (8/19/89)	Allen (8/30/02)
5069	Brent Lewis	Algonquin (7/3/99)	Allen (8/31/02)
5070	Louise Turcotte	Cascade (4/1/00)	Couchsachraga (8/31/02)
5071	Charles Wasicek	Algonquin (1992)	Allen (8/31/02)
5072	David Heidecorn	Cascade (7/67)	Cliff (8/31/02)
5073	Carol Moran	Marcy (9/15/01)	Marshall (8/31/02)
5074	Brandon Bendura	Porter (6/14/98)	Big Slide (9/1/02)
5075	Michael J. Bendura	Cascade (6/14/97)	Big Slide (9/1/02)
5076	Randy Bendura	Cascade (6/14/97)	Big Slide (9/1/02)
5077	Christopher Leonard	Algonquin (6/6/98)	Big Slide (9/1/02)

Heaven Up-h'isted-ness!

	Member	First Ascent	Forty-sixth Peak
5078	Ethan Leonard	Cascade (6/14/97)	Big Slide (9/1/02)
5079	Paul D. Leonard	Cascade (6/14/97)	Big Slide (9/1/02)
5080	Joshua L. Finkle	Seward (7/16/01)	Couchsachraga (9/1/02)
5081	Terence Finnan	Whiteface (8/48)	Redfield (9/1/02)
5082W	Steve Turon	Macomb (9/7/70)	Whiteface (9/2/02)
5083	Peter Burkhart	Marcy (7/1/02)	Phelps (9/4/02)
5084	Chris Teale	Marcy (7/1/02)	Phelps (9/4/02)
5085	Sam MacNaughton	Gothics (summer 1991)	Colden (9/5/02)
5086	Linda Lou Steiner	Algonquin (8/31/00)	Haystack (9/5/02)
5087	Robert L. Steiner	Algonquin (8/31/00)	Haystack (9/5/02)
5088	King Milne	Cascade (5/20/01)	Tabletop (9/6/02)
5089	Daniel Battin	Algonquin (9/26/99)	Lower Wolf Jaw (9/6/02)
5090	Michael Chiarella	Marcy (6/3/93)	Haystack (9/7/02)
5091	Landon K. Pelkey	Cascade (9/3/97)	Skylight (9/7/02)
5092	Erin E. Pelkey	Cascade (9/3/97)	Skylight (9/7/02)
5093	Dana L. Pelkey	Cascade (9/3/97)	Skylight (9/7/02)
5094	Bethany E. Pelkey	Cascade (9/3/97)	Skylight (9/7/02)
5095	Gregory F. Pelkey	Cascade (9/3/97)	Skylight (9/7/02)
5096	Charley Town	Marcy (7/10/99)	Whiteface (9/8/02)
5097	Dennis G. Wood	Marcy (7/10/99)	Whiteface (9/8/02)
5098	Leonard E. Tremblay	Dix (5/27/96)	Whiteface (9/8/02)
5099W	Judy Henrich	Colden (7/25/00)	Allen (9/8/02)
5100	Leeland R. O'Neal	Marcy (8/19/97)	Skylight (9/13/02)
5101	Benoit Ste-Marie	Marcy (6/20/01)	Redfield (9/13/02)
5102	Elaine Serafini	Phelps (5/24/97)	East Dix (9/14/02)
5103	Stephen M. Ramsey	Colden (9/4/99)	Skylight (9/14/02)
5104	Isabelle Daverne	Cascade (6/10/01)	Macomb (9/14/02)
5105	Jo-Ellen Unger	Porter (9/29/81)	Macomb (9/14/02)
5106	Marsha K. Finnan	Whiteface (1/97)	Seward (9/18/02)
5107	Ronald Larsen	Big Slide (10/20/84)	Haystack (9/18/02)
5108	Dale Klanchnik	Tabletop (5/31/90)	Allen (9/20/02)
5109	Patricia M. Desbiens	Sawteeth (9/19/95)	Colvin (9/21/02)
5110	Nelson H. Harris	Marshall (3/30/69)	Marcy (9/21/02)
5111	Ralph H. Coy	Colvin (8/1/98)	Marcy (9/21/02)
5112	Eric S. Lippincott	Marcy (1985)	Whiteface (9/21/02)
5113	Wendle Lahr	Giant (5/97)	Whiteface (9/21/02)
5114	Kevin Cox	Cascade (5/96)	Basin (9/21/02)
5115	Ian McMullen	Cascade (9/12/95)	Marcy (9/21/02)
5116	Peter J. Valastro, Jr.	Phelps (6/23/01)	Colvin (9/21/02)
5117	Leon Glass	Whiteface (1960)	Cliff (9/21/02)
5118	Daniel P. Michaud	Cliff (6/24/00)	Redfield (9/22/02)
5119	Joyce B. Gannon	Porter (4/27/02)	Whiteface (9/24/02)
5120W	Sean O'Donnell	Cascade (8/10/98)	Marcy (9/25/02)
5121	Sarah Fellows	Giant (1983)	Redfield (9/26/02)
5122	Jon J. Beaulac	Big Slide (9/92)	Whiteface (9/28/02)
5123	Robert A. Silverman	Giant (8/19/00)	Skylight (9/28/02)
5124	Nancie Stone	Giant (7/22/00)	Rocky Peak (9/28/02)
5125	Kenneth L. Swayze, Jr.	Giant (7/22/00)	Rocky Peak (9/28/02)
5126	James S. Kerr-Whitt	Lower Wolf Jaw (1973)	Skylight (9/29/02)
5127	Bruce F. Alexander	Whiteface (8/63)	Esther (9/29/02)
5128	Jon Bentley	Marcy (7/8/96)	Nye (9/29/02)
5129	Matthew W. Boschen	Lower Wolf Jaw (8/25/97)	Whiteface (10/3/02)
5130	Michael Dunham	Cascade (10/9/83)	Haystack (10/5/02)
5131	Sally Price	Giant (9/25/88)	Haystack (10/5/02)
5132	Robert E. Blount	Phelps (1982)	Allen (10/6/02)
5133	Langley R. Muir	Big Slide (11/1/93)	Phelps (10/8/02)
5134	Kathleen M. Bush	Marcy (8/72)	Dix (10/12/02)
5135	F. Claire Fisher	Cascade (8/6/92)	Hough (10/13/02)
5136	Elizabeth A. Cottrell	Cascade (8/91)	Colden (10/13/02)
5137	Caitlin Gucker-Kanter	Cascade (7/90)	Cliff (10/13/02)
5138	Linda Veraska	Cascade (2/18/01)	Whiteface (10/14/02)
5139W	Danny Sanfacon	Wright (10/6/01)	Rocky Peak (10/15/02)

THE MEMBERSHIP ROSTER OF THE ADIRONDACK FORTY-SIXERS

	MEMBER	FIRST ASCENT	FORTY-SIXTH PEAK
5140	Karl Sanfacon	Wright (10/6/01)	Rocky Peak (10/15/02)
5141	Jon Hayner	Nye (6/29/02)	Whiteface (10/19/02)
5142	Raymond P. Fortman	Marcy (7/4/71)	Emmons (10/27/02)
5143	Kerry Smith	Cascade (4/24/95)	Whiteface (10/28/02)
5144	Mark E. Young	Cascade (9/97)	Blake (11/2/02)
5145W	Cara Benson	Algonquin (8/22/01)	Marshall (11/12/02)
5146W	Roger C. Binkerd	Giant (12/5/00)	Redfield (11/14/02)
5147	Michael McDermott	Marcy (11/23/94)	Esther (11/23/02)
5148	Marty Krise	Sawteeth (3/95)	Whiteface (11/27/02)
5149	William G. Olsen	Marcy (11/19/94)	Colden (12/7/02)
5150W	Erik Svendsen	Marcy (8/93)	Seymour (12/22/02)
5151	David Cross	Cascade (5/24/96)	Whiteface (12/23/02)
5152	Eric Cross	Giant (5/24/96)	Whiteface (12/23/02)
5153	Jessica Cross	Cascade (5/24/96)	Whiteface (12/23/02)
5154W	Jack Whitney	Big Slide (8/26/01)	Haystack (12/28/02)
5155	Jimmy R. Vaughn	Marcy (3/18/00)	Skylight (12/30/02)
5156	Willing L. Biddle	Cascade (10/71)	Haystack (2/1/75)
5157	Andrew J. Koerner	Colden (7/4/69)	Redfield (5/25/75)
5158	Keith J. Pedzich	Algonquin (10/88)	Dial (7/17/99)
5159	Dianne Krusen	Marcy (8/27/89)	Seymour (9/9/01)
5160	Brian J. Keller	Gray (5/99)	Allen (6/17/02)
5161	Annette Marshall	Phelps (10/12/96)	Giant (6/22/02)
5162	Edward Townsend	Porter (10/7/90)	Colden (6/29/02)
5163	Phil Masterson	Seymour (7/7/02)	Whiteface (8/1/02)
5164	Andrew L. Leighton	Colden (1999)	Whiteface (8/1/02)
5165	Peter Mellgard	Porter (6/30/98)	Skylight (8/2/02)
5166	Peter Pendergrass	Giant (10/23/93)	Cliff (8/9/02)
5167	Teri Pendergrass	Giant (10/9/93)	Cliff (8/9/02)
5168	Robert M. Butler	Algonquin (6/17/00)	Whiteface (8/24/02)
5169	Christin Liberty	Gothics (10/3/98)	Whiteface (9/2/02)
5170	Christopher Dirolf	Cascade (8/95)	Rocky Peak (9/14/02)
5171	George Dirolf	Cascade (8/95)	Rocky Peak (9/14/02)
5172	Jean Chevrier	Lower Wolf Jaw (5/10/97)	Hough (9/14/02)
5173	Phyllis A. Manziano	Algonquin (6/95)	Marcy (9/21/02)
5174	Sebastien Clement	Algonquin (7/7/01)	Marcy (9/22/02)
5175	Amy Richard	Algonquin (7/7/01)	Marcy (9/22/02)
5176	Fred Galster	Iroquois (8/9/91)	Dix (10/13/02)
5177	Bruce Kenna	Phelps (6/1/76)	Gray (10/14/02)
5178W	Lutz Heinrich	Whiteface (10/23/93)	Tabletop (10/14/02)
5179	Mary Jolly	Marcy (11/5/94)	Santanoni (10/19/02)
5180	James R. Clark	Wright (7/16/98)	Colden (10/27/02)
5181	Michael TerBoss	Phelps (5/24/96)	Whiteface (11/27/02)
5182W	James J. Knapp	Sawteeth (1/5/02)	Cliff (3/15/03)
5183	Nathan Winters	Cascade (3/92)	Haystack (4/2/03)
5184	Matthew J. Young	Cascade (9/5/97)	Allen (5/31/03)
5185	Thomas L. Myers	Phelps (10/9/93)	Santanoni (6/1/03)
5186	Mark H. Rolerson	Phelps (5/29/76)	Allen (6/15/03)
5187	Todd R. Williams	Phelps (1985)	Emmons (6/19/03)
5188W	Nan Giblin	Giant (9/4/99)	Seward (6/28/03)
5189W	Suzanne Knabe	Marcy (5/27/00)	Seymour (6/28/03)
5190	David M. Galvin	Marcy (7/91)	Sawteeth (7/3/03)
5191	Norman Swift	Cascade (9/9/98)	Blake (7/4/03)
5192	Margaret F. Flynn	Macomb (8/89)	Haystack (7/5/03)
5193W	William W. Elinski	Cascade (7/24/77)	Seymour (7/7/03)
5194W	Sheila Joly	Cascade (9/2/01)	Seymour (7/13/03)
5195	Seth Coates	Lower Wolf Jaw (7/15/97)	Whiteface (7/15/03)
5196W	Rick Balboni	Algonquin (8/1/99)	Haystack (7/19/03)
5197	Charles M. Patton	Marcy (8/93)	Whiteface (7/19/03)
5198	Keith Powell	Wright (9/89)	Algonquin (7/19/03)
5199	Jeremy M. Patton	Marcy (8/93)	Whiteface (7/19/03)
5200	Robert Campbell	Marcy (8/93)	Whiteface (7/19/03)
5201	Luke Ambrose	Algonquin (8/88)	Sawteeth (7/19/03)

HEAVEN UP-H'ISTED-NESS!

	MEMBER	FIRST ASCENT	FORTY-SIXTH PEAK
5202	David Charles	Marcy (10/7/79)	Skylight (7/21/03)
5203	Kenneth W. Henneberry	Lower Wolf Jaw (9/4/93)	Seymour (7/26/03)
5204	Leigh-Anne Webster	Giant (5/20/00)	Marshall (7/26/03)
5205	Steven L. Kelley	Giant (7/17/98)	Santanoni (7/27/03)
5206	Gary Steinberg	Gothics (8/23/96)	Seymour (7/28/03)
5207	Joan Kelly	Cascade (4/18/98)	Haystack (7/30/03)
5208	Richard Kelly	Cascade (4/18/98)	Haystack (7/30/03)
5209	Munib P. Jalali	Cascade (8/12/84)	Dix (7/31/03)
5210	Alexander F. Tilton	Colden (8/93)	Dix (7/31/03)
5211	James Giambrone	Marcy (8/1/92)	Haystack (8/2/03)
5212	Robert Pedzich	Tabletop (1/27/62)	Sawteeth (8/2/03)
5213	C Michael Robinson	Lower Wolf Jaw (7/19/95)	Sawteeth (8/2/03)
5214	Caitlin M. Livsey	Cascade (6/96)	Skylight (8/3/03)
5215	Duncan K. Holley	Cascade (1997)	Wright (8/3/03)
5216	Bar Aiken	Big Slide (7/11/72)	Skylight (8/4/03)
5217	Alex Kinsey	Big Slide (7/17/99)	Sawteeth (8/7/03)
5218	David Rudd	Algonquin (5/24/97)	Iroquois (8/8/03)
5219	Brian H. Schutz	Cascade (9/95)	Whiteface (8/9/03)
5220	Nicholas Gaffney	Marcy (9/85)	Phelps (8/10/03)
5221	Jan Carlson	East Dix (9/30/01)	Skylight (8/10/03)
5222	James M. Holley	Cascade (1998)	Allen (8/10/03)
5223	Jeremy Peterseil	Wright (7/27/99)	Allen (8/11/03)
5224	Rebecca Vogel	Cascade (8/96)	Whiteface (8/13/03)
5225	Andrew Bergman	Porter (6/26/01)	Iroquois (8/15/03)
5226	Beth H. Edgley	Cascade (1966)	Nippletop (8/16/03)
5227	Sandra Weber	Phelps (7/2/88)	Nippletop (8/16/03)
5228	Nathan E. Peters	Big Slide (2/94)	Marcy (8/17/03)
5229	Peter F. Hedglon	Marcy (5/18/96)	Redfield (8/17/03)
5230	Richard Warham	Dix (7/8/97)	Redfield (8/17/03)
5231	Roger Felske	Giant (8/8/93)	Marcy (8/17/03)
5232	Roberta Taggart	Big Slide (7/98)	Dix (8/18/03)
5233	Margaret Wooster	Giant (8/17/91)	Santanoni (8/21/03)
5234	Michael A. Strich	Cascade (6/11/94)	Panther (8/22/03)
5235	James Hunt	Giant (6/12/99)	Redfield (8/23/03)
5236	Michael Schwarzchild	Cascade (7/64)	Marshall (8/23/03)
5237	Christopher R. Sausville	Gothics (6/91)	Whiteface (8/23/03)
5238	Michael C. Loner	Big Slide (9/82)	Iroquois (8/26/03)
5239	George B. Herder	Marcy (8/31/97)	Allen (8/28/03)
5240	Daniel P. Callahan	Whiteface (3/15/00)	Hough (8/29/03)
5241	William L. Weber, III	Phelps (7/2/88)	Skylight (8/30/03)
5242	Peter Lane	Cascade (6/28/91)	Iroquois (8/30/03)
5243	Edward P. Bonner	Algonquin (8/29/87)	Whiteface (8/30/03)
5244	Roger J. Couch	Algonquin (8/29/87)	Whiteface (8/30/03)
5245	Carole Stanbro	Giant (8/27/83)	Marcy (8/30/03)
5246	Edward Elinski	Wright (8/23/76)	Redfield (8/31/03)
5247	Linda S. Field	Cascade (7/28/01)	Whiteface (8/31/03)
5248	Thomas Field	Algonquin (6/29/01)	Whiteface (8/31/03)
5249	Brendan Molloy	Porter (8/9/01)	Saddleback (8/31/03)
5250	James Molloy	Porter (8/9/01)	Saddleback (8/31/03)
5251	Anthony Molloy	Porter (8/9/01)	Saddleback (8/31/03)
5252	Sean Molloy	Porter (8/9/01)	Saddleback (8/31/03)
5253	Danny Paquet	Algonquin (3/20/96)	Allen (8/31/03)
5254	Elliott A. Lacki	Marcy (8/30/99)	Dix (9/1/03)
5255	Richard B. Lacki	Marcy (8/30/99)	Dix (9/1/03)
5256	Larry B. Battles	East Dix (10/1/00)	Macomb (9/1/03)
5257	Eileen Clarke	Cascade (9/16/94)	Whiteface (9/1/03)
5258	John Clarke	Cascade (9/16/94)	Whiteface (9/1/03)
5259*	James DeLorenzo	Giant (8/19/00)	Saddleback (9/4/03)
5260	Jack Garrison	Marcy (8/27/93)	Rocky Peak (9/5/03)
5261	Scott Rasnake	Marcy (9/18/00)	Panther (9/5/03)
5262	Bob Langston	Big Slide (1970)	Whiteface (9/5/03)
5263	Steve Miller	Marcy (8/27/93)	Rocky Peak (9/5/03)

The Membership Roster of the Adirondack Forty-Sixers

	Member	First Ascent	Forty-sixth Peak
5264W	Robert Scaife	Algonquin (10/9/99)	Wright (9/6/03)
5265	Sally Hart	Marcy (5/16/98)	Seymour (9/6/03)
5266	Bruce McAlpine	Marcy (11/10/95)	Emmons (9/6/03)
5267	Judith Teuber	Marcy (11/10/95)	Emmons (9/6/03)
5268	Paul Rightmyer	Cascade (8/3/96)	Skylight (9/6/03)
5269	Judy Rightmyer	Phelps (7/3/95)	Skylight (9/6/03)
5270	Gary Clarke	Giant (9/23/95)	Whiteface (9/6/03)
5271	Susan Hoff-Haynes	Marcy (9/15/01)	Tabletop (9/6/03)
5272	Jay T. French	Giant (9/23/95)	Whiteface (9/6/03)
5273	Patricia M. Hurlburt	Street (1/2/02)	Algonquin (9/7/03)
5274	Mike Sala	Marcy (5/79)	Gray (9/9/03)
5275	Thomas A. Lizzio	Skylight (9/88)	Macomb (9/10/03)
5276	James Racquet	Marcy (9/23/96)	Gray (9/11/03)
5277W	Lori Clark	Cascade (8/23/95)	Colden (9/13/03)
5278	Kathy Cronin	Lower Wolf Jaw (7/29/95)	Iroquois (9/13/03)
5279	Brian Richardson	Big Slide (7/93)	Whiteface (9/13/03)
5280	Thomas E. Zebrowski	Colden (9/2/89)	Emmons (9/13/03)
5281	Tom Urell	Marcy (7/20/01)	Allen (9/14/03)
5282	Joan Marcher	Algonquin (7/13/98)	Seymour (9/18/03)
5283	Christopher H. DeVoe	Big Slide (5/22/80)	Whiteface (9/20/03)
5284	Eric R. Richardson	Marcy (7/21/77)	Whiteface (9/20/03)
5285	Sarah N. Krebs	Porter (7/29/97)	Marcy (9/21/03)
5286	Robert C. Krebs	Porter (7/29/97)	Marcy (9/21/03)
5287	Mick Giroux	Cascade (10/79)	Marshall (9/21/03)
5288	Ray Blair	Giant (9/13/97)	Marcy (9/21/03)
5289	Bob DeSantis	Giant (9/13/97)	Marcy (9/21/03)
5290	Bess Arden	Gothics (6/20/96)	Whiteface (9/21/03)
5291	Elaine Schwartz	Marcy (8/49)	Allen (9/21/03)
5292	Paul Coarding	Whiteface (10/8/97)	Marshall (9/24/03)
5293	William Brandow	Marcy (6/7/90)	Skylight (9/26/03)
5294	James Hogan	Algonquin (8/88)	Skylight (9/26/03)
5295	Janet Priest Jones	Colvin (8/17/99)	Marcy (9/26/03)
5296	Gina L. Hazen	Giant (7/23/00)	Esther (9/27/03)
5297	Todd G. Harris	Giant (7/23/00)	Esther (9/27/03)
5298	Patrick D. Pline	Marcy (7/2/96)	Allen (9/27/03)
5299	Susan L. Pline	Marcy (7/2/96)	Allen (9/27/03)
5300	Amy P. Hartman	Algonquin (9/24/95)	Iroquois (9/30/03)
5301	Richard O. Hartman II	Algonquin (9/24/95)	Iroquois (9/30/03)
5302	Ruben Marshall	Marcy (8/9/93)	Marshall (10/3/03)
5303	Richard J. Lightcap	Giant (9/2/91)	Marshall (10/3/03)
5304	Fred Breglia	Giant (1991)	Allen (10/4/03)
5305	Gregory J. Schaefer	Algonquin (8/15/63)	Esther (10/5/03)
5306	Susan F. Sliva	Cascade (4/97)	Marshall (10/5/03)
5307	Geralyn M. O'Reilly	Giant (10/15/87)	Haystack (10/6/03)
5308	Susan C. Smith	Giant (5/11/02)	Whiteface (10/9/03)
5309	Dan Curtin	Giant (8/23/93)	Whiteface (10/11/03)
5310	Donna Anderson	Algonquin (7/25/99)	Porter (10/11/03)
5311	Walter B. Barney	Marcy (9/3/98)	Whiteface (10/11/03)
5312	Roy M. Keats	Giant (8/23/92)	Whiteface (10/11/03)
5313	Sarah L. Keats	Giant (8/23/92)	Whiteface (10/11/03)
5314	David Ports	Santanoni (8/4/01)	Colden (10/11/03)
5315	Augusta Wilson	Dix (8/18/95)	Marshall (10/12/03)
5316W	Mary Warchocki	Marcy (6/22/00)	Rocky Peak (10/18/03)
5317	Michael LaPorte	Marcy (9/87)	Colden (10/18/03)
5318	Alan Hight	Phelps (8/7/94)	Colden (10/18/03)
5319	Madeline Morrissey	Tabletop (9/97)	Redfield (10/18/03)
5320W	Spencer Morrissey	Colvin (9/11/95)	Redfield (10/18/03)
5321W	Brian Yourdon, Jr.	Marcy (9/14/91)	Redfield (10/18/03)
5322	Christopher J. Devaney	Marcy (8/14/91)	Couchsachraga (10/19/03)
5323	Paul Demers	Giant (10/26/96)	Haystack (10/25/03)
5324	A. J. Lednor	Dial (5/31/03)	Sawteeth (11/1/03)
5325	Don VanWely	Porter (6/13/92)	Seymour (11/8/03)

Heaven Up-h'isted-ness!

	Member	First Ascent	Forty-sixth Peak
5326W	Russell Raymond	Cascade (8/22/02)	Haystack (11/24/03)
5327W	Philip Schlosser	Tabletop (10/22/00)	Nye (12/23/03)
5328	Joshua Cohen	Marcy (summer 1967)	Esther (8/30/82)
5329	Larry Cohen	Marcy (8/51)	Esther (8/30/82)
5330	Charles K. McCarthy	Wright (8/22/76)	Upper Wolf Jaw (8/16/85)
5331	Ina J. McCarthy	Cascade (7/25/64)	Upper Wolf Jaw (8/16/85)
5332	Adam K. Hovey	Cascade (1/20/90)	Haystack (5/30/92)
5333	Scott McClurg	Dix (9/82)	Rocky Peak (8/01)
5334	Merle Longwood	Cascade (6/14/97)	Whiteface (8/18/02)
5335	Nicolas Gerold	Lower Wolf Jaw (8/72)	Allen (9/20/02)
5336	Herb Terns	Wright (summer 1997)	Whiteface (9/23/02)
5337	Peter Caradonna	Porter (7/00)	Haystack (7/5/03)
5338	Erik Font	Tabletop (7/19/99)	Haystack (7/11/03)
5339	Euan Reid	Colden (2001)	Big Slide (8/18/03)
5340	Kathleen Fazioli	Rocky Peak (8/15/98)	Basin (8/31/03)
5341	Teresa E. Ritzel	Cascade (7/3/95)	Allen (8/31/03)
5342	Susan M. Carpenter	Cascade (7/3/95)	Allen (8/31/03)
5343	Alexander F. Durant	Cascade (7/22/97)	Sawteeth (12/30/03)
5344W	Rick E. Bush	Marcy (12/26/97)	Allen (3/13/04)
5345W	Michael C. Magnani	Algonquin (3/3/01)	Whiteface (3/13/04)
5346W	Richard P. Dabal	Giant (1/6/03)	Allen (3/14/04)
5347W	Edward A. Deno	Cascade (8/14/92)	Couchsachraga (3/20/04)
5348	Frank Deno	Algonquin (7/92)	Couchsachraga (3/20/04)
5349	Keith A. Deno	Marcy (9/15/93)	Couchsachraga (3/20/04)
5350W	Cindy H. McLean	Marcy (8/00)	East Dix (3/21/04)
5351	David N. Nichols	Marcy (1989)	Colden (5/2/04)
5352	Joshua Nichols	Phelps (5/25/97)	Colden (5/2/04)
5353	Donna Tuttle	Marcy (6/9/90)	Allen (5/22/04)
5354	Rich Merritt	Cascade (1974)	Emmons (5/27/04)
5355	Christiane Mulvihill	Big Slide (9/15/01)	Dix (5/29/04)
5356	Gail Sanders	Giant (5/22/99)	Haystack (6/3/04)
5357W	Robert Van Hise	Cascade (5/6/00)	Emmons (6/10/04)
5358	Braden Houston	Giant (8/4/00)	Iroquois (6/12/04)
5359	Jean Roy	Whiteface (7/21/01)	East Dix (6/12/04)
5360	Benjamin Campbell	Giant (9/22/02)	Allen (6/15/04)
5361	Bruce R. Terbush	Dix (4/77)	Emmons (6/23/04)
5362	Karen B. Terbush	Algonquin (10/77)	Emmons (6/23/04)
5363	Brian Connors	Wright (8/22/97)	Redfield (6/25/04)
5364	Pat Connors	Wright (8/22/97)	Redfield (6/25/04)
5365	Tim Connors	Wright (8/22/97)	Redfield (6/25/04)
5366	Stuart A. Buchanan	Wright (7/14/02)	Whiteface (6/26/04)
5367	Ali Buchanan	Wright (7/14/02)	Whiteface (6/26/04)
5368	Eric Maughan	Cascade (10/5/97)	Marcy (7/2/04)
5369	Mary Sue McCarthy	Dial (1975)	Colden (7/3/04)
5370	Richard Droscoski	Gothics (7/11/00)	Gray (7/4/04)
5371	Ryan Fick	Dial (1/25/03)	Sawteeth (9/5/04)
5372	Rebecca Pollard	Haystack (7/8/02)	Santanoni (7/6/04)
5373	Gretchen Stark	Big Slide (6/27/91)	Hough (7/10/04)
5374	Margaret Gaertner	Cascade (unknown)	Seymour (7/10/04)
5375	Frederick S. Chick	Giant (spring 1990)	Allen (7/17/04)
5376	S. Garen Szablewski	Haystack (9/23/01)	Allen (7/17/04)
5377	Kevin Zagorda	Colden (7/82)	Allen (7/17/04)
5378	Dan Bell	Giant (summer 1998)	Couchsachraga (7/17/04)
5379	Matthew Bell	Seward (7/6/01)	Couchsachraga (7/17/04)
5380W	Douglas Hillman	Marcy (9/16/97)	Basin (7/17/04)
5381	Joseph T. Burchenal	Cascade (9/4/94)	Whiteface (7/24/04)
5382	Kate Burchenal	Cascade (5/26/96)	Whiteface (7/24/04)
5383	Wells Landers	Cascade (7/31/93)	Whiteface (7/24/04)
5384	Philip W. Arnold	Marcy (11/91)	Cascade (7/24/04)
5385	Richard Reichman	Algonquin (7/15/90)	Hough (7/24/04)
5386	Thomas V. Stellato	Giant (7/17/98)	Cliff (7/24/04)
5387	Stephanie B. Mason	Marcy (1960)	East Dix (7/25/04)

The Membership Roster of the Adirondack Forty-Sixers

	Member	First Ascent	Forty-sixth Peak
5388	Clark E. Hayward	Giant (7/10/78)	Hough (7/25/04)
5389	George W. Miller	Giant (7/2/95)	Hough (7/25/04)
5390	Sarah Hoskinson	Marcy (7/24/96)	Emmons (7/25/04)
5391	Hank Schiffman	Algonquin (7/65)	Sawteeth (7/25/04)
5392	Steve Schiffman	Wright (1963)	Sawteeth (7/25/04)
5393	John M. Chapman	Dix (7/2/98)	Hough (7/29/04)
5394	Rodney G. Bashant	Marcy (9/4/99)	Nippletop (7/30/04)
5395	Lanny R. Bashant	Marcy (9/3/99)	Nippletop (7/30/04)
5396	William R. Tyra	Giant (6/73)	Redfield (7/31/04)
5397	Luke Bucciarelli	Dix (7/6/00)	Hough (7/31/04)
5398	Lawrence Mele	Algonquin (8/16/98)	Seymour (8/1/04)
5399	Mary Chartier	Giant (8/12/92)	Colden (8/1/04)
5400	Scott Chartier	Giant (8/12/92)	Colden (8/1/04)
5401W	Randy P. Caldwell	Macomb (8/5/00)	Emmons (8/1/04)
5402	George R. Bailie	Wright (7/89)	Haystack (8/2/04)
5403W	George E. Banks, V	Cascade (10/25/96)	Seymour (8/5/04)
5404	Albert Laubinger	Cascade (4/18/98)	Whiteface (8/7/04)
5405W	Stephane Dubois	Phelps (1994)	Rocky Peak (8/7/04)
5406	Nathalie Menard	Algonquin (8/5/01)	Allen (8/7/04)
5407	Terry H. Moore	Cascade (8/8/01)	Seward (8/8/04)
5408	Jeff Williams	Wright (6/10/01)	Whiteface (8/9/04)
5409	Dan Forget	Marcy (9/92)	Allen (8/9/04)
5410	Summer Reed	Blake (7/9/01)	Redfield (8/10/04)
5411	Benjamin J. Kallman	Wright (unknown)	Allen (8/11/04)
5412	Joshua Higgins	Saddleback (10/11/92)	Marcy (8/11/04)
5413	Andrea Robinson	Wright (1975)	Dial (8/12/04)
5414	Allison Emery	Algonquin (7/13/00)	Allen (8/13/04)
5415	Emma Whitman	Algonquin (7/27/00)	Allen (8/13/04)
5416W	Wayne Gray	Big Slide (6/7/03)	Lower Wolf Jaw (8/14/04)
5417	Ian Fitzmorris	Algonquin (8/97)	Whiteface (8/14/04)
5418	Ronald F. Gordon, Jr.	Colden (6/73)	Whiteface (8/14/04)
5419	Ed Wheeler	Giant (unknown)	Skylight (8/14/04)
5420	Tessa Wheeler	Big Slide (1993)	Skylight (8/14/04)
5421	Michael Taptick	Phelps (7/91)	Giant (8/14/04)
5422	William B. Russell	Algonquin (7/74)	Iroquois (8/15/04)
5423	William Holland	Cascade (7/14/00)	Iroquois (8/15/04)
5424	Miles Johnson	Cascade (7/14/00)	Iroquois (8/15/04)
5425	Brendan Wilson	Marcy (10/11/86)	Whiteface (8/15/04)
5426	Thomas Hoffman	Giant (7/92)	Allen (8/18/04)
5427	Colin F. Hunt	Cascade (8/25/93)	Santanoni (8/20/04)
5428	Anika James	Cascade (8/25/93)	Santanoni (8/20/04)
5429	Alexander Welles	Big Slide (7/6/90)	Rocky Peak (8/20/04)
5430	Kevin B. MacKenzie	Cascade (10/2/02)	Couchsachraga (8/21/04)
5431	James R. Ackerman	Wright (9/24/88)	Whiteface (8/21/04)
5432	Bradford Shaw	Algonquin (7/92)	Skylight (8/22/04)
5433	Hollie Shaw	Wright (10/15/94)	Skylight (8/22/04)
5434	Raymond H. Palmer	Algonquin (5/12/93)	Haystack (8/24/04)
5435	Sandy Kuhn	Algonquin (9/80)	Redfield (8/24/04)
5436	Marlene Wegman	Marcy (5/24/98)	Marshall (8/24/04)
5437	Dick Hihn	Marcy (8/92)	Haystack (8/25/04)
5438	Joanne Hihn	Marcy (8/92)	Haystack (8/25/04)
5439	Jeff Byers	Big Slide (6/87)	Seward (8/25/04)
5440	Glenn H. Chapman	Cascade (9/19/98)	Allen (8/28/04)
5441	Mark S. Davis	Marcy (summer 1975)	Allen (8/28/04)
5442	Adrian M. Payeur	Big Slide (6/14/03)	Iroquois (8/28/04)
5443	Dawn Hamilton	Panther (7/14/01)	Whiteface (8/28/04)
5444W	Tom Rankin	Nye (9/1/01)	Whiteface (8/28/04)
5445	Richard Hoskinson	Marcy (1968)	Redfield (8/28/04)
5446	E. Gray Watkins	Marcy (8/95)	Haystack (8/28/04)
5447	Edward C. Bermant	Marcy (8/21/94)	Sawteeth (8/29/04)
5448	Ryan Silvius	Big Slide (7/24/00)	Haystack (9/1/04)
5449	Kathleen Silvius	Big Slide (7/24/00)	Haystack (9/1/04)

Heaven Up-h'isted-ness!

	Member	First Ascent	Forty-sixth Peak
5450	Raymond J. Bazydlo	Dial (9/28/02)	Haystack (9/2/04)
5451	Danielle Besso	Cascade (5/16/04)	Colden (9/4/04)
5452	Howard G. Thompson	Wright (7/5/96)	Allen (9/4/04)
5453	Julie Thompson	Wright (7/5/96)	Allen (9/4/04)
5454W	Nancy Donohue	Marcy (7/79)	East Dix (9/4/04)
5455	Lynne M. Anderson	Marcy (1980)	Dix (9/4/04)
5456	William M. Medeiros	Porter (3/4/00)	Cliff (9/4/04)
5457	Michael Yergeau	Cascade (3/4/00)	Cliff (9/4/04)
5458	Carol A. Renninger	Algonquin (6/22/85)	Hough (9/4/04)
5459	Ashley K. Dubois	Cascade (8/1/99)	Whiteface (9/5/04)
5460	Katie Dubois	Cascade (8/1/99)	Whiteface (9/5/04)
5461	Nicholas Dubois	Cascade (8/1/99)	Whiteface (9/5/04)
5462	Timothy J. Dubois	Cascade (8/1/99)	Whiteface (9/5/04)
5463	Marilyn E. Rees	Marcy (9/9/00)	Sawteeth (9/5/04)
5464W	Daniel E. Russell	Dix (7/3/94)	Couchsachraga (9/5/04)
5465W	Jean C. Russell	Algonquin (1972)	Couchsachraga (9/5/04)
5466	Paul A. Dobrzynski	Marcy (9/9/00)	Sawteeth (9/5/04)
5467	Eugene Allen	Upper Wolf Jaw (1970)	Whiteface (9/5/04)
5468	Ken Allen	Lower Wolf Jaw (1970)	Whiteface (9/5/04)
5469	Mary Chayka-Crawford	Nippletop (8/12/00)	Colden (9/5/04)
5470	Daniel E. Crane	Giant (8/93)	Rocky Peak (9/6/04)
5471	Susan Cowles	Cascade (8/12/98)	Rocky Peak (9/7/04)
5472	Nancy Skiff	Upper Wolf Jaw (6/20/92)	Macomb (9/7/04)
5473W	Jason E. Chlopecki	Dix (9/16/98)	Basin (9/11/04)
5474	Charles Lutomski	Cascade (8/7/93)	Nippletop (9/11/04)
5475	Thomas Austin	Marcy (6/21/97)	Santanoni (9/11/04)
5476W	Lyle Montgomery	Gothics (10/13/97)	Sawteeth (9/11/04)
5477	David Bureau	Marcy (6/1/79)	Santanoni (9/11/04)
5478	Mary Jane L. Meier	Macomb (9/5/93)	Haystack (9/11/04)
5479	Otto Meier	Macomb (9/5/93)	Haystack (9/11/04)
5480	Mark Greenwald	Haystack (8/11/92)	Allen (9/12/04)
5481	Darrel M. Vanier	Giant (9/18/96)	Allen (9/12/04)
5482	Duke Hergatt	Macomb (10/81)	Emmons (9/13/04)
5483	David C. Shuler	Marcy (7/8/95)	Seymour (9/17/04)
5484	Ellen Dwyer	Marcy (9/01/01)	Skylight (9/17/04)
5485	Michael Dwyer	Marcy (9/1/01)	Skylight (9/17/04)
5486	Frank K. Krueger	Big Slide (7/16/91)	Cliff (9/17/04)
5487	J. Robert Moman	Giant (6/15/03)	Whiteface (9/18/04)
5488	Gary W. Burns	Big Slide (6/24/92)	Saddleback (9/18/04)
5489	Benoit Cantin	Cascade (8/17/02)	Whiteface (9/18/04)
5490	Michael DiLorenzo	Big Slide (8/96)	Iroquois (9/19/04)
5491	Paul C. Mierop	Cascade (8/31/91)	Rocky Peak (9/20/04)
5492	Jim Blais	Cascade (9/1/98)	Basin (9/20/04)
5493	Will Nixon	Colden (8/5/01)	Rocky Peak (9/24/04)
5494	Peter Anderson	Marcy (3/12/77)	Esther (9/25/04)
5495	Jeffrey R. Harper	Saddleback (9/30/93)	Whiteface (9/25/04)
5496	Michael H. Semeraro	Cascade (9/19/98)	Wright (9/25/04)
5497	Martha Lawthers	Marcy (8/29/72)	Redfield (9/26/04)
5498	Gerald Beaumont	Esther (5/15/99)	Nye (9/27/04)
5499	Ravi K. Nareppa	Marcy (7/25/02)	Allen (9/27/04)
5500	Carl Aiken	Wright (10/14/00)	Nippletop (10/1/04)
5501	Scott Peak	Macomb (7/20/91)	Iroquois (10/1/04)
5502	Alison L. Widrick	Phelps (4/99)	Marcy (10/2/04)
5503	Cassius L. Jones	Marcy (10/2/76)	Wright (10/2/04)
5504	Diann Zeigler	Giant (7/18/99)	Rocky Peak (10/2/04)
5505	Bruce Gilman	Seward (fall 1974)	Whiteface (10/2/04)
5506W	Andrew Lavigne	Wright (5/10/94)	Gray (10/3/04)
5507	Markus Wandel	Giant (5/5/96)	Gray (10/3/04)
5508	Kate Mazdzer	Cascade (8/17/96)	Whiteface (10/3/04)
5509	Sara Mazdzer	Cascade (8/17/96)	Whiteface (10/3/04)
5510	Stewart Linendoll	Haystack (8/1/74)	Rocky Peak (10/3/04)
5511	Yves Lambert	Cascade (5/6/94)	Saddleback (10/3/04)

The Membership Roster of the Adirondack Forty-Sixers

	Member	First Ascent	Forty-sixth Peak
5512	Caroline Doucet	Colden (1/26/03)	Tabletop (10/3/04)
5513	Mike Ostrouch	Marcy (9/21/96)	Seymour (10/8/04)
5514	Bonnie L. Seifried	Giant (summer 1992)	Esther (10/9/04)
5515	Kevin Heckeler	Cascade (3/15/03)	Phelps (10/9/04)
5516	Irene McCarty	Whiteface (1995)	Haystack (10/10/04)
5517	Sarah Sai Kam Ip	Marcy (5/29/99)	Colden (10/10/04)
5518	Ray Lin	Marcy (5/29/99)	Colden (10/10/04)
5519	Donald W. Hoffman	Colvin (6/27/92)	Marcy (10/11/04)
5520	Dione T. Quinn	Marcy (7/19/99)	Seymour (10/11/04)
5521	Claudia K. St. John	Giant (11/5/77)	Skylight (10/17/04)
5522	Jason Broman	Cascade (1/03)	Dix (10/17/04)
5523	Michael Dashnaw	Algonquin (8/89)	Gray (10/18/04)
5524	Joel M. Dashnaw	Algonquin (summer 1990)	Gray (10/18/04)
5525W	Laurie Moore (Rankin)	Giant (2/22/99)	Rocky Peak (10/22/04)
5526	Sheldon Reeves	Phelps (8/31/03)	Marcy (10/23/04)
5527	Steve Reeves	Phelps (8/31/03)	Marcy (10/23/04)
5528	Peter Schultz	Marcy (8/92)	Whiteface (10/23/04)
5529	Lynn Choromanskis	Wright (9/17/01)	Allen (10/26/04)
5530	Jan DeGrijs	Wright (9/17/01)	Allen (10/26/04)
5531	Rodney Ziak	Giant (9/1/92)	Cliff (10/26/04)
5532W	Denise M. Mongillo	Whiteface (10/13/03)	Big Slide (10/30/04)
5533	Cameron J. Rathbun	Cascade (11/9/99)	Sawteeth (11/6/04)
5534	Bradley J. Gasawski	Cascade (10/5/02)	Colden (11/13/04)
5535W	John Casey	Phelps (3/25/99)	Marcy (11/22/04)
5536	Will Russell	Dix (1994)	Nippletop (12/31/04)
5537	Patrick McCarthy	Wright (8/22/76)	Marshall (9/1/84)
5538W	Donnabeth Stewart	Upper Wolf Jaw (5/25/96)	Dial (3/30/97)
5539	Lynn Smith	Cascade (1980)	Allen (6/26/00)
5540	Michael Shepard	Cascade (9/2/97)	Redfield (9/8/01)
5541	Eva Luderowski	Phelps (7/14/97)	Santanoni (7/30/02)
5542	Stanley W. Barnes	Cascade (9/4/96)	Allen (8/7/02)
5543	Jack LaBombard	Phelps (7/15/99)	Whiteface (8/24/02)
5544	Nicholas C. Taylor	Marcy (8/23/84)	Couchsachraga (8/29/02)
5545	Katherine C. Taylor	Nippletop (8/87)	Redfield (9/3/02)
5546	Damien J. Lazar	Giant (5/28/97)	Dix (7/18/03)
5547	Charles J. Boland	Seymour (7/20/02)	Gray (7/25/03)
5548	Kim Shepard	Cascade (9/2/97)	East Dix (7/26/03)
5549	Jeffrey Chin	Seymour (7/21/02)	Gray (7/29/03)
5550W	Tom Vartuli	Santanoni (2/27/99)	Whiteface (6/15/04)
5551W	Justin P. Lefco	Algonquin (7/96)	Skylight (7/22/04)
5552	Maria O'Connell	Giant (9/88)	Allen (8/14/04)
5553	Jacob Gittler	Porter (7/01)	Saddleback (8/18/04)
5554	Nicholas Welles	Armstrong (8/19/93)	Rocky Peak (8/20/04)
5555	Curtis G. Menton	Giant (9/5/98)	Redfield (8/25/04)
5556	Robert Ohanesian	Whiteface (8/31/98)	Skylight (9/2/04)
5557	Lisa Casey	Giant (8/24/02)	East Dix (9/4/04)
5558W	Leslie J. Knox	Gothics (7/21/01)	Whiteface (9/5/04)
5559	Daniel S. Dubois	Giant (6/1/02)	Whiteface (9/5/04)
5560	Laurel duBois	Cascade (1987)	East Dix (9/5/04)
5561	Rosemary Daley	Giant (9/13/87)	Blake (9/11/04)
5562	John Messina	Marcy (5/87)	Redfield (9/11/04)
5563	Paul Szymanski	Haystack (7/6/85)	Allen (9/16/04)
5564	Cliff Goggins	Cascade (9/21/97)	Santanoni (9/21/04)
5565	Stephen M. Abdella	Rocky Peak (8/79)	Street (9/24/04)
5566	Christopher Sekellick	Upper Wolf Jaw (9/94)	Seward (9/26/04)
5567	Thomas E. Schmitz	Gothics (10/83)	Gray (10/16/04)
5568	Holly Vollkommer	Big Slide (1999)	Whiteface (11/1/04)
5569	Bert Wilson	Marcy (1997)	Marshall (11/7/04)
5570	Richard D. McKenna	Algonquin (2/00)	Marcy (1/29/05)
5571W	Andrew J. Janz	Porter (1990)	Big Slide (1/29/05)
5572W	Mark Surman	Wright (3/16/99)	Santanoni (2/2/05)
5573W	Heath A. Rozell	Colden (2/02)	Sawteeth (3/19/05)

HEAVEN UP-H'ISTED-NESS!

	MEMBER	FIRST ASCENT	FORTY-SIXTH PEAK
5574W	Angela M. Alphonso	Giant (8/18/02)	Redfield (3/21/05)
5575	Steven L. Andrews	Haystack (9/94)	Basin (3/25/05)
5576W	Eric M. Sicard	Giant (9/30/01)	Seward (4/3/05)
5577	Denis Walsh	Marcy (5/1/98)	Seymour (5/18/05)
5578	John F. McCarty	Marcy (1983)	Whiteface (5/21/05)
5579	Elizabeth M. Kane	Esther (5/26/95)	Blake (5/21/05)
5580	Mark J. Larson	Gothics (10/8/83)	Redfield (5/21/05)
5581	Eric Fenstermacher	Saddleback (7/77)	Whiteface (5/29/05)
5582	Rachael Oberding	Big Slide (8/5/02)	Colden (6/11/05)
5583	Sheryl Oberding	Giant (6/23/89)	Colden (6/11/05)
5584	Monique van Prooijen	Giant (7/29/03)	Colden (6/20/05)
5585	Michael P. Prockton	Marcy (6/21/00)	Big Slide (6/23/05)
5586	Jacob Zoller	Algonquin (1997)	Marshall (6/30/05)
5587	James P. Resig Sr.	Cascade (5/12/01)	Marcy (7/3/05)
5588	Jean A. Laverdure	Marcy (7/4/97)	Gothics (7/8/05)
5589	Chris Freyer	Esther (7/25/02)	Rocky Peak (7/8/05)
5590	Nathaniel Severy	Wright (7/27/99)	Colden (7/11/05)
5591	Janet Bellavance	Algonquin (5/30-87)	Whiteface (7/13/05)
5592W	Donald E. Burkett	Giant (9/24/02)	Panther (7/14/05)
5593	Morgan Hislop	Cascade (8/15/96)	Hough (7/16/05)
5594	Charlene K. Shafer	Giant (7/1/01)	Gray (7/19/05)
5595	Mark Sydorowych	Wright (7/17/99)	Allen (7/22/05)
5596	Renee B. Sydorowych	Colden (8/28/99)	Allen (7/22/05)
5597	Kevin Wojcik	Algonquin (9/1/85)	Whiteface (7/23/05)
5598	Theresa Rodrigues	Marcy (6/30/93)	Whiteface (7/23/05)
5599	Alexander Lantino	Dix (8/01)	Santanoni (7/23/05)
5600	Vasily C. Cateforis	Colden (9/19/98)	Allen (7/27/05)
5601	Jerry Lucas	Giant (7/93)	Whiteface (7/27/05)
5602	Beverly R. Burnett	Gothics (8/13/85)	Nippletop (7/29/05)
5603	Kathleen Gorman-Coombs	Gothics (6/7/93)	Nippletop (7/29/05)
5604	Robert A. Mason	Cascade (7/29/94)	Whiteface (7/29/05)
5605	Kip Cassavaw	Marcy (8/13/88)	Colvin (7/30/05)
5606	Kevin Broggy	Iroquois (1994)	Whiteface (7/30/05)
5607	James P. Gatto	Cascade (6/16/82)	Whiteface (7/30/05)
5608	David J. Hathaway	Porter (8/11/02)	Saddleback (7/30/05)
5609	Jeff Clarke	Lower Wolf Jaw (6/74)	Santanoni (7/30/05)
5610	Barbara Bilins	Cascade (1995)	Allen (7/31/05)
5611	Nancy Buckley	Big Slide (8/17/97)	Allen (7/31/05)
5612	Linda Ranado	Cascade (6/96)	Allen (7/31/05)
5613	Douglas V. Fox	Marcy (10/7/72)	Haystack (8/1/05)
5614	Cuyler Holmquist	Giant (5/25/01)	Marcy (8/3/05)
5615	Lars Holmquist	Giant (5/25/01)	Marcy (8/3/05)
5616	Timo Holmquist	Giant (5/25/01)	Marcy (8/3/05)
5617	Herbert Nyberg	Dix (8/7/95)	Whiteface (8/4/05)
5618	Michael Nyberg	Dix (8/7/95)	Whiteface (8/4/05)
5619	Cal Johnson	Marcy (7/2/93)	Gray (8/6/05)
5620	Toby J. Topa	Giant (5/97)	Big Slide (8/6/05)
5621	Christopher Lehfeldt	Porter (7/14/01)	Sawteeth (8/6/05)
5622	Nancy C. Hill	Giant (9/83)	Rocky Peak (8/6/05)
5623	Maria Schollenberger	Phelps (1997)	Colden (8/6/05)
5624W	Alex Lombard	Phelps (8/8/04)	Haystack (8/7/05)
5625	Allen R. Douglass	Rocky Peak (10/11/03)	Cliff (8/8/05)
5626	April Douglass	Rocky Peak (10/11/03)	Cliff (8/8/05)
5627	Anya Bickford	Cascade (10/2/03)	Haystack (8/10/05)
5628	Matthew Kulas	Gothics (10/98)	Seward (8/10/05)
5629	Hannah Fudin	Seward (7/14/05)	Porter (8/11/05)
5630	Margot Burns	Gothics (8/26/97)	Basin (8/11/05)
5631	Joseph J. Burns	Gothics (8/26/97)	Basin (8/11/05)
5632	Matthew Gutchess	Cascade (6/97)	Tabletop (8/13/05)
5633	Alexander J. Chlopecki II	Haystack (7/8/00)	Dix (8/13/05)
5634	Jack Lewis	Algonquin (10/21/00)	Iroquois (8/13/05)
5635	James Thies	Algonquin (10/21/00)	Iroquois (8/13/05)

THE MEMBERSHIP ROSTER OF THE ADIRONDACK FORTY-SIXERS

	MEMBER	FIRST ASCENT	FORTY-SIXTH PEAK
5636	Anthony Miller	Wright (7/25/00)	Sawteeth (8/14/05)
5637	Elizabeth Diamond	Algonquin (1964)	Skylight (8/17/05)
5638	Andrew Seitz	Macomb (10/12/02)	Colden (8/18/05)
5639	Karen Ross	Porter (7/21/90)	Panther (8/18/05)
5640	Michael Curtin	Cascade (7/8/02)	Big Slide (8/19/05)
5641	William J. Curtin	Cascade (7/8/02)	Big Slide (8/19/05)
5642	Diana Strablow	Cascade (7/90)	Skylight (8/20/05)
5643	John E. Hagerty	Giant (8/1970)	Redfield (8/20/05)
5644	John M. Hagerty	Cascade (1991)	Redfield (8/20/05)
5645	John Hamm	Cascade (7/16/02)	Haystack (8/25/05)
5646	Darleen Tector	Cascade (9/2/83)	Haystack (8/25/05)
5647	A. Bronson Thayer	Giant (8/86)	Whiteface (8/26/05)
5648	Wayne E. Dewey	Wright (7/68)	Whiteface (8/26/05)
5649	Laura Dewey	Marcy (9/73)	Whiteface (8/26/05)
5650	Dale McIntyre	Algonquin (7/87)	Whiteface (8/27/05)
5651	Robert Cirone	Big Slide (5/16/91)	Allen (8/27/05)
5652	Donald J. Tate Jr.	Cascade (6/13/99)	Rocky Peak (8/27/05)
5653	Shelly M. Tate	Cascade (9/13/99)	Rocky Peak (8/27/05)
5654	David Hoeschele	Santanoni (6/95)	Iroquois (8/27/05)
5655	Carol K. Burns	Marcy (8/13/86)	Santanoni (8/27/05)
5656	William J. Burns Jr.	Marcy (8/13/86)	Santanoni (8/27/05)
5657	Karen M. McMahon	Esther (10/80)	Whiteface (8/27/05)
5658	Robert E. Garber	Algonquin (8/60)	Allen (8/29/05)
5659	Susan J. Rohrey	Cascade (8/03)	Haystack (8/30/05)
5660	Samuel A. Laden	Cascade (1967)	Cliff (8/30/05)
5661	Janice McCann	Algonquin (9/03)	Haystack (8/30/05)
5662	David Kehn	Marcy (9/74)	Haystack (8/30/05)
5663	Shannon M. Kehn	Giant (5/31/87)	Haystack (8/30/05)
5664	Laureen Gachowski	Algonquin (6/5/88)	Emmons (9/1/05)
5665	Mark D. Chamberlain	Whiteface (12/27/02)	Colden (9/3/05)
5666	Andrew Welles	Cascade (6/97)	Colden (9/3/05)
5667	Carder Welles	Cascade (6/97)	Colden (9/3/05)
5668	Darlene Chorman	Marcy (7/82)	Gray (9/3/05)
5669	Diana L. Lavery	Cascade (5/03)	Redfield (9/4/05)
5670	Mary Margaret Ong	Marcy (9/10/02)	Cascade (9/4/05)
5671	Jeff LeMonds	Algonquin (9/21/03)	Allen (9/4/05)
5672	Ciaira Shepard	Cascade (9/2/97)	Whiteface (9/5/05)
5673	Katherine Sabin	Giant (8/29/99)	Iroquois (9/5/05)
5674	John E. Fish	Lower Wolf Jaw (6/9/05)	Whiteface (9/10/05)
5675	Matthew Hager	Cascade (5/11/02)	Whiteface (9/10/05)
5676	Bonnie Birk	Marcy (9/13/04)	Haystack (9/10/05)
5677	Barbara A. Harman	Algonquin (8/80)	Iroquois (9/10/05)
5678	Willard N. Harman	Algonquin (9/62)	Iroquois (9/10/05)
5679	Shelly Stiles	Dix (7/5/85)	Whiteface (9/10/05)
5680	Audrey Jacques	Cascade (10/24/04)	Marcy (9/10/05)
5681	Elaine Buege	Cascade (8/3/93)	Saddleback (9/12/05)
5682	Jack Buege	Cascade (8/3/93)	Saddleback (9/12/05)
5683	Frank Clark	Haystack (8/16/88)	Sawteeth (9/12/05)
5684	John C. Ryan	Skylight (8/25/00)	Sawteeth (9/12/05)
5685	Laurel Beattie	Phelps (6/1964)	Basin (9/13/05)
5686	Dale Platteter	Marcy (8/27/02)	Giant (9/13/05)
5687	Kenneth Rowell	Gray (8/6/04)	Haystack (9/16/05)
5688	E. Anne Whelan	Algonquin (8/11/01)	Colden (9/17/05)
5689	Aaron A. Harsh	Giant (9/7/02)	Allen (9/17/05)
5690	Carole K. Harsh	Giant (9/7/02)	Allen (9/17/05)
5691	Alan T. Stephens	Marcy (7/19/02)	Haystack (9/17/05)
5692	Cecil Peterson	Marcy (7/14/01)	Skylight (9/17/05)
5693	Rose Peterson	Marcy (7/14/01)	Skylight (9/17/05)
5694	Ronald T. Schubin	Cascade (9/2/98)	Allen (9/17/05)
5695W	Michael S. Katz	Algonquin (1984)	Whiteface (9/18/05)
5696	Bonnie Rondeau	Cascade (10/11/01)	Marcy (9/21/05)
5697	Michael N. Kelsey	Marcy (9/01)	Colden (6/21/05)

Heaven Up-h'isted-ness!

	Member	First Ascent	Forty-sixth Peak
5698	Stephen E. Lewis	Cascade (7/14/90)	Phelps (9/24/05)
5699	Anita M. Gabalski	Couchsachraga (1/83)	Whiteface (9/24/05)
5700	Douglas S. Nejman	Colden (9/5/94)	Whiteface (9/24/05)
5701W	Gordon Reilling	Marcy (1981)	Sawteeth (9/25/05)
5702	Gail Milhomme	Big Slide (5/14/99)	Seymour (9/25/05)
5703	Cynthia Wright	Colden (1987)	Esther (10/1/05)
5704	Ed Kasperek	Marcy (3/74)	Gray (10/1/05)
5705	George Senft	Marcy (8/19/00)	Sawteeth (10/1/05)
5706	Neil Luckhurst	Cascade (7/92)	Rocky Peak (10/1/05)
5707	Peter C. Schultz	Marcy (6/3/73)	Skylight (10/1/05)
5708	Doug Weiskoph	Gothics (7/23/83)	Nippletop (10/1/05)
5709	Eric Launier	Big Slide (6/14/97)	Saddleback (10/1/05)
5710	Dominic Luckhurst	Cascade (7/92)	Rocky Peak (10/1/05)
5711	Philip Waite	Marcy (9/30/89)	Panther (10/1/05)
5712W	Pierre Lefebvre	Colden (9/13/03)	Seymour (10/2/05)
5713	Edward King	Marcy (2/1/92)	Allen (10/2/05)
5714	John Avitabile	Porter (7/30/02)	Marcy (10/2/05)
5715	Therese Avitabile	Porter (7/30/02)	Marcy (10/2/05)
5716	Dean MacGeorge	Wright (10/30/02)	Seymour (10/2/05)
5717	Valerie M. Boyd	Porter (10/20/02)	Whiteface (10/2/05)
5718	Elizabeth Fox	Wright (10/11/03)	Whiteface (10/2/05)
5719	Liana Mistriel	Big Slide (7/15/02)	Whiteface (10/2/05)
5720	Roni Mistriel	Porter (7/18/03)	Whiteface (10/2/05)
5721	James Farmer	Marcy (9/5/75)	Allen (10/2/05)
5722	Mark Havis	Cascade (10/23/04)	Esther (10/2/05)
5723	Peter Delaney	Skylight (8/73)	Rocky Peak (10/2/05)
5724	John L. Quinn	Algonquin (1/17/76)	Colden (10/3/05)
5725	Galen J. Esper	Algonquin (6/29/02)	Hough (10/3/05)
5726	David Farnsworth	Cascade (6/21/03)	Lower Wolf Jaw (10/5/05)
5727	Marianne L. Perreault	Cascade (6/4/99)	Gothics (10/9/05)
5728	Jim Reber	Algonquin (9/28/97)	Whiteface (10/9/05)
5729	Rick Gangwer	Cascade (11/11/02)	Whiteface (10/10/05)
5730	Matthew Rennells	Dix (7/3/98)	Whiteface (10/10/05)
5731	Margaret S. Maxwell	Cascade (5/21/05)	Whiteface (10/15/05)
5732	Edward J. O'Shea	Cascade (12/28/98)	Whiteface (10/15/05)
5733	Adam Sikes	Giant (6/26/05)	Big Slide (10/20/05)
5734	Beth Sikes	Giant (6/26/05)	Big Slide (10/20/05)
5735	Dianne Sikes	Giant (6/26/05)	Big Slide (10/20/05)
5736	Eric Epner	Phelps (10/73)	Haystack (10/21/05)
5737	Anne J. Busse	Upper Wolf Jaw (8/31/02)	Cliff (10/21/05)
5738	Timothy Blosser	Esther (7/2/88)	Cascade (10/22/05)
5739	Nathan J. Blosser	Nippletop (7/21/87)	Cascade (10/22/05)
5740W	Alistair Fraser	Wright (11/1/97)	Phelps (11/1/05)
5741W	Serge Massad	Marcy (11/01)	Blake (11/5/05)
5742	Shayne Paddock	Porter (10/12/2002)	Big Slide (11/19/05)
5743W	Michael Fiorentino	Wright (9/27/03)	Haystack (12/23/05)
5744	William L. Paternotte	Giant (7/10/81)	Seward (8/6/91)
5745	Denby L. Probst	Tabletop (5/29/89)	Marcy (8/11/91)
5746	Nina Christiansen	Haystack (8/61)	Tabletop (8/30/92)
5747	Pete LeRoy	Colden (8/17/78)	Redfield (11/1/92)
5748W	Jim Becker	Giant (5/17/98)	Wright (6/30/01)
5749	Kevin J. Stacey	Marcy (5/75)	Santanoni (10/13/01)
5750	Jean-Luc Charbonneau	Algonquin (10/87)	Seymour (9/13/03)
5751	Marc Daoust	Marcy (10/11/87)	Seymour (9/13/03)
5752	Iredell W. Iglehart, III	Colvin (7/68)	Marshall (8/10/04)
5753	Michael Dinan	Algonquin (8/96)	Allen (8/28/04)
5754	Gary H. Gelvin	Algonquin (10/21/72)	Wright (10/2/04)
5755	Jeremy Dunn	Marcy (9/15/02)	Colden (11/24/04)
5756	Matthew Saucier	Algonquin (7/95)	Colden (11/24/04)
5757	Nicholas M. Rosinski	Wright (10/14/93)	Big Slide (5/28/05)
5758	David S. Greenblatt	Algonquin (7/30/03)	Haystack (8/6/05)
5759	Eleanor Roberts	Porter (7/18/02)	Skylight (8/9/05)

The Membership Roster of the Adirondack Forty-Sixers

	Member	First Ascent	Forty-sixth Peak
5760	Jack Kinney	Haystack (7/1/04)	Big Slide (8/9/05)
5761	Christine E. Scheele	Couchsachraga (7/12/05)	Porter (8/11/05)
5762	Emily Hyson	Wright (8/11/98)	Allen (8/12/05)
5763	Harry J. Wolf	Marcy (10/2/99)	Lower Wolf Jaw (8/12/05)
5764	Trent Widrick	Big Slide (9/4/95)	Seymour (8/18/05)
5765	Julia Goren	Cascade (8/94)	Esther (8/25/05)
5766	Colleen Connors	Phelps (10/9/99)	Skylight (8/26/05)
5767	Joseph J. Comuzzi	Marcy (7/19/00)	Giant (8/27/05)
5768	Marjorie DiFlorio	Algonquin (7/31/99)	Saddleback (8/27/05)
5769	Christopher L. Fischer	Marcy (8/84)	Haystack (9/3/05)
5770	Donald C. Slick	Big Slide (10/92)	Seymour (9/10/05)
5771	Dana Mills	Algonquin (9/02)	Colden (9/17/05)
5772	Douglas L. Wolff	Marcy (5/26/81)	Iroquois (9/24/05)
5773	David Coleman	Giant (1963)	Haystack (10/1/05)
5774	Malcolm N. Cooke	Esther (8/2/01)	Skylight (10/9/05)
5775	Lance P. Lindner	Marcy (8/27/01)	Skylight (10/9/05)
5776	R. Graham May	Skylight (7/91)	Emmons (10/12/05)
5777	Paul Allison	Giant (1992)	Whiteface (10/15/05)
5778	Samuel B. Allison	Marcy (1959)	Whiteface (10/15/05)
5779	Justin Finkle	Couchsachraga (7/8/03)	Sawteeth (10/15/05)
5780	James Owen	Colden (10/74)	Couchsachraga (2/11/06)
5781W	John J. Hardenburg	Big Slide (12/28/93)	Whiteface (2/14/06)
5782W	Linda Perry	Big Slide (10/31/04)	Skylight (2/16/06)
5783W	Mark W. Perry	Big Slide (10/31/04)	Skylight (2/16/06)
5784W	Dale Fox	Giant (7/82)	Gray (3/4/06)
5785W	Wilfred Murnane	Phelps (10/23/99)	Santanoni (3/5/06)
5786W	Roman Laba	Sawteeth (12/26/00)	Cliff (3/11/06)
5787	Kevin P. Donovan	Cascade (8/14/99)	Haystack (3/11/06)
5788	Eugene A. Donovan	Skylight (11/9/02)	Haystack (3/11/06)
5789W	Nancy Roderick	Allen (3/7/04)	Marshall (3/11/06)
5790W	Rejean Carbonneau	Giant (1/4/05)	Seymour (3/19/06)
5791	Wayne Bedard	Marcy (6/65)	Haystack (4/22/06)
5792	Phyllis Light	Marcy (1970)	Seward (5/13/06)
5793	Zachary Wakeman	Algonquin (6/15/01)	Redfield (5/28/06)
5794	Bob Crandall	Cascade (5/74)	Allen (6/3/06)
5795	Jim Gould	Cascade (6/80)	Gray (6/10/06)
5796	Alfred E. Dunlop	Sawteeth (8/23/01)	Colden (6/16/06)
5797	Scott Larson	Wright (6/5/97)	Basin (6/16/06)
5798	Bruce Allard	Cascade (9/13/04)	Marshall (6/24/06)
5799	Ian Ellbogen	Cascade (10/95)	Whiteface (7/1/06)
5800	Andree Gaudreau	Cascade (10/95)	Whiteface (7/1/06)
5801	Margaret L. Maney	Phelps (9/20/03)	Marcy (7/1/06)
5802W	Peter B. Desrochers	Upper Wolf Jaw (6/20/81)	Colden (7/3/06)
5803W	Sharon Desrochers	Upper Wolf Jaw (6/20/81)	Colden (7/3/06)
5804	John J. Almasi	Colden (7/65)	Tabletop (7/6/06)
5805	Karen J. Irvine	Algonquin (6/29/02)	Saddleback (7/6/06)
5806	Paul V. Irvine	Algonquin (6/29/02)	Saddleback (7/6/06)
5807	Julie A. Smith	Gray (8/6/05)	Dix (7/10/06)
5808	Albert Thompson	Allen (7/30/05)	Whiteface (7/15/06)
5809	Gail W. Epstein	Cascade (7/29/89)	Porter (7/22/06)
5810	Janice Joyce	Gothics (8/00)	Whiteface (7/22/06)
5811	Carol C. Byrnes	Phelps (8/2/99)	Saddleback (7/22/06)
5812	Elizabeth McKinley	Phelps (8/2/99)	Saddleback (7/22/06)
5813	Karen A. White	Wright (9/18/94)	Panther (7/28/06)
5814W	Robert A. Ciecierega	Cascade (9/4/00)	Big Slide (7/29/06)
5815	Brian A. Reynolds	Nippletop (8/10/94)	Whiteface (7/29/06)
5816	Sam Marshall	Cascade (8/98)	Whiteface (7/29/06)
5817	Michele I. Gonzalez	Dix (1997)	Marshall (7/30/06)
5818W	John Mattingly	Colden (10/27/84)	Gothics (8/3/06)
5819	Victor L. Perkins	Cascade (7/22/99)	Blake (8/4/06)
5820	Benjamin S. Fernandez	Esther (7/10/97)	Marshall (8/4/06)
5821	Richard J. Miller	Marcy (9/60)	Allen (8/4/06)

HEAVEN UP-H'ISTED-NESS!

	MEMBER	FIRST ASCENT	FORTY-SIXTH PEAK
5822	Andrew J. Caruso	Algonquin (9/6/92)	Marshall (8/5/06)
5823	Steven E. Matkoski	Skylight (9/6/89)	Lower Wolf Jaw (8/5/06)
5824	Lisa K. Huestis	Marcy (5/13/89)	Skylight (8/5/06)
5825	Elizabeth Pasnikowski	Nippletop (11/10/02)	Basin (8/5/06)
5826	Denise Blank	Wright (5/24/86)	Panther (8/5/06)
5827	Shannon St Louis	Phelps (5/23/02)	Haystack (8/5/06)
5828	John W. Daly	Cascade (8/97)	East Dix (8/6/06)
5829	Heather Herrmann	Marcy (10/20/01)	Big Slide (8/6/06)
5830	Karin Davidson	Giant (5/21/02)	Big Slide (8/6/06)
5831	Janet M. Balaguer	Gothics (7/27/71)	Seymour (8/7/06)
5832	Tim Caradonna	Phelps (7/2/02)	Rocky Peak (8/8/06)
5833	Charlie Farrell	Haystack (7/6/04)	Panther (8/8/06)
5834	Sarah Larsen	Street (7/10/06)	Cascade (8/9/06)
5835	Brad Sale	Street (7/10/06)	Porter (8/9/06)
5836	Jared A. Desrochers	Giant (6/26/98)	Redfield (8/9/06)
5837	Harry T. Yerkes	Marcy (7/4/02)	Colden (8/10/06)
5838	Richard H. Griffith	Cascade (8/16/01)	Marshall (8/11/06)
5839	Lee H. Cliff	Cascade (7/4/02)	Whiteface (8/11/06)
5840	Julie Chevalier	Giant (3/26/05)	Big Slide (8/12/06)
5841	Phoebe Aron	Phelps (7/27/01)	Rocky Peak (8/12/06)
5842	Lydia Singerman	Cascade (8/11/01)	Rocky Peak (8/12/06)
5843	Karen A. Burns	Big Slide (10/93)	Haystack (8/12/06)
5844	Janice Miller	Cascade (8/00)	Whiteface (8/12/06)
5845	Zachary Miller	Cascade (8/00)	Whiteface (8/12/06)
5846	Erik S. Gregory	Cascade (7/25/98)	Whiteface (8/12/06)
5847W	Reinhard L. Gsellmeier	Marcy (7/20/02)	Whiteface (8/12/06)
5848	Leah Horowitz	Cascade (7/19/01)	Rocky Peak (8/12/06)
5849	Jennifer Reidy	Whiteface (6/84)	Esther (8/12/06)
5850	Charles Spinelli	Marcy (8/25/01)	Haystack (8/13/06)
5851	Craig H. Lewis	Marcy (7/10/03)	Esther (8/14/06)
5852	Joshua Bornt	East Dix (6/00)	Wright (8/14/06)
5853	William F. Diamond	Porter (8/16/99)	Dix (8/14/06)
5854	Fiona Dubuss	Gothics (6/03)	Marshall (8/15/06)
5855	Bob Reepmeyer	Marcy (8/72)	Porter (8/16/06)
5856	Adam Sibley	Giant (9/98)	Rocky Peak (8/16/06)
5857	Ray Sibley	Giant (9/98)	Rocky Peak (8/16/06)
5858	Dan Marrone	Cascade (2004)	Skylight (8/17/06)
5859	Nancy Morrill	Cascade (6/4/04)	Couchsachraga (8/18/06)
5860	Charlotte McCarthy	Wright (7/10/93)	Seymour (8/18/06)
5861	Jessie Blank	Algonquin (7/19/02)	Gothics (8/18/06)
5862	Kristina Blank	Algonquin (7/19/02)	Gothics (8/18/06)
5863	Dan Gottsegen	Haystack (1975)	Sawteeth (8/18/06)
5864	Dan Abramson	Cascade (7/68)	Sawteeth (8/18/06)
5865	Ronnie J. Cusmano	Lower Wolf Jaw (7/9/05)	Dial (8/19/06)
5866	Sam Hutchins	Cascade (7/7/99)	Porter (8/19/06)
5867	Charles D. Tracy	Marcy (5/10/05)	Esther (8/20/06)
5868	Michael Walsh	Lower Wolf Jaw (8/85)	Allen (8/23/06)
5869	Peter Bundschuh	Marcy (8/3/75)	Allen (8/24/06)
5870	Paula Silliman	Cascade (5/27/95)	Panther (8/24/06)
5871W	James J. de Waal Malefyt	Marcy (7/4/72)	Allen (8/26/06)
5872	Benjamin R. Resnick	Algonquin (7/98)	Whiteface (8/26/06)
5873	Andrew T. Colerick	Porter (5/29/04)	Haystack (8/26/06)
5874	Leon Brill	Colden (6/27/98)	Marcy (8/26/06)
5875W	Ronald Clark	Marcy (1993)	Allen (8/26/06)
5876	Daniel S. Burks	Algonquin (7/29/03)	Colden (8/27/06)
5877	Mike Miller	Marcy (8/17/98)	Haystack (8/30/06)
5878	Lawrence Telle	Santanoni (8/1/01)	Couchsachraga (9/1/06)
5879	Joanne Engelhardt	Marcy (8/30/01)	Haystack (9/1/06)
5880	Vernon A. Pilon	Cascade (8/01)	Whiteface (9/1/06)
5881	Jason Salyer	Giant (7/27/01)	Haystack (9/1/06)
5882	James H. Somerset	Whiteface (8/18/96)	Seymour (9/1/06)
5883	Eric Elinski	Esther (8/8/02)	Saddleback (9/1/06)

The Membership Roster of the Adirondack Forty-Sixers

	Member	First Ascent	Forty-sixth Peak
5884	Leslie Rasnake	Giant (7/8/01)	Iroquois (9/2/06)
5885	John C. Harris	Algonquin (8/4/99)	Cascade (9/2/06)
5886	Michael Yaros	Lower Wolf Jaw (7/5/01)	Cascade (9/2/06)
5887	David E. Hoff	Cascade (10/20/02)	Gray (9/2/06)
5888	Lisa M. Hoff	Cascade (10/20/02)	Gray (9/2/06)
5889	Dalton Castine	Cascade (10/20/02)	Gray (9/2/06)
5890	Darcy Castine	Cascade (10/20/02)	Gray (9/2/06)
5891	Glenna I. Redmond	Phelps (6/18/00)	Saddleback (9/2/06)
5892	Bruce Wentworth	Upper Wolf Jaw (7/2/00)	Cascade (9/3/06)
5893	Kathleen Sennett	Marcy (8/31/03)	Gothics (9/3/06)
5894	Graham Carter	Dial (7/23/05)	Whiteface (9/3/06)
5895	Brian E. Hyde	Whiteface (1997)	Gothics (9/3/06)
5896	Aleks Litynski	Algonquin (6/25/98)	Colvin (9/4/06)
5897	Sandra Frederick	Whiteface (6/14/04)	Street (9/5/06)
5898	Carol D. Edmonds	Gothics (9/18/99)	Marcy (9/8/06)
5899	Suzanne Dumesnil	Algonquin (9/00)	Iroquois (9/9/06)
5900	Daniel McGrath	Dix (1992)	Whiteface (9/9/06)
5901	Matthew Corsaro	Algonquin (1980)	Cascade (9/10/06)
5902	Ben Maxson	Whiteface (7/4/04)	Skylight (9/10/06)
5903	Kyle Maxson	Whiteface (7/4/04)	Skylight (9/10/06)
5904	Mark Maxson	Whiteface (7/4/04)	Skylight (9/10/06)
5905	Shawn Maxson	Whiteface (7/4/04)	Skylight (9/10/06)
5906	Barbara Hollenbeck	Donaldson (6/29/03)	Marcy (9/10/06)
5907	Deborah Y. Kopp	Big Slide (6/5/95)	Panther (9/11/06)
5908	Marc Bachand	Giant (8/99)	Haystack (9/12/06)
5909W	Kerry Shea	Seymour (1/30/06)	Saddleback (9/12/06)
5910	Paul J. Rudershausen	Cascade (12/28/91)	Gray (9/12/06)
5911W	Nancy A. LaBaff	Whiteface (5/8/05)	Esther (9/14/06)
5912	Robert Weil	Giant (1986)	Dix (9/15/06)
5913	Lisa McDougal	Cascade (9/02)	Phelps (9/16/06)
5914	David W. Martin	Big Slide (8/21/98)	Allen (9/17/06)
5915	Steven Case	Marcy (4/98)	Haystack (9/17/06)
5916	Jonathan Kelly	Phelps (3/24/00)	Haystack (9/17/06)
5917	George Dudar	Dial (6/17/06)	Cliff (9/17/06)
5918	Stephen M. Smith	Wright (6/23/02)	Marcy (9/22/06)
5919	Patrick Keough	Whiteface (9/27/81)	Gray (9/26/06)
5920	Paul W. Liberty	Whiteface (9/27/81)	Gray (9/26/06)
5921	Mark E. Sengenberger	Algonquin (6/18/03)	Dix (9/26/06)
5922	Don Jones	Wright (7/25/00)	Whiteface (9/27/06)
5923	Martin E. Gordon	Sawteeth (7/3/80)	Giant (9/30/06)
5924W	Terri Maxymillian	Marcy (9/3/03)	Big Slide (9/30/06)
5925	Rod Bauer	Wright (6/19/99)	Whiteface (9/30/06)
5926	Jim Langley	Algonquin (8/3/99)	Whiteface (9/30/06)
5927	Michael Nortman	Cascade (7/10/99)	Whiteface (9/30/06)
5928	Jean-Sebastien Roux	Cascade (10/24/04)	Marcy (9/30/06)
5929	Terry K. Myers	Giant (8/24/01)	Emmons (10/1/06)
5930W	Siobhan M. Carney-Nesbitt	Porter (6/3/06)	Whiteface (10/1/06)
5931W	Lee S. Nesbitt, III	Porter (6/3/06)	Whiteface (10/1/06)
5932	Arthur C. Rocque	Cascade (7/70)	Saddleback (10/2/06)
5933	Brian Trainor	Algonquin (8/4/90)	Whiteface (10/2/06)
5934	Christopher J. Sedlack	Wright (1993)	Iroquois (10/7/06)
5935W	Armand Turcotte	Marcy (8/19/96)	Basin (10/7/06)
5936	Kenneth G. Wehner	Cascade (9/19/05)	Skylight (10/7/06)
5937	Kyle S. Wehner	Cascade (9/19/05)	Skylight (10/7/06)
5938	Cathy Stare	Big Slide (8/95)	Whiteface (10/7/06)
5939	Michael A. Vetrano	Gothics (10/11/94)	Whiteface (10/7/06)
5940	Kent Loomis	Marcy (1972)	Allen (10/8/06)
5941	Lynn Loomis	Giant (10/25/95)	Allen (10/8/06)
5942	Michael F. Rosanio	Cascade (7/7/01)	Haystack (10/8/06)
5943	Jeffrey P. Mans	Cascade (10/13/02)	Marshall (10/8/06)
5944	John Cooley	Cascade (1998)	Tabletop (10/9/06)
5945	Warren E. Foster	Giant (1990)	Tabletop (10/9/06)

HEAVEN UP-H'ISTED-NESS!

	MEMBER	FIRST ASCENT	FORTY-SIXTH PEAK
5946	Robert J. LaMagna	Marcy (10/24/93)	Sawteeth (10/14/06)
5947	Peter B. Butryn	Marcy (7/31/80)	Haystack (10/14/06)
5948	Reid M. Porter	Cascade (9/18/99)	Colden (10/14/06)
5949	Robert P. Stelianou	Marcy (8/73)	Marshall (10/14/06)
5950	Kevin W. Lanighan	Lower Wolf Jaw (6/30/04)	Marshall (10/14/06)
5951	A. Scott Weber	Whiteface (3/6/04)	Marshall (10/14/06)
5952	John A. Affronti	Seward (9/27/96)	Tabletop (10/18/06)
5953	Howard A. Vormelker	Marcy (7/29/78)	Lower Wolf Jaw (10/21/06)
5954	Patricia S. Christian	Redfield (10/7/94)	Big Slide (11/5/06)
5955	John W. Topping	Porter (1970)	Whiteface (11/10/06)
5956	Adam Endres	Colden (6/96)	Basin (11/11/06)
5957	Jonathan D. Angus	Lower Wolf Jaw (8/02)	Allen (11/18/06)
5958	Kenneth Krabbenhoft	Wright (7/2/02)	Rocky Peak (11/19/06)
5959	Brent Pierce	Colden (6/21/02)	Seward (11/26/06)
5960	Craig Cressey	Street (4/8/06)	Allen (12/16/06)
5961	Carl R. Cressey	Nye (4/10/06)	Allen (12/16/06)
5962W	Heidi teRiele Karkoski	Giant (6/2/95)	Seward (12/23/06)
5963	Zachary L. Obbie	Cascade (7/31/99)	Marcy (12/28/06)
5964W	Todd C. Obbie	Wright (3/21/98)	Marcy (12/28/06)
5965	Julian Garcia	Dix (5/21/95)	Seymour (8/30/97)
5966	Patrick F. Giblin	Allen (6/24/85)	Colden (5/28/00)
5967W	Gregory A. Herbison	Haystack (2/26/94)	Allen (3/17/01)
5968W	Richard J. Herbison	Colden (1/15/94)	Allen (3/17/01)
5969	Richard J. Fates	Cascade (8/10/69)	Cliff (8/15/02)
5970	Janice Prichett	Cascade (5/12/90)	Haystack (7/12/03)
5971	Mark Nolan	Phelps (7/30/98)	Allen (8/11/03)
5972	Tim Engelbrecht	Dix (10/88)	Esther (8/23/03)
5973	James Reilly	Marcy (8/11/99)	Allen (9/7/03)
5974	Marion E. Macpherson	Marcy (9/10/88)	Cliff (10/26/03)
5975	Louis H. Palmer, III	Algonquin (5/29/77)	Seymour (9/4/04)
5976	Sara Swartzwelder	Sawteeth (6/00)	Wright (8/7/05)
5977	Owen S. Teach	Colvin (8/29/96)	Dix (8/17/05)
5978	Stephen J. Teach	Giant (8/83)	Dix (8/17/05)
5979	Karen Graessle	Colvin (8/92)	Colden (9/24/05)
5980	Jeffrey L. O'Neal	Marcy (8/19/97)	Haystack (7/3/06)
5981	Peter Manning	Dix (8/29/99)	Colden (7/3/06)
5982	Rebecca L. Manning	Dix (8/29/99)	Colden (7/3/06)
5983	Matt Walsh	Dial (7/5/04)	Seymour (7/5/06)
5984	Hannah Alex Younger	Street (7/11/06)	Porter (8/7/06)
5985	Michael Shelton	Dix (7/02)	Cascade (8/9/06)
5986	Elizabeth Edwards	Cascade (8/1/99)	Esther (8/10/06)
5987	Nicholas O'Keefe Edwards	Cascade (8/1/99)	Haystack (8/11/06)
5988	Travis Blank	Algonquin (7/19/02)	Gothics (8/18/06)
5989	Paul M. Barnes	Marcy (8/71)	Esther (8/20/06)
5990	Lillian VanDyke	Cascade (7/29/97)	Skylight (9/1/06)
5991	Wesley Pilon	Cascade (7/01)	Whiteface (9/1/06)
5992	Eric Livengood	Haystack (9/26/98)	Big Slide (9/23/06)
5993	Robert Andrews	Big Slide (6/1/90)	Armstrong (9/30/06)
5994	Richard C. Scott	Big Slide (9/1/84)	Whiteface (9/30/06)
5995	Charlene A. Metz	Cascade (9/18/98)	Hough (10/7/06)
5996	Brian Frederick	Porter (9/1/96)	Whiteface (10/8/06)
5997	Julie Leclair	Colden (6/9/01)	Skylight (10/15/06)
5998	David J. Staszak	Algonquin (5/31/85)	Esther (10/22/06)
5999	William K. Thurber	Marcy (2/20/77)	Cascade (10/27/06)
6000	Steven W. Hayes	Dial (7/5/04)	Porter (11/5/06)
6001W	Jeremy R. Oliver	Algonquin (11/3/05)	Colden (12/27/06)
6002W	James D. Laney	Marcy (1/84)	Tabletop (12/28/06)
6003	Rebecca Litts	Cascade (7/2/06)	Esther (1/4/07)
6004W	Christine Boyer	Cascade (10/25/03)	Allen (1/13/07)
6005	Juan E. Carro	Marcy (9/23/95)	Skylight (1/16/07)
6006	Robert E. Homan	Marcy (9/23/95)	Giant (1/19/07)
6007	Robert F. S. Roache	Algonquin (5/26/90)	Hough (1/23/07)

The Membership Roster of the Adirondack Forty-Sixers

Member		First Ascent	Forty-sixth Peak
6008W	Ray Cudney	Dial (3/15/03)	Big Slide (3/13/07)
6009W	Peter F. Martin	Marcy (2/85)	Hough (3/18/07)
6010	Kevin J. O'Brien	Marcy (9/15/94)	Cliff (6/9/07)
6011	David Gomlak	Marcy (9/21/96)	Cascade (6/14/07)
6012	Stephen C. Swensen	Phelps (9/18/03)	Gothics (6/20/07)
6013	James T. Charboneau	Cascade (10/02)	Seward (6/29/07)
6014	Dennis VanKerkhove	Marcy (8/9/81)	Allen (6/30/07)
6015	Jeffrey VanKerkhove	Algonquin (8/19/01)	Allen (6/30/07)
6016	Andy Loux	Giant (7/2/95)	Marcy (7/1/07)
6017	James Y. Boland	Phelps (7/31/95)	Allen (7/3/07)
6018	Sarah Balaguer	Cascade (7/4/00)	Rocky Peak (7/3/07)
6019	Kimberly A. Scholle	Cascade (7/7/00)	Panther (7/6/07)
6020	Beverly W. Tignor	Giant (10/28/00)	Sawteeth (7/8/07)
6021W	Tina Boadway	Big Slide (4/19/06)	Allen (7/12/07)
6022W	Paulo Marafuga	Big Slide (4/19/06)	Allen (7/12/07)
6023	Julio Braz	Marcy (8/83)	Seward (7/14/07)
6024	Martin F. Glendon	Algonquin (8/27/65)	Santanoni (7/16/07)
6025	Kenneth F. Easter	Algonquin (10/6/98)	Cliff (7/17/07)
6026	Tyler Socash	Cascade (12/22/06)	Colden (7/18/07)
6027	Scott Albert	Rocky Peak (7/86)	Emmons (7/21/07)
6028	Thomas Schiefer	Phelps (7/10/04)	Cascade (7/21/07)
6029	Michelle Caron	Giant (6/23/05)	Haystack (7/22/07)
6030	Michael Penning	Giant (6/23/05)	Haystack (7/22/07)
6031	Sebastien Tran	Big Slide (4/17/04)	Seymour (7/22/07)
6032	Michel St-Amand	Marcy (6/24/01)	Seymour (7/22/07)
6033	Matthew Hoffman	Colden (8/5/04)	Iroquois (7/22/07)
6034	Ben Stephens	Colden (9/3/94)	Whiteface (7/23/07)
6035	Cecilia L. Disney	Cascade (10/91)	Iroquois (7/23/07)
6036	Zack Lang	Cascade (7/02)	Colden (7/24/07)
6037	Kathleen D. Murray	Whiteface (6/2/88)	Haystack (7/25/07)
6038	Mark Simpson	Phelps (1983)	Haystack (7/25/07)
6039	Matthew Bacon	Lower Wolf Jaw (10/23/04)	Skylight (7/25/07)
6040	Pierce Wezenaar	Seymour (7/16/06)	Marcy (7/25/07)
6041	Eliot W. Dalton, Jr.	Cascade (7/8/85)	Hough (7/26/07)
6042	Les Meyer	Wright (7/15/88)	Hough (7/26/07)
6043	William F. Sullivan	Marcy (9/13/01)	Cascade (7/28/07)
6044	Scott Lauffer	Giant (8/16/92)	Whiteface (7/29/07)
6045	Peter D. Richards	Wright (1991)	Whiteface (7/30/07)
6046	Tim Yeskoo	Phelps (5/26/02)	Iroquois (7/30/07)
6047	Varda F. LeMonds	Algonquin (7/13/04)	Sawteeth (8/1/07)
6048	Tom Challinor	Algonquin (7/72)	Esther (8/2/07)
6049	Rumiko Doman	Haystack (8/94)	Colden (8/4/07)
6050	Erik Doman	Giant (1975)	Colden (8/4/07)
6051	Stanley B. Kocsis	Haystack (7/20/85)	Whiteface (8/4/07)
6052	Robert E. Buckley, Jr.	Porter (9/25/99)	Saddleback (8/4/07)
6053	Robert Lawrence	Marcy (8/25/02)	Big Slide (8/4/07)
6054	Lawrence R. Schaefer	Giant (9/18/76)	Haystack (8/5/07)
6055	Pati Snow	Nippletop (7/14/02)	Redfield (8/5/07)
6056	Colette Bonelli	Cascade (9/13/98)	Redfield (8/5/07)
6057	Wendy Patunoff	Cascade (9/13/98)	Redfield (8/5/07)
6058	Jae Lyn Burke	Cascade (11/69)	Hough (8/5/07)
6059	Maximilian F. Feidelson	Cascade (7/25/03)	Sawteeth (8/7/07)
6060	Evan Finkle	Street (7/9/07)	Porter (8/8/07)
6061	Matthew Magnani	Street (7/9/07)	Porter (8/9/07)
6062	William Magnani	Street (7/9/07)	Porter (8/9/07)
6063	Deborah Wong	Tabletop (3/26/05)	Saddleback (8/9/07)
6064	Lincoln (Mac) Hull	Porter (9/1/98)	Whiteface (8/9/07)
6065	Roger Hull	Porter (9/1/98)	Whiteface (8/9/07)
6066	Douglas J. Fischer	Phelps (7/04)	Wright (8/9/07)
6067	Rudi Bosshard	Cascade (10/7/05)	Marcy (8/9/07)
6068	James Eaton	Big Slide (10/1/04)	Marcy (8/10/07)
6069	Laura Gardner	Phelps (5/30/93)	Whiteface (8/11/07)

Heaven Up-h'isted-ness!

	Member	First Ascent	Forty-sixth Peak
6070	Ned Gardner	Phelps (5/30/93)	Whiteface (8/11/07)
6071W	Stephen Dunbar	Giant (7/4/06)	Skylight (8/11/07)
6072	Karen Rose	Phelps (7/4/01)	Hough (8/11/07)
6073	Beverly Clark	Cascade (6/10/01)	Whiteface (8/11/07)
6074	Russell Clark	Cascade (6/10/01)	Whiteface (8/11/07)
6075	Michael Norton	Lower Wolf Jaw (7/77)	Colden (8/11/07)
6076	Ari Silverman	Dix (7/1/06)	Wright (8/11/07)
6077	Timothy P. Timbrook	Marcy (9/23/87)	Whiteface (8/12/07)
6078	William C. Ebbott	Giant (7/1/79)	Whiteface (8/12/07)
6079W	Jay Hui	Algonquin (1995)	Rocky Peak (8/12/07)
6080	Dwight M. Hughes	Whiteface (7/2/06)	Haystack (8/12/07)
6081	David Torraca	Algonquin (1980)	Saddleback (8/13/07)
6082	Owen Mellin	Cascade (7/05)	Iroquois (8/14/07)
6083	Carl Bashaw	Giant (9/9/06)	Haystack (8/14/07)
6084	Ingrid Bashaw	Giant (9/9/06)	Haystack (8/14/07)
6085	Julia W. O'Connor	Lower Wolf Jaw (7/70)	Whiteface (8/14/07)
6086	Jonathan A. Bush	Giant (7/67)	Santanoni (8/15/07)
6087	Janne Rand	Cascade (7/8/05)	Haystack (8/17/07)
6088	Jay Rand	Cascade (7/8/05)	Haystack (8/17/07)
6089	David R. Bell	Porter (8/28/00)	Whiteface (8/18/07)
6090	Kelly M. O'Brien	Algonquin (8/11/96)	Whiteface (8/18/07)
6091	Elizabeth Trachte	Phelps (10/91)	Emmons (8/18/07)
6092	David Wright	Wright (4/74)	Hough (8/18/07)
6093	Dustin Wright	Colden (7/29/98)	Hough (8/18/07)
6094	Mary Elizabeth Alexander	Marcy (8/10/55)	Allen (8/18/07)
6095	David S. Pratt	Big Slide (7/30/05)	Gray (8/18/07)
6096	Kendra C. Pratt	Phelps (6/30/04)	Gray (8/18/07)
6097	MacGregor Hall-Wurst	Porter (8/16/99)	Rocky Peak (8/19/07)
6098	Catherine A. Bunk	Algonquin (9/6/92)	Whiteface (8/22/07)
6099	Edward J. Michonski, Jr.	Marcy (8/22/95)	Whiteface (8/22/07)
6100	Alissa M. Ferlito	Gothics (7/89)	Whiteface (8/22/07)
6101	Jeffrey A. Johnson	Algonquin (1967)	Whiteface (8/22/07)
6102	Timothy B. Segada	Colden (8/9/87)	Whiteface (8/22/07)
6103	John Antonio	Cascade (10/9/78)	Hough (8/23/07)
6104	Stephen M. Sudak	Giant (7/30/78)	Allen (8/24/07)
6105	James Lapointe	Whiteface (7/82)	Gray (8/25/07)
6106	Carol Nestor	Cascade (2/18/93)	Whiteface (8/25/07)
6107	Norman L. Mueller	Redfield (6/17/06)	Whiteface (8/25/07)
6108	James Barry	Marcy (8/30/01)	Haystack (8/25/07)
6109	Kenneth Martin	Algonquin (1979)	Allen (8/25/07)
6110	Paul Held	Cascade (5/27/06)	Marcy (8/26/07)
6111	Adam S. Morrell	Phelps (10/92)	Giant (8/26/07)
6112	Bruce P. Hudock	Giant (7/24/98)	East Dix (8/27/07)
6113	Peter Ziolkowski	Marcy (9/8/01)	Saddleback (8/28/07)
6114	Harold E. Oot	Algonquin (7/15/03)	Whiteface (8/28/07)
6115	Ken Grimble	Cascade (9/3/94)	Whiteface (8/28/07)
6116	Linda Grimble	Cascade (9/3/94)	Whiteface (8/28/07)
6117	Michele McCall	Phelps (1974)	Redfield (8/30/07)
6118	Gloria J. Wagner	Marcy (8/23/99)	Redfield (8/30/07)
6119	Norman Kuchar	Marcy (8/30/62)	Basin (8/31/07)
6120	Christopher Martelli	Colden (8/23/99)	Cascade (8/31/07)
6121	Nancy L. Hayhurst	Cascade (9/5/98)	Whiteface (9/1/07)
6122	Thomas Hayhurst	Cascade (9/5/98)	Whiteface (9/1/07)
6123	Chip Ward	Haystack (7/10/79)	Whiteface (9/1/07)
6124	Robert J. Smith	Upper Wolf Jaw (9/21/95)	Whiteface (9/1/07)
6125	Greg Paradis	Cascade (7/25/98)	Rocky Peak (9/1/07)
6126	Francis M. Gallagher	Cascade (10/95)	Haystack (9/1/07)
6127	Linda Gallagher	Cascade (10/95)	Haystack (9/1/07)
6128	Scott A. Baker	Cascade (4/18/04)	Haystack (9/2/07)
6129	Terri Baker	Cascade (4/18/04)	Haystack (9/2/07)
6130	Dana Beck	Nippletop (7/94)	Colden (9/2/07)
6131	Dan Roth	Phelps (6/14/91)	Couchsachraga (9/2/07)

THE MEMBERSHIP ROSTER OF THE ADIRONDACK FORTY-SIXERS

	MEMBER	FIRST ASCENT	FORTY-SIXTH PEAK
6132	Tim Sweeney	Whiteface (7/24/98)	Redfield (9/2/07)
6133	Susan A. Thomas	Marcy (9/11/99)	Redfield (9/2/07)
6134	Gillian V. Scott	Phelps (8/19/95)	Emmons (9/2/07)
6135	Keith J. Koster	Porter (8/23/03)	Gothics (9/3/07)
6136	John A. Slocum	Porter (7/14/03)	Marcy (9/7/07)
6137	John P. Susko	Dix (9/14/77)	Rocky Peak (9/8/07)
6138	Shannon M. Hughes	Cascade (10/17/02)	Seymour (9/8/07)
6139	Barry Matulaitis	Allen (10/12/02)	Marcy (9/8/07)
6140	Ellen M. O'Meara	Lower Wolf Jaw (7/92)	Skylight (9/8/07)
6141	Josiah J. Vincek	Algonquin (9/23/06)	Marcy (9/8/07)
6142	Carl E. Stephan	Marcy (8/20/68)	Seymour (9/15/07)
6143	Kevin McGowan	Marcy (7/74)	East Dix (9/16/07)
6144	Stephani Krzysik	Phelps (12/29/01)	Gray (9/18/07)
6145	Lisa de Waal Malefyt	Algonquin (9/5/98)	Emmons (9/19/07)
6146	Jack Abel	Gothics (8/22/03)	Redfield (9/19/07)
6147	Bill R. Ring	Macomb (6/27/07)	Emmons (9/20/07)
6148	Taylor Feldeisen	Cascade (6/12/05)	Seymour (9/21/07)
6149	Lane A. Feldeisen	Cascade (6/12/05)	Seymour (9/21/07)
6150	Renee Feldeisen	Cascade (6/12/05)	Seymour (9/21/07)
6151	Sophie Crane McKibben	Cascade (7/98)	Basin (9/21/07)
6152	Peter C. Geertz	Cascade (7/3/99)	Whiteface (9/21/07)
6153	Hank Lenney	Cascade (10/20/02)	Skylight (9/21/07)
6154	Michelle Coe Parlej	Porter (10/20/02)	Skylight (9/21/07)
6155	Dale Aliberti	Nippletop (10/11/02)	Sawteeth (9/22/07)
6156	Lynn G. Schundler	Big Slide (9/28/96)	Sawteeth (9/22/07)
6157	Betty Lou Resotka	Big Slide (9/28/96)	Sawteeth (9/22/07)
6158	Karen H. Moriarty	Big Slide (9/28/96)	Sawteeth (9/22/07)
6159	Monica Quiroga-Zaslower	Esther (5/20/01)	Sawteeth (9/22/07)
6160W	Peter B. Abreu	Marcy (9/19/04)	Esther (9/22/07)
6161	Peter R. Mennin	Cascade (8/18/04)	Haystack (9/22/07)
6162	Mark B. Mennin	Cascade (8/18/04)	Haystack (9/22/07)
6163	William Morse	Cascade (7/2/04)	Whiteface (9/22/07)
6164	Dale Becker	Giant (7/95)	Rocky Peak (9/23/07)
6165	Gerald Perregaux	Dix (6/18/05)	Rocky Peak (9/23/07)
6166	Justin MacKinnon	Wright (6/6/05)	Haystack (9/23/07)
6167	Samuel Katz	Cascade (8/00)	Tabletop (9/23/07)
6168	Joe Brubach	Marcy (1998)	Nye (9/23/07)
6169W	Bob Marcellus	Algonquin (4/28/07)	Sawteeth (9/23/07)
6170	Laurie Hopper	Big Slide (5/10/92)	Iroquois (9/26/07)
6171	Malcolm M. Hopper	Big Slide (5/10/92)	Iroquois (9/26/07)
6172	Melody Hoffmann	Cascade (10/9/99)	Whiteface (9/29/07)
6173	David Herboldt	Phelps (10/89)	Gothics (9/29/07)
6174	Elizabeth Herboldt	Phelps (10/89)	Gothics (9/29/07)
6175	John D. Miner	Seymour (6/29/81)	Whiteface (9/29/07)
6176	Nathan Andrews	East Dix (5/25/01)	Whiteface (9/29/07)
6177	Thomas C. Mitchell	Dial (5/30/97)	Whiteface (9/29/07)
6178	Michael T. Lindacher	Giant (8/97)	Whiteface (9/29/07)
6179	James Dykes	Phelps (9/95)	Iroquois (9/30/07)
6180	Adam Gendron-Mitchell	Giant (8/94)	Saddleback (9/30/07)
6181	Gregor Mitchell	Cascade (9/93)	Saddleback (9/30/07)
6182	Janet M. Farmer	Big Slide (2/12/06)	Whiteface (9/30/07)
6183	Phil Clancy	Big Slide (8/98)	Nippletop (10/1/07)
6184	Sam Lightbody	Cascade (8/96)	Nippletop (10/1/07)
6185	H. Bradley Davidson	Marcy (1978)	Iroquois (10/2/07)
6186	Susan Black	Algonquin (6/24/00)	Skylight (10/4/07)
6187	Deb Narkevicius	Wright (9/11/06)	East Dix (10/5/07)
6188	Kay Tran	Algonquin (10/4/01)	Cascade (10/6/07)
6189	Ted H. Orr	Cascade (5/7/03)	Big Slide (10/6/07)
6190	Troy M. Nelson	Marcy (2/27/94)	Phelps (10/6/07)
6191	Cindy Molloy	Colden (5/97)	Marshall (10/6/07)
6192	Peggy Wissler	Cascade (8/27/02)	Seward (10/6/07)
6193	Real Abran	Algonquin (6/10/04)	Allen (10/7/07)

Heaven Up-h'isted-ness!

Member		First Ascent	Forty-sixth Peak
6194	Frank Pollay	Wright (7/2/95)	Marshall (10/8/07)
6195	Catherine Reynolds	Wright (1/6/93)	Esther (10/9/07)
6196	Dave Wideman	Skylight (10/26/01)	Sawteeth (10/14/07)
6197	Tyler Eaton	Cascade (8/07)	Rocky Peak (10/15/07)
6198	Jodi Drennan	Big Slide (9/96)	Santanoni (10/16/07)
6199	Michael Brown	Algonquin (9/30/06)	Seymour (10/18/07)
6200	Kenneth J. Burl, Jr.	Cascade (3/31/07)	Colden (10/20/07)
6201	Kristopher Williams	Cascade (8/99)	Iroquois (10/21/07)
6202	Gary A. VanRiper	Marcy (9/8/02)	Allen (10/22/07)
6203	Barbara Northrup	Gothics (4/30/06)	Skylight (10/25/07)
6204	Bruce W. Smith	Haystack (7/16/95)	Iroquois (10/31/07)
6205	Tim Sylvester	Cascade (5/19/07)	Marcy (11/2/07)
6206	Mireille Poupart	Big Slide (10/16/06)	Esther (11/11/07)
6207	Lori Francett	Algonquin (10/10/81)	Skylight (11/11/07)
6208	Michael Francett	Algonquin (10/10/81)	Skylight (11/11/07)
6209	Matthew R. Medick	Haystack (9/9/06)	Seward (11/12/07)
6210W	Nicholas M. Siver	East Dix (12/30/06)	Seymour (11/24/07)
6211	Denis Mault	Cascade (1/7/07)	Dix (12/2/07)
6212	Jonathan F. George, Sr.	Skylight (6/20/99)	Phelps (12/30/07)
6213	Roland Morris, Jr.	Cascade (8/63)	Tabletop (7/1/72)
6214	Jennifer B. Harrington	Giant (7/80)	Whiteface (8/1/84)
6215	Elizabeth Gold	Cascade (8/26/91)	Blake (7/13/01)
6216	Karen L. Morris	Colden (7/82)	Dix (8/14/03)
6217	Nathaniel C. Doro	Cascade (6/27/89)	Haystack (8/10/04)
6218	Roland Morris, III	Cascade (8/5/93)	Algonquin (8/17/05)
6219	Valerie Bachinsky	Marcy (10/6/03)	Seymour (5/28/06)
6220	Jacob Richey	Cascade (2002)	Allen (7/17/06)
6221	Michael Weigand	Giant (5/1/04)	Skylight (9/16/06)
6222	Robert Dutcher	Marcy (8/92)	Big Slide (10/7/06)
6223	Lorrie A. Clemo	Cascade (7/18/92)	Skylight (6/30/07)
6224	Larry Trendell, Sr.	Cliff (6/17/82)	Nippletop (6/21/07)
6225	Steven P. Nicolais	Cascade (7/18/92)	Skylight (6/30/07)
6226	Alex Lowy	Phelps (7/24/01)	Colden (7/24/07)
6227	John Adriance	Seymour (7/16/06)	Marcy (7/25/07)
6228W	Susan Duggan	Marcy (6/30/87)	Gothics (8/5/07)
6229	Meg Browning	Porter (7/11/03)	Street (8/9/07)
6230	Paul N. Leitner	Cascade (7/19/88)	Allen (8/9/07)
6231	Max Milder	Whiteface (7/16/04)	Rocky Peak (8/10/07)
6232W	Richard R. Cooley	Marcy (1987)	Nippletop (9/30/07)
6233	Mitchell Forbes	Giant (8/15/04)	Haystack (10/6/07)
6234	Maureen L. Corrado	Big Slide (9/28/96)	Sawteeth (10/22/07)
6235	Richard J. Chiasson	Cascade (6/12/05)	Seymour (10/28/07)
6236	Keith J. Clark	Marcy (1973)	Seymour (10/28/07)
6237	John Coleman	Cascade (7/30/05)	Nye (10/28/07)
6238W	Paul Sheneman	Whiteface (12/23/99)	Seward (1/5/08)
6239	Benjamin W. Uris	Giant (8/5/06)	Seymour (1/27/08)
6240W	Stephen Rombach	Giant (3/17/07)	Seymour (2/10/08)
6241W	Jennifer Innes	Wright (12/12/04)	Haystack (2/23/08)
6242	Philip Prince	Cascade (10/16/82)	Haystack (2/25/08)
6243W	Gregory E. Bennett	Big Slide (12/28/01)	Saddleback (3/17/08)
6244	Jason Ferris	Dix (11/27/06)	Haystack (4/6/08)
6245W	Jennifer Danese	Cascade (5/28/06)	Whiteface (5/25/08)
6246W	John Danese	Cascade (5/28/06)	Whiteface (5/25/08)
6247	Sabrina LaFave	Marcy (5/03)	Haystack (5/25/08)
6248	Michael Calenti	Wright (9/5/87)	Haystack (6/1/08)
6249	Steffen T. Kraehmer	Wright (9/5/87)	Haystack (6/1/08)
6250	David Buys	Giant (9/5/04)	Marcy (6/14/08)
6251W	Brian Nichols	Tabletop (1/5/07)	Phelps (6/28/08)
6252	P. Alex Comeau	Porter (1997)	Rocky Peak (6/28/08)
6253	Glenn A. Paynter	Rocky Peak (6/02)	Saddleback (7/1/08)
6254	Susan Paynter	Whiteface (7/12/03)	Saddleback (7/1/08)
6255	David A. Mansfield	Cascade (3/31/07)	East Dix (7/2/08)

The Membership Roster of the Adirondack Forty-Sixers

	Member	First Ascent	Forty-sixth Peak
6256	Andrew S. Perry	Cascade (1998)	Emmons (7/5/08)
6257	David Sutkowy	Algonquin (1983)	Emmons (7/5/08)
6258	William C. Carpenter	Big Slide (7/17/05)	Haystack (7/5/08)
6259	David A. Forsyth	Big Slide (8/5/75)	Allen (7/5/08)
6260	Lurana K. McCarron	Cascade (5/11/97)	Colden (7/8/08)
6261	Thomas J. Denham	Phelps (9/26/81)	Whiteface (7/8/08)
6262	Jim Ferrari	Dial (8/22/85)	Whiteface (7/8/08)
6263	Joseph Ciecierega	Redfield (6/12/05)	Gothics (7/12/08)
6264	Yvon Daigle	Wright (9/14/02)	Dix (7/12/08)
6265	Annie Dore	Wright (9/14/02)	Dix (7/12/08)
6266	Andrew Gonzalez	Cascade (7/21/05)	Colden (7/17/08)
6267	Paul Kroth	Cascade (8/26/99)	Gothics (7/17/08)
6268	John M. Rowley	Marcy (5/9/01)	Gray (7/18/08)
6269	Glen M. Ewart	Algonquin (6/25/92)	Allen (7/18/08)
6270	David H. Cahn	Marcy (1/70)	Cascade (7/19/08)
6271	Macky Young	Cascade (6/01)	Lower Wolf Jaw (7/20/08)
6272	Michael Bernstein	Giant (8/6/03)	Hough (7/22/08)
6273	David L. Spencer	Colden (5/83)	Whiteface (7/22/08)
6274	Drew Zeccola	Cascade (7/13/05)	Whiteface (7/22/08)
6275	William C. Zeccola	Cascade (7/13/05)	Whiteface (7/22/08)
6276	Scott Millington	Giant (9/05)	Skylight (7/25/08)
6277	Anthony D'Erasmo	Marcy (7/22/02)	Cliff (7/25/08)
6278	Lorraine MacKenzie	Phelps (6/11/05)	Whiteface (7/27/08)
6279	Samuel R. Shrago	Porter (7/1/01)	Wright (7/27/08)
6280	Theresa Pilon	Cascade (7/96)	Whiteface (7/31/08)
6281	Carolyn Cyr	Marcy (7/3/05)	Whiteface (8/1/08)
6282	John Clark	Whiteface (8/3/00)	Porter (8/2/08)
6283	Tom Burns	Cascade (5/8/99)	Allen (8/4/08)
6284	Eric Jackson	Marcy (9/25/71)	Skylight (8/5/08)
6285	Megan Beckett	Street (7/7/08)	Porter (8/6/08)
6286	Katelyn Clarke	Street (7/7/08)	Porter (8/6/08)
6287	Parker A. Harris	Algonquin (8/4/99)	Cascade (8/8/08)
6288	Francis I. Henwood	Phelps (8/87)	Rocky Peak (8/9/08)
6289	Donna Dinse	Street (2/20/04)	Allen (8/9/08)
6290	Bruce Hadley	Haystack (8/10/96)	Emmons (8/9/08)
6291	Judy Immesoete	Cascade (2/19/04)	Allen (8/9/08)
6292	Joe Merrihew	Cascade (3/7/04)	Haystack (8/9/08)
6293	Matt Edwards	Lower Wolf Jaw (9/2/02)	Iroquois (8/11/08)
6294	Natalie Foote	Street (7/13/99)	Allen (8/12/08)
6295	Andrew Lowy	Cascade (7/17/03)	Wright (8/13/08)
6296	Shannon Freyer	Wright (8/04)	Panther (8/14/08)
6297	Michael J. Bergner	Cascade (7/17/04)	Redfield (8/14/08)
6298	Donald Whittemore	Giant (8/21/99)	Marcy (8/16/08)
6299	Joseph P. Whittemore	Cascade (7/24/99)	Marcy (8/16/08)
6300	Eric Singerman	Whiteface (7/13/06)	Phelps (8/16/08)
6301	Elisabeth Craven	Algonquin (9/5/01)	Rocky Peak (8/19/08)
6302	Bob Shepler	Colvin (8/90)	Marcy (8/19/08)
6303	C. Stuart Kelley	Colvin (8/6/92)	Seymour (8/20/08)
6304	Christopher L. Rose	Cascade (1995)	Santanoni (8/21/08)
6305	Jane T. Stine	Santanoni (7/77)	Couchsachraga (8/23/08)
6306	Maria Garcia	Dial (5/21/00)	Street (8/23/08)
6307	Martha Loeffler	Marcy (3/00)	Saddleback (8/23/08)
6308	Daniel J. Fisher	Marcy (1964)	Saddleback (8/23/08)
6309	Lorne F. Erdile	Giant (8/96)	Seymour (8/23/08)
6310	Simon E. Erdile	Cascade (7/97)	Seymour (8/23/08)
6311	Harold D. Barnshaw	Tabletop (1/3/02)	Allen (8/27/08)
6312	Larry Jordan	Cascade (7/11/99)	Allen (8/27/08)
6313	Glenn V. Greibus	Marcy (10/72)	Skylight (8/29/08)
6314	Sandy Yellen	Cascade (8/6/05)	Seymour (8/30/08)
6315	Philip Lance	Cascade (7/62)	Haystack (8/31/08)
6316	Nan Mullenneaux	Cascade (8/00)	Haystack (8/31/08)
6317	John A. Schatzel	Cascade (5/5/03)	Allen (8/31/08)

Heaven Up-h'isted-ness!

	Member	First Ascent	Forty-sixth Peak
6318	Joseph M. Serletti	Porter (7/4/91)	Whiteface (8/31/08)
6319	Adam M. Nicolais	Giant (8/20/94)	Saddleback (8/31/08)
6320	Annie Edwards	Cascade (5/83)	Allen (9/1/08)
6321	Jeff Edwards	Whiteface (5/17/81)	Allen (9/1/08)
6322	Linda P. Schmidt	Cascade (5/1/05)	Haystack (9/5/08)
6323	Stephanie Martin	Cliff (6/13/87)	Whiteface (9/6/08)
6324	Jeff Glans	Marcy (7/89)	Panther (9/6/08)
6325	Heide Conibear	Marcy (9/4/99)	Redfield (9/6/08)
6326	Arnie Tran	Marcy (10/12/01)	Saddleback (9/7/08)
6327	David C. Bernhard	Giant (8/27/91)	Skylight (9/11/08)
6328	Lisa Yorke	Colden (6/8/03)	Whiteface (9/13/08)
6329	Jonathan Noonan	Cascade (5/20/01)	Haystack (9/13/08)
6330	Christi Palmer	Rocky Peak (6/21/02)	Whiteface (9/13/08)
6331	Sean Greene	Cascade (8/95)	Saddleback (9/13/08)
6332	Robert J. Conti	Marcy (6/17/02)	Whiteface (9/13/08)
6333	Eric Hanson	Marcy (1986)	Emmons (9/13/08)
6334	Thomas J. Bush	Tabletop (9/11/04)	Whiteface (9/13/08)
6335	Nathan H. Mack	Porter (7/75)	Gray (9/15/08)
6336	Sharon T. Getman	Algonquin (9/19/05)	Marcy (9/17/08)
6337	James Jennison	Marcy (7/93)	Skylight (9/17/08)
6338	Bill Chriswell	Sawteeth (9/12/05)	Rocky Peak (9/20/08)
6339	Glenn Petersen	Marcy (8/68)	Skylight (9/20/08)
6340	David Gutenmann	Cascade (2/23/91)	Haystack (9/20/08)
6341	Donna Bruschi	Marcy (7/02)	Cascade (9/20/08)
6342	Keith J. Anderson	Algonquin (5/79)	Wright (9/20/08)
6343	Kathleen Maguire	Algonquin (8/99)	Cliff (9/20/08)
6344	Jessica Brubach	Marcy (2000)	Hough (9/20/08)
6345	Zachary Felix	Phelps (8/10/00)	Skylight (9/21/08)
6346	Paul Felix	Cascade (8/18/99)	Skylight (9/21/08)
6347	Susan M. Johnson	Marcy (10/25/97)	Wright (9/21/08)
6348	Daniel C. Souter	Marcy (6/30/65)	Allen (9/2/08)
6349	Craig E. Rubio	Marcy (9/94)	Marshall (9/22/08)
6350	Tracy Duffin	Marcy (10/4/98)	Big Slide (9/22/08)
6351	Peter Herrig	Lower Wolf Jaw (1/20/07)	Whiteface (9/27/08)
6352	David H. Lyons	Upper Wolf Jaw (10/22/05)	Giant (9/28/08)
6353	Jo-Anne M. Faulkner	Marcy (10/3/03)	Rocky Peak (10/3/08)
6354	Erick Klymkow	Big Slide (9/26/98)	Haystack (10/4/08)
6355	Mark T. Laske	Marcy (1969)	Gothics (10/4/08)
6356	Ken Trischuk	Whiteface (9/91)	Dix (10/5/08)
6357	Jane Husson	Cascade (7/99)	Haystack (10/5/08)
6358	Rick Day	Seymour (8/18/06)	Upper Wolf Jaw (10/5/08)
6359	Charlie Reller	Gray (8/29/04)	Street (10/6/08)
6360	Shawn J. Turner	Phelps (11/29/96)	Marcy (10/8/08)
6361	Cindy Kuhn	Gothics (1/1/06)	Basin (10/8/08)
6362	Paul Dailey	Cascade (10/11/03)	Rocky Peak (10/8/08)
6363	Robert A. Reinhart	Algonquin (6/11/08)	Colden (10/10/08)
6364	Walter J. Jackemuk	Seymour (8/7/07)	Cascade (10/11/08)
6365	Loretta Miner	Phelps (9/30/06)	Skylight (10/11/08)
6366	Genevieve Chartier	Porter (6/9/97)	Sawteeth (10/11/08)
6367	Charles W. Krueger	Marcy (7/6/01)	Colden (10/12/08)
6368	Douglas H. Morrow	Dix (7/1/02)	Colden (10/12/08)
6369	Gregory Charon	Marcy (8/6/95)	Allen (10/12/08)
6370	Gavin D. Morrow	Marcy (8/2/03)	Colden (10/12/08)
6371	Steven Altmayer	Wright (2003)	Allen (10/12/08)
6372	Mark Perrin	Algonquin (6/8/02)	Hough (10/12/08)
6373	Joseph W. Amisson	Lower Wolf Jaw (8/99)	Rocky Peak (10/12/08)
6374	Thomas J. Amisson	Cascade (8/96)	Rocky Peak (10/12/08)
6375	James Weeks	Algonquin (10/14/01)	Hough (10/12/08)
6376	Andre Trottier	Marcy (9/15/01)	Seward (10/12/08)
6377	Rick Reed	Marcy (7/80)	Whiteface (10/13/08)
6378	Michael K. Stratton	Cascade (8/3/08)	Wright (10/16/08)
6379	Matthew LaClair	Cascade (8/2/08)	Wright (10/16/08)

The Membership Roster of the Adirondack Forty-Sixers

	Member	First Ascent	Forty-sixth Peak
6380	Lorraine Clarke	Algonquin (1996)	Nye (10/19/08)
6381	Daniel Pekrol	Cascade (4/12/03)	Dial (10/20/08)
6382	Jerome Chouinard	Algonquin (5/11/08)	Skylight (11/1/08)
6383	Catherine Glorieux	Whiteface (6/3/07)	Marcy (11/1/08)
6384	Levi Sayward	Phelps (8/93)	Dix (11/1/08)
6385	Jim Costello	Algonquin (9/23/05)	Big Slide (11/22/08)
6386	Nerissa Nields-Duffy	Colvin (8/75)	Dix (8/1/93)
6387	Craig Boronow	Seymour (1998)	Whiteface (7/30/01)
6388	Joe Norden, Jr.	Colden (11/78)	Allen (7/26/04)
6389	Michael Lawler	Santanoni (6/9/73)	Couchsachraga (6/12/05)
6390	Jordyn Wolfand	Cascade (7/5/00)	Rocky Peak (6/21/05)
6391	Daniel L. Baldessari	Wright (7/02)	Marcy (7/27/05)
6392	Bryan Baker	Donaldson (7/14/05)	Cascade (8/11/05)
6393	Paul W. Orvis, IV	Gothics (7/23/83)	Nippletop (10/1/05)
6394	Mary-Pat Burke	Rocky Peak (10/6/85)	Haystack (10/6/06)
6395	Duncan F. Johnson	Cascade (7/25/03)	Blake (8/8/07)
6396	Jerry Licht	Big Slide (8/28/03)	Sawteeth (8/9/07)
6397	David C. Mason	Cascade (10/7/90)	Seymour (8/15/07)
6398	Michael H. Mason	Algonquin (10/5/85)	Seymour (8/15/07)
6399	Roman Benke	Marcy (7/15/96)	Marshall (8/23/07)
6400	Michael Wentworth	Tabletop (8/2/02)	Porter (9/1/07)
6401	Mark Glazer	Marcy (9/11/99)	Redfield (9/2/07)
6402	Donald Pasquale	Sawteeth (7/10/99)	Whiteface (9/8/07)
6403	David Putney	Marcy (9/21/03)	Big Slide (9/30/07)
6404	John M. Vergis	Sawteeth (5/29/04)	Whiteface (6/27/08)
6405	Kevin T. Kogut	Marcy (3/28/86)	Haystack (7/14/08)
6406	Rachel Bergman	Cascade (6/04)	Giant (7/26/08)
6407	Cameron Thompson	Whiteface (7/00)	Porter (8/6/08)
6408	Hans Himelein	Gothics (7/1/80)	Couchsachraga (8/13/08)
6409	Andrew W. Charapko	Cascade (7/1/03)	Wright (8/13/08)
6410	Kathryn Landers	Cascade (5/26/96)	Colden (8/13/08)
6411	Milton F. Stevenson, IV	Macomb (7/1/98)	Marcy (8/16/08)
6412	Frederick E. Hoffman	Giant (5/6/04)	Whiteface (8/17/08)
6413	Devon E. Maust	Giant (5/6/04)	Whiteface (8/17/08)
6414	Linnaea Chapman	Cascade (9/3/95)	Sawteeth (8/31/08)
6415	James D. Warfield	Cascade (6/28/03)	Santanoni (9/6/08)
6416	Rick J. Kisselstein	Whiteface (8/82)	Sawteeth (9/6/08)
6417	Debbe Demarest	Cascade (6/28/03)	Santanoni (9/6/08)
6418	John Arrigo	Cascade (9/10/00)	Marcy (9/11/08)
6419	Carol Delahunty	Giant (9/5/05)	Marcy (9/11/08)
6420	Ann Mundy	Porter (9/00)	Rocky Peak (9/14/08)
6421	John R. Tassone	Marcy (4/84)	Street (10/11/08)
6422	Séverine Parsy	Haystack (5/18/03)	Basin (11/17/08)
6423	Mark J. Thomas	Phelps (10/10/96)	Tabletop (1/30/09)
6424W	Doug Luke	Marcy (9/23/96)	Gray (2/1/09)
6425W	Paul F. Finnegan	Wright (3/3/07)	Skylight (2/21/09)
6426W	Jennifer Garcia	Wright (3/3/07)	Skylight (2/21/09)
6427	Patricia M. Pastella	Big Slide (10/81)	Whiteface (2/27/09)
6428W	Bob Liseno	Giant (1/2/06)	Haystack (3/7/09)
6429W	Eileen Liseno	Giant (1/2/06)	Haystack (3/7/09)
6430W	Tyler J. Merriam	Big Slide (1/17/00)	Colden (3/14/09)
6431W	Brian H. Merriam	Marcy (2/73)	Colden (3/14/09)
6432W	Kim Goppert	Marcy (10/01)	Marcy (3/14/09)
6433W	David Ringwall	Cascade (12/29/02)	Saddleback (3/16/09)
6434W	Donna M. Ringwall	Cascade (12/29/02)	Saddleback (3/16/09)
6435	Eric Lawler	Algonquin (6/15/03)	Seymour (4/26/09)
6436	Daniel R. Monroe	Haystack (7/5/08)	Seward (5/23/09)
6437W	Laura Gerson	Cascade (1/5/08)	Colden (5/24/09)
6438	Scott M. Farley	Algonquin (9/10/99)	Whiteface (5/24/09)
6439	Jill M. Hayes	Algonquin (5/25/01)	Whiteface (5/24/09)
6440	Colleen Kaulfuss	Cascade (10/2/05)	Basin (6/4/09)
6441	Donald Satterly	Dial (8/1/07)	Allen (6/5/09)

HEAVEN UP-H'ISTED-NESS!

	Member	First Ascent	Forty-sixth Peak
6442	Patricia Johnston	Marcy (5/98)	Gothics (6/13/09)
6443	Larry Montague	Marcy (8/5/07)	Haystack (6/19/09)
6444	Dave Meyer	Marcy (8/5/07)	Haystack (6/19/09)
6445	David Ponka	Colden (10/98)	Nippletop (6/27/09)
6446	David P. Vallette	Cascade (9/6/92)	Santanoni (6/28/09)
6447	James Daykin	Algonquin (11/77)	Santanoni (6/28/09)
6448	Mimi L. Daykin	Algonquin (11/77)	Santanoni (6/28/09)
6449	Christian A. Hanchett	Big Slide (1992)	Gothics (6/28/09)
6450	Tracy Hanchett	Cascade (9/6/03)	Gothics (6/28/09)
6451	Alison Darbee	Sawteeth (9/16/06)	Whiteface (6/28/09)
6452	Andrew Lipp	Big Slide (7/29/06)	Basin (6/30/09)
6453	Joseph H. Miner, III	Phelps (9/30/06)	Dix (6/30/09)
6454	Dave French	Giant (5/18/08)	Basin (7/2/09)
6455	Jennifer Ciecierega	Dial (9/7/05)	Whiteface (7/4/09)
6456	Shane L. Hamilton	Giant (4/19/07)	Whiteface (7/4/09)
6457	Matthew R. Jackson	Tabletop (8/17/05)	Whiteface (7/4/09)
6458	Michael Libertucci	Cascade (8/15/05)	Seward (7/4/09)
6459	Beth DeMatteo	Giant (6/11/05)	Whiteface (7/5/09)
6460	Robert Ellis	Marcy (8/86)	Allen (7/9/09)
6461	Ted Letcher	Big Slide (10/3/06)	Basin (7/9/09)
6462	Stephanie Graudons	Marcy (7/10/07)	Iroquois (7/10/09)
6463	Steven W. Duby	Esther (9/29/07)	Dix (7/11/09)
6464W	Leonard Coolbeth	Cascade (2/17/87)	Allen (7/11/09)
6465	Rupert B. Harris, Jr.	Colden (8/21/74)	Cliff (7/15/09)
6466	Kiley J. Evans	Cascade (8/9/99)	Haystack (7/15/09)
6467	Mark G. Evans	Cascade (8/9/99)	Haystack (7/15/09)
6468	Douglas J. Varney	Porter (7/29/99)	Skylight (7/17/09)
6469	Matthew Davis	Algonquin (4/97)	Santanoni (7/18/09)
6470	Kendall P. Compton	Marcy (8/26/95)	Rocky Peak (7/18/09)
6471	Scott K. Compton	Wright (5/30/93)	Rocky Peak (7/18/09)
6472	Phil Loesch	Algonquin (8/24/96)	Rocky Peak (7/18/09)
6473	Nick Underwood	Cascade (7/8/01)	Seymour (7/18/09)
6474	Mason Compton	Marcy (7/25/97)	Rocky Peak (7/18/09)
6475	Carol Fisher	Cascade (1980)	Seymour (7/18/09)
6476	Rich Alioth	Colden (8/82)	Lower Wolf Jaw (7/19/09)
6477	Dan E. Moellman	Marcy (10/27/01)	Skylight (7/19/09)
6478	James DeMatteo	Gothics (10/1/05)	Wright (7/19/09)
6479	Matthew Baldessari	Seymour (7/13/08)	Marcy (7/22/09)
6480	Colleen Porter	Marcy (7/91)	Porter (7/23/09)
6481	Christopher L. Greco	Giant (8/92)	Colden (7/25/09)
6482	David Palat	Porter (7/31/98)	Skylight (7/27/09)
6483	Gregory Brock	Cascade (7/19/72)	Seward (7/28/09)
6484	Mike McEvoy	Haystack (10/16/94)	Skylight (7/28/09)
6485	Mark Epstein	Marcy (1993)	Panther (7/29/09)
6486	Peter W. Tilton	Sawteeth (8/1/94)	Gothics (7/30/09)
6487	Paula M. Bishop	Porter (7/4/08)	Skylight (7/30/09)
6488	Deborah T. Haynes	Colden (6/77)	Seymour (8/1/09)
6489	Penny A. Hainer	Dix (8/30/80)	Wright (8/1/09)
6490	David Bagley	Saddleback (2002)	Blake (8/1/09)
6491	Peter Johantgen	Marcy (6/76)	Whiteface (8/1/09)
6492	Bradley Arnold	Colvin (8/17/04)	Gray (8/2/09)
6493	Christopher Arnold	Colvin (8/17/04)	Gray (8/2/09)
6494	Kellen P. Arnold	Colvin (8/14/04)	Gray (8/2/09)
6495	Dennis M. Kirschbaum	Giant (7/15/70)	Panther (8/3/09)
6496	Laurie Eschmann	Marcy (9/21/73)	Colden (8/4/09)
6497	Mitchell Zimmer	Marcy (7/12/90)	Skylight (8/4/09)
6498	Stephanie Zimmer	Cascade (7/6/98)	Skylight (8/4/09)
6499	Timothy J. Johnston, Jr.	Algonquin (7/5/09)	Cascade (8/6/09)
6500	Henry Richey	Cascade (7/14/05)	Panther (8/6/09)
6501	Joshua Spokes	Cascade (6/12/04)	Panther (8/6/09)
6502	Adelaide Minerva	Cascade (7/25/03)	Colden (8/7/09)
6503	David LePage	Cascade (9/1/05)	Seward (8/7/09)

The Membership Roster of the Adirondack Forty-Sixers

	Member	First Ascent	Forty-sixth Peak
6504	Dale Spring	Cascade (4/12/02)	Allen (8/8/09)
6505	David Spring	Cascade (4/12/02)	Allen (8/8/09)
6506	John B. Egger	Marcy (1983)	Colden (8/8/09)
6507	Michael R. Boyack	Algonquin (10/4/98)	Panther (8/8/09)
6508	Kenneth C. Scott	Big Slide (9/1/84)	Whiteface (8/9/09)
6509	Lana L. Christiansen	Algonquin (9/7/08)	Redfield (8/9/09)
6510	Greg Boyer	Marcy (6/15/89)	Allen (8/11/09)
6511	Max Lopez	Gothics (7/07)	Colden (8/12/09)
6512	Jeremy D. Krones	Cascade (7/14/00)	Colden (8/13/09)
6513	Mark Obbie	Lower Wolf Jaw (8/74)	Whiteface (8/13/09)
6514	Cameron Merkh	Cascade (8/12/98)	Whiteface (8/13/09)
6515	Heather Mooney	Cascade (7/02)	Skylight (8/13/09)
6516	Tammy A. Spencer	Cascade (8/26/99)	Haystack (8/14/09)
6517	Verner C. Kreuter, IV	Haystack (6/30/03)	Cascade (8/14/09)
6518	David Page	Marcy (7/86)	Colden (8/14/09)
6519	Thomas C. Dwyer	Cascade (7/04)	Whiteface (8/15/09)
6520	Stephen T. Kinney	Wright (6/30/02)	Marcy (8/15/09)
6521	Richard Carr	Marcy (8/19/02)	Emmons (8/16/09)
6522	Gregory D. Michne	Cascade (6/3/07)	Haystack (8/16/09)
6523	Jason Lasky	Marcy (8/19/05)	Emmons (8/16/09)
6524	Mary M. Austin	Cascade (7/30/97)	Haystack (8/17/09)
6525	K. Scott Lane	Whiteface (8/21/99)	Haystack (8/17/09)
6526	Michelle Lane	Whiteface (8/21/99)	Haystack (8/17/09)
6527	Maria R. Fernandez	Algonquin (6/16/08)	Redfield (8/19/09)
6528	Ron Schildge	Dix (8/20/97)	Seward (8/19/09)
6529	Phoebe Jackson	Dial (9/26/01)	Allen (8/19/09)
6530	Ann T. Horwich	Phelps (8/92)	Rocky Peak (8/21/09)
6531	Nathaniel J. Van Yperen	Big Slide (7/98)	Phelps (8/21/09)
6532	Jim Bouton	Whiteface (10/71)	Couchsachraga (8/21/09)
6533	Noelle Ohanesian	Porter (6/3/00)	Rocky Peak (8/22/09)
6534	Sarah Ohanesian	Porter (6/3/00)	Rocky Peak (8/22/09)
6535	Matthew Nuesell	Colden (8/6/01)	Skylight (8/22/09)
6536	David J. Barnshaw	Armstrong (8/02)	Rocky Peak (8/22/09)
6537	Peter M. Ely	Cascade (4/87)	Saddleback (8/23/09)
6538	Domino MacNaughton	Marcy (8/14/95)	Basin (8/24/09)
6539	David D. Lewicki	Cascade (6/27/98)	Skylight (8/24/09)
6540	Gillian Wright	Giant (1991)	Whiteface (8/25/09)
6541	Tamra Mooney	Cascade (7/02)	Rocky Peak (8/25/09)
6542	Jeff Wright	Wright (9/80)	Whiteface (8/25/09)
6543	Stephen M. Sweet	Cascade (7/94)	Gray (8/26/09)
6544	Gillian Hunt	Haystack (8/15/96)	Marcy (8/26/09)
6545	Jason J. Close	Algonquin (10/24/05)	Allen (8/26/09)
6546	Curtis Frick	Colden (10/23/94)	Allen (8/26/09)
6547	Robert Ocampo	Marcy (7/24/05)	Seymour (8/27/09)
6548	Phil McCaffrey	Lower Wolf Jaw (5/28/06)	Haystack (8/27/09)
6549	Dolores Kong	Cascade (9/3/03)	Redfield (8/27/09)
6550	Daniel C. Ring	Cascade (9/3/03)	Redfield (8/27/09)
6551	Roger Smith	Giant (7/65)	Skylight (8/27/09)
6552	Barry J. Stone	Gothics (5/02)	Seymour (8/27/09)
6553	David P. Wolff	Algonquin (9/84)	Marcy (8/28/09)
6554	Holly C. Wolff	Algonquin (9/84)	Marcy (8/28/09)
6555	B. Kelly Wilcox	Colden (7/19/03)	Seymour (8/28/09)
6556	Michael Virdone	Colden (3/12/05)	Marcy (8/28/09)
6557	Nicole A. Virdone	Algonquin (5/26/06)	Marcy (8/28/09)
6558	Carla Canjar	Cascade (8/14/03)	Saddleback (8/28/09)
6559	Jorge A. Alvarez	Macomb (8/26/89)	Rocky Peak (8/28/09)
6560	Mark Hirsch	Panther (8/25/89)	Rocky Peak (8/28/09)
6561	Michael L. Davies	Saddleback (5/5/07)	Panther (8/28/09)
6562	James Simpson	Wright (1987)	Skylight (8/30/09)
6563	Heidi Holderied	Whiteface (7/95)	Allen (8/31/09)
6564	Jennifer Webb	Whiteface (7/99)	Allen (8/31/09)
6565	Keneck E. Skibinski	Marcy (8/4/03)	Allen (9/2/09)

Heaven Up-h'isted-ness!

	Member	First Ascent	Forty-sixth Peak
6566	Adam J. Apt	Wright (8/25/05)	Dix (9/3/09)
6567	David Kozlowski	Marcy (8/31/02)	Haystack (9/3/09)
6568	Robert Kozlowski	Marcy (8/31/02)	Haystack (9/3/09)
6569	Christopher E. Miller	Marcy (8/17/04)	Colden (9/4/09)
6570	Marc D. Ginsburg	Algonquin (10/4/04)	Cliff (9/4/09)
6571	Bonnie Whitman	Marcy (10/20/00)	Haystack (9/5/09)
6572	Judy Chriswell	Sawteeth (9/12/05)	Basin (9/5/09)
6573	Erik J. Svarcbergs	Colden (8/9/04)	Big Slide (9/5/09)
6574	Juris M. Svarcbergs	Colden (8/9/04)	Big Slide (9/5/09)
6575	Matthew Melsert	Lower Wolf Jaw (8/29/71)	Allen (9/5/09)
6576	Kelly R. Arnold	Cascade (9/25/04)	Marshall (9/5/09)
6577	Michael A. Jackson	Porter (8/17/06)	Wright (9/6/09)
6578	Alisa B. Harrison	Tabletop (7/92)	Dial (9/6/09)
6579	Gregory Chambers	Lower Wolf Jaw (11/7/02)	Allen (9/6/09)
6580	Richard V. Cox	Algonquin (7/13/03)	Whiteface (9/6/09)
6581	William S. Jones	Marcy (7/4/00)	Whiteface (9/6/09)
6582	Adriana King	Cascade (9/25/04)	Marcy (9/7/09)
6583	Kirtland King	Cascade (9/25/04)	Marcy (9/7/09)
6584	LeAnne King	Cascade (9/25/04)	Marcy (9/7/09)
6585	Sarah King	Cascade (9/25/04)	Marcy (9/7/09)
6586	Doug Lavergne	Gothics (6/27/97)	Seymour (9/7/09)
6587	Suzie Belanger	Porter (12/8/07)	Iroquois (9/7/09)
6588	Austin Huneck	Cascade (4/20/06)	Whiteface (9/7/09)
6589	Timothy Huneck	Cascade (4/20/06)	Whiteface (9/7/09)
6590	John D. McMahon	Haystack (5/75)	Marcy (9/11/09)
6591	David J. Allen	Giant (1997)	Skylight (9/11/09)
6592	Kendall Phillips	Algonquin (6/20/02)	Skylight (9/11/09)
6593	Karolyn H. Moody	Cascade (10/1/05)	Skylight (9/12/09)
6594	Nicole L. Moody	Cascade (10/1/05)	Skylight (9/12/09)
6595	Eric Montz	Marcy (5/5/04)	Allen (9/12/09)
6596	Sarah Townsend	Cascade (10/7/90)	Haystack (9/12/09)
6597	Marty Boisvert	Dix (10/01)	East Dix (9/12/09)
6598	Timothy D. Decker	Marcy (1975)	Emmons (9/12/09)
6599	David P. Miller	Giant (9/17/97)	Allen (9/12/09)
6600	Seth Goodreau	Redfield (6/2/01)	Haystack (9/12/09)
6601	Charlie Czech	Porter (8/13/06)	Big Slide (9/13/09)
6602	Mary Roden-Tice	Colden (5/30/72)	Skylight (9/13/09)
6603	Jennifer Rumbutis	Cascade (4/20/08)	Marcy (9/13/09)
6604	Mike Rumbutis	Cascade (4/20/08)	Marcy (9/13/09)
6605	Joe Menzel	Marcy (8/11/93)	Whiteface (9/19/09)
6606	David H. Finley	Giant (8/92)	Iroquois (9/19/09)
6607	Alan Hull	Giant (8/24/02)	Marcy (9/19/09)
6608	Hannah Eckert	Algonquin (8/03)	Marcy (9/19/09)
6609	Sheila Delarm	Cascade (8/2/04)	Marcy (9/19/09)
6610	Mark W. Powell	Cascade (10/1/95)	Whiteface (9/19/09)
6611	Meghan Addario	Couchsachraga (6/6/06)	Dix (9/19/09)
6612	Michael Addario	Skylight (8/30/03)	Dix (9/19/09)
6613	Andréanne Surprenant	Colden (5/24/08)	Big Slide (9/19/09)
6614	Charles S. Leounis	Giant (8/9/03)	Dix (9/19/09)
6615	Wesley Bishop	Porter (5/28/06)	Whiteface (9/19/09)
6616	Allie Delventhal	Porter (9/2/07)	Whiteface (9/19/09)
6617	Paul Klippel	Cascade (7/6/06)	Whiteface (9/20/09)
6618	Shirley LaPlante	Cascade (7/6/06)	Whiteface (9/20/09)
6619	John M. Colvin	Algonquin (7/28/83)	Colvin (9/20/09)
6620	Richard R. Reynolds	Cascade (11/5/95)	Couchsachraga (9/21/09)
6621	Robert Massey	Whiteface (8/95)	Haystack (9/22/09)
6622	Susan B. Dougherty	Marcy (6/20/79)	Whiteface (9/23/09)
6623	Michael Gsellmeier	Big Slide (9/25/04)	Colden (9/26/09)
6624	Michael D. Brown	Giant (7/90)	Whiteface (9/26/09)
6625	Dirk Endres	Marcy (6/97)	Colden (9/26/09)
6626	Scott Anderson	Big Slide (6/93)	Whiteface (9/26/09)
6627	Brendan Quinn	Algonquin (8/24/02)	Haystack (9/26/09)

The Membership Roster of the Adirondack Forty-Sixers

	Member	First Ascent	Forty-sixth Peak
6628	Thomas E. Hursh	Phelps (8/01)	Blake (9/26/09)
6629	Michael Manosh	Big Slide (8/08)	Blake (9/26/09)
6630	David Paddock	Cascade (1/17/05)	Whiteface (9/26/09)
6631	Will Golden	Cascade (5/5/07)	Rocky Peak (9/26/09)
6632	Ken Anello	Cascade (8/24/00)	Whiteface (9/28/09)
6633	Peter Holderied	Whiteface (7/92)	Phelps (9/30/09)
6634	Bill Madden	Whiteface (7/95)	Phelps (9/30/09)
6635	Stacy Bunce	Cascade (10/22/01)	Rocky Peak (10/1/09)
6636	E. Andrew Mitchell	Cascade (10/22/01)	Rocky Peak (10/1/09)
6637	Jack A. Ziegler	Marcy (3/4/03)	Seymour (10/2/09)
6638	Ben Chapman	Wright (8/5/96)	Colden (10/4/09)
6639	Riley Chapman	Wright (8/5/96)	Colden (10/4/09)
6640	Gary Cederstrom	Big Slide (5/12/07)	Basin (10/4/09)
6641	Michael Korth	Cascade (4/06)	Basin (10/4/09)
6642	Lynn Benevento	Giant (7/26/83)	Santanoni (10/5/09)
6643	Stephen Wardell	Macomb (5/23/80)	Esther (10/6/09)
6644	Gary R. Snyder	Cascade (6/6/07)	Skylight (10/6/09)
6645	Lisa Weismiller	Algonquin (1/13/07)	Rocky Peak (10/7/09)
6646	Brian Lamos	Cascade (7/25/99)	Rocky Peak (10/10/09)
6647	Janet Wilson	Giant (9/4/04)	Rocky Peak (10/10/09)
6648	Cara D. Coffin	Porter (4/5/09)	Whiteface (10/10/09)
6649	Maxime Hébert	Giant (8/5/00)	Rocky Peak (10/10/09)
6650	Alexandre Lauzon	Big Slide (12/11/05)	Dix (10/10/09)
6651	Richard A. Salvarezza	Wright (7/11/08)	Cascade (10/11/09)
6652	Anthony T. Salvarezza	Wright (7/11/08)	Cascade (10/11/09)
6653	Julie M. Moran	Algonquin (2/14/04)	Cliff (10/12/09)
6654	David Bazinet	Giant (1/24/09)	Iroquois (10/12/09)
6655	Christopher A. Johnson	Cascade (9/16/06)	Iroquois (10/17/09)
6656	Carrie Denton	Cascade (9/29/00)	Iroquois (10/17/09)
6657	Shawn G. Johnson	Marcy (10/6/05)	Allen (10/17/09)
6658	John C. Reeves	Cascade (5/08)	Phelps (10/17/09)
6659	Cynthia K. Mayer	Cascade (4/24/73)	Redfield (10/17/09)
6660	Bruce H. Candiano	Giant (9/99)	Basin (10/17/09)
6661	Dawn M. Johnson	Marcy (10/6/05)	Allen (10/17/09)
6662	Kathleen Pacuk	Marcy (8/19/06)	Cliff (10/17/09)
6663	Peter Kobor	Wright (88)	Marcy (10/18/09)
6664	David A. Walls	Dix (5/11/91)	Colden (10/31/09)
6665	Wade Lawrence	Whiteface (2/08)	Dix (10/31/09)
6666	Dean Morris	Cascade (1/16/05)	Allen (11/2/09)
6667	Kelley Morris	Giant (5/15/05)	Allen (11/2/09)
6668	Rick Bennett	Marcy (6/83)	Sawteeth (11/7/09)
6669	Richard G. Black	Lower Wolf Jaw (8/97)	Sawteeth (11/7/09)
6670	Jim Bennett	Marcy (1986)	Sawteeth (11/7/09)
6671	Lucas R. LaBarre	Big Slide (7/6/08)	Gray (11/7/09)
6672	Jim Wallace	Big Slide (3/21/09)	Phelps (11/7/09)
6673W	Michael W. Siudy	Marcy (10/8/05)	Whiteface (11/7/09)
6674	Brendan G. Schaefer	Marcy (6/12/93)	Cliff (11/8/09)
6675	William White	Wright (7/95)	Skylight (11/9/09)
6676	Michael R. O'Brien	Big Slide (6/93)	Allen (11/12/09)
6677	Jeanne M. Philion-Nichols	Phelps (6/28/08)	Esther (11/14/09)
6678	Daniel A. Winkler	Algonquin (10/12/98)	Iroquois (11/16/09)
6679W	Jeff D. Wolk	Marcy (2/82)	Seward (12/28/09)
6680	Lawrence C. Stoker, III	Algonquin (8/13/08)	Whiteface (12/30/09)
6681	Robert Andrews	Cascade (7/46)	Couchsachraga (7/22/70)
6682	Hugh Neil Zimmerman	Cascade (5/1/76)	Redfield (5/24/81)
6683	Duffy F. McCarthy	Wright (8/22/76)	Marshall (9/1/84)
6684	Teresa Cheetham-Pal	Algonquin (6/91)	Cliff (11/1/98)
6685	Daniel Rillahan	Cascade (9/92)	Tabletop (12/1/98)
6686	Jim J. Jarnot	Panther (9/17/94)	Redfield (5/24/02)
6687	Dan Recinella	Colden (10/91)	Emmons (10/12/02)
6688	Dorine Peregrim	Skylight (9/5/98)	Panther (8/30/03)
6689	Dorothy M. Beatty	Marcy (7/62)	Marcy (8/10/04)

Heaven Up-h'isted-ness!

	Member	First Ascent	Forty-sixth Peak
6690	Peter G. Beatty	Marcy (7/62)	Rocky Peak (8/10/04)
6691	Chris Hunt	Big Slide (7/96)	Sawteeth (2/11/05)
6692	Marc J. Alsina	Cascade (8/28/95)	Santanoni (9/2/05)
6693	Kathryn Arquette	Cascade (5/24/98)	Saddleback (9/11/05)
6694	Steven Arquette	Cascade (5/24/98)	Saddleback (9/11/05)
6695	Devin Hall	Haystack (2002)	Whiteface (7/24/06)
6696	Ian Laing	Wright (7/99)	Emmons (8/16/07)
6697	Richard Kapune	Giant (9/1/96)	Marshall (8/10/08)
6698	Dana C. Biddle	Cascade (7/25/00)	Skylight (7/11/09)
6699	Jonathan Brumley	Wright (3/23/03)	Panther (7/11/09)
6700	Dennis Johnson	Marshall (8/19/96)	Skylight (7/14/09)
6701	Christopher M. Frielinghaus	Algonquin (8/79)	Seymour (7/18/09)
6702	William Frielinghaus	Cascade (7/8/01)	Seymour (7/18/09)
6703	Walter Bassarab	Cascade (8/25/05)	Rocky Peak (7/18/09)
6704	Eric Coners	Seymour (7/13/08)	Marcy (7/22/09)
6705	Brian Lee	Seymour (7/13/08)	Marcy (7/22/09)
6706	Kathryn Burchenal	Armstrong (7/17/82)	Allen (7/27/09)
6707	Jeffrey M. Smith	Algonquin (6/84)	Iroquois (7/27/09)
6708	Patrick J. Torosian	Giant (8/31/01)	Allen (7/31/09)
6709	Sophie Aron	Cascade (8/11/03)	Whiteface (7/31/09)
6710	Ben Huber	Couchsachraga (7/7/09)	Porter (8/6/09)
6711	Sybil Johnson	Cascade (9/20/92)	Haystack (8/8/09)
6712	Jacqueline Chelales	Phelps (7/28/05)	East Dix (Grace) (8/11/09)
6713	Ruby Lang	Wright (7/26/04)	Seymour (8/14/09)
6714	Scott Bureau	Cascade (5/26/02)	Wright (8/16/09)
6715	Joseph Voelkel	Marcy (8/98)	Giant (8/28/09)
6716	Michael F. Wypij	Marcy (3/21/95)	Allen (9/2/09)
6717	Nathalie Puppato	Algonquin (9/30/06)	Allen (9/4/09)
6718	Jonathan D. French	Cascade (8/18/03)	Allen (9/6/09)
6719	Andree V. Sapp	Marshall (7/69)	Blake (9/19/09)
6720	Everett C. Sapp	Cascade (7/30/06)	Blake (9/19/09)
6721	Maile V. Sapp	Whiteface (7/03)	Blake (9/19/09)
6722	Randolph B. Sapp	Cascade (1972)	Blake (9/19/09)
6723	Adam Rioux	Algonquin (6/9/08)	Big Slide (9/19/09)
6724	Nate Barnett	Phelps (8/98)	Skylight (10/4/09)
6725	Georg Budenbender	Marcy (8/22/92)	Rocky Peak (10/6/09)
6726	Kjell I. Christiansen	Phelps (1991)	Whiteface (10/12/09)
6727	David Colbert	Giant (7/19/86)	Sawteeth (10/17/09)
6728	Fred Tresselt	Porter (6/29/06)	Whiteface (10/21/09)
6729	Kyle Lang	Cascade (1994)	Haystack (11/7/09)
6730	Seth Lang	Cascade (1994)	Haystack (11/7/09)
6731	Brian Delaney	Cascade (1982)	Emmons (11/8/09)
6732	Karen Delaney	Algonquin (1980)	Emmons (11/8/09)
6733	Margaret O'Keefe	Gothics (9/93)	Cliff (11/21/09)
6734	Luc Tremblay	Phelps (5/16/98)	Whiteface (1/16/10)
6735	Daniel Therrien	Giant (5/28/05)	Whiteface (1/16/10)
6736	Mary Beth Lamb	Dix (1987)	Redfield (1/30/10)
6737	Debbie Chapin	Cascade (1994)	Sawteeth (2/6/10)
6738	Dan Mayland	Whiteface (1975)	Cliff (2/7/10)
6739	Kirt Mayland	Algonquin (2/97)	Cliff (2/7/10)
6740	Lisa Albrecht	Algonquin (8/15/97)	Marcy (2/16/10)
6741	Jonathan C. Sterling	Macomb (1989)	Haystack (2/20/10)
6742	Donald P. Klein	Rocky Peak (10/5/03)	Allen (2/20/10)
6743	Lou Rosati	Marcy (6/28/76)	Allen (2/20/10)
6744	Colvin Chapman	Colvin (9/18/03)	Marshall (2/20/10)
6745	Jonathan L. Kozlowski	Marcy (8/31/97)	Haystack (2/20/10)
6746	Ian Marchant	Algonquin (7/12/05)	Big Slide (2/28/10)
6747	Lloyd S. Lowy	Cascade (1968)	Dix (3/6/10)
6748	Michael J. Lyons	Giant (5/17/09)	Marshall (3/10/10)
6749	Andrew Calcutt	Colden (10/14/07)	Whiteface (3/13/10)
6750	Robert Beirman	Wright (9/17/05)	Dix (3/18/10)
6751	Clay W. Olds	Marcy (4/23/05)	Big Slide (3/20/10)

The Membership Roster of the Adirondack Forty-Sixers

	Member	First Ascent	Forty-sixth Peak
6752	Paul Eichas	Gothics (9/1/07)	Skylight (3/20/10)
6753	J. David Palmer	Cascade (8/26/07)	Seward (3/20/10)
6754	Robert L. Wright	Marcy (10/97)	Wright (3/20/10)
6755	Felix Modugno	Giant (12/27/09)	Iroquois (3/20/10)
6756	Dawn M. Mallory	Cascade (3/28/09)	Phelps (3/27/10)
6757	Richard K. Elton	Giant (8/12/73)	Gray (3/28/10)
6758	Steve Severenko	Macomb (5/30/09)	Haystack (5/22/10)
6759	Brian A. Sutherland	Algonquin (9/28/02)	Gothics (5/24/10)
6760	Annie Lepine	Big Slide (5/27/06)	Santanoni (5/29/10)
6761	Sebastien Loyer	Big Slide (5/27/06)	Santanoni (5/29/10)
6762	Sarah Hansen	Marcy (8/17/04)	Skylight (5/29/10)
6763	Morgan Ryan	Haystack (7/12/87)	Esther (5/29/10)
6764	Gregory S. Matthei	Rocky Peak (5/28/05)	Colden (5/30/10)
6765	Timothy Spinelli	Seymour (7/26/87)	Allen (5/31/10)
6766	Carol Gates	Whiteface (5/8/09)	Big Slide (6/4/10)
6767	Thomas J. Antonini	Phelps (8/03)	Giant (6/12/10)
6768	Charles Langlois	Lower Wolf Jaw (7/11/09)	Dix (6/13/10)
6769	John S. Adams	Marcy (8/5/87)	Rocky Peak (6/19/10)
6770	Bill Quandt	Phelps (6/24/95)	Whiteface (6/19/10)
6771	Kevin Quandt	Phelps (8/24/95)	Whiteface (6/19/10)
6772	Peter Rehl	Algonquin (7/3/96)	Giant (6/20/10)
6773	Thomas J. Spies	Wright (7/6/02)	Whiteface (6/24/10)
6774	Corey A. Spies	Wright (7/6/02)	Whiteface (6/24/10)
6775	Randall Olson	Marcy (8/25/97)	Allen (6/26/10)
6776	Debbie Clouthier	Big Slide (6/8/08)	Santanoni (6/26/10)
6777	Jonathan Leonard	Cascade (5/23/04)	Porter (7/1/10)
6778	Daniel Glad	Marcy (1998)	Dix (7/1/10)
6779	Paul Cerone	Cascade (9/09)	Big Slide (7/3/10)
6780	William George Laundrie	Marcy (9/11/60)	Sawteeth (7/3/10)
6781	Linda Pollock	Allen (5/21/05)	Whiteface (7/3/10)
6782	Karen Sheldon	Allen (5/21/05)	Whiteface (7/3/10)
6783	Gail Opanhoske	Phelps (1997)	Dix (7/4/10)
6784	Judith B. Sides	Giant (7/03)	Iroquois (7/7/10)
6785	Norman Kipp	Cascade (7/08)	Haystack (7/11/10)
6786	Jason Hosier	Wright (6/16/07)	Armstrong (7/11/10)
6787	Michael L. Miller	Marcy (5/4/03)	Skylight (7/11/10)
6788	Ruby Salley	Marcy (9/9/06)	Saddleback (7/12/10)
6789	Steven Bodnar	Cascade (7/7/99)	Armstrong (7/13/10)
6790	Brandon Minckler	Esther (8/3/09)	Marcy (7/15/10)
6791	Cecile Valastro	Phelps (6/23/01)	Seymour (7/16/10)
6792	Mitchell Benson	Whiteface (7/28/00)	Iroquois (7/17/10)
6793	Rebecca Kaiser	Giant (6/7/08)	Seymour (7/17/10)
6794	Valerie Scanlon	Giant (6/7/08)	Seymour (7/17/10)
6795	Jonathan Lane	Cascade (4/17/05)	Haystack (7/18/10)
6796	Brandon J. Myers	Marcy (7/20/02)	Whiteface (7/18/10)
6797	Pamela Gonzalez	Phelps (7/73)	Haystack (7/19/10)
6798	Taylor Calfee	Haystack (8/06)	Wright (7/20/10)
6799	Charles M. LaMendola	Wright (8/9/08)	Marcy (7/22/10)
6800	Jackson Brill	Cascade (7/9/03)	Whiteface (7/22/10)
6801	Matthew C. Benson	Algonquin (9/2/00)	Emmons (7/22/10)
6802	John Stubecki	Cascade (10/6/07)	Haystack (7/23/10)
6803	Kelly Murer	Cascade (8/18/07)	Marcy (7/23/10)
6804	Donald E. Harrington	Giant (9/81)	Allen (7/23/10)
6805	William Allen Harkins	Lower Wolf Jaw (3/3/10)	Whiteface (7/24/10)
6806	Sara Kaitlin Moore	Lower Wolf Jaw (4/3/10)	Whiteface (7/24/10)
6807	Mark J. Wood	Marcy (5/23/08)	Emmons (7/24/10)
6808	Jessica L. Fowler	Algonquin (8/2/02)	Marcy (7/24/10)
6809	Bill Fowler	Algonquin (8/2/02)	Marcy (7/24/10)
6810	Meghan Murphy	Cascade (7/31/99)	Basin (7/26/10)
6811	James Hatala	Algonquin (8/86)	Whiteface (7/27/10)
6812	Tom Koester	Algonquin (8/86)	Whiteface (7/27/10)
6813	John Dirolf	Wright (10/28/84)	Gray (7/30/10)

Heaven Up-h'isted-ness!

	Member	First Ascent	Forty-sixth Peak
6814	Tom Chase	Porter (3/7/04)	Saddleback (7/30/10)
6815	Mark Zimarowski	Algonquin (5/5/07)	Saddleback (7/30/10)
6816	Michael Mayernik	Algonquin (7/16/89)	East Dix (Grace) (7/30/10)
6817	Hal H. Sprague	Cliff (8/13/87)	Sawteeth (7/30/10)
6818	James Cronn	Cascade (7/4/89)	Whiteface (7/31/10)
6819	Katherine Cronn	Cascade (7/4/89)	Whiteface (7/31/10)
6820	John H. Pearson	Phelps (7/22/07)	Whiteface (7/31/10)
6821	Glenn Hall	Colden (7/30/78)	Redfield (7/31/10)
6822	Craig Andrew Maier	Cascade (10/4/08)	Skylight (7/31/10)
6823	Stacy Lena Maier	Cascade (10/4/08)	Skylight (7/31/10)
6824	Stefanie Gallina	Cascade (5/27/07)	Saddleback (8/1/10)
6825	Jonah Goldberg	Cascade (6/2/07)	Iroquois (8/4/10)
6826	Daniel Dwyer	Wright (9/12/09)	Santanoni (8/4/10)
6827	Daniel Ference	Panther (7/6/10)	Porter (8/5/10)
6828	Gabe Naviasky	Santanoni (7/6/10)	Porter (8/5/10)
6829	Lindsey Mersereau	Panther (7/6/10)	Porter (8/5/10)
6830	Max Rosenberg	Wright (7/08)	Porter (8/5/10)
6831	Aaron Glosser	Panther (7/6/10)	Porter (8/5/10)
6832	Emily C. Caner	Cascade (1964)	Hough (8/7/10)
6833	Connor J. DeSantis	Giant (8/24/03)	Haystack (8/7/10)
6834	Noah C. Sausville	Cascade (9/6/03)	Haystack (8/7/10)
6835	Dave Franzi	Wright (6/11/97)	Seymour (8/7/10)
6836	Paul D. Posson	Lower Wolf Jaw (9/22/96)	Basin (8/7/10)
6837	Spencer Posson	Porter (10/3/98)	Basin (8/7/10)
6838	Brian Anderson	Marcy (9/19/05)	Redfield (8/7/10)
6839	Gary A. Anderson	Marcy (9/19/05)	Redfield (8/7/10)
6840	Alec Gonzalez	Cascade (7/05)	Wright (8/8/10)
6841	Joseph Zimmerman	Cascade (8/05)	Colden (8/8/10)
6842	Travis Fischer	Big Slide (7/07)	Phelps (8/8/10)
6843	Ryan Mazierski	Giant (7/24/09)	Panther (8/11/10)
6844	Erika Chelales	Cascade (8/3/05)	Allen (8/11/10)
6845	Laura W. Feidelson	Cascade (8/3/05)	Allen (8/11/10)
6846	Karen Steefel	Marcy (1979)	Whiteface (8/12/10)
6847	Adam Holdredge	Cascade (7/15/96)	Allen (8/14/10)
6848	Richard Holdredge	Cascade (7/15/96)	Allen (8/14/10)
6849	Andy Shorb	Marcy (9/9/00)	Dix (8/14/10)
6850	Philip S. Winterer	Marcy (1970)	Esther (8/14/10)
6851	Joseph R. Murphy	Donaldson (5/23/09)	Blake (8/14/10)
6852	Thomas McGraw	Colden (5/25/91)	Iroquois (8/14/10)
6853	Jeffrey M. Seltzer	Haystack (6/23/94)	Cascade (8/14/10)
6854	Eric W. Wohlers	Marcy (4/92)	Esther (8/14/10)
6855	John Schoeniger	Seward (7/7/04)	Whiteface (8/14/10)
6856	Christopher J. Duwe	Marcy (3/25/05)	Esther (8/15/10)
6857	Eric Morris	Cascade (2/23/08)	Saddleback (8/15/10)
6858	Paul LaVergne	Marcy (9/4/82)	Allen (8/18/10)
6859	James Nichols	Nye (6/22/09)	Seymour (8/20/10)
6860	Denise Koskey	Cascade (7/5/04)	Seymour (8/20/10)
6861	Craig A. Matis	Gothics (8/12/88)	Iroquois (8/20/10)
6862	Karen Krauss	Giant (5/29/04)	Marcy (8/20/10)
6863	Ted Krauss	Giant (5/29/04)	Marcy (8/20/10)
6864	Geoffrey Day	Wright (7/8/05)	Allen (8/20/10)
6865	Tim J. Walz	Lower Wolf Jaw (1/26/02)	Allen (8/21/10)
6866	Adam V. S. Abbate	Haystack (8/30/86)	Allen (8/21/10)
6867	Gino Bureau	Giant (7/12/72)	Rocky Peak (8/21/10)
6868	Eric Bureau	Cascade (5/26/02)	Rocky Peak (8/21/10)
6869	Tom Sherman	Algonquin (8/10/08)	Iroquois (8/21/10)
6870	Howard Kirschenbaum	Phelps (1973)	Whiteface (8/21/10)
6871	Mary-Helen Hughes	Big Slide (5/15/10)	Santanoni (8/21/10)
6872	Pamela Cataldi Gittler	Cascade (7/75)	Whiteface (8/23/10)
6873	Gail Tremblay	Cascade (5/2/09)	Santanoni (8/23/10)
6874	D. J. Ernie Obrist	Cliff (8/12/99)	Whiteface (8/24/10)
6875	Brenda Obrist	Giant (7/1/00)	Whiteface (8/24/10)

The Membership Roster of the Adirondack Forty-Sixers

	Member	First Ascent	Forty-sixth Peak
6876	Terry Clement	Redfield (5/28/01)	Haystack (8/26/10)
6877	Michael Price	Wright (9/28/03)	East Dix (Grace) (8/27/10)
6878	Dan Michalak	Rocky Peak (7/9/10)	Whiteface (8/27/10)
6879	Mary E. Leitten	Marcy (8/87)	Emmons (8/27/10)
6880	James H. Leitten	Marcy (8/85)	Emmons (8/27/10)
6881	John A. Greacen Jr.	Cascade (2/16/05)	Marcy (8/28/10)
6882	Kimberly A. Russell	Cascade (7/5/03)	Skylight (8/28/10)
6883	Andy Chillrud	Lower Wolf Jaw (7/10/05)	Big Slide (8/28/10)
6884	Paul L. Gaeta	Cascade (1998)	Haystack (8/28/10)
6885	Theresa V. Gaeta	Cascade (1998)	Haystack (8/28/10)
6886	John A. Tinsley	Cascade (8/16/97)	Santanoni (8/28/10)
6887	Brian Geary	Cascade (4/19/09)	Panther (8/28/10)
6888	Kristen Geary	Cascade (4/19/09)	Panther (8/28/10)
6889	Taras Dejneka	Phelps (5/14/79)	Allen (8/29/10)
6890	Michael Proulx	Phelps (8/26/96)	Skylight (8/30/10)
6891	Francis X. Olscamp	Porter (7/19/98)	Skylight (8/30/10)
6892	Furman-Steve Alden	Giant (10/1/98)	Iroquois (9/1/10)
6893	Madeline Kowalik-Bova	Esther (7/27/08)	Colden (9/2/10)
6894	Jean-Marc Vallieres	Whiteface (3/24/09)	Phelps (9/2/10)
6895	David Maynard	Big Slide (7/00)	Haystack (9/3/10)
6896	Thomas M. Brittain	Big Slide (3/17/02)	Basin (9/3/10)
6897	Douglas Nixon	Seymour (8/1/00)	Haystack (9/4/10)
6898	Stephanie Konowitz	Wright (6/90)	Algonquin (9/4/10)
6899	Dan Hartstein	Dial (6/30/01)	Cliff (9/5/10)
6900	Gregory J. Sale	Lower Wolf Jaw (5/2/04)	Allen (9/5/10)
6901	Geoffrey G. Morris	Porter (7/5/87)	Allen (9/5/10)
6902	William J. Freed	Algonquin (6/24/00)	Whiteface (9/5/10)
6903	Eric Avery	Algonquin (7/17/99)	Gothics (9/6/10)
6904	Edward G. S. Miller	Marcy (9/14/88)	Redfield (9/6/10)
6905	Trish Flaherty	Giant (5/31/05)	Seward (9/6/10)
6906	Andrew Karhan	Giant (7/8/06)	Marcy (9/10/10)
6907	David A. Senecal	Giant (1989)	Marshall (9/10/10)
6908	John D. Curran	Cascade (8/14/09)	Marshall (9/11/10)
6909	Ray O'Conor	Marcy (9/11/91)	Basin (9/11/10)
6910	Dave Campbell	Tabletop (5/6/09)	Whiteface (9/11/10)
6911	Wayne Richter	Marcy (10/82)	Phelps (9/11/10)
6912	Jessica Hageman	Algonquin (9/00)	Esther (9/11/10)
6913	Louis R. Silver	Marcy (6/1/97)	Whiteface (9/11/10)
6914	Paul Schwartz	Wright (6/03)	Skylight (9/11/10)
6915	Liette Laniel	Nippletop (10/13/96)	Panther (9/11/10)
6916	Jodi L. Kubecka	Giant (9/04)	Santanoni (9/11/10)
6917	Brian Vermilyea	Giant (8/11/02)	Whiteface (9/12/10)
6918	Erin L. Burns	Algonquin (8/5/74)	Hough (9/12/10)
6919	Russell M. Marchese	Dix (8/20/84)	Esther (9/13/10)
6920	Tom J. Marchese	Gothics (9/16/95)	Esther (9/13/2010)
6921	Bob Marchese	Haystack (9/15/95)	Esther (9/13/10)
6922	Raymond J. Galvin	Cascade (9/8/07)	Haystack (9/15/10)
6923	Jerry Geiling	Lower Wolf Jaw (2/21/01)	Whiteface (9/15/10)
6924	Linda S. Leichtweis	Algonquin (1999)	Iroquois (9/15/10)
6925	Frederick T. Whalen	Marcy (9/18/86)	Allen (9/17/10)
6926	Mary D. Whalen	Marcy (9/18/86)	Allen (9/17/10)
6927	Helena Nevarez	Dial (8/21/07)	Whiteface (9/18/10)
6928	Thomas Kral	Marcy (11/81)	Whiteface (9/18/10)
6929	David Darling	Dix (8/11/90)	Allen (9/18/10)
6930	Jackson Donnelly	Cascade (11/17/07)	Rocky Peak (9/18/10)
6931	Jim Donnelly	Big Slide (9/20/07)	Rocky Peak (9/18/10)
6932	Pamela S. Youker	Tabletop (2/19/09)	Whiteface (9/18/10)
6933	Claire A. Velsey	Marcy (8/99)	Allen (9/18/10)
6934	Alice D. K. Lemieux	Cascade (7/8/06)	Whiteface (9/18/10)
6935	James Lemieux	Cascade (7/8/06)	Whiteface (9/18/10)
6936	Tom Palen	Cascade (5/16/06)	Skylight (9/18/10)
6937	Nathan Shaheen	Lower Wolf Jaw (8/31/97)	Santanoni (9/19/10)

Heaven Up-h'isted-ness!

	Member	First Ascent	Forty-sixth Peak
6938	Joe Whalen	Marcy (4/7/10)	Whiteface (9/21/10)
6939	Rick Loyst	Giant (5/07)	Haystack (9/21/10)
6940	Joseph A. McGraw	Gothics (12/01)	Haystack (9/23/10)
6941	Brian M. Colwell	Big Slide (6/19/99)	Sawteeth (9/25/10)
6942	Bill Skiff	Giant (5/21/03)	Santanoni (9/25/10)
6943	Greg Saltsman	Giant (9/18/99)	Saddleback (9/25/10)
6944	David Klee	Cascade (7/1/06)	Saddleback (9/25/10)
6945	Gary M. Klee	Cascade (7/1/06)	Saddleback (9/25/10)
6946	Henry Klee	Cascade (7/1/06)	Saddleback (9/25/10)
6947	Marshall Klee	Cascade (7/1/06)	Saddleback (9/25/10)
6948	Terry Peters	Cascade (7/1/06)	Saddleback (9/25/10)
6949	Joe Fantasia	Wright (10/15/79)	Esther (9/25/10)
6950	Tracy Gourlay	Macomb (5/12/10)	Big Slide (9/25/10)
6951	Sophie Ligier	Big Slide (1987)	Santanoni (9/25/10)
6952	Luc Massicotte	Giant (2002)	Santanoni (9/25/10)
6953	Scott N. Pedu	Phelps (2006)	Whiteface (9/26/10)
6954	James M. Barnett	Marcy (7/01)	Whiteface (10/2/10)
6955	Shane Michael LaVancher	Algonquin (7/8/00)	Whiteface (10/2/10)
6956	Dan Jablonski	Marcy (9/25/04)	Sawteeth (10/2/10)
6957	Michael Stahl	Haystack (7/25/96)	Saddleback (10/3/10)
6958	Doug Robinson	Marcy (9/13/07)	Cliff (10/3/10)
6959	Marie-Pierre Champigny	Rocky Peak (1/23/09)	Marcy (10/3/10)
6960	Peter Kohlmann	Marcy (9/24/92)	Saddleback (10/4/10)
6961	Dave Pettit	Marcy (9/9/97)	Saddleback (10/5/10)
6962	Rachel Lamb	Cascade (9/97)	Cliff (10/5/10)
6963	Peter B. Wilson	Colden (10/21/73)	Whiteface (10/8/10)
6964	Annie Dubeau	Algonquin (6/27/08)	Hough (10/8/10)
6965	Jacinthe Roy	Algonquin (6/27/08)	Hough (10/8/10)
6966	Andrew M. Cassier	Phelps (10/1/00)	Iroquois (10/9/10)
6967	Edward J. Holcomb	Lower Wolf Jaw (1992)	Hough (10/9/10)
6968	Greg Walpole	Wright (7/23/05)	Whiteface (10/9/10)
6969	Scott Dunbar	Marcy (7/10/08)	Nippletop (10/9/10)
6970	Andrew J. Blasko	Porter (4/22/06)	Saddleback (10/10/10)
6971	Cody Blasko	Porter (4/22/06)	Saddleback (10/10/10)
6972	Ron Lobur	Cascade (7/26/05)	Haystack (10/10/10)
6973	Adam Lobur	Cascade (7/26/05)	Haystack (10/10/10)
6974	Allon G. Wildgust	Giant (9/72)	Skylight (10/10/10)
6975	Charles Derecskey	Cascade (1976)	Haystack (10/10/10)
6976	Annabelle Feist	Porter (7/03)	Haystack (10/10/10)
6977	Edward Feist	Porter (7/03)	Haystack (10/10/10)
6978	Linda Feist	Cascade (7/03)	Haystack (10/10/10)
6979	Tom Feist	Giant (1988)	Haystack (10/10/10)
6980	John F. Klebes	Marcy (3/1/98)	Giant (10/10/10)
6981	Salvatore Sannuto	Panther (1/30/10)	Cascade (10/10/10)
6982	Joshua S. Valentine	Marcy (6/4/05)	Esther (10/10/10)
6983	Robert K. Campbell Jr.	Cascade (8/72)	Marshall (10/12/10)
6984	Katy Elwyn	Marshall (9/1/94)	Colvin (10/13/10)
6985	Nicolas P. Stoker	Giant (1/2/09)	Allen (10/16/10)
6986	James Woods	Cascade (4/10/10)	Colden (10/19/10)
6987	Robert Guilfoil	Cascade (9/22/06)	Skylight (10/23/10)
6988	Matthew Butler	Phelps (9/99)	Colden (10/23/10)
6989	Peter Dinolfo	Marcy (8/28/93)	Allen (10/23/10)
6990	Harold Piel	Giant (9/26/04)	Macomb (10/23/10)
6991	Brian Connell	Wright (5/10/94)	Hough (10/23/10)
6992	Jonathan Hanselman	Gothics (7/31/01)	Esther (10/24/10)
6993	James J. Lomax	Wright (6/10/06)	Marshall (10/26/10)
6994	Robert J. Richeda	Marcy (8/10/66)	Seymour (10/27/10)
6995	Simon Roberge	Wright (5/1/10)	Whiteface (10/30/10)
6996	Zane L. Davies	Phelps (12/1/07)	Wright (10/30/10)
6997	Russell T. Fisher	Cascade (10/11/08)	Whiteface (10/30/10)
6998	Robert J. Rock	Porter (7/23/06)	Rocky Peak (10/31/10)
6999	John D. Steele	Colden (1991)	Rocky Peak (11/2/10)

	MEMBER	FIRST ASCENT	FORTY-SIXTH PEAK
7000	William A. Brizzell Jr	Giant (7/12/07)	Whiteface (11/5/10)
7001	Caleb Strong	Cascade (10/9/66)	Big Slide (11/13/10)
7002	Marie-Josee Ouellet	Algonquin (6/19/03)	Haystack (11/13/10)
7003	Francois Hubert	Algonquin (9/29/07)	Colden (12/4/10)
7004	Frederick Berube	Algonquin (7/25/1993)	Basin (12/21/10)
7005	Jean Duchesne	Whiteface (10/24/93)	Basin (12/21/10)
7006	Etienne Ruel	Cascade (7/31/04)	Seymour (12/22/10)
7007	Jeff Corelli	Giant (5/17/09)	Emmons (12/28/10)
7008	Peter Rieseler	Algonquin (7/94)	Haystack (12/30/10)
7009	Bogdan Tataru	Whiteface (6/19/10)	Couchsachraga (12/31/10)

About the Compiler

Mike Becker (#1889W) has been a member of the Albany Chapter of the Adirondack Mountain Club for more than 20 years and has led many outings for the chapter. He also designed and maintains the web page for the Albany chapter and is a former editor of that chapter's newsletter, *The Cloud Splitter*. He also formerly led hikes for the Schenectady Chapter of that organization. He is an active member of the volunteer Winter Host program in the Johns Brook Valley. He has been the adopter of the Slide Brook Lean-to for more than ten years. He prepares the annual "Peeks Sketches" article for the fall issue of *Adirondack Peeks*. Mike is a New York State licensed guide, and he is an avid runner and member of the Hudson Mohawk Road Runners Club and the Albany Running Exchange. He is also a collector of Adirondack literature, including books and magazines. He has climbed the 46 high peaks five times each and became a Winter 46er in 2003 and a four-season 46er in 2009. He also enjoys traveling, kayaking, and cross country skiing.

Mike earned a B.S. degree from SUNY-Oneonta and an M.S. degree from Indiana University, both in geology. He worked for several years in the Albany area as a geologist. Currently Mike works for the New York State Office for Technology in Albany and resides in Colonie, New York with his daughter Amy.

Index

19 L P CLUB 341
1903 fire 44, 191, 396, 411, 417, 420, 431, 441, 550
1913 fire 420, 431, 441, 442
1950 Hurricane (See "Big Blow") 236
22 S.N.Y. 341
380th Bomb Wing 366
46er First Airborne Division 103
46er T-shirt 98

Abolitionists 297
Acid rain 414
Adams, Elliott 138
Ad-i-ron-dac 254, 257, 272, 273, 524
Adirondac 41, 264, 346
Adirondac (village) ... 190, 242, 251, 281, 282, 284, 345, 436
Adirondac Pass 164
Adirondac Steel Manufacturing Company 166
Adirondack Camp and Trail Club 236
Adirondack Center Museum 326, 452
Adirondack Club 261, 283
Adirondack Council, The 96
Adirondack fisher 476
Adirondack 46R Conservation Trust 42, 123, 124, 128, 135, 344, 406
Adirondack Forest Preserve ...16, 49, 58, 66, 67, 78, 105, 107, 109, 124, 130, 136, 142, 441
Adirondack Forty-Sixers, The (book) 65
Adirondack Group 312
Adirondack High Peaks Adventure Game 99
Adirondack High Peaks and the Forty-Sixers, The 77
Adirondack Iron and Steel Company 165, 166, 204, 242
Adirondack Iron Works 156, 164, 335, 394
Adirondack Life 405
Adirondack Lodge 190, 191, 192, 341, 343
Adirondack Mountain Club (ADK) 20, 27, 29, 33, 41, 42, 47, 48, 49, 52, 53, 54, 55, 56, 57, 58, 65, 66, 67, 68, 69, 71, 72, 73, 74, 79, 80, 81, 92, 93, 94, 98, 100, 109, 111, 119, 130, 131, 136, 142, 143, 144, 145, 196, 206, 262, 263, 268, 271, 307, 341, 356, 359, 381, 398, 400, 450, 453, 507, 536, 549, 557, 559
Adirondack Mountain Reserve (AMR) 93, 96, 195, 254, 397, 399, 401, 404, 441, 473, 481, 495, 509, 511, 534
Adirondack Museum 37, 270, 281, 285, 550
Adirondack National Bank 303
Adirondack North Country Association 41
Adirondack Northway 269
Adirondack; or Life in the Woods, The 160, 161, 436
Adirondack Park Agency (APA) .. 78, 79, 81, 96, 107, 264
Adirondack Park Association 41
Adirondack Park Centennial 108
Adirondack Park State Land Master Plan (APSLMP) 78, 79, 96, 136
Adirondack Pass 333, 364
Adirondack Peeks (Peeks) 71, 129, 147-149, 464
Adirondack Pilgrimage 362
Adirondack Research Center 192
Adirondack Rock and River 237

Adirondack Stewardship Award 109
Adirondack Trail Improvement Society (ATIS) 92, 177, 343, 419, 420, 424, 428, 445, 480, 513, 519, 535
Adirondacks Illustrated, The 175, 176, 282, 337, 365, 394, 408, 505, 512, 539, 548
Adirondacks, The 228
Adirondack Winter Mountaineering Manual 254
Adirondak Loj 11, 56, 64, 70, 196, 197, 225, 337, 343
Adler, Felix 424, 495
Adota of Tahawi 498
Adriance, J. William 91
Adventures in the Wilderness; or, Camp-Life in the Adirondacks 9, 499
Adventures in the Wilds of the United States and British American Provinces 162
Agar, John 304
Agassiz, Louis 288, 310, 313, 315
Ahasuerus 559
Aiken, Inge 134, 529
Akermanite 409
Alberga, Kristofer 126
Alderson, Mrs. 495
Alexander, John 555
Alfred E. Weld Trail 93, 480
Algonquin Pass 352, 357
Algonquin Peak 9, 24, 33, 42, 45, 54, 56, 81, 83, 84, 86, 94, 102, 109, 119, 124, 185, 216, 222, 233, 346-351, 381, 386-387
Algonquins (Native Americans) 347
Alioth 178
Allen, Frederick B. 256
Allen, Hank 22
Allen, Herbert 67
Allen, Nancy 125
Allen Brook 101, 265
Allen Mountain 24, 39, 45, 47, 60, 69, 80, 91, 100, 101, 128, 138, 246, 255, 256-268
Alpine goldenrod 555
Alton, Charles D. 519
Amanita 341
American Academy of Arts and Sciences 226
American Association for the Advancement of Science 250
American Journal of Science and Arts, The 251
American Philosophical Society 250
Amedore, George 148
Amedore, Jeanne 148
Ames, Dave 387
Amherst, Jeffrey 426
Ampersand Camp 281
Ampersand Lake (Pond) 287
Ampersand Mountain 22, 23, 287, 342
Ampersand Pond 289, 290
Ampersand River 287
AMR .... (See Adirondack Mountain Reserve)
AMR gate 496
Ancient Adirondacks, The 503

And Gladly Guide, Reflections on a Life in the Mountains 536
Anderson, Phyllis 63
Anderson, "Pop" 70
Andrews, William A. 58
Andrus, Dick 379
Anorthosite 199
Anthelia 467, 475
Anthony, Theodore Van Wyck 55, 359, 493
Anti-Mason 296
Appalachian Mountain Club 9, 506
Apperson, John 192, 194, 206, 207, 502, 506, 526
Arakelian, Mary 346
Archer, David 353
Arenaria groenlandica 347
Armstrong, Thomas 533
Armstrong Mountain 533-534
Arnold, D. M. 195, 401
Arnold, Douglas R. 35, 134, 209, 454, 471, 489, 499
Article VII, Section 7 .... 43, 49, 529
Article XIV 124
Artist's Falls 467, 476
"Ascent of Whiteface" 544
Association for the Protection of the Adirondacks
.... 397, 526
Association of American Geologists 251
At the Mercy of the Mountains: True Stories of Survival and Tragedy in New York's Adirondacks... 334
ATIS .... (See Adirondack Trail Improvement Society)
ATIS logo 519
Atkinson, George 86
Atkinson, James P. 510, 528
Atlas of Essex County 397
Atmospheric Sciences Research Center... 552, 562, 563
Aurora borealis 198
Ausable Club 55, 177, 186, 397, 443, 444, 478, 494
Au Sable Forks, NY 45, 293
Au Sable (Ausable) River 227, 350, 481, 496
Austin, George 405
Avalanche Camp 181, 225, 235, 236, 400
Avalanche Lake 156, 157, 171, 190, 205, 231, 233, 238, 257, 337, 345, 349, 369, 374-375, 376, 377
Avalanche Mountain 190, 369, 371, 374
Avalanche Pass 112, 190, 193, 197, 225, 236, 239, 241, 254, 337, 369, 374-375
Avalanches 175, 179, 190, 388-390, 459
Axton Landing 291
Ayres, Mr. 257
Ayres, Douglas, Jr. 476

B-47 Bomber 373
Babb, Clyde 77
Babcock, Richard "Dick" 62, 66, 67, 70, 71, 139, 148, 446
Bachli, Werner 14, 56, 60
Bailey, Anne Biesemeyer 445
Bailey, James "Jim" (Beetle) G. 73, 270, 286, 406, 538
Balanced Rocks 413
Bald Mountain 431
Bald Peak 427, 431, 467
Baldwin, Henry I. 506

Baldwin (guide) 548
Balk, Christina Lochman 520
Balk, Robert 520, 521
Balsam fir 527, 556, 561, 563
Banana Belt 420
Bandorick, Bruce 151
Banks, Russell 344
Barienger Brake 290
Bark eaters 312
Barkeater Cliff 414
Barker, Gil 254, 451, 459
Barnard, F. J. & Son 533
Barnett, Lincoln Kinnear 503, 528
Barnshaw, James 135
Bartlett Mountain 25, 175, 179, 181, 186, 394, 501, 514
Bartlett Ridge 173, 174, 500
Bartlett's Carry 22
Basin Brook 507
Basin Mountain 21, 25, 32, 33, 56, 96, 186, 220, 223, 504-506
Bassinette 511
Battle of Plattsburgh 457
Baxter State Park 87
Bayle, Francis 441
Bean, Edgar B. 70, 119
Bear Brook Lean-to 86
Bear Cub Road 340
Bear Den 472, 473
Bear Den fire (1999) 265, 473
Bearberry willow 503, 555
Bears 138
Beaver Meadow Falls 496, 535
Beaver Meadow Trail 513
Beaver Point 385
Beaver River 185
Beavers 8
Becker, Michael "Mike" 114, 116, 674
Beckhorn 214, 441, 446, 461
Bedfield, Charles 169
Beede, Charles "Charlie" 256, 559, 431, 479, 513, 559, 560, 561
Beede, Ed 473
Beede, Orlando 192, 421, 423, 437, 482, 486, 495, 504, 505, 524, 532, 533
Beede, Smith 423, 437, 482, 494
Beede Brook 494
Beede Heights 494, 495
Beede Heights Hotel 421
Beede House 439, 494, 495
Beede Pass 532
Beetle, David H. 15, 65
Behr, Christian G. 94, 101, 102, 103, 109, 122
Behr, Christian M. 94, 101, 102, 109
Behr, June 94, 101, 102, 109, 120
Bell, James Christy 506
Bemis, Samuel 528
Bemis Crew 506, 528
Benedict, E. C. 201
Benedict, Elijah Lewis 156, 281, 364, 486, 490

INDEX

Benedict, Farrand N. 159, 161, 183, 287, 301
Benedix, Agnes W. 59, 360
Benedix, Jessie 59
Benedix, Sammy 360
Benjamin, Marcus 250
Bennett, Charles "Chuck" 117
Bennett's Pond 543
Bennies Brook (slide) 11
Bent grass 199
Bergamini, Herbert 368
Berggren, Dan 122
Berle, Peter A. A. 96, 97
Berserkers 393, 396
Bicknell's thrush 199, 370
Biddlecome 404
Biddlecome Road 404
Biesemeyer, Marian 346
Big Blow of 1950 ..... 11, 63, 197, 236, 269, 271, 272, 276,
280, 289, 316, 342, 389, 399, 445
Big Slide Mountain 92, 119, 145, 220, 402-406, 509
Bigelow's sedge 199
Bilberry 471
Bissonette, Bob 387
Black cat 469, 476
Black crowberry 199, 555
Black spruce 527
Blackmar, A. Edward 138
Bladder campion 411
Blake, Mills 174, 186, 244, 307, 466, 484, 485,
486, 491, 492
Blake's Peak (Blake Peak) ... 29, 52, 53, 54, 64, 70, 96, 119,
222, 279, 307, 487, 491-494
Blanchet, S. F. 303
Blast furnace 162, 165, 204
Bleecker, Mary 317
Blinn, Nelson 339
Blinn, Robert Scott 171, 172, 174, 328, 547
Blizzard of 1899 189
Bloomgren, Rodney D. 366
Bloomingdale, N.Y. 46, 560
Bloomingdale, Phoebe 441
Blowdown 94, 100, 102, 110, 111, 112, 130, 131, 143
Blue Mountain 314
Blueberry Mountain 417, 418
Blueberries 138
Bob Marshall Wilderness Area 18
Bodman, George 502
Bolt Number 10 438
Bonfire on Nippletop 475
Bootbay Mountain 23
Booth, John Wilkes 300
Boott's rattlesnake root 555
Boquet, Henry 456
Boquet River 433, 438, 443, 444, 445, 456, 468
Boquet River Lean-to 104
Boquet Valley .... 447 (also see "Bouquet Valley")
Boreas Range 493
Boreas Ridge 494
Botterbusch, Amelia 135

Bottle, The (slide) 422
Boulder Brook 289
"Boulder Report" 129, 149
Boulders, The 35, 36, 64, 119, 123, 406
Bouncing Betty 472
Boundary Peak 8, 9, 222, 352, 358
Bouquet River 456
Bouquet Valley 442
Bourjade, Christine 197, 207, 208, 221, 248, 380, 529
Boxer, Michael 386, 388
Boy Scout Troop #709 138
Brach, Paul 138
Bradley, John 134
Bradley Pond 100, 271, 273, 275, 278
Bradley Pond Lean-to 66
Braman, W. J. 58
Brayton, Charles 270
Brenning, Lee 428
Bridal Chamber Camp 470
Briggs, Ronald "Ron" 405, 414
Broadalbin, N.Y. 233
Broadhead, Charles 8, 9, 347, 348, 401, 426, 427
Bronski, Peter 334
Brooklyn College 386
Brosseau, E. William 111
Brothers, The 92, 403, 405
Brough, Gretchen Weeks .... (See Weeks, Gretchen)
Broughton, John G. 54
Brown, Grace 537
Brown, Homer 537
Brown, Howard 426, 427494
Brown, Jeff 387
Brown, Jeffery Paul 148
Brown, John 203, 339, 344, 543, 549
Brown, Lewis 413
Brown, Mrs. John 339
Brown, W. (Walter) Scott 186, 401, 436, 478, 560
Brown, William H. 352
Brownoker, Mr. 203
Bruce, Gene 290
Bruce, Wallace 421
Bryant, William Cullen 202, 328
Buchanan, James 159
Buchanan, Roy 56
Buchanan, Stuart 111
Buckingham, Mr. 166, 167, 169
Buckley Tote Road 263
Buckley's Camp 205, 261
Buckley's Clearing 253, 260, 261, 262, 263
Bunchberry 174, 472, 507
Bunk, Ed 122, 128, 400, 407, 529
Burgoyne, General John 436
Burks, Jean 132
Burlington, VT 155, 252
"Burning of Schenectady, The" 328
Burnside, James R. 532
Burr, David H. 456
Burroughs, John 166
Burton, Hal 382

- 683 -

Busch, Joseph	117
Bushnell, Horace	256, 394, 515, 516, 518
Bushnell Falls	195, 398, 510, 514, 517
Bushnell Falls # 1 Lean-to	108
Bushnell Park	515
Bushwhacker's View of the Adirondack, A	335
Butler, Benjamin C.	165
By Foot in the Adirondacks	394
Cadbury, Warder	257
Calamity Brook	156, 162, 171, 206, 246, 261, 375
Calamity Mountain	282, 369
Calamity Pond	162, 165, 167, 170, 171, 177, 181, 187, 189, 282
Camels Hump	456
Cameron, Judy	84
Camp and Trail Club	261
Camp Dudley	422
Camp Grace	537, 538
Camp Lincoln	72, 272
Camp Maple	288, 289
Camp Peggy O'Brien	400, 507, 537
Camp Phelps	512
Camp Pok-O-Moonshine	72, 269, 270, 286, 342, 405, 406, 423, 554
Camp Santanoni	273
Campbell, Archibald	8
Camper/Hiker Building	98
Camping permits	97
Canadian Shield	7, 8
Canister (summit canisters)	11, 59, 60, 62, 63, 77, 79, 95, 96, 97, 107, 108, 110, 112, 113, 114, 115, 116, 120, 125, 126, 127, 128, 143, 147, 211, 431, 563
Canivet, Jean	192, 207
Canning, Andrew	271
Canteen at Adirondak Loj	399
Canterbury Tales, The	362
Canton, NY	356
Caribou Mountain	369
Caribou Pass	190. 369-371, 469, 471
Carleton, Thomas	334
Carleton, Mrs. Thomas	334
Carman, Carol	105
Carman, Joseph	105
Carnes, Fred	413
Carnes, Wilfred	413
Carnes Granite Company	413
Carragan, Gertrude H.	141
Carry, The	176
Carry Trail	482
Carson, Russell M. L.	9, 28, 29, 30, 47, 48, 50, 51, 52, 53, 54, 55, 57, 58, 65, 133, 134, 135, 136, 165, 171, 174, 179, 181, 186, 187, 194, 195, 199, 200 225, 233, 244, 256, 257, 307, 308, 314, 321, 344, 348, 352, 358, 359, 381, 392, 393, 398, 402, 416, 427, 431, 434, 435, 437, 449, 451, 452, 454, 455, 457, 459, 467, 477, 478, 479, 484, 485, 486, 491, 492, 494, 505, 524, 532, 535, 539, 540, 541, 548, 551, 554, 559, 560, 561
Carson Peak	134, 452-456, 499
Carter, Robert C.	381
Cartier, Jacques	541
Cascade Brook	479, 496
Cascade Falls	409
Cascade Lake House	410, 411
Cascade Lakes	409, 412, 413, 414-415
Cascade Mountain	9, 42, 92, 117, 119, 213, 408-412, 416
Cascade Pass	411, 412, 414-415
Cascade Road	410
Cascadeville	410
Case, John C.	134, 332, 406, 479
Casimir, John	343
Castle, The	49, 551, 555
Castle Column	175
Cat Eyes	400
Cat Pond	415
Catalano, Jay	239
Catamount Roost	357, 363
Catell, Harry	510
Cathedral Rocks	496
Catskill 3500 Club	120
Catskill Forest Preserve	16
Catskill Mountain House	9
Catskill Mountains	156
Cedar Point (Port Henry)	436, 476
Cedar Point Road	468
Cedar River House	64
Centennial lean-tos	108
Certificates of Accomplishment	99, 117
Chalmers, Stephen	303
Champlain, Samuel de	7, 353
Chapel Pond	419, 442
Chapel Pond Cliffs	420
Chapel Pond Pass	419, 436, 439
Chaucer, Geoffrey	362
Cheetham, Sam	550
Cheney, Horace Bushnell	515
Cheney, John	157, 159, 160, 161, 162, 163, 164, 165, 200, 233, 242, 259, 282, 315, 348, 354, 365, 376
Cheney, Mary Bushnell	515, 516
Cheney Cobble	358, 365
Cheney's Camp 1	57, 200
Cherry Herring	407
Chicken Coop Brook	507, 522
Chicken Coop Lean-to	510
Chiltosky, Mary	342
Chimney Cliff	414
Chipman, Priscilla	59, 360
Chrenko, Elsie	119
Chrenko, Richard	119
Chubb River	156
Church, Rick	138
Church of the Good Shepherd	478
Circle of Doom	400
Citizen's Advisory Committee	107
City of the Sick	302
Civil Air Patrol	340, 368
Civil Rights Congress	140
Civilian Conservation Corps (C.C.C.)	276, 445, 461

INDEX

Clark, Elizabeth Marion Spence 21
Clark, Francis Vincent 22
Clark, George Thomas 22
Clark, Gertrude Marion 22
Clark, Herbert "Herb" 9, 15, 21, 22, 23, 24, 25, 27, 29, 30, 52, 53, 54, 65, 135, 139, 142, 144, 193, 194, 244, 258, 259, 275, 277, 307, 308, 314, 315, 327, 335, 342, 356, 358, 360, 363, 381, 392, 398, 399, 403, 443, 444, 449, 451, 453, 459, 472, 478, 503, 513, 551, 555
Clark, Herbert John 22, 23
Clark, Irene Elizabeth 22
Clark, James 22
Clark, John 21
Clark, Loris 135
Clark, Mary Jane 23
Clark, Mary Jane Dowdle 22
Clark, Mrs. B. Preston 256
Clark, Robert 205, 235
Clautice, Steve 511
Clean-up Day 86
Clear Lake 190
Clear Pond 436, 437, 439, 466, 468
Clements, Rudy 14
Cliff Mountain 29, 64, 80, 112, 131, 137, 208, 244-249, 252, 253
Climbing in the Adirondacks: A Guide to Rock and Ice Routes in the Adirondack Park 447, 532
"Climbing the Adirondack 46" 70, 72, 336
Clinton, Bill 122
Clinton, DeWitt 201, 351, 357, 472
Clinton, George 318
Clintonia 472, 508
Closed gentian 472
Cloud Splitter, The 41, 43, 48
Coal land 8
Co. B. 3 Infantry 421
Cobble, The 377
Cobble Hill 427
Cock's Comb 534
Coeyman's cemetery 492
Coffin, Jan 118, 125
Coffin, Tris 536
Coggeshall, Almy D. 91
Colby, Jack 31, 32, 350, 505
Cold Brook 361
Cold Brook Pass 352
Cold River 39, 41, 45, 69, 269, 272, 275, 279, 287, 292, 295, 315, 335
Cold River City 270, 280
Cold River Horse Trail 273
Colden, Cadwallader 376
Colden, David C. 157, 231, 232, 242, 251, 376
Colden, Mrs. David 201
Colden Interior Ranger Station 103, 238-239, 240, 384-386
Cole, Thomas 163, 202, 365
Collier, Patricia 453
Collier, Steven L. 383, 384, 385
Collins, Bob 254, 451, 459
Collins, James W. F. 70, 119
Colvin, Verplanck 10, 16, 54, 160, 164, 171, 174, 177, 178, 179, 181, 182, 183, 184, 185, 186, 189, 190, 193, 194, 205, 207, 225, 226, 230, 237, 244, 245, 249, 252, 254, 258, 274, 275, 277, 287, 304, 305, 307, 314, 316, 320, 327, 334, 337, 339, 343, 351, 353, 358, 369, 375, 376, 392, 394, 397, 419, 424, 425, 435, 437, 438, 439, 440, 448, 457, 465, 467, 471, 473, 476, 482, 483, 484, 485, 486, 487, 488, 491, 492, 500, 501, 504, 508, 513, 530, 531, 532, 533, 538, 539, 541, 542, 548, 550, 554, 561
Colyer, Mary .... (see Dittmar, Mary)
Combs, Abigail 560
Combs, Ann 560
Combs, Emily 560
Combs, Harriet 560
Combs, Rosetta 564
Combs, Thomas and Harriet 560, 564
Combs (family name) 560
Comeau, Jules 85, 92, 105, 110
Common buttercup 556
Compton, Alfred G. 169
Comstock, Andrew 202, 203
Comstock, Fritz 525
Cone Mountain 358, 448
Conservation Patch 90
Conservation Service Award (CSA) 94, 105, 147
Constable, John 458
Cook, Mary 165, 170, 176, 204
Cook, Russ 389, 390
Corduroy 145
Corell, Jay 286
Corell, Mark 286
Corell, Mary 286
Corell, Phil 84, 85, 105, 111, 114, 121, 122, 125, 132, 135, 286, 529
Corey's, NY 46, 280
Cornell Outing Club 254
Corsaro, James 118
Corson, Marilyn 116
Cotter, Lawrence E. 84
Couchee (Couchsachraga) 41
Couchsachraga Mountain ... 8, 24, 29, 41, 52, 53, 54, 55, 60, 62, 64, 81, 100, 141, 194, 278-279, 293, 294, 335
Couchsachraga ("dismal wilderness") 8
Courthouse, The (cliff) 405
Cram, Spencer 405, 409
Cranberry Pond 433
Cranston, Pamela 422
Craver, Clarence 33, 50, 51, 558
Crossfield, Stephen 52
Croton-on-Hudson, N.Y. 225
Crystal Brook 173, 174
Crystal Falls 191
Cunningham, John L. 327
Cupola furnace 165, 204
Cuyler, Theodore L. 485

Da-Yoh-Je-Ga-Go 363
Dana, Richard Henry 165, 203

Dannehower, Bill 525
Dark Cup, The 498
Dark-eyed junco 199
Darwin, Charles 226
Davis, Albert Tatum 273, 452
Davis, Arthur K. 60
Davis, Greg 114
Davis, Mary 33, 38
Davis, Stephen 452
Davis, Theodore R. 169, 204, 274
Davis (proprietor of Elk Lake Lodge) 444
Davis Mountain 452
Dawson, Louis W. 192, 206
de Forest, Robert W. 500, 512, 528
DeLong, Robert 197
Dean, William J. 506
Death angel 341
Deer's hair sedge 555
Democratic Party 296, 316, 317, 435
Dennis, Anne E. 138
Dennis, Clara 484, 486, 492
Denniston, Robert "Bob" 14, 272, 405
Department of Environmental Conservation (DEC) ...
  15, 79, 81, 82, 83, 85, 86, 87, 88, 89, 90, 91, 94, 96, 97,
  98, 100, 101, 102, 103, 104, 106, 107, 108, 109, 110, 111,
  112, 115, 125, 126, 128, 129, 130, 131, 137, 144, 145, 146
*Descriptive and Historical Guide to the Valley of Lake
  Champlain and the Adirondacks, A* 440
DeSormo, Maitland C. 77
Dewey, Melvin 193, 304, 343
Diagonal (slide) 422
Dial Mountain 60, 96, 465-477
Dial Pond 433
Diamant, Rachel 151
Diamond, Henry L. 82
Diapensia 228, 527, 555
Dibble, Norman 513
Dickens, Charles 202, 231, 376
Dickinson, Don 67
Dick's Peak 379
Dimarco, Dexter 385
Dingman, Lester F. 54
DiNunzio, Michael 208
Dipper, The 420
Discover the Adirondack High Peaks 372, 453, 473
Discovery 377
Disney, Walt 553
Dittmar, Adolph G. "Ditt" 14, 57, 59, 60, 61, 67, 68,
  69, 70, 77, 84, 99, 105, 108, 115, 122,
  132, 197, 270, 280, 292, 293, 327, 452, 480
Dittmar, Brooke (Barbara) 70
Dittmar, Charlie 69
Dittmar, David 68, 70
Dittmar, Elizabeth 70
Dittmar, James "Jim" 60, 70
Dittmar, Katharyn 70
Dittmar, Mary 14, 56, 68, 69, 117, 132, 197, 270, 280,
  292, 293, 294, 481, 536
Dix, John A. (Adams) 156, 297, 328, 434

Dix/Elk Lake/Hunters Pass Trails 94
Dix Mountain (Peak) 32, 33, 45, 82, 83, 112, 134, 138,
  185, 196, 197, 215, 216, 311, 434-448
Dix Mountain Wilderness Area 131, 132, 433
Dix Pond 433
Dix Range 36, 51, 52, 55, 130, 131, 433-464
Dix/Round Pond Trail 94
Dix Unit Management Plan 460
Dixon, Joseph 166, 204
Doherty, Paul 52
Dolly 338
Donaldson, Alfred Lee 28, 189, 191, 205, 287, 301,
  303, 304, 307, 321, 395, 404, 416, 456, 486, 491, 495, 540
Donaldson, Elizabeth 309
Doolittle, Susie 529
Douglas, William O. 346, 347
Dragon Tooth 455
Duck Hole 40, 270, 272, 275, 284, 287, 292, 335
Duck Hole/Bradley Pond Trail 100
Duck Hole Lean-to 272
Dudley Brook 263
Dumers, Jeaneen 121
Dunham, Miss 521
Dunham Plateau 515
Dunning, Alvah 287, 303, 314, 394
Dunning, Sam 431
Duquette, John 454
Durand, Asher B. 202
Durant, Kenneth 258
Durant, William 304
Durkee, A. W. 306
Dwarf birch 555
Dwarf willow 199

Eagan, Daniel 133, 149, 215, 434, 464
Eagan, Melissa 133, 149, 464
Eagan, Patrick J. 383, 384
Eagle (slide) 422
East Dix 24, 43, 45, 60, 123, 126, 134, 194, 433, 452-456
East River (Opalescent River) 156, 375
East River Trail 247, 496
East Trail 431
Eastman, Ann 503
Eaton, Amos 201, 311
Ed Hudowalski Memorial Lean-to 74, 110
Edmonds, Adrian 525
Edmonds' Ponds 409, 410
Edwards, Jody 235, 241
Edwin Ketchledge Summit Steward Endowment . 124
Elba Iron and Steel Manufacturing Company . 156, 343
Eldred, Frank 292
Eldridge, Harry Jr. 91
Elements of Botany 226
Elevator on Whiteface 552
Elijah Lewis .... (see Benedict, Elijah Lewis)
Elizabethtown #4 433
Elk Lake 225, 328, 433, 436, 437, 439, 444, 468
Elk Lake/Dix Trail 112
Elk Lake House 444

Elk Lake Lodge 64, 444, 446
Elk Lake Preserve 433
Elk Lake Trail 225
Elk Lake-Marcy Trail 94
Elk Pass 471, 472, 487
Ellis, Alexander John 202
Elms, The 491
Ely, W. W. (William Watson) 337, 342, 440
Emancipation Proclamation 299, 300
Embler, Chris 138
Embler, William "Bill" 120, 138
Emerson, Edward 423
Emerson, Ralph Waldo 288, 423
Emmett, Daniel 279
Emmons, Ebenezer ... 9, 61, 155, 156, 157, 159, 160, 171, 177, 193, 194, 200, 201, 233, 234, 249, 250, 251, 263, 287, 288, 301, 309, 310, 311, 312, 321, 348, 354, 434, 435, 436, 466, 467, 500, 539, 541, 542, 555
Emmons, Ebenezer, Jr. 157, 200, 348
Endicott, Bill 61, 404, 406
Endicott, Eloise 404
Englehard Peak 377
Englehart, Steven 556
Enoch (servant) 156
Ensworth, George 331
Erie Canal 297
Ermine Brook 273
Essex County Republican 394
Estes, Otis 402
Estes, Uncle Joe 540, 560
Estes (family name) 560
Estes family cemetery 394
Estey, George 58, 174, 501
Esther (in the Bible) 559
Esther Centennial 49
Ethical Cultural Society 424
Étude sur les Glaciérs 288, 310, 315
Exploring the 46 Adirondack High Peaks 532
Eyebright 556

Fabian, Maxine 149
Fairy Ladder Falls 210, 470, 471, 489-490
Fantod 23
Faust, Mildred 347
Fearon, Chris 294
Feldspar Brook 44, 157, 171, 178, 181, 225, 229, 230, 236, 245
Feldspar Camp 157
Feldspar Lean-to 108, 265
Fenton's Tavern 437
Fiegl, Jason 400
Field, Darby 7
Fielding, Matilda 337
Fielding, Mr. 337, 338
Filler, Andrew 135
Fillmore, Millard 355
Finch Pruyn & Co. 100, 101, 205, 253, 261, 263, 271, 278, 441

Finger (slide) 422
Finnin, Vikki 138
Fire towers 550
Fires 550
First Brother 403
First formal trail 546
Firth, George 331
Fish 414, 415, 420
Fish, C. Peter "Pete" 85, 87, 91, 104, 198, 208, 334, 336, 388, 528
Fish, Dorothy 79
Fish, Glenn 3, 76, 79, 80, 81, 82, 83, 86, 87, 90, 91, 92, 105, 122
Fish Hawk Cliffs 496, 498
Fiske, Rufus 439
Flag 2 330
Flat Top 397
Flat top asters 472
Flat top Mt. 393
Fleming, J. R. 250
Fletcher, G. 360
Flick, Hugh M. 52, 53
Flickinger, Katherine "Kay" .. 14, 56, 57, 63, 65, 119, 382
Flood (1856) 481
Flora of North America, A 201, 226, 250
Flora of the State of New York, A 250
Flowed Lands 187, 189, 206, 246, 247, 248, 260, 361, 369
Flowering raspberry 411
Flume, The 496
Flume of the Opalescent 171
Fogel, Steve 239
Foley, Ed 63
Follensby Pond 287, 288, 423
Foote, James E. "Jim" 56, 143
Footsteps Through the Adirondacks, The Verplanck Colvin Story 482, 492
Ford, Christina 389, 390
Ford, Michael 331
Forest and Crag 533, 546
Forest fire observation posts 550
Forest Preserve Association 526
"Forever Wild" 16
Fortune, Harold 553
Forty-Sixer Song 44
Forty-Sixers of Troy 11, 33, 38, 43, 49, 56, 69, 214, 359, 406, 448, 452, 557
Foster, Burns 535
Four Corners 171, 179, 181, 225, 229, 230, 245
Four Corners Lean-to 37, 96, 509
Fourth Brother 405
Fowler, Barnett (Barney) 526
Franklin, Sue 134
Franklin Falls, NY 549, 559
Freedom in the Wilderness 420
Freeman, Jack 538
Freidow, Ernest 105
French, Russell 549, 561

French, Samuel 549, 561
French's Hotel 561
Frenette, William C. 77
Fresn, Marion 84
Freud, Sigmund 423
Friend, Eleanor 346
Friendly Adirondack Peaks 246, 275, 443, 514
From the Black Forest to Tibet: One Woman's Mountains .. 71
Frontenac 328
Frostfish 414

Gabriel, Peter 332
Galeski, Pat 529
Gallos, Phil 394, 395, 428
Garden, The 32, 225, 403, 404, 411, 417, 537
Garrand, R. H. 385
Gates, Dan 165
Gazetteer of the State of New York, A 156, 251, 540
Gebhard, Michael 117
"Geologic Story of the Mountains, The" 521
Geology 409, 417, 473, 496, 521, 540
Geology of New York, Part II, Comprising the Survey of the Second Geological District 159, 233, 234, 466, 539, 555
Gettysburg Address 299
Giant Mountain 7, 8, 9, 11, 12, 55, 70, 73, 92, 94, 104, 112, 119, 214, 219, 419-429
Giant Mountain Unit Management Plan 420
Giant Mountain Wilderness Area (GMWA) 131, 132, 425, 427, 428
Giant of the Valley 156, 427
Giant Ridge Trail 419
Giant's Basin 419
Giant's Wife 431, 432
Giardiasis 103
Gibbs, John 403, 404, 536
Gibbs, Margaret 529
Gibson, Charles "Chuck," Jr. 432
Gibson, Dave 207
Gilchrist, Thomas B. 381
Gill, Kathleen 133
Gill Brook 467, 469, 476, 487, 496
Gill Brook Trail 487
Gilroy, Howard P. (Leslie Wickes) 270, 276
Gittinger, Mildred "Millie"; N. Clark 117
Glaciers 418
Glanda, Jeanine 414
Glanda, Jeffrey 414
Glens Falls Rotary Club 10, 28, 559
Glider, Victor 82
Glover, Bill 525
Glover, James M. 16, 17, 55, 505
Glover, Ruth 525
Glover, William "Will" 506, 515, 521, 524, 525
Goff, Alphonso 431
Goark, Louise 46
Goodman Mountain 454
Goodspeed, Wallace 559, 560
Goodwin, Howard 518

Goodwin, James A. "Jim" 70, 72, 73, 77, 92, 94, 100, 101, 122, 148, 152, 176, 166, 195, 196, 237, 264, 271, 272, 276, 327, 329, 332, 342, 402, 419, 445, 459, 472, 479, 480, 490, 500, 506, 509, 519, 522, 523, 529, 532, 533, 534, 535, 536, 538
Goodwin, James, A. "Tony" 12, 89, 93, 94, 132, 196, 242, 264, 330, 400, 421, 431, 476, 507, 519, 529, 535, 536
Goodwin, Peter 353
Goodwin, Scott D. M. 186
Gooley Dam 75
Gooseberry Mountain 510
Gordon Cornwell Seminary 330
Gore 375
Gorge of the Dial 328, 435, 437, 465, 467, 468, 474
Gothics Mountain (Gothic) 9, 11, 25, 26, 33, 56, 71, 93, 96, 119, 530-532
Gothics cables 537
Gothics Camp Lean-to 510
Gothics Trail 535
Gowie, Catherine 47
Gowie, Orville C. 31, 32, 33, 45, 47, 48, 50, 52, 57, 66, 279
Grace Camp 507, 538
Grace CD 133
Grace Committee 116, 117
Grace Methodist Church 30, 40, 41, 47, 64
Grace Peak 43, 134, 194, 452-456, 499
Grace Peak Committee 134, 344, 406, 454, 499
Grades, Liz 537
Grant, Ulysses S. 317
Gravestone Brook 441
Gray, Asa 201, 225, 250
Gray Peak .. 10, 29, 33, 44, 54, 131, 178, 225-230, 339, 542
Great Basin 478, 479, 504
Great Circle Trail 444, 459, 507
Great Forest of the Adirondacks, The 411
Great Purchase 8
Great Range .... (see Lower Range, Upper Range)
Great Slide 174, 542, 545
Great Trail Circle 258
Greeley, Horace 295, 298
Green Mountains 176
Greene, Don 428
Greenwich, NY 312
Gregory, Dudley S. 166, 204
Gregory, Elizabeth 204
Gregory, George 204
Grenville Province 417
Griffith, Ernest S. 56, 143
Grimm, Bob 538
Grinnell, Lawrence I. 506
Grossman, Bernard 138
Grossman, Christine 138
Grossman, Zack 138
Grubbs, Len 109, 113, 117, 446, 451, 563
Guide to Adirondack Trails 49, 242, 459, 519, 561, 562
Guide to Adirondack Trails: High Peaks Region 196

INDEX

Guide to Adirondack Trails, Northeastern Section 54, 196, 236, 356, 398, 427, 549
Guide to Adirondack Trails, Seventh Edition 272
"Guide to the Natural History of Mt. Jo" 81
Guide-Boat Days and Ways 258
Gunks, The 406
Guyot, Arnold 315, 320, 427

Haeusser, Dorothy O. "Dot" 14, 65
Hagar, Johanne 138
Hale, Barbara 176
Hale, David 481
Hale, Ed 176, 177, 205
Hale, LaGrand 474
Hale, Melissa 331
Hall, Harrison 189
Hall, James 155, 157, 200, 232, 242, 250, 251, 309, 310, 311, 312, 314, 348, 541
Hall, Ramon "Ray" 14
Hall of Fame 226, 230
Hall of Records 45, 279
Hammett, Dashiel 140
Hancock, Winfield 320
Hand, A. C. 164, 202
Hanging Spear Falls 9, 156, 168, 247, 260, 375, 376
Harmes, Edward "Ed" 14, 56, 57, 65
Harmes, John "Jack" 57
Harper, Henry 305, 306
Harper's Ferry, Virginia (now West Virginia) . 339, 543
Harriman, Edward H. 557
Harriman, W. Averell 553
Harris, Barbara 127, 128, 129, 133, 134, 135, 138, 190, 344
Harris, Charles 533
Harris, Roger 459
Hart, Kimball "Kim" 254, 259, 382, 506
Hartis, Gerald 336
Harvard Forest College 560
Harvard University 226
Haskins, Tom 529
Hathaway, Mel 195, 404, 509, 535, 536
Hayes, Ellsworth "El" 543, 548
Haystack Brook 503
Haystack Mountain 27, 28, 33, 37, 42, 56, 58, 70, 96, 119, 124, 138, 172, 174, 175, 176, 179, 182, 196, 197, 199, 208, 217, 225, 423, 500-503, 530
Hayward, Barbara Alden 353
Hayward, Robert 353
He-no-do-aw-da 333
He-no-ga 347
Headley, Joel T. 160, 161, 162, 163, 173, 201, 436
Heald, David 534
Heald, Frank 474
Healy, Bill 173, 175, 176, 257, 393
Healy, George 71
Healy, Karen 446
Healy, Susan 152
Healy, Trudy B. 67, 70, 71, 77, 81, 88, 134, 144, 148, 405, 446, 451, 455, 480

Heart Lake 190, 342
Heart Pond (Lake) 327, 393
Heart Pond Trail 399
Heartbreak Hill 235
Heaven Up-h'isted-ness 3, 65, 173, 400
Hedgehog 534
Hein, Fred 61
Held, Ray 95, 138
Helenek, Robert "Bob" 105, 120
Helms, Andy 405
Henderson, Archie 162, 204
Henderson, David 156, 157, 162, 165, 200, 201, 204, 206, 231, 232, 235, 242, 246, 251, 252, 263, 281, 282, 283, 348, 364, 375, 376, 380, 394, 486, 490
Henderson, Margaret 204
Henderson Lake 8, 167, 203, 283, 284, 330, 335
Henderson Monument 162, 171
Henry Goddard Leach Trail 441, 472, 473
Henry Young Crew Cabin 538
Herbert Brook 40, 53, 359, 360, 453
Herbert Peak 52, 53, 54, 142, 358, 359, 360
Herdpaths 1, 15, 39, 62, 71, 72, 73, 74, 75, 76, 77, 79, 82, 91, 95, 97, 100, 101, 108, 109, 110, 111, 112, 113, 114, 115, 120, 130, 131, 136
Herman, George 385
Hermit of Cold River 295
Herreshoff, Mr. 304
Herrod, Walter "Wally" 92, 94
Herz, Ken 242
Hewitt, Steuben 163
"Hi, Hiker!" 61
Hickey, J. R. (Jean René) 341, 537
Hickey, John 422
Hickey, Peter "Pete" 132, 341, 537
Hickock, Andrew 546, 547
High Bank 428
High Peak of Essex 155, 156, 157, 199, 249, 312
High Peak Task Force 91, 92
High Peaks Advisory Committee (HPAC) 91, 97, 109, 110
High Peaks Citizens' Advisory Committee (CAC) .. 109, 110
"High Peaks of Essex, The" 173, 175
High Peaks of Essex, The Adirondack Mountains of Orson Schofield Phelps, The 257, 393
"High Peaks of the Adirondacks, The" 27, 28, 30, 134, 194, 244, 275, 277, 278, 356, 357, 392, 397, 399, 403, 410, 417, 452, 478, 503
High Peaks Unit Management Plan (HPUMP) 100, 106, 107, 108, 109, 110, 111, 112, 114, 115, 124, 125, 126, 127, 147, 253, 255, 264, 341
High Peaks Wilderness 100, 109, 110, 127, 136
High Peaks Wilderness Area (HPWA) 428
High Spots 21, 23, 29, 41, 49, 54, 55, 142
High Valley 157
"Hiking Partners, Mountain Stewards" 122
Hillard, Miss 495

Historical Sketches of Northern New York and the Adirondacks 347
History of Essex County 409
History of the Adirondacks, A 189, 191, 205, 302, 307, 395, 404, 416, 456, 495, 540
Hitch Up, Matilda 338, 375
Hitch-up Matildas 337, 338, 345, 369, 375
Hixson, Edward 388
Hobblebush 472
Hocheloga 541
Hochschild, Harold K. 78, 166, 204, 453, 463
Hodge, Hugh 510
Hodgson, Gary 83, 91, 368, 385, 387
Hofer, Robert D. 145
Hoffman, Charles Fenno 9, 159, 160, 163, 194, 200, 312, 365, 436
Hoffman, Donald J. "Don" 92, 98, 102, 105, 453
Hoffman, Michael 332
Hoffman Mountain 36
Hogan, Peter 138
Hogback Brook 510
Hogback Lean-to 510
Höhenrauch 184, 205
Hokirk, Lawrence "Larry" 112
Hollingsworth, Elizabeth Sherwood 303
Holt, Charles 512
Holt, Harvey 157, 165, 200, 233, 242, 348, 482
Holt, Hiram 437
Holt, James 411
Holt, Monroe 513
Holt's Camp 157, 200
Holton, David P. 164, 165, 202
Honeywell, Martha 138
Hongo, Lyle 265
Hopkins, Arthur S. 50, 195, 208, 235, 244, 248, 258, 262, 381, 401, 427, 493, 507, 509, 558
Hopkins, Erastus 424, 478
Hopkins Hump 195, 392
Hopkins Lean-to 196
Hopkins' Peak 394
Hopkins Trail 195, 196, 510
Horan, Joseph R. 36
Horn, Charles "Charlie" 31, 32, 33, 46, 57, 452, 505
Horwich, Mike 243
Hotel Whiteface 548
Hough, Franklin B. 52, 448, 449, 456, 483, 564
Hough Peak 24, 45, 52, 53, 91, 126, 128, 216, 433, 448-451, 493
Houghton, A. S. 536
House Un-American Activities Committee 140
Howard, W. (William) G. 52, 53, 93, 450
Howard Mountain 397
Hoy, Jennifer 472
Hoy, Kate 477
Hoy, Sally 477
Hudak, Bob 228
Hudda, David "Dave" 109, 112, 451

Hudowalski, Edward "Ed" 14, 30, 31, 32, 33, 44, 45, 50, 57, 58, 60, 64, 67, 74, 93, 111, 138, 154, 228, 243, 244, 259, 278, 280, 321, 329, 349, 371, 396, 407, 448, 452, 505
Hudowalski, Grace Leach ... 12, 14, 27, 29, 30, 32, 33, 34, 35, 36, 37, 38, 39, 40, 42, 45, 46, 49, 51, 52, 53, 54, 55, 57, 58, 64, 65, 67, 68, 69, 70, 75, 77, 80, 82, 83, 93, 98, 99, 108, 116, 118, 122, 123, 124, 129, 132, 134, 138, 139, 143, 144, 146, 148, 149, 194, 196, 197, 198, 259, 262, 270, 276, 279, 280, 293, 329, 341, 371, 399, 406, 431, 449, 450, 452, 453, 454, 498, 557, 558, 559, 563
Hudowalski Essay Contest 135
Hudson from the Wilderness to the Sea, The 166
Hudson River 225, 227, 251
Hunt, Fred 84, 400
Hunter, David "Dave" 190, 274, 320, 494
Hunter, Mrs. Robert 171
Hunters (Hunter's) Pass 328, 433, 436, 438, 439, 440, 445, 465, 467, 469
Hurley brothers 411
Hurricane Belle 241, 242
Hurricane Floyd 12, 112, 124, 130, 236, 247, 265, 270, 328, 340, 343, 389, 405, 447, 459, 473
Hurricane Mountain 92, 185, 413, 417
Huyck, Dale 125
Hypersthene 235
Hypothermia 383-388

Ice caves 479
In the Wilderness 257, 393, 467, 468
Indian cucumber root 342
Indian Falls 86, 192, 193, 197, 224, 225, 294, 345, 394, 395, 397, 400, 401
Indian Falls Lean-to 86, 96
Indian Head 211, 496, 497
Indian Pass 93, 155, 156, 165, 170, 171, 190, 193, 203, 327, 328, 332-335, 339, 341, 345, 363-365, 375, 383, 436
Indian Pass, The 171, 328, 332, 413, 468, 533, 546
Indian Pass Brook 327, 330, 341, 342, 363
Indian Pass Trail 92, 94, 192, 330, 331, 332, 334-335
Indian pipe 342, 472
Ingham, Charles C. (Cromwell) 157, 163, 200, 201, 311, 333, 348, 365
Ingram, Mason T. 74, 76, 82
Ingrid (Norwegian girl) 442
Inlet Camp 186
Interbrook Lodge 92, 195, 403
Iron Dam 171
Irondequoit Club 64
Iroquois (Native Americans) 347
Iroquois (Mount Marshall) 24
Iroquois Peak 24, 33, 53, 54, 91, 119, 222, 351-353, 382
Irving, Washington 202
Isham, Ed 513, 524
Isham, Gavin 529

J. & J. Rogers Company 206, 393, 397, 399, 400, 404, 411, 441, 512, 535, 562, 563

Index

J. H. French map of Essex County 560, 561
James, Alice 424
James, Henry 424
James, Sam 138
James, William 423, 424, 501
Jamieson, Paul F. 77, 89, 362, 363
Janeway, Willie 400
Jatulis, Mindaugus "Mindy" 117, 118
Jay, John 493
Jensen, Jerome W. 91
Jensen, Kenneth R. 366
Jerry, Harold 96, 97
Jersey City, NJ 156, 166, 204, 231, 476
Jewelweed 472
Jewett, E. 314
Johannsen, Herman Smith "Jackrabbit" 502, 506
Johns Brook 225, 392, 398, 402, 531, 536
Johns Brook Lodge (JBL) 69, 74, 89, 145, 195, 398, 403, 404, 472, 509, 531, 536, 537
Johns Brook Trail 513
Johns Brook Valley 194, 195, 397, 399, 403, 404, 508, 535, 538
Johnson, Andrew 300
Johnson, Bill 446, 529
Johnson, Fred 98, 99, 105, 116
Johnson, Israel 436
Johnstone, Phil 111
Jones, Pell 461
Jordan, Al 368
Journal of the Society for Industrial Archeology ... 285
Jumpers 404, 406
Junction Camp 179, 181, 186, 205
Jung, Carl 423

Kandetski, Albert W., Jr. 366
Kapitzke, Alan Robert 118
Karaka, Harold 331
Kasch, Howard 248
Kate Smith Trophy ski race 402
Keating, Margaret "Peggy" 59, 360
Keene Central School 98, 122, 125
Keene Flats (Keene Valley) 328, 394, 403, 439, 482, 504, 518
Keene Heights 495
Keene Heights Hotel Company 495
Keene Kids Climbing Club 406
Keene Valley, NY 9, 225
Keene Valley Guides Association 512
Keeseville, NY 21, 288
Keizer, Ted E. "Cave Dog" 129
Keller, Jane Eblen 143
Kellogg, Orlando 164, 202
Kennedy, John 138
Kenney, Ransome N. 564
Kerr, Randy 83, 87, 89
Ketchledge, Edwin H. "Ketch" 3, 76, 79, 80, 81, 83, 84, 89, 90, 91, 92, 93, 95, 96, 97, 102, 103, 105, 106, 109, 110, 122, 124, 129, 197, 208, 342, 347, 379, 428, 526, 527, 528, 555, 558

Ketch's Point 379
Kilburn (slide) 11
Kilkenny Lodge 427
King, Ruth Prince 280, 294
King Hendrick 539
Klondike Notch 145
Knauth, Arnold W. 506
Knollwood 16, 20, 21, 22, 485
Knollwood Club 20
Kobak, James III 231, 241, 400
Koch, Gary 428, 529
Koch, George 360
Konowitz, John 230, 405
Konowitz, Lauren 389, 390
Konowitz, Ron 134, 138, 389, 390, 406
Kozel, William "Bill" 98, 105, 121, 122
Krakauer, Jon 241
Krummholz 425

L. Morgan Porter Trail 235, 236
Labrador tea 228, 532
LaCasse, Noah 189
LaFarge, C. Grant 186, 187, 188, 193, 194, 206
LaFarge, John 206
Lafayette, Marquis de 201
Lake Arnold 225, 235, 236, 243
Lake Arnold Crossover trail 92
Lake Arnold Lean-to 86, 96
Lake Champlain 245, 251
Lake Colden 25, 63, 68, 155, 156, 157, 159, 162, 167, 170, 171, 179, 181, 184, 187, 189, 190, 192, 200, 206, 208, 219, 225, 231, 232, 233, 235, 238, 239, 251, 252, 349, 351, 369, 375-376, 377, 385
Lake Colden Gore 253
Lake Hamish 263
Lake Henderson 380
Lake Jimmy 263, 375
Lake Kiwassa 304
Lake Marie Louise 431
Lake Perkins 178, 205
Lake Placid 541, 542, 546, 554
Lake Placid, NY 9, 408, 554
Lake Placid Club 191, 192, 304, 337, 343, 380, 399, 410, 415, 509
Lake Placid Memorial Hospital 239, 240, 281, 368
Lake Placid News 238
Lake Placid Snow Birds Ski Club 502
Lake Placid Trampers Guide, The 261, 262
Lake Road 472, 473, 476, 487, 496
Lake Sally 263, 375
Lake Sanford 8, 49, 155, 163, 194, 261, 282
Lake Stevens 557
Lake Tear Lean-to 96
Lake Tear-of-the-Clouds 38, 131, 171, 178, 179, 181, 182, 183, 184, 185, 187, 189, 192, 205, 225, 229, 245, 253, 254, 260
Lake-side Inn 439
Lamb, Adella 125
Lamb, Levi 179

Lamb, Pete 502, 513, 519
Lamb, Vern 89
Lamb, Winifred "Winnie" 84, 90
Lance, David 101, 103, 133, 149
Lance, Herbert "Herb" 38
Lance, Suzanne 11, 99, 101, 116, 133, 135, 147,
                149, 198, 329, 395, 449, 501, 529
Lance, William "Bill" 31, 32, 33, 330, 505, 556
Land of Makebelieve 553
Langdon, Warren 248
Lange, John 123
Langen, Tom 415
Langmuir, Irving 192, 206, 207, 502, 506, 526
Lanman, Charles 160, 162, 163, 164, 202, 435
Lansing, Wendell 164, 203
Lapland rosebay 503, 555
Last Chance Ranch 341
Laverty, Bill 431
Leach, Alice Luella Dolbeck 35
Leach, Henry Goddard 477
Leach, James Casper 35
"Leave No Trace" 125, 128, 147
LeBoeuf, Fred 290, 291
Lee, Day 422
Lee, Nancy 422
Lee, Tom 105, 116
Legg, Douglas 273
Leggett, E. H. 456
Leonard, Ray 83
Leveling 530, 542
Levine, Peter 225
Lewis, Will 70,
Lewis, NY 560
Lillian Brook 131, 433, 447, 459
Lillian Brook Lean-to 104
Lillypad Pond 433, 456
Lily Pad Pond 436
Lincoln, Abraham 202, 298, 299, 300, 318, 319, 435
Lindsay Brook 433, 456
Lintner, Joseph Albert 226, 230
Litter Bags 87, 95
Little, Elizabeth, "Bess" 57, 69
Little Dix 358, 448
Little Flume 538
Little Haystack 32, 56, 508, 520
Little Marcy 177, 195, 392, 398
Little Porter 417
Little Tabletop 392
Little Wolf Jaw 56
Lockwood, S. R. 455
Loeb, William , Jr. 190
Logbooks 84, 114, 126
Logging ...195, 253, 260, 285, 289, 400, 425, 441, 509, 533
Long Lake 274, 287
Long Pond 410
Long Pond Mountain 408
Long Range Planning Committee (LRPC) 125, 128
Longfellow, Henry Wadsworth 288
Longstreth, T. Morris 28, 261, 302, 485, 514

Lookout Mountain 131, 548, 561, 562
Lookout Mountain shelter 563
Lookout Point 365, 548
Loope, P. F. "Fay" 14, 55, 57, 67, 198
Lossing, Benson 166, 167, 168, 169, 170, 172, 196, 204
Lossing, Mrs. Benson 166, 169
Lost Overlook Trail 496
Lost Pond 335
Lost Pond Mountain 259, 335, 453
Lost Pond Peak 329, 335
Lowe, John T. Carr 48
Lowell, James Russell 288, 547
Lower Ausable Lake 93, 173, 174, 176,
                183, 257, 479, 487
Lower Ausable Lake dam 481
Lower Cascade Lake 414, 415
Lower Range 530-537
Lower Twin Brook 264
Lower Wolf Jaw 56, 96, 533
Lower Works (village) 160, 242, 246, 282, 283
Lowrie, Walter 506, 510, 513, 517, 519,
                521, 522, 523, 524
Luck, M. E. 402
Ludlow, Margery Nash 45, 50, 59, 141, 276, 558
Lumbering .... (see Logging)
Lure of Esther Mountain, Matriarch of the Adirondacks, The 549, 560, 561
Lycopod spores 476
Lycopodium Pond 471
Lyndsey's Tavern 162
Lynch, Daniel 277
Lynx 138

MacDonald Shelter 67, 80, 143, 196, 197
MacDonald, Pirie 143, 196
Macdonough, Thomas 457
MacIntosh (family) 513
MacIntyre, Archibald 263
MacIntyre (Mount Marshall) 54
MacIntyre .... (see Algonquin Peak)
MacIntyre Falls 131, 367
MacIntyre Mine - From Failure to Fortune, The 166
MacIntyre Mountains 345
MacIntyre Range 25, 52, 53, 54, 63, 224, 345
MacKenzie, Kevin B. 210, 211, 213, 214, 218, 219,
                220, 221, 222, 223, 224
MacKenzie, Mary 343
Macklin, Philip Alan 143
MacLaren, Malcolm 521, 523
MacMartin, Duncan 263
MacNaughton, James 189, 204, 206, 335
MacNaughton Cottage 189, 284
MacNaughton Mountain 223, 335-336
Macomb Mountain 11, 65, 215, 433, 457-460
Macomb, Alexander, Jr. 8, 457
Macomb, Alexander, Sr. 457
Macomb (family name) 560
Macomb's Purchase 8
Macready, William Charles 231, 376

INDEX

Malcolm, Herbert L. "Bert" 14, 55, 143, 555
Mallinson, Chai-Kyou 92
Mallinson, Richard 92
Manual of the Botany of the Northern United States 226
Map of the Adirondack Wilderness 561
Marble Mountain 552, 562, 563
Marcinowski, Ken 209, 211, 212, 214, 215, 216, 217, 218, 219
Marcinowski, Nilde 217
Marcy, William Learned 156, 158, 159, 165, 297, 309, 311, 317, 435
Marcy Brook .. 111, 173, 175, 179, 186, 206, 373, 394, 397
Marcy Dam 74, 84, 86, 92, 103, 110, 112, 190, 192, 197, 206, 225, 237, 369, 371
Marcy Dam Ranger Station 107
Markert, Ervin H. 91
Marshall, Elisabeth (Betty) Dublin 19
Marshall, Florence Lowenstein 16, 19
Marshall, George 9, 10, 11, 15, 16, 19, 20, 22, 23, 24, 25, 26, 27, 30, 50, 52, 53, 54, 55, 56, 62, 63, 65, 66, 67, 74, 75, 76, 77, 89, 122, 129, 135, 142, 143, 144, 193, 200, 207, 244, 258, 275, 277, 307, 308, 314, 315, 320, 327, 335, 336, 342, 352, 356, 358, 363, 381, 392, 398, 399, 403, 443, 451, 453, 455, 459, 472, 478, 485, 492, 493, 503, 513, 524, 532, 536, 555
Marshall, James 16
Marshall, Louis 16, 20, 526, 557
Marshall, Robert "Bob" .. 9, 10, 15, 16, 17, 18, 20, 21, 22, 24, 25, 26, 27, 28, 30, 34, 36, 49, 50, 52, 53, 54, 55, 56, 65, 89, 129, 134, 135, 139, 142, 144, 193, 194, 207, 244, 253, 258, 259, 275, 277, 278, 308, 314, 315, 327, 335, 342, 356, 357, 358, 359, 363, 381, 392, 397, 398, 399, 403, 410, 413, 417, 421, 424, 425, 443, 444, 448, 449, 450, 451, 455, 459, 472, 478, 480, 485, 493, 503, 505, 513, 532, 555, 559
Marshall, Ruth "Pootie" "Putey" 16, 19, 139
Martens, Joe 283
Martin, Homer 328, 468
Martin, Newell 479, 506, 513, 523
Martin, Steve 289
Masten, Arthur H. 166
Masten House 284
Maters, Andrea 529
Matteson, Letha 30
May, Harry 31, 32, 505
Maynard, Ashley 551
Mazeppa 338, 343
McComb (Macomb), Alexander 8
Mc.Comb Mt. 459
McComb, Esther 49, 50, 51, 235, 248, 558, 559, 560, 563
McComb (Macomb) Mountain 45
McCombe's Mountain 457, 459
McCook, Alexander 317
McEntee, Jervis 165, 203
McGinnis, Joseph "Joe" 23, 154
McIntyre, Archibald 155, 156, 157, 164, 166, 203, 204, 232, 233, 242, 251, 281, 335, 348, 364, 380
McIntyre, John 156
McIntyre (peak) 181, 184, 185, 187
McIntyre (village) 156, 164, 200, 202, 281, 284

McIntyre Furnace 285
McIntyre Iron Company 187, 254
McIntyre Iron Works 155, 159, 231, 232, 235, 242, 259, 468
McIntyre Range 345-391
McKenzie, Jack 14
McKenzie, Lil 14
McKenzie, Roderick 227, 530, 533, 538
McKinley, William 189, 190, 524
McMartin, Barbara 91, 263, 357, 372, 411, 413, 428, 430, 453, 473
McMartin, Christine 233
McMartin, Duncan 156, 157, 232, 233, 242, 281
McMartin, Malcom 156
McMullen, Donald 133
McMullen, Ian 131
McRae, George 159
Meek, Mr. 313
Meigs, Ferris J. 290, 292
Mellor, Don 405, 447, 532
Melvin family 273
"Membership Roster of the Adirondack Forty-Sixers, The" 565-674
Menz, Helen 14, 57, 116, 270, 280, 294, 327, 382
Merchandising Clerk 132
Mercy 173, 393, 395, 500
Merle-Smith (family) 513
Merrill, Loyal A. 171, 172, 173, 174, 328, 547
Meschinelli, Mark 389
Middle Dix 24, 358, 448, 449, 450, 453, 493
Middlebury College 354
Military and Civil History of the County of Essex, A 440, 550
Miller 348
Miller, Alexander W. 381
Miller, Ellen Goff 410
Miller, Frances 296
Miller, Nicaner 410
Miller (first name unknown) 493
Minerva Camp 445
Mirror Lake 543
Mitchell, Frederica 58
Mitchell, Paul 336
Mitchell, Roger 436
Moccasin flower, pink 562
Moffat, George 441
Monaco, Arto 553
Moody, Harvey 540
Moore, John 439
Moose 315, 325
Moose Pond 273, 330
Moose River 287
Morgan, Alice 65
Morgan, J. P. 526
Morris, Irving 305
Morrison, George 494
Morrison, Mrs. 200
Morrissey, Spencer 378, 511
Moss Lake .... (see Moss Pond)

Moss Pond 179, 182, 205, 225, 227, 229, 230, 252, 433
Moulton, Mimi 407
Mount Adams 283, 285, 369, 375
Mount Algonquin .... (see Algonquin Peak)
Mount Allen .... (see Allen Mountain)
Mount Ampersand 23
Mount Armstrong 56, 96
Mount Baker 23
Mount Clinton (Mount Marshall) 54, 351, 358, 360
Mount Colden 11, 27, 42, 56, 63, 65, 82, 83, 94, 112, 119, 124, 133, 168, 171, 172, 190, 205, 208, 212, 230-242, 247, 254, 509, 539
Mount Colvin 96, 307, 482-489
Mount Dix 466
Mount Donaldson 29, 47, 91, 123, 233, 301-308, 315, 316
Mount Emmons 15, 29, 52, 54, 60, 61, 123, 127, 233, 278, 309-314, 315, 316
Mount Emmons (Blue Mountain) 184, 185
Mount Esther . 37, 40, 49, 50, 123, 126, 131, 208, 557-565
Mount Henderson 272, 277
Mount Herbert 24, 52, 53
Mount Iroquois 358
Mount Jo 56, 85, 191, 194, 331, 341
Mount MacNaughton 334
Mount Marcy 7, 9, 24, 25, 26, 29, 30, 31, 32, 33, 37, 41, 42, 48, 51, 55, 56, 61, 63, 66, 67, 68, 69, 77, 78, 80, 86, 92, 94, 102, 109, 119, 124, 131, 133, 136, 138, 141, 143, 144, 154-207, 209, 210, 225, 226, 232, 233, 245, 249, 309, 311, 314, 348, 491, 542
Mount Marcy, The High Peak of New York ... 170, 192, 198, 201, 202, 206
Mount Marcy Ski Trail 400
Mount Marshall 24, 40, 52, 53, 54, 112, 128, 130, 142, 219, 221, 222, 279, 357-361, 368, 449, 493
Mount Marshall (Hough) 45, 52, 53, 55
Mount McDonough 457
Mount McIntyre 234, 349
Mount McMartin 233
Mount Morris 550
Mount Phelps 27, 44, 54, 72, 73, 74, 254, 392-397
Mount Porter House 411
Mount Redfield 60, 71, 80, 112, 130, 179, 227, 245, 246, 249-256
Mount Santanoni 27, 100, 113, 223, 274-277
Mount Seward 29, 45, 131, 218, 295-301, 314-315, 316, 482
Mount Seymour .. 47, 69, 91, 113, 119, 131, 218, 316-321
Mount Skylight 179, 210, 225-230
Mount Van Hoevenberg 411
Mount Washington 7, 9, 155, 163, 201, 541, 551
Mount Wright .... (see Wright Peak)
Mountain alder 556
Mountain laurel 472
Mountain lion 339
"Mountain Manners" 82, 88, 89, 128
Mountain Pond 330
Mountain sandwort 555
Mountain Tales 133, 270, 276

Mr. Van Trail 94, 102
Mud Pond 328, 465, 468, 469, 474
Mud Preston 335
Mulholland, William D. 435, 444
Mullin, Robert Bruce 515, 517
Mulverhill, Gary 331
Munyan, E. Addis 368
Murray, Amelia 318
Murray, William H. H. "Adirondack" 9, 499
Murray's fools 9
Murray's Rush 499
Myers, Bill 94
Myers, John 404
Myers Memorial Lean-to 86
"My Mountains!" (poem) 43

Nansen, Fridtjof 552
Nash, C. Howard 34, 49, 52, 59, 60, 141, 262, 279
Nash, J. V. 543
Nason, Richard "Dick" 100, 101, 264, 271
National Academy of Sciences 226
National Lead Company 49, 242, 263, 273, 285
National Outdoor Leadership School 128
Nature Conservancy 273, 283, 284, 347
Neilson, William G. 441, 494, 534
Nejmeh, Al 528
Nelson, Peter 352
New Russia, NY 431
New Topographical Atlas of Essex County 255
New York Folklore Society 41
New York State Forest Preserve (also see Adirondack Forest Preserve) 123
New York State Library Manuscripts and Special Collections 118
Newcomb, NY 233, 263, 273, 276, 364
Newcomb Farm 163
Newhouse, David L. 91, 264, 453
Newkirk, Arthur E. 91, 347, 521
Newman, Charles 169
Newton, Fannie 165, 170
Niagara Brook 436, 437
Niagara Falls 191
Niagara Mountain 456
Nicoll, John 121
Nipping 404, 406
Nippletop Mountain 27, 96, 213, 233, 312, 437, 443, 445, 465-477
Nixon, Edgar B. 65, 143
NL Industries 267, 283, 284
Nolan, Charlie 238, 239, 240, 384, 385
Nolat, Henry 412
No Man's Mountain 195
No Name Mountain 195
Non-conforming structures 79, 96, 127
Noonmark (mountain) 9, 55, 112, 132, 437, 441, 442, 472, 473, 477
Noonmark Lodge 494
North Carolina 313
North Creek, NY 49, 283

North Dial 473, 477
North Elba, NY 155, 156, 343, 356, 364
North Elba Mountains 327
North Pole, NY 553
North River Mountain 194
North Seward (Mount Donaldson) 29, 308
North Tabletop (Tabletop Mountain) 392
North Trail to Giant 94, 104, 112, 131
Northbrook Lodge 64
Northeast 111 120
Northern Adirondack Ski Tours 400
Northern Light 328
Northern Sentinel, The 539
Northville-Placid Trail 145, 272, 295, 342
Norton, Robert 83, 87, 89
Nubbins 536
Nubble, The 419
Number Four, NY 291
Nye, Jane 117, 118, 123, 125
Nye, Spencer 474
Nye, William "Bill" 190, 191, 226, 337, 339, 394, 543
Nye Mountain 24, 27, 60, 64, 78, 93, 112, 113,
 114, 119, 130, 190, 244, 337-344
Nye Ski Trail 330
Nye Wolf 340

O'Brien, Gail 353
O'Brien, Peggy Goodwin . 73, 91, 403, 405, 472, 480, 537
O'Brien, Wally Dog 353
Obrist, Alfred 91
"Ode to Joy" 138
Of the Summits, Of the Forests 121, 135, 459, 532
Office of the Historian 97, 116, 117, 118, 121,
 123, 124, 126, 128, 132
O'Kane, Walter Collins 261, 275, 350, 356,
 444, 446, 450, 459, 514
Old French Trail 549
Old Military Road 494
Old Military Tract 8, 347, 402, 426
Old Nye Ski Trail 330, 337, 341
Oliver, Almeron 58, 174, 501
Olympic Regional Development Authority 553
Olympics 78, 337, 408, 552, 553, 557
Opalescent River 9, 44, 100, 137, 155, 156, 157,
 162, 166, 167, 168, 169, 171, 179, 181, 184, 187,
 190, 194, 202, 203, 206, 225, 230, 231, 245, 246,
 247, 256, 258, 259, 261, 263, 264, 282, 370, 375
Open Space Institute (OSI) 267, 271, 283
Opening of the Adirondacks 561
Orebed Brook 513, 525
Orebed Brook Trail 537
Orebed Trail 507
Orra's Knob 379
Orson 393, 396
Osborne, Lithgow 47, 48, 52, 53, 450
Osgood, Dillon C. 532
O'Sullivan, Timothy 458
Otello 553
Otis (dog) 241

Otis, J. H. 410
Otis, J. W. 186, 206
Otis, John 119
Otis, Rob 474
Otis, Wesley 473
Ou-no-war-lah 539
Ouluska Lean-to 269
Ouluska Pass 45, 270, 280, 287, 290
Ouluska Pass Lean-to 104
Outdoor Leadership Workshop (OLW) 85, 113,
 123, 125, 133, 136, 147, 128, 286
Owl Head 427
Owl's Head 413-414

Paaske, Max 192, 207
Pack baskets 412
Pack-horse mountain 561
Painted trillium 211
Palen, Ann 121
Palen, Ed 237, 238, 405, 436
Palen, Teresa Cheetham 406
Pambamarca 467, 475
Panther (cougar, mountain lion) 497
Panther Brook 100, 270, 278
Panther Gorge 25, 26, 144, 165, 172, 173, 174, 175,
 176, 178, 181, 183, 186, 195, 196, 199, 205, 217,
 225, 228, 245, 246, 258, 394, 488, 500, 504, 508, 524
Panther Gorge Camp 260
Panther Mountain 8, 41, 71, 100, 119, 223, 277-278
Paper birches 527
Paradiso 511
Paradox Pond 543
Pardee family 557
Parker, Arthur 160
Parker, Cecil 403
Parker, Hank 274, 320
Parker, William J. 506
Parks, O. Kenneth 48
Parson, Elsie Clews 206
Passamande, Steve 405
Path Adopter Program 130
Patterson, Fred 431
Patterson, William L. 140
Peacock, Riley 165
Peacock, William 165
Peaks and People of the Adirondacks 10, 28, 29, 30, 47,
 51, 52, 54, 55, 57, 58, 133, 134, 165, 174, 181,
 187, 195, 199, 200, 225, 244, 256, 307, 344, 348,
 352, 358, 359, 392, 402, 416, 452, 477, 478, 479,
 484, 485, 491, 505, 524, 532, 539, 551, 559
Peck, Bill 138
Peck, Charles H. 208, 227, 356, 437
Peeks .... (see *Adirondack Peeks*)
"Peeks Sketches" 129
Peel Jones Lodge 518
Pelkey Basin 380
Penn State Outing Club 405
Pepper, Jerold 529
Peregrine falcon 199, 419

Perkins, Frederick S. 170, 204, 225, 504, 532
Perkins Peak 504
Peruvian Mountains 156, 200, 251, 541
Pettis, Clifford 536
Petty, William "Bill" 83, 87, 90, 422
Pharaoh Lake Area 104
Pharaoh Mountain 476
Phelps, Ed 181, 195, 394, 416, 417, 431, 473, 478, 482, 493, 504, 511, 513, 522, 530, 532, 533, 534, 538
Phelps, Orin 396
Phelps, Orra 14, 57, 58, 64, 65, 84, 121, 160, 196, 208, 346, 347, 372, 379, 398, 549
Phelps, Orson Schofield "Old Mountain" 9, 48, 58, 65, 66, 164, 165, 173, 174, 175, 177, 179, 181, 194, 199, 204, 205, 225, 227, 229, 233, 256, 257, 303, 306, 340, 392, 393, 394, 396, 397, 416, 424, 425, 427, 440, 467, 469, 470, 477, 479, 482, 486, 490, 500, 501, 504, 510, 512, 513, 516, 517, 521, 531, 532, 533, 559
Phelps Brook 394
Phelps Falls 522
Phelps Lean-to 86, 394, 400
Phelps Mountain .... (see Mount Phelps)
Phelps Trail 32, 176, 195, 196, 511, 513, 537
Philadelphia vireo 206
Philosophers Camp, The 288, 310, 313, 316, 423, 547
Phonotypes 164
Phonotypy 202
Picnic tables 86
Pierce, Franklin 159
Pierce, W. W. 191
Pilcher, Edith 441
Pinchot, Gifford 186, 187, 188, 189, 193, 194, 206
Pine martin 138
Pinnacle Ridge 440, 472, 487, 494
Pinnacle Ridge Trail 494
Pirie MacDonald Shelter .... (see MacDonald Shelter)
Pitchoff Mountain 412-413
Pitman, Isaac 202
Pittman, H. H. 478
Plains of Abraham 156, 341, 344, 348, 364, 381, 404
Plane crash 340
"Plants of North Elba" 208
Plateau 157, 192, 198, 400
Plateau Lean-to 31, 32, 86, 96, 196, 197
Plattsburgh Air Force Base 366
Plattsburgh Press-Republican 331
Pleasure Dome 395
Plug of tobacco 156
Plum, Eleanor M. "Nell" 14, 57, 61, 65, 138, 557
Plunz, Richard 423
Poe, Edgar Alan 159, 201
Point Balk 511, 520, 521
Pok-O-MacCready Camps 135, 230, 243, 269, 286, 377
Polaris 178
Polk, James Knox 159, 355
Poll tax 19, 140
Pond, Benjamin 119, 186
Pond, Byron 164, 203
Pony Trail 548

Porcupines 423, 534, 538
Porter, L. Morgan 60, 66, 143, 477
Porter, Noah 394, 416, 458, 516, 518
Porter Ledges 92
Porter Ledges Trail 92
Porter Mountain 92, 119, 416-418
Poser, Carl 24, 555
Possons, Charles H. 411, 514
Potentilla tridentata 347
Pough 433, 451
Poulette, Jim 114
Powell, Lewis 300
Pratt, Sarah 339
Precheur, Martha 125
Presidential Range 10
Preston, James O. 87
Preston, William 166
Preston Pond 138, 290
Preston Ponds 8, 283, 284, 330, 335
Preston Ponds Club 283
"Primitive Man, The" 393
Prince, Ruth .... (See King, Ruth P.)
Prindle, Patti 529
Privies 104
Proctor, Nancy 387
Professor, The 548
Pruyn, Robert C. 273
Puddling furnace 165, 204
Puffer, Louis B. 57, 266
Pugh, James 128
Purim 559
Putnam, James 423
Putnam Brook 423, 494
Putnam Camp 423, 424
Putnam Pond state campground 104
Putnam Pond trail system 94
Pyramid Brook 496
Pyramid Peak 478, 480, 535

Queen Victoria 318
Question Mark, The (slide) 422

Radmanovich, Alex 529
Railroad Notch 402, 403, 404
Rainbow Brook 481
Rainbow Falls 210, 479, 480, 535
Ralph, Alexander 205, 235
Randolph Mountain Club 9
Random Scoot 48
Randorf, Gary 431
Range Trail 513, 514, 537
Ranney, Waitstill 202
Ranney Trail 525
Raquette Lake 314
Raquette River 287, 289, 291, 318
Rarey 338, 343
Ratcliff, Alan 119
Ratcliff, Lyn 353
Ratowski, Wayne 138, 407

INDEX

Ravens 168, 182, 199, 205, 415
Raymond, Lyle 265
Recor, Mary Lou 125, 538
Red spruce 528, 561
Red-throated loon 138
Redfield, John Howard 255
Redfield, William C. 8, 9, 155, 157, 171, 177,
   193, 194, 200, 231, 232, 242, 247, 249,
   251, 274, 309, 311, 313, 348, 350, 375, 376
Reed, Willard 428
Reidel, Arthur 385
Reiss, Julian 553
Reitz, Scott 138
Rensselaer Polytechnic Institute (RPI) 35,
   200, 266, 382
Rensselaer School (later RPI) 311
Report of the Geological Survey for the Second Geological District 263
Report of the Topographical Survey of the Adirondack Wilderness of New York for the Year 1873 .... 178, 230, 465, 485
Republican Party 297, 318, 435
Resagone 479
Resagonia 478, 479
Resigonia 479
Reynolds, Charles 331
Rhododendron Pond 433
Richards, John 375, 402, 540
Richards, T. Addison 165, 203
Ridge Trail 92, 417, 421, 426
Rifle Notch 479
Rimany, Ken 207
Rimrock Trail 402
Ringlee, Robert 91
Roaring Brook 259, 335, 422, 494
Roaring Brook Falls 419, 421
Roaring Brook Trail 421, 422
Robbins, Edythe 117
Robeson, Paul 140
Robertson, Archibald 166
Robinson, Beverley 189
Robinson, Dan 537
Robinson, Herman 189
Rock and River Guide Service 406
Rock Climber's Guide to the Adirondacks 71
Rock climbing 405, 413, 420, 447, 532
Rockefeller, Nelson A. 78
Rockefeller, W. G. 526
Rockwell, Landon 346, 411
Rocky Falls 330, 331, 334
Rocky Peak Ridge 7, 55, 73, 258, 420, 429-432
Roddiger, Brian 271
Roecker, Jeff 353
Roger, Donald 413
Rondeau, Noah John 37, 39, 41, 45, 69, 77, 133, 244,
   268, 269, 272, 279, 280, 292, 294
Roosevelt, Franklin D. 49, 551
Roosevelt, James 552
Roosevelt, Theodore 189, 190, 194, 283, 483, 492, 524
Roosevelt, Mrs. Theodore (Edith) 189

Rooster Comb 92, 534
Root, Russell 440
Rooted in Rock 412
Roster of Members of the Adirondack 46ers .. 565-674
Round Lake 343
Round Mountain 419, 437, 441
Round Pond 433, 446
Round Pond/Dix trail 112
Route 73 .... 31, 193, 408, 413, 419, 422, 433, 472, 494
Route 9N 435
Roy, Rohan 389, 390
RPI .... (see Rensselaer Polytechnic Institute)
Rudge, Bill 387
Runyon, Jennifer 454
Rupp, Joe 387
Rush (assistant to Mills Blake) 186
Rustic Lodge 542
Ryder, Dorothy 33
Ryder, Ernest R. 4, 30, 32, 33, 44, 45, 195,
   228, 321, 396, 448, 452
Ryder, Harold T. 46
Ryder, Janet 33
Ryder, Lethe 33
Ryder, Willis 46
Rykert (first name unknown) 434, 436

Sabael 490
Sabael (Elijah Lewis) .... (See Benedict, Elijah Lewis)
Sabattis, Mitchell 156, 166, 167
Sabele 486
Sabille 486
Sackett's Harbor and Saratoga Railroad 166
Saddle Mountain 505
Saddleback Brook 522
Saddleback Mountain 25, 26, 32, 56, 96, 217, 504-506
Saint Anthony 274
St. Armand, NY 559, 561, 563
St. Bernard's Rock 479
St. Hubert's Inn 494, 495
St. Huberts, NY 437, 441, 472, 495
St. Lawrence River 227, 251
St. Louis, Robert 382
Sanders, Samuel 439
Sandoz, Ernest 315, 320
Sanford, Reuben 375
Sanford Lake 246, 261, 375, 476
Santa Clara Lumber Company 279, 275, 287, 289,
   290, 292, 293, 322, 326
Santanoni Brook 271
Santanoni Preserve 273
Santanonis (range) 100, 101, 131, 269-286
Santa's Workshop 553
Saranac Lake 287
Saranac Lake, NY 301, 303
Saratoga and Sackets Harbor Railroad 282
Saturday Night Club 288
Sawteeth Ledge 482
Sawteeth Mountain 215, 478-482
Sawtooth Range 287, 321

Sawyer, George 179
Scalp Mountain 231, 539
Scanlon, Jennie 306
Scenic Trail 479
Schaefer, Carolyn 352, 361
Schaefer, Paul 194, 206, 207
Schniebs, Otto 382
Schofield, Josephine .... see Scofield, Josephine
Schofield, Peter F. 181, 205, 554
Schofield Cobble 181, 188
Schottman, Ruth 347
Schueller, Gretel H. 418
Schwankert, Patti 125
Scofield (Schofield), Josephine 190, 191, 341
Scofield, Ruth 396
Scott, Alexander (Sandy) 419, 428
Scott, Edmund 128
Scott, Jeffrey 128
Scott, Robert G. 334, 339, 410
Scott, William 339
Scott, Winfield 201
Scott's Clearing 94, 334, 335, 387
Scott's Pond 334
Scudder, David 331
Search and Rescue Unit 86, 87
Sebille 486
Second Brother 403
Second Geological District 251
Secret Service 331
Seely, Bruce 285
Seelye, L. Clark 478
*Seventh Annual Report on the Progress of the Topographical
Survey of the Adirondack Region of New York to the Year 1879*
.... 487, 561
Seward, Frederick 300
Seward, Samuel Sweeney 296
Seward, William H. 287, 295, 297, 300
Seward Mountain 311
Seward Pond 293
Seward Range 287-326
Seward's Folly 300
Seymour, Horatio 287, 297, 316, 317, 318, 483
Shanty, The 423
Shanty Brook 173, 174, 480, 481, 501, 504
Shaw, Gordon "Big Axe" 92
Shepherd's Tooth 212, 352, 361-363
Shorey, A. T. 38, 402, 405, 444, 445, 459, 519
Shorey Short Cut 503, 520
Shorey's Mountain 510
Shoumatoff, Alex 412
Shurtleff, R. (Roswell) M. 458, 477, 486
Siau, John 66, 76, 91, 103
Sierra Club 20
Simmonds, Elijah 436, 437, 440, 474, 475, 485
Simmons, William 474
Simmons, F. Peter 368
Simple Speling 304
Singer, Tim 243
Ski area 552

Ski to Die Club 241, 389, 502
Ski-T Farmhouse 337
Ski Troops 382
Skiff, J. Victor 58
Skiing 78, 138, 192, 208, 400, 405, 502, 506, 511, 552
Skylight Brook 101
Skylight Camp 518
Skylight Mountain 25, 33, 44, 56, 138, 178, 210,
225-230, 252 (also see Mount Skylight)
Skylight Notch (Four Corners) 258
Slack, Nancy 347
Slant Rock 195, 196, 503, 510, 511
Slide Brook 131, 404, 433, 459, 531
Slide Brook Lean-to 104
Slide Mountain (Cakskills) 9
Slide Mountain 531
Slide Rules (slide) 405
Slides 11, 70, 112, 174, 372, 402,
409, 422, 427, 447, 459, 540
Sloan, George .. 39, 116, 117, 118, 125, 135, 147, 213, 329
Smith, Chauncy 438
Smith, Clyde H. 228, 229, 230, 405
Smith, Gerrit 344
Smith, H. P. (Perry) 199, 409
Smith, Henry B. 173, 205
Smith, Paul 303, 306
Smith, R. Pearsall 456
Sno Birds 380
Sno-Bird 502
Sno-Bird Lean-to 32, 96, 509
Snow, Joseph 534
Snow (mountain) 534
Snowberry 174, 555
Snow birds 181
Snow bunting 205
Snowshoe hare 138
Snowshoeing 119, 186, 187, 405, 502, 528
Snyder, Roy 14, 60, 61
Snyder, Tone 162, 165
Solomon, Anton "Tony" 117, 125, 529
Somers, Ellen 105
South Dial 473, 477
South Dix 24, 45, 126, 128, 134, 433, 452-456
South Elbow 157
South Fork 456
South McIntyre 358
South Meadow(s) 24, 25, 72, 191, 192, 193
South Meadow Mountain 393, 396
South Meadows Brook 403, 404
South Peak 444
South Seward (Mount Emmons) 29, 314
Southside Trail 195, 403, 536
Spafford, Horatio Gates 156, 199, 251, 540, 541
Spaniards 469, 476
Spanish Cave 471
Spencer, Melvin 366
Sphagnum 245
Spotted Mountain 433, 445, 455
Spring Camp Fire 47

Index

Sproule, Nora 35, 57, 504
Stagecoach on Whiteface 552, 556
Stagecoach Rock 413
Stanley, Edward 237
Stanwood, Tom 92, 94
Steeple-climbing 479
Steiniger, Hans 455
Stepp, Dick 511
Stevens, Curtis 557
Stevens, George 556
Stevens, J. Hubert 557
Stevens House 556
Steward's Cobble 379
Stillman, William 288, 423
Stoddard, Seneca Ray 175, 176, 190, 236, 282, 306,
  337, 365, 394, 408, 421, 482, 505, 512, 531, 539, 548, 561
Stoney Creek Mountain 23
Stoop, The 423
Stores Mountain 560
Storrow, James J. (Jackson) ... 437, 438, 504, 505, 532, 533
Storrow Pass 532
Story of Adirondac, The 166
Stott, Sliny 23
Stowe, Harriet Beecher 518
Strauss, Anna 506
Strauss, Marjorie Lord 506
Street, Alfred Billings 160, 171, 172, 173, 174,
  193, 205, 231, 235, 327, 332, 341, 365, 413,
  436, 437, 468, 474, 475, 533, 539, 543, 545, 546
Street, Alfred W. 328
Street Mountain 24, 27, 41, 93, 112, 113, 130, 327-332
Striped maple 471
Strobel, Rudolph W. "Rudy" 145, 272
Strode, Elly King 148
Strong (man's name) 348
Strong, George Templeton 299
Strong, Leah 518
Sturner, Sally 105
Suitor, Jim 399
Sulavik, Stephen 8
Summit canisters .... (see Canisters)
Summit Registers 11, 60, 61, 62, 63, 76, 77, 89,
  95, 96, 114, 138, 143, 563
Summit Rock 334, 365, 384
Summit Stewardship Program (SSP) 109, 124
Summit Water 178, 377
Sundew 174
Sunrise Mountain 433, 456
SUNY College of Environmental Science and Forestry
  284
Swan, Jack 406, 527
Swan, John "Sharp," Jr. ... 85, 105, 121, 135, 196, 208, 242,
  326, 399, 406, 423, 459, 547
SWAT team (Special Willingness and Temperament)
  103
Sygman, Steven 386, 388
Sylvester, Nathanial Bartlett 347

T Lake Falls 422

Tabletop Mountain 8, 9, 60, 111, 112,
  130, 138, 395, 397-402
Taconic Hiking Club 34, 47, 59
Taconic System 313, 314, 321
Tahawian Association 164
Tahawus (false name for Mount Marcy) 9, 159, 160,
  161, 163, 164, 165, 168, 169, 171,
  174, 175, 176, 187, 193, 204, 233, 312
"Tahawus" (song) 64
Tahawus (village, mine site) 100, 163, 190, 242, 262,
  263, 271, 274, 275, 276, 281, 283, 364
Tahawus Cabin 191
Tahawus Club 186, 187, 189, 193, 206, 253, 261, 274,
  275, 276, 283, 552
Tahawus House 169
Tahawus Tract 284
Tate, David 332
Taylor, Devon 99, 116
Taylor, Nancy 99
Taylor, R. C. 457, 466
Taylor (family) 513
Tefft, Tim 113, 114, 116, 121, 122, 135
Terrie, Philip G., Jr. 54, 200, 244, 453, 455, 532
Terry, Guy 402, 403
Thei-a-no-guen 539
Theodolite 177, 179, 182, 185, 439, 467, 485
Thistle Dhu 537
Thomas, Almon 533
Thomas, Bob 144
Thomas, George 441
Thomas, Lowell 557
Thomas, Marilyn 144
Thomas, Steven 144, 400
Thomas and Armstrong Lumber Company .. 441, 512
Thomas-Train, Betsey 447
Thompson, Dauphin 543, 545
Thompson, Dyer 156
Thompson, William "Will" 135, 543
Thoreau, Henry David 393, 423
Three Years with the Adirondack Regiment 327
Three-toothed cinquefoil 555
Thunder Bridge 496
Ticknor, Robbie 176
Tight-Nipping 404
Tilden, Samuel J. 316, 320
Timbuctoo 344
Times Square 113, 272
Tip-top house 551
Titanium 242, 282, 283
Toboggan shelter 562
Todd, John 490
Tolles, Bryant F., Jr. 410
Topographical Survey of the Adirondack Wilderness 485
Torrey, John 157, 200, 201, 226, 250, 348
Totten, Joseph 352
Totten and Crossfield 305
Totten and Crossfield Purchase 8, 195, 401, 434, 441
Town Hall 45, 279
Township 11, Old Military Tract 540

- 699 -

Township 12	402
Township 27	291
Township 45, Totten and Crossfield Purchase	244
Township 47	375
Township 48	195, 401, 434, 441, 534
Township 49	434, 435
TR Mountain	380, 454
Tracy, Henry	186
Trail Blazer Award	43
Trail crew	92
Trail maintenance	112
"Trail Workshop"	83
Trailless Peaks	27, 30, 34, 37, 39, 42, 45, 56, 59, 60, 62, 63, 66, 71, 72, 73, 74, 75, 76, 77, 82, 84, 91, 95, 96, 97, 107, 108, 109, 110, 111, 112, 113, 114, 115, 117, 119, 120, 121, 125, 126, 127, 128, 130, 131, 143, 146, 562
Trailless Peaks Committee	111, 112
Trailmaster	92, 93, 95, 101, 102, 109, 111, 112, 113, 120, 132
Trails and Summits of the Adirondacks	261, 275, 350, 356, 444, 450, 514
Trails Maintenance Manual	145
"Trails to Mount Marcy" (map)	42
"Trails to Mount Marcy" (pamphlet)	30, 208, 262
Trap Dyke (Dike)	133, 233, 236, 238, 240, 241, 243
Trapp, Charles	14, 57
Trapp, Charles, Jr.	14, 57
Trapp, George	14, 57
Trees of the Adirondack High Peaks Region	81
Trent, The	299
Trilobite	312
Trowels	104
Troy Record	33
Trudeau, Edward Livingston	301
True North (slide)	11
Trumbull, Mel (Melville)	41, 225, 257, 458, 459, 472, 482, 496, 504, 505, 533
Tubby, Joseph	165, 203
Tubby, Josiah	203
Tuberculosis (TB)	190, 302, 550
Tulip (slide)	423
Tupper Lake, NY	289, 291
Turner, Breck	529
Turner, John L.	121
Turner, Joseph Mallord William	458
Turner, Julie	529
Turner, Mark	115
Turon, Joseph "Joe"	148, 229
Tuthill, Sidney P. Jr.	91
Twain, Mark	518
Twichell, Burton P.	515
Twichell, Joe	518
Twichell, Joseph Hopkins	256, 394, 515, 517, 518, 521
Twin Brook	138, 244
Twin Brook Lean-to	101, 104, 247, 248, 255, 256, 260, 263, 265
Twin Brook Trail	247
Twin flower	174
Twin Mountain	403
Twin Pond	433
"Two Visits to the Mountains of Essex County, 1836 and 1837"	348
Two Years Before the Mast	165, 203
Ulloa, Antonio de	475
Ulloa's halo	476
Ulloa's Rings	554
Ulrich, Anthony	105
Ulrich, Ferdinand	105
Union College	192, 296, 317, 448, 534
Unit Management Plans (UMPs)	79, 100, 132, 137
United States Board on Geographic Names	54, 134
United States Steel	283
University of Vermont (UVM)	159
Up the Lake Road	441
Uphill Brook	44, 155, 157, 183, 194
Uphill Brook Lean-to	101, 108, 138, 254, 255
Uphill Lean-to	247, 263
Upper Ausable Lake	165, 173, 174, 175, 176, 179, 181, 183, 184, 185, 186, 190, 193, 256, 257, 393, 394, 472, 486, 511
Upper Ausable Pond	512
Upper Cascade Lake	408, 414, 415
Upper Range	500-529
Upper Twin Brook	260, 261
Upper Wolf Jaw	56, 145, 533
Upper Works	156, 162, 166, 171, 173, 181, 186, 187, 189, 190, 242, 246, 248, 256, 261, 282, 284, 328, 383, 476
Urbanczyk, Joe	103, 105, 109, 113, 117, 123, 125, 132
Urbanczyk, Marilee	117
UVM Outing Club	240
V-Badge	119, 382
Vallandigham, Clement	317
Van Buren, Martin	355
Van Dyke, Paul	254, 451, 459
Van Hoevenberg, Henry	190, 191, 192, 195, 339, 341, 351, 381
Van Hoevenberg Trail	32, 94, 191, 192, 195, 225, 394, 400, 401
Van Ness, Myron R.	414
Van Santvoord, Abraham	242, 376
Vanderbilt, A. G.	526
Vandrie, Chuck	284
Van Norden, L. John	99, 118, 125, 133, 134, 454
Vermilyea, David A.	77
Via, Alan	134
Victory Mountain Park	198, 397
Viscome, George	239
Vracarich, Toma	389, 390
W. A. White Trail	92, 258, 496, 535
Wa-ho-par-te-nie	539
Wagner, Richard	303
Wallace, E. (Edwin) R.	191, 410, 439, 440, 459, 482, 500, 514, 539
Wallace Falls	191

Index

Wallface Mountain 8, 9, 165, 177, 332-335, 341, 345, 349, 363, 365, 550
Wallface Ponds 93, 177, 334, 335
Wallface Pond Trail 102
Wanakena (Ranger School) 83
Wanika Falls 330, 342
Ward, Peter A. 58, 66, 77
Wardell, Helen 529
Warden Camp Trail 479
Warden's Camp 176, 481
Warner, Charles Dudley 173, 205, 256, 257, 306, 393, 394, 458, 467, 468, 469, 470, 516, 517, 518, 521
Wart of Iroquois, The 362
Washbond's Flume 92
Washbowl, The 419, 420, 531
Washbund, Marvin 165
Washbund, William 165
Watch Rock Hotel 411
Waterhouse, Alice 73
Waterman, Guy and Laura ... 11, 419, 448, 459, 533, 546
Watson, Winslow C. 252, 436, 440, 456, 550
Webb, Nina 176, 482, 484, 492
Webb, W. S. 526
Weber, Sandra 170, 176, 181, 192, 198, 201, 202, 203, 204, 206, 549, 560, 561
Webster, Daniel 202
Wedge Brook Cascades 535
Wedge Brook Trail 535
Weed, Elizabeth 328
Weed, Thurlow 296, 297, 301
Weeks, Barbara 238, 239
Weeks, Gretchen 238, 239
Welch, Thomas R. 129
Weld, Alfred E. 535
Weld, Frank 502
Weld, Paul W. 72
Weld, William Floyd 480
Wells, Alfred 403
Wells, Nathaniel "Nat" 111
Wells, Sylvanus 534
Wendell, Chrissie 14
Wendell, David 37
Wendell, Mrs. Roland 37
Wendell, Richard "Dick" 14, 37
Wendell, Roland 14, 37, 58
Werner, Bob 138
West, Alton Clinton "Clint" 208, 372
West, Charles "Charlie" 29, 307, 308
West Cobble 427
West Mill Brook 433, 456
West Mountain 416
West River Trail 496
Weston, George 548
Weston, Harold 420, 426, 436, 439, 442, 496, 509, 519
Weston, Mr. 412
Weston, Sidney 548
Weston, W. F. 410
Westport, N.Y. 245
WGY (radio station) 37

Whale, The 379
Whalen, Mike 456
Whale's Tail 380
Whale's Tail Ski Trail 402
Wheeler, Eileen 268
Wheeler, George 458
Wheeler, Matthew 268
Wheeler, Tom 268, 335
Wheeler, William 483
Whig Party 297
Whistletricker, Jacob 23
White, A. L. 526
White, Harold 502, 519
White, Theodore 165
White, W. (William) A. 494, 495, 519, 535
White Brook 562
White Falls 543
White Lily Pond 246
White Lily Trail 260
White Mountains 7, 9, 10, 77, 165, 175, 198
White Ribbon, The 546, 547
Whiteface Brook 557
Whiteface Mountain 9, 15, 24, 30, 33, 40, 49, 50, 119, 123, 155, 156, 164, 177, 184, 185, 224, 251, 328, 339, 539-557, 561, 562
Whiteface Mountain House 548
Whiteface Mountain Ski Center 553, 562
Whiteface Mountain Tract 540
Whiteface Veterans Memorial Highway 549, 552, 556, 561, 563
Whiteface-Wilmington Lean-to 562
Whitefish 414
White-throated sparrow 199
Whiting, Brad 346
Whitney, Nettie Holt 200
Whitney, W. C. 526
Wickes, Thomas P. 431, 513, 534, 535
Wickham, Robert S. 246, 275, 276, 443, 444, 459, 514
Wiessner, Fritz 332, 405, 406
Wiggs, Leslie A. .... (see Gilroy, Howard P.)
Wiktorek, Penny 150
Wild Scenes in the Forest and Prairie 160, 436
Wilderness Ethic 76, 86, 88, 114, 120
Wilderness First Aid 128
Wilderness Leadership Workshop (see also Outdoor LeadershipWorkshop) 11, 84, 85, 97
Wilderness Original: The Life of Bob Marshall, A 505
Wilderness Paths 74, 76, 77, 82, 110, 130, 136, 144, 248, 255, 327, 328, 329, 340, 341, 342, 343, 401, 446
Wilderness Preservation ... 15, 16, 17, 18, 19, 20, 72, 144
Wilderness Society, The 18, 53, 142, 143, 207, 559
Wiley, Bob 65, 66
Wiley, John 120
Wilkes, Charles 299
Williams, Andrew 440
Williams, Frank 192
Williams, Henry G. 98, 106
Williams College 309, 541
Wilmington, NY 177, 293, 542, 559, 563

Wilmington Reservoir 562
Wilmington Road 553
Wilmington Trail 561, 562, 563
Wilmington Turn 552, 556, 562
Wilson, Augusta 243
Wilson, Franklin H., Jr. 59, 93, 141, 329
Wilson, Woodrow 420
Wilson's snipe 182, 205
Wing, Yung 518
Winkler, John E. 138, 335, 350, 378, 455, 529
Winter Camp 537
Winter 46ers 70, 119, 120, 121, 130
Winter Mountaineering School 254
WMHT (television station) 37
Wolf Jaws Notch 92
Wolfe, Doug 556
Wollastonite 409
Wollenberg, Peter 240, 241
Wood, Charles 356
Wood, John 104
Wood, Willis D. 502
Wood sorrel 471
Woods, Edward A. 261
Woods and Waters: or, The Saranacs and Racket 328, 543, 547
Woods' farm 26

Wright, Jack 165
Wright, Silas 297, 353, 354, 356
Wright Brook 373
Wright Peak 42, 54, 78, 83, 84, 124, 138, 218,
    353-357, 366-367, 372-374, 380, 382, 388-390
Wright Peak Ski Trail 402
Wrong Peak 377, 378, 379
Wrong Slide 218, 372, 373, 374
Wuillermin, John 138
Wyant, Alexander H. (Helwig) 458, 504, 505, 533

Xerxes 559

Yale University 416
Yard, Robert Sterling 53, 142
Yard Mountain 405
Yellow-rumped warbler 199
Young, Brigham 548
Young, Ed 335
Young, Miss 189
Young, Wally 243
Yourdon, Brian 511

Zabinski, Robert 133
Zahniser, Howard 207
Zander Scott Trail 419, 421
Zika, Peter 528

917.475
Heaven up-h'isted-ness!: the history of the Adirondack Forty-sixers and the Hight Peaks of the Adirondacks.
9/11 $29.95

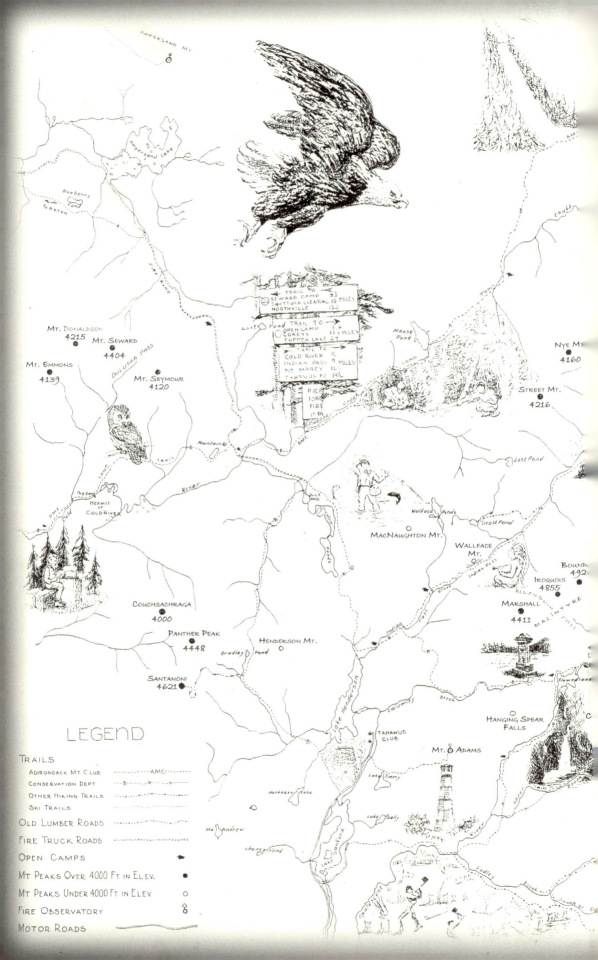